Queen's University

Volume III

*To Carmel, Arts '72
with fond memories
of Queen's
Duncan
Arts '72*

Queen's University

Volume III

1961–2004: Testing Tradition

Duncan McDowall (signature)

Duncan McDowall

Cha Gheill!! (signature)

Published for Queen's University
by
McGill-Queen's University Press
Montreal & Kingston • London • Chicago

© McGill-Queen's University Press 2016

ISBN 978-0-7735-4696-7 (cloth)
ISBN 978-0-7735-9876-8 (ePDF)

Legal deposit first quarter 2016
Bibliothèque nationale du Québec

Printed in Canada on acid-free paper.

McGill-Queen's University Press acknowledges the support of the Canada Council for the Arts for our publishing program. We also acknowledge the financial support of the Government of Canada through the Canada Book Fund for our publishing activities.

Library and Archives Canada Cataloguing in Publication

Queen's University

Includes bibliographical references and index.
Contents: v. 3. 1961–2004 : testing tradition / Duncan McDowall.
Issued in print and electronic formats.
ISBN 978-0-7735-4696-7 (bound : v. 3).
ISBN 978-0-7735-9876-8 (ePDF : v. 3)

1. Queen's University (Kingston, Ont.) – History. I. McDowall, Duncan, 1949–. 1961–2004, testing tradition.

LE3.Q32N34 1978   378.713'72   C2015-906747-2
                                          790025787

Dedicated to the memory of the Rev. Robert McDowall (1768–1841), who glimpsed the potential of Queen's, and Professor Frederick Wellington Gibson (1920–1992), who helped realize that potential.

Contents

Foreword by Daniel Woolf ❖ ix

Introduction ❖ 3

1 In the Fall of 1961 ❖ 14

2 "Deliberate Speed":
Alex Corry and the Modernization of Queen's, 1961–1968 ❖ 49

3 "Uproariously Busy":
John Deutsch and the Codification of Queen's, 1968–1974 ❖ 93

4 "A Puzzle of Patterns":
Student and Faculty Life, 1961–1974 ❖ 135

5 Challenging Limestone Liberalism:
The Edwards Affair and Hotel Hobbit ❖ 188

6 "A Pretty Taste for Paradox":
Ron Watts and the Art of Compromise, 1974–1984 ❖ 223

7 An End to "Effortless Superiority":
David Smith, 1984–1994 ❖ 279

8 "The Life of the Greater Queen's":
The Challenge of Diversity ❖ 341

9 Town, Gown, and the World Beyond ❖ 399

10 "To Chart a Different Course":
William Leggett and the New Millennium, 1994–2004 ❖ 437

Afterword: In the Fall of 2004 ❖ 504

Acknowledgments ❖ 533
Illustration Credits ❖ 537
Notes ❖ 539
Index ❖ 567

Foreword

Daniel Woolf

Principal and Vice-Chancellor

The president of a great university was once asked: "What does it take to make a university great?" "Time," the president responded with a smile.

By the standard of many American and European universities, Queen's has had a relatively short life. Yet we are among the oldest of Canadian universities, and mark our 175th anniversary in 2016–17. From its humble beginnings – at the initiative of local Kingston leaders who saw the need for an institution of higher learning in the eastern reaches of the newly reorganized Canada West (of which the city had become, that year, the capital) – Queen's has grown and prospered into the mid-sized university that we have inherited and which we will, in turn, hand on to our successors.

As an alumnus of our department of history, and now as one of its professors, I have long taken a personal interest in the history of our institution and will make the following observation: our path has virtually never been a smooth one. The fledgling college of a small cohort of students and a tiny faculty complement – without even its own building for a few years – could easily have been a failed venture through much of its first half-century. The threat of absorption into larger Ontario schools hung over our predecessors like a sword of Damocles, its fragile suspending thread frayed, little by little, by a series of financial challenges. Under our sixth principal, Rev. William Snodgrass (1864–77), a measure of stability was restored following a major Canadian banking failure. The foundations of the university's strong relationship with, and reliance on, its alumni, were thereby laid, with no better early example of alumni loyalty than Robert Sutherland, Queen's first black student, whose generous legacy in 1878 would prove a game-changer. Moreover, during Snodgrass's tenure, Queen's became the first university west of the Maritimes to admit women as students.

The visionary seventh principal, Rev. George Munro Grant (1877–1902) continued and extended Snodgrass's work during a principalship of a quarter-century. Closely tied to Canada's founders, including Sir John A. Macdonald and CPR builder Sir Sandford Fleming (later our Chancellor), Grant energetically pursued a bold vision of a national institution that would produce not merely a well-informed local citizenry and clergy, but

Canadian leaders of the highest moral and intellectual fibre. An empowered student government, the Alma Mater Society (AMS), was a significant component of his strategy. This first juncture or fork in our road, from local college to national institution, complete with schools of medicine and engineering, had been taken by the time Grant died. His immediate successor, Rev. Daniel Miner Gordon (1902–17) saw Queen's through most of World War I and the separation of the Theological College from a newly "rebranded" (a modern bit of jargon that Grant and Gordon would have neither understood nor liked) "Queen's University at Kingston." It was during this period that the "pipeline to Ottawa" was laid – that steady flow of Queen's professors and students into the upper ranks of the federal public service that continues today. Two subsequent principals, geologist Robert Charles Wallace (1936–51) and economist William Mackintosh (1951–61) – the latter an alumnus, professor, and veteran of the Ottawa mandarin class – brought Queen's safely through the turbulent times of the Great Depression, World War II, and the war's 1950s aftermath. And, of course, this was also the era of Queen's legendary registrar, Jean Royce, who, among her many achievements, decided to admit, in 1941 (in the middle of term!), a young Austrian-born Jewish student, recently freed from internment as an enemy alien, named Alfred Bader, who had just been refused admission by two other Canadian universities.

What happened next is captured in Duncan McDowall's fascinating chronicle of a second juncture in Queen's path, between 1961 and 2004 – the period of Principals Corry, Deutsch, Watts, Smith, and Leggett. In this era, the university became not merely a great undergraduate institution, but built up its graduate school and joined the ranks of leading Canadian research universities. Queen's increased dramatically in student numbers and in faculty complement, added new programs, and began, cautiously, to venture on to the international scene. It also struggled with an unprecedented pace of change, one that has only accelerated since the turn of the millennium. Indeed, one of the great achievements of Duncan's volume is that, while great respect is accorded to Queen's leaders, this third volume of our institutional history ranges much more widely than its two predecessors, written by the late Hilda Neatby and the late Frederick Gibson respectively. Volume 3 is a history of the university as a whole, of its faculty, staff, and students – with a special emphasis on the kaleidoscopic experience of *being* a Queen's student. That experience is often drawn here from the memories and lips of student leaders, as well as faculty and staff, during those decades. Professor McDowall has balanced the use of oral history with the sound archival source work for which he was trained in our very own department of history.

I observed at the outset of these remarks that our path has never been free of rocks and obstacles. This was as true during the period of Prof McDowall's study as it was during the mid-nineteenth century. In particular, Queen's found itself constantly challenged by profound social change. Universities tend by their very nature to be rather conservative institutions in many ways: they can also be both inward-looking and defensive of their traditions and practices. Queen's has been no exception to this predilection, and as one of Canada's oldest universities bears a proportionately richer – and heavier – "burden of history." At many points in the forty-three years between 1961 and 2004 described by Duncan McDowall, the university (itself an increasingly complex community of different constituencies) was repeatedly forced to ask itself which traditions were fundamental, which were perhaps ephemeral (or even noxious when weighed against modern social expectations), and which had simply become obstacles to progress and to maintaining a leader's, rather than a follower's, role on the Canadian educational stage. Because we are a university and not a corporation, ideas and debate flow freely, and often heatedly. "Tradition" was tested repeatedly during these years, and that testing has provided the perfect theme and subtitle for this book.

The testing continues to this day, but it is paradoxically tradition's strength that it is not static and unchanging but constantly evolving. It must be thus, or how would there ever be opportunity for new generations to create their own traditions?

One of the many traditions that *has* continued to stand us in good stead is that of the generous support, advice, and encouragement of our alumni. Thousands over the years have supported Queen's, from the smallest annual gift or bursary to an academic department, to the seminal contributions of Dr Alfred Bader, Joseph Stauffer, Britton Smith, the Chernoff family, Mel Goodes, Robert Buchan, Stuart Lang (lead donor for the refurbishment now under way of Richardson Stadium), and most recently Stephen Smith. All gifts are meaningful, regardless of amount, and we owe the success of our recent Initiative Campaign to thousands of expressions of individual gratitude for a past Queen's experience, as well as to the broader appreciation by corporations and foundations of the university's special place among Canadian universities and, above all, to a shared love of our alma mater.

Among our most steadfast supporters over the last century has been the Richardson family, whose firm originated in Kingston and is now based in Winnipeg, my own hometown. Several generations of the family have attended Queen's, and two family members, father James and daughter Agnes, have served as Chancellor. The family has also contributed significantly to the renovation of the Stadium. And I note here, with my profound thanks, their generous and unswerving financial support for the writing of this volume of the Queen's history.

❖ ❖ ❖

History, like tradition, is an unfinished story. We have reason to take great pride in our achievements of the past 175 years. But, as our predecessors knew very well, we cannot stand still. Our best way of honouring the students, faculty, staff, and alumni who have built a great university is not to rest on our laurels, but to strive to make the next decades an era of continued, and even greater, achievement as a leading Canadian – and global – university.

Daniel Woolf (Artsci '80), PPhil, FRHistS, FSA, FRSC
Professor of History and Principal and Vice-Chancellor
Queen's University

Queen's University

Volume III

Grant Hall, the iconic centrepiece of Queen's identity. Built to commemorate the pivotal principalship (1877–1902) of Rev. George Munro Grant, the hall was completed in 1905 and funded by contributions from students, faculty, and alumni. Dean of Practical Science Nathan Dupuis, a polymath of invention, designed the tower's clock. Romanesque in style, Grant Hall embodied many Queen's traditions: the university's signature use of limestone, its sylvan campus with a canopy of spreading elms, and its cohesive collegiality.

Introduction

He who would forecast the future of Queen's must cast a shrewd eye over its past.
Principal Bruce Taylor, *Queen's Review*, 1927

The chief service of universities and their chief glory is not the piling up of useful knowledge to support the material side of our lives. It is rather the protecting and nourishing of the traditions of civility on which all civilization in the end depends.
Principal Alex Corry, 1970

We drink from wells we did not dig.
AMS Information Officer Greg McKellar, paraphrasing Deuteronomy 6:11

What Is a University?

This appears at first to be a simple question to answer. Dictionaries offer bald, functional definitions. The magisterial *Oxford English Dictionary* tells us that a university is "an institution of higher education offering tuition in mainly non-vocational subjects and typically having the power to confer degrees." Most such definitions also invoke the idea of a "community" of scholars and learners, the former dedicated to the making and transmission of knowledge and the latter to its digestion and application to life. Explication of the Latin word *universitas* – meaning "the whole" – is often cited to furnish etymological legitimacy. Other definitions deploy history to underline the university's deep roots in western civilization, citing the existence of guild-like enclaves of scholars and students as early as the eleventh century in such European cities as Paris and Bologna. The European parentage of the university has been challenged in recent times by Islamic scholars, who argue that *madrashas* – from the Semitic word "to learn" – were active as early as the ninth century in North Africa.

For those who favour a less mechanistic rendering of the university's purpose, the eloquence of that formidable Victorian evangelical and Oxford academic Cardinal John Henry Newman (1801–90) frequently provides sustenance. "A University," he assured students in Dublin in the 1850s, "is a place where enquiry is pushed forward and discoveries perfected and verified and rashness rendered innocuous and error exposed by the collision of mind with knowledge." Newman's 1858 *The Idea of a University* has long been the friend of academic speech makers. It allows them to isolate the utility of a university education as "a habit of mind is formed which lasts through life, of which the attributes are freedom, equitableness, calmness, moderation, and wisdom ... a philosophical habit." This radiating influence has pulsed through Western society since the Enlightenment. The university, for Newman, was "a place for the communication and circulation of thought, by means of personal intercourse, through a wide extent of country."

Many universities have adopted mottos that strive to convey this purpose. Harvard University proclaims its purpose under a bold and simple dedication to *Veritas* – "truth." Across the Atlantic, Cambridge University commits itself to the motto *Hinc lucem et pocule sacra* – "from this, enlightenment and precious knowledge." In the 1840s, the Presbyterian founders of Queen's University – the subject of this chronicle – drew on the Book of Isaiah for their Biblical inspiration: *Sapienta et Doctrina Stabilitas* – "Knowledge and wisdom shall be the stability of thy times."

The modern university, however, often confounds the clear-cut nobility of such definitions. The cloistered, guild-like scholastic communities of late medieval Europe have been superseded by what, in modern academic argot, have become *multiversities* – sprawling, disjointed communities of scholars and students that process knowledge, ranging from the broad socialization of adolescents to the fine-tuning of professional expertise in more mature adult minds. In doing so, the multiversity strains the communitarian quality of university life so prized by Cardinal Newman. What indeed is the modern university "community"? Universities have become distended communities, seemingly held together by shared fiscal arrangements, campus geography, and loose, collegial governance. What, for example, supplies cohesion to academic communities that span pedagogy stretching from the contemplation of North Italian Baroque art to the durability of asphalt? Clark Kerr, president of the University of California in the turbulent 1960s, once quipped that universities had become communities of scholars bound together by little more than a "common grievance" over parking policy. Famous for his dry wit, Kerr also suggested that his role as his university's principal administrator was "to provide sex for the students, sports for the alumni, and parking for the faculty." Despite such quips, Kerr was profoundly committed to the university's autonomy in society: he resisted outside pressure to extinguish student demonstrations and political activism on his campuses. Ultimately, under pressure from then–California Governor Ronald Reagan, the university's regents dismissed him in 1966. Long remembered for his championing of academic freedom, Kerr is credited with coining the term "multiversity."

The modern university – "multi" or otherwise – has thus become a protean, yet curious, social and intellectual construct. It has evolved into a compendium of starkly diverse intellectual communities, bound loosely in sustained symbiotic relationship. At one end of any university's demographic spectrum lies its largest constituency – its student body, that polyglot of predominantly young adults striving to find their orientation in life. Their lives are marked by an uneasy mixture of uncertainty, experimentation, deference, and rebellion. The university serves as their life laboratory. At the other end of the spectrum, the university community embraces an ever-accumulating reservoir of alumni – generations of one-time students who have travelled through life and are now inclined to project their life experience and acquired values back onto their alma mater. Thus, while the student tends to frame his or her definition of the university out of *expectancy*, the alumni define their sense of the university's utility through a filter of *nostalgia*.

Between these two poles of attachment to the university lie the faculty and staff, who deliver education and seek to craft new knowledge. Faculty and staff define their attachment to the university in terms of *careers* within their respective spheres of expertise. While they find some commonality in fulfilling the basic functions of the university – teaching, maintenance, and administration – they are just as likely to shape their identity in intellectual and practical specialization beyond the campus community – being a biologist or processing admissions or providing maintenance services. This dispersion of focus is perhaps most evident in university faculties of arts and science, where scholars today find themselves under an imposed common umbrella that encompasses everything from the humanities to the life sciences.

Beyond their Newmanesque mission of broad pedagogy, universities today thus defy easy generalization as "communities." In the words of Irish poet W.B. Yeats, "things fall apart; the centre cannot hold." The historian seeking to "tell the story" of a particular university is confronted with the daunting challenge of identifying the bonding agent or overarching motivation in that institution's existence. There can be exceptions. Washington's Howard University can, for instance, be closely associated since its inception in post–Civil War America with the desire to advance the well-being of black Americans. The London School of Economics, that echo of Fabian socialism, can be associated with the study of social demographics and public policy. Its motto – *Regnum cognoscere causas* – betrays the school's technocratic devotion "to know the causes of things." Such association of institution and purpose does not, however, come readily to most modern universities. Hortative Latin mottos have little resonance in modern societies that have at best only an inkling of that "ancient language." Most universities today instead attempt to project their purpose by embracing bland slogans that "brand" their university as if it were a soft drink. Indeed, many American universities, in the absence of meaningful common denominators, take refuge in Clark Kerr's "sports for the alumni" dictum by hanging their identity on their gridiron prowess as "Bulldogs," "Cornhuskers," or "Nittany Lions."

The Centrality of Tradition

This history of Queen's University in the late twentieth century seeks to construct a narrative built around denominators that rise above this commonplace. More than any other word, "tradition" punctuates the perception of Queen's since its founding in 1841. Whether in the columns of its student newspaper, in its admissions literature, or in its ivy-covered architecture, tradition abounds. *"Queen's colours we are wearing once again!"* Queen's habitually projects itself as a place of tradition. Pipe bands, Gaelic tartans, the singing of the school's warlike *Oil Thigh* chant, leather jackets emblazoned with year crests, and football Saturdays all colourfully convey a sense of "Queen's spirit," but are often in reality only outward or superficial projections of Queen's *inner* tradition.

Historians in recent decades have written about the way in which societies and nations construct or "invent" tradition to bolster their sense of togetherness and purpose. "'Invented tradition' is taken to mean a set of practices," British historian Eric Hobsbawm wrote in *The Invention of Tradition*, a book that he and Terence Ranger published in 1983, "normally governed by overtly or tacitly accepted rules and of a ritual or symbolic nature, which seek to inculcate certain values and norms of behaviour by repetition, which automatically implies continuity with the past."[1] Tradition can thus be a powerful agent of continuity and cohesion. Other scholars have extended the analysis.

Social philosopher Benedict Anderson of Cornell University has suggested that all societies can be best understood as "imagined communities," bound together by carefully constructed notions of past achievement and purpose. Echoing the belief of nineteenth-century French historian Ernest Renan that nationalism is the remembrance of great moments of communal action, Anderson's 1983 *Imagined Communities* argued that "members of even the smallest nation will never know most of their fellow-members, meet them, or even hear of them, yet in the minds of each lives the image of their communion."² At its best, tradition can accentuate the positive elements of any society – "*Loyal she began. Loyal she remains*," Ontario's motto reminds us. At its worst, this inclination to instill a shared heritage can lend itself to nefarious manipulation and collective belligerence. "We dream of a Roman Italy ... wise, strong, disciplined, and imperial," Mussolini declared in 1922.

There can be no doubt that Queen's has over the decades "invented tradition": its adoption of Highland Scottish folklore and ritual speaks to the conscious grooming of tradition useful to the building of cohesion and a clan-like sense of community. Take, for instance, the *Cha Gheill* – "no surrender" – war cry chanted by Queen's students in pseudo-Gaelic aggressiveness at football games. Tradition's potency as means of promoting social cohesion has long echoed in Queen's culture. The 1903 *Queen's Song Book* captured this artificial durability by printing the words of "On the Old Ontario Strand," a ditty then popular with students:

> *For has she not stood,*
> *Since the time of the Flood*
> *On the Old Ontario Strand?*³

But Queen's has a culture that rests on *more* than invented tradition. Even Hobsbawm acknowledged that societies can rest on deeper, more intrinsic traditions than those of "wilful creation." There can also be *organic* tradition, tradition that evolves out

The *Queen's University Song Book*, published in 1903 by Whaley & Royce in Toronto, perpetuated university tradition in oral form. Its pages contained such rollicking favourites as "Queen's College Colours," "Queen's College Is a Jolly Home," and "On the Old Ontario Strand."

of actual experience. Such tradition reflects values rooted in the lived experience of an institution. America's seemingly unshakable belief in the second-amendment right to bear arms is, for instance, no invention. It is instead genetically tied to the legacy of colonial revolution, when a "well-regulated militia" seemed the difference between colonial oppression and "the pursuit of happiness." Similarly, the Canadian rubric of "peace, order, and good government" echoes British North America's dedication to crafting a society in which English and French might live peaceably under the rule of law and responsible government.

In 1941, as Queen's celebrated its centenary, a graduate of Arts '02 took pen in hand to write the first history of the university. Dileno Dexter Calvin, scion of a prominent Kingston shipping family, wrote in *Queen's University at Kingston, 1841–1941*, that Queen's was "a Canadian university, not a local one … part of the life of the Dominion, not one section of it."4 Commissioned by the Board of Trustees, Calvin's book was cast in an onward-and-upward, Whiggish style, and lacked access to documentation beyond the university's official minutes. With the birth of the Queen's archives in 1961, a more investigatory and contextualized history of Queen's and its traditions became possible. By the end of that decade, Principal Alex Corry's thoughts turned to the prospect of a more professional approach to the history of the university. Queen's first two official university historians – Hilda Neatby and Frederick W. Gibson – consequently strove to discover that inner, organic tradition. Neatby, a scholar of post-Conquest Quebec, who came to Queen's in the early 1970s from the University of Saskatchewan, chronicled the fledgling college's precarious beginnings from its founding in 1841 to the appointment of Principal R. Bruce Taylor in 1917, amidst the trauma of the Great War. A complete outsider to the Queen's culture, Neatby initially regarded all the talk of "Queen's spirit" and "tradition" as so much hokum, crafted to attract promising undergraduates. She quickly discovered otherwise. Queen's College, she told the readers of the *Queen's Quarterly* in 1973, emanated out of the "Scottish fact" in Upper Canada, and that flinty Presbyterian mindset reverberated through the institution's first eighty years. There was no coincidence in her choice of a line from Tennyson's "Ulysses" as the title of her volume: *To Strive, to Seek, to Find, and Not to Yield*.5

Neatby characterized the years from 1841 to 1917 as a time of unrelenting precariousness for the small college. In his foreword to her 1978 volume, then-Principal Ronald Watts described nineteenth-century Queen's as "an experiment in survival," as a place "beset by misfortune after misfortune." Fractious relations with the provincial government and the Presbyterian Church left the young college perennially on the verge of bankruptcy. Queen's Presbyterian orientation also at times impeded its progress. The young medical faculty, founded in 1856, rebelled at having to oblige the charter's obligation of professors pledging allegiance to the Presbyterian faith. Consequently, the faculty bolted into an arm's-length relationship with the college, eventually to re-affiliate in 1892. The stronger and better-endowed University of Toronto always lurked on the western horizon, hovering, it was feared, to seize just the right moment to swallow up its struggling eastern-Ontario rival. Amid all this uncertainty, Neatby chronicled the laying down of tradition. There were, much as Eric Hobsbawm would later suggest, adopted traditions. In 1882, the college began playing rugby football, a manly game that seemed, almost in parallel with the college's own struggles, to accentuate a Darwinian survival of the fittest. Students reinforced this gridiron contest by adopting vigorous Gaelic rituals – sword dancing, warlike chants, the wearing of kilts on chilly autumn days – to craft a distinctive student culture. *Oil Thigh na Banrighann gu Brath! … Queens' forever!* In the early 1880s, student leaders and the football captains struck a committee to give this emerging tradition a visual identity: a tricolour of gold, red, and blue was selected. On the gridiron, gold soon dominated the footballers' jerseys and knickers (as they were then called), hence the adoption of yet another Gaelic tradition – Queen's players would be dubbed Golden Gaels, the athletic personification of fierce Highland raiders.

But Neatby drew her readers' attention to other more-fundamental, structural traditions in the making in Queen's society. Given the fiscal tightrope walked by the fledgling college, assertive leadership was imperative. Queen's, in the Scottish tradition, had a *principal* – a first among equals – who faced the delicate challenge of shaping consensus through the force of his character rather than by executive fiat. In this respect, two clerics emerged as the epitome of Queen's resilience: Rev. William Snodgrass,

Principal George Munro Grant (1835–1902) infused Queen's tradition with a Presbyterian dedication to making education a force of social betterment. Grant's flinty determination to make Queen's a *national* institution echoed through the twentieth century.

principal from 1864 to 1877, and his successor down to 1902, Rev. George Munro Grant. Through their hard-nosed bargaining with province and Church, vigorous fundraising, and the embracing of a Scottish model of hands-on, flexible teaching, Queen's persevered. The term "Grantian dedication" has come to be the highest compliment payable to a Queen's principal.

Queen's forged its initial pedagogic traditions in these hardscrabble years: teaching that bonded teacher and student, dedication to public service, and a connection to the nation at large. Queen's drew heavily on a Scottish tradition that focused on excellence in the classroom – well-crafted lectures and close mentoring of students by professors. Queen's professors such as English scholar James Cappon, philospher John Watson, astronomer James Williamson, and theologian William Jordan etched their ideas into the minds of generations of young Canadians. Perhaps the university's greatest pedagogic polymath was Nathan Fellowes Dupuis, who down to his death in 1917 excelled as astronomer, mathematician, natural scientist, and chemist, not to mention stints as a librarian and the university's first dean of Applied Science. In 1893, the college displayed its dedication to practical education by inaugurating the province's first school of mining and was soon populating the Ontario northland with its graduates. Queen's was thus first and foremost a *teaching* university.

Empirical inquiry was not, however, absent. Political economy became a forte at Queen's, with pioneering Canadian political scientists such as Adam Shortt and Oscar "O.D." Skelton delving into such questions of national significance as the workings of the banking system and socialist ideology. Such scholarship made Queen's a "national" university from an early date. Principal Grant epitomized this unfolding national tradition. A muscular Christian, once described as a "locomotive in trousers," Grant had in the early 1870s joined engineer Sandford Fleming (who would serve as the university's first chancellor from 1880 to 1915) on an arduous coast-to-coast expedition in search of a route for a transcontinental railway that would bind the young nation together. In 1902, a joint effort of students, faculty, and alumni raised the funds to build Grant Hall in his memory. The ever-inventive Nathan Dupuis designed the tower's clock. A few Queen's women – such as pioneering social worker and controversial future mayor of Ottawa Charlotte Whitton – reinforced Queen's impressive national orientation. Queen's, nonetheless, remained a fundamentally male institution in the nineteenth century, a tradition that would prove doggedly durable.

Situated as it is in eastern Ontario on the margin of central-Ontarian growth, Queen's perforce became an inward-looking community, sustained by its own consensus building and camaraderie in the bosom of a small, provincial city. Since 1858, the incubator of much of this dedication and talent was the Alma Mater Society, the body that began a tradition of student self-governance on the Queen's campus. A student newspaper, the *Queen's Journal*, followed in 1872. In 1912, the university confirmed the inclusion of students in its decision-making by grafting the Scottish tradition of a rector onto its governance structure. The rector was elected by the students to represent their interests before the university's Board of Trustees. The rector elaborated another Scottish tradition transplanted into Queen's from Scotland: bicameral governance that allocated academic regulation to a faculty-dominated Senate, and bricks-and-mortar concerns to a Board of Trustees made up of outsiders. The presence of the principal at the deliberations of the trustees and as chair of the Senate ensured ongoing connection and dialogue across the spectrum of university governance. The rector gave students a voice in this dialogue. Scottish precedence supplied two other distinctive facets of Queen's governance in the 1870s: a Chancellor to act as the university's ceremonial head at convocations and a University Council, a kind of annual meeting of the Queen's clan – trustees, alumni, and senators – in an advisory capacity. Queen's thus developed a balanced, practical form of governance – one of its most enduring traditions.

Hilda Neatby died in 1975, before her charter volume of the Queen's history was complete. Completion fell to two Queen's historians, Roger Graham and Frederick Gibson, who brought the book to fruition in 1978. Collectively, the three historians portrayed Queen's as an institution that had evolved its own distinctive traditions by 1917. Collegiality, a bent for practical education, a respect for students' innate good judgment, and a dedication to national service had given the once frail college a *national* reputation. The report of Ontario's 1921 Royal Commission on University Finances caught the essence of the achievement: Queen's, it concluded, had "a marked individuality," one anchored by a "noteworthy contribution to the life of the Province" and "a student tradition of hard work, thrift, and maturity." In this sense, early Queen's coincided exactly with Cardinal Newman's notion of a small, collegial community.

It fell to Frederick W. Gibson to carry the story of Queen's and its traditions forward. A scholar of Prime Minister Mackenzie King's long mastery

Introduction 9

of Canada's fragile body politic, Gibson was, unlike Neatby, Queen's born-and-bred. He had graduated from Queen's with an honours BA in history in 1942, followed by an MA in 1944. As such, he had personally witnessed momentous events at Queen's – American President Franklin D. Roosevelt's receipt of a Queen's honorary degree at Richardson Stadium in 1938 and, a year later, the royal visit of King George to the campus. He acted as D.D. Calvin's research assistant for the centennial history. After graduate studies at Harvard, Gibson returned to his alma mater to teach history, eventually serving as the vice-principal, academic, in the mid-1960s. A meticulous researcher, Gibson was an avid supporter of the university archives, which became the designated custodian of Queen's history in 1960. The Queen's Archives in the Douglas Library thus became a crucial transmitter of Queen's tradition, a repository of artifacts, such as the signature-covered football used by the Queen's Golden Gaels to capture the 1923 Grey Cup, as well as the meeting-by-meeting record of the proceedings of the Board of Trustees and the Senate. Here Hilda Neatby mined the university's records to produce her history of the intrepid early decades of Queen's. In 1982, generous support from Ottawa broadcaster and Queen's economics BA Kathleen Ryan (sister of Charlotte Whitton) afforded the archives quarters of its own in a grand 1907 limestone building on the historic medical quadrangle. A year later, Professor Gibson's volume chronicled Queen's evolution down to 1961.

Like Neatby, Gibson chose an uplifting, resolute title: *To Serve and Yet Be Free*.[6] Promising a "candid, honest historical inquiry," including "warts and all," Gibson picked up many of Neatby's themes, thereby tracking Queen's tradition in evolution and adaptation. The tradition of "practical" men grappling with parlous financial resources through the lean 1920s and the catastrophic Dirty Thirties once again accentuated "a certain Scottish determination to survive." The university's treasurer through the Depression and later vice-principal, William Everett McNeill, epitomized the Presbyterian frugality that sustained Queen's through adversity. Gibson similarly underscored Queen's dependence on forceful principals, such as classicist William Hamilton Fyfe (1930–36) and geologist Robert Wallace (1936–51), whose role Gibson likened to that of a "sort of Governor-General." While George M. Grant had been Canadian-born, Gibson argued that the princi-

Queen's has also instilled its traditions in material objects – here, the football used by Queen's to capture the 1923 Grey Cup. The team flanked the victory with similar triumphs in 1922 and 1924. Team members, including renowned running back Frank "Pep" Leadlay, signed the ball, now preserved in the Queen's Archives.

palship of William Archibald Mackintosh (1951–61) heralded the indigenization of leadership at Queen's. Born in the nearby eastern-Ontario town of Madoc, Mackintosh was cut from the same cloth as the majority of Queen's students – recruits from rural Canada eager to advance in Canadian society. In this sense, Queen's traditional reliance on Scots and Britons for leadership and pedagogic skill began to diminish.

In Gibson's mind, Mackintosh also epitomized Queen's "national character." In the tradition of O.D. Skelton, Mackintosh had applied his training in political economy at Queen's to the challenges of Canada in depression and war. In 1945, Mackintosh's blueprint for Keynesian price and employment management had launched Canada on its postwar baby-boom prosperity. Together with other Queen's graduates, such as economist John Deutsch, Kingston-educated civil-service mandarins formed the core of what became known as the "Ottawa men," advising the Liberal government of Mackenzie King on the making of the social-welfare state. Political columnists quipped that Canada's welfare state was "born by King, out of Queen's." Gibson's volume also celebrated the perpetuation of "the Grant tradition" of "liberal humanists" at Queen's, who inculcated their students with the notion that education must prepare them to be "useful" in society. Amongst many in the university's growing faculty, Gibson wrote of history professor Arthur Lower's stalwart defence of civil liberties and of political scientist Alex Corry's insistence on the rights of the individual in the face of rising state power. For Principal Ronald Watts – to whom the task again fell of writing the second volume's foreword – "excellence in undergraduate teaching and responsiveness to national needs" seemed to be paramount in the Queen's tradition.

Watts also isolated Gibson's insistence on the university's "organic institutional vitality." To study, teach, or otherwise work at Queen's was, for Gibson, to be part of "a clan." In its governance, the university behaved as "one big fraternity," with "no

Principal Ronald Watts and Professor Frederick Gibson share a lighthearted moment at the 1984 launch of the second volume of Queen's history – *To Serve and Yet Be Free* – covering the years 1917 to 1961. Queen's, Gibson said, was "a living, human organism" propelled forward by its "traditions and loyalties."

rooted rancours." Consensus invariably emerged from the delicate tensions of bicameral decision making, with the principal as the crucial "narrow isthmus," to cite the metaphor invoked by Principal Mackintosh, between the two islands of academic regulation and fiscal authority. Students were accorded a wide measure of self-rule under the Alma Mater Society. The place consequently evoked lasting loyalty in faculty and graduates. Having promised warts and all, however, Gibson was not shy in citing the shortcomings of Queen's happy insularity. Perhaps because of its persistent scrapes with insolvency, its principals acquired the attitudes of Scottish "chieftains" eager to have their own way. Governance at Queen's had a tendency to become "more authoritarian than democratic." At other times, the Board of Trustees became imperious and found itself at loggerheads with the principal. Such power struggles had by the late 1950s, Gibson argued, reduced the Senate to a "rubber stamp body."

Furthermore, Gibson argued that Queen's determination to protect its distinctiveness and autonomy had at times produced an "ingrained conservatism and pessimism" that bound it too closely to the received wisdom of its traditions. "At Queen's," he warned, "the strong sense of community can at times degenerate into parochialism," citing Principal Mackintosh's 1953 admonition that "it is possible to be cosy but second-rate." In effect, *To Serve and Yet Be Free* left readers with the realization that Queen's had persisted – "prospered" seldom seemed to apply to the university's first 125 years – on the strength of its traditions, but that it also possessed the intuition of knowing when to modify, or even to abandon, those traditions when they became dysfunctional. In 1912, for instance, Queen's had surrendered the Presbyterian exclusivity guaranteed in its original charter in return for unimpeded access to the provincial purse as a secular institution. Under a federal amendment to its charter, Queen's College thus became a "university," with its Theological College assuming an arm's-length affiliation with its one-time parent. This fundamental break with tradition opened the little college in Kingston to the secularizing ethos of the twentieth century. At other junctures, Queen's shored up its traditions in order to preserve their stabilizing influence. In 1934, a mass meeting of the Alma Mater Society voted to prohibit fraternities on campus, thereby preserving the Presbyterian-inspired egalitarianism that had prevailed on campus. Prompted by the prospect of American-style fraternities in the medical faculty, Queen's students acted decisively to protect their clan from the invidiousness of exclusivity and privilege.

❖ ❖ ❖

This volume of the history of Queen's University encompasses the years 1961 to 2004, years in which Queen's grew sevenfold, from a small, collegial campus of 3,100 students into a sprawling multiversity of more than 20,000 students engaged in undergraduate studies on through to graduate and professional programs. This history employs as its principal point of interrogation a *testing* of the durability and utility of tradition at Queen's.

How did Queen's, long possessed of a keen sense of its own distinctiveness, adapt and survive in the face of a Canadian society that was engaged in dramatic social, political, and economic alteration predicated on diversity, inclusion, and globalization?

How did a university that had traditionally drawn its strength from Anglo "poor boy" stock in rural Ontario adjust to a Canadian society that was becoming urban, multicultural, and multiracial?

How did Queen's, a campus once so indelibly male in its ethos – "*So, boys, go in and win*" – accommodate shifting attitudes to women's place in Canadian society? How did these pressures alter *what* was taught on its campus and *who* delivered that teaching? To what degree could tradition be bent to such new circumstances – credentialism, employment equity, Charter Rights? When does tradition become dysfunctional? Indeed, in the last half-century what traditions has Queen's jettisoned and what traditions has it invented to fill the void? How has tradition bolstered Queen's distinctiveness as a "national" institution? And what does the process of testing Queen's tradition tell us about its agility and openness in matters of intellect and governance?

It can be argued that the tension between the tug of tradition and the impulse to move forward drove the history of Queen's University in these years. Tradition is usually conceived of as a conservative force, a brake on precipitate action. Throughout his *To Serve and Yet Be Free*, Professor Gibson frequently returned to the notion that Queen's was a place of "ingrained conservatism and pessimism," both of which were attitudes forged in the course of its storied battles to survive fiscal starvation, war, and sectarian difference. Many recalled that Principal Grant, forever condemned to drum for money for his university, often remarked that his epitaph should be taken from Luke 16:22: "And it came to pass that the beggar died." But the beggar never did die, principally because, as Gibson noted, the university was populated by "practical men with a practical object in view," who acquired a knack for modifying tradition. Queen's thus entered the 1960s as a conservative institution bent in liberal directions – to national service, to dynamic teaching, and egalitarianism in its precinct. *To serve and yet be free.*

While the university had long since shed its overt Presbyterian affiliation, strong Presbyterian impulses still shaped its social and educational dedication. One went to Queen's to elevate oneself and to "do good" for society. This was the "Queen's spirit." "As an institution of Scottish origin," Queen's Principal Alex Corry would write to former Ontario premier Leslie Frost in 1963, "you can see that, like the Scots generally, we have a good conceit of ourselves." Queen's in the late twentieth century would thus proceed by cautiously – perhaps at times too cautiously – testing the physics of its traditions under the pressure of rapidly changing times. Through all this, Queen's was ever conscious that the knowledge and wisdom ingrained in its traditions provided a modicum of stability in tumultuous times. But there was a keen awareness that reluctance to yield to the imperatives of change could court instability and irrelevance. Historian Arthur Lower, a Queen's scholar never shy with his opinions, sensed the tension and would lecture Board of Trustees chairman J. Douglas Gibson some years later: "There is always a large element in Queen's that can be depended upon to fight for a rough present expediency. It is unfortunate when it is yielded to, as thereby the University turns traitor to its own excuse for existing." For Queen's, the late twentieth century would be a contest of expediency and tradition.

1

In the Fall of 1961

Dear old Queen's. Her 100 years have brought rich rewards to one and all … to you who lead, we gladly say: 'we follow!' and to Queen's our Alma Mater: 'lang may her lum reek.'
William J. Russell, BA 1900, to W.A. Mackintosh, September 1961

Our decent, homely limestone.
Principal William Hamilton Fyfe, 1937

We are concerned to maintain the balance and compactness of the University and we are concerned to maintain the quality of its instruction.
Principal W.A. Mackintosh to minister of education, Toronto, 1956

A happy place, no rooted rancours … the inherited values we still honour.
Principal J. Alex Corry, installation speech, October 1961

One Autumn Afternoon …

Queen's new principal had never been an avid football fan. As a Rhodes Scholar at Oxford in the 1920s, James Alexander Corry had kicked a soccer ball around and, as was expected of Canadians studying in Britain, had played on the university hockey team. Indeed, Corry could boast of bringing a hockey championship back to Oxford from a tournament in Switzerland. Since then his interest in sports had waned; occasional treks in the Alberta foothills with the Alpine Club and Sunday-afternoon walks to sort out the week's cares were the closest he came to athletic endeavour. Since arriving at Queen's in 1936, Corry had applied himself to the classroom as the architect of Politics 2, the foundation course in democratic governance given by the department of economics and political studies. His stature had grown with his appointment as the university's Hardy Professor of Political Science and the publication in 1946 of his seminal book *Democratic Government and Politics*. Soon after William "Bill" Mackintosh, a departmental colleague and prominent Keynesian economist, assumed the principalship in 1951, Corry became his de facto understudy, serving as the university's vice-principal. Excellence in scholarship and academic administration, to Corry's mind, did not require his attendance on fall Saturday afternoons at Richardson Stadium, Queen's hallowed playing ground.

That changed on 20 October 1961, when Corry – the product of a one-room school in Perth County, Ontario, and of the University of Saskatchewan law school – was installed as Queen's thirteenth principal. Corry had taken the helm of a university that perhaps more than any other in Canada plotted its course from the chart of tradition. Queen's principals were expected to be genetically attuned to tradition on their campus; tradition must be honoured, nurtured, and also constantly modified, if they were to succeed. Football was central to that perpetuation at Queen's. The sport had been played at Queen's since the 1880s; its nature had evolved from the rough and tumble of "rugby football" into the modern game of football, with its forward passing and alternating squads of defensive and offensive players. It had been a glorious evolution: in 1922, right in its own Richardson Stadium, Queen's had captured the Grey Cup, emblematic of national football supremacy, by drubbing the Edmonton Elks 13–1. To reinforce the point, they won the cup again in both 1923 and 1924. In 1923, Queen's newly founded, student-run radio station, CFRC, treated the campus to a pioneering play-by-play broadcast of the Gaels' battle with McGill, and a myth sprang up that the station's call sign stood for "Canada's Famous Rugby Champions."[1] Over the

Football Saturday: the Queen's band marches onto Richardson Field to initiate another autumn afternoon of football. First formed as a brass band in 1905, the Queen's bands grew into an ensemble of pipers, drummers, colour guard, Highland dancers, majorettes, and cheerleaders, all accompanied by Boo-Hoo, the university's bear mascot. After World War II, military-style uniforms were replaced by the Stewart tartan.

years, the names of football stalwarts like Guy Curtis and Frank "Pep" Leadlay (who led Queen's to twenty-six consecutive victories in the twenties) became embedded in the university's folklore.[2]

The English social historian Eric Hobsbawn once famously suggested that societies "invent" tradition to bolster their cohesion and self-confidence. Invented tradition reflects both actual, lived experience – battles, persecution, discovery – and elements that are consciously groomed and introduced to that identity. Early in its history, Queen's had learned the power of invented tradition. Much of that invention took place on the gridiron. Football at Queen's wore

In the Fall of 1961 15

a Gaelic uniform; the team played as *Gaels* – the storied Celtic raiders – and the fans urged them on with the Gaelic yell *Cha Gheill!* – "No Surrender!" Since 1925, the Scottishness of Queen's football had been accentuated by one of the country's finest pipe bands, which paraded to the stadium and marched at half-time clothed in their Royal Stewart tartan kilts. The Queen's bands had become roving ambassadors, epitomizing the university's ethos at convocations and projecting it to the world beyond at Grey Cup and Santa Claus parades. Sword dancers and acrobatic cheerleaders completed the ensemble. Moreover, gridiron fervour begat its own songbook. By the early twentieth century, Queen's students were belting out lyrics to songs like "Queen's College Colours": "Queen's colours are the dearest in the world / So, boys, go in and win."[3] And, well into the post–Second World War era, football at Queen's had its vivid "mascots" – a succession of bears, all named "Boo-Hoo," and the renowned cheerleader Alfie Pierce, said to be the progeny of a runaway American slave, who urged the crowd on from the sidelines dressed in a John Philip Sousa–like bandsman's uniform.[4]

Thus, just weeks after his ritual installation, Corry found himself bundling up in a woollen overcoat on a brisk mid-November day and heading across campus from his new home at Summerhill, the 1839 neoclassical stone villa which served as the principal's residence, to the walled bastion of Richardson Stadium. Tradition beckoned. As principal, Bill Mackintosh had relished his role as the university's most prominent football fan. He seldom missed a game; in the fall of 1955, when the university had given an honorary degree to American presidential hopeful Adlai Stevenson, Mackintosh had arrived late at a ceremony, which had inconveniently coincided with a more vigorous ritual at the stadium. At half-time, Mackintosh would hurry down to the Gaels' locker room to urge "his boys" on to victory or to encourage them to regroup in the face of unexpected opposition. Every fall, he wrote a "Principal's Message" to the team, an exhortation to players and fans alike to excel. His Monday-morning correspondence to bureaucrats and fellow academics often concluded with a Queen's sports update. Mackintosh also became a confidant of the Gaels' redoubtable head coach, the cigar-chomping Frank Tindall. A crew-cut American, Tindall had come to Queen's in 1947 from the University of Syracuse, where he was an All-American, and delivered Yates Cup championships, emblematic of intercollegiate supremacy, in 1955 and 1956. To his devoted players, Tindall was already affectionately dubbed "Kindly Old Coach" and "The Mentor."

Mackintosh had fashioned his own small addition to the football culture at Queen's. The university competed in a small, yet intensely competitive, league against McGill, Toronto, and Western, so football tribalism ran deep. It was, Mackintosh often wrote, a league of "worthy rivals and old companions." Whenever Queen's played in a crucial playoff game, Mackintosh invited the president of the rival university to come to lunch and then attend the game as his guest; he expected the same invitation when the Gaels played on enemy turf. A ten-dollar wager was always placed on the outcome. In November 1960, the principal had been obliged to surrender a ten-dollar bill to Principal Cyril James of McGill after the Redmen humbled the Gaels 21–0. "It's a black day in Kingston-town as a foreign mob march down Princess Street," the *Queen's Journal* captioned a photo of celebrating McGill fans.[5]

The fall of 1961, however, saw a string of Queen's victories. The team seemed headed for an undefeated season and automatic possession of the Yates Cup. The stands roared when quarterback Cal Connor connected with wingback Bill Sirman and the score rose. But then, on 11 November, the Redmen toppled the Gaels 15–7 behind the quarterbacking of Tom Skypeck, a talented American golden boy who was studying dentistry at McGill. Skypeck stymied Queen's with a shotgun offence, which the Tricolour had never seen before. Queen's fans were stunned; local sports writer Paul Rimstead, who had breezily predicted victory for

Gaels coach Frank Tindall displays the fruit of his team's 1961 Yates Cup intercollegiate victory. Syracuse-born Tindall first coached Queen's in 1939 and then returned after the war to the Queen's gridiron in 1947. By the time he retired in 1975, the Gaels had accumulated eight intercollegiate championships. Most pictures of Tindall depict him on the sidelines, chomping a cigar and locked in intense discussion with his players, players who revered him for his leadership.

Queen's, was obliged to eat a copy of the *Whig-Standard* in contrition. Even the *Queen's Review* grudgingly admitted that Skypeck was "brilliant."[6] Now a sudden-death playoff for the Yates Cup was in order.

So, on Saturday, 18 November, Corry of Queen's, James of McGill, and eight thousand other fans crammed into Richardson Stadium for the season's finale. Through the end-zone gate came the band and the cheerleaders. Student constables frisked fans in a largely vain attempt to keep liquor out of the stands. A large contingent of McGill fans was in a cocky mood, and McGill halfback Willie Lambert tossed around a ball with "*Oil Thigh Beware*" inscribed on it. A CBC crew geared up to televise the contest, with the quick-lipped Fred Sgambati as commentator. Queen's fans quietly prayed that coach Tindall had beefed up his defence against the vaunted Skypeck shotgun. On a campus where football had become the central organizing cultural value, tradition seemed to hang in the balance.

Two hours later, Alex Corry was ten dollars' richer. "YATES OURS ... They Came, They Saw, We Conquered" screamed the headline in the *Queen's Journal*.[7] The 11–0 shutout hinged on a first-quarter McGill fumble, which Queen's defensive back Kent Plumley scooped up and carried to the McGill thirteen-yard line. On the next play, quarterback Cal Connor broke the huddle in Queen's own version of the shotgun, fooling McGill and allowing Connor to dance his way unscathed into the end zone for a lead that was padded by a field goal in the third quarter and a single in the last quarter. Statistically, McGill was the superior team, but Skypeck's inability to find the end zone decided the day. As the clock ran down at the game's end, pandemonium broke out on the field. Hundreds of Queen's engineering students poured onto the field to uphold another

Queen's tradition: protecting the school's goalposts from marauding out-of-towners. The engineers were clad in their yellowy-gold nylon faculty jackets, new "traditional" attire at Queen's. Many of them also wore gold-painted construction hard hats adorned with horns, beer cans, and decals. Corry was somewhat discomfited by the spectacle, especially with the venerable principal of McGill at his side. Corry would spend much of the next week replying to indignant letters from alumni and townsfolk perturbed by the sight of young men, who looked more like a paramilitary unit than high-minded young students, running amok. All in good fun, he bravely assured them.

Down in the locker room, champagne filled the Yates Cup and line coach Hal "Moose" McCarney was given a "beer shampoo." Sportswriter Rimstead was thrown fully clothed into the shower. Coach Tindall was even said to have cracked a smile, although his own son, Frank junior, had seriously injured his neck in the game. Outside, Queen's fans quickly emptied the stadium, leaving the goalposts to McGill souvenir hunters. Later in the day, Skypeck's uniform and helmet mysteriously disappeared from the bus en route to the Montreal Street CNR station. Like Corry, the Alma Mater Society student government spent the next week issuing apologies and recovering Skypeck's apparel. The Kingston Bus Company, on the other hand, dispatched a bill for $470.10 to McGill for damage to its buses. As the afternoon receded into November darkness, thousands of Queen's students, headed by an impromptu band, funnelled into the downtown, where they performed a huge "snake dance" down Princess Street. The exuberant procession wound its way in and out of Princess Street landmarks, including Woolworth's, Loblaws Groceteria, the Odeon Theatre, and the Bowladrome.[8] There were few complaints; Kingstonians chalked up such behaviour to youthful exuberance and tended to merge Queen's success with that of their limestone city. Although the Redmen would take their revenge and win the Yates the next year, Tindall and his Gaels were in fact on the verge of a glorious decade of gridiron success.

A Sense of Tradition

Prowess on the football field was hardly the only core ingredient of Queen's sense of tradition. Football was instead more a reflection of deeper strengths in a university that had been evolving since its founding in 1841. Indeed, much of the tradition displayed that November afternoon was either invented or predicated on dubious grounds. Queen's, for instance, had been founded by a coterie of lowland Scottish Presbyterians, who spoke English, not Gaelic. Gaelic at Queen's was largely a pretense. In 1937, former principal Fyfe had told the BBC that Queen's was "fortunate" to have a belligerent Gaelic yell for its football fans, but he admitted that "it is little understood and universally mispronounced."[9] Well into the twentieth century, the university had offered the Cameron scholarship for the best Gaelic scholar or speaker on campus, but few ever possessed the credentials to claim it. If Gaelic had withered, the spell of Scottish music had not. Queen's radio station 9BT (later CFRC) launched its inaugural broadcast in 1922 with fourth-year engineering student George Parsons playing "The Bluebells of Scotland" on his cornet.[10] Years later, in 1964, when Marvin McInnis arrived to be interviewed for a professorship in economics, he was captivated by the skirl of the bagpipes floating across the campus. It was Burns night, and he was hooked on Queen's tradition.

The skirl of the pipes and the fling of sword dancing were Highland Scottish traditions that Queen's had over time appropriated for its own identity building. Throughout the year, Queen's students continued to wear their tams daily to demonstrate their commonality (frosh being required to demonstrate their inferiority by pulling the rim of the tam down over their ears). The university's adeptness at *inventing* useful tradition was further

Frosh wash cars for charity in downtown Kingston, introducing them to a Queen's tradition of service to the community. A dapper "Vig" (short for vigilante) ensures the quality of the job.

exhibited on that November Saturday, with the donning of faculty jackets by the engineering faculty. The jackets – first fashioned out of silk and cloth, then out of nylon, and eventually out of leather – were a postwar phenomenon rooted in the tastes of the flood of young engineers who arrived on campus in the late 1940s. Many had wartime experience with uniforms and now sought the same kind of visual identity in their daily academic life. In the 1950s, engineering students also intensified the initiation rituals of their faculty by inventing a greasepole ceremony, using a looted University of Toronto goalpost slathered in lubricating oil and offal to test the dexterity of each year's freshmen. And the goal of this slippery exercise? To remove a woollen tam – another emblem of life in the Scottish Highlands – from the pole`s apex.

At some primordial level, members of the Queen's community had come to understand that tradition and its rituals provided them with a bonding agent, a means of building cohesion and smoothing the ongoing operation of their closed society. The American sociologist Edward Shils has remarked that "in all the rational calculation and cognition [of a society], there is thus much that is traditional. This does not mean 'wrong'; it does not mean 'right'; it means only 'traditional' in the sense that the end and the technique have been learned from others who taught or exemplified them ... Tradition enters into the constitution of meaningful conduct by defining its ends and standards and even its means."[11]

At Queen's in 1961, that introduction to "meaningful conduct" began for incoming students at an evening ceremony early in their freshmen initiation week. The "tradition service" commenced with a torch procession to Grant Hall, followed by pipes, drums, and Gaelic dancing, and culminating with the almost-sacred "donning of the tams." For the first time, newcomers to Queen's locked arms and belted out an *Oil Thigh* in kick-line fashion. To emphasize this "laying on" of the faith, the principal, deans, and university chaplain all graced the service. "You have to be weaned from the milk of parental clucking and teachers' solicitude," Corry would tell the frosh in 1964. "University teachers are not going to hover and fuss over you." But, it was implied, everything about the place would from now on mold your character and conduct.[12]

For faculty, the acculturation to Queen's began less ritualistically. Political-studies professor John Meisel recalls that his interview for a position at Queen's in 1949 began when he was met at the train station by Alex Corry, then Hardy Professor, and taken to the Corry home, where over the next forty-eight hours he sensed that he was "giving Queen's the chance of assessing whether I was worthy of an offer." Having passed the test, Meisel quickly melded into the collegiality – "excessive interdisciplinary schmoozing" – of the faculty.[13] Meisel's fellow political scientist Ted Hodgetts, who had been at the university since 1945, saw Queen's as "a kind of club."[14] For others, the tradition of teaching on the Kingston campus unfolded just as informally and convivially: when Brian Osborne arrived at the university as an assistant professor of geography in the mid-1960s, he was immediately struck by the ingrained "family" nature of the place. To his astonishment, Principal Corry invited him to his office to welcome him, and later personally introduced him at the next faculty board.[15] In 1949, a faculty dining room had been squeezed into a corner of the Students' Memorial Building, and there faculty bonded over fifty-cent lunches and "ice cream for all."[16] James Leith, a young historian of the French Revolution, hired in 1961, was struck by the egalitarianism of the faculty club: an unwritten rule obliged single diners to join an already occupied table rather than dining alone.[17] For morning coffee, many Queen's professors wandered over to the Queen's Tea Room, a convivial greasy spoon run by a Greek-Canadian named George Sakell at the corner of Division and Union, where cigarette smoke and academic gossip swirled. On a somewhat higher plane, one Saturday evening a month during the academic year, select members of the faculty convened as the "Saturday Club," a kind of essay society, at which members presented papers on topics of general interest. The Saturday Club had roots into the 1890s and offered faculty a chance to air their intellects over coffee, cake, and cigars.[18] For less high-minded scholars, there was always the allure of an evening of poker with M.C. "Mac" Urquhart, the bachelor head of economics, who spent his days unravelling the national accounts and his evenings dealing cards. To teach at Queen's was to be part of a chummy, male-centric camaraderie. Few ever forgot its comfortable rhythm.

In 1951, a faculty association had been formed, but its function was hardly confrontational. Instead, it simply facilitated dialogue and common purpose between faculty and the administration. The phrase "very kindly" habitually surfaced in its newsletter to describe the actions of the principal towards the professoriate.[19] At the annual faculty dinner in the spring of 1962, association president Hugh Thorburn caught the copacetic nature of the teaching establishment at Queen's: "Enduring communities of effort, whether universities or whatever, do not consist of physical things or even organizational charts ... The real fabric of such communities is woven of the lives of the persons that do their work." At

Queen's, he concluded, the "university teacher gives himself freely." Shortly after Corry took office, Thorburn assured the principal that "Queen's is not a university like the others."[20] In their reminiscences of their experience at Queen's in the fifties and sixties, Thorburn and many of his faculty colleagues almost invariably employed the word "family" to describe the university that surrounded them.

The Queen's community inherited by Alex Corry in 1961 was thus largely cohesive, convivial, and guided by the received wisdom of tradition. Corry would later remark in a memoir that he found the university "in good heart, well-staffed for the most part, and free from debilitating strife and jealousies."[21] Queen's was, by virtue of its situation, a small, manageable community, amenable to the conditioning of tradition. It found itself in a modest, eastern-Ontario community of just over sixty thousand people, removed from the dynamic pulse of the so-called Golden Horseshoe at the other end of Lake Ontario. Kingston was, as many historians have remarked, a constellation of self-contained enclaves – Loyalist Kingston, military Kingston, working-class Kingston, academic Kingston, and penal Kingston – within the larger urban shell.[22] Each of these enclaves in the so-called "Old Ontario Strand" tended to be introverted and activated by its own values. United Empire Loyalists in the city saw themselves as "the old stones of Kingston." The Royal Military College, founded in 1876, lived in its own hermetic world of martial ritual. When English author and literary critic C. Day Lewis visited Queen's in the 1950s, he likened Kingston to "the Boston of Canada, without Boston's complacence and starchiness."[23]

Queen's, with its well-honed traditions typified the pattern: in the fall of 1961, the Queen's community comprised just over 3,000 mainly undergraduate students in daily communion with 215 professors, a relationship intensified by the university's constricted precinct. That precinct was neatly contained in a box bounded by Stuart, University, Barrie, and Clergy streets, a configuration that echoed the university's original nineteenth-century land endowment, which had been carved out of the two-hundred-acre Loyalist land grant given to the Reverend John Stuart. Solid limestone buildings set the aesthetic tone of the campus. In the late 1950s, the campus had jumped westward across University Avenue to allow construction of the university's first dedicated administration building, Richardson Hall, as well as Dunning Hall for the bulging commerce and political-economy programs and Macdonald Hall for the fledgling law faculty. By 1961, space was at a premium at Queen's. The daily rhythms of the Queen's community were consequently played out in the closely packed geography of classrooms, residences, playing fields, and administrative buildings. At nightfall, faculty would filter into residential areas around the campus and some students – mainly upper-year males – would seek out the boarding houses of Sydenham Ward. But the overall culture of Queen's was inward-looking. Most undergraduates trooped to nearby residences for cafeteria food or to the Douglas Library for study or to the Bews gym for a sweat. Only the university's support staff – secretaries, janitors, gardeners – enjoyed an easy reciprocal relationship with the greater Kingston community.

By the early 1960s, Corry would have had little difficulty in identifying the core values of the university's sense of identity and self-importance. All principals of Queen's inherited a dossier of tradition as they assumed their appointment, tradition that would both sustain them and at the same time demand progressive nurturing. Future principal Ron Watts would sense the same endowment two decades later: "Queen's had developed an organic institutional vitality, which could transcend the vicissitudes occasioned by external fortunes or by internal tensions which surfaced from time to time in her own family."[24] This vitality had carried Queen's through times of adversity – such as the struggle of Principals William Snodgrass and George Grant to pull the university back from the financial abyss in the late nineteenth century, the painful adjustments provoked by two world wars, and the catastrophic global depression of the thirties. Queen's administrators were fond of quoting the words of 1930s professor of civil engineering Sandy Macphail: "Queen's has the stubbornness of all living things."[25]

Unshakable Values

That stubbornness rested on what seemed a set of unshakable values that permeated the university. First and foremost, Queen's was a teaching university dedicated to undergraduate excellence. Secondly, it prided itself that the education offered benefited not just the immediate recipient, but also the broader society it served: a Queen's education was decidedly about public service. And, thirdly, if Queen's was to help fashion the society around it, it must conduct its own affairs in an egalitarian and effective manner. Thus, over time the university had devised a workable and harmonious system of university governance that allowed its trustees, senior administrators, faculty, and students to find common ground and at the same time enjoy a generous measure of autonomy in their affairs. This was jointly epitomized by the presence at Queen's of Canada's longest-extant student government, the Alma Mater Society, and by the carefully balanced jurisdictional divide between the Board of Trustees and the Senate in the strategic governance of the university. The administrative tradition at Queen's was one of *shared*, *consultative* power, not of power from on high. Out of these priorities, autonomies, and tensions the university had been able to fashion a rich communal life, the last lodestar of Queen's received culture. When Alex Corry took the podium in Grant Hall on the day of his installation in 1961, he was quick to project his respect for "the inherited values we still honour." Under Bill Mackintosh's principalship, "standards have been defended – and raised, wise appointments made, and new ventures auspiciously launched." His task, Corry noted, would be to protect this patrimony of tradition, while at the same time adjusting it to what he called "the rapid thrusting of the universities into greatly enhanced responsibilities in our society" in the era of the "electronic and rocket revolution."[26]

Above all else, teaching was the lifeblood of Queen's. On its founding in 1841, the college had been powerfully shaped not only by a denominational urge to project Presbyterian values into Upper Canadian society, but also by an impulse rooted in the eighteenth-century Scottish Enlightenment to impart useful knowledge. When the Catholic cleric John Henry Newman delivered his famous lectures on "the idea of a university" in Dublin in 1852, he noted that there were many routes to the "broadening of knowledge." One of them was the "Scotch" method "for lecturing." Lectures in places like the University of Edinburgh were seen as the principal means of conveying knowledge and thereby provoking students into a rational, empirical, and yet humanistic exploration of themselves and their world. Such knowledge, Newman advised, promoted "an acquired illumination … a habit, a personal possession and an inward endowment." Through lecturing and interrogation of the matter at hand, the professor might equip a student with "a habit of mind" that would last through life, "of which the attributes are freedom, equitableness, calmness, moderation, and wisdom … a philosophical habit."[27] This conception of education was carried across the Atlantic to the colonial college in Kingston by many of its Scottish-trained professors and through such things as books donated by Edinburgh to the college's puny library. As late as 1966, the Queen's student-elected rector, Leonard Brockington, reiterated this philosophy: a university should never be "a factory of diplomas, but a forge of character and an armoury of citizenship."[28]

By the 1850s, the syllabus at the fledging college (as it would be officially called until 1912) reflected the Scottish inclinations of its founders. Lectures were offered in theology, the sciences, medical practice, moral philosophy, Latin, Greek, and mathematics. In its 1853–54 report of its activities, the college catalogued its offering to students, noting that "on each of these subjects a pretty full course of lectures was given. During the afternoon, however, the students were regularly examined on the lectures of the morning."[29] Students were called to synthesize their knowledge in essays; theological students wrote practice sermons. This tradition was successfully transmitted through the university's subsequent evolution. Whether it was Adam Shortt teaching political economy, James Cappon teaching English literature, or Nathan Dupuis expounding on chemistry and mathematics, Queen's made its mark as a *teaching* university. Queen's reputation for teaching extended well beyond the predictable orthodox syllabus. Since 1942, the Queen's School of English had taught English to nuns from Quebec and, later, to international students. The Department of Extension had carried Queen's learning, either by mail or by roving professors, to communities, largely rural, spread across the nation. A summer school every year gave schoolteachers an opportunity to upgrade their qualifications on the leafy campus. The School of Business reinforced the pattern, offering extramural courses to accountants and bankers (almost four thousand of them in 1961–62).

Queen's had thus nailed its colours to the mast of teaching. Faced with the greater size and geographic centrality of the University of Toronto, and with its frequent financial droughts and relatively isolated situation in eastern Ontario, excellence in pedagogy afforded Queen's a distinctive edge. A 1949 brief to the provincial minister of education pleading for more generous annual support concluded, for example, with the bold assertion: "*Queen's is by a wide margin the second in size and range of the Ontario universities. It was the first to begin teaching.*"[30] Many fell into the habit of describing Queen's as "the Princeton of the North," where the grooming of bright young undergraduates was the primary and dedicated aim.[31]

There was, however, a downside to this devotion to teaching undergraduates. Research and the teaching of graduate students at Queen's lived in the shadows. Professorial reputations at Queen's rested on classroom performance, not on the shelves of the university library. Research was to be shoehorned between other duties. With few sources of research funding available in Ottawa and Toronto, professors could apply for support from the university's Committee on Scientific Research or its Arts Research Committee. But funds were tight, often dependent upon the generosity of benefactors such as Oshawa automotive mogul and philanthropist Sam McLaughlin. What money there was tended to go to senior, established scholars. For instance, George Whalley's research on Coleridge's marginalia and John Meisel's analysis of the 1962 federal election were funded by the R. Samuel McLaughlin Trust Fund. Graduate studies lived a similar shadowy existence at Queen's. There was no dedicated faculty of graduate studies, only a Board of Graduate Studies set up in 1943. In the fall of 1961, Queen's registered only 203 graduate students.

Nonetheless, a freshman student arriving at Queen's in the fall of 1961 soon encountered a remarkable array of professors, whose talents in the classroom would indelibly impress them. Classes at Queen's were small, and contact with professors was frequent and constructive. Soon after he arrived to begin studying politics, John Rae (BA '67) of Ottawa picked up on the "intimacy" of the Queen's campus and the "dialogue and respect" that existed in the classroom.[32] Laboratory work, field schools, and honours seminars all enhanced this intimate pattern. Throughout the term, the Politics Club brought professors and students together to discuss the latest trends in national governance. The pages of the *Queen's Alumni Review* through the late decades of the twentieth century yield a harvest of reminiscences of Queen's professors who lingered in students' minds long after graduation. Take, for instance, Alfred "Fred" Jolliffe in Geology. Since the founding of its School of Mining in 1893, Queen's had nurtured generations of geologists and mining engineers under the tutelage of renowned professors such as Willet Miller and William Nicol. In 1950, just when the department changed its name to Geological Sciences, it acquired the services of Jolliffe, who was in many ways "a geologist's geologist." His undergraduate training at Queen's in mineralogy and chemistry had been followed by a Princeton doctorate and field work with the Geological Survey of Canada. As the atomic era dawned, Jolliffe spent a decade scouring Canada's North for uranium, becoming so familiar in the area that an island near Yellowknife was named in his honour. A much-published expert on ore formations and Precambrian geology, Jolliffe filled his spare time preparing the first English translation of the work of sixteenth-century German geologist Georgius Agricola.

In the classroom, Jolliffe took charge of the department's introductory course, Geology 100. For him, geology was not simply the study of rocks and their physical characteristics. Instead, it was the study of man's relation with the rocks, a *cultural* history of geology. Man must be seen as an "integral part" of nature: "the study of man in nature is essential for understanding the nature of man."[33] In the lecture hall, the bow-tied Jolliffe mesmerized his students. A chain smoker, he began his hour by opening a window on the fourth floor of Miller Hall and lighting a cigarette. As each cigarette expired, he lit another from its tip and neatly expelled the butt out the window. But it was the portrait of Canada's landscape that stayed in students' minds. Ned Franks, a mid-1950s undergraduate in Geology 100, never forgot what he learned. Franks went on to become a Queen's professor and an expert on Canada's political landscape and would impress colleagues on government commissions by pointing out cuestas – slopes of sedimentary rock – in the Arctic landscape.[34]

Franks's gravitation into political economy was largely the result of magnetic professors in that field. There was, of course, Alex Corry, presiding over his famous Politics 2, but Corry was not a stylish lecturer, preferring to regurgitate chapters of his well-regarded treatise – *Democratic Government and Politics* – on the need for democracies to resist

Professor A.W. "Fred" Jolliffe lecturing to Geology 010 students in Miller Hall. With chalk in one hand and a cigarette in the other, Jolliffe conducted students through what he called "4,600,000 years of earth history."

all-powerful collectivist states. More highly regarded was Frank Knox in Economics 4. Knox was a "boy from rural Ontario," who had trained as a schoolteacher, served in the Great War, gone on to graduate studies at Chicago and Harvard, and then joined the faculty at Queen's in 1924. His ECON 4 was intended to be an introduction to the new-fangled discipline of economics. Instead, on most days it became a rumination on whatever theme Knox felt like pursuing – the gold standard, the efficiency of tariffs, monetary policy. His agenda was often influenced by something he had seen in the morning papers, something about which he felt students would need to understand in a broader context. Always meticulously prepared and punctual, he perched on a desk on the lecture-hall stage, scratched out a crude outline on the board, folded his hands, and then launched into a monologue. Many students complained that it was impossible to take notes; others were stunned by how Knox's intellectual peregrinations jolted their world views. His final examination always posed just one broad-ranging question and asked students to supply both a positive and negative reaction to it. He taught senior-year classes on the business cycle and monetary policy, and edited *The Canadian Banker*, in which Knox freely editorialized on economic issues in his monthly column. His students went off into the world of modern economics and policy making as apostles well versed in, for instance, the implications of Bretton Woods and the mechanics of Keynesianism. A future dean at the university, Duncan Sinclair, who grew up around Queen's, where his father was a biochemist, recalled that Knox was "absolutely a master of awakening curiosity."35 Years later, in 1989, the Alma Mater Society would name its new faculty teaching award after the boy from Peterborough who never got around to completing his American graduate degrees.

Small-town Ontario also supplied Queen's with an outstanding English professor. George Whalley was Kingston-born, the son of the dean of St George's Cathedral, who went to Bishop's University before winning a Rhodes Scholarship to Oxford's Oriel College in 1936. He brought a vigour to his life reminiscent of Queen's muscular Christian of a principal, George Grant. He loved music and messing about in boats, but, above all else, he loved words and their ability to convey human emotion. War brought out the Anglo-centric patriotism in Whalley, and for five years in the Royal Navy he experienced the fear and adventure of combat at sea. In 1960, he would describe to readers of *The Atlantic* his small role as junior officer on a British destroyer during the chase of the German battleship *Bismarck*. With peace, he became a specialist in the poetry of Coleridge. A doctorate from the University of London led to a job in the Queen's English department in 1950. Whalley cut a wide swath in Kingston: he commanded the local naval reserve unit, read poetry on the local

English professor George Whalley, pondering his Coleridge scholarship. Queen's graduate student Michael Ondaatje would admiringly write that Whalley was "never merely bookish … He liked to bring knowledge into the real world of daily life."

radio stations, kept a parrot as a pet, walked the streets absent-mindedly with a book in hand, and sailed Lake Ontario like some sort of Canadian Hemingway. He conducted a crusade against the incursion of jargon into the language: "This is a godforsaken and desolate zone, as deadly as uranium 235, to be avoided at all costs if what we have in mind is the civilized study of 'English.'"36

But it was in the classroom that he left the largest wake. Unlike Knox, Whalley was seldom well-organized and often arrived late for class. Once there, he seemed to go into a kind of transcendent trance to summon up an appropriate theme for the day's contemplation. As one student later recalled: "Shuffling students, institutional green walls, the smell of wet wool and galoshes faded before the luminous vision of George, seated on the lip of a great alabaster half shell with legs dangling down, ascending into universal light whilst engaged in an exposition of Shelley's 'To a Skylark.'"

For an hour, students sat fixated, enthralled, and overawed by Whalley's ability to bring poetry to life. As the class ended, a timid student might often ask: "Please, sir, are we responsible for *that*?"[37] Few could resist Whalley's way with words. His exposure on the CBC widened the net of his influence. Aspiring poets came to Kingston to feed off the Whalley aura. One of them, the celebrated poet and novelist Michael Ondaatje, who did graduate studies at Queen's, would later salute his mentor as "this fabulously wise man."[38]

Queen's professional schools had their own galvanic personalities. The education of doctors had long relied on demonstration and exposition. The cluster of medical buildings behind Summerhill all possessed steep-sided lecture halls with overhanging observation galleries. Dissection rooms allowed lectures to feature grim anatomical demonstrations. Like all medical schools, Queen's small medical school – 330 pre-medical and full-time students in 1961 – relied on a mélange of full-time academic staff and local medical practitioners to impart the foundations of medicine. By the early 1960s, it was becoming difficult to maintain this balance between academic and clinical obligations. A relatively small regional hospital, Kingston General, strained to provide enough "beds" to sustain clinical instruction, while local doctors tended to resist the medical school's need to teach students in the wards as an intrusion into their daily business of tending to their patients. Nonetheless, the faculty had its classroom stars. Dr Walter Ford Connell, known by his middle name so as not to confuse him with his father, Walter, a bacteriologist who had headed the department of medicine at Queen's until 1941, was a student favourite. The younger Connell had been born on Arch Street in Kingston, in the shadow of Kingston General Hospital. Graduating from Queen's in 1929 with the gold medal in surgery and medicine, Ford then filled his father's shoes, replacing him as department head in 1941. To the post, Ford brought training in Europe, where he had mastered German, and a determination to establish cardiology as a distinct function at the hospital. This he did, buying the hospital's first cardiograph machine. His days revolved around teaching, clinical demonstrations, private practice, and consultations. He stocked his department with promising young cardiologists like John "Jack" Milliken and H. Garfield "Gub" Kelly, and haematologist Malcolm Brown. His colleagues came to regard him as the "good shepherd." To his students, he stressed the importance of compassionate patient care. They reciprocated with a fierce loyalty. "I would walk fifty miles in my bare feet for Ford," Dr Bruce Cronk, a Belleville lad from Meds '46 would remember students affectionately saying.[39]

Over at Queen's new-born law school, lively, committed teaching was also of the essence. Founded in 1957, the school sought to teach the practice of the law in a social context. Until new law schools were established at Queen's and Western, lawyers in Ontario were educated at the knee of the Law Society of Upper Canada through its chosen instrument, Osgoode Hall in Toronto. There, the emphasis was on mastering the mechanics of legal practice. Under the deanship of constitutional lawyer William Lederman, Queen's set out to place the law in a broader social context. The law, Lederman believed, must be "both humane and social."[40] To do this, he recruited professors who brought a humanistic and academic bent to their teaching.

One of the charter members of the faculty was Stuart Ryan. A practising lawyer since graduating from Osgoode in 1933, Ryan had spread his interests widely. He had served as chairman of the Board of Education and mayor of Port Hope, Ontario. Like Whalley, he was a devout Anglican, who allowed his religion to act as a prod to social action; he was, for instance, exercised by conditions in local prisons and was active in the John Howard Society. Once engaged by a cause, Ryan was dogged in championing its virtue. It was Ryan who gave the faculty its motto: *Soit Doit Fait* – "Let right be done." He was, in short, a polymath: he could speak Latin and had a lexicographer's ability to parse the precise meaning of words. Ryan was, in

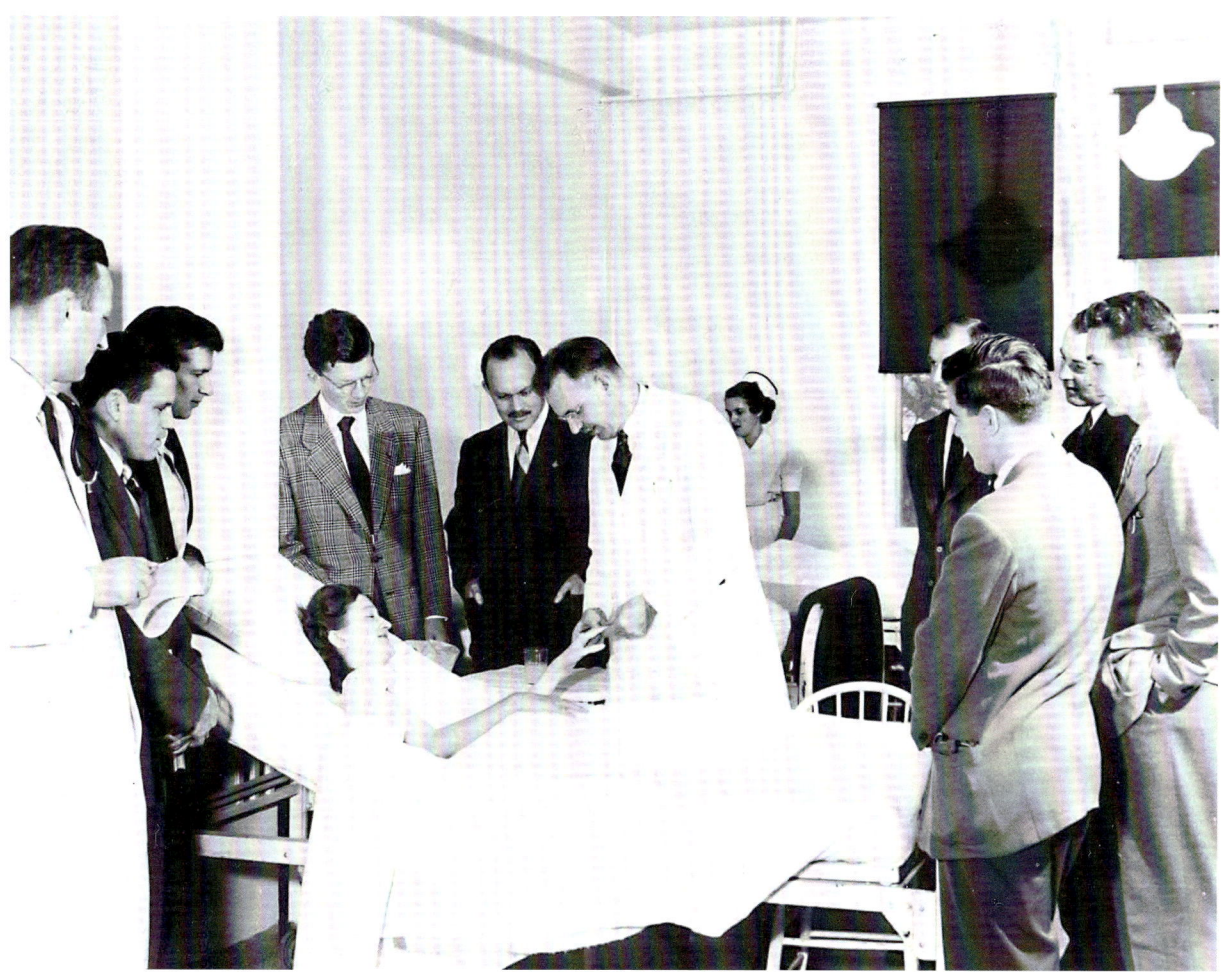

Cardiologist W. "Ford" Connell takes his students on rounds in Kingston General Hospital. A Queen's medicine graduate of 1906, Connell followed in the footsteps of his father, Walter, who taught in Queen's medical faculty for fifty-five years. Nationally renowned for his heart research, Ford headed the department of medicine from 1941 to 1968.

fact, more engrossed by the intellectual challenge of the law than its day-to-day practice. He stressed that the teaching of the law should be about ruminating about the law, not just the rote learning of it. He was, Lederman would say, "our Renaissance man." All these traits were quickly evident to Ryan's students, who took courses from him that ranged from criminology to legal history. They came to think of him not only as "a human encyclopedia of the law," but also as a professor whose door and wisdom were ever open to them.[41]

Professors such as Ryan, Whalley, Knox, Connell, and Jolliffe earned Queen's its reputation as a teaching university. There were many other worthy instructors too. Men such as the Edinburgh-trained Arts and Sciences dean, A.R.C. "Sandy" Duncan, whose Philosophy 1 introduced students not just to the names of the great philosophers but also to the utility of their ideas. Duncan reserved his highest grade – an "Edinburgh Alpha" – for those few students who mastered both the intricacies of philosophy and the majesty of the English language. Much the same could be said of George Harold "Curly" Ettinger, the dean of medicine, whose lectures and research in embryology inspired generations of students. And there was the inimitable Campbell "Pappy" Plewes, head of chemical engineering, who brought his experience in thermodynamics gained in the wartime Manhattan Project to his popular undergraduate lectures. Plewes's popularity perhaps also reflected the rich store of jokes with which he salted his lectures, thus drawing students from other faculties to pack his classroom. Students in the postwar decades perhaps found an eccentricity – a licence to wander off-topic, to indulge personal foibles – in their professors, something that some found memorable, others annoying. Plewes was wont on certain restless days to post a simple notice on his door: "Gone fishing." There were undoubtedly professors at Queen's who lacked the pedagogic golden touch, but on the whole, students at the university came to discover that the classroom would have a formidable influence on their emergence as educated citizens.

That teaching instinct spilled outside the classroom into the after-hours life of Queen's students. The university's political scientists, for instance, formed the Politics Club, which met at professors' homes to enable honours students to mingle with their mentors and engage in topical discussions or meet prominent visitors to campus, among them Robert Oppenheimer, the father of the nuclear age. John Isbister, an Arts '64 honours history and economics student, showed even more initiative. Exasperated by the rowdiness of residence life, he moved to an apartment and began inviting professors to join him in a kind of *salon* to discuss ideas. Historian Arthur Lower came to discuss civil liberties in Canada. So did Principal Bill Mackintosh, who dissected the ideas of Marx one evening before a dozen students in Isbister's tiny living room.[42]

As if to reciprocate, Principal Mackintosh, as did his successors, began inviting bright undergraduates to Summerhill to meet prominent honorary-degree recipients on convocation days. The faculty facilitated other types of extracurricular stimulation: they coached the Debating Union and oversaw model parliaments. Politics student Ned Franks relished the latter opportunity, running in a model parliament presided over by Corry in Grant Hall as head of the "Queen's Communist Party," and later reorienting himself as head of the Reactionary Monarchists.[43] Faculty fashioned other invitations to learning for their undergraduate charges. The annual Dunning Trust Lectures, funded by a generous 1946 bequest to honour Chancellor Charles Dunning (chancellor from 1940 to 1959), brought distinguished thinkers to campus to discuss "the freedoms and responsibilities of the individual in society." Students were involved in the planning of the series and the hosting of the annual visitor. In 1954, for instance, George Whalley used the Dunning Lecture to bring English literary critic C. Day Lewis to Queen's, and in 1963 invited poet W.H. Auden to the Dunning podium. Such visits helped to spark what was to become a vibrant colony of young poets that included Michael Ondaatje and Tom Marshall.

Service to the Nation

Fuelled by the instruction they had received at Queen's, graduates were expected to make themselves useful to the broader society. While the university had surrendered its denominational status as a Presbyterian institution in 1912, strong Presbyterian elements remained in its psyche. The worldly work ethic of the church's Shorter Catechism echoed through Queen's didactic rhetoric of education: an education should be a platform for social involvement. At its spring convocation in 1961, Queen's gave an honorary degree to the American ambassador in Ottawa, Livingston Merchant. A "Princeton man," Merchant flattered his Canadian audience by noting that Queen's shared his alma mater's dedication to teaching. What is more, he added, Princeton had a reputation for "service to the nation," something that he also saw as "a bond in common between your university and mine."[44]

If Princeton's contribution to America had been shaped by the vision of those like Woodrow Wilson, then Queen's commitment to Canada's betterment was typified by such men as engineer Sandford Fleming, the university's chancellor (1880–1915), and a contemporary of Principal George Grant. Fleming had helped to frame the young dominion by supplying Prime Minister John A. Macdonald with a coast-to-coast railway route (a trip chronicled by Grant in his famous 1873 book *Ocean to Ocean*) and by devising standard time to remove the chaos from railway scheduling. In the mid-twentieth century, Queen's constructive engagement with the nation at large continued in the person of Principal W.A. Mackintosh. Hailing from rural Madoc, Ontario, Mackintosh had polished his intellect with a Queen's degree in political economy and had gone on to a stellar career as an economic historian and wartime planner in Ottawa. His 1945 "white paper" on employment and income, advising Ottawa to stabilize national income through its program spending, monetary policy, and social spending, served as the capstone of the Canadian welfare state. Now in 1961, the time had come for Mackintosh to pass the torch. "The University sends you out with its blessing and high hope," the outgoing principal told the graduating class that spring, "not to conquer but to serve, not to acquire, but to achieve, not as a multitude blinded by a doctrine, but as a few freed by understanding."

By 1961, Queen's could boast of a diverse and illustrious gallery of graduates who had gone on to serve society with great distinction. Probably most prominent in this panoply were the so-called

A triumvirate of Queen's "Ottawa men": W.A. "Bill" Mackintosh (left), J.A. "Alex" Corry, and John J. Deutsch (right). Throughout the twentieth century, Queen's political economists not only applied their talents to the shaping of the modern social-welfare state in Ottawa, but also served as principals of the university, from Mackintosh's arrival in the office in 1951 to Deutsch's retirement in 1974. Ronald Watts and David Smith would perpetuate the tradition until 1994.

Ottawa "mandarins," graduates of Queen's storied political-economy program. Mackintosh had been preceded in Ottawa by "Queen's men" such as O.D. Skelton, one-time dean of Arts at Queen's and from the mid-1920s the architect of Canada's Department of External Affairs.[45] Ottawa, in fact, abounded with Queen's voices. As Liberal Prime Minister Mackenzie King cautiously unrolled the Canadian welfare state in the 1940s, the joke in Ottawa was that Canada's new federal state was bred "by King, out of Queen's." One of Skelton's recruits to his fledgling department, Elizabeth MacCallum (BA 1917; MA 1919), had become a world-renowned expert on the tangled Middle East, advising the United Nations and becoming the first woman to head a Canadian diplomatic mission, in Beirut in 1954. As the civil service grew in the 1950s to handle the new duties of the Keynesian state in Canada, Queen's graduates from economics, politics, and history classrooms headed north after graduation and began to follow the tracks of Skelton and Mackintosh. In the fall of 1961, history and politics honours student Derek Burney (BA 1962; MA 1964) acted the lead role of Willy Loman in the Queen's production of *Death of a Salesman*; on graduation he would join External Affairs and soon, like MacCallum, find himself a head of mission, in Kenya, and ultimately a negotiator of free trade with the United States.

Across town in Ottawa, the outspoken and at times irascible Charlotte Whitton (BA 1917; LLD 1941) had served as mayor of Ottawa since 1952. Whitton had honed her intellect and limbs at Queen's, serving as editor of the *Queen's Journal* and playing on the women's hockey team. Another Queen's alumnus, H. Lorne Greene (BA 1937), by 1961 had left Ottawa, where he had used his Drama Guild experience at Queen's and his sonorous voice on the wartime CBC to build a reputation as "the Voice of Doom." Now, Greene had turned to television, in 1959 taking the lead role as uber-rancher Ben "Pa" Cartwright in the NBC hit show *Bonanza*.

The diaspora of Queen's graduates stretched far beyond Ottawa. Across the Atlantic in London, a Queen's medallist in political economy and philosophy, Sir Edward Peacock (BA 1894), had brought lustre to the City of London, where he had found fame and fortune as a director of the Barings merchant banking firm. Born in Glengarry County in Queen's hinterland, Peacock had "come down to Queen's," as they used to say in the Ottawa Valley. There he acquired a probity in youth that guided his career through teaching school at Upper Canada College, working in investment banking at Dominion Securities, and eventually serving as a financial advisor to the Royal Family. The same vein of determination was evident in the career of Canadian publisher Lorne Pierce (BA 1913), another Queen's recruit from eastern Ontario, who had vaulted out of Queen's into a Methodist ministership and, by the early 1920s, the editorship of Canada's largest English-language publishing house, the Ryerson Press. Almost single-handedly Pierce used his presses to establish the canon of English literature in Canada, publishing poets and novelists, and employing Canadian artists such as C.W. Jefferys to adorn the covers and pages of his prodigious output.[46]

The march of Queen's talent was also evident in business. The 1936 Queen's gold medallist in economics, Earle McLaughlin, would in 1961 be appointed president of Canada's leading bank, the Royal Bank. Ernest Gill (BA 1923) headed Canada Life Assurance and now lent his executive talent to his old university as the chairman of its trustees. Queen's engineers could be found all across Canada's scattered mining frontier, and in the head offices of companies like Alcan in New York. John B. Stirling (BA 1909; BSc 1911) headed one of Canada's largest construction companies, Cape Construction, and had returned to his alma mater in 1960 to become its eighth chancellor. Not surprisingly, politics had drawn on the social-service ambitions of Queen's graduates as well. The Ontario New Democratic Party in 1961 had chosen Donald C. MacDonald (BA 1938) as its leader. In Ottawa, John Matheson (BA 1940) was elected to the federal house as a Liberal that same year. Pauline Jewett (BA 1944) would soon follow. It was not coincidental that in 1960 it was to the Queen's campus that the federal Liberal Party came to rethink its ideological bearings and policy prescriptions. The "Kingston Conference" would echo through the sixties after the Liberals unseated John Diefenbaker's government in 1963.

Queen's medical men also enjoyed prominence: Dr John Hammett (MD 1919) was one of New York's top surgeons and doctor to the likes of Joe DiMaggio and Marilyn Monroe. Dr Jason Hannah (MD 1928) thrived in Toronto as a neuropathologist and provided a prime example of the blending of private ambition and broader social purpose that Queen's had tried to inculcate in its graduates. In the depths of the Depression, Hannah pioneered non-profit health insurance for Canadians; his Associated Medical Services was doctor-operated and allowed patients a prepayment plan to cover major medical expenses. It thrived.

Any respectable university can draw up a flattering listing of its successful graduates. Queen's in 1961 would have been no exception to this desire to preen. Such lists can be artificial constructs, implying more than can be realistically demonstrated. One could argue, for instance, that many graduates behave atomistically, applying their educations according to their own idiosyncratic agenda rather than obliging some imposed grand altruism. Nevertheless, a Queen's undergraduate education in the first half of the twentieth century did seem to contain a strong impulse towards a purpose beyond individual gratification. When Bill Mackintosh died in late 1970, the university's memorial service in Grant Hall was built around a theme taken from Psalm 90: "So teach us to number our days, that we may apply our hearts unto wisdom." The impulse to push graduates in the right direction after graduation persisted: John Rae, former editor of the *Journal*, remembers political scientist John Meisel calling him to his office in his fourth year and telling him that his talents were in demand in Ottawa. Months later, Rae became a speechwriter for up-and-coming Quebec politician Jean Chrétien.

A Generous Loyalty

For Queen's, the "wisdom" carried away by its graduates had also created lasting benefit for the university in the form of a devoted alumni. By 1961, there were 17,973 of them. At convocation, all Queen's graduates took an oath "to cherish a generous loyalty to this university." Over the years, that loyalty manifested itself in many ways. Alumni attached themselves to their alma mater by ritual, attending the annual fall reunion weekend with its hoopla of a Saturday-morning parade, football game, tea with the principal, a grand dinner, and a Sunday church service in Grant Hall. Individual class reunions highlighted the proceedings. During the year, the Alumni Association, founded in 1926, connected the activities of Queen's alumni branches spread across the continent from Halifax to San Francisco. In New York, Dr Hammett had organized Friends of Queen's Inc. to coordinate the university's nearly fifteen hundred Yankee alumni. In 1961, Queen's personalities – among them Principal Mackintosh, the university's chaplain, Marshall Laverty, and outspoken historian Arthur Lower – spoke at branch meetings, where they stoked the coals of nostalgia. The *Queen's Review*, first published in 1927 and long edited by the association's secretary-treasurer Herb Hamilton, found its way nine times a year to alumni mailboxes, part of the 292,506 mailings made by Queen's to alumni in 1961. Queen's women graduates maintained their own alumnae association, which in fact predated the umbrella organization by a quarter-century; its membership overlapped with the broader alumni group, but in many ways the women had a more vigorous and activist culture than their male counterparts.[47] In the 1920s, for instance, the women had conceived and financed the university's first on-campus residence for women, Ban Righ Hall.

In return for their reunion weekends, branch sherry parties, and magazines, Queen's alumni sent money. In 1961, 5,965 alumni donated $151,210 to their alma mater. Companies where Queen's alumni worked, Ford and IBM among them, matched their employees' donations. The result of this ongoing generosity, together with bequests and non-alumni giving, financed scholarships and fattened the university's endowment, which by 1961 stood at a then-handsome $17,481,000. On a per-capita basis, this was one of the largest university endowments in the country and was managed with Presbyterian vigilance by the Board of Trustees. The endowment at times aroused talk of making Queen's a private university, free and clear of any government support – like many American Ivy League colleges. Mackintosh and Corry celebrated alumni generosity, but advised that it was not so fulsome as to warrant abandoning the largesse of Toronto and Ottawa in times of expansion.

Alumni gave back more than money. They sent their progeny back to Kingston. Well into the 1960s, the *Queen's Review* ran a story late each fall, entitled "My Father Sent Me Down to Queen's." In 1961, the registrar, Jean Royce, reported that, of the almost 850 first-year arrivals at Queen's, 131 were second-generation Queen's people. Take, for instance, Robert Little, the president of the student government. Little had earned his BA in 1958 from Queen's and was, in his AMS presidential year, a final-year law student. His father, Walter, had emerged from Arts '28 as a champion debater (coached by Frank Knox) and became an Ontario judge in Parry Sound. The Arts class of 1928 had also included Bob's mother, Marjorie (née McDonald, born in Lanark in Kingston's hinterland). When the time came for Bob to ponder university, Queen's seemed the inevitable choice. His brother, Bruce, would make the same decision a few years later.[48] Other families similarly had attached themselves to Queen's well back into the nineteenth century.

Alumni loyalty was not just a generational affair. It was also a regional matter of the sending new faces "down" to Queen's. The university's annual intake of new students drew heavily on Ontario and, in particular, eastern Ontario. In 1961–62, of the 3,449 students registered at Queen's, 2,849 were from Ontario, and of these a majority were eastern Ontarians, with Frontenac County, embracing Kingston, providing the richest harvest of 494 Queen's recruits.[49] Ottawa was also fertile ground. By way of example, five of the key players on Queen's Yates Cup–winning Gaels team in 1961 came from Ottawa: the Quinn brothers, Pete and John; the Rasmussen brothers, Don and Laird; and Bill Edwards. Other Queen's recruits came from central Ontario, however Queen's reach dwindled beyond this bailiwick; Quebec sent just 213, and only 6.26 per cent were from abroad, with the United States in the lead with 43 students.[50] Between 1951 and 1974, Queen's would be overseen by two principals boasting rural roots and a Queen's BA – Mackintosh from Madoc, near Peterborough, and John Deutsch from Quinton, Saskatchewan. Sandwiched between Mackintosh and Deutsch was another rural boy, Alex Corry from Millbank, near Stratford. Queen's affinity for rural Canada was strong.

Eastern Ontarians flocked to Queen's for various reasons. Success begat success. The university had a rich network of graduates – high-school teachers and principals, lawyers, and doctors who had studied at Queen's and were quick to push promising high-school graduates towards Kingston. Similarly, Queen's mining engineers scattered across the northern-Ontario frontier served as unofficial salesmen for their alma mater's well-regarded mining-engineering and geology programs; in 1961–62 there were 394 students from northern Ontario. For others, Kingston was also simply closest at hand and was the only university in the St Lawrence valley; the University of Ottawa and Carleton College (a university after 1957) competed to the north.

The magnetic effect of Queen's on eastern Ontarians fostered the persistent notion that Queen's was a "poor boys' university." This impression was widespread. Bob Crandall, an early 1950s commerce student from the Maritimes, recalled that to him Queen's seemed to be "emptying out the country" in that hinterland. In doing so, it acted as a "way station for rural boys," who, with a bit of pedagogic polishing from Queen's, were then pointed in the direction of Canada's burgeoning urban professional class.[51] An early 1960s commerce student, Merv Daub, concluded that his undergraduate home was a "lunch-bucket university."[52] "It used to be said," Duncan Sinclair, the son of a Queen's faculty member in the decades before Corry's arrival, recalled, "that you would come to Queen's with a small bag of oatmeal over your shoulder, and that was it!"

In the absence of reliable socio-economic data on the background of Queen's students in the first century of its existence, it is difficult to probe the reality of this caricature. Certainly, Queen's was situated in the poorer eastern region of a prosperous province and drew its feedstock from this hinterland. Queen's "success" stories, such as those of financier Edward Peacock or publisher Lorne Pierce, featured a motif of farm and village beginnings. The public perception of Queen's also tended to be coloured by its Presbyterian beginnings: here was a place that emphasized frugality and hard work, a supposed training ground for Canadian Horatio Algers. Queen's reliance on a rural catchment area had also unfolded since the late nineteenth century against a massive transition in Canadian life, as the fulcrum of Canada's national income shifted from the farm to the city. Queen's was, in effect, staking its admissions policy on the segment of the Canadian population that was progressively being marginalized. This did not, however, mean that Queen's freshmen were in fact reduced to eating oatmeal and living in constant penury. Circumstantial evidence – a reading of the *Queen's Journal* or student government debates – seemed to indicate that Queen's students in the decades before 1961 came from respectable and comfortable, if seldom affluent, backgrounds, and that the idea they were "poor boys" is fanciful.

The Ontario-centric pattern of the Queen's student body also gave the institution a somewhat schizophrenic reputation. In terms of its student demographics, it was clearly a regional Ontario university and profited handsomely from that linkage. At the same time, Queen's styled itself a prominent "national" university, with its heritage of "Ottawa men," its nation-wide extension programs in banking and accountancy, its theological imprint on churches across the nation, and the quality of its teaching and scholarship. Mackintosh was, for instance, regarded as pre-eminent in understanding the country's economic development. Similarly, historian Arthur Lower enjoyed national respect as a defender of civil liberties. Ford Connell was acclaimed for his cardiology work. Thus, Alex Corry had inherited the challenge of maintaining Queen's role as a bulwark of higher education in eastern Ontario, while at the same time extending its national reach and renown. This central tension in the university's existence would colour its deliberations on everything from admissions policy to the expansion of graduate and professional studies. Queen's, for instance, developed a system of regional scholarships designed to ensure that it could pull students from all reaches of the Dominion.

A Tradition of Student Self-Autonomy

Two more sturdy timbers of Queen's tradition would support the new principal in this mission: the empowerment of students to govern themselves and carefully balanced decision making by its Board of Trustees and Senate in matters of academic purpose and of bricks and mortar. Collectively, these two traditions had evolved to provide a sturdy – and, in many ways, a nationally unique – architecture of governance at Queen's. Student self-government was almost as old as the university itself. In the 120 years since the university's chartering in 1841, Queen's students had seen their daily existence on campus move from being under the *in loco parentis* sway of university administrators to the looseness of the most autonomous student culture in the country. In the beginning, the university's Senate exercised all power over students' college life. In 1850, the sternly named Committee of General Superintendence devised guidelines for the "general deportment of students," which the university Senate duly put into place to govern Queen's small student body. Students were warned off "all impure and profane language … the playing of cards … the keeping of dogs … the use of gunpowder, and of firearms." They were further urged not to bother the kitchen servants in the boarding houses where they lived, the doors of which would be bolted each night promptly at 10:00 p.m.[53]

Despite the Senate's heavy Presbyterian guiding hand, students soon began constructing an associational life that served as a platform for an increasing degree of self-control over their own affairs. A debating or dialectical society emerged in the 1840s. It necessitated students organizing debates, lectures, and an annual conversazione, which was a kind of day-long open house, at which students sang and danced before an audience of their professors, the local citizenry, and the college's tiny alumni community. Other informal organizations, such as the Glee Club, provided the kernel of a club tradition at Queen's. In 1858, these first stirrings solidified in the founding of the Alma Mater Society. The Society's Latin name perhaps best conveyed its initial purpose: it was to be the students' *nurturing mother*. Its mandate was a mixture of student self-interest and altruism: the AMS was "to preserve the attachment of the Alumni to the University … to serve as a bond of union between the different classes of students … to cultivate a literary taste … to further the general interests of the University" and to provide communication between the students and the administration.[54] Spurred by this purpose, Queen's students soon found themselves holding business meetings, taking minutes, exacting fees, and carrying their concerns to the corridors of power at Queen's. An elected council emerged as the arbiter of these activities and, in 1872, the student voice found printed expression with the appearance of the *Queen's Journal*, the student newspaper.

Through the last quarter of the nineteenth century, the Senate progressively surrendered authority to Queen's students. While it zealously guarded its jurisdiction over the academic life and outcomes of students, the Senate was prepared to yield jurisdiction over what came to be labelled "non-academic matters." What seemed to lie behind this gradual empowerment was a belief that the virtues of a formal education might be enhanced by the encouragement of initiative in a student's daily collegiate life. Thus, the focus of the AMS tended to gravitate away from sustaining the filial bond with alumni towards the building of a student culture on campus. The society's Saturday-morning business meetings served to define that culture. In the 1880s, the AMS dedicated itself to improving athletic facilities for students: in 1886 the Senate agreed to collect an annual one-dollar fee from all Arts students to finance a gymnasium, a building that finally materialized in 1907 with the opening of the Jackson Hall gym and pool. Long before that, in 1898, all student athletic activities were placed under AMS control. Soon there emerged a rich culture of intramural sports clubs that continues to this day.

Central to this unfolding of student control was the notion that student services would be in large part funded by fees approved by the students themselves. All this was reflected in 1898 when the AMS incorporated itself as "the Alma Mater Society of Queen's University," and armed itself with a constitution that focused on the provision of student services and the building up of a cohesive student *esprit* at Queen's. The AMS sat on a pyramid of authority: the AMS president and council executive were drawn from and approved by clusters of student faculty societies. The first of these was the Arts Society of 1868, followed in 1872 by the Aesculapian Society for medical students and the Engineering Society of 1897. In 1889, the handful of women in Arts seceded from the Arts Society, arguing that women had particular associational needs that were best served by a separate society. For this, they also turned to Latin for a name – the Levana Society would honour a Roman deity who aspired to elevate human aspiration towards heaven. A Theological Society gave voice to the theology students embedded in the larger university, until its 1912 secularization.

These societies projected and protected the particular interests of each faculty (and gender), while at the same time linking them to the organic needs of the wider student body. Like the imposition of a fee-for-service culture on Queen's students, the AMS also embodied a strong impulse towards inclusion at the university, an aversion to any hint of exclusivity or privilege. This was perhaps genetically rooted in Presbyterianism's egalitarian impulses: a distrust of hierarchies and a belief in broad consultation through the election of elders. In the fall of 1959, AMS President Bruce Alexander welcomed the new crop of freshmen by telling them that they were about to become members of the "oldest self-governing student body in Canada." Their years as students at Queen's would put them in touch with "liberal democratic processes" that would filter into their broader citizenship.[55]

The growing prerogatives of the AMS extended beyond the orchestrating of sports, clubs, and dances and into the realm of policing student deportment. By the late 1870s, students began to resist the university's paternalistic authority over their deportment. At first the impulse was more hedonistic than legalistic. Senior-year students set up ad hoc tribunals – *concursus iniquitatus et virtulis* – at which they indicted guileless freshman on some trumped-up infraction (a tradition that would be perpetuated well into the next century by initiation week's "frosh courts") and then exacted a penalty, one usually calibrated by the price of beer. By the end of the century, however, the *concursus* had evolved into a more formal system of student-regulated justice.

The AMS court system – and courts similarly installed in the faculty societies – were rooted in the concept of natural justice, not the formal, precedent-driven law of society beyond the campus. The court had structure – a chief justice, a prosecuting attorney, defence counsel, and a jury of peers. Court officers tended to be drawn from senior-year undergraduate ranks and, after 1957, from the common room of the new law faculty. The court's judgments and subsequent penalties were rooted in the intuitions of natural law – what seemed appropriate to the crime. The quality of Queen's student justice was infused with a sense of reasonableness and a didactic desire to prevent further incidents of the same ilk. A pliable article of the AMS constitution forewarned students that they might be charged with behaviour "unbecoming a member of the AMS."[56] Many bylaws followed. Nonetheless, fines and punishments were usually light and tokenistic; loss of face usually took a heavier toll on the guilty. The court also served as the final interpreter of the AMS constitution and as final arbiter of disputed student referenda and election results.

In 1936, the AMS equipped the court with enforcement muscle by creating a system of constables. Paid, quasi-uniformed students began to police campus events involving students. The constables could frisk, direct, and, if necessary, charge a fellow student. While it was never clear where the court's jurisdiction held sway – certainly anywhere on campus, but not so clearly on Princess Street when a football snake dance was in full swing – the system worked well in once again instilling in adolescent undergraduate minds that they were not just receiving an education, but were also in some measure fashioning their own destiny. There was thus real import in Principal Mackintosh's warning to 1959's incoming frosh that "aimless" and "tiresome adolescent" students were not welcome at Queen's, and that misbehaviour in residence would "bring summary action" from their peers.[57] Not everybody, of course, heeded such advice. In 1958, nine Queen's undergraduate women raided the Royal Military College's Stone Frigate, the college's signature building, in search of masculine booty. Although the so-called "naughty nine" won a lasting place in Queen's folklore, the Levana court was not amused and sentenced them to ten hours of community work each. In the fall of 1961, Queen's students on a football train to Toronto were alleged by the CNR to have done $514.97 in damage. While the CNR police supplied the names of nine alleged miscreants, the court investigated and concluded that the evidence against the individuals was circumstantial. Rather it concluded Queen's students were *collectively* guilty, and a general levy on each faculty society should make right the damage. The court also ordered that two AMS constables be on future football trains. Similarly, when a partying Science '66

❖ Thinking Outside the Box ❖

For centuries, universities have lived in the midst of the communities that surround or abut them. One thinks of storied scholastic enclaves such as the Sorbonne, Padua, Cambridge, Oxford, Bologna, and Salamanca. While these medieval universities looked upon the communities surrounding them as a kind of hard shell of shelter, they at the same time asserted the right to conduct their own affairs. Hence, the tradition emerged of scholars wearing an academic gown as a uniform to provide outward differentiation of scholars from townsfolk. This symbiotic relationship has come to be politely described as "town-and-gown" relations. Towns thrived off the daily commerce generated by scholars and universities benefited from the infrastructure of the town. But each party could easily find reason to resent the other – cocky, entitled scholars rubbing up against the prerogatives of local property and commerce. In 1355, for instance, an argument in an Oxford tavern erupted into a two-day running street battle – the Battle of St Scholastica Day – that saw death and destruction.

In the years down to 1961, Queen's enjoyed largely placid relations with Kingstonians. Local clerics, lawyers, and businessmen such as John A. Macdonald and Alexander Pringle had, after all, been instrumental in establishing the college in 1841. Queen's sat comfortably in a box fashioned mainly out of the old Loyalist land grant of Lot #24. For its first century, this endowment afforded a cushion of comfort with the city that lay to its immediate north and east. The trustees abided by an unwritten commitment not to expand the university east of Barrie Street or north of Clergy Street. No longer worried about losing taxable land, the city responded with benevolence. In 1903, for instance, it underwrote the cost of building Kingston Hall. In the 1950s, the city council subscribed $150,000 to the university's capital campaign. The university extended its own influence in the Limestone City. From 1948 to 1952, Queen's political economist Clifford Curtis sat as the city's mayor. Curtis later helped establish an institute of local government at the university. Queen's principals Mackintosh and Corry delivered campus news to Kingstonians on the "Queen's Quarter Hour" on radio station CKWS. In 1964, the university estimated that its payroll pumped $5.5 million annually into the local economy; each Queen's student spent $1,000 a year. Local law firm Cunningham & Cunningham served as university solicitors. *Whig-Standard* publisher Arthur Davies sat on the Board of Trustees. Queen's professors such as F.R.C. Clark played local church organs; others contributed to the founding of the Kingston Symphony in 1953. When it opened in 1957, the Agnes Etherington Arts Centre on campus gave all Kingston an artistic focal point.

There were frictions. When Queen's students painted the City Park statue of Sir John Macdonald in the red, blue, and gold of Queen's signature tricolour, Corry sent the city a cheque for $107. "I doubt that I can stop pranks and horseplay entirely," he wrote, "and probably it would be wrong if I did." The gentle city-university relationship attracted the satirical pen of journalist and former student Robertson Davies, whose 1951 novel *Tempest-Tost* poked fun at "Salterton" and its resident "Waverley College." Waverley graduates, he wrote, loved "their Alma Mater as the disciples of Socrates loved their master."

student commandeered the Wolfe Island ferry in 1963, crashing it into the dock, an AMS prosecutor was put on the case.[58]

The purview of the AMS did not end with the operation of a justice system, the publishing of a newspaper, and the perpetuation of a crowded annual cycle of sports and social events. The role of the AMS extended to defining the very nature of student society at Queen's. Article IX of the AMS constitution explicitly forbade Queen's students from belonging to any outside, "oath-taking" organization; their loyalty was to be exclusively devoted to their alma mater. In the 1920s and the 1930s, the issue had come to a head. In the United States and on some Canadian campuses, fraternities had grown dramatically. They fulfilled a basic sociological need for identity and a sense of belonging. At Queen's, that impulse had always been satisfied by attachment to the broadest definition of community. But the allure of a more exclusive affiliation was tempting, especially in faculties such as medicine, where the whole ethos was elitism. When Queen's medical students formed their own fraternity, Psi Delta Phi, and moved to affiliate with the American fraternity Sigma Nu in 1934, student government was thrown into a tempestuous debate over the nature of loyalty to the university. A coalition resting on support from Arts, Levana, and Theology passionately argued that the linchpin of Queen's culture was the inclusive, organic ethos of the place. They argued that allegiance to an internal coterie rooted in exclusive membership and tied to fraternal authority beyond the university's reach was antithetical to the whole evolution of Queen's as being a democratic, egalitarian campus society. Through a series of task forces, mass meetings, and votes, students wrestled with the question. What is striking in retrospect is that the students themselves decided the issue, the trustees and the Senate assuring the AMS that they would uphold the student consensus. When the AMS court ruled that Psi Delta Phi had contravened the student constitution and meted out one-year suspensions from student activities to twenty-four would-be frat boys, the die was cast – Queen's would have no fraternities.[59]

Ironically, vestiges of exclusivity lingered at Queen's. The Aesculapian Society was permitted to maintain a house on Bagot – later on King – Street as a residence, Medical House, for some of its members. Similarly, one could argue that, by 1961, the Queen's bands, with their pipers, drummers, horn players, cheerleaders, and colour guard, had evolved into a quasi-fraternity. The pipe and brass bands developed an elaborate internal hierarchy – pipe major, chief cheerleader, publicity manager, head highland dancer, and so on – and drew a substantial annual budget from the AMS. And, of course, they had a distinctive uniform that set them apart from non-bandsmen. So, too, did their secretive rituals, such as the tot of "scary sherry" on the bus before every performance.[60] One could also argue that the Levana Society was a giant sorority, which allowed – some would soon say, *obliged* – women to enjoy their own cloistered culture on campus.

A woman's life on Queen's campus began with a series of initiation rituals. On a Sunday evening early in the fall term, first-year women, robed in academic gowns, were paraded to Grant Hall, where, serenaded by organ music, they filed past candle-holding senior students, who had arranged themselves in a preordained pattern. In this Masonic atmosphere, the freshettes were told of Levana's 1889 purpose – "so that they will be fitted to take their place in the larger society of the world with dignity to themselves and credit to Queen's" – and then, as if passing the faith from one generation to the next, seniors pressed their lit candles to the unlit candles of the initiates. Various mythologies grew up around the ritual. Some suggested that the pattern of wax droplets on the tricolour ribbon on each candle would foretell which faculty would furnish the freshette with an educated doctor, engineer, or "artsie" for a husband – *and* how many children that union would produce.[61] However secretive and idiosyncratic the rituals of the bands and Levana might seem, however, they were predicated on life at

Queen's rather than compliance with some external code of exclusivity and, therefore, were tolerated within the AMS sphere.

Principal Mackintosh had witnessed this AMS cohesiveness first hand. In 1959, the society had initiated a campaign to provide the university, and greater Kingston, with a presentable concert and theatre hall. Grant Hall, so emblematic of Queen's, was in reality a miserable venue for concerts. In the winter, it was notoriously cold. In the 1950s, the university had inaugurated a Grant Hall concert series. Artists of the calibre of jazzman Oscar Peterson now played Queen's. But when the young Canadian prodigy Glenn Gould came to play the piano, there was a problem. The brilliant, but famously neurotic, Gould refused to play – too cold. The panic-stricken organizers dispatched Esther Russell, the wife of one of the concert organizers, to fetch a hair dryer. Twenty minutes later the keyboard was sufficiently warmed for Gould to perform his magic.[62] Enough, said the AMS. A building committee was formed, fund-raising plays and concerts were staged, and the trustees were promised that the mooted fifteen-hundred-seat theatre would be self-financing. Montreal architect Fred Lebensold was invited to lecture on theatre design. By 1961, a modest-but-encouraging $12,300 was in the bank.[63] At Queen's, the student horse on occasion led the administrative cart. The theatre project would persist through the next decade, culminating in a design by Lebensold, a design that proved too rich for Queen's pocket. Nonetheless, Queen's students had displayed a willingness to dig into their pockets to support their university, a tradition that went back to the erection of Grant Hall six decades before and would stretch into the future.

In the spring of 1961, Mackintosh had another brush with the collective will of Queen's students. In February, desperate for space on the cramped campus to shoehorn in a much-needed new physics building, the trustees – who oversaw the bricks and mortar of Queen's – concluded that they had no other option but to construct it on the Lower Campus, opposite the picturesque Arts building. The Lower Campus had long been a place where students tossed footballs, lounged in the sun, and met sweethearts. It also offered a swath of green in a campus that was increasingly filling up with limestone buildings and concrete walkways. Once a student at Queen's himself, Mackintosh agonized over the decision, but in the end yielded to the trustees' belief that at times tradition must yield to expedition. On the evening before the crucial meeting of the trustees in February 1961, Mackintosh sent the university chaplain, Marsh Laverty, to knock on the apartment door of the AMS president, Bob Little, in the Students' Memorial Union building. Would Little meet with the principal and Rector Leonard Brockington? Later that evening, the three met over a drink. How would the student body react to the placing of a shiny new physics building on the Lower Campus, Mackintosh inquired, hoping that the promise of new facilities might sway the point. Little demurred; since he had not consulted the AMS executive on the issue, he really could not say. But, speaking for himself, he regretted any loss of open space on the campus and suspected that he was not alone. Chagrined, Mackintosh decided to proceed regardless. The next morning the trustees cast the die.

The campus reaction was almost immediate. A groundswell of indignant student protest emerged. The *Queen's Journal* spearheaded the attack, editorializing against the loss of a prime piece of the university's sylvan heritage. The paper urged alumni and faculty to join the cause – and they did. The AMS mailed offprints of the editorials to alumni, who needed little prompting. "Back in 1903 it was the students who built Grant Hall," Arts alumna Shirley Ross (BA 1953) warned Mackintosh, "and the spirit that functioned then is still functioning now, or the Lower Campus wouldn't matter to us."[64] "If it goes," wrote the Kingston alumni branch, "part of the Spirit of Queen's will go with it."[65] The faculty association quickly chimed in. Its president, Stuart Ryan of Law, told Mackintosh that

the faculty appreciated the "complexity" of the issue, but nonetheless thought the decision "unbalanced." History professor Arthur Lower, never shy with his feisty opinions, told the principal that the loss of green space would make Queen's look like Columbia University in New York – a huge slab of concrete in the middle of a city. The decision would "split" the campus community and would ruin "his reputation before history." There were petitions and even demonstrations, with picketers hoisting signs reading "Spare the Lower Campus!"

Bob Little's intuition had been right. One didn't meddle lightly with tradition at Queen's. On 21 March, Mackintosh and the trustees backtracked. While Mackintosh told the trustees that he felt the opposition was "somewhat annoying" and ill-informed, he privately wrote to heir-apparent Corry: "Let this be a lesson to you. Never let the Board of Trustees make up its own mind."[66] Tradition had been sustained; Queen's students had rallied to preserve the university's leafy heritage. Deeper divisions had been avoided and, Mackintosh consoled himself, a "good atmosphere" had been created for his successor. Fortunately, an astute local realtor and former student, Graham Thomson, had quietly bought up five residential homes on nearby Queen's Crescent, and now offered them to the university as an acceptable alternative location for the new physics building. The bulldozers moved in. Within a year, Ball Brothers Construction had begun con-

"Keep Queen's Green": students, faculty, and alumni protest the trustees' decision to construct the new physics building on the Lower Campus. Their victory and the placing of the physics building on nearby Queen's Crescent led to a break from Queen's addiction to limestone. Stirling Hall was not only circular, but it employed glass and concrete interspersed with limestone panels.

struction on a striking circular building nestled between Queen's Crescent and Stuart Street. The architects of what would soon be called Stirling Hall, after the university's new chancellor, John B. Stirling, seemed conscious that the "new" at Queen's must accommodate the "old." Despite their bold embrace of curvature and generous use of glass and aluminium, the new physics building was wrapped with a broad coursing of Queenston limestone.

The View from Richardson Hall

Corry inherited more than a "good atmosphere" from Bill Mackintosh. He inherited the principal's office in Richardson Hall. Opened in 1954, Richardson Hall, with its reliance on limestone and the Collegiate Gothic style, was the first purpose-built administrative building on the Queen's campus. When Mackintosh became principal in 1951, he occupied a small office in the Douglas Library, with a single secretary supporting his activities. By the time Corry took over in late 1961, newly completed Richardson Hall had become the fulcrum of administrative power at Queen's. Decisions emanated from its offices, and people went there to stake their claims. In many ways, power had become highly centralized in postwar Queen's. In an era that increasingly venerated the organizational chart as the key to understanding how power flowed, Richardson Hall sat at the apex of Queen's "org. chart." Queen's steady growth in the 1950s – the addition of a thousand students since 1951 – had provoked scrutiny of the university's administrative mechanics. A 1958 report by Toronto consultants Price Waterhouse stressed the need to break down the constant flow of matters large and small across the principal's desk. The old informality of making decisions by bumping into the principal at the faculty club or by quick telephone calls or hasty notes, the consultants reported, needed "to be revised in keeping with its transition to the full-fledged university it has become."[67] In effect, academic and administrative affairs at the university should be segregated.

In 1959, Mackintosh appointed a vice-principal of administration to act, in effect, as the chief operating officer of the university. Mackintosh picked a quietly brilliant bureaucrat, John J. Deutsch, a Queen's commerce graduate, former wartime mandarin, financial journalist, and professor. Deutsch was horrified by what he found: no systematic budgeting and poor lines of control. Decades of financial stringency had made Queen's a place of neurotic penny-pinching, a trait honed to perfection by its one-time English-professor-turned-bursar and vice-principal, William McNeill. Although he had retired in 1947, McNeill's mentality and methods had moved comfortably into Richardson Hall. Now at least, Mackintosh had bequeathed Corry a competent technocrat to ease the transition to more rational management. To further smooth the transition, Mackintosh agreed to stay on as vice-chancellor (an appointment that required a cumbersome federal amendment of the university's royal charter)[68] to oversee matters of planning and finance. Corry would direct his energies to the university's academic affairs. Thus, an – albeit light – breeze of reform had blown in the front door of Richardson Hall.

In the fall of 1961, day-to-day operational control of the university rested squarely in a handful of Richardson Hall offices. Corry, with advice from his close friend Mackintosh, now manned the principal's office. Down the corridor, John Deutsch approved expenditures, crunched the numbers, and engaged in rudimentary strategic planning. If Deutsch measured the outputs at Queen's, the university registrar, Jean Royce, managed its most crucial input – the annual admission of undergraduate students. Royce (BA 1929) personified dedication to Queen's: she had joined the registrar's office in 1931 after a stint as a teacher and librarian. In 1933, she became the registrar, and for three decades had vetted the admission of thousands of students. Few ever forgot her kindly attention to their ambition, and often, to ease their initial confusion in arriving at Queen's, Royce pointed students in academic directions likely to capitalize on their potential. A "Jean Royce letter of admission" was, for many, many students, the first bond they formed with their future alma mater. Royce's annual report on registration late every fall provided Queen's with a barometer of its fortunes. She was, in the words of her biographer, "the university's main gatekeeper."[69] Royce lived in a walk-up apartment on Queen's Crescent (later on Stuart Street), but it seemed to most that her real home was just steps away in Richardson Hall.

The control room of the university contained one other, often unheralded, personality: Ralph Hinton, the director of the physical plant. From stocking the small mountain of coal at the university's lakeside power plant to the upkeep of its high-maintenance and drafty limestone buildings, Hinton guarded the physical foundation of a Queen's education. Under his watch, a small army of janitors, carpenters, and boiler men kept Queen's up and running. One of them, Bud Cornelius, had joined Hinton's team as a carpenter in 1955; his grandfather before him had worked at Queen's for forty-five years. He loved the camaraderie of working for Queen's. Cornelius recalled that Principal Mackintosh greeted the maintenance crews with a cheery "good morning, boys" as he made his way from Summerhill to Richardson Hall each day. At Christmas, Mrs Mackintosh reinforced the message by distributing cartons of cigarettes.[70]

While the power to sign cheques and to stoke the university boilers may have resided in Richardson Hall, power over the university's long-term material and academic well-being was much more diffuse. The Royal Charter bestowed on Queen's in 1841 was full of canny Scottish pragmatism. The governance of the university was constructed around a complex system of checks and balances intended to preserve a strict demarcation of the academic and material management of the institution, while at the same time promoting ongoing consensus. Some years later, political scientist Ron Watts, principal from 1974 to 1984, addressed the perplexing symmetry of governance at Queen's. Many, he warned, might form the impression that "a neat and tidy mind is a crippling disability in any effort to understand the processes of internal governance at Queen's … While the processes of governance at Queen's are not simple, they avoid the rigidities of a precise hierarchical structure."[71]

The Board of Trustees thus had purview over the university's financial health, its bricks and mortar, and the approval of all senior appointments, both academic and administrative. Its membership had been almost entirely drawn from the world beyond Queen's; only the principal sat at its table as an insider. A formula dictated the election of thirty-five trustees to ensure representation of key university constituencies, ranging from its benefactors to its graduates. Meeting three times a year, the trustees were supported by committees, which deliberated over such crucial matters as buildings, finances, and investment of the endowment. Strategic guidance was provided by an executive committee, which met frequently. The success of the Board depended not only on the recruitment of a broadly representative membership but also on the pivotal working partnership of its chairman – by 1961, always a prominent businessman – and the principal.

The Collins Room in Richardson Hall also provided a monthly venue for the university Senate. Empowered in 1841 to "exercise Academic superintendence" of the fledgling college, the Senate until 1913 was comprised of *all* the faculty members. Since then, its membership was representatively drawn from the university's burgeoning faculties. Its purview was wide. It debated and approved curriculum, controlled registration standards, approved scholarships, deliberated on the awarding of honorary degrees, policed student probity and behaviour, approved the annual list of graduating students, and vetted new courses and programs. Like the trustees, the Senate sat at the top of a pyramid of committees that pondered academic matters ranging from the delivery of public lectures to cases of alleged plagiarism. The Senate also relied on the sounding board provided by an array of five faculty boards. The faculty boards debated academic life in specific precincts, thus providing the Senate and their respective deans with a grassroots perspective on the university's academic direction. Many departments fed into this progressive filtration of academic life by maintaining Committees of Department. The principal acted as Senate chairman, thereby affirming that he was in fact *primus inter pares*, who continued to share the concerns of his colleagues.

Connecting these two solitudes of authority at Queen's were a number of bodies and offices designed to promote mediation and communication. In 1874, Principal Snodgrass had urged the university to create the office of chancellor, a feature of many Scottish universities. The chancellor was in some ways intended to act as a head of state, relieving the principal of ceremonial duties at convocations and generally adding lustre to the university's prestige. The arrival of John Stirling as chancellor in 1960 typified the utility of the role. "Bert" Stirling had built two Queen's degrees – a BA in 1909 and a BSc in 1911 – into the presidency of E.G.M. Cape & Co., a Montreal-based construction firm. Stirling brought a natural vivacity to the university's convocation dais, while at the same time contributing an engineer's insights to the trustees' deliberation on new buildings. The chancellor also played a key role in selecting the university principal; he headed a joint Board-Senate search committee and was expected to steer its deliberation towards a unanimous selection of a new principal.[72]

Once appointed, a new principal looked to the chancellor not only to alleviate his workload, but also to help project the university's image to the outside world as a kind of roving ambassador and fund raiser. The chancellor's ceremonial and bridging role was echoed in another 1874 creation, the University Council. Drawing an elected membership in equal measure from the Board of Trustees, the Senate, and the alumni, the council had few specific powers – although it did oversee the election of the chancellor, for instance. Meeting usually only once a year, the council was designed to function much like a Scottish clan meeting, at which the "well-being" of the university might be discussed by its vital constituents. Its role was to act as a sounding board for issues affecting university life. With ninety-six members, the council was a cumbersome body, but, when chaired by an able chancellor like Stirling, it opened "a window on the world" for Queen's. At its 1961 session, for instance, the council debated how Queen's should respond to the surge of baby-boom registration headed towards its classrooms in the upcoming decade. Discussion was vigorous: when Corry cautioned that unbridled expansion of enrolment would jeopardize the "character" of Queen's, an engineering alumnus countered by urging Queen's to become an American-style "super university." Chancellor Stirling worried that capping enrolment might penalize Queen's in the eyes of its government funders.[73] The University Council seldom arrived at a cohesive conclusion; its utility lay more in prompting the exchange of opinions and perspectives across jurisdictional boundaries.

In 1912, a final Scottish touch was added to the canopy of governance at Queen's. The position of Rector was created to provide the student body with a conduit of influence to the university hierarchy. The idea was that a prominent outsider would act as the students' champion in the corridors of power. The rector was technically elected by the students, but in reality the AMS presented only a single candidate for the post, and so the appointment was by acclamation. Distinguished politicians and journalists were favourites; they were eloquent and practised in persuasion. Former Tory prime minister Richard Bennett and Ottawa mandarin O.D. Skelton each served as rector in the 1930s. Journalists also fit the bill as rector – *Saturday Night* editor B.K. Sandwell in the 1940s and then, in 1947, broadcaster and labour negotiator Leonard Brockington. Brockington brought an activism to the role, appearing at convocations and giving voice to such student concerns as the Lower Campus fracas in 1961. His Welsh origins seemed to equip him with a talent for spellbinding rhetoric; students flocked to his annual address. "The history of this university," he is famously remembered as telling them, "is the story of a fire that would not be quenched."

For all its Scottish structure and protocol, the governance of Queen's in the end came down to a question of personality and consensus. The principal at Queen's possessed little raw power, but he was crucially positioned to exercise an immense power of suasion. He was the only person to sit on both the Board of Trustees and the Senate. "The Principal is at times a very narrow isthmus between these bodies and carries a heavy responsibility," Mackintosh responded to an inquiry about the key to governance at Queen's from McGill. "I am not very enthusiastic about elaborate and precise organization. I am keen to encourage initiative, though how successful I am, I do not know."[74] An effective prin-

The Board of Trustees, c. 1967: a solid phalanx of male competence and authority. Vice-principal John Deutsch (front right) briefs the trustees. Principal Corry, Board Chair R.D. Harkness, Chancellor Bert Stirling, and former principal Bill Mackintosh sit at the far end of the Collins Room. The sole woman present is trustee Mrs D.W. Boucher, a Queen's graduate in science in the 1920s and a prominent horticulturalist.

cipal should always act as a buffer between the academic prerogatives of the Senate and the administrative oversight of the Board. University historian F.W. Gibson, having studied Queen's principals in action since 1917, concluded that a good principal should act like a ringmaster, gently orchestrating all the loosely connected elements of the university community, "breathing into the corporation the spirit of a clan and making the principal a kind of chieftain."[75] By 1961, most agreed that Bill Mackintosh had fulfilled this prescription with avuncular competence and that Corry's experience as acting dean of Law and vice-principal had equipped him with "a velvet glove" when it came to drawing consensus out of his colleagues.[76]

But this did not mean that all was well in the governance of Queen's. What was meant to be a self-balancing machine had been knocked out of alignment by a steady accumulation of influence by the trustees and the principal as the university had struggled its way through the Depression, the exigencies of war, and the first pangs of postwar expansion. Fred Gibson concluded his history of Queen's in the years down to 1961 by noting that "government at Queen's has been more authoritarian rather than democratic,"[77] the financial straits of the university tending to privilege the power of the purse, and allowing the Board of Trustees to take the commanding heights of the university.

Even in 1961, the Board still had vestiges of the flinty, eastern-Ontario Presbyterianism that had given birth to Queen's in 1841. There was, for instance, the Rev. George Brown, an Arts and Divinity grad from the first decade of the century, who had become minister at Chalmers United Church in Kingston and would serve a redoubtable forty-two years in total on the Board. He began every Board meeting with a prayer, and by all accounts could be relied upon for a parsimonious reaction to issues placed on the agenda. Despite such persistence, it was a newer breed of hard-nosed, business-oriented WASPs who now dominated the Board and brought

In the Fall of 1961

their considerable prowess in matters of money and management to Queen's. These were men who had cut their teeth in the hothouse wartime economy and the postwar corporatization of the Canadian economy. Many were Queen's grads who had done well on Bay Street or St James Street, men such as Board chair Ernest C. Gill, the president of Canada Life Assurance, and Colonel Robert D. Harkness, president of Northern Electric. Others had no previous Queen's connection. One of them was hard-driving Donald Gordon, who brought experience in banking, war management, and railroading to the Collins Room. Gordon was also known to arrive in Kingston in his private car, attached to a CNR train. And after Friday-evening Board meetings he would invite the inner sanctum of the Board to the car to sample his favourite Scottish export. Lawyer-politicians such as Tory MP James M. Macdonnell added another national perspective, while distinguished medical professionals like the aforementioned Dr John Hammett from New York rounded out the professional perspectives. The Board was thus a powerhouse of talent, full of men (and they were almost all men, with only four women sitting in their midst) who were used to getting their way.

The trustees applied their expertise through an array of committees that oversaw the long-term planning of Queen's, the investment of its endowment, its annual budget, and the construction of new buildings. The Board also ratified the appointment and salary of every new faculty member and administrator at Queen's. They may have been modern businessmen, but their deliberations were still marked by a Presbyterian financial vigilance to ensure the university received, penny-for-penny, good value for its money. For instance, it became dogma for the Board that no new building be commenced until its capitalization was completely secured. Not surprisingly, preparations for the Board's spring, fall, and winter meetings became major logistical exercises – briefing papers, committee reports, and registration updates crowded the agenda and usually pushed the meetings from Friday evening well into Saturday afternoon. The principal regarded his meetings with the trustees as a kind of command performance, at which the true course of the university would be decided. Savvy principals and Board chairmen quickly learned to orchestrate Board meetings in advance to ensure that desired outcomes were likely to materialize.

The ascendancy of the Board had tended to diminish the weight of the Senate. In an era when the undergraduate curriculum was still rigidly limited (first-year Arts students were offered a narrow range of compulsory courses), and when graduate studies were in their infancy, there was little call on the Senate to engage in intense pedagogical discussion. Instead, its quick-paced meetings revolved around approving graduation lists and honorary degrees, reviewing the plight of those students who had failed examinations, and applying academic discipline and admission standards. Historian Fred Gibson noted the decline in Senate utility: "the Senate acted for the most part as a rubber-stamping body for decisions taken elsewhere."[78] The same emaciation was evident downstream in the faculty boards. In Arts and Science, the Board largely undertook academic housekeeping. In newer faculties like Law and Business, there were more substantive discussions about curriculum and new academic directions. In Medicine, perhaps the exception, the faculty board acted as the focus for discontent over the whole functioning of the faculty. But, in general, the faculty boards played a passive role, transmitting little of scholastic consequence to the Senate.

Academic change at Queens's instead flowed through informal channels that had evolved between the principal, the deans, and department heads. Many deans brought their dogs to their weekly meeting with the principal (Dean Douglas Ellis of Applied Science in the 1950s even insisted that Buster, his collie, appear in his official university portrait). Decisions to hire new faculty, grant sabbaticals, employ contract instructors, and conduct annual salary reviews were directly negotiated by heads of department with their deans. History professor Arthur Keppel-Jones likened a visit to the dean's office to a visit to the dentist. "Are you here for a filling or for an extraction?" attendees on the dean would quip.[79] Departmental heads were appointed by the deans and often served indefinitely. John Coleman, appointed head of the mathematics department in 1960, would serve until 1980, building the department tremendously. His colleagues, half-affectionately and half-disparagingly, referred to him as "the lord of the manor" and the "dictator."[80] Some defended this chummy approach to getting academic things done at Queen's as being expeditious and in the best interests of the place. Many excellent appointments were made as the result of a quick consultation of head, dean, and principal. But others thought it smacked of cronyism. Mechanical-engineering professor W. B. Rice likened Queen's to "a family company."[81] When physiology professor Vivian Abrahams arrived at the university in 1963, he would reach much the same conclusion: "Queen's is a funny old place. It's heavily inbred. There's an Old Boys' system that is very active looking after itself, which has a hard time accepting outsiders."[82]

The Reality of '61

Thus, Queen's in the fall of 1961 was far from an Elysian institution. The storied strength of its dedication to teaching, its self-powered student government, its careful husbanding of its resources, and its ongoing connection with "the national good" had all polished its lustre. In October 1962, the federal Historic Sites and Monuments Board unveiled a historic plaque on the lawn of Summerhill, honouring Queen's emergence as "one of Canada's leading universities." But beneath the majestic flow of tradition there were worrisome currents of dysfunction. At times, Queen's tended to slip into a comfortable, self-justifying conservatism, as if numbed by the ever-present celebration of its traditional ways. In 1953, Bill Mackintosh had sensed this danger: "It is possible to be cozy but second-rate."[83] Thirty years later, university historian Fred Gibson's exhaustive research brought him to the same conclusion: "At Queen's the strong sense of community can at times degenerate into parochialism."[84] Soon after he took office, Principal Corry received a briefing from Registrar Jean Royce on the "changing character of the University." The demographic and socio-economic ground was shifting under Queen's feet, she cautioned, and traditional values would have to be adjusted. "The gentleman scholar belongs to the past," she poignantly suggested.[85]

Tradition, it seemed, could be either a stimulant or a sedative. This ambivalence lurked just below the surface at Queen's, in its ethnic composition and gender arrangements. The census taken across Canada in the spring of 1961 revealed that small towns and cities such as Kingston largely reflected Canada's established racial balance. Canada was still a predominantly white nation, drawn largely from European stock. Immigration flows into Canada were, however, shifting; "new" Canadians were arriving from untraditional lands – the Caribbean, the Pacific Rim, and Central America – and they flocked to the big urban centres where access to the ladder of advancement was more assured. Neither Queen's nor Kingston appealed. When Merv Daub arrived on campus from Kitchener in the early 1960s to study business and play football, he did, however, find the campus "white diverse" – an intriguing mixture of WASP Canada drawn from rural reaches and urban centres. "There was always a lot of stuff about 'you dumb' Polack and you know this stuff floating around."[86] But there was little hint of the new Canada. When Jamaica-born civil engineer Barry Batchelor arrived to teach at Queen's a decade later, he found the campus a pleasant change from the overt anti-black bigotry he had encountered during his graduate studies in England. Nonetheless, he found Kingston "a very lonely place ... even my children at school were looked on as curiosities."[87]

Women at Queen's in 1961 also had good reason to believe that they were curiosities. The entire power structure at the university was patriarchal. There were only two women of any administrative stature on campus. Jean Royce's long innings as registrar and secretary of the Senate had given her a formidable reputation. And, since 1918, the university had had a dean of women. The current incumbent, Beatrice Bryce, had inherited a mandate quite unlike that of her male compatriots in the academic faculties. Her purpose was maternal: to nurture the daily lives of young women students. Her position was "one of influence rather than of authority."[88] She oversaw the residences women lived in, structured their cultural life, and dispensed caring advice. In terms of bureaucratic weight, she brought little to the table at the weekly meeting of deans; she managed on a meagre budget and small staff. There were only four women on the Board of Trustees. Mrs James Richardson, widow of the university's chancellor in the 1930s, embodied the Richardson family of Winnipeg's splendid benevolence towards Queen's. The others were women in the tradition of Charlotte Whitton – women who had proved themselves in a man's world, such as Dr Florence Dunlop, a special-education expert, and the novelist Grace Campbell.

Women were sparse in the ranks of the faculty too. Only 5 per cent of tenured faculty in 1961 were women. This, of course, represented the broader Canadian fact that women of the day were marginalized in the professions and in graduate education. However, there were women of real distinction in the Queen's faculty – women like Alice Vibert Douglas, a world-renowned astrophysicist and dean

Registrar Jean Royce oversees registration in the late 1950s. From 1933 to 1968, Royce served as the formidable and benevolent first point of contact for thousands of incoming Queen's students, steering them into programs best suited to their potential. She left an indelible mark on many of them.

of women from 1939 to 1959. Only one woman – Hilda Laird in German – had ever headed a department. Women professors who persevered at Queen's tended never to marry; there was an unwritten understanding that faculty men were breadwinners and that women should not impinge on this obligation. A noticeable number of the women who did carve out careers at Queen's were related to prominent males at the university: English professor Wilhemina Gordon was the daughter of Principal Daniel Gordon, and Classics professor Mary Macdonnell was the sister of Board chairman James Macdonnell. Queen's males were steadfast in preserving their exclusivity. That lofty Saturday Club contained no women colleagues; wives of members were relegated to the kitchen, where they readied coffee and cakes for the male participants.

In 1939, a Faculty Women's Club was formed to provide "a means of social intercourse" for women in some way connected to Queen's – wives, widows, women professors, and administrators. Its teas and lectures at its Union Street home usefully raised money for scholarships. Members served tea to parents and newly minted alumni at every convocation. By 1961, the club had 218 members.[89] It steeped its tradition as carefully as its tea. Novelist Janette Turner Hospital later penned a withering short-story portrait of the club's culture of "baroque silver teapots" and white gloves: "'It's always been done this way, dear,' the woman on the telephone said to Juliet [the fictional wife of a new faculty member]. There was only the gentlest hint of frost in her voice. 'I don't think it would be very nice for a new young faculty wife to upset tradition, do you?'"[90]

In every respect, women at Queen's were in a minority position. A heavy, opaque glass ceiling hung above their heads. By 1961–62, the student body included 1,034 women, almost a third of overall registration. However, 677 of them were clustered in Arts and Science. Only in nursing and Physical Education were women in the majority. The closer one got to the professional faculties, the fewer women there were: only 11 of 103 in Business and 36 in the Medical faculty, which had 330 students. Masculinity ruled almost supreme in Applied Science – one woman amid 885 men. A male frosh in Science '61 recalled a manifesto by his professor in his first class in mining engineering:

Before we go any further, there is something I want to make clear [long pause for effect]. There is absolutely no place – none whatsoever – for a woman in the field of mining engineering! He paused again, glaring out at us, stern-faced and almost angry, and then, without further comment, began his lecture.[91]

Most male engineering students soon picked up the message. The unsigned engineers' column in the *Journal*, dubbed the "Steamshovel," delivered a weekly dose of talk about the "Glorious Fac," "booz," and the comely "lemonz" in "artz."[92]

In matters of student governance, women were segregated in their own precinct, the Levana Society. Women students lived in residences such as Ban Righ and Chown Halls, which were off-limits to males. There, under the eye of the dean of women, they constructed a rich woman-centred life of teas, fireside chats, lectures, and evening meals, to which they were obliged to wear skirts. This "Levana culture" should not however automatically be seen as something antediluvian: it did provide Queen's women with a measure of control over their lives and nurtured a slow progressivism that could at times challenge the broader culture of the university. In early 1962, a woman, Jane Matthews, was elected president of the AMS. Nonetheless, once away from their residence, women were surrounded by a gender culture that at every turn reflected a powerful, male-defined set of values that pervaded the campus. Only in Susie-Q week were they entitled to turn the tables on male dominance, enjoying what the *Journal* dubbed "male hunting season," when they could stage their own dance and ask a male to be their date. The rest of the year proceeded according to a cycle of formal dances, winter carnivals, and beauty contests reflecting the strong heterosexual and bourgeois ethos that permeated the social background of Queen's students. As with other aspects of Queen's procrustean culture, those swayed by other values – sexual and cultural – quickly learned to conform or lie low.

Thus, when he arrived in his new office in Richardson Hall in the fall of 1961 Alex Corry could hardly have been aware that western societies, nursed by almost two decades of postwar prosperity, were about to experience incredible social upheaval, a world that Corry naively foresaw as the "electronic and rocket revolution" in his installation address. Old norms were about to be questioned, disparaged, and rejigged. "Tradition" in many minds would come to be seen as an obstacle rather than a handrail of stability and gradualism. Universities would be arenas of this transformation. At Queen's, over a century of distilled tradition would now come under seismic pressure to change and embrace a wider definition of purpose. It would be obliged to become, in the words of University of California President Clark Kerr in 1963, a "multiversity," an agent of change serving reaches of society hitherto unconnected to the university. From his chilly perch in Richardson Stadium, Corry could scarcely have been expected to anticipate second-wave feminism and agitation for affirmative action, bilingualism, or enhanced human rights. But his training as a political scientist and his persistent championing of individual rights did precondition him to navigate the changes that would break so dramatically over his tenure as principal. Two decades later, when his thoughts turned to writing a memoir, Corry would liken the eight years of his life as principal of Queen's, starting in 1961, to "running the rapids."[93]

2

"Deliberate Speed"
Alex Corry and the Modernization of Queen's, 1961–1968

The universities are short of everything, except students ... They are now outside the gates for everyone to count and cannot be wished away.
John J. Deutsch, 1961

I urged that self-discipline on the inside was the best way to avoid discipline being imposed from outside.
J. Alex Corry to R.S. McLaughlin, 1967

I regret the decision to expand Queen's and, although I am not optimistic about your plan to maintain a small university character, good luck.
Olive Caldwell, Arts '56, to Corry, 1963

Prelude to the Rising Tide

They gathered in a Toronto hotel in the late spring of 1955. In their business suits, white shirts, and dark ties, the presidents and principals of Canada's universities and colleges were a sober-sided group. The official photographer caught them with coffee cups and cigarettes in hand, their sameness varied only by a handful of clerics in religious garb. Sister Francis d'Assisi, president of Mount St Vincent College, broke the male monopoly. Since 1911, the National Conference of Canadian Universities (NCCU) had tried to unfurl an umbrella of consensus over the disparate concerns of post-secondary institutions across Canada. By 1955, it had thirty-seven university and college members. Observers from the federal and provincial governments and research agencies, such as the National Research Council and the Canadian Association of University Teachers (CAUT), swelled attendance at these annual NCCU meetings. American philanthropic foundations like the Carnegie Corporation came north to watch – and sometimes fund – Canadian developments in higher education.

Prominent among the 1955 attendees were Queen's Principal Bill Mackintosh and his vice-principal, Alex Corry. Not only was Queen's one of the nation's oldest universities, but a reputation as a "national" institution endowed its opinions with gravitas. Mackintosh could count on making other connections at that Toronto gathering. During coffee breaks, he would have quickly fallen into conversation with old friends from the wartime Ottawa bureaucracy, men such as Queen's-educated John Deutsch, who was now head of the economics department at the University of British Columbia, and R.B. "Bob" Bryce, one-time deputy-minister of finance and now clerk of the Privy Council. All were men who had steered Canada through a perilous war and into a prosperous peace. Now they were turning their attention to bolstering a system of post-secondary education that was being overwhelmed by demographic change.[1]

The members of NCCU had come to Toronto in 1955 to hear what that they already suspected: postwar Canada was enjoying sustained prosperity. The bogeyman of depression had been vanquished by the managed growth of what economists were calling a "mixed economy" – a state and private-sector partnership, one foretold by Mackintosh's seminal 1945 "white paper" prescription for the state to orchestrate a high level of employment and economic stability. Unlike the situation after World War I, post–World War II Canada had not stumbled into recession. Instead, fifteen years of depression and war had given way to a demographic and economic surge. Immigrants flowed into Canada. Agricultural exports flowed out. Industry diversified. Investment flourished. Cities grew. Indeed, the Queen's Board of Trustees boasted men such as Donald Gordon of the Canadian National Railway and Hazlett Lemmon of Canada Life, who sat in the Bay Street and St James Street control rooms of the surging economy.

Average Canadians did not need corporate annual reports or census data to confirm what they saw all around them: suburban sprawl, highways, new cars, television sets, and a daily consumerism that was making food "fast" and pleasure affordable.

Above all, Canada was becoming *youthful*. The Baby Boom was under way. In 1952, for example, the country saw more than four hundred thousand babies born for the first time in its history, a number that would not slip below that until the mid-sixties. A baby boom is usually calibrated by historians as a birth rate of twenty-four per thousand; by this measure Canada witnessed unprecedented growth again right into the mid-sixties. As Queen's-educated historian Douglas Owram would later observe, this was a generation "born at the right time."[2] The flood tide was reinforced by other powerful urges in Canadian society: the hunger of parents who had known depression and war to enjoy the normalcy of family life and social respectability and by a surge of veterans eager to better themselves in a society now increasingly self-assured and affluent. In the late 1940s and early 1950s, for instance, Queen's Faculty of Applied Science had been swamped with veterans and young men intent on equipping themselves for boom times in the mines, factories, and infrastructure building of the nation. So great was the squeeze in Applied Science that classes were accelerated and degrees sped to completion; 1948 saw two graduating classes of engineers troop to Grant Hall – Science '48 and Science '48½.

The challenge for Canada now became one of looking *forward*, not backward on the fading traumas of privation and war. In 1955, for instance, the Liberal government in Ottawa had convened a royal commission to examine "Canada's economic prospects" over the next twenty-five years. Following a familiar pattern, Queen's scholars, such as economist David Slater (who had studied in the 1940s at Queen's under Frank Knox and Mac Urquhart), headed to Ottawa to crunch numbers and build economic models that would reveal Canada's prospects. Their 1957 report would note that Canadians were becoming consumers who would fuel their buying with credit and an unfolding array of goods and services. New manufacturing and boundless resource exports would pay the national bill. Sensing that post-secondary education was increasingly perceived as an input – to adopt the terminology of economists – that Canadians would regard as a key driver of future prosperity, the NCCU dedicated its 1955 conference agenda to the prospective – and daunting – expansion of enrolment as the baby boom surged from crib to college. To give precision to their anxieties, the NCCU called in an Ottawa economist, Edward F. Sheffield from the Dominion Bureau of Statistics, to extrapolate the impact of the baby boom on Canada's universities and colleges. From a base of 72,737 full-time undergraduate and graduate students in 1955, Sheffield delivered the startling news that, by 1965, the country would require 128,900 university places. By 1971, as most baby boomers hit adolescence, capacity would have to stretch to 229,100.[3]

Alarmed by the magnitude of Sheffield's prediction, the NCCU reconvened in November 1956 to ponder "Canada's crisis in higher education." Led by President Claude Bissell of Carleton College (soon to become a university), the NCCU dedicated itself to assessing the "points of pressure" that a doubling of capacity would create on Canadian campuses. What was needed, Bissell urged, was a "sober, realistic analysis of minimum needs" if the surge was to be successfully met. And, at the same time, there must be a "systematic and intensive campaign to acquaint the public with the urgent national nature of educational problems." Sheffield, who would soon become the conference's research officer, began spreading the message. He would tell readers of *Canadian Business* magazine in 1959, for example, that $400 million would be needed for bricks and mortar by 1963. If the teaching ratio of professor to students was to be preserved at one professor for every 14.3 students, Canada's professoriate would have to expand from 6,610 in 1958 to an astonishing cadre of 16,020 by 1970.[4] For those funding Canada's universities – Ottawa, the provinces, corporate Canada, and university alumni alike – Sheffield suggested, purse strings would have to be generously loosened. Growth was the order of the day. "To sum up," University of Toronto President Sidney Smith told the NCCU at its 1956 confab, "there are two watchwords for the universities in the next ten years: flexibility of structure and tenacity of purpose … We cannot meet the country's needs for university graduates by dropping our standards and shoving everybody through. That would be simply an attempt to fool ourselves and cheat the public."[5]

Nobody could have agreed more than the two Queen's delegates listening to Smith's message. As an economist, Principal Mackintosh was by no means oblivious to the input of education to national growth, but he was also acutely attuned to Queen's reputation as a small teaching university known for its quality and intimacy. Queen's, he announced, with its student body of 2,498 in 1957, "cannot do its best work with a doubled enrolment" and would cap future growth at 4,000.[6] Vice-principal Alex Corry, displaying his political-science sensitivities, worried that the universities might sell their academic integrity for a mess of potage. If expansion necessitated ever-larger subsidization by the state and other powerful outside interests, universities would soon see their dedication to objective inquiry and disinterested social service eroded. Corry's anxieties were somewhat assuaged by the conference's keynote speaker, Liberal Prime Minister Louis St Laurent. After announcing a $100-million dollop of federal support for Canada's universities, the prime minister was quick to assure his learned audience that Ottawa would not "tamper" with academic freedom, because this was what brought out "the nobler side of our human nature."[7]

Despite St Laurent's rosy assurances, a tectonic tension in Canadian post-secondary education was beginning to reveal itself as the baby boomers began to gaze longingly beyond high-school classrooms to the campuses of Canada's universities. On the one

Alex Corry (left) awaits his installation as Queen's thirteenth principal on the stage of Grant Hall in the fall of 1961. Overseeing the ceremony is Chancellor John Bertram "Bert" Stirling. Stirling was steeped in Queen's tradition: a BA graduate of 1909 and a founder of the Queen's bands, Stirling became a mogul of Canadian construction and served as chancellor from 1960 to 1970.

hand, there was the broad desire to make Canada's post-secondary educational institutions an engine of social change and economic betterment. Many impulses lay behind this. Foremost among them was the urge to manage what Canadian-born economist John Kenneth Galbraith had dubbed the "affluent society" in his influential 1958 bestseller; education could be a force for *both* income growth and its redistribution. Many also believed that universities could bolster Western stamina in the Cold War; the startling launch of Sputnik in 1957 underscored the message that prowess in mathematics and physics was fundamental to ideological supremacy. In 1961, Queen's new physics building – Stirling Hall – bespoke this expectation, and the arrival of John Coleman from Toronto a year earlier to head the math department marked the start of a concerted effort to reinvigorate Queen's ability to teach mathematics and statistics (over the twenty years of his headship, Coleman would expand the department from ten to forty-eight members).[8] Universities were also being called upon to bolster the professions in Canada: an affluent society needed more lawyers, doctors, teachers, physical-education instructors, social scientists, business managers, and engineers to oil the wheels of the modern industrial state and the burgeoning welfare state it supported. As soon as Sir John A. Macdonald Hall was opened in 1960 as the Law faculty's home, for instance, Dean Bill Lederman began lobbying the principal's office for an extension and for the creation of graduate programs in law.

Politicians across the nation sensed this mood of expectation and dedicated themselves to maximizing accessibility to the income enhancement implicit in university education for Canadians. In retrospect, there was a streak of naïveté in this: national productivity and well-being depended on factors more complex than simple injections of post-secondary dollars. But the heady mood of rising affluence and social entitlement of the late 1950s tended to encourage simplistic expectations. Education began to be conceived of in quantitative, not qualitative, terms. In the words of Paul Axelrod, the historian of Ontario's postwar university system, "[h]igher education was valued *not* for its ideals, but primarily for its products."[9] In 1965, Gordon Garbutt, one of the first public-relations experts hired to guide the university's external relations, warned Principal Corry that pleas for "'Quality, not quantity' have fallen on deaf ears ... Queen's, in common with many other universities, is being pushed farther and farther along the road to becoming an 'education factory,' a glorified vocational school, rather than an institution dedicated to scholarship."[10]

Rationalizing Disparate Goals

Ontarians and their politicians thus entered the sixties dedicated to an expansion of post-secondary education that would be the system's "most glorious voyage to date."[11] Slumping economic performance and creeping disillusionment with education's payoff would erode this optimism severely by the time the decade ended, but there would be one unshakable legacy of this initial infatuation: the dedication of Ontario politicians – and the voters behind them – to the notion of accessibility. If there is one word that captures successive Ontario governments' attitude to universities down through the remaining decades of the twentieth century, it would be *accessibility*. Like the "universal" health care that was being unrolled before Canadians in the same decade, the allure of accessibility would have long-lasting political implications. To offer broad access to universities was politically expedient, but to curtail its application would prove political heresy.

Universities, however, regarded the principle of accessibility with ambivalence. There was, of course, undeniable comfort in the kind of largesse that Prime Minister St Laurent dispensed at the 1956 NCCU annual meeting: the capital cost of bricks and mortar as the baby boom approached was daunting. Beyond that, there was concern that the state was assuming the role of predominant paymaster of the university system and that the processes of implementing accessibility were as yet not systematized. Boldly put, university presidents shared a primal fear that whoever "paid the piper" would also want to call the tune. Universities were prisms of liberal societies, not mirrors of a procrustean state. As such, they must zealously protect their academic freedom, their right to self-determination, and their individuality. In this respect, Queen's was supremely well-served by the selection of Alex Corry as its principal in 1961. Corry's reputation rested on his dogged championing of individualism in the face of the postwar megastate. "Thus," he had written in his seminal 1946 treatise *Democratic Government and Politics*, "we believe in freedom and social equality, not for themselves alone but rather because they are both needed in varying proportion to create the best environment for the development of individual personality." Social equality – accessibility – was a commendable goal, but it could not be attained at the expense of trammelling individual liberty, which was the quintessence of western societies and their universities. The key, for Corry and now for his fellow university presidents, was to work out the mechanisms of compromise by which universities could embrace the baby boom but not at the same time surrender their academic liberty. "Procedures," Corry concluded, "are almost as important as the ideals themselves. The means used to reach an end cannot be divorced from the end desired."[12]

The sixties would thus see the gestation of a new diplomacy between Ontario's universities and their political facilitators at Queen's Park – and to a lesser degree in Ottawa. Under the British North America Act, the provinces controlled education spending; Ottawa contributed indirectly through per-capita grants to the provinces for post-secondary education and by its direct funding of research on campuses. As a result, the primary tension in this symbiotic diplomacy would be the reconciliation of Toronto's quest for accessibility and financial accountability with the universities' insistence on their autonomy and individuality. This contention would become the leitmotif of Queen's external relations with Toronto and Ottawa over the next four decades. Fiscal conditions, the ebb and flow of federal-provincial relations, wavering economic prosperity, and social attitudes towards higher education might stiffen or ease the tension over time, but the central dialectic remained. As Corry would every year remind his students in Politics 2, "[F]undamentally, the democratic political process is one of discussion, accommodation and compromise."[13]

Over the years 1961 to 1974, Queen's was fortunate to be guided in this process of rationalizing accessibility and financial security with autonomy and individuality by two of the shrewdest and most prescient strategists in Canadian university diplomacy: the suave and persuasive Alex Corry, principal until 1968, and his successor, the less-charismatic but tactically brilliant John Deutsch (1968–74). Their mastery of the art of policy adjustment would allow all Ontario universities to regularize their relations with Queen's Park, while at the same time allowing Queen's to guard its distinctiveness as a national university with a reputation for quality teaching – and simultaneously unfolding new graduate and professional studies.

In the 1950s, there was more caprice than system in Queen's relations with Queen's Park and Ottawa. The Conservatives had seized the political centre in Ontario in 1943, and by the fifties had pushed the Liberals and Co-operative Commonwealth Federation (CCF) to what seemed the perpetual margins of Ontario politics. Since 1949, the premier's office had been occupied by Leslie Frost, whose avuncular, prosperity-based style had brought him the nickname "Old Man Ontario." Coincidently, Frost's brother Grenville had taught chemistry at Queen's until his retirement in 1960, although this seemed to confer no special privilege on the university. Instead, Frost's dealings with Queen's and the handful of other Ontario universities – Toronto (long favoured as the "provincial university"), McMaster, Western, Ottawa, Carleton, Waterloo, and, after 1959, York – were marked by ad hoc informality. There was, in effect, no cohesive, articulated provincial policy on post-secondary education. Frost inherited the instincts of his Tory predecessor as premier, the combative George Drew, who, when it came to the province's universities, pursued a policy described by Brian McKillop, another Queen's-trained historian, as "ad hoc and unsystematic, with universities left to provide their own direction and to articulate their individual financial needs." As early as 1949, the *Globe and Mail* had editorialized that Ontario's university presidents had to become "executive salesmen, leaders of delegations, and beggars," desperately trying to keep their institutions viable.[14] Paul Axelrod concurs: the Ontario government's approach to its universities "remained largely responsive, and its responses were *ad hoc* in nature. As specific problems arose, it responded in a piecemeal fashion."[15] To this, Premier Frost brought a grudging, utilitarian attitude: "If we were to do everything the universities wanted us to do," he wrote in 1958, "there would be no money for anything else … I think it [funding] should be based upon utility and the training of the best minds and aptitudes … we should cut off all of the frills … and get down to essentials."[16]

University presidents in the fifties were consequently obliged to approach Queen's Park cap in hand when it came to funding their operations. Such short-term supplication had the added debility of denying universities any sense of stability, let alone the luxury of long-term planning. Late each fall, the Queen's principal boarded a Toronto-bound train, clutching his wish list for the next year's operating budget. These submissions were sparsely detailed and depended mainly on the principal's powers of persuasion at Queen's Park. In 1956, for instance, Principal Mackintosh reported to the provincial minister of education that Queen's would spend an estimated $2.87 million in 1956–57, of which $775,000 came from the provincial coffers and $335,000 from Ottawa. Thus, only about 30 per cent of Queen's annual expenditures in the fifties was covered by government; fees, philanthropy, and endowment-based revenue made up the rest. But with the baby boom around the corner, Mackintosh stressed that government would have to contribute more. He estimated that the provincial "maintenance" grant would have to grow by 7 to 10 per cent a year for the next five years, even with the university itself trying to raise $4 million in donations on its own. Despite his financial predicament, Mackintosh felt compelled to remind the minister that the piper would not necessarily play Queen's Park's tune: "We are concerned to maintain the balance and compactness of the University and we are concerned to maintain the quality of its instruction."[17]

By the time Corry became principal in 1961, the pressure for a more systematized and less politicized means of financing the university had intensified. As Mackintosh's understudy, Corry already knew the arithmetic, although, as a political scientist, number crunching had never been his forte. The Corry years were to be marked by an inexorable increase in universities' dependency on government for support. Not only were annual operating costs ballooning, but so too was the capital cost of expanding the university's physical plant in a decade marked by steadily rising inflation. To this fiscal crescendo, Queen's brought its own peculiar demands. Mackintosh – and now Corry – complained that Queen's Park favoured the sprouting new universities in the province, like Carleton and Waterloo, where infrastructure was being hurriedly installed, to the detriment of those campuses established in the nineteenth century. In 1960, Mackintosh alleged, Carleton received $1,717 from Toronto for every student it had, and Waterloo luxuriated with $4,895 per capita, while older Queen's skimped by on $895.[18]

Corry perpetuated Queen's sense of grievance. Queen's, he lectured John Robarts, provincial minister of education, was a "high cost" university. Its limestone buildings were old and expensive to maintain. Its relatively isolated location in eastern Ontario deprived it of economies of scale enjoyed by newer, red-brick universities clustered around booming Toronto. Furthermore, Queen's was a small institution dedicated to quality teaching, which meant higher faculty costs, especially in professional faculties such as law and medicine. In 1960–61, 53 per cent of Queen's 3,000 students were in intensive programs like medicine, law, honours arts, and engineering, whereas only 32 per cent of Western students were in similar programs. The age of low-cost liberal-arts colleges was over, Corry argued. "It is clear that the present maintenance grant to Queen's falls considerably short of an equitable arrangement," Robarts was told, "and we again ask that further progress be made to rectify the discrepancy in the grant for the coming year."[19] Corry did not spare Ottawa in his quest for financial stability and fairness either. In 1964, he wrote Kingston Liberal MP and one-time Queen's commerce lecturer Edgar Benson, urging the continuation of federal per-capita support of students and infrastructure funding of universities: "The truth is that university-educated people serve the nation and it is, therefore, entirely appropriate that the National Government should carry a significant part of these costs."[20]

All the while though, Corry kept up his vigilance about university autonomy. Queen's, he insisted, would expand and diversify according to its own agenda. In 1958, in an attempt to end the capriciousness of cap-in-hand budgeting, the Frost government had created the Advisory Committee on University Affairs (ACUA), which was intended to provide the government with an arm's-length evaluation of university budgets and strategic plans. Shortly after Education Minister John Robarts took over the premiership in 1961, he asked outgoing Premier Frost to take over chairmanship of the advisory committee. Frost donned the mantle of an elder statesman: "To meet the university problem is not going to be easy ... We are all going to have to show our ingenuity in finding ways and means of meeting the enormous expenses involved in accommodation [of students] and maintenance."[21]

Ontario's universities reciprocated in 1962 by creating their own Committee of Presidents of Provincially-Assisted Universities of Ontario (CPUO) to serve as a consensus-grooming body for the universities in their Queen's Park diplomacy. For the first time, a structured dialogue between government and providers of higher education was available. Not surprisingly, Corry, with his grounding in constitutional and administrative law, took a leading role in the CPUO.[22] When, in 1964, Robarts proposed folding the administration of the provincial universities into the Department of Education, Corry and the CPUO vehemently resisted. The universities, they argued, would not take dictation as the primary and secondary system did. Obligingly, Robarts created a separate Department of University Affairs under William "Bill" Davis, a rising Tory politician who would quickly attach his star to delivering a broadening foundation of universities to appreciative Ontarians. However, despite the new channels of communication, the fundamental problem remained. As the presidents' committee informed Premier Robarts in late 1963, "the basic problem … is to reconcile the expenditure of public funds with the autonomy that a university must have in order to fulfil its task."[23]

Back at Queen's, Corry found things going from anxious to tense: costs were rising and the university's revenue was losing its race with expenditures. Enrolment was already feeling the first of the baby boom: by early 1963 total enrolment had grown to 3,492, up 400 from 1961. To protect the university's reputation for quality teaching, Corry kept his foot lightly on the brakes, telling Queen's Park that Queen's might grow to 5,600 by 1971, but absolutely no more. Let the new universities, such as Brock, Trent, Guelph, York, and Carleton, move with the tide of new students. "No, it is the province that is demanding, not I," he testily told Leslie Frost early in 1963. "Queen's is not pushing big ambitions at all." He reiterated that the province was unduly favouring the newcomers with more generous annual operating grants than Queen's.[24]

Nonetheless, Queen's was rapidly shifting into expansion mode. Long-term planning began to dominate the trustees' deliberations, with constant talk of architects' plans, budget inflows, and returns on the endowment fund. The new physics building had to be completed. Extensions to Nicol, McLaughlin, and Gordon halls were needed to allow growth in the Faculty of Applied Science. A new biology building seemed unavoidable, as did some expansion of the picturesque, but antiquated, buildings around the Medical Quadrangle. The Douglas Library was bursting at the seams, a concern made doubly worrisome by the province's new-

found interest in expanding graduate studies. Graduate and professional study programs depended on a broad foundation of library and research facilities. There was also pressure to expand the Agnes Etherington Art Centre beyond the lovely, but cramped, Neo-Georgian house where it had opened in 1957.

Behind all this, other problems lurked: the need to provide better accommodation for humanities professors, many of whom were crammed into attic offices in Kingston Hall, sharing desks and telephones. And, as more students arrived each September, more residences were desperately needed – a double challenge, since the provincial government refused to consider capital grants for residences. All the while, Queen's older buildings, like the handsome Romanesque Ontario Hall, dating from 1903, demanded, because of their Gibraltar-like facades, constant upkeep. Last, but hardly least, new professors and support staff had to be paid and their benefits made competitive.

Under these pressures, the Board of Trustees clung to ingrained Presbyterian behaviours.[25] Buildings would not be commissioned until their financing was secure. The endowment might be tapped, but was never to be drained. When Corry reported in the fall of 1963 that the university would need an estimated $25 million by 1969 to digest its swelling enrolment, the trustees hired Canada's premier fundraising consultants, G.A. Brakeley & Co. Brakeley suggested that a capital campaign for $5 million seemed feasible and advised that Queen's sell itself as a "national" university. Royal Bank President Earle McLaughlin (BA 1936) agreed to chair the campaign. As money became tighter, relations with former premier Frost as head of the government's advisory committee on university affairs became increasingly fraught: Corry repeatedly charged that Queen's was being shortchanged in its annual operating grant at the expense of much younger universities. For his part, Frost retorted that Queen's figures were "always reliable … but that there just wasn't that much money available for distribution."[26] The fiscal pain intensified with the realization that

Expansion in the 1960s was not just about students, faculty, and buildings. Queen's cultural presence also expanded: the Agnes Etherington Art Centre, opened in 1957, was for instance expanded and benefited from handsome additions to its collections. Here, Toronto financier Samuel Zacks (second from left) and his wife Ayala present the gallery with works of contemporary Canadian art in 1962. Kingston-born and Queen's-educated, Zacks was an avid and incisive art collector. Centre director and artist André Bieler (left) looks on.

federal transfers to the province were distributed on a per-student basis, so that the more Queen's enrolment lagged behind that of the province's burgeoning new universities, the less it reaped.

In March 1963, Corry balked. Queen's was chronically underfunded and felt systematically discriminated against by Queen's Park. John Deutsch, the university's vice-principal, administration, had crunched the numbers and could see only two options: fee increases or running a deficit. Higher fees would mean paying out more endowment monies as scholarships to deserving but cash-strapped students. Corry lectured Frost: "This is a Scots Presbyterian institution in origin and it holds fast to its traditions. You know enough about the frugal, cautious Scots to know how repellant a deficit would be to the Board of Trustees. Queen's University has survived only by paying its way all the time. It has never run a substantial deficit in its history. When the Board asks me who will carry the deficit, I will not be able to answer that one."[27] That fall, that unpalatable question did indeed come up. Corry reported to the trustees that the university's request for an operating grant of $2.8 million from Toronto for 1964 had been whittled back by the ministry to $2,365,000. Queen's was now in deficit: when the accounts were finally reconciled, the books showed a deficit of $39,000 in 1963, rising to $109,000 in 1964.[28] But, just as the fiscal clouds grew darker, Queen's storied reputation for public-policy ingenuity came to the rescue.

"Deliberate Speed"

Queen's Leads the Way on University Funding

Jarred by having to ask the trustees to dip into the precious endowment for $75,000 to help cover an operating deficit in 1963, Corry decided to force the issue. "The experience of the last year has convinced me that substantial changes in the present organization for examining and judging requests for support from the Government must be made," he told Premier Robarts.[29] He had a proposal in hand. By 1963, Corry was wearing two hats: as Queen's principal he pushed the interests of his campus at Queen's Park and as chairman of the NCCU he spoke for *all* Canadian universities. He was also an influential voice in the CPUO, of which he would become chair in 1966. While there were tensions between Ontario's old and new universities, there was shared ground between them when it came to negotiating their operating grants with the province. (The CPUO was similarly working towards the creation of a centralized admissions centre for all Ontario universities and interlibrary loan services for its members' libraries.) With this in mind, the CPUO struck a research subcommittee and tasked it with studying the financing and planning of the Ontario university system down to 1970–71. Heading the committee was Queen's vice-principal, administration, John Joseph Deutsch.

Deutsch was an astute choice. Mackintosh had brought him to Kingston in 1959 in the wake of a Price Waterhouse consultants' report a year earlier that had concluded that the university's administrative structure was holding it back from the challenge of becoming a modern institution. In some ways, Deutsch was cut from the same cloth as Mackintosh: each had emerged from rural Canada and each had found their professional prowess as students at Queen's. Deutsch was the eldest of seventeen children on a Quinton, Saskatchewan, farm. Educated in local Catholic schools, Deutsch himself trained to be a teacher at Campion College in Regina in the dark early days of the Depression. Deutsch aspired to a university education and enrolled as a Queen's extension student in commerce. In 1934, he came east and enrolled full-time at Queen's for his final year, paying his way by teaching math for $55 a month at Kingston's Regiopolis College. He would later recall his enervating daily schedule: up at dawn, trudge up Division Street to Regiopolis, and then to classes in the afternoon at Queen's. He impressed his professors and had little trouble being admitted to a year of graduate study on graduation in 1935.

Deutsch's ability to extract useful patterns from masses of economic statistics proved an attractive talent in the depths of the Dirty Thirties, when economists struggled to dissect the failings of capitalism. Deutsch was thus recruited to the research department of Canada's fledgling central bank in Ottawa. Queen's had sent other gifted researchers to Ottawa in the interwar years: one-time political-economy professor Norman McLeod Rogers sat in Mackenzie King's federal cabinet as labour minister; former dean of Arts, Oscar "O.D." Skelton, served as undersecretary of state for external affairs; and, economist Bill Mackintosh was researching the economic structure of the federation for the Rowell–Sirois Royal Commission on federal-provincial relations. Deutsch soon joined Mackintosh at the royal commission, providing seminal input on the creation of a distinctly Canadian set of national accounts, economic statistics that allowed Canadians to look inside their economy for the first time.[30]

With the coming of the war in September 1939, Deutsch joined the ranks of senior bureaucrats who rallied to manage the war crisis.[31] He quickly won a reputation for calmly getting to the heart of an issue in the face of excruciating pressure. Deutsch never undertook doctoral studies; the real-world crisis of depression and war provided ample schooling. Nor did he ever lack for challenging work. After the war, he moved with facility from the bureaucratic world of the external affairs department and the Treasury Board, to journalism, where he advised the *Winnipeg Free Press*, then finally to the academic world, where he became head of the economics department at the University of British Columbia in 1956. All the while, Deutsch was becoming a much-sought-after advisor and royal commissioner on issues as varied as the finances of Newfoundland and natural-gas distribution. In 1959, Mackintosh could see that a man of Deutsch's experience was ideally suited to dragging Queen's into the modern age.

From 1951 to 1974, Queen's would thus be forcefully led by three boys from Canada's "back forty," two of them polished as undergraduates at Queen's into skilled political economists and sent off into the world at a time of global crisis, one day to return to their alma mater. The third, Alex Corry, had the same rural roots, but came to Queen's as the product of the University of Saskatchewan and Oxford. Through the 1950s, Mackintosh and Corry had become close friends, together through the working day and into many an evening. When Corry became principal in 1961, Mackintosh stayed on until 1965 as his vice-chancellor, where he kept an informed eye on Queen's stretched finances. Corry had never been strong on financial matters; Mackintosh, the economist, was. Despite their friendship, by day they abided by the stiff protocol of Queen's management, referring to each as "Dr" in memos. Away from the office, Mackintosh relished his collegiate football, bridge, and fishing at the posh Five Lakes Club outside Ottawa. There was bonhomie about Corry: he was a great raconteur, always ready with a witticism or a telling anecdote. To be a university president, he once quipped, one had to face the "slings and arrows of extravagant youth." And he mixed a memorable martini.[32] He dressed and acted like a seasoned diplomat, smooth and smiling, although, as some would learn in the challenging times of the sixties, there was a decisive steeliness beneath his friendly demeanour.

Deutsch was outwardly different. He lacked any obvious charisma. He presented a deceptive surface; at first contact, many misread his bashful facade.[33] Invariably dressed in a dark suit (his wife, Stephanie, would joke that her husband had only two suits: one

Principal Corry's convivial personality, and his reputation as a raconteur and martini-maker, is evident as he chats with James Richardson, Liberal MP and scion of Winnipeg's Richardson family. The Richardsons, whose commercial fortunes were rooted in nineteenth-century Kingston, had long been generous benefactors of the university, providing Queen's with facilities as varied as football stadiums and art galleries.

at the cleaners, the other on his back), he projected a rumpled, almost downcast, persona. He tended to listen rather than orate, to digest information until he could discern a course of action. There was a gentleness about him, a willingness to take in others' viewpoints without revealing his own inclinations. University secretary John Bannister remembered him as a "gentleman's gentleman."[34] Yet Deutsch possessed a keen intellectual edge. If by day at Queen's he concerned himself with parking spaces and balancing accounts, by evening he kept up his knowledge of economics as the discipline diversified in the heady sixties. When the university gave Pierre Trudeau an honorary degree in 1968, he saluted Deutsch for possessing a wry wit uncharacteristic of those in the dismal science. By the late 1950s, Deutsch's peripatetic career had given him a broad base of experience that few Canadian academics could rival – his contacts stretched from university campuses, to the inner sanctums of power in Ottawa, to the editorial offices of the national press, and to corporate boardrooms.

When Deutsch arrived at Queen's in the fall of 1959, he was appalled by what he discovered. Queen's administration ran along casual, largely undefined, lines. At a time when organizations were discovering what business schools called "organizational theory and practice," Queen's still operated as a chummy, catch-as-catch-can entity. Deutsch immediately realized that, if Queen's was to efficiently capitalize on the upcoming surge of baby-boom revenue, it would need systematic organization. He hired an executive assistant, Bob Crandall, a chartered accountant with experience at the prestigious Wood Gundy firm in Toronto. Like Deutsch, Crandall was aghast at what he saw. Neither Deutsch nor Crandall could figure out how the university negotiated its crucial annual operating grant from Toronto. It simply seemed to be "arrived at arbitrarily," usually after Mackintosh had gone on a plaintive excursion to the premier's office. "We sort of had to live within what we were given," he recalled. Neither Deutsch nor Crandall could fathom the hazy lines of financial authority within the university. When a request for a copy of the upcoming year's budget was dispatched to one department, the answer came back that the department waited to the *end* of the fiscal year to crunch its numbers; it was easier that way. Crandall recalled an exasperated Deutsch holing up in his office, where over several days, with pencil in hand, he sketched a new, rational accounts system for Queen's on a university exam booklet.[35]

Deutsch's "new broom" swept change through Queen's. With more and more Queen's employees driving to work, Deutsch scrapped the old preferential parking system, which assigned dedicated slots on the basis of seniority, arguing that pooled parking offered more efficient allocation. Work in civil-service Ottawa and consulting in the private sector told Deutsch that computers had tremendous organizational potential. Queen's seemed only dimly aware of the promise of the new machines. One slim file on computers exists in the office records of Bill Mackintosh; it is archaically labelled "computers (electric)." In 1960, Deutsch ordered Queen's first mainframe computer – an IBM 1620 – and challenged administrators and academics alike to explore its application to management and teaching.[36] It was a tough sell; Crandall recalled that the campus had many obdurate "Luddities." But Corry backed Deutsch and in 1961 set up an interdepartmental advisory committee on computing, soon followed by the creation of a centralized computing centre.

Deutsch threw himself into the challenge of modernizing Queen's. Most Saturdays found him in his office. While Corry busied himself contending with the university's external relations, Deutsch made himself the master of every nook and cranny of Queen's finances and bricks and mortar. So it was hardly surprising that Corry, as a persuasive member of the CPUO executive, would recruit his vice-principal of administration to head a CPUO committee inquiry into the way the province funded its universities. The CPUO was not the first body to recognize Deutsch's prowess. In 1962, the provincial government of New Brunswick had called on him to chair a royal commission on higher education. Universities in New Brunswick existed in a politically charged atmosphere, as tensions between anglophone-Protestant and francophone-Catholic citizens surfaced over the way provincial universities were chartered and funded. For thirteen months, Deutsch and his commissioners wrestled with the delicate situation. Their report had many dimensions, principally a recommendation that francophone higher education be consolidated on one campus. In 1963, the University of Moncton was thus created.

The report also hatched an idea that was to serve as the kernel of a solution to the concern of Ontario universities with buffering themselves from government interference while allowing longer-term fiscal planning and accountability. Drawing on a British model of scheduling state support for universities on a five-year horizon, Deutsch suggested the adoption of a formula-driven scheme, whereby universities would receive their annual operating grant according to a formula that awarded a per-capita "basic income unit" (BIU), based on the resources required to sustain particular programs offered on a campus. Governments would at the same time award an annual "block" grant to support universities' long-term strategic goals – new buildings, the start-up cost of new programs. They would also annually dispense a payment that would reflect the number of BIUs a university's programs had generated. While the province would retain the right to initially approve and periodically review academic programs by means of arm's-length panels, BIU monies, once received, could be spent as the university saw fit. By gearing payments to quantitative benchmarks, the proposed system offered fairness and equity among campuses and would facilitate financial planning well into the future. Like large corporations and government bureaucracies, universities could now enter the age of planning.[37]

Deutsch carried the BIU proposal in his intellectual baggage back to Queen's, where Corry could immediately see its utility. Formula funding offered stability and autonomy to the universities, and at the same time assured government that its spending on higher education could be metered and made accountable. This had been Corry's goal for years. In particular, formula funding would compensate Queen's for its high-cost programs such as honours and medicine, and at the same time make its fledgling graduate program less financially onerous.[38] The CPUO stoked the debate by releasing a report in the fall of 1963 that projected enrolment at Ontario universities soaring towards a projected total of 91,600 by 1970–71, a ceiling that suggested at least another five to seven hundred faculty members would be needed across the province.[39] Corry estimated that every new faculty member added $12,000 to his university's bottom line. The magnitude of this expansion alarmed politicians. In 1963, Toronto had generously hiked its support for universities from $45 million to $70 million, but CPUO enrolment estimates indicated that even this would not be enough. At the advisory committee, Leslie Frost despaired. It would be "impossible" to satisfy higher education's appetite. Ontario's universities, he told the chairman of the Queen's trustees, Colonel Harkness, "are a pretty hungry family."[40] Corry argued that, even if provincial coffers became strapped, formula funding would at least be fair and equitable, since it replaced the old piecemeal funding with a mechanism that would encompass the whole Ontario university system with one global payment scheme.[41]

Corry quickly became the chief salesman of the Deutsch scheme. In November 1963, he wrote to Premier Robarts advocating a "university grants commission," which would disperse metered aid to the universities, while at the same time proffering advice to the cabinet on the overall budget apportionment and priorities of higher education.[42] Invited to Dalhousie University the next February to lecture on "the university in the modern state," Corry took the BIU proposal public. A "double-decked device is almost certainly called for: fixed block grants of varying amounts depending on the circumstances of each university, topped off with a system of uniform grants per student," he told his Halifax audience.[43] Back home in Ontario, reaction was positive. "I read your Dalhousie speech," Frost wrote to Corry. "Excellent – but I wish you would make an outline of its application here – we need a Solomon."[44] Corry's fellow university presidents concurred and agreed that the CPUO research staff should be set to work in conjunction with senior officials at the ministry of university affairs to fine-tune the scheme. In its classic style of liberal investigation and judicious prescription, Queen's had acted as a "Solomon" in reaching a workable consensus on how Ontario's universities should be soundly funded and intellectually protected.

Then, in the final stretch, there was a glitch. Queen's was not the only Canadian institution trying to plot a more predictable and sustainable future. In Ottawa, the Liberal government of Mike Pearson was becoming increasingly technocratic, believing that a balanced mix of econometrics, policy analysis, and regulation would guide Canada to the plateau of stability and prosperity first glimpsed by Mackintosh in his 1945 "white paper." To do so, objective advice was needed. In 1963 the federal government created the Economic Council of Canada to furnish arm's-length economic advice. John Deutsch (who had worked with Pearson at external affairs in the late 1940s) seemed a natural choice for the chairmanship of the new council. In September 1963, he broke the news to Corry, telling him that he hoped to return to the academic life "in a few years." The trustees granted Deutsch a two-year leave of absence. Deutsch's place as vice-principal, administration, was taken by Hugh Conn, a mechanical engineer who had been dean of Applied Science since 1955 and brought a crisp military style to the modernization campaign initiated by Deutsch. To maintain the momentum, Conn was inclined to import retired military men to administrative posts – men such as George Wattsford, a retired general who became director of university services and who set about bringing discipline, and profit, to the university's conference programs. These senior recruits introduced precision and process, but lacked Deutsch's finesse for policy formulation. The academic staff soon dubbed them "Conn's commandoes."

Perhaps more importantly, Corry needed somebody to fill Deutsch's shoes as the university's man on the CPUO research committee, where the BIU system was being drafted. Corry had also come to the conclusion that the Queen's principal could no longer operate on an administrative shoestring. Mackintosh had managed with a single secretary in a small office in the Douglas Library, but with the university's executive centre now in Richardson Hall and his span of control widening, Corry concluded that he needed an executive assistant. That assistant, he realized, had better be worldly wise. And in Bernard Trotter, a CBC public-affairs expert, he found that man. Although his father taught history at Queen's, Trotter had pursued his 1945 degree in history at McMaster. An MA at Queen's in history followed, despite the fact that it was Corry's political-science lectures on the constitution that most fascinated him. A succession of field postings for the CBC followed, culminating in his appointment as general superintendent of public affairs in Ottawa. Trotter knew his way around the corridors of power and, as it turned out, he was remarkably adept with figures for a history graduate.

For his part, Trotter had been drawn to Corry's style – which he described as one of "deliberate speed" – when he observed the latter on the CBC's board of governors.[45] Trotter proved a productive addition to the university's new management ethos. He acted as Corry's factotum, preparing briefing notes for the principal's frequent trips to Queen's Park and the CPUO. Before he departed for Ottawa, Deutsch had urged Queen's to establish an office of academic planning, an idea, Trotter believed, that was inspired by the "institutional research" nostrum of American auto executive, later defence secretary, Robert McNamara. This function unfolded around Trotter as the decade progressed, with university statisticians learning how to massage enrolment and government grant data to project a critical path for Queen's. Most crucially, Trotter played a formative role over the next two years, working in Toronto with other university planners and provincial University Affairs bureaucrats such as Douglas Wright to calibrate the BIU system. By 1967, it was ready. Central to the system was a table of weights which assigned a monetary weight to the range of academic programs delivered by Ontario universities. An Arts and Science student in a general BA garnered a single BIU, whereas an honours student brought a double BIU. Doctoral students, drawing down more faculty labour and research support, brought in a lucrative six BIUs each.

Corry regarded the BIU system as a crowning achievement. "The features of the formula probably eased Queen's financial situation more than any other university," he wrote in his memoirs.[46] From now on, the Senate committee on academic development would each year project enrolment goals for all Queen's programs. As the fall term progressed, the university registrar would report enrolment totals as they gelled, and then in November the final tabulation was dispatched to Queen's Park. Early in the new year, a BIU-driven cheque would arrive. However, the negotiation of the annual block grant for capital expenditure remained more contentious and subject to the fiscal prosperity and policy preferences of the government. Ontario, for instance, remained resistant to direct funding of university residences, arguing that they were not academic facilities, but instead were self-financing entities. Nevertheless, a fundamental stability had been established in university-government relations.

The system was by no means without its shortcomings. It could, for instance, encourage ambitious universities to aggressively recruit undergraduates, knowing that they could reap an immediate harvest of BIUs – but the danger here was that any downturn in enrolment would leave the university obliged to sustain an expanded infrastructure on diminishing BIU income. In 1966, Corry assumed the chairmanship of the CPUO from Claude Bissell of Toronto, a post he described as "delicate and often agonizing."[47] On the one hand, there were ongoing bones of contention with Toronto – library funding, residences, the vetting of new programs, and the need to ensure accessibility – while, on the other hand, maintaining consensus in the corral of expanding Ontario universities often proved daunting, as individual universities were easily tempted to pursue their own interests at the expense of their confreres. However, the channels of communication were now established, and the buffer between academic freedom and government oversight was now acknowledged. The CPUO would eventually rechristen itself as the Council of Ontario Universities (COU) as the universities' lobbying voice. For its part, in 1973, the provincial government would turn its old Frost-era advisory committee into the Ontario Council on University Affairs (OCUA).

Throughout the sixties, it became apparent that the provinces were a growing factor in Canadian university life. Nevertheless, a powerful undertow of federal-provincial conflict and co-operation continued to flow through Canadian university affairs. In 1964, at a time of transition, Corry was elected president of the NCCU. That year the group reconfigured itself into the Association of Universities and Colleges of Canada (AUCC) and dedicated itself to adopting a more activist role in pressuring Ottawa on university funding. In this vein, an AUCC commission led by Toronto political economist Vincent Bladen and funded by the Ford Foundation presented a projection of dramatically escalating costs for higher education down into the 1970s, thereby prompting Ottawa to boost its transfer payment to the provinces from two to four dollars per student.

Similarly, 1964 saw the birth of the Canada Student Loan Program as a federal-provincial initiative. Corry and the AUCC pushed two agendas in Ottawa: the need for Ottawa to alleviate the strain on the provinces of financing the universities and the need for an acknowledgement that Ottawa would directly consult with the universities on such a matter. Corry was dogged in these respects. In November 1964, he bearded the prime minister in his den, telling Mike Pearson that the universities objected to "the adventurism of the Government on building telescopes, oceanographic institutes and what not without any consultation with the universities and without any apparent concern as to whether these facilities would be used for the training of graduate students."[48]

As the first president of AUCC, Corry, a constitutional lawyer by training, had set the style for what was to be the ongoing pattern of vigilant university diplomacy. Whether through the COU or the AUCC, universities were now active participants in what Corry described as the "deeply entangled" politics of Canada's federation. It was no coincidence that in 1965 Queen's (urged on by former Ontario premier Leslie Frost, who agonized about the fraying of the union) would create an Institute of Intergovernmental Relations, capably directed by former Manitoba deputy-minister of finance Ron Burns, to provide objective investigation of the central constitutional tension in Canadian political life – federal-provincial relations. In doing so, Queen's provided further evidence that it was a "national" university, one that once furnished Ottawa and the provincial capitals with many of their mandarins and now brought objective analysis to the pragmatics of Canadian policy-making.

Ensuring a systematic and predictable fiscal foundation was, in fact, the *sine qua non* of Queen's modernization in the sixties. Without a sustainable budget, Corry could not have orchestrated a thoroughgoing renovation of the university's ability to deliver academic services faculty by faculty. As the arrival on campus of the children of the baby boom loomed, universities such as Queen's were being pushed towards becoming "multiversities," that is campuses offering an array of educational options tuned to the needs of a complex late-industrial society. Professionalization and specialization infiltrated almost every branch of knowledge. "In the older, simpler society," Corry told the graduating class of 1965 at the University of Western Ontario, "a skill once perfected would fill a niche for a lifetime. That society is gone. Everything is now entangled in intricate relationships."[49] As the sixties unfolded, Ontario thus experienced a proliferation of universities. Indeed, one of the recommendations of John Deutsch's CPUO research committee in 1962 had advocated the conversion of liberal-arts colleges into full universities and the outright creation of other universities. Guelph, Trent, Brock, Lakehead, and Laurentian soon appeared on the Ontario university map. This expansion challenged Queen's in two ways: it broadened the options for undergraduate education in Ontario – Queen's traditional forte – while at the same time obliging Queen's to sharpen its appeal as a mature university offering focused programs in law, graduate studies, business, and medicine. On this latter front, Queen's was feeling vulnerable in the early 1960s. Its professional and graduate offerings were all too often narrow and antiquated. This was particularly acute in the case of the Faculty of Medicine, and here Corry first desperately focused his attention.

Crisis on the Medical Quadrangle

Public demand for more accessible universities in the sixties coincided with a national groundswell of demand for inclusive medical coverage. This would culminate in 1966 with the passage of the federal Medical Care Act, which gave Canadians "single payer," universal health care, generously subsidized by Ottawa, but administered by the provinces. By 1972, all provinces had signed onto the program. Medicare had unfolded at first slowly in Canada, dating back to co-operative health-insurance schemes in the early decades of the century, and then rapidly in the late 1950s, when Ottawa and the provinces had agreed to cover the diagnostic and hospitalization costs of all Canadians. A royal commission under Saskatchewan Justice Emmett Hall, appointed by the Diefenbaker government in 1960, not only shunted Canada towards taxpayer-financed medicare, but also underscored the challenge of new medical technologies and specialties for the education of medical practitioners. While some interests vociferously resisted "socialist" medicine, it was clear that the paradigm of Canadian medical services and research was shifting quickly and irrevocably.

In January 1962, when the researchers from the Hall Commission visited the Queen's medical faculty, they found its programs in parlous shape. Queen's was one of the smallest of Canada's twelve medical schools. With an intake of 64 pre-medical (i.e., students without a qualifying degree) and 51 first-year students, the school could count only 330 students in its program. Despite a rich heritage of teaching medicine since 1854, the faculty of medicine at Queen's by the late 1950s had found itself ruled by expediency and increasingly operating on the margins of Canadian medical education. Many factors conspired against it. Situated in a small provincial city with a thinly populated hinterland, the faculty often found itself short on both financial and human resources. Medical education rested on two pillars: the imparting of theoretical knowledge in the basic sciences, such as biochemistry and pathology, and on in situ clinical teaching in hospital wards at the bedside of patients. The picturesque limestone buildings clustered around the elm-treed Medical Quadrangle contained Queen's expertise in the basic sciences, an expertise dispensed by professors under the university's direct control. There was, for instance, the anatomy department, with its dissection room and grim reservoir of cadavers, under the capable headship of Turkish-born Armenian John Basmajian, whose seminal textbook, *Primary Anatomy*, was widely used in medical schools.[50] Across the grassy quad, biochemistry was taught in the Craine Building, a 1930s gift from Dr Agnes Craine, a Smiths Falls woman who had come to Kingston (not Queen's, because the medical college for women was not affiliated with Queen's) in the 1880s to become a pioneering female doctor.

The Achilles heel of medical education in Kingston lay in the clinical area. Queen's had no university hospital, instead relying on a loose affiliation with the two local hospitals: nearby Kingston General Hospital (KGH) on the waterfront and the Catholic Hotel Dieu Hospital (HDH) on Brock Street.[51] Dating from the 1830s, KGH is Canada's oldest public hospital. Over the years, the hospital had developed a culture of zealously defending its autonomy and, as a consequence, conservatively managing its affairs. In the pre-medicare era, it had come to depend heavily on revenue from private patients, delivered to its doors by local doctors who came to regard the hospital in proprietary terms. At the same time, relations between KGH and Hotel Dieu, a sectarian institution with roots going back to the 1840s, had long been standoffish.

The city had never captured the synergies of consolidating the delivery of its medical services. KGH's post–World War II ambition had been to build itself into a regional – not a just a city – hospital, and thereby make itself an adequate base for clinical teaching for Queen's. But progress had been slow. New wings were added for veterans, children, and cancer care, and finally, in 1960, an extension was built named for bacteriologist Walter T. Connell, patriarch of one of Kingston's leading medical families. Hotel Dieu Hospital pursued its own agenda, all too often duplicating the services of KGH. As a result, KGH offered an increasingly unsatisfactory liaison for the Queen's medical school. Intensifying the situation was the fact that Kingston's sparse hinterland often did not produce a sufficient range of patient maladies to support the varied hands-on experiences that a modern medical student needs. By the 1950s, medicine was rapidly specializing, and medical schools were increasingly channelling their students into specialty streams – specialties that were becoming more and more dependent on expensive technologies. The 1950s had seen breakthroughs in diagnostic techniques, such as radioisotope scanning and echocardiography. The decade had also seen new life-support mechanisms like pacemakers, which were perfected along with machine-supported therapies such as cobalt teletherapy. As Queen's medical historian Jacalyn Duffin has noted, hospitals were no longer simply places for treating those already ill; they were becoming places for medical investigation and diagnosis.[52] As such, they were also becoming ever more capital intensive and more and more in need of sophisticated centralized administration. And here again, Kingston's hospitals were falling behind the pace. The usefulness of the KGH wards for medical education had been steadily eroded by two powerful trends.

The 1957 federal-provincial agreement to underwrite the cost of hospitalization led to the 1958 creation of the Ontario Hospital Services Commission. With government now paying 94 per cent of Ontarians' hospital bills, the availability of what had been rather cruelly called "indigent patients" (that is, reliant on the hospital's good will for treatment) on hospital wards dropped dramatically, thereby depriving medical students of easy access to patients who had no option but to serve as medical guinea pigs. Access to indigent patients had never been easy at KGH; they had been scattered throughout the hospital, requiring clinicians and their students to scurry from ward to ward in search of teachable cases. With little daily "walk-in" medical traffic to supplement these cases, KGH was becoming a poor training ground for would-be doctors. To remedy the decline in patients available for teaching purposes, many medical schools had been moving towards the creation of "clinical teaching units" – wards populated by patients all suffering from similar maladies and all amenable to inspection by medical students.

The situation was worsened by Kingston doctors' dogged defence of their admitting privileges. In effect, patients with serious problems could be admitted to hospital only by their general practitioner, who retained the right to deny or grant better-trained specialists access to their charges. Clinical teaching units, they feared, would erode the lucrative income generated by their admitting privileges. This chronic balkanization of medical services meant that little progress had been made in Kingston towards the integration of medical services – the smooth interconnection of primary and specialist medical expertise – that now lay at the heart of modern medical treatment. Queen's was not oblivious to this impasse. The principal sat on KGH's board of management and frequently conveyed the worrisome news that the medical accreditation teams sent by the American Association of Medical Colleges (to which Canadian hospitals turned) to inspect the Queen's medical school were reporting that KGH was on the road to becoming a "cottage hospital," out of sync with modern medical training. The dean of medicine, Harold "Curly" Ettinger, repeated the message: clinical teaching units and outpatient clinics, plus the physical facilities to support them, were the way of the future. In 1961, he reported that, with the unfolding of medicare, the Canadian Medical Association had projected that by 1980 Canada would need to produce five hundred more doctors each year. However, Ettinger, a distinguished-but-aging physiologist, who had been dean since 1949, was running out of steam. "The implementation of these recommendations," he urged, "will require money, good will, and mutual trust."[53] In 1961, these seemed in short supply in Kingston.

Ettinger's exasperation was heightened by problems with his own faculty. As in any medical school, medical faculty members – often referred to as "geographically full-time" appointments – were usually given the right "to attend" in local hospitals. Attending physicians were expected to balance their working lives between lecturing students, undertaking research, and ministering to patients in local hospitals or at their local practices.[54] The problem facing Queen's by the early 1960s was that teaching and research were being submerged by the profitability of private practice. Attending physicians were setting themselves up as specialists in competition with local generalists, or else they were positioning themselves for referrals from the local medical community. Consequently, many attending faculty members began to give short shrift to their university obligations and the mentoring of interns. "It was the student opinion that some of the staff were too busy with private practice to do much research or publishing of papers, as in other centres," a 1962 external report concluded. "They don't get enough bedside teaching and too many lectures. They get little outpatient teaching."[55]

Perhaps the most notorious example of this slippage was provided by Dr Dermid Bingham, an acclaimed British surgeon who, after arriving at Queen's in 1945, had risen to the headship of the department of surgery. Born in Ceylon, Bingham had trained in England and Switzerland, honed his skills as an army surgeon, learned French, and initially displayed a keen interest in research. Soon after coming to Queen's, he had been appointed chief surgeon at KGH. Such kudos allowed him to open a private practice, which flourished. He became conspicuously successful, driving the only Rolls-Royce in the city and projecting a lofty sense of hauteur to both his colleagues and students. Around his neck, Bingham wore a stethoscope intended to draw attention to his service in the North African campaign of the last war – the listening bell was fashioned out of a shell case. His presence in the lecture hall became infrequent, his research tailed off, and his clinical tours through the wards became perfunctory. As early as 1956, Principal Mackintosh wrote to Bingham about the "profound and widespread dissatisfaction with your contribution to the teaching of the medical school and the hospital … [and] the low priority which you attach to your teaching work."[56] Bingham grew shirty, arguing that the informally negotiated terms under which he was hired in 1945 stipulated no obligation to give teaching priority. Although Bingham attracted some new talent to the medical school, such as a promising young anesthetist from Toronto, Stuart Vandewater, other members departed in disgust.

Bingham was the most prominent example of the staff woes at the Queen's medical school. And by the early 1960s, the effect had become cumulative. Not only was there swelling resentment among talented younger members of the faculty, who felt that they were being held back by well-heeled "old guard" types such as Bingham, but the interns and residents who came to Queen's and KGH to polish their skills also expressed their ire. The interns faced practical problems: shoddy and inadequate residences, stingy stipends, and too few patients to study. More fundamentally, interns discovered that KGH and Hotel Dieu lagged far behind hospitals in Toronto and Ottawa in offering full access to all the specialities that were now deemed necessary by the Royal College of Physicians and Surgeons for professional accreditation. As yet, KGH had paid little attention to the growing need for ambulatory care or emergency medicine. Up in the wards, beds were not assigned with any thought to clinical teaching. Not surprisingly, each year saw fewer applications for residency at KGH: in 1961–62 the hospital was able to fill only fifty-four of its sixty-seven available residency positions, and many of those went to foreign students. In March 1961, the interns rebelled. Hearing rumours that the interns were agitating to move the Queen's medical school to the bilingual University of Ottawa, the committee overseeing interns at KGH created an ad hoc committee to investigate their dissatisfaction.[57]

The committee was headed by a young specialist in metabolic disorders, Laurence Wilson, one of Ford Connell's promising catches for the department of medicine. Wilson was one of the young guard who sensed that medical education at Queen's was teetering on the edge of collapse. His committee pulled no punches, reporting early in 1962 that nothing short of a root-and-branch reorganization of the medical program was acceptable. Above all else, clinical teaching units must be introduced. The KGH board of management grimly accepted the news, and Principal Corry conveyed it to the Board of Trustees. He candidly told the trustees that men such as Bingham had fostered "years of acute dissatisfaction,"[58] and that the future of the faculty hung in the balance. The organizational disorder now exposed, KGH and Queen's moved to seek a remedy – the medical consultancy firm of Agnew, Peckham and Associates was hired to map the way forward to a better future.

Founded by Dr Harvey Agnew, a University of Toronto grad who had pioneered the art of health-services consultancy from his New York office, the firm had a sterling reputation. Agnew would later acquire the nickname of "Dr Hospital." Working out of his Toronto office, he and two colleagues produced a scathing analysis of the situation in Kingston: intern applications were down, the teaching and clinical program was poorly resourced, specialties were not supported, and morale was poor among students and staff. The KGH might at most support the ambition of young doctors to enter general practice, but those wanting to specialize would be disappointed. The geographic full-time staff was too involved in private practice; there were no caps on their private earnings. "Although the programs of certain departments look adequate on paper," Agnew, Peckham reported, "they are in fact not being carried out." Teaching had become "didactic," with students receiving little one-on-one "personalized" instruction. Bingham was singled out as a goat, his remarkable ratio of private to "staff" patients castigated. Better housing for residents was imperative, as was an enhanced medical library. Above all else, clinical teaching units must be introduced, and faculty members must reorient themselves to more intensive teaching and research. Queen's must attach itself to "modern concepts of medical education" or wither. The report concluded with a clarion call: "To cope radically with practical problems is more rewarding at certain times in history than at others."[59]

So scathing was the Agnew report that no copies were made or circulated to the hospital governors. The only copies available were kept in a room at a motel on upper Princess Street, where a small committee headed by the chair of the board of governors' management committee, local accountant Bruce Matthews, secretly deliberated on the findings.[60] They quickly concluded that clinical teaching units and a mechanism to cap the private income of the full-time teaching staff were inescapable reforms. Corry carried this message to the university's Board of Trustees, telling them that a "sufficient staff of interns" must be attracted and a new era of cooperation between the hospitals and the university inaugurated.[61] An accord was soon reached between KGH and Queen's: four hundred beds at KGH would form the core of clinical teaching units, ambulatory clinics were established, private practice was strictly regulated, new specialty departments, such as family medicine, were established, and clinical teaching by teams of clinicians, interns, and students were inaugurated. All that remained was to convince the university and hospital staff that this was the path to be taken.

Sensing what a tall order this would be, Corry pre-empted the whole process. Despite his affable, gradualist persona, there were times when Corry knew that university principals are obliged to act decisively. In the case of the medical faculty, he knew that only dynamic and no-holds-barred leadership would ensure reform. Dean Ettinger, an honourable, but now weary, administrator, wanted to take his leave. So, in the fall of 1961, Corry convened a search committee for a new dean and stocked it with members well-attuned to the new world of medicine. Almost immediately, their attention was drawn to Edmund Harry Botterell, a much-respected neurosurgeon at the University of Toronto. Ettinger had known him for almost thirty years and extolled his talent. The dean of medicine at Toronto lavished praise on him, saying that Botterell was "dynamic, imaginative, and highly intelligent." Others concurred: Harry was "a man of unusual ability and energy." He was, some cautioned, "somewhat mercurial in temperament."[62] The young anesthetist Stuart Vandewater, who had agitated for change at KGH, remembered Botterell from his days at Toronto and admired his managerial charisma.

Vancouver-born and Manitoba-educated Botterell had built his career on medical innovation and intellectual pushiness. He had honed his surgeon's skills at hospitals in Winnipeg, at Johns Hopkins University (there following in the footsteps of the great Canadian physician Sir William Osler), and in Toronto, London, and Montreal. He developed a keen interest in the treatment of paraplegic patients, specializing in the prevention of pressure sores and the treatment of spinal-cord trauma. During the war, he had managed a neurology hospital in Basingstoke, England, where, amongst many war-torn patients, he had removed shrapnel from the head of Queen's graduate John Matheson (BA 1940), who was by now a Queen's trustee and a federal MP. After the war, Botterell returned to Toronto, where he brilliantly continued to balance the demands of teaching, research, and practice as a surgeon.⁶³ In effect, he possessed exactly the modernizing touch that Corry knew Queen's needed. Interviewed in November 1961, fifty-five-year-old Botterell accepted the deanship in January 1962. He reported for duty that summer, just as the Agnew report laid out its blueprint for change.

Botterell arrived at Queen's with a half-affectionate, half-fearful nickname he had acquired in Toronto: "Harry the Horse" (probably taken from the 1955 hit musical *Guys and Dolls*). He often signed his memos with a stick figure of a horse. His reputation for decisiveness intensified in Kingston. He did not suffer fools gladly. A folklore grew up around his determination to remake the faculty. His favourite riposte to those who quibbled about his agenda was to ask: "What am I paying you for today?" If the person persisted: "What is your hurry? Here is your hat."⁶⁴ Botterell lacked any appetite for the usual give and take of academic collegiality. Bernard Trotter remembered him as a "very, very tough character ... not a diplomat ... He wanted things done yesterday."⁶⁵ While Botterell lacked polish, Corry had no problem with Botterell's style. Through the next decade, Corry consistently backed Botterell's decisions, defended him to the trustees, and went to bat for him in Toronto when it came time to seek funds to modernize the faculty. In effect, Harry the Horse became the principal's stalking horse, doing his bidding and, in the end, saving the Queen's medical faculty from what in 1960 seemed like an imminent demise. When a young neurophysiologist from England, Vivian Abrahams, arrived in the faculty in 1963, he immediately picked up the mood of change: "Principal Corry was just full of fire: Harry Botterell was going to create a *real* medical school, not the sleepy place it had been."⁶⁶

Change on the Medical Quadrangle came quickly and dramatically. Botterell was determined to wean many of his faculty from their lucrative pursuit of private practice onto a system that em-

Dean of Medicine Harry "the Horse" Botterell, probably Corry's shrewdest senior appointment. A world-renowned neurosurgeon, who had honed his skills in wartime England and at Toronto General Hospital, Botterell was given a mandate by Corry to modernize the Queen's medical faculty in 1962, a task to which he brought an imperious personality and a keen vision for the teaching and researching of medical science.

phasized teaching, clinical instruction, and research. Central to this was the plan to cap the outside income of the "geographical full-time" (GFT) faculty members. A formula was devised to place a ceiling on private income. Fees collected by a faculty member past this ceiling would be diverted into a departmental fund to be applied to the broader needs of the faculty.⁶⁷ Despite the fact that similar schemes were being adopted in other medical schools, many Queen's faculty members saw this as an erosion of their professional liberty, and they did not surrender willingly. Not surprisingly, Dermid Bingham in surgery put up the stiffest fight. He called in lawyers to argue his claim. In the wake of the Agnew report, Bingham had stepped down as head of the surgery department and chief surgeon at KGH, but he stayed on as a professor of surgery. He refused to see his income capped.

Botterell and Corry instinctively knew that if Bingham could not be brought into line their campaign would be lost. When the Ontario College of Physicians and Surgeons gave its sanction to the GFT scheme, the board of trustees convened a special committee to force Bingham's hand. The committee was headed by the hard-headed railroader Donald Gordon and included the renowned New York surgeon Dr John Hammett. Bingham was told that the issue did not revolve around his professional competence but his compliance with a new administrative order. Bingham remained litigious. (The legal correspondence generated by the Bingham affair are the only sealed, confidential documents in the entire run of the pre-2004 Board of Trustees minute books.) On 2 December 1965, Bingham was summoned to the principal's office to confront Gordon and his committee. Corry and Botterell attended. No minutes of the encounter were kept. Gordon had a notoriously abrasive style as a businessman. After twenty minutes, Bingham sheepishly emerged. He had signed a GFT agreement. Bingham would linger at Queen's until 1971, when he commendably moved to Ghana to establish a surgery clinic. A bright, younger surgeon from McGill, James McCorriston (a Queen's graduate of 1943), was appointed to head the surgery department. McCorriston painstakingly put an efficient clinical teaching unit in place.

Clinical teaching units (CTUs) had a fractious inauguration at Queen's. At a tumultuous faculty meeting that lasted well past midnight, the faculty ratified the CTU principle in November 1962. Local doctors resisted. The two local hospitals were similarly resistant. Although the CTUs would allow specialists more immediate access to patients, it was not until December 1965 that KGH actually signed an agreement with Queen's setting aside 50 per cent of its beds for clinical teaching. At times, Botterell grew exasperated by the parochialism around him, confiding to Corry that KGH's slow acceptance of CTUs "make me wonder if the 'brave new world' which was envisaged two and a half years ago is not being nibbled to pieces."[68] But progress there was. Hotel Dieu Hospital signed onto the CTU agreement. Teams of clinicians, interns, and residents now moved about the wards, directed to CTU patients by red dots pasted on their files. In 1966, an associate dean of medicine for clinical matters was appointed; Garfield "Gub" Kelly, a Queen's-trained local boy with a keen interest in rehabilitation medicine, was appointed to the post. Ambulatory clinics were established that gave patients walk-in access to specialists. In 1967, a family-care unit was opened at KGH, reflecting the emerging trend towards the provision of interdisciplinary general medical care; a department of family medicine at Queen's followed.

Botterell recognized that the teaching and provision of medical care increasingly demanded centralized administration and delivery. This extended from prosaic matters such as billing on through to huge capital-intensive projects like the provision of new equipment and space. The term "health sciences" and "health services" began to creep into the vocabulary of health care at Queen's. With medicare in place by the late 1960s, centralization, with its attendant economies of scale and coordination, came to dominate health planning. Botterell insisted that his department heads participate in the collective planning of the faculty. In 1965, a Medical Advisory Committee was established. Botterell came to rely on a restricted circle of department heads – Don Hatcher in physiology, Nate Kaufman in pathology, David Rosen in ophthalmology, and Stuart Vandewater in anaesthesiology – as a kind of inner cabinet that would back his actions. People quietly labelled them "Harry's henchmen." And, as a new norm of cooperation with the local hospitals fitfully emerged, discussion turned to the need to break out of the charming, but now chronically antiquated, buildings of the Medical Quadrangle. Botterell initiated discussion of a "medical sciences centre," convincing the Board of Trustees in late 1967 to sanction an agreement with Kingston General Hospital that set aside twenty-seven acres of land along Stuart Street as the future precinct for such a complex.[69] Considering the frictions of the last few years, there was no doubt that such a project would have to endure a thicket of negotiations with the local hospitals and the provincial government. Like Corry, Botterell began to board the Toronto train frequently, in order to proposition and inform the bureaucrats and politicians on whom such crucial decisions hinged.[70]

Above all else, Botterell understood that it was *people* who made a faculty viable. As the old guard began to fade, he sought out new staff who would reinforce his drive for clinical and academic excellence. In 1965, for instance, James Low, a University of Toronto graduate and specialist in perinatal asphyxia, arrived to head the obstetrics and gynaecology department. Botterell showed no hesitation in bringing talented Jewish physicians, like Kaufman and Rosen, into his faculty, a trait not evident in every Canadian medical school. He also was prepared to look well beyond the Canadian border for talent. When John Basmajian reported that he had spotted a promising specialist in rehabilitation medicine at the University of Washington, Botterell hired him. David Symington quickly convinced the dean that the faculty needed not only a department of rehabilitative medicine but also a School of Rehabilitation Therapy. Occupational and rehabilitation therapy had never been considered as mainline medical activities; practitioners were seen as lowly technicians. Symington argued that, as the national net of health services expanded, therapy must be reconsidered as a serious medical pursuit. Botterell had seen the effectiveness of rehab therapy at his wartime clinic in Britain, and needed little convincing. In 1967 the School of Rehabilitation opened at Queen's with Symington as director, first offering

diplomas and, after 1972, a full four-year degree program. New blood brought new ideas.[71]

During the Botterell years, a similar modernizing spirit of reform touched the training of nurses at Queen's. If the training of doctors had been set in a national context, nursing had always been construed in intensely local terms. Nurses were not seen as professionals, but simply as necessary accessories for any hospital – a pair of competent hands ever ready to do a doctor's bidding. Consequently, nurses were trained on the job, in schools attached to the hospitals. Kingston General Hospital had schooled its own nurses since the 1880s, and Hotel Dieu Hospital since 1913. Only under the pressure of World War II did Queen's broaden its medical net to include nurses. The School of Nursing was established in 1941 and housed in Kingston Hall, and later in the west wing of Summerhill, near the medical students. Since the mid-1930s, the Canadian Nurses Association had been agitating for the adoption of national standards for nursing, thereby suggesting that nursing was a profession, not just a technical service. In 1945, Queen's appointed a director, Jennie Weir, to the school and put in place a five-year training program for registered nurses. The so-called 1:3:1 program was narrowly focused on preparing nurses for a closely prescribed set of duties. An initial year was spent on campus gaining exposure to the basic sciences and humanities, followed by three years of practical training in a local hospital, and crowned by a final year of specialization and a smattering of courses in administration and politics. The faculty were trained nurses themselves, few possessing higher academic degrees. In 1961, the school awarded twenty-nine nursing degrees and had more than a hundred full and part-time students.

The 1964 report of Emmett Hall's Royal Commission on Health Services called for a recognition that nurses were not just medical accoutrements, but should be a part of integrated medical teams. Their training should be broadened. The old in-house hospital nursing schools were too parochial to meet this challenge. In 1961, Weir similarly reported that many students were dropping out of the Queen's program because it lacked "intellectual stimulation." She proposed a more professionally and intellectually vigorous four-year program leading to a bachelor's degree in nursing science.[72] She wanted separate faculty status and a teaching faculty with graduate credentials in what was now being called "nursing science." Although he did not oversee the nursing school, Dean Botterell was sympathetic to Weir's ambition, because it complemented his vision of integrating all medical education and services at Queen's. In 1965, Queen's nurses had joined Queen's doctors in staffing a community hospital in northerly Moose Factory, Ontario. For his part, Principal Corry lobbied provincial health minister Matthew Dymond (a Queen's-trained MD) to support an autonomous nursing faculty at Queen's that would provide "better clinical training" for nurses.[73] Queen's Park agreed and applied a quota of two BIUs per student to Bachelor of Nursing Science programs in the province. When Jennie Weir retired in 1966, Botterell (who was generally wary of females infringing on male medical prerogatives) chaired the selection committee for her successor. The appointment of Dr Jean Hill, the product of graduate programs at Kansas and Yale, as *dean* of nursing, signified what the *Principal's Report* called "a new era of progress" for nursing at Queen's. In 1967, nursing became a separate faculty. More academically qualified staff were hired, and in 1969 a new four-year BNSc program was launched, focusing on community-based nursing. Hill built working alliances with local hospitals and community groups and became an active participant in Botterell's planning of a health-sciences complex. Nursing was no longer an afterthought at Queen's; it had entered the medical mainstream.

The galvanic arrival at Queen's of people such as Harry Botterell and Jean Hill provokes reflection on what was to become a perennial dilemma at Queen's: where does leadership best come from and what ensures its effectiveness? Traditionally, Queen's had tended to be an introverted community. Relatively isolated in eastern Ontario, it had come to rely on its own intrinsic rhythms. Leadership at Queen's tended to be organically developed, with capable academics, already inured to Queen's idiosyncrasies, smoothly moving into the university's administrative cadre. True, many of the early principals were imported from Scotland and England, but this reflected a residual colonialism that lasted into the 1936–51 principalship of Orkney-born Robert Wallace, who had masterfully guided Queen's through the exigencies of depression and war. Bill Mackintosh in the fifties had demonstrated that Queen's could thrive with a native son at the helm, just as George Munro Grant had done a half-century before. At Queen's, there was a genetic predisposition to allow staff already in situ to percolate up through the university hierarchy. Indeed, from 1951 to 1974 the principal's office was occupied by Queen's men almost born and certainly bred – Mackintosh, Corry (at Queen's since 1936), and Deutsch – who were steeped in the university's culture long before they got the call to Richardson Hall. Similarly, deans rose out of the professoriate to take charge of faculties with which they were already intimately familiar. Arts and Science dean, Sandy Duncan, emerged from the philosophy department. Applied Science dean, Hugh Conn, took on that mantle after serving as head of mechanical engineering since 1946. As deans, they continued to sit as members of the Senate, joining their confreres to collectively approve the university's academic course. Registrar Jean Royce had been on the job since 1933 and knew the vast majority of professors and students who had passed through Queen's portals. Similarly, well into the late 1960s, department heads held baronial sway over their colleagues, retaining their posts at the grace of the principal, sometimes for decades. George Whalley in English commanded respect and attention largely because he could trace his Kingston roots back to his 1913 birth in the shadow of St George's Cathedral, a lineage he reinforced with his superb Coleridge scholarship.

In short, there was a powerful inclination at Queen's to promote from within, to trust the "trustable," and to regard outsiders with skepticism, to cling to the "Queen's way." Harry Botterell and Jean Hill had demonstrated that there were times, particularly as the imperatives of modern management took hold of the university, when outsiders might import much-needed, but hitherto alien, expertise and willpower to the campus. As Botterell almost daily demonstrated, outsiders could challenge Queen's sometimes too complacent, too gradualist culture. They could bring change and resuscitation, as Botterell so dramatically had delivered to the Faculty of Medicine. In subsequent decades, this new tension between home-bred familiarity and outside expertise would persist in decisions of succession at Queen's. Modernization provoked such decisions.

The modernizing and diversification of the university in the sixties also eroded Queen's heritage of centralizing power in the principal's office. A more-complex, technocratic university necessitated decentralizing decision making out into the offices of deans and vice-principals, where new talent incubated change. Deutsch's selection as the university's chief administrator in the early 1960s gave Queen's the perfect hybrid: a man steeped in Queen's culture since his undergraduate days, yet imbued with experience from the modern, outside world. This dexterity, heightened by his stint as chairman of the Economic Council of Canada, virtually predetermined his stature as Corry's heir apparent.

Other Faculties Feel the Modernizing Touch

The tension between the established and the modern also played itself out at Queen's School of Business in the topsy-turvy sixties. "Much is heard today about the need for enterprise in both the domestic and world markets," wrote Richard Hand in the *Queen's Quarterly* in 1961. Hand had arrived at Queen's with an MBA from the University of Chicago and had found alarming the narrowness and fading orthodoxy of the School of Commerce and Business Administration at Queen's. "Much is also heard about our failure to fit education to the needs of our society ... Business, like music and medicine, calls for disciplined artistry at the level of application. Although artistic judgments have always been required in practice, rational analysis is now increasingly important."[74] Hand was part of a new breed of business professors – trained, usually in the United States, in specialties such as marketing and organizational planning. His older, tenured colleagues at Queen's came out of accounting, finance, and economics backgrounds. The school, as it had been known since 1937, had been offering BComm. degrees since 1919, but its bread and butter had been the offering of extension and summer courses in accounting and banking procedure to legions of young Canadian accountants and bankers. In 1961, for instance, the school had 103 undergraduates on campus and 4,851 off-campus students in non-degree courses. It was not a faculty unto itself, but instead was folded, along with industrial relations, into the conglomeration of disciplines under the banner of the Department of Economics and Political Studies. With the opening in 1959 of Dunning Hall on University Avenue, the polyglot department was finally afforded some breathing room.[75]

But the school's director since 1958, Lawrence Macpherson, an accountant by training, realized that more than a change in venue was in the air. Postwar prosperity had been orchestrated by the concerted macroeconomic planning of western governments; business responded by embracing its own brand of planning – planning through the expertise of specialists in marketing, product development, and a myriad other specialties that stretched well beyond the skill of totting up numbers and mastering the Bank Act on which Queen's had traditionally staked its reputation. Business education became mingled with other disciplines that illuminated the way in which modern capitalism functioned. Mathematics enabled statistical analysis of sales and costs; psychology and sociology shed light on consumer behaviour and employee satisfaction. Macpherson began hiring specialists schooled in these perspectives. Most came from graduate schools in the United States, where the cult of the business school had much deeper roots. For instance, Dan Monieson, who boasted a doctorate in business administration from Ohio State and experience at the Wharton School of Business in Philadelphia, was hired to teach marketing and "foreign commerce." At the same time, Macpherson linked the school to the new Queen's computing centre so that its students could run computer business models developed at the University of California at Los Angeles on Queen's new IBM computer. In 1960, the simpler title of School of Business was adopted. The old finance and banking courses were wound down.

Macpherson realized that, if Queen's was to make its educational wares more relevant to the business community, it would have to close the distance between its campus in isolated eastern Ontario and the bastions of Canadian business in Toronto and Montreal. In 1959, the school began offering "executive education" seminars that brought business executives to campus for intensive courses on management trends. At the same time, Macpherson created an advisory council for his school, attaching Queen's to current trends in Canadian business. A year later, the study of industrial relations at Queen's was hived off from the political-studies department and, under director Donald Wood, began offering similar seminars and conferences on Canada's industrial-relations outlook for those charged with what was now becoming known as "human resources" in Canada's corporations. As at many other business schools in North America, theory was in the ascendancy. To succeed in the day-to-day hurly-burly of the business world, managers needed the stabilizing perspective of the theory that lay behind their decisions. This meant infusing business schools with a dedication to research, whether driven by Harvard-style case studies, MIT science-inspired instruction, or Chicago-style insistence on methodology. In 1959, Macpherson unveiled Queen's own Master's of Business Administration, a two-year program that would groom "mature students" into practitioners or managers conditioned to the demands of finance, marketing, industrial relations, personnel management, production management, and operations research. Thirty-seven students – all male – enrolled.

In 1963, the business school became a separate faculty, although economists still provided business students with their fundamental grounding in economics. Macpherson continued to diversify his faculty, with the goal of making the school a reflection of the "mosaic of disciplines" that business administration had become. Bob Crandall, the chartered accountant Deutsch had hired as his assistant, succumbed to the new ethos of teaching business and headed to Berkeley in 1965 to earn a doctorate in business, returning in 1969 to join the faculty.[76] Nonetheless, Queen's business school was still playing catch-up. "To suggest that the faculty of about fifteen people," Merv Daub and Bruce Buchan argue in their history of the school, "was spread a bit thin is an understatement."[77] Then, in 1965, Macpherson switched his academic hat for an administrative one, taking over the newly created position of vice-principal, finance. The appointment provided a microcosm of what was happening in the business world: the university had become an enterprise that needed constant, hands-on financial management.

In 1966, Macpherson was replaced as dean by Richard Hand, who now represented the new wave of business education at Queen's. Hand quickly proved a canny leader of the expanding School of Business. He realized the danger of a rift opening up between the faculty's old guard – accounting and finance types – and the new cadre of specialists in quantitative and methodology-driven business administration. There was also a growing tension in the faculty between those who taught and those who researched. With this in mind, Hand allocated offices in Dunning Hall on a mingled basis, so that the old and the new would have to interact. Departmental roundtables were organized to oblige his now-diverse faculty to share perspectives. Unlike Dean Botterell in medicine, Hand adopted a hands-off style of shepherding his faculty. He tended to be reclusive and hard to corner. To avoid what he considered time-consuming daily interaction with his colleagues, he sometimes secreted himself in a janitor's closet in Dunning Hall, where the intrusions of the day might be avoided. Younger members of the faculty, anxious for decisions from their dean, took to calling him "the Invisible Hand."[78]

Despite such quirks, Hand was popular with his faculty, because they recognized he was pursuing Macpherson's vision of a business school that was intimately connected to the needs of businessmen on the street. Typically, he devised a three-week, intensive, MBA-style course for middle managers, who might use the experience on their way up the corporate ladder. Closer to home, he built bridges with the Kingston business community, turning their problems into case studies for his students. And, aware that no Canadian university yet offered a doctorate in business, he kept his eye peeled for promising talent in business schools south of the border. Once a year, Hand made a flying trip through the big-name American business schools, seeking out promising young Canadians studying there. Over lunch or dinner he urged them to direct their ambitions homeward when they graduated and hinted that Queen's wanted them. One such catch was Ed Petersen, a Stanford and CalTech graduate, originally from Olds, Alberta, who joined the faculty in 1968. Petersen's solid research and teaching backstopped the school's operational research area for decades to come, especially in the field of transportation. By the early 1970s, not surprisingly, Hand was agitating for a doctoral program in business at Queen's. Thus, in the space of a decade, a parochial school of business had been transformed into a faculty with national aspirations. Sensing the change in their faculty, Queen's commerce students formed their own society in 1967 and – as was the Queen's tradition – donned distinctive jackets, in this case, burgundy leather.

A gust of modernization blew through other Queen's programs as well. Since 1946, the School of Physical and Health Education had prepared students to be elementary and high-school physical-education teachers. The program reflected an old-fashioned Canadian approach to what was universally called "Phys Ed." As an early 1960s director of athletics commented, the administration at Queen's regarded Phys Ed as a straightforward, sweaty business of "bouncing basketballs and throwing footballs," and nothing else. By 1961, there were 140 students in the school's four-year program. Since its creation, the school's director had been Fred Bartlett, who had emerged from a career at Jarvis Collegiate and a stint in the provincial department of education. Bartlett regarded his position at Queen's as a "plum" and, while he had a knack for public relations, he had never mustered any vision for the program beyond the high-school locker room.[79] Despite the fact Queen's boasted a vibrant network of intramural and intercollegiate sports, staff morale in the school was low. By the 1960s, physical education was beginning to be construed in a much more activist context. It was no longer seen as a simple matter of throwing medicine balls around a gym, but instead as part of a broader, societal "fitness" initiative. Effective physical education now entailed linkages with other disciplines, such as psychology, anatomy, and sociology. Governments were becoming involved in encouraging citizens to be more physically active; in the sixties Canadians started to be haunted by the spectre of robust, seventy-year-old Swedes, radiating good health.

This transformation seemed to escape Fred Bartlett, thereby handicapping the Queen's program in attracting a new generation of Phys Ed students. Belatedly, Bartlett did encourage his students to take one of Queen's early sociology courses, realizing that sociology provided insights into society beyond the locker room. In 1964, the head of the anatomy department, John Basmajian, nonetheless dispatched a confidential memo to the principal. While other schools were remodelling their Phys Ed curriculum, there had been "no outward sign that a fresh and vigorous scientific approach is in the offing" at Queen's. Bartlett was a fine fellow, but without change the school was "in danger of sinking into the depths of mediocrity and anti-scientism."[80] Corry did not need much prompting. The school must be modernized. Outside consultants reinforced the message: "May I begin by being perfectly frank and saying that the Queen's physical education program is in need of modernization," wrote an expert from the University of Alberta.[81]

When Bartlett took retirement in 1965, Corry chose as his successor Dr Donald Mackintosh from the University of Calgary. Mackintosh dedicated himself to revitalizing the old teacher-training stream in the school, but at the same time he also introduced a more academic bent to the hiring of new staff and their subsequent pursuit of research. Like Hand and Botterell, Mackintosh brought dramatic change. In 1967, a new combined BA-BPHE degree was introduced to provide would-be physical-education teachers with a more rounded and academic education. With its students now studying biological and social sciences, the school began cross-appointing its staff to relevant departments, such as physiology, so that physical education could mingle with life sciences and medicine in its instruction. At the same time, Mackintosh abolished Queen's age-old requirement that first-year students undertake obligatory physical education; the gym would now cater to voluntary "recreation" through intramural sports and individual fitness. Pleased with Mackintosh's headway, Corry formed an ad hoc committee of users of the university's physical-education infrastructure. In early 1966, the committee urged the university to enlarge and modernize its gym facilities and playing fields. Five years later, the old 1930 Bews Gym on Union Street found itself wrapped into a new Physical Education Centre, which offered three gyms, a pool, and an arena.[82]

The imperative of connecting academic preparation with the changing world beyond the campus was also keenly felt in the Faculty of Applied Science. Postwar Canadian prosperity sat on a foundation of applied science. The iconic monuments of the new industrial Canada – the gleaming skyscrapers, the St Lawrence Seaway, bush planes, trans–Canadian highways and pipelines – all required the touch of the professional engineer. Yet, after a surge of enrolment in the immediate postwar period, admissions into applied science at Queen's had slumped. By 1964, Queen's had 300 available first-year spaces in engineering, but only 237 were taken up (it had been 238 until the lone female fresh-"man" dropped out). Since taking up the deanship in 1954, Hugh Conn had grappled with the waning appeal of his faculty. In essence, the problem seemed to lie in a curriculum that had become detached from the practical needs of engineers in the field. Engineering students were obliged to take set-piece courses that thwarted their ambition to specialize in particular fields. First-year students were, for instance, all obliged to take a surveying course, even though such skills had no relevance to, say, chemical engineering. Students complained that there was little flexibility in the scheduling of courses; applied science students were locked into full-year courses that allowed little latitude in choosing courses that intensified specialization. Grades were governed by an antediluvian set of regulations. The dropout rate was high. There was too little emphasis at Queen's on graduate programs dedicated to actual industrial needs.

By the early 1960s, industrialists on the Board of Trustees, like Roy Gordon of Inco, complained that their companies found young engineers poorly prepared for the workplace. They reflected that other universities, like the recently founded University of Waterloo, were finding success with co-operative programs that mingled classroom learning with intervals of on-the-job experience. In 1965, the Canadian Council of Professional Engineers instituted an accreditation system that obliged engineering schools to submit to periodic external evaluation of their curriculum. The profession would be looking for change when it came to Queen's.

Back at Queen's, Dean Conn, universally known as "the Colonel" as a result of his wartime service and his crisp, decisive manner, strove to refresh his faculty in Ellis Hall, which had been opened in 1958 as a new home for civil engineering. Although attitudes about the sanctity of the curriculum proved resilient, Conn managed to work more pure science and mathematics – crucial determinants in the Sputnik age – into the curriculum. He insisted that engineering students begin taking courses in economics, politics, English, and business, so as to better prepare themselves for their professional life. But attracting new faculty to Kingston also proved difficult: the allure of working for industry was strong, and Kingston was outside the Canadian mainstream. Reform was slowed by the fact that Conn himself continued as head of mechanical engineering and an active professor; he was, in effect, a part-time dean. When Conn replaced John Deutsch as the vice-principal, administration, in 1963, Corry decided that the times required seismic change in the Faculty of Applied Science. This would begin with a full-time dean. And it would be driven by an outsider. That same year, a thirty-four-year-old Canadian metallurgist, Jim Brown, had been offered a professorship in the Queen's metallurgy department. He had a doctorate from MIT, where his studies had connected him with the latest technologies and exposed him to the unfolding developments in business management and applied economics as well. Brown turned down the offer. He was happily employed at US Steel and liked the corporate ethos. But when Conn called a year later to entice him into the deanship, Brown was interested. He wanted to return to Canada and egotistically – by his own admission – believed that he could effect change in lethargic academic structures by applying a corporate style of leadership. He liked quoting American steel magnate Clarence Randall: "Every organization is the extended shadow of the man at the top."[83]

Brown arrived in the dean's office in September and launched what faculty historian George Richardson would describe as the "first wholesale" reform of the faculty since the turn of the century.[84] His style was bullish and impatient; Brown had little time for the habitual give and take of academic discourse. The process began with student admissions. Brown pulled engineering admissions out of the registrar's office and set up his own admissions process, one which weighed not just secondary-school grades but also a student's non-academic interests. First-year curriculum was then liberated from its rigid structure. Students were offered more courses in the humanities in a bid to polish the role of the engineer in society. Courses were cut in length from a full year to a term; more optional courses were offered. Grading was made less arcane and fairer than the unforgiving system that had tended to drive down retention rates. In a bid to moderate the steep learning curve of students trying to cope with the intensity of university courses, mathematics professor Jim Whitley pioneered "J section" courses, which stretched instruction of difficult material over more than a standard term in order to make it more digestible.[85] Courses in FORTRAN computer programming were made mandatory. Brown pushed hard for the introduction of "information science" into the curriculum and for parallel research support. In 1967, the Senate approved the creation of a department of computing and information science, although it was attached to the Arts and Science faculty (but located in an engineering building). To maintain the momentum of curriculum reform, Brown pulled Professor Reg Browne out of the department of mechanical engineering to act as his executive assistant. Results were impressive: by the fall of 1968, Applied Science welcomed 374 first-year students (three of them being women).

Brown's "new broom," as Richardson called it, swept through the faculty. Research was emphasized, reflecting not only the appetite of industry for useful scientific knowledge but also the increasing importance of federal granting agencies, especially the National Research Council, as sponsors of research. Brown instigated the annual *Research in Progress* to showcase faculty research. He also became the faculty's ambassador, making contacts with government officials and industry leaders. In the department of mining engineering, for instance, he insisted on a "highly technical undergraduate curriculum," so as to groom its undergraduates for work "breaking rock" on the mining frontier. He courted McIntyre Porcupine Mines and other companies for research money and advice, thereby reawakening Queen's long association with the Canadian mining frontier.[86] Similarly, as Hand had done in the business school, Brown encouraged departments to form advisory councils that channelled industry's priorities into curriculum development and employment guidance. More attention was paid to securing outside benefactors; in 1965 geological sciences (a hybrid department that straddled both Applied Science and Arts and Science) received a generous endowment of $100,000 from nickel promoter Thayer Lindsley. Partnerships for research and continuing education were formed with Bell Canada and other companies and government agencies such as the Defence Research Board. In 1968, the Centre for Metal and Mineral Sciences was established under the department of metallurgy to incubate research at the intersection of chemistry and physics. A partnership with government and Canada's railways similarly hatched the Canadian Institute of Guided Ground Transport in a bid to develop high-speed trains.

The pulse of Brown's reformation was felt in every Applied Science department. Chemical engineering provided a fine example. When the redoubtable-if-eccentric Argyle Plewes died suddenly in 1962, his role as head of chemical engineering was ably taken by Reg Clark, an English-born biochemist. With the baby-boom economy devouring an ever-growing array of chemically engineered products, the department rode a wave of expansion in the 1960s. Clark grew the faculty to a complement of twelve professors by the decade's end, adding promising young members like Henry Becker, David Bacon, John Downie, and James Hsu to its roster. Doctoral studies began in 1963, with the first graduate emerging in 1966.

That same year, the department moved to new quarters in Dupuis Hall. Undergraduates were offered new elective courses that allowed them to specialize in their senior years. Reflecting Dean Brown's inclination to link engineers with the broader sensibilities of society, Clark in 1969 pioneered a course – "Nature, Science, and Man" – that reminded engineering students that their actions could reverberate into the ecology and the structure of society. For the first time at Queen's, professors from departments as disparate as English, political studies, and chemical engineering preached an environmental message. Did man, the course asked, have a God-given right to have "dominion" over the earth? Clark and his colleagues packed the lecture hall and the course was soon televised.[87]

Jim Brown was one of the most impatient and brusque of the men Alex Corry brought to his side in the sixties to refresh the way the university conceived of itself and delivered its services. Brown's memos to the principal, his sermons to the Applied Science faculty board and to department heads were full of "radical revision" and similar terms. His style was unnecessarily abrasive for many, but Corry backed him, in the belief that the complacency of the fifties had to be rooted out. Nonetheless, post-secondary educational institutions habituated to gradualist change, like universities, cannot indefinitely sustain the kind of command leadership seen in Applied Science in the sixties. When his first term as dean ended in 1969, Brown agreed to a two-year extension and then slipped into other less-transformative administrative functions at Queen's. There was an unexpressed sentiment that the Applied Science faculty needed a breather from the frenzy of the Brown reformation.

Other faculties enjoyed more normative times than Business, Applied Science, and Medicine. The Faculty of Law, for instance, was a work in progress. Founded in 1957, it carried no baggage in terms of ingrained curriculum or faculty entitlement. Ably led by Dean William "Bill" Lederman, the faculty had dedicated itself to approaching the law from a more academic perspective. Stress was placed on the social and constitutional implications of the law. For instance, Professor Stuart Ryan focused his students on the appropriate sentencing of offenders, often taking his class en masse to the Kingston prisons for some personal exposure to the human consequences of the law.

Saskatchewan-born Lederman enjoyed the enthusiastic backing of Saskatchewan-educated Corry in this broadening of legal education. Like many professional programs incubated by Canada's post-war boom, the school surfed a wave of demand in Canada for more lawyers. By 1961, there were 105 students enrolled (three of them women), catered to by seven full-time professors, aided by three local barristers as adjuncts. Throughout the sixties, Lederman pushed for more students, more faculty, more books, and more space.

In 1960, the faculty had moved out of its temporary home in a brick house on University Avenue into the new Sir John A. Macdonald building on Union Street. Prime Minister John Diefenbaker cut the ribbon, no doubt a sweet moment for Lederman, who would have seen in Dief's reputation as a battling small-town Saskatchewan defence lawyer an echo of his own purpose in the law. Lederman would also have relished the fact that Diefenbaker's government had just delivered a Bill of Rights to Canadians. Now comfortably housed, Lederman almost immediately launched a campaign to expand the faculty. In December 1962, he informed Corry that his plan for the school had been "too modest" and that he would require at least twelve full-time professors by 1970. And, he added, he wanted to offer more competitive salaries in order to attract the best talent, pointing out that good candidates were reluctant to leave the bright lights of Toronto for provincial Kingston. Furthermore, the relatively small Queen's law library, with just forty thousand volumes, must be expanded, because it was "the very heart and centre of a law school."[88] Lederman also turned his attention on Vice-Principal Conn: the Macdonald Building would have to be expanded "very soon – much sooner than we anticipated when the present building was constructed." Then he headed for Toronto, where he lobbied the Law Society of Upper Canada to expand his enrolment and liberalize his curriculum, suggesting that Queen's might handle as many as three hundred students by the mid-1970s, some of them engaged in graduate studies.

Lederman's persistence paid handsome dividends. The Faculty of Law grew steadily through the sixties, not only deepening its front bench of teachers, but also broadening the scope of its offerings. By 1968, there were nineteen full-time professors, now buttressed by five Kingston part-timers. Some of the new recruits boasted impressive credentials. Albertan Bernie Adell arrived, fresh from a Rhodes Scholarship and boasting labour-law expertise. Hugh Lawford brought an interest in the compilation of legal information, while Ron Delisle was hired to teach criminal law and evidence. Delisle's hiring was a milestone of a sort – a 1964 Queen's law grad (and Gaels football player), he was the first law-school alumnus to return to teach at his alma mater. Delisle proved a popular teacher with students, who came to quip that "if Delisle says it is so, it must be so." Another Queen's graduate, Mary Alice Murray (LLB 1960), was appointed secretary of the law faculty Board. Until Irene Bessette was hired in 1969 as head law librarian and lecturer in civil and Quebec law, Murray remained the only woman in an all-male faculty.

Lederman's hiring was also informed by a desire to reach out to other disciplines. The law, he believed, must be linked to other fields of intellectual endeavour; it could not simply be an isolated island of dry legal procedure. "A law school must operate as a faculty in the interdisciplinary environment of a university," he argued, "so that legal issues can be illuminated by reference to the natural sciences, the

Prime Minister John Diefenbaker opens Sir John A. Macdonald Hall in late 1961. Chancellor Stirling (left) and Dean of Law William "Bill" Lederman and Principal Mackintosh watch as the law faculty gets its first designated home. Established in 1957, the Queen's law school was dedicated to teaching law in its broadest social and constitutional aspects. Alex Corry, then vice-principal, had recruited Lederman to Queen's in 1958; both had had first studied law at the University of Saskatchewan.

social sciences and the humanities generally, and vice versa."[89] With this in mind, in 1965 Lederman wasted no time (the interview and offer were made in one swift afternoon) in hiring David Bonham, who boasted credentials as both a chartered accountant *and* a lawyer, plus graduate study at Harvard. Bonham was deployed to classrooms in both the law and business schools.[90] Elsewhere on campus, links were made with the political-studies department in the area of constitutional and administrative law, Corry's lifelong areas of interest, and with the economics department and Institute of Intergovernmental Relations.

When Denis Magnusson arrived to teach business and contract law at Queen's in 1968, he found the law school "a very optimistic place."[91] Construction of additional floors on the Macdonald Building was nearly complete. The law library now topped 60,000 volumes, and 275 students now crowded the school's lecture halls. New courses on human rights and on psychiatry and the law were unfolding, and negotiations with the Law Society in Toronto were under way to liberalize the overall curriculum by reducing mandatory core courses and increasing optional courses for upper-year students. Plans for a master's degree in law were about to bear fruit in 1969. The first successful LLM granted – to Toni Pickard (wife of law professor Michael Pickard), for a thesis on psychotherapy in the prison system – reflected the social commitment of Lederman's law school. The faculty were also increasingly active in research: Hugh Lawford, in partnership with IBM, had launched QUIK/LAW, a project to construct a computer database that would place an inventory of past legal decisions at a lawyer's fingertips. In his dean's report at the end of 1967, Dean Lederman had rather modestly concluded: "All in all, it has been a busy ten years." A year later, such dedication took its toll. Lederman was felled by a stroke and, although he recovered, he lost the stamina to be dean. Such was the richness of Lederman's recruitment over that decade that a worthy successor was readily at hand. Associate Dean Dan Soberman, a specialist in business law, stepped up, took the dean's chair, and clinched the final details of Lederman's plans for curriculum reform and graduate studies. If there was a story of onward-and-upward progress at Queen's in the sixties, it emanated from the law faculty. In 1970, when Magnusson returned from a year away completing his master's degree, he rejoiced in the "tightly-knit community" he found there. It was, he concluded, "a good home."

Corry's unswerving belief that a first-rank, national university must be equipped with cutting-edge professional programs reverberated in the creation of a Faculty of Graduate Studies in 1963. "I agree," he wrote to Professor Robert More, head of pathology, in 1963, "that we must have deep concern now that we do not become simply a small regional university in eastern Ontario. To counter this effect, we do need to develop high-class graduate work in at least a few fields." Sterling graduate programs in departments of traditional Queen's strength, such as economics and political studies, would have "considerable drawing power."[92] Yet, in 1961, Queen's supported only a flimsy shell of graduate studies.

A motley collection of post-undergraduate options had existed at Queen's through the century, most oriented to the sciences, although Queen's first PhD was awarded in 1904 to a candidate in philosophy. In 1943, the Senate had centralized control of these programs under a Board of Graduate Studies. This board had a chairman, the slimmest of staff, and a miniscule budget. Financial support of graduate students depended on a smattering of endowment-driven scholarships and the piggy-backing of graduate supervision on grants obtained by faculty. By 1961, the university had 219 students enrolled in graduate studies and graduated ten doctoral and fifty-one master's students. But, in that year, the chair of the graduate studies board, chemistry Professor James Beveridge, reported that change was imperative. The baby-boom surge was beginning to wash into undergraduate programs, in turn creating a demand for more professors in university classrooms. And there was the broader demand for professional training coming from a society that increasingly functioned on credentialed expertise. As noted above, the launch of the Queen's MBA in 1959 had given the first hint of this.

In April 1960, the Board of Graduate Studies struck a committee under Beveridge to study the prospect of a dramatic expansion of graduate studies at Queen's under the centralizing umbrella of a single faculty; deans from the major faculties participated. Its report in early 1961 called for a wholesale remaking of the graduate enterprise at Queen's. A "school" of graduate studies should be created, with a dean served by a constitution, a sustaining budget, and systematic regulations.

Over the next year, the intricacies of constructing what was in fact a new faculty were painstakingly worked out. Early on it became apparent that Queen's would adopt a unitary graduate structure – as was the case at most North American universities, the graduate faculty would enjoy an autonomous existence, floating above the undergraduate faculties below it. While undergraduate departments would be consulted, the spigot of admission and financial support would be controlled by the graduate faculty. Such centralization would allow the university to mould its graduate program as it saw most fit. Corry worried that "the glitter of graduate work," if unregulated, might erode the quality of undergraduate teaching, as professors flocked to the allure of graduate supervision from the seeming banality of the burgeoning undergraduate lecture hall.[93] A centrally controlled graduate office could also act as the "overseer of academic standards" and manage fees, financial assistance, and the quality of professors admitted to graduate teaching. In February 1963, the Senate approved the creation of the School of Graduate Studies. Its constitution divided the school into four divisions – biological sciences, humanities and social sciences, engineering sciences and mathematics, and physical sciences – and established a council to guide faculty affairs.

Growth came quickly and steadily. The fall of 1962 saw an enrolment of 293; a year later it was 351. Government accelerated the pace. Post-secondary education had become palatable political policy. Pundits flippantly noted that every university place that was opened up brought two votes from appreciative parents. Until the Ontario government created the Department of University Affairs in 1964, Premier John Robarts, conscious of the political capital to be reaped, wore two hats: premier and minister of education. Historically, Canada had had a chronic deficit in the production of graduate degrees, and now that new venues for undergraduate education were unfolding across the province, thoughts turned to bolstering post-BA options. In September 1962, Robarts announced the Ontario Graduate Fellowship (OGF) program, under which MA and PhD students might qualify for up to $2,000 in annual support. It was, he said, "one of the most imaginative and unique [programs] in the history of higher education in this country."[94] At the same time, the federal government, through the National Research Council, the Canada Council, and other agencies, enhanced its support of graduate students. Queen's devised its own inducements – through R. Samuel McLaughlin Fellowships, for example – for top-notch graduate students. Corry talked about the need to attract "blue-ribbon" graduate students. For the first time, universities began competing vigorously for graduate students.

Worried that graduate studies in the province lacked an overarching strategy and were becoming costly and overlapping, the Council of Ontario Universities and the Committee of Presidents of Ontario Universities in 1965 asked University of Saskatchewan President John Spinks to investigate. Spinks reported that a master plan was indeed missing, and went so far as to recommend the creation of a University of Ontario to coordinate all provincial graduate studies. Fearful that Queen's Park might impose procrustean politicized control through such a mechanism, Corry, who was CPUO chairman, and other university presidents recoiled. To shore up their autonomy, the CPUO in late 1966 took the initiative and established the Ontario Council of Graduate Studies (OCGS), which was empowered to accredit new graduate programs and periodically vet existing ones.[95]

Through the mid-decade, the new graduate faculty gelled. An elaborate rubric of regulations, ranging from thesis specifications to thesis defence procedures, had to be set in place. When Beveridge left to become president of Acadia University, the deanship was first filled by Clifford Curtis, former head of economics and political studies, and then in 1967 by David Slater, the bright young Queen's-trained economist who had returned from policy work in Ottawa some years earlier. Under these men, the graduate program broadened and matured. In 1965, the Senate, for instance, approved a doctorate in the French department, but turned down one in mining engineering, arguing that it was "premature." Master's programs, like the one approved for geography in 1965, multiplied. Competition for program approval was intense; there was indeed "glitter" in graduate teaching. Before stepping down as dean, Curtis boasted that Queen's graduate school was finally "an organized entity," but warned that interdisciplinary co-operation must prevail. "Internal bickering over power," he warned, "can only destroy it."[96] Sensing the same need, Queen's graduate students organized the Graduate Students' Society in 1962. Corry privately noted that he thought graduate students a "distinct and different kind of animal," worthy of special attention.[97]

In the fall of 1967, Corry asked Dean Lederman of Law to chair a broad-ranging study of the burgeoning graduate faculty. The committee reported that it was overwhelmed by how complex the young faculty had grown and underlined that strong central control was in order to steer it forward. The Faculty of Graduate Studies was destined to be a constantly changing thing, continually subject to internal strains and external demands for ever-changing types of expertise. For Corry, the new faculty was the capstone of making Queen's modern and comprehensive. At his last Queen's convocation as principal in 1968, Corry proudly watched as 171 graduate degrees were awarded. An honorary degree was given that day to Ernest Sirluck, dean of graduate studies at the University of Toronto, who counselled against "an unplanned proliferation of graduate programs" but assured the graduates sitting before him that Ontario's dedication to graduate studies "is why this province seems to me about as exciting a place as I know for a university man to be."[98] And, he concluded, it was Corry of Queen's, who as CPUO chairman had most formatively moulded Ontario's "tenable pattern of graduate work."

Growth Pains

Alex Corry's drive to shunt Queen's out of its old, comfortable ways into a crisper, more modern configuration did not always go as smoothly and convivially as it did in law and graduate studies. On two occasions, he reluctantly resorted to root-and-branch tactics to affect dramatic change, tactics that bruised the loyalty that some had developed over decades.

In any university, the registrar's office and the library occupied central functions in ensuring the efficient servicing of students initially seeking to gain admission to the university and later wanting to feed their appetite for knowledge. Both functions at Queen's were forcibly recast in the sixties. Since 1924, the linchpin of the Queen's library system had been the Douglas Library, an imposing collegiate-Gothic building at the corner of Union Street and University Avenue. The gift of Queen's-trained mining promoter James Douglas, who had made a fortune in copper mining, the library had been a state-of-the-art facility in the 1920s, but by the sixties the growth of the university had stretched it to capacity. A library designed for 85,000 volumes was now buckling under 450,000 volumes. Its beautiful reading room, with its stained-glass windows and oak desks, could seat only 200. Its rules and procedures seemed almost Dickensian. The stacks where books were shelved were closed, necessitating the cumbersome retrieval of material by request. The reference staff were competent, but formidable; for years, reference librarian Melva Eagleson stoically sat at the reference desk in the main reading room, acquiring the sobriquet of "the dragon lady." "QUIET" signs adorned the walls. On football Saturdays, the library closed.[99] A quaintly titled Board of Library Curators oversaw the library's policies.

The library operated by dint of manual effort, largely performed by teams of women who engaged in the busy-hands work of ordering books, cataloguing them, and then managing their circulation. Their skills were often acquired on the job or through a stint at library school in Toronto. Queen's was fortunate to be able to staff its library in large measure by drawing on the increasing number of intelligent women whose husbands had been taken on as faculty. The library offered a job when there was little else available in Kingston, either for the long term or for intervals between childbirth. Such was the case with a young British immigrant, Lin Good, who came to Kingston in the late 1950s, when her husband joined the staff at the Royal Military College. After acquiring a diploma in library science in Toronto, she was hired at Queen's as an order librarian. Principal Mackintosh quizzed her personally at her interview about her mathematical ability;

he quipped that he did not want her pushing the university into deficit through sloppy addition. Good found the Douglas Library systems "very primitive," but found the woman-centred culture of the place "collegial."[100]

If the library was a convivial enclave of women, it was still managed by a male: H. Pearson Gundy, the University Librarian. Gundy was much admired by his staff, remembered by one as "a gentleman of great wit and warmth." He roamed the library, greeting staff and patrons and ensuring that service was attentive. He often answered his phone with similar outgoing goodwill: "Your friendly banker here," he greeted callers, implying that he was in the business of satisfying their desires. He served as the perennial secretary of the Saturday Club, recording its minutes in verse. But Gundy was in reality a bookman, not a librarian. His MA degree was in English literature, a subject he had taught at various colleges until 1944, when he took a library course at Columbia University in New York City. Even after he became Queen's University Librarian in 1947, his abiding passion was the study of books and publishing. His erudition on such Canadian poets as Bliss Carman and Kingston's own Charles Sangster was impressive. So was his industry in building up Queen's "Special Collections" – books and papers donated by prominent Canadian literati such as Lorne Pierce.

However, as the sixties unfolded and growth engulfed Queen's, Gundy seemed overwhelmed by the challenge of adapting the library to new needs. Studies commissioned by the National Conference of Canadian Universities and Colleges all indicated that university libraries had to adjust to burgeoning demands on their resources and to rapid advances in library systems. In particular, provincial approval of graduate studies in any field would depend on a demonstrable base of library resources. Every new doctoral field, it was estimated, would have to be supported by 24,500 library volumes. By the early 1960s, the Douglas Library simply did not have the space to house such resources. Nor was it addressing the emerging professionalization evident in many libraries. Libraries were increasingly seen as *systems*, not just repositories for books. Librarians were coming to see themselves as professionals, not technicians. Ultimately, this shift would convert "librarianship" into "information science." But Pearson Gundy appeared to prefer the old world of books to the new world of systems.

There were some changes in the early sixties. Under Gundy, Queen's enhanced its reputation as one of the finest troves of Canadiana in the country, with holdings like the Edith and Lorne Pierce Collection, which was placed under the expert care of custodian William Morley. The university archives were put on a professional footing under archivists Charles Beer, John Archer, and Ian Wilson, and began accumulating holdings of national import. Historian Fred Gibson had a canny instinct for capturing papers of pivotal national figures – among them novelist and governor general John Buchan and journalist Grant Dexter. In 1962, the trustees approved an aggressive expansion of the library itself. Three underground floors and a new north wing were added along Union Street, enlarging the capacity of the library to 800,000 volumes. While the Gothic facade was retained, a sunny reading room was placed in the new north wing. Finished in purple carpet and upholstery, the comfy room quickly acquired the student nickname of the "purple passion pit." Open stack access was allowed, and new labour-saving devices such as photocopying machines began to appear in the early 1970s.

But such change proved exponential. In February 1965, Gundy announced that he was retiring. His decision was probably partly driven by his own intuition that libraries were changing in ways uncongenial to him and partly by pressure put on him by the Board of Library Curators, which, predictably, transmitted the agenda of the principal and trustees. As was his wont, Gundy went gracefully. To his delight, he was taken on by the English department and became editor of the *Queen's Quarterly*, thereby playing out his innings surrounded by the books he so loved.[101]

As Gundy's replacement as Chief Librarian, the university hired Donald Redmond, a Nova Scotian with a library-science degree from the University of Illinois and experience as assistant librarian at the University of Kansas. Redmond was a "systems man," who understood what had to be done to make a library complement its university's expansion. He recognized that professionalization was permeating library work. He brought in up-to-date talent: Ted Phillips, with American library training and IBM experience, became assistant chief librarian, and Diana Blake, with experience in industry and government libraries, was made head of acquisitions. Redmond argued that his staff should not be seen as part of the university's administrative apparatus, but instead as part of the academic establishment. In 1967, Queen's librarians were consequently given professional job classifications.

Redmond also pinned his colours to the centralization of all library functions at Queen's, alleging that the university's system of scattered branch libraries was costly and antediluvian. Here he faced vehement opposition from the English and mechanical engineering departments, among others long accustomed to having their own libraries. Within the library, Redmond inaugurated a regime of crisp, business-like management: staff received weekly "all staff" memos, which discussed problems and set goals. If Gundy had been the genial bookman, Redmond was a systems man in a grey flannel suit. With the library by 1966 consuming 8 per cent of the university's annual budget, the transition was unavoidable. "Give us the tools; the job will never be finished," Redmond wrote in 1967, "but give us the funds, and the library will come closer to satisfying its users."[102]

If the university library felt the pressure of Queen's swelling population in the sixties, so too did the registrar's office, the portal through which every new student arrived on campus. Since 1933, that office had been filled by the redoubtable Jean Royce, as devoted a servant of Queen's as had ever lived. She was students' first point of contact with their future alma mater and was thus in a position to inoculate them with the university's culture. Once admitted, a student's passage through Queen's was traced on student records that were kept in Royce's office. These cards captured grades, distinctions, and, on occasion, indiscretions. Royce poured maternal devotion into her duties; she remembered names and faces and could winnow a student's potential out of high-school grades and letters of recommendation long before they materialized on campus each autumn. She was, in the words of her biographer, Roberta Hamilton, "the university's main gatekeeper" and "a superb talent scout."[103]

Royce's devotion to Queen's and her function in perpetuating that devotion in future generations of students was rooted in her own undergraduate studies at Queen's in English and history in the 1920s. After a brief career as a librarian and schoolteacher, Royce had returned to Queen's in 1931 at the bidding of the vice-principal, William McNeill, who had detected her organizational ability when she had worked briefly at the Douglas Library. In the almost hermetically male world of Canadian universities, the post of registrar sometimes fell to a woman, a reflection of contemporary belief that women were somehow genetically better suited to the busy work of keeping track of paperwork and dispensing maternal guidance. When the incumbent registrar, Alice King, died in 1933, Royce smoothly slipped into the role. Her reputation rested on her beneficence and her diligence.

For thousands of students, Jean Royce was both the guiding and guardian angel of their unfolding academic careers. In an era when the undergraduate curriculum tended to be predetermined – and not selected by the student – Royce dispensed advice about academic direction. She seemed to have an uncanny ability to discern where a student's strengths lay, pushing them into the arms of a department that would nurture their potential. Since the registrar's office also coordinated the dispensing of the university's scholarship funds, Royce was also in a position to accentuate a student's academic performance. Royce took to describing the role of a registrar as a "craft," not a job. Given the relatively small and stable student body at Queen's through the fifties, Royce was able to maintain a bird's-eye vigilance over the student body. No other figure at Queen's acquired such devoted admirers. An issue of the *Queen's Review* seldom passed without transmitting an anecdote about some act of kindness or sage advice dispensed by Royce. For some it was more than a passing kindness. In late 1941, as mentioned, she had used her discretion to admit a young Jewish refugee from Vienna, Alfred Bader, into an undergraduate program in chemistry. She did so midway through the academic year. McGill and Toronto had turned a blind, prejudiced eye to his application. Through Royce, Bader thus learned that, for all its flinty Presbyterianism, Queen's harboured tolerant instincts. Other Jews followed Bader's wartime path to Queen's. Bader himself would never forget the tolerance and benevolence of Royce's decision and over time demonstrated his gratitude to Queen's in many generous ways.[104]

Royce's competence soon spread beyond the registrar's office. She extended a helpful hand to many newly hired faculty, offering them a friendly dinner and some sage advice on the faculty syllabus. Her penchant for orderly procedure saw her drafted into many administrative functions. Over the years, she variously served as the secretary of the Senate, the Board of Graduate Studies, the Board of Library Curators, and the Faculty of Arts and Science. Agenda preparation and minute taking are activities shunned by most, but those seated in the secretary's chair are afforded a unique perspective at the crossroads of an organization's culture. When Royce stepped down years later from her role as Faculty of Arts and Science secretary, Principal Corry praised her "unstinted thought and effort." She possessed, he noted, "a full knowledge of its rules and practices, and its lack of rules and practices, her peculiar province."[105] Corry, who had interacted with Royce since his own arrival at Queen's in 1936, formed a warm appreciation of her skills and dedication. When, in Canada's centennial year of 1967, Ottawa called for nominations for the celebratory Centennial Medal, Corry was quick to make Royce one of Queen's nominees.

However, the sixties changed the university's landscape. On campuses across the continent, the registrar's role began to shift. Quantitatively, the number of applications soared. Entrance to university became less of a process of *registration* and more a complex business of *admissions*. As the base of potential applicants widened and politicians unfurled the banner of accessibility, entry to university ceased to be a largely automatic entitlement. Thus, in 1961, Queen's abandoned its old commitment to admitting any Grade 13 student with an average of 60 per cent. That threshold was raised to 65 per cent, and henceforth students in the 60-to-65-per-cent bracket were to be scrutinized by a special committee to decide their possible admission. The principal's report declared that this was a "stopgap" and that "properly designed controls" were needed if Queen's was to have "manageable" growth.[106] This meant that not only the volume of paper flowing through the registrar's office was going to steadily increase, but also that decisions on subsequent entry or denial would be more onerous. Queen's would now have to *pick*, rather than *accept*, its incoming students.

At the same time, other factors came into play. Universities were now *competing* for students, so that admission acceptances had to be hastened to high-school students who were placing multiple university bets. And, as undergraduate studies became more complex – arts students now pondered honours *versus* general degrees – individual departments sought to pitch their own wares to would-be students, rather than leaving this crucial come-hither to the registrar's office. In effect, there was strong pressure for registrars to confine themselves to administrative matters, leaving academic guidance to the academics. Similarly, should scholarship allocation be left in the hands of those who did not teach? And finally, as the number of applications burgeoned, the old methods of sorting and evaluating applications manually sagged as their volume exploded. Nice, neat piles of cards and applications had worked in the fifties, but now the computer promised quicker and easier results. In 1967, as a first step towards more efficient processing of admissions, Ontario's universities banded together to create a Central Admissions Office.

As the baby-boom years unfolded in the sixties, Jean Royce began to feel the pressure. Knowing that Queen's had to become more worldly wise, Principal Corry hired public-relations experts to ensure that Queen's was attuned to the external world, with its high expectations of universities. Queen's storied reputation now needed constant grooming. One such expert, Toronto-based Gordon Garbutt, immediately detected problems. "The Registrar's Office is the perennial pitfall," he reported to Corry in 1965. "It is almost impossible to maintain an effective working relationship with Miss Royce on almost any matter within her jurisdiction (the boundaries of which are of her own making and subject to frequent revision), such as the release of results, admission bulletins, faculty calendars, information about enrolment. No part of the work of the [Public Relations] Department has been done under more unpleasant conditions, nor with such unsatisfactory results."[107] There were other symptoms of stress. A high-school principal, for instance, wrote to complain of the "patronizing" tone adopted by Royce in advising him.[108] Corporate donors complained that they were not being informed of how their scholarship funds were being disbursed.[109] Hugh Conn, the vice-principal, administration, joined the chorus of critics: Royce did not answer his memos, the scholarship committee never met, student files were misplaced, and unnecessary stationery was ordered.[110]

Corry was quick to defend Royce. She was "overrun with work." The university had, he argued, got it "wrong through pressure of too rapidly increasing burdens in the Registrar's Office which we were not, for some time, adequately organized to handle."[111] Royce concurred. Her budget had been drastically cut and she was short-staffed. "The workload is already so heavy," she told Conn, "that overtime is inevitable, the present equipment is being used to the fullest degree, and present indications are that there will be a substantial increase in registration next year."[112] As the burden grew, some changes were made to ease the strain. In 1962, a brilliant young maths professor, Ralfe Clench, was appointed as Royce's assistant to help sort out the paper flow through the office at crunch times of the year. Clench also turned his quirky intelligence to rationalizing the cobweb of the university's examination schedule. That same year, Margaret Hooey was also hired as an assistant registrar. Hooey began work on the first day of registration, when organized pandemonium broke out as the new students arrived in Grant Hall to register. Hooey learned quickly and became devoted to Royce. Like many before her, she marvelled at Royce's devotion to her work and the "Geiger counter she had for students' potential."[113]

But the ground continued to shift. Dean Brown in Applied Science successfully pulled the admissions function over to his office, arguing that his faculty were more sensitive to what it took to pick out the best and brightest engineers. Although Royce had long argued that her office was the "focal point for the academic housekeeping of the University," she complied with the move. More broadly, students in the liberating sixties were becoming less inclined to being told by a registrar what was deemed to be in their best interest. Rightly or wrongly, students wanted to make their own choices about their education, not be handed their schedule on a sheet of paper by a kindly senior administrator. Just as had Pearson Gundy in the library, Royce began to feel overwhelmed by the need for change.

In June 1966, Corry commissioned Robin Ross, the registrar and director of student services at the University of Toronto, to undertake a review of Queen's registration system. A month later, Ross reported that the registrar's office at Queen's had fallen behind the times. Too many functions had been heaped on its shoulders. The registrar's office was "overloaded and understaffed." It had failed to adopt the "accepted Canadian pattern" of breaking its staff into functional sections – records, admissions, financial aid, examinations, and ceremonials – and placing each under an assistant registrar. Ross recommended Hooey for the key role of admissions officer. In short, Ross concluded that Royce was "greatly overburdened," and without rationalization of her function, there was "a lively possibility that the office may simply be unable to deal in future with the mounting complexities that face it immediately and in the future."[114] Ross noted that Royce had not resisted his prescriptions, even saying that she would welcome the advent of computers. Corry, too, pointed out that Royce had only "minor" objections to the report, mostly arising out of "standing under dignity on the principle that she knows more about the Registrar's Office than anyone else."

But the die was cast. By August, she and Corry were engaged in a dialogue about grooming an heir apparent. Royce said that her successor should be someone younger, someone capable of guiding the office through a period of change. The assumption underlying this calculation was that Royce would coach her successor while reforms were set in place and then make a dignified exit into retirement. Corry soon announced that he had a possible candidate: a fifty-five-year-old retired brigadier-general, George Leech. Queen's had fallen into the habit of employing ex-military men in the sixties, believing that they brought decisive management skills. Indeed, Royce was impressed by Leech, praising him as "a man of great competence," but wondering whether he was a bit too old for the challenge at hand. Nonetheless, Leech was hired. Most liked him. Hooey found him a "really good guy." But all noted his complete lack of experience as a registrar. Once again, Royce's devotion to Queen's shone through. She worked closely with Leech to draw up a blueprint for the new registrar's office based on Ross's report. By January 1967, it was ready. A functional division of responsibilities would take place, with the registrar installed at the centre of a constellation of assistant registrars, each assigned to their own bailiwick. Hiring new staff began, and Leech initiated plans for a computer-based student records system. He would learn on the job as de facto registrar, with Royce acting as his éminence grise until her sixty-fifth birthday and retirement arrived, when she would exit amid a chorus of tribute.

Unfortunately, this lovely, gradual sunset never arrived. Sometime in the fall of 1967, Corry decided to accelerate Royce's departure and, in February 1968, he called her into his office to announce that she would retire that August. Royce was stunned. Not only had she been completely blindsided by the decision, but she had to immediately inform Corry that her sixty-fifth birthday did not fall until 1969. Unable to deny this fact, the principal fell back on the argument that he could hardly inform George Leech that his apprenticeship would be stretched out over another year. This stance would seem to indicate that Corry had already briefed the new registrar on Royce's premature departure. Royce took all this in stoically. She discussed the fateful meeting with only her closest friends. To one, she ruefully revealed: "I am going to retire. I'll be replaced by ten brigadiers and fifteen lieutenant colonels."[115] As if conforming to a military metaphor, Royce then fell on her sword. It was officially announced that she would retire on 31 August that year, and would then linger as a consultant and on paid leave until her 1969 birthday rolled around.

The departure of Jean Royce from the active service of Queen's has become a *cause célèbre* in the annals of the university's history. Tellingly, it

Chancellor Stirling presents Jean Royce with her honorary degree at the fall convocation of 1968. Students at the convocation gave Royce a standing ovation. The registrar's function came under tremendous pressure of growth in the 1960s and some began to question Royce's ability to cope with an enrolment that was tripling in size. Nonetheless, her "retirement" was not graciously handled.

remained a repressed memory for many years. Royce concealed her wounded feelings and the university continued to celebrate her devoted service. On the surface, Corry and Royce remained cordial. That spring, as he prepared to depart his own office, Corry nominated her for an honorary degree. She told him that she was "shaken" by his gesture, particularly since she would receive it on the same day as Pierre Trudeau received his LLD. from Queen's. At convocation that fall, the students gave *both* the prime minister and former registrar a standing ovation. Corry also eagerly nominated Royce as the Queen's representative to conferences on post-secondary education. But the puzzle remains: why was Royce dealt with in such a summary and insensitive manner? It seems inconceivable that the principal – a lawyer by training and a man imbued with respect for the dignity of the individual (he had just undertaken a report for the federal government on hate literature) – would have not checked his facts before delivering a career-ending blow to an erstwhile friend. Significantly, Corry did not recount the episode in his memoir *My Life and Work*, suggesting retrospective unease about his handling of the situation.

In the absence of such candour, Royce's treatment can possibly be understood from two perspectives. In much the same way as he had approached the need to renovate the management of the university library, Corry regarded the situation in the registrar's office in functionalist terms. The registrar's office was a front-line department in the university he was remodelling. Its role as gatekeeper was paramount if Queen's was to continue to attract the best and brightest students; on its choices the lustre of the Queen's brand rested. Knowing that his second term as principal was winding down and that his successor was waiting in the wings, the thought may well have come to Corry in his last winter in Richardson Hall that he should tidy up loose ends before handing over the reins of power. Like Gundy, Royce seemed to have accepted her fate. Why, therefore, leave the final act of the transition to the incoming principal? Why not simply close the file?

Corry's desire to do so was also probably conditioned by the gendered framework within which Queen's at the time operated. At some almost primordial level, Corry and the men at the top were possessed of an attitude that university management was a male precinct and that the handful of women

❖ *Many Happy Returns: Queen's and Canada, 1967* ❖

Every 16 October, well into the twentieth century, Queen's honoured its founding by celebrating University Day, a day marked by a Grant Hall ceremony. While Queen's had obtained its charter on 16 October 1841, its first classes were not in fact offered until April 1842, when the doors of its first humble abode on Kingston's Colborne Street opened. To celebrate its hundredth anniversary in 1941, the university chose to commemorate the charter date with the publication of *Queen's University at Kingston: The First Century of a Scottish Canadian University, 1841–1941*, by Queen's grad and trustee D.D. Calvin. The ensuing three-day celebration was built around praising the "great men" of Queen's and defining the modern utility of universities in war and peace.

The temptation of aligning the university's 125th anniversary with the centennial of Canadian nationhood in 1967, rather than the charter centenary in 1966, was too great to resist. The celebration began in Grant Hall in January, when Queen's faculty, students, and dignitaries, including Prime Minister Lester Pearson, massed to honour the birthday of Sir John A. Macdonald and the advent of Canada's centennial year. Queen's, Principal Corry noted, was a quarter-century older than the country, and its history bore the same canny touch of Scottish pragmatism that informed Sir John's deft shaping of Confederation. Queen's had something, he argued, to teach the nation at large: "crises overcome have sharpened her wits, toughened her fire, and enlarged her sympathies." Later in the year, Corry nominated nineteen of his colleagues for Ottawa's Centennial Medal. Included were artist André Bieler, registrar Jean Royce, Student Union janitor Alfred Plumb, and German scholar Hilda Laird.

Intent that the anniversary leave a lasting mark, Corry asked former university librarian Pearson Gundy to write an overview of Queen's evolution. The result, *Queen's University at Kingston*, was more coffee-table book than incisive history. "It has been said," Gundy wrote, "that a university, unlike a woman, takes pride in her age and observes anniversaries as soon and as often as possible." Stereotypes aside, Gundy's central message was that Queen's was "a national rather than a local university." The student yearbook for 1968, the *Tricolor*, echoed the theme that Queen's was a "small, select community that grew gradually." Across Canada, newspapers tipped their editorial hats to Queen's. "Well Done," declared the Arnprior (Ontario) *Guide*, deep in Queen's traditional hinterland.

Queen's 125th culminated in a grand celebration in October, when no less than twelve luminaries received honorary degrees at a single grand convocation. Queen's had never seen such a constellation of talent in Grant Hall. Economist John Kenneth Galbraith, industrialist H.R. MacMillan, central banker Louis Rasminsky, composer Godfrey Ridout, and humanitarian Pauline Vanier appeared on the stellar list. That evening, a black-tie dinner, the largest in the university's history, was held in Leonard Hall. The toasts and speeches made much of Queen's Celtic roots. Scottish cleric Dr Arthur Black gave the toast to the university, noting the "debt which Queen's owes to the Scottish manse." Corry responded that Queen's was "deeply affected by the sound of praise in a Scottish voice." The evening left other memories. Corry, the modernizer, waived Queen's long-time inhibition about liquor at formal gatherings. The wine and port flowed freely that night. "I have had many compliments on the menu, the decorations," Corry wrote to organizer George Wattsford, "and, of course, the wine!"

who had penetrated its perimeter were there on sufferance. However devotedly Royce had served Queen's, there was an attitude that women, even hyper-competent women, were, in the end, anomalies in the university's inner circle. Indicative of this skewed perspective was the fact that, after thirty-five years as registrar, Royce's annual salary by 1968 had risen to $10,334. Brigadier Leech, untutored in the ways of a registrar, signed on at a salary of $17,000.[116] In the language of the feminists who would begin to assault such discrimination in the decades ahead, Jean Royce lived out her career beneath a "glass ceiling," and in the end failed to break through the constraining mentality of the men with whom she daily worked. Alex Corry's insensitive treatment of her in the winter of 1968 was not the product of some long-standing personal malice, not the product of some "plot,"[117] but rather a reflection of attitudes deeply engendered in society. In this important sense, the principal had failed to modernize his university.

Unfinished Business

Alex Corry left other unfinished business at Queen's. The sprawling Faculty of Arts and Science, for instance, had been left largely untouched by Corry's reformation. It had grown immensely, soaking up many of Queen's baby boomers. New departments, such as geography, sociology, and Russian, had been added. Faculty ranks had swollen. The opening of Watson Hall in 1968 would allow many humanities departments to cluster together. But for all its three thousand students that fall, the Faculty of Arts and Science still offered much the same curriculum as it had in 1961. There were emerging issues – an important one being the balancing of resources between general and honours students – but so far there had been no seismic movement in the way teaching and learning in the faculty proceeded. Similarly, Corry may have dramatically altered the superstructure of faculties such as medicine and engineering, but he had barely addressed the way the university governed itself. Sensing the demand of the sixties that power belong "to the people," Corry in 1966 had asked history professor Fred Gibson to don the novel hat of vice-principal, academic, and to study how the Senate might take a more participatory (to borrow a word from Pierre Trudeau) role in university affairs in the wake of the Duff-Berdahl Report, an inquiry sponsored by all Canadian universities into the modernization of their governance. That report was still in gestation in 1966. Corry also sensed that Queen's students would inevitably demand similar inclusion, but events had not as yet pushed him into giving much priority to what he flippantly described to Senator Grattan O'Leary as "the slings and arrows of extravagant youth."

Still, when Corry delivered his last principal's report to the trustees in the late spring of 1968, his achievement was unmistakable. Queen's had been transformed. He had "run the rapids." Queen's had been largely shaken out of its old complacency and attached to new rhythms and attitudes that attuned it more to the boisterous society surrounding it. With John Deutsch, Corry had devised the transformative BIU funding formula, which allowed Queen's and Ontario's other universities to govern themselves without fear of direct government dictation. The BIU also allowed universities to measure their financial performance and plot their future operations with some financial confidence. Inside Queen's, Corry had decentralized power, finding forceful men who renovated crucial faculties and then ran them with his backing while asserting their own initiative. Deans such as Harry Botterell, Rich Hand, Jim Brown, and others became masters of their own turf. Medicine, in particular, had been pulled back from the edge of extinction. Behind the front lines, Queen's had cast off from its antiquated style of managing its affairs along chummy, informal lines. Planning was now possible. The registrar would supply the raw numbers, while the planners would now plot the parameters of future expansion. Most importantly, Corry ensured that Queen's would

Watson Hall, completed in 1967, was designed as a compendium home for humanities departments. Its interior design was much influenced by English professor George Whalley, who believed that departments should have strong collegiality. Common rooms were provided on each floor. Watson Hall's use of pre-cast concrete slab construction heralded a radical departure from Queen's limestone heritage.

govern the pace of its own expansion and thereby protect its hard-earned image as a national university with deeply local roots. Under Corry, Queen's had nearly doubled in size, to six thousand students.[118] Corry had acted with "deliberate speed," but left behind a commitment that Queen's would never place quantity over quality. He had harkened to University of Toronto President Sidney Smith's 1956 admonition that "flexibility of structure and tenacity of purpose" would be the key to success in baby-boom post-secondary education. If the BIU had an Achilles' heel, it was its seductive ability to encourage headlong expansion driven by per-capita mathematics. When asked, Corry suggested that Queen's might grow to about ten thousand students.

After that point, it might, he said, be difficult to perpetuate some of the traditions that made Queen's Queen's. Few on campus disagreed.

In the end though, some traditions at Queen's needed little modernization. Through the fall of 1968, Frank Tindall and the Golden Gaels rushed and passed their way to the first truly national football championship, the newly christened Vanier Cup. Paced by quarterback Don Bayne and backs Keith "Skip" Eamon and Heino Lilles, the Gaels demolished Waterloo Lutheran 42–14 in Toronto before twenty thousand fans in Varsity Stadium and a national television audience. One could perhaps excuse Alex Corry for missing the game.

3

"Uproariously Busy"
John Deutsch and the Codification of Queen's, 1968–1974

These days of ferment and bewilderment.
John Deutsch to Pierre Trudeau, November 1968

Inherent conservatism and rigidity will not, in the circumstance of today, prevail against either governments or revolutionaries.
John Deutsch's installation speech, 1968

The only people who should be university presidents are the friendless, the orphaned, and bachelors.
John Deutsch, 1968

Facing "Puzzling" Times

The fall of 1969 delivered another bumper crop of students to Queen's. A total of 7,378 full-time students settled into residence rooms or off-campus apartments, a jump of almost 600 from the previous year. Throughout Alex Corry's tenure as principal, which had ended a year earlier, Queen's had been stymied in its attempts to cap its enrolment. In 1962, Corry had agreed with Queen's Park that his university would aim for 5,600 students by 1970. Even though Queen's growth rate trailed that of other Ontario universities, that benchmark had been passed by 1967, as Queen's was inundated with top-quality applicants it could not turn away, even as falling drop-out and failure rates kept Queen's brimful with students. While the BIU system rewarded such expansion, it placed seismic stress on both Queen's confined geography and its dedication to quality teaching. There were already worrisome signs of that stress. Through the Corry years, for instance, the ratio of professor to students had slipped somewhat from 1:11 to 1:13.

John Deutsch, Corry's successor, would warn the trustees that the pressure to get into Queen's was likely to intensify. He added: "We are attempting to work out a system to deal with the problems that will arise."[1] Like Corry, he began to muse about a new ceiling on growth at Queen's, after which the university enrolment would potentially plateau in size. Deutsch had a reputation for getting things done. Across the campus, his image as the soft-spoken, yet authoritative, technocrat was already well-established. He looked and sounded, at first glance, like a charter member of the national power elite – soon to be dubbed "the Canadian Establishment" by his journalist friend Peter Newman – which, in the obstreperous sixties, seemed so much the object of public opprobrium. But students picking up the first issue of the *Queen's Journal* that fall of 1969 were treated to another, unexpected, perspective on the man in Richardson Hall – John Deutsch as a man of the "people." There on the front page was their principal, portrayed as a guitar-strumming troubadour, hair flowing in the wind, clothed in a loose hippiesque tunic, strolling across a field. Aided by a bit of camera trickery, the *Journal* editors had doctored a photo of one of the Bee Gees, the hugely popular Australian rock group, superimposing the principal's head on a Bee Gee body. The intention was affectionate, not satirical. To clinch the point, the portrait was captioned with the lyrics of a Bee Gees' song: "There is no reasoning or asking why / Simply to prove / I love you deeply with the sun in my eyes."[2]

In a year that had seen the sacking of Sir George Williams (later Concordia) University's computer centre by student activists and the bitter faculty upheavals at Simon Fraser University, it seemed that Queen's enjoyed a softer, gentler approach to the angst of the sixties, orchestrated by a principal well suited to guiding it through troubled times. "While we have a few nihilists and extreme activists," Deutsch wrote to Prime Minister Pierre Trudeau, "I find that the great majority of our students are highly responsible, sincere and intelligently concerned about the bewildering problems of our time."[3] Deutsch knew that the odds against university presidents maintaining their equilibrium in the topsy-turvy sixties were daunting. Early in 1969, he had seen his old friend, the climatologist Kenneth Hare, driven from the presidency of the University of British Columbia by campus turmoil. A university president, Hare forlornly told the Vancouver *Province*, is "in the position of the neck of an hourglass."[4] For John Deutsch, the sand in the Queen's hourglass at times slowed, but it never stopped. As a result, his university was able to establish a new, more inclusive, and more codified culture in the six years of his tenure as principal. In this respect, Deutsch's tenure as principal neatly dovetailed with that of his predecessor Alex Corry, whose vigorous renovation of the university's superstructure made Deutsch's remodelling of its inner governance possible.

To most people familiar with Queen's, John Deutsch's arrival in the principal's office in the summer of 1968 was preordained. He had been associated with the university since his student days in the 1930s. As vice-principal, administration, in the late 1950s, he had built up an understanding of the bricks and mortar of the university and where the money came – or did not come – from. After three years away as chairman of the Economic Council of Ottawa, he had returned in 1967 with his public-policy wits sharpened and his respect for the stimulative role of universities heightened. For his part, as he prepared to leave the principal's office, Corry told the trustees that the university needed "fresh thinking."[5] This Deutsch brought. As the *Tricolor*, the student yearbook, pointed out, Deutsch, with his Bavarian-Canadian lineage, was the first principal with "New Canadian" roots.[6] His early years on the Depression Prairies had given him an enduring empathy for the broad Canadian population. His time as an Ottawa mandarin instilled in him an understanding of the challenge of harnessing public policy to social and economic ends. This was particularly

Principal John Deutsch portrayed as rock star. Soft-spoken and undemonstrative, Deutsch won the affection of Queen's students, who nicknamed him "Johnny Dutch," for his dedication to the university's distinctiveness.

evident in the yeasty sixties. At the Economic Council he had, for instance, warned Prime Minister Pearson, that Canada was facing a "very serious" housing crisis as the baby boom began to demand a roof over its head.[7] Deutsch's former colleague at Queen's, commerce professor Edgar Benson, was Pearson's national revenue minister. He was equally well connected to corporate Canada; he sat on the boards of Inco, the nickel giant, and the Canadian Imperial Bank of Commerce. He had also trotted his public-policy expertise around the world, advising the Bermuda government on taxation, for instance. Deutsch, in essence, brought a cosmopolitan worldliness to Richardson Hall, a valuable dimension for an institution tucked away in small eastern-Ontario city.

When Pearson announced his intention to step down in late 1967, Deutsch quickly shifted his loyalties to Pierre Trudeau. He had known Trudeau for twenty years and, he later admitted to Peter Newman, was one of those who urged him to seek the Liberal leadership. Deutsch supplied Trudeau with economic position papers during his successful leadership bid. "We are now at a new road of Canadian development," he wrote to Trudeau aide Gordon Gibson, "both as a people and as a nation."[8] Trudeau's narrow leadership triumph and subsequent landslide at the national polls in June 1968 buoyed Deutsch. The news that Benson would take the finance portfolio enhanced the good news for Queen's and Kingston.

Deutsch's own ascendancy to the principal's office at Queen's proved more expeditious than Trudeau's to the prime ministership. He had said when he left for Ottawa in 1963 that he would return to Queen's intent on once again becoming an economics professor. But once Corry's exit loomed, the pressure on Deutsch to occupy the corner office in Richardson Hall mounted. In February 1967, the trustees established a joint committee of trustees and senators to seek a new principal. While its deliberations were confidential, all eyes seemed to turn on Deutsch. Influential trustee Donald Gordon confided to Corry that Deutsch seemed the "obvious and logical" successor.[9] Deutsch initially demurred: did the university want another member of the economics and political studies department as its head after seventeen years of Mackintosh and Corry? Then, with typical shrewdness, Deutsch quietly canvassed the deans and prominent department heads to test their reaction, and thereby build legitimacy around his selection. When, in May 1967, the selection committee announced that an "overwhelming majority" had endorsed Deutsch, it was apparent that the university had found the right man for the times.[10] Deutsch moved into Richardson Hall on 1 September 1968.

Deutsch's willingness to abandon the classroom for front-line duty in the principal's office was rooted in his belief that universities were closely connected to the society around them. "It is an exciting time in universities," he wrote to former Australian prime minister Francis Forde. "There is much ferment and the universities face large problems of adjustment to the new attitudes in the world."[11] For Deutsch, the university could not afford to stand on the margins of social change. In his inauguration address that November, he described the times as "puzzling," as two decades of prosperity clashed with an insurgency of youthful skepticism. Reflecting on the long-standing Queen's tradition of liberal engagement with the society it served, Deutsch quoted one of the regents of the protest-tossed University of California: "[I]f a campus is completely unruffled in these tense times, you can be sure that it is sliding downhill."[12]

For his part, the new principal dedicated himself to building "balance" on and off campus, something that would be not achieved through "inherent conservatism and rigidity" but by constructive engagement and consensus. As if to drive the point home, Deutsch's installation was accompanied, not by a lot of pomp and circumstance, but by a symposium on "The University and the Ethics of Change." All classes were cancelled so that faculty and students could crowd into Grant Hall to listen to outspoken journalist Arthur Koestler, literary guru Northrop Frye, microbiologist René Dubos, and urban planner Martin Myerson expound on the dilemmas confronting a society fuelled by prosperity but tormented by choices. Deutsch insisted that two students join the discussion panel after each speaker's presentation.[13]

Winds of Change

Even as he took up his position, there were encouraging signs that the university, preconditioned by Corry's transformative rejuvenation, was forsaking rigidity and aligning itself with the times. That fall, for instance, the university unveiled its new department of computing science. Students could now prepare themselves for the world of what would soon be called "information science." Boasting a state-of-the-art IBM 360, the computing centre in Dupuis Hall, under its director Mers Kutt, dedicated itself not only to administrative data-processing but also to enhancing teaching and expediting research in fields as disparate as English professor George Whalley's compilation of bibliographies and the economics department's embrace of the so-called "Samuelson revolution" of quantitative econometric analysis.[14] The age of mainframe computing had dawned at Queen's. Students and professors, juggling tall stacks of computer punch cards and heading for Dupuis Hall, at all times of the day, now became a familiar sight on campus.

The burgeoning discipline of sociology provided another bridge to change. It highlighted the fact that Canadians were living in an increasingly pluralistic society, a fact that was beginning to register on the rather closed community at Queen's. If computers allowed universities to aggregate and disaggregate the data underlying society, then sociology allowed them to look inside societal rhythms, structures, and mores. Although sociological inquiry could be traced back into the nineteenth-century investigations of Durkheim, Marx, Spenser, and Comte, the social activism of the sixties propelled sociology onto university campuses as a mainstream discipline. At Queen's, sociology had been a subsidiary of the political studies department since the 1950s. Professor John Meisel had long contended that sociology offered a crucial insight into how society functioned. Year after year, Meisel offered Sociology 080 to undergraduates as an introduction to the discipline. The sixties, with its ethos of questioning authority and asserting that Canada was perhaps not the mythologized classless society, incubated demand for the subject. In 1965, for instance, sociologist John Porter at Carleton University published his groundbreaking study of the social stratification of Canadian society, *The Vertical Mosaic*. At Queen's, enrolment in sociology soared. Meisel needled his dean for more faculty. Jayant Lele, with his newly minted PhD in sociology from Cornell, arrived on staff in 1965 and was immediately thrown into the frontline of Sociology 080. Enrolment skyrocketed from 70 in 1975 to 700 two years later. The cry "70 to 700" became a chant for departmental status.

The sociological perspective crept into other courses: political scientist Richard Van Loon offered political sociology. More young sociologists were hired. British-born Robert Pike arrived and, in the spirit of the sixties, went to work on a demographic

Computers made their first appearance on campus in the Deutsch years. Their utility was at first narrowly conceived of – as an aid to administration and as a means of compiling data for research projects. Such data had to be laboriously committed to punch cards, and processing time on the mainframe computer was booked by appointment on an around-the-clock schedule.

study for the Association of Universities and Colleges of Canada (AUCC), *Who Doesn't Get to University – and Why?*[15] Because sociology had no male "old guard," its ranks soon contained more women than existed in established departments, women like Kay Herman and Mary Maxwell. Finally, in the fall of 1968, sociology bid farewell to economics and political studies and became a separate department. There was stiff opposition from naysayers in some humanities departments like history and classics – sociology, they said, was too presentist, too bent towards the whims of today, too full of would-be rabble-rousers – but Corry, Deutsch, and the faculty board at large could see the folly of "inherent conservatism and rigidity" blocking so timely an initiative. Over the next decade, sociology became a workhorse of the Faculty of Arts and Science, and, in doing so, acted as a promoter of new attitudes at Queen's.[16]

The unfolding range of sociology courses at Queen's included courses on the "sociology of modernization." A prominent vein of sociology was functionalism, the belief that society was best analyzed by breaking down the alchemy of the customs, norms, and traditions at the core of its institutional life. In the heady sixties, there was much fascination with the concept of "modernization." How did stable societies perpetuate themselves? Was conflict or consensus a better mechanism for propelling change? Such questions provide a persuasive framework for understanding the Corry–Deutsch years at Queen's. Alex Corry had tackled the often-creaking structure of Queen's in the early sixties, renovating and modernizing the formal structural components of the university. Harry Botterell, by this measure, was a structural engineer, shunting the medical faculty into the age of medicare. Now it fell to John Deutsch to renovate the customs, norms, and traditions that underlay the governance of Queen's day-to-to-day life – matters like academic appointment, tenure and promotion, discipline on campus, the delivery of teaching, and the process of decision making. He would also strive to set the parameters of growth at Queen's – with an ambition to achieve, in what he would describe with a sociological bent, a "steady state" for the university. In short, the challenge before Deutsch was how to codify – that is to say, make predictable and accessible – the rhythmic life of the university, so that the old informality of the place could be displaced by a more inclusive, self-perpetuating system of governance. This cultural transition had begun on Corry's watch; Deutsch would complete the transformation of the modus operandi at Queen's.

Participatory Democracy Comes to Queen's

In 1963, the Association of Universities and Colleges of Canada (AUCC) and the Canadian Association of University Teachers, sensing that many students and faculty wanted more sway over university decisions, commissioned British educational administrator Sir James Duff and American educational theorist Robert Berdahl to tackle the central question of where decision-making authority should lie in universities. Although Principal Corry sat as president of the AUCC in 1963–64, Queen's brought to the Duff-Berdahl inquiry expectations that were somewhat different than those of other universities. At Queen's, student discontent was diffused by the century-old tradition of student self-government by the Alma Mater Society and by the existence of a rectorship. Drawn from the Scottish tradition of empowering students, the rector at Queen's was elected by students to convey their concerns to the university's trustees. The rector had traditionally been an outsider who possessed sufficient *gravitas* and eloquence to command the trustees' attention. Since 1947, that person had been Leonard Brockington, labour lawyer, loquacious broadcaster, and CBC governor. Brockington's forceful personality, coupled with the wide measure of AMS control over student life at Queen's, tended to diffuse student discontents.

If there was a problem at Queen's, it lay with the Senate, the supposed fulcrum of academic policy at Queen's. Most agreed that, by the sixties, its authority had become lethargic and its influence over the direction of the university atrophied. Power had, it was widely felt, accrued to the Board of Trustees and to the faculty boards. In a pattern prevalent in universities across Canada, there was widespread belief that the Senate needed waking up. With legions of young faculty being hired to teach the baby boom, professors wanted greater sway over how the institutions to which they had attached themselves were governed. At the same time, student opinion across Canada began to question boards of university trustees and governors who seemed to have unchallenged control of policy. Trustees, they alleged, owed their allegiance more to corporate Canada than to "the people." As one proponent of greater power-sharing on campuses told Deutsch, it was not a question of "how to challenge the Board of Governors' authority, but whether the Board of Governors holds any true authority in the first place."[17]

In early 1966, the Duff-Berdahl Report proposed to relieve these tensions by advocating a considerable widening of university decision making. Central to its recommendations was an expansion of faculty representation on university boards of governors and of an invigoration of university senates to give faculty firmer control over academic policy. Duff-Berdahl also persistently stressed the need for better channels of communication among faculty, students, and university administrators. A small contingent of senators should be allowed to sit on university boards to give voice to faculty concerns and, since the line of authority between senates and trsutees was often blurred, joint senate-board committees should be utilized to build consensus on matters that straddled the administrative and academic precincts. The report did not, however, throw the doors of university decision making wide open. Students were ill-equipped for board membership, it argued. Too many decisions involved long-term financial commitments or touched on confidential issues, such as salaries and promotions. Instead, students should be invited to join committees that oversaw matters that had an impact on their years on campus – library, scholarship, admissions, and curriculum policy, for instance. Students should also be able to elect a rector as their ex officio voice on the board.

Duff-Berdahl gave Canadian universities an opportunity to act pre-emptively in the face of growing campus activism. Many did. At Queen's, the reaction was more restrained. Principal Corry told the trustees that "many of the recommendations have little application" to Queen's. The university had built good relations with its students by devolving power onto the AMS over many decades and, of course, Queen's already had a rector who did sit ex officio at each board meeting. Corry also reported that he sensed little enthusiasm for board membership on the part of faculty and students. The university's ingrained bicameral structure of authority may have stood in need of perking up, but, he argued, it had served the university well since 1841. Besides, any move to admit faculty to the Board of Trustees would require a cumbersome amendment to the university's federal charter, which explicitly forbade the inclusion of professors in the trustees' bailiwick. But, Corry wisely concluded, it would be foolish to stonewall any desire by faculty or students to extend their entitlement to the way the university was governed. "I think it would be a mistake to man the barricades for the purpose of resisting a request for such representation," he advised. The trustees generally agreed, suggesting that three senators might be admitted to their deliberations, as long as they bowed out when matters of salaries and promotions came before them.[18]

Queen's thus adopted what Corry would describe as "a cooler approach to matters of university government."[19] The university would rely on its genetic predisposition to gradualism to affect change in its governance – a belief in what might be called limestone liberalism, the art of painstaking consultation and careful consensus-building across the campus, dedicated to the betterment of the whole community. Central to this approach was an appreciation that the trustees did not in reality "govern" the university, but instead served as a body which consulted and facilitated decisions on resource allocation and on maintaining "the confidence of the general community."[20] As the only person taking a seat on each body, the principal's pivotal role was to act as a bridge – the "narrow isthmus," in Bill Mackintosh's famous phrase – between the Board of Trustees and the Senate, and now increasingly with the student body. Corry believed that his role was to act as "an effective link" between all interested parties. It was a role that John Deutsch would readily perpetuate.

Moreover, in the spring of 1966, Corry took initiatives that would work their way through the next decade of the university's culture of governance. Two new positions in the university's senior management were created to smooth the process of consultation and reform. In February, the trustees approved his appointment of a dean of student affairs. Queen's had had a dean of women since 1911, but this new post was conceived as an umbrella over *all* students' lives on campus. It was intended to serve as a "listening post," which would connect grassroots student concerns with the administration. The new dean would fill a line function, reporting directly to the principal. To fill the post, Corry brought in Stewart Webster, a Queen's undergraduate of the 1940s and, more recently, a history professor at the University of Manitoba. Webster was easy-going and empathetic. He and his wife, Joan, moved into the west wing of Summerhill and began pursuing an open-door policy with their student neighbours on campus. Joan Webster quickly perfected a standard Sunday-evening dinner of ham, roast beef, and apple pie; every weekend in the term, twelve Queen's students got to dine and talk with somebody who talked with the principal every Monday morning.[21]

Corry's next appointment was more momentous. In March, sensing the need to distance the administrative and academic spheres of university life, he created the post of vice-principal, academic. He again turned to a historian to meet the challenge. It was, perhaps, that historians were inured to the messiness of the human condition and conditioned to the dynamics of consensus building. In this case, Corry turned to Frederick Gibson, the Queen's historian who had specialized in studying that greatest of Canadian consensus builders, Mackenzie King. Just as Canada in the sixties wrestled with its unity and harkened to Trudeau's call for "participatory democracy," Gibson fretted that Queen's was losing its internal integrity and inclusiveness. The month of his appointment, he sent Corry an excerpt from a speech by the president of Cornell University, James Perkins: "University integrity, then, is involved not with preserving things as they are, but rather with maintaining the coherence of its various parts, and the harmony with which it is able to pursue its aims – whatever their specialized nature ... It follows that the real integrity of the university is violated when large decisions in one area do not consider the impact on the other two."[22] While Webster's function was to smooth student relations, Gibson's was to guide the "academic implications of long-term expansion" and to facilitate inclusion on campus.

In January 1967, Gibson's energies came to be focused on the formation of a Senate committee, chaired by himself, to examine the "structure and procedures of the Senate." Corry was worried about the "fuzzy edges" surrounding decision making at Queen's. He hoped the Gibson committee would provide a clearer delineation of this authority and, in doing so, invigorate the Senate's oversight of academic matters at Queen's. Gibson picked a small, tight committee: physicist, and dean of Arts and Science, George Harrower; law professor Richard Gosse; philosophy professor Martyn Estall; and civil engineering professor Arthur Brebner. To bolster Gibson's mandate, Corry distributed copies of the Duff-Berdahl Report to the AMS, the university council, the faculty association, and the faculty boards, asking for their reaction to its blueprint for change. The summer of 1967 thus became a season of internal deliberation – a group pondering of whether Queen's traditions of governance were drifting out of touch with the temper of the times.

In its January 1968 report, the Gibson committee concluded that governance at Queen's was indeed out of kilter with the times. The Senate needed reform. It had failed to keep pace with the growth of the university since its functions had last been codified by the trustees in 1913. The growth in size and complexity of the university had progressively drawn power over the academic life of the university away from the Senate, a fact that Corry's administrative shakeup in the sixties had accentuated. Power had devolved onto faculty boards and the deans and department heads who now micromanaged the academic life of the university. This had given the university short-term intellectual nimbleness. But it had come at a broader cost: "the sacrifice of the real, though not the formal, power of the Senate." The Senate had come to occupy "a position somewhat akin to that of a constitutional monarch possessing full *de jure*, but little real, power and discharging functions which in the Senate have become formal rather than substantial in nature."

In other words, the Senate had become a rubber-stamping authority. At the same time, the Gibson committee pointed out that post-secondary education had become a crucial necessity in "the complex and volatile society in which we live." This meant that universities must undertake "more effective, more systematic, and more comprehensive planning of their affairs" if they were devise effective curricula, attract top-notch scholars, and garner research funds. The report noted that, despite their recent empowerment, all the feedback from faculty boards and the faculty association had favoured a reconvergence of coordinating power on the Senate. Only the Senate could act as the academic prism of the university.

The Senate should sit at the crossroads of all academic planning at the university, the Gibson committee urged. Its suzerainty should embrace the establishment of new academic programs, the awarding of scholarships, examinations, honorary degrees, policies for the appointment of deans and heads of department, and oversight of library and computer policies. The committee acknowledged the long-established right of the AMS to discipline students and to promote their "well-being" – the so-called Senate function #11 – but did assert the Senate's right to act as the final court of appeal for student discipline. Furthermore, the Senate should take a central role in "planning the development of the university" – for instance, the approval of major buildings and oversight of its operating budget – in conjunction with the trustees. Ex officio presence on the Senate by deans and senior administrators should be controlled to ensure that elected faculty members always enjoyed a 2:1 majority.

To execute this expanded mandate, the report advocated using the nine standing committees of the Senate as crucibles of policy formation. The committees would be stocked by members appointed to staggered two-year terms, thereby ensuring that "fresh ideas" would constantly be brought to their debates. The crucially important committee on academic development, with its mandate of reviewing programs and standards, would, for instance, have a broad membership of eight, under the chairmanship of the vice-principal, academic. And, in a last clarion call, the Gibson report recommended the inclusion of student voices on the Senate: "Student representation on the Senate would be an appropriate recognition of the aspirations of a large and vitally important segment of the University."[23]

The report of the Gibson committee thereby opened the way for a new model of consultation on university policy. While it had been a committee of the Senate, its mandate and catholic deliberations had suggested a recognition of more-inclusive consultation on policy at Queen's. A year earlier, Corry had signalled that this was his own inclination, when he broke precedent by inviting the Senate to join the Board of Trustees in the search for his own successor. This ended the trustees' cozy, long-held prerogative of relying on their own wisdom to select principals.[24] What Corry had initiated and Gibson had confirmed, Deutsch and future principals would emulate. Queen's would now instinctively turn to the mechanism of "principal's advisory committees" and ad hoc Senate and Board committees to flesh out the parameters of strategic issues and to foster consensus on their handling. This process would at times prove annoyingly glacial, but it had the redeeming virtue of soaking up campus-wide opinion and moulding it into a broad, actionable consensus that would keep the university in tune with the times. As the Gibson group neared the end of its investigation, Corry again engaged and broadened this approach, using his prerogative to create a Joint Committee on University Government to shape Queen's overall reaction to the Duff-Berdahl Report. The breadth of the committee's membership was precedent-setting. With Corry in the chair, committee membership was stretched to include the chairman and vice-chairman of the trustees, Colonel R.D. Harkness and Bill Mackintosh; the president of the AMS, George Carson; and university council member Ian Rogers, a Toronto lawyer representing the alumni. Other members of the student government, professors from every faculty, Vice-Principal Gibson, and Principal-Designate Deutsch joined the round table. The inimitable Jean Royce sat as the joint committee's secretary.[25]

Echoing Gibson's interim report, the Corry committee noted the "rapid social change" surrounding the university, as well as swelling student dissatisfaction with universities' ability to act as "significant agents of social change." Acknowledging that sixties students wanted their universities to be "self-regulating" communities – not top-down, authority-driven quasi-business corporations – the committee once again noted that, more than most Canadian universities, Queen's already had a long tradition of delegating power to its faculty and students. This delegation of "the main lineaments of the self-regulating community" were "of daily familiarity to us." The problem at Queen's was that this "slow accretion of custom" had "not been deliberately and solemnly affirmed." The challenge now was to codify and extend the informal spirit of Queen's governance into a vital system that would bind the interests of all constituencies of the university.

The committee saw no reason to tamper with the established jurisdiction of the AMS or the faculty boards; they already suited the new decentralized sharing of authority on campus. But the Senate urgently needed invigorating, as the Gibson inquiry had emphasized. Centralized supervision of academic life must be regularized and vigilantly managed. To legitimize that role, Senate membership had to reflect the interests of *all* parties tied to the Queen's academic community. The Corry committee therefore endorsed the Senate's January decision to expand its membership to fifty-one members. The fulcrum would rest on the thirty members of faculty elected to the Senate, proportionate to the strength of various faculties. Arts and Science would get eight members, for instance, while nursing and the theology college would each get a single senator. The perspective of the senior administration would be secured by seventeen ex officio deans, vice-principals, and other directors. The principal would continue to chair the Senate, thereby placing himself in a position to connect the academic deliberations of the university with the more practical preoccupations of the trustees. The seismic shift came with the arrival of four student senators: John Buttars, a theology student; John Gray, a medical student; Barry LeRoy, a commerce student; and Craig Aitkins, a doctoral student in botany. These neophyte senators were selected by an AMS committee, mainly because the regular student elections had already been held in February. Future student senators would have to run for their seat in the Senate. Nonetheless, for the first time in the university's history, students had been admitted into the inner sanctum of decision making.

It would be inviting to link the opening up of university governance at Queen's to more renowned and galvanic movements of political reform in the mid-sixties – social and political acting out in the streets of Detroit, Paris, and Prague, for instance. But change at Queen's was more calibrated, more graduated, than that. At Queen's, there was a reluctance to sever traditional bonds, a desire to preserve the useful elements of a received culture, a culture rooted in student self-government since 1858 and the conviviality of faculty and administration in a small-town university. Again and again, Corry stressed that he detected no burning desire on his campus for radical change. "The number of students at Queen's who were pressing strongly for 'participatory democracy' and 'joint decision-making' was relatively few," he would write in his memoirs. "The great majority was either indifferent, only mildly interested, or well enough satisfied with what was being provided for them."[26] So there were natural limits to the reform of governance at Queen's. Senate meetings were to remain closed, and student senators were bound to respect the body's confidentiality. The door of the Collins Room where the trustees met was still to remain firmly barred to would-be faculty and student participation. Corry's

The expanded Senate meets in the Collins Room in 1971. Its fifty-one-person membership still held a faculty majority, but one now joined by elected students and a larger contingent of ex officio administrators. The principal chaired the Senate, the only member to also sit on the Board of Trustees.

committee on the structure of university government reiterated the argument that faculty membership on the Board of Trustees would betray the original spirit of the university charter; professors would trespass on the long-respected demarcation of academic issues from administrative decisions. At most, faculty inclusion might be worthy of "careful review" before any attempt was made to seek a parliamentary amendment to the charter. This would take time. More emphatically, the Corry committee believed that students had no innate affinity for the affairs of the trustees; their academic interests were best pursued in the Senate, where they now had status. If matters concerning students did emerge before the trustees, AMS officials might be "invited" to present their perspective to the Board. Otherwise, the rector would continue to be the students' sentinel before the trustees.

As he prepared to step down as principal, Corry – a lifelong student of constitutional development and rights – took pride in his remodelling of university government at Queen's, describing it as "the most comprehensive and searching in the history of the university."[27] "I think that we have settled the issues raised by the Duff-Berdahl Report for some time to come," he proudly wrote to trustee Donald Gordon late that spring.[28] The old bicameral governance of Queen's had been preserved, but its operation had been rebalanced and broadened. Students now sat in the Senate, and professors had the assurance that their academic activities were under the sway of a body that they dominated. Beyond this newly redrawn jurisdiction, the emphasis in governance at Queen's remained focused on collaboration, accommodation, and gradualism, not hierarchy and leadership by fiat. This would prove a durable and flexible culture. Some twenty years later, when asked to distill governance at Queen's, one-time Queen's Principal Ron Watts concluded in 1988 that "collegiality" was "the Queen's Way." Queen's, he reflected, had avoided the "rigidities of a precise hierarchical structure" and relied on "pragmatic and flexible decision-making processes," which facilitated "the achievement on most issues of a broadly based consensus."[29]

Within this latitude, many procedures and tolerances remained to be worked out, a task that in 1968 would fall to John Deutsch as principal. In the short term, Corry's renovation had allowed Queen's to anticipate, possibly pre-empt, the kind of disintegrative activism that would overtake many Canadian campuses in the late 1960s. Students at Queen's had been given a voice in high university affairs even before they had demanded it, and faculty were now in large part masters of their own academic fate. The next decade would thus mark the high noon of influence for the Queen's Senate; it would become a lively crucible of change for students and professors alike. And, as principal's advisory committees and Senate committees habitually thrashed out problems and groomed university regulations, life at Queen's assumed a prescribed quality unknown in earlier, less-regulated decades. For many professors and students, the words "committee work" now took on a creative, if at times onerous, meaning as their campus became a truly self-regulating community. This new equilibrium would not, however, go untested. John Deutsch would soon agonizingly learn that when, a year into his tenure in 1969, Queen's brand of limestone liberalism found itself under assault by a small, but vociferous, group of student activists, who dismissed all the talk of inclusion and collaboration by Corry, Webster, Gibson, and Deutsch as liberal window dressing. More of this in the next chapter.

Getting Down to Work

At Christmas 1968, Deutsch wrote to his old professor Frank Knox, now retired from Queen's and basking in the Florida sun, to report that his first months as principal had been "uproariously busy."[30] Deutsch possessed a remarkable ability to cope simultaneously with a panoply of issues. To those dealing with him, he was disarmingly laconic, preferring to communicate in economical sentences and relying on deliberate silences. Yet, at the climax of any meeting or exchange, Deutsch could convey the gist of any matter with clarity and precision. He had an uncanny knack for managing multiple points of policy and sorting out what priority each deserved. Deutsch had the kind of lateral vision that characterizes an effective leader; he could see any university issue from multiple perspectives – faculty, alumni, student, political, and Kingstonian sensibilities all had a place in his policy arithmetic. Ross McGregor, who had almost daily contact with the principal when he was AMS president in 1969–70, never forgot the principal's 360-degree appreciation of situations: "Deutsch played chess when everybody else was playing checkers."[31] Moreover, Deutsch was not so fixated on the university's strategic course that he lost sight of the more mundane side of university life. His door was always open to all comers with a problem or an insight into the way Queen's was proceeding. Student politicians sensed that he was their friend, not their adversary. With only one exception,[32] Deutsch dispatched a letter late every March to the outgoing AMS president, reflecting on the progress or intransigence of issues

Deutsch's effectiveness in leadership reflected the breadth of his experience. Experience as an Ottawa mandarin, economist, journalist, corporate director, and royal commissioner gave him a balanced perspective on the Canadian community. Here he talks with humanitarian Jean Vanier in 1971, when Vanier came to McArthur College to lecture on prison reform.

in the past year and wishing him or her future success. The outgoing presidents always warmly reciprocated, and many kept up the acquaintance as their careers unfolded.

To maintain order in his office life, Deutsch had insisted that his trusted personal secretary, Mary Medland, accompany him to Queen's from the Economic Council. She had been with him since his days at the University of British Columbia. Every day, Medland performed triage on those appearing outside his door seeking his indulgence. Over at the AMS offices, students took to affectionately calling the principal and his efficient gatekeeper "Jack Dutch and Mary Mudlark."[33] On the other side of the campus at Summerhill, where the principal lived, Deutsch's wife, Stephanie, oversaw the social underpinnings of the principal's harried life – the annual fall welcome cocktail party for new faculty, entertaining visiting academic dignitaries, and feeding the trustees, to name just a few pleasant, if inescapable, social obligations. Together, the Deutschs worked to preserve the conviviality of the Queen's community. In later years, Stephanie Deutsch recalled that her husband was always quick to venture his fervent belief that Queen's should remain "a small place … the Harvard of Canada … quality first."[34] Over at the AMS, Ross McGregor concluded that, under Deutsch, Queen's was going through a "transformational" experience and that the principal's style of low-key openness and strategic anticipation was the essence of the "Queen's way." Deutsch, he believed, was supplying the "institutional glue" that helped the university's cohesion and progressiveness.

In the late 1960s, Deutsch pushed Queen's over many transformational frontiers. The campaign began almost as soon as he took office in July 1968. Sensing the mood of discontent that gripped many campuses across the continent, he convened a "principal's committee" on the way teaching and learning was conducted at Queen's. The new principal possessed superb strategic vision: the surging baby boom was starting to swamp the complacent, cohesive values of North American society in the fifties and, he concluded, shrewd institutions were best served by anticipating, not belatedly reacting, to shifts in public expectations of the university system. As the values of fifties normalcy began to crumble, the largest adolescent cohort in Canadian history began to question the legitimacy and efficacy of institutions like universities. "I must say that the universities nowadays are far different than they used to be," Deutsch wrote to a Montreal friend. "It is an entirely new attitude. What the implications are for the universities themselves, and for our society in the future are very puzzling."³⁵ Whether prompted by Quebec's Quiet Revolution or a nationalistic and ideological critique of the "military-industrial complex," youth in the sixties did share a common belief that the university could be a nexus of social change and that, if quality and purpose of life on campus could be altered, then life thereafter in the broader society might be similarly enlightened. Many concluded that the university classroom was antediluvian territory, where the values of the older generation were force-fed to students and the aspirations of youth were starved. John Deutsch determined to respond to this "puzzling" discontent and, in doing so, to hold Queen's teaching and learning up to scrutiny. But, in the same spirit that the Senate had been modernized, such inquiry would take place in an inclusive atmosphere of deliberation and objective analysis, rather than as a hurried acceptance of unexamined demands for change.

The process had begun under Corry, when Queen's faculties oriented to the professions had been steered closer to the needs of the practical worlds of law, medicine, nursing, and engineering. The introduction of clinical teaching units had, for instance, allowed medical students to gain bedside experience in diagnosing patients' maladies. Similarly, nursing students were now exposed to physiology and psychology, so that they had greater comprehension of what was going on *inside* the body. But, by 1968, Queen's students in the liberal arts had good reason to question whether their education had felt the same regenerating impulse. Little had changed since the beginning of the decade. Arts and Science students were given little latitude in course selection in their initial years of study. First year was tightly prescribed by a limited list of introductory courses in established disciplines, such as English 2 and Politics 2, topped off by a mandatory two hours of physical education a week. Early on, however, Arts and Science students faced a defining decision about whether to embark on a four-year honours program leading to an honours BA or BSc. Honours programs tended to be labour-intensive – the history department, for instance, prided itself on its small, combative seminars – while the general-degree program rested more on mass lectures. In the ambiance of the sixties, such differentiation smacked of elitism and of a perpetuation of the inequality in Canadian society. To many, however, the honours degree was the shining epitome of "quality" education at Queen's. Through the early to mid-sixties, this orthodox approach to curriculum in Arts and Science thus remained largely untouched. This stasis was paradoxical, since the faculty itself had ballooned from 1,339 students in 1960–61 to 2,996 in 1967–68.

At the same time, the faculty had added new departments, such as geography, computing, and sociology, had grafted new film courses onto English, split economics and politics apart, and stretched music into a four-year degree to cater to the teaching of music in secondary schools. Paralleling this diversification, there had been unbounded hiring of new faculty: in 1968–69 eighty new professors arrived in the faculty, bringing its total complement to 375. Yet, despite all this exponential growth, there had been little pedagogic innovation. This Deutsch recognized: "Change is not easy to introduce into a university," he wrote. "A university is a massive structure and has, therefore, considerable inertia."³⁶

Nonetheless, on 21 October, Deutsch created his Committee on Teaching and Learning. In keeping with the new spirit of allowing students a voice in academic affairs, four students, representing both undergraduate and graduate studies, were appointed. Four faculty members joined them, and the dean of Arts and Science, George Harrower, an astrophysicist, was in the chair. Harrower had taken over as dean from Sandy Duncan in 1964 and had displayed a willingness to entertain the ethos of the sixties. "I think we accept very fully," Harrower told student journalist Jeff Simpson on CFRC Radio, "that the university is responsible to the society

❖ *Swash Q: Building Brand Identity* ❖

The postwar boom in Canada rode on a tide of consumerism. Canadians bonded with brands that delivered predictable and satisfying results – Canadians "refreshed" with Coca-Cola and made a "getaway" in their Chevrolet. Successful brands boosted market share and cemented customer loyalty. The same would be true for universities. Since the 1880s, Queen's had tried to build a visual image. The initial impetus came from intermural sports teams and their fans wanted something that made them stand out. In 1884, the AMS and Queen's footballers agreed that a tricolour of red, blue, and gold – to represent Arts, Applied Science, and Medicine – would inspire school spirit. In the 1930s, an official Queen's blazer followed, with a crest bearing the St Andrew's cross and the "Sapienta et doctrina stabilitas" motto taken from the Book of Isaiah. In the 1950s, Principal Mackintosh had the crest registered with the College of Heraldry. A tricolour flag was approved by the trustees in 1965. A tartan followed. (Curiously, the student yearbook, *The Tricolour*, employed the American spelling of the word – *Tricolor* – until 1978.)

But as consumerism flourished in the sixties, Queen's had no overall visual symbol to project its identity. Deutsch determined to change this; in 1969, he struck a committee on graphic symbols, chaired by art-gallery director Ralph Allan, to create a paramount image. In May 1970, the committee reported that Queen's was failing to transmit its values because of "the fragmented and undistinguished work done in graphics by the university." For example, the university had at least seventy different letterheads in use. The solution: hire an "on the spot" director of graphics and task him with building an all-embracing "typographical image." That man was Peter Dorn, a German immigrant who had arrived in Canada in 1953 and found sales work in Eaton's hosiery department before moving up to the store's graphics department. There he learned the power of a well-designed catalogue to move retail goods. Scouted by Toronto designer Allan Fleming, creator of the iconic CN worm logo, Dorn went on to study at the Ontario College of Art.

Dorn brought a breath of artistic fresh air to Queen's. He ended the chaos of individual faculties preparing their own calendars and pulled the design of promotional material out of the registrar's office, centralizing all graphic design in one office. Many objected – tradition was being abandoned. Others rallied to the cause; George Whalley in English loved calligraphy and could see Dorn's talent. Dorn's boldest stroke came with the creation of the "swash Q" – a graceful, stylized Q with an elegant, wavy tail. Dorn cast the new image in Palatino font; he liked its "humanistic" aesthetic. Dorn's swash Q tagged university signage and alumni memorabilia, and adorned all university publications. The new McGill-Queen's University Press seized on Dorn's artistic genius to design its books, thereby shedding the visual fustiness of most academic publishing. Dorn's masterful eye for display surfaced in Agnes Etherington exhibitions and the *Queen's Quarterly*. In the 1980s, Dorn guided the university graphics shop through computerization. Retiring in 1996, Dorn was celebrated with a Distinguished Service Award.

which has nurtured it."[37] Sensing this, Deutsch gave the committee a free-ranging mandate: examine degree programs, the structure of curriculum, methods of instruction, academic support for teaching, and any issues, such as student services, pertinent to enhancing the quality of teaching at Queen's. Through the fall of 1969 and into the next spring, the committee held open meetings on the state of Queen's curriculum in Arts and Science and then met privately with students and administrators. Individual faculty members submitted their own nostrums. Harrower proved a forceful chair, remembered by a senior Arts rep on the AMS council as "quietly persuasive, smart, and highly regarded by students, the principal, and, I believe, his faculty colleagues."[38] The committee culminated its deliberations with a two-day retreat at a lodge north of Kingston on Lake Opinicon, to which interested students and faculty were invited. One of the speakers lightheartedly referred to it as a "Deutsch treat." The get-together was very much in the spirit of the sixties: free-speaking and free-wheeling. Ideas poured out in a fashion that defied the usual stuffiness of faculty boards and Senate meetings. Despite much prodding from Dean Harrower, who wanted fundamental change, many present concluded that the status quo was satisfactory. Harrower bullishly persisted, spinning the final report to his own inclination.

In October 1969, the committee presented its blueprint. Readers quickly dubbed it the "Blue Book," for its blue cover, or, given the dean's guiding role in its deliberations, the "Harrower Report." The report was infused with the libertarian rhetoric of the sixties. The university, it argued, was a community in which "personal fulfillment" and "mutual education" should flourish. To remain vital, universities must engage in a "constant re-examination of conventional wisdom." They must respond to society's "cry for relevance," abandon their recidivistic, cloistered ways, and build a "total environment" for learning. The report contained a good deal of prescient analysis: students came to university for varied reasons – for intellectual stimulation, for vocational preparation, and for social engagement. Most undergraduates arriving at Queen's came in the expectation of building a broad platform of intuitions for life. With this in place, they would move on to some avenue of specialized expertise. With this orientation, the committee was quick to fault the existing undergraduate program. It lacked flexibility and demanded that students commit themselves to particular programs long before they had found their intellectual bearings. Why should students be obliged almost as soon as they set foot at Queen's to decide between the proto-professional training of an honours degree and a general "pass" BA? Throughout the report, there was a persistent implication that honours programs were elitist, while the general BA was more democratic and in touch with the tenor of the times. The critique continued to indict the slide of undergraduate education into the mediocrity of large-lecture teaching and criticized the loss of small-group teaching. The report pointed to a failure to focus on the student "as an individual," a failure to offer students choice in shaping their own education. The dilemma for Queen's was to engage in forward thinking that would allow it to fashion a more "progressive" undergraduate education, while at the same time retaining its storied reputation as an undergraduate educator.

The solution offered by the Harrower Report was to abandon the honours degree and to infuse the first three years of the BA with flexibility that allowed students to prepare for the life-committing decisions that followed. Students should not be locked into concentrated compartments. They should also be exposed to more small-group teaching, write fewer examinations, and obtain the benefit of innovations in pedagogy, like filmed lectures. After three years, they might exercise the option of continuing into a more-focused honours-style program that would culminate in an MA degree. After three years, they would, however, be better prepared to make a commitment to training in the professions or to pursue academe with a doctorate. Yes, the committee acknowledged, their prescription might be construed as "too permissive," but the Harrower Report believed that the time had come to empower students with the right of self-determination. Not to act was to court "serious problems" in the future.[39]

The Harrower Report's authors soon came to the realization that there was a formidable gap between conception and reality. Any academic reform at Queen's was subject to the prerogative of the Senate. In July 1969, even before the report was tabled, George Harrower had moved on to fill the shoes of the outgoing vice-principal, academic. Fred Gibson, having shepherded Senate reform to its conclusion, wanted to return to the history classroom. Harrower's shoes as dean were in turn filled by a young member of the political studies department, Ronald Watts. Watts had come to Queen's in 1955 as a philosophy professor, but had gravitated into the fractious field of analyzing Canadian federal-provincial politics. His collegial manner seemed to suit him for the delicate task of finding consensus in a faculty made up of nineteen disparate departments. The faculty had just been through the trauma of admitting "departmental student committees" into their decision making. A report penned by English professor George Whalley had advocated that students be consulted on matters such as curriculum, appointments, and evaluation, which had hitherto been solely under the purview of their academic superiors.[40] Some departments had accepted this with equanimity, but others were recalcitrant. In addition, for the first time, student representatives had been admitted into the inner sanctum of the faculty board itself. Now the Harrower Report demanded more upheaval. The report's proposals trod on the turf of established programs and seasoned academic careers. Many considered the honours degree the quintessence of Queen's excellence in teaching. Indeed, Watts reported that there was a pronounced trend in the faculty towards honours and away from the general degree; Queen's students seemed to value early specialization. He also warned that the heyday of faculty expansion was over, since the cooling provincial economy indicated that a period of stringency was at hand.[41] The Harrower proposals tended to be labour-intensive. Where would the troops come from to man the mooted "total environment"?

When focused debate of the Blue Book began in the Senate in December 1969, committee member Fred Euringer, a drama professor, admitted to "how difficult it had been to ascertain and weigh consensus." Nonetheless, there seemed to be general agreement that Queen's needed to provide better support for undergraduate teaching, and had to embrace ongoing pedagogic adaptation. Beyond such broad-brush agreement, dissent materialized. There was disagreement as to what exactly had been agreed to at the heady Opinicon meeting. Practical problems were raised: how could art history or music be taught as "general" subjects? Would Queen's students be at a disadvantage with their three-year generalist degree when it came to applying to graduate schools? Would wily students be able to assemble enough general courses to fashion a de facto specialist concentration? More fundamentally, many came to the defence of "elitist" honours. Arthur Keppel-Jones of the history department argued that honours not only focused intelligence, but at the same time promoted "a general education of the mind."[42] History department head Eric Harrison chimed in, citing a letter from a Queen's honours graduate who had gone on to graduate work at UCLA: small seminars had equipped him with the ability to undertake "intensive scrutiny and criticism." Physics professor David McLay issued a clarion call to preserve the distinction between honours and general as a reflection of students' varied ambitions and abilities. Some students, like Arts and Science Society president Andy Pipe, countered the defence of the status quo by arguing that most students wanted a generalist education. Harrower weighed into the debate, returning to the "cardinal difficulty" of making students specialize too early.

Watts again cautioned that the deteriorating financial situation militated against any dramatic redeployment of resources into small-group teaching.

By mid-1970, the Harrower Report had lost momentum. The honours system proved resilient against populist assault and remained in place. To many long-time professors the report appeared a direct threat to the university's reputation for quality teaching as they construed it. Queen's habitual inclination to gradualism thus remained intact. As Keppel-Jones concluded, the faculty ethos at Queen's was "not favourable to radical revolution."[43] Other universities, like the University of Toronto, asked the same questions, arrived at the same critique of the honours programs, and then jumped, a decision they later came to regret in an age that increasingly exalted credentialed specialization over generalization.[44] The Harrower Report was not, however, a cul de sac for Queen's. To adopt the rhetoric of the sixties, discussion of the report "raised consciousness" over the centrality of undergraduate teaching at Queen's. Harrower's Blue Book did prompt piecemeal pedagogic changes – the introduction of course packs, the factoring of teaching skills into departmental hiring, more resources for graduate teaching assistants, better course counselling of students – but its most lasting legacy was to remove the complacent belief that good teaching at Queen's was inherently excellent, rather than something that required constant adjustment to the tenor of the times. In that sense, the spirit of that weekend Chautauqua beside Lake Opinicon lived on in the minds of those committed to making Queen's a more progressive place.[45] It is, however, difficult to discern John Deutsch's reaction to the Harrower Report adventure. He had welcomed the combative Senate debate as "timely," but his initial desire to renovate the Arts and Science curriculum seemed stillborn. "Trying to change a curriculum," he would laconically admit to his close friends, "is like trying to move a cemetery."[46]

If the Harrower Report indicated that Queen's was not a place habituated to seismic change in its culture, the deliberations of innumerable Senate committee meetings and plenary Senate meetings through the Deutsch years did demonstrate the emergence of a new participatory approach to academic governance. Through the early 1970s, the Senate asserted its primacy in deciding the academic course of the university; the days of cozy consultation between deans, trustees, and the principal in academic matters – hiring, promotion, tenure, curriculum design, and grievances – were over. In these matters, the principal increasingly took on the role of a forceful, persuasive coach, who highlighted the strategic goals and challenges before Queen's and then called on his team to join in plotting appropriate tactical responses. The resultant mechanism for building consensus often proved laborious, but it legitimated the codification of university policies, ranging from the seemingly mundane – parking and library fines, for instance – on through to primal codes that governed who was hired, how they were evaluated, and what they taught. All nine Senate committees participated in this gestation, but the Academic Development (SCAD) and the Appointment, Promotion, Tenure, and Leave (SCAPTL) committees sat at the fulcrum of the new governance culture at Queen's. Deutsch would first turn to the academic development committee for guidance.

Managing the University

As an economist, John Deutsch had directed his energies to the emerging field of macroeconomics – the contemplation of economic performance in its broadest context. He had, for instance, been instrumental in introducing the key concept of the gross national product to Canadian economic management. As a university principal, his attention was naturally drawn to discerning the optimal productivity of the educational establishment under his sway. At what size and with what inputs would the university thrive and thereby retain its market advantage over its competitors? Soon after he settled into Richardson Hall, Deutsch began describing his ambition to make Queen's the "Harvard of the North" – small, prestigious, dedicated to quality education, and thereby selective in its offerings and admissions. To do so, he realized, he must be able to isolate the various inputs into a university's well-being – capital, infrastructure, personnel, physical space – and, from this analysis, put the university in a position to manage its outputs – that is to say, its reputation for teaching and research and the willingness of students, governments, and benefactors to subsidize its operations. In the fall of 1968, he directed the Senate Committee on Academic Development to delve into this educational calculus. In effect, the committee was asked to divine an ideal balance for Queen's between its intrinsic endowment and the external demands exacted on it by government and the increasingly competitive world of Ontario universities.

Officially, the committee, which Deutsch himself chaired, took the title of the "Senate Report on Enrolment to 1975–76." Unofficially, it quickly acquired the sobriquet of the "steady state" committee, reflecting its early predilection to protect Queen's distinctiveness by closely regulating its growth. From the outset the committee rejected Queen's ingrained faculty-to-faculty, department-by-department, "willy-nilly" approach to planning its growth. The concept of long-term planning had hitherto never been broadly rooted at Queen's. An "integrated" approach to university planning was now imperative, so that every individual academic activity could be construed in light of the university's overall resources. That approach also had to be "flexible," because, as the Harrower group was discovering, universities were being called upon to deliver "new knowledge," and would have to be adept in responding. For instance, resources had to be apportioned between departments that provided "service teaching" (the inculcation of knowledge prerequisite to other disciplines) and those providing a specialized focus. Here, Deutsch benefited from a seed he had sowed before he had departed

for Ottawa in 1963. Queen's now had an Office of Academic Planning. Deutsch deployed Corry's one-time executive assistant, Bernard Trotter, to direct the small planning group of four. Trotter recruited people who were good with numbers, people like chemist-turned-statistician Mario Creet, who immersed himself in the ebb and flow of registration, BIUs, and research-grant statistics, numbers that could be extrapolated into the future.

To enhance the university's ability to probe its physical limits, Deutsch appointed a University Campus Planner, civil engineering professor Graham Andrews, in December 1968. Queen's had never devoted much attention to its built environment, trusting instead that limestone and grass would somehow continue to exert their spell over the campus. A 1961 attempt at a campus master plan by Montreal consultants Barott, Marshall, Merrett and Barott had exposed such naïveté: the Queen's campus was tending to become "an informal hodgepodge of buildings of various sizes, heights, shapes and masses forming a variety of irregular intervening spaces."[47] The expertise now offered by Trotter and Andrews provided the perfect complement to the work of the Senate's "steady state" committee.

By March 1969, the Senate Committee on Academic Development (SCAD) had its preliminary enrolment projections and strategies ready to lay before the Senate. Three subsequent reports over the next two years fine-tuned the new, managed approach to enrolment at Queen's. Two fundamental control factors would govern the university's growth: its limited geography and capital availability. In each case, the committee's advice was not to strain the envelope in which Queen's found itself. A restricted supply of student accommodation presented a formidable limitation on growth. The boxed-in campus was reaching the limits of expansion: new residences on Queen's Crescent and on Leonard Field had provided new beds, but, overall, the university's ability to house its undergraduates was being outstripped by its annual growth. The situation was exacerbated by the province's refusal to fund residences as it did academic buildings. Residences, Toronto argued, should be financed and amortized more like commercial ventures. Furthermore, it was unclear how much accommodation was available off campus to soak up the on-campus surplus. More apparent was the fact that a shortfall in accommodation might tarnish Queen's reputation as a generally happy, campus-oriented community. Indeed, the unfolding housing shortage was the first bone of contention Deutsch encountered with the Alma Mater Society when he took office in the fall of 1968. Headlong growth, such as that being pursued by some of Ontario's newer universities, therefore might well strain the physical fabric of Queen's, while at the same time eroding its core values. The committee also expressed caution over fiscal recklessness. Provincial post-secondary-education funding contained the built-in temptation to couple enrolment to the automatic per-capita reward of the BIU. But, the committee pointed out, university budgets were sprawling things, which had to cover a myriad of expenditures – from salaries to the purchase of research equipment – and there was danger in allowing bloated enrolment to multiply the university's ongoing fiscal obligations. If enrolment stalled or fell, a university could readily fall into deficit, unable to meet its fixed costs. In a sense, the university's old pattern of Presbyterian frugality had resurfaced.

By the fall of 1969, the committee had honed its analysis into a workable prescription. Queen's would expand its enrolment to a ceiling of 10,200 students by 1975–76, and thereafter "remain relatively stable."[48] This goal would be tinkered with annually as financial and academic circumstances shifted. At the same time, SCAD would be the university's enrolment metronome, every year furnishing the Senate with a reassessment of the mid-seventies target. To ease Queen's passage to this goal, the committee outlined ways in which the university might adjust its resources. More interdisciplinary programs would allow faculty capabilities to be deployed across once-rigid disciplinary lines.

Professors should similarly be cross-appointed. Departments should co-operate more in the provision of common research facilities. The benefits of "service teaching" in areas of broad academic application, like statistics, should be explored. A year-round teaching schedule should be considered, and graduate supervisors should encourage their charges to complete their studies within the limits stipulated by their degree requirements.

The allure of the "steady state" scenario rested on its deceleration of the university's 1960s annual growth rate of 9.6 per cent to a more manageable 3.8 per cent down to 1975, after which it would theoretically plateau. Within this managed growth, certain favoured programs could be expanded and others reduced. Graduate studies, with its rich pay-off in BIUs and kudos, was plotted to grow by 16 per cent down to 1975. The projection of undergraduate growth made by SCAD placed Queen's well below the average provincial projection. While this scenario tended to annoy planners at Queen's Park, it proved a shrewd strategy for Queen's: by restricting places at the university, the steady state would constrict admission to Queen's, drive up its entry standards, and thereby enhance its hereditary brand as a teaching university. By closely guarding its admissions gate, Queen's would be in a position to take only the best and the brightest. This also positioned Queen's advantageously if and when the post-secondary boom of the sixties ebbed, something that Deutsch, with his mandarin antennae, was beginning to suspect by 1970. Queen's would therefore not be caught overexpanded if the stream of BIUs ever slackened. The "steady state" scenario would also, in theory at least, allow the university to anticipate its needs. For instance, the hiring spurt of the sixties had left Queen's with a remarkably youthful contingent of 638 faculty. The problem was that they would all grow old together: how, under a "steady state" regimen, could they be renewed? What would be the effect of this demographically homogenized cohort on tenure, on promotion, on the intellectual climate? Consequently SCAD concluded that a "no-growth" environment would necessitate departures from traditional academic norms: new criteria for evaluating faculty performance that segregated teaching and research, the increased use of sessional teachers to promote a more healthy turnover of faculty, and other such measures. In short, there was a great deal of the unknown in the "steady state" scenario, something symptomatic of the hubris of planning that was so prevalent in the technocratic late sixties.[49] But Deutsch had at least crafted a steadying, rational plan that gave Queen's an advantageous orientation that respected its physical limitations and reputation for quality after a decade of headlong growth.

Deutsch could also see that a large measure of reason and predictability was called for in the internal academic affairs of Queen's. The old, informal manner in which faculty were hired and shepherded through their careers had been overwhelmed by the surge of growth in the sixties. "Our present arrangements for promotion and tenure are pretty informal," the principal confided to his counterpart at the University of New Brunswick in 1968. "What really happens is that the heads of department discuss these matters with the Deans and the Deans in turn discuss them with the Principal."[50] Professors' initial appointments to the university were thus surprisingly casual. Well into the sixties, department heads would seek to convince their dean that new expertise was needed in a particular area of their discipline. If successful, they would be commissioned to go on the hunt for the requisite faculty members. Each summer, deans dispatched department heads to Canadian and American learned societies to comb the job market. Some were even flown to Europe. Once candidates were identified, the prospective professor struck a deal on salary – usually by telegram or phone call – with the dean or the principal. There was no prescribed interview process; there was a powerful tendency to rely on the comfortable old boys' networks. The university, for instance, refused to pay the travel expenses of any candidate interviewed on campus for a position below the rank of an associate professorship, meaning outside candidates were at a disadvantage.[51] All this informality culminated in the principal presenting the trustees with a list of proposed appointments, a list they consented to with little questioning. Political scientist Stewart Fyfe, who had been hired for Queen's local government institute in the 1950s, remarked on the "clannishness" of the whole process, its "glad to see you when you show up" ethos.[52]

The casualness of Queen's recruitment and retention policies before the sixties was indeed striking. Philosopher Albert Fell was hired on the spot by Arts dean Sandy Duncan after a pleasant chat over lunch and a walk in an Edinburgh park. Fell's starting salary and the offer of a donship in the men's residence seemed to be pulled out of a hat. Later, in the early 1960s, the dean used his discretion to give Fell a two-year leave of absence to complete his Columbia doctorate.[53] Biologist Madan Joneja was working on his doctoral thesis in a Queen's lab one evening, when his supervisor, Hans Stich, unexpectedly arrived. "The anatomy department would like to offer you a job," he announced. Joneja demurred; he had hopes of returning to India. Stich countered: "Why don't you try a few years and if you don't like it you can still leave." Joneja would, in fact, stay for thirty-seven years.[54] That same year, 1965, David Bonham, a Saskatchewan-trained accountant then studying at the Harvard Law School, came to Kingston to visit a friend, who had surreptitiously arranged interviews for Bonham with Bill Lederman, dean of Law, and Lawrence Macpherson, dean of Business. In the space of one afternoon, Bonham was interviewed and offered a joint position in the two faculties. He, too, happily stayed for the long haul.[55] Macpherson's successor as dean, Richard Hand, acquired a reputation for "bagging" promising graduate students at American business schools – over dinner.[56] Politics professor Ned Franks was hired over a drink with Principal Corry (who had run the idea past his colleagues John Meisel and Ted

A cartoon from the *Queen's Alumni Review*: the surge of student enrolment was not alone in making Queen's markedly more youthful in the 1960s.

Hodgetts beforehand) in the Hotel Saskatchewan. When a startled Franks reminded the principal that he had only obtained a B in his Politics 2 course, Corry responded that this did not matter, since he believed Franks had a "first-class mind."[57] There is no denying that this chummy way of hiring brought some tremendously dedicated and talented scholars to the campus. But it also revealed some alarming blind spots in the way that Queen's saw itself. Inevitably, the process produced "the new man," as innumerable memos described the new addition to staff. But it tended to be oblivious to candidates, particularly women, who did not show up on the Queen's "old boys'" radar.[58]

The same coziness prevailed in the selection of deans and departmental heads. Heads of departments enjoyed their tenure at the pleasure of their dean and the principal. There were no prescribed procedures for their selection or the review of their performance. In September 1967, Principal Corry simply telephoned Arthur Keppel-Jones and asked him to stay on as head of the history department. Keppel-Jones agreed, saying that he "saw no reason for sending the history department members notice of his continuing."[59] This, of course, could work in a department's favour when a forceful head won the ongoing approbation of his dean. John Coleman, the dynamic head of mathematics, oversaw his department with baronial vigour from 1960 to 1980. His colleagues half-admiringly, half-fearfully, tagged him "the Lord of the Manor." Even the principal enjoyed an open tenure in Richardson Hall, the assumption being that he would step down at the mandatory retirement age of sixty-five.

Although he was himself the product of this inside-track culture, John Deutsch was savvy enough to realize that times were changing and that recruitment and retention of university faculty must become more inclusive and equitable. "Although Queen's University has been fortunate in avoiding any serious disagreements in the relationship with academic staff," he told the trustees in 1969, "it is highly desirable that a formal policy be adopted on the granting of tenure, dismissal and grievance procedures."[60] Just as SCAD assumed oversight for the university's pace of expansion, under John Deutsch matters pertaining to the recruitment and retention of academic staff increasingly gravitated to the Senate Committee on Appointment, Promotion, Tenure, and Leave. What had hitherto been governed by a convivial idiosyncrasy now became codified and regulated.

The transition had been foreshadowed in Corry's years when faculty sabbaticals became institutionalized. Hitherto, under a 1937 policy, sabbaticals were regarded as a "permissive" right of the university, not an "unconditional right" of faculty. Times were fiscally tough, and the principal obligation of faculty was teaching, not research. The right to grant sabbaticals, Bill Mackintosh always insisted, was not "contractual" and was governed by the power of the trustees over the university purse strings. "The number of such leaves which can be provided for in one year is limited," Corry later wrote to a philosophy professor in 1961. "I had to establish priorities and could not place you high enough on the list."[61] Those lucky enough to win the sabbatical sweepstakes were expected to leave town and to have some money tucked away. Given that, professors with six to nine years' service could expect only 50 per cent of their nominal salary. After fourteen years, those going on sabbatical received 80 per cent of salary.

University employment was now a seller's market, and the terms of employment needed sweetening if young scholars were to be attracted. Research was at the same time becoming an obligation of university life, while teaching had become more onerous as enrolments grew. Professors needed time away to refresh themselves and restock ideas. Early in the decade, the Canadian Association of University Teachers advised its members to push for the transformation of sabbaticals into an entitlement. At Queen's, the faculty association accordingly formed a committee. Corry did not resist. He told the trustees that the university's rapidly expanding faculty deserved "better provision" for sabbaticals, since the burden of work was growing. To ensure that Queen's did not differentiate itself too much from other universities, he discussed the matter with the Council of Presidents of Ontario Universities. Then, in September 1966, he announced a new policy that made sabbaticals an entitlement for all faculty and set out a formula for their allotment.

As principal, John Deutsch accelerated this codification of faculty rights. In April 1969, the Senate ratified a *Statement on Academic Freedom and Tenure*, which upheld the "freedom of a faculty member to study, to teach and to record knowledge to his best professional judgement." Tenure, and the probationary period leading to tenure, was the embodiment of this freedom. "Tenure entails the right of fair consideration for increases of responsibility and salary and promotion in rank."[62] The document set out a universally applicable process for probationary appointments to faculty, the granting of tenure, possible dismissal, and a grievance procedure if tenure was denied.

Once ratified, these regulations fell under the oversight of the Senate Committee on Appointment, Promotion, Tenure, and Leave (SCAPTL). In the 1970s, for instance, SCAPTL elaborated the initial appointment procedure – positions must be advertised in at least one national publication – and broadened it to embrace the expanding number of term appointments.[63] As an example, 1971 saw the Senate's adoption of guidelines for the regularization of the appointment of deans and heads of department. Deans and heads would now serve a mandated five-year term. Deans would be selected by a broadly representative advisory committee, which would begin its search fifteen months before the outgoing dean departed. Similar search committees for departmental heads would have nine months to make their own selection. Deans and heads might be reappointed.[64]

Having set out the entitlements of faculty and invited students into its decision making, the Senate turned its attention to the tricky question of policing the behaviour of the university community. The sixties had acted as a solvent on the established boundaries of behaviour at Queen's. The surge of baby-boom entitlement had washed away the last vestiges of *in loco parentis* authority at Canadian universities. Paternalistic control had been superseded by the notion that students, like the faculty who taught them and the university staff who maintained the fabric of the university, were now *citizens*, with normal rights and responsibilities. This distinction was more complicated than it seemed. Where, in a self-regulated community like a university, was the jurisdictional division between outside civil authority and internal, customary control of the institution's own affairs? Similarly, what distinguished the adjudicating of academic discipline – be it a matter of student plagiarism or faculty tenure – and non-academic discipline, such as breaches of town-gown etiquette? Historically at Queen's, the Senate had the charter-ordained right to oversee all aspects of student life on campus, but had delegated oversight of non-academic discipline to the Alma Mater Society, which had vested its authority in the AMS Court and its student constables. The sixties ethos of protest and self-realization tested these arrangements. Students had become more assertive, more eager to question the status quo and its inherited authorities. Similarly, faculty and staff were less willing to be acted upon, rather than acting. Concomitantly, with new, less paternalistic, entitlements eroding the ingrained habits of university life, demand for appeal and grievance procedures rose. Members of the university community not only wanted recognition of their rights, but also mechanisms by which to seek redress if the system, in their opinion, went against their behaviour or fortunes.

John Deutsch trod these shifting sands with sagacity. As he said at his 1968 installation, "Inherent conservatism and rigidity will not, in the circumstances of today, prevail against either governments or revolutionaries."[65] The decorum and discipline of campus life must move with the times, not stand in their way. And in the spirit of the Gibson Report, Deutsch concluded that change in the rubric of campus discipline and grievance should not come about by top-down fiat, but by broad consultation. And the Senate would be the fulcrum of such change. In January 1970, the principal therefore created the Senate Committee on Grievance, Discipline, and Related Matters. Membership on the eleven-member committee was nicely balanced to reflect the new inclusive nature of the Queen's community. Chaired by Ron Watts, dean of Arts and Science, the committee had five student members, including meds student David Walker and student senator Jeff Simpson. Conscious that the issues at hand had a crucial legal aspect, Deutsch included both a law student and law professor on the committee. The committee was instructed to make the rights and responsibilities of faculty, students, and staff "clear and explicit."

The difficulty of achieving this ambition was evident in the fact that the committee's final report, presented in May 1971, required twenty-one pages of dense print to convey its message. While praising "the existing informality and multiple channels for handling cases of grievance and discipline," the committee argued for a more explicit statement of rights and responsibilities on campus. Every disciplinary agency on campus, from residence councils to faculty boards, should review and explicate its jurisdiction. A code of conduct for faculty and students alike should set out what constituted "unacceptable conduct" on campus. At the same time, the university community should not see itself as exempt from the constraints of the broader Canadian legal code. The constables of the AMS should confine their purview to matters of decorum related to normal university life. By the same token, the presence of external police, especially RCMP surveillance officers, should be strictly prescribed and monitored, to protect intellectual freedom on campus. The confidentiality of all documentation relating to members of the university community should be tightly guarded.

And then, in great and quasi-legalistic detail, the committee set out an elaborate system of appeals for both students and faculty caught in the courts of campus discipline, ranging from the AMS Court to library fines. Even issues of faculty salary, promotion, and tenure might be grieved. The process would be constructed like a ladder of appeals, culminating in an Ultimate Tribunal presided over by an "outside arbitrator," who would operate at arm's-length from the Senate. One rung below the Ultimate Tribunal, a "filter" committee composed of equal numbers of student and faculty senators would screen potential appeals to the Ultimate Tribunal.[66] Appeals deemed to be without substance could be denied access to the Ultimate Tribunal. The Senate duly ratified the proposed discipline and grievance procedure in April 1972. In practice, the process soon proved cumbersome. For instance, it expected students and faculty appointed to the filter committee to assume a quasi-legal function, for which they were ill-equipped. Furthermore, there was the question of whether those appealing their fate at the hands of a campus justice system might avail themselves of outside legal counsel, and, if so, who would pay for those services. Not surprisingly, the process also proved time-consuming, a problem exacerbated by the fact that cases involving students tended to stall once students migrated off-campus in the spring.

From Deutsch's perspective in Richardson Hall, responsibility for these matters had now been transferred to the university community itself. Attitudinally, the Corry and Deutsch years saw Queen's move into an age of inclusion, away from the tight, top-down suzerainty of the principal and trustees. Queen's was becoming a self-regulating community in word and deed. Senate committees and principal's advisory committees now became the crucible of policy and consensus at Queen's. The latter – PACs, as they soon became known – and Senate committees advised on matters as disparate as athletics and long-term planning. Faculty and students began spending long hours in committee rooms. The process was often slow, sometimes prolix and pedantic, but somehow eventually connected to the broad sociology of Queen's. Members of the Queen's community now came to understand that they could be masters of their own fate. The Senate office became a central crossroads of opinion at Queen's, a choice place to work. Margaret Hooey, Jean Royce's one-time understudy in the registrar's office, was appointed to the crucial post of secretary of the Senate. Hooey ran a tight ship, insisting that her office play an absolutely neutral role in facilitating the deliberations of Senate committees. Having studied politics at Bryn Mawr, Hooey was intrigued by Deutsch's "new" university: "I've always been intrigued about how things worked, politically. I've always had a passion for fairness." One of her assistants, Jill Harris, revelled in her work for the Senate: "[Y]ou got to see the whole thing," she recalled.[67]

As if to underscore the new importance of communal discourse, Deutsch in 1969 launched the *Queen's Gazette* as a weekly university-published compendium of decisions upcoming and decisions made. This spirit embraced campus life from the sublime – one's promotion to full professor – to the mundane – the unveiling of Queen's first parking regulations in 1970.[68] For his part, Deutsch revelled in his *primus inter pares* role as the chairman of the Senate; in many ways he sensed that more transpired there than in his Richardson Hall office. His role as principal was to anticipate problems and issues, feed them into the arena of the Senate, and then nudge them to conclusion. David Bonham, the lawyer-accountant who served as Deutsch's executive assistant, recalled that Deutsch took the Senate's function "so seriously" that one day the principal rose early, was driven to Queen's Park in Toronto for a meeting with university bureaucrats, hurried back to Kingston to chair the scheduled Senate meeting in the afternoon, then was driven back to Toronto to deliver an evening speech before returning home to his bed in Kingston.[69]

Second-Wave Feminism Comes to Queen's

Reform is seldom complete in its sweep. As with economies, there are leading and lagging sectors in university life. Corry, Deutsch, and their cabinet of progressive deans had pulled Queen's into the age of the multiversity – academic diversity, social responsiveness, and accountability now characterized the structures and culture of Queen's. But their reform zeal was not all-embracing, especially when it came to the sense of inclusion felt by one conspicuous, yet historically almost invisible, segment of the campus community: women. In the classrooms and residences of Queen's, there was no mistaking the presence of female students at Queen's. In 1967–68, for instance, women students found themselves in the majority in programs such as nursing, rehabilitation, physical education, and Arts and Science. But their presence was much less pronounced in traditionally male-oriented programs like Applied Science, where a lonely band of 12 women pursued degrees in the midst of 1,123 males. The more oriented towards professional accreditation a program was, the fewer the women: 17 women pursuing a commerce degree against 216 men. In graduate studies, the ratio of men to women was six to one. Overall, males outnumbered women students at Queen's by a margin of 4,129 to 1,869. But there was an irony buried in the statistics. Throughout the sixties, women students surged onto university campuses, pushed by baby-boom demographics and by what feminists would come to call "second-wave feminism," the urge felt by women to move beyond first-wave political entitlements into realms of equal employment and social equity. Hence, the numbers of women coming to Canadian universities in the seventies and eighties would continue to swell, particularly as barriers to entry to one-time male preserves like engineering and law crumbled. This shift in registration underscored a paradox at Queen's: while women asserted their right to post-secondary education, women on Queen's faculty and staff largely remained caught in a backwater, denied access to academic and administrative power and often frozen out of the cultural ethos of the place. Thus, while women who came to study at Queen's rode a tide of expanding rights and recognition, women who looked to Queen's for the fulfillment of an academic career continued to stare in frustration at what feminists would come to describe as a "glass ceiling" of discrimination and obliviousness. It was a glass ceiling invisible to most males at Queen's, but one which John Deutsch at least recognized and determined to alter.

It is difficult to quantify the frustrations of women at Queen's in the sixties. Only a handful of women enjoyed any administrative power or traditionally defined influence on campus. The dean of women – Beatrice Bryce from 1959 to 1971, followed by Evelyn Reid through the seventies – had for decades been the only woman at senior management meetings at Queen's. But the dean of women did not have the clout of the male deans; her portfolio lacked a big budget and her influence resided in the soft power of moral suasion and daily contact with women students. The arrival in 1967 of Dr Jean Hill as director, later dean, of nursing, followed in 1976 by Dr Alice Baumgart, doubled the number of women at the weekly meeting of principal and deans. A few women academics at Queen's had been able to fashion reputations that stood up in the manly world. Astrophysicist Dr Vibert Douglas, for instance, had not only ably served as dean of women for twenty years down to 1959, but also built world renown as an astronomer, serving as president of the Royal Astronomical Society. Dr Hilda Laird had served as head of the German department. But otherwise there were huge lacunae for women on campus. The hiring of Mabel Corlett into the geological sciences department in 1969 brought the first women on staff in Miller Hall, indeed in the whole engineering faculty, where she taught by cross-appointment. Even though Corlett boasted a doctorate from Chicago (and a father who had been a long-time geologist at Queen's), she was initially given only a technician's position.[70] In fact, so few women taught at Queen's in the sixties that no effort was made to track their numbers, their compensation, or their progress through the ranks. There was no paid maternity leave, and pension arrangements were skimpier for women than for Queen's men. Many campus buildings, especially those serving applied science, contained few, if any, women's washrooms. In fact, one young scholar, taken on to teach English, later learned that there had been some concern about her hiring, because she would have to share a washroom with the secretaries – something that mattered not a whit to her.[71]

There were enclaves of influence for women at Queen's, but they were in areas traditionally deemed to be "woman's work." The library, with its hands-on routines of book ordering, cataloguing, and circulation, was almost exclusively a female domain – except ironically for the senior male librarians. As we have seen, when Queen's hired legions of young male professors in the sixties, the university library reaped a windfall of intelligent spouses eager to supplement the family income.[72] And, since turnover was high and supply abundant, the university could keep salaries low. Library work demanded some training, but this could be acquired at library school in Toronto or through on-the-job training. Similarly, administrative staff work beckoned women, attested to by the expansion of the Senate office around Margaret Hooey. Indeed, the achievements attributed to Queen's principals often rested on the stalwart, behind-the-scenes orchestration of their secretaries, women like Katharine Mein for Mackintosh and Corry and Mary Medland for Deutsch. Queen's was thus a place that depended on the labour of women but dispensed few kudos in their direction. Nonetheless, perhaps reflecting the gendered divisions of labour in Canadian society at the time, most women at Queen's regarded the place, as Jill Harris recalled, as "a very good people place."[73]

But women did not have to wander far from the library or the Senate office to discover that Queen's construed itself in narrow, sexist terms. When, for instance, Elizabeth Greene arrived in 1969 to teach Chaucer in the English department, she found the university "very male," a place where a woman professor was seen as "an oddity on campus." There was, she recalled, a "very chilly climate for women at Queen's." Her office did not have a phone. The department head often forgot her name, and later, after she married, would contact her husband, also an English professor, to discuss *her* teaching assignments.[74] At the same time, Queen's benefited from what Marion Meyer, hired to teach sociology in 1966, described as a policy of "hiring wives of [male] academics for more or less pocket money." Meyer, who admittedly lacked a doctorate, was paid a meagre $375 to teach a tutorial for eight months. Indeed, the ranks of adjunct professors – sojourning professors who enjoyed no security – were predominantly female.[75]

Much the same male-centric culture was encountered by a woman whom we have seen would later rise to prominence as Queen's tried to overcome its gender imbalances: Lin Good, the British-born wife of a newly hired RMC maths professor, who arrived at Queen's in the fifties. Advised to take a three-month library course in Toronto by Eleanor Tett, head of the library's order department, she returned to Kingston and was hired by Pearson Gundy. While she found her work and colleagues as an order librarian sympathetic, she yearned to return to the doctoral work in history she had begun at the University of London. Jean Royce suggested that she drop a note to Arthur Lower, the distinguished Canadian historian at Queen's. Lower invited her to his office. On her arrival there, Lower looked up in surprise but not delight and exclaimed, "Oh, you're a woman." Lower had misread the "Lin" on her note as "Jim." "And," Lower added, "you're English … I don't like women students and I don't like English students." Summoning both her courage and indignation, Good responded: "I'm not sure that I like you." Lower received a dressing down from the redoubtable Royce, but Good decided to forego history and dedicate herself to what would become a successful career as a librarian – and an advocate for women's rights at Queen's.[76]

Chauvinism surfaced in virtually every aspect of the university's life. When Bev Wilson (née Baines) began the study of law at Queen's in 1970, she found herself in a very male-centric world. The graduating law class that year contained a daunting cohort of ninety-nine men and a single woman (Mary Jane Mossman, who would go on to a distinguished legal career at Osgoode Hall). In her course on legal advocacy, Wilson was startled to hear the prominent local lawyer who was teaching the course pronounce with pontifical certainty that women were genetically unsuited for legal advocacy.[77] Wilson persevered and graduated in 1973, by which time women were a more visible minority in the law school. While Wilson studied law in 1971, a young Kingston woman, Bettyanne Gargaro, applied for an administrative job at Queen's. She passed the typing and office-skills tests in the personnel office and was given a job. Personnel told her to keep her salary to herself and not to discuss it with anybody – a ploy to stop female support staff from comparing notes on compensation. She was told that she would be working in the office of the dean of Arts and Science, given a folded note of introduction (written by a *woman* in human resources), and told to report for duty. En route to the dean's office, Gargaro peeked at the note and read: "Here's a beautiful blue-eyed blonde for your office." It was, she later recalled, "just the way things were."[78] Pulchritude even entered the admissions process at Queen's: in 1964, the president of Brandon College, writing in support of one of his students eager to do graduate studies at Queen's, appended the following to his reference letter: "an attractive blonde ... but I omitted this fact from my statement, as being beneath your notice."[79]

Such anecdotes invite the question: did gender relations at Queen's deviate from the national norm? Was the gender backwater at Queen's deeper and more entrapping than elsewhere? In all probability, women at Queen's experienced much the same climate of gender-based segregation and denied ambition as they would have in any large sixties institution. Many commercial employers, for instance, still expected women employees to resign as soon as they became pregnant. Nonetheless, one senses that male-derived values at Queen's were perhaps more deeply rooted than in, say, a big city such as Toronto. Queen's sat in a small, eastern-Ontario city, which in its own right had developed conservative ways. Furthermore, Queen's culture tended to be introverted and in many ways impervious to trends that pervaded more progressive, more urbanized, reaches of Canadian society. And the cult of "tradition" at Queen's tended to inoculate the place against hasty change: until 1967, for instance, women undergraduates inhabited their own sphere – the Levana Society – with its nineteenth-century notions of gender separation. Since 1939, the Queen's Women's Association had strived to create "a collegial atmosphere" for women both employed by Queen's and married to Queen's through a spouse. Thus, well into the sixties, relations between the sexes at Queen's rested on a complacent and uneven base of largely unexamined values. It was a relationship that mirrored broader attitudes embedded in western society and, for most, lacked a sharp consciousness of male power asserted or full female equality denied. In 1963, for instance, John Deutsch confided in Corry that he felt it "desirable" to have three or four women on the Board of Trustees. Corry concurred; it was "very desirable."[80] But there was never any thought given to placing a woman at the head of the trustees' table or even as chairman of a board committee.

The sixties disturbed this inequity. Early in the decade, second-wave feminism, with its focus on systemic barriers to women's broader empowerment in society, began to permeate Canadian thought. Canadian women avidly read Betty Friedan's *The Feminine Mystique* (1963), with its call for women to shake off the complacency and manipulation of suburban life and begin to demand equality of access and treatment in the corridors of power, whether they led through the corporate hierarchies or university admission offices. Groups like the Voice of Women were formed to deliver a feminist perspective on issues like nuclear disarmament. Women began to make a small dint in the male power bastion of parliament. Women politicians like Queen's-trained Liberal MP Pauline Jewett (BA 1944; MA 1945) increasingly sat in the House of Commons. In 1967, Secretary of State Judy LaMarsh oversaw the federal role in Canada's centennial celebration. That year, Queen's gave an honorary degree to humanitarian Pauline Vanier, a small shift away from its traditional inclination to celebrate male achievement.

In 1967, Prime Minister Lester Pearson, never much attuned to feminist perspectives but acutely aware of his minority government's precariousness, created the Royal Commission on the Status of Women to explore the dynamics of gender exclusion and preference in Canada. Sensing Canadians' desire for equality, Pearson's successor, Pierre Trudeau, the next year pitched to the electorate the message of a "Just Society," with its implied message of opening up opportunity for all Canadians, and danced to a majority government. In 1970, the report of the royal commission unveiled academic data on what many Canadian women already suspected was their subordinate lot in life. Pay inequity, sexist entry barriers to the professions, lack of social support for maternity, and a myriad of other attitudes and policies had crept into Canadian society and needed rooting out. Heartened by this validation, women's groups coalesced into the National Action Committee on the Status of Women, determined to maintain the pressure on what soon became widely known as "patriarchy." Back at Queen's, Professors Mary Maxwell and Kay Herman in the fledgling sociology department began offering a new course: Sociology 331 – the Sociology of Women.

With his many connections in Ottawa and his commitment to inclusion at Queen's, John Deutsch was not oblivious to the message of second-wave feminism. Moreover, as was often the case, Queen's students were a step ahead of the faculty and administration: in the last years of the sixties, a small band of feminists had been active on campus, lampooning the heterosexual rituals of Queen's student culture – beauty pageants, prudish segregation of student residences, and out-of-date oversight of women students. Deutsch was also aware that members of staff were increasingly forthright in complaining about how gender framed, and at times disrupted, their careers. Over at the library, the technicians, perhaps the largest congregation of women working at Queen's, were so disgruntled by low pay and male-defined management that they were agitating for a union under the auspices of the newly formed Canadian Union of Public Employees. Indeed, the library technicians would become the first Queen's employees to win union certification under the flag of CUPE 1302. Librarian Lin Good, for instance, recalled how an arrogant male graduate student refused to pay an overdue fine at the library front desk: "Oh God," he complained, "is this place run only by women?" "Well," the feisty Good replied, "unfortunately for you, it is." She phoned the principal's office, a move that prompted the recalcitrant student to reach for his wallet. "I see you listen to males," Good remarked.[81]

Late in the spring of 1972, Lin Good received a call asking her to come to the principal's office. This seemed to reverse the usual line of communication she had had with Richardson Hall, one of channelling the complaints of women librarians to the personnel office. When she entered Deutsch's office, the principal asked Good if she recognized the neat pile of memos on his desk. She didn't. These, he informed her, were all the missives she had sent over from the Douglas Library about the concerns of women working there. As he had done with Senate reform, Deutsch wanted to get out in front of feminist concerns on campus. Would Good head a principal's committee to investigate the status of women at Queen's? She could choose the members of the committee, and there would be no constraint on its inquiries. Sensing Deutsch's sincerity, Good agreed. Good did not see herself as a feminist in the sixties sense, although she was quick to point out that her grandmother had been a British suffragette. By temperament, she was a gradualist: "If you can get it with honey, don't use vinegar."[82] Deutsch now seemed to be offering constructive engagement to women at Queen's, something Good took on faith. She drew up a list of eight committee members – six women and two men. Eveline Flint from the personnel office, for instance, brought a more urgent feminism to the assignment; she had witnessed the capricious way in which the university listed jobs so as to favour some and exclude others. Jean Hill came from nursing. Gail Brent came from the law faculty, and Marney Cousins of Arts '73 gave voice to the students. Since data gathering was likely to be at the heart of the investigation, Ida Smith from the academic planning office would serve as secretary of the committee. Electrical engineering professor Jim Bennett and economist Alan Green rounded out the committee. Deutsch accepted the nominations.

The committee in many ways emulated the federal royal commission on the status of women. It was not "a grievance committee," but instead an investigatory project. It harvested statistics on the gendered nature of work at Queen's. Public sessions were held to listen to and provoke campus dialogue. Private one-on-one sessions were held with senior administrators and faculty. Past and present deans of women were sought out. Confabs were held with university staff, ranging from residence cleaners to deans. Informal coffee sessions were held with students in residence. Good displayed dogged and outspoken leadership; she spoke with clarity and vigour to alumni, to the trustees, and to her campus colleagues. The message was always the same: Queen's needed to raise its gender consciousness and the new spirit of inclusion at the university had to embrace women.

The magnitude of that change became apparent in February 1974, when the committee presented a substantial thirty-two-page report. There was no rush to judgment. First, it got at the facts. The report began by laying down an authoritative foundation of empirical fact that demonstrated that men and women at Queen's inhabited two distinctly unequal spheres. Of the 732 faculty at Queen's only 61, or 7.7 per cent, were women, and they were predominantly clustered at the low end of the faculty ladder as lecturers and assistant professors. There was only a single woman full professor – Hilda Neatby, the university historian[83] – on the whole campus. Remarkably, among 85 professors in Applied Science, there was not a single woman. One lone woman taught amidst 31 men in the business school. Only in the relatively small nursing and rehabilitation programs were women in the majority. Women faculty fared badly on paydays too. The median salary of women on faculty was a substantial $4,800 below that of their male colleagues. Fringe benefits and pension entitlements were calculated differently and less generously for female faculty. This systemic differentiation between what men and women were paid and how they were hired and promoted echoed into the ranks of the university's support and administrative staff. For instance, 93.7 per cent of women in non-academic positions earned less than $10,000 annually, whereas only 67.3 per cent of men fell into this range. The committee pointed out that these differentials matched those prevalent across eastern Ontario, and thus did not indicate that the university was in itself guilty of "discriminatory action." But it did indicate that Queen's was guilty of conforming to a broad pattern of systemically treating women inequitably and paying them less for comparable types of labour performed by men. In contrast to this sadly bifurcated world of male and female professors and support staff at Queen's, the committee was quick to point out that the number of women *studying* at Queen's was making considerable progress towards equity. By the fall of 1972, 39.6 per cent of undergraduate students at Queen's were women, and that total had been steadily swelling since the mid-sixties. All the statistics made one thing abundantly clear: even for women lucky enough to have a teaching post at the university and those aspiring to such employment or admission as students, Queen's was in a gender time warp.[84]

The Good Committee advocated root-and-branch change. Student admissions should be governed by "positive" criteria that did not differentiate on the basis of race, gender, marital status, or place of origin. In particular, "positive admission" policies should be developed and given prominence in the medical, law, and business faculties. Similarly, "male bias" should be weeded out of all student recruitment and orientation literature; Applied Science should not be portrayed as a club for males alone. Women faculty members should hereafter sit on all admissions and awards committees. Admission applications should no longer require a photograph. Vigorous effort must be applied to expanding the number of women professors. All hiring committees should contain a woman. All salary differentiation between men and women should be abolished, and deans and department heads should annually validate the enforcement of this policy. To ensure that women moved up the ranks of the faculty, a review committee appointed by the principal should monitor all appointments and promotions. The university should endeavour to appoint women to senior administrative posts. The same strictures should be applied to non-academic positions: salary inequalities between men and women must be levelled, and a staff-liaison officer appointed to act as a kind of ombudsman to help allay outstanding grievances. Similarly, women in staff positions should be afforded greater job mobility, so as to escape from existing enclaves of female employment. All gender-driven differentiation in the university benefits and pension plan must be ended, and, since so many women were in part-time and instructor posts, benefits must be broadened beyond the mainstream ranks of those tenured. The university should work with the city to provide better daycare facilities, so that women could balance their work and domestic responsibilities. The committee even addressed the need for attitudinal reform: women's studies was affirmed as a "legitimate" area of academic study. Instructors who exhibited sexist behaviour before their students should be held accountable under the university's new grievance procedures. And, although other universities were dispensing with the post, Queen's should retain its dean of women as a clearing house for women's concerns on campus.

In his foreword to the report, Deutsch stressed that it was "a beginning, not an end." To reinforce the point, Good presented the report's agenda to the Board of Trustees, who seemed receptive to its import. There were soon some encouraging signs. Deutsch appointed committee member Eveline Flint to the new post of Staff Liaison Officer. Flint became an enforcer of the emerging new gender consciousness at Queen's. It was, she recalled, "a very hands-on period, because we were just beginning to do things that allowed women an easier time in the workplace." There were, she added, "many knockdown, drag-out fights with people."[85] A year later, in 1975, a Principal's Review Committee on the Status of Women was appointed to provide ongoing statistical tracking of the recruitment and promotion of women at Queen's. But the reality was that bringing gender balance to Queen's was far more daunting than the Good Committee's well-argued list of recommendations might have foretold. Much conspired against expeditious reform. The male-dominated professoriate was entrenched by tenure; they were relatively young and unlikely to make way in the near future for female replacement. There was also, Good sadly recalled, dogged opposition to any thought of women's empowerment, particularly in parts of the law and medical faculties. Why train women doctors, some in the medical faculty contested, since they would only get married, have babies, and leave the profession? Years later, when asked why his department of forty-eight members contained so few women, John Coleman in mathematics answered point blank that there were "hardly any good women mathematicians."[86] Even more fundamentally, the mid-1970s proved a financially difficult time to rebalance gender representation on campus. The economy was slow and university budgets were consequently constrained, thus decreasing the university's effective leverage on new appointments. So Deutsch would inadvertently be proved right: the Good Report was indeed only the beginning of a problem that would simmer and at times boil over at Queen's as second-wave feminism worked its way into Canadian society.

However, despite this intractability, consciousness of the gender imbalance had been brought into the open at Queen's. Women at Queen's had been "given voice." Two events in 1975 illustrated that empowerment. Before the Good Report, women academics on campus tended to lead atomized, cloistered lives, holed up in their separate departments. They got on with their workaday duties and had little sense of any campus-wide women's agenda. The Good Committee hearings and the general ethos of second-wave feminism now connected them. Elsewhere on campus, women students were finding their voice, organizing "bitch-ins" and weekend seminars on women's issues. In 1974, monies garnered over decades from the astute management of the women's residences were pooled into a foundation, the Ban Righ Centre for Continuing University Education, to connect mature women with the possibilities of higher education.

Women at Queen's thus began to recognize common experience and grievances. Over lunches and through telephone calls, woman professors at Queen's began to caucus. Not surprisingly, sociology professors like Mary Maxwell, Mary Morton, and Kay Herman, who worked in a department where teaching and research tended to emphasis collective effort, took a lead in activating the group. At a meeting on 6 June 1974 (which they feistily nicknamed "D-Day"), they organized themselves under the banner of the Association of Women Teaching at Queen's (AWTAQ). The group remained informal, seeing its role as unflinching advocacy. For instance, AWTAQ urged women professors to make their views on salary and benefits loudly known at the faculty association. It sponsored guest lectures on women's issues. And, once the principal launched his review committee on the status of women in 1975, the AWTAQ became, like early suffragettes, unceasing in demanding an annual statistical accounting of the recruitment of new female colleagues. The AWTAQ thus chose to stay inside the tent of policy-making at Queen's, engaging the university's culture of decision making, while at the same time voicing exasperation at its lethargy. Its impatient agenda would pulse through the next fifteen years.[87]

Early in December 1975, women at Queen's welcomed another recognition of their place in society. The Agnes Etherington Art Centre opened an exhibit of eighty-two paintings created by forty-five Canadian women artists over the two centuries down to 1970. The centre's director, Michael Bell, had come to Queen's from the picture division of the National Archives in Ottawa, and possessed a keen eye for the alignment of art with contemporary social issues. Bell determined to bring an artistic perspective to the demand for "women's liberation."

He took the exhibition's title from Shakespeare's *Love's Labour Lost*: "From women's eyes ... doth spring the true Promethean fire." Dedicated to the upcoming International Woman's Year, the exhibit was opened by Gabrielle Léger, wife of the governor general. The *From Women's Eyes*' curators, Dorothy Farr and Natalie Luckyj, made it clear that their intention was to elevate women artists in Canada out of a kind of de facto second-class status. Women brought a different perspective to the world they observed, one of equal validity. The male artists of the Group of Seven painted the rugged Canadian landscape; women artists tended to paint the people of that landscape. Painters like Depression-era painter Paraskeva Clark, Farr and Luckyj wrote in the exhibition catalogue, "have been more willing to grapple with the presentation of delicate human relationships and strong emotions than have other Canadian artists."[88] For many, the exhibit implied that just as women painters had countered discrimination at the hands of the stuffy male bastion of the Royal Canadian Academy by creating their own Women's Art Association, so too could Queen's women chart their own course. Beyond being a persuasive, if accidental, companion to Lin Good's report on the status of Queen's women, the exhibition was an immense success in attendance and national kudos, a symbolic watershed.

Vestiges of Tradition

Sweeping as change was at Queen's in these years, it should be noted that John Deutsch's determination to radically alter tradition at Queen's was not automatically applied to every received trait in the culture of the university. Nowhere was this truer than in Deutsch's defence of the Theology College, the most venerable branch of the tree of education at Queen's. The education of a Presbyterian ministry had been Queen's primordial purpose in 1841. In 1880, Theological Hall – or the "Old Arts Building," as it had originally been called – had been built in

The 1975 Agnes Etherington Art Centre's *Through Women's Eyes* exhibition not only aroused national awareness of the work of Canadian women artists, but also paralleled a growing awareness at Queen's that women lived in the shadows. Centre director Michael Bell (left) welcomes Madame Léger, wife of the governor general, who opened the exhibition. Exhibit curators Natalie Luckyj (second from right) and Dorothy Farr look on. A painting by Emily Carr hangs behind the group.

Romanesque Revival style, its limestone solidity serving to anchor the small campus. For years, the hall was simply known as "the college." Its convocation hall was etched into the memories of many alumni as a place of graduation and, sometimes later, a site for marriages. But through the twentieth century, theology at Queen's had contended with a rising tide of secularism. In 1912, the provincial government had decreed that it would no longer directly fund denominational university education. Queen's responded by altering its charter to sever its affiliation to the Presbyterian Church, thereby secularizing itself and pushing the Theology College into an arm's-length, quasi-autonomous relationship with the university. In the mid-1920s, when church union melded a majority of Methodists and Presbyterians into the United Church of Canada, Queen's Theology College became one of the feedstocks for the new church's ministry. Queen's maintained an active engagement with the college, supplying it with an annual stipend (in return for furnishing the main campus with courses on religion) and administering the small provincial grant the college received. The Theology College was represented by a single seat on the Board of Trustees and, once students joined the Senate in the late 1960s, elected a single senator. Rev.

Gordon Brown, a Queen's BD graduate of 1907 and long-time minister of Chalmers United Church in Kingston, epitomized this connection, serving on the Board of Trustees for an astonishing forty-two years until 1968, providing each meeting with an opening prayer. The principal reciprocated this filial connection by sitting on the college's board of management.

Under these arrangements, the Queen's Theology College built a respected reputation for its Bachelor of Divinity and Bachelor of Theology degrees. Like Queen's of old, it pulled its enrolment out of eastern Ontario and the Quinte region. Queen's-trained ministers were renowned for their attention to pastoral care and community service. That reputation was paralleled on Queen's campus by the presence of a university chaplain, an office ably occupied since 1947 by Rev. A.M. Laverty. "Padre" Marsh Laverty's background was that of a military padre and United Church minister; he learned quickly to adopt the role of a spiritual advisor and students' friend, an adroit adjustment in an age when Queen's was moving towards secularism from its storied reputation as a place of muscular Christianity in the days of Principal Grant. Over at the Theology College, similar adjustments became increasingly necessary. Since 1955, Dr Elias Andrews, by training an iron-willed Methodist, had acted as the college's principal. Andrews worked hard to shore up the college as enrolment fell, debts rose, and relations with the United Church became strained. In the early sixties, Principal Andrews successfully led an appeal to raise $150,000 in outside support. He negotiated with Queen's for additional space in Theology Hall, a building now shared with academic departments, such as biology and drama. He augmented his small five-member faculty, adding such talent as Dr Donald Mathers, a Scot trained at St Andrew's University and steeped in the Student Christian Movement tradition of social engagement. Mathers quickly earned a reputation as a magnetic liberal theologian and engaging lecturer in world religions, a topic of growing appeal in the latitudinarian sixties. (Deutsch was so impressed with Mathers that he tried to lure him over to the main campus with an offer of the vice-principalship, academic: Mathers declined.) In all his innovations, Andrews found an unlikely ally in John Deutsch, a Catholic. In 1962, when he was still vice-principal, administration, Deutsch had boosted the university's annual stipend to the college to $20,000. As principal, Deutsch re-engaged with the college, sensing that it reflected a core Queen's value – the connection of community outreach and social service with personal actualization through education.[89] Furthermore, Mathers's Religion 131 "Introduction to World Religions" course was attracting legions of Queen's students, a welcome quid pro quo for the university's loyalty.

Things were less rosy within the United Church of Canada. Demand for places in its theology colleges across Canada was dropping precipitously. Church membership peaked in 1966. In 1964, for instance, there were 382 would-be ministers enrolled in these colleges across the nation; by 1970, there were only 172. At Queen's, BD and BTh enrolment sagged to 38 students by 1970.[90] The United Church responded to this decline in two ways. It sought to close theology colleges outside of densely populated urban areas and to make its curriculum more ecumenical, so as to attract other denominations to its clerical training. Under this vision, there seemed little room for the narrowly dedicated Queen's divinity and theology degrees. In 1968, the United Church's board of colleges voted to transform the Queen's Theology College into "an ecumenical centre for specialized ministries." Queen's would devote itself to training chaplains for prisons and the armed forces. In response, Principal Andrews went on the offensive. He asserted that the university must not "lightly abandon the Queen's tradition in theology." The college would accommodate the training of chaplains, regardless of denomination, but to abandon its established programs in divinity and theology would erode its core purpose and its ability to supply religion courses to the university at large and thus pay its way. Ending these programs would also jeopardize Ontario's BIU support to the college for BAs supplied.[91] Again, Deutsch was supportive of Andrews, seeing the United Church's agenda as an assault on Queen's heritage and an erosion of its financial viability.

In the midst of this crisis, Andrews retired as principal of the college and was replaced by Donald Mathers. With his reputation for liberalism, Mathers was in a tight spot. He worried that stiff opposition to the church's agenda might provoke an end to the life-sustaining United Church subvention to the college. "The ecumenical age has arrived and we must take full account of it," he told his small faculty in 1971. On the other hand, he feared that the once-proud college was in danger of losing its charter mission. Deutsch continued to be supportive; he assured Mathers even before he became principal that he would fight to block any cessation of existing degree programs. This hard line registered at the Toronto headquarters of the church. In 1971, Father Edmund Roche, a respected member of the Canadian Catholic Conference, was commissioned by the United Church to divine the future of the Queen's Theological College. Would it become simply a service centre or maintain its heritage as a fully fledged centre of divinity?

Then tragedy intervened. Shortly before becoming principal of the college in July 1970, Donald Mathers became anemic. The diagnosis was incurable leukemia. With daunting fortitude, Mathers forged ahead, determined to devise a strategy to save his college. By late 1972, it came down to a race between Mathers's illness and Roche's deliberation. Death came first: on 12 September 1972 Queen's lost a dynamic teacher, a valiant Christian, and an able administrator. Two months later, Roche submitted his report, *Queen's Theological College Faces the Future*. Roche offered a palatable compromise: the college should be allowed to continue its grooming of ordained minsters, but at the same time should recognize the possibilities of continuing education for clergy in the realm of pastoral care. The United Church, he recommended, should financially support this mixed mandate, at least until its success could be evaluated a decade later. Through the winter months, United Church mandarins in Toronto hotly debated the recommendations. A hard core still favoured extinguishing Queen's right to grant degrees in divinity and theology. The matter came to a head in April 1973, when the Division of Ministry of the church met to resolve the issue. Deutsch determined to bring Queen's full prestige to bear on the decision. To fill Mathers's shoes, he had supported the appointment of Dr Charles Parker, an Old Testament specialist, as acting principal. On 28 April 1973, an unlikely delegation of Deutsch (the Catholic), Parker (the theologian), dean of Arts and Science Ron Watts (the son of an Anglican missionary to China and Japan), and Bob Little (the university lawyer and United Church member) motored to Toronto to appear before the Division of Ministry. Their purpose was clear: to demonstrate that the university was adamantly behind its theology college. The day was won. The division voted down a motion to curtail the divinity and theology degrees at Queen's by a vote of 19 to 9. To clinch its argument, the university lawyer argued that the church had no right to act unilaterally in any matter that touched the university's charter rights.[92] Back in Kingston, Deutsch was blessed for his preservation of a central Queen's tradition. Queen's men, and now women, would continue to find their way to the pulpit. But the challenge of an increasingly secular world had not been banished: the funding and sustenance of the college would remain problematic.

Deutsch's resolve to preserve elements of the Queen's tradition that he believed viable and relevant in a changing world surfaced in other spheres. The principal's own career had epitomized a deep-rooted tradition of Queen's graduates going out into the world of public service as "Ottawa men," a tradition that stretched back a half-century to Adam Shortt and O.D. Skelton. Deutsch himself had stretched this tradition, not only by feeding ideas into the federal finance department and Treasury Board, but also by supplying his insights to foreign governments and major corporations, as a consultant and corporate director. Other Queen's academics, such as political scientist John Meisel and dean of Law Bill Lederman, had close informal ties with the bureaucratic-business-legal world of Toronto.

But by the 1960s, Deutsch and other observers at Queen's began to realize that the old informal lines along which Queen's influence flowed into public policy were being superseded by the formalization of public service in Canada. The postwar growth of the welfare state had prompted a surge in public-sector employment and had made policy formation an intricate, consultative process. While there would undoubtedly be continuing opportunities for outstanding individuals of the ilk of Skelton and Mackintosh, Deustch realized that rank-and-file civil servants now needed regularized training for the business of public administration. Since the forties, Queen's had offered such input on labour economics and municipal administration through its Institute of Local Government and Institute of Industrial Relations and its economics summer school. In 1969, the university launched its Institute of Inter-governmental Relations with financial support from the McConnell Foundation and lumberman H.R. Macmillan. It would not offer degrees, but would instead act as a think tank to stimulate policy debate on issues like tax reform and Maritime union (a subject on which Deutsch reported in the mid-sixties). A former Manitoba deputy-minister, Robert Burns, was made its director. The institute organized seminars and policy studies, boasting in its literature that it was carrying on "Queen's tradition of marrying academic excellence with public administration."

The problem was that "public administration" did not fall into a neat academic compartment. As Deutsch's executive assistant, Donald Gow, himself a former federal civil servant, wrote: "There is no body of revealed truth for which we should be seeking."[93] Public administration was instead an amalgam of many disciplines. Deutsch was enthusiastic. Queen's could teach would-be public servants how to manage complex issues so as to take into account "the aspirations of the relevant sectors of society before them." They would come to realize that "there is no 'one best way.'" Instead, the focus must be on "comparative administration" and optimum "policy choice." By late 1968, the new School of Public Administration began to take shape, not as an undergraduate program but as a master's program for those with a foot already in the bureaucratic door. They would be brought to Queen's, "decompressed" from their work anxieties, and then exposed to intensive, problem-oriented policy workshops. Faculty from departments as disparate as history, law, and sociology would guide the discussions.[94] Senate approval was forthcoming, and in the fall of 1970 the first Master's of Public Administration students – many down from their jobs in Ottawa and Toronto – arrived for eleven months of insight into how policy was made and administered. Donald Gow, now director, and his faculty, along with many distinguished visitors, began delivering seminars on topics ranging from science policy to Arctic sovereignty. An old Queen's tradition found itself donning new academic garb.

The Deutsch years saw other bridges built between the academic and the applied worlds. In 1970, a School of Urban and Regional Planning was opened under the direction of civil engineer Stanley Lash. Just as Queen's had appointed Lash's colleague Graham Andrews as its planning officer, so too were Canadian towns and cities turning to planners to shape their growth. A two-year master's program was under way by 1971, offering interdisciplinary courses on such topics as urban aesthetics, human ecology, and data handling. Other centres and institutes in resource studies and guided ground transport paralleled developments in urban planning and public administration. They all catered to the growing demand for credentialed people and targeted research to guide Canada's burgeoning urban-industrial society. In the days of Bill Mackintosh, a well-placed phone call would usually turn up a promising candidate for a government opening or a research inquiry. Now a formal degree was the expectation, and Queen's would supply these. Institutes also provided a vehicle for fundraising, thereby enabling corporate and governmental backing to be built into their mission from inception. Queen's was, however, always careful to ensure that institute boards of directors or advisors always had a majority of academic appointees in order to ensure that the university's independence was protected.

Deutsch also transposed another Queen's tradition into a more structured framework. Academic careers had always been benchmarked by publication. Promotion, especially in the humanities, was geared to publication, particularly of books. But Queen's faculty had always been obliged to seek academic publishers away from their campus. There was the venerable and much-praised *Queen's Quarterly*, founded in 1893 by Principal Grant, but its focus lay in literary commentary, poetry, and short, opinionated essays. Amongst universities, there was an unspoken sense that to be a *real* university, there ought to be a university press to project the output of resident scholars. Alex Corry had sensed this need, but had also sensed that Queen's alone could not sustain such an expense. Deutsch persisted. In

September 1968, he announced that negotiations were under way for a consortium university press with the fledgling McGill University Press. Marketing studies suggested that, despite the dominance of the University of Toronto Press, there was room for a newcomer in Canadian academic publishing. Besides, Deutsch noted, the arrangement would "enhance our scholarly reputation." The McGill-Queen's University Press was thus launched in 1969 with a $60,000 annual subsidy from Queen's,[95] and editorial offices were opened in Montreal and Kingston. The new press's first publication, a study of East African multicultural states by British anthropologist Audrey Richards, appeared in 1969. Eager to feed more manuscripts in its direction, Deutsch clinched another initiative begun by Corry: as we have seen earlier, he secured the services of a senior Canadian historian, Dr Hilda Neatby of the University of Saskatchewan, to come to Queen's to write the history of its early years. Deutsch assured the trustees that Neatby would provide a "vivid account of the part that Queen's has played in the development of our country."[96]

Deutsch would see one other Corry initiative to fruition, one that would both carry Queen's one step further to being a multiversity and at the same time expand its geographic footprint. Once again the baby boom was the locomotive of change. If university classrooms were bulging in the sixties, it was because the secondary schools had already felt the swelling flow of postwar adolescence. The law decreed that children had to attend primary and secondary schools. This exerted a bedrock demand for teachers in the province. Since the mid-nineteenth century, that demand had been met by a series of "normal schools," situated in major centres like Toronto, London, and Ottawa, where the rudiments of teaching were imparted. From those days of Ontario's first superintendent of education, that zealous Methodist Egerton Ryerson, the provision of teachers had been firmly dictated by Toronto, a right embedded in the provincial government at Confederation. An early attempt to educate teachers at Queen's succumbed to Toronto's suzerainty in 1920.

However, the postwar baby boom threatened to overwhelm the province's ability to educate its own youth. Ontario became a seller's market for teachers; every spring school boards convened in Toronto's Royal York Hotel to sign up would-be teachers at what students called "the cattle market."[97] Not only was enrolment growing exponentially by the early sixties, but education was becoming a more sophisticated affair, abounding with theory and reflecting complex demands now placed on it by society – social studies, physical fitness, and even sex education. In 1951, the Ontario College of Education began offering graduate programs for teachers, followed in 1965 by the Ontario Institute for Studies in Education (OISE) as a graduate campus for the training of teachers who taught teachers. At the same time, Ontario had to devise a way to enhance its basic supply of qualified teachers.

In 1961, John Robarts, Ontario's minister of education, announced that Ontario would sponsor two new colleges of education, and that they would not be affiliated to existing teacher education in Toronto. Kingston and London were the favoured locations. Principal Mackintosh and Western's President Edward Hall were cautious. They fretted that the new teachers' colleges would have strings attached that would entail dictation from Toronto. They insisted that the new colleges be "placed within the framework of the Province." Thus began what would become a long and arduous negotiation between the politicians and bureaucrats at Queen's Park and university administrations. Although Mackintosh expressed his "warm approval" of the concept, a myriad of details, many outside the usual sphere of relations, bogged down progress. In 1964, Queen's formed a negotiating team of senior administrators – Corry, Conn, and Harrower – to strike a deal. Problems persisted. Where could already-cramped Queen's locate the college? How could it be integrated into the academic life of the university?

By 1965, a deal was struck: the province would honour the university's academic autonomy and would supply the college with an annual subsidy. A university-appointed advisory board would provide oversight. A fundamental decision was taken to locate the college away from the established campus on fifteen acres of land acquired along Palace Road, about a kilometre west of the main campus. While Queen's had planted operations away from main campus before – such as its biological research station on Lake Opinicon north of Kingston – this new, rather unimaginatively named, "West Campus" was to be a year-round academic community in its own right. Given the pressures of the start-up, understandably little thought was given at the time to connecting the fledgling campus with its mature partner seven blocks to the east. The $6.5-million education college was to be named for Duncan McArthur, a Queen's history professor who had left Kingston in the 1930s to become a highly regarded deputy-minister of education in the provincial government. McArthur College would open its doors to an anticipated throng of six hundred would-be teachers in the fall of 1967.[98]

The rosy optimism did not last long. While Toronto had agreed to regard the new college as an "integral" part of the university, the building of the large new facility entailed endless consultation with Toronto bureaucrats in two provincial ministries, a process unfamiliar to university administrators. Everything had to be referred to Toronto. Building approvals were slow in coming. Financial oversight was cumbersome. All the while, the politicians kept up the pressure for new teachers. In 1966, the new minister of education, William Davis, complained that the question of the supply of elementary teachers had become "vexatious." That same year, Queen's appointed Vernon Ready (BA Hons 1944) as the dean of the new college. Ready was a product of the normal-school tradition: a Lanark County boy, he had been pushed towards Queen's by a school inspector who noticed his bright, sunny personality. He then became a teacher and eventually principal at Kingston Collegiate Vocational Institute before joining the staff at Althouse College at the University of Western Ontario. Ready began hiring faculty, tending to select former normal-school instructors, who were proficient in imparting the day-to-day skills of teaching but possessed little interest in educational research. Most had only a BA. Ready complained about the cumbersome channelling of all his dealings with Toronto through the office of the vice-principal, administration. He also sensed that the incipient West Campus had no real connection with the main campus and that his growing group of faculty members were beginning to feel that they were in exile from the culture of the university.

It soon became apparent that the new campus, with its sprawling main building and residence complex, was woefully behind schedule. Architects were replaced and costs mounted. The initial opening date of 1967 slipped by unrealized. As the fall of 1968 crept nearer, a desperate search for temporary quarters began. The first forty students finally arrived that September and found themselves shoehorned into an old house off the main campus, and with lectures in borrowed halls. Problems continued. Construction of the college's main building – a low-slung, precast-concrete modernistic edifice that was a stark departure from main-campus limestone – was not completed until 1971, rising in cost to $8.2 million. The residences opened a year later.

There were squabbles with the province over the BIU rating of a bachelor of education degree (most students would eventually generate two BIUs for Queen's). Queen's found itself caught in the middle ground in turf wars between the ministries of education and of university affairs in Toronto. "We seem never to be out of the woods with regard to funding McArthur College," Ready dolefully confided to Deutsch in 1971.[99] That same year, in order to emphasize the college's identity as part of Queen's, it was redesignated as the Faculty of Education, and the McArthur name reapplied to the college's main building, social centre, and student street. Some progress was made: a master's degree in education was approved and an experimental program in science education was introduced. However, through the early 1970s, unresolved tensions pervaded the new faculty. Older faculty, steeped in the normal-school tradition, found little in common with Ready's younger faculty, who boasted doctorates in education and wanted to research educational theory rather than teach teachers.[100] Students complained that the curriculum was uninspired, less challenging than the honours undergraduate degrees that most had just completed. The faculty, they maintained, contained too many old mediocrities and young free spirits and too few inspiring mentors.[101]

The inchoate character of the education faculty was further undermined by a sudden downturn in enrolment in the early 1970s as the provincial hunger for new teachers sharply contracted. In the spring of 1972, Dean Ready reported to the Senate that a "sizable number" of his BEd graduates would not find employment that fall. A year later, Deutsch told the Senate that education had been the only program offered by the university where enrolment was below target.[102] Designed to take as many as nine hundred teacher candidates, the faculty would experience a steady fall in demand through the mid-seventies, dropping to as low as five hundred admissions by mid-decade. In retrospect, university planners realized the folly of blindly pouring resources into fields that seemed to hold irrepressible future promise. There were too many factors to control in these fields – stiff competition from other universities, demographic twists, shifts in public attitude – and a university could easily find itself carrying heavy overheads for programs in which demand was cyclical or vulnerable. Deutsch had thus helped to assist in the rebirth of Queen's Faculty of Education, but he never managed to work the faculty into a completely viable and relevant entity. The West Campus largely remained *terra incognita* to those on the main campus. By 1971, Deutsch's mind had necessarily shifted to other, more fiscally challenging, matters. The Faculty of Education was left as unfinished business.

Deutsch accompanies newly elected Ontario premier Bill Davis at the opening of McArthur College of Education in 1971. As education minister, Davis had placed persistent pressure on Queen's to create a college of education. In the background, students protest inflation-driven fee increases.

The Public Mood Begins to Shift

As chairman of the Economic Council of Canada in the mid-sixties, John Deutsch had commissioned studies on the economic impact of education. Influenced by the work of American economists like Gary Becker (later a Nobel laureate), Canadian economists attempted to plot the impact of education on economic productivity and living standards. The news, they reported, was largely positive. Higher education not only boosted national economic output, but it also brought "private returns to educational investment."[103] At some visceral level throughout the sixties, the broader public embraced this belief and transmitted it to politicians. A university degree was a ticket on the train of upward mobility or, as a young, Princeton-trained economist at Queen's, David Dodge, put it, a degree was as good as a "union card." As the decade wore on, that simplistic creed began to lose adherents. Vietnam-generated inflation, rising unemployment, and the faltering of Keynesian economic management into stagflation tarnished the allure of higher education and prompted questioning of whether its soaring cost was merited. Others alleged that universities were hardly social equalizers, but instead bastions of entrenched privilege. Student radicals attacked their universities as captives of big business and the state power. Academics themselves began to cast aspersions on their own bailiwick. By 1972, David Dodge, himself a former Queen's undergraduate, could bring cruel cost-benefit analysis to the proposition: "At first glance it appears that public investment in higher education should be curtailed on purely economic grounds, since the social returns calculated at a reasonable approximation of the social rate of discount (ten percent) are negative."[104] For the public, the glow of a college degree also seemed to fade. Whether prompted by news that a bachelor of education had not automatically translated into classroom employment or the suspicion that an arts degree fit few identifiable employment niches, university education was losing some of its lustre. As Judge Walter Little warned his fellow trustees in 1971, there was "an increasing resentment by the public against the high percentage of tax dollars which are being spent on education."[105] As if to drive Little's point home, the trustees at the same meeting learned that Queen's most-recent capital campaign, with its goal of $6.5 million, had fallen well short of expectation. Even the alumni were having second thoughts.

Deutsch was quick to sense that the landscape around secondary education was changing. In 1971–72, he had served as a member of the Commission on Post-Secondary Education in Ontario, the so-called Wright Commission. The commission's report, *The Learning Society*, took stock of Ontario's gains in post-secondary education over the last decade. The report did not forsake the goal of broad public access to university education, even going so far as to advocate an "open university" for the province. But it also came down emphatically in favour of greater accountability of universities to the government and people of the province. There should be "more scholar for the dollar," to quote historian Paul Axelrod. The commission set out mechanisms for tighter control of the universities, while agreeing that university autonomy should be "buffered" from the homogenization of tight state control. Like many commissions, the Wright Report provoked much discussion and only a modicum of action, but it did mark a watershed, and the Ontario Council on University Affairs did materialize to mediate between scholarly and political agendas. Nonetheless, the halcyon days of post-secondary growth were clearly over. Very quickly, the "sixties" would work their way into the reminiscences of Ontario academics as days of unbridled growth and boundless expectations. By contrast, universities now entered a period of constantly contested existence. Politicians began to demand accountability and to attach strings to BIUs, while at the same time reciting the sixties mantra of accessibility.

Deutsch had spent enough years around the corridors of power to detect the changed message. By 1972, he was warning the trustees and the Senate that lean times lay ahead. On one flank, inflation – climbing steadily into double digits by mid-decade – gnawed at Queen's spending power. It also created pressure on the university's fee structure. On the other hand, Queen's Park, which was by now the predominant payer of the university's operational costs, was itself pinched by a contracting provincial economy and being pushed into austerity budgeting. Here the fundamental governor on support of the universities was the annual setting of the BIU, the key denominator of provincial post-secondary subsidization. And, of course, the BIU was in a fiscal dance with enrolment: any combination of falling enrolment and BIU stinginess spelled hard times for the universities. The drama was heightened by the fact that Queen's Park did not usually reveal its BIU equivalent until mid-winter, well after the universities had been obliged to prepare and set their budgets for the upcoming academic year. University finances in the seventies thus became an ongoing high-wire act, with a constantly churning calculation of BIU input, fees, faculty salaries, and capital costs reducing university planners to a state of perpetual anxiety. Here Queen's would be well served by its cautious "steady state" strategy: having avoided the temptation of headlong expansion, it was now left with its top-notch reputation intact and, consequently, a very high take-up rate on admissions each spring and a strong ongoing retention rate.

Deutsch – a Prairie boy who had seen how the Depression had derailed a whole society in the Dirty Thirties – had positioned Queen's well for the downturn, but he was still obliged to deliver worrisome news. In the spring of 1972, for instance, he grimly informed the trustees that Queen's costs were rising about 7 to 9 per cent annually, but that George Kerr, the minister of colleges and universities, had belatedly informed him that the BIU would increase by only 2 per cent, to $1,765, for the upcoming year. Kerr had also reminded the principal that the province was facing a $600-million deficit, perhaps to cushion the news that the province was also freezing funding of all capital projects on Ontario campuses – news that particularly hit Queen's slowly unfolding plans for the integrated health-sciences complex that Harry Botterell had insisted was the future of medicine at Queen's. When Toronto reduced funding for graduate fellowships and stipulated that graduate students pay fees through the summer, Deutsch announced that Queen's ambitious plan to expand its faculty would likely be crimped. Ironically, Deutsch pointed out, any contraction in graduate studies would hobble efforts to Canadianize faculty across the country, a much-desired goal in the sixties. The financial squeeze was intensified by a 3.5-per-cent salary increase for faculty, a boost Deutsch argued was necessary to retain quality instruction and research. The only mitigation of this intensifying financial gloom was a small $100 increase in fees for 1973, the first since 1964 and one that only marginally offset growing costs. The words "uncertainty," "discouragement," and "deficit" began to punctuate the narrative at Board of Trustee and Senate meetings.[106] The *New York Times* dubbed Deutsch "an affable male Cassandra."[107] No doubt, trustees and senators must have at times conjured up the memory of Principal Grant and wondered if the history of Queen's was indeed cyclical and whether the bad times might return.

At the 12 October 1973 meeting of the trustees, Deutsch had some good news: Queen's enrolment was holding up well. While province-wide admissions had dropped, Queen's enrolment that fall was up 5 per cent, to 9,150, on course for the "steady state" ceiling of 10,000. At the same time, the percentage of women enrolled at Queen's had continued to grow, to 40 per cent. But there was no avoiding the fact that a deficit in the neighbourhood of $500,000 loomed, to be offset by accumulated surpluses. Queen's, it seemed, was making the best of a worsening situation. But then Deutsch surprised the trustees: he had decided to retire. He was, he told them, in his sixty-fourth year, and he felt that his policies were "coming to completion." It was time for a "younger man." The job of principal was "very challenging but demanding."[108] And indeed it was. Deutsch had allowed the job to devour him. His reputation for judicious policy management was paralleled by his unflagging devotion to the office he occupied. One Christmas morning, for instance, assistant registrar Ralfe Clench popped into his Richardson Hall office to collect some papers. Clench, a brilliant-but-quirky mathematician, had a knack for untangling classes and examinations, a valuable talent in an age before computers sorted these things out with a bit of astute programming. As he packed papers into his satchel, Clench heard noises upstairs. A burglar? He went to investigate, only to discover the principal working in his office. Pouncing on the opportunity to get the principal to himself, Clench asked for ten minutes. Ten minutes, Deutsch replied. The compulsively punctual Clench pulled out his stopwatch and proceeded to bend the principal's ear for exactly the allotted time.[109] By 1973, such relentless toil had taken its toll. Deutsch's driver, an ex-military man named Raymond Teepell, recalled that, early in his pricipalship, Deutsch had used his frequent trips to Toronto and Ottawa to wade through correspondence and reports. Now, Deutsch dozed in the back seat.[110]

In an age of mandatory retirement, the trustees had assumed that Deutsch would remain in office until 1975. Many, like Board chairman James Gibson and Chancellor Bert Stirling (men who had seen how Deutsch had lifted Queen's prestige beyond its campus), pleaded with Deutsch to remain, but he would not change his decision. Reluctantly, the Board struck the now-standard joint committee of sixteen senators and trustees, chaired by Chancellor Stirling, to select a new principal. There was an added poignancy to the search, in that Stirling himself had announced his intention to step down as chancellor after over a decade of stalwart and popular service. In January, Deutsch announced that former governor general Roland Michener, one-time lawyer and federal Conservative MP, would assume the chancellorship that April. A month after that colourful installation (at which the university awarded an honorary degree to Michener's wife, Norah, a political scientist), the joint committee reported that it had found its man. Eighty-five nominations had been received and short-list candidates had been interviewed over four days. Many speculated that Vice-Principal Harrower, with his broad experience, was the man. But the nod went to Dean of Arts and Science Ron Watts. In 1978, George Harrower became president of Lakehead University.

Watts knew Queen's, having taught philosophy and political studies there since 1955. His expertise in federal-provincial relations seemed to suit him for the give-and-take of university governance, particularly since, if Deutsch was right in his prognostication, tough times were ahead. Many remarked that Queen's political economists seemed to own the keys to Richardson Hall. Few, however, could deny that Mackintosh, Corry, and Deutsch had modernized and codified the university and that the wand of political science had been formatively waved over the campus. Watts also fit the bill as the "younger man" that the outgoing principal urged the university to seek. He was only forty-five years old, over a decade younger than Deutsch had been in 1968. He was so young, in fact, that he had to query the trustees whether they wanted him to linger in the post until he turned sixty-five. Probably not, they conceded, and offered Watts a five-year, renewable term. Watts took over on 1 October 1974. The next issue of the *Queen's Alumni Review* carried a cover picture of the new principal, with a devil-may-care grin on his face, racing around the football stadium track on a tricolour-draped bike in a United Way fundraising race. It would probably be the easiest contest that Watts would encounter over the next ten years.

Queen's new principal Ronald Watts races around Richardson Stadium.

134   TESTING TRADITION

4

"A Puzzle of Patterns"
Student and Faculty Life, 1961–1974

Will Queen's rise to the challenge, or will she shout another coarse
'Oil Thigh' and head for The Chalet?
John Isbister, *Queen's Journal*, 17 October 1961

The old informal, paternalistic (in the good sense) position of the university
is passing away as the university grows, and the newer relationships
based on contract replace the older ones relying on usage and custom.
J.A. Corry's 1963 address to faculty association

Never again, quite possibly, will limestone loyalty of the last few years exist.
Chris Redmond, *Queen's Journal*, 9 February 1971

A World We Have Lost

Everyone agreed that it was a capital place to live. Since 1927, Miss Bertha Bailey, a spinster with United Empire Loyalist roots, had maintained a rambling rooming house and small apartments at #135–39 Union Street, which she filled each year with Queen's students. The picturesque Victorian row house was fashioned in so-called Carpenter Gothic style, with bay windows and gable board aplenty. To land a room with Bertha Bailey meant that classes, the library, the gym, and the Students' Memorial Union were all just minutes away. Bill Sirman, the fleet-footed wingback on Frank Tindall's Yates Cup–winning football team, had, for example, an apartment at the front of #139, just a short forward pass away from his daily practice venue at Richardson Stadium across the street.[1] Miss Bailey loved to chat with her boarders and was always there to supply tea and a sympathetic ear. Late in the evening she would announce that her famous banana cream pie and cookies were available for snacking. Bertha the landlady seemed to be straight out of Stephen Leacock's famous "boarding-house geometry": "an oblong angular figure … which cannot be described, but which is equal to anything." Bertha's boarders proved a loyal lot. They once formed an intramural hockey team in her honour – "Bertha Bailey's Battling Bearcats" – and trooped down the street to play at the venerable Jock Harty Arena. Rooming at Bertha's remained a Queen's tradition until she died in 1974.[2]

Bailey had lots of competition. Kingston's Sydenham Ward, to the east and north of the campus, was dotted with rooming houses dedicated to the men of Queen's. Many supplied regular meals. "Ask for Wilmots Dairy milk in your boarding house," ran an advertisement in the *Queen's Journal*. On average, in the early sixties, a room cost between $12 and $14 a week. Just across the street from Bertha Bailey's boarding house, for instance, at the corner of Union and University, stood the famous – some would say *infamous* – "Hotel Austin," a boarding house run by Miss Margaret Austin, sister of one-time Queen's surgery professor Dr L.J. "Blimey" Austin. Austin's boys lived student life to its fullest; the house was largely furnished with items purloined from local taverns and hotels. Miss Austin's end-of-term sherry party must have seemed a rather tame affair to most of her roomers.

In the fall of 1961, only 612 of the 2,219 male students at Queen's were accommodated in campus residences. Housing men on campus was a belated initiative at Queen's. In 1955, McNeill House had opened, followed by Morris Hall in 1958 and Leonard Hall in 1959, all of which were situated on a six-acre plot generously donated by Col. R.W. Leonard. Slowly, Queen's was adopting an English model of accommodating its students: housing them on the edge of the academic precinct in the hope that the residences would become places of "informal education."[3] In the interim, however, most Queen's men lived under the sway of the matrons of Sydenham Ward or, if they were lucky, they were accepted into Science Co-op '44, a cluster of student houses run on co-operative principles. Room and board there was $15.50 a week.

Males enjoyed other gender prerogatives around Queen's. Since 1889, all male students in Arts and Science were banded together in the Arts Society, women students having broken away into their own Levana Society in that year. And for the male student in search of a game of billiards, a cup of coffee, or a meal, the Students' Memorial Union on the corner of University and Union was an exclusively male bastion. Rebuilt after a 1947 fire, "the Union" grudgingly allowed women access to the business offices in the building, but continued to let the boys enjoy their dining room and smoking lounge. Well into the 1960s, Queen's males might also don a martial persona by parading at the weekly army, navy, and airforce "university training" unit musters on campus.

A ten-minute walk south from the Union brought one to the campus's female precinct. Women at Queen's in the early sixties were far more cloistered than their male counterparts. Since the late-nineteenth century, women at Queen's had lived a tightly bound associational life. Since 1911, there had been an "advisor" to women students, the post becoming designated dean of women in 1918. Still very much in a minority in the student body, women passing through Queen's nonetheless formed a lasting affiliation with the place. As early as 1900, women graduates had formed an Alumnae Association, dedicated to promoting "any scheme for the special benefit of women students."[4] One such early scheme was the provision of modern residence accommodation for women. Hitherto, women students had resided in scattered off-campus boarding houses, including the legendary "Hencoop" at 174 Earl Street. By the 1920s, the association's assiduous fundraising made possible the construction of Ban Righ Hall – *ban righ* meaning "wife of the king" in Gaelic – opposite the Lower Campus. Other residences followed – Adelaide Hall (named for the wife of General Motors mogul Sam McLaughlin) in 1952 and Chown Hall

Bertha Bailey's Union Street boarding house in the early 1990s, about to be moved from its original Union Street location around the corner onto Alfred Street. Heritage activists argued that the house could not be sacrificed to make room for the new Stauffer Library. Queen's would win a heritage award for its relocation of the gabled and fabled old building.

(named for May Chown, the long-time treasurer of the Ban Righ board, which in 1960 oversaw the women's residences). Six converted homes on the edge of campus also accommodated female students. The Science '44 Co-op even maintained Boucher House as a women-only residence. Thus, by the early sixties, half of Queen's women lived on campus: in 1961–62, 440 of the 870 female students registered at the university lived in a residence.

Under the watchful and benevolent eye of Dean of Women Beatrice Bryce, women undergraduates in residence lived a measured life. Men were banned from the dormitory floors, but were allowed in the common rooms at prescribed hours. There were curfews, "quiet hours," and high-table dinners. Skirts – never pants or jeans – were worn to dinner. Sunday-afternoon teas were served. A nurse was always on duty. Bryce issued edicts on proper deportment: in the evening, women students were advised "to go in twos." In her 1963 report to the Ban Righ board, Dean Bryce described her dedication to "the practical routine of settling some four hundred intelligent, normal young women into a pattern of living that will be an integral part of their University life ... We operate on the principle of rather careful supervision of Freshettes in their first year, with extended privileges in the second."[5] Perhaps the key word here was "pattern." Cathy Perkins, a late 1950s Arts student, caught the mood in Adelaide Hall: "More often than not, one could find a quiet game of bridge in the common room, or perhaps some maths and physics genius trading his 'know-how' for some tutoring in English or French, or again a more casual group absorbed in TV, Coke, and one another in the basement games rooms."[6]

Hovering over these two gendered spheres of student life at Queen's was the Alma Mater Society, Canada's oldest system of student self-government. The AMS drew its authority from faculty society representatives delegated to sit on the society's executive council, its main deliberative body. The council, in turn, elected the president of the AMS out of its own ranks. Lacking a direct electoral connection to the student body, the AMS executive was clubby and self-regulating, not to mention prone to perpetuating the received tradition and policies of Queen's student government. As if to anchor student decision making, a non-student, Herb Hamilton, the editor of the *Alumni Review*, served as the permanent secretary-treasurer of the AMS. Frequent referenda were employed to seek student approval of myriad fees, which were added to their tuition to cover the cost of student-oriented services, ranging from support of the radio station CFRC and the *Queen's Journal* to dues paid to the National Federation of Canadian University Students. The AMS executive also vetted the constitutions of, and subsidized, a constellation of student clubs, embracing activities from sports-car rallying to the Student Christian Movement. Committees of the AMS oversaw an annual cycle of social events stretching from alumni reunion weekend in the fall to Snowball and Susie-Q weeks in mid-winter. The AMS also acted as the impresario of student concerts, bringing the Oscar Peterson Trio and renowned Spanish guitarist Andrés Segovia to campus in 1961–62.

On the whole, the AMS dedicated itself with great efficiency to what might be called the *associational* life of Queen's students.[7] Dances, bands, Colour Night athletic banquets, and even its own justice system ran like clockwork year-in, year-out, all celebrated in the AMS-funded *Tricolor* yearbook. But the culture of student government at Queen's was at the same time introverted and self-satisfied. Social and political issues unfolding beyond the campus seldom entered campus dialogue. Snowball ice sculptures in 1962 featured Kennedy and Khrushchev going nose to nose over Cuba, and the annual model parliament debated issues of national import, but these were more pastimes than commitments. In the fall of 1961, AMS President Stewart Goodings complained that the AMS had fallen into the habit of addressing day-to-day issues to the exclusion of "broader issues."[8] As if to make his point, Goodings and two colleagues went on a three-day "starvation diet" to draw attention to world poverty. The *Journal* covered the fast, but few students seemed much interested.[9] "Will Queen's rise to the challenge," John Isbister editorialized, "or will she shout another coarse 'Oil Thigh' and head for The Chalet?" Most, it seemed, opted for The Chalet, where draft beer was fifteen cents a glass, or Wilmots Dairy Bar on Bath Road for a milkshake.

Queen's faculty inhabited much the same cozy, parochial world as the sixties dawned. Older faculty had become inured to the rhythms of life in the Limestone City, integrating with life there through amateur dramatics, choirs, and poetry readings on radio CKWS. They had also grown comfortable with their colleagues who had risen in the ranks to deanships and offices in Richardson Hall. Newly hired younger faculty initially found the campus and city attractive in a kind of Ivy League manner, but regarded life in Kingston as stale and claustrophobic. Many had arrived from graduate studies in places renowned for their academic glamour – Oxford, Cambridge, and even Toronto. Life in Kingston and at Queen's seemed like a prosaic deceleration. When Christiane Fleig-Hamm arrived from France in 1963 to teach French and later manage the language labs, she was horrified by her football-player students with their T-shirts and "hairy legs." They were "a circus," she recalled. "I thought I was in the far west. I thought, you know, this is not civilization."[10]

A few years later, Welsh-born Brian Osborne arrived at Queen's after a stint of teaching in Colorado. He liked Queen's limestone and his new geography department, which was expanding rapidly under Richard Ruggles's dynamic headship. But Kingston depressed him: it was a "very, very internal-looking community with few social facilities."[11]

Similarly, Roy Walmsley, who joined physical therapy in 1967 from England, initially found Kingston "a little hick town"[12] with poor shopping. In 1959, Queen's reached out to the French fact in Canada by hiring Québécois writer Gérard Bessette. Some years later, Bessette penned a *roman á clef* about life in his adopted city, which he dubbed *Narcotown* – a place of sullen monotony.[13]

Remarkably for most, this jadedness soon wore off as newcomers themselves relaxed into the comfort of small-city academic life. Osborne quickly came to relish the "family" feeling at Queen's. Roy Walmsley, having found the Queen's rehabilitation program "very congenial," stayed thirty years. Carlos Prado, arriving in the philosophy department from California and Hawaii, was immediately impressed by a campus "totally focused on first-class undergraduate education."[14] English professor David Helwig and his wife, Nancy, quickly connected with the local literary scene. Nancy became involved in the Domino Theatre, a local amateur troupe, and the Faculty Players, while David attached himself to a small Bohemian colony on West Street, just across City Park from campus, where aspiring poets like Tom Marshall and Michael Ondaatje contributed work to *Quarry*, Kingston's literary quarterly.[15] Back in the departments, young faculty generally melded into the established common-room culture of the faculty – morning coffee in the lounge, lunch in Wallace Hall, and play rehearsal or sailing on the lake in the evening. They also began to alter the culture of the place: drama professor Fred Euringer arrived from the Stratford Festival and immediately revitalized theatre at Queen's with plays by Albee and Sartre.[16]

In the buoyant sixties job market, many newcomers to Queen's chose to move on to what they imagined were greener academic fields, but many stayed. Nowhere was this more apparent than in the quiescence of the faculty association, the Queen's University Faculty Association (QUFA), formed in 1951. To adopt a word popular in the sixties, QUFA enjoyed a copasetic relationship with the university administration. Each year, the principal addressed the annual dinner of the association, and the QUFA president enjoyed the ear of Richardson Hall. The rhetoric on both sides was reverential and cooperative. Principal Corry was an enthusiastic member, as were his deans. Queen's faculty also took a keen interest in national academic affairs, voicing its concerns through the Canadian Association of University Teachers (CAUT). When the CAUT-sponsored Duff-Berdahl Report on university governance arrived at Queen's in 1966, Principal Corry immediately relayed it to QUFA for its reaction. The administration was desperate in the hot academic employment market of the baby-boom years to attract and retain staff. Although QUFA was affiliated with CAUT, it tended to be resistant to the more demanding agenda of that body's more urbanized academics. The ethos of academic life at Queen's thus remained collegial and non-confrontational. If there was an incipient bone of contention, it was salaries. Measured on grids supplied by CAUT, Queen's salaries lagged those of big-city universities. In 1963, for instance, a full professor at Queen's earned $13,000, about $2,000 less than the national average. The phrase "catch-up" began to enter, however politely, the faculty-administration dialogue.[17]

In fact, the relative tranquility and self-satisfaction of student and faculty life at Queen's in the early sixties was in its twilight. Over the next decade, inexorable changes would occur. They would work to fragment the once-tight, homogeneous campus life of Queen's and force the university to address the increasingly pluralistic society that surrounded it. Much of what would transpire in the years down to the mid-seventies would defy easy description. In the words of the 1970 *Tricolor*, "a puzzle of patterns" emerged. The AMS would be jolted alive by the shifting social and intellectual sensibilities of the topsy-turvy decade. It would fundamentally alter its constitution, acquire the status of an incorporated enterprise, and alter its central purpose from being the organizer of happy times on campus to being the coordinator of *services* relevant

AMS Clubs' Night, 1968. Student clubs have a deep tradition at Queen's; the AMS itself emerged out of a debating society in the 1850s. Each year clubs, funded by student-approved fees, gave student passions outlets as varied as the radio club CFRC (pictured here) and the Queen's Young New Democrats.

to the daily life of students. The tradition of student self-government would persist, but the purposes of that autonomy would become more utilitarian and responsive. "Queen's is a university in transition," the *Tricolor* would reflect in 1971. "It is a slow transition, sometimes protested, but more often accepted and familiar, marked by meticulous planning and execution." Faculty members, too, would adjust their attitudes and purposes in the university community, away from the expansive mood of the sixties to a more defined and negotiated stance in the seventies. As early as 1963, the prescient Corry saw the change coming: "the old informal, paternalistic (in the good sense) position of the university is passing away as the university grows, and the newer relationships based on contract replace the older ones relying on usage and custom."[18]

Exiting the Flabby Fifties

The ground began to shift under the AMS as the sixties progressed. The complacent attitudes of what the *Queen's Journal* labelled the "flabby Fifties" were increasingly found wanting by the standards of the more socially conscious new decade.[19] Early in the decade, the *Journal* preached traditional sermons to the student body, exhorting them to be "good citizens" and abide by AMS bylaw #12, which sought to keep liquor out of the [football] stadium.[20] The tenor of student government was timely and efficient internal housekeeping: a Meds student was, for instance, fined by the AMS court for sporting an unapproved athletic "Q" on his jacket.[21] But soon more pressing worldly issues began to infiltrate the student dialogue. As English-Canadians began to take note of Quebec's socio-economic awakening – a surge of modernization dubbed the "Quiet Revolution" by the *Globe and Mail* – some at Queen's took notice. "Most French-Canadians feel themselves limited, humiliated, and even oppressed by their position as a minority in Canada," the *Journal* reported after two Queen's students returned from a conference at Laval University.[22] This stimulated the AMS executive to propose adopting a bilingual letterhead for its stationery. The purpose was "to strike a blow against Quebec separatism" by sending an empathetic message that Queen's, a supposed bastion of Anglo-Canada, cared.[23] Few seemed to agree, however. A wag on AMS council countered by proposing that Gaelic would be a more appropriate bilingual gesture, since Queen's in fact was more closely tied to Scotland than Quebec. The issue went to a student referendum, where a large majority voted for familiar unilingualism. There were, however, a few islands of interest in Quebec's awakening: political scientist John Meisel offered a course on the province's political culture, and French professor Gérard Bessette introduced Queen's students to the literature of his native province.

A growing restlessness among some Queen's students persisted. A cartoon – "Missing the Boat" – in the *Journal* in late 1963 took aim at student apathy. The good ship Queen's, packed with carousing students, sails through the "cool sea" over an "undercurrent of apathy," ignoring a nearby isolated island where a socially and politically engaged student makes a bid for their attention.[24] Ironically, the AMS's subsidization of clubs like the Young Liberals, New Democrats, Progressive Conservatives, the debating union, and the Student Christian Movement served to sustain this dissident opinion. Confronted with lethargy on campus, such groups connected with like-minded activists spread across the country. A branch of the Student Union for Peace Action (SUPA), a group dedicated to opposing the horrific prospect of a nuclearized world, sprung up at Queen's. On Remembrance Day 1965, SUPA's president at Queen's, an articulate Arts student named Bronwen Wallace, circulated a petition against the Vietnam War. Soaking up thinking from the New Left, with its strident critique of capitalism and the "military-industrial complex," Wallace said SUPA was "the only rebellion in town."[25] Peace activism, she argued, had "a strong idea of what should be, and a clear sense of what is."[26] But SUPA remained a fringe movement at Queen's, with its adherents eventually spinning off in various directions. For instance, some continued to resist the Cold War, blockading the Wolfe Island and Thousand Islands border crossings to protest American nuclear testing in Alaska. Others opted for social-welfare activism. In the summer of 1965, for instance, a contingent of Queen's students, including Wallace, ventured into North Kingston, the city's poorest precinct, to act as social workers and advocates for the powerless in society. Given moral backing by Principal Corry and politics professor John Meisel, the project was intended to "spectacularize" Kingston poverty and assail slum landlords.[27]

New Left perspectives surfaced elsewhere on campus. As the decade progressed, the *Queen's Jour-*

A cartoon from the *Queen's Journal* of 19 October 1963. A boatload of partying Queen's students sails blithely past an island of political awareness from which bottled messages of political import are cast into the seas of apathy.

nal increasingly shed its "good times" demeanour and became the impatient voice of change. "The central political value of the New Left," the paper editorialized in 1966, "lies in its concept of participatory democracy." By this measure, it concluded, Queen's students suffered from "intellectual castration."[28] There was, however, a problem: the editor of the *Journal* was appointed by the AMS executive and the AMS collected the fees that subsidized the paper's production – and, on occasion, its deficits. Throughout the decade, tension grew between the mother society and the editors it appointed. The society believed that the *Journal's* principal function was to propagate its news – football, social events, council debates – while the editors increasingly sought to look beyond the campus. Wilf Day, editor late in the 1960s, liked to say that news was not about what *had* happened, but instead was about what *about to happen*; a newspaper was in the business of making things happen.[29] Students could be agents of change. To make the point, Day ran a picture of protest folk singer Phil Ochs on the front page of the

Journal with a caption that was a quotation from one of his songs: "When I've got something to say, sir, I'm gonna say it now."[30] This sentiment was often echoed in the work of *Journal* writers.

Krista Maeots, an undergraduate from Alberta with a keen eye for social justice and a fierce pen, argued that a Queen's education was more about socializing young Canadians to the status quo than promoting "self-realization and individualization." Queen's, she concluded, was "one of the most class-oriented" campuses in the country, one that had been "suckled in the bosom of a community that once harboured what passed for an aristocracy in Canada."[31] Another Queen's student, James Laxer, in the history graduate program, carried such sensibilities to a broader audience when he became the head of the Canadian University Press, the news agency of the National Federation of Canadian University Students.

Throughout the decade, *Journal* editors such as Robert Crown, John Rae, Tony Tugwell, Krista Maeots, and Day enjoyed hot-and-cold relations with the AMS. At heart was the issue of journalistic freedom: whether the paper followed orders or its own instincts. Crown was, in fact, fired from the editorship in 1963 for failing to toe the AMS official line. Day in 1968 took the offence, upping production to two issues a week and adding a weekly magazine, *Focus*, to showcase long, thematic articles. When the pressure of his law studies obliged Day to step down, the new editors, Bill Martin and John McIntyre, adopted a satirical approach to the Queen's status quo, describing the students as "sheep" and whimsically advocating the erection of a "crystal pleasure dome" and the purchase of the Green Bay Packers football team as a sop for their sensibilities. The ongoing frustrations felt in the *Journal*'s cramped basement offices in the Union seemed to bear witness to the smug solidity of Queen's student culture in the sixties and early seventies. After only ten people showed up at a campus rally against the Vietnam War in 1967, organizer Tom Beckett woefully admitted that "it looks like the Gaels are a better drawing card than we are."[32]

George Anderson, a politics student who had been Queen's representative to the Canadian Union of Students, similarly reported his dismay at the complacency of his home campus. A university, he urged, "should be dedicated to more than the perpetuation of its own customs." Like Maeots, he came to see Queen's as "the saddest sort of intellectual community, that which has a prior conception of truth."[33] Almost as if to confirm the point, the Queen's engineering society in the fall of 1967 sponsored the birth of its own campus newspaper, *Golden Words*. Often prone to juvenilia, *Golden Words* dedicated itself to celebrating the seemingly tried-and-true at Queen's: beer, wenches, and the macho maleness of engineering, not to mention lampooning the "peaceniks." Few took it seriously.

Anderson, Maeots, and Beckett perhaps underestimated the impact of sixties' controversy on their fellow students. The appearance of protest on campus, discontent with the prevalent campus culture in the *Journal*, and the ongoing debate over Queen's attachment to national student lobbies such as the Canadian Union of Students with its impatient agendas, all served to soften the shell of Queen's traditional student culture. Students at Queen's were being obliged to shed their introverted self-satisfaction and look to wider horizons. Campus dialogue started to reflect the broader Canadian dialogue over social participation and the quest for a more inclusive "just society." In particular, student activism in Quebec, fanned by the birth pangs of the Quiet Revolution, mesmerized students in English Canada. The process at Queen's, perhaps predictably, would be slow and conservatively paced. But the broader agitation would serve to reawaken an old, if slumbering, Queen's tradition: a conviction that education was about social utility, about combining individual ambition with social betterment. By the early 1970s, the hard-edged social activism of SUPA had largely spent itself and percolated into the formation of the Queen's Student Volunteer Bureau, which dispatched students into the Kingston community to "do good."

Goodbye Susie-Q

The shell of student tradition at Queen's was also fractured in these years by dramatic shifts in gender relations. Queen's students had always lived in a powerfully heterosexual culture. "What's the sport of kings?" went the chant at football games. "Queen's, Queen's, Queen's" came the answer. Overt sexism abounded. "Cheerleaders defeat Western 36–22–36," the *Queen's Journal* boasted in 1961.[34] *Journal* reporting frequently lapsed into blatant sexism: "This week, the *Journal* news staff has been stretched thinner than Jayne Mansfield's leotards, trying to cover the multitude activities of Susie-Q Week."[35]

In orientation week in the sixties, "freshettes" were required to print their name and telephone number on the back of their frosh uniform. Senior-year engineers rated the new females on a faux Olympic-style rating system and put the "stunners," who earned an "8" or higher, on their "bull sheet." Science '69 furthered this process by publishing the *Freshette Book*, a compendium of the names, addresses, and phone numbers of all incoming female students.[36] When Ralph Clench, not only the university's systems man in the sixties but also the honorary president of the AMS, was asked to design student ID cards suited to the computer age, he came up with pink cards for girls and blue cards for boys. (When the blue cards ran out, theology students were asked to make do with pink.)[37]

Once a year, during Susie-Q Week, roles were reversed, and the girls could chase the boys. "Susie-Q Cannibalette Courting Procedures" were set out in the *Journal*, and the week culminated in a Grant Hall dance at which "prize captives" could be paraded.[38] In late 1968, the *Journal* editorialized that Queen's was locked in a time warp in which women were "expected to set the 'moral standards' of the university." Almost as a counterpoise to such notions of campus femininity, Queen's men established their own demonstrations of rugged maleness. In 1956, for instance, Chief FREC (short for the menacing Frosh Regulation Enforcement Committee), Ron "Porky" Eady, erected a football goalpost stolen from the University of Toronto in a pit full of grease and offal and required the exclusively male freshman of Applied Science to remove a tam from its top. Upper-year engineers complicated the task by hurling "missiles" – tomatoes, rotten fruit, and even dung – at the would-be male engineers of Science '60.[39] For much of the sixties, Queen's thus remained a place where "boys were boys and girls were girls."

The principal bulwark of female sanctity at Queen's, as we have seen, was the Levana Society, founded in 1889 to provide coed students at the university with a point of convergence and mutual support. It is inviting to portray the Levana Society as some sort of throwback, a recidivist backwater. However, at a time when women were a conspicuous minority at Queen's, Levana provided them with considerable sway over their own destiny on campus. The Levana chant hinted at this autonomy: "Arts forever / Queen's forever / Women's rights or war." Levana governed women's athletics, orchestrated women's social activities, and provided a forum for the discussion of women's issues. Beauty contests, fashion shows, and afternoon teas punctuated the Levana year. Women graduated from Queen's en masse as "Levanites," appearing as a separate section of BA's in the yearbook. Levana "girls" invariably resurfaced in the industrious Alumnae Society, raising funds and awareness that eased the way for future women coming to Queen's or leaving it for graduate study elsewhere.[40] Such gendered traditions remained strongly entrenched: in 1977, when asked in an AMS referendum whether Susie-Q Week should go, 82 per cent of voters said "keep it."

"A Puzzle of Patterns" 143

Two "freshettes" (left) during initiation in the late 1960s. Incoming females, the vast majority of whom were entering Arts, were in effect put on display for their male counterparts. During orientation week, women students were obliged to display their name and telephone numbers on their backs for ready identification by potential suitors. Grease-pole mayhem (right) in 1963

But, by the late sixties, this utility nonetheless began to grate against second-wave feminism and its impatience with preconceived notions of women's trajectory in society. The very fact that women at Queen's found themselves defined and organized by gender, rather than by their academic ambition, ran against the grain of sixties' feminism, which sought to liberate women from constraining compartments (or, in later terminology, from living under "glass ceilings"). "The Levana Society," Dean of Women Bea Bryce noted, "is no longer a small group fighting for recognition and privilege."[41] The existence of Levana invited stereotyping of women: "Are Levanites Aggressive?" wondered the *Journal* in 1963.[42] Women at Queen's were, however, by the early sixties increasingly shifting their sense of identity to their faculties and the career vistas that they opened up in life. Dr. Vibert Douglas, dean of women from 1939 to 1959, had, after all, been a world-renowned astrophysicist and role model, who saw her gender as an important, but not a defining, factor in her career motivation. In reality, Levana had been easing its way into the mainstream at Queen's since the 1930s. Three Levana representatives had sat on the AMS executive since 1939, giving voice to women's concerns alongside the other constituencies of the Queen's community. In 1967, after several years of negotiation, the exclusively male Arts Society and the Levana Society voted to merge into the Arts and Science Undergraduate Society (ASUS). Levanites were permitted to carry forward certain of their traditions and a budget to sustain them.[43] But the traditions did not wear entirely well in an era of heightened feminist sensibilities.

A 1969 *Journal* article focused on the growing constraints on the life of "Susie Q. Student BA (MRS)" and "the cultural exploitation of women in our society." "Clearly," it concluded, "Susie's whole life has been defined by men's needs rather than her own."[44] The most prominent, and increasingly deplored, ritual of Levana life was the annual candle-lighting ceremony in Grant Hall. Conducted in an atmosphere of academic solemnity and Masonic secrecy, candle-lighting symbolized the bonding of senior women students with their neophytes each fall – a passing on of the "light" of femininity. The organ played as the inductees filed into the hall, gowns were transferred from senior to junior, and, climatically, a senior student lit each junior's candle. Rumour and myth swirled around the ceremony. Many alleged that the disposition of the melted wax on the tricolour ribbons below would foretell whether a doctor, engineer, or artsie lay ahead in the student's marital future. A motion put before AMS council in 1969 condemned the ceremony as "a dehumanizing fertility rite which perpetuates the concept of university women as charming and cultured accessories who are being prepared for careers as wives and mothers of university men, without consideration of their development and value as human beings."[45] The motion was defeated. In 1971, the ceremony was disrupted by intruders chanting: "Bow down to the power of the mighty cock."[46] Some, however, championed the event, arguing that it actually heightened women's self-esteem and solidarity.

By the early 1970s, it was clear that the existence and perception of women students at Queen's had shifted: they had left the cloister and entered the mainstream of student life. Over in the residence precinct, men and women were now allowed to visit each other's rooms, and skirts were no longer *de rigueur* for women at dinner. Running for AMS vice-president in 1968, Arts student Jan Lichty made it abundantly clear that she had not come to Queen's to become a "glorified secretary." The next fall Lichty, Bron Wallace, and four other women staged a piece of guerilla theatre, entering the Homecoming

The candle-lighting ceremony in Grant Hall. The location and numbers of drops of wax falling on the tricolour ribbons tied around the base of the candle were said to foretell the faculty of the freshette's future husband and her fecundity. The ceremony persisted until the early twenty-first century, but increasingly emphasized women's solidarity over their marital prospects.

beauty contest in clown customs and loudly denouncing the ritual for "objectifying" women. At the same time, the AMS, mimicking the student movement elsewhere, began offering "counter courses" on birth control, the image of women in literature, and (paralleling new courses offered in the sociology department) sexual theory. Second-wave feminism had come to Queen's.

While women on campus asserted a new definition of their role in student life, the acceptance of gender diversity and equality only lightly touched the lives of non-heterosexual – or "homosexual" or "homophile" in the parlance of the times – members

"*A Puzzle of Patterns*"

of the Queen's community. In an atmosphere as intensely heterosexual at Queen's, gays and lesbians instinctively suppressed their orientation in public, where they might be seen as "queers." This obliged them to construct their own secretive community, one that stretched well beyond the usual boundaries imposed by academic and class sensibilities. That community embraced academics, Kingstonians, and members of the military who sought non-heterosexual companionship. They learned where to find each other: in downtown bars like The Cat's Meow, amongst the stately elms in City Park (cruelly nicknamed "Pervert Park" by many Kingston residents), and at house parties, often discreetly hosted by gay and lesbian Queen's faculty members.[47] From the historian's perspective, it is difficult to chronicle the existence of a segment of society that lived such a furtive and undocumented life; gay and lesbian history resides in the memory of those who lived it and in the often vituperative actions of those who resisted that culture. Letters to the *Journal* by non-heterosexuals complaining about their oppression were, for instance, invariably signed with a pseudonym.

Early in the seventies, Kingston's queer community, as gays now ironically and proudly label themselves, began to find a public voice. Perhaps inspired by a new mood of gay activism in the wake of the 1969 Stonewall riots in the Greenwich Village district of New York City and the birth of gay-pride marches in big urban centres, the Kingston gay community began to "act up." They pushed back against prejudice. When *Golden Words* columnist "Fred Fudpucker" informed his readers that "a sure faggot test" was to "tweak his bum," "three campus homophiles" complained to the *Journal*, noting that the Kinsey Report had conservatively estimated that 10 per cent of the North American population was homosexual and, by this measure, probably a thousand students and staff at Queen's fell into that category.[48] They also alleged that gay patrons of a downtown bar had been beaten up and, in one case, forced to leave town. The tide began to turn slowly: the *Journal* announced that it would no longer publish unsigned homophobic letters. Emboldened, Queen's gays and lesbians formed the Queen's Homophile Association later that fall and committed themselves to a "come out, come out, wherever you are" philosophy.[49] Such openness drew attention from wider audiences. "Kingston, Ontario, is for Canadian gay people," the *Body Politic*, a Toronto gay-liberation magazine, wrote the next spring, "what Little Rock, Arkansas, was for American blacks prior to their civil rights struggle."[50] Sensing the shifting wind, the AMS gave the new association club status and a subsidy of $250.[51] The 1974 *Tricolor* noted the shift: "Gays Surface," it announced.

No More *in Loco Parentis*

If ideological restlessness and gender diversity pushed the Queen's student body hesitantly in new directions in the sixties and early seventies, the social imperatives reflected deeper, more categorical, shifts in that culture. The old introverted, self-satisfied, and homogenized student culture of Queen's became more outward-looking and worldly wise in these same years. Born into a world of growing prosperity and social stability, a world denied their Depression-bred parents, students coming up to Kingston in the sixties brought more cosmopolitan expectations with them. These would manifest themselves in pressure for a renovated student government more dedicated to servicing the immediate daily needs of students, rather than decorating Grant Hall for formal dances and perpetuating good times.

It is, of course, dangerous to engage in sweeping generalizations about "Queen's students," but it did seem that, by the early 1970s, the demographics of studying at the university had been transformed. The once-dominant Queen's catchment area of eastern Ontario had swung magnetically to the wealth and numbers of urban Canada. Thanks to the success of John Deutsch's "steady state" approach to growth and admissions, Queen's was now attracting the best and the brightest, not only from the high schools of rural Ontario, but from the comfortable middle-class enclaves of urban Canada.

In 1970, the University Council, usually a rather reticent presence in university governance, took the initiative of creating a committee to investigate the university's admissions policy and its outcomes. Chaired by Bruce Alexander, a former AMS president, the committee reported that, by 1970, a Queen's student was likely to be a somewhat different species. The gist of their fall 1971 report was well reflected in the *Journal* headline: "On the average we're urban, male, and quite well-off." While the committee's methodology was rather loose (it compared a 1970 questionnaire survey of Queen's students with 1967 and 1968 data garnered from the national census and the Canadian Union of Students), it did suggest that 41.3 per cent of Queen's students came from families with annual incomes over $15,000, whereas only 15.7 per cent of students in other Ontario universities could boast the same affluence. They came from "educationally advantaged" families, where parents tended to be professionals and managers. And 90 per cent came from urban areas; Queen's now attracted fewer rural students than the provincial average. There was one continuing link with the past: 36.4 per cent of respondents had a relative who had attended Queen's, indicating that wealth and power had made a transition to the city in the postwar boom. Echoing the ideology of many of its sixties' editors, the *Journal* concluded that Queen's was anything but an "everyman's university."[52]

More than demography was altering the student ethos at Queen's. By the seventies, there was little vestige of the traditional *in loco parentis* role left on Ontario university campuses in general. The age of majority in Ontario dropped from twenty-one to eighteen in 1971; students were now regarded as adults, and consequently began to harbour adult expectations. Queen's students became more footloose. Reflecting the population at large, they now owned or had better access to cars. Highway 401 opened in the late sixties, making Toronto, Montreal, and Ottawa easy, four-lane destinations. Bus and train service improved. There were, in short, fewer reasons for regarding the Queen's campus as an hermetic zone, which one inhabited without interruption for the term's entire duration. And each trip to, say, Toronto exposed Queen's students to the wider world of student experience in the sixties – "What was this Rochdale College?" As student curiosity and experience expanded, so did their entitlements in the modern welfare state. Queen's students now stood on a carpet of programs that ministered to their health, their summer employment prospects, and their ability to borrow to finance their education. In Ottawa, for instance, the Trudeau Liberals created Opportunities for Youth and Katimavik summer-job opportunities to open the world to students. Since the mid-sixties, the provincial government had offered the Ontario Student Assistance Program to those who could not shoulder the cost of university education. It was hardly surprising, therefore, that students began to adopt a more activist attitude towards the postsecondary education now on offer to them. When Principal Corry asked for the AMS's response to the Duff-Berdahl Report in 1967, the student government was quick to emphasize that students were no longer simply grateful recipients of education, but that they now wished to be *participants* in the process: "We do not visualize students as customers in a supermarket of learning ... We are an integral part of the community and as such have a legitimate claim to participation in its government."[53]

Reform began at home, in the basement offices of the AMS in the Students' Union. As the decade unfolded, students came to expect more from their government. They sought to expand the century-old tradition of student self-government at Queen's into something more encompassing and progressive. In September 1965, AMS President Gordon Watt confided to Principal Corry the view that students were shedding their "sandbox approach" to life. And this meant rethinking their hitherto narrow participation in university governance, while at the same time making the internal structure of their own self-government more relevant to student needs.[54] Watt and his successor presidents in the mid-sixties, Edwin Chown and George Carson, all reached the same pivotal conclusion: the workings of the AMS were too incestuous, too self-perpetuating, and, consequently, poorly connected to the student body it served. Anticipating such criticism, *Journal* editor Robert Crown had voiced his disparagement of the AMS "establishment" in the fall of 1962, a move that cost him his job. Two aspects of the AMS grated against the sensibilities of a decade that increasingly emphasized participation and equity. The AMS president continued to be elected by an electoral college constituted of representatives sent up by the faculty societies to sit on the AMS executive. Late every January, they went into a Vatican-like caucus and selected one of their number to carry the AMS torch through the next year. The student proletariat had little say in the succession; there were no party platforms and few policy promises, just the assurance that power had been passed to someone who knew the ropes. Also grating was the fact that the AMS secretary-treasurer was in fact a member of the university administration, alumni director Herb Hamilton. He had held the post for years and clearly fulfilled the paternalistic role of overseer – the set of administration eyes on the students' internal affairs. Hamilton countersigned all AMS cheques.

In 1964, things began to change. The shadow of administration oversight was lifted from the AMS; Hamilton resigned and was not replaced. Under criticism from *Journal* editorials that it was disconnected from issues like housing that were pressing on students, the AMS executive created a Student Government Commission under AMS Chief Justice Barry Earle to ponder reform. How, for instance, was the AMS to cope with the rapidly growing student population at Queen's? Each new student swelled AMS revenue, but at the same time stretched local housing and campus services to the limit. How was this to be managed and apportioned? Adding to the surge, Queen's rapidly growing graduate-student population had organized in 1962 as the Graduate Students' Society and, a year later, affiliated with the AMS. The relationship was delicate. Graduate students had little bond with the Queen's culture (they complained about paying fees for bands and football), but they would abide by the AMS's overall jurisdiction.

A New Student Democracy

The Earle Report made no dramatic suggestions for democratizing the AMS, but it did argue that it desperately needed better management and recommended the hiring of a full-time, paid business manager. Mrs Dorothy Williams was consequently hired to bring some order and continuity to the AMS. With AMS executive teams in the saddle for less than a year, continuity was constantly fractured; Mrs Williams would help to connect one year with the next, and ensure that the bills were paid and budgets sensibly constructed. Other problems remained: the Earle Report pointed to the antiquated committee structure at the AMS – too many committees to organize dances and too few to find housing. Communications with Richardson Hall were poor, predicated on personality, not regular channels. In 1966, Principal Corry sought to remedy this shortcoming by appointing a dean of student affairs and the AMS reciprocated by appointing a communications officer.

When Edwin Chown took over as AMS president in 1966, he immediately realized the need to loosen the almost autocratic grip of the inner circle of the executive council. Just as Corry was decentralizing academic power to deans and departments, Chown wanted to push power out closer to the students. Without this, students would increasingly feel disenfranchised and disconnected, and the executive would remain immune from democratic responsibility. That October, Chown castigated "the lack of preparedness on the part of the Executive."[55] At the same time, the AMS outer council – the broader grouping of faculty reps who were not directly given specific responsibilities – showed signs of apathy. Council attendance was poor. Chown launched another student-government commission to explore a more dramatic restructuring of how students governed themselves at Queen's. In the interim, piecemeal initiatives were made: a student-centred survey of housing needs, better student counselling, and active planning of the campus theatre for which students had been agitating since the late 1950s.

Looming above all these practical concerns was the more strategic issue of how students were to engage the Duff-Berdahl Report's prescription for greater student-faculty participation in overall university governance. Complicating this calculation was the deteriorating credibility of the Queen's student rector. Since 1912, the rector at Queen's had acted as the students' advocate in the university's corridors of power. In an era of student deference, the role had always fallen to a well-placed and forceful outsider. Former prime minister R.B. Bennett had served in the 1930s. Since 1947, the loquacious broadcaster Leonard Brockington had ably carried student concerns to the Board of Trustees. He regularly visited the campus and chummed around with the student body. In 1966, Brockington died, and, although he was universally remembered for his "single-minded and adroit advocacy of his clients," students began to question the role.[56]

Usually, a new rector was identified by an AMS committee and then nominated, unopposed, for the position. Times were, however, a-changing and some wondered, as the *Journal* did, whether in an age of youth empowerment, the rectorship had become what a *Journal* writer termed a "tokenistic ... relic."[57] A fall 1967 referendum asked students if the rectorship should be retired or reformed. In the spirit of student gradualism at Queen's, students voted to make the rectorship a more structured part-time position, as opposed to keeping its previously loosely defined mandate. Two students timorously said that they might be interested in taking on the role. In the end, tradition prevailed, and Senator Grattan O'Leary, another silver-tongued Ottawa journalist and one-time editor of the *Ottawa Journal*, agreed to take on the position. Interestingly, O'Leary was described as a "candidate" for the post. He seemed to say the right things, praising Queen's for its "rich, old Conservative background."[58] Applied Science students responded with the new mood of sixties irreverence by hauling a huge banner up the side of Grant Hall: "SUPPORT YOUR RECTOR."[59]

However, from the outset there were problems. O'Leary seemed to regard the assignment as a sinecure. He seldom made contact with the students and seemed poorly briefed at trustees' meetings, which he attended sporadically. At a time when students everywhere were pushing for a more activist participation in university affairs, O'Leary seemed more attached to a fading culture of cronyism. Dissatisfaction grew. Some council members suggested the senator never understood that his was meant to be a "working rectorship." The rub lay in the fact that, while the university council made the official appointment of the rector, there was no mechanism for obliging a rector to step down or smarten up. In the fall of 1968, a small AMS delegation, headed by Arts and Science rep Andy Pipe, was dispatched to Ottawa to drop hints that, if he did not perk up in his duties, there was talk that he might be impeached. O'Leary fobbed the students off.* A November referendum sent a clearer message: 2,480

---

*At the end of the uneasy meeting, O'Leary attempted to appease the student politicians (some of whom were in political science) by asking if they would like to see "the Senate in action." The students politely agreed. O'Leary trooped them down the corridor to the Members' Gallery, but the doors were locked. Not to worry, O'Leary assured them, there was always the public gallery overlooking the Red Chamber. But, to the Senator's consternation, those doors were also locked. A commissionaire approached to offer assistance. O'Leary told him that he wanted to show "his boys from Queen's" the Senate in action. "But Senator," the commissionaire announced, "the Senate sat down three weeks ago." Author interview, Alan Broadbent, 6 Nov. 2012.

students voted to ask O'Leary to step down in light of his "poor record."⁶⁰ In December, O'Leary finally took the hint (probably after a little subtle pressure from John Deutsch). The rectorship had reached a low ebb; few remained to defend it, and most now believed it irrelevant. For the next year, there would be no rector, the trustees agreeing to let the AMS president attend their meetings as an observer.

As the rectorship slowly went into a hiatus, the AMS continued to probe its own future. In fact, two student dynamics would unfold over the next few years at Queen's. The first, set in motion by Chown and his predecessors, sought to accelerate the reconfiguration of the AMS, to shunt it into alignment with modern student needs – housing, entertainment, health care, and services supporting daily student needs. Here the emphasis was on constructive engagement and progressive improvement, something that had been implicit in the Queen's student experience since the 1850s. A second and narrower stream sought to reject such gradualism, and instead assailed the very purpose of "liberal" university education and the society it served, using student government as a tool of root-and-branch change. The latter conformed to the stereotype of the impatient late-sixties student radicalism that swept across North American and European campuses – accusatory rhetoric accompanied by bold demands for social re-engineering. Students at Queen's would engage both dialogues, making the years 1968 to 1970 the most tense and argumentative in the student history of Queen's. Student politics on campus consequently became polarized as never before. Queen's students began to discuss – and contest – issues that resonated beyond the campus and the annual cycle of administrative and social affairs. The central pivot was the tension between internal reform and worldly crusading. Briefly in the fall of 1968 and then again through the fall and winter of 1969–70, radicalism seemed to win out, and Queen's seemed poised for a Berkeley-like disintegration. Those fractious events, their personalities, and ideas would serve as a case study of how

Queen's coped with calls for change that came at it with an unprecedented vociferousness. Beneath this turmoil, much like a musical continuo, more-orthodox student politicians continued to write a less-antagonistic, more-pragmatic, prescription for change at Queen's.

Ed Chown's successor as AMS president, George Carson of Meds '68, embodied that pragmatism. Just months into his tenure in November 1967, and after two weekend AMS retreats on Wolfe Island, he proposed a bold leap: making the AMS president a full-time, year-round position, supporting the office with a full-time assistant and, most dramatically, electing the president in a campus-wide open election.⁶¹ Council debates that fall had been alive with heated exchanges over whether Queen's should maintain its membership in the increasingly radical Canadian Union of Students (CUS), with its inclination to use student power to restructure western society. One vocal faction, openly identifying with New Left ideology, urged the council to condemn the Vietnam War and to sponsor "a seminar on radical doctrine."⁶² The *Journal* increasingly echoed this line. The university was conceived as an instrument of social change, not a grooming experience for life *after* graduation. Another group focused on more-immediate issues: the need for a survey of Kingston's off-campus housing capacity, the adequacy of student health services, and the possibility of a student pub. Here there were some innovative ideas: for instance, could the AMS take an activist role in alleviating the housing situation by underwriting the cost of co-operative student housing? Amid this cacophony of opinion, Carson concluded that direct democracy alone would bring discipline and constructive, long-term change. George Carson was intent on incubating a cadre of "young politicos" at Queen's, who would galvanize the way students managed their own affairs.⁶³ It was, as Liberal leadership hopeful Pierre Trudeau was telling the nation, an era of "participatory democracy." Let the students decide for themselves what they wanted and end the closed-circuit decision making of the AMS council and its inner cabal.

Carson proved to be forceful in his leadership. When the *Journal*, in his opinion, persisted in pursuing a New Left bent in its stories, he faulted editor Krista Maeots for the paper's "lack of news coverage on campus." In January 1968, the AMS countered and launched its own newsletter, a rather prosaic and amateurish vehicle, for its own rendition of campus life. Top of the news was the revision of the AMS constitution late that month. By that blueprint, Queen's students would in future elect their AMS president in an annual, mid-February election that offered competing "tickets" of presidential and vice-presidential candidates. Candidates could be nominated on the strength of two hundred signatures on a petition. Campaign spending would be capped at $50, and the AMS Court would arbitrate any contested results. The *Journal* would be obliged to provide free advertising to candidates. Voters would have the right to remove elected AMS officials through an impeachment referendum. Only the *Journal* editor was spared such abrupt recall, but was instead tied on a tight leash to the authority of the AMS publications committee. At the AMS general meeting on 5 February, the new constitution was approved and a new democratic era dawned at Queen's.[64] What had begun as a student debating society – a *conversazione* – in the 1850s had evolved into a modern, direct democracy.

Now the race was on. Two teams vied for the presidential prize. Charles "Chuck" Edwards, a graduate student in chemical engineering and chair of the AMS finance committee, offered himself as president, with Arts student Jan Lichty, an outspoken feminist and chair of the AMS building committee, running for vice-president. They presented themselves as reformists who knew the AMS ropes, promising an activist agenda of chivvying the administration into better health care, housing services, new athletic facilities, and more student participation in university governance. Their tone was gradualist, not radical. Opposing them were law student Rob Nelson and Dave Rose, an economics undergraduate. Their platform largely echoed that of the Edwards ticket. The campaign passed without rancour or, seemingly, much heated debate. The *Journal* interviewed the candidates but carried few campaign ads. The mid-February vote saw a 36-per-cent voter turnout, with the nod going narrowly to Edwards 1,095 to 988. The neophyte electorate, it seemed, preferred the AMS insiders.

The winter of 1968 thus proved a seminal moment in the life of Queen's students. They had for the first time elected their leaders directly. At the same time, in the wake of the Duff-Berdahl Report and under pressure from prescient Principal Corry, the university had announced that four students would be admitted to the Senate. Given the lateness of the academic year, a special committee of the AMS would select the first four incumbents; future student senators would be elected. Students in Arts and Science were also being called to departmental student committees, where for the first time they would have some input into their curriculum. Over at the *Journal*, the new editor, Wilf Day, seemed engaged with campus issues such as the housing shortfall and the need for counter courses that challenged prevailing academic orthodoxy. Day also used his podium to attach Queen's students to the world around them – describing conditions of the Kingston working class. Down the corridor in the AMS offices, the new executive seemed focused on the practical concerns of students. A committee was struck to investigate a student-run pub on campus. The AMS began to distance itself from the CUS, whose outspoken radicalism seemed to be troubling many Canadian campuses. Other committees engaged the prospect of co-op housing to alleviate the student housing crunch. Coeducational dining in the existing residences was discussed, as was the need for guidelines to police illegal drug use on campus. "Nothing replaces the face-to-face relationship with the students," Lichty told the *Journal*.[65]

There were, however, already signs that this golden moment would be fleeting. There was intensifying resentment over O'Leary's dilatory performance as rector. And, already, an outspoken minority expressed their opinion that four seats in Senate and departmental committees were not enough. Demands were made that more students be members of the Senate and that hitherto-closed Senate and Board of Trustee meetings be opened to students. The AMS VP Jan Lichty leaned in this direction, resigning from the committee to select the first four student senators. It was, she said, "elitist" for the society to arrogate the function of selection; they should be elected no matter what the circumstances. Sensing the danger of ideologically driven student politics, George Carson used his valedictory address as AMS president to warn against being seduced by the agenda of the "idealists."[66] Yet that is indeed what happened through the summer and fall of 1968: impatience for change overwhelmed discussion of incremental reform. Under Edwards and Lichty, the AMS leadership veered dramatically towards the radicalism so prevalent on other university campuses in that most incendiary of years of student protest. At Queen's, such radicalism proved a squall rather than a storm, perhaps largely due to its adroit handling by Principal John Deutsch and the resilience of student politicians at Queen's, who clung to, and at the same time adapted to, the vital AMS tradition of student self-government.

AMS Inc.

George Carson's ambition of repurposing the purpose of the AMS and then handing its operation over to a cadre of competent political administrators was realized when Queen's students returned to the polling stations in February 1970. Two political-science students – Ross McGregor for president and Peter Griffiths for vice-president – handily won the mid-month AMS election. McGregor had cut his teeth in student affairs as the editor of the 1968 *Tricolor* and then had headed the AMS publications committee in 1969. He was not oblivious to the world down Highway 401. That year he had picketed on the Thousand Islands Bridge to protest American nuclear testing in Alaska, and had guided the executive's decision to seek incorporation as a commercial corporation. As a corporation with a continuing board of directors, the AMS Inc. was better able to hold property and apply itself directly to student needs. Incorporation also reflected the fact that, as Queen's had grown, so too had the inflow revenues garnered from student-sanctioned fees. Many noted that the society had suddenly become "a million-dollar enterprise." As a corporation, the AMS would be better equipped to apply and account for this largesse. Furthermore, a board of continuing directors would allow the society to better engage in long-term planning and accountability. The 1969 incorporation thus indicated that the AMS had ceased to exist simply as the organizer of the associational life of Queen's students, but now conceived of itself as a manager of an enterprise, an enterprise that delivered services to students.

McGregor played strongly to this transition in the 1969 election. He promised practical things – a pub, a bank, an employment service, better housing, and a university centre – knowing that the mass of students had wearied of the ideological turmoil of the last year and wanted a return to normalcy. The AMS, McGregor argued, had "to step up to the plate" and make itself relevant to its constituents.[67] McGregor also made it clear that his inclination was to work *with* the university administration, rather than against it. He sensed that Principal Deutsch, who was equally anxious to avoid any return to the previous year's rancour, was ready to work with the revised AMS; indeed McGregor suggested that the principal was "ahead of us" on such issues as alleviating the housing crisis. If elected, McGregor envisioned his role as one of "brokering solutions" between various student factions and the administration. In later years, he would describe this as "constructive bridging" and suggest that he had recon-

President Ross McGregor (right) votes on a motion at an AMS meeting, while AMS Speaker Bob Buller presides. "Railroad Ross" galvanized the way the AMS delivered services to its membership. Buller would go on to become the manager of the Queen's pub system, one of the new areas of student enterprise.

nected the AMS with "the Queen's way" – careful grooming of a centrist consensus. Consensus was, he believed, the "institutional glue" of Queen's. When the votes were counted (although turnout dropped to about 20 per cent of the now-less-agitated student body), McGregor and Griffiths won in a trot. Accompanying referenda questions saw students vote to elect their university senators each spring on a staggered-term basis and to withdraw from the Canadian Union of Students. Queen's, it seemed, had returned to an even keel.

McGregor set a blistering pace of reform, quickly acquiring the nickname "Railroad" Ross. (When he left office, the AMS council saluted their outgoing president with taped sounds of locomotives and, incongruously, a rousing rendition of "Anchors Away"). Indisputably, his most lasting innovation was the introduction of a "commission" system of student government in the spring of 1969. Governance at the AMS would be broken into two chambers: an outer council composed of all the traditional faculty society representatives and an inner council composed of the elected president and vice-president and seven presidentially appointed commissioners.

McGregor had faulted the old AMS as "an amalgamation of ad hoc committees without coherent direction." In effect, the commissioners would now act like cabinet ministers, given jurisdiction over designated portfolios: education, services, external affairs, communications, judicial affairs, budget and finance, and campus activities. McGregor, a political-science honours student, reasoned that the Canadian federal government seemed to function well under such a defined dissemination of power. Commissioners were to be paid a small honorarium.

Each commissioner would be expected to draw up policy objectives, manage a budget, and deliver results. Student government at Queen's would thus mimic what Principal Corry had done with the academic administration of the university: decentralize power and decision making out from Richardson Hall to the deans and department heads, closer to rank-and-file students and professors.[68] To take one example, the first education commissioner, Glenn MacDonell, used his mandate to focus student dialogue on contemporary issues. "Teach-ins" were staged in Grant Hall – some held overnight with sleeping bags and snacks. The Laura Secord

"*A Puzzle of Patterns*"   153

Memorial Teach-in, for instance, focused on the "Americanization of Canada." The Vancouver Street Theatre was brought in to introduce Queen's students to street theatre as a form of social commentary. The education commission also extended funding to counter courses and held forums to discuss the Harrower Report's controversial blueprint for democratizing undergraduate education. The commission also drew up briefs in support of the AMS's claim for a "fair share" in university governance. The thrust of all this was that students be afforded a structured means of demonstrating their campus citizenship and daily concerns.[69]

Under the ethos of the commission system, the AMS inner-council meetings became more like corporate board meetings, with each commissioner presenting weekly updates on their mandates. This put an edge on the debates and, at times, introduced frictions and competitiveness among the respective commissioners. This tended to politicize the internal workings of the AMS, as commissioners with their eyes on the prize of the next year's presidency vied against each other. Each January, nominations were called for the upcoming presidential election. "Teams" emerged, offering loose platforms with predictable promises of better communication, responsibility, and services. Once the votes were counted, attention turned to the selection of a new slate of commissioners. As with any democratic system, some administrations proved activist, others quarrelsome and ineffectual. "Railroad" Ross fell squarely in the activist camp. Some criticized his "up-tight," top-down style of pushing the AMS forward; McGregor responded by saying that he was trying to conquer student apathy. The *Journal* agreed, editorializing that "student power" was now "dead" and that a new era of "student responsibility" had dawned.[70] Believing that it was discovering its own brand of homegrown student empowerment, Queen's dropped out of the CUS in February 1969. When other campuses emulated the move, the CUS collapsed that spring.

McGregor's activism delivered results. On a day-to-day level, Queen's students got more for their money. On a campus that constitutionally forbid fraternities, every student was obliged to belong to the AMS and consequently to contribute six dollars a year to its sustenance. Now there was more tangible evidence of the society's spending. In November, a student pub, The House of Commons, opened in the basement of the Students' Memorial Union. It joined the Bitter Grounds coffee house, which already reflected the folky ambiance of the sixties. The AMS started a housing service, which tried to connect students with the Kingston rental market by publishing lists of available apartments and providing telephones to facilitate quick action by students seeking a place to lay their heads. It also supported the opening of a day-care centre in the Union. The AMS services commissioner joined with the university administration to begin planning for a new university centre to replace the cramped and antiquated Students' Memorial Union. A university-owned house at 51 Queen's Crescent was taken over to serve as a one-stop centre for students seeking counselling and to give advocacy groups a place to meet. Space in the Grey House quickly became prized. The AMS, sometimes after heated council debates, got itself into the advocacy and counselling business. Pressure was brought on the university to accelerate its own slow support of birth-control counselling, to update its parking policies, and to introduce meaningful teaching evaluations. The spirit of progressive reform trickled down into the faculty societies. Andy Pipe, the president of the Arts and Sciences Undergraduate Society, for instance, launched a campaign to temper the horseplay and humiliation of frosh week with activities more aimed at readying students for the academic and social challenges ahead. There was resistance, almost costing Pipe his job by impeachment, but there was no mistaking the new "take charge" mood of Queen's students. "If you have a complaint or an idea, don't whisper it in the dungeon room of McNeill House or Adelaide Hall," McGregor advised, "shout it – somebody is listening."[71]

The People's Rector

The McGregor administration's shouting and listening extended to two more strategic issues. Since Grattan O'Leary had resigned in late 1968, the AMS president had acted as de facto rector, sitting in on Board of Trustees meetings and speaking on student issues before the trustees. In reality, the rectorship had tended to slip from student consciousness; it seemed closer connected to the old paternalistic student culture than the new style of student engagement. McGregor seemed to place little emphasis on the post, and there was an unspoken belief that it would simply fade out of existence. Under the terms of the university charter, the rector could only be elected in November, and as that date neared in 1969, there was little discussion of initiating an election. Then, early in November, a rump of New Left activists, still vocal in student politics after the tumult of the previous fall's radical outburst, saw an opportunity: nominate one of their own as a candidate for the rector's post, elect that person, and gain access to the inner sanctum, as they saw it, of university power. They nominated Jacqui Good, a fourth-year Arts student and AMS rep-at-large, who ran on a platform of agitating for the dissolution of the "illegitimate" Board of Trustees if elected. Other "radical" candidates followed, including dislodged AMS President Charles "Chuck" Edwards. Few paid any attention to the upcoming election. And then, on the last day for nominations, the penny dropped in McGregor's office. The backdoor had, in effect, been left open to the student-power advocates. Desperately, McGregor and his inner circle looked for a last-minute candidate to foil the scheme.

They found their man in Alan Broadbent. He was a new face on campus, a recent graduate from the University of British Columbia who had come to Queen's in the fall of 1968 to upgrade his degree in political science. His father had been at Queen's in the 1920s and had been AMS president in 1928. Broadbent had quickly settled in at Queen's, becoming a reporter and columnist at the *Journal*. His "Dormouse" column furnished readers with the often wry observations of a newcomer to a campus with deep-set traditions. He was personable and worldly wise. It was perhaps his bad luck on an afternoon in late November to leave the *Journal* offices in the Union basement and walk by the AMS offices, where McGregor and company were scurrying to find a candidate for the rectorship in time for that day's nomination deadline. McGregor beckoned Broadbent into his office and within minutes had persuaded him to throw his hat into the ring. He would run on the McGregor-inspired platform of bringing pressure on the university to acknowledge a "fair share" for students in the institution's governance.[72]

What followed was a double-barrelled referendum and election. The level of interest was low. When asked if the rector's position should be retained, a strong majority voted "yes." But when students were then asked to select a candidate, interest dropped. Broadbent won, but with only a meagre 129 votes. Edwards, Good, and others were close on his heels. Indeed, if the radicals had not split their vote by fielding so many candidates, the rectorship would have fallen to them. Broadbent immediately took up his seat in the Collins Room and became the first student in Queen's history to sit on the Board of Trustees. A three-year term lay before him. From a small office in the Union, he began to fashion the rector's function to the needs of the "new" student. Gone was the ceremonial style practised by outsiders Brockington and O'Leary, replaced by a hands-on, ombudsman-like dedication on the part of a fellow-student rector. Broadbent acted as a "fix-it" man for students with problems, administrative and academic. Like McGregor, he quickly understood that Principal Deutsch wanted to be his partner, not his adversary. The principal, Broadbent recalled, was "full of wisdom about how the world works." This said, the new rector did not relent in championing the call for more student inclusion in the governance of Queen's. "It must be recognized by Senate," he warned, "that students are not interested in fruitless efforts. Students feel they must have something real to contribute to the decision making process at Queen's."[73] Through such advocacy and attention to individual students, over the next three years Alan Broadbent reinvented one of Queen's most distinctive traditions.

McGregor echoed Broadbent's belief in broader student inclusion in university governance. With his credibility enhanced by his reformation of the internal structure of the AMS, McGregor now turned to pushing the door of the Senate wider. With the first four student senators now at the table in the Collins Room, McGregor began arguing that, to adequately represent the full panoply of student concerns, more student senators were necessary. How could just four students stretch themselves across all the issues before the Senate, let alone make their presence felt on all the Senate committees? If more faculty were being allowed a voice on Senate, why shouldn't students be given parity? As posters that started appearing on campus put it: what was fair about "Lions 44, Students 4"? Drawing on intuitions gained in his political-science studies, McGregor approached the situation not with obdurate rhetoric, but with the subtlety of an Ottawa politician. He asked his vice-president, Peter Griffiths, to chair the President's Committee on University Governance. Almost immediately, it acquired the nickname of the "Fair Share" committee. The committee deliberated into the winter term of 1970, reporting just as the McGregor–Griffiths mandate drew to a close and as students elected a law student, Rod Follwell, and Arts student, Janet Rogers, as their new president and vice-president. Follwell proved somewhat less headlong than "Railroad" Ross, but stayed the "fair share" course.

Give Us a "Fair Share"

The report advocated the creation of another ten student senators. Fourteen students on Senate, it argued, would ensure the satisfactory projection of the views of a student body now totalling more than seven thousand. "The underlying premise of the Fair Share Report," the *Alma Mater Matter* editorialized, "is that no one should have the right to control or determine the life of another ... They must have this voice, not just because they are students, but because they are and are affected by the decisions of its government."[74] Hence, there should be parity between faculty and students on the Senate, and the hitherto closed meetings of the Board of Trustees should now be open to all members of the university community. The report conceived of university governance in terms of constituency representation: equal blocks of faculty, administrators, and students, all vying to forward or protect their positions. The report even suggested that students should elect their Senate representatives on a faculty basis, not on a campus-wide basis. This line of argument ran counter to the long-standing understanding that the Queen's Senate was a forum for broad, non-aligned *participation* in the academic governance of the university, not an arena for the pursuit of narrow advantage. Similarly, the Fair Share prescription for open trustee meetings seemed oblivious to the fact that the bricks-and-mortar management of Queen's required a degree of confidentiality and candid access to outside expertise in financial affairs and external relations. Despite students' insistence on questioning the broader ethos of western society, John Deutsch remained determined to contain student agitation inside the tent of university discourse. He forwarded the report to the Senate Operations Committee (with its oversight over the mechanisms of Senate governance) for consideration. The operations committee had, in fact, already been examining the delicate balance of Senate elected and ex-officio membership since the fall. Now a joint nominating-operations committee would review both the Fair Share and Senate findings. On a shrewd motion by Dean of Medicine Harry Botterell, the committee was instructed to examine only the "principles" at hand, not the specific Fair Share recommendations.[75]

Through the late winter of 1970, arguments swirled. English professor George Whalley vehemently resisted any notion that senators were constituency watchdogs; the Senate, he insisted, was a body where a varied membership applied its expertise to the best interests of the whole community. Participation was its central virtue. In May 1970, the joint committee reported that the Senate should be expanded to a total membership of sixty-two. Students should be allotted fourteen elected seats, but not at the expense of faculty membership, which would grow proportionately to thirty-one. Other students would be empanelled as members of Senate committees. Students, the report conceded, could bring "knowledgeable criticism" to Senate deliberations. Senior university administrators, including the deans and vice-principals, plus the AMS president, would add sixteen ex-officio senators, while the principal would continue to sit as the Senate chairman. All senators would vote, with the principal only voting to break ties. Senate meetings would also now be open to the public, although seating would be limited and subject to prior reservation. Constables from the AMS would be called upon to ensure that decorum was maintained. The committee was, however, adamant in insisting that all senators should regard their duty as one of participation, *not* representation. In subsequent decades, the principal would echo this sentiment every September when he welcomed new members to the Senate's first fall meeting: Senators were to place the general interest of the university before that of their immediate constituency. On 28 May 1970, the senators approved the new blueprint for the Senate.[76] The decision coincided neatly with the wrapping-up of the Senate's thorough and laborious investigation of former AMS president Chuck Edwards's allegation that ideological prejudice had blighted his academic freedom at Queen's. Thus, just as the Senate dismissed a radical indictment of Queen's culture, it judiciously opened the door to wider democratic participation in university governance by students.

That door would, however, open only so wide. The Fair Share Report had also called for student participation in the deliberations of the Board of Trustees, either through direct membership or by making the Board meetings open to the public. At this, the trustees balked. The university charter clearly stipulated that the only active member of the university community entitled to sit on the Board of Trustees was the principal; the onus was on applying outside expertise to the non-academic administration of the campus. Many Board deliberations involved matters of money and confidence, and these could not be bandied about the campus. There was also the perennially awkward and uniquely Queen's fact that any alteration in the university charter required approval by the federal parliament, a cumbersome and time-consuming affair. Nonetheless, the Board struck a committee under Toronto lawyer Norman MacLeod Rogers (BA '43) to explore the possibility. Rogers reported that parliamentary approval of a charter change might "provoke other difficulties." Furthermore, the Queen's faculty, also barred from Board membership, had expressed no interest in gaining entry to trustee deliberations, but would probably demand as much if students were admitted. Rogers suggested a compromise: allow three student observers – the current AMS president and the past two presidents – to attend Board meetings and invite the rector to join the Board's executive committee. Meetings would remain closed, but non-confidential Board minutes would be published in the *Queen's Gazette*.[77] In the emerging mood of expanding participation, this easing of tradition seemed acceptable to students.

The early 1970s witnessed a new exuberance in student life at Queen's. Given a voice in Senate and a presence before the trustees, the AMS used its new corporate structure to make itself more relevant to its constituents. Under AMS presidents Rod Follwell, Patrick Riley, Greg LeBlanc, and Steve Brereton, the AMS increasingly conceived of itself as an "enterprise" devoted to supplying students with services and empowering students as members of civil society. Many of these activities came to be clustered under the label of Queen's Student Services. The AMS, for instance, became a landlord.

The AMS Housing Service was intended to ease the tight student-accommodation situation in Kingston by leasing university-owned houses adjacent to the campus, tidying them up, and then renting them to students. By 1972, it had eighty houses in its inventory. At the same time, the AMS provided financial backing to the reinvigorated Science '44 Co-op and the Elrond College apartment tower, a student-managed initiative (featured in the next chapter). To promote a student diaspora away from the densely populated campus and adjacent Sydenham Ward, a "Bus-It" scheme was introduced to allow students to ride Kingston buses for "free" after the payment of a lump sum by the AMS to the local transit company. The House of Commons pub in the Union gave students an on-campus drinking spot for the first time, while at the same time providing employment for bartenders and waiters. A typing service and copy shop were opened. The AMS even sponsored the opening of a shop, Heffalump, on Princess Street, dedicated to selling crafts. At the 1971 AMS general meeting, President Patrick Riley mused that the society had "abandoned academics to the faculty Societies" and in effect no longer had an interest in "educational development." Others suggested that the AMS had become a "service organization." Others noted that the expansion of such services was regulated by student referenda, which either approved or quashed AMS fee increases to cover the cost of any new service. In 1970–71, the student activity fee, covering the operating costs of everything from the band to the Union, amounted to $55.50.

The AMS nonetheless did maintain a broader altruism. It remained engaged in social and political issues. Six thousand copies of the famous *McGill Birth Control Handbook* were purchased and distributed on campus. Another brochure – "You and the Law" – was prepared by Queen's law students to advise students on their rights and responsibilities in civil society. A Student Volunteer Bureau was organized to connect Queen's students with local social needs. There was discussion of starting a food co-op to challenge the hold of local supermarkets. A motion was passed deploring Canada's laws on cannabis use. An ongoing debate unfolded on the relationship of Queen's students to national student bodies and their politics. On the whole, the AMS took a conservative – one observer called it "introverted" – line on student activism on the national stage, arguing that Queen's students were better served by engaging the participatory potential of their own campus government than by pursuing placard-waving protest in front of the provincial legislature. Queen's shunned the outspokenly radical student politics of the hawkish National Students' Union, while embracing the more moderate Ontario Federation of Students.

Even then, there were tensions over how to confront the Conservative government of Premier William Davis, who in 1972 announced a one-hundred-dollar hike in post-secondary tuition in Ontario. In reaction to this, the AMS was not inclined to in-the-street protests, instead favouring the withholding of fees in the fall of 1973 to bring pressure on the government. Supported by strong referendum approval, the AMS won support from the trustees, who agreed to waive the usual five-dollar late-payment fee if students withheld their fees that fall. And 2,500 of them did just that. The fee strike did not result in a fee rollback, but it did help to nudge the Davis government (which had just taken delivery of the Wright Report on Post-Secondary Education, with its message of building a "learning society") to improve university accessibility through higher student-loan ceilings and beefed-up BIU payments.[78]

The fee strike of 1973 underlined a growing reality of post-secondary student life at Queen's, and in

Ontario as a whole: education increasingly entailed financial strain. As Queen's catchment area for students reoriented itself from rural, eastern Ontario to the burgeoning cities of eastern Canada, the university shed its image as a "poor boys' university" and began acquiring a reputation as a dormitory for "rich kids" from the city. For some this was perhaps true. Queen's, for instance, did well recruiting promising undergraduates from Toronto and Montreal private schools like Upper Canada College. But student-aid statistics tended to erode this impression. In 1972–73, for instance, the Queen's Student Awards Office oversaw the distribution of $4,540,000 in student assistance, some from provincial and federal student-loan programs and the rest as bursaries and loans from university endowment funds. Thus, 3,963 of Queen's 9,412 students were deemed worthy of financial assistance that year by federal, provincial, or university officials.[79]

A Steep Learning Curve for the New AMS

The "new" AMS did not, however, take flight with Phoenix-like perfection. The learning curve was steep. There was a fundamental failure to appreciate that new services for students took not only vision, but also careful planning. The AMS tended to plunge into new activities without thinking through their financial and administrative underpinnings. Take, for instance, the craft store on Princess Street. Was Heffalump meant to offer a venue for local artisans? Or was it an opportunity to employ students or to enhance community relations? Should it endeavour to make a profit? None of this was ever thought through, and, consequently, the store began to pile up debts. Heffalump staff seemed oblivious to commonplace retail practices: Christmas stock was not ordered until late November, only to arrive in time for the January sales. When asked why the shop never made a profit, the manager, Jane Corkin, announced: "Somehow, that doesn't seem to be the sort of thing a Heffalump should do."[80] The store was finally closed in 1972. The typing and copy service similarly floundered; there seemed to be no systematic way of keeping track of pages typed or copies made. Concerts run by the AMS, usually moneymakers, lost $4,000 in 1972–73. The *Journal* was failing to collect its advertising revenue and was in debt. Even the student pub could not make money. While sudsy sales were strong, profits were drained by poor inventory control and what was called "slippage" (meant to convey the idea that some beer was spilled on the floor, but had in fact gone down waiters' throats). When the manager, who tended to hire his friends, boosted the pub's hourly wage to $1.80 without AMS permission, he was fired. The folly continued: draft beer at the House of Commons retailed at 30 cents, well below the downtown price of 55 cents. Despite its woes, the pub became a campus hot spot and stayed open.[81]

As the AMS council pondered its wonky entrepreneurial record, there were moments of unintended revelation. In 1973, the campus activities commissioner, who oversaw the booking of campus concerts, reported strong profits on concerts by Blood, Sweat and Tears and Genesis. This was happy news to the cash-strapped society. How had he done it? Well, he answered, the stage crew had been paid in "dope and booze," far cheaper than the going rate of $2.50 for stage crew. "Some members: gasp," read the minutes. The practice was abandoned.[82] By the spring of 1973, the coffers at the AMS were virtually empty. Office staff was laid off. The business manager reported that the society was "not only broke but was in danger of going bankrupt." AMS vice-president, Bruce Trotter, was consequently obliged to go cap-in-hand to Vice-Principal David Bonham to seek a bridging loan until the annual harvest of student fees could be taken in that fall. Bonham extended an interest-free loan of $20,000, continuing evidence of the administration's willingness to give Queen's students plenty of latitude, but to backstop them when tight occasions arose.[83] The crisis continued and, in the fall, AMS Education Commissioner Marv Bloos personally undertook a thorough investigation of the AMS's descent into deficit.

Bloos's report, bluntly titled *How to Lose a Million: A Report on* AMS *Business Practices and Other Matters*, pulled no punches. The post-McGregor campaign to enhance student services had proceeded with little planning, little professional advice, and a diminishing pool of leadership. The AMS had failed to realize that it was now "a million-dollar operation" and had naively believed that part-time amateurs could manage complex enterprises. There was too much cronyism. And, Bloos argued, the AMS council had neglected its oversight responsibility and was prone to spending most of its time "navel-gazing."[84] Many students called for its abolition. Bloos's report delivered a stinging indictment, but it helped the AMS turn the corner to a new maturity. The pub was closed, pending new control systems being implemented. AMS accounting was centralized. A restructuring committee studied the AMS and urged the creation of a second vice-presidential office to oversee operations, with the original vice-president handling university affairs. Honoraria were approved to allow the AMS executive trio to work through the summer to keep constant tabs on the society. For the first time in its history, the AMS had become a truly year-round operation. The AMS board of directors was at the same time expanded to include two worldly wise faculty members and a student with no ties to the AMS's inner circle. A heated debate took place over whether membership in the Ontario Federation of Students was money well spent. Accountability and strategic focus became the order of the day. AMS elections consequently became more politicized. Candidates' platforms now emphasized focused goals and policies. Voters expected results and alacrity in response to their needs. "Remember Heffalump" became a popular chant as the presidential election of 1974 drew near.[85]

By the time Steve Brereton's term as AMS presidency ended in the spring of 1974, the AMS was on more stable and accountable financial ground.

While the new president, Tony Wolman, was obliged to raise the student fees in order to fatten revenue, it seemed that the AMS had regained its purpose and direction. It now seemed to understand what its normative boundaries were and, while there would be good and bad years ahead, how to address the needs of the modern Queen's student. The pub, for instance, reopened, and, after a bit more spilled beer, hit its stride, renaming itself "The Underground" in 1976 and, three years later, "Alfie's," in honour of Alfie Pierce, Queen's beloved, if racially stereotyped, football "mascot" of yore.

The Student as Consumer: Putting Heads on Pillows

Through the AMS's mid-1960s reformation, the university administration had initiated its own program of adjustment to changed student sensibilities. This extended well beyond the inclusion of a student voice in university governance. It reflected a broad recognition that students at Queen's were no longer wards of the administration, but rather were young adult citizens, whose rights and responsibilities merited constant attention. They were also becoming "consumers," not just recipients, of education. As competition grew among Ontario universities for the best and brightest undergraduate recruits, the quality of a university's student services increasingly weighed in the balance of a student's decision to come to and stay at Queen's. This began with student accommodation, always a thorny issue on Queen's increasingly cozy campus.

Principals Corry and Deutsch were acutely aware that Queen's could not grow towards a "steady state" of around ten thousand students without a massive expansion of student accommodation. The 1950s had seen sizable expansion of on-campus residences: McNeill, Morris, and Leonard residences had been opened to cater to male undergraduates, and Chown Hall had bolstered women's on-campus accommodation. But, as enrolment

The 1960s saw Queen's triple in size. Given the relatively small size of Kingston, the university adopted the de facto policy of guaranteeing a residence bed for every first-year student. Boxy, monolithic Victoria Hall residence for women opened in two stages in mid-decade.

surged in the 1960s, demand for beds quickly outstripped supply. Several factors compounded the problem. The simple trust that surplus demand would be soaked up by Kingston boarding houses and rental accommodation proved naive. The venerable boarding-house tradition á la Bertha Bailey withered. The introduction of government income supplements, such as the Canada Pension Plan and state health care, reduced the dependency of widows and single women on boarders. And, at the same time, students acquired an appetite for living on their own in rented accommodation. A rented apartment seemed so much more sophisticated and liberating. (The term *lifestyle* gained currency in the sixties.) The problem here was that the stock of rental accommodation in Kingston was limited, old, and consequently expensive. At the same time, students found themselves competing for housing with the swelling number of young faculty arriving in Kingston. Thus, the onus shifted back to the campus, where new beds had to be squeezed onto the already-crowded venue.

New residences were more easily imagined than built. Provincial post-secondary education budgets did not encompass non-academic capital projects. New residences had to be funded out of endowments (never a preferred route at Queen's) or made possible by commercial-style capitalization through agencies such as the Canada Mortgage and Housing Corporation and the Ontario Student Housing Corporation. This required careful financial planning to ensure that income from the residences would service their amortization. Throughout the 1960s, the trustees found themselves caught in the agonizing dilemma of meeting student demand for beds and not unduly extending the university's indebtedness. Nonetheless, the results were impressive. A huge new women's residence, Victoria Hall (named for the monarch who had made Queen's possible in 1841), was opened in two stages in 1965 and 1968, adding 750 beds. Over on Leonard Field, conjoined Gordon and Brockington halls were constructed, following an expansion of Leonard Hall. In 1969, Harkness Hall on Clergy Street opened to provide close-to-campus accommodation for upper-year and international male students. The Students' Memorial Union was also expanded to afford rooms for graduate and visiting students.

"A Puzzle of Patterns"

As the graduate school grew, a premium developed on accommodation for married students, pressure that intensified with the opening of the education college. In the early seventies, a married-students residence for 260 people was built in Calvin Park near the West Campus, followed by a 450-bed residence tucked in behind McArthur College. All in all, it was an impressive expansion. In 1964, 27 per cent of Queen's students lived on campus; by 1968 that total had risen to 33 per cent.[86] But it was not enough. Principal Deutsch repeatedly told the trustees that Queen's inability to house its entire student body was a "serious" issue, one likely to erode student trust in their institution's administration. In November 1968, he warned the trustees that the university had a chronic 850-bed shortfall, and that as many as 1,500 beds might be needed over the next five years.[87] Student housing thus emerged as a problem in lockstep with the university's creeping growth in enrolment. Late every summer a predicable crisis materialized as the administration tried to shoehorn the ever-burgeoning freshman class into the tight supply of residence beds; every year a handful of new Queen's students found themselves temporarily bivouacked in local motels or double-bunked in single residence rooms.

At Queen's, student accommodation provoked constant pragmatic adjustment. As the pressure for space grew, the old administrative division between men's and women's residences was done away with in the interests of centralized oversight of all the residences. The venerable Ban Righ Board, which had so ably managed the women's residences since the 1920s, was merged with the Men's Residence Board, although the dean of women retained control of daily life within the women's residences. The new Residence Board reported to the Senate, an indication of how closely the issue of student accommodation was tied to students' overall academic success at Queen's. The Board was thus put in a position to lay out a strategic blueprint for the residences. In the early 1970s, two high-rise apartment towers for married and older students – *An Clachan* (Gaelic for "the village") and John Orr (in honour of biochemist John Orr, who had ably directed the men's residences until his 1965 death) – were erected on the new West Campus, which had given the university some breathing room. In 1974, Jean Royce Hall opened adjacent to the new educational college, providing rooms for education students and some main-campus overflow. While the West Campus provided a new frontier for residence expansion, living away from the main campus generally did not appeal to undergraduates, who saw main campus as a the epicentre of campus life and the West Campus as a kind of Siberia (even though it was only a brisk walk away to the west). Compounding the problem was the insatiable demand for more parking spaces on or near the main campus. "Parking or Housing?" a *Journal* headline asked in 1968.[88]

The 1970s also saw the end of gender segregation of the university residences. The old residences had quarantined males and females. A strict code of gender deportment prevailed – women wore skirts to dinner and observed evening curfews. Men might only visit the common rooms of women's residences on Sunday afternoons. A tradition of panty raids and midnight escapes through residence windows testified to the dictum that rules were meant to be broken. In the 1970s such rules were largely abandoned for good. Egged on by the AMS, the Residence Board inched towards making the residences coeducational. Referenda on the issue revealed that male students were far more eager to cohabit with women than women with men. Nonetheless, in 1972, Morris Hall became a coeducational residence. Other residences followed. Some floors remained reserved for unisex occupancy. The residences were brought into sync with the more permissive times of the 1960s in other ways. Lounges where couples could listen to popular music were added. Snack bars and a coffee house opened. In Victoria Hall, a floor was set aside for students wishing to speak

French. Counselling services for birth control and rape awareness were encouraged by Dean of Women Evelyn Reid (1971–80). In short, the residences became not just places to sleep and eat, but places to round out a formal education.[89]

Faced with a perennial squeeze in accommodation, the university progressively surrendered to the Kingston rental market, trusting that local landlords would somehow supply the needed extra capacity. Late in 1967, a hopeful Principal Corry confided in the trustees that the growing trend of students moving into off-campus apartments after their first year would alleviate the strain on campus and allow the university to concentrate on furnishing sufficient space for first-year students in the residences.[90] Despite the Bus-It service, Queen's students favoured the walkable residential areas immediately adjacent to the campus, particularly Sydenham Ward. Where the old boarding houses once thrived, apartments now multiplied. By 1978–79, 65 per cent of the roughly five thousand Queen's students living off-campus found their accommodation in a cluster around the campus in Sydenham Ward. This migration brought more and more Queen's students into daily contact with Kingstonians. As the student density grew in Sydenham Ward, friction developed between exuberant adolescent hormones and middle-class respectability. The AMS and the principal's office increasingly found themselves in correspondence with irate citizens over issues such as noise bylaws and orientation-week hijinks.[91]

Through the 1970s, Sydenham Ward gradually filled up with students. Sometime late in the decade, parts of the ward just to the north of Queen's acquired the nickname "the Ghetto," perhaps in emulation of the famous student enclave attached to the eastern flank of Montreal's McGill University. The term was descriptive, not pejorative. Neighbourhood relations remained generally harmonious, although the exuberance of orientation – house parties and street parades – created complaints each autumn. As the residential density and balance began to tip in favour of students, the problems and stresses began to mount – though the real frictions still lay in the future. In the interim, Kingston's business leaders reminded themselves that the Queen's students represented a tremendous economic shot in the arm to the local economy. (There was, at the same time, simmering resentment that beds in campus residences escaped the net of city taxes. In the mid-decade, the province began compensating the city for taxes lost on university-provided accommodation – the so-called "heads and beds" tax rebate.) For their part, Queen's students began to think of the Ghetto as *their* ward. "Yeah – but without Queen's, you know," read the caption on a 1968 *Journal* cartoon depicting students cavorting in the streets, "this city would be broke."[92] This creeping sense of entitlement hinted of problems ahead.

A Healthy Mind and Body

The 1960s witnessed a revolution in the way Canadians tended to their health. The federal Medical Care Act of 1966 marked the culmination of Canada's decades-long, slow march from private to publicly funded health care. "Medicare" was becoming a core value of Canadian society. In its microcosmic way, Queen's reflected this watershed transition. Queen's students in the early 1960s received minimal medical attention. The university maintained an infirmary and appointed a University Health Officer, but the service was, as one doctor remarked, little more than a "Band-Aid and Aspirin dispensing unit."[93] There was a daily military-style sick parade. The university also set certain health standards for its undergraduates – well into the sixties, freshman applications had to be accompanied by an X-ray to demonstrate healthy lungs. (First-year students also had to pass a swimming test.) However, if a student became seriously ill, outside medical assistance was necessary. To cover this contingency, the AMS negotiated collective medical

❖ *Hazing: From Initiation to Orientation* ❖

"Is initiation a carry-over from our tree-swinging days?" wondered the *Tricolor* in 1968. A member of the newly created Queen's sociology department might have answered that initiation – the rite of inducting a person through various rituals into a group culture – was a centuries-old compulsion. Initiation, or "hazing" or "rushing," as colleges often called it, can build cohesion and purpose in a group. Sociologically, hazing seeks to employ personal debasement – humiliating acts, bizarre garb, or grovelling subservience – to reduce an individual to a point at which group allegiance might be inculcated. "Tradition" justifies initiation's perpetuation. The problem lies in determining the boundary between inflicting lasting damage on a person's ego and fostering healthful social purpose.

Initiation had been a facet of student life at Queen's since the 1850s. Rituals such as obliging freshman to measure playing fields with sausages and chanting Gaelic ditties – *Cha Gheill!: No Surrender!* – were aimed at building school spirit and interfaculty rivalry. While the Senate had ultimate authority over student life on campus, practical orchestration of initiation was delegated to faculty societies. The tendency was for initiations to drift into ever-more-demeaning antics and for the Senate then to apply a corrective. The sixties witnessed such a tussle. For freshmen and freshettes arriving on campus in the fall of 1961 there was a good deal of fun to be had in initiation: dances, silly games, school songs, parades down Princess Street, and charity drives. A "frosh court" dispensed rough justice on trumped-up charges like molesting squirrels. Beer was tasted, sometimes for the first time. The rite of passage for "plumbers" (as engineering students were often lightheartedly called) was less frivolous, probably because theirs was an all-male fraternity. The hair of freshmen was shaved and their week culminated with an assault on the grease pole under a fusillade of eggs and tomatoes. For medical students, the week usually entailed an initiation involving cadavers. These hallowed rituals were administered by second-year students, sinisterly dubbed "Vigilantes."

By the mid-1960s, things seemed to be getting out of hand. Principal Corry talked about the "problem of initiation": too much rough stuff and not enough acculturation to the normal life of the university. In one frightening incident, an engineering student was thought to have been drowned when his whole class was "baptized" in Lake Ontario. The Senate passed a motion prohibiting "undesirable initiations involving personal violence, personal indignity or interference with personal liberty." This proved difficult to enforce, although the engineers stopped shaving heads. Arms were now dipped in purple dye. The demand for initiations less predicated on horseplay and humiliation and more on preparation for academic life continued to grow. The AMS endorsed a more "useful and friendly welcoming of newcomers." The term vigilante was dropped and replaced by Gael (Arts and Science), FREC (Applied Science), and Boss (Commerce). The *Tricolor* noted "a realization that first-year students are people is slowly gaining strength."

By the late decade, the Arts and Science faculty attempted a thorough rethinking of initiation. The president of ASUS, Andy Pipe, called for the abolition of hazing and the adoption of an "orientation" program which would downplay group behaviour and focus on the individual. Outlandish costumes and boozy antics would be replaced by activities that would tutor newcomers on their integration into academic and residence life. Pipe asked for too much, too soon. An attempt to impeach him failed, but a subsequent referendum strongly backed the continuation of some moderate hazing in what was now called *Orientation* Week. The trend to a more humane rite of undergraduate passage continued, especially in the arts. Gaels, for instance, stopped wearing military-style red armbands. Students uneasy with the whole orientation experience were allowed to opt out. The AMS imitated a post-mortem process every year to fine-tune orientation to student needs. In a farmer's field in Barriefield, however, young engineers continued to find themselves every year at the wrong end of a hail of rotten tomatoes.

coverage with a private insurer and required students to support this coverage with an annual ten-dollar payment, collected with their fees.

In 1964, the AMS expressed "growing dissatisfaction" with this flimsy scaffold of student health care. That spring, a conference on student mental health and the growing inner stress of life on university campuses was held at Queen's. Again, the AMS complained that little was available for students suffering from such pressures. The Senate responded by asking Dr John Read, head of the department of preventative medicine, to investigate. Read advocated the placing of all student health care under the control of the university administration. A health council would monitor policies. The deans endorsed the proposal, pointing out that a vast majority of Queen's students came from out of town and lacked a local doctor. The medical needs of the growing number of married and foreign students coming to Queen's also warranted better university-centric health care. Principal Corry told the trustees that the university must respond, especially in the area of mental health. Dean Botterell of medicine eagerly backed the plan, arguing that it was in line with the general drift towards centralized medical services in Canada, and that it would provide his students with a steady flow of hands-on experience. The trustees voted $39,000 to beef up student medical services.[94] Group coverage for Queen's students was negotiated with a major insurance company, for which students continued to pay an annual fee.

In August 1964, Dr Donald Upton, a Queen's-trained psychiatrist practising in Montreal, was appointed director of what was now called the Student Health Service at Queen's. Operating first out of a house on Union Street and then from larger facilities on Stuart Street, the new service offered students an array of medical and psychiatric services. Nurses orchestrated the daily routine of a morning clinic and subsequent referrals. Two infirmaries tended to the longer-term care of students. The service was an immediate success; in 1965–66 Upton reported that more than seven thousand students walked through the clinic's door.[95] Upton himself proved an able ambassador for the service, giving interviews to the *Journal* on topics such as "sex, suicide, and students." Seventy per cent of students coming to the clinic, he reported, did not have any diagnosable illness, but were there instead for assistance in "coping with the stresses of the educational process."[96] The service also reached out across campus to spread its message, with Upton, for instance, advising the residences on food safety.

There were problems. While the university took pride in the fact that it now had "an integrated, comprehensive health service," not all the service's policies were clearly thought through. This became acutely apparent when women students appeared at the clinic seeking birth-control advice and the Pill. At the heart of second-wave feminism was women's assertion that they alone should control their reproduction rights. Books with titles like *Our Bodies, Ourselves* circulated freely and spoke to this empowerment. In Canada, large metropolitan universities were the first to experience this wave of liberation. The *McGill Birth Control Handbook* became not just a source of practical information but also a feminist manifesto. In provincial Kingston, such liberation came more slowly. Given the university's reliance on local medical practitioners to support its medical faculty and student health service, the student clinic on Stuart Street tended to reflect the varied attitudes of its staff on the propriety of birth control, rather than any uniform policy on its accessibility. Doctors were left to the dictates of their own consciences, often oblivious to the notion that women now considered birth control their *right*, not the moral prerogative of a doctor. One Queen's student recalled that, in 1968, she went to the clinic and asked for a prescription for the birth-control pill from the doctor on duty. The agitated doctor pulled a recent clipping from the Kingston *Whig-Standard* from his pocket and waved it in front of her. The article appeared to link birth control and loose sexual behaviour. "I suppose you too think that this is a 'sex clinic'?" he said. She persisted. So did he, and she left empty-handed.⁹⁷ Other doctors were more accommodating and less moralistic. Nurses in the know at the clinic, like Marilyn Bennett, directed women seeking the Pill to sympathetic staff doctors like Hans Westenberg and James Day, who dispensed the Pill after an objective professional discussion.⁹⁸ The university's capricious approach to birth control was reflected in the deliberations of the health council, where some board members, like the university chaplain and the dean of women, vocally opposed distribution of the Pill, arguing that it was "immoral." It would fall to the AMS to push the university into a consistent policy of complying with student demand for the Pill. Copies of the McGill handbook were handed out free, and student politicians pressured the Senate to get with the times. By the early 1970s, the clinic acquiesced.

The emergence of integrated student health services at Queen's reflected the new definition of student as citizen and consumer. The old student passivity was fading. From the moment that a student applied for admission to departure from campus with degree in hand, the student was now increasingly regarded as an active participant in all aspects of his or her education. Thus, front-line student services became crucially important. A dissatisfied student might decamp or spread the word to potential applicants that Queen's was not up to the mark in catering to students' needs. The awkwardly executed dismissal of Jean Royce from the registrar's office and Pearson Gundy's shunting out of the University Librarian's office are explicable in this light: the university could not afford to have bottlenecks in these crucial front-line functions. The same fate awaited Donald Upton in the Student Health Service. Although he had pioneered research on the ability of psychotherapy to improve academic performance, Upton's daily administration of the service was deemed to be lackadaisical and prompted complaints from students that the clinic was inefficiently run. Upton himself suffered from personal distractions. Sensing that a failure to deliver crisp medical services to students would tarnish the university's ability to retain undergraduates, Principal Corry and Dean Botterell "redesignated" Upton in 1967 and appointed surgeon Dr Herbert Greenidge as the new director. Upton remained a professor of psychiatry, but soon left Queen's.⁹⁹ Under Greenidge, the Student Health Service quickly righted itself.

The "Just Society" Comes to Queen's

Queen's responded to the changing sensibilities and expectations of its students in other ways during these heady years. Anachronisms were tidied up. The university had very loyal and generous alumni, who had kindly displayed their gratitude by funding scholarships so that others might follow in their footsteps. Many of these donations and bequests reflected the values of their creators, values which often proved out of kilter with the liberalized ethos of the sixties and seventies. Queen's had, for instance, been handsomely endowed by Colonel Reuben Wells Leonard – ironically, an RMC graduate – who, since the 1920s, had donated land and money to the university. The Leonard Field residences stood on land that he had donated. The scholarships which he also endowed contained, however, a worm in the apple. Leonard, who had died in 1930, stipulated that the scholarships be awarded to young Canadians who would work towards "the preservation and development of civilization," goals that were "primarily functions of the white race." Leonard instructed that clergymen's offspring be given the inside track, especially if they seemed ready to uphold the cause of Empire.¹⁰⁰ Other benefactors favoured stout Presbyterian lads from eastern Ontario, and specifically ostracized French-Canadians from their beneficence. One specifically excluded any student who was "a Communist, Socialist or a Fellow Traveller" from his largesse.¹⁰¹ Principals Corry and Deutsch instantly realized the injustice of such conditions and, working with the university lawyers and fundraisers, rooted out old prejudice and barred its perpetuation in new benefactions.¹⁰²

The redefinition of the Queen's students along more inclusive and democratic lines manifested itself in other ways. The folding of the Levana Society into the Arts and Science Society in 1968, for instance, removed gender demarcations in the student body. That same year saw the end of a venerable link between the Canadian military and Queen's male students, a link that stretched back to the raising of a World War I student contingent. After World War II, male students at Queen's had been able to combine their education with weekly officer-training programs offered by the Canadian army, navy, and air force under the Canadian Officer Training Corps program. Beyond weekly parades at HMCS *Cataraqui*, the program offered summer employment and a convivial annual cycle of mess dinners and balls. Although the decision to kill the program came from cost-conscious Ottawa (which was also educating would-be officers at the nearby Royal Military College), the melding of universities and the military was increasingly regarded with skepticism in a decade increasingly jaded by the Cold War and Vietnam.

The student citizen at Queen's in these years also experienced an ill-defined transition from the paternalistic world, in which their daily behaviour was governed by a loose partnership of university and AMS, to a world in which jurisdiction over student deportment in society seemed increasingly to fall between two stools of jurisdiction. The natural justice dispensed by the AMS Court and the "law" enforcement provided by the AMS constable system had worked well in days of what was construed as adolescent misbehaviour – beer at football games, raids on RMC dormitories. Fines were dished out and wrists were slapped. By the late 1960s, as we have seen, students were increasingly regarded as fully fledged citizens in the broader Canadian society, and the question of what was called "student non-academic discipline" became enveloped in jurisdictional haze. Where did the campus end and where did civil society begin? The 1970–71 deliberations of the Senate Committee on Grievance, Discipline, and Related Matters agonized over this dilemma.

"Students are fully accountable and wholly responsible individuals," their report concluded, setting out a broad range of rights and responsibilities they might enjoy and exercise. There was, however, a practical problem of actually spelling out "ascertainable rules of conduct." The report suggested a code of conduct, which would apply not just to students, but to all members of the Queen's community. The proposed code sought to demarcate "acceptable" and "unacceptable" behaviour on campus.¹⁰³ Some of these clearly fell in the sphere of external civil and criminal justice. Others relating to social conduct on campus seemed to fall within the ambit of university bodies, ranging from resident boards to the Senate, which had traditionally been the ultimate authority over non-academic student discipline. The issue was thorny. Who, for instance, policed student conduct in the burgeoning student ghetto? Constables of the AMS had policed football trains en route to Toronto, but did they have the right to intervene in house parties on Frontenac Street? As the AMS brief to the Senate committee in 1970 stated: "Another problem we have faced for a long time is the ambiguity and insufficiency of detailed material in the AMS constitution, concerning just what actions by students are considered to be problems resolvable by the AMS Court … The Court needs a much more detailed coda of both penalties and offences to be maximally effective."¹⁰⁴ Elsewhere, the AMS complained that too many of the rules governing the Queen's community were "rather amorphous and helter-skelter, written and unwritten."¹⁰⁵ Nonetheless, the AMS contended that its surveys indicated that students wanted to be policed by their own peers, rather than outside authorities. Even here there were problems: wages for the corps of eighty AMS constables were said to be low at a time when constables complained that they faced an ever more unruly and liberated student body. Compounding this was the charge that the constable system contained few women – only 20 of 120 in 1971 – and that quotas kept women out of the force.[106] Policing the conduct of the modern student aware of his or her "rights" at Queen's would be an ongoing, and at times excruciating, problem.

Even the nature of athletic life at Queen's changed its complexion in these years. For years, the Athletic Board of Control, a panel of appointees including the director of athletics, Al Lenard, had overseen students' participation in intercollegiate and intramural sports at Queen's. The Athletic Board tilted its budget and deliberations towards the perpetuation of Queen's prowess in intercollegiate competition, particularly on the gridiron. The AMS reinforced this culture by exacting an annual athletics fee from students and at the same time applying student funds to the band and the cheerleading corps, the celebratory props of Queen's football. The annual Colour Night crowned this cycle, as awards were handed out to each year's outstanding athletes. Each year, the Johnny Evans Memorial Trophy went, for instance, to football's most valuable player. Below this crust of intercollegiate excellence lay a layer of intramural sports usually organized around clubs and interfaculty team competition. By the late 1960s, about 40 per cent of Queen's students participated in such informal sports, a number probably kept low by the poor quality of athletic facilities. Particularly galling to students was the loss of the venerable Jock Harty Arena in 1968, a loss necessitated by the inexorable expansion of the academic precinct.

Participaction Comes to Queen's

The creeping mood of broader participation in Queen's culture in these years was soon felt in campus athletics. With the emergence of a structured physical-education program at Queen's under Donald MacIntosh, agitation grew for a more thoroughgoing and systematic approach to Queen's athletics. A 1966 report by Dean of Graduate Studies Clifford Curtis had called for a centralizing of control over Queen's athletics. In the spring of 1969, Principal Deutsch followed up by asking Queen's cardiologist Jack Milliken to head an advisory committee on athletics at Queen's. Almost immediately, there was opposition in some quarters: football stalwarts feared that the new School of Physical Education would be given preference over the star sports. Milliken's report did indeed prescribe a dramatic change of course for athletics at Queen's. Student athletics at Queen's should, the report advocated, become more centralized, with the School of Physical Education overseeing both intramural and intercollegiate sports. The ethos of student sports at Queen's should be rooted in participation, not competition. The Athletic Board of Control, soon to be renamed the University Council on Athletics, would cease to be a standing committee of the AMS, but would continue to manage the athletics budget. Playing a sport at Queen's would no longer mean being a quarterback before a roaring crowd, but instead might mean bumping a volleyball back and forth every Tuesday evening. The subsequent opening of a new, multi-purpose athletic complex with a series of gyms and workout rooms, and an arena, precipitated the shift to a broader base of athletics at Queen's.

The recognition of broad athletics participation as an integral, rather than a peripheral, part of a Queen's education served to accelerate something that had been incipient in the Queen's culture for over a century: that Queen's was a place of amateur-sports enthusiasts. In the wake of the Milliken Report, a panoply of more than forty intramural sports opened up on campus. The new Bartlett Gym complex became heavily used, and student athleticism became a strong selling point for Queen's, as running, curling, badminton, and a myriad other sports flourished on campus. Some remarked that this transformation had come at a price: the decline of Queen's vaunted football tradition. The Golden Gaels had been splendidly triumphant in the 1960s, but had slipped steadily as the 1970s unfolded.

Coach Tindall still commanded immense admiration from his players, but the days of recruiting brawny linebackers and swift receivers from small-town Ontario seemed gone. Some suggested that Queen's ever-rising admission standards were making it difficult to attract promising athletes, students whose grades might not be up to Queen's mark. Ceilings on scholarship levels set by the intercollegiate sports bodies made it difficult to attract promising footballers. Rising academic standards also militated against the retention of players who found it hard to juggle both academics and football. Old-time players had boasted that they could devote the fall to the gridiron and the winter to their books and manage to squeeze through the year. This was now less possible. Football's slide was perhaps precipitated by the demise of hallowed Richardson Stadium, another victim of academic expansion on the main campus. The advocates of participatory sports at Queen's, like Arts and Science Dean George Harrower, pursued a double agenda: by squeezing football and hockey out of their old venues, they created precious new space for academic expansion. The new stadium was thus erected on the West Campus. On 18 September 1971, Liberal cabinet minister James Richardson, latest scion of the Richardson family that had so faithfully supported Queen's growth, inaugurated the new Richardson Stadium. In a bit of Queen's kitsch, cheerleaders, accompanied by the band, carried a lump of sod from the old stadium down Union Street to the new stadium, where Richardson implanted it in the new gridiron.

Centring Student Life at Queen's

The new stadium did not, however, draw the same crowds as its predecessor. It lacked the atmosphere of the old walled stadium. Despite what Harrower and his ilk believed, football had worked itself into the sociological fabric of Queen's and the distant new stadium seemed too much on the margins to perpetuate the tradition. It was a hike from the

Westward ho! The opening of the West Campus to accommodate the education faculty provoked other geographic shifts. In 1971, Queen's relocated its gridiron to a new Richardson Field, tucked in behind McArthur College. Here Queen's cheerleaders transport the sacred sod of the old stadium to the new stadium. The 1923 Grey Cup football went along for the ride.

main campus, especially for the carless football fans living in residence. And the scores were not what they used to be. The nadir came in the 1974 season, when the Gaels won two and lost five. "The sad thing is that what is being lost is not just an athletic tradition," former AMS president and trustee Bruce Alexander wrote the principal, "but a significant Queen's tradition ... the unique social role this Saturday afternoon outing played for Queen's, bringing together as it did various constituents of the Queen's community."[107] In 1975, coach Tindall announced his intention to retire. His had been a truly remarkable record since his coming to Queen's in 1955: nine Yates Cups and a national Vanier Cup victory, not to mention success in coaching the Queen's men's basketball team to several intercollegiate championships. At a hugely attended farewell dinner in the spring of 1976, Tindall – "the sage of Syracuse" – bid farewell to Queen's. He had, he said, hoped to go out in "a blaze of glory," but, he noted with wit, that this had not done Joan of Arc "much good." Football would not, however, disappear at

To provide a social centre point for faculty life, the university purchased and refurbished the 1845 Herchmer House on King Street as a faculty club for its burgeoning faculty. The club became a gathering spot for lunches and dinners, lectures, and the occasional beer.

Queen's, as a new winning formula would emerge under succeeding coaches.[108]

The newly evolved ethos of student life at Queen's was by the early 1970s lacking a crucial element: a modern student centre to act as a crossroads of student life on campus. Since 1927, Queen's had had the student union at the corner of Union and University, but, despite being rebuilt after a 1940s fire, the Students' Memorial Union was now bursting at the seams. The AMS and *Journal* offices were crammed into its rabbit-warren of a basement. Upstairs, there were traditional elements of Queen's student life, such as the Memorial Room, commemorating the university's war dead, and the Wallace Hall dining room, but some of the newer elements of that culture, like the pub and coffee house, had to share space. In 1969, Principal Deutsch told trustees that he considered more breathing space for the students a "high priority."[109] He worried, however, that government would be unwilling to fund such expansion. Nonetheless, he believed that the building might be undertaken as a partnership between the administration, the AMS, and the alumni. At the time, most universities were allowing student governments to proceed with their own autonomous student centres, entirely under student sway. Queen's would adopt a hybrid model, a centre under multi-party control. A users' committee was formed, chaired by math professor Dan Norman, with AMS and alumni participation.

Deutsch initially suggested that the whole block bounded by Union, University Avenue, Alfred, and Clergy streets (now the site of the Stauffer Library) would serve as an ample footprint for the centre, but as austerity came over the horizon in the early 1970s, this was scaled back to an add-on to the existing Union. This, however, entailed demolishing two classic, Queen Anne–style brick houses on University Avenue. One of these housed the fledgling Queen's birth-control centre. Advocates of that centre argued that nervous young women would be unlikely to venture into a big, impersonal building in search of such intimate advice. Others noted that Queen's was rapidly acquiring a reputation as a brutish developer, knocking down heritage homes in the name of progress. (A huge seven-hundred-space underground car park being built under the Lower Campus was disrupting life at the other end of campus.) The houses were nonetheless sacrificed to the bulldozer. Finally, in early 1974, a plan for the new

University Centre was unveiled. The old Union would first be renovated, and then a modern addition, designed by Arthur Erickson, would be tacked to its rear. Controversy continued. Plans to chop the lovely wood-panelled Wallace Hall into separate spaces were successfully opposed by members of the art history department who argued that Wallace Hall was a focal point of Queen's life.

Indicative of the inherent bond between the AMS and the administration, Queen's students ratified a $10 annual fee to support the construction of the new centre, a pledge that would eventually amount to a $500,000 contribution. Students also became party to the hybrid, tripartite management committee that oversaw the running of the centre as a kind of arm's-length university corporation. A general manager was hired to supervise the centre and a supervisory board installed. The finished centre was by no means a success. Architecturally, Erickson's ugly, concrete-clad addition clashed with the collegiate-Gothic limestone of the original Union. The concrete was soon stained and made grimy by pollution and rainwater. Inside, despite the inclusion of a central *ceilidh* (Gaelic for "place of gathering"), the building was a warren of dark passages and staircases. The AMS soon became resentful of its only partial control over the building, feeling handcuffed by its non-majority role on the management council. The centre's budget seldom balanced, and little provision was made for renewal and change. Nonetheless, the facility did unavoidably become a *ceilidh*: a place where a student might go to the bank, have a meal, attend an AMS meeting, buy some sundries, and, of course, have a beer at Alfie's. It would all have been a pleasant surprise to a student of 1961.

By the early 1970s, one traditional denizen of the Union was forever gone: the faculty. Wallace Hall's sacredness had in part rested on its role as a kind of de facto dining club for faculty. Nothing fancy was on offer, just sandwiches, a daily special, ice cream, and academic gossip. Tradition insisted that professors not sit alone; they were expected to join their colleagues for lunch. Much the same could be had a block down Union Street at the Queen's Tea Room, the privately owned greasy spoon. But by 1973 the Tea Room was also a memory, another victim of the Queen's bulldozer. By that time, the faculty had migrated across the campus to a handsome lakeside home that the university had purchased in 1965 and subsequently hired local architect Andrew Connidis to renovate.

"The Profs Are Getting Younger"

The opening of the faculty club in 1969 provides a telling metaphor for the transformation of Queen's faculty in the years down to the mid-seventies. Expansion was the byword for Queen's faculty in the 1960s. In 1961 it was more like a clique, a convivial clique whose members came to know each other well fraternizing (the word is deliberate) over lunch, sharing desks in their cramped academic quarters, rehearsing with the Faculty Players in the evening, and, for a chosen few, intellectualizing at the highbrowed meetings of the Saturday Club. This homogeneity was diluted by the massive expansion of the faculty in the 1960s. In 1960–61, Queen's had 226 full-time faculty; by 1970–71 there were 680. In 1968 alone, 50 new professors in Arts and Science were hired, a high water mark. This floodtide was swelled by the university's growing addition to adjunct and part-time professors. In 1961, faculty demographics revealed a postwar cohort of males – there were few women on staff – who had often served in the war and then settled into a comfortable academic existence after graduate work in England or America. They were by now middle-aged and middle class. The average faculty salary in 1961, it bears emphasis, has been estimated at $9,000. Through the 1960s, the faculty became remarkably younger. In 1968–69, the median age of an assistant professor at Queen's was thirty. For an associate, it was thirty-six, and for a full professor it was forty-seven. By 1970–71, the average professorial salary was $16,764, an 86-per-cent boost over the decade.¹¹⁰ So great was the rush to get bodies behind lecterns that many newly hired junior faculty still lacked a completed doctorate.

The 1960s were thus the best decade in the century to aspire to a career on a university campus. It was a seller's market. With this in mind, university administrators worried about both attracting and retaining faculty. Kingston was a small town with little of the allure associated with big-city universities. Many, in fact, liked the city; its limestone and lakeside ambiance beguiled many grown jaded by exposure to graduate studies in impersonal, metropolitan universities. Department heads nonetheless fretted that ambitious young academics would merely "park" at Queen's before seeking a greener academic pastures. Richardson Hall therefore conspired to "bait the hook" in an effort to induce new faculty to think of Queen's as a long-term employer. The new faculty club fit this ambition. The hope in renovating the King Street West home into a handsome facility, with dining room, lounges, bars, and a splendid lake view, was to make it the kernel of a faculty social culture. It seemed to work. A lunch crowd materialized, others gathered after work for a drink, and Friday evenings became renowned for liquid good times. Other inducements were devised to build faculty loyalty. Low-cost mortgages were offered to new faculty to enable them to penetrate the tight Kingston housing market.¹¹¹ Departments developed their own mechanisms for bonding with new colleagues. Political-studies professor John Meisel related that, on his arrival at Queen's in the late 1940s, Alex Corry delivered a hand-me-down "departmental couch" to the new junior member to help make a sparse apartment more habitable. "The collegiality in the department was palpable," he remembered, "and, to my astonishment, was immediately extended even to the lowliest of the low on the totem pole – me."¹¹²

This collegiality infected newcomers to Queen's in the boom years of the 1960s. When economist John Hartwick arrived at Queen's in 1969 from his

No one professor can epitomize an era, but mathematics professor Ralfe Clench still strides through the memory of those who worked and studied at Queen's in the 1960s and 1970s. A true eccentric, Clench possessed a brilliant mind for organization: he mapped out, for instance, all the permutations of the university's class and examination schedule in his head. Everywhere he went, Clench sported a belt of tools, which seemed to meet every contingency, including unlocking the jammed door of Grant Hall one convocation day. He wore galoshes every day of the year to preserve shoe leather. Clench fitted out his University Avenue home with pulleys and remote controls to make domestic life effortless.

doctoral studies at Johns Hopkins, he initially lamented that he had landed in an "academic wilderness." He saw himself as "a chippy guy with large ambitions." Fortunately, the head of his department, future principal David Smith, possessed a "delicate touch in interpersonal relations," and Hartwick was soon won over to the "family culture" of Queen's. Smith had dextrously balanced the department's old-guard economists with young recruits steeped in the esoterics of microeconomics and econometrics. Hartwick liked the blend and served his career at Queen's.[113]

Rapid growth changed the ethos of Queen's faculty in many more ways than where it ate lunch. Individual departments expanded not just quantitatively, to keep up with Queen's surging student population, but also qualitatively, to encompass the intellectual diversification and intensification of their disciplines. Most professors in 1961 were expected to be jacks-of-all-trades when it came to teaching. They may have been hired at Queen's for their expertise in a particular field – George Whalley for his knowledge of Coleridge, for instance – but they quickly discovered that the department would deploy them in undergraduate survey courses designed to cover huge swaths of foundational knowledge.[114] From 1946 until the 1960s, the music department had been a one-man show, with Graham George serving as resident university musician and instructor. After 1959, George was supplemented by organist-composer F.R.C. Clarke, whose talents had to be shared part-time with the theology college. Graham and Clarke were obliged to spread their talents widely, from teaching music and musical theory on campus to playing church organs and to building up the Kingston Symphony Orchestra off campus.

Intellectual Diversity and the Dawn of Funded Research

The 1960s altered departmental chemistry dramatically. With the university expanding relentlessly through the decade, departments were able to structure themselves and fashion a repertoire of course offerings that reflected the growing sophistication of their disciplines. Take the geography department, for instance. Founded in 1960, it initially consisted of two professors – neither of them a full professor – and a map librarian. Courses were predictably limited to physical geography, cartography, and a smattering of human geography. Under the forceful leadership of Richard Ruggles, geography emerged over the next fifteen years as a diverse modern department. By 1975, it boasted a complement of seventeen professors and offered a panoply of courses reflecting the broadened pedagogic horizons of the discipline – geomorphology and spatial, cultural, industrial, economic, urban, and environmental geography. Graduate studies leading to an MA were now on offer and a PhD program was in preparation.

While some departments expanded and diversified within traditional parameters, other departments emerged *de novo*. Sociology hatched out of political studies and economics in 1968. In the Faculty of Medicine, the 1960s witnessed a growing recognition of the importance of family medicine – the delivery of primary care by front-line general medical practitioners. In the age of medicare, preventative medicine offered a way of pre-empting costly treatments by specialists once disease took hold. Family medicine required the drawing together of medical staff from disparate specialties – community health, epidemiology, paediatrics, and medicine – into a new cluster of skills. At Queen's, the family-medicine initiative was focused on preparing doctors for primary-care delivery in small communities, like Kingston and its environs. Beginning in 1967, Queen's created a Family Care Unit as an adjunct to the Kingston General Hospital's outpatient and emergency departments. In 1971, the Senate approved the creation of a fully fledged department of family medicine. A dedicated Family Care Centre was soon opened near the Hotel Dieu Hospital, allowing in situ family-practice clinics and supporting the placement of residents throughout eastern Ontario.[115]

Such maturation was common to almost every Queen's department. This had the effect of turning departments inward on their intrinsic culture and that of the discipline to which they belonged. Faculty became in this sense introverted, fixated on the structuring of their department into a pyramid of specialized knowledge and on interaction with specialists in their field away from Queen's – at conferences and through research projects. Two things accelerated this compartmentalization of departments. First, as Queen's grew and became codified in the way it managed its affairs, more and more faculty time had to be devoted to administering the departments and faculties to which they belonged. Departments now became "managed." Their growth could now be plotted through deliberate hiring decisions. Defining and realizing such vision required special leadership skills; academics do not come easily to consensus agreement. Interestingly, Queen's departments retained their established tradition of calling the person in charge the "head" of department. At most universities, the term "chairman," or more latterly "chair," was adopted to connote the fact that the affairs of the group could no longer be overseen in the cozy, self-perpetuating fashion that prevailed up to the 1960s. After 1971, heads of department were peer-elected, no longer appointed by order of the dean, and they also served for set terms, usually a period of five years.[116] Also, as graduate studies grew at Queen's, new positions of administrative importance, such as the supervisor of graduate studies, emerged in departments. Beyond their departments, professors began to find their lives encumbered by duties – on Senate committees and principal's advisory committees – linked to the broader campus community. In the 1970s, the phrase "committee work" acquired an increasing ring of opprobrium in professors' vocabulary.

Secondly, faculty began to recalibrate their academic ambitions away from teaching towards research. This would be a slow, but inexorable, transition. The primacy of good teaching remained paramount at Queen's: from 1960–61 to 1970–71 the ratio of full-time students to faculty fell from 25:1 to 22.3:1. Research was hitherto something to be done on the periphery, to be fitted into a teaching schedule, and usually only if the dean condoned the effort with funds at the university's disposal. Slowly, however, research and the competition for research funding asserted itself, another reflection of the intensifying sophistication of individual disciplines. Opinion polls showed that Canadians expected professors not only to educate their progeny, but at the same time to solve the problems of society. The inauguration of Queen's graduate-studies faculty in mid-decade intensified the realization of and competition for the kudos to be gained by faculty from research. In 1964, the university's entire expenditure on research was a mere $1,480,400. By 1968, it had ballooned to $3,637,600. Medical research dominated the list, followed by arts and sciences, with applied science trailing with a meagre $492,100.[117] While constitutional control of post-secondary education in Canada largely fell under provincial sway, the funding of research – construed to be in the national interest – fell to Ottawa. By the late 1960s, federal agencies such as the Canada Council, the Medical Research Council, and the National Research Council provided almost three-quarters of the research funding at Queen's. The province, corporations, foundations, and individual benefactors supplied the rest.

The effect of departmental diversification and the incipient hunt for research achievement tended to reorient the faculty away from campus approbation towards external accreditation. While friendships persisted, it no longer mattered so much what the fellow across the faculty-club table thought of you and your teaching. What mattered now was your success with external granting agencies or the editorial boards of academic journals. Credentialism was working itself into the culture of Queen's, especially as the process of tenure and promotion was codified by the Senate in the early 1970s. A faculty member's curriculum vitae now weighed heavily in the balance of tenure, promotion, and research-grant decisions – more heavily than the good impression that individual had made on the dean or departmental head. In terms of rooting out the "old-boys' culture" so prevalent in pre-1960s Queen's, this was, of course, a progressive turn, but it also had the effect of putting an edge of competitive meritocracy on faculty life at Queen's. Against the hard benchmark of publications and research dollars harvested, teaching paled as a yardstick of performance. Effective teaching was difficult to calibrate. In the early 1970s, efforts were made, largely under student pressure, to introduce a system of teaching evaluations at Queen's. Ironically, many faculty opposed such evaluation on the grounds that their performance in the classroom was a "confidential affair." In the early 1970s a number of AMS-sponsored course-evaluation reports – often dubbed "anti-calendars" – appeared, but in matters of tenure and promotion, teaching scores increasingly took a back seat to publications and research. (In the 1990s, the AMS would revive its advocacy of standardized teaching evaluations, co-operating with faculty and the administration to create the QUEST evaluation system.)

In an effort to polish the lustre of its faculty, Queen's in the late 1970s attempted to attract a handful of star professors who, it was hoped, would burnish the reputation of some of its departments and spearhead their quest for top-notch graduate students and research dollars. In 1968, for instance, political scientist David Easton came to Queen's as the inaugural Sir Edward Peacock Professor of Political Science. Although Canadian-born, Easton had built a reputation at the University of Chicago on his application of behavioural and systems theory to policy-making. He had also served as a consultant to Ottawa's Royal Commission on Bilingualism and Biculturalism. Principal Deutsch saw Easton as a welcome addition to Queen's long tradition of feeding expertise to Ottawa. Unfortunately, the appointment's potential never fully materialized. Easton continued to spend much time in Chicago, and the cachet he was supposed to bring to Queen's never left the Windy City. Far more successful was the 1970 appointment of economist Richard Lipsey to Queen's as the Sir Edward Peacock Professor of Economics. With experience at the University of Essex and the London School of Economics, Lipsey arrived with a brilliantly inquisitive interest in econometrics and how societies economically adapt. He was immensely popular as an undergraduate lecturer and found international fame as the author of a bestselling economics textbook that became a staple in the teaching of undergraduate economics. Other departments benefited from the infusion of dynamic new talent. In 1971, Hungarian-born composer Istvan Anhalt arrived to take up the headship of the newly created School of Music; new degree programs, a new music building, and the embrace of modernist musical tradition followed. Anhalt, one student recalled, was "very academic" and imparted "a very high level of professionalism" to the school.[118] Over in the Faculty of Medicine, Dr Harry Botterell recruited a bright pathologist, Nate Kaufman, away from Duke University to spearhead teaching, cancer research, and clinic work in the department of pathology.

The arrival of Easton, Lipsey, and their ilk underscored the growing internationalization of the university faculty. Postwar prosperity had built Canadian national confidence, but by the 1960s it also excited certain primal anxieties. Principal among these was the worry that we were letting control of our economy and culture slip into the hands of foreigners. In reaction, a loose movement of what was soon called the "new nationalism" emerged in Canada, often most vocally expressed on university campuses. All sorts of demands were put forward: ceilings on foreign ownership, government-funded cultural programs, and aid to Canadian publications and music among them. As Canadians became satiated by consumerism and invaded by new technologies, there was also the fear that our culture was being submerged by a tidal wave of "Americanization."[119] With fledgling Canadian graduate programs unable to meet the demand for home-grown university teachers, universities had little choice but to hire non-Canadians, or at best Canadians educated abroad, especially in hot, emerging disciplines such as sociology. Nationalists queried whether such interlopers, as they saw them, were inculcating proper "Canadian values" in the young minds open before them in the lecture hall. Many responded that such attitudes were the antithesis of what a liberal university should represent.*

Whatever the merits of the "struggle" to protect Canadian universities from foreign influence, the debate arrived at Queen's in 1968. The trustees, who read their newspapers and saw the issue of Americanization gathering momentum, asked Principal Deutsch whether the invasion had reached the shores of Lake Ontario. When one trustee fretted that too many American professors on campus in the topsy-turvy world of civil-rights and anti-war protest would "create discontent on campus," Deutsch replied that a university should not attempt "to control political beliefs" in its intellectual community. The principal also suggested that Queen's salaries were not sufficiently attractive for many Americans to apply.[120] The issue persisted. In 1970, Deutsch produced statistics that went against what appeared to be the national grain. Only 11 per cent of applicants for teaching posts at Queen's that year were American. In fact, of the existing faculty, only 9 per cent were American. Some 61 per cent of Queen's professors were Canadian-born.

The surprise was that 17 per cent were British, a reflection of the fact that, in the 1950s, many British academics, disgruntled with British austerity and budget cuts, opted to migrate to the "colonies." Most bonded with the expansive possibilities of Queen's and Kingston. Chris Crowder, who arrived to teach history in the mid-1960s, initially thought that crossing the Atlantic to a small Ontario town was like "walking the plank." Crowder quickly bought into the "more egalitarian" way of academic way of life at Queen's; he found the new faculty club "a focus of the faculty sociability."[121] Despite Deutsch's trepidation, Americans also joined the faculty. Geoff Smith, a Californian-trained specialist in American diplomatic history arrived in 1969 and was shocked to find the university so out of touch with the tumult that was engulfing many US colleges. Smith was struck by how "Anglo" Queen's seemed – afternoon tea was served at the faculty club, for instance – but soon learned to chivvy his seminar students with peppery questions about America's pretensions on the world stage.[122] The closest Smith came to being a Trojan Horse of Americanization was his avid interest in promoting better basketball at Queen's. The reality, Deutsch seemed to be hinting to the trustees, was that the Queen's faculty in these years of heady expansion was becoming what any good faculty should be: cosmopolitan, tolerant, and worldly wise, not chained to parochialism and exclusion.

A New Sense of Faculty Identity

For all the talk about faculty-club conviviality, the sheer scope of faculty growth and diversification in the years into the seventies doomed the old informality that had prevailed in relations between faculty and staff at Queen's. Speaking to the faculty association annual dinner in 1963, a very clear-sighted Principal Corry predicted that "the old

---

*Was a Canadian with three foreign university degrees still a "Canadian"? Was an American who had done two graduate degrees in Canada still an "American"? How did one characterize a candidate for a teaching post at Queen's if he/she had been born in England, educated in France, and then taught for a decade in the United States?

informal, paternalistic (in the good sense) position of the university is passing away as the university grows, and the newer relationships based on contract replace the older ones relying on usage and custom" asserted themselves.[123] As Queen's modernized its structures and codified its procedures under Corry and Deutsch, it was inevitable that the relationship of those who managed the university and those who taught there would become more sharply defined. Queen's was becoming a "multiversity," to use a word that gained currency in that decade. Its faculty was now stretched from professional faculties such as Medicine and Law on through to Arts and Sciences and Applied Science. Such diversity did not lend itself to the old informality that saw hiring, promotions, tenure, and salary setting conducted in a chummy fashion, in which faculty tended to trust that their efforts were both appreciated and fairly rewarded. Hence, the fact that the principal was perennially invited as keynote speaker at the faculty association's annual dinner. Nonetheless, for most professors at the time, the notion that the association might act as a union seemed alien to the idea that academics were intellectual workers removed from unseemly confrontation with those who paid them. The demands of unionization, many argued, would erode academic freedom by obliging professors to put aside their individuality to man the barricades of class interest. An "association" was, however, palatable as a channel of communication with the administration. As the 1960s unfolded, inflation annually gnawed at salaries, the university's rapid growth fostered growing anonymity in the faculty, and the hot academic job market bred a broadening awareness that other universities offered different terms of employment.

There were also external pressures shaping faculty self-consciousness. The multiplication of university campuses across Canada was creating a sense that university teachers were a *national* class with national interests. In 1950, the Canadian Association of University Teachers (CAUT) had been formed to give voice to this incipient solidarity. Late in that decade, the arbitrary dismissal of Harry Crowe, a professor at Winnipeg's United College whose privacy had been invaded by the college administration, galvanized Canadian professors into a defence of their right to due process in matters of tenure and dismissal. At Queen's, professors stepped out of their regular lecture routine to brief students on the serious implications of the Crowe case for academic freedom. After his ejection from the Manitoba campus, Crowe was offered a sessional position at Queen's for a year. Early in the sixties, other common issues surfaced, such as the need for a protocol governing the presence of the RCMP as a Cold War surveillance presence on campus. Professors were also obliged to come together to find consensus on matters such as access to federal funding of research and Canada's embrace of a bilingual and bicultural culture. In many instances, Queen's faculty were able to consult CAUT background studies to calibrate their relative position in the spectrum of Canadian faculties. In 1966, for instance, newly appointed University Librarian Donald Redmond argued that librarians across the country were increasingly being regarded, not as glorified technicians, but as a professional grouping to be considered on a par with professors. The following year the entire librarian staff was reclassified as "professional."

Given this emerging group cohesiveness, Queen's faculty were willing, indeed expectant, participants in the university's campaign to codify the culture in which it operated. As described earlier, Principals Corry and Deutsch realized the need to regularize the way Queen's operated and related to its employees. Sabbatical policy became a faculty entitlement, ending the capricious awarding of leaves by deans and department heads. Faculty now "earned" their sabbatical according to a formula. Throughout the 1960s, the university pension plan was progressively reformed. What had once been a rather parsimonious deposit pension plan was enhanced by the advent of the Canada Pension Plan in 1966 and the subsequent adoption by Queen's of a money-purchase pension plan in the early 1970s. The plan was acknowledged as one of the best Ontario university plans in 1972,[124] although it still contained a systemic bias against women faculty members, who were not seen as principal breadwinners and therefore not assumed to require the same retirement support as a male breadwinner.

The fulcrum of change for faculty in these years rested on issues of tenure, promotion, and grievance, all of which moved from the realm of informality to codification. A large faculty simply could not be sustained, or attracted in the first place, without the laying out of specific processes and entitlements. In 1969, the Senate set out a "Statement on Academic Freedom and Tenure." The statement began with the primordial proclamation of the "freedom of a faculty member to study, to teach and to record knowledge according to his best professional judgment is a prerequisite for a university to fulfill its role in society." From this flowed the right to a transparent process of initial appointment and eventual securing of tenure, the road to which was laid out in detail. A Tenure Appeal Committee would be established to review cases of denied tenure. Standardized tenure was seen as a prerequisite lever on academic productivity: "Tenure entails the right of fair consideration for increases of responsibility and salary and promotion in rank."[125] On this foundation, the Senate Committee on Appointment, Promotion, Tenure and Leave (SCAPTL) was able to adjust faculty's basic employment rights. When, for instance, fiscal restraint in the seventies resulted in a startling increase in the number of term and sessional appointments, SCAPTL addressed the question of defining the rights of term appointees to ensure that they were not condemned to a permanent loop of insecure employment. Such adjustments would continue as the seventies unfolded. The point was that such adjustments were now in effect *negotiated* by faculty in the forum of a Senate committee and not determined at the whim of administration. Many complained that such fine-tuning often proved arduous and time-consuming ("the afternoon of the living dead," some joked), but most understood that academic employment was now crucially a matter of regulation and transparency.

Beyond appointment, tenure, and promotion, it always came down to money. And here the Queen's University Faculty Association (QUFA) came to the fore. Throughout the 1960s and early 1970s, unprecedented inflation and a growing awareness of what universities elsewhere were paying their staff put an increasingly sharp edge on the annual cycle of negotiating what professors would take to the bank each month. The tone of the negotiation tended to remain friendly and consultative – "warm and sympathetic" as Richard Gosse, the QUFA president put it in 1965[126] – but the willingness to give and take became less evident over time. The faculty association maintained a series of committees – salary, pension, and fringe benefits – and research groups that groomed its position on financial matters. Throughout the 1960s and early 1970s, two issues persisted in relations with the university administration: gnawing inflation and the idiosyncratic timing of the province's annual support of the university system. Propelled by a strong Vietnam War–fuelled economy, Canadian inflation rose steadily to the 10- to 12-per-cent range in 1973–74. This, of course, affected more than the university's wage bill; capital projects such as the new residences consistently exceeded initial cost projections. But for a predominantly young faculty anxious to buy homes and settle in Kingston, salary was the only relevant yardstick. From the perspective of Richardson Hall, however, the university's budget had to be stretched in many directions, especially in a period of rapid growth. This challenge of this delicate division was compounded by the fact that the province's annual operating grant to the university seldom arrived when promised. The university endeavoured to finalize its budget for the upcoming academic year in the late fall of the preceding year, but the province often dallied in announcing its annual operating grant until mid-winter. Thus, the crucial governor of growth in the university's budget was left up in the air until the last minute. In the summer of 1965, for instance, Principal Corry apologized that the announcement of the annual salary increase – 7.5 per cent – and promotion list had been delayed by the "ambiguities in the provincial grant."[127] A year later, the salary increase reached a whopping 13 to 14 per cent.

The QUFA used its affiliation with the Ontario Confederation of University Faculty Associations to point out that Queen's, in their opinion, was lagging behind other universities in its faculty salaries. Post-secondary educators cast an envious eye towards secondary-school teachers, arguing that school teaching was becoming a more lucrative career choice than university teaching. Richardson Hall was acutely aware of the threat of a salary-induced exodus of faculty, something that would undermine Queen's reputation for teaching. In 1970, David Dodge, the young Queen's economist, presented statistics indicating that certain areas of faculty expertise, such as economics and chemistry, were being denuded by the pull of higher salaries in the civil service and private sector.[128] On the whole, the willingness to find common ground prevailed in relations between the faculty and the administration. When the Duff-Berdahl Report arrived on campus in 1965, Principal Corry immediately dispatched it to the faculty association for its input. Corry and Deutsch each instinctively understood that confrontation with faculty would corrode the greater sense of community on campus. By 1974, a solid majority of Queen's faculty – 628 professors – belonged to QUFA, but its ethos was non-confrontational and gradualist. (Annual meetings were, for instance, thinly attended.) Sensing this, the principals were conciliatory in the face of faculty demands. The QUFA Salary Committee was, for instance, allowed access to select trustees, so that the hard realities of the university's financial situation could be discussed frankly. Still, Corry wrote candidly in 1965, "We all know that members of university staffs feel their oats these days, because their bargaining position gets stronger every year ... Here at Queen's, we have conceded a good many things."[129]

This mood of mutual engagement persisted into the 1970s, even when government-imposed austerity began to bite deeply into the university's operating budget. There was a willingness to talk to the other side, even if the news from the principal's office was increasingly grim. Even when the minority of female faculty decided in 1974 to protest the beleaguered status of female faculty by forming the Association of Women Teaching at Queen's, they urged their crusading membership to turn out at QUFA meetings, in effect to stay inside the tent, to bring pressure on the administration for more progressive policies. As Ron Watts took over the principal's office in 1974, it could legitimately be asked just how long this tradition of mutual consultation and respect could be maintained as the university slipped deeper into financial hard times. Perhaps ominously, QUFA in 1975 established created a committee to investigate "alternative mechanisms of salary negotiations."[130]

From Limestone to Concrete and Aluminum

One aspect of life at Queen's unavoidably united faculty, students, and administration in these years: the "built environment" at the university. Those familiar with Queen's in 1961 would have hardly recognized the place in 1974. Queen's had slipped westward across University Avenue throughout the sixties, displacing the football stadium and pushing one-time residential homes out of its way. To the east, it had expanded hard along Barrie Street by City Park, respecting the university's understanding with the City of Kingston that the park was sacred green space. To the north, Queen's had crept towards Clergy Street, buying up residential homes and expanding existing buildings along Union Street. Even the waterfront to the south, vigilantly guarded by the City, had seen a Queen's presence – the new faculty club – and there were plans for a huge new medical building overlooking the lake. Within these boundaries, the university learned to squeeze buildings into existing nooks and crannies in the name of academic expansion. It had also devoured once-familiar buildings like the venerable Jock Harty Arena and the hallowed Richardson.

Given the degree to which Queen's hung its image on the solidity of its limestone architecture, one might have expected that all this expansion emanated from some sort of master plan, or at least a set of guiding design criteria. But such was not the case. The "new" Queen's that unfolded in these years was guided by little other than expediency – a hurried scramble to create space for the great swelling of the student and faculty bodies. As early as 1961, just before the great surge hit, a Montreal consulting firm had urged the adoption of a more concerted approach to planning Queen's. If one looked beyond the curtain of lovely elm trees and abundance of limestone facades, the campus had "no formality of symmetry, nor balanced, designed symmetry."[131] Despite the report's call for a "well-defined, well-designed" approach to Queen's development, the Board of Trustees embarked on an ad hoc campaign of expanding the university. Admittedly, Queen's was perennially walking a financial tightrope, with the exigencies of hiring staff and putting students in classrooms and beds always trumping the aesthetics of campus development.

One might have thought that a policy of "limestone forever" might have given the university some physical and aesthetic stability. Queen's and the City of Kingston had invariably associated themselves with limestone. If Queen's had an abiding icon, it was Grant Hall, the 1905 Romanesque Revival building and tower constructed in limestone with contributions from students, faculty, and alumni. Life at Queen's routinely and metaphorically revolved around Grant Hall. (In 1973, the annual engineer's April Fool's prank entailed placing a huge Mickey Mouse watch face on the tower's clock.) But limestone had its limitations. Buildings made of it were solid, but inflexible, and they were formidably expensive to maintain. Classrooms in buildings such as Kingston and Ontario Halls were romantically picturesque with their high ceilings. But they were poorly insulated and difficult to retrofit to new teaching needs. They had often been built to a one-size-fits-all formula and, by the early 1970s, Queen's classes stretched from small graduate seminars to sprawling undergraduate courses in psychology.* Beginning in the 1970s, the trustees annually heard from their building committee that the list of deferred maintenance projects on the university's limestone buildings was burgeoning. The trustees, faced with more immediate needs, usually put such work on the back burner.

The crux of the problem was that the planning of new buildings required input from both the academic side of the university and the equally important financial- and physical-planning side of operations. And here the dialogue between the trustees and the Senate was often inarticulate. Each body had a long-term planning committee, but each also pursued different criteria. At a late-1967 trustees meeting, Principal Corry decried this chasm, arguing that "orderly planning" was the only way that the university could convince Queen's Park to fund the much-needed expansion of the campus. The two long-term planning committees were consequently merged. From this amalgamation emerged one guiding concept that Queen's would embrace over the next decade: the clustering of academic buildings into academic precincts. Arts and Science dean, George Harrower, argued that Queen's could better deliver its education if the services of each faculty

---

*One attempt to alleviate the space problem at Queen's entailed an exploration of television teaching. A prototype system in the early 1970s had allowed Professors Maurice Yeates in geography and Harold Good of biology to televise their lectures. Bernard Trotter, the principal's executive assistant, who had CBC experience, produced a report on television in 1972, but there seemed little sustained interest in the idea.

could be clustered in designated pockets of the campus, so that students could enjoy an economy of proximity in attending their classes and consulting with their professors. Social sciences, he suggested, should be concentrated in the area of the old football stadium. Applied Science could spread out from its existing quadrant along and to the north of Union Street. Medicine should gravitate to the southeast section of the campus south of Summerhill; to this end, the trustees endorsed the Kingston General Hospital's setting aside of 27.5 acres of land along Stuart Street as a precinct for the mooted new medical-sciences building. And the humanities would cluster north of Queen's Crescent.[132] As his campaign to reform the Queen's honours program was also revealing, Harrower had been acquiring a reputation as a progressive around Queen's, so his clustering proposal won loose approval as a lodestar for future building development.

Clustering did over time segregate the campus into academic precincts. It did little, however, to dictate the *quality* and *aesthetics* of new building at Queen's. In an environment of hurried expansion and financial belt-tightening, buildings were approved that were only loosely associated to each other or to any master aesthetic. Full-dressed limestone was abandoned as too expensive and inflexible. In its stead, cast and precast concrete dressed with Queenston limestone became the accepted style of Queen's buildings. Architects hired by the university embraced the Modernist style, but never with much verve. Here the problem was that the university tended to fall into the habit of using the same architectural firms, and therefore never reaped the benefits of a vigorous design competition at the conceptualization stage of any new building. Thus, the Modernist credo of "form-follows-function" came to Queen's, with its reliance on strong verticals and horizontals, little ornamentation, materials applied in their natural state, and exposed structural elements. This dominated Queen's expansion down to the 1990s. The results were usually not aesthetically pleasing. The only redeeming feature of the period was the unwritten dictate that no building should be higher than Grant Hall.

Beginning with Ellis Hall in 1958 as the new home of civil engineering and continuing through buildings like the Macdonald Building for law (1960), Stirling for physics (1961), Earl for biology (1966), Dupuis for chemical engineering (1966), John Watson for humanities (1967), Humphrey for psychology (1969), Jeffery for mathematics (1969), the new Harty Arena (1970), Goodwin for mining engineering, Harrison-Levine for music (1973) and concluding with the Mackintosh-Corry Building in 1974, Queen's largely forsook limestone for concrete. The buildings did provide space for the teachers and the taught, but the campus acquired a brutalist character, redeemed only by the remaining bastions of limestone.[133] Some of the buildings were dated in concept. Watson Hall (built with precast concrete slabs) as the hub of the humanities was heavily influenced by a committee headed by George Whalley, which argued that departments should be set out along long corridors, with full professors getting larger offices than junior faculty and with a faculty common room at the end of each corridor for afternoon tea and chit-chat. Jeffery Hall was obliged to crouch down in the shadow of Grant Hall. Obliged to go down as well as up, Jeffrey Hall ended up with awkward and seldom-used features, such as a sunken interior court and a charmless rear podium.

Queen's infatuation with Modernist architecture was epitomized by the design and construction of the Mackintosh-Corry Building in the early seventies. Modernism's appeal partly lay in its seeming flexibility – the fact that concrete could be poured to accommodate any function. In 1965, the idea of massing academic functions in one mega-building surfaced. At first, two ten-storey towers were proposed. The hiring of architect Ronald J. Thom in 1969 brought matters back to earth. Thom had won kudos for his designs of Toronto's Massey College

The Mackintosh-Corry building, completed in late 1974, forsook limestone altogether and embraced modernist concrete. Budget austerity and souring relations with architect Ron Thom crimped the project. Students found the building a bewildering maze. The elements soon began soiling the building's facade.

and Peterborough's Trent University campus with its constellation of colleges. Thom's inclination was to build a sprawling mall-like building of modular units connected by a central concourse or "street." He wanted "to allow the intermingling of staff and students from various disciplines."[134] Thom worked with a university planning committee headed by political scientist Ned Franks, and the project rapidly assumed an unprecedented dimension for Queen's: a 400,000-square-foot edifice capable of accommodating several Arts and Science departments. Space in the building was to be "fluid and re-assignable" so that pedagogic change over time could be accommodated. The building would be nestled in behind Dunning and Richardson halls, leaving space for 1,600 parking spaces on the footprint of the old football stadium immediately to the west. In 1971, the university told Queen's Park that the bill for the complex would be almost $6.5 million.[135]

Given its novel scale and scope, problems soon plagued the project. Construction coincided with the onset of a harsh austerity. The university began to cut corners on the budget; one whole wing – Block D – was cancelled, and the music department, initially a charter tenant, was shifted to a separate building. Architect Ron Thom grew testy, arguing that the university was undermining the "nobility" of his design. Lawsuits ensued, and Thom essentially abandoned his lead role in the project. In October 1974, the building, named in honour of former principals Mackintosh and Corry, was opened, with its central streetscape containing coffee shops and student-service offices. Most were intrigued by the design. Many, however, complained that the building, with its spin-off modules and warren of corridors, was counterintuitive and difficult to navigate. "Mac-Corry," as it instantly became dubbed, defied the logic of users habituated to buildings with long, straight corridors. Others disliked the monotonous use of drab concrete, which clashed with its limestone companions. Some liked all the open space and the absence of oppressive corridors. Numbering the rooms in the complex in a "one-up" fashion proved impossible, given its meandering footprint. A graduate student summed up the general reaction: the building was "cheap and efficient, but not attractive."[136] There was one other irritant: old-timers around Queen's did not like seeing Principal Mackintosh's name contracted to "Mac" in student argot.

The year after the building opened, the annual Susie-Q dance was held on the Mac-Corry "street." In effect, the old met the new. Nearly a decade and a half of pressured growth had changed the way Queen's looked and acted. The landscape had lost its limestone monochrome; concrete, aluminum, and glass now varied the campus. The students looked different. The crewcuts and bouffants of the early sixties were gone. The *Tricolor* graduation gallery was now dotted with scruffy, bearded men and women with long, straight hair. The campus was a sea of denim. If they wore skirts at all, women wore them short. Amid all this sartorial change, some things persisted: Queen's students still wore their leather faculty jackets, festooning them with their pass crests, class year, and departmental affiliations. And while social traditions such as Susie-Q Week were fading in an era of assertive feminism, the core of student tradition at Queen's proved durable. The university's celebrated pipe and brass bands, for instance, marched forward throughout these years as perhaps the most widely recognized symbol of "Queen's spirit." From alumni weekend reunions to the Grey Cup parade, Queen's bands projected the image of the university. When Allan Armit of Brighton, Ontario, arrived for his first year at Queen's in 1966, he found life in his boarding house dull and isolating. But when he joined the band to play the tuba and sousaphone, his life changed. The bands became the "glue" of his years at Queen's. The camaraderie of weekend bus trips to away games with football players and cheerleaders – including the inimitably beautiful and athletic "Cartwheel Jane" Campbell – anchored his Queen's experience, rounding out his enjoyment of time in the classroom with history, English, and philosophy professors. He emerged from his "Brighton shell" and revelled in what he described as Queen's "egalitarian society."[137]

A "New Queen's Spirit"

Allan Armit was hardly alone in acquiring the Queen's spirit in these years. Fewer students at the university now came from small-town Ontario; more now called urban centres like Toronto, Ottawa, and Montreal home. They, too, acquired Queen's traditions. In 1968, a group of thirty Queen's students from St Catharine's rented a billboard – replete with football motif – in the city and announced to passersby that "Queen's is the *only* university!"[138] The campus radio station, CFRC, epitomized such transmitted – both literally and metaphorically – tradition. Founded in 1922, the station was the second-oldest radio station on the air in Canada. Run by student and staff volunteers, CFRC had been briefly affiliated with the Kingston *Whig-Standard* and the CBC, but since 1957 had been managed by a paid general manager, the redoubtable Margaret Angus, and operated by the volunteer CFRC Radio Club. In 1953, it had obtained an FM licence, which also allowed it to broadcast its AM programs on the FM band. In 1961, the station initiated year-round programming, and by 1968 was offering 37.5 hours of shows a week. A year later, separate FM programming was launched. Live broadcasts of content as varied as football games and Vaghy String Quartet concerts were introduced. The station moved with the times: public-affairs programs with such provocative names as "Drugs and You" were aired. Overseen by a subcommittee of the Senate Committee on Fine Arts and Public Lectures, the station received financial support from the administration and the AMS, plus the avid support of its volunteers.

Nonetheless, its continued existence required constant vigilance and inventiveness. Costly new transmitters to upgrade the FM signal were needed. In 1972, the federal Canadian Radio-Television Commission questioned the station's licence status, arguing that it was in fact a "provincial institution." The broadcasters at CFRC fought back. Principal

Despite a decade of unprecedented growth, "Queen's spirit" proved effervescent. In 1968, a group of graduates dug into their own pockets to sponsor a billboard in St Catharine's to attest to their choice of university.

Deutsch, drawing on his federal connections, secured a renewal in Ottawa by pointing out the station's contribution to the public interest in the Kingston area. In this manner, CFRC perpetuated that deeply rooted Queen's tradition of doing public service. It spread knowledge and prepared young citizens to go out into the broader world. Music professor Fred Clarke described his CFRC show, "The Music Department," as an attempt to play "all sorts of obscure music which I liked and I felt other people should know about." His control-room operator, art history student Shelagh Rogers (BA '77), would soon move behind the microphone herself and, from there, to a distinguished career in the CBC.[139]

Such tradition could rebound on Queen's in positive ways, as alumni grateful for their education found ways to reciprocate for what Queen's had given them. Take the university's art gallery, for instance, established in 1957 by Agnes Richardson Etherington, sister of the 1930s Queen's chancellor, James Richardson, and wife of the dean of medicine, surgeon Frederick Etherington. The Richardson family had generously endowed the university since Agnes's other brother, George, had perished in the Great War: Richardson Stadium commemorated the loss of that soldier-athlete. Agnes's love of the arts was reflected in her formative role in the Kingston Arts and Music Club. Before her death in 1954, she established the George T. Richardson Memorial Fund to cultivate art and music around Queen's. She bequeathed her brick home on University Avenue to Queen's, and as we have seen, there, under the directorship of Swiss-born artist André Bieler, a fledgling art centre took shape. Expanded into seven exhibition galleries and an artist's studio in 1962 with aid from the Canada Council, the Agnes Etherington Art Centre, like CFRC, became a cultural beacon – not just for Queen's, but also for the eastern-Ontario region.

The art centre also quickly became a focal point for the philanthropy of other alumni eager to bolster the university's involvement in the arts. André Bieler proved an able ambassador for the centre, drawing attention to its potential through his own art and his outgoing personality. When he arrived in 1936, many regarded Kingston as an "artistic backwater."[140] By the time he retired as director in 1964, the Queen's art centre was acquiring a vibrant reputation. Locally, it offered community art classes. Nationally, it provided a repository for an astonishing collection of highly regarded art donated by Queen's graduates. In 1963, Samuel Zacks (BA 1924), a Toronto mining promoter and avid art historian, donated more than ninety contemporary Canadian paintings and sculptures to the centre. The donation was widely covered in the national press. That same year, insurance executive and one-time chairman of the trustees Ernest Gill donated a splendid collection of watercolours by nineteenth-century artist Daniel Fowler, who had painted on nearby Amherst Island. Two Queen's-trained doctors, Stuart and John Houston (MD '24 and '20) endowed the centre with a fine collection of early English silver.[141] What would become the most generous and long-lasting benevolence in the arts at Queen's began in 1967 when Alfred Bader (BSc 1945; BA 1946; MSc 1947) presented the gallery with an early sixteenth-century *Salvador Mundi* painting by Venetian painter Girolamo da Santacroce. Bader, the Jewish refugee admitted to Queen's by Jean Royce in the 1940s, who had prospered after graduation as a supplier of research chemicals in the United States, would become a frequent contributor of early Italian and Dutch masters to the centre's permanent collection, thereby broadening the foundation and reputation of the centre. By 1970, the trustees would note that Bader had established himself as "our most substantial benefactor."[142] Such was the growing prowess of the art centre that, in 1973, it spearheaded Queen's contribution to the celebration of the three-hundredth anniversary of Kingston's founding. An extensive exhibit at the centre – *Heritage Kingston* – on Kingston's evolution as seen through the artist's and photographer's eye accompanied by a handsome catalogue, ran through that summer.[143] As a tercentenary gift to the City, the centre cleaned more than fifty of the City's official paintings, a precursor to the art-conservation program that was about to begin at Queen's.

Radio and love of art were but two of the ways in which Queen's indelibly marked its graduates. The web of fealty between the university and its graduates grew in both breadth and complexity in these years. In 1961, Queen's had an alumni population of about eighteen thousand. A decade later, there were twenty-seven thousand alumni and, even with Deutsch's carefully regulated "steady state" growth, that number was growing by more than a thousand every year. The alumni anchored Queen's sense of tradition. They were vociferous in decrying the loss of the Harty Arena and Richardson Stadium. They faithfully appeared each year for the festivities – parade, football, principal's tea, dinner, and church service – on reunion weekend in the fall. In essence, "Homecoming" was intended to allow the alumni to mingle with the current undergraduates, as if to ensure that traditions were smoothly transmitted. At other times during the year, local alumni branches and the *Alumni Review* spread the Queen's gospel. Ironically, Queen's alumni exhibited a Presbyterian flintiness when it came to giving to their alma mater. While the university's 1964–65 capital campaign raised $4.5 million, mostly from corporations and foundations, alumni gave a meagre $392,000.[144] Some attributed this to the looseness of the Alumni Association, which was spread out across the country and difficult to effectively marshal. The Queen's alumni effort seemed more dedicated to what some called "friend-raising" than fundraising. In 1969, the campus alumni office was bolstered with more staff, and Herbert Hamilton, long-time editor of the *Queen's Review* and a man steeped in Queen's lore, was appointed its director. A year later, an outsider was brought in to revitalize

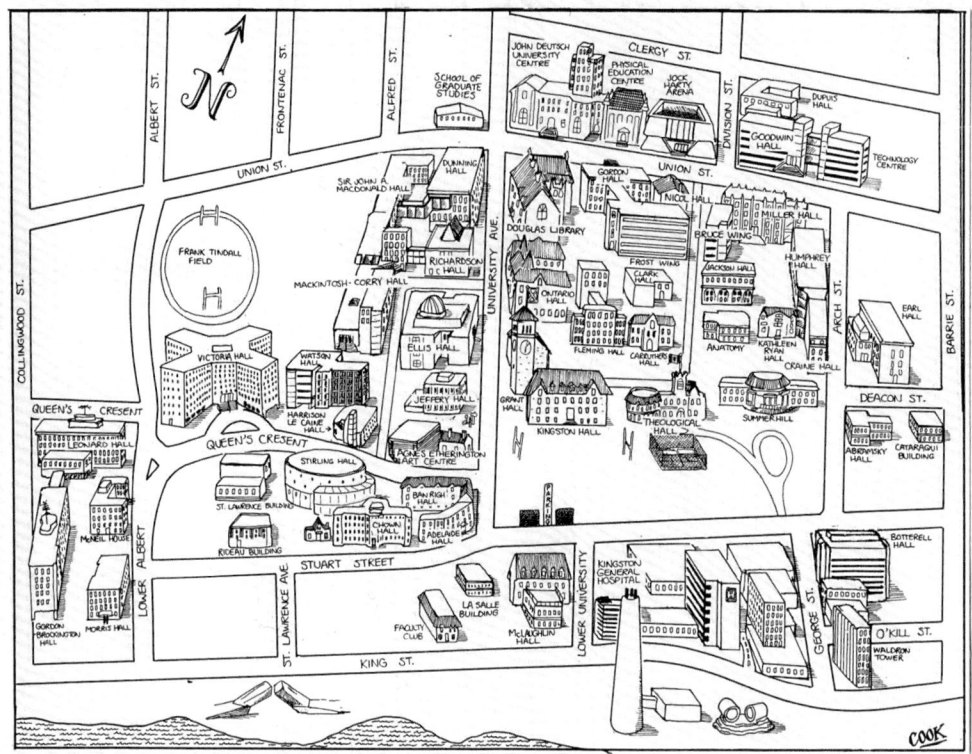

The new geography of Queen's: a map of the campus from the mid-1970s shows the dramatic expansion of the university west of University Avenue, with new residences and new academic buildings. Other buildings, such as Botterell Hall and the Jock Harty Arena, had been shoehorned into the old campus. The West Campus (not shown) opened a new frontier beyond Queen's 1840s precinct.

the whole alumni exercise. Indeed, the term "development" first appeared to describe a more-rounded and concerted effort to attach alumni hearts and wallets to their old alma mater. Former Shell Oil executive Jim Courtright (BSc 1941) was named vice-principal, development and information. A 1936 Olympic athlete, Courtright pulled Queen's into the modern age of image building, corporate communications, and fundraising.

Courtright's arrival reflected the reality of what the university had become since 1961. Queen's, now truly a multiversity, had become an enterprise spread over many faculties and catering to widely different expectations on the part of its administration, students, and faculty. Prolific *Queen's Journal* writer Chris Redmond caught the essence of the "new Queen's spirit" in a 1971 article. Queen's, he said, had become "a very complex place, as a community of ten thousand [students] must be." The compactness, ad hocery, and paternalism of the old Queen's were fading. In its stead, regulation, the pursuit of professional status, and a landscape of "stark concrete and glass" had emerged. "The only kind of unity that will come is recognition of this disunity and its good points," Redmond concluded. "Never again will Queen's be a homogeneous college as it was forty years or even ten years ago. Never again, quite possibly, will the limestone loyalty of the last few years exist." As a community, Queen's had seen a progressive devolution of power through the 1960s. Power had flowed from the principal and the deans to the Senate and into the departments. Faculty had moved away from the complacency of a reactive association toward a more assertive sense of their collectivity. At the same time, Queen's students had reconfigured their self-government into a more participatory, service-oriented democracy, one more synchronized with the times. Queen's was thus now more a community of self-identifying constituencies, each more aware of its prerogatives and ambitions. Not everybody thought this progress. University historian Hilda Neatby unburdened herself to the Newman Club one evening in 1971: the professors were becoming selfishly "careerist," she complained, and it entailed a "vast amount of pretence" to think that students had much to contribute to university governance.[145] Many thought otherwise: traditions had been modified and a new pluralism admitted on campus, but the central cultural values of communal compromise and dedication to social utility had been preserved. In this, Chris Redmond trusted: "a loyalty to Queen's can continue. It will only come from recognition that there is no value in 'loyalty' to walls and a name, but to people and the four years spent among them."[146]

5

Challenging Limestone Liberalism
The Edwards Affair and Hotel Hobbit

Limestone will burn!
Protestor's placard outside Richardson Hall, fall 1968

It's time we stopped messing around with the liberals.
Mark Elliott, *Queen's Journal*, 15 October 1968

I don't find confrontation useful as such. I like to deal in reasonable discussion and dialogue. Confrontation is not my way of doing things.
Principal J.J. Deutsch, November 1969

Radicalism on campus – Queen's was the last to get it and the first to lose it.
AMS vice-president Victor Bradley, *Queen's Review*, Jan.-Feb. 1972

The Fall of Our Discontents

The *Queen's Journal* said that he "whirled through Kingston." The *Globe and Mail* reported that Pierre Trudeau had arrived in town that chilly November morning in 1968 to open a new hockey rink, where he told the young skaters that his next stop was Queen's University for an afternoon of "speechifying." He advised them to stay where they were, because hockey was "much more fun" than speeches. At Queen's, it was indeed to be an afternoon of speeches, for the new principal, John Joseph Deutsch, was being installed amid much fanfare and the parallel awarding of honorary doctorates to an illustrious list of intellectuals, politicians, and servants of the university. An academic procession of 505 notables filed into Grant Hall to the sound of a brass flourish composed by resident Queen's composer Graham

George. Deutsch, always an earnest if not flamboyant speaker, assured his Queen's colleagues that it was his desire "to do everything I can do to help us to continue forward in this rational and civilized way to deal with our problems in this time of explosive change and tension – to establish appropriate participation of students." With that, the AMS President Dave Pakrul and the longest-serving member of faculty, Harold Stewart of electrical engineering, hooded the new principal.

For all the academic regalia and ritual that day, Trudeau, as Canada's newly elected prime minister, stole the show. Despite the fact that he told the Queen's audience that he had long marvelled at their new principal's storied prowess as an Ottawa mandarin, Trudeau mesmerized the crowd. An awestruck *Queen's Journal* noted that the prime minister wore his academic garb "like a superman robe."* During the convocation, the audience rose to its feet in applause only twice: once for the university's long-cherished registrar Jean Royce and then for Trudeau. After the convocation, Trudeau agreed to attend a bear-pit question-and-answer session with Queen's students in Grant Hall. His only condition was that the event be organized by the students. Chaired by AMS vice-oresident Andy Pipe, the bear-pit attracted fifteen hundred students. That year's *Tricolor* reported that there was a "little heckling" and "much applause." Trudeau told the audience that he was far more worried about world poverty and civil unrest on the streets of North American cities than he was about "the bomb." As he headed to his limousine after the session, Trudeau apparently said that he had expected a rougher interrogation by Queen's students. They were, he thought, too polite.¹ For its part, the *Whig-Standard* scoffed that the "bear pit" had turned out to be "a lamb fold."² Indeed, many students that day seemed more concerned with that weekend's Science Faculty Formal, with its Middle Eastern

---

*Queen's now maintains a policy of not awarding honorary degrees to serving Canadian politicians.

Prime Minister Pierre Trudeau in Grant Hall at the installation of Principal John Deutsch in October 1968. After receiving an honorary degree, Trudeau attended a bear-pit session with fifteen hundred Queen's students. Trudeau expressed surprise that the students were so respectful and non-confrontational.

Al-Ashar theme, and Saturday's football contest with the University of Toronto for the Yates Cup than they were with Grant Hall ceremonies.

Certainly, Trudeaumania had not conquered the whole campus. As he entered Grant Hall, the prime minister was jeered by workers on the construction site of Jeffery Hall across the street. They shouted that rampant inflation was eroding their wages and waved New Democratic Party banners. Student activist and journalist Krista Maeots reminded readers of the *Queen's Journal* that, for all the Trudeauesque talk of a "just society," their university was "class-oriented," and was in fact pandering to the "wrong class." Another *Journal* writer, Jacqui Cocks, contributed a caustic account of the gala dinner after the Deutsch installation under the headline "Let Them Eat Cake."[3] While the new principal would later confide in a letter to Trudeau that there might be a "few nihilists and extreme activists" at Queen's, he was confident that the "great majority of our students are highly responsible, sincere, and intelligently concerned about the bewildering problems of our time."[4] This indeed would be Deutsch's quietly held credo throughout his tenure in Richardson Hall. Whatever students' concerns, he would endeavour to engage them in the governance of their university, even if it meant shifting the ground rules. For John Joseph Deutsch, those ground rules at Queen's, the university from which he had graduated in the mid-1930s, were encapsulated in what might be called "limestone liberalism."

There was, however, a good deal of anxiety lurking beneath the principal's breezy assurance as he donned the principal's mantle. The fall term of 1968 would give the administration at Queen's a few tense moments and reason to ponder the future stability of the "Queen's way." The daily media brought news of rampant student disenchantment in the United States. Prestigious campuses such as Columbia and Berkeley had become embroiled in student sit-ins and walk-outs, as issues of war, racial discrimination, and the military-industrial complex spilled onto campus. This jagged dialogue was tinged with violence, not just because Martin Luther King and Robert Kennedy had been gunned down that spring, but also because student radicals like the Students for a Democratic Society (SDS) were preaching that liberal values were a sham and must be forcefully exposed. Such rhetoric was already evident on Canadian campuses: the spirit of the SDS had migrated north from American campuses to McGill and Simon Fraser universities and, by the fall of 1968, was advocating militant student action against the "powers that be" in academe. At Queen's, students in the fall of 1968 began to take a bead on their institution's liberal instincts.

Cracks in Limestone Liberalism

Universities are great sprawling communities that generally defy easy intellectual labelling. By their very nature, universities succeed because they tolerate and encourage divergence and diversity of opinion. Queen's was no exception. By the 1960s, it was inhabited by scholars, graduate students, and undergraduates dedicated to ideas and perspectives scattered over a vast geography of ideology and methodology. Over the decades, Queen's had, however, come to see itself as a *liberal* institution, with a dedication to the organic interests of society. This had become Queen's brand, its message of distinctiveness, which gave it its overriding bearings as an institution. Reduced to its essence, this limestone liberalism had three central values rooted deep in the nineteenth-century genesis of the institution.

First, there was Queen's commitment to the power of personal empowerment through education. Being a student at Queen's was about being part of an egalitarian society in which there were no fraternities, where students had, since 1858, governed their own daily behaviour through the Alma Mater Society, and where students enjoyed close proximity to their professors. It was a campus where the influence of memorable professors like Frank Knox in economics and Arthur Lower in history rolled through the lives of the students they taught. Lower had won publishing and journalistic acclaim for his celebration of liberalism as "this most famous stream" in Canadian life and the need to recognize the "two ways of life" in Canada – the French and English cultures.[5] Queen's students were encouraged by such mentors to think and act for themselves. For instance, in 1961 they sent an emphatic message to the administration that they did not want the green expanse of the Lower Campus blighted by a new physics building. A pugnacious Professor Lower led their assault on Richardson Hall. The trustees got the message and built Stirling Hall elsewhere.

A second tenet of limestone liberalism was the belief that progressive change in society was the outcome of education. By improving themselves through education, Queen's grads were put in a position to improve the society into which they graduated. Much has been made of the tremendous contribution of the so-called "Ottawa men" who left Kingston to inhabit the Ottawa bureaucracy, a tradition begun by Oscar Skelton in the 1920s. It is striking to note that the two of the men who sat in the principal's office from 1951 to 1974 – Mackintosh and Deutsch – were farm boys from rural Canada who were taken in at Queen's to be polished with the grit of political economy and sent out into the bureaucratic world to help to win the war and build the welfare state. It was Mackintosh who in Ottawa crafted the famous 1945 "white paper" on employment and income that would serve as the Magna Carta of Keynesian postwar Canada. Queen's graduates were encouraged to believe that the world could be improved through conscious effort. If they could run their own justice system on campus, they might bring justice and equity to the broader society outside college precincts. Whether it was Lorne Greene behind a CBC microphone or Charlotte Whitton in the Ottawa mayor's chair, Queen's grads believed they could alter the world.

A third and last attribute of limestone liberalism was a belief in critical inquiry. Universities were intended to be the detectives of modern society, charged with prying apart the inner workings of the world beyond the campus. Open and unbiased inquiry was crucial to progressive societies. Adam Shortt pioneered systematic inquiry into the Canadian economy in the 1890s at Queen's. Others picked up the tradition. In the 1930s, Bill Mackintosh and a young John Deutsch played a central research role in the famous Rowell-Sirois Royal Commission on Federal-Provincial Relations, an inquiry intended to deliver Canada from the Great Depression. Since the war, Queen's scholars such as

Queen's Journal editor Krista Maeots at her desk. Maeots used her columns in the student newspaper to question – some would say assault – the complacency of Queen's liberalism. She was joined in her critique by other remarkable Queen's women undergraduates, notably writer Bronwen Wallace and student politician Jan Lichty.

John Meisel and Hugh Thorburn had made themselves the nation's leading experts on the workings of federalism. There were other initiatives in local government, industrial relations, and ground transport. The corollary of critical inquiry was transparency – a belief that openness was imperative in any investigation of society's problems. Due process mattered as much in governance as it did in research. The Deutsch papers in the Queen's archives are cramped with the documentation of the many royal commissions and inquiries in which he participated.

As was often the case at Queen's, it fell to onetime principal Alex Corry to capture the essence of Queen's liberalism in his 1981 memoir, *My Life and Work: A Happy Partnership*. The university's reputation, he would write, was rooted in a "tradition of teaching, fearless inquiry and loyal service to Canada."[6] Education was about social utility – about improving the individual and, through him or her, improving society as a whole. Now, under the seismic pressures of the 1960s, the nature of that utility and the values it reinforced came under intense scrutiny. Across North America, many arrived at the conclusion that liberal society was but a facade, a smokescreen for selfish interests bent on promoting their interests. In the United States, student radicals assailed the liberal political values of their country. They attacked the hierarchy and manipulation of power by elites. In effect, they called for a return to real liberal values: equality and openness. In their hortative 1962 Port Huron Manifesto, the Students for a Democratic Society called for "participatory democracy," a phrase that would eventually filter into Pierre Trudeau's youth-oriented political vocabulary. Yippie leader Abbie Hoffman wrote of the need for an "alternative society" stripped of the buildup of bourgeois hypocrisy dressed up as liberalism (and at the same time urging his readers to "steal this book"). At Queen's, the pressure point would be a *cause célèbre* occasioned by Charles "Chuck" Edwards, the graduate student in chemical engineering, already active in student politics, who cast the liberal vision of a university's purpose into question, and in doing so, obliged Queen's to defend, and contemplate, its core values in a way that it had not done for decades.

Queen's liberalism had remade itself before. Historian Barry Ferguson has demonstrated that at the turn-of-the-twentieth century such Queen's thinkers as Shortt, Skelton, and W.C. Clark had repositioned liberalism at Queen's to encompass the complexity of the unfolding urban-industrial world. In the nineteenth century, liberalism at Queen's tended to reflect the rights of the individual and to celebrate the atomistic creativity of individuals. Broader society, loosely regulated by the state, was seen simply as the arena in which the interplay of these two worked itself out. Aggregate economic progress was society's lodestar, and untrammelled individualism was its generator. Students at Queen's in the late-nineteenth century, when the indomitable John Watson headed the philosophy department, would have been schooled in such "classical" or "market" liberalism. The rise of an urban-industrial society and all the concomitant ills – poverty, rapacious capitalism, Gilded Age conspicuous consumption – called forth a new relationship between the individual and society. The so-called "new liberalism" or "social liberalism" – the liberalism with which Mackintosh and Deutsch would soon imbue Queen's classrooms – attempted to rebalance the relationship of individual and state. It encouraged scholars and students "to serve as brokers between the class and interest-group affinities in the nation." It was a creed dedicated to social and economic progress through equality. "The new liberalism," Ferguson has written, "was an argument for the provision of equal conditions for all men and women and the extension of the measure of well-being to include the totality of social, economic, and political life."[7] Liberalism was now predicated on regulation, income distribution, and government intervention, and in this Queen's and its "Ottawa men" had excelled.

By the dawn of the 1960s, this dedication appeared becalmed. The welfare state was comfortably ensconced in Canada. Times were good. Queen's students consequently seemed lulled into a comfortable complacency. Their AMS government ably delivered an array of services, ranging from a splendid pipe band to Susie-Q dances. But there was little engagement with the outer world, beyond the annual clashes with the McGill, Western, and Toronto football teams. In a world full of Cold War tensions and awakening Canadian nationalism, Queen's students cocooned themselves in a small eastern-Ontario city, away from the mainstream ideas of the day. Second-wave feminism only faintly beckoned. Comfortably Anglo in orientation, Queen's seemed oblivious to the Quiet Revolution upheavals in Quebec. Only a handful of student journalists and student politicians seemed capable of seeing over the horizon. Queen's affiliation to the Canadian Union of Students and national bodies such as the Student Union for Peace Action (SUPA) at least opened a dialogue on broader issues, but few seemed interested. In a 1966 *Queen's Journal* editorial, student activist George Anderson accused Queen's of being "the saddest sort of intellectual community, that which has a prior conception of truth."[8]

It would take a practical, not a philosophical, issue – the housing of students – to reactivate the liberal conscience of Queen's students. As the agitation for a student co-op apartment tower has already revealed, the scarcity of beds for students provoked a debate over – indeed, for some, a rejection of – the adequacy of liberal values at Queen's. Here was the rub that would bring student activism at Queen's to life. For the university administration, the housing crisis was largely seen as a crisis of *policy*. The provincial government refused to finance residences as it did academic buildings, where 85 per cent of the cost was covered by the provincial government. This meant that the university either had to face the unsavoury prospect of dipping into its endowment funds or seeking long-term financing through CMHC mortgaging. The students, on the other hand, quickly came to see the housing crunch in more immediate practical terms. They needed a place to live – one that was affordable and close to their studies. Kingston's housing stock was old and limited, its rents consequently high. The old boarding houses of bygone decades were dwindling. Rightly or wrongly, local landlords were viewed as uncaring and rapacious. At the same time, Kingston's woeful housing situation tended to connect students with the elements of the broader Kingston population, elements also contending with inadequate accommodation. The university responded to this festering problem with stop-gap solutions: motel rooms were rented and school buses hired to transport students from the boondocks to campus. It also bought up old houses on the periphery of campus and became a landlord itself. Plans for new residences on Leonard Field had been accelerated. However, by the fall of 1968, in many students' eyes, it all seemed a case of too little, too late. The crisis shunted the AMS into action. Its meetings that fall were full of talk about housing. Local pressure groups sprang into existence. The most vocal of these was the Association for Tenants' Action in Kingston (ATAK) headed by local housing activist Joan Newman.[9] On campus, the ad hoc Emergency Committee for Student Housing materialized and demanded action from the principal's office. Various solutions were proffered by the AMS: rent control, a student-conducted survey of Kingston housing, and more co-operative housing.

An Incendiary Moment

The fall of 1968 would prove to be an incendiary moment for student activism at Queen's. It served to connect a practical problem – decent, affordable accommodation – with two possible courses of action: a liberal embrace of co-operation or a resort to the politics of confrontation. One path led to Elrond College, a multi-storey, student-owned high-rise on Princess Street; the other to defamatory rhetoric, sit-ins, and distrust of traditional authority. One option connected Queen's with student co-op movements across the country and continent; the other drew militant inspiration from the rhetoric of the New Left radicalism that had been percolating through campuses in Europe and North America. Each reaction fed on a coincidence of need and ideology that served to penetrate the insularity of student politics at Queen's. The problem of putting students in beds was no longer just a question of juggling policies and finances; it was instead a reflection of much deeper ideological possibilities and failings in western society. Capitalism and its alleged handmaidens, the universities, were in the eyes of a vocal minority unable to serve the needs of "the people." Others would argue that students themselves might remedy the situation by less-imperative means. The stage was set. Now the actors began to enter, stage left.

In the spring of 1968, Queen's students did something they had never done before – they had elected the AMS president by direct vote. Hitherto, the AMS president had been selected by a cabal of faculty society presidents. In this, Queen's was reflecting the same mood of participatory democracy that was sweeping through Canadian democracy that year. Pierre Trudeau had captured the prime ministership that June with promises of a "just society." At Queen's, the ticket of Chuck Edwards and Jan Lichty, a third-year Arts student, took the presidency and vice-presidency on a reformist platform of better communications with the administration, action on housing, and the selection of the first four student members of the university Senate. Edwards's tone was reformist, almost populist. He criticized the outgoing AMS council for consuming coffee and donuts at student expense.[10] At the same time, he advocated a student "sit-in" to protest the loss of any more green space on campus. In all this, he appeared to operate within the bounds of existing student politics. He had ably occupied the AMS's budget and finance portfolio in the previous year and had initiated a detailed survey of Kingston's housing stock. In the February election, he had been narrowly voted in on a 36-per-cent voter turnout, hardly the sign of radical enthusiasm on the part of most students. However, by the time classes resumed in September and the annual cycle of AMS business began, Chuck Edwards was a changed man, ready to test the tenets of Queen's liberalism.

Edwards was born in Arvida, Quebec, in 1943. From his father, a research scientist with Alcan, he acquired the steadfast belief that the physical sciences were the surest way of comprehending society. After a comfortable childhood in the suburbs of Montreal, Edwards arrived at Queen's in 1961 as an Applied Science freshman. The red English sports car he drove suggested that he was in tune with the easygoing culture of the campus. He served on the executive of Science '65, at one point inviting the "girls" of Levana to bring a feminine touch to the decorating of the engineers' Christmas tree. In the summers he worked as a research assistant in industry. Edwards proved a solid "A" student, considered clever, but not brilliant. He fixed on chemical combustion as his principal academic interest. After a year in private industry, in 1966 he returned to Queen's to begin an MSc in chemical engineering.[11]

Edwards had chosen a burgeoning field. Fuelled by demand generated by the Cold War and booming consumer spending, the chemical industry was hungry for young engineers. Queen's responded by growing its small chemical-engineering department. The sudden death in 1962 of long-time departmental head Campbell "Pappy" Plewes opened the door to change. Plewes was replaced by Reg Clark, an English chemist trained at Imperial College in London. In 1966, the department moved to new digs in Dupuis Hall and that same year graduated its first PhD. In advance of other Applied Science departments, chemical engineering sought out women students and soon acquired the nickname of "femeng." In short, the department was collegial and progressive.[12] Clark would expand the department to twelve professors by 1970.

One of the promising new professors was a MIT doctoral graduate, Henry Becker, a Saskatchewan boy with Mennonite family roots and an inclination to CCF/NDP politics. Becker had taken a minor in moral philosophy and saw himself as "basically a socialist." But as a professor he saw his role as apolitical and eagerly joined in Clark's effort to expand the graduate program. Their strategy here was to identify promising Queen's undergraduates and recruit them into graduate studies.[13] Chuck Edwards was such a recruit in 1966. Becker supervised his master's thesis on flame resistance in cellulose. In the spring of 1968, just as he was being elected AMS president, Edwards was accepted into the doctoral program.

In the iconic spring and summer of 1968, Chuck Edwards's dedication to science began to slacken. Not surprisingly, his time became dominated by AMS matters. A student pub was under consideration. There was the issue of coeducational dining in residence. In the wake of the Gibson report on Senate reform, four student senators had to be selected. Future senators would be elected, but this first batch would be selected in the interests of expedition. Edwards's vice-president, Jan Lichty, saw the process as elitist and quit the selection committee.[14] Hovering menacingly above all this was the housing issue. Edwards kept up the pressure here, calling for telephones in the housing office for quick contact with prospective landlords and the promise of a student action plan for housing by December.

To this juncture, Edwards was simply pushing the envelope of student politics. He was, after all, the first elected president of the AMS. His stance was reformist and impatient, but stayed within the bounds of established practice. He was pleased, for instance, to take a role in planning the November induction of new Queen's principal, John Deutsch. But then he caught sight of new horizons. That July, his supervisor, Henry Becker, offered to take him to a conference on thermal combustion in Paris. Becker believed it would whet Edwards's appetite for research. In Paris, Edwards instead encountered the embers of the student revolution of the spring of '68. He talked with student agitators and, in one galvanic episode, was chased through Parisian streets by the gendarmes.[15] Back in Canada, he headed the Queen's delegation to the annual convention of the Canadian Union of Students in Guelph. There a fractious debate unfolded over the ideological orientation of CUS. Was it to be in the vanguard of social change or simply a clearing house for more mundane matters? Many delegations averse to a radical turn withdrew. In the end, CUS dedicated itself "an anti-capitalist and anti-imperialist critique of society." Only one Queen's delegate – Ted Parnell of the Arts and Science Society – voted against the platform. Parnell felt that a "majority of students on this campus would not be in favour of making the commitment." The rest of the AMS executive, however, had taken a radical turn.[16]

Back on campus, the students were arriving for the fall term. The housing shortfall was acute. On 27 August, Edwards and other members of the Emergency Committee for Student Housing wrote to Deutsch, complaining that the university's housing service was "useless." They demanded that the university put up $50,000 in debentures for co-op housing. From the outset, Deutsch adopted a conciliatory tone.[17] The university rented more motel rooms and hired more buses. The emergency committee was partially mollified but still impatient. "You have the means at your disposal to implement all of our proposals," they told Deutsch, "it only remains for you to enforce your words with deeds."[18]

A few days later Edwards told the *Whig-Standard* that student housing was just the tip of a much broader issue – the place of the student in society. "I want the students to come into agreement with what the CUS has said, because I think they are right … People aren't committed to burning buildings, but they are committed to raising urgent issues."[19] If the university was incapable of housing all its students, why should it also be in a position to dictate what and how students should study? Here Queen's students began drawing on student activism elsewhere. They demanded "counter courses" on subjects of their own choosing. "University is simply the icing on a school system," Edwards told *Journal* editor Wilf Day, "which makes learning drudgery instead of fun and stultifies creativity of the young."[20]

To remedy this, students therefore demanded parity in university and departmental decision making. They wanted "openness" and a "fair share," phrases that would quickly install themselves in the lexicon of student politics at Queen's over the next year.

Assaulting the Liberal Bastion at Queen's

Capitalizing on this mood, the Emergency Housing Committee transformed itself into a broad-front organization, the Students for a New University – the SNU. Its aim was "to destroy the existing authoritarian structures of society and the university and replace them with institutions which are democratic, dedicated to humanistic values, and fit for a free people." All else was deemed liberal tokenism. "It's time we stopped messing around with the liberals," SNU member Mark Elliott, an Arts student from Britain, wrote in the *Journal*.[21] The university was, he wrote, "just a machine turning out students like bottles of Molson to be consumed by capitalist corporate society."²² To drive home the point, the SNU distributed around campus a booklet, drawn from the Californian student movement. It was entitled *The Student as Nigger*.

Almost immediately, the SNU embraced the politics of protest. On the night of 13 September, they attached themselves to a "tent-in" on the lawn of Summerhill, the principal's home – "Deutsch's lawn," they snidely called it. From the outset, the mood was lighthearted, not menacing. Photos captured an atmosphere that was more picnic than protest. About seventy people showed up, but only fifteen to twenty actually camped out overnight. The AMS president Chuck Edwards and his vice-president Jan Lichty were among the campers. Also present was a Kingston tenants' action group. A tent was reserved for "Dr Deutsch."²³ The *Journal* was obliged to describe the event as "only a partial success." *Journal* editor Wilf Day did, however, lend his editorial support, arguing that the university's housing record was a "history of waffling and inaction."²⁴ John Deutsch, already de facto principal since July, was annoyed, describing the tent-in as a "stunt." He was doubly annoyed that his dean of student affairs, historian Stewart Webster, and his wife, who actually lived in Summerhill, had conveyed coffee and donuts to the campers through the night. Deutsch was prepared to negotiate, but not to pander.²⁵

The SNU was a shadowy affair, its membership always rather amorphous. Like many student movements, it eschewed a hierarchical structure: there was no obvious leader, just a series of spokespersons. But it was clear that Edwards and Lichty were in its forefront and, in effect, wearing two hats – one as elected AMS leaders and the other as outspoken radicals. The SNU was not in any way an arm of the AMS, but it often arrogated to itself the role of "voice of the students of Queen's." AMS vice-president, Jan Lichty, would declare that the SNU was "the only hope for meaningful change in the university."²⁶ This conflation of roles would underlie the traumatic events of the next few months and ultimately be the undoing of Edwards and Lichty.

Throughout September and October, student politics became polarized at Queen's in a way never seen in the comfortable days of Susie-Q and football pep rallies. Early in October, an AMS referendum gave solid support for greater "openness" in university governance, in particular the demand for even more elected student senators. But SNU-oriented members of the AMS council soon started to push the limits of Queen's students' desire for change. Motions were brought to council that called for AMS support for striking workers at the Proctor-Silex factory in nearby Picton, monies to help unionize Kingston high-school students, and subsidized buses to out-of-town protests against the Vietnam War. Housing activist Joan Newman was brought into council to lecture on rents in Kingston, after which Edwards proposed a blacklist of landlords who evicted tenants in order to hike rents. Old values were disparaged: the Snowball Queen was told that she would have to attend beauty contests at her own expense. Members of the SNU went to local high schools to put on didactic skits that portrayed Queen's as an autocracy ruled by King Deutsch, who was cut off from the real world. (At some Kingston high schools, the SNU got a rude reception from students, some of whom pelted the university activists with eggs.)

By mid-October, resistance to the scope and pace of the Edwards-Lichty agenda began to materialize. There was growing concern that they were pulling the AMS away from its primary duty of ministering to the immediate needs of the student body. *Golden Words* attacked the SNU for its "total lack of interest in negotiations or in compromise."²⁷ The melding of the AMS and the SNU troubled others, as did the increasing engagement of the *Journal* editorial staff with off-campus issues. The growing tension became starkly evident when the SNU announced that it would stage a sit-in in the Collins Room to pressure the Senate into admitting more student

Accommodation-starved Queen's students stage a "tent-in" on Summerhill lawn in September 1968. While there was genuine anxiety over the lack of beds for students in Kingston, the protest appears more like a hootenanny than a Berkeley-style uprising.

members. A majority of the AMS council opposed the tactic and instructed Edwards, who had voted for it, to inform Deutsch of their opposition.

On the evening of October 21, the pot boiled over. Before a crowd of 250 students, Edwards and Lichty stood their ground in council. Four AMS constables were deployed to insulate the AMS president from his constituents. Just before midnight, Edwards and Lichty slipped out of the room and took pens in hand. "A heated debate is going on among Queen's students," they wrote, "over the policies and actions of the President and Vice-president of the AMS. We are pleased by this fact, since debate can lead to much greater awareness of the issue on campus." With that they resigned and invited the students to prepare for "an issue-oriented, not personality campaign."[28]

On 6 November, Queen's students went to the polls for the second time that precedent-setting year. Against Edwards and Lichty's call for student parity in university governance, full disclosure of the university budget, and counter courses, other candidates offered more-moderate reformist proposals that were closely focused on student needs. David Pakrul and Andy Pipe told voters that their focus was on "means," not lofty goals. "Student government at Queen's," they told the *Journal*, "has become an illegitimate farce in light of the irresponsible and provocative actions of our previous leaders."[29] In the end, 2,150 voters agreed with this prescription. Only 746 chose to stay the course with Edwards and Lichty.

Within days, Deutsch was installed, Pierre Trudeau visited the campus, and the Golden Gaels won the Yates Cup. But it would be foolish to conclude that the short Edwards-Lichty era was simply a boisterous aberration and that Queen's student life was again on an even keel. In fact, for all their disregard for due process, Edwards and Lichty had reawakened the old vitality of student liberalism at Queen's. Pakrul and Pipe did not look backward. They took an option on a building lot on Princess Street, where they planned a student-owned residence. The university housing service was brought under AMS control. They pulled Queen's out of the Canadian Union of Students and appointed an editorial team at the *Journal* more dedicated to satire than political activism.* In February, a new full-term AMS president, Ross McGregor, had taken on the mantle of moderate reform. "Railroad Ross" brought vigour to student government such as it had never before seen. A new student centre, a student pub, the building of a student co-op residence on Princess Street, and the adoption of commission government, which divided student government into portfolios all unfolded under McGregor. Not all of

---

*The new *Journal* editors, Bill Martin and John McIntyre, had in fact run for the AMS presidency that October on a platform that seemed, on the one hand, to satirize the lofty goals of campus radicals and, at the same time, castigate the apathy of many on campus. They promised to declare "a new golden age" and to construct "a crystal pleasure dome, with caverns measureless to man." Queen's would also buy the Green Bay Packers football team. Unsuccessful at the polls, they transferred their wit to the *Journal* editorial board.

Challenging Limestone Liberalism 197

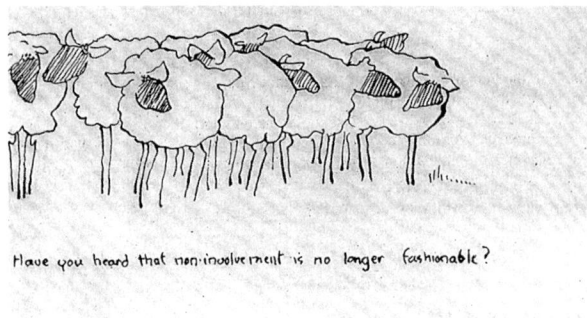

Sheep became a persistent visual metaphor at Queen's in the fall of 1968. Student activists and journalists projected their impatience with what they saw as the apathy of the majority by invoking sheep-like docility.

Railroad Ross's initiatives succeeded, but there was no doubt that Queen's students had rediscovered their limestone liberalism. As a *Journal* cartoon put it: "Psst! Have you heard that non-involvement is no longer fashionable?"[30]

The events of the fall of 1968 were not lost on Richardson Hall. To respond to student demands, the new principal drew on his own years of experience at Queen's as a student, professor, and administrator. Deutsch had spent enough time in Liberal-dominated Ottawa to appreciate the virtue of consultation and consensus. Despite his sang-froid, it is clear from his papers in the archives that John Deutsch was worried and at times frightened by the unfamiliar events at Queen's. Newspaper clippings describing the latest student outbursts at Berkeley, Harvard, Columbia, and Paris interleave his working files from these tense months. In October, students "liberated" the faculty club at UBC, where Deutsch had once taught. Within a year, his old friend Kenneth Hare would be driven from the presidency of UBC by student militancy. Closer at hand, Vice-Principal Fred Gibson, the history professor whose report had just advocated the admission of students to Senate, sternly warned his fellow administrators: "There has been no irrational activity on either side. We have done our homework [on the committee] here. Either universities are going to change or they are going to blow up."[31]

Deutsch's response was to seek compromise through consultation. "I don't find confrontation useful as such," he would tell students later in the year. "I like to deal in reasonable discussion and dialogue."[32] It was an attitude shared by most Queen's faculty and administrators. Even at the height of the Edwards turmoil, that inclination for inclusion remained manifest. Most departments passed motions to create student-faculty committees for the discussion of curriculum. In late November, the Senate embraced "openness": in future its meetings would be open to student and faculty spectators. Within a year, another ten student senators would be admitted to the Senate and other students would be invited onto Senate committees. Also within a year, the AMS president would be admitted to trustees' meetings as an observer. Richardson Hall, the trustees, and the Senate were rediscovering the old Queen's tradition of progressive governance.

But what of Chuck Edwards? History is by no means a seamless affair. The radical commotion of 1968 was not snuffed out at the ballot box. Student radicalism still rattled Canadian campuses; in February 1969, most spectacularly, students at Montreal's Sir George Williams University sacked the university computer centre. At Queen's, the SNU, shunned by the majority, transformed itself into a more strident organization – the Free Socialist Movement, or FSM. It was difficult to pin down the actual membership of the FSM. It represented itself as a collective, with no regard for traditional political hierarchy, and thus had no conspicuous leader. However, Edwards and Lichty were prominent, as were a number of other student politicians such as precocious second-year Arts student Terry O'Hara and graduate students Tom Good and Glenn MacDonell. The FSM nettled the AMS on issues such as housing and women's rights on campus. In October 1969, for instance, Lichty entered herself in the annual Homecoming beauty pageant and proceeded to lampoon the affair by appearing in a clown costume. The group launched a newspaper – *This Paper Belongs to the People* – as a vehicle for its opinions.

Richardson Hall, where Board and Senate meetings took place, became the epicentre of student protests in the late 1960s. Discontent focused on housing shortages, exclusion from university decision making, and a broader critique of Canada's social and economic arrangements. For a minority, Queen's embodied these shortcomings. Here one protester (centre) carries a sign declaring "Limestone will burn."

For all their theatricality, the FSM existed on the fringes on student life at Queen's. Then Chuck Edwards carried the radicals back to centre stage.

Academically, Edwards was changing course. In September 1968, he had defended his master's thesis and had only narrowly scraped through. One of his examiners noted that his work did not reflect "eighteen months of serious study and experimental effort."[33] Nonetheless, Edwards began work on his doctorate under Henry Becker and began lab work on flame turbulence. But his faith in the physical sciences was wavering. His focus was shifting from the laboratory to the streets.[34] History and sociology now seemed a surer way of explaining society's ills. He audited History 020, a course on revolutions. His professor there, James Leith, would later say that he sensed that Edwards regarded the textbook not so much as a studying aid but as a how-to manual on revolution.[35] Edwards began to soak up non-scientific critiques of society. He embraced Marxist analysis that suggested professional engineers were the handmaidens of capitalist exploitation. Engineers, he wrote, were oblivious to the real needs of society. Writing in *Golden Words*, he quoted from Bertolt Brecht's play about Galileo: "I have betrayed my profession. Any man who does what I have done must not be tolerated in the ranks of science."[36] Edwards concluded his dissection of professional engineering by saying that he himself faced three options in life: becoming schizophrenic and learning to segregate life and work, suicide, or dedicating himself to "knocking down the wall." When, in late October 1969, department head Reg Clark asked Edwards to present an informal update on his research to his fellow graduate students, Edwards used the occasion to present a denunciation of American mining companies, under the title "Why Jack Can't Get a Job in Canada."[37]

Henry Becker watched his student with growing dismay. In his opinion, Edwards's lab work was becoming fitful and negligent. Students complained that, as a teaching assistant, Edwards was inattentive. Becker was aware of his student's political activities and, given his own socialist inclination, was sympathetic. He even went so far as to read some of the authors, like Herbert Marcuse, who seemed to be the guiding lights of Edwards's radicalism. But, according to Becker, he never brought political issues

Challenging Limestone Liberalism

into his relationship with Edwards. His concern lay entirely with Edwards's declining academic performance. He believed that Edwards's doctoral-thesis proposal was shoddy and unlikely to gain support. There were problems with Edwards's research apparatus. With all this in mind, Becker called Edwards to his office on 8 November and voiced his concerns. Becker later emphatically insisted that the conversation never touched on Edwards's political views. The bottom line in Becker's mind was that Edwards must decide between dedication to his studies or dedication to his personal crusade.

The Mounties Come Calling

But another issue had reared its troubling head on that day in early November. On 30 October, two RCMP officers had come to the chemical-engineering department to see departmental head Reg Clark. Their purpose was straightforward: to obtain information for a security clearance for an Israeli graduate student who has just been offered a job in a federal laboratory. Such interviews were commonplace. Few contested the right of the state to vet the credentials of its employees, especially during the Cold War. What troubled Canadian academics were the parameters of these investigations. As early as 1963, the Canadian Association of University Teachers had sent a delegation headed by lawyer Bora Laskin to lobby Prime Minister Pearson for a clearer definition of the bounds of Mountie privilege on campus. The universities did not want any infringement of their freedom of speech and thought. Pearson was evasive. Then CAUT issued a set of guidelines that urged professors to be wary when the Mounties came calling. Back at Queen's, Principal Corry, a great champion of the individual's rights before state power, told the faculty association that the ambiguity of the line between state security and personal liberty worried him, and he wondered what the university would do "when such a case turned up."[38] In November 1969, that case turned up.

What exactly happened in Reg Clark's office that day is contested. Clark alleged that as the Mounties were putting on their coats, one of them asked if there were any other students they might be interested in. Clark recalled that he mentioned that Edwards had been prominent in student activism. The Mounties would allege that it was Clark who *volunteered* the tipoff. Whatever the genesis of the alert, Clark later that day encountered a colleague in the corridor and mentioned that the RCMP had asked about Edwards. Shortly thereafter, that colleague spread the news in the common room, from where it quickly reached Edwards. In retrospect, there can be no denying that Clark acted unprofessionally in allowing the news of the RCMP interest in one of his graduate students to spill out so publicly. But, then again, as far as he knew, the incident might have been a fleeting matter.[39]

Two things need elucidating at this point. First, the university in 1969 had absolutely no formal procedures for dealing with student and faculty grievances – no instructions on whom to go to if you sensed your rights had been infringed upon. Justice in such matters at Queen's had always been dispensed in an *informal* manner. A frank discussion with the departmental head or perhaps the dean would suffice to clear the air. Principals Corry and Deutsch each prided themselves on the notion that "their door was always open" for those with grievances. And indeed it was, but the process had to be initiated by the student and, for many reasons, it took a good deal of temerity to seek an audience with the principal. Of parallel concern was the absence of any explicit policy on how the university handled matters of student discipline. Since the nineteenth century, the Queen's Senate had delegated authority over student misdemeanours to the AMS Court and its constables. The Senate retained the ultimate power of disciplining students, but this had very seldom been exercised.

By the 1960s, the nature, or at least the perceived possible limits, of student misbehaviour at Queen's had moved beyond beer bottles on trains and panty raids. What if a university building were occupied by "radicals"? What if classes or university events were blockaded? With the daily news reporting such events in the United States and Europe, this anxiety was felt across Ontario university campuses. In the fall of 1969, a task force of the Council of Presidents of Universities of Ontario suggested some tough guidelines on the way universities should respond to student indiscipline á la Berkeley. Their report, *Order on Campus*, argued for draconian punitive measures for those guilty of "illegitimate" actions on campus. At Queen's, the reaction to the report was one of instantaneous and widespread objection. Student discipline belonged in the hands of the students themselves, except in cases which flagrantly breached the broader Canadian civil and criminal code. The AMS regarded it as a dangerous trespass on its authority. The Senate Committee on Student Affairs condemned the report, its chairman, physicist David McLay, saying that it should be "thrown in the waste basket." Deutsch shared the concern that Queen's' ingrained tradition of communal justice attuned to the university's unique circumstances could not be abandoned in favour of some procrustean provincial code.[40] The report died in the CPUO committee room.

Secondly, from this point onwards in what was soon to be called the "Edwards affair," the Mounties volunteered nothing to elucidate their interest in Queen's affairs and stood silently behind the facade of state security. The university was on its own. Ottawa remained resolutely mute, an affront to the university that had done so much over the years to export its liberalism to the corridors of Ottawa power.

At his 8 November meeting with Becker, Edwards voiced his concern about the Mountie visit. Becker told him not to worry, that the RCMP were only concerned with gangsters and subversives. Two days later, Edwards went to see AMS president Ross McGregor to share his news. McGregor recalled that Edwards seemed "confused and uncertain." Then, on 19 November, Edwards dropped off a handwritten letter telling Becker that he was discontinuing his thesis work so that he could devote more time to studying sociology and various personal matters. The tone of the letter was polite and non-confrontational. Two days later, Becker informed the associate dean of graduate studies that he assumed Edwards had dropped out of his doctoral studies, describing his student as "a mixed-up person with little capacity for self-discipline or hard work."[41]

Edwards did little else through official channels. He did, however, turn to his allies in the FSM at a meeting on 23 November. There, the decision was made to turn Edwards's predicament into a *cause célèbre* – a clear-cut instance of political repression on campus. The next day Edwards went to see Clark about the police visit. Clark gave him his recollections of the event. Later, Edwards would allege that Clark called him a "dangerous revolutionary" at that meeting, but strangely Edwards did not bring this up in his initial account. In retrospect, some Queen's observers have suggested that Edwards at this juncture ceased to play the lead in the controversy that was about to unfold. They suggest that, in his bewildered state, Edwards allowed himself to be used or "manipulated" by other, more hard-line, members of the FSM, who recognized the powerful potential of the story that Edwards had related to them.

The FSM went to work quickly. On 28 November, Stuart Ryan (son of Queen's law professor Stuart Ryan), who styled himself a reporter for *This Paper Belongs to the People*, came to Clark's office to discuss Edwards's situation. He did not interview Becker, nor was there any fact checking. The 3 December issue of *This Paper* blared the headline "Cops on Campus" and went on to allege that Becker and Clark were guilty of political persecution. Clark was quoted as saying he was "willing to talk about anyone" with the RCMP. Becker recalls that he was completely blindsided by the allegation and found it "preposterous."[42] An "open letter to John J. Deutsch" from the FSM appeared on the same page; it demanded a "special committee" be struck to investigate the allegation and that RCMP activity be banned from campus. The same day the paper appeared, Good and Glenn MacDonell, FSM members who sat on the AMS council as reps of the graduate society, issued a letter on AMS letterhead and sent it to eighty other student governments and newspapers. The letter repeated the claim that Edwards had been "pressured out of his doctoral studies" by his department. Edwards's fate was not, it argued, "an isolated event," but was "part of a pattern of political repression which is developing on university campuses across Canada."[43] To reinforce the point, the envelope contained an FSM flyer.[44] The allegation and its to-the-barricades tone immediately caught press attention. Berkeley, it seemed, had come to Kingston.

A "Full and Open" Inquiry

But Queen's – both the student government and Richardson Hall – responded with alacrity. The AMS council immediately met and reprimanded Good and MacDonell for acting without official sanction. A telegram was dispatched to the same mailing list rescinding the previous day's message. AMS president Ross McGregor then won unanimous support for his suggestion that a Senate committee investigate Edwards's treatment. The committee should be comprised of representatives of the four parties directly implicated in the affair – Edwards, the chemical engineering department, the university, and the AMS – and be presided over by an impartial chairman. McGregor walked the resolution over to the principal's office and within minutes received Deutsch's assurance that the committee had his blessing. The principal agreed with McGregor that this was an issue that touched not only the rights of students at Queen's but also the integrity of its faculty and administration. At a hastily called Senate meeting that afternoon, Deutsch's motion for a special committee was endorsed with a mandate to "fully and openly" get to the truth of the matter. The parties were given a week to name their representatives and then chose a chairman. A report would be expected early in the new year.

The FSM was not happy. It wrote to Deutsch saying that the inquiry should have a broader mandate; it should unravel the whole issue of students' freedom from police surveillance and universities' complicity in such activity. Deutsch responded that Queen's would investigate Queen's issues alone. Fortuitously, the Senate had just a week before established a student-faculty-administration committee to review the whole spectrum of "grievance, discipline and related matter" on campus, a reflection of Deutsch's determination to codify procedures at Queen's. The Mounties, Deutsch argued, were just such a "related" matter. The FSM baulked and said that they would not participate in the committee and directed Deutsch to direct any further communication to them through their spokesperson, Bronwen Wallace, the English department grad student who had earlier become involved in peace activism.

For two tense weeks the principal waited and pondered whether the inquiry could proceed without FSM participation. In the interim, most of the other pieces fell into place. The AMS delegated Val Traversy, a fourth-year Arts student, as its representative. The principal turned to Professor Gordon Simmons of the Faculty of Law as his proxy and the department of chemical engineering selected David Canvin, a biology professor and president of the faculty association, as its point man. Deutsch supplied a list of plausible chairmen. Finally, the FSM announced that it was on side and that Terry O'Hara, a rotund, eloquent and quick-witted Arts student, would represent Edwards. Sensing the legalistic nature of the upcoming inquiry, chemical engineering retained a lawyer – law professor

Morley Gorsky – to represent Clark and Becker, who were – given the career-threatening allegations made by Edwards – in effect on trial. The FSM reciprocated, naming a senior law student, Don Kuyek, as their legal "spokesman." Finally, on 19 December the inquiry panel met for the first time and, over the objection of O'Hara, selected law professor Bernard Adell as their chair. Adell was a labour law specialist who had arrived at Queen's in 1964 from a Rhodes scholarship in Oxford.[45] If there was one striking characteristic of the Edwards panel, it was its youth. Adell was under thirty. O'Hara was still in his teens.

Through late December, all of January and part of February, the inquiry took its evidence. Adell proved an adept chairman. Meeting in a lecture hall in Macdonald Hall with a staff of secretaries recording every word, the panel heard seventeen witnesses over twenty-eight sessions and ninety hours of testimony.[46] To accommodate student and faculty class schedules, sessions were usually held in the evenings, with secretaries working late into the night to produce transcripts of that day's proceedings. The tense, at-times-theatrical, sessions drew large, attentive audiences. The national press covered the story.[47] The level of interrogation was incisive. Gorsky proved doggedly effective in getting at actual details underlying Edwards's allegations. Edwards undermined his own credibility by reversing some of his testimony, particularly the worrisome omission of any mention of Clark's assertion that he was a "dangerous revolutionary" that was not raised until his second round of giving evidence. Edwards was also stymied in his contention that chemical engineering was awash in defence-related research; it wasn't. Gorsky also successfully demonstrated Edwards's sliding academic achievement as the crucial determinant of his treatment at the hands of his supervisors. Edwards was hard-pressed to present any credible evidence of Becker's purported condemnation of his political activities. Good, Ryan, and MacDonell were also raked by Gorsky

Charles "Chuck" Edwards, wearing a Free Socialist Movement armband, testifies at the Adell inquiry into allegations that Edwards's graduate supervisor brought political pressure to bear on his graduate studies.

for the recklessness of their journalism and their irresponsible use of the AMS authority. Gorsky found the task so onerous that he resigned and was replaced by Kingston lawyer Stu Willoughby.

The FSM, for its part, tried to take the moral high road. Sensing that Edwards was on shaky evidential ground, Kuyek and O'Hara tried to cast the whole episode in the broadest possible context. Edwards, they argued, was a victim of a malfunctioning of liberal society. The power of the state had co-opted the university, obliging it to carry on a "concerted campaign" against Edwards. The refusal of the RCMP to even appear at the inquiry tended to heighten this impression of collusion. Around campus FSM supporters posted signs that tried to connect John Deutsch's presence on the boards of Inco and the CIBC with the behaviour of Kingston landlords. One poster read "6th Big Week – Trial – Tonite's star Jovial John Deutsch (also appeared at Inco, the Canadian Bank of Commerce – Hear John's hilarious monologue."[48] But however much the FSM castigated the "narrowness of the liberal myth," it could muster little specific evidence of actual collusion. Weak on evidence, the FSM played the part of campus radicals, wearing armbands and berets and saluting each other with fist pumps. In one dramatic instance, Edwards reached into his pocket, pulled out a hand grenade, and placed it on the witness desk. A startled Stu Willoughby immediately objected. Adell examined the grenade and determined that it was a World War I antique and likely harmless.

A Verdict Delivered

By late February, the report was ready. It boldly concluded that Professors Becker and Clark were "utterly innocent" of any political persecution.[49] Much was made of the inconsistency in Edwards's testimony. Why was his note to Becker on 19 November so matter-of-fact in tone if he believed that he was a victim of political harassment? The Adell Report did scold Clark and Becker for their "error in judgment" in so freely spreading the news of the RCMP visit and not directly informing Edwards of it. The report then reprimanded Good and MacDonell for their "misuse of the trappings of the AMS." In general, the FSM was guilty of using the concept of academic freedom as a shield for their reckless accusations of persecution on the part of two professors, accusations for which they had virtually no hard evidence. (Years later, looking back on the hearings through the lens of long years teaching the law, Adell now suggests that any judge would have early on dismissed the "case" for lack of substantive evidence on the part of the complainant. The inquiry, he now believes, provides an object lesson in showing that "you cannot gratuitously ruin people's reputation" by hurling false accusations at them.[50]) And, last, the report acknowledged the wider context of the affair by urging the Senate to hasten its inquiry into the role of police on campus.

And what was to become of Mr Edwards? The report did not mince words about the "gross wrong" that Edwards had done the university's reputation. The report could see no plausible way by which Edwards could proceed with his doctoral studies in chemical engineering and urged him to voluntarily withdraw before the university acted against him. But, it added, he should be allowed to apply for entry in another graduate program and in doing so be evaluated for admission as any other student would be. Despite its dismissal of Edwards's claims, the report expressed recognition of his innate potential. He was "a highly intelligent man who is a sensitive critic of the absurdities of our society and of the professional narrowness and complacency that our universities far too often inculcate, but who at the same time has become so thorough and zealous a convert to Marxism that he lost the capacity to discern degrees of radicalism and reaction and to distinguish those who are of good will and able to help him from those who are predatory or hidebound." Edwards, it concluded, was "a paradox of social concern and individual callousness."

The report was not unanimous. The FSM's representative, Terry O'Hara, refused to endorse its judgments and instead appended a minority report that alleged the university had exploited the secretaries who had laboured on meagre wages every evening to prepare the daily transcript of evidence.

Now the Senate had to act. Senate reform the previous fall had opened its meeting to newly elected student senators and to students who wished to observe that body's hitherto-closed-door meetings. All they had to do was reserve a ticket at the Senate Office. The Adell Report was slated to be read onto the record at the 3 March 1970 meeting. Interest on campus was intense and it was obvious that the Collins Room would be filled to capacity. And, at this sensitive juncture, John Deutsch uncharacteristically faltered. If Edwards wanted to attend, Deutsch pronounced, he would have to get a ticket like any other student. This seemed vindictive to the FSM, since Edwards was the central figure in the whole episode. He was, in effect, the accuser, who had provoked the uproar and who now deserved to hear the committee's verdict. When the meeting convened, the ticketless Edwards was out in the corridor.

A crowd gathers outside Richardson Hall as the Senate prepares to discuss the Adell Report and the fate of Chuck Edwards. Near the front door, FSM supporters rally in support of Edwards. Other students endorse the report's findings with placards proclaiming "Give Edwards the boot!" From afar, Applied Science students pelt the FSM with snowballs. One window in the hall was broken.

Deutsch opened the meeting and immediately called upon Adell to read his entire report onto the record. As he began, Terry O'Hara interjected, saying that this was a kangaroo court at which the "accused" was denied the right to be present. A shouting match ensued. Deutsch ruled that O'Hara was out of order and must leave the room. He refused. The AMS constables present moved in to perform the eviction. "I am quite heavy," the burly O'Hara warned them. The constables began their onerous task. "It can't happen here," O'Hara yelled. "Oh, yes it can!" he concluded.[51] Six constables later, the meeting resumed and Adell set to his task. Out in the corridor, FSM supporters chanted "Ho, Ho, Ho Chi Minh, the NLF [National Liberation Front in Vietnam] is gonna win." When Adell finished reading his report onto the record, initial reaction was hostile to Edwards. Dean Brown of Applied Science and Dean of Graduate Studies Slater were hawkish. Edwards had tarnished the reputation of their bailiwicks and they wanted justice. Edwards should be expelled. Yet, almost immediately, there were voices of moderation. Student Senator Jeffrey Simpson called for compassion: "everybody has lost and lost appreciably," he sermonized.[52]

A little over a week later – on 11 March – the Senate reconvened to deliberate on the report's findings. Again, the mood was tense. In the intervening week, there had been angry outbursts, with spontaneous rallies in the residence cafeterias at which some students chanted, "Let's go up and get them [the FSM]." A petition signed by 748 students proclaimed support for the Senate's authority. Now, outside Richardson Hall, a small group of FSM supporters, styling themselves the Edwards Defence Committee, picketed the main entrance. They held hand-lettered signs: "Apathy is pleasant" and, ominously, "Limestone will burn." Other students gathered to shout down the FSM. By a deliberate coincidence, a larger group of chemical and electrical-engineering students converged for what their posters had advertised was to be a friendly snowball fight. Their aim proved mischievously inaccurate and snowballs began hitting the radicals in the no-man's land. A Richardson Hall window was broken. Inside, the meeting convened. Twenty-four hours earlier, Dean Slater had given notice of a three-part motion calling for action on the report. The motion reiterated the finding that Becker and Clark were

Challenging Limestone Liberalism   205

"utterly innocent." It went on to censure Good and MacDonell for issuing unverified allegations and failing to seek redress through normal channels.

Dean Slater then electrified the Senate by calling for Edwards to be expelled from Queen's on account of his "groundless" attack on the reputation of the university. Slater said that he was acting out of a sense of "fair play, compassion, openness, and due process." Again, not everybody agreed, especially given the very short notice Slater had provided the Senate. Dean Soberman of the law school immediately pointed out that the Senate had authority only over academic matters and that Edwards's misbehaviour in dinting the university's reputation lay outside their power. The AMS, he said, was probably the appropriate policeman for such behaviour. Many expressed the view that the Senate was proceeding with undue haste. Sensing this, student senator John Gray moved that deliberation of the Slater motions be postponed. When this motion was defeated, an uproar engulfed the Senate chamber. As if by prior arrangement, about fifty FSM sympathizers broke through the doors of the Collins Room, bowling over AMS constables, and installed themselves around the Senate table. Amid the chaos, Deutsch declared the debate "disrupted" and adjourned the meeting.53 Once the senators hastened away, the FSM occupied the room and held a mock Senate meeting, passing a resolution proclaiming Queen's liberalism a myth.

The university had come to the edge of the abyss. The national press reported events on its campus that many found hard to reconcile with their impression of "good old Queen's." But at this delicate juncture, Queen's instinctively reasserted its old liberalism. Few sought to exonerate Edwards. But many now tried to mitigate his behaviour and thereby suggest more-subtle forms of punishment that might mend the breach in the cohesion of the Queen's community. Contrary to the hawkish notion that Edwards had knowingly concocted the whole scenario out of some misplaced ideological conviction, others suggested that he was a confused and rattled young man who had been startled by the news of the RCMP's interest in him. Edwards had acted in the honest conviction that people were out to get him. He had fallen into the arms of hard-line radicals who had manipulated him into making reckless allegations. (Looking back on the affair forty years later, Professor Henry Becker came to the view that Edwards had been "manipulated" by other members of the FSM eager to stage a piece of political theatre. Bernie Adell, the young law professor who had chaired the inquiry, has come to share this view too, seeing Edwards as a young man "genuinely distressed" and understandably "confused."54) Similarly, AMS president Ross McGregor could not conceive that Edwards had perpetrated a "malicious, predetermined attack"; he was more simply "confused and afraid" and should not be the only one to pay the price for a broader system that had failed.

Viewing the rubble of the aborted 11 March meeting and sensing the dangerous diversity of opinion, John Deutsch determined to bring the whole issue out into the open by calling a special meeting of the Senate, at which all parties might speak and the case be brought to resolution. One senses reading his correspondence from these nervous days that Deutsch realized that the vindictiveness of the Slater motion had to be defused and that a full airing of the issue was imperative.

Other encouraging signs appeared. Late that March, an unprecedented voter turnout of 50 per cent saw second-year law student Rod Folwell elected AMS president. Folwell and his running mate, Janet Rogers, had run on a slogan of "We listen." At the same time, the Senate embraced the AMS's "Fair Share" report with its recommendation of an additional ten student senators. In addition, the special Senate Committee on Grievances and Discipline was beginning to construct a protocol to help the university systematically cope with just the sort of issues that the Edwards conflict had illuminated. On 13 March, the AMS council had endorsed the Adell Report, but only after making it very clear that it regarded Slater's motion as overly harsh and punitive. At the same time, petitions raised by faculty urged the Senate to avoid taking a hard line with Edwards, fearing that it might set a deadly precedent that could be applied whenever students believed they too had a valid grievance with the university. Other professors complained that the hard line drawn by Dean Slater flew in the face of Queen's long tradition of "debate and discussion."[55] The Student Christian Movement at Queen's petitioned for leniency. History professor Fred Gibson confidentially warned the principal that the Senate might be in danger of exceeding its authority to regulate the academic life of the university; Edwards was guilty of a non-academic transgression, and the AMS alone should deal with the issue.[56] To all this, Deutsch listened. The university was, in short, reconnecting with the art of compromise.

High Noon in Wallace Hall

Deutsch booked Wallace Hall for the afternoon of Friday, 3 April, believing that an open meeting in a larger hall was a way of "rebuilding trust and confidence." Tickets would be made available for 45 faculty and 155 students. Non-Senate members who wished to register their views were asked to indicate their desire in advance. To avoid another gate-crashing incident, student senator Jeff Simpson arranged for CFRC to broadcast the proceedings. And then everybody waited.

Those arriving in Wallace Hall that Friday afternoon were greeted by FSM members dressed as clowns chanting: "Free Edwards, free popcorn, free show!" But the clowns did not have tickets and obligingly departed to listen to the proceedings on the radio. For the next three hours, it is no exaggeration to say that the entire campus was fixated on Wallace Hall. Deutsch moved the Senate into a committee of the whole. Dean Slater then addressed the intent of his motion. The university lawyers had told him that they were all within the powers of the Senate. A bad sign. But Slater immediately added that he would "support more compassionate treatment than the motion allowed."[57]

Send in the clowns. FSM members dressed as clowns and carrying balloons parade outside Wallace Hall chanting "Free Edwards, free popcorn, free show." Unlike their actions at the March Senate meetings, the FSM members did not disrupt the final meeting in the Edwards saga.

An avalanche of opinion followed. The tendency was towards compassion for Edwards. Some returned to the argument that Edwards had acted out of naive confusion. Others stressed that the Senate's power was indeed solely academic. History graduate student John Smart castigated the RCMP for its shadowy role in the whole affair. Another grad student, Michael Larass, urged the Senate to construe Edwards as "an agent to reduce the lethargy in our society" and objected to the university taking "a God-like attitude of meting out punishment."

Challenging Limestone Liberalism 207

3 April 1970: the final working out of the Edwards allegations in an open meeting in Wallace Hall. Principal Deutsch and dean of Arts and Science George Harrower are front centre. A CFRC soundman captures the debate and FSM spokesman Terry O'Hara walks to his seat.

In 1898, the Senate delegated all non-academic discipline to the AMS. Since 1936, the AMS had maintained its own constabulary. Throughout the entire Edwards affair, AMS student constables maintained order; no city police were ever called.

An FSM spokesperson Judith Weikum concluded with a twenty-five-minute peroration, labelling the administration and AMS as lackeys of capitalism.[58]

Slater announced that he was prepared to entertain amendments to his motions. And then, student Senator John Buttars, a fourth-year theology student, cut the Gordian knot. Let the absolution of Clark and Becker stand, he argued, and the scolding of Good and MacDonell. But remove any talk of expelling Edwards. Focusing on Edwards's academic potential, Buttars suggested that Edwards be given a second chance. But not in chemical engineering. Let him submit an "alternative plan of academic study" at Queen's. This he must do by the end of May. After that date, he could apply for admission to Queen's as any other applicant might.

Slater said that he would accept the amendment, as did other senior administrators. Only the hawkish Dean Brown of Applied Science wondered whether Edwards's lack of respect for the reputation of members of his faculty was being unduly condoned. Sensing that all opinion had been aired, Deutsch called for a vote. The Buttars amendment was unanimously passed with only Dean Brown abstaining.

It was finally over. "Almost everyone seemed to leave the Student Union smiling," the *Journal* observed. AMS President Folwell concurred. "This meeting reaffirmed the belief," he said," that students can act reasonably."[59] Deutsch said little in public, but writing to friends he expressed immense relief and the belief that he had delivered what he had promised three months before – an inquiry that would "fully and openly" get to the heart of the matter. The principal's only disappointment would be his inability to get the federal government to budge on defining exactly what the RCMP's role was on Canadian university campuses. As historian Arthur Lower (who was long used to prodding the consciences of Queen's principals) reminded Deutsch, "It seems to me that we Canadians are extremely innocent about the role of central police forces."[60] Time and again federal solicitor general, George McIlraith, gave the Queen's principal the polite brush-off whenever he raised the issue.[61]

As with any contentious issue, there were codicils to the Edwards affair. Who would pay the legal bills? All parties had approached the inquiry as if it were a quasi-judicial proceeding. Lawyers were retained on all sides. In April 1970 the legal bills began to appear. Edwards, the AMS, and the two chemical engineering professors all sought financial relief from the university. Deutsch's response was that the university had tried to maintain a neutral stance throughout the inquiry. It would not, therefore, foot the legal costs of Edwards or the AMS.[62] They were, in keeping with the new codified persona of the university, independent parties, who must assume the cost of their interaction with other constituencies. When the faculty association asked about Becker and Clark's $7,000-plus legal fees, Deutsch agree that, as university employees whose reputations had been assailed, their defence costs should be covered by the university, their employer. At the same time, QUFA turned to CAUT for support, and soon garnered $1,500 from that quarter. Deutsch himself quietly sent along a personal cheque for $1,000 to QUFA.[63] The university covered the rest. But, as QUFA, pointed out, the university had no declared policy on its responsibility to professors under attack from outside parties. Fortunately, the Senate committee investigating the handling of grievances on campus was in the process of addressing this thorny issue and would a year later suggest the adoption of a tribunal system of handling grievances involving professors – one supported by university financing.[64] Through all the high drama of the Edwards affair, in a kind of ironic commentary on its essence, Queen's students continued their often desperate search for a place to rest their heads each night.

Building a "Perfect House" at the Corner of Division and Princess

At Queen's, the precipitating issue for student discontent had been housing. Society's failure to provide sufficient accommodation had sparked the New Left's critique of Queen's as a liberal institution, but in the end its agitation did little to actually alleviate the problem. Other students were at the same time prompted to devise a *practical* solution to the problem. Consequently, the Emergency Committee for Student Housing, headed by grad student Tom Good, sprang up and won tacit support from the AMS. Deutsch tried to placate the members by pointing to the university's own emergency housing measures.[65]

Unsatisfied by this, the emergency committee took a page from student tactics elsewhere and proposed the "tent-in" on the slope outside Summerhill, the principal's official residence, to highlight that the "system" had failed to provide for one of a student's fundamental needs. Behind the call for immediate action was a broader and more sweeping call for a "new university," one not so beholden to the power structure and the values of Canadian society. Overt student protest was hardly a novel development at Queen's – there had been a general student strike in the 1920s and the furor over Stirling Hall's displacement of green space in 1961 produced a grassroots student uprising. But the tent-in in the late sixties suggested that Queen's students were associating themselves with a more root-and-branch rejection of mainstream ideological values.

As the term settled in, the housing situation eased somewhat, as homeless students shoehorned themselves into whatever nooks or crannies they could find. Its political resonance, however, lingered. By October, Deutsch believed that enough beds had been found, but warned that space for another 1,750 single and 750 married students would have to be found in the upcoming years. Queen's had, in fact, just made a submission to a federal task force on urban development, stressing its belief that student demand for better-quality accommodation was not likely to slacken in the near future.[66] At the Board of Trustees meeting of 25 October, the issue made its way to the Collins Room and the attention of the trustees. A delegation from the Students for a New University (SNU) had the temerity to ask to make their case before the trustees. The request was unprecedented. Student concerns were traditionally brought before the trustees by the rector. But the rector at this point was Senator Grattan O'Leary, who seemed blithely disconnected from student sensibilities. The SNU was not an official arm of the AMS, and therefore had no claim on the trustees' time. The Board chairman, R.D. Harkness, probably after conferring with Deutsch, took a liberal line. There would be "some merit," he advised, in allowing the group to make its presentation. It was an organization which "might capitalize on a refusal to be heard." In the students came, headed by its president, Robin Ryan, and supported by Tom Good and Jacqui Cocks. They "accused" the university of being "negligent" on the housing front and demanded measures to alleviate the situation. Deutsch suggested in response that the administration had already taken measures to correct the situation. The trustees nonetheless took the SNU's ideas in, thanked them, and said that any response to their agenda would be communicated through the official channel of the AMS. The Queen's trustees thus had their first encounter with radical student politics.

Later in that same meeting, a delegation from the AMS, led by AMS President Dave Pakrul, was also invited to speak to the trustees on the housing problem. Pakrul said that his presence was provoked by concern that the SNU was usurping the AMS's legitimate role as representative of Queen's students. The AMS, he insisted, was "the authoritative body in these matters." Pakrul's tone was less confrontational. The AMS, he said, had a proposal for the trustees, a proposal emanating out of Queen's long tradition of student empowerment. Let students, he argued, play an active role in solving the housing problem. The concept of cooperative student housing had been gaining credibility across North America. Indeed, Queen's had known the concept since 1941, when a group of students bought a house on Earl Street, and ran it as a co-operative residence. Students formed the co-op executive. Residents performed assigned duties like stoking the furnace and chopping wood. A paid cook provided meals. Social activities – canoe and ski trips – emerged out of this culture of sharing. Women began joining the co-op in 1945. The Science '44 Co-op culture was vigorously transmitted through the postwar period. In the late 1960s, the Co-op, assisted by the university, engaged in a wholesale financial restructuring that enabled it to acquire more houses and, in its way, help to alleviate the housing crisis.[67]

In the participatory, "people"-oriented ethos of the 1960s, the co-operative philosophy found fertile ground. Co-operative living quickly blended with ideas of "free learning," of breaking the regimentation of the multiversity. Co-op colleges sprang up on or near Ontario university campuses in Waterloo, Ottawa, and, most prominently, in Toronto on Bloor Street, where the eighteen-storey Rochdale College – named for a nineteenth-century English weavers' commune – opened in 1965. Given intellectual credence by philosophers like George Grant (whose grandfather had been principal of Queen's) and Howard Adelman, Rochdale was, in the words of poet Dennis Lee, "edgy about authority."[68] It offered freely structured learning programs and would even award a doctorate for $100. Rochdale sadly soon lost its utopian gloss, and by 1968 had piled up debt and slipped into drug- and hippie-induced mayhem. Queen's, Pakrul assured the trustees, could chart a different co-operative course than Rochdale, but it would require a bit of help from the trustees.

In its frustration with the university's slow and awkward handling of the housing situation, the AMS now proposed to take matters into its own hands. It had taken a $178,000 option on a car-dealership lot downtown, at the corner of Division and Princess streets. A Toronto architect had been commissioned to work up a feasibility study for a tower building on the site. Dan Burns, a geography student sitting as an Arts rep on the AMS council, who had participated in the Science '44 restructuring and had spent the summer working at the Central Mortgage and Housing Corporation (CMHC) in Ottawa, pointed out to the AMS Building Committee that the National Housing Act had recently been amended to permit 90-per-cent financing of student residences over fifty years. The question now, Pakrul told the trustees, was where would the AMS get the 10-per-cent down payment? A loan of $50,000 would overcome this obstacle and cover start-up costs. The trustees were interested. Harkness, the chairman, even "congratulated" Pakrul for his initiative and urged his colleagues to "approve the proposal in principle in order to give the AMS encouragement to proceed with its feasibility studies." The finance committee of the Board would review the numbers in that study. After a brief discussion, the motion to lend the AMS $50,000 was passed. Pakrul left the meeting with new purpose.[69]

Although no one sensed it at the time, that October 1968 meeting of the Queen's trustees symbolized in microcosm a powerful provocation of the "Queen's way" in those tumultuous late 1960s. The challenge went to the genetic roots of the university. If there was one abiding intellectual thread that ran through Queen's history, it was the notion at the core of limestone liberalism that a university education was about personal empowerment and social improvement. A Queen's education still smacked of Presbyterian practicality and moral improvement. To adopt the argot of the 1960s, one "found oneself" through education, by realizing that the purpose of university was to inform the delicate trade-off between self and society. In essence, the two student delegations – one bold and overtly critical and the other somewhat deferential yet still adventurous – that appeared before the trustees that October projected two embryonic prescriptions for limestone liberalism in transition. The SNU proffered a systemic rejection of Queen's heritage, arguing that it was nothing more than a facade for a social and economic system that served some but exploited others in Canadian society. The AMS also agitated for change, but its prescription was for change *within* the system – progressive change. Over the next few years, each came to fruition, one in a bitter and time-consuming investigation of alleged political persecution on campus and the other in the construction of Elrond College, a massive, drab apartment tower that still dominates the Kingston skyscape. Each prescription would throw open a window on Queen's culture in transition. Each would leave a mark – some might say, a scar – on the university's evolution. One would unfold brick-by-brick, dollar-by-dollar on Princess Street, and the other witness-by-witness, allegation-by-allegation, in a lecture hall of the law school.

Student Developers Learn Their Trade

The bricks-and-dollars story of Elrond College seems perhaps a more straightforward tale to relate than the convoluted Edwards case. In some ways, Elrond embodied the naive appeal of the "come on people, smile on your brother" ethos of sixties culture. It was not, however, to Jefferson Airplane that Dave Pakrul and his AMS colleagues turned for inspiration for their student co-op tower. Instead, they turned to J.R.R. Tolkein's 1950s trilogy *Lord of the Rings*. They aimed to construct a Hobbit-inspired alternative way of student life around Queen's. They would build, in Tolkein's words, "a perfect house, whether you like food or sleep, or story telling or singing, or just sitting and thinking, or a pleasant mixture of them all." And they would name it after the resident of that serene palace – Elrond, Lord of Rivendell. Just when the ambition actually gelled is uncertain, but throughout 1969 four Arts students – Michael Vaughan, Dave Peters, Dan Burns, and Ross McGregor – drew inspiration about co-operative effort from disparate sources: the co-op experiments elsewhere in the province, Science '44 co-op's recent revival at Queen's, and the ethos of the heady "summer of '68." From California, there was, for instance, *The Whole Earth Catalogue*, the bestselling prescription for more ecologically friendly lifestyles. At the same time, Austrian philosopher Ivan Illich was urging society to "de-school" and design "plug-in teaching." Early on, certain preconceptions therefore installed themselves in the thinking about the Elrond initiative. It would reject the sterile design model of high-rise apartment buildings, with their dingy, linear corridors and cubbyhole apartments. The emphasis at Elrond would be on communal association and communal management.[70] The old landlord-tenant relationship would go; tenants would govern their own destiny. Residents would live and learn together, while presumably heading off to Queen's by day to indulge in a little formal learning. Looking back on the whole Elrond experiment in 1973, the Kingston *Whig-Standard* would note that, from the outset, the project was "a mixture of whimsy and business sense."[71]

Through the winter of 1968–69, the Elrond project percolated through the student government. In February, Ross McGregor won the AMS presidential election on a reformist platform that gave prominence to the housing issue and catering to student needs. The AMS immediately began negotiations to take over the campus housing service from Richardson Hall, arguing that it was closer to student needs. The AMS then funded its architectural study of what a co-operative college on Princess Street might look like. For this, it turned to Toronto architect Irving Grossman. Grossman had made his name as a designer of modernist homes and apartment buildings in Toronto. The 1960s had attracted star architects to campus design – Ron Thom to Trent University and Arthur Erickson to Simon Fraser University, for instance – so it seemed fitting that Queen's should seek prestige and innovation in its choice of architect. Grossman's design of the 1957 Betel House in York Downs – a cantilevered in the crowded Kingston housing market. When freshman Bill Young arrived at Queen's in late August 1972, for instance, he was desperate to put a roof over his head. He looked to Elrond out of expediency, not philosophical commitment. Young was slotted into a twelve-person "house" in the tower. He liked what he saw. The place was run by its inhabitants; a student, Jane Lindsey, sat as president of the college. Young went on to sit on the college board for three years, but came to sense that the original élan of the place was dissipating. The routine of communal service broke down, especially since resident turnover (especially in the summer doldrums) disrupted any sense of continuity. Soon, only a handful of residents were doing the weekly chores.[82] The building became dirty, and maintenance problems mounted. There were water leaks and heat loss at a time when Canada was experiencing an unprecedented "energy crisis." With revenues faltering, repairs were put off. As the co-op ideal faded, social decorum inside Elrond deteriorated. There were problems with drug trafficking and rowdyism. Elrond seemed to be drifting into Rochdale territory. Kingstonians began to regard the ungainly tower on Princess Street as a liability, not as a beacon of new-age urban living.

The accountants completed the gloomy picture. By late 1974, the college owed a $2.4-million first mortgage to the CMHC, a $832,000 second mortgage to Queen's, and $30,000 to the AMS. The Elrond board of directors, now headed by Bill Young, reluctantly reported the next year that the college had lost $139,000, but continued to whistle into the wind, predicting a financial break-even point in five years. But lower-than-expected occupancy and costly attempts to adjust the building's configuration obliged the Board to add annual deficits to the CMHC mortgage, thereby expanding debt-servicing costs and further attenuating the college's long-term viability. Over at Richardson Hall, university administrators agonized over the situation. Principal Ron Watts inherited John Deutsch's empathy for the project, but could not ignore the obvious. By 1977, the college was $3.86 million in debt and Vice-Principal David Bonham (an accountant by training and lawyer by trade) warned that Elrond would likely not be able to meet its mortgage payments that summer. Watts told the trustees that a short-term fix would "simply postpone the moment of truth."[83] Throughout the late 1970s, the college engaged in frantic negotiations with the CMHC for some kind of financial life-saving ring. Queen's remained standoffish, although its almost one-million-dollar liability from loans to the college caused deep anxiety in these years of campus austerity. The university adamantly dismissed one option: it would not take over the faltering college. It did not want the additional financial burden, especially since Elrond would require costly retrofitting into a "normal" residence and because the Kingston housing situation had stabilized. As Elrond's debt to Queen's crested over the million-dollar mark in 1978, Principal Watts admitted that the university had gone "as far as it can go."[84]

By 1979, Elrond began to sound a death rattle. The CMHC refused to allow the college's deficits to be rolled over into its mortgage. The college directors fought valiantly to shore up the occupancy rate, while at the same time desperately appealing to the federal public works minister for a helping hand. A 1980 Price Waterhouse study held out little hope of redemption: the building had too many "unique features" to allow it be modified into a less-communal residence. Late in 1980, the unavoidable happened – the CMHC took ownership of the building, and the dream of a "perfect house" died. A year later, the CMHC offered the building to Queen's for $950,000. Queen's said "no thanks," and thereby quietly ate its million-dollar-plus investment in the project. The building was subsequently sold to a developer, who did remodel it into a more conventional apartment block. Hotel Hobbit became the Princess Towers.

It is inviting to dismiss Elrond as a fiasco for student and university alike. One could easily portray it as a case study in sixties naïveté – a starry-eyed exercise in seeking to defy the hard, cold realities of the marketplace. Aesthetically, it bequeathed Kingston a building that is almost universally disparaged as an eyesore of discoloured concrete and ugly rooftop antennae. From any angle, "Elrond" dominates the Kingston skyline, in jarring contrast with the shapely limestone domes and steeples bequeathed by the nineteenth century. Financially, Elrond cost Canadian taxpayers, Queen's, and its student government dearly. But perhaps there is an inner beauty to the place. Architecturally, Elrond explored new frontiers. Irving Grossman and his student collaborators acted out a critique of contemporary architectural practice. Elrond was designed from the *inside out* – it was predicated on a sociology that suggested that those who were to inhabit a building should be party to its design. Jack Smith, a social-science student involved in the project, later produced an insightful analysis of the Elrond experience. "New design should facilitate rather than frustrate the desires of people to seek communities of association," he wrote. Urban architecture should dedicate itself to producing "more humanitarian micro-environments which will 'soften' the impact of rapid mechanized change on man, and allow him to retain the spontaneous associations which generate forms of community." Buildings such as Elrond result in a "constantly changing public schemata of architectural perception." They explore "frontiers of new cultural innovation."[85] None of this places Elrond in the same realm as the work of Buckminster Fuller (geodesic domes) or Moshe Safdie (Habitat '67), but it does situate it in a context that extends far beyond the corner of Princess and Division streets in Kingston.

Elrond had other redeeming features. When all was said and done, it did add four hundred beds to the stock of Kingston accommodation at a time when beds were scarce. More importantly, it tested and extended the storied relationship of the university with its students. Since the 1850s, the university had steadily relaxed the paternal leash of control it once held on its students. The AMS embodied the Queen's belief that students could be trusted to oversee many matters governing their own fate. It had been clear to all concerned in the late 1960s that the orthodox approach to housing Queen's students was faltering. The university was unable to build sufficient residence capacity, while local landlords either shared this failing or abused the shortfall by imposing usurious rents or becoming slum landlords. So Queen's students acted on their own initiative. What is remarkable is the alacrity with which Principal Deutsch, the trustees, and other members of the Queen's community, such as Ned Franks and Jim Whitley, bought into the idea and actively supported it with time, money, and advice. As Elrond's general manager, John Blanchard, told the *Whig-Standard* in 1973, John Deutsch had been "our most important helper."

Yet, the university always sat in the back seat of the project's direction. It was the students who dealt with the architect, went to court to battle the contractor, and travelled to Ottawa to deal with politicians and bureaucrats. Deutsch might have lent a helping hand – a telephone call to Ottawa, a legal opinion from the university's Kingston lawyers – but the onus was left to the students, even as the university's financial exposure climbed. Deutsch was thus trusting in the Queen's tradition that students should learn both inside and outside the classroom. Elrond was just such a training ground for the world beyond the prescribed life on campus. Even as a costly failure, Elrond prepared its supporters for the knocks and sometimes outrageous fortunes of life. There were no courses at Queen's on the pitfalls of building a sixteen-storey apartment building. Elrond supplied such a tutorial, a lesson in teamwork and working "the system."

Many of the early student promoters of Elrond went on to distinguished careers after graduation – graduating, as it were, from both Queen's and the Elrond experiment. Dan Burns and Dave Peters became prominent in Toronto urban planning. Burns would later return to his alma mater to serve on the Board of Trustees, where he became outspoken in advocating the adoption of a long-term campus plan and better architectural design at Queen's. Ross McGregor left Queen's and went on to a high-profile career in public affairs and fundraising. Bill Young became a successful consulting engineer and investor in the United States, who would later return to Queen's to chair the Board of Trustees early in the next century. Queen's supplied such graduates with the intuitions they needed for life. Elrond, with all its expensive travails, supplied them with an understanding of what was worth striving for and what was in the end possible. In this sense, the eccentric concrete tower on Princess Street provided the latest iteration of Queen's culture of inclusion and public service. In doing so, it re-established and extended the bond of trust and mutual support between the university and its students through a decade more laden with change than any other in its history.

Radical Queen's?

Throughout the Edwards affair and the laborious unfolding of the Elrond, there was an irony lurking just below the surface. Much of the social and economic critique levelled at Queen's and the broader Canadian society by the Free Socialists was superficial and even jejune in its analysis. In many ways, the FSM simply aped the anti-establishment rhetoric of student-protest movements elsewhere. The tone was sensationalist and the analysis shallow. Its dynamic relied solely on negativism. There was little attempt to suggest alternatives. Elrond, for all its congenital problems, at least offered the long-pursued ideal of social co-operation. The FSM ultimately failed, not just because its claims against Becker and Clark proved hollow, but because it promoted nothing constructive for Canadian society. Ironically, a more progressive prescription for Canada's future was, in fact, being quietly drawn up *elsewhere* on the Queen's campus in the late 1960s, a prescription more in keeping with Queen's long-standing tradition of nurturing the governance

of Canada. Just as John Deutsch and his ilk at Queen's had contributed to the construction of a liberal welfare state since the 1930s, others now pondered the extension of that social-democratic impulse. The federal Co-operative (that word again) Commonwealth Federation had remade itself in 1961 as the New Democratic Party (NDP). The NDP endeavoured to reorient itself away from its agrarian roots towards the more urban and industrial challenges of postwar Canada – income security, affordable housing, universal health care, and macroeconomic policies. These instincts resonated on the Queen's campus.

In this respect, Kingston – a small city with an industrial and service-industry base – proved fertile ground. North Kingston, for instance, was a district of entrenched urban poverty. The presence of a network of federal prisons reinforced the message that all was not well in Canadian society. In the mid-sixties, the campus NDP Club at Queen's came alive to these realities and soon struck an alliance with social reformers in the city. Queen's graduate students in history and French, such as James Laxer, John Smart, and Pat Smart, joined with student activist Krista Maeots and professors such as George Rawlyk in history to engage what they saw as Canada's pressing social and economic problems. Laxer, in particular, stressed that their energies must be dedicated to rewriting what he construed as the NDP's too-moderate social-democratic agenda; constructive change, he insisted would only come from working *within* the party system, not by toppling it. This strategy resonated beyond the campus, where Kingston social activists such as Joan Newman and Bronwen Wallace saw common cause.

The Kingston NDPers soon connected with the wider Canadian social-democratic community, and by the end of the decade were instrumental in writing a far-left, but still social-democratic, prescription for Canada – the Waffle Manifesto. The manifesto urged, amongst other things, state ownership of key economic sectors of the economy and the necessity of warding off foreign ownership of Canada's patrimony. The Waffle Movement gained its real momentum in Toronto and central Ontario, where University of Toronto economist Mel Watkins shaped the movement into a powerful faction within the NDP urging a sharp turn to the ideological left. But much of the intellectual spadework for the manifesto was done in graduate-student lounges and apartments in Kingston. Through the Edwards affair, the Kingston "Wafflers" paid lip-service support to the FSM, but intrinsically distrusted its reckless behaviour and simplistic prescriptions. Laxer, now a history-department lecturer and soon to be married to Queen's journalist Krista Maeots, mounted a serious underdog run at the NDP leadership in 1971, only narrowly losing to the more moderate David Lewis. Nonetheless, Waffle ideas served to push the beleaguered Trudeau minority government of the early 1970s into greater state intervention – PetroCanada, foreign investment screening, most typically – by the mid-seventies. Laxer himself succumbed to the big-city pull of NDP politics and left Queen's for York University.[86] Few would associate Queen's with the radical chic – to take a Tom Wolfe term – of the age, but beyond the transitory theatre of the FSM, the Queen's NDP was in its way living up to Alex Corry's belief that Queen's was all about "loyal service to Canada."

Curtain Call

So what are we to make of Charles "Chuck" Edwards and Queen's brush with student radicalism in the late 1960s? It might be tempting to dismiss Edwards and his antics as misplaced adolescent behaviour – kicking out at the system, a system that seemed beyond his control. But this would do a disservice to the whole episode. Yes, Edwards and his ilk acted irresponsibility, levelling fallacious accusations at good people. But beyond the gratuitous injury, the Edwards affair played a *constructive* role in accelerating the pace of change at Queen's. It forced the university to attach itself to the times, to reconnect with its liberal roots. As Dean Slater reluctantly admitted at the climactic April Senate meeting, Edwards had obliged Queen's "to re-examine its philosophical basis." To the immense credit of John Deutsch and Ross McGregor, Edwards was shown the full power of liberalism – an open inquiry, fair representation, and a second chance. If there is a defining moment in Queen's modern history, it came on the morning of 3 December 1969 when AMS president Ross McGregor met his council, gained support for the idea of an unfettered inquiry into the Edwards allegations, and then walked down University Avenue to the principal's office, where Deutsch immediately gave the proposal the nod. When the Senate endorsed the proposal that afternoon, it seemed that Queen's had obliged its heritage of "fearless inquiry." Yes, other forces were pushing Queen's forward – the Gibson Report on Senate reform, the recognition that the university needed a grievance and discipline process, and the emergence of a modernized AMS. But Chuck Edwards forced this pace and, whenever that pace slackened in the 1970s, the phrase "the Edwards affair" inevitably surfaced in the dialogue of change and focused the debate.

In the late 1980s, students asked the American student radical Abbie Hoffman to speak at Queen's. Hoffman had gone nose-to-nose with the American Establishment, going to jail for his role in the tumultuous protests at the 1968 Democratic Convention in Chicago. "Sacred cows," Hoffman liked reminding his followers, "make the tastiest hamburger." In 1974, however, Hoffman had run afoul of American drug laws, was arrested, skipped bail, and went into hiding in the Thousand Islands. Thus, when he arrived at the podium at Queen's shortly after emerging from his exile in 1986, Hoffman had a passing acquaintance with the university just down the way from the Thousand Islands. His talk that evening was a rambling reflection on the world as seen by an aging Yippie. For his purposes, the Queen's student culture provided a convenient foil for his assault on entrenched conservatism. In his mind, students at

In 1985, American activist Abbie Hoffman spoke at Queen's. The former Yippie intoned that "Queen's is a hotbed of social rest." In his expectation of brick-throwing radicalism, Hoffman probably underestimated Queen's age-old and at times tardy reliance on liberal gradualism.

Queen's had never lived the sixties. "Queen's," he proclaimed, "is a hotbed of social rest." It was a great line and drew much laughter.[87]

But Hoffman's quip missed the mark. There was no denying that Queen's students had never en masse embraced the placard-waving, building-blockading ethos demonstrated by many North American students in the 1960s. Queen's one brush with that style of student activism – the Edwards affair – proved transitory, deflated by objective inquiry and a steadfast refusal by university authorities to stonewall student opinion. Instead, Queen's students in the 1960s had rediscovered the university's genetic liberalism. They had reinvented their student government, making it more relevant to modern student needs. They had graduated into the ranks of the Senate, the senior body of academic policy at the university. They had elected one of their own to serve as their rector on the Board of Trustees. They had devised their own solution to the city's chronically tight housing market. And, while Elrond College may have faltered under the weight of adolescent inexperience, it spoke volumes of Queen's students' determination to set their own course and reflected their intuition that co-operation rather than confrontation (so often the attitude on other campuses) was the best way forward. Far from what may have appeared as "social rest" to some outsiders, Queen's was in fact a "hotbed" of what Brian Rogers, an Arts student at the time and one of the first AMS education commissioners, described as "creeping liberalism."[88] John Blanchard, the business manager at Elrond, similarly praised the "progressive conservative" mentality of Queen's students. Other AMS participants came to identify a vein of "pragmatism," to quote long-time AMS business manager Claude Sherren, in the way Queen's students looked on the world. In the end, it turned out that limestone did not "burn" and that limestone liberalism continued to be a most durable, and yet flexible, foundation for life.

Whether it was holding a referendum to secure student funding for a university-wide project such as a new university centre or deploying their own constables to enforce campus discipline, the student culture was radical only in its commitment to progressive change based on consultation and consensus. On the other side of the fence, the university administration (so often headed by Queen's graduates) had the good sense to work *with* and not *against* the students on the creeping liberal frontier. There was, therefore, much wisdom in Alex Corry's belief that an education at Queen's should be about personal empowerment, not just about book learning and conformity. As a result of experiences such as Elrond, the Edwards inquiry, editing the *Journal*, or, indeed, managing the Queen's band, many students graduated from Queen's with one foot already confidently planted in the world beyond.

Queen's alumni from the late 1960s and early 1970s strode off in many directions. To draw up a list of such achievement would involve too-selective and perhaps dangerously invidious distinctions. The student names that have punctuated this chapter's narrative – Burns, McGregor, Simpson, Broadbent, Young – perhaps impart a flavour of that achievement. Each carried away from Queen's a commitment to constructive citizenship, whether through bureaucracy, journalism, business, or public advocacy. Each in their way had imbued the spirit of limestone liberalism. And what of Chuck Edwards? Where did his path lead? Edwards never took up the offer to return to Queen's in a graduate field unrelated to chemical engineering. Instead, he drifted about for several years working in filmmaking in Montreal and even driving a cab. But then, in the language of the 1960s, he "found himself" and returned to the love of his earlier life – engineering. He found work as a mining engineer in Canadian frontier mining towns such as Flin Flon. Over the years, he built a national reputation as an expert in uranium mining, working for well-regarded companies such Cameco and AMEC (ironically an American-owned enterprise). Edwards's expertise has echoed globally through his contributions to international bodies such as the International Atomic Energy Agency in Vienna. In 2011, he was elected president of the Canadian Institute of Mining, Metallurgy and Petroleum – an illustrious honour for a man who once predicted that "Jack" would never get a job. Other youthful participants in the Edwards inquiry found their métier after Queen's. Terry O'Hara became a dogged and much-respected criminal lawyer in Kingston. Stuart Ryan kept the faith, becoming a union organizer in Ottawa and frequent candidate for the Communist Party of Canada in federal elections. Tom Good became a professor of economics.

And back at Edwards's alma mater, his one-time mentors Henry Becker and Reg Clark returned to their classrooms and research labs, winning esteem in the eyes of their colleagues and, in doing so, building their department into a bastion of chemical engineering. Dean David Slater went on to be the ill-starred president of York University. Professor Bernie Adell became the Dean of Law at Queen's. For all concerned, those long evenings of the Edwards inquiry not only rejuvenated Queen's liberalism, but also stamped the personal trajectory of those involved. There was perhaps an irony in the fact that the man who never finished his doctoral thesis on combustion ignited so much at Queen's.

6

"A Pretty Taste for Paradox"
Ron Watts and the Art of Compromise, 1974–1984

At Queen's, things do not rage as much as simmer.
Maclean's columnist Allan Fotheringham, March 1980

A neat and tidy mind is a crippling disability in any effort to understand the processes of internal governance at Queen's ... collegiality has traditionally been the essence of the style of governance at Queen's.
Ron Watts, 1988

We are operating on goodwill and the high morale of the staff, but we cannot continue on this basis for long.
Applied Science Dean David Bacon, 1983

Minding the Federation

In the fall of 1977, the McGill-Queen's University Press published a book with a disarming title: *Must Canada Fail?* After a decade of centennial euphoria fuelled by a buoyant economy, Canada sank into a slough of national despondency in the early seventies. Stagflation, soaring energy costs, and fractious relations between Ottawa and the provinces soured the Trudeauesque optimism of the late sixties. Anxiety turned to near-panic in November 1976, when Quebec voters elected the Parti Québécois with its separatist agenda. "As a political entity," an alarmed *Queen's Journal* editorialized, "Canada is thought to be perilously close to dissolution."[1] But, as they had done since the days of Adam Shortt, O.D. Skelton, and Bill Mackintosh, Queen's political economists reacted with alacrity and with insight into the national crisis. Orchestrated by political-studies professor Richard Simeon, seventeen authors – only two of whom had no connection with Queen's – produced essays on the fragmentation of the national mood and its potential consequences. "This is not an optimistic book," Simeon darkly wrote in his introduction.

The essays did not shy away from the worst-case scenario: Canada breaking apart. Law professors John Whyte and John Clayton discussed the legal ramifications of Quebec separation. History professor George Rawlyk underscored the dire consequences that separation would spell for the Atlantic provinces. Edwin Black from political studies countered that a "workable rearrangement" of the constitution might save the day. His colleague John Meisel, long an advocate of *bonne entente* with Quebec, was more upbeat: "*J'ai le goût du Québec.*" Meisel counselled Anglo-Canadians to have more empathy with Quebec's cultural aspirations. Joining this more positive chorus was their fellow political scientist Ron Watts, principal of Queen's at the time. Watts added a global perspective, providing examples of federations around the globe that had buckled under pressure. Federations, he concluded, survived when they mastered the art of compromise and learned to adjust their ways.[2] In the days immediately after the momentous PQ victory, Watts had told a hastily convened symposium in Dunning Hall that, without the elasticity of compromise, Canadians could expect "violence if the Québécois separate."[3]

Must Canada Fail? arrived in the bookstores at a troubling juncture for the McGill-Queen's University Press. Barely eight years old, the publishing partnership was feeling the pinch of the austere seventies.[4] Deficits and staff cutbacks haunted its editorial offices. *Must Canada Fail?* did not top the bestseller list in Canada, but it was widely reviewed and much debated by policy-makers and Canadians at large. It reminded the nation of Queen's storied dedication to what had once been called "political economy." A year later, Prime Minister Trudeau appointed Watts to his Task Force on National Unity, set up in an attempt to get at the root causes of national disquiet.[5] Like many Queen's scholars before him, Watts willingly headed to Ottawa to help guide the nation in a time of duress.

During these fractious years, national unity surfaced in other ways at Queen's: in 1975 the Dunning Trust lecture series brought eminent Canadians like politician Stephen Lewis and historian Donald Creighton to campus to discuss "Canada: Towards the Year 2000." In 1976, Quebec publisher Claude Ryan spoke as the Brockington Visitor. Three years later, the university gave an honorary degree to labour economist and ardent federalist Eugene Forsey. Forsey warned the convocation against the temptation of loosening the bonds of the federation, of letting Canada become a society of "ten jackasses eating leaves off a single maple tree."[6]

The problems of maintaining the national federation not only reverberated in the scholarly life of Queen's, but also found echoes in its own cohesion and governance. It was no coincidence that Watts was the fourth political economist in a row to occupy the principal's office. Like the selection of Mackintosh, Corry, and Deutsch before him, Watts's appointment reflected the belief that a man who could probe the intricacies of a decentralized federal union like Canada was probably well predisposed to tackle the challenge of overseeing a loose academic federation like Queen's. However, Watts, unlike Mackintosh and Deutsch, was neither born on Canadian soil nor Queen's bred. He was born in Japan in 1929 to Anglican missionary parents. The bloody invasion of Manchuria in 1932 soon provided the first indication that Japan was pursuing imperial ambitions. By the fall of 1940, the unnerving prospect of war eventually obliged the Reverend Watts to dispatch his family to the safety of Ottawa, from where Ron subsequently set off to undertake a bachelor's degree in philosophy at the University of Toronto. A Rhodes Scholarship followed, allowing him to undertake a second honours degree at Oriel College, from which he graduated in 1954. After a brief stint as a fledgling accountant in Toronto, he caught the eye of Queen's philosopher and dean of Arts and Science Rollo Earl, who persuaded him to come to Queen's as a lecturer in philosophy. Watts was conscious that he was at a fork in the road; Earl told him to try university life for a year and, if it did not whet his intellectual appetite, then he would be free to balance books in Toronto. Watts would stay at Queen's.

Watts was typical of many of the junior faculty arriving at Queen's in the fifties and sixties; the university was desperate to attract faculty to meet the swelling tide of undergraduates, and consequently took on young scholars with great potential but as-yet-incomplete academic curricula vitae. To make ends meet, Watts became a residence don in the newly opened McNeill House. There, he became an advocate of the "significant relationship between academic results and membership in a good residence," arguing in the Queen's Quarterly that *life* in residence should reinforce a student's mainstream academic development.[7] Dean Earl could see Watts's potential, and in 1959 urged him towards graduate studies, offering a leave of absence as an incentive. Oxford again beckoned. There, he fell under the spell of the renowned Australian constitutionalist Kenneth Wheare. The intellectual imprimatur stamped on Watts in those years is suggested by the titles of Wheare's best-known monographs: *Federal Government* (1946) and *Government by Committee* (1955).

By 1962, Watts had his DPhil from Oxford and was welcomed back to Queen's by the new dean of Arts and Science, philosopher A.R.C. "Sandy" Duncan. Given his graduate research, Watts now found himself more closely aligned to the department of political studies, where he became an assistant professor. He quickly learned to balance pure academic research with the giving of hands-on advice. In 1963, he advised the fledgling and ultimately doomed East African Federation. His first book, *New Federations: Experiments in the Commonwealth* appeared in 1966.[8] His timing was auspicious: Canada was locked in a constitutional crisis, as Quebec sought to redefine its status within

Former principal John Deutsch (left) and his successor, Ronald Watts, with his wife, Donna, head for Richardson Stadium in the fall of 1975. Sadly, Deutsch would succumb to cancer the following spring, an immense emotional blow to the Queen's community. Watts, a specialist in federal-provincial relations, would perpetuate Deutsch's attachment to the processes of governing Canada.

the federation. The unfolding of the welfare state in Canada, with its health, educational, and pension benefits, further strained the dated fabric of the British North America Act. In 1965, Queen's responded to all this flux by creating the Institute for Intergovernmental Relations, a clustering of academic expertise dedicated to hands-on comparative analysis and exposition of what made federations work – and, at times, fail. On a personal level, Watts was also well situated to observe the scrum of federal-provincial politics. Bill Davis, a friend from University of Toronto undergraduate days, was, for instance, now a rising star in the "Big Blue Machine" Conservative government at Queen's Park and was, perhaps more significantly, Ontario's minister of education.[9]

Watts's academic involvements at Queen's mirrored his scholarly expertise: the give-and-take of successful federations could well be applied to governance of an academic community. In 1964,

Watts became an assistant dean of Arts and Science. From that perch, he observed Dean George Harrower's aggressive expansion of the Arts and Science faculty list; the faculty became young and vital. In 1968, he himself became dean of Arts and Science. His low-key approach to dealings with his faculty colleagues was shaped by a belief that he was no more than *primus inter pares*. He continued to attend Senate meetings, believing that he was uniquely positioned to wear two hats – one as a continuing, tenured faculty member and the other as the lead member of faculty, whose responsibility was to broker consensus and to connect his faculty with the broader Queen's community.[10] He applied the same philosophy to his dealings with students, citing Cardinal Newman's famous definition of a university as "not a foundry, or a mint, or a treadmill," but "an Alma Mater, knowing her children one by one."[11]

Succession in Richardson Hall

In late 1973, John Deutsch's unexpected decision to retire early triggered the creation of a joint Senate-trustees committee to select a successor. Eighty-five candidates were nominated for the post. The committee's deliberations were hermetically secret, but the campus scuttlebutt suggested that George Harrower, astrophysicist, former dean, and now vice-principal, academic, was the odds-on favourite. For all his galvanism in expanding his faculty, however, Harrower lacked a collegial charisma; he was rather stiff and frontal and tended to see his responsibilities in terms of numbers, not personalities. Earlier, Harrower had established his reformist inclinations by forcefully trying to jettison the faculty's honours program in favour of a more populist generalist approach to the undergraduate curriculum, but had been largely turned back by opposition in the ranks of his faculty. Whatever the undisclosed wisdom of the selection committee, Watts emerged as the new principal of Queen's.[12] Harrower remained vice-principal, academic, before returning to the physics department, usefully serving the university until 1977, when he was called to the presidency of Lakehead University.

Watts made two immediate impressions. First, at forty-five, he was a remarkably youthful choice to lead Queen's. A tall, well-framed man, with a broad, winning smile, Watts looked the part of an academic now comfortably competent in mid-career. His three immediate predecessors had assumed the principalship well into their fifties. Indeed, it had been clear that, for Mackintosh, Corry, and Deutsch, the appointment was the crowning achievement of their careers. For Watts, it seemed more like a mid-career benchmark, so much so that the principal-elect had to remind the trustees that, given his relative youth, it would be in the university's interest to limit his tenure to a five-year, renewable term. Secondly, Watts brought a demonstrable sense of collegiality to his assignment. His record and his demeanour suggested that he was not going to force issues, but instead would endeavour to act as an amicable ringmaster trying to orchestrate harmony on campus. Decision making would be decentralized. Senate committees would be employed to "talk out" – a phrase he often used – issues. He would conduct himself as a diplomat, who courteously took in disparate points of view and groomed them into some kind of binding conclusion. Tellingly, he instructed the editor of the university news department not to employ the term "the administration" in its publicity material. The term, he argued, "tends to suggest a remote and inaccessible group." In his mind, Queen's had "always tried to foster a sense of community" in projecting its image.[13] To emphasize the point, Watts made a habit of regularly lunching at the Faculty Club and of taking an active role in Senate meetings, which he now chaired but at the same time still attended as a continuing faculty member. Every Wednesday morning, before he met his deans and vice-principals, Watts met the AMS president for coffee and a catch-up on student concerns.

But, for all his convivial inclinations, the new principal quickly found himself working against the

grain of the times. The first sentence of Watts's installation address in November 1974 caught that mood: "Universities the world over feel themselves on the defensive; Canadian universities are no exception." He pointed out that, on every side, university presidents found themselves "squeezed" by shifting realities and expectations. The expansive sixties were over, replaced by sputtering economic performance and fiscal constraint. Governments found themselves with much less money to spend on post-secondary education, yet they continued to embrace the dogma of accessibility, to which they now added overtones of accountability, rationalization, and productivity. Whereas Corry and Deutsch faced the challenge of channelling, and at times even constraining, growth in the sixties, Principal Watts would face the seas of seventies constraint. After ten years in office, Watts would sum up his innings as principal as being "marked by constraint, consolidation and constructive evolutionary development."[14] If governments were placing new demands on universities, they were in large part transmitting a shift in the broader public attitude towards universities. A college degree was no longer deemed to be the ticket to worldly success. Persistent high unemployment dogged the seventies. Students consequently began to cast a more vigilant and critical eye on its cost and the quality of higher education.

At the same time, students sought curricula better tailored to society's needs. They started to act

Although a cloud of austerity descended over the Ontario university system in the 1970s, the mood of youthful exuberance unleashed by the 1960s persisted. Here, Queen's men "streak" down University Avenue. Elsewhere on campus, medical students continued their raucous tradition of staging an annual medical variety show.

much more like *consumers* of education rather than its *recipients*, quick to demand better and more-extensive services in support of the university life. Faculty and staff on campuses experienced similar shifts. Were they now little more than civil servants, expected to shape adolescent socialization and produce socially useful research, or were they guardians of academic freedom, free to follow their intellectual consciences? And, if they were in fact public servants, did they have the right to collective bargaining, something Ottawa and the provinces were rapidly conceding to their respective civil services? Watts used his installation address to express his bewilderment at the Hydra-headed nature of Canadian university life in the seventies. "At the root of this situation lies a lack of consensus in our contemporary society about the purposes and role of the university," he concluded. He admitted to feeling

"*A Pretty Taste for Paradox*" 227

somewhat like the "very model of a modern Major-General" in Gilbert and Sullivan's *Pirates of Penzance*, who, when confronted by contradictory pressures, developed "a pretty taste for paradox."[15]

Watts's premonition of paradox was soon reinforced by other disjunctures with the sixties. In the spring before Watts's installation, Bert Stirling had stepped down as chancellor, a post he had capably filled since 1960. A successful engineer (BA 1909) and construction magnate, Stirling had provided expert guidance to Principals Corry and Deutsch during the building boom of the sixties. He had also been an effective ambassador to the alumni. Stirling was replaced by outgoing Governor General Roland Michener, who brought tremendous affability to the chancellor's role, but as yet lacked his predecessor's depth of knowledge of university ritual and tradition and, not having gone to Queen's himself, lacked a natural affiliation with the alumni. Similarly, the chair of the Board of Trustees, the banker-economist J. Douglas Gibson, stepped down early in 1975, to be replaced by Ottawa publisher Robert W. Southam. Ominously, Gibson used the occasion of Queen's awarding him an honorary degree to remark on the "wave of sentiment against universities" prevalent in Canada. Universities, he noted were "no longer the darlings of politicians." Sharing Watts's sense of paradox, Gibson urged "more adaptation to the facts of the world in which we live. But I hope we do not make a fetish out of change: change for change's sake is a dubious philosophy."[16] Watts thus settled into his new Richardson Hall office knowing that both the neophyte chancellor and Board chairman were also feeling their way into new responsibilities.

Anxiety turned to sorrow when John Deutsch died in the spring of 1976. During their principalships, Corry and Deustch had each benefited from the continuing presence of Bill Mackintosh near at hand for guidance and a second opinion. Skilled in financial analysis, Mackintosh had, for instance, shepherded the university's endowment investments through the seventies. Watts, having served as a dean under Deutsch, had looked forward to Deutsch's ongoing guidance, especially in navigating the corridors of power with Queen's Park and Ottawa. It was not to be. In the winter of 1975–76, Deutsch was diagnosed with a perniciously fast-paced cancer and died in March. Queen's, and the nation at large, were stunned. The *Montreal Gazette* praised Deutsch as a skilled practitioner of the art of "constructive compromise." He was "what the ancients would have called a sage, but a most effective and functional sage in the dominant Canadian power conglomerate of the post-war years."[17] Watts reminded the Senate of Deutsch's abiding faith in "rational and civilized" university governance.[18]

Queen's was prominently represented at Deutsch's funeral in St Mary's Cathedral. Corry noted that his long-time colleague never "seemed to be hampered by the psychic wear and tear which often afflicts those carrying enormous burdens of responsibility." Douglas Gibson said that Deutsch's "approach was catholic in the broadest sense." Music for the service was furnished by philosophy professor Norman Brown at the cathedral organ, as well as the Queen's Choral Ensemble and piper major Peter Richards, who piped Deutsch's coffin out of the cathedral to the strains of "Flowers of the Forest."[19] In the weeks before his demise, the trustees, backed by the AMS, had voted to attach Deutsch's name to the nearly complete university centre at the corner of Union and University; the "JDUC" – as students quickly dubbed it – became a daily reminder of a man who had taken much from Queen's as a youth, then given more than equal measure back. Toronto artist Helen Frances Gregor fashioned a tapestry for the atrium of the JDUC out of the seventeen honorary-degree hoods that Deutsch had been awarded. Later in 1976, the John Deutsch Institute for the Study of Economic Policy was founded to perpetuate Deutsch's – and Queen's – commitment to the making of sound national policy.

John Deutsch left other instructive legacies. In the last two years of his tenure as principal, he had repeatedly warned the trustees and the Senate that the halcyon days of the sixties were quickly fading. His economist instincts told him that the glory days of expansion were being displaced by an unfamiliar mixture of inflation and slow growth. Old Keynesian policy mechanisms offered little leverage on stagflation. As a dean, Watts would have heard these gloomy prognostications. Now he faced their reality as principal. Since the 1950s, the role of paymaster of Ontario's university system had steadily shifted towards Queen's Park. In 1967, the Federal-Provincial Fiscal Arrangements Act had created what were soon called "established programs" to transfer monies from Ottawa to the provinces, using transfer of personal and corporate tax credits to support the provinces' operation of social and educational programs. Out of this and their own revenue streams, the provinces funded the universities of Canada. For Queen's, this meant that the annual operating grant from Queen's Park constituted the university's lifeblood. While student fees, investment income from the endowment, bequests, and revenue from externally funded research supplemented Queen's revenue, the provincial operating grant, largely calculated on the basis of the enrolment-driven basic income unit (BIU), was the university's financial aorta.

Throughout the seventies that vital BIU injection was progressively constricted: first by inflation, which constantly eroded a university's purchasing power, and secondly by Queen's Park's determination to control its costs at a time of flagging revenues and locked-in fiscal commitments to a myriad mandated programs. In this respect, Queen's was penalized by its own success: Deutsch's "steady state" policy, dedicated to holding Queen's enrolment to a ceiling of about ten thousand students, had the effect of capping Queen's draw on the BIU system, especially at a time when other Ontario universities were deliberately expanding enrolment so as to reap a harvest of BIUs. Hovering in the background was an ongoing uncertainty over Ottawa's willingness to extend its hefty established program

In the wake of Deutsch's death, the new university centre at the corner of Union and University was named the John Deutsch University Centre. Students immediately dubbed the building "the JDUC." Its central foyer became a gathering place for campus life. Concerts frequently enlivened it. A wall tapestry displayed the colourful academic hoods that came with Deutsch's many honorary degrees.

transfers, transfers for which it received little direct political credit. All the while, Ontario's ruling Conservatives, who had and would continue to hold power through the Mackintosh, Corry, Deustch, and now Watts principalships, clung to the mantra of "accessibility" – Ontario's universities must continue to be instruments of social advancement, even if inflation and austerity dramatically diminished their ability to deliver on the promise.

"*A Pretty Taste for Paradox*" 229

"Learning with a Little Oatmeal" Again

For province and university alike, the word "deficit" assumed a worrisome place in the public fiscal discourse. Almost immediately upon assuming office, Watts perforce acquired the perennial role of being the bearer of bad news. Deutsch's last year, 1973–74, had been marked by "severe cost cutting," which had reduced many functions at Queen's to "minimal staff." Reluctantly, the university had been obliged to disburse an additional $625,000 to shore up the inflation-ravaged salaries of faculty and staff. The trustees faced the unsavoury prospect of raiding the university's endowment to make ends meet. The university thus endured a fourth straight year in which its operating grant had not kept pace with inflation. Despite intense lobbying by the Council of Ontario Universities, James Auld, minister of colleges and universities, had announced that the BIU increase for the upcoming year would be 7.4 per cent, which by any measure was well below a national inflation rate that was running above 10 per cent. Despite this dismaying news, Watts counselled that there was a need to avoid "hasty and ill-considered adjustments" in policy.[20] When physiology professor Viv Abrahams angrily complained directly to the minister about this debilitating gap between income and expenditure, he received a polite-but-firm fiscal lecture from Auld: "Universities should recognize that they remain in a valued position and emphasize their merits to the public and make the best of the numerous resources they have. Universities, like all other sectors of society, must bear some of the brunt of inflation. However, I can assure you that their load is no heavier than anyone else's."[21]

In April of 1975, the *Globe and Mail* reported a testy exchange that had allegedly taken place between the minister and the new principal. Auld had called upon Ontario's universities to tighten their admission standards and not let their enrolments drift upwards. When Watts queried this, he received an earful from the minister: "Goddammit, a few years ago you were saying you were going to stay at 6,000 and now you have almost 10,000." When Queen's BIU-preserving "steady state" philosophy was explained to Auld, he apologized for his outburst.[22] Nonetheless, underfunding became the abiding bone of contention between Queen's Park and Richardson Hall throughout the decade. Whenever the annual calculus of determining Queen's operating deficit became grimly necessary, Watts harkened back to the "learning on a little oatmeal" tradition established by Principal Grant in the lean 1890s, when the university was nearly submerged by debt.[23] Grant, who was said to donate $2,500 of his $2,700 salary back to the university every year, crimped expenditures and cajoled benefactors with Presbyterian vigour into balancing the university's books. Grant, Watts pointed out with black humour, liked to remind audiences that his epitaph should be taken from Luke 16:22 – "And it came to pass that the beggar died and was carried away by the angels." Grant's own brother Charles saluted him as "the Prince of the Pocket Pickers."[24]

The Queen's of Ron Watts was, of course, a far more financially and managerially complex institution than Grant's lean operation of the 1890s. Watts quickly perforce became a master of financial expediency. Just weeks after his installation, he wrote to all staff to say that diminished financial support from Toronto constituted "a major and radical reduction in the proportion of real resources per student." He would avoid short-sighted expediency but stressed that long-term strategic changes were unavoidable. As the deficit mounted throughout the fall and winter of 1974–75, Watts set before the trustees, the Senate, Queen's students, and alumni a series of broad principles by which, he hoped, the university would navigate the seas of austerity ahead. These principles would prove remarkably prescient. Queen's, he argued, in an *Alumni Review* article entitled "Moderating Disaster," must tackle the crisis as a community, drawing on a tradition of "cooperation, mutual support, and rational accommodation."[25]

Before his departure in December 1974, Deutsch had appointed a Principal's Committee on Financial Constraint to explore "approaches" the university might adopt in the face of fiscal austerity. Chaired by Lawrence Macpherson, vice-principal, finance, the committee was stocked with deans, including Watts, and senior administrators. Its report the next spring pulled no punches and equipped Watts with a blueprint for tackling hard times. Ontario's universities were, the report concluded, entering "a period of severe stringency" that demanded "a process of cutting back that is much more than 'trimming the fat.'"[26] Without corrective action, the university's accumulated deficit would balloon to a crippling $11.3 million by the spring of 1980. If there was one Presbyterian instinct that persisted at Queen's, it was an almost pathological dislike of debt.

The bedrock reality of Queen's finances was that 80 per cent of expenditures went on wages of all types. In this climate of stringency, Watts's unshakable commitment would be to maintain the vitality of Queen's core faculty at all costs. The constraint report revealed that this need was already recognized; since 1971 the proportion of the university's budget devoted to faculty salaries had in fact risen, from 47.9 per cent to 51 per cent. This was higher than the provincial trend; other Ontario universities allocated an average of 46.3 per cent of their budgets to faculty salaries. Salaries for administrative staff at Queen's had remained steady at just over 30 per cent of the overall budget for the same period. At Queen's, the axe had instead fallen on non-salary expenditures. These fell from 21.5 per cent to 18.5 per cent over the same period.[27] Budgets across the campus for everything from maintenance to pencils were snipped and dramatically slimmed down. Watts elected to stay this course, favouring a policy of "limited salary improvement" rather than layoffs for faculty; in 1975 he announced salary increases – 12.5 per cent on the first $10,000 in salary – that were especially geared to helping junior faculty cushion the impact of inflation.[28] While these raises did not entirely close the inflation gap,

they did, he assured faculty, allow the university to avoid layoffs.

Again and again over the rest of the decade, Watts appealed to the loyalty of his faculty, to their willingness to endure salaries that were steadily eaten into by the rising cost of living. Embedded in this appeal was the notion that employment at Queen's was somehow special and that, in accepting sub-inflation pay increases, faculty were not only protecting their jobs, but were also protecting the Queen's brand of quality teaching. Implicit in this strategy was the reality that there would be little new hiring of faculty until the financial clouds cleared; adjunct faculty and term positions would be relied upon to take up any increase in teaching demand. If faculty would buy into this social contract, Watts argued, Queen's would be able to take a strategic view of its shape after the fiscal storm cleared. In return for such loyalty, the principal repeatedly promised "to seek full discussion and consultation within the university community" before fundamental decisions were taken.[29] Such mutual deliberation would allow Queen's, as the crucial Senate Committee on Academic Development readily agreed, to choose "carefully what we want to do, and [do] it to the best of our ability."[30] The Watts years would thus be marked by a seemingly endless succession of advisory committees and special task forces, each designed to preserve this culture of consultation and consensus.

There were crucial codicils to this overarching fiscal strategy. Queen's, through its presence on the Council of Ontario Universities (which Watts would chair in 1979) and its representations to the advisory Ontario Council on University Affairs (OCUA), was committed to maintaining a buffer zone between its government paymaster and its right to academic freedom. Within this dialogue with Queen's Park, Queen's would strive to demonstrate the need for some revision of the BIU funding system, which was by the seventies still too geared to the growth mentality of the sixties. At the same time, Watts and the trustees determined to become more assertive in explaining the role of the university to the society it served. In particular, Ontarians must be made to realize that their province was underfunding its universities, and that a threadbare post-secondary system jeopardized their social and economic future. Within that provincial university system, Queen's would also have to protect and enhance its reputation as a *national* institution with a reputation for quality undergraduate teaching, while at the same time shielding its now well-rooted graduate school from government-imposed rationalization.

There was also the challenge of transforming the medical faculty at Queen's into an integral part of the health-sciences complex that Harry Botterell had envisaged. The challenge of bringing the university libraries into the computer age also loomed. But here again was the paradox that Watts had identified at his installation. Even treading water academically, let alone refurbishing programs, would take capital, capital that Queen's Park was reluctant to provide. Thus, Watts's strategic plan necessitated diversifying the university's revenue stream away from the preponderant contribution of government. Government funding of the provincial university system, which had so generously expanded in the sixties, was now beginning to arc downward. Consequently, Queen's would have to become more self-starting in raising capital, not just for its operating budget but for its capital expansion. In short, Queen's would have to become more entrepreneurial.

Bolstering Leadership

By the spring of 1976, Watts was ready to crystalize what he believed would be a distinct Queen's approach to tough times. In an effort to show that Queen's austerity program would affect *all* levels of the community, Watts had moved in late 1975 to rationalize the senior management of the university. The three existing central-administration vice-principal positions – finance, administration, and academic – were condensed into a more streamlined dual structure of finance and services. With the departure of George Harrower and Russell Kennedy from the academic and administrative portfolios, Watts was left with the considerable talent of lawyer-accountant David Bonham in the all-important finance slot and Morris Love as vice-principal, services, overseeing a gamut of functions ranging from student services to the physical plant of the university.[31] This contraction of executive authority promised greater decisiveness and economies of scale. While the position of vice-principal, health sciences, held by the indubitable Garfield "Gub" Kelly, remained in place to oversee the university's medical endeavours, many remarked that the loss of the position of vice-principal, academic, sent a telling signal that financial expediency was now paramount at Queen's.

As the pressure of financial austerity became the central and abiding reality of managing Queen's, Watts was able to bolster the leadership of the university's academic divisions with resilient new talent. Queen's had long had a tradition of appointing its deans from familiar ranks; academic leadership at Queen's had tended to be an organic affair. Talent was spotted early on, and potential candidates for deanships were moved up the ladder of advancement through departmental headships and associate deanships until a deanship beckoned. Such succession worked especially smoothly when departmental headships depended more on the dean's approval than on departmental consensus, a process that finally wound down in the early seventies, when departments began electing their heads for five-year terms.

Watts obliged this ingrained organic grooming of talent, but he also showed no compunction in reaching beyond the campus whenever he felt the need for some outside stimulus. Senior management at Queen's thus assumed a pattern that would persist through the rest of the century: establishing a delicate hybrid balance between home-grown talent and imported, fresh faces. When it came to filling his own shoes as dean of Arts and Science, Watts went for the tried and true: physiologist Duncan Sinclair had served as his associate dean and had roots at Queen's that extended back to his own father's graduation from the university in 1924 and subsequent employment as a biochemist. Sinclair himself vividly remembered taking Frank Knox's memorable Economics 4 course as an undergraduate, before going on to graduate studies in physiology and veterinary science. Sinclair was tough and opinionated, well-suited to guiding a faculty that sprawled over disciplines ranging from fine arts to hard science and was the biggest undergraduate catchment in the university. Paradoxically, while Arts and Science was the workhorse of enrolment, it was also the faculty most often taken for granted when decisions were made. A vigilant and dogged dean was a necessity.

The medical portfolio was also restocked from within. In 1973, Deutsch had split responsibility for the medical faculty in two: vice-principal, rheumatologist "Gub" Kelly, was redeployed as a vice-principal to mind the faculty's strategic interests, while a dean, pathologist Douglas Waugh, would tend to the daily operation of the faculty. When Waugh departed in 1975 to head the Association of Canadian Medical Colleges, the deanship passed to Tom Boag, a British-born psychiatrist who had come to Queen's in 1967 after teaching at McGill and the University of Vermont. Similarly, in 1977 Dan Soberman's long and productive tenure as dean in the Faculty of Law came to a close, and an insider, labour-law scholar Bernie Adell, was appointed in his stead. Succession matters in the law faculty were always hotly debated, some favouring the importation of outside talent – a judge, for instance – and others leaning towards teaching and research credentials. The choice was never easy, and faculty cohesion therefore often fragile.

Elsewhere, Watts looked further afield. When dean of Education, Vern Ready, announced that he would step down in March 1976, a search began for a replacement who would broaden the faculty from straightforward pedagogic instruction to a more research-driven and academically-engaged enterprise.

Whereas Ready had oriented the faculty to the day-to-day needs of local school boards, the need for wider horizons was now evident. It found this in the appointment of Tom Williams as dean. Williams had a doctorate in educational administration from Michigan and had done research on school governance in gritty urban Chicago before going on to the Ontario Institute for Studies in Education. Williams was given a mandate to professionalize the faculty and to close the gap between the West Campus and the mainline academic departments on the central campus.[32]

Much the same shift in focus took place in the School of Business. Richard Hand, who had so vigorously transformed his faculty from a narrow school of commerce into a diversified faculty attuned to the needs of corporate Canada, was initially reappointed to his deanship in 1975. But when Hand moved to vice-principalship, resources (redesignated from services), in 1977, a Watts-chaired search committee selected John Gordon as the new dean. Although Gordon, a mechanical engineer by training, had a Queen's MBA, he also had an MIT doctorate in academic administration and wide-ranging experience teaching at MIT, Western, and RMC, and in Switzerland at the prestigious IMEDE management school. Gordon, who published in stellar journals like the *Harvard Business Review*, was tasked with getting the faculty's new PhD in business up and running and with connecting the relatively isolated eastern-Ontario faculty with a big-city business culture that was becoming increasingly international.[33]

Watts's early years in office saw other new faces arrive on campus. Just as Hand had transformed the business school, Dean Jean Hill had built Queen's School of Nursing into a modern medical training program centred around a four-year degree program. Hill's decision to retire in 1975 kicked off a search for a successor. Once again, an outsider took the post: Alice Baumgart, who epitomized the new professionalization of nursing. She was completing a doctorate at the University of Toronto on patient compliance, and had years of teaching experience at the University of British Columbia. Over at the Douglas Library, the departure of Donald Redmond from the chief librarian's office opened the door to the appointment of Margot McBurney in 1977. Redmond had modernized the administrative structure of the library. Now it would fall to McBurney, with senior library experience at the University of Alberta, to embrace the computerization of library catalogues and circulation, while at the same time imposing some rationalizing of the central library's relation with its scattered branch libraries.

Only three senior roles in university management did not change in the years of the Deutsch-Watts transition: dean of Applied Science, Robert Uffen; dean of Graduate Studies and Research, Robert McIntosh; and dean of women, Evelyn Reid. In some ways, Uffen presaged a new, outgoing style for an engineering dean. A geophysicist, he had come to Queen's with three-ply experience as a dean at Western, as an advisor on science issues to the Privy Council Office in Ottawa, and as a government research scientist. As dean of Applied Science at Queen's since 1971, he had remained busy off campus, involving himself in global ecology with the Club of Rome and sitting as chairman of Ontario Hydro after 1975. Some complained that he spent too much time away from his office, but, given the prevailing austerity, Watts tended to favour deans who could see beyond the perimeter of government support into the professional worlds into which their graduates passed. In 1975, Uffen was appointed for a second five-year term.

Dean McIntosh of Graduate Studies and Research lived an uneasy existence: while the graduate-studies faculty had expanded dramatically in the late sixties and early seventies, its dean had little sway over the health of his own faculty. That is to say, appointments to graduate faculty were made by the departments themselves, and Queen's overall budget for graduate studies was never an integrated affair but instead the aggregate of downstream departmental budgets. The dean lived and died by his power of persuasion with the departments. History professor George Rawlyk cruelly described the graduate dean as "an academic eunuch." This was ironic, for, as the decade unfolded, it would become apparent that external funding for graduate students and funded research offered one inviting means of fattening the university purse. In 1979, geographer Maurice Yeates would succeed McIntosh; the committee selecting him expressed the wish that the new dean establish "effective leadership" in his sphere.[34]

As had long been the case, the dean of women also occupied an anomalous position. The elevation of the head of the School of Nursing to the status of dean in the sixties finally ended the lonely existence of the dean of women as the only woman in the university's inner circle. First appointed in 1971, Reid confronted not just assertive demands from second-wave feminists that women be freed from bailiwicks such as, they alleged, deanships predicated on gender, but also from those who, on the other hand, wanted her office turned into a vehicle for affirmative action for women. Already, for instance, the dean's direct control over the women's residences had passed to the unisex director of residences. Reid tried to tread a delicate middle path, using her office as a kind of centre for women's experience at Queen's. She, for instance, championed the provision of birth-control information and abortion referral on campus. She encouraged the compiling of oral histories of women who had passed through Queen's, and tried to elevate the cultural side of residence life. But Reid's lack of formal academic credentials tended to work against her (she had experience with the United Church, but no university degrees). After protracted deliberations by a committee appointed by Watts, Reid was reappointed for a shortened three-year term in 1976. Queen's became one of the few universities left with a dean of women. It seemed clear that an ultimate decision on the utility and appropriateness of the dean's role had simply been put off, perhaps because, in the deep freeze of mid-seventies austerity, decisions concerning an office with a modest annual budget of $40,000 could be postponed.[35] In the midst of so many pressing problems, this one might usefully be pushed into the future.

Walking the Deficit Tightrope

With an impressive cadre of administrators in place or falling into place, Watts announced in June 1976 that he would perpetuate Deutsch's "financial constraint" advisory initiative. He created the Principal's Advisory Group on Resource Planning (PAGORP – the university was rapidly becoming a place of acronyms). Chaired by a bright young economist, Rod Fraser, its mandate was to advise the university on the macro implications of coping with austerity. It would conduct incisive analysis of the costs and impacts of "alternative policies and measures" that might be pursued by Queen's as it tried to eke maximum advantage out of its beleaguered budget. Watts had prepared the way for this draconian mandate shortly after taking office in late 1974 by writing to all his deans asking them to outline the "implications" of severe budget cuts in their precincts, so that he could pass their surveys on to the Ontario Council on University Affairs. Their responses were strikingly similar. The phrases "no frills," "loss of good faculty," "steady and drastic decline," and "big classes" punctuated their replies.[36] These anxieties would now be systematically addressed and worked out by the new resource-planning group. Watts's instinct for broad inclusion in PAGORP was evident in the presence on the committee of AMS president James Avis, along with other well-positioned university officials like Registrar Ken Gunn and rank-and-file professors like Bob Crandall of the business school.

The creation of PAGORP allowed Richardson Hall an arm's-length mechanism for examining the dramatic impact of adjusting the university to tough times *and* at the same time transmitting that analysis to all Queen's constituencies. The group was free to investigate all university operations and policies – space use, early retirement, external research funding – in an effort to determine where money might be saved, where new money might be found, and what trade-offs might be activated. Criteria would be established to benchmark the introduction of such policies. In its first progress report in July 1977, PAGORP drove home the message that Ontario was now one of the least-generous provinces in its funding of post-secondary education. By most accounts, Ontario now ranked eighth in the ranking of Canada's ten provinces in its support of universities; in 1970–71 the province had devoted 0.98 per cent of its gross provincial product to post-secondary education, and now in 1976–77 that support had dropped to 0.88 per cent. In a constant-dollar calculation, Ontario's support of university students had fallen from $1,693 per capita in 1971–72 to $1,466 in 1976–77.[37]

In the late seventies, in this deteriorating fiscal environment, Queen's financial affairs fell into an annual pattern of managing with less. Year after year, the cycle began with either Vice-Principal Bonham or Hand informing the trustees that the financial outlook was dismaying. Like any large institution, Queen's maintained *two* budgets: an annual operating budget, which encompassed all the expenses in *operating* the university that year, and a *total* budget, which reflected the university's accumulated fiscal position. A deficit in one year's operating budget surfaced as part of the accumulated deficit in the university's total budget. At Queen's, the trustees had developed an almost-pathological fear of deficits. This proved very difficult to maintain in the austere seventies. Early in 1976, for instance, Bonham told them that, even though Queen's Park had boosted university operating grants by 14.4 per cent, Queen's would receive a hike of only 13.5 per cent, because its enrolment was tightly controlled and lagged behind the provincial average. The end of special grants to the fledgling education faculty and the government's decision to freeze tuition would further decrease the all-important operating grant to an increase of 11 per cent. All this, combined with Canada's rampant inflation, would leave the university, he predicted, mired in an operating deficit of $800,000 on an overall budget of $52 million.³⁸ As the university pushed towards the end of its financial year on 30 April, an accumulation of factors – slightly higher-than-expected enrolment, retirement of staff who were not replaced, deferred maintenance – served, deliberately and accidentally, to whittle down the initial worst-case scenario. Nonetheless, by the end of the fiscal year in April 1976, Bonham reported that the annual deficit had instead climbed to $873,000, boosting the university's accumulated deficit to an unprecedented $534,000.³⁹ The years 1976 to 1982 would thus be marked by a seesaw of slowly declining operating deficits and small surpluses that would cumulatively push the university into surplus by the time Watts left office in 1984.⁴⁰ At times, he felt as if he had taken on the frugal habits of Principal Grant as he battled to keep the university afloat in the grim 1890s.

There was little escaping this grip of deficit financing through the rest of the decade. When the Trudeau government unexpectedly imposed wage-and-price controls in 1975, the universities were able to cite outside legitimation for the capping of wages at 10 per cent and then progressively down to 6 per cent. Many economists, however, claimed that such controls did little to moderate the gallop of inflation. At the same time, the Conservative provincial government in Toronto dedicated itself to balancing its books. In May 1978, Watts reported to the trustees that provincial treasurer, Darcy McKeough, had adopted the tough-minded stance of keeping spending on universities 3 to 4 per cent below the rate of inflation until the province balanced its books. The financial situation would, he reported, "remain bleak for several years."⁴¹ The prediction was borne out by events. Watts frequently joined his university president confreres in lobbying Queen's Park for some relief from the systematic underfunding of their campuses.

Indeed, Watts – with his suave command of meetings and his mastery of Canadian federalism – often found himself the leading spokesperson of the Council of Ontario Universities (COU), the consortium voice of Ontario universities, and as an eloquent advocate of more generous government support before the Ontario Council of University Affairs (OCUA), the crucial advisory buffer between the universities and Queen's Park. The OCUA in fact listened intently. In 1978, it produced a brief, *The Ontario University System: A Statement of Issues*, which chronicled the problems besetting Ontario campuses: fees lagging behind inflation, retardation of professional programs, inability to replace a now-ageing faculty. A year later the OCUA followed up with another report, bluntly titled *System on the Brink*, which squarely indicted underfunding as the universities' most insidious weakness. The problem was not only one of accumulating debt, worn-out equipment, and deferred maintenance. There was also the demographic fact that the baby boom was petering out and that enrolment would plummet in the eighties, leaving universities with fewer students and crippling debts. In good academic fashion, the report set out various scenarios of decline. If 1978–79 funding norms were extrapolated to 1983–84, the report suggested, Ontario universities would face a cumulative operating deficit of $228 million. If this shortfall were to be addressed through salary and benefit cuts, the province would have to shed 2,684 academic positions. The report ominously concluded that "the funding outlook for the universities indicates a future of precipitous decline and turbulence as universities grapple with immense resource allocation problems."⁴²

The OCUA's prediction of universities at the brink failed to sway Queen's Park. There were piecemeal concessions – a $100 undergraduate fee increase in 1976, for instance – but no fundamental shift away from parsimony. Other concessions were less welcome: the government's decision to impose higher, differentiated fees on international students

promised to boost revenue, but also went against the grain of Queen's stated policy of trying to attract a greater foreign presence on its campus. There were adjustments to the calculation of the BIU payment to universities: the annual operating grant would now reflect a three-year rolling average of enrolment, rather than the more erratic one-year calculation, an adjustment that would discourage some universities from taking a windfall from sharp increases in admissions. Three-year averaging would also facilitate steadier planning. Beyond this adjustment, Queen's Park made pragmatic adjustments – one-time boosts in library support, special grants for bilingual programs. But intransigence largely prevailed: on advice from the OCUA, a freeze was imposed through the late 1970s on the creation of

The combination of government austerity and untamed inflation put immense fiscal strain on the university and its students, staff, and faculty in the 1970s. Faculty obliged Queen's tradition of collegiality by joining Principal Watts's "consultative group" to broker issues of salary. Students took to the streets, appearing here in 1978 outside Queen's Park.

new graduate programs across the province, accompanied by talk of "rationalizing" these programs on a province-wide basis.[43]

On the issue of fees, Queen's Park clung to its ingrained dedication to broad accessibility to post-secondary education, but increasingly – and somewhat paradoxically – began suggesting that some deregulation of fees might allow individual universities to differentiate their student intake and manage revenues. In September 1979, for instance, Premier Bill Davis, flanked by Treasurer Frank Miller and Education Minister Bette Stephenson, called the university presidents to Toronto for a now-familiar confab, this time to discuss the *System on the Brink* report. The meeting turned testy when John Panabaker, the chairman of McMaster's board of governors, complained that a "sense of drift" characterized the Davis government's post-secondary education policy and that provincial universities were tumbling in national prestige. Watts reported to his own board afterwards that the premier admitted the situation might improve if universities were allowed to set their own fee levels, especially since he felt students had hitherto "not paid enough of a share of the cost of their education."44 A year later, Toronto allowed universities the discretion to raise their fees 10 per cent above the declared provincial norm. Queen's immediately bumped its fees to 110 per cent, knowing that its province-leading admission standard could stand up to the difference. This brought in a welcome fillip of $150 per student, but, as Watts pointed out, tuition covered only 15 per cent of Queen's operating costs.45 The halcyon days of Leslie Frost and the free-spending sixties were gone. The universities were now obliged to sustain themselves within a system that their province was no longer willing to productively fund – but at the same time was unwilling to rationalize.

Austerity's Toll: "The Agony and the Ecstasy"

Back on the home front, battling the deficit exacted a terrible toll on Queen's. Each round of austerity cut deeper into the university's vitality. Department heads were instructed to comb their budgets for the savings on items as small as stationery and conference travel. The library cancelled journal subscriptions and cut back on book orders, intellectual necessities that had already been eroded by inflation.

Not unexpectedly, every area of the university defended its turf tooth and nail. Watt's circle of forceful deans did not hold back in challenging every item removed from their budgets. "We are attempting to meet our most urgent needs as cheaply as possible," Sinclair in Arts and Science bluntly told the principal, "by offering 8 or 9 month appointments, allowing replacements at the salary floor for Assistant Professors, and by hiring part-time faculty members using casual academic funds. In short, we are living on our future capital of human resources and reputation, apparently mortgaging our longer-term future because our present circumstances leave us no other choice."46 Over in the law faculty, things were little different. Dean Adell advised Watts in late 1978 that, although "it could not be claimed that any other law faculty has been lavishly financed this year, we appear to have been among the most tightly squeezed and to have suffered some overall deterioration in our relative position ... Given that we will always have what in our field is the very substantial handicap of being outside Toronto, I think there is a real danger that if we face further disadvantage of being underfinanced year in and year out, with unavoidable implications for our program, and everything else we do, we will run the risk of faring badly in our endeavour to have the best students and the best faculty members"47 Other deans weighed in with similar vehemence.

Watts responded to such resistance by encouraging his senior colleagues to think *strategically*. These were years in which the corporate world was embracing strategic planning as a way of judiciously positioning companies for future growth and adjustments. Companies should think, not in myopic terms of the next financial quarter, but instead of the long-term horizon. Watts believed that universities should adopt similar perspectives. In June 1977, he initiated what would become an annual retreat for all vice-principals, deans, and associate deans at the Opinicon Lodge, often used by Queen's as a retreat from day-to-day decision making. Fed with background papers by the Senate committees on academic development and the university budget, the attendees focused on "strategies for enduring the seventies and enhancing the eighties – *the Agony and the Ecstasy*."[48] Watts urged his colleagues to think in "quinquenniums," a rather elaborate way of saying five-year periods. The retreats proved useful for identifying emerging issues – the need, for instance, to attract young faculty and to enhance the flow of external research funding – but they also revealed fundamental differences of strategy. Watts's inclination was to coordinate policy-making from Richardson Hall, where centralized control could be best wielded to find economies of scale and rationalize programs. Many deans, however, believed that the decentralization of authority that had flowed in their direction in the sixties was more conducive to keeping a university inclusive and supple.

The reality was that universities were loosely structured communities that did not lend themselves to tight, disciplined corporate visions. As Watts himself would later reflect on the nature of governance at Queen's, "a neat and tidy mind is a crippling disability in any effort to understand the processes of internal governance at Queen's. It is not based on a clear and simple hierarchical structure, but on the dispersion of decision-making among the multiple bodies at various levels and upon complex and interlocking [interrelationships] between these bodies which involve the whole range of constituent communities within the university."[49] But viewing things from the abyss of debt in the late seventies, Watts yearned for more of a common pull on his campus, for a widespread willingness to see Queen's in its global context, rather than from scattered parochial perspectives. In exasperation, he scribbled at the end of a long memo from Dean Sinclair decrying centralization at Queen's: "A heavy dose of rhetoric from Dunc. Basically doesn't yet accept reality of the financial pressures requiring reduction. Hence resistance to reduction in any field rather than an identification of priorities and strategy."[50] Whatever Watts's exasperation, his reaction captured the useful dialectic between Richardson Hall and the deans scattered across the campus. Out of the tension over contested policy, consensus emerged.

Watts's retreats in the Rideau Lakes did leave a legacy, even if the participants were unable to arrive at a long-range blueprint for Queen's. By the early eighties, strategic questions were at least being asked. Beginning in 1982, the Board of Trustees was given a strategic briefing built around a classic strengths-and-weaknesses analytical framework – a consideration of what Queen's did well and what threatened its success. Queen's, for instance, had a larger endowment than most Canadian universities and had a knack for being a pioneer of specialized programs in such areas as public policy, but, the analysis revealed, this edge was being undermined by financial constraints blocking the hiring of new, young faculty. Watts urged the trustees to adopt a "dynamic," not a "static," attitude to how these tensions could be managed. Then, he somewhat ruefully concluded by quoting John Deutsch to the effect that university presidents were never in a position to give orders.[51]

Preserving Faculty Loyalty through Consultation

Ron Watts not only instinctively understood that he could not give orders, he perfectly understood his role in maintaining campus cohesion. Whatever frictions emerged with his vigilant deans over the big picture at Queen's, Watts knew that he had to keep his faculty – 837 of them by 1975–76 – solidly on side as the deficit steadily diminished Queen's possibilities. With over 50 per cent of his annual budget dedicated to paying the rank-and-file professoriate, and with so much of Queen's reputation resting on the prowess of its teachers, Watts dedicated himself to keeping the faculty consulted and co-operative. As a faculty member in the late fifties and sixties, he had experienced the close relations that had prevailed between the administration and the Queen's University Faculty Association (QUFA) in those years. The rhetoric of that relationship projected an image of Queen's as a family, and the sense that it was a unique sort of place, detached from the hurly-burly of large urban universities. The annual salary negotiation between Richardson Hall and QUFA was a chummy process of information-sharing and mutual concession. Each negotiation seemed to reflect the sense that working at Queen's involved more than a paycheque; it also carried intangible benefits, such as teaching above-average students in the company of above-average colleagues. A glance around the faculty club any day at lunch would have conveyed the impression that no barriers existed between faculty and those who administered Queen's. By the seventies, the principal adopted the practice of appointing an "academic colleague" from the ranks of the faculty, a person with whom he could share the burden of attending on- and off-campus meetings pertaining to the academic policy. Embedded in this trusting bond between faculty and administration was an unspoken belief that QUFA was a *professional* association, and that any idea of unionization would corrode campus collegiality.

The onset of tough fiscal times in the mid-seventies destabilized this equilibrium. As retrenchment bit into Canadian campuses, a gulf of differences grew between professor and administrator at many Canadian universities. Both Deutsch and Watts nervously reported a growing trend towards faculty unionization. In Quebec, where both inflation and the heady empowerment of the Quiet Revolution affected teaching staff, there were faculty strikes at Laval and the Université de Montréal. Closer to home, Ontario universities like Carleton saw their staff associations seek union certification. Sniffing the wind, QUFA in 1976 established a committee to investigate an "alternative mechanism for salary negotiations." There was, the committee reported, little enthusiasm for collective bargaining at Queen's. But, sensing that a financial squeeze was taking hold, QUFA expressed a wish to "regularize" the hitherto-casual negotiation of faculty salaries. A relieved Watts told the trustees that "there is still a strong feeling at Queen's that collective bargaining and the adversarial processes involved therein are not in keeping with the collegial relationship that should exist at a university."[52] But, he added, it was "difficult" to predict the future. Law dean Dan Soberman noted that the prolonged strike at Laval was likely the result of that university's rigid unicameral governance structure, whereby there was no check on the administrative will of the institution. Queen's bicameral governance, which gave faculty a powerful Senate voice, was by definition predisposed to negotiation. Queen's did not have "a cadre of senior administrators who are viewed as 'they' by non-administrators." Each side, he suggested, understood its share of the "shrinking pie" now on the table.[53] "There is no escape from all the trends around us," Dean Sinclair told Watts, "and I think there is a need to become somewhat more formal than we have been in the past about salary 'negotiations' ... [it offers] some benefits from a bit more formality in procedure while avoiding the potential cost of a decrease in collegiality."[54]

In September 1976, QUFA and Watts struck a deal to regularize salary negotiation. A memorandum of understanding outlined the creation of a Consultative Group on Faculty Compensation. The group would be constituted of eight senior administration and QUFA officials – four on each side. The principal would chair its monthly meetings, and would indeed retain the ultimate authority over salary disbursements each year. The intent was, however, that the panel would dedicate itself to finding a consensus each year through frank discussion of the university's financial condition and a sympathetic hearing of faculty's concerns about pay, benefits, and "related matters." That consensus would be non-binding, but the hope was that it would carry "considerable weight" on both sides of the salary fence.

The group got off to a collegial start. Richardson Hall freely shared its analysis of the university's financial situation. The principal kept up the tradition of annually addressing the QUFA general meeting. By March 1977, agreement was reached on the 1977–78 salary settlement – a 9-per-cent overall salary boost, which would encompass a 5.5-per-cent scale increase (that is, an across-the-board upward adjustment for all those in a particular rank to reflect the erosion of inflation), with the rest left to merit increase for actual performance and various anomalies. There were bones of contention: QUFA sometimes queried the candidness of administration statistics and exactly what constituted "merit." But, on the whole, there was remarkable unanimity of perspective on Queen's perilous financial condition. A note of black humour sometimes crept into the group's deliberations: "General agreement was expressed on the desirability of a major oil discovery under Mackintosh-Corry."[55]

While the cumulative effect of the consultative group's deliberations was to retard faculty salaries behind the level of inflation in the broader interests of institutional solvency, its role was not entirely reactionary. Each year, a deliberate effort was made to skew salary increases towards junior faculty by boosting wage hikes on the lower portion of salary foundations and tapering off increases at the higher end of the scale, so that across-the-board increases did not unduly favour senior staff. In the early 1980s, for instance, it had negotiated the introduction of paid maternity and adoption leave and the removal of gender discrimination from the pension plan. Recognizing that the imposition of procrustean salary settlements sometimes failed to adjust compensation for pockets of employment where the nature of work had changed, Watts devised an "anomalies fund," which gave him discretionary monies to adjust salaries that no longer reflected the duties at hand.

Watts found other expedient ways of easing the fiscal pain: shortly after taking office, he invited "Rainbow Proposals" from all members of the Queen's community. These proposals were intended to keep creative initiatives alive on the campus – political-studies internships, an organ in Grant Hall, and expansion of Queen's biological research station in the Rideau Lakes won support. In 1980, Watts initiated the Principal's Development Fund to allow him to devote unrestricted endowment funds to needy projects that might not otherwise be considered in times of austerity. None of these moves fattened paycheques, but they did give some sense of overall momentum. Other initiatives were brought in on the employment front: in 1976, a staff training and development coordinator was appointed to provide all Queen's staff with personnel counselling.

Given the financial stress that besieged the university and its faculty down through the early eighties, the consultative group was a remarkable success. It preserved the collegiality that Watts believed lay at the heart of a successful university. Most agreed. In its 1980 salary brief to its membership, QUFA reported that the group's ability to find the middle ground was "a matter of satisfaction to most, but of frustration to some." Nevertheless, confrontational labour relations had been held in abeyance. "Management" at Queen's was perceived as "forwarding the interests of the entire university, the Board, the students and the faculty, and the community at large."[56] The group allowed Watts, on the one hand, to stay his course of avoiding massive faculty layoffs, while not, on the other, pitching the campus into labour wars. When he stepped down from his office in 1984, Watts could reflect with considerable pride that, while Queen's that year received only 76.4 per cent of the level of support from Queen's Park that it had received in 1974–75, its faculty had shrunk by only 5 per cent.[57]

By late 1981, the financial situation was beginning to improve. Watts proudly told the trustees that Queen's was one of only four Ontario universities that were in surplus (Waterloo, Toronto, and Laurier being the others), but cautioned that Queen's slim surplus was equivalent to only one day's operating budget.[58] As the 1982–83 financial year drew to a close, Vice-Principal Hand held out the prospect of a somewhat larger surplus, even though revenue growth of 6.2 per cent was still outstripped by expenditure growth of 7.2 per cent. By October, Watts could bring the trustees happier news: Queen's had come out of 1982–83 with an operating surplus of $306,000, and the dreaded accumulated deficit of $286,000 had been pushed into the black – with a surplus on the books of $20,000. The trend continued in 1983–84 with a surplus of $68,000, which swelled the cumulative surplus to $88,000.[59] Queen's had snatched victory out of the jaws of financial defeat.

But the price of victory was steep and, in many instances, lasting. As the eighties dawned, faculty's willingness to toe the austerity line began to slacken. Much of Queen's return to financial stability had been paid for by restraint of staff and faculty wages. Late in 1979, QUFA President Peter Hennessy spoke with pride of his colleagues' willingness to share the financial stress at Queen's. QUFA had, for instance, strenuously endorsed the OCUA *System on the Brink* report. But an undercurrent of discontent was coming nearer the surface. "We shall be bitter in the extreme," Hennessy warned," if the Government ever channels a larger fraction of the available funds to those who have not exercised such restraint."[60] As the new decade dawned, QUFA began crunching numbers and reported that its analysis revealed that Queen's faculty salary floors (that is, the base salary platform for each faculty rank) had fallen below 1961 levels when expressed in constant, inflation-corrected dollars.[61] By 1981, the tone of the faculty association became more strident: "Why haven't we had real increases in 10 years?" asked QUFA President Grant Amyot, who pointed out that Ontario's GDP had risen by 20.8 per cent over the last decade, while the income of a Queen's associate professor had shrunk by 23.7 per cent.[62]

Issues beyond money also troubled faculty. The meagre growth of tenured faculty in the lean seventies had been outstripped by the hiring of temporary adjunct faculty, who cost much less to employ and entailed much less of an impact in terms of benefits and pensions. Many uneasily sensed the emergence of a two-tier professoriate. In 1978, adjunct staff and assistants took up 11 per cent of the university's total academic budget. On the one hand, adjuncts were perceived as a threat to the mainstream tenured faculty's traditional role, while, on the other hand, there was growing concern that adjuncts should not be treated as second-class academic citizens. Similarly, procedures for announcing the results of promotion deliberations needed clarification. So did the matter of whether the university would pay the legal costs of a faculty member contesting a tenure refusal.

There was also the thorny matter of redundancy: under what conditions of financial duress did the university have the right to dismiss staff? And QUFA was expanding. In 1984, Queen's professional librarians, hitherto represented by their own association – PLAQ – affiliated with QUFA, adding to the menu of bargainable issues. In short, the consultative group's approach to maintaining cohesion at Queen's was becoming freighted with an increasingly complex agenda of issues and frustrations. Perhaps not surprisingly, in the spring of 1982 the group failed to reach an amicable consensus on salary adjustments for the first time, when QUFA balked at the university's offer of an 11-per-cent increase in scale to a maximum of $5,000, citing "the intense frustration over the salary issue felt by many QUFA members." Principal Watts consequently ratified the 1982–83 salary package by fiat.

Sensing the faculty's growing disquiet, QUFA polled its membership (645 of Queen's 900 faculty members belonged in 1982) in January 1983 about the viability of the consultative process. Of the 49 per cent who responded, a majority – 64 per cent – indicated that some adjustment of the process was in order, but that radical change was unnecessary. The next month, a more structured poll set defined options before the membership. On a turnout of 314, 37 per cent favoured maintaining the status quo, but another 36 per cent plumped for an adjustment of the 1976 memorandum of understanding to give faculty an expanded presence in university decision making. A minority of 20 per cent advocated QUFA pursuing collective bargaining via certification. Despite the reservoir of frustration, the poll provided an endorsement of Queen's unique approach to consultative labour relations.

A year earlier, a federally funded survey conducted by researchers at UBC and the University of Calgary had revealed the resilience of the loyalty of faculty to Queen's. When asked whether their university was a "very good place for me," 64 per cent agreed, compared to 54 per cent of respondents in a national survey that embraced seven other universities. The same study showed that only 42 per cent of Queen's faculty favoured collective bargaining, as opposed to 82 per cent in the overall national survey.[63] Such sentiment surfaced again in January 1984, when the university and QUFA ratified a modified version of the 1976 memorandum of understanding. The agreement maintained the original "good-will" framework by broadening the scope of faculty participation in university decision making. The consultative group was expanded to ten members, five from each side. Three faculty members would now sit as observers at Board of Trustee meetings, and others would sit on crucial campus committees such as health and safety and on tenure-and-dismissal arbitration committees. The principal would consult the QUFA president in making these appointments. The association president would also be given a one-third release from teaching duties to compensate for his role in university governance.[64]

Lean Times in the Administrative Front Line

The consultative engagement of Queen's faculty through the dark fiscal days of the late seventies reflected their powerful leverage on the university. They were the indispensable ingredient in the institution's existence. Holding their loyalty was imperative. Principal Watts's reports of faculty strikes on Quebec campuses and the trend towards collective bargaining and compulsory arbitration on other Ontario campuses rattled the Queen's trustees. The same inclination to inclusion did not, however, colour the administration's perception of the university's support staff, the people who day-by-day oiled the administrative machinery of the campus and ensured its efficient physical operation. Through the early decades of the twentieth century, Queen's clerical and maintenance workers – the "support staff" in the parlance of the times – had evolved in much the same way as their academic confreres into comfortable, collegial bailiwicks. Unlike the male-dominated academic precinct, gender was often the determining factor in organizing Queen's support staff. Males dominated the physical trades, like cleaning and maintenance. Women staffed the more clerical functions, such as processing applications in the registrar's office, typing correspondence, or cataloguing books in the library. The men were generally seen as lifelong Queen's employees, and the women, more often than not, as more temporary sojourners at the university. Bud Cornelius, for example, the carpenter who came to Queen's in 1955, typified the pattern. His grandfather had worked as a carpenter at Queen's for forty-five years. It was, he recalled, "like a family thing."[65] Cornelius worked out of what was called the "maintenance shop," from which teams of maintenance workers oversaw the upkeep of dedicated districts of the campus. Furthermore, maintenance managers were often ex-military types, and their maintenance workers had, since 1955, been unionized, something that began to introduce an element of friction into the daily workplace.

Women support staff remained largely non-unionized, in enclaves scattered across the campus. They were almost unconsciously regarded by the administration as replaceable; Kingston had a ready supply of young women to draw upon, many of them young high-school graduates and others the wives of professors in search of a wage to

Tough fiscal times built alliances on campus. In 1981, the AMS organized a "study-in" in support of the university library's financially beleaguered condition. Students "occupied" the library stacks and slept there overnight. Principal Watts, Kingston Mayor John Gerretsen, and federal MP Flora MacDonald spoke in support of the students.

supplement family income. The Queen's personnel office simply sorted available talent into available openings. Only minimal skills – typing, dictation, "good with numbers" – were required. There was little thought to career development through training. Eveline Flint, who joined Queen's in 1969 as an administrative assistant in the university secretary's office, described Queen's approach to personnel management in the late 1960s as being "in the dark ages."[66] In partial reaction to this state of affairs, the Queen's University Staff Association (QUSA) was formed in 1972. Like the faculty association, its ethos was associational and informational, not confrontational.

Assurance of readily available administrative support coloured Queen's relations with its staff as the lean seventies crept onto campus. There was an assumption that administrative staff could be squeezed to wring out budget savings and that any resultant staff loss could be easily filled. In the fall of 1975, all administrative staff were, for instance, sent on a course, "Cost Reduction at Work," that rather insensitively schooled them on how to make budget dollars go further. Such insensitivity was reflected in the fact that there was never any thought given to admitting the support staff to the Consultative Group created for faculty in 1976. Nonetheless, QUSA began surveying the Kingston labour market so as to statistically situate Queen's in the local wage economy. The news was seldom flattering to Queen's; the university seemed to lag rather than lead the local labour market in compensation. There were at most small concessions: in 1974 the first on-campus daycare facility was opened on Queen's Crescent, and in 1975 staff were allowed to take two Queen's courses a year at their employer's expense. A year later, in 1976, the Staff Liaison Officer, whose function had been reactive in fielding workplace complaints, was transformed into the more proactive Staff Training and Development Coordinator, whose function was to facilitate staff skills.

Consequently, the support staff fared far worse than faculty as Queen's lurched into deficit territory. Not only were wages depressed and positions left unfilled, but in the atmosphere of contraction there was little opportunity for career advancement or even lateral movement. In 1975, for instance, an angry Eveline Flint, who was serving at the time as staff liaison officer, wrote to Flora MacDonald, the local member of parliament, who herself had worked at Queen's as the administrator in the department of political studies before winning her seat in Ottawa in 1968. Flint told her MP and one-time colleague that many non-academic staff members at Queen's had incomes below the poverty line. She cited a female secretary with three children who earned a meagre $5,800 annually. Similarly, a male clerk with a wife and two kids earned $6,300 a year. "The result can only be a state of virtual serfdom for the young and unskilled – food and a place to sleep, but that's about all," Flint concluded.[67] There was little MacDonald could do but sympathize; labour relations were in the provincial bailiwick.

Throughout the decade, QUSA and the administration played statistical games with Statistics Canada data over what wage levels at Queen's actually were. A confidential personnel-department memo in the spring of 1981 candidly acknowledged that Queen's clerical and secretarial salaries trailed comparable Kingston salaries by 16 to 23 per cent, and worried that the university stood in danger of losing key staff as new government offices – like the OHIP processing centre – opened downtown.[68] Remarkably, through all this compression, Queen's administrative staff remained broadly loyal to Queen's and took a non-unionized approach to their situation. The "family" spirit so prized by Bud Cornelius generally held. However, in the fall of 1981, a minority group within QUSA agitated for a union-certification vote to open the door to affiliation with the Canadian Union of Public Employees. Although a majority of the QUSA membership opposed the idea, an appeal to the Ontario Labour Relations Board allowed the vote to be taken. Certification was, however, handily rejected.[69] Throughout these years, some quietly remarked on the "inherent conservatism and perhaps paternalism" of Queen's human-resources culture. While many others took pride in the abiding "loyalty" of Queen's employees, by the early 1980s there could be no denying that such loyalty had entailed a hefty cost to this group.

Over in Richardson Hall, senior administrators were beginning to express their own anxieties about the wear and tear of austerity. In the spring of 1982, Vice-Principal Hand, who bore much of the brunt of whittling down the deficit, broke the news to the trustees that the prospective deficit for the upcoming 1982–83 financial year was likely to be $690,000, and that salary increases would average 13 per cent. All the while, he noted, inflation was playing havoc with his calculations. The "support base," he concluded, "cannot take much more cutting. We are doing our best to keep quality up, while paying close attention to morale. It is a very depressing exercise."[70] Others worried about what recessionary times were doing to the psyche of Queen's. Dean Sinclair concluded that all the penny-pinching had created a "bunker mentality" that was cutting the university off from its future prospects. "I regret to say," he said in reaction to the 1983–84 budget projections a year later, "that I see around us an increasing preoccupation with the here and now, with preserving what we have, and an unwillingness to look imaginatively to the future … Our forebears would be disgusted! … Queen's has been characterized by its innovativeness in developing the foundations of the new strengths in the face of financial adversity that makes our present problems look pretty small."[71]

Pursuing Selectivity, Not Stagnation

Amid all the expedient financial barrel-scraping, strategic planning, faculty consultation, and morale management, Ron Watts never lost sight of his primordial function: the preservation of Queen's distinctiveness and reputation. In the fall of 1978, he told both the trustees and the Senate that he had read the just-published first volume of the Queen's history, covering the years down to 1917. He reported that Hilda Neatby's volume was "fascinating and inspiring." In its rather ungainly title – *Queen's University Volume I, 1841–1917: To Strive, to Seek, to Find, and Not to Yield* – he said he found a gospel relevant to the present: resiliency through adversity.[72] When called upon by the OCUA a year later to report on Queen's reaction to the financial drought in provincial post-secondary education,

Watts again chose to stress his institution's determination to steer its own course. Queen's, he said, was a "modest-sized" provincial and national institution with demonstrated competences, "responding in its own way to well-defined needs."[73] He echoed his predecessor John Deutsch's dedication to perpetuating Queen's mission: "A policy of selectivity cannot be a policy of stagnation. We will choose to do those things which we can do well and will do as well as we can the things we have chosen."[74]

But in an environment of shrinking finances and with a faculty insulated by tenure and programs mandated by provincial academic regulation, universities had little free play to pursue such selectivity. How, for instance, did a university redirect its resources from an area of fading academic demand to an emerging discipline? And by what criteria could one balance the interests of, say, the Classics department against the newly hatched imperatives of the computer age? And over what strategic timeline? Classics had been central to Western intellectual life for centuries, while "information science" might be a will o' the wisp. Similarly, how important was old-fashioned, bricks-and-mortar civil engineering in the face of the computer revolution and all its implications for electrical engineering? Unlike a corporation, a university could not readily redeploy its resources or realign its structure to suit shifts in consumer preference. Universities contended with justifiable rigidities imposed by academic freedom and by bodies such as the Ontario Council on Graduate Studies, which initially approved and subsequently reviewed graduate programs. So, if Watts was to effectualize his policy of selectivity for Queen's, a premium would have to be placed on inventiveness and persistence to ensure that the university's distinctiveness was preserved. This effort would encompass everything from maintaining quality undergraduate enrolment to broadening the university's revenue base away from the spigot of government support.

The central thrust of perpetuating Queen's select status lay in quality undergraduate teaching. Here the lodestar was Deutsch's dedication to a "steady state" enrolment – Queen's dedication to remaining a modestly sized, well-rounded university offering a competently delivered array of professional programs, ranging from medicine and law on through to an array of undergraduate programs. By explicitly constricting growth, Queen's was not only able to maintain its sense of community and dedication to a relatively small student body, but it was also able to attract the highest quality of applicant and thereby very precisely regulate its undergraduate intake.

The policy worked brilliantly, especially in the early seventies when overall demand for access to post-secondary education in Ontario became more volatile. While many other universities were obliged to drop admissions standards to fill their classrooms, Queen's continued to hold the bar of admission very high and thereby take the pick of the crop. Each year, the Senate Committee on Academic Development (SCAD) drew up a blueprint for the next year's enrolment that set out quotas for each faculty. Given the carefully groomed Queen's brand, the targets were invariably met with precision. In 1977, for instance, Watts reported to the Senate that, while enrolment province-wide had declined for the first time in years, Queen's had exceeded its target by 63 students and was dead-on the "steady state" boundary with a total enrolment of 10,324 students. Better still, demand for entry had been intense: 13,000 applications for 2,300 first-year places.[75] A year later, registrar Ken Gunn delivered similar glad tidings: while university enrolment was down across the province by 3 to 4 per cent, Queen's was in "a remarkably strong position," coming in just a tad below the SCAD target, at 10,313.[76] This pattern continued through Watts's entire tenure as principal. In 1983, for instance, he could tell the Senate with considerable pride that 63.1 per cent of Ontario entrants to Queen's were Ontario scholars who had graduated from high school with an average of above 80 per cent.[77]

Success begat problems. The recruitment of premium students resulted in what came to be called "the pipeline effect." Students admitted on paper to Queen's tended to show up every September; "no-shows" were the bane of university registrars. Similarly, they tended to stay the academic course; Queen's enjoyed a very high retention rate in its undergraduates. Students did not "drop out" at Queen's. Consequently, Queen's experienced an enrolment creep that slowly served to puncture the ceiling of the "steady state." By 1983–84, total Queen's undergraduate enrolment had inched up from 8,668 when Watts took office to 9,845. When a 50-per-cent swelling of the university's graduate students during these years, from 1,044 to 1,523, was added, Queen's overall enrolment arrived at 11,368 in 1983–84. While this incremental growth tended to slowly erode the rationale of the "steady state's" dedication to quality control through manageable numbers, it did every year bring a slightly larger harvest of BIUs from Toronto.

Within the enrolment numbers, there were shifts that allowed Queen's to reorient its mission. In the late seventies, the gurus of post-secondary education had predicted that the coming of the baby boom to adulthood would tend to dry up post-secondary intake. What they missed was a dramatic shift in the once male-dominated participation rate in post-secondary education. Propelled by postwar prosperity and the liberation of second-wave feminism, women arrived on university campuses in increasing numbers. At Queen's, this meant that, while women represented 43.7 per cent of undergraduates in 1974–75, they had become a majority of 51.9 per cent by 1983–84. Within certain faculties, the women's spurt was dramatic: in Applied Science, women went from a puny 5.1-per-cent enrolment to a more substantial, although still small, 16.6 per cent. In the School of Business, women doubled, to 52.9 per cent of undergraduates by 1983–84. In the same years, female participation in the Faculty of Law rose to 37.2 per cent.[78]

Queen's attempted to groom its enrolment in other ways. Eager to enhance its reputation as a national university, it used aggressive canvassing – relying, for instance, on the university's coast-to-coast alumni branches as recruitment venues – to attract out-of-province students. Endowment funds were used to fund special national scholarships and bursaries to bring non-Ontario students to Queen's. A similar ambition pertained to international students, who were increasingly seen as a new frontier of growth for Canadian universities in the seventies. The administration set a goal of 6-to-7-per-cent international enrolment at Queen's, but found that hard to meet. Foreign students tended to be attracted to big-city universities, and Queen's in eastern Ontario, with its image as an Anglo-centric institution, perhaps did not always appeal. A more fundamental obstacle was the introduction of higher fees for foreign students by the Ontario government. Vehemently opposed by administrations and student governments alike, the fees stuck, obliging the trustees to apply endowment funds to a set of fee rebates and special international scholarships to entice foreign students to Queen's. These soothed the situation. By 1978, Queen's had 471 foreign students, the largest contingent – 22 per cent – from Hong Kong.[79] But the goal of internationalizing Queen's remained daunting and often elusive.

Teaching under Duress

For an institution that had long prided itself on the quality and intimacy of its teaching, there was an implicit threat in the conjuncture of a slowly increasing enrolment and a slowly decreasing faculty complement. By 1984, there were 1,200 more undergraduates on Queen's campus than there had been in 1974, while in the same time the size of the faculty had contracted by 5 per cent. The usual benchmark of teaching proficiency was the much-watched student-professor ratio. The essence of a Queen's undergraduate education in the days of George Whalley and Frank Knox had been small classes and the intimacy they generated. (As principal, Ron Watts honoured this tradition by annually continuing to teach a seminar in federal-provincial relations.) The rapid growth of Queen's in the sixties had pushed up class sizes, and now the stringency of the seventies endangered this teaching tradition. The financial calculus of running the university hinged on an agonizing trade-off between maintaining faculty salaries, morale, and class size, while at the same time ensuring the overall quality of a Queen's degree. When Watts, as a new principal, canvassed his deans in late 1974 about the condition of their faculties, almost all of them drew attention to the climbing teaching ratios in their bailiwicks. Dean Uffen in Applied Science, for instance, complained that, at 16:1, his ratio was the highest it had been since 1967. Throughout the seventies and into the early eighties, Queen's did manage to keep its overall teaching ratio hovering around 15:1. The ratio varied from faculty to faculty and from year to year. In 1979, for instance, Vice-Principal Hand reported to Watts that overall the number of professors at Queen's had fallen 1 per cent since 1976, from 727 to 719, but that the full-time equivalent student-professor ratio had somewhat perversely improved from 15.2 to 14.7.[80]

Despite the stringency and diminished hiring of the 1970s, Queen's faculty remained remarkably young and dedicated to the university's tradition of quality teaching. In 1975, the Alumni Association instituted an award for excellence in teaching. One of the first winners was New Zealand–born David Mullan, an expert in administrative law and a perennial favourite among law students.

The ratio was, as the foregoing figures suggest, often a deceptive benchmark. It failed, for instance, to reflect the *quality* of the teaching or the status of the "professor." In the seventies, with so few new, tenure-stream faculty being hired, more and more teaching duties passed to part-time teaching staff. By 1977, the Senate Committee on Appointment, Promotion, Tenure and Leave (SCAPTL) reported that Queen's had 154 term appointments. This was not to suggest that term appointees were inferior teachers, but it did draw attention to the fact that an increasing proportion of Queen's teaching was being done by academics with no long-term commitment to Queen's (who tended to be younger and, therefore, had less teaching experience). Subsequently, SCAPTL, backed up by QUFA, contended that students at Queen's were increasingly being taught by a two-tier professoriate and urged that all teaching appointments at Queen's be reduced to a tenure stream, and, in fairness to sojourning adjuncts, a fixed, five-year term stream, at the end of which the university would either convert the term appointee to the tenure track or part ways.[81]

The issue of the quality of teaching at Queen's in the seventies surfaced frequently in the discussions of the consultative group. Faculty contended that larger classes were wearing down their ability to teach effectively, and that, with few new faces appearing in departments, a staleness was consequently creeping into their pedagogy. This concern was often echoed in the deliberations of the Senate and the trustees, where any perceived deterioration in the Queen's brand as a teaching university aroused concern. The quality of any educational output has always been a slippery topic. Did, for instance, the hesitant beginnings of computer-assisted teaching in the seventies in fact enhance the quality of teaching, thereby reducing the significance of the ratio of "live" professor to student? In 1975, Watts responded to such unease by appointing a Principal's Advisory Committee on Teaching Effectiveness with one-time dean and renowned teacher Sandy Duncan at its head. The committee would institute a program of grants to facilitate pedagogic improvement – the application, for instance, of computers to the teaching of respiratory physiology – and recommend the creation of a Teaching Centre to promote better teaching by faculty and learning by students. That same year, the Alumni Association created the Alumni Award for Excellence in Teaching to celebrate excellent teaching.

Despite such initiatives, there was a recurrent concern in all quarters of the Queen's community that austerity was taking a toll on teaching. At a Senate meeting in early 1977, student senator Margaret Churcher, a 1975 BSc and now medical student, complained that budget scrimping at Queen's had strained its teaching ability "well beyond the point at which students could maximally benefit from their stay at university." Queen's had drifted from its storied reputation of producing "well-informed, thoughtful individuals," and was now dedicating itself to processing "large numbers of mediocre students in an attempt to conform to a government policy of accessibility."[82] As if to reinforce Churcher's critique, a young filmmaker at Queen's, Michael MacMillan, produced a film essay on the Queen's undergraduate experience in 1976. *The Academic Cloister* was not kind in its assessment. With a voiceover of Dean Sinclair intoning the message that Queen's was a place where the "critical mind" and "leaders" were nurtured, the film suggested that post-secondary education had become "a chase for marks" and that "repetition" and "conformity" were now its guiding qualities.[83]

Student government at Queen's took a less caustic line but was nonetheless quick to rally in support of the quality of their education. In 1981, for instance, the AMS orchestrated a day-long, study-in at the Douglas Library as part of provincial day of protest against government underfunding of their education. (Eager to support the initiative, the library left its doors open at midnight, brewed coffee, and allowed sleeping bags into the stacks.) Larger classes, overstretched faculty, and library cutbacks featured prominently in the AMS list of grievances. The latest reduction in established federal support for universities would, the AMS loudly complained, "hack away at the very sinews of an already financially disabled system." As if to demonstrate the worth of acquired erudition, the AMS statement ended by citing Lewis Carroll: "I weep for you, the Walrus said, I deeply sympathize."[84]

Faculty joined the chorus of concern. In 1983, universities minister, Bette Stephenson, visited the campus and, in response to students' complaints of underfunding and high fees, suggested that either the university look to private support for its budget or the government would "rationalize" Ontario's universities. The provincial government also dropped hints that universities running persistent deficits might be placed under direct provincial control. The president of QUFA, Dan Norman, took umbrage and fired off a letter to the minister, hammering home the message that Toronto's persistent underfunding of the universities had brought a "real decline" in the quality of education. To make his point, Norman cited the cutting back of undergraduate chemistry labs at Queen's from a weekly to a biweekly basis.[85] Other professors took a more systemic perspective, arguing that the whole edifice of education in Ontario had been eroded by the parsimony of the seventies. Standards in the high schools had fallen. The number of prized Ontario Scholars entering Queen's rose steadily through the seventies, indicating to some that secondary-school standards were being inflated. Others complained that Queen's ability to provide a quality education was being hampered by the low skills its undergraduates possessed upon arrival. English Professor Colin Norman surveyed eight hundred Queen's undergraduates in 1975–76 and reported that a quarter of the first-year class was not "adequately literate." As a consequence, Norman went on to write a primer on basic grammar and writing skills, cleverly entitled *The Queen's English*, for use in campus classrooms.[86]

Queen's Thick Glass Ceiling

The delivery of effective teaching at Queen's in these years was never simply a mathematical matter of per capita productivity. Good teaching also depended on a sympathetic connection of teacher and student that reflected cultural, gender, and demographic understanding. In a Canada that was in the throes of surging immigration, with a baby boom rapidly coming into adulthood and second-wave feminism's assault on the glass ceilings that was hanging above women in the workplace, Canadian university faculties looked increasingly out of kilter with the rest of Canadian society. Canada's professors projected a demographic, racial, and gender homogeneity that increasingly set them at variance from the broad tendencies displayed in the national census. They preponderantly conformed to a WASP, native-born, and middle-aged male profile. At Queen's, there were telltale signs of social change that accentuated the disjuncture of the faculty with the society it served. In 1974, the year Watts took the reins at Queen's, 58.3 per cent of students in the Arts and Science faculty were women. Across the entire undergraduate program, 43.7 per cent of students were women. Since the 1960s, women now frequently served as AMS president. By the time Watts stepped down in 1984, 51.9 per cent of all Queen's students were female. Female participation in post-secondary education was surging. Even that traditional bastion of maleness, the Faculty of Applied Science, had tripled its intake of women – admittedly to only a modest 16.6 per cent, or 279 students, by 1983–84. Yet, in that same year, only 13.7 per cent of Queen's faculty were women. Applied Science had *no* full-time women faculty members at all. Over the past decade, the quotient of women professors at Queen's had only inched up from 11.3 per cent.[87] If the strategic trajectory of Queen's under John Deutsch and Ron Watts was indeed one of selectively adapting Queen's to the times around it, then the glacial entry of women into its faculty ranks constitutes an unflattering tale of arrested development.

Ron Watts was hardly oblivious to the ambitions of women on campus. As dean of Arts and Science, he had watched Deutsch appoint the 1972 Status of Women at Queen's Committee. That committee's deliberations had exposed a yawning gender gap at Queen's between its male and female employees. In the spring of 1975, as the new principal, he had delivered a twenty-one-page report card on the implementation of the so-called Good Committee, named after Lin Good, its librarian chair. The thrust of Watts's remarks was on "what remains to be done." Admissions policy would be altered to stress the opportunities for women in hitherto male-oriented programs, such as business, law, and engineering. Explicit statements of gender equality would be implanted in university promotional literature. Women faculty members would sit on all admissions committees to ensure there was no gender bias. Scholarship policy would be rejigged to enhance the inducement to female students. Initiatives such as these would prove efficacious and largely explain why the gender balance at the undergraduate level swung so noticeably in the Watts years. As if to underscore the principal's good intentions, the Dunning Trust Lecture committee brought three prominent women lecturers to campus that spring. One of them, the dynamic editor of *Chatelaine* magazine, Doris Anderson, chose to speak on the topic of "Women's Role: A Time of Redefinition." That redefinition was slow coming in Queen's faculty ranks.

Watts devoted half of his report to the trustees and the Senate to the recruitment and retention of more women professors. Here his support of the Good Committee was softer, less inclined to affirmative action. He reported that the (predominantly male) faculties had reacted strongly to the Status of

Women Committee recommendation that all future recruitment notices carry the message that "women are especially encouraged to apply." This, he said, had been found "not essential" and even "distasteful." Appointments should be "based primarily on quality of credentials." To address the salary differentials that the Good Committee had identified between males and females already on staff, Watts announced that, where gender-based gaps had been identified, salaries had been adjusted. A system of "peer-pairing" had been introduced to allow the equitable comparison of male and female salaries in future. Thus, the small contingent of women professors on staff in 1975 received small, one-time salary adjustments of 0.2 per cent above the faculty average.

Other Good recommendations were dampened with caution: the hope of more women in senior management positions at Queen's was commended but qualified by the thought that "it was not realistic to expect quick results." In response to the recommendation that the university explicitly modify its appointments policy to favour the hiring of women for probationary and tenured positions, Watts demurred. This would deny "opportunity to equally qualified men." To ensure equal opportunity in the administrative ranks of the university, no attempt would be made to dislodge acquired male seniority rights, but future appointments would reflect a job-classification system – the Hay Evaluation System – that would treat job qualifications in a gender-neutral fashion. Other nods were made in the direction of pension reform and daycare. The thrust of Queen's newly aroused awareness of gender was thus to trust that awareness and suasion would gradually alter the tidal flow. Queen's would shy away from deliberate affirmative action.

On one level, Watts's embrace of gender gradualism reflected reality. The university was financially stifled by provincial austerity; it had little fiscal discretion to leverage the gender balance in its faculty. Tenure paralyzed any attempt at a radical realignment of faculty responsibilities or composition. Precious notions of academic freedom and peer-reviewed competency similarly threatened to thwart any attempt to impose ulterior objectives onto academic hiring. If the halcyon days of sixties expansion ever returned, then there would be hope of sufficient new hiring to turn the tide. Beyond these dollars-and-cents barriers, there were other, less-tangible attitudinal impediments to change. The university had grown inured to a male-based perspective on its affairs. With only Evelyn Reid, and latterly Alice Baumgart, at the deans and vice-principals meetings, there was little to correct an instinctive male inclination in campus decision making.

Ron Watts hardly created this mindset, but he reflected it. When, for instance, he announced his Principal's Advisory Committee on Financial Constraint in early 1975 as his crucial agent in getting a grip on spending and the university's strategic direction, former registrar and now trustee Jean Royce scolded him for appointing ten men and not a single woman to its influential membership.[88] Three years later, the same ingrained maleness surfaced in Watts's state-of-the university address, his useful annual summation of Queen's health. Drawing attention to Queen's venerable evolution, the principal noted in the second sentence of his remarks that "it has been said that a university, unlike a woman, takes pride in her age and observes anniversaries as soon as and as often as possible." In an age of second-wave feminism, such stereotyping raised hackles. A biochemistry professor, Arlene Crowe, upbraided the principal for his "stereotyped and gratuitous" depiction of women. Watts retracted. The offending phrase was subsequently blacked out in all printed copies of the address.[89]

Crowe was not, however, a lonely voice. She spoke with the backing of the Association of Women Teaching at Queen's (AWTAQ), the group formed in 1974 to give voice to the scattered minority of women professors at Queen's. As an organization, AWTAQ performed two seminal functions. It provided a forum – a sense of female togetherness –

for women academics who hitherto had found themselves at Queen's leading isolated lives in departments heavily dominated by males. The association, through its informal get-togethers, lectures, luncheons, and, eventually in 1981, its newsletter, for the first time gave women professors a critical mass that enabled them to define and act on their collective interests. In effect, AWTAQ formed a feminist lobby that both empowered women at Queen's and at the same time allowed women to bring pressure to bear on the university's decision-making councils. From the outset, AWTAQ shrewdly operated *inside* the Queen's culture of collegiality. Its members may have had a deep-seated sense of grievance about the halting progress of women at Queen's, but AWTAQ never forsook the process of bringing its demands to the established central decision-making arenas of the university and thereby striving to broker change.

Ron Watts, a political scientist by training, recognized AWTAQ for what it was: a lobby group with legitimate interests. Through the late 1970s, AWTAQ played a monitoring role, watching for progress or miscues in the administration's pursuit of the goals it had set itself in the wake of the Good Committee. They monitored the *Queen's Gazette* to ensure that all hiring committees contained at least one woman. (Here there was a downside consequence; a handful of women like Beverley Baines in law and Dean Baumgart of nursing soon found that their time and energies were drained by sitting on so many search committees, many in disciples completely unrelated to their own interests. Baines eventually baulked, telling the principal that she no longer wished to be considered a "token" woman.) The AWTAQ urged female faculty to caucus within QUFA in the belief that their professional association would champion their cause. They resolutely brought their concerns about benefits – daycare, pension equality for men and women, maternity leave – before the administration. They showed no temerity in delivering their agenda to Richardson Hall, bearding the principal in his den. In 1978, for instance, Crowe and Kay

In February 1977, feminist Germaine Greer spoke in Grant Hall. Her presence symbolized the growing awareness and frustration of women on Queen's campus. Although more than half Queen's undergraduate students were now women, only slightly more than 10 per cent of tenured faculty were women. The Association of Women Teaching at Queen's became vocal in demanding change.

Herman of sociology drew Watts's attention to the fact that Queen's adjunct professors – untenured and predominantly female – were especially "vulnerable" in times of economic downturn and should therefore be afforded better job security.[90] A year later, Arlene Crowe, as chair of the group, urged that all hiring committees be instructed to quiz candidates about their "long-range attitude" towards women entering graduate studies in their particular discipline. In 1979, AWTAQ told Watts that it was "shocked and dismayed" that no woman had been placed on the committee to select a new associate dean in the business school.

Watts responded. Late in 1975, he asked art historian Kathleen Morand, the only female department head at Queen's, to chair a principal's committee to review the patterns of appointment and promotion experienced by women faculty at Queen's. When Morand was obliged to move away from Kingston, leadership of the committee passed to Marie Surridge, the head of the French Studies department. Surridge was inured to the marginalization of women at Queen's – most people entering the departmental office assumed she was the secretary, not its head. Her committee's March 1978 report bore some good news: peer-pairing analysis revealed "no demonstrable differential" remained in salaries between male and female professors. There was, however, concern that women might be moving through the academic ranks more slowly than their male counterparts. The committee did not speculate why this should be so, although maternity absences from campus would seem the likely reason. The problem of *qualitative* discrimination on the basis of gender thus seemed to have been largely alleviated, the committee concluded.

What remained was a *quantitative* problem: there were simply not enough women in the faculty, and without this critical mass, the faculty was unlikely to reflect the demographics of Canadian society. The paucity of overall hiring was prohibiting an inroad being made into the male dominance of Queen's faculty. The problem was, in short, a "problem of numbers." There were, for instance, precious few women in full professorships. In some faculties, such as Applied Science, and some departments there were no women faculty whatsoever. While the committee understood the dampening effect of the university's "steady state" policy and its debilitating deficit, it advocated greater dynamism in the challenge of bringing gender balance to the Queen's faculty. Search committees should be encouraged to actively seek out female candidates, and advertisements should explicitly invite applications from both males and females.[91] The Surridge Committee advocated greater activism: the principal must maintain the pressure, keeping records to track the progress of women faculty and promising to revisit the issue within five years.

Inching Towards Gender Parity

Watts listened. He now understood that the challenge of gender balance at Queen's was no longer something to be episodically revisited, but instead something demanding constant vigilance. On various levels, women were given more voice in the councils of university governance. Watts nominated Lin Good to sit as a Queen's delegate on the Ontario Council of University Affairs; Good also gave voice to women's concerns as a member of the Ontario Council on the Status of Women. When Good stepped down from the OCUA, her place was taken by Jill Harris of the Senate office, who had been involved in the staff association and prominent in establishing a grievance procedure for Queen's staff. One outcome of such pressure was the 1982 appointment of Wilma Bernabei as Queen's first Equal Employment Opportunity Officer. Bernabei immediately began taxing the administration over the slow progress towards gender parity in the ranks of Queen's staff. Other forceful women appeared on the Queen's scene. Traditionally, women had been a distinct minority on the Board of Trustees, appointed for tokenistic reasons – eastern-Ontario women novelists and women known for their philanthropy were favourite choices. During the seventies, women with professional experience and well-informed views were appointed, notably Mary Collins (BA 1962), a Calgary business consultant, and Shirley Carr, executive vice-president of the Canadian Labour Congress.

Perhaps most significantly, Watts chaired the committee that led to the 1980 appointment by the university council of Agnes Benidickson as the university's first female chancellor. Benidickson brought not only a family connection with the Richardson family, which had so generously supported Queen's for decades, but, more importantly, she brought formidable organizational skills and an incredible zeal for Queen's well-being. Married to an Ottawa politician, Benidickson had served on the Canadian Council on Social Development and as a director of James Richardson & Sons Ltd., the Winnipeg-based grain-and-investment corporation built up by her father, James, who had himself been Queen's chancellor through the 1930s. Benidickson had joined the trustees in 1969 and had chaired the Queen's Fund as a feedstock for the university's endowment. As chancellor, Benidickson became a vivacious ambassador for Queen's. Across Canada, she beat the drum for Queen's with alumni and donors, while back on campus she took on projects such as the furnishing of Summerhill with period furniture, turning it into a charming venue for visiting worthies.

Watts also converted the advisory committees on the status of women, which had been periodically reporting since 1974, into an ongoing advisory group. The first of these advisory groups, chaired by Professor Jean Alexander of paediatrics,* reported familiar news in the spring of 1980: that there had been precious little headway in hiring women. Women continued to have transitory experience at Queen's as adjuncts, the university's favoured method of acquiring teaching staff in times of budgetary stringency. The committee offered evidence to illuminate the situation – the supply of women holding doctorates paled in comparison with men (in 1977 Canadian universities graduated 294 PhDs in social sciences, of which only 65 were awarded to women). The Alexander Committee urged consideration of ways to deflect women in adjunct positions into tenure-stream appointments in areas that were in woeful need of gender balancing. But the fundamental problem remained: "a significant number of women do not have long-term career prospects at Queen's."[92] In 1981, Watts broadened this incremental approach to gender at Queen's by appointing Jill Harris, a staff employee, to chair the status of women committee, a committee that was now also fleshed out with student representatives, such as AMS President Sue Rooks. He also added the dean of women and the new equal employment opportunity officer to its roll. The committee was tasked with collecting data and providing an ongoing report card on women's progress at Queen's.

Patience with the university's gradualist approach to women's issues was, however, wearing thin by the early 1980s. Society beyond the Queen's campus was reflecting a pronounced shift in gender values, which would culminate in 1982 with the passing of the Canadian Charter of Rights and Freedoms, a document that enshrined gender equality as a national norm. Two years later, Jeanne Sauvé would be appointed Canada's first woman governor general. Terms like "employment equity" were becoming commonplace in the national dialogue. The Canadian Association of University Teachers established its own committee on the status of women. Queen's law professor Beverley Baines became a much-sought-after commentator on women's rights under Canada's newly patriated constitution, while at the same time introducing a course on women and the law in her own faculty. But the composition of Queen's faculty still a lagged in this transformation. The rhetoric of an increasingly exasperated AWTAQ became assertive. "The problem is unam-

---

*Professor Alexander's career typified the marginal status of many women academics at Queen's in the decades before the seventies. A pediatrician educated in Australia, England, and the United States, Alexander arrived as a pediatrics instructor at Queen's in 1967. Even though she would become the first woman appointed as a geographic full-time medical professor at Queen's, her salary in her early years in Kingston was too low to qualify for the university pension plan. When Aberdeen-educated Janet Sorbie arrived to teach family medicine in 1977, she had the clear sense that she had only been reluctantly hired because "no suitable man" had applied. When, in 1986, she became that department's first woman head, she recalled arriving at her first departmental meeting and hearing a colleague comment: "Well, guys, I guess we can't tell our jokes." See Jacalyn Duffin, "Feminization of Canadian Medicine: Voices from the Second Wave," in *Canadian Bulletin of Medical History*, 29, 1 (2012), 83–100.

biguously one of numbers," it wrote in rejecting the gradualism of the Alexander Report. "There has been and continues to be a vicious cycle of few women professors, thus limited attraction for women to enter many fields of study, thus few women graduate students, thus few women professors. Unless the problem of numbers is addressed squarely, we submit, few of the other recommendations of future committees will have the slightest chance of success."[93]

By the early 1980s, AWTAQ had a considerable following: an estimated membership of 141 early in 1981. It hosted luncheon discussion groups, collected membership dues, ran a lecture series, and frequently carried its message of "the abysmally *low* number of women faculty in our universities" as far afield as Queen's Park. Then AWTAQ took the plight of the adjunct professors under its wing, arguing that adjuncts deserved better benefits and a chance at permanent employment. It also broadened its scope to encompass the very conspicuous gender imbalances of the support staff at Queen's. Here Wilma Bernabei proved a valuable ally: her first annual report on employment equity in 1982 revealed that 97 per cent of clerical secretarial support at Queen's was female and that their pay was between 1 per cent and 11 per cent less than men in comparable positions.[94]

The association also turned its attention on what was taught about women at Queen's. Feminists across North America had castigated the male-centric bias of academic disciplines and argued that women's experience had to be "centred" in the structuring of what was taught to students, a majority of whom were now women. In 1982, for instance, AWTAQ members in departments such as French, English, sociology, and law began drawing up a compendium list of courses that might be clustered into a women's-studies program at Queen's. Similarly, there were demands that sexist language that implied that certain fields of study were genetically male in orientation be expunged from faculty calendars and replaced by gender-neutral descriptions.

Outgoing Chancellor Roland Michener (1973–80) peforms the ceremonial kickoff at a Gaels game in Richardson Stadium in 1980. Agnes Benidickson, the incoming chancellor, holds the ball. In the late-twentieth century, Queen's was served by a succession of imaginative and energetic chancellors who enhanced not just its ceremonials but also boosted fundraising and its external image.

"*A Pretty Taste for Paradox*" 255

❖ *"Women Investing in Women": The Ban Righ Foundation* ❖

It is tempting to cast the history of "women" at Queen's in terms of distinct feminist phases. First-wave feminists secured women's rights on campus by asserting them through the 1889 Levana Society. "Arts forever / Queen's forever / Women's Rights or War," went their chant. Second-wave feminism in the sixties strived to end the sequestering of women at Queen's, for instance by merging the Levana enclave into an Arts and Science mainstream in 1967. Statistics seem to illustrate this pattern of restraint and challenge. They show the ascendancy of women as the majority of Queen's students by the early 1980s, while in those years their female mentors in the faculty bumped their heads on a resilient glass ceiling that denied them any more than 13 per cent of the professoriate. Women's points of grievance at Queen's were real – gender quotas in medical-school admissions, for instance – and the tactics brought on to counter such obstruction were clever and persistent – for example, the establishment of the Association of Women Teaching at Queen's. One could, however, also argue that women's experience at Queen's was characterized by continuity and constant adaptation. Some Levana traditions – the candle-lighting ceremony, for instance – lingered well past the sixties as a simple testament of sorority without its dated fertility rites. The creation of the Ban Righ Foundation in 1974 provides another such an instance of transformation.

In 1902, a small group of alumnae at Queen's began agitating for better accommodation for women students. Their campaign led to the purchase of houses near campus where women might live together. These scattered homes away from home nurtured a distinct feminist culture. The most famous of these "residences," at 174 Earl Street, acquired the nickname of the "Hencoop," with its eat-in residents called "grubbers." From the outset, financial support from Queen's alumnae sustained the effort, so much so that by the twenties Queen's women launched a concerted effort to sponsor the erection of a modern, on-campus women's residence. In the face of much skepticism from the male-dominated Board of Trustees, $80,000 was raised, and Ban Righ ("wife of the king") Hall was opened in 1925. Until 1969, women managed their own residences at Queen's, so well that the Ban Righ Board overseeing them steadily reported surpluses. Additional residences – Adelaide, Chown, and Victoria halls – reinforced the tradition. The men's residences lagged in both decorum and profitability. But, in 1969, arguments of efficiency and gender equality saw Queen's amalgamate all its residences under one unisex umbrella. However, the Ban Righ Board refused to surrender the fruits of its labours – an accumulated nest egg of $420,000. A subcommittee of the Board, headed by the former registrar Jean Royce, was struck. Its advice was to invest the capital in a foundation dedicated to the needs of a relatively new breed of Queen's woman – the mature female student returning to university or coming to her studies later in life. In 1976, more than four hundred women at Queen's were older than twenty-six.

In 1974, the Ban Righ Foundation for the Continuing Education of Women was born to assist women to "continue" their education on a campus that hitherto had done little to support older students. To project its welcoming image, the centre shunned accommodation in a formidable limestone building, opting instead for the comfort of an arts-and-crafts-style home at 32 Queen's Crescent (the one-time home of Queen's treasurer William McNeill). The centre offered cups of coffee, fireside chats, counselling, bursaries, and programs ranging from assertiveness training to women in literature. Helen Mathers, its first director, likened all this to a "curtain ... rising on a new Queen's woman." Kingston writer Bronwen Wallace suggested in the *Queen's Alumni Review* that it was simply a case of "women helping women." She cited the experience of Margaret Teertsta, a divorced mother of four, who had always been told that she was "only a girl," unsuited for university. With trepidation, she enrolled at Queen's and was "petrified." But the "homey atmosphere" of the Ban Righ Centre was "heaven sent." In 1985, Margaret became a Queen's BA, one of many such Ban Righ success stories.

Building a Faculty Bridge to the Nineties

The main thrust of the group became a steady agitation for what it called "a strategy of structural change." A new AWTAQ subcommittee appeared before the influential Senate Committee on Academic Development to advocate the creation of a "mechanism" that would explicitly give priority to the hiring of women faculty. To achieve this, a "special programs officer" should be appointed. AWTAQ drew attention to the need for better grievance procedures for faculty to contest tenure and promotion decisions that might reflect gender bias. By the mid-1980s, such persistence finally began to bear fruit. Two related factors provided the final impetus for change: the overall "greying" of Queen's faculty and the availability of capital that was free of the tight grip of the provincial operating grant.

On the first front, the university's planning staff began pointing with growing alarm at the bulge of middle-aged professors at Queen's, the legacy of the hurly-burly of hiring in the sixties. These professors were now well into middle career and, with the drought in seventies hiring, there was concern that the Queen's faculty was becoming an inverted pyramid, one that would topple by the nineties, when a spate of predictable retirements would decimate its upper echelon. Over and above the demographic challenge of renewing "manpower" at Queen's, there was the parallel challenge of intellectually renewing the faculty, opening it up to new ideas and methodologies. Watts dubbed this challenge one of "bridging": the need to incubate a new generation of professors before older faculty departed en masse over the next decade. Coincidentally, bridging might also provide an opportunity to diversify the faculty away from its engrained maleness. A first hint of this approach to faculty renewal came early in the eighties, when monies from the Webster Foundation were used to offer two annual research fellowships to junior professors. The Webster Fellows were intended to bolster beleaguered departments in the humanities and social sciences. In 1983, for instance, Roberta Hamilton, a bright young sociologist with a PhD from Concordia in Montreal, arrived as a Webster Fellow and immediately reinforced the growing interest in women's studies at Queen's.

But bridge building required more than two short-term research appointments. Here Watts and the trustees showed their ingenuity. By the late seventies, it had become clear that the provincial government in Toronto was not going to loosen its purse strings for post-secondary education until its books were balanced. There was little likelihood that this would happen soon. Traditional, tenure-stream appointments seemed likely to remain a trickle. Egged on by the university's dynamic vice-principal, development, Jim Courtright, and advised by alumni such as executive Walter Light (BSc 1949), the trustees decided to dramatically diversify the university's income through aggressive fundraising. Paradoxically for a university that had such an ingrained sense of tradition, Queen's had never enjoyed above-average financial support from its alumni compared with other established universities. Indeed, it had taken Presbyterian zeal to build up a comparatively large endowment over the years, an endowment that had been usefully drawn upon in the lean seventies to supplement the university coffers.

Under Courtright, the university began to consider fundraising as a systematic, as opposed to periodic, activity. A professional fundraiser, Donald Duff, was hired. A more-vigorous administration was brought to alumni relations. The old, branch-by-branch looseness of the Alumni Association was tightened and centralized. A new director of alumni affairs, Murray Gill, was appointed, and the records of Queen's 35,000-plus alumni were computerized. From a strategic point of view, there was also the growing awareness that Queen's was graduating more students than ever before and that the ranks of the alumni were yearly swelling. On the other hand, there was also the realization that Ontario's burgeoning university sector had made the quest for donor dollars a competitive endeavour. The term fundraising "campaign" now had almost military resonance.

In 1977, Queen's girded for such a campaign. The Queen's Quest set an ambitious goal of $10 million over a six-year span. Such money would alleviate the university's deficit, while at the same time diversifying its revenue stream. Chaired by Walter Light, the CEO of the up-and-coming Canadian telecommunications corporation Northern Telecom, the Quest campaign was brilliantly executed. Large corporate donors like Alcan set the initial tone, thereby creating the momentum that encouraged smaller donors to fall into line. An AMS referendum saw students pledge $7.50 each annually over ten years, for a total of $750,000. Staff and faculty joined in, pledging over $400,000. The City of Kingston pledged $150,000. Within a year, Light could report that the campaign was already halfway to its goal. Such beneficence allowed Principal Watts to announce in December 1979 that $875,000 of the largesse would be applied to a Queen's Quest Visiting Scholars scheme that would bring out-of-town scholars and "fresh ideas" to Queen's over the next four years.[95] The Queen's Quest rolled successfully into the eighties, raising an astonishing $14 million by 1983. Almost immediately, this achievement prompted the birth of the Queen's Appeal in 1984 with, for Queen's, the dizzying goal of raising $25 million over five years. This time the chairmanship was taken by William Mulholland, CEO of the Bank of Montreal – and, interestingly, a non-Queen's grad. Aided by bank vice-chairman and former diplomat Jake Warren and the Bank of Montreal's communications staff, the Queen's Appeal faced a tougher environment – the nation was contending with persistent inflation and sky-high interest rates. Nonetheless, Mulholland's team began by approaching over three hundred potential corporate donors. The campaign stressed Queen's tradition of excellence in teaching and the loyalty of its alumni. "Give for Excellence," the literature urged. Such generosity would "reinforce existing strengths." It worked. The City of Kingston, for instance, once again generously gave $500,000. By the spring of 1985, Mulholland could report that $21.3 million was in the kitty, with more arriving daily.

The real bounty of the Quest and Appeal campaigns was that it furnished Watts with unencumbered money that gave him, for the first time in years, considerable budgetary discretion. Since 1983, almost in anticipation, Watts had worked up a plan to apply some of the Queen's Appeal funds to offsetting the greying of his faculty. As his term as principal neared completion in late 1984, Watts had no trouble converting his heir apparent, economist David Smith, to the necessity of recruiting young, new talent to Queen's. Bolstered by Mulholland's good financial news early in 1985, Smith unveiled the Queen's National Scholar (QNS) scheme as an initiative to revitalize Queen's faculty. The program, he said, would reinforce Queen's "existing strengths in teaching and research," thereby allowing it to differentiate itself from other universities, which were often still mired in deficit and unable to reach out to new talent.

The insertion of the word "national" cleverly accentuated that differentiation. The QNS professors would be the cutting edge of a new, replenishing generation of Queen's professors. The principal retained the prerogative of allocating QNS positions to faculties which could demonstrate dire need or a strategic opportunity for such talent. Other QNS appointments would be open to interdepartmental competition, with the best departmental bid getting the position. There would be two types of appointments: short-term three-year posts, and longer-term appointments, designed to deliver younger faculty to the mainstream faculty by the nineties. Once the principal's annual allocation had been made, departments would conduct the recruitment under standard hiring procedures. When Smith presented his innovative scheme to the Senate early in 1985, AWTAQ was there to remind him that, for the first time in years, the university had a flexible mechanism to leverage the gender balance. From the outset, Watts had seen the potential of the QNS scheme to tilt the gender balance towards better representation of women in Queen's faculty. Smith initially presented the QNS proposal as a means to "provide an opportunity" to hire more women scholars. At the Senate meeting, law professor Bev Baines, speaking for AWTAQ, said that this lacked decisiveness. The phrase was dropped and replaced by the more assertive "to improve the proportion of women" on faculty.[96]

The QNS program proved a brilliant stroke. The first "outstanding young scholars" started arriving on campus in the fall of 1985. Rena Upitis, a Canadian trained in epistemology and art education at Harvard, was, for instance, lured away from her post at MIT back to her old alma mater to join the Faculty of Education. A year later, Christine Overall, a philosopher with an interest in feminist theory, who had arrived at Queen's in 1984 as a Webster Fellow in the Humanities, secured a QNS in the philosophy department.[97] Other QNS appointments would follow across the campus, ranging from rehabilitation therapist Cheryl King to feminist legal scholar Kathleen Lahey. Finally, there was momentum. Not all the QNS appointments were female. In 1986, a clever chemical engineer with industrial experience at DuPont, Tom Harris (BSc 1975), was recruited to the department of chemical engineering. Over in music, composer John Burge arrived. Nonetheless, a gender realignment was slowly emerging in the Queen's faculty. By 1991, sixty-two QNS appointments had been made, thirty-three of them going to women.[98]

As if to highlight this turning of the corner, the university in 1984 celebrated the hundredth anniversary of the first women – two in Arts, three in Medicine – to obtain a Queen's degree. The June 1984 convocations honoured no less than four prominent women: Anne Bodnarchuck, a Queen's grad and the first woman vice-president at Air Canada; Kathleen Shannon, a Montreal filmmaker; Christine Rice, a bacteriologist; and Lois Wilson, moderator of the United Church. That fall, the university sponsored a symposium, "The Prism of Change: University Women in the 1980s," to probe the change status of women at Queen's. Lin Good, who epitomized the gradualist inclination in campus feminism, used her keynote address to rejoice in the advances experienced by women on campus since the sixties – a boom in female enrolment and the end of conspicuous segregation of women. But for many of the other delegates the word "struggle" still predominated in their description of woman's place on the Queen's campus. Dean of Nursing Alice Baumgart concurred: "There is still a lot of work for us to do."[99] Baumgart was closer to the truth: Queen's had finally budged in its complacent attitude and policies towards women, but significant results remained to be seen. The Queen's National Scholars constituted a bold initiative that was finally gnawing away at the once-almost-procrustean maleness of the university. But lurking just below the surface there still existed sexist attitudes that suggested that Queen's suffered from non-financial kinds of deficits. These, as Principal Smith would sadly discover, would come payable later in the eighties.

Nurturing Graduate Studies and Funded Research

Fundraising had demonstrated what the injection of money garnered from generous donors could do for Queen's – new faces and new ideas. The same became increasingly true of Graduate Studies and Research at Queen's in the late seventies and early eighties. Graduate programs meant generous BIUS – six BIUs per doctoral student, for instance, as opposed to the one or one-and-a-half units for undergraduate students. This revenue stream could thus be fattened by the addition of new graduate programs. Such programs were, however, subject to rigorous approval by the Ontario Council on Graduate Studies, and in the late seventies, the cash-strapped Ontario government had frozen the approval of all new graduate programs and was in fact talking of the need to "rationalize" existing ones. Some universities, such as Trent, actually surrendered graduate programs in return for improved support of other operations. At Queen's, the freeze put the School of Business's ambitious plan for doctoral studies in management in limbo; approved in 1977, the management PhD did not receive provincial funding until 1983.

Nonetheless, growing the graduate program offered an attractive strategic opportunity to both broaden the prestige of the university and enhance its financial foundation. There was also pronounced sentiment on campus that Queen's had not seized the potential of expanding its graduate capacity in years when the country was crying out for more expertise – to run industry, advise government, and teach future generations. Just as he took office, Watts received an indignant letter from a doctoral candidate in history, who complained that the graduate faculty suffered from "complacency," and that some departments needed to be dragged "kicking and screaming into the twentieth century." There seemed to be an attitude amongst many faculty that graduate studies would poach resources from Queen's hallowed devotion to undergraduate teaching. Dean Sinclair, with characteristic bluntness, chimed in: the graduate school was "too bureaucratic, and removed from the mainstream of research activity centred on departments and faculties."[100]

At Queen's, graduate studies and faculty research huddled under one umbrella: the School of Graduate Studies and Research. This double-headed structure reflected the relatively recent origins of the faculty; its administrative structure and constitution were not even a decade old. The school's bifurcated nature also reflected the traditionally subsidiary role of research unrelated to teaching at Queen's. There had, of course, been significant research done at the university. To take one illustrious example: in 1972, English professor John Matthews and history professor Don Schurman began editing the sprawling correspondence of nineteenth-century British prime minister Benjamin Disraeli. Queen's thus built up world-leading expertise in the life of one of Britain's greatest leaders. Additional grants from the Social Sciences and Humanities Research Council and new impetus from another English professor, Mel Wiebe, and from political scientist Jock Gunn, saw the publication of the project's first volumes of collected letters in 1982 under the imprimatur of the University of Toronto Press.[101] The Disraeli Project pointed the way to the future: growing the university's reputation, intellectual capacity, and financial well-being through externally funded research. At a time when the main input to university revenue was tightly regulated by Queen's Park, the pursuit of external research monies, often sourced from the federal government, the private sector, and foundations, opened up a promising area of discretionary revenue growth for the university. The pursuit of more external funding, combined with a concerted effort to expand graduate studies at Queen's, seemed ideally suited to Watts's inclination towards "selective" growth.

The drive to expand began in earnest in 1978. Hitherto, the dean of Graduate Studies and Research occupied a rather ambiguous place in the Queen's senior-management structure. In the staffing of graduate programs, he was at the mercy of individual departments, where faculty appointments were made. The departments also held sway over the deployment of graduate teaching assistants. Graduate Studies consequently had little financial leverage over the entire graduate program beyond the dispensing of scholarships. It did oversee the interaction of departmental graduate programs with the provincial accreditation bodies like the OCGS and advisory bodies like the OCUA. In 1977, for instance, chemist Robert McIntosh, the school's dean, was asked by the OCUA to provide an overview of graduate studies at Queen's at a time when provincial austerity was biting deeper into post-secondary education. McIntosh reported that "hard choices" lay ahead, and that

Queen's Park wanted more strategic planning on the part of individual campuses before any further expansion could take place.[102]

The report seemed to crystallize the sense that Queen's had been too passive in developing its graduate studies and research effort. Certainly, the McIntosh Report provoked a lively debate about missed opportunities. The head of the physics department, William McLatchie, complained to Watts that it was a "disgrace" that the university put so low a priority on science and the research it invited. Science at Queen's had "always been a tender plant, tended before mass education came about by the occasional outstanding scholar and more recently by an active group of young people who are now beginning to develop national and international clout." Without more support, scientific research at Queen's would, he concluded, wither.[103]

The Research Boom

Watts sensed that an opportunity lay before Queen's and acted quickly. He oversaw the appointment of Maurice Yeates to the deanship in 1978. Yeates, a geographer who specialized in urban growth, had capably headed the geography department and now brought his dynamic personality to his new office. In some ways, Yeates assumed office at an auspicious moment. While the provincial government was putting brakes on its commitment to graduate studies, the federal government was awakening to its role as a sponsor of university-based research. Having retreated from any role in providing direct operating revenue to the universities, Ottawa now donned the mantle of research master. Ottawa had since the 1950s sponsored research in the humanities and social sciences through the Canada Council. In 1977, this effort was centralized in the new Social Sciences and Humanities Research Council of Canada (SSHRC). Since 1960, medical research had been funnelled through the federally financed Medical Research Council of Canada in Ottawa (whose first head was former Queen's professor of medicine Malcolm Brown). In 1978, the Natural Sciences and Engineering Research Council (NSERC) was established as the central clearing house for graduate studies and research on Canadian campuses.

Yeates immediately recognized the potential of these granting agencies. (His colleague Dean Uffen in Applied Science had served as an advisor on science policy in Ottawa before coming to Queen's.) Yeates appointed an associate dean, John Beal of electrical engineering, to invigorate the school's clearing house for grant applications, the Office of Research Services (ORS). For the first time, Queen's began not only to encourage applications for external research funds but also to coach faculty on how best to style themselves for such support. At the same time, the university began to explore the possibility of exploiting the commercial possibilities of carrying research findings out into the world of manufacturing and services. A patents officer was appointed to help professors and the university capitalize on their intellectual capital. This provoked a protracted discussion of intellectual property rights: how would the profits of research be split between its originator and its facilitator, the university?

Hand-in-hand with the accessing of research funding, the school developed ethical guidelines for researchers whose work involved living subjects. Through all this effort, a parallel effort was undertaken to broaden interdisciplinary research at Queen's. By drawing the synergy of various disciplines into consolidated research projects, the potential of research could be pursued in various directions and with granting agencies spread across many disciplines. The Disraeli Project had shown the way. Throughout the late seventies and into the eighties, interdisciplinary projects ranging from plant-cell biology to population studies blossomed at Queen's. Professors Henrik "Hank" Wever and Tim Bryant of the mechanical engineering department, for instance, joined a bioengineering research team and were able to draw on the orthopaedic expertise of Queen's medical faculty to study joint movement and produce artificial replacements.

The results were impressive. In the six years after Yeates took office, externally funded research at Queen's ballooned by 168 per cent, to just under $28 million by 1984. By 1982–83, Queen's had risen to third amongst Ontario universities (behind Guelph and McMaster) in terms of total sponsored research as a fraction of operating revenues. The university also showed well in terms of national granting-council awards as a fraction of operating revenues.[104] Such effort brought kudos to Queen's faculty. In 1982, Dr Adolfo de Bold of biochemistry was, for instance, celebrated for his work on cardionatrin, a peptide acid central to the operation of the heart. De Bold's findings were the product of years of funded research. A year later, his research team received an $800,000 grant from Ontario's IDEA Foundation (created to bolster innovation in the province) to continue its work on cardionatrin and the health of the heart.[105] Similarly, Dr W. Bennett Lewis of the department of physics was awarded the Enrico Fermi Prize by the American government for his role in the development of the CANDU nuclear reactor.[106]

Watts pushed the research frontier at Queen's beyond individual achievement. In late 1981, he visited Japan, where he had spent his earliest years, and reported, like so many others in the decade of Japan's "economic miracle,"* his admiration of that country's National Universities as sites of pooled scientific research supported by government and conducted by academics.[107] Influenced by this synergy, Queen's, with much encouragement from Walter Light of Northern Telecom, was in 1983 designated by the federal government as the site of the Canadian Microelectronics Corporation, a non-profit enterprise with initial funding of $3 million from NSERC dedicated to coordinating electronic design at all Canadian universities.[108]

The exponential growth of research activities at Queen's was not, however, without either problems or long-term implications. The flow of government grants and external research contracts seemed to handsomely fatten the university's bottom line. In 1983, the trustees, long accustomed to bad financial news, were told the good news that funded research now constituted 26 per cent of Queen's operating budget, or about $20 million. University planners and accountants, however, reported that the numbers were deceptive. Most government grants in support of research were predicated on the assumption that the host institution would cover the overhead costs of the research – everything from heating the labs on through to alleviating the researcher's teaching load. The failure of external funding to reflect these costs in calculating research stipends in effect penalized the host institution and, not surprisingly, became a bone of contention with Ottawa granting bodies and other external funders. In 1980, Queen's therefore arbitrarily introduced its own policy to claw back overhead costs from research funds flowing onto its campus: 30 per cent on on-campus research and 2 per cent of travel costs off-campus.[109] Once this slice was taken, the problem arose as to how much of this "payment" went into the university's central coffers and how much should trickle down to individual departments. In 1986, a 50:50 split was decided upon.

The age-old question of academic freedom illustrated another problematic aspect of funded research. By its very nature, externally funded

---

*The 1980s saw Queen's, like much of the western world, begin to look westward to the Pacific Rim for economic inspiration. From 1978 to 1981, Prince Takamado of the Japanese imperial family had studied law at Queen's. On his 1981 visit to Japan, Watts spent Christmas Eve with the prince's relatives at the Imperial Palace in Tokyo. Over the next decade, Queen's would introduce a number of Japan-oriented initiatives. Japanese language courses were first taught in 1987, and in 1991 David Anderson, dean of the business school, visited Japan with the hope of establishing teaching linkages. Interestingly, when Watts reported his admiration of Japan's progress to the trustees in 1982, Trustee Shirley Carr promptly reminded him that women's rights in Japan lagged far behind those enjoyed by Canadian women.

research implied some acquiescence to outside authority in setting the purpose and framework of research to be done by academic staff, staff who had traditionally cherished their right to pursue their own intellectual inclinations. In 1983, for instance, the Bank of Montreal generously underwrote the establishment of a chair in the School of Business dedicated to the study of banking and finance. Was the incumbent to be expected to do the bidding of the bank, or was the endowment simply a foundation to allow the holder of the chair to pursue an independent agenda? When the principal presented the news of the new chair to the trustees, one of their number, the former student rector Alan Broadbent, wondered whether the university's freedom to follow its own conscience was being undermined. No, Watts answered, all research units were controlled by management committees that had a majority membership of members of the university community, not outsiders.[110]

From Mainframe to Microcomputer

The expansion of funded research created other pressure points on campus as well. With cash-strapped Queen's Park releasing little financial aid to university capital projects during the eighties, research often had to be shoehorned into existing labs and had to rely on underfunded facilities like the library. Even more pressing was the need to equip Queen's researchers with up-to-date computer support, something that was becoming the *sine qua non* of research. Watts's tenure as principal paralleled a seismic revolution in the way Canadians conceived and applied computer intelligence to their daily needs. Not only was the processing capacity and speed of computers exponentially expanding, but the application of computers to work was shifting dramatically from a paradigm of central control into a diaspora of microcomputing. When Watts assumed office in 1974, the bulky mainframe computer ruled at Queen's. Computing was seen as a facilitator of administrative work – payroll and the computerization of alumni files, for instance – with certain peripheral applications to teaching and research. The computing centre in Dupuis Hall was the round-the-clock mecca for all computer users on campus. By 1976, the rapid advance in microelectronics was challenging the rule of the mainframe. That year, the Senate Committee on Computing predicted that Queen's was shifting to a system of "distributed computing."[111]

A year later, the committee was complaining that computing was being starved by austerity at Queen's. The campus computer system was "outdated" and "haphazard" in its design. Watts desperately applied what discretionary funds he could muster for the library and computing services, the two crucial information conduits on campus. He also launched a broadly consultative process on what direction Queen's should take in addressing its computing future – and with what equipment. The crux of the debate was whether the university should rely on Burroughs or IBM equipment. As was characteristic of the Watts approach, a long deliberation ensued. Finally, in 1984, the decision went to IBM, and a large, state-of-the-art IBM 3081 was purchased.[112]

The ascendancy of the computer was nowhere more evident than in the Douglas Library. Margot McBurney, the university's chief librarian, had been brought to Queen's in 1977 to accelerate the transition from an old-style, busy-hands library to a library in which cataloguing, accession, and circulation were assisted by technology. The problem of cataloguing new accessions at Douglas had become so serious that a huge backlog of uncatalogued books had built up in a wire cage in the library's basement. The overwhelmed cataloguing staff placed a sign on the outside of the cage: "Please do not feed." With the university's expanding graduate program, and now enlarged undergraduate foundation, it was imperative that books and periodicals be placed in the hands of professors and students as quickly as possible. In 1979, McBurney therefore hired Gene Clevenger as an assistant librarian in charge of systems and development. The word "systems" was installing itself in Queen's lexicon.

Clevenger had up-to-date library experience in the United States, and most recently at York University. He invited the vendors of new automated library control systems to peddle their wares at Queen's and, in 1979, selected GEAC, an Ontario computer company specializing in computers that facilitated repetitive processing, to supply a computer that would automate the library's circulation system. This would entail the laborious challenge of manually converting the library's existing punch-card-driven circulation system into a readable-barcode system. A GEAC 8000 computer, purchased with funds from the Queen's Quest fundraising campaign, was installed in a data-processing office on the first basement level of the library. News coverage of the event frequently employed the image of "space-age" technology. Library staff, however, nicknamed the mainframe and its disk-drive storage companion as "Archie" and "Bunker." The subsequent RECON retrospective conversion took the next five years and ate up huge amounts of labour (forty-seven staff positions over the life of the project), but by 1985 the main library catalogue was complete and work was under way on cataloguing Queen's branch libraries. The cost of converting a punch card to a barcode that was readable with a light wand: $1.18 per record.[113]

Despite the new central capacity, there was still a fundamental decentralizing drift in Queen's computing policy. With almost every meeting, the Senate Computing Committee discovered some rapidly unfolding electronic innovation – the use of computers for "text editing" and their potential as a surrogate for the university's internal mail system. One thing seemed clear: computing was heading in a decentralized direction. Work was begun on a computer-training facility for first-year students, the belief being that they would constitute the first wave of a new computer-savvy generation of students. To position itself for their arrival, Queen's tried to make its campus computer friendly, leasing laser printers, planning computer "work stations," and developing its own operational system – QUIX – dedicated to Queen's needs alone.

Much of this recognition seemed to emerge out of the Applied Science faculty, where computing seemed so closely related to the career aspirations of its undergraduates. Dean David Bacon was an early convert. In 1983, he struck an ad hoc committee on microcomputing. Guided by the director of computing services at Queen's, D.T. Bernard, Bacon's group reported that microcomputing must be seen as a "fundamental component" of his faculty's undergraduate program.[114] To this end, first-year engineering students beginning in 1985 would be expected to arrive on campus with a personal computer, or "PC," in hand. The other faculties were not far behind. In 1982, a Dean's Committee on New Information Technology in Arts and Science, chaired by William Nichols of film studies, urged that "computer literacy" should now be regarded as a core faculty objective. Over in the Faculty of Education, Dean Tom Williams reported that fifteen of his faculty were undergoing intensive training in the application of microcomputers to teaching teachers.[115]

In preparation for the micro-revolution, the university signed a three-year, $2-million contract with IBM to help it develop the protocols for the widespread use of small computers on campus. The trustees then jumped in with enthusiasm and approved the development of a "campus information network," which they hoped would supplant the campus phone system as a means of moving data around the campus. For this, it turned to Northern Telecom with a $3.5-million contract.[116] To facilitate the transition to the personal computer, the Senate Computer Committee devised a Computer User Code of Ethics. Shadowing these developments, the Department of Computing and Information Science, hesitantly founded in 1969, now burgeoning in size, added a master's degree in the mid-1970s and a doctoral degree in the early 1980s. The department began attracting pioneering scholars, such as

Stanford-trained Mike Jenkins, who arrived in the seventies as a specialist in programming languages and immediately galvanized his new department. While computing and information science remained an Arts and Science department, the department of electrical engineering in Applied Science spearheaded that faculty's computer revolution, striking research liaisons with Northern Telecom and Bell Northern Research. Not surprisingly, the department would in 1993 restyle itself as the department of electrical and computer engineering.

By the time he stepped down as principal, Ron Watts took considerable pride in having overseen a computer revolution at Queen's. At the Association of Universities and Colleges annual meeting in 1984, Watts, drawing on Queen's close ties with Northern Telecom, helped to shape the agenda – "Universities in the Information Revolution: Leaders or Laggers?"[117] Queen's itself had gone from being a laggard in computing to a leader in building a computing strategy that balanced central administrative needs and a broadening decentralized demand for electronic support of teaching and research. Capacity since 1980 had multiplied fortyfold.[118] Computers continued to lubricate the central operations of the institution, but they were also now arriving on the desk – "work stations" – of individual faculty members and researchers. In a departure from previous technological shifts in pedagogy, this was a very democratic transition, with students immediately expected to share in the unfolding computer networks on campus. Perhaps most importantly, Queen's had abandoned the old notion that computers were somehow a static fixture in the way the university functioned. By the mid-1980s, computing and all the electronic marginalia it entailed were now conceived of as an ever-changing frontier – and the quality of Queen's teaching and research would crucially depend upon keeping abreast of that frontier. Artificial intelligence would now supplement Queen's storied reputation for human intuition and acquired learning.

Meanwhile, in the Graduate-Student Lounge

With the infrastructure and financial support of research falling into place, Queen's was in a position to expand its graduate-studies program. Graduate studies went hand-in-glove with a more dynamic research effort and fattened the university's revenue stream with more dynamic and lucrative research efforts. Given the Ontario government's reluctance to return to the headlong sixties' expansion of graduate studies, Watts and successive deans of graduate studies realized that expansion of graduate studies at Queen's would have to be shrewdly designed. In keeping with its philosophy of selective growth, Queen's centred its ambitions on areas where there was demonstrable demand and little overlap with existing programs at other universities. Such a strategy heightened the chances of a program being approved by the tough-minded Ontario Council of Graduate Studies adjudicators in Toronto. A salient example of this came in 1982 when Queen's successfully argued that its long-standing Industrial Relations Centre, founded in 1937 to bring labour and management to annual round-table conferences discussing labour-market trends, should be upgraded to a year-round graduate program. An MA in industrial relations would not only reinforce the centre's outreach and research activities, but it would also create a more stable BIU-driven revenue stream. The centre consequently became the School of Industrial Relations.[119]

Similar extensions and innovations were made to other graduate programs. In 1974, the department of art introduced a master's degree in art conservation under the direction of Canada's leading art conservator, Mervyn Ruggles. With the proximity of the expanding collection of the Agnes Etherington Art Centre, art conservation made eminent sense, especially since Queen's would have the only such program in Canada. The program quickly established close working ties with Canada's national museums and galleries in nearby Ottawa. (In 1975, the "Agnes," as it was widely called on campus, was able to add a wing containing conservation labs with financial assistance from the National Museums Corporation in Ottawa.) In the eighties, the art-conservation program was expanded to embrace paper conservation. There were other carefully targeted additions to Queen's graduate offerings in the Watts years: proposals, for instance, for doctoral studies in fields as diverse as historical geography and biochemical engineering.

From Watts's personal point of view, the crowning moment came in 1984 when a preliminary proposal to consider the creation of a School of Public Policy was placed before the Senate. The rationale here was to capture the synergies of hitherto-separate Queen's centres and institutes dedicated to fostering constructive public policy in Canada – a perpetuation of the storied "Queen's men" tradition in Ottawa – under one, coordinating roof. The school would probably not offer formal degrees, but would serve to ensure the public-policy whole at Queen's was greater than the sum of its parts. Under Dean Yeates's guidance, the proposal to combine the Queen's Centre for International Relations, the Institute for Intergovernmental Relations, the Deutsch Institute for the Study of Economic Policy, the School of Industrial Relations, the School of Public Administration, and the Centre for Resource Studies was worked up. In unity, there would be strength. Once again, there seemed to be strong external interest in the project: in Ottawa, the department of the Secretary of State was eager to underwrite the cost of "centres of excellence" on selected university campuses. There was also the sense that prominent private donors and foundations might join in to reinforce Queen's renowned place in Canadian public policy.[120] Like all university initiatives, much delicate negotiation lay ahead – turf would have to be surrendered, responsibilities split, and new rules created – but there was the sense that, once again, graduate studies at Queen's had found a unique niche.

In 1983, the Senate Committee on Academic Development, the metronome of Queen's enrolment growth, outlined its "Strategies for the 1980s." Prominent among them was the continued expansion of graduate studies at Queen's. In 1979–80, the university's 1,048 full-time graduate students had constituted 10.1 per cent of Queen's student population. By 1983–84, that proportion stood at 13.2 per cent, reflecting a spurt to 1,502. Measured in degrees granted, Queen's awarded 436 graduate degrees in 1974–75. By 1983–94, that tally had swollen to 559. Late in 1983, Dean Yeates used the word "booming" to describe his bailiwick. He also revealingly took to describing graduate studies and research at Queen's as "enterprises."[121] Mindful of such optimism, SCAD recommended that Queen's push the target for its graduate population to 15 per cent of total enrolment. Despite the pressures generated by such forced growth, the same sense of collegiality that could be found among their supervisors seemed to pervade the ranks of Queen's graduate students. There were problems over imposing standardized rates of pay for graduate teaching and research-assistant positions, but when the Canadian Union of Public Employees attempted to unionize Queen's graduate students in 1982, the certification vote was strongly rejected.

A Shifting Sense of Excellence

Behind the crescendo of growth in research and graduate studies there was a creeping but profound attitudinal shift in the way Queen's saw itself in the educational marketplace: research was starting to push teaching into the shadows. In 1982, Watts asked Dr Allan Bromley, a world-famous nuclear physicist at Yale, to visit Queen's and report on the progress of research in the Applied Science and computing-and-information-science fields at Queen's. As a Science '49 graduate from Queen's himself, Bromley quickly recognized the high quality of undergraduate teaching at Queen's. The problem, he reported, was that there was "a fundamental ambiguity towards research in the minds of a substantial number of faculty." If Queen's was to garner an international reputation as a place of top-notch graduate study and research, the faculty would have to take a "quantum leap" onto a more prominent research plane. He concluded that the "critical issue" facing Queen's was that "of deciding exactly what the long term goals and aspirations of Queen's are, in terms of research as contrasted to teaching, and then the articulation of these goals."[122] Watts was somewhat taken aback by the provocative nature of Bromley's prescription. He liked the direction, but noted on his copy of the report that he favoured "accelerated evolution" as a less-dramatic alternative strategy. But Bromley had the direction right: the ascendant benchmark of academic life at Queen's, as it was on many other Canadian campuses, was passing from teaching to research. With operating budgets constricted by cash-strapped provincial governments in the seventies, and undergraduate programs rigidly mandated, universities had understandably identified funded research and the cultivation of lucrative graduate programs as the path of most flexibility and differentiation.

Faculty soon intuitively responded to this shift in the centre of academic gravity. Kudos in terms of tenure and promotion seemed to come more and more from research and from success in the competitive scramble for external support. The university encouraged this trend. The minutes of the Board of Trustees and the Senate from the mid-seventies onwards reveal a progressive privileging of news from the research front. The reports from the dean and associate dean of Graduate Studies and Research became an early and prominent feature on the agenda of these meetings. In terms of calibrating the university's success, funded research appealed because it was a *quantifiable* commodity that could be presented as a barometer of Queen's progress in comparison with other universities. Funded research also bore the legitimization of outside granting agencies. Pedagogic success in the lecture hall, still held up as a Queen's trademark, was less tangible, less measurable. This shift in emphasis was also evident in the way the university presented itself to its alumni and the world beyond the campus; publications such as the *Alumni Review* and press releases from the department of communications increasingly projected the harvesting of funded research as the talisman of the university's future.

In 1984, Maurice Yeates announced his intention to step down from the graduate deanship. The committee appointed by Watts to seek his successor pondered pulling the research function out of the deanship and creating a separate vice-principal, research. In the end, the committee opted to maintain the status quo, but did favour giving the office of research services a more autonomous role. The nod for the deanship went to David Canvin, a plant biologist who had served as head of that department and had considerable experience in university governance. That same year, as he prepared to exit the principal's office, Watts took evident pride in what he described as Queen's "dramatic" rise as a research-oriented institution. Queen's stood second in the province in graduate enrolment and, over the period from 1977 to 1983, recorded the fastest rate of growth in sponsored research funding among Ontario's five research-intensive universities.[123]

Fewer Bricks and Less Mortar

The campus that Principal Watts inherited in 1974 saw remarkably little physical change over the next decade. The great spate of sixties building had almost run its course by the time austerity started to bite into the university budget in the early seventies. All the new construction had altered the look of the campus. The completion of the Bruce Wing of Miller Hall, the John Deutsch Centre, Mackintosh-Corry and Goodwin Hall (plus, of course, Elrond College on Princess Street) seemed to signify the new suzerainty of concrete architecture at Queen's. At its worst, the style, with its strong, unadorned verticals and horizontals, lapsed into Modern Brutalism. Queen's soon discovered that rain and snow dirtied concrete and imparted a sombre dullness to these paradoxically newest additions to its built environment. The effect was heightened by the university's liberal application of interlocking brick on many of its pathways. The overall impression of concrete challenging limestone was accentuated by the steady devastation from Dutch Elm disease of the elegant trees that had so long majestically lined the university's avenues and accented the Gothic grandeur of the limestone buildings behind them.

Watts had little financial leverage to alter this aesthetic drift. Queen's Park was in a budget-trimming mood and shunned any suggestion of costly capital projects on university campuses. After all, Queen's had committed itself to "steady state" growth and could hardly argue that expansion was the order of the day. The completion of Mackintosh-Corry had been blighted by penny-pinching on construction costs that had led to an acrimonious parting with architect Ron Thom. Budget stringency stifled new initiatives. In 1975, the Senate Campus Planning Committee boldly proposed that the university develop a dormitory area for students immediately north of the campus. The "Block V" project would encompass a block-large area bounded by University, Alfred, Union, and Earl streets and would be gradually assembled out of university-owned residential housing. By 1977, the project had withered when high interest rates undermined its financing.[124] (In retrospect, one can speculate how much this project, if realized, might have allowed a more regulated emergence of what soon came to be called the student "Ghetto" in Sydenham Ward.) There were small exceptions to the rule: the period restoration of Summerhill in 1982 (made possible by a provincial heritage grant) and the tasteful extension of the Etherington Art Centre (largely made possible by federal support). But beyond this, the campus seemed frozen.

Compounding the stasis brought on by austerity was the understandable, but ultimately costly, failure to maintain Queen's existing buildings. Many of these were made of limestone that needed costly repointing and were in need of energy-saving retrofitting in an era of soaring energy costs. In this environment, there was little time, money, or will to consider Queen's built environment from any long-term or holistic perspective. The joint Senate–Board of Trustees Campus Planning Committee seldom looked at the campus in any kind of strategic fashion. In 1977, Campus Planning Committee chairman Dan Norman complained that "planning' at Queen's had become little more than a series of expedient decisions with little reference given to overarching consideration of a "campus which serves its community, physically, socially and economically in a more satisfactory manner."[125]

By 1984, Watts could point to one solitary, yet significant, capital project that both changed the campus landscape and at the same time secured the well-being of a crucial Queen's faculty. Despite the fact that Harry Botterell had stepped down as vice-principal, health sciences, in 1971, his dynamic legacy reverberated into the Watts years. Implicit in Botterell's modernization of the medical faculty at Queen's was the recognition that the convergence of modern medicine and national medicare in Canada spelled an unavoidable integration of medical education and the provision of health care. Even as he scrambled to reinvent his faculty through enhanced clinical teaching and salary arrangements, Botterell, as usual backed by Alex Corry, sought to position Queen's, and the local hospitals adjacent to it, to capitalize on the benefits of size and integration. The prospect of an integrated teaching, research, and medical-care facility could also be held out as an inducement to prospective new staff, staff that Botterell knew were needed to replenish his faculty. In 1963, he asked Donald Hatcher, the head of the physiology department, to chair a planning committee that would look into the concept of a "medical-sciences complex," which would facilitate the integration of clinical training with the teaching and research of the basic health-related sciences, while at the same time forging affiliations with the four nearby hospitals in Kingston.[126]

The auspices for such conflation were promising: the federally appointed Hall Royal Commission on Health Services would soon report in 1965 that the integration of medical education with the delivery of services was crucial to the efficiency of medicare. Ottawa reinforced this by creating a large pool of capital – the Health Resource Fund – that would fund the kind of integration that Hatcher was investigating. Queen's Park joined this push for integration with its own pool of capital. Closer to home, the Kingston District Chamber of Commerce rallied to the idea of a health-sciences complex, believing that it would provide the optimum regional level of health care. From the perspective of the Queen's medical school, one of the nation's smallest, the notion of attaching itself to a vibrant regional medical complex appealed powerfully as a strategy for long-term survival.

From Medicine to Integrated Medical Sciences

The idea of a medical-sciences complex in Kingston, however, was more easily contemplated than realized. Botterell's dogged struggle to establish clinical teaching units on the floors of the local hospitals gave a foretaste of what lay ahead. Kingston's four hospitals – Kingston General (KGH), Hotel Dieu, St Mary's of the Lake, and the Kingston Psychiatric Hospital – each had a deep-seated identity rooted in local heritage and, in the case of Hotel Dieu (HDH) and St Mary's, religion.[127] Within each hospital, there were also departmental loyalties that tended to construe any talk of integration with similar nearby groups of clinicians or researchers as a threat to their autonomy. Much the same antipathies existed within Queen's, where the prospect of integration touched not only the medical faculty, but also reached into those Arts and Science departments that furnished students interested in what was coming to be called "life sciences." Over in Richardson Hall, senior administrators faced similar cross-currents of approval and resistance. Not only were dealings with the local hospitals fraught with jurisdictional jealousies, but approvals from the provincial government involved negotiations with *two* ministries: the ministry of colleges and universities and the ministry of health.

Despite this potentially fractious landscape, the Board of Governors at Kingston General Hospital voted in 1965 to initiate negotiations with Queen's for an integrated complex dedicated to medical teaching, research, and patient care. Hatcher's planning committee was now joined by anaesthesiologist Stuart Vandewater, with his strong clinical ties to Kingston General, who would represent the hospital's interests. A "project control office" was established to initiate preliminary planning. As if to bait the hook, the Queen's trustees in 1967 set aside twenty-seven acres in the southeast corner of the campus along Stuart Street as a possible site for the complex. Things did not, however, go smoothly. Despite the fact that Kingston was in a de facto race with medical schools at McMaster, Toronto, Western, and Ottawa to curry provincial approval of what would clearly be a limited number of health-sciences complexes, parochialism prevailed. Late in 1968, with virtually no headway in planning the complex made, Vandewater lost his patience. There was, he angrily scolded KGH executive director, Donald MacIntyre, a "smoldering fire of unrest and suspicion" between the university and KGH on the subject of the mooted complex. A "clash of personalities" had led, Vandewater alleged, to "a complete lack of trust between individuals although each, presumably, had a common goal." "Must," he concluded, "history, custom, and parochial viewpoints preclude an integrated Health Sciences Complex?"[128]

The early seventies witnessed little headway. In 1969, in a bid to break the deadlock, an umbrella committee embracing the potential partners in the complex had been created under the ungainly acronym QUAFHOP – Queen's University and Affiliated Hospitals Council. Desperate to make progress, QUAFHOP called in outside consultants, Booz, Allen

& Hamilton, to advise on the possible structure of the health-complex organization. Their 1971 report advocated greater coordination and led to the conversion of QUAFHOP into the Queen's–Kingston Health Sciences Complex Council. The mandate of the seventeen-member council, to which Queen's appointed four delegates, encompassed six medical centres clustered around the Queen's campus. The Queen's medical school, Kingston General Hospital, Hotel Dieu Hospital, St Mary's of the Lake, St Lawrence College (with its nursing program), and Kingston Psychiatric Hospital. The council finally provided a workable platform for consensus and, in 1972, basic agreement was reached for the federation of the six parties: the "complex" would be centrally planned and financed, but its individual constituents would retain operational autonomy.

This looseness reflected the wariness of the council's partners about surrendering any of their jurisdictional turf. To handle this delicate politic, Queen's split its medical deanship in two, with the new vice-principal, health services, "Gub" Kelly, charged with strategic overview of the unprecedented project, while the dean of medicine, Douglas Waugh, minded the day-to-day shop. What brought discipline to the overall quest for a health-sciences complex was the imperative need to secure provincial financial support. The Health Sciences Council estimated that the total cost of the Kingston project would be $106 million, the bulk of which would go to the construction of an eleven-storey, seventy-thousand-square-foot building on the Stuart Street site, with secondary spending on the renovation of facilities at Hotel Dieu and St Mary's. Although the Kingston project was perhaps the slowest in making its case to Queen's Park, in 1973 it got the nod from the provincial minister of health to proceed, along with other centres in Ottawa, Toronto, London, and Hamilton.

This came as very welcome news at Queen's. Dean Waugh had been reporting that morale in his faculty was sagging. There was a growing sense that the golden years of Botterell expansion were dwindling. Medical education at Queen's was still largely confined to a cluster of nineteenth-century buildings on the quadrangle behind Summerhill. With over three hundred medical students in its program and growing demand for life sciences in other faculties, the medical school found itself squeezed into outdated accommodation. There were not enough laboratories and large lecture halls to service a curriculum heavy in basic sciences and hands-on laboratory and anatomy instruction. The medical library, situated in the nearby Theology Building, fell well below national standards in terms of its holdings and periodicals. To alleviate the pressure, the trustees would later vote monies for the renovation of medical labs and lecture halls in Richardson House, in Etherington Hall, and in the LaSalle Building, but these were clearly stopgap measures and tended to scatter medical instruction across the campus.[129] The fundamental problem of expansion and the regional coordination of medical services remained. This dilemma confronted Ron Watts when he assumed the principalship in late 1974.

Initially the news was encouraging. The Health Sciences Council was gingerly negotiating the intricate details of coordinating everything from bed allocation to the assignment of responsibility for specialty services. At the same time, the five designated health-complex locations in the provinces began to synchronize their planning and their dealings with Queen's Park. The Ontario Council of University Health Sciences was born, under the auspices of the COU, with Dean Waugh on its executive. Back in Kingston, initial design work on the complex was initiated. So eager was Queen's to see spades in the ground that the trustees took the unusual step of dipping into university operating funds to provide $5 million in bridge financing for the start-up of the project. Watts described this as a "calculated risk," a departure in habit for a university that throughout the sixties had refused to lift a hammer until the financial wherewithal for any capital project was firmly in place. Colleges and universities minister, Harry Parrott, confirmed in principle that the province would pledge $50 million for the construction of the Kingston medical complex. The first tranche of $10.3 million would be delivered the spring.[130]

But then the clouds rolled in. Parrott became the bearer of bad news: the province's soaring deficit had obliged Queen's Park to freeze all capital projects on the books. Queen's anticipated first instalment on the health-sciences complex would be reduced to $4.9 million. The minister assured the university that the complex was still a priority with the government, but could not say exactly when it would be in a position to honour its share of the cost. In the interim, the university had the province's permission to secure bridge financing to keep the project alive. Queen's thus found itself in a devilish position – either to halt construction and let inflation drive up the ultimate cost when work resumed or to stay the course.

Fearful of what time and inflation would do to their project estimates, Watts and the trustees chose to stay the course. Early in 1976, Parrott visited Queen's, met with Watts, and confirmed that Toronto would make its final payment towards funding the Mackintosh-Corry building and was fully behind the emerging health complex, which Toronto would now treat as an exception to the freeze on capital spending. An elated Watts reported the news to the trustees: "Dr. Watts stated that, when he mentioned that it had taken four Deans and three principals to bring this matter to a successful conclusion, the Minister pointed out that it had also taken six Cabinet Ministers."[131]

Provincial support for the complex was soon echoed by generous private donors. Dr Franklin Bracken, a New York City eye specialist who had come to Queen's from the eastern-Ontario hamlet of Seeley's Bay and graduated from Medicine in 1911, came forward in 1976 with an offer to modernize Queen's medical library. The new library would be embedded in the new health-sciences complex, readily available to students and faculty. The Bracken Library would also be equipped with up-to-date audiovisual equipment to help the faculty cope with the exploding universe of medical literature. A bust of Bracken by another Canadian who had found fame in the United States, doctor-sculptor R. Tait Mackenzie, would adorn the library's foyer.

Bracken's beneficence towards his old alma mater was matched by Dr Jason Hannah, a Meds graduate of 1928 and a neuropathologist, whose company, Associated Medical Services Inc., had prospered by providing Canadians with a form of contributory health insurance since the 1930s. The arrival of one-payer, universal medicare made Hannah's insurance scheme superfluous, forcing Hannah to wind up his once-lucrative enterprise in 1972. Hannah then redirected his energies to the philanthropic support of medical research, creating a foundation in 1976 that, among other activities, endowed chairs in the history of medicine. Queen's received a Hannah chair in 1975, and appointed Dr Ruth Hodgkinson, a social historian of medicine, to the post. Hannah money also supported medical lectures and book buying for the faculty. Eventually, all five provincial medical schools building health sciences complexes in the late seventies were endowed with Hannah chairs.[132]

Tenders on the project were finally called in the late spring of 1976. Work on the health-sciences complex proceeded fitfully. Inflation persistently pushed up costs. Corners were cut: the sensible idea of linking the complex and Kingston General by means of a walkway across George Street was dropped to save money. The province, still desperately battling its deficit, would commit itself to financing only Phase I of the complex – the first nine floors. As construction unfolded, there were continuing squabbles over the academic configuration of the building. For instance, Professor Tony Travill of anatomy strenuously argued that the faculty's medical museum reinforced the day-to-day teaching of medicine, and therefore should be placed beside the dissection room where students did their anatomy labs. Others complained that planning both the building and the curriculum that it would support had become a time-consuming process. Dr David Symington in rehabilitation complained to Watts that "the decision-making process in the faculty has become too complex and cumbersome." William Powles in psychiatry was more blunt: medicine had become "a faculty of committees."[133] Dean Tom Boag became a frequent briefer of the trustees, each time trying to convey the complexity of the task before him, one that obliged him to operate variously as an agent of financial constraint, a construction boss, and a diplomatic emissary to the other members of the Kingston health consortium, all the while trying to manage his faculty.[134] Even Watts at times showed the strain of it all. In his 1979 "State of the University" address, he told the joke of the university president who died and found himself in a room in hell that looked exactly like his earthly office. He told the devil that his job had never been a bed of roses but that he had never equated it with hell. "Ah yes," replied the devil, unmoved by the complaint, "but here you will have two medical faculties."[135]

Finally, in the fall of 1978 the building was ready for its first occupants. A relieved Board of Trustees had already voted to name the building in honour of Harry Botterell. The official opening was held in October 1979, arranged to coincide with the 125th anniversary of the Queen's medical faculty. A gala dinner attended by Premier Bill Davis (whose government had reiterated its unwillingness to fund Phase II of Botterell Hall until 1980), Kingston-born Health Minister Dennis Timbrell, federal MP Flora MacDonald, and Kingston Mayor Ken Keyes highlighted the ribbon cutting. The faculty historian provided a retrospective lecture on the "gentlemen of 1854," while Associate Dean Stuart Vandewater, who had been with the project since its inception fifteen years before, organized a symposium on what the delivery of medicine would look like in 2004, when the faculty celebrated its 150th anniversary.[136] Almost as an afterthought to the festivities, the Davis government gave the go-ahead for the $3.75-million completion of Botterell Hall in February 1979.

Botterell Hall was by any measure a significant step forward for medical teaching and research at Queen's. It made Queen's look like a modern medical school rather than a collection of handsome-but-outdated limestone buildings. Students and researchers quickly understood this. In December 1980, Dean Boag reported to the trustees that his faculty was brimful of students, ranging from undergraduate doctors-in-training on through to postgraduate researchers. He boasted of a faculty of 96 full-time professors, bolstered by 137 geographic full-time appointments, that linked Queen's medicine to the practising medical community in Kingston.[137] Botterell Hall had also given the long-awaited health-sciences centre a tangible hub, a nucleus from which its services could radiate. The challenge ahead, Boag concluded, was to broaden the regional catchment area of the complex, so that it could don the mantle of eastern Ontario's dominant medical centre. To expedite this ambition, a retired naval admiral with a Queen's doctorate in public administration, Sam Davis, was hired to head and bring a sense of urgency to the Queen's-Kingston Health Sciences Council. Early evidence of the synergy produced by the new facilities had come a year earlier when the Queen's School of Rehabilitation had been integrated into the medical faculty, moving into the nearby Louise D. Acton Building on George Street. On the research side, the complex allowed a broadening of the base of medical research at Queen's: in 1978, for instance, the department of pathology's Cancer Research Group, capably led by Professor Nathan Kaufman, moved into new laboratories in Botterell Hall.

Sadly, Botterell Hall was by no means a ringing success. Aesthetically, it was a pedestrian edifice. In style, it perpetuated the drift away from limestone. Precast concrete horizontal bands, accented by anodized aluminum and tinted windows deprived the building of any architectural flair. Functionally,

Botterell suffered from its long, painful gestation. It was conceived in an era when medical education still emphasized the delivery of basic science knowledge in large-lecture format, with intensive lab work in areas such as anatomy. Even as the cranes were assembling the building, the medical faculty had revamped its curriculum in 1979 to reflect the drift of medical education to small-group teaching, less reliant on animal- and human-cadaver anatomy and more focused on clinical training in the hospital wards.

Botterell Hall was thus designed to satisfy an approach to medical education that was by the time of its inauguration already passé. Even then, there were glitches. The first-floor lecture halls were too small to accommodate the swelling number of medical and life-sciences students attracted to the faculty. And not all departments found immediate accommodation in the new building. The anatomy department was, for instance, obliged by the retarded completion of Phase II to wait until 1986 before settling into its new quarters on the hitherto-unfinished top two floors of the new complex. And finally, the lack of a fixed link with Kingston General meant that there was a lingering sense of separation between those learning medicine and those practising it.

However, Bottterell Hall did, when all was said and done, mark a fundamental shift for medicine at Queen's – the medical centre of gravity at Queen's had immigrated from the picturesque, ivy-walled Medical Quadrangle, where it had existed for over a century. Concrete-sided Botterell Hall signified the arrival of "new" medicine at Queen's, even if was not ideally configured to accommodate it.[138] There was, in passing, one immediate beneficiary of this geographic shift: the New Medical Building on the old Medical Quad (ironically also subsidized by the Ontario government back in 1907 and inaugurated by Ontario's lieutenant-governor) was vacated and, with the generous support of alumna Kathleen Ryan (BA 1926, and wife of Ottawa radio entrepreneur Frank Ryan, BA 1927), renovated by 1982 into a new state-of-the-art home for the university archives.

With Great Enthusiasm

On 10 September 1982, Ron Watts reminded the executive committee of the trustees that the end of his second term as principal in mid-1984 was approaching. He told them that he had thought about seeking a third term, but had decided that a return to teaching was his priority. He was still relatively young and could see a full decade in the classroom and many challenges to Canadian federalism – his abiding academic interest – ahead. Canada had a new patriated constitution and was still smarting from a Quebec referendum that had seen the Québécois ponder the virtue of separation from Canada, only to pull back at the polls. Throughout his time in Richardson Hall, Watts had found time to engage the broader concerns of the nation. In 1977, he had agreed to serve on the Task Force on National Unity (the so-called Pépin-Robarts Commission). Both campus and country seemed in need of his mediating skills. In 1978, returning from a cross-country session of listening to the concerns of Canadians with his fellow commissioners, Watts wryly told the trustees that he had come "to the conclusion that it is Queen's graduates who hold this country together."[139] More seriously, he shared the view taken by his political-scientist colleague Richard Simeon that Queen's had a long tradition "of marrying academic excellence with public opinion."[140] By way of inducement, the Institute of Intergovernmental Relations beckoned, and there was now also the prospect of a school of policy studies at Queen's. Having always insisted as principal that he was simply *primus inter pares*, Watts chose to revert to a *pares* role in the faculty.

More importantly, Watts's decision to step down as principal reflected the accumulation of nearly ten years' wear and tear on the job. With a joint

In 1983, the Alma Mater Society celebrated its 125th anniversary. Here Principal Watts and his wife, Donna, visit the AMS offices to meet with President Sue Rooks (centre, with back turned). Watts made a point of having coffee every week with the AMS president in order to connect with the mood of Queen's students.

committee of the trustees and Senate deliberating over the choice of his successor, Watts began to reflect on the travails of being a university president in the seventies. His predecessors, Alex Corry and John Deutsch, had faced the challenge of managing expansion, of channelling growth in constructive directions, while at the same time holding true to Queen's traditions. To Watts fell the more onerous challenge of managing contraction, of cutting up an ever-shrinking pie. By the time he took office in 1974, the trajectory of his mandate seemed grimly evident. Deutsch had sternly warned the Queen's community that hard times were on the way. Despite this, Watts signalled his intention to emulate Deutsch's "rational and civilized" approach to university affairs once in office. The odds of success seemed daunting. Deutsch and Watts had, for instance, grimly watched the ignominious demise of their former colleague David Slater as president of York University in 1973; Slater, one-time dean of Graduate Studies and Research at Queen's, was overwhelmed in his attempt to find common ground between rebellious students and fractious faculty.

But Watts stayed the course. Now as he prepared to exit university administration, Watts liked to point out that the average North American university president stayed in office six years, a benchmark he had bettered by four years. Like George Grant in the late nineteenth century and Robert Wallace through the stress of thirties' depression and wartime disruption, Watts lived an arduous life as principal. In his last months in office, he liked to quip that he had accepted the job in 1974 "with great enthusiasm," and that he now embraced the thought of leaving it "with great enthusiasm." The key to understanding the Watts decade lies in understanding, not his policies, but his *style* of leadership. Like a suave provincial premier (his University of Toronto schoolmate Bill Davis comes to mind) or successful federal prime minister (Mackenzie King's twenty-two years as national leader had inspired much scholarship at Queen's), Watts instinctively understood that the preservation of a sense of central purpose provided the best foundation for action. Time and again, Watts punctuated his speeches and correspondence with talk of "collegiality." When, in 1988, the trustees asked him to reflect on the essence of Queen's governance, Watts told them that "collegiality" was "the Queen's way."[141] He realized what every good principal of Queen's had realized: that the principal's only real power lay in the power of persuasion. Hence the concepts of "pragmatism" and "flexibility" were his hallmarks and his benchmark of success was "a broadly based consensus." To this end, Watts often cited the wisdom of long-time Harvard President Derek Bok that universities were places of "genial anarchy."

Watts accordingly exercised his power in a decentralized fashion, pushing the discussion behind decision making out into faculty boards, Senate committees, innumerable principal's advisory committees, Wednesday-morning coffees with the AMS president, and consultative groups with the faculty association. Change and the preservation of Queen's tradition would only be possible if all parties in the Queen's community felt that they had been consulted. Watts hardly invented the style, but he brought a deft and patient touch to its practice. At times, he seemed more diplomat than university president. Jim Courtright, Queen's dynamic vice-principal, development, through many of the Watts years, understood the style and its benefits: "At our university there is a civility and openness to differing views on internal and external questions of the day and a polite unwillingness to be bullied by strident voices from any single sector."[142] Much the same conclusion was reached by Maclean's magazine columnist Allan Fotheringham when he visited Kingston in the spring of 1980. After quaffing beer with Queen's students at Alfie's and wandering the campus, Fotheringham concluded that Queen's abiding virtue was its "galloping egalitarianism."[143]

The Watts style was seldom fleet of foot. Consultation took time, particularly in lean times when consensus often meant more the surrender of entitlements than their acquisition. Consequently, proposed changes in academic policy and curriculum found themselves being initially introduced in the full Senate, sent for massage by a Senate committee, then returning to the full Senate for further deliberation, only to be returned to committee for final polishing. At times, the building of consensus at Queen's was glacially slow. But it was habitually consensual. Watts liked to quip that "a Watts pot never boils." When setting out his expectation of a committee's mandate or tweaking a change in policy to the Senate or the trustees, Watts frequently salted his instruction with phrases like "a talking out of the university's problems" or a "thrashing out of issues." Some found this infuriatingly slow, but for Watts the goal was always to foster a sense of inclusion and input by all parties. The rhetoric that accompanied such elaborate discussion usually came wrapped in talk of "loyalty" to Queen's, but there was always a more profound and more structured purpose in such appeals – the preservation of a community of shared interest.

Watts's diplomatic style of leadership thus kept Queen's on a stable, if slow, course through a decade of financial duress and crimped expectations. Perhaps the most outstanding success of such gradualism and inclusion was the consultative group on faculty salaries, which managed to perpetuate loyal faculty attachment to the greater purpose of the university at a time when inflation and government austerity was sapping the financial viability of Queen's. Consultation and assiduous consideration of cost and consequences did not necessarily always check or retard progress at Queen's in these austere years. In 1981, for instance, the university took a big step towards greater transparency in university governance when Board of Trustee meetings were opened to all members of the university community as observers. Under Watts, the university welcomed an Equal Employment Opportunity Officer into its midst.

Unfinished Business

There was, however, a downside to the Watts management of consensus at Queen's. His delicate calculation of consensus making often failed to fully register the concerns of those on the margins of the Queen's experience. In lean times, it was difficult enough to maintain cohesion and equilibrium among the existing parties to the Queen's compact. The acknowledgement of new interests or the accommodation of emerging problems threatened to create disequilibrium, especially when there was so little fiscal grease to apply to the squeaky wheel. So, the natural inclination was to postpone addressing such dysfunction. There was no better example of this predicament by 1984 than the still-yawning gender gap at Queen's. Despite clever initiatives, such as the preponderant appointment of women to Queen's National Scholar positions, the university found itself in the mid-eighties with a dramatic gender imbalance in its faculty and, all too often, attitudes that could only be described as sexist.

As a consequence of such halting progress, old attitudes and Queen's innate conservatism lingered.

"At the risk of sounding like a male chauvinist, I cannot think of any female member of Faculty who should be appointed to the Committee [to appoint a new dean]," one department head wrote to the principal.[144] Similarly, while the consultative group on faculty salaries worked brilliantly in holding the budgetary line and at the same time preserving faculty loyalty to a cash-strapped institution, by 1984 it was becoming apparent that that loyalty was fraying, as inflation's toll became cumulative and as other points of friction – promotion and grievance procedures – became increasingly out of kilter with professional expectations. How long could the much-touted goodwill on Queen's campus hold out?

Much the same was true of the administration's relationship with the university's rapidly changing student culture. The late years of Watts's tenure had seen more and more students detached from the old inward-looking intimacy of studenthood at Queen's. Rowdy street parties in the emerging student "Ghetto" north of campus indicated that the university's relations with its students in issues of discipline and the precious tradition of student self-government was under pressure of change. In effect, the university's list of unfinished or unaddressed issues was growing, and it called out for a response that went beyond the well-oiled, but increasingly out-of-date, system of brokerage at Queen's. The Watts years had two foretastes of this shifting world of values – controversy over the social responsibility incumbent on the university when investing its endowment in places like Chile and South Africa and the appropriateness of "religious elements" that smacked of Queen's Presbyterian origins embedded in its annual convocations (events to be addressed in a future chapter). Queen's was beginning to encounter the modern pluralistic Canada and, in many ways, was ill-prepared for the challenge.

Many nonetheless watched and admired the Watts style. In 1976, Ken Snowdon, a young graduate of Queen's with his master's of public administration degree, was taken on staff by the university's department of financial planning. Launched by Bernard Trotter in the Deutsch years, the planning office was Queen's inner sanctum of strategy. It crunched enrolment and expenditure numbers and thereby came to understand the complex and arcane workings of the BIU system, the mainstream of the university's operating budget. Snowdon came to understand the mathematics of Ontario post-secondary education better than anyone else at the university. His data and projections were the raw ingredients of the annual projection of enrolment made by the Senate Committee on Academic Development. But, beyond the all the numbers and cross-tabulations of fees, enrolment, and BIUs, Snowdon quickly came to admire the principal's overarching "core values" which all these calculations supported. Queen's excelled because Watts had sustained a campus culture that perpetuated "quality" in teaching and research. This entailed as much decentralization of decision making as possible – shared power was always better than imposed power.

Watts had thus perpetuated the "good model" of governance at Queen's. His deans were his "sectoral champions," capable of carrying his message of cohesion in tough times, but not afraid to push back if the medicine was too harsh or precipitous for their faculty.[145] Out of this chemistry, Queen's had been able to find niches and gambits by which it had been able to move forward in the Watts years and capitalize on its inherited strengths. The Queen's National Scholars, the adroit use of fundraising, and the invention of the Principal's Development Fund epitomized the gains to be made out of Watts's style of leadership.

Snowdon was not alone in admiring the Watts style. Late in 1982, the Ontario government asked Watts to join a three-member commission to study "the future development of the universities of Ontario." Heading the commission was Toronto businessman Edmund Bovey, renowned for building up the huge energy company Norcen. Bovey and Watts were joined by Fraser Mustard, a dynamic medical researcher from McMaster University. The commission's mandate was framed by the decade-long slippage in Ontario's support of its universities. In 1981, a previous report on the "future role" of the provincial universities conducted by H.K. Fisher, the deputy-minister of education, colleges and universities, had been ignominiously set aside by the Davis government when it became apparent that the politicians and universities were at loggerheads over the degree to which Toronto could exert central control over provincial campuses and the educators' strident demand that Ontario's chronic underfunding of post-secondary education be reversed. The Bovey Commission was now asked by Premier Davis to examine "practical" issues surrounding the universities: how they might bolster "quality, how they might enhance access to professional programs, and how they might differentiate their profiles." As a quid pro quo for their wisdom, the premier gave the assurance that the aggregate level of provincial spending on the universities would not be allowed to slip below current levels. Davis's minister of education, Bette Stephenson, simultaneously conveyed the message that the government was committed to action. Thus, Watts's last year as principal was heavily encroached upon by the bringing of his expertise to the broader forum of post-secondary education in Ontario.

The Bovey Report of January 1984 bore a prescriptive resemblance to Queen's journey through the last, lean decade. Ontario's universities, the report argued, must retain their autonomy at all costs and resist an encroachment on their authority by central agencies such as the Ontario Council of University Affairs. Universities should be empowered to "differentiate" themselves by becoming more competitive. Quality must be restored. To do this, there must be an immediate injection of capital. Capital projects must be approved. Library neglect of the last decade must be addressed by the injection of $25 million. Core values, such as the provision of humanities and social-science instruction must be maintained, but new frontiers of learning in areas like computing and information science must be incubated. Centres of excellence in specific disciplines were held up as accelerators of difference and competitiveness. Funding formulas needed to be freed from the sixties rigidity of the BIU system. Universities should be able to structure their enrolment within "corridors," which allowed them latitude in setting the pace of their growth.

The report acknowledged that the future of Ontario's universities was not just dependent upon more money and autonomy from Toronto. Perhaps most controversially, the Bovey commissioners recommended that tuition in Ontario become "tiered," so as to reflect the market value of the service rendered and the benefit received. Fees for professional education should be weighted to reflect the cost-benefit of the degree received. If this scenario were accepted, the report suggested that college tuition in Ontario should be allowed to increase by 25 per cent over the next five years.

Queen's liked what it read in the Bovey Report. Because Watts was a member of the commission, the university's response to the report was coordinated by dean of Nursing Alice Baumgart and later by dean of Arts and Social Sciences Rod Fraser. The Bovey recommendations, they concluded, flattered Queen's long tradition of distinctiveness: "the quality of its students" and its persistent ability "to adapt to new circumstances and changing needs." To support this alignment, Queen's official response to the report set out many instances of the university's pedagogic and research success – from the recent creation of a Biotechnology Board to the Humanities House support of research in the humanities. Above all else, Queen's welcomed the suggestion of differentiated fees, less central control, and the adoption of some new type of "block funding" as a means of breaking down the roadblock of underfunding that had plagued the Watts years.[146] Sadly, the Bovey Report brought little immediate relief. Its talk of tiered and rising tuition fees triggered an immediate public debate that deflected any discussion of constructive reform into a predictable revisiting of the issue of accessibility. Having embraced accessibility as the lodestar of post-secondary education in the sixties, Ontario now found itself trapped in the populist implications of the doctrine. Any contemplation of rejigging the financial underpinnings of Ontario university education was almost automatically cast as a betrayal of basic rights, rather than as a progressive adjustment of existing principles. In this case, the paralysis was reinforced by the fall of the province's Progressive Conservative government – "the Big Blue Machine" – after four decades of uninterrupted power. The emergence of an NDP-supported minority Liberal government under David Peterson made any fundamental rearrangement of provincial-university finances politically unpalatable.

Back at Queen's, initial optimism quickly turned to frustration. Walter Light, the new chairman of the Board of Trustees, urged his fellow trustees to go on the offensive and lobby Queen's Park directly for change. Otherwise, the university would study the report "to death." Dean Fraser concurred, grimly quoting Fraser Mustard's view that in Ontario the health and education budgets had become "ghetto budgets."[147] For Ron Watts, the only silver lining on leaving office was that since 1982 cooling inflation and a slow loosening of the provincial purse strings had seen Queen's receive annual boosts in its operating grant that exceeded its battered expectations and often included one-time special grants for such things as library upgrades and bilingual teaching.[148]

On 6 July 1983, the Board of Trustees were called together on short notice to consider a single agenda item: the selection of Queen's new principal. Despite its size, the joint committee of senators and trustees had expeditiously reached a unanimous decision, earlier than most had expected. They had been charged to seek out a "reputable scholar" who could command the "respect of his colleagues" and who "should be able to proceed in a collegial fashion and was sensitive to the various groups in the community." The mandate seemed to uncannily reflect the attributes Ron Watts had displayed as principal. Anticipating this reaction, Chancellor Benidickson, as chair of the committee, assured the trustees that every effort had been made "to identify candidates in disciplines other than Political Economy." Forty-nine applications had been received and five candidates interviewed. In the end, the committee seemed moved by the notion that the challenge of running a modern multiversity was best left in the hands of someone schooled in understanding the social, political, and economic rhythms of contemporary society. Their choice was David Smith, an economist at Queen's since 1960. On the surface, there were striking parallels with Ron Watts. Each had been born to missionary parents in faraway places – India in Smith's case. Each had careers woven into the making of public policy in Ottawa, Smith most recently as an advisor to the Royal Commission on the Economic Union. In praising Smith's "soft-spoken and approachable manner," Chancellor Benidickson seemed to hint that, as of 1 September 1984, the Watts style would continue to work its way at Queen's.[149]

7

An End to "Effortless Superiority"
David Smith, 1984–1994

*Queen's shouldn't worry about having to become too jazzy. There is
a place and necessity for a very solid, dependable place like Queen's ...
This is not a negative quality.*
Margaret Atwood, The Mission of the University, 1984

*The gap between responsibility and authority in the principalship
seems at times unfairly large.*
David Smith, quoting John Deutsch, Values at Queen's, 1990

*We now seemed to be faced with a government that has simply
discovered the "well is empty."*
Principal David Smith, 1992

Traditions under Pressure

There seemed an irrepressible quality to Queen's tradition. As preparations began for his installation as Queen's sixteenth principal, David Smith had one request: could the ceremony be staged in the capacious Jock Harty Arena? It was important, he argued, that as many people as possible attend. No, he was told, "old tradition" dictated that small-but-storied Grant Hall be the venue. So on the afternoon of 26 October 1984, more than a thousand invited guests squeezed into the grand old hall with its Corinthian columns, stained-glass windows, and wood panelling.

Perpetuating another tradition, Dr Fred Clarke of the School of Music serenaded the audience on the organ, accompanied by a forty-piece ensemble. Ominously for the incoming principal, Clarke chose to play Scott Joplin's "The Strenuous Life." Less scripted was the

arrival in the middle of the ceremony of the Queen's Bands and its troupe of cheerleaders. Down the main aisle they marched, cheerleaders perched on male shoulders – to the amazement of those unfamiliar with Queen's ways. Before departing, the drum major sprinted up onto the stage and planted a Queen's tam on Smith's head. As the band retreated, a spontaneous *Oil Thigh* broke out on the stage and spread to the floor of the hall, academic robes flailing in the midst of the kick line. "It has probably now become part of the tradition," the *Journal* suggested, "that the unexpected happen during an installation."[1]

On the preceding day, Smith had had his way. Eager to set his stamp on Queen's, he had asked for a symposium on the "mission of the university." Chaired by history professor George Rawlyk, the symposium featured an impressive array of opinion-makers. Each was asked to ponder the role of the university in the context of such challenges as increasing globalization, the contemporary relevance of the arts and humanities, and the increasingly

A spontaneous Grant Hall welcome for the new principal.

complex relationship between campus and the state. Here Grant Hall was undeniably the perfect venue. On its stage, novelist Margaret Atwood, historians Jill Conway and William McNeill, labour leader Shirley Carr, and constitutional expert David Johnston, amongst others, wrestled with the challenge of how best to connect the university with the broader needs of society. Queen's voices included economist Richard Lipsey, Fred Euringer of drama, Vivian Abrahams of physiology, and John Meisel of political studies.

The new principal used the symposium to provide a hint of his vision for Queen's: the university must become less hidebound in order to dedicate itself to a more flexible definition of quality education. This meant taking new directions in research and teaching, and fashioning a new relationship with the state, thereby asserting Queen's distinctiveness as a top-tier, national university. Queen's, he argued, must break out of the fiscal straitjacket that had constrained it for more than a decade and find a way to differentiate itself in a post-secondary culture that put universal accessibility before all other considerations. This transition provoked debate amongst the panelists. Margaret Atwood cautioned that Queen's should not abandon its old reputation as "a very solid, dependable place" by becoming "too jazzy." John Meisel, on the other hand, saw transition as unavoidable: universities were in dire danger of becoming "too complacent," he argued. Smith agreed and threw down the gauntlet: "Queen's is not a centre for the quiet contemplation of our tranquil consciousness of effortless superiority," he said. Queen's must, in short, resist "pressures for less openness."[2] It must instead attach itself to the protean society surrounding it.

David Smith's first months in office would provide jarring evidence that some of Queen's ways had to change. The annual September rite of initiating first-year students seemed, for instance, to be drifting away from acculturating newcomers to the norms of university life and instead towards hedonistic self-indulgence. On the first Saturday of term, the grease-pole climb, the culmination of Applied Science's orientation since the 1950s, had gone sadly awry. On that cold, windy, and wet day, freshman engineers had plunged into a filthy pit in a farmer's field in Barriefield in a quest to snatch an elusive tam from the top of the pole. Second-year FRECS hurled verbal abuse – and detritus ranging from tomatoes to beer bottles – at the novitiates. Mayhem ensued. Twenty-four frosh emerged from the ordeal with injuries varying from cracked ribs to hypothermia. The entire ambulance service in eastern Ontario had to be mobilized. After nearly three hours of futility, the pursuit of the tam was abandoned. Back on campus, there was outrage. John Stackhouse, the editor of the *Journal*, editorialized that the grease-pole event was "nothing more than sheer barbarism unquestionably blessed with the name 'tradition.'"[3]

Things got worse. Two weeks later, buses bore a horde of Queen's student up Highway 401 to Montreal, where, in a "Kill McGill" mood, many Queen's students drunkenly invaded Molson Stadium. On the field, the Gaels, under quarterback Peter Harrison, ran roughshod over the Redmen, 59–30. In the stands, however, Queen's students behaved with such abandon that the Montreal riot squad was summoned. At halftime, there was mock, on-field fornication with the McGill mascot. After the game, Queen's students took their usual trophy of the opponent's goalposts, but then moved on to tear up strips of Astroturf. That evening, Montreal's downtown streets were full of carousing Queen's students. The press coverage of the incident was not flattering. Barely in office, David Smith was obliged to send a letter of apology to McGill Principal David Johnston (who was soon to be his guest at the installation symposium). When outraged trustees demanded that the AMS discipline its errant members, AMS president John Lougheed shared their disgust but wondered whether the judicial arm of the student government reached as far as Molson Stadium. Nonetheless, the AMS sheepishly sent McGill a cheque for $750 to pay for stadium damages. The AMS council passed a motion dedicating itself to changing "the attitude that exuberance and intoxication are excuses for public disturbances, obscene language, or petty vandalism."[4]

Three weeks later, similar boorish behaviour enveloped Homecoming, the much-cherished annual reconnection of alumni with their alma mater. Some elements of the weekend lived up to the traditional conviviality of Homecoming: Science '83's imaginative Robin Hood float took top honours in the Saturday-morning parade before appreciative alumni. That afternoon at Richardson Stadium, the Gaels obliged the festive mood by flattening the University of Ottawa Gee-Gees 52–1. It was only when the sun set that the mood shifted from excited to reckless. On both Friday and Saturday evenings, spontaneous street parties sprang up along University Avenue north of the campus. Beer flowed and an open-air rock concert fractured the night. When Vice-Principal Duncan Sinclair and AMS President Lougheed moved into the crowd in an attempt to calm the turmoil, they were jeered and jostled. Kingston police laid sixty-four charges for disorderly behaviour. The police blotter later revealed that only a quarter of those charged were Queen's students. A handful of the scofflaws were alumni, but the majority of revellers were not associated with the university. "I've had enough, I really have," complained Kingston mayor, John Gerretsen, who promptly sent the university a bill for police overtime. *Journal* editor Stackhouse found street parties "disgusting and embarrassing," and again called for reform. Kingston *Whig-Standard* publisher Michael Davies later put his finger on the problem: Queen's was incubating "an instant tradition" that must be nipped in the bud.[5]

Homecoming excess was the most obvious sign of shifts taking place in the ethos of the Queen's community, some of it transmitted into the university by outside social, economic, and demographic pressures, and others morphing spontaneously on campus. David Smith was the first principal to take office in Canada's new era of Charter rights. Students were now indisputably full citizens, whose personal lives at Queen's would be lived completely under their own cognizance. Queen's administrators were left armed only with moral suasion, something that was becoming increasingly difficult to exercise. As enrolment edged upwards, the student community increasingly infiltrated Sydenham Ward north of the campus, beyond the traditional bailiwick of the university. This state of affairs not only tested the broader reputation of the university, but more immediately challenged the storied self-governance of Queen's students. Did, for instance, the jurisdiction of the long-effective AMS Court – now dubbed the "AMS Judicial Committee" – extend into the so-called Ghetto? Did its mandate supersede or complement that of the civil authority that prevailed in residential areas throughout Kingston? Did Charter rights trump Queen's long-standing Code of Conduct? Could the university still aspire to shape the non-academic deportment of its students? An early 1980s attempt to add a clause to the Code of Conduct proscribing any behaviour calculated to bring Queen's into "disrepute" had, for instance, been quashed on account of its amorphous ambition in an age of defined rights.

Similar pressures were obliging the Alma Mater Society to reorient itself. Few questioned the student government's established servicing of quotidian campus life, but in an age of rights, many asked whether the AMS should increasingly turn its attention to external affairs. The provision of adequate housing off-campus was an obvious and pressing issue. But there were other areas of concern, such as exerting social responsibility in the investment of the university's endowment. In short, was Queen's to remain a pleasant, somewhat introverted, place of *preparation* for life, or was it to serve as a venue for student *participation* in broader socioeconomic debates stretching from the apartheid townships of South Africa to the abortion rights in Kingston?

The bold strategic challenge facing David Smith was thus twofold. As the raucous events surrounding his installation had vividly demonstrated, the social mores and values of campus life needed to be adjusted to a world that no longer tolerated universities living a cloistered existence, detached from the society that supported them. Immigration, Charter rights, and social pluralism had changed Canadian society dramatically since the 1960s. The time had come for universities, particularly those such as Queen's – with its sense of ingrained superiority – to align themselves with the new Canada beyond their campuses. Inclusion, not subtle exclusion, was the new byword. This would encompass everything from building better town-gown relations to attuning campus discipline to an age of Charter rights. Principal Smith would also face the challenge of shifting the corporate culture, attitudes, and policies underlying Queen's administration. For all its magnificence, the traditionalism and habitual gradualism of Queen's was slipping out of kilter with the increasingly contractual and confrontational society that surrounded it. Queen's was losing its old organic culture. David Smith would find himself at times awkwardly resisting this shift and at other times acting as its handmaiden. This began with the challenge of administrative transition and would flow though into Queen's adjustment to the new pluralism and diversity in Canadian society.

Queen's Faces a New Strategic Landscape

If student culture at Queen's was experiencing dramatic shifts, so too was that of the faculty and staff. Ron Watts had bequeathed Smith a relatively cohesive academic establishment, one bound in co-operative consensus by the Consultative Group. That body, now a decade into its existence, had been successful in brokering the salary expectations of the faculty association against the budgetary limitations of the administration. More recently, however, that compromise had become increasingly frayed by inflation and freighted with society's stepped-up expectations of employers – notably policies imposed from off-campus requiring greater equity, accountability, and social justice. Internal pressures accentuated the growing strain on the relationship – the need to accelerate the entry of women to faculty ranks, updating grievance procedures, and regularizing the tenure and promotion process. Could the centre hold? Could Queen's ingrained collegiality embrace so many new dimensions in the relation between professor and administrator? Or would the first tentative calls for a more formalized relation – perhaps even collective bargaining – that had been heard under Watts grow into a chorus? Moreover, much the same drift towards a more formalized communal relationship was evident in the ranks of Queen's administrative staff and even its graduate students.

Behind this increasingly nervous partnership there were emerging pedagogic pressures. How could a faculty locked into place by tenure and deeply rooted departmental autonomy be reconfigured to accommodate the demands of a society vaulting into an age of information technology and globalization? How could new disciplines of social relevance, such as women's and environmental studies, be worked into the university's curriculum? Such questions invariably begged further questions about finding the financial wherewithal to pay for such reconfiguration, let alone to expand Queen's bricks and mortar. In 1984, neither the provincial nor the federal government seemed in an expansive mood. Ronald Watts and his vice-principals had deftly succeeded in running Queen's on a shoestring, often reluctantly sailing into deficit waters. The 1983–84 financial year had produced a small mercy: a slim surplus of $68,000. Queen's Park nonetheless showed every sign of clinging to its mantra of accessibility, while at the same time preaching frugality in the public sector. Ontario continued to slip in the national rankings of provincial support to post-secondary education. This despite the fact that the Bovey Report on the "future development" of Ontario's universities had preached the need for the restoration of quality post-secondary education through enhanced funding and a willingness to let universities differentiate themselves through competition. Queen's had backed this reformist prescription, but David Smith did not seem sanguine about the post-Bovey world. At his first Senate meeting, he flatly stated that Queen's hope for an end to chronic underfunding and freedom to pursue its own distinctiveness "could not be satisfactorily dealt with by fiddling with the system in a minor fashion."[6]

Smith carried much the same uninspiring message to the trustees in the fall of 1984: his expectation of better funding from Toronto was "not very high," and, he added, he also worried that Ottawa might reduce the Established Programs Financing it poured into provincial coffers to support universities.[7] Post-secondary education once again seemed at the mercy of federal-provincial political gamesmanship. Trustees shared the new principal's gloomy fiscal prognosis. Toronto financier James Leech, a recent Queen's MBA (and future chancellor), told his fellow trustees that he despaired of Queen's ever becoming "world-class" under such stingy circumstances. "The Provincial Government," he protested, "the major source of funds, has no interest in creating a world-class institution, but only in keeping voters satisfied."[8] It seemed ominously clear, therefore, that Queen's was going to have to devise a new revenue strategy, one that diversified revenue and one that had the temerity to break the orthodoxy of provincial university funding by broaching the idea of market-driven fees unfettered by political constraint.

If forbidding fiscal challenges lay ahead, so did nagging concerns about the internal governance of Queen's. The Board of Trustees had traditionally played a reactive, contemplative role in guiding the material well-being of the university. Now, under the chairmanship of Toronto lawyer Norman McLeod Rogers (until 1985) and then Queen's-educated Walter Light of Northern Telecom, there was pressure for the Board to become more assertive in carrying the university's agenda into the broader Canadian community. Light urged his fellow trustees to become more involved with "people in government," suggesting that they seek interviews with Queen's Park politicians. He worried that outside decision-makers had an ill-informed perception of the universities' predicament, one partially the result of financial reporting systems that did "not make their problems clear."[9] For its part, the Board, he argued, should engage in strategic planning sessions that explicitly set out the university's goals. Other seasoned business executives on the Board – such as David Leighton of the Banff Centre and David Rigsby of Alcan – joined the chorus, Leighton stressing that "quality" would be an elusive goal until Queen's achieved a more diversified financial base. Leighton also embodied a feeling among many of the business-oriented trustees that Queen's needed more forceful leadership, leadership less beholden to academic consensus. Endless committee meetings, he suggested, "might be the price universities have to pay for a collegial governing structure," but this often deflected attention from the "'real challenge' of 'effective leadership.'"[10] The necessity of putting a more assertive face on Queen's governance was reinforced by the activism of Chancellor Agnes Benidickson, who saw herself as an advocate for Queen's well beyond the traditional ceremonial boundaries of her post. First appointed by the university council in 1980, Benidickson was not only the first woman chancellor, but was also the first to have had a family member – her father, James – precede her in the post. (She recalled her father singing "Queen's College Colours" each morning as he shaved.) She was regularly reappointed, a reflection on her assiduous coast-to-coast work with Queen's alumni and her constant burnishing of Queen's national brand. (Tellingly, in Ottawa Benidickson drove a white Cadillac with custom "Queen's One" plates.)

If there was an expectation that the Board make more of its external-affairs role, there was also growing concern that the Senate needed reawakening to its pivotal oversight of Queen's intellectual well-being. After its burst of energy in the sixties and seventies as the arbiter of academic procedure at Queen's, the Senate, many felt, had slowly slipped into quiescence. Students, for instance, seemed to lose their enthusiasm for sitting on the Senate and its committees. From the faculty perspective, the Senate's power seemed to have been diminished by the growing power of departments and deans in governing academic life. Some went as far to suggest that the Senate had returned to its fifties' status as a "rubber stamp."[11]

Others remarked that the pendulum of "power" on campus seemed to be swinging back towards Richardson Hall, where the ethos of planning and externally mandated policy was slowly aggrandizing the central administration. Principal Smith, as Watts had done before him, nonetheless reminded the Senate every fall that it was the central representative crucible of university opinion and that its members' function was to participate in that process, not simply to voice the narrow concerns of one particular Queen's constituency. All too often, however, the Senate seemed to be bogged down in interminable debate that sawed back and forth among its many committees and its plenary meetings. If Queen's were to successfully restructure its academic programs, entitlements, and procedures, the Senate would have to be revivified.

Principal Dave

In the fall of 1984, David Smith found himself uncomfortably caught in all these currents of change. A cartoon in the *Journal* captured his situation. "Welcome to Queen's, Dave," the caption read, while the image showed members of the Queens' community, ranging from fuzzy-haired students to sombre professors, draping the new principal with robes inscribed with "Bovey Commission, street parties, non-academic discipline, tuition fees, Homecoming, and grease pole."[12] "Dave" was,

"Welcome to Queen's, Dave!" A *Queen's Journal* cartoon reminds the new principal that his mantle of responsibility was already weighed down with issues that suggested the university could no longer blithely rely on its storied traditions to automatically guide it.

of course, no stranger to Queen's; he had arrived there as a young economist two-and-a-half decades earlier. And, if there was one thing he understood about Queen's culture, it was that it aspired to be a consensual place. The principal possessed little power beyond that of elucidation and moral suasion. Smith would frequently cite John Deutsch's remark that "the gap between responsibility and authority in the principalship seems at times unfairly large!" Like Watts, he pledged allegiance to the "Queen's tradition of a non-authoritarian approach," a tradition that made "it difficult always to know how to act promptly and decisively without at the same time flouting legitimate demands for consultation, democratic decision, and due process."[13] This predicament, then, would be the abiding dilemma facing the new principal: promoting a dramatic shift in Queen's culture, and then managing that change without fracturing the university's sense of community.

Remarkably, David Smith was the fifth principal to be drawn from the pool of political-economy talent at Queen's. Although the economics department had formally separated from political studies in 1964, there seemed to be a penchant at Queen's to draw on these first cousins as a reliable reservoir of

Dave Smith was no stranger to Queen's. Eight years after joining Queen's in 1960, he became head of the economics department, helping to adjust it to the rapidly changing world of the "new economics." Low-keyed and convivial, Smith was a believer in walking about, stopping to chat with colleagues and students alike. Queen's principals seldom adopted haughty demeanours; the campus was too intimate and convivial. Here Smith chats with an attentive freshman in 1972.

leadership. Political scientists and economists were schooled in the dialectics of society – the brokering and aggregation of individual interests for the greater good. While the selection committee chaired by Agnes Benidickson made a point of denying any such predisposition, in the end it chose Smith because he seemed to hold out such convivial potential. David Smith himself did not, in fact, apply for the position. He was instead nominated by admiring colleagues. They did so because Smith, as its head from 1968 to 1981, had ably guided the economics department through its own dramatic transition.

A labour-markets specialist with a Harvard doctorate, Smith had come to Queen's in 1960 with no previous exposure to its culture. His university roots reached back to a 1953 BA from McMaster, followed by additional undergraduate and graduate studies at Oxford. Before Queen's, he had taught briefly at Berkeley in California. There, the first stirrings of American student radicalism were evident, events from which Smith drew the lesson that problems were better talked out than acted out. Smith's family roots spread even farther. His father had been a quixotic Baptist minister, who had served as a missionary in India. When war came in 1914, Smith senior forsook the cloth and became the commander of a Sikh cavalry regiment. At war's end, he headed for Mesopotamia, where he fought alongside T.E. Lawrence (the renowned Lawrence of Arabia) in the campaign to capture Damascus and establish an independent Arab state. When the French capture of Damascus from King Faisal in 1920 dashed that hope, he returned to the pulpit in India, where son David was born in 1931. In 1939, the Smith family returned to Canada. Although David Smith did not retain his father's formal devotion to the Baptist faith, he did retain a "strong Baptist conscience," the cardinal feature of which was the discipline to remain "very focused" on goals.[14] His graduate study on how labour markets worked seemed to reinforce a belief that problems should be addressed in a deliberate, rationalist fashion from initial encounter to eventual solution, in much the same fashion as an economist formulated theories of economic behaviour.

When he took on the economics headship in 1968, Smith found both his discipline and the Queen's department in transition. The old world of economics, with its focus on macroeconomics and economic history, was fast being overtaken by a growing interest in the so-called "New Economics," with its focus of quantification and theory. Perhaps symbolic of the transition, venerable Frank Knox had retired from the department in 1964, leaving behind the powerful legacy of ECON 4, with its sweeping view of the economic landscape. Many of the new appointments in the department reflected the much-celebrated "Samuelson Revolution" (named for Paul Samuelson, the MIT economist who would win the Nobel Prize in Economic Science in 1970), with its bent for microeconomics and arcane methodologies such as econometrics. The dilemma at Queen's was how to blend old-school economics – with its storied record of teaching and input to national decision making – with the quantifying bent of the New Economics. Much the same tension existed across the hall in Dunning Hall in the School of Business, where the old orthodoxies of accounting and banking practice were being challenged in the sixties by clever new approaches to business management and planning.

Thus, just as Dean Richard Hand had deftly blended the old and the new in the business faculty, David Smith created, as one of his colleagues, John Hartwick, noted, "a department in the modern idiom."[15] He recruited many promising young economists – Dan Usher, Rod Fraser, Doug Purvis, David Dodge (another future chancellor), James McKinnon, to name a few – but was at the same time careful to ensure a macro-micro balance within the department. He demonstrated, Hartwick recalled, "a very delicate touch in interpersonal relations." Smith disliked confrontation and sought to build a "compatible staff." His focus was on making the economics department a stellar national group. To crown this ambition, Queen's appointed Richard Lipsey its Sir Edward Peacock Professor in Economics in 1970. Lipsey, with his globally bestselling survey text in economics, brought star quality. The sixties thus proved a restless decade in which to head an economics department. Many young academic economists, for instance, left for better-paying work in the public and corporate world. Fellow labour economist David Dodge, for instance, left Queen's to take up a career in public policy in Ottawa. Smith nonetheless built the department into a national powerhouse, one that was "intellectually vibrant" and full of "camaraderie."[16]

Despite his success in the economics department, Smith was inclined to see himself as an "outsider"[17] in the Queen's hierarchy; he had never been a dean and had spent his career within his department. Shortly after stepping down as department head in 1981, Smith accepted an invitation from former federal finance minister Donald Macdonald to become director of research for a royal-commission inquiry into the competitiveness of the Canadian economy in the emerging global economy. Created by soon-to-retire Prime Minister Pierre Trudeau, the awkwardly named Royal Commission on the Economic Union and Development Prospects for Canada was to be a broad-front investigation of Canada's economic strengths and weaknesses. In accepting the position, Smith was perpetuating Queen's formative role in shaping Canadian public policy: in the thirties, Mackintosh and Deutsch had gone to Ottawa as researchers for the ground-breaking Rowell-Sirois Royal Commission. In Ottawa, Smith helped the royal commissioners to identify research needs, and then farmed out the actual empirical work to academics across the nation.

The call from Benidickson's search committee came as a surprise, but Smith quickly responded. Interviewed off-campus in an old stone house on Emily Street, he was "ignited" by the prospect of the principalship.[18] He told the committee that his vision for Queen's hinged on arresting what he believed had been the slow erosion of its distinctive reputation for quality education. Mediocrity, he sensed, was creeping onto the campus; there was a worrisome gap at Queen's between what many construed as its preternatural superiority and its sagging ability to deliver on that reputation in a climate of perpetual fiscal constraint. Smith told the search committee that his focus as principal would be on internal matters, rather than external issues. While this ingenuously overlooked the increasingly unavoidable external relations of the university – something that Watts had discovered demanded frequent trips to Toronto and Ottawa to lobby decision-makers and cheque-writers – Smith would dedicate himself to mending fences on campus before all else. He would strive to restore Queen's "effortless superiority," yet alter its parameters and values. His determination to preserve the fabric of the university community put him squarely on the path trod by his predecessor, Ron Watts. Smith already had a reputation for strolling about the campus, making friendly contact with students and faculty he encountered. But his simultaneous desire for reconstruction and ongoing cohesion would require innovative solutions and a sensitivity to the nuances of an increasingly complex community. The unruly events of the fall of 1984 on Queen's campus provided David Smith with the first indication of how hard it would really be to maintain that balance.

Adjusting the Old Order

Defining Queen's Vision

In the mid-1980s, the corporate world embraced the "mission statement" as a means of focusing the vision and energies of an organization. Up-and-coming high-tech companies such as Apple Computer set out mission statements – "making tools for the mind that advance mankind" – that put a progressive edge on what they aspired to do. Mission statements were prisms of "corporate culture," another passion of business in the eighties. Corporate culture was framed as the distillation of day-to-day values in a successful organization. Customers and employees alike would thus be under no illusion as to the enterprise's dedication to its products and the society it served. Critics remarked that mission statements tended to be vacuous or clichéd. Nonetheless, they became a pervasive trend, spilling over into non-profit organizations such as Canada's Terry Fox Foundation, and inevitably into the world of higher education. Harvard, for instance, rather smugly hinted that its 1636 motto – "*Veritas*" – was the first post-secondary mission statement in North America. Arriving at a mission statement was in itself seen as a focusing exercise, a winnowing of the inessential from the essential within an organization. Around that definition, all other operational aspects of university operation – revenues, curriculum, faculty development – could theoretically be calibrated. For David Smith, that calibration would revolve around the *quality* of a Queen's education and the *values* embedded in it. As if to underscore his determination, Smith immediately activated Watts's scheme of renewing the faculty by recruiting Queen's National Scholars, but added a decisive strategic twist to its purpose: women (and later visible-minority) candidates would be given preference, all other things being equal, in any competition. Consequently, Queen's was soon able to recruit some women professors to its faculty ranks, women such as philosopher Christine Overall and epistemologist Rena Upitis. The gender tide was finally turning.

However bright, new faces in departmental corridors did not constitute a thoroughgoing strategic remaking of Queen's mission. That would take time, and consultation. From the outset, Smith sought greater, more activist, input from the Board of Trustees. Walter Light, of burgeoning Northern Telecom, who became Board chairman in 1985, proved a strong ally. Light was direct, and impatient with the glacial pace of academic deliberation. At the end of each Board meeting, he would, for instance, make a show of throwing the thick dossier of briefing documents given each trustee into the wastebasket as he departed, as if to indicate that it was time to move on to new matters. Smith and Light formed a close kinship, one often conducted through long-distance telephone calls. Joined by other like-minded trustees, Smith and Light engaged the Board in an effort to map a revitalized strategic path for Queen's.

Trustee James Leech, drawing on his Bay Street expertise, undertook to head a task force on "revenue enhancement"[19] to build a broader and more stable financial base for Queen's, one less dependent on the largesse of government. Its May 1987 report broached the thorny challenge of convincing Queen's Park to deregulate university tuition fees. All agreed that this would be difficult, with politicians unwilling to forsake the creed of accessibility. There was also the sense that, while the province's older, well-established universities would welcome an opportunity to break out of the grip of government-mandated fees, the province's smaller, newer campuses would resist such a drift to what most perceived as a two-tiered post-secondary system. But increased fees, the Leech task force pointed out, would allow Queen's to bolster its distinctiveness: at current enrolment – 15,335 full- and part-time undergraduate and graduate students in the fall of that year – every $100 hike in fees would garner an extra million dollars for Queen's. Beyond fatter fees, the Leech Report advocated higher discretionary, non-tuition fees, enhanced overhead payments on funded research, and more-aggressive fundraising, especially from the university's 65,000 alumni.[20]

Other Board task forces investigated the need to raise awareness of Queen's in the public mind. To accentuate this necessity, a new vice-principal, institutional relations, had been created in 1984, and former dean of Arts and Science, Duncan Sinclair, with his long familiarity with Queen's, was slotted into the position. A 1986 task force on external relations subsequently examined the image of the university outside its long-comfortable Ontario hinterland and concluded that Queen's "was not yet a national university" and that "some means must be found to make Queen's better known."[21] A follow-up study on the "perception of Queen's" reported that the university department of public relations should be bolstered.[22] Consequently, in 1986, Tom Williams, with his dynamic record as dean of Education, took over the institutional-relations role when Sinclair moved to the post of vice-principal, services. The institutional-relations mandate rapidly expanded to embrace everything from harmonizing town-and-gown relations through to elevating Queen's profile nation-wide. Working with the director of the Alumni Association, Bob Buller, Williams began to model a new communications strategy for Queen's, one involving everything from its image in the media through to the creation of advisory groups to assist in the placing of Queen's in the national dialogue.[23]

In an effort to refocus the trustees on Queen's long-term strategy, the Board began devoting the last part of their weekend meetings to "theme sessions," focusing on big-picture issues. These sessions were primed with detailed statistical analysis and expert opinion. Ken Snowdon, as the university's director of research, briefed the Board on a series of "university indicators" that his department had developed.[24] How, for instance, did Queen's compare in terms of Ontario Scholars attracted into first year? Similarly, in conjunction with the annual meeting of the university council in 1987, the Board listened to Hannah Gray, the president of the University of Chicago (and the first woman president of a major American university) tell them that a university's reputation for quality rested primarily on having quality faculty, something that Queen's already seemed to be getting right with its National Scholars program.[25] Cumulatively, the Board of Trustees in the late 1980s thus took on a more corporatized purpose – digesting facts and figures, balancing the long view against short-term necessity, and setting a "mission." The rub would lie in conveying such perspectives to a broader university community that traditionally regarded itself as self-regulating and calibrated its productivity by less-objective, less-responsive criteria. The challenge would also lie in convincing Queen's Park to allow the university to pursue a path of its own defining.

New Fiscal Corridors

In support of this new mission, many trustees heeded Light's advice and became activist ambassadors for the university. In 1985, after four decades of Tory government, Ontario electors elected a Liberal government headed by David Peterson. The next year Light joined the chairs of other Ontario university boards in lobbying the new premier for enhanced funding. Peterson suavely assured them that his government placed a "premium" on university education, but that other "priorities and rationalization" needed to be respected. A chagrined Walter Light reported the news to his own board, arguing strongly that Queen's would have to forcefully fashion its own strategy for differentiation.[26] This realization was reinforced when the Board vice-chairman, *Whig-Standard* publisher Michael Davies, buttonholed Lyn McLeod, colleges and universities minister, and asked what chance there was that university tuition might be freed from strict regulation. McLeod immediately trotted out the accessibility mantra.

Queen's Park did, however, yield some ground. Queen's and other established universities had argued through the seventies that the basic income unit (BIU) formula for funding Ontario's universities, for all its equitability, had an Achilles heel. The BIU system was predicated on growth, and rewarded individual universities for each student that passed through its portals. For universities such as Queen's – with its "steady state" commitment – the BIU system in effect penalized them for not growing. The Bovey Commission had acknowledged this dilemma, citing the concept of the "the tragedy of the commons," an idea made popular by environmentalist Garrett Hardin in the sixties. Hardin pointed out that communally held pasture could be infringed upon by aggressive private landowners, thereby aggrandizing their turf, while at the same time depleting the broader society's well-being. In the context of Ontario's universities, the province's newer universities, eager to establish their footprint in postsecondary education, were doing much the same thing – drawing down on a fixed budgetary allocation at the expense of universities already operating satisfactorily within their self-determined sphere.

Queen's had generally welcomed the Bovey Report because it had recognized this conundrum. In shaping Queen's response to the report, Smith and his colleague in economics (now dean of Arts and Science) Rod Fraser, argued that the report's

Queen's students protest the Bovey Report and its recommendation that fees be raised by 25 per cent over the next five years. The late-twentieth century would see a fundamental tension emerge between university administrations, eager to grow tuition at a time of shrinking government support, and students, who felt increasingly pinched by the above-inflation rise in the cost of their education.

recommendations held out the prospect of a more stable funding base, while at the same time allowing the university the fiscal security to diversify into new areas, such as biotechnology, and to intensify its research efforts. Briefing the Senate on Queen's response to Bovey, Dean Fraser argued that "block funding" tailored to an individual university's distinct mission would allow Queen's to concentrate on quality rather than quantity. A block-grant system offered stability, simplicity, and predictability. Within its own fiscal bubble, Fraser wistfully suggested, a university might be allowed to set "differential tuition fees."[27] In the wake of the Bovey Report, a discussion paper entitled *Strategy for 1985 to 1990* was circulated to the trustees and the Senate. It underscored a dedication to "particular institutional objectives," thereby pointing to an agenda of "qualitative standards" for projects ranging from accelerating of new information technologies in the library to the recruitment of more women scholars.[28]

In 1987, the Peterson government finally modified the BIU formula by introducing a "corridor" system of managing enrolment. That is to say, each university would negotiate a corridor, which would place an upper and lower limit on its enrolment. The corridor would reflect the "planned capacity" of that campus to deliver post-secondary education. In any year, a university would aim for the "midpoint" in that corridor when recruiting new students, and would receive appropriate BIUs to sustain that enrolment. The system allowed a discretionary zone of plus or minus 3 per cent of midpoint enrolment; any university straying out of its corridor would be penalized in its BIU payout. Universities wishing to add new academic capacities could negotiate for an adjustment in their corridor basement and ceiling. Universities could also apply for one-time special funding to introduce new fields or programs. Every autumn, university administrators would trek to Toronto to negotiate their university's corridor. This approach allowed for the fine tuning of enrolment. In 1989, Queen's, for instance, negotiated to stabilize its Arts and Science admission, while at the same increasing admission into the Faculty of Education by 145 and seeking permission to expand the Faculty of Law from 450 to as many as 540 by 1994.[29]

The new system had the virtue of reducing interuniversity bidding wars for students, while allowing individual universities to adjust their programs to new opportunities. Queen's Park welcomed the scheme, because it promised to cap the overall growth of universities, while preserving the notion of accessibility. Principal Smith both helped to fashion and supported the corridor system because it allowed Queen's to stay within parameters appropriate to its capacities and ambitions – an undergraduate enrolment of about 10,500 and a graduate-student cohort of 1,800. Each year the Senate's Academic Development Committee, aided by Snowdon and his researchers, established Queen's midpoint target within the corridor for the upcoming year's enrolment. Given the high quality of applicants to Queen's, that benchmark was annually met with uncanny accuracy.

The Liberal government in Toronto also loosened a fiscal belt that had long been constricting the universities. In 1985, David Smith had chaired a Council of Ontario Universities (COU) task force on fees, where his expertise in the relation of prices and labour markets was turned on the fees paid by Ontario university students. The government seemed to entertain the COU argument that there was too much rigidity in university tuition. That year, it began allowing individual universities to exceed the "formula fee," set under the BIU system, by 10 per cent. In the past, any university that hiked its fees over the mandated BIU level saw that gain clawed back out of its operating grant. Now, as long as increased revenue did not exceed 110 per cent of the overall grant, the gain stayed with the university. Thus, for the first time in decades, an element of price competition appeared in university recruitment. Trusting in its sterling reputation and persistently high application rate, Queen's adopted a policy of annually setting its fee structure at 110 per cent of the provincial average. This eased the fiscal situation, while allowing politicians to maintain their general, if somewhat loosened, commitment to accessibility.[30]

But the corridor system controlled volume, not quality, given that it did nothing to alleviate the per-capita underfunding of post-secondary education that had persisted in Ontario since the grim seventies. Without some upward per-BIU financial adjustment, Queen's ability to pursue any further definition of quality was limited. In the spring of 1985, vice-principal, resources, David Bonham had reported that the university's $103-million operating budget from the previous year would likely see a slim surplus, but the surplus had been made possible by the transfer of one million dollars from the university's endowment and the generous use of the Principal's Development Fund. The budget situation was also alleviated by a trend to targeted financing of university education. Queen's began, for instance, to seek out dedicated funding for endowed chairs. In 1986, chairs in cancer research, supported by the Stauffer Foundation, and marketing research, funded by Nabisco Limited, were established. In 1986, sensing this trend towards niche financing of post-secondary education, the Liberal government in Toronto unveiled its University Excellence Fund, which invited universities to tender proposals for one-time funding of specific programs. From this initiative, Queen's garnered just under three million dollars in support of library and research enhancement.[31]

Beyond these targeted enhancements, however, there was no fundamental structural adjustment to address underfunding. Queen's still ran on a financial shoestring. In the spring of 1986, Smith frankly told the trustees that he saw no sign whatever of Toronto acceding to the Bovey Report's call for tuition fees to be boosted from 15 to 25 per cent of university operating expenses. With his keen business eye, Walter Light pointed out that, over the last decade, inflation had steadily reduced the proportion that students contributed to university running costs. Students were, in effect, getting less for less. On the academic front line, Applied Science dean,

David Bacon, would, for example, report that his faculty was falling behind in the provision of all-important classroom teaching equipment. His faculty needed $12 million to refurbish its teaching aids, but was able to spend a meagre $250,000 a year. "We are spending less per student than almost all other engineering schools in Ontario," Bacon complained. "It means that our students are getting less than a first-class education."[32]

"The Qualities of a Queen's Education"

In one very direct way, David Smith perpetuated the style of governance practised by his predecessors John Deutsch and Ron Watts – the consensual identification of intrinsic Queen's values and the most appropriate strategy for protecting and extending them. The favoured instrument for such explorations was the principal's advisory committee. Much as the federal government in Ottawa fell back on royal commissions to delve into (and, some suggested, delay solution of) matters of national importance, so too did Queen's resort to broad-based deliberation to delve into its problems and the options available to it. The process was predicated on consensus building, but it was also time-consuming and tilted towards gradualism. And, given the rigidities of tenure and the need to respect academic freedom, such inquiries did not necessarily lead to decisive strategic correction. The Smith years would thus be characterized by all-too-familiar attempts to spell out the "Queen's way," punctuated by periodic attempts to invent new policies to perpetuate such "values."

Queen's latest attempt to define its mission and attach it to a viable revenue stream culminated in 1989, when David Smith issued a special Principal's Report that crystalized the "qualities of a Queen's education."[33] The report read like a sales pitch. Smith set the stage by utilizing many of the "performance indicators" developed by Snowdon to demonstrate the strength of the Queen's brand. Bar graphs and statistical tables were employed to quantify the quality of a Queen's education. More than 70 per cent of entry-level Queen's students were Ontario Scholars, the highest such entry rate in the province. Other benchmarks – such as sponsored research as a percentage of general operating funds and the growth of doctoral studies – reinforced the message that Queen's exceeded national averages in much of its student academic performance. Queen's student-faculty ratio, after deteriorating in the cash-strapped seventies, had levelled off at about 15.5:1 by 1989, thanks largely to Queen's National Scholar hires.

Smith then sketched the qualities of the education that made this performance possible. In terms of undergraduate enrolment, Queen's appeared "to be about right" in size. That is to say, it was just large enough to offer a broad array of academic programs, but not so large that it incurred any of the drawbacks – anonymity, lack of contact with professors – evident on larger campuses. At the graduate level, Smith saw room for Queen's to expand to about 20 per cent of full-time enrolment, especially since there would be growing demand in Canada for young professors to replace the aging sixties cohort nearing the end of their careers. Queen's was also "national" in the composition of its student body; 14 per cent of its student body came from outside its home province, more than at any other major Canadian university. Smith acknowledged that, by contrast, Queen's lagged in attracting international undergraduate students – although it did have students from thirty-five other countries on its campus. Overall, the entrance qualifications of students coming to Queen's consistently bested national averages.

Scholarship expenditures per student were among the highest in the country. Special efforts were being made to adjust the university's admission policies to accommodate such demographic realities as the need to welcome mature students and accommodate students with disabilities. Faculty was being diversified through programs such as the Queen's National Scholars; by 1989, 35.7 per cent of tenured faculty were women, a significant breakthrough. Smith rounded out his portrait of Queen's as a "quality" institution by setting out statistics suggesting that its expenditures on computing and library support were well above the national average.

Smith crowned his hortative sermon on Queen's virtues by asserting that the university possessed "a set of characteristics distinctive among Canadian universities: it is medium size; the academic quality of the students and programs exceptionally high; a strong sense of spirit and loyalty to the institution develops among the students and graduates; the high quality of the undergraduate work is accompanied and reinforced by strong and growing professional and graduate programs, by impressive research and scholarship, and by an advancing of the University's tradition of service."[34]

Queen's Goes on the Offensive: A "Blueprint for Action"

Rhetoric could lead to action. Smith's sermon came with a kicker: Queen's mission of quality could not be maintained under the present financial arrangements with the province. The "meeting of Queen's educational goal requires a level of expenditure per student," Smith declared, "above the average provided by public funding."[35] With government financial support now constituting only 50 per cent of university operating budgets, "the case for new funding initiatives" was "strong." And for that, Queen's had another, more assertive, document: a *Blueprint for Action*. This was designed to shake up Queen's – and hopefully other universities' – fiscal relationship with the government and the broader Canadian community. It drew its momentum from the trustees' Task Force on Revenue Enhancement. As mentioned earlier, that task force had reported in May 1987 on what it considered Queen's desperate need to diversify its revenues, especially as government subsidization of universities continued to shrink.

The Leech Report, however, harboured little optimism that Queen's Park would entirely surrender its prerogative to set tuition-fee levels, thereby allowing a university such as Queen's to match its revenues with its ambitions. Politically, such deregulation would invite cries that the government had breached the dike of accessibility and thrown post-secondary education open to invidious competition. The Leech Report therefore argued that Queen's might still push for higher tuition, but it should also become much more entrepreneurial in seeking new revenue streams. Accordingly, more campaigns such as the just-completed and highly successful Queen's Appeal would be needed; fundraising would have to be treated as an active, ongoing function. The university's endowment would have to be fattened. In 1987, Queen's endowment provided a cushion of $65 million, the ultimate guarantee of the university's viability. As a rainy-day fund, Queen's endowment paled in comparison with that of McGill and Toronto – $160 million and $236 million respectively – and was miniscule in comparison with Harvard's $4 billion. The Leech Report's prescription for financial diversification provoked a free-wheeling discussion among the trustees. Why not, one adventurously suggested, build a domed stadium on the West Campus and rent it out?

The ideas of the Leech task force took prescriptive form in the *Blueprint for Action* in the spring of 1989. The full title of the proposal – *Ontario Universities: Blueprint for Action*[36] – underscored Queen's ambition to take the lead among provincial universities in finding a way out of the financial thicket. The initiative was reminiscent of the manner in which Queen's spearheaded the adoption of the BIU in the sixties as a means of introducing equity and arm's-length regulation to Ontario's post-secondary funding. The central plank of the

Blueprint was a proposal to raise undergraduate tuition by $625 in one-time annual increments of $125 (plus any adjustment for inflation) over a five-year period. This increase would raise student support of university operating costs to 25 per cent of their total. The hikes would be phased in as new students arrived each year and enrolled; any one student would thus face only a single fee adjustment over their stay in an undergraduate program: cumulatively the hike would return students' share in the cost of their education to its early seventies level. To restore government's proportion of support to its seventies level, the *Blueprint* advocated a phased-in, per-student hike of $1,875 in its operating grant over the same five years. Government's share would be calibrated at a three-to-one ratio to student tuition. As student and government support expanded, universities would intensify their fundraising and funded research to augment operating budgets, thereby enhancing the universities new-found "margin of excellence."

Anticipating the charge by critical observers that higher fees would raise the threshold of entry to university, the *Blueprint* argued that universities should take on more responsibility for student assistance. It wanted 30 to 40 per cent of the new revenue harvested from higher fees and government grants recycled into better student assistance and student services. Ontario Student Assistance loans would thus be topped up with the new revenue, while enhanced bursaries would be extended to aspiring students coming from under-represented and underprivileged segments of the population. Other monies would be used to bolster student counselling, career planning, and athletics. The tone of the report was that of a "win-win" solution. Universities would finally have the wherewithal to pursue the excellence glimpsed in the Bovey Report, and, at the same time, politicians could still point to their holy grail of accessibility. The tone was also altruistic – the report seldom mentioned Queen's, but instead adopted the collective voice of all "universities."

The *Blueprint* was an explicitly political document. It was intended to rally support from other universities, while at the same time providing a basis for consultation with the students who would pay the higher fees, as well as with politicians who would up their ante in the interest of resuscitating provincial post-secondary education to the "glory days" (a phrase now frequently and wistfully employed) of the sixties. If adopted, the *Blueprint* would herald better libraries, new instructional equipment, renovated buildings, and an end to the scrimping and saving of the previous decade. At the trustees meeting of March 1989, Board Chairman Walter Light urged his fellow trustees to go out and sell the *Blueprint* to the broader public. The proposal must be made "saleable to all." Vice-Principal Fraser seconded the sentiment, saying that the plan was founded on "the concept of partnership."[37]

Crucial in this respect was the support of Queen's students, who, like students across the province, had long opposed any talk of increased fees. The key here was to demonstrate the link between higher tuition, increased university revenue, and better-quality education, while guaranteeing needy students that loans and bursaries would be more plentiful. Students were assured that the $625 rise in fees would be phased in and strictly governed. In March 1989, vice-principal, resources, Rod Fraser carried this message to the AMS annual general meeting. The AMS listened sympathetically and passed a resolution endorsing the *Blueprint*. "Quality is what we're concerned about," AMS President Scott Nowlan confessed. "We can't rely completely on students, we can't rely entirely on the government, and we don't support deregulation. So the cooperation on the *Blueprint* is extremely important and we support it heartily."[38]

There were other hopeful signs. The *Blueprint* was debated by other Ontario universities, with the boards at Waterloo, York, and Guelph endorsing it. The Council of Ontario Universities fell into line with an endorsement, and the Ontario Council on

University Affairs – the crucial advisory panel that buffered relations between the universities and the government – began debating the proposal. Not content to rest on its assembly resolution, the AMS carried the *Blueprint* to the Ontario Federation of Students, urging it to forsake its long-standing opposition to fee increases in favour of graduated fee hikes in return for better-quality education. On the political front, there was hope that a sympathetic ear would be lent to the proposal by Sean Conway, the new minister in the Peterson administration with responsibility for education, skills development, and colleges and universities. Conway held a Queen's MA in history and, as one of the youngest members of the cabinet, had recent ties with post-secondary education in Ontario.

As if to demonstrate its readiness to diversify its own revenue stream, Queen's had hired a Toronto public-relations firm, Ketchum Ltd., to assess its ability to raise outside capital. The Ketchum Report, written by its president and former AMS president, Ross McGregor, argued that a more systematic approach to fundraising – or "advancement" as it was increasingly being called – would allow Queen's to raise $50 to $60 million. The key, Ketchum urged, was to treat advancement as a permanent, ongoing university function, not just as an episodic endeavour. Heartened by this prognosis, Queen's unveiled its ambitious Challenge Fund campaign, headed by Royal Bank CEO Allan Taylor, in the fall of 1989, with a goal of $70 million. The sense of light on the financial horizon was heightened in the spring of 1990, when the provincial government agreed to contribute $26 million to Queen's proposed "library of the twenty-first century," and the federal government funded a multiuniversity project to build a neutrino observatory deep in a Sudbury mine.

Diminishing government support for post-secondary education obliged Queen's to become more systematic and aggressive in its fundraising (soon to be dubbed "advancement"). Supplementing the university's budget with alumni, corporate, and foundation donations could no longer be an unsystematic, episodic affair. The Challenge Campaign launched in 1989 aimed for a total of $70 million, but by 1992 peaked at just over $100 million. Here Principal Smith and campaign chair, Royal Bank CEO Allan Taylor, celebrate Queen's success.

Tough Times Return

Unfortunately, just as Queen's bold proposal seemed to find a consensus, the tide of hope ebbed. In the 1987 provincial election, Premier David Peterson converted his precarious minority coalition into a solid majority, the first enjoyed by Ontario Liberals in almost half a century. To observers, this change seemed to offer a stable platform for reformist initiatives. But then, in the fall of 1990, as Canada grappled with constitutional showdowns over Quebec's sovereigntist ambitions, Peterson, much against the advice of his caucus and cabinet, called a snap election. Voters, annoyed that they had been called to the polls a mere three years after the last election, scolded Peterson by handing an unprecedented 74-seat victory to the New Democratic Party (NDP) under Bob Rae. Two years of assiduous consensus building by Queen's for reform of university funding seemed to hang in the balance. This jeopardy was intensified by a sharp global economic downturn in 1989. Presaged by the stock-market collapse of late 1987 and the pricking of a commercial real-estate bubble, western economies began to wobble. Central banks were obliged to battle rising inflation with higher interest rates. Unemployment rose and the dreaded word "deficit" resurfaced in discussions of government fiscal policy. The Gulf War in Kuwait then prompted a spike in energy prices. In Ontario, this increasing volatility was inherited by the newly elected New Democratic Party, which initially reverted to a Keynesian formula of spending into adversity in the hope of sparking an economic turnaround.

David Smith was initially hopeful that the new government's expansive ways would redound to the university system's betterment. In October 1990, he told the trustees that he was heartened that a McMaster history professor, Richard Allen, had been appointed minister of colleges and universities. Allen had acknowledged that post-secondary education in Ontario had "serious problems in the funding level" and might therefore be expected to look favourably on Queen's *Blueprint*.[39] At a meeting in March 1990, the new minister told the chairman of the Queen's Board, Richard Stackhouse, that he recognized that universities were seriously underfunded and that tuition was "substantially behind inflation." Allen said that that he had accordingly created an advisory group on university funding. Shortly thereafter, Queen's Park gave the universities a 7.3 per cent boost in their operating grant, plus a one-time $15-million payment to ease the implementation of pay equity.[40] At the same time, however, Toronto announced a hike in the provincial health-care premium paid by employers and employees alike, a direct addition to the universities' bottom line.

Very quickly, however, it became apparent that the NDP was less concerned with the financial sustainability of the provincial universities than with issues of equity and accountability surrounding their operation, an interest more in line with the party's social-democratic ethos. In the spring of 1991, Allen wrote to Smith, and to all provincial university presidents, telling him that the government was committed to promoting educational equity and, having already discussed the matter with the Council of Ontario Universities, now wanted feedback. How could universities better demonstrate their "accountability" to the public they served? Allen suggested that accountability might best be built by placing provincial appointees on university boards, and also by opening up their membership to students and university staff.[41] Smith was understandably perplexed. He wrote back to the minster that universities did not lend themselves to hard-and-fast notions of corporate accountability. University outputs were by their very nature soft and qualitative, not hard and measurable. How, for instance, could one calibrate the performance of a professor teaching a large undergraduate course, beyond established means such as annual teaching evaluations, when even these were regarded as dubious by many? Smith also countered the minister with the argument that Queen's long tradition of tripartite governance – Board of Trustees, Senate, and University Council – had already given Queen's a "distinctive" form of accountable self-government, one that was buttressed by a copasetic relationship with the AMS student government. Besides, since Queen's 1916 merger with the provincial mining school, the provincial government had had the right to place four appointees on the Board of Trustees, a right it had never exercised.[42]

Allen's embrace of accountability was soon reinforced by a fiscal *volte-face* by the Rae government. With the provincial deficit soaring as a result of copious Keynesian injections into the economy, and little sign that the recession gripping the province was slowing, Premier Rae adopted draconian austerity measures. Vice-Principal Fraser conveyed the bad news to the Board: Queen's was in relatively good financial condition (the Challenge Campaign was already topping $50 million), but inflation and

Amid the stress of fiscal austerity and academic realignment that the early 1990s brought, there was reason to celebrate at Queen's. In the fall of 1991, the university marked its 125th anniversary, an event highlighted by the royal visit of Prince Charles (who received an honorary degree) and Princess Diana. The next fall, the Gaels football team won its second Vanier Cup national championship under coach Doug Hargreaves – a 31–0 thumping of the St Mary's Huskies. Hargreaves (affectionately dubbed the "Professor of Pigskin") carried on the winning ways of Frank Tindall for nineteen years.

cumulative underfunding had created "a demanding set of challenges." Cutbacks were all but unavoidable. Trustee, newspaper columnist, and political realist Jeffrey Simpson reiterated the message: "severe" government cuts were going to continue, and Premier Rae was "resistant" to any idea of a unilateral tuition increase. Accessibility and frugality were now the NDP's lodestar – all too sadly familiar words to university administrators.[43]

Through the fall of 1991 the financial news grew more ominous. On 13 September, Vice-Principal Fraser met with Minister Allen in Toronto and was told that the government was determined to hold the provincial deficit under $10 billion.[44] The news had immediate implications. Foremost, it was the death knell of Queen's *Blueprint for Action*. Ontario's government was in no mood to contemplate catch-up financial adjustments for post-secondary education. Behind the scenes, Board Chairman Richard Stackhouse lashed out at Premier Rae: "We believed that your word was your bond ... However, if you continue to promise the people of the Province that their children will have unlimited access to a university education then, Mr. Premier, you will be promising something that we can no longer deliver."[45]

An End to "Effortless Superiority" 297

Whatever interuniversity consensus had been built up by Queen's diplomacy on funding reform was now overwhelmed by introversion, as universities separately faced the reality of austerity and took the paring knife to their budgets, the unavoidable outcome of Queen's Park's parsimony. The old fiscal bugbear of underfunding, so oppressive in the era of Principal Watts in the seventies, reasserted itself. Vice-Principal Fraser told the Senate that, while the university's total budget of $281 million had controllable inputs from funded research and endowment investment, the university's operating budget of $155 million was highly dependent on government inputs. This was ominous news for faculty and staff, whose salaries constituted 83 per cent of that budget. Fraser frankly told the Senate that the university had several grim options before it: ride out the austerity by simply increasing its deficit; try to impose constraint on its spending, especially on salaries; or explore new diversified revenue sources, even if it meant privatizing certain services. The agony of making these choices was heightened in January 1992 when Queen's Park announced that it would only increase the universities' operating grant for the 1992–93 academic year by a meagre 1 per cent, followed by two subsequent years at 2 per cent. In effect, the government was clawing back money from the universities, obliging them to maintain previously approved programs on budgets now pared by provincial stringency and eroded by inflation. A year later, the Rae government upped the austerity ante by reneging on its 1-per-cent operating-grant boost and imposing a zero-per-cent ceiling on its annual obligation to the universities.[46] Times had turned very tough.

In February of 1992, Queen's administration dispensed all-too-familiar medicine. With only a 1-per-cent increase in the provincial grant, Queen's was projecting a deficit in its operating budget of $820,000 for the 1992–93 academic year – this on top of an accumulated deficit of $4.8 million. Then, with even-handed equity, Fraser announced that there would be a 1-per-cent budget cut across all faculties in the upcoming year. On 3 February, Principal Smith circulated "a letter to faculty, staff, and students" which did little to disguise the university's financial straits, but did extend an assurance that everything would be done to protect jobs and arrest any deterioration of teaching quality.[47] That spring Queen's students learned that their tuition would rise 7 per cent in the next year, the maximum increase allowed by the province.[48]

Scrambling to find a financial Band-Aid that would stretch across all of Queen's diverse communities, Smith reconvened the Task Force on Revenue Enhancement and tasked it with identifying new revenue sources. Here, there was some encouraging news: the Challenge Fund in 1992 surged past its initial target and was now pushing towards $80 million. There were other positive signs of financial innovation: in 1987, Queen's had established an arm's-length enterprise, PARTEQ Innovations, designed to commercialize intellectual property developed by faculty and various regional academic partners. Although a not-for-profit agency in itself, PARTEQ was positioned to transfer royalties derived from successful patents back to their originators and into university coffers. Ably managed by its chief executive, John Molloy, PARTEQ quickly established a sterling record of commercializing patents, incubating spin-off companies to capitalize on those patents, and finding venture-capital partners to extend their business reach.[49]

Meeting the Challenges

The glad tidings of the Challenge Fund and PARTEQ did not diminish the fundamental fiscal problem now confronting Queen's: managing with less and finding a way to align itself with new opportunities in the face of the fiscal rigidity of Ontario post-secondary education. Queen's was hardly alone in sensing the magnitude of this challenge. In fact, the post-secondary squeeze was being felt across the western world. In 1990, the OECD in Paris had issued a report, *Financing Higher Education: Current Patterns*, which had noted seismic shifts in the public perception of higher education. Gone everywhere was flush sixties spending, replaced by a tension between the state's expectation that universities would be held accountable to "national needs" and the universities' desire to preserve their autonomy.[50] Closer to home, the Association of Universities and Colleges of Canada (AUCC) issued its own report in 1992. *Prosperity in the Knowledge Age* underscored the message that universities could no longer "continue to struggle with an untenable triad of pressures – higher quality, increased accessibility, and less funding."[51] Awareness of the squeeze on post-secondary education spread beyond lobby groups and think tanks. *Time* magazine produced a theme issue on the "College Crunch," while the *Toronto Star* pointed out that the federal government's transfer payments for education were at their lowest level in a decade.[52] Political columnist Jeffrey Simpson spoke at the AUCC annual meeting in the spring of 1992, telling delegates that all the talk of making universities more accountable to the public purse was not a passing fad, and that that purse was likely to become even smaller in the final years of the century.[53]

To face this erosive challenge, Smith once again fell back on Queen's inured habit of broad collegial deliberation of strategies of change. In January 1992, he unveiled a Principal's Advisory Task Force on Resource Issues (PATFORI). Smith gave the group a sweeping mandate – to look twenty years out at the way Queen's should define itself and how it should deploy its resources to sustain its core values. This mandate had an impatient and decisive tone. The task force must be acutely conscious of "the need to make choices" in "severely resource-constrained times." Its recommendations should reflect a realization that "not all things we do can be accorded equal priority" and that "downsizing" (argot made popular by the struggling business sector in these same years) and even elimination of academic functions were legitimate outcomes of their deliberations. If Queen's could not force change in its circumstances at the provincial level, then it must forge selective change in its own bailiwick.

Chairing the task force himself, Smith stocked it with a membership from the entire Queen's community. Three trustees, including Anne Bodnarchuck (BA 1957), the highly regarded Air Canada executive who was guiding the airline into the electronic age, joined Vice-Principals Fraser and Williams, Dean Carl Humacher of Applied Science, and various associate deans, professors, and AMS and Grad Society reps, as well as administrative staff members, to ensure every segment of the Queen's community had a voice in the upcoming candid dialogue. Smith even added the well-known journalist Peter Trueman to the panel to ensure an external perspective in its deliberations. To support the investigation, Smith appointed Ken Snowdon from research services, registrar Alison Morgan, as well as his own executive assistants, history professor Alan Jeeves and physiologist Chris Chapler, to act as resource staff for the task force. In contrast with Queen's often slow-paced deliberations, Smith moved the inquiry along briskly: Queen's Park had made it plain that any future additional monies for the operating budget required tangible evidence of change. As if to drive home the point, the advent of the university's 1992–93 financial year on 1 May heralded the sudden drop to a 1-per-cent increase in the annual operating grant. At the same time, Smith was being pressured by some of his colleagues to resist Queen's institutional conservatism. Its vaunted traditions, they argued, were a brake on reform. Dean of Medicine Duncan Sinclair, never shy in his opinions or loyalty to Queen's, sagely warned his fellow senior administrators that they were spending more of their "scarce energy attempting to preserve those traditions and practices than we are in figuring out how to change them and better serve our 'customers' – our students and the society that supports them and us."[54]

The Beginnings of a Paradigm Shift

September 1993 brought the task force's recommendations. *Meeting the Challenges* began by reaffirming Smith's previous distillation of the "qualities" of a Queen's education: top-quality undergraduate and graduate instruction, stimulating research and scholarship, and exemplary service to the broader community. Those values now had to be expanded. Queen's would have to persist in its effort to ensure equity and access to all comers, something that had troubled it over the last decades as women and groups on the margin of its traditional culture sought inclusion. Queen's must also respond to a world that was rapidly globalizing by finding ways to internationalize its established national reputation. It must also be more responsive to demographic trends and dedicate itself to offering continuing education to Canada's maturing population. In short, Queen's could no longer rest on its laurels. The days of "effortless superiority" were inevitably fading.

Having reasserted familiar core values and identified challenging new goals, the report moved into more unfamiliar territory. Adopting the language of corporate strategic planning, it argued that Queen's must learn to integrate its decision making and resource utilization by means of tangible "indicators of performance." It must adopt processes that measured its productivity and thereby calibrate its spending decisions with demonstrable outcomes. Ken Snowdon at the Office of Research had already been moving in this direction. Queen's, for instance, now administered an "exit poll" of its graduating undergraduates, quizzing them about their perception of the value they received in their education, the results of which were fed back to the trustees and the Senate. (This polling mimicked the prevailing practice evident in publications such as *Maclean's* and the *Globe and Mail*, which published annual ratings of Canadian universities, rankings based on criteria ranging from class size through to residence accommodation.) Now the *Challenges* report advocated the application of other, more focused, indicators to demonstrate Queen's productivity and thereby bring substance to its financial dealings with the provincial and federal governments. The report listed twenty such "critical factors" that meshed the university's priorities with available resources. These encompassed success in winning outside awards such as Rhodes Scholarships by students and Killam Fellowships by faculty, the gender ratio of faculty, class size, and "research intensity."

The university had long, of course, employed statistics to demonstrate its activities, but these were usually after-the-fact markers of enrolment and faculty publications. The *Challenges* report now required that quantification become an aspect of making future decisions at Queen's. To take a word from contemporary corporate culture, universities had to become "proactive" in making a case for their livelihood. For many, this was alien to the traditional culture of collegial governance at Queen's. While some would even see it as evidence of the corporatization of university life, Smith and his task-force colleagues reasoned that the university had no option but to respond to the ethos of accountability and value-for-money that prevailed beyond the campus.

With the tools of ongoing assessment now at hand, the report moved on to suggest their application. Flexibility and precision would now be defining practices at Queen's. Financial austerity would no longer be automatically met with egalitarian across-the-board cuts – equal pain regardless of strategic importance. Money should in future flow where need could best be demonstrated. Such selectivity was already embedded in the successful Queen's National Scholar program, which invited departments to bid for preferment in seeking new faculty members. Although such language was never used, it was now implicit that there would be "winners" and "losers" in decision making. Emerging opportunities and criteria imposed from beyond the campus might now be privileged over long-entitled academic bailiwicks. Emerging disciplines with strong student or social demand behind them, such as women's studies, computing science, biotechnology, and environmental studies, should be privileged. Any new hiring, regardless of discipline, the report urged, should make criteria such as gender equity and intellectual innovation a deciding factor.

With such flexibility in mind, the report suggested that Queen's could now be in a better position to reconfigure itself in the face of the austerity emanating from Queen's Park and Ottawa. At the same time, such shifts would serve to shunt the university towards greater non-governmental funding. The university must become more nimble and less lethargic in governing its affairs. Once again, Dean Sinclair put his finger on the necessity of this shift: "We are no longer the incubators of innovation, pushing the pace of societal change. Rather we have become reactive to changes in society around us and far more resistant to change than impatient at the slowness of society to accept our ideas and change in accordance with them."[55]

True to its mandate, the report then delivered *choice* – five "options for action" designed to help Queen's weather the fiscal storm and to alter its course. First, the university should not abandon its broad-front campaign with other universities to bring pressure on government for an acknowledgement of underfunding and slipping quality. A year earlier, Queen's had endorsed a wistful "recovery plan," set before the provincial government by the Council of Ontario Universities. It called for an injection of $410 million to restore the quality and accessibility of Ontario's universities to 1977–78 levels.[56] That pressure had to be kept up, even if the Rae government was retracting its spending. At the same time, the universities must continue to push for greater freedom in setting their fees. Why should specialized professional programs, with a lucrative potential for students in terms of future salary and job security, be held under the same constraint as undergraduate programs designed for broad social acculturalization? If fees could be more directly linked to life outcomes, then universities might harvest more variegated tuition, which reflected different personal and societal benefits.

The liberalization of fees echoed a larger theme in the *Challenges* prescription: universities must diversify their income away from reliance on governments. Ontario's creed of cutbacks in the early 1990s was the latest reminder that the province's educational largesse had been steadily shrinking for two decades. The university's income must therefore be diversified to provide a more stable foundation for future development. The same month that *Challenges* was tabled, the report by consultants Ketchum Canada underscored the message that Queen's must gird itself for more concerted fundraising. The days of episodic fundraising were over. Ketchum argued for an ongoing, systematic approach to the soliciting of voluntary financial support. The Alumni relations – "friend-raising" – and the development function – that is, fundraising – at Queen's must "work more efficiently, cooperatively, and synergistically." Fundraising should no longer emanate from the principal's office; the principal had too many other obligations. Instead, the university's "advancement" should be decentralized to reach down as far as the faculties, where departments could attach their needs to potential outside sponsors. In the spring of 1993, Queen's would regularize the role of advancement, with the creation of a vice-principal, advancement. Florence Campbell, formerly with Ottawa's Conference Board (an organization that subsisted on fees from a broad base of member organizations), was appointed to the post.

The fourth option set before Queen's by PATFORI was hardly unexpected: expenditure control must be intensified. If the university was to sell itself as an "accountable" entity, then it must be able to demonstrate fiscal self-control. It must practise a better stewardship over its affairs than simply imposing across-the-board policies, such as the 1-per-cent ceiling on expenditure it imposed in response to the Rae government's draconian cuts. In future, the report concluded, Queen's must face the fraught prospect of selectively restructuring its programs and policies. Procedures must be developed to enable "downsizing" of units that failed to satisfy objective, university-wide performance benchmarks.

While it is inviting to conclude that the Smith years were marked by much talk and little action, the corporate-style prescriptions embedded in the PATFORI report augured a fundamental shift in the culture of Queen's. Unlike its predecessor, the *Blueprint for Action*, which was dedicated to systemic change for the whole Ontario system, the *Challenges* report focused on workable options for Queen's alone – deregulated fees for market-oriented professional studies, the pursuit of academic niche markets, internationalization of programs – options that might be capitalized upon to restore Queen's distinctiveness. Few expected fast-tracked reform. Most sensed that the road ahead would require dextrous navigation. Respect for the cardinal virtue of academic freedom meant, for example, that any attempt at "downsizing" could not proceed without due respect for professors' entrenched rights. Would decisions to abandon established programs bring the Board of Trustees into loggerheads with the Senate? Did financial imperatives trump academic prerogatives? And, perhaps most crucially, how would the pursuit of flexibility and accountability affect Queen's long tradition of collegiality? After listening to Vice-Principal Fraser's worrisome prognostication of university finances under NDP austerity, trustee Alan Broadbent wondered aloud about the impact of such lean times on Queen's "heavy reliance on collegial decision making."[57]

Fraying the Cord of Loyalty: The Consultative Group Begins to Unravel

Queen's collegiality was most clearly manifest in the Consultative Group, which Watts had bequeathed his successor. The group had been remarkably successful in helping Queen's weather the retrenching seventies and early eighties. Even though the ultimate prerogative in setting faculty salaries remained with the principal, consensus between the administration and QUFA, the faculty association, had almost always been arrived at in each salary negotiation. Despite steady erosion by inflation and the realization that Queen's faculty salaries were falling below provincial averages, a negotiated settlement on salaries emerged almost every year. The group rested on a foundation of mutual trust, which reflected a belief that administration and faculty were bound by a loyalty to the overall well-being of the university. In 1988, for instance, Smith hailed the conclusion of that year's salary agreement as "strong evidence of our shared commitment to Queen's." That bond not only produced fiscal savings, but also brought about occasional advances in labour relations at Queen's. In 1983–84, for instance, it facilitated the introduction of a salary-calculation system that bifurcated each professor's performance by merit and progress through the ranks (PTR). Each year's salary increase thus would now reflect merit and career development, multiplied by the percentage raise (usually reflecting inflationary pressure) negotiated by the faculty association and the administration.

The group also acted as a forum for leveraging other aspects of employment at Queen's. Maternity leave and better on-campus daycare had, for instance, been negotiated. In 1984, the group had agreed to boost the salary floor on assistant professors' salaries, citing the fact that across-the-board percentage salary increases unduly penalized assistant professors, who garnered fewer dollars from, say, a 2-per-cent increase than their full-professor colleagues. That same year, QUFA and the administration signed a new memorandum of understanding extending the original body's mandate, at the same time boosting its membership to ten members and agreeing to let it address "new conditions" in the Queen's labour market. Minutes of the group's meetings reveal a workable conviviality. Meetings and correspondence were conducted on a first-name basis and, while there were tensions, there was seldom acrimony.

The late eighties, however, witnessed a steady decline in the civility of the Consultative Group. The insidious effect of inflation was becoming uncomfortably cumulative. By 1989, for instance, civil engineering professor Barry Batchelor reported to QUFA that Queen's salaries ranked sixth out of the fifteen universities in the province and sixth out of seven research-intensive universities.[58] University administrators contested this stark comparison. Ken Snowdon, director of resource planning, warned QUFA that such comparisons were simplistic and ignored differences between campuses and professions: "It is clear," he wrote to QUFA President Marvin Baer, "there is no one answer to the rather complex question of faculty compensation. In fact, given past experience, it is likely that no amount of data – no matter how convincing one way or the other – will alter the perception of some faculty."[59] Not surprisingly, the air of civil give-and-take began to desert faculty-administration relations. "In my over 20 years at Queen's," one faculty member angrily wrote to *QUFacts*, the newsletter of QUFA, "my experience is that it is *always* the faculty that has to bear the brunt when there are financial problems."[60] Part of the problem was that the group had become increasingly freighted with matters that extended beyond direct dollars-and cents compensation. For many generations at Queen's, employment culture had been a hermetic affair. Now, as the welfare state achieved maturity, society-at-large began obliging universities to conform to broader, all-inclusive agendas aimed at social betterment.

A good example of this came in 1987, when Ontario passed a Pay Equity Act that mandated equal pay for equal work through all spheres of the Ontario labour market. The process entailed the setting of benchmarks and reporting procedures that required compliance from all employers, including universities. The equal-pay-for-equal-work challenge at Queen's was daunting. There were conspicuous gender imbalances in both the academic and administrative staffs. To ease the transition, the Ontario government made one-time payments to Ontario's universities to lubricate the adjustment. At the same time, the federal government imposed its own equity agenda on campuses. The 1987 Federal Contractors' Program, for instance, stipulated that Ottawa's funding of university research would hitherto be tied to the existence of campus employment equity.

Queen's responded by trying to adapt to the world of employment equity. It appointed an advisor of employment equity, backed by a Council on Employment Equity to monitor progress and proffer advice. Principal Smith highlighted the necessity of such conformity by issuing a statement of *Values at Queen's*, which, in mission statement style, put on record that the university would not tolerate any form of "coercion and exploitation" and that it was "morally objectionable to prevent human beings from fully exercising their humanity."[61] To bring practice to principle, in 1989 Smith struck an agreement with QUFA to investigate whether there was systemic salary discrimination in the ranks of Queen's faculty. Headed by economist Nancy Oleweiler and mathematician Joan Geramita, the resulting panel reviewed "women's salaries" at Queen's. The Alexander task force in the mid-1970s had concluded that the university's one-time bias against women in compensation had been virtually eliminated. When the new group reported in 1990, it concluded that women professors were still in fact discriminated against, and that an across-the-board corrective hike of 4.35 per cent for women was warranted. Other recommendations were made: promotions should be geared to "years of experience" rather than being a straight linear calculation of years since previous appointment (thereby acknowledging years taken for maternity). Of particular concern was the university's cohort of adjunct professors, a group heavily populated by women. The difficulty of such calculations was made evident by complaints from the deans that the panel's methodology was faulty. The panel revisited its findings and, in 1991, convinced the principal to make a one-time 3.5-per-cent corrective hike in the salaries of female faculty.[62] To drive home their impatience for change the report quoted the principal's own words from his *Values at Queen's* manifesto: "The university cannot flourish if some members are made to feel their concerns and needs rate lower than those of others." By the early 1990, the long-standing gender imbalance in Queen's faculty began to fade as a perennial irritant. The Association of Women Teaching at Queen's, so effective in raising consciousness of the imbalance, began to lose its insistent edge and met less frequently. However, problems in gender relations and attitudes in the student body, Smith would painfully discover, still lurked close beneath the surface of university life.

Staff Relations in Transition

The issue of pay equity also reverberated through the ranks of Queen's administrative staff. Here the challenge was more convoluted. By 1988, the university had 1,435 staff appointments arranged around 500 different job descriptions. Unlike the linear, rank-by-rank progression of faculty, staff employment at Queen's was more a messy mosaic of tasks and career paths. Dissatisfaction with this chaotic structure was rising. Since the late fifties, staff at Queen's had been dividing into unionized and non-unionized ranks. The predominant point of contact had been the Queen's University Staff Association (QUSA), founded in 1972 as the bargaining agent for non-unionized staff. However, in more recent years, the Canadian Union of Public Employees (CUPE) had made inroads at Queen's; CUPE locals 229 and 1302 now represented maintenance workers and library technicians. There were indications that efforts were under way to bring teaching and research assistants into the CUPE fold and to woo the remaining non-unionized workers into national affiliation.

Richardson Hall, long used to a collegial relationship with the university's staff, preferred working with the Queen's University Staff Association rather than face what it believed was the more hard-line approach of national unionism. Paternalism had traditionally shaped the university's approach to its staff: from Principal Mackintosh's cheery "good morning" to groundskeepers to Principal Corry's nomination of the janitor in the Memorial Union for a 1967 Centennial Medal, the attitude had always been familial – you take care of us and we will take care of you. Principal Smith certainly wished to perpetuate this tradition, often hinting to administrative staff that unionization would break the "family" bond at Queen's. In this spirit, QUSA and the administration in 1985 established their own consultative group to facilitate monthly discussion of employment issues. The designation in 1988 of former dean of Nursing Alice Baumgart as the bluntly titled vice-principal, human services, indicated the university's heightened concern with its well-being on the labour front. The introduction of pay equity now complicated this chemistry. "The support staff are not 'at peace' regarding compensation issues," Jack Hughes, the associate director of personnel services, reported in 1988. "Our rude arrival at the portals of the equity era has coincided with the gathering into the CUPE fold of our two previously independent union locals, establishing an extremely strong CUPE presence on campus."[63]

The Senate Budget Committee picked up this sentiment: in 1989, it noted that, while Queen's student population had grown by 12 per cent in the last decade, the university's administrative staff supporting campus operations had expanded by only 2 per cent.[64] Bud Cornelius, the carpenter who had worked at Queen's since 1956, daily experienced the difference. In a bid to reduce costs, the university, he recalled, had hired ex-army "dudes," who had tried to cut costs by creating maintenance "zones" across the campus. The resulting overburden of regimentation stripped the pride of work from the maintenance staff. "Stress" dominated the workplace. Working for Queen's no longer, Cornelius lamented, felt like "family."[65]

In the spring of 1989, Baumgart had the dubious distinction of weathering the first strike in Queen's labour history – a brief falling out with CUPE unions 1302, 229, and 254 that resulted in a two-year agreement that awarded staff annual hikes of 4.3 per cent, plus enhanced benefits.[66] Later that year, a gingerly negotiated agreement with CUPE and QUSA initiated a wholesale attempt to create a new, more egalitarian, job-evaluation system at Queen's. Consultants from Price Waterhouse were hired to facilitate the process. When the evaluation group was unable to agree on an acceptable universal system for Queen's, the decision was made to live with a dual system, one for unionized workers and the other for non-unionized staff, excluding teaching assistants.[67]

As the nineties dawned, it was thus increasingly apparent that staff relations at Queen's had acquired an assertive edge. Members of the CUPE local staged information pickets outside Richardson Hall, and there were surreptitious discussions of certification votes under the Ontario Labour Relations Board.[68] As Toronto imposed budgetary cuts on the universities, job security became a pervasive concern. Early in 1992, for instance, the presidents of the CUPE unions on campus wrote to Principal Smith demanding that their membership be given the right to nominate their own delegates to university committees overseeing issues such as health and safety: "We reiterate once again that the Unions are equal partners within the University community and that partnership will work best when respect is exercised in the democratic choice of Union representatives."[69]

Drifting Apart: QUFA Looks for a Dispute-Resolution Mechanism

Similar strains were enervating the faculty Consultative Group. A swelling agenda of negotiable issues – pay equity, grievance procedures, promotion, and tenure criteria – now encumbered the traditional bargaining issue of compensation – all of this unfolding against a backdrop of debilitating financial austerity. The viability of the Consultative Group was compromised by other disintegrative tendencies. In 1989, QUFA President Marvin Baer, a law professor specializing in commercial law, outlined three trends that he believed were militating against the old collegiality. Professors were, he suggested, being increasingly regarded as "entrepreneurs," expected to rake in funded research. Consequently, "external market forces" were being allowed to determine the assessment of faculty. And, last but not least, a growing cadre of "full-time career administrators" dedicated to bottom-line performance had been inserted between the faculty and the senior administration. The ethos of university governance, Baer argued, had thus shifted from widespread collegial participation and decentralized decision making to a highly centralized "elaborate game of three card Monte designed to defuse issues and disguise responsibility." The university was in the thrall of a "siege mentality" brought on by the administration's blinkered fixation with its finances.[70]

A year later, the succeeding president of QUFA, political scientist Grant Amyot, picked up Baer's analysis. There was "an iron law of oligarchy" overtaking the governance of Queen's, he suggested. The old consultative spirit of the Duff-Berdahl Report, with its empowerment of the Senate and its acknowledgement of faculty and students' right to inclusion, was evaporating.[71] "Increasingly," Amyot and his QUFA executive reported, "members have commented to us that we seem to be losing control of our working environment, that collegiality is a thing of the past, that decisions that vitally affect us are being taken without our having had a say."[72]

The drift into an increasingly confrontational relationship with Richardson Hall was also a reflection of the arrival of a new generation of scholars at Queen's. The great bulge of sixties hiring was beginning to fade into retirement. Departments were being restocked through programs such as the Queen's National Scholars – sixty-two of them by 1991 – with new mental attitudes. With this shift, the symbiotic coexistence of faculty and administrators, once so prevalent at Queen's, began to wane. The university was now a much larger institution, less familial and more variegated and anonymous. New scholars taking up their duties had no genetic predisposition to compatibility with the administration. Most had done their graduate studies at other universities, often abroad, where faculty unions were commonplace and where better progress had been made on issues such as gender equality. When, for instance, Annette Burfoot arrived in 1989 to take up an appointment in sociology after her doctoral studies at England's University of Sussex, she thought Queen's was in a "time warp," twenty years behind the times. Salaries were low and faculty had little leverage over salary bargaining and lacked certain rights that were a given on other campuses, such as a stipulated right to appeal a promotion denial.[73]

Other new faculty shared Burfoot's impatience with what seemed like Queen's immovable status quo. Librarian Janny Eikelboom, QUFA president in 1991, reported "a high level of frustration and unhappiness amongst the faculty" over the administration's expectation that faculty should bite the financial bullet for the greater good.[74] Other QUFA presidents, such as Allan Manson in 1994, emerged out of the law school, bringing with them a desire to place faculty-administration relations on a more contractual, less deferential, basis. The youthful mood for change was perhaps epitomized in 1995 when Burfoot took over the QUFA presidency, the first non-tenured president of the association in its history.

But faculty opinion was not monolithic. Of Queen's nearly 1,000 faculty members in 1991, only 580 were QUFA members. The association newsletter frequently appealed to its membership to recruit recalcitrant colleagues. As austerity enveloped university finances in the early nineties, some faculty members overtly supported the administration's call for salary suppression as a means of shoring up Queen's reputation for quality. In January 1990, Dean Bill McCready of Arts and Science, for instance, called a special meeting of Arts and Science department heads to ponder the impact of cutbacks. Here there was vocal support for faculty restraint on the salary front, and for respecting the established collegiality. James Stayer of history declared that he and his colleagues would prefer to see their salaries drop than see their programs debased. He did not share the "salary-oriented viewpoint of the QUFA," suggesting that many did not see QUFA as "our natural leaders."[75] Peter Baxter of film studies believed that "the continuing problems of inadequate infrastructure for teaching and research" should outweigh salary demands.[76] Similarly, economics professor Doug Purvis wrote to QUFA President Marvin Baer, scolding the association for its unwillingness to acknowledge that Queen's was indeed at a "critical juncture" financially.[77] On the surface, therefore, Queens' faculty seemed to be divided into two camps: an outspoken and impatient group of generally younger faculty eager to use QUFA as an instrument for change and an older guard who clung to the comfortable collegiality that had prevailed on the campus for decades. Below the surface, there were other, more fundamental, fissures: the professional faculties, such as business and engineering, tended to shun collective bargaining, seeing themselves as academic extensions of professional communities rooted in individual performance. There were exceptions: some members of the law faculty (perhaps exemplified by one-time QUFA president and criminal lawyer Allan Manson) rallied to the collective-bargaining cause. Professors in Arts and Science tended to favour collective bargaining, although even here there were departments, such as economics, which preferred individuality to collectivity. Since QUFA votes were secret, it is, of course, impossible to definitively track faculty support for a departure from the established norm of consultation at Queen's.

As the nineties unfolded, two factors would tip the balance towards greater militancy. First, as the NDP government veered away from its initial Keynesianism and embraced Dickensian austerity, the Consultative Group found precious little room for give-and-take. With Queen's Park dictating no increase in universities' operating grants, Principal Smith addressed the "very grim" financial situation at Queen's by hiking fees 7 per cent and holding the line on faculty salaries. With so little leeway in 1992, the Consultative Group found slim prospect of compromise and broke off its negotiations. Principal Smith therefore imposed a settlement containing no adjustment for scale and a paltry 1 per cent for merit and PTR. From QUFA's point of view, this starkly revealed that, when all was said and done, ultimate power over compensation resided in Richardson Hall. The forced settlement also accentuated the accumulating belief that salaries at Queen's were in dire need of "catch-up." The salary committee of QUFA alleged that Queen's 1992–93 salary package was "the lowest in the province." The same committee raised the flag of reform: "Is it now appropriate for QUFA to press for the adoption of a dispute resolution mechanism?" The rights of the faculty, the committee suggested, must be recognized and vested in a formal and entrenched bilateral process of salary negotiation.[78]

As QUFA soured on the Consultative Group, the association's executive sought a mandate for change. In January 1993, it surveyed the entire faculty for possible options. The central issue revolved around whether, in rejecting the voluntarism of the existing arrangement, Queen's faculty favoured an in-house dispute-resolution mechanism or one that drew its authority externally from union certification under the Ontario Labour Relations Act. The survey revealed that almost 80 per cent of respondents favoured *some* form of mechanism. The favoured option was a "special plan" tailored to Queen's needs alone. Only a minority favoured attaching Queen's to a provincially mandated scheme of labour negotiations that hinged on the formation of a certified union and the possibility of binding arbitration. At the other extreme, a minority wanted to stay the course. Professor Charles Beach of economics, for instance, noted that only 34 per cent of eligible faculty (416 of 1,207) had participated in the survey. Two other economists, Lorne Carmichael and Peter Roeder, expressed their disdain for the idea of a "union." Academics, they said, did not go out on strike, and even the threat of a strike "demeans our work."[79] Others suggested that a "mechanism" in itself would not solve faculty compensation frustration. "In calling for a 'dispute resolution mechanism,'" Duncan Sinclair wrote, "you propose to take out of our hands the power to make our own decisions. Do you really believe that once gone, external decision-making would stop disputes about rates of pay?"[80]

Nonetheless, the QUFA executive now believed that it was armed with a mandate for change. In April 1993, it voted for a one-year exploration of the idea of a Queen's-designed dispute mechanism. This, they hoped, could be "achieved in a collegial rather than a confrontational spirit and that the result will be beneficial not only to faculty but for Queen's as an institution." Such a "special plan" was seen as a tonic "to heal the divisions and improve morale among faculty."[81] Richardson Hall was cool to the idea. Vice-Principal Fraser expressed his skepticism that a salary mechanism alone would solve Queen's problems. In an exchange with QUFA President Amyot, Fraser reiterated the need for a "balanced" approach to salary negotiation, one that would reconcile budget austerity, job cutbacks, the need for new revenues, and new strategic goals in the interests of all Queen's parties. Amyot replied that faculty relations had come to such a point that the exchange of statistics and strategic planning would not in itself save the day. The faculty wanted confirmed rights: "Only a dispute resolution mechanism can give us that voice."[82]

Principal Smith, who in the spring of 1993 was entering his final year in office, acknowledged this groundbreaking shift. He told Amyot that a dispute mechanism was an "important issue," but begged for time. The search committee for his successor had just begun its work and had asked that "no sweeping changes" be adopted before the new principal took office. That said, Smith suggested that initial discussion of a new salary process could at least begin, and then might proceed in "several stages." But, he added, with the caution often displayed by Queen's principals, this was "a time of great uncertainty and change at Queen's" and that undue haste might do more damage than good.[83]

The "great uncertainty" that Smith alluded to was the second factor tipping the balance of Queen's labour relations. Once again, the unease emanated from Queen's Park. In the spring of 1993, just as QUFA attempted to place its dispute-resolution mechanism on the university's agenda, the Rae government in Toronto was discovering the snowballing magnitude of its fiscal problems. Inflation and an economic slowdown that drove unemployment up and government revenues down had pushed the province into a $13-billion deficit, a deficit that advisors told provincial treasurer, Floyd Laughren, might burgeon to $17 billion. Faced with such a liability, the Rae government abandoned its trust in Keynesian counter-cyclical budgeting and announced that a policy of "real and enduring restraint," shared equitably by all elements of provincial society, offered a better route to social and economic betterment. All Ontarians would be expected to subscribe to a "social contract" designed to inflict short-term pain in the hope of long-term gain. The public sector would be the front line of this campaign. Wage freezes, unpaid days of leave, early retirements, and roll-backs of entitlements would, the April budget promised, save Ontario $2 billion. In return, there would be no public-sector job layoffs. The social contract would extend to all agencies of the state. This included the provincial university system, which was informed that the already-harsh days of zero-per-cent budgeting were over, to be replaced by a regime of budgetary clawbacks. The budget announced that $118 million would be stripped out of the post-secondary education allocation. The number crunchers at Queen's quickly calculated that this would wash down to their university as a painful $9-million reduction in its provincial grant. The Queen's medical faculty, so dependent on the provincial health budget, might see its budget fall by 30 per cent.

The social contract caused a political earthquake in Ontario. The province's two largest public-sector unions – CUPE and the Ontario Public Service Employees Union – regarded it as an act of betrayal by their erstwhile social-democratic ally, the NDP. The business sector, once vocal in its opposition to what it perceived as the government's profligate ways, warmed to its new gospel of restraint. At Queen's, the impact was less seismic. Principal Smith, after consulting Cunningham, Swan, Carty, Little, and Bonham, the university solicitors, announced that the clawback would be administered in "a consultative fashion" by a "cabinet" of vice-principals and deans shaping the impact of the cuts.[84] To ensure faculty sensibilities were taken into account, the Senate Committee on Academic Development would provide faculty feedback, while the Board of Trustees would convene a task force to study the university's long-term resource-implementation policy.

This multilateral approach bore immediate fruit. The Social Contract Act that instituted the province's new fiscal regime contained an incentive designed to ease the pain of implementation: if all parties in a "sub-sector" of the public service could expeditiously agree to comply with the social contract, then the clawback in their sector would be reduced. By July 1993, that consensus – backed by QUFA, QUSA, and CUPE – was in place, with the effect that the provincial clawback on Queen's was reduced by 20 per cent, to $7.4 million. Queen's students fell into line. When the administration announced that it would bolster its income by imposing a three-year Student Assistance Levy designed to skim an additional fee off tuition – $10 per undergraduate half-course and $33.33 for each graduate course – the AMS insisted that the student body must first be consulted. Katherine Philips, AMS president, nonetheless urged students to support the levy as a means of enhancing the quality of their education, but only after she had successfully negotiated for a halving of the levy.[85] An AMS referendum produced a 78-per-cent endorsement of the levy.

Ironically, the social contract produced the last great common pull in labour relations at Queen's. Smith was acutely conscious that the social contract must land equitably on all shoulders at Queen's. To allay anxiety, he set out several overarching assurances: that the "learning environment" would be protected, that everything would be done to avoid permanent layoffs, and that all sectors of campus life would be treated equally. The administration demonstrated its determination to cut costs while maintaining equity by redeploying pension-fund surplus monies and by protecting faculty and staff in lower salary brackets from the full brunt of the social contract. Nonetheless, Queen's entered the 1993–94 budget year looking at a shortfall of $11 million. Members of the Board of Trustees connected with the Toronto business and political world warned that the social contract augured a fundamental shift in Queen's Park's attitude to post-secondary education. Words such as "accountability" and "productivity" began to enter its post-secondary vocabulary. In May 1993, for instance, a provincial task force had called for a "strengthened framework" of accountability for provincial universities. The implication seemed to be that universities would have to empirically demonstrate their productivity if they wanted continued access to the public purse.[86] Some complained that a "value for money" approach was hardly applicable to the world of learning, especially in universities, where decision making was split between a bricks-and-mortar Board of Trustees and an academic Senate. Others nonetheless warned that, without better centralized accounting, better strategic planning, and enhanced financial support from alumni and the private sector, the government would deliver more social contracts to university doorsteps.[87]

The social contract thus foreshadowed a new culture of governance at Queen's. On a practical level, faculty and staff with salaries above $30,900 were now taking five-and-half days of unpaid leave each year, while within departments and service units, budget paring was limiting future possibilities. Despite its willingness to join in a common response to the social contract, QUFA realized that it now lived in a world where outside forces could arbitrarily dictate its fate. In early 1994, the president of QUFA, Allan Manson, remarked that there were still "those in our community who honestly believe, or want to believe, that we live in an age of the rarified academy, removed from worldly issues, homogeneous in composition, seeing life through common eyes. In that world, the administration spoke for everyone. But that nostalgic image of the privileged university no longer exists."[88] David Smith was hardly the handmaiden of this shift; rather he and his colleagues at Queen's had been caught up in changes transmitted from beyond the campus by forces as varied as inflation, government austerity, and employment equity. They had found that once-tried-and-true mechanisms of consensus at Queen's could no longer encompass such diverse pressures. Smith's successor in the principal's office would arrive on the threshold of this transition. By default, in his second term as principal, Smith therefore determined that if he could not fundamentally alter the university's fiscal foundation, he would instead attempt to open up breeches in the wall of provincial-funding uniformity. Subsequently, his modernization initiatives – ranging from a blanket formula for paying the medical faculty to "privatizing" parts of the MBA program – would allow Smith to tailor the university's finances to its particular strengths and needs.

Harmonizing the Medical Faculty

If QUFA and the administration provided an example of the slow disintegration of a salary culture reaching the limits of its utility, the Queen's Faculty of Medicine pointed the way to the future by revamping the way it delivered its teaching and research services in the early nineties. Harry Botterell's galvanization of Queen's medicine in the sixties had carried the medical faculty through the seventies. The new health-sciences building was completed, new departments such as family medicine and community health were built up, and an ever-stronger liaison with the Faculty of Arts and Science for the teaching of life sciences was developed. Under the leadership of Deans Douglas Waugh, Tom Boag, and Laurence "Larry" Wilson, the faculty spread. The Cancer Research Centre and the Clinical Learning Centre were opened, each adding to the faculty's breadth of research and clinical teaching. Closer ties were developed with the Schools of Rehabilitation Therapy and of Nursing, reflecting the growing recognition that teamwork was fundamental to the delivery of medical services. Typical of this trend was Queen's staffing of the local hospital in the northern-Ontario Cree community of Moose Factory. Under an initiative launched in 1972, the hospital each spring welcomed Queen's nursing and medical students, who used the experience to perfect their nursing and community-health skills, while at the same time enhancing Queen's community outreach.[89] But it was this same ever-broadening sophistication of modern medical education that by the late eighties began to expose an Achilles heel of the Botterell reforms of the early sixties.

Botterell had regularized the staffing of the medical faculty under the concept of "geographic full-time" (GFT) appointments designed to compensate faculty in such a fashion that they might equitably conduct research, undertake clinical teaching, perhaps administer their faculty, and at the same time pursue private practice. The system was fuelled by financial injections – so-called "Treatment and Rehabilitation" or T & R grants – from the Ontario ministry of health and by fees garnered from services dispensed. To prevent more lucrative fee-for-service earnings (now paid for by the state under medicare) squeezing out their clinical teaching and research responsibilities, medical faculty agreed to cap their private earnings at a predetermined ceiling. If their earnings exceeded this ceiling – dubbed "overage" – the surplus earnings were to be deposited into trust accounts dedicated to supporting the hiring of new clinicians and the adoption of new medical specialties. The GFT system had been an admirable fix for the problems of medical staffing in the sixties, but under the strain of seventies austerity and the exponential progress of medical science, the GFT system begat its own crisis of inequality.

Under the "one-payer" system of medicare, medical faculty were increasingly drawn into fee-for-service clinical work. At the same time, government austerity in the seventies and eighties squeezed the annual operational budget of medical schools. By 1989, only $12.5 million of the medical faculty's $72-million budget was directly funded through the university. In this environment, the trust funds built up in clinical departments became crucially important. Departments with a heavy emphasis on procedural clinical work, such as cardiology, succumbed to the logic of fee-for-service and were therefore able to build up sizable trust funds, but did so at the expense of minimizing their research and teaching time. Other departments, with less exposure to fee-for-service OHIP revenue, saw their ability to deploy trust funds to attract new talent and to support their teaching and research crimped. Thus, invidious distinctions grew throughout the faculty: by the early nineties, certain departments, such as medicine, with its strong commitment to undergraduate teaching and the continuing education of established practitioners, found that their trust funds could no longer sustain their expenditures.[90]

Other problems plagued the GFT system. The reporting of earnings beyond mandated ceilings by clinicians hinged on an honour system that allowed the deduction of expenses from OHIP billings, thereby allowing at-times-questionable reductions in transfers into the trust funds.[91] Some clinicians simply failed to pay their overage and fell into serious arrears. Morale in the faculty consequently sagged; gaps grew between "have" and "have-not" departments. All this dysfunction took hold against a backdrop of a massive expansion in demand for medical education and services in Canada. As Jacalyn Duffin, Queen's Hannah Professor of the History of Medicine, was telling each year's arriving cohort of would-be doctors, medical knowledge was exponentially multiplying as new microspecialities, such as medical "informatics" (how information is processed by computers), emerged and old specialties, such as surgery, reinvented themselves by embracing new technologies that allowed non-invasive surgery.[92]

In 1988, Duncan Sinclair had assumed the roles of dean of Medicine and vice-principal, health sciences. Sinclair, a physiologist by training, typified the tradition of organic leadership at Queen's. Since joining the faculty in 1965, he had served as dean of Arts and Science, and then in the mid-eighties had stepped into vice-principalships overseeing the university's institutional relations and then the deployment of its resources. This catholic curriculum vitae gave him a broad view of the complexity of academic organization. Sinclair was also candid and impatient for change. By the early nineties, he could see that the old Botterell system was "broken." Sinclair wrote to the principal, "As you know, things are happening very fast in the health-care system. There is a high degree of uncertainty and it is apparent that we have to make very major changes very soon. Clinical trust budgets are close to bankruptcy and we will be at the point of being unable to meet the payroll during the course of the current fiscal year." Without such reform, the faculty would be unable to replace its retiring faculty, respond to the demands of emerging areas such as epidemiology, community health, and biochemistry, and modernize the Bracken Library. There was, he concluded, a need to "renegotiate the whole business on which health professional education is funded."[93]

Towards an Alternative Funding Model for Medicine at Queen's

In February 1991, a task force chaired by Sinclair reported that the faculty had become "unbalanced" in its ability to deliver on its three central missions: clinical services, teaching, and research. The cardinal problem was "the lack of a centralized, integrated system of governance over all three functions." Financial inputs to the faculty were uneven and, as the OHIP fee schedule felt the pinch of provincial austerity and hospitals closed critical-care beds, even the front-line clinical departments were becoming underfunded. To remedy the situation, the Sinclair Report suggested severing the direct link between faculty income and fee-for-service payments. A steadier, more predictable, and equitable revenue stream was needed. Professors providing instruction and research in basic sciences such as biochemistry should, the report recommended, continue to be treated as salaried members of the university, able to draw on research funds from outside agencies. Members of clinical departments, such as surgery, psychiatry, and medicine, should however fall under a new financial arrangement that bound Queen's, the ministry of health, the three local hospitals – Kingston General, Hotel Dieu, and St Mary's (soon to become the Providence Care campus) – and the clinicians working in these facilities into a new integrated local health-care, teaching, and research partnership.

This partnership would be called the Southeastern Ontario Medical Organization (SEAMO). It would manage the financial affairs of the partnership by, on the one hand, negotiating with the ministry of health for a predetermined annual injection of operating funds that would reflect both the contribution of the old T & R grants and an imputed amount to compensate the School of Medicine for the clinical services performed throughout the year, but no longer directly billed to the ministry. On the other hand, SEAMO would regulate the income of the over five hundred faculty members working under its supervision. Each faculty member would earn a small base salary (large enough to ensure coverage under the university's benefits plan) and then a larger "income" (clinicians do not like the term "salary") that reflected their day-to-day provision of care to patients. Like their colleagues in the basic sciences, clinicians would also be able to enhance their income with "soft" money from funded research. Every three to five years, SEAMO would renegotiate the ministry's grant to reflect changing cost structures.[94] In effect, the entire faculty would now operate under what Sinclair called "a single funding envelope," with the dean acting as a kind of de facto chief executive officer.

Sinclair conceived of what he dubbed the "alternate funding plan" (AFP) as part of a broader-front renovation of his faculty. After widespread consultation painstakingly led by the vice-dean of Medicine, Bob Maudsley, the Medical Faculty Board adopted a new undergraduate curriculum in 1991, one that tailored a Queen's medical education to recent shifts in the nature of medical practice. Undergraduate medical training was broken into three phases: a foundation of biomedical sciences, followed by clinically based learning and capped by a medical clerkship. The delivery of these phases would stress small-group learning and would at the same time promote "information literacy" in a profession that was increasingly dependent on the transmission of electronic data.[95] Medical education at Queen's would, Sinclair declared, abandon its old "sausage-stuffing" ways in favour of a more intimate, hands-on pedagogy.[96] Hitherto, the faculty had instructed its students along traditional subject lines – anatomy, pathology, and so on – relying on mass instruction in large-hall lectures. Now instruction would be geared to understanding how the body's systems – heart, lungs, brain – functioned, and would rely on case studies discussed in small-group format. Such teaching was more labour-intensive than lecturing, thereby underscoring the need to pull faculty back towards their teaching duties by breaking the drift towards billable clinical service.

Later in 1991, Sinclair wrapped his curriculum changes and funding reforms into a "strategic plan," one designed to guide his faculty into the mid-decade. The plan conveyed the image of the faculty unfolding like an umbrella over an expanding array of health-sciences activities. Sinclair had always taken a keen interest in incubating Queen's expertise in the life sciences, which by the late 1980s had become a hugely popular feedstock of students seeking entry into medical schools or into the burgeoning biotechnology industry. (By 1989, only 40 per cent of students taught in the faculty were pure medical students.) Given the exploding growth of medical knowledge, the faculty would also increase the continuing education of established physicians eager to update their skills. Masters and doctoral programs would be expanded in the faculty and funded research would be encouraged. Emphasis would be placed on instilling a sense that medical services relied on team effort. Rehabilitation therapy, long regarded by the medical faculty as a poor cousin, would now be an integral part of the faculty and was slated by Sinclair to expand to 320 students, who would learn to work closely with physicians.

Special emphasis would be placed on community-based rehabilitation. In 1991, for instance, the Canadian International Development Agency (CIDA) in Ottawa gave funding to Queen's for an outreach program in community-based rehabilitation, one that would eventually reach as far afield as Bangladesh. Similarly, the School of Nursing would be drawn closer into this holistic approach to medical teaching and delivery. Rita Maloney, dean of Nursing since 1989, pushed strongly for the professionalization of nursing, urging more emphasis on nursing theory and research by her faculty and students. By the early nineties, Maloney was advocating that an academic-style BSc in nursing be approved for students wishing to upgrade their community-college diplomas in nursing. A master's degree in nursing science was approved by the Senate in 1991.[97]

Compared with the growing disjuncture over salaries in the mainstream Queen's faculties, approval of the AFP moved along swimmingly, possibly because each party to the agreement saw its unavoidable necessity. Although the medical faculty escaped falling under the social contract,* in the spring of 1991 Queen's Park did freeze the size of the crucial T & R grants to all medical schools, a hint that government favoured SEAMO-like initiatives, which rationalized expenditure. In effect, SEAMO was a stand-alone "sub-sector" agreement. Every member of the medical faculty was sent "a letter of offer," which set out their regularized income – composed of a small base "salary" and a larger imputed income for medical services rendered. A well-attended meeting of the medical-faculty board hotly debated the plan, but in the end, over 90 per cent of the faculty took up the offer and signed a contract with the university. There were small pockets of resistance in departments such as surgery and anaesthesiology, where fee-for-service income had been lucrative.

In 1992, the School of Medicine received an accreditation visit from the American and Canadian medical association committees, which periodically vetted the quality of university medical programs. Accreditation reports could make or break a medical school. (Canadian medical schools were still, in a strangely neo-colonial way, obliged to submit to American scrutiny.) The previous accreditation visit in the eighties had resulted in only provisional approval of the school – the curriculum was said to be outdated and faculty morale poor. Now the American report gave Queen's unconditional "full accreditation" for the next seven years. The Canadian report found that the school had been "revitalized" in spirit and culture by the adoption of its new curriculum, its strategic plan, and the AFP.[98] Less than a decade earlier, in 1984, an outspoken Ottawa health economist had told the Parliamentary Committee on Health, Welfare and Social Affairs that the Queen's medical school was superfluous to Canada's medical needs and should be shut down. Local MP Flora MacDonald dismissed the idea as ludicrous, Dean Larry Wilson described the idea as "preposterous," and Dean Sinclair decried it in the *Whig-Standard* as groundless. Nonetheless, the controversy suggested a perception of trouble at that time.[99]

A decade later, any suggestion of malaise had evaporated. Queen's had developed a dynamic model of delivering medical service and education that was soon adopted by other Ontario medical schools. That model had allowed the university to take direct charge of the quality of its medical offerings, while at the same time harmonizing the culture of the faculty inhabiting that culture. David Smith had spent much time in the late eighties stressing that Queen's must privilege its "values" and the "quality" of the education it provided. The medical school now seemed to epitomize that ambition. Reform had set it on a course with its cousins in rehabilitation and nursing to ultimately amalgamate as the Faculty of Health Sciences in 1997. When asked to address alumni on Homecoming weekend that fall, Dean Sinclair proudly pointed out that Queen's medicine was now very comfortable in its own skin: "As a deliberately modestly-sized medical school," he noted, "we do not pretend to be all things to all people. We do not aspire to be Toronto in microcosm."[100]

---

*Since the Ontario Medical Association (OMA) negotiated all Ontario physicians' compensation under OHIP, medical faculty were deemed to already be in a collective bargaining relation with the government. The Clinical Teachers' Association at Queen's in effect acted as the OMA's agent on the Queen's campus and hence was in a position to sign on as a partner in the SEAMO agreement.

Preparing for the New Order

From "Steady State" to Privatized Niches

From a fiscal perspective, the SEAMO arrangements of the medical faculty pointed to a way of solving the fundamental dilemma of the Smith years: reconciling constrained financial resources with the exigencies of quality education. Politicians' dogged adherence to the creed of accessibility and their unwillingness to entertain funding models that would allow individual universities to differentiate their brands had long stymied Queen's ambitions. Since the Deutsch years in the sixties, Queen's had therefore embarked on its "steady state" strategy of constricting its admissions, so as to ensure that it inducted the best and brightest into its undergraduate ranks.

By the mid-eighties, however, the "steady state," with its ceiling of roughly ten thousand students, was becoming increasingly difficult to maintain. It was, in the first place, the victim of its own success. High entrance standards tended to beget students who excelled, did not drop out or transfer to other universities, and, consequently, intensified the sense of achievement of attending Queen's. It also allowed Queen's to garner extra income by capitalizing on the province's willingness to let universities exceed the stipulated tuition formula by up to 10 per cent. This so-called "pipeline effect" produced a slow creep in enrolment at Queen's, even when the overall volume of provincial university applications sagged. In 1984, a new pressure materialized: Ontario announced that it would abolish Grade 13, replacing it with a system of Ontario Academic Credits (OAC), which would enable a diligent student to clear high school in four years. Universities were warned by the provincial government to expect a possible "double cohort" arriving on their doorstep in 1988. In 1987, Principal Smith told the trustees that this would probably result in a 10-per-cent surge in enrolment over the four to five years after 1988. Lurking behind this surge were other demographic projections that suggested demand for university placement would naturally grow late in the decade.

By 1988, that pressure became evident. The Senate Committee on Academic Development (SCAD), the monitor of admissions, reported that applications to the province's universities had increased by 10.8 per cent over the previous year, but that applications to Queen's were up by 12.5 per cent. Both the Senate and the trustees therefore engaged in a debate as to how far Queen's might accommodate the double cohort and at what cost to its "steady state" creed. Most agreed that it would be "irresponsible" for Queen's to rebuff the government's alert. Outright refusal would hardly curry favour in Queen's Park, and would be financially foolish. Additional students would bring in more BIUs, regardless of the shortcomings of the current funding model. Queen's Park was also offering a one-time boost of $88 million in operating grants to be shared by campuses willing to expand. Therefore SCAD recommended piecemeal increases in enrolment across the board: Applied Science might accept an additional 425 new undergraduates and Education another 30, for instance.

There was agreement that Queen's should avoid general headlong expansion. Too much militated against such growth: already-stretched library resources, the off-campus student-accommodation squeeze, and limited financial assistance for students, plus the worry that class sizes would buckle under the strain. In short, quality would suffer. As Smith told the trustees: "Queen's decision is that it cannot increase numbers greatly." The Senate Committee on Academic Development concurred: Queen's would abide by a policy of "moderate and controlled growth."[101] Nonetheless, even this modest concession to provincial trends spelled an end to the "steady state" rubric of the last two decades. Queen's would no longer be a "small town" university. By the fall of 1988, Smith reported that an extra 349 undergraduates had pushed undergraduate admissions up 3.5 per cent, and graduate enrolment had swelled 10 per cent, to 1,819, with the result that Queen's now had an overall, full-time enrolment of 12,214. By Smith's last year as principal in 1993–94, the university would add another 1,100 students.

Pioneering New Frontiers: A Full-Cost MBA in the School of Business

A strategic question now faced Queen's: how to reap the maximum advantage from this grudging acceptance of growth? How to maintain quality, enhance income, and yet not overtax faculty, staff, and facilities? How to capitalize on new learning opportunities without breaking the creed of accessibility and at the same time underscoring the distinctiveness of the institution? The School of Business, long obliged to adapt to shifts in its external market, led the way in solving this challenge. Under Dean John Gordon (1978–88), the school had tried to adjust itself to changing times – the globalization of commerce, the advent of the "new economy," with its galloping electronic culture, and the proliferation of specialized business knowledge. Gordon arrived in Kingston as a specialist in academic organization, with experience in prestigious European business schools and strong connections with business education in the United States. He thus returned to the business school in Kingston where he had done his own MBA and found it parochial. For Queen's under Gordon, this impatience meant reaching out from the confines of its relative isolation in eastern Ontario towards Bay Street and beyond.

Gordon revitalized the school's advisory council, drawing in the expertise of cutting-edge business leaders. (Paralleling this, successful School of Business graduates such as Melvin "Mel" Goodes, CEO of the pharmaceutical giant Warner-Lambert in the United States, and Toronto financier Jim Leech were recruited to the Board of Trustees.) In 1981, an in-residence executive-education program was initiated. Energy was poured into small-business consulting in the Kingston region. Continuing-education programs were developed for public-sector executives. Both the undergraduate and MBA curricula were revised to align the school's teaching with emerging trends in the business community, such as information technology. To reflect the arrival of a second-wave feminist consciousness in the business world, more women – five by 1990 – were brought into the tenured faculty. Other new appointments allowed the school to bring in expertise in developing trends in the rapidly deregulating world of finance – the use of derivatives and the blending of retail and investment banking. Across Canada, business schools were reinventing themselves, drawing closer to their principal constituency – the business sector. Symptomatic of this affiliation was the trend towards close sponsorship of "b-schools" by prominent business leaders. In 1995, Western's business school became the Richard Ivey School of Business, while in 1997 the University of Toronto's business school became the Rotman School of Business. More systematic change followed. In 1998, for instance, the Ivey school opened a branch in Hong Kong.

But, for all this diversification, the Queen's business school still felt constrained. Budgets were tight in the late eighties and, like every other faculty at Queen's, business had to vie for the wherewithal to explore its ambitions. The school was still crammed into Dunning Hall and desperately needed new space, preferably a building of its own. Principal Smith quashed that idea as unaffordable. When David Anderson assumed the deanship of the school in 1988, he immediately sensed the mood of frustration. Anderson, a resource economist with an interest in the Canadian mining industry, had come to Queen's from Saskatchewan. He, too, immediately saw the need to increase the school's connection with the outside business world. With two hundred students enrolled in the school's existing two-year MBA program – one geared to aspiring young managers just emerging from their undergraduate degrees – the crucial challenge would be to develop offerings that brought added value to both the school and to those already established in their business careers. The hope here was to target managers in mid-career through programs that were self-funding – outside the bounds of formula funding, and therefore capable of carrying enhanced fee structures.

In 1991, Anderson briefed the Senate on the school's ambition to launch an executive MBA that focused on public-sector management. Times were tough in the public sector. In Ottawa, the Mulroney government had embraced the creed of deficit reduction and (as the "value for money" doctrine in Ontario illustrated) private-sector nostrums for leaner, more-effective management were, perhaps naively, being directed at the public sector. Anderson thus proposed an intensive, part-time MBA program in public-sector management. The program would aim at attracting managers in the thirty-five to forty-year-old cohort, who were well-established in their careers. So as not to disrupt those careers, the degree would be offered part-time, with students coming to Queen's for intensive weekend sessions and at other times connecting through coast-to-coast video-conferencing.[102]

Anderson turned to Gordon Cassidy, a mathematics-trained business professor with a dynamic, outgoing personality, to work up the new program. Beyond its closely defined niche market, the new "executive" MBA's principal attraction was its promise of being self-financing. It would not be cross-subsidized out of existing university resources, but would instead pay for itself through its $16,000 annual tuition. At this rate, it would probably be a money-maker. It was assumed that most students' fees would be covered by their employers. The prospect of self-financing courses thus found strong resonance at Queen's: the trustees had just launched a task force on "revenue enhancement," headed by Toronto businessman Donald Rickerd. There was much talk of bolstering the university's "bottom line," so a self-financed degree that catered to a specific need, while not compromising the code of undergraduate accessibility to universities, immediately appealed. The proposal was strongly supported by Tom Courchene, director of the school of policy studies, who argued that the new MBA perpetuated Queen's long-standing ties with the Ottawa bureaucracy. Indeed, many classes in the new program would be held in Ottawa, not Kingston. In late September 1991, the Senate approved the innovative program, and the first students in the intensive twenty-three-course program began their studies the following fall.

The sense of constraint pervading the business school quickly dissipated. The school's historians, Mervin Daub and Bruce Buchan, have described in dramatic terms Dean Anderson's second term as dean, beginning in 1993: "the lid blows off." Harkening back to the school's early years of pioneering courses for bankers and accountants, they concluded that "the School was again an innovative path breaker for the rest of the schools in the country."[103] Other initiatives followed: a twelve-month master of science in management and the Canada-Asia Business Relations Centre. But the immediate success of the new executive MBA prompted a more-ambitious gambit. Late in 1993, marketing professor Ken Wong, himself a Queen's MBA graduate from 1976, appeared before the Senate with a proposal to extend the executive MBA into a full-time, full-cost-recovery MBA focused on the managerial requirements of the science-and-technology sector. Two impulses lay behind the initiative, which almost immediately became labelled a "privatized" MBA. First, it reflected the esteem in which the MBA degree was held in the business community. The MBA degree was seen as a key ingredient in business success and was increasingly being rated along lines of international comparison. At a time when there was much talk of responding to the "new economy" and its global dimensions, business schools hankered to give their MBAs something of global appeal, something "world-class." At the same time, Queen's sought to tailor its new MBA to the needs of a particular industrial sector – the hot science-and-technology, or "high-tech," frontier on which Canadian companies like Nortel, Bombardier, and CAE seemed so well-positioned.

Vigorously backed by his dean, Wong proved a passionate and persuasive missionary for the new program. The old two-year MBA would end. The emphasis would now be on accelerated learning: Queen's broke ground by offering Canada's first one-year MBA. At the faculty board meeting that debated Wong's blueprint, there was a palpable sense that the school was taking a big risk, but that it was a risk in tune with the times. The new MBA would be punishingly concentrated into twelve months, half the time of an ordinary MBA. Tuition would be set at a stunning $20,000. The program was designed to appeal to ambitious young business managers, who more than likely had already been baptized in business but wanted to add depth to their skills and velocity to their careers. Given this, the Queen's proposal was rooted in the belief that such courses stood apart from the ethos of accessibility that underlay most Ontario university programs. This was a program serving the interest of healthy private-sector enterprise, which could quickly refund higher tuition costs to its graduates in handsome salaries paid upon graduation. Wong predicted that the "world-class" degree would add nothing to the university's deficit and would in fact contribute $850,000 to its bottom line.

As with all new academic programs, the science-and-technology MBA was sent to the Senate Committee on Academic Development for review. The committee, with its mixed faculty and student membership, found the proposal "revolutionary." Almost immediately, an ideological debate sprung up. Student member Alison Young wondered whether such a full-cost degree would make post-secondary education a "private good" that would send a signal to government that education was no longer "solely a public matter."[104] Others remarked that university education should not be "market-driven or niche-oriented." When the proposal reached the Board of Trustees, faculty observer and QUFA president Allan Manson worried that many would not be able to afford the tuition and that revenue generation at the classroom door might be "a vision of the future." Given the pioneering nature of the new degree, the debate soon spilled into the national press. The *Globe and Mail* suggested that the Queen's scheme epitomized the dilemma of balancing accessibility to education against ensuring its quality. *Canadian Business* put the story on its cover under the title "Class Warfare," noting that Wong had "declared open season on every aspect of the traditional MBA."[105]

Anderson and Wong nevertheless stood their ground. Without "privatization," the new degree, they argued, would generate a $400,000 deficit in the school's budget. Critics of the idea needed to take a "total cost" view of its implications. Wong pointed out that, by condensing the degree into twelve months, degree takers would be back in the labour market eight months before those in the traditional MBA programs, and thereby able to reap the benefit of the higher salary that the degree would support. The short, intensive program might also be better suited to the needs of older candidates, whose time was at a premium. Young mothers in business careers might welcome the opportunity to upgrade their skills with minimum disruption of their domestic lives. In this way, Wong suggested, the new MBA might actually enhance the accessibility and quality of professional training, making it available to groups which might otherwise not be able to break away from existing commitments. Furthermore, the school would guarantee interest-free loans to anyone lacking the tuition on admission, loans that would only be called when the newly minted MBA had secured employment on graduation with a salary in excess of $50,000. Beyond such individual considerations, the degree would bring prestige to Queen's, heightening its national and international recognition. It would also serve to halt the brain drain of promising young Canadians to US business schools and thereby push Queen's near to the top of globally-ranked business schools. As Wong assured Queen's graduates in the alumni magazine, the new degree was "more than just a price tag."[106]

Once approved by the Senate and the trustees, the new MBA needed a nod of approval from provincial accreditation officials and, perhaps most importantly, the politicians. The NDP government's education minister, Dave Cooke, was skeptical. The program seemed elitist and a Trojan horse at the gates of accessibility. Wong bearded the minister in his Queen's Park office, arguing again that the program would enhance accessibility to professional training, improve educational quality, and help alleviate stretched university finances. Cooke relented. So did the Ontario Council of Graduate Studies. With approval from the American Assembly of Collegiate Schools of Business (AACSB), the new program was ready to go in the fall of 1995.

The two new MBAs offered by the School of Business had been launched with surprising alacrity in an institution that was predisposed to slow deliberation and skepticism about hurriedly responding to the external pressures of change. But a combination of forceful advocacy and financial timeliness had carried the day. The new MBAs were instantly popular. In 1998, the all-important AACSB gave the Queen's business school an "unconditional" accreditation, and the business press began to mention the school in the same breath as prestigious American and European business schools. Early in the new century, Queen's began negotiations to push its MBA activities across international borders, with talk of an affiliation with Cornell University's Johnson School of Management. (A joint Queen's-Cornell MBA would indeed be launched in 2005.) Income from these innovative programs proved a boon to the university;[107] within a decade, tuition for the executive MBA had risen to a lucrative $55,000 per year. As the new century unfolded, MBA fees crested over $100,000, and Queen's annually found itself favourably ranked by prestigious publications such as the *Financial Times* against prestigious business programs around the world.

Perhaps the most lasting legacy of the new Queens MBAs was the message they sent to the rest of the campus. They offered a new, bolder solution to the university's decades-old dilemma of accessibility and quality. They identified areas of pressing opportunity in the society beyond the campus, and tied them to the university's potential. And they did so by devising a viable model for sustaining such initiatives. While the fundamental dilemma of reconciling accessibility and solvency remained embedded in its underlying strata of undergraduate education – as the failure of the *Blueprint for Action* had revealed – Queen's was, at the graduate level, finding a path to distinctiveness that upheld its reputation as a crucible of innovative learning. These initiatives on the Kingston campus echoed shifts in Canadian public policy: in the last decade of the twentieth century, cash-strapped Canadian governments sought to target their educational policy and spending on niches of opportunity where evident need could be matched with evident expertise. Queen's would thus respond to federal initiatives such as the Canada Foundation for Innovation or the Ontario Research and Development Fund in much the same way the Executive MBA had responded to public- and private-sector needs for managerial excellence.

This dawning recognition of a synergy between academic and societal need would reverberate through many other Queen's start-ups in the last decade of the century: a School of Environmental Studies in 1994, a Centre for Studies in Molecular Neuroscience in 1996, a Centre for Knowledge-based Enterprises in 1998, and a Centre for Automotive Materials and Manufacturing in 1999, to mention just a few. Each of these had a different mandate, a different clientele, and a different academic structure, but collectively they all spoke of a new flexibility in the way the university conceived of its purpose.

New Frontiers: Internationalizing Queen's

The advent of privatized degree programs and the loosened regulation of tuition reflected a new dedication at Queen's to tailoring post-secondary education to the shifting sensibilities of Canadian society. By the late eighties that also came to mean responding to broader international tendencies. The North American free-trade deal of 1988, coupled with an awareness of the dynamics of globalization, arguably pushed Canadians into abandoning their protectionist inclinations and into thinking strategically beyond their borders. In some superficial ways, Queen's had always conceived of itself as an international university. Its campus had long drawn students from abroad, often from countries that shared Canada's Commonwealth sensibilities. Bermudian and Caribbean students had for decades, for instance, been amply represented on Queen's campus, as had American and British students. At the same time, Queen's had sent its own abroad; the Theological College had for years exported many of its graduates to foreign Protestant pulpits. Other off-shore affiliations were maintained with Scottish universities in Edinburgh and Glasgow, in celebration of Queen's earliest pedagogic ties with the "old country." Since the award's inception in 1902, Queen's had had an admirable track record of securing Rhodes Scholarships for its most stellar students. In 1987, by way of example, Queen's impressively dispatched two of its students – chemical engineering student and football captain Charles Galunic and Arts student and musician Stephen Beke – to take up Rhodes awards in Oxford. In total, Queen's secured an impressive fifty-one Rhodes Scholarships from 1905 to the end of the century.

But these were only hesitant, periodic appearances on the world stage, which did little to transform Queen's traditional reputation as a leading *national* university, into a reputation for international excellence. Since the seventies, the university had indeed dedicated itself to making itself more international. The Senate and trustees had endorsed the goal of drawing at least 6 per cent of admissions from beyond Canada's borders. This goal would prove elusive. After a brief initial spurt that saw "foreign" students, as they were described, peak at 5.9 per cent in 1982–83, non-Canadian enrolment steadily declined until, by 1985, foreign students constituted just 3 per cent of undergraduate enrolment and 19 per cent of graduate students.[108] Queen's was, in fact, below the national average in attracting international students. By 1988, Queen's had only 610 full-time international students out of an overall undergraduate and graduate enrolment of 12,214.

Despite the faltering numbers, the international fact at Queen's had put down some roots. Since 1962, the International Centre in the Students' Union, generously supported by a Kingston couple, Ed and Anna Churchill, and the local Rotary Club, had eased the transition of overseas students into the life of a small Canadian city and a tradition-bound university. In its early years, the centre focused on intercultural events and drop-in friendliness (sometimes with the result that foreign students came to feel uncomfortably exotic at Queen's).[109] The centre proved especially helpful in assisting newcomers to find accommodation in the tight Kingston housing market. By the eighties, the centre's director, Wayne Myles, had diversified the centre into a facilitator of *two-way* international student exchanges. As with many trends, Queen's students were quick to sense the possibilities of international education. In 1985, only four Queen's students spent a term away from the university on international exchange; by 1992 that number had grown to seventy-four.[110] As with its willingness to connect its MBA program to the globalizing economy, the Queen's business school pioneered the university's international outreach: throughout the 1990s, the faculty put together an international exchange program for its undergraduate students. Guided by international business professor David Rutenberg, the exchange program initially offered third-year students the opportunity to study abroad in countries as disparate as Switzerland and Taiwan. Responding to the unfolding world of North American free trade and a globalizing world economy, the program would quickly expand in numbers and destinations to the point that 80 per cent of Queen's undergraduates in commerce would pursue studies abroad by the new century.

At the same time, other students undertook to work as volunteers in the developing world under the auspices of organizations such as faith-based Crossroads. Principal Smith obliged this trend by signing academic exchange agreements with universities in Korea, China, Japan, Australia, and Guyana. This allowed course credits taken abroad to count towards a Queen's degree. Not surprisingly, Japan with its "miracle" economy in the eighties held a magnetic attraction for Queen's. In 1988, Queen's began teaching Japanese, and two years later it joined the Japan Society, an American non-profit foundation dedicated to building cultural bridges. Back in Kingston, the international student presence began to take root on Queen's campus: for instance, a Chinese Students' Association and an Indian Classical Dance Club were founded and, in 1992, an umbrella International Students' Association was born with AMS blessing. Despite these initiatives, Queen's still struggled to attract foreign applicants.

Many factors explained Queen's slow uptake on the international front. The national census suggested that newcomers to Canada, even if as transient students, preferred large urban environments to small provincial enclaves that seemed cut off from big-city dynamics. Similarly, Kingston's eastern-Ontario location necessitated an additional leg on the journey of any foreign student arriving in the gateway cities of Montreal and Toronto. Attracting international students was made more complicated by the provincial government's determination to apply higher fees to foreign students. The university, having committed itself to its 6-per-cent goal of foreign enrolment, tried to offset this by supplying bursaries to foreign students, but this tended to bite into the funds available for domestic students. In 1994, Toronto withdrew Ontario Hospital Insurance medical coverage from foreign students attending provincial universities. Such financial stringency made it difficult to attract foreign students. There can be little surprise, therefore, that international enrolment became volatile, and that Queen's never achieved its 6-per-cent target for international admissions.

Internationalization was, of course, about more than attracting foreign students. It also extended to the university's intellectual endeavours. In this sense, Queen's had myriad international connections that drew its expertise across many borders. Academic conferences annually took Queen's scholars around the globe; Queen's professors took their expertise in areas as disparate as glacial formations and the workings of federalism throughout the world. But there was little concerted effort or structure behind these activities. David Smith assumed the principalship with a determination to make Queen's a more internationalized place. This was not just a fanciful ambition to see Queen's achieve an aura of international engagement. Instead, it reflected a realization that internationalization was an imperative option for late-twentieth-century universities. Introducing his long-term blueprint *Queen's University: Strategy, 1985–90* to the Senate in 1986, Smith underscored the plan's "ambitious program for Queen's development, urging it to compete in an international sense."[111] That same year, an Office of International Programs was established in the Graduate Studies faculty to coordinate Queen's effort to link its expertise with international opportunity. From 1986 to 1991, for instance, the Education faculty undertook a $6.3-million project to mentor teacher training in Kenya. Other faculties took up the quest for foreign affiliations: in 1991, Dean David Anderson of the School of Business toured Japan, hoping to make connections for Queen's recently created Canada-Asia Business Centre. Medicine offered its community-based rehabilitation expertise. David Eastham, director of the International Programs Office, argued that Queen's should centralize its efforts to establish an international beachhead. The office's 1991 publication *The International Dimension of Queen's University* moved in that direction. But, on the whole, Queen's ambition to move more forcefully onto the international stage was a fitful and uncoordinated affair. International initiatives offered attractive opportunities outside the usual regimen of financing and administering the university. Grants from agencies such as CIDA brought money to Queen's with no provincial strings attached. International projects, and students from abroad, also leavened Queen's culture by connecting it to multicultural diversity. All the while, however, uneasy trade-offs had to be made between Queen's urge to internationalize itself and the exigencies of maintaining its established domestic orientation.

A Castle of International Dreams

In 1992, Queen's international aspirations received a powerful, unexpected nudge. Out of the blue, the university was offered a medieval castle in the English countryside south of London. For years, top-flight American universities had maintained prestigious footholds in Europe, seeing them as a means of stretching their intellectual endeavours and adding lustre to their reputation. In 1959, for instance, Harvard had been bequeathed millionaire Bernard Berenson's beautiful Tuscan villa, I Tatti, turning it into a centre for the study of the Italian Renaissance. Closer to Queen's, upstate New York universities Cornell and Syracuse had each established branch operations in Italy. There students streamed each summer, not just to immerse themselves in Europe's culture, but also to study its social, political, and economic affairs. Now that possibility presented itself to Queen's. On 7 October 1992, David Smith surprised the weekly meeting of his vice-principals and deans by announcing that a donor had approached the university with an offer to buy Herstmonceux Castle in Sussex and donate it to Queen's as a "European Study Centre."[112] The

castle, built by Sir Roger Fiennes, dated from the late-fifteenth century and was reputed to be one of the oldest brick structures in Europe. It had fallen into disrepair in the late-eighteenth century, but had been restored early in the twentieth to be inhabited by a succession of private owners before, after World War II, becoming the home of the Royal Greenwich Observatory. When the observatory moved out in 1989, the castle fell into the hands of a developer who began looking for a modern-day lord of the manor. With 140 rooms, a moat, a formal garden, and a sprawling 532-acre park, Herstmonceux, a relic of an aristocratic world long in decline in Britain, promised to be a tough sale. That is, until it fell under the eye of Queen's-trained chemical engineer, Alfred Bader, the same refugee student who years earlier, in the midst of the war, Jean Royce had admitted to Queen's, who was now willing to don the mantle of Bernard Berenson and use this formidable piece of English heritage to coax his alma mater across the Atlantic.

Alfred Bader had a deep love for Queen's – and not just on account of his intellectual debt to the university. Born in Vienna of Czech-Hungarian parentage in 1924, Bader fled Austria in 1938 when the Nazi annexation of his homeland obliged relatives to send him to safety in England on a *kindertransport* train. There, when war came the next year, seventeen-year-old Bader was cruelly caught in the trap of technically being an "enemy alien" (the citizen of a country at war with Britain). Even though they had demonstrated repugnance towards the Reich by fleeing Austria, Bader and other European Jews in Britain were interned on the Isle of Man. Realizing the folly of confusing the victims of war with its perpetrators, Britain prevailed upon Canada and Australia to absorb its interned Jews. Canada agreed, even though its own record of welcoming Jews within its borders in the interwar years had been niggardly and tragically exclusionary.[113] Sadly, Bader's first memory of Canada was of jeering Canadians as he and the German prisoners-of-war disembarked from the same ship in Quebec

Moated Herstmonceux Castle in the Sussex countryside. Alfred Bader's unexpected and generous offer provided a platform for Queen's accelerated emergence as an international university. Here Principal Smith showcases Queen's new real estate.

City. To add injury to insult, his suitcase, containing all his worldly possessions, promptly went missing, probably stolen. Bader soon found himself incarcerated in an only-slightly-more-hospitable Canadian internment camp. Here, at least, he was able to write the matriculation examination for McGill University, scoring handsomely. Finally, after fifteen months, Bader was released in late 1941 into the oversight of a caring Montreal Jewish family, the Wolffs of Westmount.[114]

Freed from the evil threat of Nazism, Bader nonetheless soon discovered some of the limitations of his Canadian freedom. He was required to renounce any financial claims he might make on the Canadian government and was obliged to report weekly to the Royal Canadian Mounted Police. And, despite his strong matriculation results, he discovered that his chances of university entrance at McGill were slim. Situated in the largest Jewish community in Canada, McGill had always quietly capped Jewish admissions to its programs, a phobic reflection of the racist fear that clever and ambitious Jews might overwhelm the WASP culture of Montreal. Much the same policy prevailed at Canada's other leading university, the University of Toronto. The surge of wartime Jewish refugees, like Bader, exacerbated the prejudice. Words such as "swamped" came to punctuate the discussions of university admissions policy. Queen's was not immune to this dialogue. As the war took hold, Jewish enrolment at Queen's had more than doubled – from 45 in 1938–39 to 127 in 1942–43, and this at a time when overall Queen's enrolment was contracting in wartime. Principal Wallace wrote that the relative influx to Queen's was the by-product of McGill capping its intake of Jewish applicants, obliging those excluded at McGill to seek other academic pastures.

To consider the "problem" of the spike in Jewish students at Queen's, a joint Senate-trustees committee was struck. The ensuing debate ranged dangerously close to blatant racial discrimination – there was talk of an outright restriction of Jewish admissions. Others wrapped their anxiety over Jewish students at Queen's in more expedient terms – the concern that any overt exclusion would tarnish Canada's wartime image and might provoke a divisive "blow-up" on campus. To his lasting credit,

Principal Wallace resisted all talk of overt restrictions and played for time as the issue worked its way through the deliberations of the Board, the Senate, and the faculty boards. Finally, as the war neared its end, the university decided to upgrade its admission standards, hoping that if they raised the bar of admission, Jewish applicants unsuccessful at McGill would similarly fail to gain entry to Queen's. With the peace, the pressure eased and the issue waned, allowing Queen's to revert to an unspoken wariness about Jewish admissions and a surreptitious system of quotas in faculties such as medicine.[115]

Alfred Bader arrived at Queen's in November 1941, before the issue of the Jewish incursion became a matter of open debate. Shunned by McGill and Toronto, Bader had turned towards Queen's both because one of the Wolff daughters, Rosetta, was taking an extramural degree there and because her father, Martin, had befriended an engineering professor at Queen's. As with almost all neophyte undergraduates, Bader's first stop on the Queen's campus was Royce's office. There, she opened the gates of the university to him, sending him over to the chemical engineering department.[116] Bader would never forget this act of faith in his abilities. Through dint of hard work, he crammed a full term's work into a few weeks and passed his Christmas exams. Bader quickly bonded with Queen's. In 1945, he earned a B.Sc. in engineering chemistry, winning a university medal. Then, to demonstrate that his mind was not narrowly compartmentalized, Bader took a BA in history, before rounding out his Queen's education with a M.Sc. in chemistry in 1947. En route to these achievements, Bader imbibed Queen's student culture, especially its expectation that students should leave a mark on their alma mater. In 1945, he led the drive to establish a Queen's branch of the Hillel Foundation, an organization dedicated to the well-being of Jewish university students. In this mission, he approached Principal Wallace (who was by this time, of course, acutely aware of the Jewish presence on his campus) with a request that he approve the constitution of the fledgling group. Wallace gave his nod, delighted with Bader's assurance that Hillel at Queen's would never be an exclusivist group, but instead one dedicated to "understanding and co-operation with other religious organizations."[117]

From Fine Chemicals to Fine Art

The brilliant Bader had graduated into the right industry at the right time. The postwar economy was fuelled by chemical innovation. "Better things for better living ... through chemistry," DuPont's sales pitch promised North Americans. Another master's degree, followed by a 1949 doctorate in chemistry from Harvard, landed Bader in this hot job market. Turning away from the prospect of an academic career, Bader began his industrial career as a research chemist with a paint company and, when that company was taken over by the Pittsburgh Plate Glass Company, he moved to the Milwaukee labs of his new employer. Increasingly, Bader became fascinated by the production of high-grade organic chemicals such as bisphenolic acid, which were crucial to meticulous research. In 1951, Bader and a Milwaukee attorney incorporated Aldrich Chemical as a challenge to established makers of fine chemicals, such as Kodak. Through a combination of brilliant innovation, aggressive marketing, and cohesive corporate culture, Aldrich prospered. In 1954, Bader left Pittsburgh Glass to concentrate on his fledgling firm and thus began his ascendancy as one of America's leading purveyors of fine chemicals.[118]

Alfred Bader was a man of many dimensions. He indulged a passion for art. In later years he would lightheartedly confide to friends that he suffered from "an incurable disease" – that he was "uncontrollably consumed by an overwhelming passion for art."[119] From the time he wandered through the galleries of Vienna as a boy, Bader developed an appetite for the Dutch masters of the seventeenth century. In adulthood, his taste broadened to the Italian Baroque. The walls of his home and office became galleries reflecting his taste. He pursued particular artistic themes in his collecting: the iconic depiction of the Bible in paintings and bold characterizations of the human figure. Bader was no run-of-the-mill wealthy businessman in search of art that would advertise his worldly success. Instead, he became a shrewd buyer, who framed his acquisitions with a connoisseur's instinct. He, for instance, applied his chemist's knowledge to the analysis and restoration of paintings. At the same time, he made himself into an art historian, speaking and writing knowledgeably about seventeenth-century Dutch and Italian art. He approached each acquisition like a hunter, sizing up his quarry from afar and then deftly moving in for the capture. He loved, as one Queen's art historian would later note, "the puzzle of buying and the egotism of discovery."[120]

Bader also deeply believed that the inspiration generated by art should be shared. He began to donate paintings to galleries such as the Fogg at Harvard and the Milwaukee Art Centre. His generous impulse turned Bader's thoughts to his alma mater. This had first been evident in 1967, when he donated an early sixteenth-century *Salvador Mundi* ("saviour of the world") portrait of Christ to the Agnes Etherington Art Centre, a bold painting that would later be attributed to the Venetian painter Girolamo da Santacroce. His giving continued. He candidly admitted that it was his desire to turn Queen's into "the Oberlin of Canada in the academic art world," Oberlin being the small Ohio college renowned for music and art.[121] In 1970, the trustees put on record that Bader had become Queen's "most substantial benefactor."[122] The mutual affection of donor and recipient never flagged. By the early 1990s, Bader had given Queen's more than 120 paintings. "You know," Bader wrote to art centre director David McTavish in 1993, "how paintings have affected my life. I get such enormous pleasure when I look at a really great painting – it is quite indescribable."[123] Moreover, Bader's wife, Isabel, shared in this delight, focusing her enthusiasm on the art centre's large costume collection.

Rembrandt's *Head of an Old Man in a Cap*, painted about 1630, acquired by Alfred Bader in 1979 and first displayed at the Agnes Etherington Art Centre in 1984. The portrait reveals Rembrandt's mastery of the human face as an interplay of light and expression. Since his initial donation of art to the centre in 1967, Bader (later joined by his wife, Isabel) had been unstintingly generous to his alma mater and, in doing so, had helped the "Agnes" become not just an outstanding university gallery, but also a cultural hub of regional and national importance.

Now Bader's love for Queen's manifested itself in real estate. At first, Bader had toyed with the notion of moving into Herstmonceux Castle himself, but Isabel had balked at the suggestion, saying that the place would overwhelm them. Bader quickly converted his ambition into making the castle a "European study centre," a cultural gangplank for Queen's into the rich cultural heritage of Europe. The offer took Principal Smith by surprise. His first reaction was to run the proposal past a "broadly based group" of Queen's administrators and trustees. Their response, he told the vice-principals and deans at that October 1992 meeting, was "enthusiastic." Having little sense of what the property actually looked like, Smith headed across the Atlantic to survey the potential gift that Bader had put before them. He took with him Sam Blyth, a Toronto tourism impresario, an indication that Smith initially saw the castle in terms of cultural tourism – something on the periphery of Queen's academic purpose. Together, Smith and Blyth quizzed five British architectural firms for their assessments of the possible capital needs and operational costs of so strange an addition to the university's campus. Back in Kingston, David Barnard, the associate to the vice-principal, resources, warned the principal that the castle would probably require a "major expenditure after purchase," and much would depend on the business plan developed to guide the castle's operation. Not surprisingly, it was clear that no one at Queen's had much expertise in operating a distant medieval castle. By now, most on campus understood that the mystery donor was Queen's old friend Alfred Bader and understood that Bader had always displayed resolution in his enthusiasms. Smith indeed reported that "the donor is not interested in committing equivalent funds to other purposes in the University."[124] Furthermore, Bader intimated that, as is often the case in real-estate transactions, a decision had to be taken quickly.

Bader's offer put Smith and his close advisors on the horns of a dilemma. The gift of a castle valued at approximately $10 million seemed like a godsend, a heaven-sent response to Queen's unfolding urge to internationalize itself. On the other hand, there was a palpable sense that all this was virgin territory. Sensing this dilemma, Smith asked the executive committee of the trustees to hold a special meeting in Toronto on 14 November. There he showed the trustees a video of the castle before setting out three principles that he considered should guide the university's response to Bader's offer. Privately, Smith feared that, if the castle offer was rejected, Queen's might alienate Bader and his long-standing benevolence towards the university. Bader was at the same time in the process of sponsoring a chair in organic chemistry at Queen's. If acquired, Smith argued, the castle should never constitute a drain on Queen's operating budget. Herstmonceux must also maintain the university's "tradition of excellence in education" and, thirdly, it must be developed as "a genuine, accessible international study centre."

In response, the committee expressed "unanimous enthusiasm and gratitude" about the offer. Nonetheless, there was a hesitancy about the implications of accepting ownership of the castle. There was worry about the legal and zoning implications of converting an English country estate to educational purposes. To this end, Smith asked a recent Queen's graduate, Jane Whistler (MEd 1980) who lived nearby in Sussex, to act as his unofficial agent in England and report on all the idiosyncrasies of acquiring an ancient building in a foreign land. A savvy British lawyer was retained to elucidate the process of establishing ownership. The trustees all seemed to realize that the castle presented an "entrepreneurial" challenge that would require the "strong leadership of a very able, senior official of the University."[125]

Smith reported that the Blyth Company in Toronto had expressed an interest in managing the castle. There was vague talk that Herstmonceux might make an inviting venue for Queen's art-history courses and its executive-development programs. The Baders themselves met with the committee the next day. Alfred Bader made two generous commitments that seemed to win the committee's confidence: he was prepared to provide additional funds for renovations and, if the university at any point decided that the project was not academically or financially viable, he would not block its sale. Hearing all this, the executive committee unanimously voted to accept Bader's offer. Queen's had its own castle.[126] The first students, it was excitedly announced, would arrive in the fall of 1993.

The full Board of Trustees duly approved the executive committee's resolution at its May 1993 meeting. Planning for the castle's future unfolded on the trot. Smith reported that it would be operated as a charitable foundation, held at arm's-length from Queen's normal operating budget. Money for its operation would be garnered from donations by Queen's alumni living in Britain, and from handsome fees reaped from courses offered to students from Queen's and other institutions. At $5,500 per half-course, fee revenue would be outside the pale of BIU funding, yet would still be less than the steep tuitions levied by American colleges in Europe. To make it all come together, Smith appointed one-time graduate studies dean Maurice Yeates as director of what was now being called the "International Study Centre." A heady optimism surrounded the whole project – there was a sense that Queen's had broken out of its parochial bailiwick and was stepping onto the world stage. At the same Board meeting, Chancellor Benidickson announced that a joint Senate-Board committee had been struck to seek a successor as principal for David Smith, who would now leave a legacy as the man who had taken Queen's across the Atlantic.

Dreams, however, do not always magically come true. Herstmonceux proved an ungainly addition to the Queen's family. Foremost, there was the awkward conjuncture of financing the launch of Herstmonceux in the lush English countryside with the brutal onset of "social contract" austerity on Queen's campus, where the mood could only be described as beleaguered. However flattering the acquisition of a castle may have initially been to Queen's self-image, Herstmonceux quickly became an object of invidious comparison. While Vice-Principal Rod Fraser valiantly sought to convince faculty and staff that $6 million would have to be squeezed out of the university's operating budget, and students dug deeper into their pockets to pay the new Student Assistance Levy, the castle quickly established itself as a drain on university finances.

By October 1993, Fraser's associate David Barnard reported that there was still a shortfall of $5.5 million in covering its start-up and operating costs – that over and above the $12 million the Baders had generously provided for the castle's purchase and renovation.[127]

Renovating a medieval castle was outside the usual cost expectations of North American budgeters. Queen's had never, for example, owned a building with a moat. Asbestos had to be removed from walls. Plumbing and heating systems were truly medieval. Building codes were Byzantine. British construction work seemed lethargic and sloppy. At the same time, initial projections of student interest in taking courses at Herstmonceux proved overly optimistic. Student accommodation was inadequate, so an old observatory building had to be converted into a residence at considerable expense (and christened Bader Hall). A year later, Maurice Yeates reported that only 47 students had registered for the fall courses in Sussex. To break even, he reported, Herstmonceux needed 175 students in each of its three terms. Rector David Baar voiced student concern that the fees were out of reach for most Queen's students and wondered whether the castle was only "marginally associated with the Queen's mission."[128] Early projections that the castle would break even after its first year of operation evaporated. Alumni in Britain proved stingy and unexcited about the castle in their backyard. Reluctantly, the Board of Trustees voted to approve a $12-million line of credit so that the yawning gap between expenses and revenues at Herstmonceux could be covered.

Ironically for a university that was in the throes of modernizing its MBA offerings, the fundamental flaw in the rollout of Queen's International Study Centre was the lack of a compelling and viable business plan. On the academic side, projection of the castle's role in catering to Queen's students was only fancifully conceived. Students proved resistant to an expensive, if exciting, program that bore little relationship to their mandated degree program back in Kingston. Many students wondered whether they could dovetail Herstmonceux's half-courses into their main campus programs. Faculty by and large proved reluctant to take on the challenge of transatlantic teaching at a time when salaries were capped. Little effort was initially made to connect Herstmonceux with the potential demand of students at other universities.

Moreover, on the operational side, Queen's experience in maintaining stately buildings such as Ontario Hall on the Kingston campus was no preparation for taking on the challenge of a medieval castle on the other side of an ocean. Cumulatively, Herstmonceux began to tarnish Queen's image. Faculty, staff, students, alumni, and, increasingly, the broader public began to think of the castle as Queen's white elephant, an expensive act of folly. All the while, there was genuine anxiety over retaining the goodwill of Alfred Bader as one of the university's best-intentioned friends. Through all the initial agony, Bader did keep the faith. So, too, did David Smith, who resolutely stood by his vision of Herstmonceux as an instrument of internationalizing Queen's. When Benidickson's search committee called McGill Vice-Principal William Leggett to Queen's in the late autumn of 1993 to be interviewed for the principalship, they were brutally frank about the castle and its problems. To his credit, Leggett immediately saw beyond the sheaf of bills and realized Herstmonceux's potential. It was "a window of opportunity" that beckoned Queen's to shed its comfortable eastern-Ontario identity and to step onto the world stage.[129] Leggett would get the job and inherit the problematic challenge of making Herstmonceux work.

Cow-paths, Concrete, and Congestion: Modernizing a Neglected Campus

Herstmonceux was hardly the first building to command Principal Smith's attention. The years spanning his principalship witnessed Queen's slow awakening from a long slumber of neglect of over what people were coming to call its "built environment." Even under the regulation of Deutsch's "steady state" policy of growth, Queen's ninety-three-acre campus had been saturated with new buildings and parking lots. Cars had squeezed green space into ever smaller pockets of lawn and shade. Old Richardson Stadium was gone. So were the tennis courts. Dutch elm disease intensified the deforestation: every year groundsmen buzz-sawed dead trees, leaving conspicuous gaps in the university's once-substantial canopy of green. As campus density went steadily up, a daily traffic of students and staff etched footpaths – "cow-paths" they were colloquially called – across once-pristine lawns. In an attempt to discipline this chaotic wandering, the university put down a network of lock-stone paths across the campus. Little thought was given to the way *people* actually moved around the campus; much more was devoted to the arterial flow of automobiles and their parking. And hovering over this warren were the new buildings that had sprung up – been shoehorned might be a better term – in wherever space could be found.

Many of these buildings contradicted Queen's long-standing image of a limestone campus. For decades, Queen's had styled itself in its promotional literature as a shady, stone-walled sanctuary, where architecture and intellectual purpose somehow seamlessly blended. In reality, for the last two decades, campus expansion had proceeded by expediency, a reflection of an era when space and money were in short supply. In the late sixties, the Board and Senate had sensibly joined forces to create a campus planning committee. The trustees, however, maintained a separate building committee, which held ultimate financial authority over all campus infrastructure. There was, in short, no central oversight of campus growth.

Given the excruciating austerity of the seventies, planning was done on the run whenever money became available. The result was a kind of accumulating jumble. Building design became a prosaic affair, with the university falling into a cozy relationship with familiar architectural firms, seldom demanding excellence in design, and often receiving uninspired, mediocre buildings in return. Mackintosh-Corry Hall, for many, epitomized this deterioration, a fate precipitated by the university's financial woes and by a falling out with architect Ron Thom. Other aspects of campus appearance, notably maintenance of its existing limestone buildings and landscaping, were simply allowed to become an afterthought. The topic of "deferred maintenance" put in a regular awkward appearance at most trustees' meetings, and was always pushed down the road.

By the mid-1980s, critics of this neglect of the Queen's aesthetic began to emerge. Alumni returning to campus remarked on their alma mater's drift away from any consistent architectural style. One typical critic was Alan Broadbent, Queen's first student rector in the late sixties and now an established voice in Toronto's financial and urban-reform communities. Members of the trustees' finance and building committees similarly remarked on the all-too-frequent cost overruns on Queen's construction projects; new buildings seldom lived up to expectation or met budget. Two mid-eighties' buildings in particular – the new Policy Studies Building and the Technology Centre on Union Street – seemed to bring the issue to a head. The Policy Studies project was executed hastily, as the university scrambled to secure a subsidy from the Secretary of State in Ottawa and at the same time induce the generous financial support of the Stauffer Foundation. Complicating the process was the fact that the school was to be an amalgam of several institutes, therefore entailing delicate discussion of space and purpose.

Almost immediately, there were problems. The school's footprint on Union Street placed it on the flank of the law faculty's Macdonald Hall. No one took into account the fact that law was planning its own project, a library expansion. "It appears," Dean Dan Soberman wrote to Vice-Principal Bennett, "that we have had a serious failure in campus planning at Queen's both in the quality of the work done here and in the participatory processes that have evolved as the strength of Queen's over the past two

Queen's School of Policy Studies, a compendium of all its policy-oriented programs, such as industrial and intergovernmental relations. The school's 1989 building represented a triumph of concrete-and-glass brutalism. Its central atrium chronically leaked. The building provoked a heated debate over the university's architectural integrity and heritage.

decades."¹³⁰ Construction intensified the dissatisfaction. The building's Brutalist use of concrete, metal ribbing, and glass complimented nearby Mackintosh-Corry Hall, but little else. The glass staircase rising up its front facade immediately began fogging up. The offices were cramped, the classrooms oddly shaped, and the air conditioning wonky. When the cost of the building topped $7.6 million, the Board's building committee said that it was "embarrassed" and made its displeasure known to the architect.

The new Technology Centre proved little better. Approved in 1985 to allow the university to react to the dramatic computer revolution that was breaking across the globe, the building was to be a "no frills" edifice which would allow the electrical-engineering department much-needed room to grow. A hurry-up ethos propelled the project. Again, the Stauffer Foundation displayed its generosity by contributing $2.3 million to the building's $4.9-million budget. Few demands were put on the architects, who once again employed concrete and glass in strongly horizontal window pattern, or fenestration. Brutalism seemed to be taking over Union Street. In 1987, Vice-Principal Sinclair, whose job it was to sign off on completed projects, was horrified by the quality of the building. Windows leaked and admitted drafts. The floors were uneven, and the tile work "shoddy." To make the point, Sinclair met with the builder on site, took a marble out of his pocket, dropped it, and watched it roll to the corner. Sinclair estimated that it would take $250,000 to rectify the shortcomings. He demanded restitution. He worried that Queen's was acquiring a reputation for accepting any architect, any builder, and any standard of work.¹³¹ Ironically, the building was three years' later named in honour of Walter Light, the stalwart Board chair and cutting-edge electronics executive who arguably deserved a more graceful memorial on campus.

Trees, Walkways, and Buildings: Queen's Discovers Campus Planning

Under such pressure, attitudes began to shift. Early in 1986, Vice-Principal Bennett retained a firm of Toronto planning consultants, Berridge, Lewinberg, to assess "the state of the Queen's campus." Their conclusions were damning. The Queen's campus, they reported, presented "two images." The first was the stereotypical Queen's aesthetic: "a place of some order, quality, and graciousness" – a limestone university in a limestone city. The second, more-modern image was "one of being tired, scruffy, and comprised by bad new buildings, landscaping, and parking." Three particular tendencies blighted the campus: shoddy, inattentive landscaping; modern buildings designed with no relation to "the remarkable qualities of the older building stock"; and "too much large size litter on the campus, in the form of car parking and garbage containers." At root, it all boiled down to "the lack of any overall strategy and guide for the myriad decisions that make up the management and future development of the campus." Queen's was becoming a campus where the needs of cars outweighed those of pedestrians, little attention was paid to off-street lighting, too much lock stone was put down, and "a series of very bland bulky modern buildings with rather harsh fenestration patterns" soured the view.¹³²

The report had immediate resonance. Speaking on behalf of the Campus Planning Committee, Helen Cooper, a Kingston city councillor from Sydenham Ward and a Queen's science grad from the sixties, told the Board that a working group had begun developing a long-term campus plan that would encompass green space, parking allocation, and the aesthetic objectives of architectural design. There was a recognition that the university had operated under "the mistaken impression that, once Queen's had reached a steady state in enrolment, the physical development of the campus was completed."¹³³ Similarly, the building committee turned its attention to the way the university negotiated

❖ *"Where Have All the Green Trees Gone?"* ❖

If there was ever an iconic image of Queen's, it was that of shady, elm-tree-lined streets, with limestone walls peeking through verdant foliage. As early as the 1860s, special care was taken to groom the campus forest. Natural-history professor George Lawson, who founded the Botanical Society of Canada, celebrated the fact by maintaining a botanical garden on the slope to the south of Summerhill. (To this day, exotic trees still occasionally sprout unexpectedly on that lawn.) As the university put its own roots down over the next century, a perennial favourite image for promotional literature was the sylvan beauty of University Avenue. But that image was slowly undermined both by nature itself and by man's expansionist and parsimonious instincts.

As the human and built density of the campus intensified during the building boom of the sixties and seventies, trees found themselves at risk. In 1945, there were 60 people for every one of Queen's 93 main-campus acres; by 1970 that ratio had surged to 130 people per acre. At the same time, Queen's paid a price for its dangerous monoculture reliance on Dutch elms, as beetles carried a deadly fungus under the bark of the stately elms. Through the seventies, buzz saws felled the victims. The financial austerity of that same decade pushed landscaping and sylviculture to the bottom of Queen's operating-budget priorities. Architect Arthur Erickson's mid-1970s sketches of the John Deutsch University Centre showed planters and window boxes. None were ever installed. The sprawling Mackintosh–Corry Building had only $20,000 budgeted for landscaping, and consequently lacked anything natural to soften its brutish concrete. "Where have all the green trees gone?" asked the *Queen's Journal* in 1976.

With Pete-Seeger-like alacrity, Queen's students took up the cause. Arts '75 launched "Queen's Green Forever" as a class project: $1,300 was raised to replace fallen elms. In October 1974, David Gordon of Science '76 launched Project Green, a more sustained effort to green the campus: if the administration was not prepared to groom the Queen's forest, then the students would. Project Green was a voluntary effort – it consisted of students with rakes, saws, and spades. Gordon had been a student member of the Campus Planning Committee and had been dismayed by the university's ecological parsimony. He used an AMS referendum to win a dollar-a-year levy from every Queen's student in support of Project Green for the next five years. Advised by groundskeeper Karl Duttle (who personally ached over the loss of trees and the lack of money to replenish them), Gordon and a crew of stout volunteers drove to Shawville, Quebec, to uproot pines, which they brought to Queen's and planted behind Grant Hall. Their actions were inspirational: Trustee Robert Dunsmore (BSc 1915) donated crabapples to line lower University Avenue. Project Green brochures reminded the Queen's community: "Civilization is when old men plant trees in the shade of which they'll never sit." Each year, usually around Arbour Day, Project Green members picked up their shovels and put a little more green back into their alma mater's campus.

Project Green was a small affair, but it set a powerful example. It tweaked the conscience of the community. The 1994 Campus Master Plan had a strong tinge of green in its recommendations. The project itself was wound up in the early eighties, bequeathing its accumulated surplus of $27,000 to a Tree Fund, which would annually feed saplings into campus ground. To this day, alumni honour their university by planting young trees around the campus at Homecoming. Gordon never lost his ecological devotion; he would return to Queen's to become the director of its School of Urban and Regional Planning and a champion of the "new urbanism."

Project Green student volunteers and Queen's grounds staff lower a conifer (transplanted from the Ottawa Valley) into place beside Grant Hall in 1976.

with architects.¹³⁴ This impetus was picked up by Alan Broadbent, who had joined the Board of Trustees. Returning to Queen's after a decade and a half, Broadbent was struck by the "shoddy" look of the place and quickly realized that "nobody cared" about the situation. What, he wondered, would this deterioration mean for Queen's ability to entice would-be students and faculty to come to Kingston?¹³⁵ Broadbent had urged the university to employ Berridge, Lewinberg. In the fall of 1987, he convinced the trustees to create a Task Force on Physical Planning, a group he would chair. Broadbent quickly became a prophet of change. His group dedicated itself to getting "aesthetic qualities within the budget." This did not mean, Broadbent insisted, "endless replication of limestone architecture." "Good design," he said, "had to work on its own and in the context of the environment." For this to happen, Queen's needed "a continually evolving plan."¹³⁶

Trustee David Leighton, an arts administrator and marketing expert, seconded the opinion: Queen's diverse and collegial style of decision making had left it open to "amateur leadership in the area of physical planning." Broadbent had other disciples. Stewart Ladd, an Alcan executive interested in strategic planning, began to push the Board's building committee towards a more vigorous approach to the selection of architects. Competition would be the key – to make the architects vie for the university's business with imaginative proposals. In 1989, these ideas and personalities began to coalesce in the newly created Campus Planning and Development Committee, which not only drew its membership from the Senate and the Board, but also – at Broadbent's insistence – had four outside members, whose presence was intended to connect Queen's with outside design and planning expertise. Toronto architect Dan McAlister joined the committee, bringing much experience in designing university facilities suited to new multidisciplinary and "people" uses. Similarly, Dan Burns, a senior official with the Toronto Housing Commission, whose own career had begun as a leading proponent of Elrond College, arrived on the Board and took up the crusade for change in the way Queen's configured itself.

In the gradualist world of universities, change seldom arrives dramatically. But in the early nineties, thanks to the aesthetic agitation of the preceding years, startling changes occurred in the way Queen's plotted its physical future and executed its capital projects. In 1990, a Director of Campus Planning, Jeanne Ma, was appointed to coordinate the university's stewardship of its built environment.

An End to "Effortless Superiority" 331

Ma had two degrees in landscape architecture and was soon working closely with Stewart Ladd and the trustees' building committee. There was alacrity and vigour in their deliberations. They discussed everything, from installing better lighting and security telephones on campus to ensuring handicapped access to all campus buildings. There was a clear sense that Queen's had to be made a people-friendly campus. The dedication was to long-term planning and hard-and-fast guidelines, not to short-term fixes. Furthermore, the process was not oblivious to the fact that Queen's sat in the midst of one of Canada's most-revered urban heritage cores. In 1966, local historian and Queen's employee Margaret Angus had published a survey of Kingston's magnificent architectural heritage, *The Old Stones of Kingston*, which had flagged the intrinsic value of the city's limestone vernacular architecture.[137]

Now official Queen's thinking caught up to that realization. That became evident in 1991 when the university bought the old Victoria School on the corner of Alfred and Union streets. Designed in 1892 by renowned local architect Samuel Newlands, Victoria School was eyed for its potential as a new, more-commodious home for the university's alumni and development offices of its registrar. There was little talk of sending in the bulldozer: instead the challenge was construed as one of marrying a heritage building with the modern pedagogic needs. Similarly, as other construction plans unfolded further east on Union Street, the university reluctantly agreed to relocate three Newlands-designed Victorian row houses to a new location on Alfred Street in order to save them from the wrecker's ball. The decision needed considerable shunting by local heritage advocates (including Margaret Angus, who told Principal Smith that it would be a "rude shock" to see the houses demolished) and by Helen Cooper, now mayor of Kingston.[138] The relocation thus restored some substance to Queen's long-standing rhetoric about its storied past being a limestone campus at the centre of Ontario's Old Strand.

Queen's new instinct for planning its aesthetics culminated in 1994 with the unveiling of the Campus Master Plan by the Campus Planning and Development Committee. The plan was the product of much consultation and a determination to provide the university with a template by which it could frame its future physical growth – "the need for a co-ordinated, planned approach to campus development," so as to improve "the spatial structure" of the campus. Aided by planning consultants Du Toit, Allsopp, Hillier and chaired by Ma, the committee cast a very wide net. The resultant plan balanced the myriad demands for space placed on Queen's tightly-hemmed campus by its academic, athletic, residential, health and safety, cultural, and transportational functions. Systematic planning and predetermined priorities would enhance the *genius loci* – the spirit of place – at Queen's. To do this, the campus would be divided into precincts or "spaces" – green space, residential, and academic quads, and so on. "Mid-range and long-term possibilities" would be applied to each precinct according to established principles and "planning foundations." Pedestrians and their fluid movement around campus would, for instance, be given priority over cars. Thought would be devoted to opening up walking "corridors," so that the daily life of the campus might flow between "spaces" rather than squeeze its way between buildings or cars. By this measure, University Avenue would become "the heart of the campus." To alleviate pressure on the main campus, the West Campus would be "enhanced" with new athletic, residential, and maintenance facilities. The plan in effect invited the Queen's community to think of their campus in holistic terms, not as a plain for a zero-sum contest between its occupants. To ensure that a complacent status quo never again asserted itself, the plan would be revisited every five years. "Preserve the Best, Enhance the Rest" was the plan's parting clarion call.[139]

Crowning Glories: New Buildings for New Times

By the time that David Smith, now looking careworn by nearly a decade of confronting change on his campus – some manageable and some unmanageable – prepared to hand over the reins of office in the early fall of 1994, there was a conspicuous change in the campus skyline, a change that symbolized Queen's transition to the new means and modes that had marked his principalship. A towering new university library – built with post-modernist flair tinged with hints of the neo-Gothic – stood at the corner of Union and University streets. Its prosaic predecessor buildings of the last two decades further along Union Street paled in comparison. Since it was but a twinkle in a committee's eye, the Stauffer Library had been conceived of as "the library of the twenty-first century." Delivered on time and under budget at $42 million, the five-storey library with its modernistic flying buttresses straddled the old and new: its exterior was clad in 285,000 pieces of split-face Bruce Peninsula limestone accentuated by aluminium finials, all supported by an inner structure of 1,000 cubic meters of concrete. Inside, a 24-metre-high atrium accommodated spiralling, mahogany-trimmed staircases, while, in cherry-wood-panelled reading rooms off the soaring atrium, gas fireplaces flickered. The library won instant popularity with students and faculty, students coming to regard it as a campus hub – a convivial crossroads of their daily intellectual and social life. Some years later, "Club Stauff" found itself the subject of a student blog. In promotional literature and visitors' eyes, the new library quickly established itself as the visual image of the "new" Queen's.

The Stauffer Library experience provided a most persuasive example of the new paradigm at Queen's. The old library system had been buckling under the strain of the university's growth and fundamental shifts taking place in the way that knowledge was transmitted and stored. The venerable Douglas Library, built in the mid-1920s with monies from former Chancellor James Douglas, a Queen's-trained mining engineer who had prospered in copper-rich Arizona, was stretched to the limit, despite a sixties expansion. The spread of undergraduate programs, the surging expansion of graduate studies and research at Queen's, plus the exponential expansion of knowledge across the board had filled the Douglas to the brim. To some degree, the strain was alleviated by the university's extensive network of branch libraries, which pushed material out into individual departments. The installation of computer cataloguing and circulation tracking in the early eighties had also alleviated the pressure. Nonetheless, in the fall of 1985, Acting Chief Librarian Lin Good reported that Queen's had the "most heavily used" post-secondary library in the province. Furthermore, it was also the most decentralized university library in Ontario, something that appealed to many departments but drove up the library system's overheads. In 1989, library consultant Margaret Beckman, an Ontario-based, globally respected consultant in library design and management, toured the Douglas Library and reported that its shelves, designed to hold 576,209 volumes, were now crammed with 908,000. Combined with deficit-battling cuts to the library's budget, Queen's library system was falling behind in the challenge of feeding information to the scholars and students surrounding it. Rankings done by the prestigious *Chronicle of Higher Education* showed that Queen's was slipping in comparison with other North American university libraries; by 1988, Queen's occupied an unflattering 82nd place in the *Chronicle's* ranking of 118 North American college libraries.[140] Given that provincially-sanctioned reviews of undergraduate and graduate programs invariably placed crucial emphasis on a library's ability to sustain teaching and research, Queen's library was in parlous shape.

By the mid-eighties, libraries began to sense that their traditional mandate of putting books and journals on shelves was being challenged by new forms of information transmission and storage. This had been hinted at in 1984, when a contract was signed with Bell Telephone to install a campus-wide Campus Information Network System, which would allow every computer-savvy person on campus to communicate over what would soon be dubbed "the internet." In faculties such as Commerce and Applied Science, undergraduates were now required to arrive at Queen's with a personal computer ready to connect with their professors and fellow students. By the early nineties, Queen's was developing systems that would allow students to register electronically each fall, thereby ending the age-old (and much-complained-about) fall ritual of standing in queues in the arena waiting to register in person. Across campus, just as across Canada, the letter "e" was being prefixed to all sorts of normative processes – e-mail, e-commerce, etc.

Libraries were arriving at the same threshold. Since the sixties, Ontario university libraries had been working out collaborative arrangements for the physical exchange of material – such as the 1970 Inter-Library Loan agreement – but now there was the tantalizing possibility of digitally exchanging information at virtually no cost across borders far beyond Ontario. Libraries were setting off down the so-called "information highway." Many possibilities beckoned: consortia purchases of electronic databanks and the sharing of digital journal subscriptions, for instance. These offered not only almost instantaneous accessibility, but also the prospect of financial economies. However inviting these opportunities, a daunting challenge lay in renovating libraries so as to preserve their traditional functions, but at the same time allowing them to develop systems and digital literacy that would open new horizons. At Queen's, this goal became embedded in the term "the library of the twenty-first century." The guiding impulse here was to move Queen's from being a laggard in library systems to a proactive position of being a leader in new library technology. The potential payoff was not just a state-of-the-art integrated library, but also a chance to revamp Queen's reputation as a research-oriented university and a premier teaching institution. At the same time, the new library might serve as the hallmark of a new architectural aesthetic on campus. The task ahead was therefore much greater than simply renovating the library's function; instead, it was something that touched every corner of the Queen's community, and therefore had to be founded on inclusion and consensus.

The process began in the Arts and Science faculty in 1988 with an ad hoc committee on the library of the twenty-first century. It quickly expanded into further task forces struck by Vice-Principal Sinclair, reports by outside library and architectural consultants, and input from as many as twenty "working groups," which fleshed out the actual needs and impacts of a new library from the perspective of students, faculty, and librarians. The breadth of this inclusion was in sharp contrast with the narrow path to architectural design that had delivered so many pedestrian buildings to Queen's in recent decades. While there was constant pressure from trustees such as Dan Burns to get the building aesthetically and practically right, the undeniable guiding spirit behind the design of the new library was Alan Green of the economics department, whose dynamism permeated the whole process.

Green had come to Queen's in 1963 from doctoral studies at Harvard, where he studied economic history under the renowned Simon Kuznets. Asked to head the initial Arts and Science committee on the library in 1986, Green continued to bring an enthusiasm, and in many ways a very unacademic impatience, to the configuration of the new library. Given its breadth of inclusion, the process was by its very nature highly political. Tough decisions – reeling in the scattered branch libraries, for instance – had to be made. But Green brought vision to his chairing of the linchpin Library of the Twenty-first Century task force in 1989. "The size of this project will dictate that it has a major impact on the life of Queen's University," he stressed. "It must be done correctly since there is no second chance." The 1989 report of his task force confirmed the university's commitment to "a new integrated library system" and set out a timetable for an architectural design competition and construction and fitting out of the new library, together with the refitting of the old Douglas Library as a centre for science and engineering reference, special collections, and study.[141] All this would culminate in 1994 when Queen's would turn towards the new century with a cutting-edge library.

Throughout the whole design and construction campaign, Green assembled a broadly representative and knowledgeable team. Faculty members teamed up with librarians and senior administrators, such as Vice-Principal William McLatchie and his assistant, David Barnard, to provide a sounding board for every aspect of the project. On the user side, for instance, they listened to the AMS Gender Issues Committee, which insisted that the new library have open, well-lit stack areas that would diminish any chance of women being harassed. On the technical side, there was at the same time endless input on the electronic linking of the building to the information highway and the provision of computer access for students, a dedication that would eventually manifest itself in an electronic "learning commons," where digital learning would supplement book learning. On the aesthetic side, much time was devoted to getting the placement and look of the new edifice right. Late in 1989, Green's building committee invited Montreal architectural-conservation champion Phyllis Lambert to visit Queen's and lend her expertise to the process. Lambert was outspokenly dedicated to imaginative modern architecture in appropriate urban settings. Shepherded by the principal, art historian Pierre du Prey, and Green, Lambert walked the campus and pronounced with characteristic assurance that the corner of Union and University was the undeniably best location for the new library – there it would be a hub for campus daily life, a place where knowledge and socialization would intersect.

Other experts followed, such as Margaret Beckman, who had already been retained to advise on systems development for the new library. Similarly, Bill Truch, a congenial Calgary engineering consultant, was brought in as project supervisor to facilitate the dialogue between the building committee and the builders. Later, Nancy McAdams, a Texas-based library-design specialist, was retained to help explain the peculiar user needs inside a modern library – electronic wiring, study space, shelving, and so on – to the architects. Green thus found himself at the head of a broad-front design endeavour, with his building committee at its apex supported below by the Senate Library Committee and other groups focused exclusively on the technology and space utilization of the new building. In an academic world habituated to drawn-out debate and jealousy, Green proved "masterful" at chairing his committee and brokering parties to the process as varied as cosmopolitan architects and library technicians.[142]

The selection of an architect for the new library emerged naturally out of this process. The cardinal principle here was that the successful architect would be chosen by competition. The days of a telephone call to a familiar architectural firm and a hastily designed conceptual sketch followed by a handshake were over at Queen's. By 1990, Green's building committee had forty-eight conceptual submissions before it. Suddenly, designing for Queen's had some kudos. Architects as renowned as Moshe Safdie expressed interest in the new library. The field was narrowed first to eight, and then to five finalists, each of whom was asked to submit a maquette of their vision. The maquettes were put on display in Wallace Hall, so that the reaction of potential users could be garnered. In the end, the contract went to the Toronto firm of Kuwabara Payne McKenna Blumberg (KPMB), a young firm founded in 1987 that worked as a collaborative "hybrid" studio. Its design for a new city hall in Kitchener had won praise as the firm sought to build a reputation for designing civic, educational and office buildings. Their design for Queen's library offered a blend of old and new – Gothic solidity married to modern openness. Trustee Alan Broadbent, an outspoken proponent of beautifying the campus, liked what he saw: the new library would be a "landmark, a new focal point and gathering place … [that] embodied the best of tradition, expressed in modern idiom."[143] The design was also clearly imaginative – quiet study rooms with fireplaces – and exuded a feeling of attention to quality – slate floors and spiral staircases, cherry-wood trim, and ample natural light. Observers well beyond the Queen's campus were also enthusiastic. The *Globe and Mail*'s architectural correspondent Adele Freedman described the KPMB plan as "a stunning scheme."[144]

Ground was broken for the new library in September 1992. Symptomatic of Queen's new holistic approach to its built environment was the decision to preserve heritage brick-and-wood homes that stood on the site of the new library. The moment the new library was announced, local heritage advocates voiced concern that the mammoth new building would impinge on the quaintness and scale of Sydenham Ward. Mayor Helen Cooper reminded the university that the Local Architectural Conservation Advisory Committee, the provincial heritage watchdog, took a dim view of historic architecture being bulldozed in the name of progress. (Cooper shrewdly pointed out that Queen's had invited Charles, Prince of Wales, to its campus that fall. Did the university want, she implied, this outspoken critic of modern architecture vilifying the new university library for trampling on the city's heritage?) Sensing the potential friction, Principal Smith appeared before Kingston City Council and pointed out that the new library was as much to the city's advantage as it was to Queen's. Nonetheless, Queen's asked for, and received, City permission to move a lovely Victorian row house at 135–139 Union – Bertha Bailey's famous boarding house – around the corner onto Alfred Street. The relocated row house would later garner Queen's a heritage conservation award. The next spring three substantial brick houses on the University Avenue side of the library sold to Corrections Canada. Their transport on enormous flatbed trucks to a new home on Macdonald Boulevard gave Kingstonians a memorable spectacle one Saturday morning.

Alan Green proved as adept at fundraising for the new building as he had been in finessing architects. The projected $42-million price tag for the new library was daunting. The Ontario government generously assigned $14.5 million to the project. Additional monies could be squeezed out of the university's operating budget. In the long-standing tradition of students supporting university initiatives, an AMS referendum approved a $515,000 student contribution to the project. But a project of such magnitude and potential prestige needed a lead sponsor, a supporter whose faith in the idea would instill confidence in other donors. Green found that sponsor in a man who had been dead over a decade. Joseph S. Stauffer, who had taken an Applied Science degree from Queen's in 1920, had – much like mining engineer James Douglas in Arizona – parlayed his engineering skills into a fortune rooted in supplying telephone companies and developing fuel cells. Stauffer once self-deprecatingly quipped that his career had been one of "limited successes and plenty of failures." Although his career took him as far afield as Mexico and England, Stauffer, like Douglas and Alfred Bader, never forgot his alma mater. He lived frugally, indulging few passions beyond his work, and when he died in 1978, he left a fortune that was installed in a charitable foundation. Oversight of that foundation fell to his widow, Annabelle (until her death in 1983), and his trusted Toronto lawyer W. Dennis Jordan, a Queen's Arts grad from the thirties.

In life, Stauffer had proved magnanimous to Queen's. He had, for instance, anonymously topped up the meagre pensions of widows of retired faculty who had left before the 1962 pension plan was adopted. Stauffer even bought an old theatre organ for the Jock Harty Arena. The foundation perpetuated that benevolence by applying millions to projects such as the Policy Studies and Technology Centre, as well as endowing chairs in cancer research and public policy. Advised by David Smith that Jordan had strong personal ties with Queen's and a record of directing Stauffer monies to the campus, Green contacted him on a trip to the Carolinas in 1989. Green's enthusiasm for the new library was easily contagious. He convinced Jordan to accompany him on a week-long tour of state-of-the-art American college libraries. This, he argued, is what Queen's desperately needed if it were to enter the twenty-first century. An initially reluctant Jordan was soon won over, and committed the foundation to a $10-million pledge to the nascent library. A grateful Board of Trustees voted to name the library in Joseph Stauffer's honour. Across the street in the renovated Douglas Library (also supported by the Stauffer Foundation), Queen's would later christen the new home of its esteemed collection of Canadiana after Jordan.

As the bricks and mortar rose on the corner of Union and University, a last crucial ingredient was added to the new library. New buildings demanded fresh talent. In 1991, Paul Wiens, arrived at Queen's as its new University Librarian. His predecessor, Margot McBurney, who had capably done so much to introduce the library to the age of computing, had departed after failing to see eye-to-eye with Green and some of the off-campus consultants on the problems confronting the library. With experience in public and academic libraries in Ontario, Manitoba, and Saskatchewan, Wiens brought solid expertise in books-on-shelves library science, but was also impressively well oriented to the rapidly emerging world of electronic knowledge delivery. He understood that, while the new library would have an impressive wooden door leading in from the campus on its ground floor, it would also have many equally-important "portals" connecting with the invisible electronic channels through which knowledge now coursed. A library of the twenty-first century could not stand still, it needed constant updating to stay abreast of what everyone described as

The completed Stauffer Library in the fall of 1994, a triumph of neo-Gothic architecture and the visionary leadership of economics professor Alan Green and Chief Librarian Paul Wiens, propelled by the generosity of the Joseph Stauffer Foundation. Behind the limestone facade, Queen's had a "library for the twenty-first century."

an age of "rapid change." The internet, Wiens liked to quip, was "the new volume on the shelf." Wiens was not just a prophet of the electronic age. He fought doggedly to increase the library's overall budget allocation, arguing that inflation and "social contract" austerity had diminished the library. Faculty rallied to his side; John Meisel in political studies contended that a library starved of knowledge "would be the last straw in my mind and would lead to Queen's being a third- or fourth-rate institution of learning." Between 1991 and 2004, Wiens would ratchet the library's acquisitions budget up from $4.4 million to $9 million.[145]

An End to "Effortless Superiority" 337

The new library, as noted above, built on schedule and under budget, was officially opened on 28 October 1994. (Three weeks earlier, Green, Wiens, and librarian Barbara Teatero had informally cut a ribbon at the main door, thereby admitting the first wave of eager users.) With typical Queen's élan, a piper led the dignitaries into the library's spacious foyer. Alan Green welcomed the dignitaries; in most minds it was "his" library. Ontario Premier Bob Rae spoke. The new principal, Bill Leggett, fresh from his installation that afternoon, quoted Thomas Carlyle: "The true university of these days is a collection of books." The whole project, the new principal enthused, had been "a magical success." Paul Wiens's sister, the well-known Canadian soprano Edith Wiens, serenaded the gathering with renditions of Rossini, Foster, and Gershwin. (Queen's had another special guest musician that day: Premier Bob Rae entertained the dignitaries with his keyboard accompaniment of Ms Wiens.) When his turn to speak came, Paul Wiens reflected on Cardinal Newman's words when, in the nineteenth century, he first cast his mind to the great libraries of antiquity: libraries served as "oracles of the world's wisdom." The *Globe and Mail* chronicled the day, reporting that Queen's new library was "an imaginative synthesis of space, light and purpose."[146] Only weeks into his retirement from the office of principal, David Smith took his place with the dignitaries. The new library epitomized his dedication to the "qualities of a Queen's education" he had so often championed. The road to the Stauffer seemed to indicate a new readiness to plan, consult, and execute at Queen's, and a recognition that such excellence required sustained diligence. Smith could take added satisfaction that the Stauffer was by no means an aberration.

It is worth noting briefly that another building was helping to transform Queen's campus. Not yet visible in the Queen's skyline by 1994, but rising in its consciousness, was the new biosciences building. It was soon to be appended to Earl Hall, existing home to Queen's biology department, on the southeast corner of the campus adjacent to the medical precinct. In the mid-eighties, Queen's had determined to accentuate studies in the biosciences – the application of biological knowledge to practical outcomes, such as biotechnology and molecular science. Such interaction required architecture that transcended traditional academic design predicated on individual disciplines in sealed compartments. Synergy was now the order of the day in biosciences. With this in mind, the trustees had empowered the Campus Planning and Development Committee to devise a building that would marry academic and physical requirements into "a laboratory and science building for the next generation." Like the Stauffer, architects were obliged to bid on the project. By late 1993, the committee had thirty-nine design proposals before it. An initial budget allocation of $25.7 million was fast inflating; by opening day it would swell to $52.2 million. Once the architectural competition was decided, the bulldozers and high-hoes would arrive and another hallmark building would begin to rise.

Design of the $52.5-million Biosciences Complex, prospective home to the department of biology and PARTEQ, was eventually assigned to the firm of Shore, Tilbe Irwin + Partners and Darling and Downey in Toronto. Echoing the Stauffer process, there was talk of light-filled atriums and state-of-the-art biotechnology facilities. The funding formula for the multipurpose facility drew support from Queen's Park and the City of Kingston. Elsewhere on campus, discussions were under way with celebrated Canadian architect Raymond Moriyama for an addition to the Agnes Etherington Arts Centre. The Campus Master Plan now provided a long-term framework in which a new-look Queen's might unfold.

The Art of Managing a Multiversity

Buildings were not the only ingredient adding to a university's vitality. In ten years as principal, David Smith had discovered the protean challenge of guiding what had come to be called a "multiversity." The Stauffer Library, for example, was hardly the product of Queen's old-style "effortless superiority." Its creation recognized that fiscal, demographic, and technological shifts beyond the campus had to be reflected in the way the university did its business. As the late-twentieth century faded away, Queen's comfortable trust in its parochial customs and habits had become increasingly out-of-kilter with the times. Smith's tenure as principal thus presented an ambivalent mixture of rearguard defence of ingrained values and practices at Queen's (keeping Queen's, in the words of Margaret Atwood's admonition, from being "too jazzy") and, at the same time, a vigorous advocacy of new orientations. By 1994, it was, for instance, obvious that the old culture of collegiality among administrators, faculty, and staff was nearing exhaustion. Matters of compensation and employee entitlements had become too complex to be contained in a simplistic, bilateral relationship based on goodwill and friendly give-and-take. Some form of collective "dispute resolution" was now unavoidable. On the other hand, Smith and his vice-principal, health services, Duncan Sinclair, were able to rationalize the way in which the Queen's medical faculty was compensated under the SEAMO formula. Through all this redefinition of relationships, Principal Smith was hesitant and at times awkward, as the next chapter will show, in adapting Queen's to the burgeoning diversity of Canadian society. In a decade in which Canadians sought to give daily meaning to the citizenship rights acknowledged in the 1982 Charter of Rights and Freedoms, Queen's was slow to adjust its attitudes to sexual, racial, and ethnic diversity, first on its periphery and then increasingly in its midst.

Smith's legacy by 1994 displayed strong progressive streaks. His *Blueprint for Action* had brought ingenuity to the perennial conundrum of freeing the university from the stiff harness of government funding predicated on accessibility and universality. Like Watts before him, he had learned that talk of fundamental reform of the way the state funded post-secondary education seldom translated into action. The political sacredness of accessibility, rooted in the heyday of the sixties, seemed genetically implanted in the province's politics. When systemic reform escaped him, Smith turned to more opportunistic adjustments. Once the province allowed some latitude in setting post-secondary fees, he moved Queen's fee schedules to the maximum allowable provincial ceiling, capitalizing on the Queen's brand of quality education to maximize revenue. At the same time, the university helped to devise and then use the new provincial "corridor" system to bring stability and predictability to Queen's enrolment. Conscious that these policies courted the charge that Queen's offered an elitist education, student assistance was boosted to ensure access to Queen's for deserving applicants. Moreover, David Smith made Queen's think in international terms. Whether it was the signing of student exchange agreements in the Far East or the fortuitous acquisition of a castle in the English countryside, Smith urged Queen's to think beyond its comfort zone in eastern Ontario and beyond its national reputation in Canada, and to fixate on global horizons. Finally, and perhaps most dramatically, Smith engineered the "privatizing" of professional programs at Queen's, calibrating their fees to what the external job market would bear. By 1994, Queen's MBA students were assembling in electronic classrooms across Canada and as far away as Bermuda for seminars that allowed them to combine their weekday careers with weekend professional development.

Faced with implacable attitudes and hard-line austerity at Queen's Park, Smith also pushed to diversify Queen's revenues. He worked hard to break the mindset that the state was the sole fiscal support for the university. Aggressive fundraising could diversify income. "Advancement," as it was now called, was more than simply attracting the generosity of lead sponsors such as Alfred Bader and Joseph Stauffer; it was also about broad-front fundraising, reaching out to individuals, foundations, and corporations in concerted campaigns. The Challenge Fund crested over $100 million in donations just as Smith left office; other targeted campaigns for the bioscience building and the Agnes Etherington Art Centre expansion were revealing that capital could be raised through similar concerted effort. In the end, the Smith years saw Queen's weather the turbulence of seismic government cutbacks and emerge in relatively stable shape. In the university archives, a file of pleading "dear colleague" letters from Smith to his colleagues points to how arduous the business of allocating, and often crimping, the university's tight budget was throughout these years. Nonetheless, when Smith left office in 1994, Queen's $180-million annual budget was showing a deficit of only $389,000, an amount that the vice-principal, finance, suggested might be squeezed out of existence by the spring of 1995. At the same time, the trustees' investment committee reported that the university's endowment fund had grown to $144 million. If Queen's financial bed at times produced some sleepless nights, at least the university had a relatively plump pillow under its head.

When Smith's appointment as principal was announced in 1983, his friend geographer and graduate-studies dean Maurice Yeates wrote to congratulate him with a caution: "The schedule you have set yourself can be completed only by a person with a stout heart and quick legs."[147] Smith, a morning runner and occasional 10K racer, had soon learned the limitations of a principal's power at an institution steeped in a tradition of gradualism yet increasingly subject to interdiction from impatient external agendas, public scrutiny, and pure fate. Asked by the venerable Saturday Club (which had finally admitted women professors into its esteemed ranks) to speak at its jocular annual meeting in 1987, Smith admitted he had become somewhat more worldly wise about his ambitions since taking office. Like Harvard president Derek Bok, he had come to see university culture as one of "genial anarchy," over which his only power was suasion and consensus building. He likened the university's power structure to that of an inverted pyramid, in which the apex of administrative action was delicately balanced below a broad, teetering base of faculty and students, with politicians and public opinion pushing on its sides. Consequently, Smith sometimes bemoaned the fact that decision making at Queen's moved with the "speed of a centipede." Courting mixed metaphors, he likened his role to that of "an air traffic controller for a swarming beehive."[148] By 1994, he could nonetheless take satisfaction from the fact that he had in many ways forced Queen's out of its comfortable ways, preserved its core values, and, as epitomized by the Stauffer Library, turned its attention to the new century. The task of maintaining this hesitant momentum would now fall to William Leggett, his successor.

8

"The Life of the Greater Queen's"
The Challenge of Diversity

*Some values deserve preservation. Other traditions require changing –
and some changes, as Queen's has learned the hard way, are overdue.*
Cathy Perkins, *Queen's Alumni Review*, 1990

"We" must be an inclusive "we."
Toni Pickard, Faculty of Law, 1990

*You can't remain in the era of the 1850s. This is a different kind
of generation, a different time, a different climate.*
Pradeep Kumar, School of Industrial Relations, 1980s

A Minister with a Mission

He was always in action, but the autumn invariably brought his schedule to fever pitch. The Reverend A. Marshall Laverty – "Marsh" to his campus colleagues, "Padre" to generations of Queen's students – had been the University Chaplain since 1947. He epitomized the familiar, old-style paternalism of Queen's that was to persist unchallenged until the dying decades of the century. In the summer, Laverty travelled to his cottage on Manitoulin Island for a much-needed holiday, but September found him back in Kingston, ready to welcome the students. A handsome man with a neatly trimmed moustache, Laverty was dapper in blue blazer, grey flannels, and clerical collar. He was grandiloquent both in and out of the pulpit and possessed a dazzling Dale Carnegie–like ability to remember names and faces. Many a frosh was stunned when a silver-haired man unexpectedly called across University Avenue: "Aren't you the son of Bob … of Science '51? How's your sister Wendy doing in nursing?" On Sunday evenings, Laverty and his wife, Frances, invited batches of Queen's newcomers to their Albert Street home for an evening of snacks and games. Many of the students initially thought the invitation a bit odd. Little did they suspect that Padre would administer the Harvard undergraduate-admission test as an icebreaker. "When I got back to residence that night," went a thank-you note to the Lavertys from an Arts '77 student, "I had four second-year students trying to figure out your game with the cities and not one of them had the faintest notion how it is done."[1]

For Laverty, the autumn cycle began in Grant Hall, where he participated in the "tradition ceremony" inducting frosh into Queen's Gaelic culture of tams and the *Oil Thigh*. Throughout the academic year, Laverty returned to Grant Hall every Sunday morning to conduct the university's weekly church service. Although he was ordained in the United Church, Laverty's services were ecumenical. He intoned the invocations and benedictions at every Queen's convocation, presided over Remembrance Day commemorations and the spring baccalaureate service, and married innumerable Queen's graduates in the Morgan Chapel in Theology Hall. He brought a dignified grandeur to all these roles.

In between such duties, he travelled tirelessly as Queen's chief booster, speaking at high-school commencements, career days, and university nights from Kapuskasing to Orillia. In 1961, he attended a staggering 218 high-school events. In between, he attended "smokers" and sherry parties at alumni branch meetings across the nation, bringing the latest news of the alma mater and drumming up donations and admission applications from the faithful. Out of these connections he created his own "Friends of Queen's Fund," an endowment fund which allowed him to promote pet projects.

Laverty's peripatetic routine also allowed him to build up a coterie of Queen's supporters, prominent citizens who had never darkened a Queen's lecture hall, but who had come to value the university's mission. In fact, for many visitors to Queen's, Padre Laverty was the face of the institution. His circle of contacts was immense. For example, after the university gave a special honorary degree to black American singer and civil-rights activist Marian Anderson in 1962, Laverty received a signed photograph from the singer, one he proudly displayed on his desk. Perhaps most prominent of all Laverty's admirers was the General Motors auto mogul R.S. "Colonel Sam" McLaughlin. Laverty brokered much of the high-spirited McLaughlin's munificence towards Queen's – buildings, scholarships, the purchase of the papers of novelist John Buchan. Also numbered among Laverty's circle was William "Bill" Davis, Ontario education minister and later premier. Laverty and Davis, pipe smokers both, frequently exchanged pouches of Amphora and Enmore. Laverty bonded with some of Queen's most ardent supporters; in 1953, trustee and Toronto investment banker D.I. McLeod went so far as to underwrite Laverty's purchase of one of McLaughlin's Buicks as a token of his work for Queen's. Closer to home, Laverty sat on the local board of education and connected Queen's to the community through his work for the Rotary Club and a local kids' camp.

From Padre to Pluralism

In point of fact, in 1946, when Principal Wallace had convinced the trustees to appoint a chaplain as a permanent university staffer, he was setting a precedent for Queen's. Queen's had deep denominational roots reaching back to the Presbyterian agitators who had won a royal charter for the college a century before. But since the revamping of the university's charter in 1912, Queen's had been avowedly secular, albeit with a strong residue of Presbyterian values. Quietly, however, as the spiritual latitude of the university broadened, the Protestant monopoly over Queen's dissipated. For instance, Roman Catholics found a vibrant life on Queen's campus through the activities of Newman

House, especially under the forceful guidance of Father John Hanley (until 1958) and later under Father Bob Burns (a street priest with a passion for human rights). Similarly, many Jews on campus celebrated their identity at Hillel House.

Sensing this growing diversity, Principal Wallace conceived of the role of the Queen's chaplain, not so much in denominational terms but more as that of "a friend and counsellor to students." Laverty fit the bill admirably. Toronto-born and University of Toronto–educated, he had served as a wartime chaplain to Canadian signals and artillery units in Europe. That experience seemed to equip him for dealing with a variegated university population, especially at a time when the Queen's campus was crowded with veterans. "Just come and do whatever has to be done," Wallace is said to have instructed the new "Padre."[2] Laverty set up his office in the athletics complex and made sure his door was always open. Students brought their problems to him – the need for a loan to tide them over the term, a bout of homesickness, an uncongenial residence mate. When a Queen's student met an untimely

Padre A.M. "Marsh" Laverty in action. From 1947 to his retirement 1983, "the Padre" acted not only as the university's spiritual mentor, but also as a fixer of student problems and facilitator of their Queen's experience. He was present in their lives from the festivities of frosh week until the formalities of their convocation. Here, on the left, he presides over his annual sunrise service on the shores of Lake Ontario and, on the right, he is outraced by Arts and Science Dean Duncan Sinclair in a United Appeal fundraising bike race.

death in the midst of summer, Laverty made the long drive from Manitoulin south to comfort his grieving family. The Padre supplied solutions – be it a call to "Colonel Sam" for a few hundred dollars or a note of explanation to the dean of women. He was as much an ombudsman as a preacher. He quickly seemed to have a contact for every need. His became the most familiar face on campus, appearing with regularity in the *Queen's Journal* and *Alumni Review*, for example, whether it was being propelled down Princess on a rickety bedstead by engineering students as part of the YMCA Bed-a-thon or receiving a medal from the Montreal or Toronto alumni.

"The Life of the Greater Queen's"

For all his heartfelt bonhomie and utter dedication to Queen's, the Padre embodied and actively projected a set of values – an institutional persona – which by the 1980s many sensed was out of sync with changing Canadian values. By the time David Smith became principal in 1984, immigration, secularization, and Charter-driven liberalism were imparting strong pluralism to Canadian society. "Multiculturalism" had become a political mantra. The WASP rituals and rhetoric of Queen's, which the Padre so masterfully practised, began to strike many as being out of kilter with the times. Laverty's highly personalized way of doing things unwittingly smacked of a coziness and paternalism that some regarded as selective and that demanded deference to Queen's established culture. Take, for instance, the way the university conducted its high-school recruitment every fall – a campaign that Laverty, in company with a corps of high-school liaison officers, spearheaded.

Conscious that the university had long attracted top-notch candidates from mainstream Anglo-Canadian society, the recruiters automatically headed for high schools in the prosperous urban enclaves of Toronto and Montreal. Private schools such as Branksome Hall, Upper Canada College, and Havergal were particularly inviting hunting grounds. (Queen's had for years appointed two members to the board of Montreal's posh Trafalgar School.) Queen's consequently harvested the best and brightest, but, as the French say, this approach to admissions suffered from "the defects of its virtues." Queen's unwittingly fell into the comfortable habit of replicating itself, which made for poor connection with the new, multicultural Canada. In 1985, a Senate committee examining Queen's admissions policy reported that, while conscious of the need to broaden admission criteria, the university had done well by following what Vice-Principal Sinclair labelled "an elitist policy." But, he added, elitism was based on achievement, and in that the university need make no apology."[3] This was a dangerous attitude in an era of cultural change if Queen's was ever to align itself with changing Canadian demographics.

Queen's thus found itself caught between two worlds. Alumni clung to the comforting nostalgic residue of Gaelic and Presbyterian ritual which had for so long infused the place, an ethos still treasured by many incoming undergraduates (who were often the progeny of alumni). However, many newcomers to Queen's in the eighties felt marginalized by this ethos. The newcomers' world view was often secularized or shaped by quite different religious and ethnic sensibilities. Thus, while the Ottawa politicians talked of multiculturalism and pluralism, Queen's still seemed to speak the language of WASP predominance. Laverty, for instance, opened convocations by intoning the Christian supplication: "Almighty God, unto whom all hearts are open." He also called the audience to honour its duty of loyalty to "our liege lady, the Queen." As in other areas of cultural adjustment – such as bringing gender balance into faculty ranks – Queen's with its comfortable, introverted, eastern-Ontario culture tended to lag behind mainstream Canadian values. For some, this conservatism constituted the essence of Queen's appeal. Others found it wanting.

Padre Laverty's bravura performance as university chaplain in many ways insulated him from the powerful shift of Canadian society towards secularism and multiculturalism. It also kept him in his job well past the university's mandatory retirement age of sixty-five. In 1978, the trustees happily allowed the Padre to stay on in his office past retirement age. This licence was extended until 1983, when Laverty turned seventy and could boast thirty-six and a half years of service to Queen's. Now a replacement had to be found. There was no hint of criticism of the outgoing chaplain in the trustees' decision to seek out a new incumbent who would be more in tune with the times. They found that man – it might well have been a woman by the mid-eighties – in Brian Yealland.

Yealland also emerged from the United Church. If Laverty had been schooled in human nature by wartime service, Yealland had been schooled by the rough-and-tumble of serving as a prison chaplain in Kingston for Corrections Canada. Initially educated in philosophy at the University of Toronto, Yealland had done a master's degree in divinity at the Queen's Theological College in the early 1970s at a time when then-principal Donald Mathers was infusing the curriculum with the need to endow the United Church with more liberal attitudes. Yealland soaked up the message, seeing himself as the "first longhair" at the college. Initially dedicating himself to the needy, he became a parole officer in Kingston in 1972. At the same time, he preached as an associate minister at Chalmers United Church in Kingston, hard by the campus, and sat on the Board of Management at the Theological College. After Donald Mathers's untimely death in 1972, Robert Bater had become principal at the college. He perpetuated Mathers's liberalism, arguing that the notion of "Christian hegemony" no longer served the spiritual needs of many Canadians.[4]

Yealland was doubtful about applying for the chaplain's post at Queen's; Marsh Laverty cast a long shadow. Nevertheless, Queen's insiders, such as principal Ron Watts, Applied Science dean David Bacon, and university lawyer Bob Little, urged him to reconsider, sensing that he possessed the skills to connect with a new generation of Queen's students. Yealland came round, tempted by the thought of "getting back in the front lines." Appointed in 1983, Yealland immediately altered the chaplaincy's course. "We have a university," he told the trustees in 1985, "which is pluralistic, secular, culturally mixed, and with a number of faiths … The work of the chaplain [therefore] should be human-centred."[5] In Yealland's mind, the chaplain should be akin to a spiritual ombudsman on campus, promoting religious pluralism and dialogue. In 1990, this culminated in the establishment of an Inter-Faith Council at Queen's, a plenary group of local ministers of all faiths dedicated to breaking down "dogmatic, narrow, or sectarian insistence on campus."[6] Catering to students' spiritual needs now became a team effort. Yealland also stimulated respect for religious pluralism at the practical, day-to-day level: he convinced the residence kitchens to provide kosher and Halal food for Jewish and Muslim students. During Ramadan, for example, Halal food was made available late in the evening when daily fasting concluded with sundown. Examination schedules were also adjusted to accommodate the holidays of other religions.

In God We Trust?

The challenge of increasing the religious and ethnic diversity of Queen's entailed much more than rejigging menus and exam schedules. It required bedrock shifts in the university's culture and sensibilities. Even before Yealland moved into the Padre's office, Queen's had been convulsed by a fractious debate over what religious "elements" appropriately belonged in one of its central academic rituals – the annual convocation of new graduates. Convocation represented the ceremonial high-water mark of a Queen's student's achievement. It was intended to resonate with the institution's culture, a culture that echoed back to the ambitions of the cabal of local Presbyterian ministers who agitated in the 1840s for a seat of higher learning in eastern Ontario. The ceremony was consequently adorned with Gaelic trappings – pipers, tartan, and frequent spontaneous *Oil Thighs* – and framed with Christian observance. An opening invocation and closing benediction were supplied by the Padre. The participatory centrepiece of the ceremony was a lusty signing of the hymn "O God, Our Help in Ages Past." "God Save the Queen" rounded out the Christian tone of the day.

Indeed, the Christian deity was present in almost every aspect of Queen's ceremonial – the chancellor took an oath to proceed with the "strength which God shall give me." The trustees began their meetings with a prayer. Indeed, the university's revamped 1912 charter instructed the trustees to ensure that "the University shall continue distinctly Christian"

"*The Life of the Greater Queen's*" 345

and that staff hired be of "Christian character." (This injunction had quickly slipped into abeyance, as Queen's hired Jews, Hindus, and Muslims, although never in great numbers.)

Historically, the infusion of Protestant rhetoric and ritual into Queen's convocations had been seen as a sacred, symbolic element in the bonding of its students with their alma mater as they began their transformation into alumni. Over the years, the Gaelic/Protestant aura of convocation seemed to be embraced by all comers as an unquestionable part of the "Queen's way." Principal John Deutsch, a devout Catholic, seemed quite comfortable presiding over what amounted to a Protestant legitimization of a Queen's education. After all, this logic went, the "God" of Christianity appeared in well-known national rituals off-campus, such as the national anthem and citizenship and court oaths, which were sworn on Bibles.

Nevertheless, it is difficult to divine what members of the Queen's community who were neither Christians nor believers in any faith made of these rituals. Until the 1980s, any dissenters remained silent or, possibly, simply did not attend convocation. That changed as Canada entered a world of Charter rights and multiculturalism. In November 1979, the Law Students' Society executive passed a resolution calling for the removal of "the elements of religious observance in the Convocation ceremony." The resolution did not seem to reflect any powerful groundswell of opinion in Macdonald Hall: no referendum had been held to canvas broader opinion, and the executive appeared to be acting on a complaint from a handful of law students. There were, however, a number of Jewish professors in the faculty, including Bernard Adell, its dean, who would assert that they had always felt discomfited by Queen's overt Christianity. Prompted by the Law Students' Society, Adell brought the matter of religious elements before the law faculty board. The board endorsed his motion to expunge religion from convocation, and Adell urged that the proposal be sent on to the Senate for university-wide deliberation. Recognizing that the issue was contentious, the faculty board tacked a codicil to its motion, stating the desire to remove religion from convocations was passed "without prejudice to appropriate acknowledgement in other ways of the great contribution of the Presbyterian Church to the foundation and development of Queen's University in its earlier years."[7]

When the resolution reached the Senate in March 1980, Adell proposed that it be referred to the Senate's Committee on Academic Procedures (SCAP) and that the opinion of the AMS and other faculty boards be canvassed. Civil-engineering professor Barry Batchelor added that it would be "offensive" not to solicit the views of alumni and the university council. The university council, after all, held ultimate jurisdiction over university ceremonials. There was an immediate edge to the debate. Professor Mark Weisberg of law acknowledged that the matter aroused "strong feelings for and against." Principal Watts said that he had already received letters from law students opposed to the proposal. A law student present alleged that there had been no systematic surveying of faculty and student opinion in his faculty. Principal Bater of the Theological School was inclined to favour the proposal, but suggested that the word "removal" be altered to the "moderating" of religious elements at convocation, because the former was "too drastic." Bater's amendment was defeated, and the Senate dispatched the matter to the academic procedures committee.[8]

Throughout the summer and fall of 1980, SCAP, chaired by electrical-engineering professor C.H.R. "Chuck" Campling, deliberated. When it reported early in 1981, Campling reminded his academic colleagues that his committee had been charged with the straightforward decision of removing or retaining religion from convocation – not tinkering with it. The committee, Campling reported, had done due diligence: every constituency of the Queen's community had been canvassed. Many unsolicited submissions had been received. The verdict was clear: "No individual or group except the Faculty of Law and the Law Students' Society has declared in favour of the proposal. The committee itself is not disposed to disagree with the widely-held majority view." Religious elements, with all their resonance for Queen's tradition, should remain.[9]

Reaction was immediate and heated. This issue was not, removal advocates insisted, a matter of the will of the majority, but rather a question of values and tolerance. The Law Students' Society went on the offensive. Terry Ellen Markus of the society vigorously laid out its case. Publicly funded institutions – such as Queen's had been since 1912 – should stage secular ceremonies. Any retention of Presbyterian elements would make Queen's look like an "historical anomaly" in Canada's pluralistic society. Furthermore, convocation was the culmination of an *academic*, not a *religious*, experience. Retention of religious elements would show "insensitivity" to non-Christians. Spirituality had many guises, so why not allow convocations a minute of silence so that attendees could each make their introverted oblation? Dean Adell reinforced Markus: this issue was not a matter of "counting noses." Morality should not be related only to Christian values. Contrary to SCAP's hope of putting a finish to the issue, it now broke out into open debate. The AMS reported that it supported retention. History professor James Nuechterlein warned that it was impossible to discuss the issue in an "unemotional way," but nonetheless concluded that the Senate owed it to the alumni and the majority not to meddle with tradition.

Robert Bater begged to differ. Despite his position as head of an institution affiliated with the United Church, he felt "uncomfortable with a discussion which seemed to reveal so little sensitivity to the minority." Modern Canadian society required more pliability on these matters. He said that he found himself feeling "something between embarrassment and unreality." Bater advocated "moderate" reform, culminating in an end to "Christian triumphalism" at Queen's. The use of the Lord's Prayer, he wrote to the *Globe and Mail* "trivialized" the prayer by turning it into an element of a secular ritual.[10] Padre Laverty took the opposite tack, arguing that foes of religious elements were unreasonably pulling stones from Queen's arch of tradition to the past: "As for 'things offensive' in the ceremony," he wrote to Vice-Principal Russ Kennedy, "what if someone [who] is offended by the monarchy takes exception to the degree being granted by authority of the Royal Charter?"[11] Laverty had plenty of allies: Professor Stuart Ryan, long a voice of social justice in the law faculty, confided in the Padre that he was "sorry" that his colleagues had moved against tradition.[12] Buffeted by all this contention, SCAP chairman Chuck Campling reiterated that his committee had not been asked to consider alternatives or modifications to the convocation. Attempting to pour oil on troubled waters, Dean Sinclair pointed out that this was not an "all-or-nothing" issue. The Senate responded by asking Campling to go back into committee to consider the religious elements of convocation on a one-by-one basis. In the interim, the status quo would be maintained at convocation.

The mail flooded in. Alumni were largely convinced that their alma mater was selling its birthright. Judge John Matheson (Arts '40, LLD '84), one-time MP and father of Canada's maple-leaf flag, thought the whole matter of proposed change "monstrous" and decried the "games people are playing at the Theology College." History professor Fred Gibson wrote a letter to the *Whig-Standard* haughtily urging Bater and Adell to "accept with good grace a residuum of Christian observance in the public ceremonies of the university which they serve."[13] Others tried to finesse the issue, arguing that the "Our Father" could be construed as anybody's deity. Similarly, Jesus Christ was never named in "O God, Our Help in Ages Past" and convocation invocations and benedictions contained no Trinitarian – "Father, Son, and Holy Ghost" – reference. In a similar vein, the argument was made that nobody was obliged to sing the hymns or recite the prayers at convocation. The mail brought contrary opinions. Alfred Bader wrote from Milwaukee that Queen's needed to wake up to the fact that Canada was now a pluralistic society. Bader noted that the Queen's that had taken him in so willingly in 1942 had exhibited the tolerant and humane side of Christianity, but that same Christianity back in Nazi Germany had been synonymous with hatred and persecution, so best to set religion aside in civil ceremonies.[14]

As the mail flooded into Richardson Hall and the *Alumni Review*, university officials grew worried that the controversy was generating bad press for Queen's. The story made the CBC news. The *Toronto Star* reported "University split over Lord's Prayer."[15] The press framed the story as a collision of nineteenth-century values with those of the late-twentieth century. Having committed itself to a more vigorous approach to development, university administrators fretted that the publicity was damaging the crucial Queen's Quest fundraising campaign. Seeking insight into the seminal "Christian character" clause of its 1912 charter, the administration turned to the university's lawyers in Kingston for clarification. Lawyer David Bonham, a one-time Queen's professor and vice-principal, rendered the firm's opinion: any obligation to ensure that the university be "distinctly Christian" was now overridden by the 1962 Ontario Human Rights Code, which mandated secular neutrality.[16] (Ironically, the province of Ontario remained constitutionally bound to maintain a separate school system for Catholics.) When made public, the legal opinion bolstered the reformers. History professor Gerald Tulchinsky told Principal Watts that the shedding of the 1912 rubric would prompt the university to "open its mind – and perhaps even its heart – to the diversity of modern Canada" and thereby push Queen's towards a "new self-definition for this University community."[17]

In March 1982, the Campling committee was back with its reconsideration of the thorny issue. The faculty, they generalized, were subject to "many misconceptions" about the ceremony. Many, they suggested, had never attended convocation. Nonetheless, the committee dissected each "element" of convocation and found that the whole ceremony was "less specifically Christian than some people had thought." The Lord's Prayer could stay, because it had demonstrable roots in Judaism. "O God, Our Help" had similar roots, and made no direct reference to Christ. Furthermore, it was installed in campus lore as a university tradition. The Trinitarian invocation had not been used in a decade. Noting that all faculty boards, except law, and the AMS, had expressed satisfaction with the present convocation liturgy, the committee concluded that "no changes be made at the present time." Nine other Canadian universities, it pointed out, had religious elements in their graduation ceremonies.

The report was instantly challenged. Student senator Margot Schwartz contended that convocation should reflect "the values of today's society." Mark Weisberg from law was dismayed by the report's majoritarian tone and the implication that Christian values alone were the keys to a moral life. Believers in other faiths who were teaching and studying at Queen's might easily get the message that they were "here on sufferance." Bater voiced his concern with the report's "insensitivity," and made a motion that the Lord's Prayer be replaced with a moment of silence. When this was defeated, the Senate moved to accept the report by a margin of 22–11.[18] Tradition seemed to have trumped modernism.

At the heart of the Senate debate lay a malfunctioning of Queen's long-standing consensus culture. On the surface, an issue had been investigated and thrashed out in debate before being brought to a vote. Usually such careful grooming produced – albeit slowly – a palatable consensus. But with the religious-elements debate, no centre ground had materialized. A determined dissenting minority remained fixed to its purpose. This unbending resolve became apparent early in the fall of 1981, when Dean Adell appeared back in the Senate with news that the law faculty board had voted "by a large majority" to request that the university allow it to stage its own convocation, one at which no religion would be privileged and no spiritual discomfort felt by attendees. This was, he said, a "matter of principle." Law students were keenly aware of human rights and wanted to see tolerance in their graduation ceremony. Given such high purpose, Adell said, the issue must be decided by the whole Senate and not shunted off to a committee. Nonetheless, the Senate did just that, throwing the ball back to SCAP.[19]

The issue spilled over into 1982. The law faculty, while not resigning its claim to an autonomous convocation, voted on 4 February to again take up the cause of reforming the mainstream convocation so as to make it reflect "the diversity of the university community." Again, the idea of a minute of silence replacing the Lord's Prayer was mooted. The SCAP, now chaired by philosophy professor Norman Brown, was again in the hot seat. In April, it reported its reluctance to allow the "private beliefs" of a minority on campus to dictate the identity of the "corporate body." The committee suggested that giving in to the notion that a publicly funded college must always reflect the "pluralistic values of modern society" could set a "dangerous" precedent. Universities at times had a mandate to resist some ideas that had become prevalent in society. Queen's had ensured that religious and political convictions in its classrooms were open to free discussion, but at the same time it had the right to preserve ceremonial elements of its "traditional and cherished religious values." These values were never "imposed" on the community. The idea of separate convocations could therefore not be condoned.

Finally, however, the committee offered a glimpse of compromise. It dismissed the idea that the Lord's Prayer had non-Christian utility, or that it was a simple theistic oblation open to varied interpretation. It was instead declared as clearly Christian and, as such, the prayer might "cause real embarrassment" to some at convocation. Therefore, the university chaplain should make it clear that recitation of the prayer was voluntary. But the prayer itself should be retained. Societies naturally sought a "religious dimension" in their ceremonies. Perhaps someday Queen's would come to see religious elements as "hypocrisy," but "that time is yet to come."

Sensing a compromise, the Senate reconvened four days later. Dean Sinclair set three motions before his colleagues. The Senate was first invited to retain the Lord's Prayer, with the proviso of making its recitation voluntary. Or, it could once again refer the matter to SCAP. Or – and here Sinclair was conspicuously joined by his fellow dean Bernard Adell – the Senate could move to delete the prayer from convocation. Sinclair supported the third option, saying that he sensed a feeling that the Queen's community favoured the retention of the "traditional" over the "religious" in convocation. The Lord's Prayer was undeniably religious, whereas "O God, Our Help" was traditional, a Christian hymn secularized into a school song. Deleting the prayer, Sinclair argued, would be a "gracious compromise" that would end two years of the Senate being "harassed" by the issue. Swayed by Sinclair's logic and probably exhausted by the perseverance of the matter, the Senate voted to delete the Lord's Prayer from convocation. A month later, a motion to reinstate the prayer until such time as an "alternative ceremony" was devised met with quick defeat.[20]

All in all, the religious-elements controversy provides a remarkable example of forced change at Queen's, an institution habituated to gradual, gently negotiated change. A determined minority, emerging out of the law school, put its hand on the back of the majority and pushed firmly for the university to adjust its ethos in a way that would make a minority feel culturally accommodated. Historically, Queen's rituals must, they argued, shed their exclusivist aura and project a more inclusive message. In short, Queen's must close the gap between the values embedded in its rituals and those of contemporary Canadian society. A university must have resonance in the society it served. Not to do so meant that it risked becoming an anachronism. In effect, a university must make new traditions.

In the face of this logic, Queen's ingrained and conservative tradition put up a stiff fight. "Queen's owes its founders more respect," the *Whig-Standard* editorialized. "Must it surrender the last, final, historic fragments of its Founders' souls in the name of spiritually-neutral tax bucks?"[21] The alumni offered the stiffest resistance. One could detect in their opposition to the removal of the Lord's Prayer from convocation a reflection of a broader *angst* in Canadian society, one brought on by the nation's shift to a multicultural definition of itself. Secularization accentuated the anxiety. Church attendance in established religions, for instance, had peaked in the mid-1960s. Older WASP Canadians feared that they were being stripped of their essential (and heretofore dominant) identity. In its small way, alteration of the convocation injured their sense of security and well-being. "No money for the ungodly," one alumnus scrawled across a fundraising pledge card. Another wrote, perhaps with some deeper understanding of the role of tradition: "Tradition comes from countless years of holding on to what might otherwise slip away unnoticed."[22]

Embracing Pluralism

It is clear from the foregoing that institutions such as universities absorb change slowly. Their cultures are anchored with Burkean steadfastness by the very things that give them stability and longevity. For example, while academic tenure protects an academic's freedom of speech and thought, it can also have the tendency of insulating pedagogy from shifts in society beyond the campus boundary. Similarly, the compartmentalization of academic inquiry into departmental structures and programs can introduce rigidity into the way knowledge is defined and shared. The accumulation of printed knowledge in libraries is also a prism of the curiosity of past generations who have taught and studied on the campus. A university's composition and orientation is powerfully influenced by the mindset of its faculty and alumni to impart a certain dedication and social attitude on its recruitment of the next generation of students. Universities are thus prone to a self-defined perpetuation, with an accompanying propensity for the exclusion of participants and perspectives that do not readily conform to the institution's stereotype of itself. Queen's undoubtedly succumbed in many ways to this pattern. Among Canadian universities, it boasted, for instance, a very high rate of generation-to-generation loyalty – "my father sent me down to Queen's … on the Old Ontario Strand," so the old song went.

At the same time, Queen's location in a relatively small eastern-Ontario city tended to diminish its contact with Canada's metropolitan culture. Indeed, Queen's has always tended to be an introverted community in many ways. As the Padre's annual recruiting sorties illustrated, it became very adept at tapping into promising nodes of undergraduate material in big-city Canada, but these conduits were often sealed off from other increasingly significant segments of Canadian society. Queen's, in short, had prospered from a selective homogeneity. This homogeneity was apparent in its annual listing of faculty and students, in its alumni magazine, and in the image it projected to the nation at large. The formula had turned George Grant's struggling university of the 1890s into a national university. But the formula was now isolating the campus from Canada as a whole.

That is to say, the postwar surge in immigration, the maturing of the baby boom, the reaffirmation of Canada as a deeply rooted bicultural culture, and the recognition that the country was becoming multicultural were by the seventies and eighties undermining Queen's dedication to its version of national excellence. The university was oblivious to these tendencies. These decades were punctuated by tentative attempts to connect Queen's with the "new" Canada. In the sixties, the turmoil of the Quiet Revolution provoked some at Queen's to connect with

Quebec; student exchanges with Laval University were established. The International Centre opened in 1962 to give foreign students a home away from home. For many summers, Queen's School of English had attracted non-English speakers to campus, a trend given greater breadth by the emergence of English as a Second Language (ESL) courses. In 1976, the Senate, under prompting from the Council of Ontario Universities, had adopted an admissions policy dedicated to promoting greater diversity in its student body.[23] These initiatives tended to be predicated on geographic diversity, on stretching the university's catchment area.

Other inchoate initiatives recognized that Queen's needed to encompass difference in terms of race, religion, and ethnicity. In 1975, for example, the university unveiled a plaque honouring Robert Sutherland, the Jamaican who came to Queen's in 1849 and became not only its first black graduate but also later a successful Toronto lawyer and benefactor of his alma mater.[24] A year earlier, the university had belatedly named its physiology building on Arch Street after Harry and Ethel Abramsky. The Abramskys, a successful local Jewish mercantile family, had generously supported the building's construction in the 1950s, only to discover that the university was reluctant to put their name above the door. The "official" explanation was that Queen's did not name buildings after living people. In reality, the decision smacked of anti-Semitism. McLaughlin Hall, home of mechanical engineering, had been named for its benefactor, Sam McLaughlin, as early as 1949, as had the Craine Building, which was named in the 1930s for its benefactor, Dr Agnes Craine. When one-time Chancellor Charles Dunning and former Dean of Arts and Science Rollo Earl died, the university moved with alacrity to christen buildings after them. Remarkably, the Abramskys kept up their generous financial support of Queen's and finally, in 1974, the trustees gave them their due by putting their name on the door. There were other hints of diversity on campus by the eighties, often made possible by the AMS's inclusive policy of supporting student clubs – a Chinese Students' Club, an Indian Dance Club, an Hispanic Club. There were thus encouraging signs of multiculturalism taking root at Queen's. In 1987, Queen's B'nai Brith Hillel Foundation invited the Queen's Islamic Association to a Shabbat dinner. "We have a great deal to learn," Hillel President Howard Crosner told the *Journal*, "We should try, in university, to do that."[25]

But these were all small dents in what was still a very monolithic campus culture. In early 1985, a special Senate committee on admissions suggested that the existing admissions policy, by focusing on academic achievement in high school, provided Queen's with superb undergraduates, but did so at the price of sidelining those who emerged out of less-privileged socioeconomic circumstances. Chaired by Vice-Principal Duncan Sinclair, the committee concluded that it was "probable that the student body at Queen's is less representative of socially and economically disadvantaged Canadians than some other universities, especially those in large urban centres." Queen's policy was "elitist and unabashedly so!"[26] The national census suggested that, if Queen's chose to set its admission bar at such a high mark, then certain social and ethnic groups would always be underrepresented at Queen's, a reflection of systemic social and economic inequities present in Canadian society. This effect was heightened by the fact that Queen's was a residential university, where students incurred higher living expenses than "commuter universities," such as York and Carleton, situated in large urban areas.

Two years later, Sinclair's replacement as vice-principal, institutional relations, Tom Williams, carried the same message to the trustees. The problem, he said, was a *recruitment* problem, not an *admissions* problem. The university had a poor socioeconomic mix because it had "not really tried to recruit in certain areas."[27] The university had, to a degree, brought this problem on itself by focusing its urban recruiting efforts on older – often private – schools and overlooking schools in the burgeoning, newer metropolitan areas. Ironically, Williams remarked, every other university in the province was trying to emulate Queen's traditional, cream-of-the-crop approach to admissions. Queen's inability to break out of its traditional shell was given popular credence in the pages of the bestselling 1987 *Guide to Canadian Universities*. Using somewhat impressionistic evidence, the *Guide* portrayed Queen's as party-loving country club for WASP adolescents.[28] In part to reverse this perception, Queen's began appointing recruitment officers in Toronto and deploying them to a more demographically diverse range of schools.

David Smith's years as principal thus became the fulcrum for social and cultural change at Queen's. In all likelihood this was because the adjustment had been postponed through the seventies as the university fixated on its fiscal problems and remained too beholden to its consensual culture.

Change would arrive on three fronts: through *sui generis* new processes and programs, through externally mandated policies, and by shock treatment. New academic programs tended to reflect agitation within the university for learning that connected Queen's with broader social sensibilities – women's studies, Aboriginal studies, and Jewish studies – of demonstrable relevance to students. Other new programs and practices – the imposition of equity policies and human-rights guidelines – arrived on campus as the result of state-imposed mandates. In an era of Charter rights, the universities were increasingly obliged to conform to nationally imposed codes of conduct that brooked no exclusions. In 1984, for instance, a royal commission conducted by Ontario Justice Rosalie Abella had emphasized the need for "employment equity" in the workplace, an objective soon evident in federal legislation and contracting practice. Queen's responded to such mandates by embracing the idea that it could socially engineer not only the composition of the university community but also its day-to-day behaviour and attitudes. Procedures were established, offices opened, and appointments made to instill an understanding across the campus that diversity hinged on undifferentiated respect of rights. The incremental introduction of such policies worked towards synchronizing Queen's with the mores and expectations of the wider Canadian society.

There were, however, conspicuous points of friction in this adjustment, friction which flared up on campus as starkly different renditions of gender rights, racial relations, and a university's social responsibility overwhelmed Queen's usual collegial atmosphere. In 1988, for instance, Marilyn Hood, the Principal's Advisor on Employment Equity, quit her job, arguing that senior administrators were excluding her from the inner sanctum of policy making, thereby sending the message that Queen's was not really taking equity seriously.[29] It would take four dramatic, unprecedented crises on campus – a "gender war" in the Faculty of Law, a misogynistic sexist sign incident in the residences, a bitter debate over the university's investments in Chile and South Africa, and an inquiry into alleged racism at Queen's – to provoke real change on the equity front at Queen's. These crises would at the same time catch the nation's attention and rightly sully the university's national reputation, while at the same time ultimately jolting Queen's out of its complacency into a new, more activist and inclusive definition of self.

Moreover, by revealing Queen's ineptitude in brokering and remedying such contentious situations, these crises startled governance at Queen's into both a new vigilance and a new responsiveness. The trustees, for instance, created a social-responsibility committee, while the AMS initiated a Committee on Racism and Ethnic Relations. For David Smith, principal through this tumult, managing this transition proved the most draining challenge of his years in Richardson Hall. Even more than the challenge of walking the financial tightrope strung by Queen's Park or edging the university into new international and professional orientations, Smith found the task of seeing Queen's over the watershed of cultural change in the late eighties excruciating. His primal fear was that, under his watch, the fabric of the university might be irreparably rent by its inability to bridge opposing perspectives that had opened among its members. If rancour replaced consensus at Queen's, he feared, the university ran the risk of detaching itself from the expectations of the society it served, thereby betraying its long tradition of social service.[30]

Classroom Inclusion: Recognizing the Jewish Fact at Queen's

Commendably, pressure for better accommodation of Canada's diversity in these years often arose out of the ranks of Queen's faculty. Queen's had never, for example, been hermetically sealed to Jews as students and faculty. Despite the university's official dedication to being "distinctively Christian," a few Jewish scholars had been taken onto faculty. In 1938, anatomist Ben Kropp had joined the medical faculty. A brilliant, Princeton-trained mathematician, Israel Halperin, was recruited in 1939, albeit to face bitter career controversy. After wartime service researching explosives, Halperin had been caught up in the infamous Gouzenko spy investigation. Like many who had observed the social and economic carnage of the Depression, Halperin had been attracted to alternate ideologies. This inclination, plus allegations implicating him in the passing of secret technological information to the Soviets, led to his immediate tarring in mainstream Canadian opinion with the label of "communist."[31]

Halperin, however, was acquitted of charges of violating the Official Secrets Act and conspiracy. Despite pressure from some trustees that Halperin, as a "fellow-traveller," had no place in a Queen's classroom, he was welcomed back to campus. In their defence of Halperin, Chancellor Charles Dunning and Principal Robert Wallace asserted that Queen's durable traditions of liberalism and due process applied to Halperin as much as they did to any other member of the university community. He would remain at Queen's until 1966.[32] While Halperin's longevity at Queen's was more a reflection of ideological tolerance than ethnic accommodation, it does speak to a degree of latitude on a campus generally known for its narrow WASP personality. This latitude in fact continued. In 1968, when he became Dean of Law, for instance, Daniel Soberman became the first Jewish dean at Queen's, followed in 1977 by another Jew, Bernard Adell (who would take a leading role in the campaign to remove religious elements from convocation).

However, Queen's was by no means immune to the anti-Semitic attitudes broadly prevalent in twentieth-century Canadian society. In her research into "Queen's Jews," Hannah Professor of Medical History, Jacalyn Duffin, has concluded that none of the Jewish members of the medical faculty she interviewed "felt personal discrimination, although several said that a 'vague anti-Semitism lurked in off-the-cuff remarks (e.g., several cited the verb 'to Jew'), smoldering, as Moussa Cohanim [a bone specialist in the department of medicine] said, 'like a flame under the ashes.'"[33] There were indications that some Jewish students at Queen's encountered subtle discrimination: in the late 1930s, medical student Ben Scott found his graduation blocked for a year by an anti-Semitic professor who failed him in his oral examinations (knowing that there would be no written record of his interrogation of the student).[34] When history professor Gerald Tulchinsky arrived at Queen's in 1966, he was immediately struck by the collegiality and "accepting attitude" of Queen's. He had little sense of being perceived as Jewish in his department. Colleagues did, however, pass along tales of WASP students naively inquiring whether a professor with a name ending in "sky" could communicate effectively in English. Over in the faculty club, Tulchinsky sometimes detected a "genteel anti-Semitism" in some of his fellow faculty.[35] When the issue of "religious elements" at convocation arose in the early 1980s, Tulchinsky acknowledged that he always felt uncomfortable taking part in a ceremony redolent with Christian ritual and rhetoric and joined the agitation for change.

Harry and Ethel Abramsky were generous benefactors of Queen's. Harry, a successful Jewish merchant in Kingston, in 1955 donated funds for a physiology building on campus. The university gratefully accepted the money, but relegated the Abramsky name to a plaque inside the door. In 1974, Principal Watts rectified the slight by naming the building Abramsky Hall. Abramsky generosity also touched medical labs and the Agnes Etherington Art Centre.

If Queen's had never entirely excluded Jewish faculty, neither had it ever shut its doors to Jewish students. Canada's big-city universities, notably McGill and Toronto, notoriously established quotas on Jewish admissions, quotas that, while not overtly publicized, were broadly understood in the communities that surrounded them.[36] At Queen's the idea of limiting Jewish admissions never took on a quantifiable dimension, perhaps because, unlike Montreal and Toronto, Queen's in Kingston did not have a sizable Jewish community on its doorstep. Quotas at McGill and Toronto were often predi-cated on the anti-Semitic belief that allegedly "pushy" Jews would "take over" the campus. (Jews in Montreal and Toronto in these same years were obliged to establish their own hospitals.) Such was seemingly not the case in Kingston.[37] In fact, the university enjoyed a strong and trusting relationship with the local Jewish community, a relationship typified by the generosity of the Abramsky family in the 1950s. Only once – at the height of World War II – did Queen's toy with the idea of consciously restricting Jewish entry to its programs. Worried that Jews were unable to gain entry to McGill because of its quota, some trustees embraced the phobic notion that a surge in Jewish attendance at Queen's would unbalance the place.

The alleged "problem" was dressed up as a question of academic standards and, after much study by a joint Senate-Board committee, the university raised its senior-matriculation entry standard as it applied to *all* applicants, in the hope that this would screen out Jewish students unable to satisfy McGill's entry bar who might therefore consider Queen's. Through all this, Principal Wallace stoutly reminded the trustees that overt action against Jewish applicants would court charges of discrimination and unsavoury publicity at a time when Canada was sacrificing men to vanquish the Nazi menace. Peace in 1945 alleviated the "problem," as the spike in Jewish interest in Queen's diminished. In his sweeping history of Jews in Canada, Tulchinsky concluded that Queen's, through its hiring of Jewish faculty and its avoidance of rigid entry quotas, was "mildly more liberal than either McGill or Toronto."[38] The experience of Alfred Bader, turned away at McGill and Toronto but accepted by Queen's in 1941, supports this judgment, as does the establishment of Hillel House on campus in these same wartime years.

Prejudice is impossible to quantify. Its deceitful stratagems are seldom documented in obvious ways for the historian. One window on the experience of Jews at Queen's is offered by the medical school, with its emphasis on professional education and its narrow, measurable admissions portal. Until 1980, students admitted to Queen's medical school were required to reveal their religious denomination. A collation of the student records of the 4,173 students admitted to the Queen's medical school between 1912 and 1980 by Jacalyn Duffin reveals that 212 – or about 5 per cent – of Queen's medical students over these years were Jewish. While Queen's medicine countenanced an absolute prohibition of black medical students and shunned most women applicants well into the post–World War II period, it never utterly excluded Jews. Nonetheless, willingness to admit the latter varied over time.

In the 1920s, Jewish students began appearing at Queen's, many from Kingston, but others from bigger cities and even the United States. During the 1930s – paradoxically at a time when the federal government quietly did its best to push refugee European Jews away from Canada's shores – Queen's proved willing to accept Jews into its medical program. In 1936, for instance, eight of a graduating class of forty-six were Jewish. Once at Queen's, Jewish students and the small number of Jewish faculty gravitated to Kingston's Beth Israel synagogue, which had served the city's Jewish community since 1897.[39] Hillel House, after 1941, also enhanced a sense of Jewish community around Queen's. The graduating class of Meds '47 represented a high-water mark for Jewish grads in the Queen's medical school, with 20 per cent of its fifty-one members being Jewish. The postwar period, however, saw a decline in Jewish student admissions to Queen's, a reflection of phobias and anxieties brought on by the emerging Cold War, the controversial birth of Israel, and a misplaced belief that Canadian Jews were being endowed with privileges out of proportion with their minority status. Between 1944 and 1949, applicants to Queen's were, for the first time, obliged to state their "racial origin." Despite the confusion of race and religion, this categorization tended to isolate Jews, the closest Queen's came to a formal quota. By the class of 1955, only three of sixty-eight medical students were Jewish. Then, in the 1960s, as Canada embraced human rights – with Diefenbaker's Bill of Rights in 1960 and Ontario's Human Rights Code of 1962 – equity returned to medical admissions and numbers reverted to the long-term average of about 5 per cent each year.

It is perhaps only of semantic significance to debate whether Queen's ever imposed identifiable "quotas" on Jews coming to Queen's. Less debatable is the realization that that there was a *persistent consciousness* of the Jewish fact on campus – a sense, at times a wariness, that Jews were different. As he sought to acculturate to his new academic surroundings at Queen's in the late 1960s, Gerald Tulchinsky sensed this cultural tension and attributed it to the "pronounced insularity" of a relatively small university situated in the hinterland of eastern Ontario. Queen's, he sensed, suffered from an ill-informed smugness that at times, despite its tradition of liberalism, blinded it from seeing the full diversity of the Canadian people. Brantford-born Tulchinsky had begun his academic career studying the dynamic bicultural Montreal business community in the mid-nineteenth-century glory years of that city. Over time his interest in cultural pluralism drew him into the study of North American Jewry. By the mid-1980s, that focus had broadened to embrace European Jewry, a shift that inevitably entailed addressing the Holocaust. The Holocaust, he sensed, had a paramount place in postwar western liberal consciousness. Yet few non-Jews understood the dynamics of the evil that precipitated this blight on twentieth-century history. There was certainly not a hint of Jewish experience in his department's offerings.

In 1986, Tulchinsky therefore approached his dean, Rod Fraser, with the idea of a dedicated course on the Holocaust. His department head, Jim Stayer, had already "warmly" approved the idea. Fraser was enthusiastic. There were obstacles – a lack of library resources, for instance – but, with the assistance of the Principal's Development Fund, the course came to life in 1989. In preparation,

Tulchinsky went to Israel for a workshop on teaching Jewish civilization. He was aware of the delicacy of the subject matter, but told Principal Smith that he was "resolved to focus on the intentions of the perpetrators with detachment and rigour, though – to be frank – I know that this is extremely difficult material to deal with."[40] The course – History 295: The Holocaust – The Destruction of European Jewry, 1933–1945 – was immensely popular with students. Tulchinsky went on to reinforce Queen's new-found reputation as a welcoming place for those interested in Jewish culture by writing two books on the Jewish experience in Canada, *Taking Root* and *Branching Out*.[41] This popularity was soon reflected in a concerted effort to create a chair of Jewish Studies at Queen's, an effort spearheaded by the department of religion and generously given financial wherewithal by Irving and Regina Rosen of Kingston. By 1989, $400,000 had been raised towards establishing the chair. In 1993, the chair was ratified by the trustees.[42] Classes in the Hebrew language and the possibility of taking courses in Israel followed. Paralleling this implanting of Jewish studies in the faculty's expertise was the creation in 1988 of the annual Rosen Lecture. Also generously supported by Irving and Regina Rosen, the lecture's focus on the Jewish experience reinforced the bridge between Queen's and Kingston Jewry.

In these years, the advent of Jewish studies at Queen's was symptomatic of a broader cultural awakening. In 1989, Principal Smith's special report on the "qualities of a Queen's education" gave priority to the development of so-called "ethnic studies" at Queen's. Two years later, when asked to investigate alleged racism at Queen's, psychology professor John Berry and his committee concluded that racism could not be examined in isolation, but must instead be framed by a much larger discussion of diversity in Canadian society. Race, gender, and ethnicity were all "inextricably linked." Only a handful of political-science and sociology courses addressed the central Canadian reality of biculturalism and multiculturalism. Among the Berry committee's recommendations was the need "to establish a more balanced curriculum" that reflected "a multi-cultural and multi-racial Canadian society" and which prepared Queen's students "to work in a diverse population."[43] As a result, departments, particularly in Arts, began rejigging their curricula to broaden the scope of their intellectual inquiry from one fixated on the evolution of western civilization and Eurocentric values.

As the nineties unfolded, academic hiring began to reflect this pattern. To cite one example of many, scholars such as Reena Zeidman and Justin Lewis were hired to bring depth to Jewish Studies at Queen's. Eventually, Howard Tzvi Adelman, a specialist in Judaism's relations with the Islamic and Christian world, was hired in the history department to perpetuate Tulchinsky's initiative by becoming the director of the new interdisciplinary Jewish Studies Program at Queen's. Indeed, the history department provided an excellent barometer of the university's embrace of diversity. Over the next decade, the department, traditionally dedicated to Canadian, American, and European history (often along political, diplomatic, and economic lines) welcomed into its midst scholars focusing on race and sexuality, while at the same time expanding its global perspective to include the South Asian diaspora, the Islamic world, and multiracial societies.

Towards Greater Diversity: Aboriginals

The ability of the concept of diversity to reorient Queen's intellectual compass was evident in other areas as well. Two examples will suffice here: acknowledging Aboriginal status and women's studies. Like most Canadian universities, Queen's had historically maintained only a peripheral encounter with Canada's First Nations. Ironically, Queen's stands on land that is part of the traditional lands of the Haudenosaunee and Anishinaabe peoples. Kingston's hinterland still contains vital Native communities, such as the Tyendinaga Mohawks along the Bay of Quinte. On occasion, Queen's had taken its skills to Canada's Aboriginal peoples: since the 1960s, Queen's nurses and medical students had rotated through the community hospital at Moose Factory on the shores of James Bay. Over time, a handful of Aboriginal peoples had come to Queen's for an education: notable Native graduates included Dr Marlene Brant Castellano (BA '55), later an acclaimed Native-studies proponent at Trent University, and psychiatrist Dr Clare Brant (MD '65). The chasm between the culture of Queen's and that of Canada's Native peoples, however, remained wide. An equity census of Queen's employees in early 1992 revealed that only 0.4 per cent of the university's workforce was Aboriginal, well below the national average of 2.1 per cent – and even below the Kingston-area average of 1.7 per cent.[44] Most Native students who ventured to Queen's hit a wall of cultural difference – the challenge of conforming, for instance, to rigid class timetables and deadlines for assignments, as well as that of adapting to residence life – and found little guidance in negotiating so Eurocentric an environment. The drop-out rate was consequently horrendous.

The early nineties brought a shift in attitude. A federal royal commission on Canada's Aboriginal peoples was created in 1991 to study the woefully marginalized existence of the First Nations. Its investigations raised national consciousness of the plight of the Native peoples. The commission's 1996 report would, amongst other things, recommend the creation of a First Nations university. This consciousness resonated at Queen's. First and foremost, there was recognition that Native students needed a central point of reference and coordination as they were adapting to university. The university, for its part, had at the same time to adapt to their needs. Beginning in 1991, plans were laid for an Aboriginal Council at Queen's "to ensure that for generations hereafter Aboriginal peoples will have access to higher education at Queen's University, and that the institution will be responsive to the broader needs of Aboriginal peoples." Wide-ranging discussions with Ontario Native communities led to subsequent formal agreements that linked Queen's with potential Native constituencies. Approved by the Senate, the Aboriginal Council was composed of representatives from Ontario Native councils, senior university representatives, and representatives of Native students actually attending Queen's. Provincial funding supported its oversight.

The Aboriginal Council initiated an "action plan" to facilitate Native needs on campus – alternative methods of delivering post-secondary education to people whose cultural background contained little exposure to higher education. Conscious that Native students needed mentors and role models, the council invited Native elders to take up residence on campus and thereby provide a daily, near-at-hand link with traditional Native culture. In 1992, a Native Educational Council was established to vet undergraduate applications to Queen's by Natives, so that the cultural predilections of Aboriginal Canadians, hitherto invisible to the Queen's admissions policy, could be weighed in the balance. The law faculty announced that it would similarly treat minority status as a "positive factor" in scrutinizing its applications. At the same time, the law school began integrating topics such as Native land claims into its curriculum. For its part, the education faculty launched its Aboriginal Teacher Education Program to foster the development of better Native secondary-school teachers. Dr Cecil King, an Odawa from Manitoulin Island and an academic specialist in indigenous languages, was hired to direct the program. Finally, the general student body at Queen's became more responsive to the Native fact. The AMS, for instance, invited former Prime Minister Joe Clark to speak at Queen's on the challenge of reforming the governance of Natives in Canada. At the same time, a Native Student Association sprang up, and in 1996 the Four Directions Aboriginal Centre opened in a house on Barrie Street to provide Native students with a focal point for the balancing of the spiritual, physical, emotional, and academic needs of their new university

The 1990s saw the Aboriginal fact embraced by Queen's. An Aboriginal Council was established and, in 1997, the Four Directions Aboriginal Student Centre opened. Efforts were made to connect the Aboriginal and white cultures on campus. Here photographer Greg Black captures an autumn powwow taking place on Benidickson Field. At convocations, the principal welcomed graduates by reminding them that Queen's sits on territory once occupied by the Anishinaabe and Haudenosaunee peoples.

lives. In true Queen's fashion, the centre started its own traditions: a weekly Three Sisters Feast of Native food for both Native students and curious Queen's non-Natives.[45]

There was, however, no overnight Aboriginal revolution at Queen's. In 1995, Registrar Alison Morgan reported that Queen's still lagged behind the provincial average in attracting Native students.[46] By 2000, there were about sixty Aboriginal students in Queen's mainstream academic programs. The Aboriginal Teacher Education Program (ATEP), offered in conjunction with Trent University, took root more

quickly: by 2003, philosophy professor Christine Overall, co-chair of the Aboriginal Council, reported that there were 116 students in training. Medicine had introduced its own affirmative-action policy for Aboriginal applicants. Overall remarked that, while progress in promoting an Aboriginal presence at Queen's was slow, at least a workable academic and social infrastructure had been put in place and that the council now therefore needed to devise a "new action plan." Queen's, she argued, still faced the challenge of making itself "a more welcoming place for Aboriginal students."[47] The council almost immediately gave evidence of its new determination: in 2004, the Senate approved a policy to annually admit ten Aboriginal students into Arts and Science under separate admission criteria.[48]

Diversity at Queen's did not come unopposed. A faculty and student body that was overwhelmingly WASP in its orientation was bound to contain those who defended the status quo. When, for instance, the 2004 separate-stream admissions protocol was approved by the Senate, some members of the campus Progressive Conservative Club protested that the policy was a quota system based on racist principles.[49] In the Senate, the arbiter of academic programs, new initiatives aimed at promoting greater social inclusion at Queen's at times encountered the argument that programs designed to promote greater inclusion at Queen's inevitably led to a dilution of quality in both teaching and scholarship, leaving Queen's with a mess of multicultural pottage.[50] Similarly, some argued that the stretching of the faculty's scope of scholarly interest entailed a dissipation of the university's intellectual integrity. Queen's, they argued, was never meant to be all things to all comers. To force the university to bend to outside social predilections was, they contended, a breach of academic freedom. In vote after Senate vote, such reasoning was firmly countered by a liberal-minded majority that equated academic excellence with broad social inclusion. In time, Native rituals would find a place in the university's convocation ceremony and Queen's students would be offered the opportunity to take a minor in Aboriginal studies. Queen's innate liberalism thus rose to the challenge. The Berry committee on racism arrived at the same destination: "Excellence is a quality that pertains to institutions, not just to individuals. In a multicultural and multiracial society, it is plausible to argue that a culturally and racially diverse institution is superior to a homogeneous one."[51]

Towards Greater Diversity: Women's Studies

In these same years, Queen's belatedly adjusted its academic culture to acknowledge the new position of women in Canadian society. In 1984, the university had celebrated the one-hundredth anniversary of the graduation of its first women students. The occasion was marked by a slew of honorary degrees given to women, by much journalistic writing on nostalgic topics such as Levana candle lighting, and by the celebration of feminist milestones at Queen's – women were now regularly, for instance, elected as AMS and Engineering Society presidents. On the faculty front, the persistence of the Association of Women Teaching at Queen's (AWTAQ) was finally beginning to pay dividends: initiatives such as the Queen's National Scholars program had started to right the historic gender imbalance in Queen's faculty. As one of its prime movers, law professor Beverley Baines, has noted, AWTAQ had "a power to give voice" beyond its numbers.[52]

Thus, in parallel with the rise of second-wave feminist consciousness across the continent, AWTAQ members became prominent in a growing agitation on Queen's campus for women to be brought to the centre stage of academic study – a demand that centuries of curricula permeated by male perspectives now be offset by scholarship centred on female experience (that is, viewed through a feminist lens). If Queen's was to have a more gender-diverse faculty, it was argued, then it must also foster greater gender diversity in its curriculum. Women's studies courses had been appearing elsewhere for over a decade – Cornell and the University of Toronto leading the way in 1969. Such scholarship necessarily stretched across the neat boundaries of traditional academic disciplines – after all, women's experience could be found in everything from physics to art history. As had been the case in the campaign for the feminization of Queen's faculty during the Watts years, the campaign for the introduction of women's studies was a collective effort involving women from disparate departments, all united in a belief that Queen's students were being denied a feminist perspective on their lives.

At Queen's, initial interest in women's studies emerged in the early 1980s as a result of efforts in the Deutsch and Watts years to promote the "status of women" on its campus. The Principal's Advisory Group on the Status of Women lobbied hard on strategic issues such as the more equitable treatment and promotion of women professors and staff,[53] while a subcommittee of the Status group agitated for the establishment of women's studies on campus. Indeed, Queen's was a laggard in this respect, as many other Ontario universities already had such programs in place. In 1982, the subcommittee, chaired by Mary Maxwell of sociology and composed of both faculty and students, published a list of courses addressing women's experience already available at Queen's. Workshops on women's studies were organized and faculty boards were urged to recognize women's studies in their curriculum deliberations. The work of the subcommittee galvanized campus opinion. A petition calling for formalized women's-studies courses was signed by over a thousand students and presented to Principal Watts. Watts proved sympathetic, dipping into his development fund to facilitate the subcommittee's investigation. A scheme for hosting visiting speakers was initiated to expose students to prominent women.

Out of this conjunction of broad student enthusiasm and effective coordination by a strong interdisciplinary group, Queen's initial women's-studies course emerged in 1985. As was the case in any new curricular initiative, the women's-studies advocates faced the question of where their pedagogy would be lodged in the university's panoply of disciplines and, equally importantly, who would foot the bill. A creative solution was found in making the course interdisciplinary and appointing two paid coordinators for the course – English professor Elizabeth Greene and historian Katherine McKenna. Together they orchestrated the efforts of seventeen women professors who volunteered – that is, contributed their energies as a teaching overload – to provide lectures conveying women's experience in fields as disparate as art history, film, law, and nursing.

Introduced in the fall of 1985, the course – Interdisciplinary Studies 200 – "Introduction to Women's Studies" – was an instant success. Beyond its appeal to existing undergraduates, the course drew many women from the broader community, women anxious to place their experience in a meaningful theoretical framework. The *Queen's Alumni Review* pronounced the course "a hit" and wrote an article on it that focused on a young mother from Seeley's Bay, north of Kingston, who religiously attended the course with baby in arms. "I would drive for hours just to take this course," she enthused. Lisa Moore, chair of the AMS Women's Issues Committee, added further praise: "For three years I have been educated to see my experience as too subjective. Here [in IDIS 200] my experience is validated, and I am made to realize that *everybody's* perspective is subjective."[54]

The groundswell grew. In the spring of 1985, an ad hoc committee of about fifty students had spontaneously sprung up, motivated by Queen's "poor record in hiring women faculty and its lack of a multidisciplinary Women's Studies program." "To ignore half of the world's population," they warned, "is a serious distortion of reality." To remedy this, they advocated a fully fledged program in women's studies, crowned by the appointment of a chair in the field. The cost, they estimated, would be a million dollars.[55] Spurred on by this initiative, thirty-two women faculty members from numerous departments caucused under the guidance of sociology professors Mary Maxwell and Mary Morton to bring forward a proposal for a "special field concentration" in women's studies. While not a formal honours program, a field concentration would allow a student to cluster fourteen courses over the four years of an undergraduate degree. The women's-studies concentration would offer core courses and the possibility of an honours thesis. Dean Rod Fraser was enthusiastic, making it known that he could find the resources to support the program and would provide a release from teaching for the program's coordinator. Perhaps the most striking aspect of Queen's embrace of women's studies was its grassroots promotion – by a determined group of well-focused women academics, backed by enthusiastic student opinion eager to see Queen's step into line with other campuses across the continent.

By November, the women's special-concentration proposal had cleared the Arts and Science faculty curriculum committee. At each stage of its incubation, the proposal was shepherded by forceful and articulate champions – Bev Baines of law, Susan Dick of English, and Joy Parr of history, in this instance – who ensured that it would not be derailed by critics. On 13 December 1985, the proposal arrived in the full Arts and Science faculty board for final approval. The room was packed and the atmosphere tense. Ably explained by sociologist Roberta Hamilton (a newly appointed Queen's National Scholar) and forthrightly supported by Dean Fraser, the proposal nonetheless encountered some opposition. A handful of male professors, although paying lip service to the necessity of "reshaping traditional structures," argued that women's studies was not in fact worthy to be treated as a distinct discipline. Philosophy professor Norman Brown opined that women's studies lacked "a cohesiveness due to the wide range of departments involved." It lacked a "specific methodology of learning." Hamilton countered that women's studies had "a unity based on work of the organizers who have been involved in the field for up to fifteen years." North America, she noted, was embroiled in debate over feminist theory as vigorous as that in any other academic discipline. Without further ado, the proposal was passed by a large majority of faculty and sent to the Senate for final approval.[56]

The Senate smoothly approved the new program early in 1986. Principal Smith's first year and a half in office thus witnessed substantive progress – as opposed to a study of the problem – in righting the gender balance at Queen's. In an instructive coincidence, law professor Beverley Baines drew the

A full lecture hall welcomes the arrival of Queen's first course in women's studies in the fall of 1985. Within a decade, women's studies would establish itself as a full academic department.

Senate's attention to the anachronistic way in which its female members were addressed at Senate meetings and in its minutes. Whereas male senators were simply given a genderless set of initials – N.J.P. Brown of philosophy – female members were invariably labelled as "Miss" or "Mrs." This discrepancy, Baines pointed out, was sexist. The Senate acquiesced. Hitherto all women would be known as "Ms" (later changed to initials alone).[57] Women's studies continued to gain momentum at Queen's. With Roberta Hamilton as coordinator, new courses were developed in feminist theory, an introductory first-year course in women's studies was created as the foundation of the program, and new cross-listed courses were added to the special concentration. The pool of willing teaching talent expanded, adding promising names like Suzanne Fortier in chemistry and Bronwen Wallace in creative writing. In 1989, the program created the Kathleen Herman Prize in Women's Studies to honour the sociologist who had taken so prominent a role in helping Queen's women to challenge the academic glass ceiling. By 1993, women's studies offered five core courses and a choice of twenty-seven cross-listed courses for its students. That year, reflecting this strength, women's studies became an institute within the Arts and Science faculty with a director, geographer Audrey Kobayashi, named to the post in 1994. Within a decade, women's studies would become a fully fledged department.[58]

Change by Crisis: Gender and Sexual-Diversity "Wars" in Macdonald Hall

The broadening of Queen's academic horizons to encompass Jewish and women's studies and its recognition of Aboriginal sensibilities spoke positively to Queen's long-standing tradition of liberal adjustment to changing social currents flowing around and through its campus community. Queen's was by no means a pioneer in any of these fields. Its relative isolation in eastern Ontario had often tended to deny it a first-mover role in adjusting to seismic shifts in Canadian society, shifts usually first sensed in large metropolitan areas. Nonetheless, the university's primordial Presbyterian inclination to make education a matter of social utility usually asserted itself once the need for adjustment was made evident. There was nothing faddish or headlong in Queen's culture; change at Queen's often needed considerable prodding – as AWTAQ had so effectively demonstrated on the gender frontier. Queen's acute sense of excellence in what it traditionally had done well – catering to the bright scions of urban WASP Canada – tended to isolate it from groups on the margin of this fertile core.

But change always did eventually come at Queen's. Perhaps the best example of this had come almost a century before when, amid Canada's topsy-turvy spurt of growth in the Laurier years, political economists such as Adam Shortt and later O.D. Skelton had connected Queen's with the growing need for social and economic regulation through public policy. Queen's thus turned its attention to preparing its "Ottawa men," a tradition still manifest during the Watts and Smith years in the formation of the School of Policy Studies. But this storied public-policy connection with the greater Canada was now reinforced by new initiatives designed to make Queen's relevant to other segments of Canadian society – to Jews and Native people – while at the same time reinventing its relevance to Canadian women by making their experiences a subject of legitimate academic inquiry. Other initiatives in these years – a Chair of Ukrainian Studies in 1987, a School of Environmental Studies in 1994, and even a School of Music more oriented to performance music in 1987 – gave further evidence of the university's awareness of the need to reinvent itself along more inclusive, diversified lines. As a university task force looking into Canada's changing demographics concluded in 1991: "We believe Queen's should move to reflect the mosaic of Canadian society in its learning community ... [and] this should be along lines of race, age, culture, and religion."[59]

It would thus be comforting to conclude that Queen's adjustment to the pluralism and diversity of late-twentieth-century Canada moved progressively, if somewhat conservatively, forward along Whiggish lines. Unfortunately, however, not all change in Queen's in these years emanated out of faculty lobbying and consensual debate in faculty boards or the Senate chamber. At times, circumstances simply overtook Queen's ability to govern its own pace of change. Outmoded values and structures then buckled under the strain of change, and the institution succumbed to fatigue and acrimony, out of which a recognition of Canada's broadened pluralism painfully emerged. Nowhere was this truer than in the sad dysfunctioning of the university's gendered relations in the late eighties, demonstrated in the deep-seated bitterness of the so-called "gender wars" in the law faculty and the raw chauvinism of male students in the residence precinct. These events awakened it to an imperative need to construct a sexually more equitable and inclusive campus society, one that accepted sexual diversity and ensured

By the 1980s, the gender balance in Queen's faculty finally began to reflect a greater presence of women on campus. The Queen's National Scholars program, brilliantly conceived by Principal Watts, was given a deliberate feminine bent by Principal Smith. Monies for QNS allowed Queen's to attract many very capable young women scholars at a time when austerity was limiting recruitment. Historical sociologist Roberta Hamilton (left) typified the influx.

respect of such diversity by learning to police itself against sexism and harassment.

Queen's much-vaunted campus traditions had undeniably done much to sustain the university's cohesion and sense of purpose. Queen's tradition was, however, unmistakably heterosexual in its tone and trappings. From football chants – "What's the sport of *kings*? Queen's, Queen's, Queen's!" – to the annual Grant Hall candle-lighting ritual for Freshettes, with all its fecund expectations of graduating from Queen's with an "MRS," student culture at Queen's was propelled by a powerful dialectic of boy-meets-girl – in which boy has the upper hand. The faculty mirrored this in a slightly more subtle fashion: for decades women were treated as junior partners in the institution's intellectual dedication, uninvited to the Saturday Club's high-minded deliberations, given second-class pensions, and, as the Association of Women Teaching at Queen's so vehemently underscored, passed over by appointments committees.

In the seventies, Queen's progress towards gender parity had been painfully slow, partly the result of severe financial constraint, but also undeniably due to its inured male-dominated gender politic.

As noted above, by the eighties, reformist inroads were beginning to be made into this unbalanced heterosexual culture. The Queen's National Scholars program was "fast-tracking" women into faculty ranks. At the student level, the Levana Society was gone, and women now made up the majority of Arts and Science students. Pensions had been equalized, and women, such as Marie Surridge in French, headed departments. The long-standing Code of Conduct, which had been loosely applied to student behaviour, had been beefed up with a more explicit code governing sexual harassment, backed up by the appointment of sexual-harassment officers ready to act on complaints from students and faculty alike. However, as Beverley Baines has put it, Queen's was still very much a "male enterprise."[60] As late as 1989, first-year women arriving at their residences in Frosh Week were greeted by hand-painted banners proclaiming: "Don't worry, Dad, she won't sleep alone," and "Giving unwed mothers their start."[61]

In the late eighties, events in the Faculty of Law and in the residence precinct on Leonard Field threw this complacent culture into stark and unflattering light. In the summer of 1985, the unexpected secondment of a senior professor to a university administrative post prompted the law faculty to make a two-year term appointment to deliver courses in torts, arbitration, and collective agreements. The job went to a 1984 Queen's LLB graduate, Sheila McIntyre. McIntyre arrived in a law faculty that had seen no permanent hiring through the lean early eighties, making do with limited-term, non-renewable appointments. Faculty composition thus bore the mark of hiring in the decades before: from 1974 to 1981, twelve tenured posts had been filled, eleven of them by men. Queen's law faculty was thus largely staffed with seasoned-but-aging male professors. Few young – and even fewer female – scholars had been attached to its ranks. The faculty was thus a reflection of an era when males dominated the teaching and practice of law.

By 1985, only two of the faculty's twenty-six tenured professors were women – Beverley Baines and Toni Pickard. One other woman, Sheila Noonan, joined McIntyre on two-year appointment. Faculty curriculum cast only a fleeting glance at women's situation under the law, despite the fact that, since the late seventies, at least 25 per cent of first-year students were women. Baines had initiated a course on women and the law and, on occasion, sociologist Mary Morton offered a course on the sociology of the law which related the law to Canada's social structure. Elsewhere in the faculty, Mary Alice Murray, one of the first women to graduate from the school in the early 1960s, had ably served as faculty registrar, replaced in 1981 by Virginia Bartley (LLB '77). Irene Bessette, a lawyer by training, was faculty librarian and taught a single course. But, beyond this, the teaching of law at Queen's, and indeed across Canada, was a male-oriented endeavour.* The language of legal pedagogy, for instance, automatically assumed the male voice and perspective – "he" dominated case books and lecture examples.

As her first year of teaching unfolded, McIntyre discovered that male chauvinism extended well beyond textbooks. While not universally the case, there was a male jocularity about many of her colleagues, in the hallways and in the lecture halls. One well-known scholar in the faculty was said to conduct his torts course as if it were taking place in a "male locker room," punctuating his lectures with off-colour comments that seemed to be intended to discomfit the handful of female students who braved the class.[62] Another professor addressed the minority of women taking his course as if they were all of one mind – a "lump" as McIntyre reported it. Picking up on this ambiance, some male students engaged in in-class sexist banter – jokes, double entendres – with their professors. One female student, Sharon Cohen, despaired: "Maybe I don't belong here," she was quoted in the *Journal*. "Maybe it's a fluke that I even got into law school."[63]

Women's marginality in the faculty was underscored late in the spring of 1986, when a search committee was struck to find a replacement for Dean Denis Magnusson, who had announced his intention to step down. As dean since 1982, Magnusson's tenure had been marked by a watershed moment in Canadian citizenship – the invoking of the 1982 Charter of Rights and Freedoms with all its implications for equality. Yet, when the search committee for a new dean was struck, little emphasis was placed on seeking female candidates. Professor Baines lobbied hard, urging the committee to put weight on the "pedagogy of equality," and even recommending her colleague Toni Pickard as a worthy possibility. Since 1980, Pickard had been urging her colleagues to unpack the "hierarchical relationships" of men and women under the law. The committee nonetheless opted to appoint John Whyte, a constitutional expert who had studied at Queen's in the 1960s. Whyte's fair-mindedness would soon be sorely tested. Pickard, a member of the search com-

---

*Women were not the only students of law to feel they lived a marginalized existence at Queen's. Responding to the faculty's commitment to take minority status into account in its admissions, Aboriginal students began appearing in the faculty. One of them, Mohawk Patricia Monture, recoiled in shock when the professor in her first-year property-law course declared that the Crown owned all the land in Canada. It was, she said, like "running full-force into a brick wall." Monture would graduate in 1988 and move on to a prominent career as an expert on Native affairs in Canada. See Mark D. Walters, "'Let Right Be Done': A History of the Faculty of Law at Queen's University," *Queen's Law Journal* 32 (2007), 358.

mittee, expressed her dismay at the "gender-based dismissal of the idea [of a female dean] as trivial."⁶⁴

By the summer of 1986, McIntyre's frustration also reached critical mass. She had toyed with the idea of leaving academe to become a labour lawyer in Ottawa, but determined to see out her two-year contract at Queen's. Nonetheless, after wrestling with her experiences of the previous year, she also determined to speak out. In July 1986, she produced a lengthy memo that detailed her experience of two fundamental obstacles confronting a feminist legal scholar. Most immediately, there was the chauvinistic atmosphere of the Queen's faculty and its daily message that women were regarded as second-class academic citizens. Sir John A. Macdonald Hall exuded the aura of "the taken-for-granted legitimacy of an oppressive status quo." Beyond this critique, McIntyre expressed her more catholic concern that women were systematically underrepresented and misrepresented in Canadian law and its teaching. The suzerainty of a male-defined and male-centred law remained "unacknowledged, unexplored, and unexpressed," so much so that "women's interests, experiences, and perspectives will be excluded, devalued, and subverted in the classroom and the profession, and in the larger society shaped by law and legal institutions."⁶⁵ The memo was a *cri de coeur* – "a personal act of survival," as McIntyre called it. The silence had to be broken. There must be "a commitment to equality" in Canadian law schools. "When you swallow poison," she declared, "you have to purge it from your system or die."⁶⁶

After agonizing over the decision and its probable consequences, McIntyre sent the memo to her colleagues and student members of the Law Faculty Board. She quickly discovered that she had indeed broken the silence. In her own classes, she deliberately began using gender-neutral terms to describe the workings of the law. She challenged her students to question some of the patriarchal concepts embedded in case law. Did the law necessarily have to be rooted in a masculine model of power and conflict? Could a model of co-determination and communal interest be employed? Some of her male students began resisting, arguing that their professor was politicizing the law. A handful turned abusive. They conspired "to take a run at Sheila" in class, naysaying her gender-neutral language and her interrogation of male perspectives buried inside famous cases.

As the fall term of 1986 unfolded, some of McIntyre's male colleagues similarly bucked at the memo's critique. One circulated a counter-memo contesting McIntyre's rendition of events in Macdonald Hall and protested "the essential disunity of anger in our collective lives together."⁶⁷ Not surprisingly, McIntyre's memo quickly gained wider circulation, first in the *Queen's Journal* and then in the Kingston *Whig-Standard*. *Whig* editor Neil Reynolds pondered the "slowness of change" for women at Queen's.⁶⁸ The *Toronto Star* then took the story national: "Many men can't accept our equality" wrote journalist Lois Sweet in an op-ed piece.⁶⁹ On campuses across Canada, McIntyre's memo began to circulate amongst feminists and legal scholars as a kind of *samizdat*. In December, McIntyre contributed an op-ed piece to *The Lawyer's Weekly* on the "oppressive silencing" of women in the law.

Back at Queen's, the McIntyre memo prompted calls for action well beyond the law faculty. The chair of the AWTAQ, Kay Herman, wrote to Principal Smith, reminding him that the principal at Queen's had historically been expected to show leadership when such issues broke (as Deutsch had done over the status of women in the early 1970s). McIntyre's complaints, Herman noted, had "struck a common chord in all of us not simply because it is so controversial but because it is so true."⁷⁰ Strictly speaking, the issues raised by McIntyre fell within *faculty* jurisdiction. Smith nonetheless asked Dean Magnusson for a report on the situation and asked the university's Advisory Committee on the Status of Women to consult with the faculty. In Senate, Baines asserted that gender inequality was a "pervasive problem" at Queen's that demanded prompt attention.⁷¹ As if to reinforce the point, a petition signed by twenty-five women professors published in the *Journal* called on Smith to act decisively.[72]

With all this in mind, Dean Magnusson called a special full faculty meeting for late October to air the matter. At that meeting, two themes became starkly apparent. One focused on the need to address McIntyre's specific complaints – student impertinence, sexist incidents – while the other fixed on the need for a broader discussion of how the teaching of the law needed a gender rebalancing. Professor Nick Bala, for instance, urged the creation of an ad hoc committee to tackle the broader issue. Students, he insisted, must be involved in such a deliberation. Former dean, Dan Soberman, agreed, saying that McIntyre's grievances must be treated as "paradigms of value" leading to broad reform. The faculty, he warned, should avoid "speechifying" and should not expect a "flash of enlightenment."[73]

Magnusson was caught in the midst of a divided faculty. Desperate to preserve faculty cohesion and yet inclined to follow his own instinct to act, the dean advised his colleagues in early November that McIntyre had indeed raised "serious" issues, but that it would be "destructive" to investigate them in isolation. The faculty was, however, morally obliged to address the systemic issues raised by McIntyre and her supporters, even if they formed a minority. A first step, he suggested, would be for the faculty to consider passing a "motion of gender equality" and then moving onto some consideration of curriculum reform. He would also investigate whether the then-just-launched Queen's National Scholars program might be used to attract women to its ranks. Magnusson transmitted much the same message to Principal Smith and the Status of Women committee: "further debate and dialogue" would be the order of the day.

Smith accepted the advice, noting that Queen's had in recent years been moving on the gender front with such initiatives as women's studies, revised sexual-harassment and employment-equity guidelines, and an attempt to root sexism out of frosh orientation and the student press.[74] In doing so, Smith was displaying Queen's inveterate reliance on moral suasion in shaping the culture of the university: a belief in the power of elucidation on the liberal mind as opposed to hard-and-fast sanctions. This philosophy had often yielded noble results – sometimes with aggravating slowness, but usually in the end fostering workable inclusion in the making of campus consensus. However, events in the law faculty over the next few years would place such gradualism under extreme duress.

There was, however, initial progress. The faculty did endorse a "commitment of principle relating to gender issues" that obliged its instructors to reflect gender-neutral dialogue in classrooms and in written material conveying the working of the law. "Neither women nor men," it proclaimed, "should be needlessly portrayed in stereotypical, pejorative or derogatory terms." This statement was published in the 1987 faculty calendar. In addition, before he stepped down as dean in the spring of 1987, Magnusson oversaw the hiring of three women to tenure-track appointments in the department, including McIntyre and Noonan, who won open competitions and thus remained in the faculty. Magnusson was also successful in recruiting tax expert Kathleen Lahey from the University of Windsor as a Queen's National Scholar. Lahey had in fact been at Queen's the previous fall to lecture on the male bias in the training of Canadian lawyers. Although Noonan opted to spend the upcoming year studying at Harvard, the Queen's law faculty finally had a nucleus of women scholars. New courses were consequently introduced; Lahey taught "Law and Social Theory" and "Law, Gender, and Equality." There was talk of founding an institute for feminist legal studies. The newly established *Canadian Journal of Women and the Law* found an editorial home at Queen's.

Nevertheless, when John Whyte assumed the deanship in March 1987, he inherited a faculty riven by discord. Collegiality had evaporated. The faculty had become an unflattering prism of many of the gender and professional tensions wracking the broader Queen's campus. Symptoms of discontent abounded: flyers alleging rampant sexism in the school posted in corridors; obscene, accusatory graffiti on washroom walls; and ribald, anti-feminist articles in the law-student newspaper, *The Queen's Counsel*. Colleagues shunned fellow professors in the hallways. Students took sides, acting out their support for factions in the professoriate. In 1988, for instance, a group called the Queen's Law Lesbians and Gay Men's Caucus brought Sarah Salter, a leading New England legal scholar, to campus to lecture against homophobia. The outside world took note. In 1988, the *Whig-Standard* magazine ran a long and unflattering profile of the faculty under the title "Law School Confidential."[75] *Frank*, a national satirical magazine, lampooned the school's squabbling mercilessly. Alumni wrote to express their concern over the school's tarnished image.

The tension was never simplistically one of men vs women. Opinion in the male faculty ranged from outright hostility towards the feminist agenda through to cooperative sympathy. Women in the faculty were similarly fragmented. Sexuality as well as gender came into play. A fundamental schism opened up between heterosexual and lesbian female professors, each with a different perspective on the "problem." Some hard-line feminists were skeptical about male participation in their project to remake the law. In fact, an ongoing debate sprung up as to whether male students had any place in feminist law seminars. "I would like a feminist space for feminists," McIntyre proclaimed. "In my view, men can be pro-feminist, but not feminist. So I don't want them in such a place. If people want a mixed-sex seminar, go for it; just count me out."[76] Hearing such rationales, some law students began to question whether the shoe was now on the other foot – whether male students in law were being denied their rights. A petition signed by 110 people protested law courses that favoured "the inclusion of one group within the faculty and the exclusion of any or all other groups."[77]

The Queen's Faculty of Law of the late eighties thus resembled a camp of warring factions, all uneasily regarding the prerogatives and pretensions of the others. A Vesuvius-like rumbling ran through its affairs. Dean Whyte's brokering talents as a constitutional expert were daily put to the test. Yet, as faculty historian Mark Walters has remarked, the working out of these tensions was "critical to the emergence of the school as a modern institution."[78] The study of the law was, after all, predicated on the realization that there will always be conflict in society and differences have to be arbitrated. In the late eighties, Queen's "gender wars," as they came to be known, served another dynamic function. They ironically reconnected the school with the intentions of its founding "fathers" in the late 1950s. Professors such as Bill Lederman and Stuart Ryan profoundly believed that the law must be taught and practised as a "humane and social" project. That tradition had persisted at Queen's. In 1979, Dean Bernie Adell had confided to Principal Watts his ambition that courses in his faculty would "connect the students to the real world" so that they might "handle real problems of real clients" and not just be "market-oriented" purveyors of mechanistic services. Or, as one-time Queen's labour-law professor (and later dean of Osgoode Hall) Stan Beck reminded his colleagues in the Lederman glory days: "We are not running a shoe store."[79] That dedication had perhaps atrophied by the mid-eighties. Sheila McIntyre then jolted it out of its slumber.

Change by Crisis: "No Means No"

Vesuvius did not in fact erupt in the late 1980s in Macdonald Hall; the law faculty instead remained locked in a state of bitter equipoise. Instead, the eruption took place in November 1989 several blocks south on Leonard Field. To extend the geophysical metaphor, Queen's suffered a sharp release from the long buildup of tension between two tectonic plates in its campus culture, each moving in a different direction. A massive substrata of sexist behaviour, long tolerated on campus, collided with the emerging social geology of sexual equality and respect. The result would be cathartic: Queen's would suffer unprecedented public stigma and spend much of the upcoming decade adjusting its attitudes and policies to ensure that the university was no longer an enclave of privileged recidivism. A handful of sexist cardboard signs hung in residence windows in the fall of 1989 would alter the university's comfortable sense of entitlement.

To set the scene, it is clear that, throughout the 1980s, there had been some encouraging indications that Queen's was conforming to broader shifts in Canadian society. In the wake of the invocation of Canada's Charter of Rights and Freedoms and under the accumulating pressure of second-wave feminism, with its emphasis on gender equality, Queen's began to challenge its long-unquestioned culture of entrenched gender relations. Since the middle of the nineteenth century, Queen's students had been bound by a Code of Conduct intended to govern their demeanour. The code was largely focused on behaviours that might injure the "reputation of the university" – boisterous drinking, vandalism. Academic plagiarism was proscribed, but nothing was said about the student's obligation to respect the rights of fellow students. The AMS judicial system reinforced this intention, meting out fines for rowdiness and infringement of residence rules. However, Canadian society adopted a more proactive attitude to sexual and gender rights in the 1980s, and in 1985 Queen's added sexual harassment to its Code of Conduct. Much effort was directed at defining the parameters of harassment. A year later, the university established a system for handling allegations of sexual harassment for all members of the campus community. Advisors were appointed to counsel those making the complaints.

A process of mediation between alleged victim and perpetrator was established, one that might culminate in a hearing before a grievance board. The Queen's Student and Community Assault Centre subsequently opened on campus, and a student-run "walk-home" service began. The AMS Education Commission published a booklet on sexual assault. Women staged "Take Back the Night" marches. The 1989 report of a university task force on sexual assault, chaired by engineering professor Paul Gaskin, confirmed the need for such vigilance: a survey of 445 women students found that 3 per cent had been raped and another 10 per cent had been threatened with or experienced sexual violence.[80] Two years later, in 1991, after much pressure from the AMS, the university installed "blue light" safety stations across the campus.

Recognition of a problem was accompanied by evidence of other shifts in gender roles on campus. In 1986, Kelley McKinnon became the first female rector at Queen's. More student residences became coeducational; in 1987 the sprawling Victoria Hall residence was opened to both sexes. That same year, Medical House, long a males-only enclave, admitted women residents. The AMS created a press council empowered to invigilate, among other things, the depiction of sexual relations in campus publications, most notably the often-raunchy *Golden Words*. The sale on campus of magazines such as *Playboy* was also debated. AMS President Emily Moore, backed by the AMS Assembly, called for a ban on *Playboy*, arguing that it promoted pornography. The library copy of *Playboy* was sequestered in the rare-books section, where students were required to produce proof that they were over eighteen in order to peruse its baring-all pages. Eventually, citing financial constraint, the Senate Library Committee cancelled the naughty subscription (to protest this crimping of intellectual freedom, history professor Geoff Smith bought a token subscription for the university library). In the wake of initiatives such as the American Title IX proviso – mandating equal opportunity in all varsity sports – and the 1986 *Blainey* vs *Ontario Hockey Association* decision in the Ontario Court of Appeal, which knocked down males-only codes in amateur sports, the Athletic Board of Control began apportioning its annual budget equally between male and female sports. Even the storied lyrics of the *Oil Thigh* – "so boys, go in and win" – were given a more gender-neutral gloss – "so Gaels, go in and win."

There were more substantial signs of change: Dean David Bacon of Applied Science reported that his faculty, long a bastion of maleness, was strenuously recruiting women students. Senior women in engineering were being dispatched to high schools to impart the message that their profession was not just for males. In 1986, Queen's, for instance, graduated its first female PhD in mining engineering. By 1988, Bacon was able to report that almost 18 per cent of his undergraduates were women, not a stunning total but one well above the national average of 11 per cent.[81] At the same time, the Queen's campus began to discuss matters at the heart of Canada's debate on sexual rights. A women's right to abortion surfaced as a hotly contested issue in the *Journal*. When Dr Henry Morgentaler, Canada's most outspoken advocate of a woman's right to abortion, delivered a 1985 Dunning Trust lecture, 2,000 people vied for 950 tickets. The lecture provoked intense debate but no obstructive protests. Anxious that there might be upheaval, Principal Smith stayed in his office and did not attend the lecture.

As encouraging as these advances were, bedrock sexism remained firmly in place beneath Queen's. At its most benign, the attitude was captured in a plaque embedded in the steps outside Victoria Hall by Science '67: "She who is kissed by an engineer while standing on this plaque officially becomes a Queen's co-ed."[82] At its most virulent, it surfaced on Medical Variety Night as crude humour about gays and AIDS. The engineering weekly *Golden Words* took persistent adolescent pleasure out of publishing offensive stereotypes of women. Features titled "How to Screw" and "Scratch and Sniff" brought reprimands from the AMS Press Council and official complaints to the Ontario Press Council. Although conscious that *Golden Words* was a student paper, a shocked Principal Smith was on occasion prompted to complain to the Engineering Society that its features were often "offensive, disgusting, and an embarrassment to Queen's University."[83]

Male sexism had also entwined itself with racism in campus rituals: the rugby club's "Zulu ritual," consisting of naked, beer-fuelled males cavorting in Sydenham Ward, provided an annual occasion of raw sexuality and downright unneighbourliness. The Engineering Society's Clark Hall pub became an epicentre for hijinks that frequently offended. A speed bump outside the hall was, for instance, painted yellow and dubbed the "golden tit." Freshmen were obliged to kiss the tit in an initiation ritual. Once a year, the trees around Clark were decked with effigies of nurses on whose uniforms obscene comments were scrawled. Despite widespread condemnation, this cycle of offensive sexist behaviour was never effectively broken – snickering apologies were issued by *Golden Words* editors and Engineering Society presidents, but the lesson never seemed to be learned.[84]

Abrasive sexual attitudes materialized elsewhere. Gay and lesbian students on campus sometimes became the victims of verbal and physical intimidation. Alarmingly, the word "homophobia" began to punctuate the campus dialogue on sexism. The *Journal* reported ugly incidents in which members of the Queen's Homophile Association were persecuted: an association member was spat on while putting up posters on campus. Another reported being roughed up outside the Douglas Library. Other Queen's gays and lesbians reported altercations with harassers outside Princess Street bars hospitable to gay patrons.[85] When NDP MP Svend Robinson, who was openly gay, came to speak at Queen's in 1989, "Nuke all Lesbians" flyers appeared outside the lecture hall. Homophobia

❖ *A Candle in the Wind* ❖

On a Sunday evening in September 1889, the handful of women attending Queen's inaugurated a tradition that was to last for well over a century. That same year, female students in arts and medicine recognized the need for some sort of organization that would centre their existence on campus. Women had, in fact, been admitted to Queen's only since 1880. They formed the Levana Society, named after the Roman goddess of childbirth and its rituals, as an exclusive sorority. The society would provide women with a sense of identity and mutual support amid Queen's powerfully male-oriented culture. Rituals followed – teas, dances, lectures, rings, and, most memorably, the annual candle-lighting ceremony. Early in the fall term, black-robed first-year women were shepherded into a hall – Grant Hall after 1905 – by their second-year sisters. Masonic-like secrecy prevailed. Oaths were taken. Traditions and duties were transmitted. The climax of the rite came when the senior girls transferred the flame of their candle to that of their new Levana sisters. Much folklore grew up around the ceremony: wax droplets on the tricolour ribbon tied around the candle was said to predict a future husband's faculty and the number of prospective children.

Such candle lighting was predictably found wanting by sixties feminism. In the words of one Queen's feminist, it was a "dehumanizing fertility ritual." In 1967, Levana voted itself out of existence, combining with the male Arts Society to form the Arts and Science Undergraduate Society. But candle lighting survived by adapting to the times. The secrecy diminished and the dedication to fecundity and male-obliging femininity disappeared. The ceremony was transformed into a welcoming ritual, in which women discovered their commonality. Candles were still lit, but the emphasis shifted to practical guidance through post-secondary life. Influential women were invited to impart their wisdom. In 1991, for instance, black politician, human-rights advocate, and Queen's trustee Rosemary Brown spoke. In 1997, men were allowed to attend. Slowly, however, the ceremony flickered out of existence. By the new century, the tradition had exhausted itself. Whenever, however, Queen's students gathered to commemorate the fourteen women killed in the 1989 Montreal massacre, candle lighting symbolized their grief and solidarity.

Male traditions at Queen's also faced the test of shifting gender values. The lewd and blatant sexism of male student culture at "good old Queen's" persisted through the baby boom. "Sport humping," "golden tits" painted on roadways, panty raids, and ribald chanting ingrained themselves in male campus culture. But, as women acquired second-wave consciousness and became the majority of undergraduates by the mid-seventies, crises such as the "No Means No" imbroglio would strip away any residual legitimacy granted this "boys-will-be-boys" attitude. Gender equity and respect for diversity became the ideal of acceptable behaviour. Queen's was thus learning to bend, and at times abandon, its once-hallowed traditions. Long-established bastions of male prerogative broke down: for example, women were elected president of the Engineering Society. In 1986, mechanical engineer Genevieve Dumas became the Faculty of Applied Science's first women professor. The transition was not entirely smooth – *Golden Words*, a tongue-in-cheek newssheet published by the engineers, occasionally lost its balance and plunged back into adolescent sexism. But other engineering traditions passed the test of social relevancy and continued to play a solidifying role in campus life. Every Christmas, as it had since 1946, the Engineering Society continued to host its carol-singing service. Every spring, teams of geology students and faculty competed for the Fur Cup, a hockey tradition dating back to the fifties. April Fool's Day continued to see cars hoisted in trees. And, oh yes, the beer continued to flow: the engineers' annual brewing contest – "Barium Enema Brew" was the 1996 winner – raised money for Bridge House, a residence for wives of penitentiary inmates.

was evident well beyond student ranks. An assistant professor wrote to the *Journal* noting that, "in a conservative city like Kingston, homosexuals live almost totally invisible and secret lives."[86]

Behind this unfriendly facade lurked another obstacle to change. The university's ability to police and reform unsavoury student sexual behaviour rested on a disjointed, and at times ineffectual, scaffold of student non-academic discipline. Queen's had a multilayered system of student discipline stretching from the residence councils all the way through to the Senate, which stood as the last court of appeal for any non-academic misdemeanour. The university had traditionally been unwilling to exercise its last-resort authority, preferring to allow student self-government to hold sway over such matters. This commendable intention tended, however, to be undermined by the ramshackle nature of student non-academic discipline at Queen's. The recently appointed sexual-harassment advisors were a step in the right direction, but the positions were staffed by volunteers, usually professors, who lacked the expertise and time to deal with an issue as slippery as sexism. There were also often poor lines of communication and procedural disjunctures in the discipline process. Some levels saw their role as educative and advisory; others took on a more punitive role. In 1985, the old AMS Court had been renamed the AMS Judicial Committee. In many ways, it functioned smoothly, processing misdemeanours sent to it by AMS constables and residence councils. However, its first annual report warned that there was "a lack of coordination amongst all of the various levels and branches of non-academic discipline which operate in some fashion on campus."[87]

The *Journal* identified other shortcomings. The AMS Judicial Committee was obliged to initiate prosecution proceedings within thirty days of an incident taking place; this was problematic at the end of the academic year in April, when students tended to disappear for the summer. By the fall,

Members of the Queen's Homophile Association picket the Kings' Lounge on Princess Street in 1977 after the bar's owner forbade same-sex dancing. Gays and lesbians at Queen's, and in greater Kingston, often faced parochial hostility to their sexual orientation. By the 1980s, they became more assertive and open; the university responded by adopting anti-homophobia policies.

cases had gone cold. There was also the problem of knowing exactly who was and who was not a Queen's student in off-campus situations, and whether the AMS justice system had any jurisdiction over non-students apprehended on campus. The increasingly tenuous position of the student justice system would be exacerbated in the next decade, when the Law Students' Society exited the AMS, thereby depriving the system of personnel with rudimentary legal skills. Even without the legalists, the court still managed to find able judges, prosecutors, and defenders. One problem was, however, clarified: in 1987 the Ontario Supreme Court ruled in a case pertaining to York University that universities did have the right to discipline their students for incidents taking place off campus when their actions redounded on the university at large.[88]

Resistance to the established gender balance at Queen's began to assert itself. In 1986, a group styling itself the Coalition for Voices against Sexism sent a petition bearing 104 signatures to Principal Smith demanding action on the "salient sexism" on the Queen's campus.[89] Others went on the offensive. The Queen's Homophile Association changed its name to the Lesbian and Gay Association of Kingston and began to come out of the closet, contributing a weekly column to the *Journal* entitled "The Third Text." The AMS created a Lesbian and Gay Issues Committee. "Other dances" were staged for gays and lesbians. Frosh events were organized for gays and lesbians, and in 1990 a thousand people participated in Queen's first gay-and-lesbian pride week. In 1989, gay Queen's alumni staged their first reunion in Toronto, thereby sending a powerful signal back into the Queen's community.

A more militant anti-sexism materialized in a periodical called *Surface*, financed by the Arts and Science Undergraduate Society and produced by "wimmin" to give voice to its contempt for the "bland, pudgy, and limp" attitude towards sexism at Queen's.[90] Whatever the tone, there seemed to be widespread acknowledgment that Queen's had a sexual culture that was dangerously out of kilter with broader Canadian values. One-time *Journal* editor John Stackhouse recalled from his *Globe and Mail* office in Toronto the "conformist atmosphere" and sexist attitudes he found so prevalent at Queen's in the mid-1980s.[91] This pervasive and permissive culture, all too prone to dismissing sexist attitudes and actions as little more than the trappings of a "boys-will-be-boys" tradition, coupled with a disjointed system of student discipline, finally encountered reality just after Thanksgiving 1989.

Signs of the Time: The Gordon House Incident

As the fall term of 1989 unfolded, Queen's students turned their attention to sexual politics. An AMS referendum asking whether abortion should be recriminalized got under way; a 47-per-cent turnout would strongly reject the idea.[92] Dr James McSherry, director of Student Health Services, warned students that they were oblivious to the risk that AIDS posed on campus. At the same time, the Queen's Women's Centre, the Sexual Assault Centre, and the AMS Gender Issues Committee took up advocacy of a cross-country campaign initiated by the Canadian Federation of Students to raise awareness of date rape. "In every way, in every language," the campaign slogan went, "No Means No." Posters were distributed across the campus. Some of the posters were ripped down, others were defaced. And then, over on Leonard Field, where male students still predominated in residences, a series of roughly lettered signs began appearing in the windows of Gordon House. "No Means Maybe," "No Means Have Another Beer," and "No Means Tie Me Up," their counter-message proclaimed. There was an immediate reaction. Some women on the opposite side of the field retaliated with their own signs: "No Means It's Too Small."

Other women had a much less jocular response: they emphasized that the signs were offensive and showed utter disregard for a serious social issue.

Sexism on display: anti-feminist sign in a window of Gordon House male residence in the fall of 1989. Days passed before the signs were ordered removed.

Their reaction was underscored by the appearance of other, more virulent, signs in Gordon House windows, such as "No Means Kick Her in the Teeth." Elspeth Baugh, dean of women, was alarmed by reports of these events and asked the president of Gordon Hall to have them removed. Residence dons reacted by instructing nine Gordon House residents to remove the signs from their windows, and then convening floor meetings to discuss the matter. Remarkably, the *Journal* initially took a dismissive approach to the story; the sign men were simply trying to "lighten up" the anti-rape campaign. The campus, they reported the perpetrators as saying, had been inundated with too much date-rape information. There were "too many pamphlets."93

The Main Campus Residence Council, the first line of vigilance over student discipline, took the episode more seriously. Briefed by the dons on the incident, the council concluded that "some action" should be taken, but debated whether it should be punitive or educational. The council dithered over the constitutional powers put at its disposal and whether it could pin down with judicial certainty exactly who might be held responsible. In the end, the council decided that punitive action was "not the most effective route" and launched a gender-awareness campaign in Gordon House. Anything

harsher, they concluded, might undermine their "community building" role on Leonard Field.94 And there the matter rested. News of the incident, or at least its potential import, never seemed to reach Richardson Hall, a striking illustration of the looseness of Queen's chain of student discipline. Only Dean Baugh had reacted, but oddly she did nothing to convey the troublesome news to her colleagues at the weekly meeting of the deans and vice-principals.95

Not everybody was satisfied by this lackadaisical response. Some of the sign perpetrators began receiving threatening phone messages denouncing their sexism. And then some of their parents (whose addresses would have been readily available in *Who's Where*) began receiving unsigned letters castigating the behaviour of their offspring. Then, more dramatically, spray-painted graffiti appeared on the walkways of Leonard Field: "No Means No" and "ROFF is Watching." ROFF? Most assumed that this was something connected with the Queen's Women's Centre, but Natalie Quinton of the centre said that ROFF was "an independent collective of militant feminists whose purpose is to eradicate misogyny on campus."96 Its acronym projected its impatience with Queen's complacency; it stood for "Radical Obnoxious Fucking Feminists."97 ROFF

"The Life of the Greater Queen's" 373

was a small, informal coalition of women who had become exasperated by Queen's supine attitude to sexism. Formed in the spring, the group's indignation had been fuelled by the spectacle of frosh kissing the golden tit and derogatory statements – "Florence Nightingale had AIDS" – inscribed on nurse effigies outside Clark Hall. Sexism, they believed, was "poisoning" Queen's. They had concluded that Queen's traditional resort to tempered dialogue seldom resulted in more than slapped wrists and educational campaigns. In reaction, they embraced civil disobedience and styled themselves radicals. One night the group painted over the golden tit, leaving their name in its place. Many women on campus began to share ROFF's frustration, if not their tactics. Jennifer Tipper of Arts '91 told the *Journal* that punishing the sign men by "educating" them to better gender awareness "was not a satisfactory measure." "It wouldn't be the same if they had said something about 'niggers,'" another woman added.[98]

The situation festered. Nothing was heard from Richardson Hall. The Main Campus Residence Council confirmed its decision not to discipline the nine sign men. The signs had been posted "in ignorance, not malice." Gordon-Brockington residence would instead stage its own gender-awareness week. There was a lingering sense that the matter was simply an ill-timed "joke." But the issue was beginning to seep off campus. The Advancement Office began to receive messages from alumni expressing displeasure that attitudes at their alma mater seemed so out-of-sync with notions of gender equality in their workplaces and communities. Such messages finally began to wake up the administration; the Queen's brand was in danger, as was alumni response to the university's ambitious $50-million fundraising campaign. A student-made sign on University Avenue reflected the shift: "Bad press means no Queen's." Perhaps sensing this, the nine male students at the centre of the incident dispatched a letter of apology on 3 November to the Kingston *Whig-Standard* and *Toronto Star*, expressing regret for their "immature actions" and promising in future to treat "moral and gender issues with the serious attitude they deserve." But there was still no official university response to the matter. "No means soon," some students scoffed. Tempers became frayed. The *Journal* was criticized by some for "censoring" ROFF and its demand for more vigorous action. Finally, on 8 November, Principal Smith sent a letter to the *Journal*, "deploring" the Gordon House signs and expressing his trust in Queen's "well-developed" student-justice system. It was too little, too late.

Making "Herstory" in Richardson Hall

At 9:45 a.m. on 9 November (before Smith's letter appeared in the *Journal*), while the principal was on the phone, a group of some forty women poured through the door of his office and announced that they were "occupying" it. Their behaviour was peaceable, but most had wrapped their heads in scarves. Smith stayed put, offering to listen to the group's demands. A photographer caught the scene: women ensconced in armchairs and sitting on the floor, while Smith, arms defensively folded, looks on apprehensively. The women, who projected no formal affiliation (although AMS education commissioner Caroline Jones joined their sit-in) but who seemed to contain elements of ROFF, presented the principal with a list of seven demands. Their tone was accusatory and categorical. The administration had to stop "hiding behind its bureaucracy" on the signs issue. Senior administrators had remained "appallingly silent" for three weeks. Action must be taken to root sexism out of Queen's rituals like orientation. The golden tit must be eradicated. The dean of women must be bolstered as a voice of women at Queen's. The Main Campus Residence Council must be stripped of its autonomy in student disciplinary matters, as it had proven itself "incompetent" in handling the mess at Gordon House. The residents of Gordon House must organize a campus-wide campaign against sexual assault and donate $5,000 to organizations that assist victims of sexual assault. And, finally, Queen's administration must fund a branch of the Kingston Sexual Assault Crisis Centre on the campus.[99] The demands were in some respects unrealistic – they implied that *all* Gordon House residents must pay for the sins of a handful – but they were an understandable outcome of a lassitude that had prevailed for too long at Queen's. "I hear your frustration," Smith quietly replied and left the room. The group then placed "No Means No" posters in the window of his office.

After twenty-nine hours, the protesters left Richardson Hall. "This is just the beginning," one of the women told the *Journal*. "We have made Queen's 'herstory.'" No charges were levelled against the women. Their action had elevated the issue onto the national stage. The national press seemed to revel in juxtaposing the incident and the paralysis besetting it with Queen's sterling reputation as a seat of higher learning. Alumni took indignant notice. Daniel Woolf of Arts '80 made his displeasure known to the *Alumni Review*: this was not "an isolated incident of puerile behaviour"; instead it was endemic and continued because of the "apparent indifference shown by the administration in refusing to take a firm stand."[100] There seemed to be an immediate understanding that what happened at Gordon House was in fact a microcosm of a campus-wide problem. In a late-November letter to Principal Smith, Queen's gays and lesbians, showing solidarity with their feminists sisters, urged a "strong stance" against all sexual violence, because such malevolence tainted "the life of the larger Queen's."[101]

Now, at least, there was action. The AMS Assembly asked the Judicial Committee to review the Residence Council's decision not to mete out punishment to the "Gordon nine," as they were now tagged. There was talk of beefing up the Residence Council's constitution with more explicit powers. The AMS debated dovetailing the student-discipline processes more efficiently and providing better communicating options to complainants. But

Counter-offensive: masked feminist occupiers of Principal Smith's office in Richardson Hall reiterate the message that "No Means No," while at the same time sending a message to the world beyond Queen's that the university needed to change its ways.

problems quickly materialized: could the Judicial Committee muster sufficient evidence to prosecute the Gordon nine? When four women from the occupation group lodged an official sexual-harassment complaint, alleging that the signs "created an intimidating, hostile, and offensive working environment for women," it was uncertain whether such complaints could be levelled against a *group* as opposed to an individual.

On 23 November, Smith briefed the Senate (the body with final oversight of student discipline). Vice-Principal Tom Williams first outlined the judicial possibilities, suggesting that a Grievance Board hearing might offer a resolution of the sexual-harassment aspect of the incident. Smith took a broader perspective, arguing that the university was faced with the seismic challenge of changing its attitudes. He cited Rosabeth Moss Kanter, author of the bestselling book *The Change Masters* and Harvard's well-known expert on managing change in gender relations within large organizations. Smith underscored her insistence on empowering the *entire* community in such change. When asked why he had taken so long to act, Smith said that he had been reluctant to intrude on the student justice system's autonomy and that he had regarded Dean Elspeth Baugh, who was also Director of Residences, as his "point person" during the incident.

With all this in mind, Smith announced that he would establish a Principal's Working Group on Gender Issues, chaired by Baugh, to re-engineer Queen's gender culture. On 1 December, the principal carried much the same message to the Board of Trustees. He enumerated the sensitive areas he had mandated the Baugh group to investigate: better counselling, better campus security, better definition of judicial powers held by residence government and the AMS, and stepped-up educational programs. At the same time, the principal's Standing Committee on the Status of Women would be called upon to root sexist attitudes and rituals out of orientation and alumni weekends. All in all, Smith was offering the predictable, if belated, Queen's response to the pressure of change – broad consultation and cautious adjustment.[102] Perhaps as a hint of things to come, the trustees willingly voted on a motion of rector, Charis Kelso, to match student fees supporting the local sexual-assault crisis centre. Looking back on her role in the climactic occupation of Smith's office twenty years later, protester Penelope Hutchinson of Artsci '90 expressed no regrets: "I believe we played a small part in helping to initiate some of the changes that have made Queen's a more welcoming place for women."[103] Kam Rao, the outspoken AMS education commissioner, agreed:

women acting up in the face of the "No Means No" backlash had "destabilized the idea of where the [gender] centre was" at Queen's.[104]

And then the landscape shifted dramatically once again. On the evening of 6 December, a gunman crazed with the belief that feminists had "ruined" his life massacred fourteen women at the École Polytechnique de Montréal. The event shocked not only Canada but also the world. Beyond the immediate sense of collective grief, the effect at Queen's was to extinguish any hint that the "No Means No" events and the reactions to them over the last month had been some sort of aberration, some sort of forgivable, adolescent prank gone awry. A thousand people gathered in Grant Hall to grieve the tragic loss. Principal Smith told them to work "together against violence, discrimination, and divisiveness." The Polytechnique deaths accelerated Queen's willingness to tackle sexism. By February, Baugh's group – a group including prominent female members of the Queen's community such as Margaret Hooey of the Senate Office, vice-principal Alice Baumgart, and rector Charis Kelso, as well as males such as Chaplain Yealland – tabled an interim report, one that emphatically urged Queen's to shed its "preppie-WASP community" image. All members of the university must admit that the "present realities of sexism, racism, and homophobia" existed on campus. The inoculation against these viruses must begin in the first week a student set foot on the campus. Lewd inscriptions on the overalls worn by frosh must, for instance, be banned. *Golden Words* must stop publishing offensive sexism such as its "Slut of the Week" feature. An emboldened Principal Smith wrote to the Engineering Society president, informing him that the university would no longer collect its student subsidy if the ribald journalism persisted. The report went on to stress the need to streamline non-academic discipline, bolster security, and, most significantly, question whether some of its traditions were "contrary to our goal in human relations."

"Rim Ram, Goddam, Son of a Bitch …"

The momentum continued. Almost everybody agreed that sexism was incubated in Queen's undergraduates during their first week on campus when they were herded through the intensive orientation activities orchestrated by upper-year students. Much fun was to be had in these first days of university life – for decades Queen's traditions, ranging from memorizing the incomprehensible Gaelic of *Oil Thigh* lyrics to bonding with one's faculty society had been passed on to the frosh. But there had been increasing alarm that orientation had drifted away from its original purpose of acculturating newcomers to the ethos of university life. Chanting lewd slogans, excessive drinking, and boisterous house parties in Sydenham Ward seemed to betray this intention and validated such sexist and anti-social behaviour through the upcoming four years of campus life. If you had been schooled in orientation to consider Queen's as "the sport of kings," there could be little surprise that date rape might not be taken too seriously as a social issue.

Like student discipline, orientation had long been the prerogative of the faculty societies and not the administration. Throughout the 1980s, faculty societies had made a conscious effort to reconnect orientation with the real culture of university life. Under the AMS's auspices, an Orientation Activities Review Board (OARB) had been established with a mandate to review each year's orientation week later in the fall and to recommend future fine tuning. The general drift was towards more academic orientation and less beer and tribalism. But the Gordon House incident and University Avenue street parties had revealed how resilient sexism and rowdyism proved in an adolescent culture. The "No Means No" fiasco once again impelled the university to adopt a more integrated, systemic approach to its problems, a determination to bond administration, faculty, and students in common action. Consequently, in March 1990 Principal Smith asked business-school professor Rick Jackson and senior administrator Kathy Beers to head a joint faculty-student task force to look into the culture of student orientation.

The Jackson Committee report in November read like a case study in sociology. The rhetoric and role modelling by which second-year students transmitted Queen's values – wholesome and unwholesome – to each year's crop of freshmen set up a self-perpetuating cycle of normalized behaviour. The report followed fictitious Queen's newcomer "George" through his week of orientation: "by the end of orientation week, George could be excused if he concluded that, as a Queen's student, he could do just about anything he wants."[105] Queen's storied "spirit," the report argued, had mutated from a catchword for personal empowerment into a "we are the best" tribalism. "We submit that this instantly created brand of 'Queen's spirit' is unthinking, shallow, narcissistic, and arrogant. In point of fact, it's not Queen's spirit in its true sense at all. It is, rather, the inevitable result of a clumsy and unthinking attempt – very self-congratulatory in itself – to make the students feel they are a part of Queen's."

The cycle had to be broken. Jackson offered hands-on recommendations. Second-year group leaders must pledge not to perpetuate a culture of alcohol. Indeed, they should sign contracts obliging them to deliver only certain constructive behaviours. The Code of Conduct should be explicitly applied to obscene behaviours. Orientation should also build consciousness of the link between actions and their consequences; the student justice system must be "tightened." More attention should be devoted to introducing freshmen to life in residence and their new life of university study. More faculty should attend the orientation events. Queen's should develop a mandatory "University 101" course designed to smooth the post-secondary transition. Faculty rivalries ("We are, we are, we are the engineers; we can, we can demolish forty beers … an artsie queer") must be moderated.

Self-criticism: the cover of the spring 1990 issue of the *Queen's Alumni Review*. Artist Charlene Janzen captured the distemper of the times at Queen's.

The Jackson Report prompted real change – at an unusually fast clip for Queen's. The 1991 orientation week reflected many of its recommendations. It was a "kinder, gentler" orientation, reduced in duration from nine to six days. First contact with Queen's for frosh came at a university-wide welcome party. University 101 was launched early in the week. Kingston police briefed students on city bylaws. An "other dance" was staged for gay and lesbian frosh. When AMS education commissioner Kam Rao complained that the Toronto band The Phantoms, notorious for its sexist lyrics, had been booked for the climactic frosh-week dance, the contract was cancelled. Observers sensed the shift in orientation culture. Kingston mayor Helen Cooper wrote to commend the orientation committee for doing a "superb job in recognizing many of the deeply rooted problems that had become so-called traditions in the past."[106] Cathy Perkins, another Queen's graduate and one-time editor of the *Alumni Review*, reached much the same conclusion: "No.

It's not the Queen's many of us knew, just as it's not the world we grew up in. Some values deserve preservation. Other traditions require changing – and some changes, as Queen's has learned the hard way, are overdue."[107]

"No Means No" provoked unprecedented self-criticism at Queen's – a willingness to hold once-sacred tradition up to the harsh light of modern reality. Throughout the Gordon House controversy, the alumni office had been inundated with mail from alumni almost universally angered by what they saw as Queen's apparent detachment from contemporary social values. Jim Bennett, the director of alumni affairs, decided that candour was the best response, especially with a large fundraising campaign under way. He urged Ken Cuthbertson, Perkins's successor as editor of the *Alumni Review*, to give the matter frank treatment. Cuthbertson, himself a Queen's graduate, had taken the editorship with a determination to put a critical edge on the publication, thereby moving away from the "rah-rah" tone of many alumni magazines. "No Means No," Cuthbertson concluded, demanded an outside assessment. He commissioned Toronto novelist Katherine Govier to visit Queen's and report on her assessment of the recent upheaval.

Govier's essay, "A Time To Be Just," pulled no punches. She condemned the old sexism prevalent on the campus. Queen's, she sensed, seemed to be in a time warp. "We have a tradition of privileging people," law dean John Whyte admitted to her. "It is the focus of a number of students ... the idea is, if you're here, you're important ... Queen's students sometimes have the attitude of the British in India. I don't think Queen's is nearly enough concerned with the justice of the enterprise."[108] But Govier ended on a positive note: change seemed to be afoot at Queen's. There was a "possibility here for quantum leaps forward." Queen's must not only change, she argued, but it must learn to be "just" to all who walked its campus. Principal Smith did not like the article's frankness and, advised by his public-relations staffers, wanted it suppressed. But Bennett sent it to press. Alumni readers reacted positively to the article's candour. The magazine's cover added a visual edge to the message. Charlene Janzen, the *Review's* graphic designer, produced a cover portraying dignitaries at a university convocation. The university principal looks remarkably like Principal Smith. Beside him sits a perky female academic and down on the floor a female student, presumably about to graduate, looks askance back at the artist as if signalling her disapproval of the event. That face was in fact the face of Alison Holt, a Queen's graduate of 1987 and then assistant editor of the *Review*. Holt had been appalled by the university's lethargic response to sexism; Janzen reinforced her critique by painting her into the scene.

There were other encouraging shifts in the wake of "No Means No." The AMS Gender Issues Committee reinforced the Jackson inquiry with its own prescription for uprooting sexism. The editors of *Golden Words* attended a conference for engineering newspapers at which new guidelines for more palatable content were discussed. The Queen's law Lesbians and Gays hosted a conference at which the need for a better legal definition of same-sex marriage and the "family" were discussed. A gay man was elected as president of the Law Students' Society and widely praised for his work. Elsewhere on campus, the student-run non-alcoholic pub in the Union – Na Banrighinn – reported a profit for the first time.[109]

Not everything fell into place. The judicial attempt to discipline the Gordon House nine petered out after eighteen months of legal jostling. First, there was the problem of sustaining the case, which had fifty potential witnesses on its docket. The AMS was repeatedly obliged to extend its statute of limitations for the case. A reference was even sent to the Ontario Supreme Court to clarify the boundaries of AMS justice. Some suggested that the case might be more appropriately tried under the university's sexual-harassment grievance process. But was there also a problem of double jeopardy if the case was shunted on to another jurisdiction? Through all this, the principal and the AMS were persistently heckled by the parents of the Gordon House nine. Their sons had suffered enough and had themselves become victims of "a malicious vendetta," so much so that the tables had been turned and their boys were now the target of "gender-based harassment."[110] Finally, in March 1991, the AMS Judicial Committee abandoned the case, a clear acknowledgment that student-discipline procedures were inadequate in the litigious environment that now enveloped Canadian campuses, especially in matters of sexual harassment. Sensing this, Smith struck another panel – a joint committee on non-academic discipline, containing students, administrators, and faculty – to examine the university's lack of "a more formal body to deal with cases involving complex legal issues."[111]

That logic provoked another reform: making the university's sexual-harassment procedures responsive and effective. For this, Smith turned to two people. First, he asked Claudette Mackay-Lassonde, a trustee, consulting engineer, and corporate executive, to spearhead a task force dedicated to making Queen's a more "secure and hospitable place for women students." Her 1992 report called for many adjustments in campus security and, more importantly, for the university to become more proactive and less reactive in dealing with matters of diversity on its campus.[112] Secondly, Smith approached law professor David Mullan with a mandate to bolster the handling of sexual harassment at Queen's. Mullan was not only a popular teacher in the law school and past president of QUFA, but he had built a considerable reputation as a scholar of public law. In a 1983 paper to the secretaries of Ontario university senates he had noted that, as their *in loco parentis* role had receded in the sixties, universities had acquired new, more-formal legal obligations as public institutions. The courts in an age of Charter rights were increasingly looking to the universities for "procedural fairness" in matters of student discipline and rights. "Much as some people might regret the passing of the small, clubbish, intimate and near monastic-type institution in which certain standards were understood and universally accepted," he warned, " that situation has clearly changed with the advent of the open, secular, pluralistic institution that characterizes even our smallest universities today."[113]

Mullan's working group now sought to place sexual-harassment policy into this framework. A more encompassing definition of sexual harassment was developed. A more rigorous and responsive system of sexual-harassment advisors was called for, one that gave assurance to all Queen's staff, faculty, and students that "overt, unsolicited, and unwanted" sexual harassment was subject to complaint. Mullan's group nonetheless noted the slipperiness of the matter – what, for instance, divided sexual harassment from sexual discrimination? There was also the problem of knowing which university grievance procedure most appropriately fit a particular case – what if a student was alleged to have harassed a faculty member? One thing was, however, certain: the sexual-harassment process must be overseen by professionally trained staff, operating out of a dedicated office. The voluntary system of the eighties neither instilled confidence in victims of alleged harassment nor ensured objective adjudication.[114]

After the upheaval of "No Means No," there was little opposition to such advice. The Mullan Report's recommendations were adopted by the Senate, and a Sexual Harassment Complaint Board was established and equipped with powers ranging from loss of salary for university employees to expulsion for students. As Mullan had foretold, the university now found itself operating a litigious process based on defined rights and arbitrated justice. Consequently, the Senate now must fulfill a role as the last court of appeal for cases involving student sexual indiscretions, a task that often involved the traumatic recitation of the circumstances that had brought a student to the verge of expulsion from the university.[115] From the perspective of Richardson Hall, this process meant that such vexatious matters would no longer inexorably end up on the principal's desk, each one requiring an excruciating deliberation. With luck, the existence of reliable channels of redress would reduce the likelihood of further student sit-ins in the principal's office. Like the rest of Canadian society, Queen's was moving to a mandated, systemic approach to the challenge of ensuring inclusiveness and rectifying the marginalization of women. The institution's old predisposition to paternalism and vaguely defined notions of "fairness" was being supplanted by statements of principle, procedural manuals, and professionally administered grievance processes.

Not everybody agreed. Even with the wound of "No Mean No" still healing, there were voices arguing that Queen's was entering an age of debilitating political correctness, in which individual freedom would be crimped by endless pandering to minority pretentions. Smith's mail contained missives from disgruntled faculty who complained that Queen's was being held captive to "a lot of specious special pleading" which would prove "deleterious to the institution."[116] However, the new system and ethos at Queen's withstood such backsliding, even in painful incidences. When, for instance, in 1993 it came to light that a mathematics professor at Queen's had been convicted of molesting his daughter, in an incident that had taken place off campus ten years previously and for which he had gone to jail for thirty days, there were loud calls and graffiti calling for his dismissal. Even the AMS Assembly endorsed this mood. As the faculty association pointed out, their colleague had paid his debt to society and had performed his academic duties without complaint from students. Although forced by the furor to take a temporary leave, the professor retained his tenure.[117] As the Mullan Report had suggested, sexual harassment and assault were slippery matters that could not be separated from other societal rights and obligations.

Opening the Umbrella of Human Rights

Given the expanding complexity of Queen's obligation in matters of equity, harassment, and diversity, Smith raised the prospect in the fall of 1991 of creating an umbrella agency to coordinate all matters of human rights on Queen's campus. Such a body would not only bring clarity and predictability to human relations on campus, but would also simplify and centralize the process. From the principal's point of view, such centralization had the distinct benefit of distancing his office from all the agonies that another "No Means No" incident might bring. Smith turned to Madan Joneja, an India-born professor of anatomy, to head a small task force to sketch out what such a compendium human-rights office might look like. By 1992, the office was taking shape. It would have a broad mandate to tackle sexism, racism, and homophobia, and to promote anti-heterosexism (that is, challenging the belief that heterosexual values are the only acceptable way to frame a social perspective), both by means of arbitrating complaints and by educating members of the Queen's community to the values of a more tolerant and diverse society. The initiative seemed auspicious. In 1990, Ontario, building on the tradition of its 1962 Code of Human Rights, mandated pay equity in the province. Earlier, in the late 1980s, the federal government had begun attaching similar provisos in its constitutional bailiwicks, demanding, for instance, that federal contractors build equity into their tenders for work. Indeed, many remarked that Canada was well-embarked on its transition to a rights-driven, multicultural society. For instance, Board of Trustees member Rosemary Brown, a Jamaica-born, British Columbia politician, would soon be appointed as chair of the Ontario Human Rights Commission.

Back at Queen's, in the wake of the "No Means No" imbroglio, the kaleidoscope of new grievance and advocacy bodies was causing some confusion. Where exactly did one turn to exercise a grievance or anxiety over sexual harassment or employment equity? Rector Antoinette Mongillo complained to the Board of Trustees in 1992 that her job had become more like that of an ombudsman than a representative of student perspectives on university governance. Much of her time, she reckoned, was now consumed in directing students to appropriate offices on campus for counselling and advice. What was needed, she suggested, was a "peer helper system." Smith reached the same conclusion. Early in 1992, he told the Senate that he was looking for an "outstanding person" to take charge of a "human-rights office." (Poignantly, at that same meeting, the Senate voted to cancel classes every 6 December for the next five years in commemoration of the women slain in the 1989 Montreal massacre.) Smith found the person he was looking for in Irène Bujara.

Bujara had spent her early years in bicultural Montreal and had attended the bilingual University of Ottawa, where she had taken a BA in modern languages and cultural studies. A law degree followed in 1988. Uninterested in the practice of law, she involved herself with the National Association of Women and the Law, with its focus on gender and rights. This led to full-time work as an organizer with the Human Rights Research and Education Centre at the University of Ottawa. Bujara's duties entailed activities ranging from organizing courses on human rights (something that many employers were now mandating for their employees) to outreach programs designed to spread awareness of human rights. Bujara took from this experience the understanding that human rights was not just about adjudicating one-off complaints, but was also about "systemically ingraining" awareness of a rights culture in society. This philosophy coincided with Principal Smith's new-found respect for human rights at Queen's. He had told the Senate that he now saw a central human-rights office as "an evolutionary step in developing Queen's system for handling human rights issues," thereby building the university into a "harmonious community."[118] Bujara was hired and the Human Rights Office (HRO) opened in the fall of 1992.

The dawn of the nineties was thus a watershed in Queen's social culture. There was finally a coherent philosophy and institutional structure supporting a more inclusive and responsive campus society. The Human Rights Office was eventually not only closely partnered with the Equity Office, but the university soon also opened a Special Needs Office to foster better accessibility on campus. Vigilance over occupational health and safety was stepped up, with an "officer" appointed for every operational unit on campus. Echoing these commitments was Chaplain Yealland's new Inter-Faith Council, which gave interdenominational voice to all religions present on campus. The crucial motivating factor behind all this activism was leadership. David Smith had found his road to Damascus and was determined to never again find himself, or the university, in such a situation.

Irène Bujara immediately sensed this resolve on her arrival at Queen's. In her interview for the position of director of the Human Rights Office she told Smith that there would be times when she would expect him to stand behind her in trying and delicate situations. There would be times, she said, when the opposition would be obdurate. (Early in her tenure, Bujara was described by some naysayers as the "Czar" of human rights at Queen's.) Smith, and his successor, Bill Leggett, understood the need for a solid human-rights front. Such leadership, Bujara came to realize, was the "determinative factor" in building a new diverse culture at Queen's. When she accepted the job, Bujara signed on for a five-year stint, although she suspected, given Queen's recent upheavals, she would be gone in two. Indeed, when she took up her duties she was "stunned" by the reactionary attitudes she encountered around human rights on campus.[119] The university seemed to comfortably exist in an unquestioning, narrow WASP ethos. Nonetheless, Bujara would stay the course well into the next century.

Although Bujara was savvy enough to realize that cultures do not change overnight, signs of movement were soon evident. The office began publishing an annual report so that, for the first time, Queen's had some quantitative impression of the size of the challenge facing it and the progress made in addressing it. In her first report in 1992, Bujara reported that her office had handled thirty-nine sexual-harassment complaints, of which twenty-six were informally resolved, while the rest went to formal grievance hearings.[120] Bujara's stressed that her office was not just about meting out punishment for human-rights abuses, but also about resolving conflicts and raising awareness. By 1993, the Equity Office became more proactive in measuring Queen's progress towards becoming a more inclusive society. Its 1991 employment-equity census revealed that, while visible minorities represented 6.3 per cent of the national population, visible minorities at Queen's constituted 7 per cent of those working on campus. Law, where a conscious effort had been made to boost minority admission, boasted an 11.8-per-cent minority quotient. However, only 24 of Queen's 421 full professors were from visible minorities.[121] Bujara's office became staffed with specialists who could delve into such cases and ensure that all members of the Queen's community could expect open and objective treatment of their rights and grievances.[122] By 2000, the Human Rights Office would work up an all-encompassing Harassment/Discrimination Complaint Policy. Bujara was adamant that her mandate also involved promoting *systemic* change: "Finally," she concluded her report to the Senate in 1993, "we must be clear that systemic issues must always be addressed in conjunction with the individual issues." To this end, the HRO sponsored lectures – by Sunera Thobani of the National Action Committee on the Status of Women, for instance – and arranged workshops on diversity. Once QUFA unionized, faculty contracts began to include provision for mandatory sessions on campus diversity. Other policies and training procedures were directed at creating "positive space" on campus where gay, lesbian, and transgendered people might gather, study, and work in a respectful environment.[123]

By the mid-1990s then, Queen's was engaged in a more open dialogue about the challenge of diversity. In marked contrast to the decade that preceded it, issues of sexism, diversity, and equity were now out in the open, subject to debate and rectification. The debate was not always pleasant, but at least it was not kept down, chancing another outburst of the suppressed frustration that the signs in Gordon House windows had provoked in 1989. When, for instance, the ASUS-sponsored magazine *Surface* published intemperate radical lesbian-feminist articles – "How to make love to a white boy" and "You can't rape a .38" – a campus-wide debate on their propriety followed. There were angry, unsigned letters attacking "dykes," but elsewhere there was reasoned discussion in the AMS Assembly and its gender-issues committee. Students were offered the referendum option of withdrawing *Surface*'s ASUS annual subsidy. When the *Globe and Mail* questioned the taste of *Surface*'s content, Principal Smith wrote to tell *Globe* editor William Thorsell that, while many found *Surface* tasteless, the university did not believe in censorship, and pointed out that "a broad consensus is emerging in support of our policies on human rights and race relations."[124]

Queen's was indeed finding a new sense of its identity, one far less predicated on its old sense of preppiness and now more open to diversity and difference. Most students took this shift in their stride, for, after all, their world view reflected the high-school milieu from which they had just hatched. Instinctively, this generation of students understood the tolerances and trajectory of the new, multicultural Canada. They could sort out what was important – respecting human rights, tackling sexism – from matters on the margin. When, for instance, the South-East Asian Womyn's Collective complained about the "insensitivity" of naming a local coffee shop the Chinese Laundry Café, the *Journal* ran the story as an interest piece rather than an outrage. Others greeted the new ethos at Queen's with tongue in cheek: "I am extremely offended by everything," a doctoral student wrote to the *Journal* in 1991. "I feel terribly marginalized by the vast majority of not-like-me's who surround me."[125] "Welcome to PCU [politically correct university]," the 1993 *Tricolour* proclaimed. Beneath the banter, however, one could sense that the tide had turned at Queen's.

But no revolution in values moves with even momentum. While the student culture of the university seemed to embrace diversity in a boisterous, if at times contested, spirit, there were still back-eddies of sexism and recalcitrant behaviour in the more-mature ranks of the community. Here, the early nineties brought a last catharsis. Nowhere was this truer than in the troubled corridors of Macdonald Hall.

Acting Out in the Law Faculty

As the numbing news of the Montreal massacre burst onto the newscasts late on the evening of 6 December 1989, students in the Queen's law school gathered around televisions in the lounges and took in the grim news. It was a scene repeated across the campus – in residence common rooms, pubs, and apartments in the student ghetto. But in the law school, the news had a unique resonance, for it landed in the midst of a community of students and scholars which had, for half a decade, been locked in divisive sexual politics. The issue of gender had invaded almost every aspect of the school's culture, from hiring policy to admissions to the teaching of the law. The faculty had to a disquieting degree broken into sullen, antagonistic factions, factions often reinforced by similar fissures among the student body. Students acted out the tensions they sensed in their professors and in the law at large. In the late 1980s, for instance, a group of male students branding themselves the "Hound-dogs" spread misogynist sentiment around the faculty, scrawling graffiti on billboards. Other issues, such as differing perceptions between mature and fresh undergraduate students, exacerbated the tension. Since the initial furor in 1986 over the McIntyre memo, Dean John Whyte had thus presided over what might be called an armed truce – courses were taught, faculty pursued their research interests – but there was virtually no sense of commonality. The Montreal massacre and the impending need to appoint a new dean now broke that fragile tension.

On the morning after the massacre, law students began assembling for their morning lectures. According to a report carried in the *Whig-Standard* the next day, a male student arrived in one classroom as his classmates chatted and readied their notes. Then, without warning, he ran down the classroom aisle mimicking the action of someone dodging a barrage of bullets. Another report alleged that a male student leaving the room had aimed his finger, gun-like, at a female student. The *Whig* based its version of the incidents on a telephone interview with Professor McIntyre, who admitted that she had not been in the room during the incident, and with her colleague Beverley Baines, who told the reporter that she was not sure the story was anything more than a rumour. In fact, no professor had been in the room at the time – not that professorial authority was necessary to verify the details. What was undeniable was that a rumour indicating some such behaviour spread like wildfire through Macdonald Hall. The distraught atmosphere on campus that morning was ripe for such contagion. Certainly, no names were ever attached to the alleged perpetrators and precise details of the actual incident varied. Some said that there were in fact two make-believe "gunmen." There was also confusion as to whether the pantomime involved mock shooting or mock dodging of bullets. There were additional stories of tasteless jokes about women being bandied about the corridors. Not surprisingly, given the pre-existing tensions in the faculty, the allegation demanded immediate and serious investigation. This did not seem forthcoming, symptomatic of the paralysis that had initially stalled action during the "No Means No" incident. Like so much else at the law school, the incident sank into the surreptitious currents of gossip and accusation already so prevalent in its culture.

Over the next week, the incident percolated. The *Whig-Standard*, realizing that it had rushed to judgment in the wake of the sensational events in Montreal, backtracked somewhat on its original story. Its 11 December issue admitted that Baines had advised the reporter that she could not vouch for the fact that the incident was anything more than a rumour. Meanwhile, the university's public-relations department tried to put a cap on the publicity, suggesting the whole matter was simply an aberration. The *Globe and Mail*, for instance, reported on 14 December that a university publicist had passed off the whole incident as seemingly inconsequential, attributing it to an unnamed student who was "a bit of a character." That same day, the Senate convened for its scheduled meeting. Principal Smith alluded to the "so disturbing" events in Montreal, but his remarks predominantly focused on the mandate he had given Dean Baugh's gender-issues working group. In the ensuing discussion, the principal three times described the *Whig's* initial report of the morning-after incident in the law school as "false." The implication of the university's official stance seemed to imply that one could not read anything more into the alleged incident – that it contained no larger implication of rampant sexism in the law school. Indeed, Dean Whyte had told the *Whig* on 9 December that he felt that the classroom pantomime had been an "insensitive act," but that he did not "interpret it as misogynous."

And there the matter rested over the Christmas break. But within the women's caucuses now so highly activated on campus the issue festered. Deliberations of the Association of Women Teaching at Queen's and the Queen's Women and the Law readily concluded that the incident and the university administration's stonewalling were yet another manifestation of misogyny at Queen's.[126] Throughout January of the new year, they voiced their concern over Smith's 14 December pronouncement that reports of the mock shooting were "false," especially because it seemed to shut off any possibility of further addressing the issue of misogyny. Dean John Whyte heard their message. On 5 February, he circulated a memo to his faculty, admitting that he now "regretted" his earlier statement that he could not see misogyny in the incident. He also acknowledged the attitude of denial that permeated the university's official reaction to the event and the implication that the issue had been stirred up by a small group of irritable feminists. Whyte's forthright admission ended with a clarion call: "I think it is important that we recognize failures (especially our own) and express our sense of a better way."[127]

Whyte's about-face provoked a trenchant reaction from Vice-Principal Tom Williams, who came to the defence of the university's senior administration. At a tense Senate meeting on 24 March, Williams recalled that, on the morning of the "strafing," the principal had been out of town, so it had fallen to him to investigate the purported incident. Throughout the day, he had worked with Whyte's office to locate eyewitnesses to the event. That proved difficult – rumours abounded, but hard fact was elusive. By the end of the day, a single law student came forward and reported that he had witnessed a fellow student enter the lecture hall that morning. That student had moved "erratically" and kept looking around "furtively." He uttered not a word and sat down. Later in the morning, the witness told Williams that he had pondered what he had seen and had reached the "personal interpretation" that his fellow student "had been imitating being shot at." Williams stressed that this was the student's "*personal* view." The witness had shared his interpretation with colleagues over coffee. From there, the interpretation was launched into the fast current of faculty rumour. Once the rumour had been spun into quasi-fact by the newspapers and radio, the university tried to correct the facts – albeit belatedly, Williams admitted – by pointing out the flimsy relation of the facts to the surging rumours. This corrective effort, Williams vehemently charged, did not amount to a disparagement of feminism or an obliviousness of misogyny. He concluded by echoing Smith's earlier recitation of "educative" efforts on campus to address sexism. He believed that the issue was now "out of the closet" and that policies were now in train to improve the culture of the campus.

The controversy did not abate at this point. The motion before the Senate was to accept onto its record the various memos and depositions that had surfaced around the classroom incident of 7 December. Before that motion was put to a vote, two law professors – Meredith Cartwright and Michael Pickard – voiced their concern over Vice-Principal Williams's interpretation of the incident. Cartwright objected to the implication that it had been her colleagues who deliberately had put the rumours into circulation. She also suggested that the administration's assertion that "nothing" had happened that morning did not negate the possibility that "something" implicit in the whole uproar had indeed pulled back the curtain surrounding misogyny at Queen's. Pickard said that the administration had wrapped itself in a "punctiliousness about fact" that had blinded it to the broader magnitude of the incident. He preferred Dean Whyte's "more generous vision of what it meant to try to tell the truth." With that, the Senate passed the motion.

The prolonged debate over the "strafing" episode did nothing to calm the tensions in the law faculty. Whatever the reality in that classroom that sad morning in December, Queen's senior administration had done an awkward job of handling the situation. While Vice-Principal Williams's quick investigation of the alleged incident may have brought clarity to the rumours, Principal Smith's poorly nuanced and seemingly categorical declaration that reports of the incident were "false" showed little sensitivity to the situation that was already alive with tensions from previous flare-ups in the law faculty. The attempt to pass the alleged perpetrator off as a "bit of a character" exacerbated the situation, leading many observers to conclude that the university was more concerned with patching up its external reputation than addressing sexism in its midst.

"Threatening, Hostile, Angry, Vitriolic, and Vicious": Law Seeks a New Dean

In the spring of 1990, the law faculty returned to what had for the last half-decade passed as normal – a hostile factionalism. Queen's was hardly alone in this respect. Through the late 1980s, the Osgoode Hall law school at York University had been enveloped in controversy when its associate dean, Mary Jane Mossman, had been passed over for the deanship. Mossman was one of Queen's early female graduates, being the only woman in the class of 1970. Mossman had taught in Australia, worked in legal aid, and had made herself a respected family-law specialist and an advocate of women in the law. Joining Osgoode in 1977, she had risen to become its associate dean in 1986. A year later, however, against much expectation, she had been passed over for the deanship. Many concluded that the "old boys'" network had triumphed. A long human-rights case unfolded, with Mossman's feminist champions arguing that she was a victim of sexism. Early in the 1990s, an out-of-court settlement was reached.[128]

Against this broader background, John Whyte, his health sagging under the strain of recent faculty tensions, announced in the spring of 1991 that he would not seek a second term as dean at Queen's. Principal Smith consequently invoked the usual practice of appointing an advisory search committee to look for Whyte's successor. The timing was inauspicious: *The Canadian Lawyer* had just published a "report card" on Canada's law schools and had awarded Queen's an ignominious C+, arguing that it was a "cauldron of dissent and bitterness."[129]

The principal had traditionally chaired search committees for the law dean, but, given the delicate chemistry of the faculty, Smith in this instance placed special emphasis on building as broadly representative a group as possible. Two students, including the president of the Law Students' Society, sat on the committee, joining two senior male members of the department, Stanley Sadinsky and former dean Dan Soberman. Vice-principal, resources, Rod Fraser, gave voice to the concerns of senior administration, particularly over the university's crimped financial circumstances. The committee contained four women, including Virginia Bartley, the faculty registrar and its associate dean. Smith rounded out the committee with Gordon Sedgwick, a senior partner with the Toronto firm of Borden, Elliot and president of the Queen's Alumni Law Association. Three outside consultants were retained for their perspectives. Almost immediately, the committee sensed the pressure it was under. In November 1991, Queen's Women and the Law wrote to the committee reasserting the wish, first evident in 1986 when Whyte had been selected, to have a woman dean. They forwarded the names of seven women, the most promising of which was Mary Jane Mossman in Toronto. Mossman had been a visiting professor at Queen's the previous year and knew the faculty's culture well.

Almost immediately, Mossman wrote to Smith to say that she admired the school but had reservations about its gender balance and its approach to teaching the law. There were other early opinions: former dean Bernie Adell wrote to say that the new dean should be committed to the school's lodestar of teaching the law in its "social context." Adell also ominously suggested that the new dean should have a thick skin. The outside consultants visited the campus and filed ambivalent reports. Constance Hunt, the dean of law in Calgary, reported that she found the school rather "insular," but that its recent divisions had given it a "lively, exciting atmosphere." Vern Krishna from the University of Ottawa reported that the faculty "was bitterly divided by intra-faculty rivalries" and that cynicism prevailed. Krishna, however, sensed "nearly unanimous support" for Mossman, but also liked what he saw in Donald Carter, a Queen's-trained labour lawyer already on staff.[130]

Throughout the fall, the committee fine-tuned its criteria. The successful candidate, it decided, must agree to live in Kingston. This had been a bugbear for the faculty for years; promising young lawyers preferred the bright lights of Bay Street and Osgoode Hall and were reluctant to step off the big-city legal escalator. Queen's at this juncture needed a hands-on, on-the-spot dean. Outgoing Dean John Whyte stressed the need for a successor who understood the need for "pluralism." By December, the committee was vetting applications and sorting candidates into internal and external categories. Smith warned that the university's finances might not support the hiring of a stellar external candidate. Virginia Bartley, perhaps anxious not to block the way to a Mossman candidacy, announced that she did not want to be considered. At the committee's bidding, Smith contacted Mossman in Toronto. Mossman was, however, not interested, principally because her lawyer spouse had a rewarding career in Toronto, the epicentre of Ontario's legal profession. Undeterred, the committee urged Smith to recontact Mossman, who agreed to reconsider. Amid all this to-ing and fro-ing, rumours about the committee's deliberation flowed freely. Many thought that the process was too secretive. Others sensed that Smith did not seem enthusiastic about Mossman, perhaps because of her recent altercation with Osgoode Hall.

In January, Mossman again withdrew her candidacy. The committee's "A-list" now came down to a handful of external and internal candidates, but there was a division of opinion over their abilities. Smith reported that there was strong student opposition to one of the internal candidates. Time was running out; Whyte's retirement loomed. The faculty was growing resentful over the protracted wait and the committee's closed-door style. Smith, Sedgwick, and Fraser responded that it was "naive" to think that such deliberations could be open. In May, two decisions were reached. Virginia Bartley agreed

Mary Jane Mossman was the only woman to graduate in Queen's law class of 1970. Despite a distinguished legal career teaching in Australia and as a family-law specialist in Toronto, her talents were passed over at Queen's in the early 1990s when the law school sought a new dean.

to step into the role of acting dean. She would not only be the faculty's first female head, but also the first women dean of law in Ontario. The committee also decided to postpone its ultimate decision until the fall in the hope that new talent might be attracted. Frustration in the faculty grew. The process of selection began to garner more attention than its intended outcome.

The committee renewed its deliberations in September. There were further, inconclusive discussions with Mossman. A short list finally materialized. It contained, as external candidates, Brian Etherington of the University of Windsor and Lorenne Clark, the deputy-minister of justice in Yukon and expert on sexual coercion, and, as internal candidates, Marvin Baer, a specialist in commercial law, and Virginia Bartley, who had won kudos as acting dean. Interviews would take place in January 1993 – now a full year and a half into the selection process. Clark withdrew, and Mossman again made it clear that she did not wish to be considered. Etherington, Baer, and Bartley were interviewed. Etherington had little administrative experience but stressed his commitment to "mutuality of respect" in the faculty. Baer and Bartley expressed similar awareness of the need "to refresh the sense of community." On 18 January, Smith polled the committee: seven voted for Etherington, two for Bartley.

Etherington was offered the deanship early in February and accepted. Although he had graduated in law from Queen's in 1982, he would be the first outsider to head the faculty since its inception in the late 1950s. The news was not universally welcomed. There were indications that details of the committee's deliberations had been leaked. The rumour mill spun.[131] Many of the feminists on staff argued that once again the patriarchy had found its man. Graffiti appeared in the washrooms: "white balls win again." A student rally protested the appointment. Several women professors openly disparaged the selection process in their classes. More disturbingly, Etherington received telephone calls at his home in Windsor which warned him off the job. Stanley Sadinsky of the search committee was appalled. He would later describe the actions of some of his colleagues toward Etherington as "threatening, hostile, angry, vitriolic, and vicious," worthy of investigation.[132] Within days, Etherington withdrew his acceptance and graciously wished Queen's well "in dealing with the future well-being of the law school."

On 15 February, the selection committee morosely reconvened. Smith said that certain members of the faculty had "no respect for process, civility or appreciation of the need for good relations with alumni and others." The whole future of the faculty, he implied, hung in the balance. Indeed, Smith's mailbox was crammed with angry missives. "The university is supposed to be one of the places that protects against mass hysteria and agendas of the moment, a.k.a. witch hunts," wrote criminal lawyer Alan D. Gold. "These days it seems you have become a breeding ground for that very disease."[133] Former dean Dan Soberman said that the outside view was that Queen's law faculty was seen as "ungovernable." Certainly, the department had succumbed to zealous intransigence on all sides of the issue. Under this pressure, the committee saw four options: offer the deanship to Bartley, who had been well-regarded as acting dean; go ahead and restrict the search to outsiders only; appoint an acting dean for two years; or place the faculty under trusteeship. There was also talk of an investigation into the whole search process. Any way the committee looked, there seemed to be chasms of difference. Smith revealed that he received sixty-nine confidential submissions about the appointment process. Committee member Patti Pepin said that what she had seen of such submissions made her "physically ill" because of their vituperativeness.

The committee then discussed putting Bartley in the deanship. She had, after all, been on the short list. "Sonny" Sadinsky argued, however, that to do so would condone the behaviour of those feminists who had harassed Etherington. Although no evidence was produced that Bartley had been in cahoots with her colleagues, Bartley was thus dealt out of the equation. The idea of a two-year acting deanship dedicated to assuaging the faculty tensions seemed to be the course of least resistance. Bartley, understandably, said she had no interest in the position, as did Marvin Baer. (At the next law convocation, many of the graduating students presented Bartley with a white rose as they received their degree on the podium.) But Don Carter showed interest – so much so that Smith was able to talk him into accepting a full five-year term as dean.

Carter's considerable reputation as a labour and employment-law expert may well have seemed ideally suited to the problems besetting the faculty. And indeed, Carter did bring a calming influence to the department. Despite austere financial times, he found money for two new appointments, renovated the law library, established a law advisory board to connect the school to the world of legal practice, and established a co-operative program in law and industrial relations.[134] In this atmosphere, the faculty slowly began to rediscover its commonality. The school reasserted its national reputation, whether through Kathleen Lahey's incisive work on gender inequality in the tax system, Allan Manson's championing of prisoner rights, or the vigorous debate of Beverley Baines and Nick Bala over whether polygamy should be legalized in Canada. Other Queen's lawyers took up administrative-law positions with the Ontario Environmental Review Commission. Others stepped onto the international stage, advising the ILO and the IMF. As if to confirm this new cohesion and productivity in 1998, when Don Carter stepped down from the deanship, there was little contention when the faculty appointed Alison Harvison Young as its dean. Trained at McGill and Oxford, Harvison Young was the first outsider to take the reins in the faculty and, following in the shadow of Virginia Bartley, the embodiment of the faculty's new feminism.

Harvison Young's arrival as dean bookended a decade of unprecedented academic acrimony in the law school. It is safe to say that the university had never witnessed so protracted a contest over the values and processes of academic life. The university's usually well-oiled apparatus of collegiality gave way to ongoing skirmishing that fuelled distrust and acrimony. Beyond the campus, the reputation of the law faculty suffered. As Gordon Sedgwick confided to Principal Smith, that reputation had fallen "both in the legal academic community and in the legal profession generally. It is perceived as having drifted out of the mainstream of Canadian legal academic life, as having isolated itself intellectually and spiritually from that life."[135] Graduating students reported that their interviews for articling positions had been punctuated by queries about "what's going on at Queen's?" But, in one crucial sense, Sedgwick misjudged the situation in Macdonald Hall. The battles over sexism, legal teaching, and deanship in the faculty were *not* about the school "drifting away" from the mainstream of legal culture in Canada, but instead about pulling it back into the mainstream of prevailing social values in Canada. However abrasive the tactics of some feminist professors and their opponents were – intimidating a nominee for the deanship, politicizing the lectures – they were waging a legitimate battle to shunt many of their male colleagues into a world of Charter rights, social pluralism, and professional equity.

After all, the study and practice of the law was quintessentially about arbitrating fairness and equity in society. The ethos of the law had always been about contestation and assertion of rights. It should have been no surprise that the same critical forces might be brought to bear on the teaching culture of the law. The law demanded an umbilical connection with the society it served. At Queen's, in this case, the gender ethos had lagged woefully behind the temper of the times over the last few decades, to such a point that only an abrupt crisis could dislodge it. Caught on the fault line of this tectonic shift were men like John Whyte, a constitutional expert, and David Smith, an economist. However clumsily he had reacted to "No Means No," that crisis had at least awakened Smith to the dire need to rebalance Queen's sexual culture. "The university cannot flourish," he wrote in his 1991 *Values at Queen's*, "if some members are made to feel their concerns are lower than those of others." The fracas in the law school unhappily completed the lesson: through the laborious search for a new dean, Smith, the rationalist economist, proceeded in the belief that any equation could be balanced out. He ultimately discovered, however, that some situations were so out of equilibrium that decisive intervention was necessary. Finally, the law school got Donald Carter – a good dean, as it would turn out – but in the process other worthy candidates were passed over and pushed away. Few forgot the "gender wars" of the law faculty, but they looked at it from a dramatically changed attitudinal perspective.

The Challenge of Racism: Putting a New Face on Queen's

In January 1966, Queen's opened its new International Centre, a handsome facility nestled beside the Union and made possible through the generosity of the local Rotary Club. A festive evening of performances by the small community of foreign students – mainly graduate students – studying at Queen's marked the occasion. Lion dances from China, Zulu dances from "Africa," a steel band from the West Indies, and a sitar raga from Pakistan found themselves sharing a bill with Queen's more traditional fare of Scottish dances. The evening had an exotic air about it – a sense of "other," as postmodernists would later label such perceptions. While the International Centre was conceived in the hope of making foreign students feel welcome at Queen's, the reality was that Queen's remained a fundamentally WASP community. Throughout the seventies, the Board of Trustees expressed an ambition to boost Queen's intake of international students – a target of 5 per cent of total enrolment was established – but the results were persistently disappointing. Indeed, most of Queen's international students came from predictable and culturally similar countries such as the United States and Britain. For many foreign applicants, Queen's in Kingston seemed a long way out of the mainstream of Canadian urban life, a low rung on the ladder of Canadian advancement.

Instead, Queen's experienced more change in its ethnic and racial composition through the front door of its domestic undergraduate admissions. In these decades, the face of Canada was changing. In the Pearson and Trudeau years, the traditional European feedstock of Canadian immigration shifted dramatically, as immigrants from the West Indies, Central America, and, most significantly, the Pacific Rim flocked to Canada. The census revealed that most of this surge of "new" Canadians washed into the nation's large cities. Kingston, with its high dependence on public-sector employment, was not a favoured destination. However, by the eighties and nineties, Queen's, with its high-profile national recognition, began to attract the interest of newly arrived or second-generation Canadians who were clearly out of the traditional WASP mold of Queen's recruitment. In a small, hesitant way, the Queen's faculty had felt this same shift since the sixties, a decade in which the university hired its first non-Caucasian professors. Unlike big metropolitan universities such as York and Concordia, Queen's tended to lag behind the shifts in national demographics. Nonetheless, as the century waned, Queen's did experience the emergence of noticeable visible minorities in its midst. There had always been racial difference at Queen's; students from Commonwealth nations like Bermuda and Barbados, for instance, had long favoured Queen's.

But now there was a critical mass, a mass often differentiated by strikingly different religious and cultural values. Race now became a denominator of life at Queen's. So did the possibility of racism – the invidious differentiation of individuals on the basis of implied racial distinctions. Did racism exist at Queen's? Did racism exist in the wider Kingston community and impinge on life at Queen's? Was racism at Queen's deliberate and predatory, or was it systemic and unknowing in its manifestation? These were all questions – often framed as accusations – that troubled Queen's through the same years as it grappled with questions of sexism and social inclusion. Racism was perhaps a more insidious challenge. It could be embodied in as little as a sneer and a turn of phrase or it could be as virulent as a street beating or a scrawl of ignorant graffiti. Or it could be unconsciously embedded in the way the university went about its daily business – in the type of food served in residence cafeterias or in the Eurocentric focus of its history courses. As a Senate committee rather dejectedly reported in 1992: "The issue of race is a notoriously uncertain category."[136] It was also by the late twentieth century in North American society a highly inflammatory subject, one that had prompted reactions ranging from riots to affirmative-action programs.

There had always been an aura of racism about Queen's. These were usually reflective of broader currents flowing through Canadian society – the nativist reaction of a predominantly white host society to the changing racial demographics of a growing population. Through the first half of the twentieth century, for instance, Queen's had revelled in its association with a local black man, Alfie Pierce. While Alfie was lavished with affection, there was no question that he was perceived as different and inferior by the white students who surrounded him. Yearbook pictures show him reclining on the floor in front of men's teams. Most regarded him as a "mascot." Yet, when he died in 1951, his body lay in state in the gym for students and alumni to pay their respects. The famous *Queen's University Song Book* contained songs by American Stephen Foster that evoked the idyll of the old American South. Queen's theatre groups produced minstrel-like shows in black face. All of these habits and practices reflected the mores of Canadian society at the time.

In 1966, Queen's hired its first black professor. Jamaican-born Barry Batchelor arrived in Kingston with a doctorate in civil engineering from the University of London and a desire to avoid the overt racism that was gripping Britain and America at the time. At conferences in the United States, he and other blacks had been obliged to register at separate desks from their white "colleagues." He found Kingston a "lonely place," where there were few other blacks. He sensed a distinct difference between his daily life on campus and that of his family in the city. His children "were looked on as curiosities" at school and came home with tales of name calling and bullying. At Queen's, Professor Batchelor developed ambivalent feelings for his new home. He enjoyed the collegiality of the place and encountered little overt racism. Yet, he always sensed that he was regarded as an oddity on campus and resented the fact that there seemed so little effort to recruit other visible minorities to the professoriate. There were, he sensed, lines of racial demarcation still in place at Queen's. Although well-respected in the classroom and on the research front, Batchelor believed that he was passed over in his bid to become departmental head – civil engineering was "not ready" for a black head of department. Others had similar experiences. When India-born Madan Joneja joined the anatomy department in 1965, he too felt emotionally isolated. There were, he noted, absolutely no ethnic restaurants in Kingston beyond the predictable lone Chinese restaurant. He too felt racially marooned, but sensed that to complain about anything tinged by race was to "shoot your career." (Joneja would nonetheless eventually become head of his department.) When Pradeep Kumar joined the School of Business in 1974, after graduate studies at the university in the sixties, he quickly sensed that tradition at Queen's acted as "a smokescreen for not doing things." Knowing that the greater Canadian society was fast becoming multiracial, Kumar recalled concluding: "You can't remain in the era of the 1850s. This is a different kind of generation, a different time, a different culture." Yet, despite their frustrations with Queen's racial narrowness, Batchelor, Joneja, and Kumar would all stay at Queen's, and in retrospect never regretted their choice.[137]

By the early 1990s, Queen's student population was shedding its WASP uniformity. Student clubs reflected the campus's new diversity; the Queen's Committee Against Apartheid depicted here revealed interracial interaction. Nonetheless, racist attitudes remained ingrained in the university's Eurocentric curriculum and in periodic nasty racist incidents.

Students from visible minorities had similar experiences. When West Indian Lamoire Alexander came to Queen's in the mid-seventies to study engineering, he found it a "not welcoming place for minorities" with "almost no persons of colour on staff including professional, technical, clerical, and janitorial staff." Although he came to believe that a Queen's education offered "significant advantages," Alexander also believed that Queen's was in "deep denial about its systemic and institutionalized racism."[138] By the mid-eighties, racial interaction began to take on a sharper edge. University admissions were reflecting the increasingly multiracial composition of the broader population. Tensions emerged. Letters to the *Journal* proclaimed that "racism at Queen's is not hidden." People "who look 'different' reported having obscenities yelled at them."[139] A Nigerian student reported to the *Journal* that, although people at Queen's were "courteous outwardly," visible minorities "get stabbed in the back."[140] Mohawk Patricia Monture complained to Principal Smith that, despite the law faculty's effort to attract and hold Aboriginal students, her time at Queen's had been "a draining and painful experience," because she felt "vulnerable."[141] In 1988, an East Indian doctoral student in history working as a sessional lecturer was shocked to discover a bar of soap in her mailbox, a message presumed to come from her students and implying that her grooming differed from theirs.

Racism usually defies quantification and categorization. Was the campus awash with virulent racism? Or was racism at Queen's episodic and rooted in ignorance rather than malice aforethought? Thomas Minde, a white student doing masters' research on racism, told the *Journal* that "racism at Queen's is of the passive kind. It seems to be born of ignorance rather than negative intent."[142] Others concurred. "Sheltered campus world breeds racism," the *Journal* concluded in 1987. Others were less certain. The president of the Queen's Afro-Caribbean Club, Johnny Ramesar, believed that there was "an undercurrent of racism at Queen's," but that it took drink or cover of darkness to bring it out.[143] Many in racially visible minorities sensed that they were living in an academic community defined by white-skinned privilege. Some felt "rage" about their situation.[144] Others countered that there was no telling where such sentiment came from. When crudely made, xenophobic flyers from the Heritage Front began appearing on Queen's telephone poles, many suggested that they represented provocation by outsiders. Nobody really knew. Irène Bujara sensed that the Heritage hatred was perpetrated by outsiders intent on seeding racism on Queen's campus, although she did assist in extricating one Queen's student from the clutches of the group.[145]

Racism's cowardice usually bore no signature. But to the student mocked as a "Paki" from across a dark street this mattered little. By the mid-eighties, racism had undeniably reared its ugly head on campus, and Queen's was ill-prepared to deal with it. Systemically, the university had done virtually nothing to promote tolerance of racial diversity on campus. Hiring of new faculty remained a departmental prerogative and, without any overarching university dedication to affirmative racial action, departments were likely to reproduce themselves. As Barry Batchelor told a conference on racism in education organized by the Multi-Heritage Collective at Queen's, "the administration is a group of WASPish people that don't have time for minorities." The attitude was replicated in classrooms: the curricula placed before students were powerfully Eurocentric.[146] Perhaps more worrisome was the absence of any mechanism that allowed members of the Queen's community to complain about racial harassment or discrimination. Complaints might be lodged with the Ontario Human Rights Tribunal in Toronto, but at Queen's there was a conspicuous chink in the university's much vaunted system of self-regulation.

Students to a critical degree set the agenda on racism at Queen's in the late eighties. Their activism provoked action. Two things preconditioned the student body to racial awareness. The AMS's long tradition of empowering student clubs gave many students from visible minorities a way to register their identity on campus. The AMS approved constitutions for clubs devoted to Chinese, Bermudian, Afro-Caribbean, and Iranian students, as well as groups devoted to cultural pursuits, such as Indian classical dance. The AMS constitution specifically stated that none of these clubs could be racially exclusive; they must be open to all comers, regardless of race, colour, or creed. (The Ontario Human Rights Code allowed exclusivity to groups dedicated to Aboriginals and specific religious creeds.)[147] A more strident form of student racial activism had been foreshadowed by student-led agitation over the university's endowment investments in South Africa and in companies that had South African subsidiaries. Vocal, persistent, and heartfelt student activists backed by the moral force of the AMS had railed against the evils of apartheid and demanded that the university wash its hands of profits made from racialized labour.

Now the disquiet came closer to home. Having come into adolescence in an era of Charter rights, Queen's students were alive to the injustice embodied in the stories of racism that seemed to punctuate the pages of the *Journal* weekly. In 1989, the AMS Assembly created a Committee on Racism and Race Relations "to organize a dramatic and forceful campaign [against racism], including both awareness programs and immediate responses to incidents on campus."[148] Within this framework, new student leaders emerged ready to tackle racism head-on. One of them was Ali Velshi, a religious-studies student who had been born in Kenya and raised in Toronto before coming to Queen's. Velshi's father was the first Indo-Canadian to sit in the Ontario legislature. In 1990, Ali Velshi was appointed Campus Activities Commissioner at the AMS and chaired its Racism and Race Relations Committee. He persistently spoke out, not just against specific instances of racism – racist graffiti on Homecoming weekend – but also about the need to erase systemic racism in Queen's routine life. "The time has come," he wrote in the *Journal*, "for our university to stop 'studying the situation' and to take decisive action against racism."[149]

To broaden the net of the AMS's campaign for tolerance, Velshi, an Ismaili Muslim, changed his committee's mandate from race relations to *ethnic* relations, so as to capture the experience of minority groups not necessarily defined by race, such as Jewish students. Joining Velshi on the 1990 AMS Council was education commissioner Kam Rao who brought a passion for social equity to her portfolio. Rao cast a scrutinizing eye over anything that smacked of sexism or racism on campus – anti-Muslim and homophobic signs, for instance – while at the same time trying to connect Queen's students with the wider context of social justice – lobbying politicians for Native self-determination and questioning the Gulf War. Throughout 1990–91, the AMS Assembly became a hothouse of debate on social issues. Some argued that the crusading of committees, such as Gender Issues and Racism, were exceeding the bounds of their authority and that the cohesiveness of the AMS was dissolving.[150] Velshi and Rao, on the other hand, were committed to jolting student consciousness of sexism and racism on their campus.

The message did get through to Richardson Hall. In January 1989, Principal Smith took a page from the university's consensus-building playbook and announced a Principal's Advisory Committee (PAC) on Race Relations. The group would study the magnitude of the problem and advise on remedies. It would instruct Queen's on principles of "equal dignity." Smith sensed, however, that racism could easily become a mare's nest of controversy. The campus was coming alive with groups crusading against racism; each brought a different perspective and agenda to the issue. Smith's intuition was therefore to give the PAC a membership of great latitude, thereby countering any expectation that this would be another panel of white male sages. Initially, Smith approached Barry Batchelor of civil engineering to chair the PAC. Batchelor, who was beginning to think that Queen's was only capable of tokenism on the race front, declined. In his stead, Smith prevailed upon John Berry of psychology to take the assignment. Berry had ideal credentials: a doctorate in intercultural relations and acculturation and plenty of experience advising governments on the demands of managing multicultural societies. Madan Joneja of anatomy agreed to sit as co-chair. The principal's office made a wide-ranging call for nominations to the committee. The hope was to capture perspectives from all constituencies touched by racism on and near the Queen's campus. By March, the committee was in place. Its membership included faculty (including Barry Batchelor), staff, senior administrators (dean of women Elspeth Baugh), students (representatives from SCAR – the Student Committee Against Racism), and the broader Kingston community (local black Jamaican poet "Winsom").

Berry was determined to cast his committee's net widely. The committee hosted open public meetings to plumb the depths of racism at Queen's. The testimony was revelatory. A black Caribbean student recounted asking his English professor whether his class might study some modern Commonwealth literature. He was told: "We don't do that sort of thing at Queen's." Barry Batchelor talked about his career frustrations at Queen's. Yet, when Batchelor's son Wayne, a medical student at Queen's, heard his father's anguish, he responded; "Dad, I don't know what you're talking about." Smith sat in on the open meetings and was on the whole "dumbfounded" by what he was hearing.[151] The open meetings were combative affairs. The Student Committee Against Racism attacked Berry's credibility. How could a middle-aged white man understand the true dimensions of racism? Few agreed with SCAR's portrayal of the advisory committee as a "white bread" exercise. Berry and many of his fellow members found such rhetoric emotionally bruising

Despite some students' insistence that the PAC sit as a judge and jury on racism, the committee quickly determined that "racism" was too narrow a focus for its investigation. They also decided that they lacked the time and methodology to compile a listing of racist incidents on campus. Their obligation was to look ahead, not back in retribution. The focus would instead be on human rights. Only by fitting racism under the more integrated umbrella of human rights could the social culture of Queen's be altered. Racism, harassment, and sexism were not hermetic behaviours. Making Queen's a society respectful of diversity and equity required a blanket strategy. Nonetheless, when the PAC issued an interim report in the fall of 1989, the immediate reaction was focused on its analysis of racism. The fact that the "No Means No" fracas was breaking over the campus at exactly the same time probably heightened reaction to the committee's prescription. Smith advised the trustees that there could be no doubt that "racism is a societal problem to which Queen's is not immune."[152] He told the Senate that he had "heard clearly" from the PAC. Indeed, he would act even before the PAC issued its final report. Two "race-relations officers" would be appointed to adjudicate complaints about racist incidents and work would begin on drawing up a grievance procedure for racism.

By January of 1990, Smith had found his race-relations officers. Not surprisingly, Barry Batchelor was approached and accepted. Smith then approached Toni Pickard, a feisty law professor activated by a desire to dismantle barriers to social inclusion. Pickard hesitated. She knew that racial discrimination had many "dimensions of difficulty" and did not lend itself to easily dispensed justice. The task would be time-consuming. Once Smith offered her some relief from her teaching duties, Pickard accepted. "'We' must be an inclusive 'we,'" she told the principal.[153] Smith reinforced the appointments in March by issuing his *Values at Queen's* declaration, in which he dedicated the university to creating an "environment in which all members may pursue their common purpose without fear of injustice, indignity, or bodily harm."

However, there were problems from the outset. As had been the case with the sexual-harassment officers, the racial-relations system relied on well-meaning volunteers who soon found themselves overwhelmed by the hours involved and the trickiness of adjudicating alleged racist incidents. For his part, Batchelor came to believe that his appointment was "a sort of window dressing appointment." Its main purpose had been to "diffuse" a tense situation. Batchelor resigned the post in late 1991, complaining that he was "carrying a torch no one wants to carry." Pickard carried on, telling Smith that her effort would not work until there was "authority, power, and unqualified community support behind their efforts."

In its final report of February 1991, the Berry Committee sought to supply that authority and power. In keeping with its intention of broadening its mandate, the committee titled its report *Towards Diversity and Equity at Queen's: A Strategy for Change*. The report was structured around a dialectic of students ("who comes to Queen's?"), faculty and staff ("who works here?"), and curriculum and library ("what is taught?"). The report then set out a broad menu of policy and attitudinal shifts that would remake the comfy, often passively biased, culture of Queen's into a society actively pursuing equity and diversity. For each thrust of this strategy, primary responsibility would be assigned to a particular campus agency – the registrar, the AMS, deans, librarians. The revolution must begin with recruitment. Queen's must learn to send a message to would-be applicants that the university was not an extension of white, urban Canada. Recruitment tours should penetrate beyond their traditional bailiwicks of WASP high schools in Toronto, Ottawa, and Montreal and push into the burgeoning suburbs. Recruitment officers should themselves reflect Canada's new diversity.

The same ethos should prevail when Queen's sought to hire new professors. A conscious effort should be made to attract visible minorities to university teaching positions. This must be written into position postings, not just loosely expressed. Departments must "*demonstrate*" this same commitment in their tenure and promotion procedures; let Queen's faculty begin to reflect the racial and ethnic diversity of the new Canada. Departments should not, for instance, overload newly hired faculty from minority groups with administrative work, thereby crimping their teaching and research and their chances of promotion. Departments should also examine their curricula, asking whether what they teach was too canted towards Eurocentric values. Queen's curriculum should reflect a "multicultural and multi-racial Canadian society." Pedagogy should also consciously embody an anti-racist intent. Students should be quizzed in course evaluations about a professor's demeanour in questions of race. The library should replicate these trends in its acquisitions, building a collection that was less Eurocentric.

The report continued with a detailed prescription for making the "climate" at Queen's more welcoming and reflective of human diversity. "Sensitivity" courses should be made available across the campus to increase awareness of social diversity. University publications should project the university's commitment to diversity. There must be continued vigilance to ensure that orientation activities and rituals sent a message that *all* newcomers had a place at Queen's. In addition, the university should partner with city and county programs to promote racial harmony. Finally, the whole renovation of Queen's social and racial culture must be anchored with a grievance process for when moral suasion failed. Here, the report called for the creation of a Race Relations Council to set a complaints process and a Race Relations Officer to deal with actual complaints. The report closed by noting that it had not compiled an inventory of racist incidents at Queen's – the cost would have been high and there was no national baseline of racism against which to set Queen's record. That said, empirical evidence left little doubt that there were "clearly identified problems of both individual and systemic racism" at Queen's.[154]

Given its strongly prescriptive content, the Berry Report was farmed out by Principal Smith to faculty, students, and university administrators for their feedback. Senate committees were on the whole positive. The Senate Committee on Academic Procedures, for instance, agreed that the university's annual calendar of teaching and examinations should take the religious holidays of other religions into account. The Graduate Student Society worried that the report might simply be "for show," but nonetheless strongly endorsed its call for the hiring of more faculty from visible minorities. The AMS was more enthusiastic, noting that it had already altered its constitution to declare that it was a "non-racist" organization and an equal-opportunity employer. Robert Buller, director of alumni affairs, reported that the Alumni Association favoured the Berry recommendations, praising their intent of connecting Queen's with "events and sentiments of today." Faculty were less unanimous. Some saw its prescriptions as an invasion of academic freedom. The drama department, for instance, held an extraordinary meeting to discuss the report. Yes, theatre should serve to make the majority aware of the "cultural background of the minority," and to this end it would introduce an Asian element to its Western theatre-history course. However, adding a question about a professor's racial biases to course evaluations was "Orwellian."

Others saw the committee's prescription as closet affirmative action. Rudy Kalin, head of psychology, wrote to say that affirmative-action programs "*cause*, rather than *reduce*, social and inter-racial conflict" and often led to "group polarization" rather than harmonization. Others wrote that their disciplines were by their very nature unavoidably Eurocentric. William Reeve of the German department, for instance, wrote "our discipline is clearly not one pursued by racial minorities." There was also a backlash against what many saw as the report's prescriptive political correctness. "I object strongly," English professor A.C. Hamilton wrote, "to the assumption that racism is so rampant that everybody is racist except those who belong to the racial minorities."[155] Despite such dissident voices, a special general meeting of QUFA reached the resolution, after hearing a recitation of racial incidents on campus from Toni Pickard, that "educational equity is the key to increasing minority representation."

Senior university administrators took a more hands-on attitude to the Berry Report. After two years of constant turmoil on the gender and race front, they sensed that there must be tangible evidence of change. Vice-principal, operations and institutional relations, Tom Williams, believed that he and his colleagues must take a "leadership role" in ensuring that the message of diversity was spread into every nook and cranny of the university. Alice Baumgart, in her human-resources portfolio, agreed. She was wary of hardline affirmative action, but did favour the kind of "mild" affirmative action that had seen more women faculty hired over the last decade. On the whole, she believed that Queen's and Kingston had been "sheltered" from national trends in diversity and equity for too long. She would now redouble efforts to ensure that employment equity worked at Queen's. Dean John Whyte in law, bruised by recent events in his faculty, endorsed the move towards greater pluralism at Queen's, pointing out that law now, for instance, offered instruction in Aboriginal land claims.

John Berry, who had chaired the racism committee, stepped back from this dialogue, believing that his role had been to report, not advocate. He would go on to enjoy an internationally acknowledged career as a consultant to governments and social agencies on the delicate management of intercultural relations and acculturation. Back at Queen's, Principal Smith asked Madan Joneja to head a small working group charged with implementing the Berry Report. The Berry Report thus acted as the final catalyst for change that had come to critical mass under the broad societal pressure to accommodate equity and diversity. Most crucially, the Berry Report converted Principal Smith into an enthusiastic advocate of the Queen's Human Rights Office, which would open in the fall of 1992. Smith had thus heeded the Berry Report's initial emphasis on diversity as opposed to racism. Diversity was best ensured through centralized and coordinated auspices, rather than committing the university to a cluster of policies and agencies for racism, sexism, equity, and diversity. Paralleling this broad, inclusive approach, the university chaplain Brian Yealland at the same time launched the Inter-Faith Council as an umbrella over the many faiths that now inhabited what had once been a bastion of Presbyterianism. Now, every spring, the convocation invocation might be delivered by Yealland or a local rabbi or a local imam. A Muslim prayer room was made available in the Deutsch Centre. Registrar Alison Morgan reported that undergraduate recruitment been broadened to include high schools more populated by visible minorities. Specially contracted recruitment officers now visited First Nation reserves.

Whatever pockets of resistance remained to these initiatives, it was apparent that the Berry Committee had pushed Queen's over a significant watershed – there was now a keen awareness that the institution must close the gap between the rhetoric of equity and diversity and the daily reality of campus life. All understood that this would not happen overnight, but that decisive steps were being taken in that direction. Sexist and racist incidents would persist on campus – the Heritage Front would periodically rear its ugly head, anti-gay graffiti would still appear on walls, and slurs would still be shouted across darkened streets. But a frank, if at times acrimonious, dialogue and avenues of redress had been opened. The debates of the trustees, Senate meetings, and reporting in the *Journal* all carried news and updates on diversity, anti-racism, and anti-homophobia as a matter of course, rather than as some sort of aberrational intrusion on traditional university life. Perhaps the greatest transition was to an understanding that equity and diversity had been normalized in Queen's culture.

Two Men from Jamaica

This was nowhere more apparent than in February 1996 when the students elected Greg Frankson, a third-year continuing-education student, as the first president of the AMS who was black. What was heartening was that race played no obvious role in the campaign. As Frankson, a first-generation Jamaican-Canadian from Toronto, told the *Journal*: "More blacks need to become involved in leadership roles on campus. That's not my sole motivator. I don't place great stock in it."[156] Frankson's platform instead emphasized a promise of practical activism on behalf of students. And that he delivered: lobbying MPPs in Toronto over the rising cost of post-secondary education, promoting inclusion of part-time students in AMS activities, and enhancing daycare services soon surfaced on his agenda. Frankson was also quick to act on reports of sexism and racism, urging the AMS Committee on Racism and Ethnic Discrimination to bolster the mandate of the Human Rights Office.

But Frankson did choose to champion one cause designed to promote racial tolerance on campus. Shortly after taking office, he reminded the AMS Assembly that Queen's had done little to honour its first black graduate, Robert Sutherland, the Jamaican-Canadian who had graduated from Queen's in 1852 and had gone on to a legal career in southwestern Ontario, where he also helped facilitate the Underground Railway. When he died in the 1870s, Sutherland left a substantial estate to his alma mater, a life-saving financial injection at a time when the university tottered on bankruptcy. Yet Queen's, locked in a nineteenth-century perception of Canada's racial identity, had done little more than unveil an innocuous plaque in his honour a century after he died. Frankson determined to give Sutherland his proper due. "It's something that's been talked about in the university community on and off now, and I think it's about time it was dealt with in a serious way."[157] That fall, Frankson created an AMS task

In March 1998, Principal William Leggett and former AMS president Greg Frankson unveil a plaque naming a room in the John Deutsch University Centre after Queen's first black graduate, Robert Sutherland, in 1852. Despite a successful legal career and considerable financial benevolence to Queen's, Sutherland was left in the shadows by his alma mater until Frankson championed his legacy. The Board of Trustees would later, and somewhat reluctantly, agree to name the new policy-studies building after Sutherland.

force to ponder ways in which Sutherland's legacy might be celebrated.

The March 1997 report of the Sutherland task force suggested a number of commemorative initiatives – naming a fireplace in the new Stauffer Library, for instance. Thanks to Sutherland were "long overdue," Frankson happily announced. "Since things have changed and racism has subsided somewhat, hopefully the university will give Robert Sutherland the recognition he deserves."[158] But the issue of campus racism still made the trustees nervous. So it was the students who took the initiative, focusing on facilities under their sway. Working through the John Deutsch Centre Council, the AMS voted to name a second-floor room in the Union after Sutherland. This the trustees approved. A visitorship, meant to bring accomplished blacks to Queen's, was also established – Nigerian activist Ken Wiwa and Nova Scotian writer George Elliott Clarke were early visitors. Lastly, a prize honouring a black student at Queen's who displayed "leadership and initiative" in fostering diversity on campus was established. When Frankson graduated and launched what would become a career as an actor and spoken-word artist, others took up the torch of Sutherland's memory. A decade later his name would grace the public-policy building. Frankson's precedent-setting AMS presidency would echo in other ways – also within a decade Queen's students would elect Muslims as their rector and student president. Down in Toronto, consulting engineer Lamoire Alexander, the black West Indian who had attended Queen's in the 1970s and found the place "unwelcoming," was astonished: "In my student days I could not, in my wildest dreams, expect a black to be elected student president."[159] "Tradition" had changed at Queen's, and would have to continue doing so.

9

Town, Gown, and the World Beyond

There are things in this world more important than serene institutional relations and social conformity in the interests of the "Queen's spirit."
James McHugh, *Queen's Journal*, 11 Sept. 1987

Once a reputation like that of the Mariposa Festival or Fort Lauderdale was acquired it was hard to get rid of it.
Jim Leech, trustee, 1987

I believe in battling from within the system in order to try to alter the shape of public policy ... symbolic acts are important.
George Rawlyk, history professor, 1980

A More Active Citizenship – Kingston and Beyond

On an autumn Saturday evening in the early 1970s, Principal John Deutsch received an unexpected telephone call at Summerhill, the handsome 1830s limestone residence of the university's principals. Summerhill offered an elegant solitude in the midst of the busy campus. Blocks to the north, however, lay the university's boisterous residence precinct. That autumn, Queen's students – mainly males – had succumbed to a fad of "streaking" – brazenly running naked through public areas. Such exhibitionism had become rampant at colleges across the continent. That particular evening, the streakers were out in full force in the student ghetto that stretched north of the campus through Sydenham Ward. Picking up his phone, Principal Deutsch was challenged by an indignant Kingston citizen who had just seen a student jog down his respectable street in the buff. *What*, he demanded to know, was the principal going to do about such behaviour? "Well," Deutsch responded drily after a pause in his inimitable way, "I'm praying for snow."[1] Beyond offering an example of Deutsch's droll sense of humour, the incident was a reminder that Queen's had neighbours – in this case just down the street – with whom it had to coexist. From its earliest days, there had inevitably been points of friction between the university and Kingstonians. Adolescent hormones, the temptations of revelry in the spirit of *gaudeamus igitur* ["Now let us rejoice"], and the pressure of academic study invariably combined to aggravate relations on the town-and-gown frontier.

Queen's has always been a university within a city. But through the first century of its existence, its relatively small size and the cloistered nature of its campus encouraged a garrison-like culture. Queen's looked inward. Boarding houses on nearby streets may have provided beds by night, but it was the campus that centred students' daily routines. The sixties altered that rhythm forever. Deutsch's carefully paced expansion of the university to nearly ten thousand students in the early seventies strained the campus, pushing students and faculty deeper into the surrounding boroughs. The boarding houses with their presiding landladies disappeared. Apartment living surged. A lower legal drinking age also pulled students towards the taverns of Princess Street and Portsmouth Village. Moreover, these were baby-boom students, floating on postwar prosperity. For many, an education at Queen's no longer meant twelve-week stints of monastic dedication on its tightly bound campus. Queen's was now fluidly connected to a wider community, not just locally but also provincially. The newly completed Highway 401 made Toronto a weekend destination. Some students now had cars, and the AMS organized weekend charter buses that every Friday whisked students away to Toronto, Ottawa, and Montreal. Thus, Queen's became more outward-looking, more conscious of the greater community in which it existed.

Queen's students had, of course, long been aware of the world beyond their campus. Model

"Tricolour" bus prepares to leave Kingston on a Friday evening. Since the 1960s, changes in transportation patterns, such as the opening of Highway 401, had tended to erode the traditionally introverted culture of Queen's campus. Students now not only increasingly lived off-campus, but they also no longer felt themselves hermetically bound to the university precinct. The emergence of students as Charter-rights citizens completed the liberation.

parliaments, political clubs, Brockington Visitors, and relations with national student organizations all bred awareness of broader horizons. But then there was a sense that such activities were *practice* for life after graduation to the "real world." The sixties – for many, a decade of adolescent questioning and protest – closed this gap. Student years were now seen as a baptism of fire, during which students formed the habits of an active citizenship. The Edwards affair in the late sixties provided an early hint that Queen's students were connecting

400 TESTING TRADITION

with issues of social justice and responsibility. For members of the Free Socialist Movement, for instance, John Deutsch was seen at that time not as a benevolent patriarch, but rather as the agent of a corporatist agenda for post-secondary education in Canada. Over the next decade, many Queen's students sought to reconnect with, if not the ideology of the Edwards imbroglio, at least its spirit of interrogation. "There are battles yet to be fought!" AMS vice-president John Koopmans wrote in the *Journal* in 1978. "Have the Seventies taken away the veil of innocence through which students used to see the world? Chuck Edwards – where are you today?"[2]

This transition to activist citizenship rippled through student life at Queen's in the late-twentieth century. It brought students into the active governance of the university as they took seats in the Senate and acquired observer status at Board of Trustee meetings. Beginning in 1969, one of their own sat as rector, thereby giving voice to student concerns in the governing councils of the university. The Alma Mater Society, having incorporated in 1969 to dedicate itself to furnishing students with better services, reflected the shift to greater activism. An external affairs commissioner carried the aspirations and frustrations of Queen's students off campus to Queen's Park, Ottawa, and the Canadian Union of Students. At the same time, the AMS education commissioner built bridges between students and the broader issues of the day. Special AMS task forces and committees – addressing matters of gender, sexuality, equity – were struck to analyze and recommend. Referenda allowed students to dedicate their money as fees to causes deemed worthy by the majority.

As a million-dollar-plus annual operation, the AMS learned in the seventies that it had weight in society, that its actions had impact not just on University Avenue but farther afield. Queen's student democracy began to construct its own social programs – in 1988, for example, a "Walkhome" service and an accessibility fund for physically challenged students. Paralleling this coming of age by Queen's students, Queen's faculty were also acquiring in these years a more engaged perspective on the world beyond the campus. Through most of the sixties, Queen's professors had resided in a cozy, collegial, campus-oriented world. But financial austerity, the growing sophistication of scholarship, and the politics of externally funded research obliged them to also turn their eyes outward. Coordinated by their faculty association, Queen's professors increasingly engaged in *provincial* and *national* dialogues.

Thus, in the same late-century years that Queen's was slowly and at times awkwardly adapting its cultural values to a more racially and ethnically diverse Canadian society, it was also obliged to construct a new framework for interaction with the broader world. This process would entail more than relatively straightforward practical decisions: it also begged consideration of the ethical and moral dimensions of living in an affluent, post-industrial society – that is, what was "right" and what was "wrong" in society? The debate would at times be agonizing, but the intellectual and political callisthenics of reaching common accord would hone the edge of Queen's democracy and, in effect, sharpen the quality of a Queen's education. Two key issues would epitomize this transition to a more responsible and engaged citizenship: first, deciding the moral and practical parameters of investing the university's endowment funds, and, second, learning to regulate the university's hitherto chaotic town-and-gown relationship. Each issue took in the entire Queen's community, involving students, faculty, alumni, and administrators. Each issue put Queen's in the public spotlight as starkly as the "No Means No" fracas of 1989 had done.

The investment issue found its roots in the university's Presbyterian genetic code. As if scripted by the Presbyterian Shorter Catechism, the Queen's charter made it abundantly clear that the Board of Trustees was entrusted with the sacred – by Scottish standards – duty of ensuring the university's financial well-being. The 1841 royal charter designated the trustees as the corporate embodiment of the university, endowing them with the right to hold its property and to make financial transactions they deemed "best for the interest of the said College." This authority came to entail overseeing the institution's annual operating budget and building up an endowment fund to serve as a rainy-day fund, as well as a feedstock for major endeavours. The trustees nurtured Queen's endowment, zealously defending it from those eager to apply it to expedient purposes. English-professor-turned-university-treasurer William McNeill built a formidable reputation down to the late 1940s for his hawkish frugality and fixation on the university's bottom line. Mindful of how the Depression had bruised the endowment, the trustees appointed stalwart financial types to its investment committee. With men such as Hazlett Lemmon of Canada Life and Earle McLaughlin of the Royal Bank guiding its portfolio, Queen's endowment was built up to a handsome $12.4 million by 1961. Through all this, the management of the endowment remained the unquestioned prerogative of the trustees. For their part, the trustees regarded the endowment in hard, cold financial terms: their abiding obligation was to support the material well-being of the university.

Defining Queen's Social Responsibility

Such prerogatives and rationales began to be questioned in the iconoclastic sixties. Across the western world, the primacy of capitalism to create national income came to be questioned. There was growing talk of the "social responsibility" of capitalism. This groundswell became a vigorous debate. Critics called for more transparency in corporate and financial dealings. Business should be obliged to acknowledge the social, economic, and cultural implications of its activities. Investment was no longer necessarily seen as an unalloyed positive. In Canada, for instance, economic nationalists argued that foreign direct investment was diluting our culture and wresting our economic destiny from our hands. Across the border, the United States passed legislation in 1977 proscribing "foreign corrupt practices" by American corporations. Opponents of this policing of corporate autonomy, such as free-enterprise champion and economist Milton Friedman, countered by arguing that "the business of business is business": bridling enterprise with regulation would only stifle profits and hence economic growth. Not surprisingly, this tension soon slipped out of newspaper op-ed columns and legislative debate into shareholder activism – and onto university campuses. In Canada, for instance, Earle McLaughlin was confronted at annual meetings by a small, but vocal, group of feminist shareholders, who demanded to know why the Royal Bank's retail front line was almost exclusively female, while its head office was a male domain. Citizens began linking corporate governance with political developments in distant countries. When, for instance, the social-democratic government of Salvador Allende in Chile was toppled by a bloody military coup in 1973, many concluded that there had been collusion between Chile's army and foreign corporations eager to shed the burden of an unfriendly, interventionist government.

At Queen's, the late sixties had seen a growing transparency around the key instruments of university governance. The Senate welcomed student senators. The trustees, while doggedly protecting their exclusivity, now allowed student and faculty observers to attend their meetings. The financial health of the university was consequently more broadly understood, as was the status of the endowment. But some students and professors began to look beyond the immediate financial performance of the university's portfolio for answers to moral and political questions. Amongst the stocks and bonds held in the endowment in the mid-seventies were shares of Noranda Mines, a Canadian mining conglomerate famous for copper mining and smelting. Although fluctuating in value, Queen's holdings in Noranda totalled about $422,000, generating an annual return of about $18,000. Noranda shared the general belief held by foreign mining corporations operating in Chile that the Allende government had ruined its all-important copper industry. In 1971, Allende had nationalized Gran Mineria; most observers reckoned that this had reduced the productivity and profitability of Chilean copper. The new military regime of Augusto Pinochet promised stability and market-oriented openness. Noranda responded by partnering with a local firm, Chilean Mining Corporation, in a $350-million project to develop the Andacollo copper field in central Chile.

Many Canadians queried the investment, pointing out that the Pinochet government had run roughshod over human rights, imprisoning and torturing Allende supporters. Church groups and human-rights advocates carried their outrage to the newspapers and demanded that Noranda reverse course. The investment seemed to sully Canada's reputation as a middle power and arbiter of fairness on the world stage. Opinions expressed in the pages of the *Globe and Mail* were soon echoed on the Queen's campus. At its May 1977 meeting, the trustees received a letter from physics professor David McLay. An associate dean of Arts and Science, McLay had taught at Queen's since 1962 and had long mixed his academic life with social activism. He had roots in the Student Christian Movement, supported Amnesty International, and, closer to home, had boosted the Queen's International Centre and worked to alleviate Kingston's chronic housing situation by helping to organize a student volunteer bureau on campus. He believed in turning anger into "positive community action," as he put it.[3] Now Queen's endowment investment in Chile troubled his conscience. He called upon the trustees to ponder the "moral dimension" of taking profits from an economy governed by the repressive regime of General Pinochet. McLay pointed out that prominent church groups in Canada had condemned Pinochet's methods and called upon Canadian companies to withdraw from Chile. He also asked the trustees to reconsider their investment committee's practice of simply voting the proxy on shares held by Queen's in favour of management.

Responding to McLay's request, the Board concluded that it was "very difficult" to judge the matter without hearing both sides of the issues, but on the whole it was not inclined to take any action unless the Chilean investment could be seen to directly impede the operation of the university.[4] Seldom do issues crystallize so quickly. On the one hand, a faculty member, soon to be joined by many students and fellow professors, construed the issue in the broad context of a university's obligation to the society it served. A university's actions must mesh with and guide the moral standards of its host society. By contrast, the Board – and university administrators – took a more legalistic position. Queen's charter had charged the trustees with the responsibility of ensuring the material well-being of the university. The sustainability of the institution was its moral obligation. Regulating the moral and intellectual health of the university fell to the Senate. Holding shares in Noranda was not illegal; it may have been questionable, but, as many Board members commented, the Board could hardly be expected to politicize its decisions. In fact, where would a veto of the Chilean investment lead? Would it lead it to trespassing on the academic freedom so sacred to the university's culture? What about, the counter-argument contended, the freedoms of Chileans who found themselves detained without due process and often tortured? As a result of all this, the polarity of what soon became known as the "divestment issue" was established. What followed was a vigorous and at times vituperative debate over the moral and practical purposes of the university – a debate that would activate a feisty new sense of citizenship on the part of many members of the campus community.

The fall term of 1977 brought evidence that a coalition of students and faculty was emerging on the divestment issue. A student petition asked the Board of Trustees to reconsider its position on Noranda. When Noranda announced that it would in fact increase its stake in the Andacolla project, AMS president Hugh Christie wrote to Noranda CEO Alf Powis to tell him that Queen's students were "outraged." "Surely," Christie insisted, "the almighty dollar is not so powerful that it can cause us to disregard everything we have fought two world wars to protect?" To confirm this stance, the AMS held a referendum in late November, asking students if they opposed Noranda's move "on the basis of the serious violation of human rights by the Chilean Government?" Some 72 per cent said "yes," they did oppose it (on a voter turnout of 33.4 per cent, about average for student elections).[5] On the heels of the referendum, a motion was introduced at the November Senate meeting, urging the Board of Trustees to exercise its right as a shareholder to voice Queen's opposition to the Chilean expansion.

A vigorous debate unfolded. Nobody claimed support for the Pinochet regime; the debate hinged on what was appropriate action. Professor Viv Abrahams of physiology advised the Senate to stick to academic governance. One man's "moral judgment" was an invasion of another man's freedom of opinion. Barry Batchelor of civil engineering said that he was reluctant to see the Senate intervene, but would act as an individual against Noranda. Tony Travill of anatomy warned that any university sanctioning of Noranda would "open a Pandora's Box which the university will live to regret."[6] Principal Robert Bater of the Theology College countered by saying the Senate already took moral decisions on matters such as student plagiarism. Others argued that the Senate was the "best forum the university had" to discuss issues of moral relevance, and that other North American universities were engaged in similar debates over their social responsibility. Sensing the divisiveness of the issue, the Senate postponed a vote on the motion, opting for a fuller discussion at its next meeting.

The Noranda issue sent an unmistakable message that Queen's usually polite and deferential approach to contentious questions was not going to bridge the gap between what seemed like two diametrically opposed viewpoints. In December, the trustees opted for the familiar response of dispatching the issue to an arm's-length body of inquiry. It asked Toronto lawyer and board member Norman McLeod Rogers to head an ad hoc Board committee on social responsibility, charging the group to come up with guidelines applicable to contentious investments. In the interim, the January Senate meeting ratified its earlier motion sanctioning Noranda. That same month, a substantial petition bearing the names of 562 members of staff and faculty was placed before the trustees and principal: it condemned Noranda's active involvement in Chile's economy. Queen's students were also becoming activated by the issue. A Student Action Committee (SAC) spontaneously emerged. Unaffiliated with the AMS, the SAC believed in direct action unfiltered by the usual consensus brokering, and thus brought pressure for action – leaflets, placards, and chanting – quite literally to the door of the Collins Room, where the trustees and Senate convened.

At the same time, the outside world began to take note of the fact that Queen's seemed to be caught on the horns of a dilemma. Toronto alderman Dan Heap, long an advocate of labour and human rights, wrote to commend the Senate for taking a stand on Chile. The *Globe and Mail*, on the other hand, reported the Senate's anti-Noranda vote as if Queen's had overnight become a hotbed of anti-corporate agitation. Other voices were heard: the Anglican Church in Chile announced that it backed the copper project, arguing that the Pinochet regime had eased its human-rights persecution, and that the mine would create a thousand much-needed jobs, with 60 per cent of its income staying in Chile. Alumni joined the debate. A mining-engineering graduate from 1959 wrote to hoist the Senate on its own petard: why reprimand Chile, when there had been a "deafening silence" on Prime Minister Trudeau's "flirtation" with communist regimes such as Cuba, where human rights were trampled every day?[7] Others asked why not condemn Canada's sale of CANDU nuclear reactors to Argentina, where the military were suppressing democracy and torturing citizens?

Sensing the delicacy of the situation, Rogers asked for more time to prepare his guidelines. Given the rising temperature of the debate, Rogers suggested that that the university in the interim not vote its proxy on its Noranda holdings. It might also, he said, be worthwhile for Principal Watts, the rector, and the chair of the Board of Trustees, Robert Southam, to seek a meeting with Noranda CEO Powis to explain Queen's anxieties over his company's Chile policy. Finally, in October, Rogers's committee tabled its guidelines for social responsibility. It chose to adhere to a clarified annunciation of the status quo. There was little hint of moralism in its view of university investment. The Board's duty was to make investments for "maximum returns with an acceptable degree of risk." The Board should take "appropriate measures" only if the activities of a corporation in which it held stock "might directly affect the well-being of the University." If there was "obvious widespread support among the constituents of the University" for sanctioning of a company held by Queen's, then the Board might convey that concern to the company. The investment committee of the Board should be empowered to use its proxy power to send both positive and negative messages at annual meetings. And, finally, recognizing that social responsibility was no passing fad, the Board should establish a permanent social-responsibility committee to screen the university's portfolio for investments that might be injurious to its integrity.[8] The Board quickly acted on this last idea, asking Calgary corporate consultant and Queen's political-science graduate Mary Collins to sit as its chair. Former AMS president – now rector – Hugh Christie joined her, along with history professor George Rawlyk (well-known for his outspoken commitment to social justice), business professor Bruce Buchan, the federal Deputy Auditor General William Muir, and mining engineer John Kostuik.

Professor George Rawlyk. A long-serving head of the history department, Rawlyk was also actively involved in local and national affairs as a member of the New Democratic Party and the Baptist church. Rawlyk perpetuated a long Queen's tradition of voicing concern over moral and ethical dilemmas in Canadian society. The politics of Chile and South Africa aroused that conscience in the late 1970s and through the 1980s.

Under the Collins committee's watchful eye, Queen's investments became less passively managed. The committee canvassed corporations in which Queen's held shares, particularly those with international operations, to assess their commitment to social responsibility. Walter Light, CEO of Northern Telecom and Queen's Board member, for instance, submitted his company's code of business conduct. Queen's became a member of the Investor Responsibility Research Centre in the United States, giving it access to reports on how companies conducted themselves abroad. In particular, Queen's became obsessed with the so-called "Sullivan Principles of Corporate Social Responsibility," a kind of checklist of acceptable corporate behaviour on foreign shores. In 1977, the Rev. Leon Sullivan, who sat on the board of General Motors, had devised the principles as a means of allowing investors to police the actions of American corporations operating in countries with dubious democratic oversight. Did they, for instance, offer the same benefits – lunchroom, health benefits, training opportunities – to their employees in apartheid South Africa as they did in their American operations? If a corporation could prove parity of treatment across international boundaries, then they received the Sullivan stamp of approval.

Queen's social-responsibility committee instructed the university secretary, John Bannister, to survey every company in which Queen's had holdings to see whether it met Sullivan standards. Almost all did. One, Dominion Textiles, refused to comply, and the committee eventually ordered the disposal of Queen's holdings in that company. The committee also wrote to other universities to ascertain their policies on social responsibility. From Harvard, for instance, they learned that a committee headed by the distinguished economist Michael Spence had concluded the university should stay with its established policy of only supporting social-responsibility resolutions introduced by others. A few years later, Harvard's forceful lawyer president Derek Bok weighed in on the subject in his book *Beyond the Ivory Tower: Social Responsibility of the Modern University*. Universities, he advised, should stick to their "normal educational functions in an effort to influence events" rather than engaging in political interventions which were likely to jeopardize their academic freedom.[9] Sharing Bok's point that political stricture and academic freedom should not be mingled in academic governance was Hannah Gray, the historian president of the University of Chicago, who would be invited to Queen's to elucidate her belief in a hands-off approach to forced divestment. Closer to home, the committee learned that many other Canadian universities were also engulfed in divestment debates. Only two – McGill and Dalhousie – would actually go so far as to sell holdings.

By early 1980, despite the committee's cautious attempt to bring clarity to the campus, fissures were opening up over the Noranda question. The trustees felt that a degree of moral transparency had been brought to the issue, thereby allowing a return to the Board's primary role of guarding the university's material well-being. "I don't imagine that any of us who have had the opportunity of an education at Queen's," Mary Collins wrote to student Kathleen Gallivan, "will ever be satisfied with the status quo and will continue throughout our lives to search for better ways and a better world." Principal Watts's executive assistant, Vernon Ready, told an inquiring *Journal* editor Drew Fagan that social responsibility was a "varied and complex" issue and that hard-and-fast guidelines were impracticable. Many disagreed, saying that the Board was engaged in a condescending exercise in "fence sitting." There had, after all, been a student referendum endorsing a clear-cut divestment. The Graduate Student Society passed a motion expressing its "profound disappointment" at the university's wavering position on Noranda; "polite platitudes and ambiguous phrases" were not enough.[10] In March, the AMS held a second referendum on the issue: once again 72 per cent of voters favoured selling Queen's stake in Noranda. Faculty joined in the call for a more assertive policy. History professor George Rawlyk wanted forthright action. "I believe in battling from within the system in order to try to alter the shape of public policy," he wrote to Collins. "The issue is a most difficult one. Yet, the committees should realize that symbolic acts are important and can help to create the kind of trust that we so desperately need at the time of crisis, disorientation, and confusion."[11]

That spring a Queen's student showed up at the Noranda annual meeting in Toronto, presented a proxy, and took the floor to deliver a forceful sermon on Noranda's involvement in Pinochet's Chile. He presented a copy of the recent campus petition protesting the investment. Noranda shareholders were unmoved, but senior management suggested that a Queen's delegation come to Toronto to discuss the matter. That meeting took place in July. Ten delegates from the university, including the

AMS president, faculty and staff members such as Rawlyk, alumni, and Vernon Ready representing Watts, met with Alf Powis in his executive suite. There was an awkwardness about the meeting – a chain-smoking, outspoken corporate executive confronted by a motley academic crew. Powis stressed the economic benefits to Chilean society from the Andacolla project – as many as seven thousand jobs and trickle-down effects such as larger tax revenues. The delegation focused on the moral implications of propping up a regime that suppressed human rights. They urged Powis to act as a "Canadian ambassador," carrying Canadian values into the southern hemisphere.

The Bay Street meeting did little to close the now-yawning divergence of opinion of campus. The debate in fact intensified. Business professor Merv Daub wrote of the difficulty of trying to reconcile the conflicting emotional and economic perspectives. Social responsibility was, he advised, "a long-suffering tale of many solitudes" that required "constant reassessment, discussion, debate, and, most importantly, change."[12] Nonetheless, pressure for decisive action grew. Former AMS president Ross McGregor, now a Toronto business consultant, wrote to scold the trustees for not being "more responsive to the apparent disposition of the university community." More, he urged, must be done "to escape the ivory tower stereotype by openly addressing the broad issues arising from its role in Canadian, indeed, world society."[13] In October, the SAC staged a sit-in outside the trustees' fall meeting, and SAC member Gary Beaton demanded that the trustees take the issue "seriously," complaining that the Board's inaction suggested that it was little more than a puppet of the "Canadian corporate elite."[14]

Early in November, the social-responsibility committee held an open meeting to address the Noranda situation. The meeting reflected Queen's habitual liberal approach to contention: air out the grievance, seek common ground, and construct a consensus for future action. Divestment had, however, become too polarized for such brokerage. On one flank, the Board held tightly to its prerogative to manage the university's investments as just that – investments. Queen's Noranda shares, they reasoned, constituted only a sliver of Noranda's overall equity. Selling them would barely be noticed and, besides, the same shares might be snapped up by a much-less-scrupulous investor, one quite willing to bolster Pinochet's regime. Queen's would, in effect, be making the lot of Chilean workers worse. Better to retain the shares, vote the proxy, and exercise at least a flimsy leverage on the corporation. On the other flank, a coalition of students, staff, and faculty construed the issue in stark moral terms. Queen's, they seemed to be implying, had blood on its hands. One problem on this flank was that its adherents ranged from impatient radicals – "neo-Marxists and politicos," Rawlyk called them – to mild-mannered United Church lobbyists. It was therefore difficult to estimate just what measures might satisfy their demands. Similarly, it was hard to gauge the depth of divestment agitation. Only 30 per cent of eligible students had voted in each of the two referenda. Nonetheless, there was no denying that a vocal and highly motivated minority wanted action.

When the November open meeting did little to clear the air, the AMS in December created its own social-responsibility committee under the auspices of the education commissioner. As if to telegraph its own determination, the trustees that same month issued a "public statement on social responsibility and investment policies." The statement affirmed that Queen's upheld "basic human rights globally." However, no shares of any company in the portfolio would be sold until all other "constructive actions" had been exhausted. The policy of influence by proxy vote would continue. To maintain the campus dialogue, the Board's social-responsibility committee would stage an annual open meeting to garner feed-back.[15] Some trustees worried that students seemed to distrust the Board and found its actions autocratic. Others suggested that they were simply ill-informed about the powers and dilemmas of the Board. One of the by-products of the divestment debate would be the opening up of the Board meetings to a wider audience. Within a year, spectators would be admitted to the Collins Room to watch and listen to the Board's deliberations. In the interim, mutual suspicion remained over the Chilean dilemma.

And then two things shifted the whole divestment debate. The price of copper plunged. Interest rates rose and economies faltered. The financial press began to speculate that Noranda and its Chilean state partner at Andacolla were scaling back their investment plans. Then development was halted. Noranda would remain interested in the property, but another Canadian company, Aur Resources, would eventually bring the rich copper-gold mine into profitable production. When the stock market began to reflect Noranda's retreat from Chile, its share price dipped. Over the next two years, the Board's investment committee steadily disposed of the university's Noranda investment, doing so, they emphasized, for financial not moralistic reasons. By early 1983, Queen's no longer appeared to be a Noranda shareholder.[16]

By this juncture, there could be no denying that Queen's had been aroused into a new consciousness and activism by the complexity of social responsibility. The issue had connected its governing bodies and significant elements of its community to ongoing socio-political debates beyond its campus. Divestment had acted in some ways as a solvent on the traditionally deferential relationship of the student body and university administrators. Students were now inclined to engage issues that stretched beyond their immediate interests – fees, student services, social activities – into the realm of effecting influence on the society that lay beyond their campus and coloured the world into which they would graduate. The issue of South African apartheid would amply illuminate this new mindset.

"Fraught with Grey Areas": Divesting from South Africa

"After Chile comes South Africa," John Bannister, the university's prescient secretary wrote in 1978 to Bruce Buchan in the principal's office. "A quick perusal of our portfolio indicates we hold the following stocks with assets in the Republic of South Africa: General Motors, Goodyear, E.I. Dupont, Eastman Kodak, Exxon, Upjohn, American Home Products, Dow Chemical, Eli Lilly, IBM, and GE."[17] Bannister's predictions coincided with a dramatic rise in western abhorrence of apartheid. The Soweto uprising of 1976 had laid bare the violent underpinnings of segregation and activated latent antipathy to apartheid into forceful, persistent opposition around the world. Condemnation of South Africa's treatment of its black citizens echoed from church halls to the United Nations General Assembly. In Canada, the Task Force on the Churches and Corporate Responsibility, an ecumenical research and lobbying coalition established in 1975, increasingly turned its attention to apartheid, arguing that activism by minority shareholders could exert pressure on companies operating in South Africa. Canadian aluminum producer Alcan became an early target. Queen's quickly reacted. Late in 1981, the Student Action Committee issued a press release alleging that 70 per cent of the companies in Queen's endowment portfolio had links to South Africa. Almost immediately, the Board's social-responsibility committee instructed University Secretary Banister to write to all companies operating in South Africa in which Queen's held shares to inquire whether they subscribed to the Sullivan guidelines. In January 1982, the committee hosted a seminar on human rights and social responsibility. Over a thousand people attended the gathering. Discussion ranged from assessing the university's responsibility to becoming involved in fighting pollution to prisoners' rights.[18]

The social-responsibility committee had become an ongoing Board fixture. It was no longer chaired

Queen's students make their concern over South African apartheid known to the university trustees outside Richardson Hall in 1986.

by Mary Collins (who would shortly launch a political career as a West Coast federal MP). Her place had been taken by Alan Broadbent, Queen's first student rector in the late 1960s, who had gone on to become a co-founder of the Toronto-based Maytree Foundation, a non-profit facilitator of community renewal. Broadbent would now have to walk the tightrope of social responsibility. He adopted much the same attitude as had Collins. The committee would keep a "watchful eye" on the broader implications of the university's investments. It would seek, to take words from Principal Watts's 1980 "State of the University" address, to "elucidate issues, not draw lines around them." Proxy votes would not be cast until a discussion of such a vote had been thrashed out. There would be more open meetings to allow the university community to air its concerns. But there were boundaries to such latitude.

Broadbent doubted the wisdom of deciding such convoluted matters by referendum vote; these situations were too nuanced to lend themselves to clear-cut "yes or no" propositions. Divestment "by fiat" was too "problematic." His committee's role was to gather and then respect opinion, while never imposing one point of view on another. He felt that Queen's should "avoid infringing on the freedom of opinion of the members of the university community, and should refrain from publicly condemning others."[19] Such dialogue would serve to "mitigate the situation," but probably not resolve it. (Over time, Broadbent came to see the challenge of weighing the pros and cons of divestment as "insoluble." Indeed, the social-responsibility committee became a hot-potato assignment on the Queen's Board. When trustee Donna Scott, publisher of Flare magazine, teasingly asked Broadbent: "how do I get off your committee?" Broadbent told her to "join the line."[20]) The AMS, at least initially, tended to agree with Broadbent's commitment to openness and dialogue: "We realize that the issue, far from being a 'black-and-white' one, is fraught with grey areas."[21]

Despite such seeming harmony, the situation soon became polarized and politicized. In the United States, the annual meetings of companies with South African operations became tempestuous affairs, with shareholder activists demanding complete divestment on moral grounds. In April 1982, for instance, Queen's social-responsibility committee decided to support IBM management in the face of an unsuccessful shareholder resolution calling for a withdrawal from South Africa. Broadbent and his colleagues based their decision on the fact that IBM conformed to the Sullivan guidelines in South Africa and a belief that IBM's presence in the republic was in fact helping to boost the black worker's lot. Many supported their decision. An Arts '56 graduate now teaching at Western wrote to the *Alumni Review*, arguing that a sale of Queen's holdings in South Africa would "only create black unemployment and hunger and drive blacks into the arms of Soviet-oriented revolutionaries." Another letter to the *Review*, this one from a recently graduated mining engineer working in Namibia, suggested that "South Africa needs guidance from countries like Canada, not a slap on the wrist. By divesting in companies that operate in South Africa Queen's will be harming the very people they wish to aid."[22]

Beyond citing such justifications of the status quo, the Board also trotted out the more practical argument that, in 1980–81, the endowment portfolio had generated $3.5 million in income, money that was farmed out to vital functions, such as student assistance, computing upgrades, and even subsidization of the McGill-Queen's University Press. In short, the Board continued to see oversight of the university endowment as its prerogative. It would consult and listen, but in the final analysis it would act in what it construed as the university's best interest. When an angry student wrote to accuse the Board of toeing a corporate line, trustee Alfred Bader responded firmly, pointing out that the Board had never been intended to be "representative" of student opinion, only "sensitive" to it. As a businessman, he too argued that foreign direct investment flowing into South Africa was actually "bettering" the lives of black Africans.[23]

Not everybody saw the issue of divestment in such positive terms. Debate over South Africa was percolating across Canada. South African wines were being boycotted. Sports visits were cancelled. In Ottawa, anti-apartheid pressure was growing and would culminate in mid-decade when Prime Minister Brian Mulroney forcefully imposed economic sanctions on the republic. Many Queen's students and faculty shared this impatience for decisive action. The *Journal* complained that "a stop-and-go game is the rule in the issue of social responsibility at Queen's."[24] An AMS-funded seminar in October 1982 was addressed by Yusuf Saloojee, the African National Congress's representative in Canada. Saloojee called for total divestment.

Another referendum was held in the spring of 1983, and once again a majority (58.8 per cent on a meagre 2-per-cent turnout) called for Queen's to exit South Africa. The AMS vice-president for university affairs (the new designation for the old commissioner post) David Duff became the chief prophet of divestment, organizing a group styling itself the Kingston Anti-Apartheid Coalition. Under his guidance, the AMS published a pamphlet entitled "South Africa: You Can Make a Difference." Duff, a political-studies student, then produced an accusatory ninety-eight-page recounting of Queen's whole approach to divestment. The Broadbent committee pointed out that Duff often played fast and loose with the facts, but this did nothing to calm the increasingly hostile tone of the debate. Its May 1983 report to the Board reiterated its belief that the university should simply aim to "influence" corporate behaviour. To become activist would entail "infringing on the freedom of opinion of the members of the university community." Some agreed. One student wrote to the *Journal*, saying that divestment had become a politically correct "witch hunt" that was stoking campus discord but doing little to help poverty-stricken people in distant lands. It was all too "simplistic." He closed by suggesting that "the AMS launch a campaign against pizzerias that serve Chilean anchovies."[25] The *Whig-Standard* thought otherwise. The Queen's committee's call for balance and influence, it felt, was in fact a "recipe for inaction." The Board should, the paper argued, respect the will of the people and divest.

Testiness increasingly marked the divestment debate, further polarizing the campus. When law professor Stuart Ryan, long an outspoken advocate of matters of social equity, wrote to the Board, accusing it of taking profits from oppression, Alan Broadbent replied that his committee was confident that all Queen's investments in South African met the Sullivan criteria. To drive home his point, Broadbent enclosed a clipping from the *New York Times* – an article by a prominent American economist entitled "Beware the Well-intentioned," which argued that the best of liberal intentions could drive poor black South Africans out of their livelihoods.[26] Broadbent similarly told the AMS education commissioner that his committee had developed "an appropriate analytical framework" that respected human rights while at the same time ensuring the university's well-being. The social-responsibility committee continued holding open meetings to air out the debate, but the rhetoric was becoming predictably repetitive. "Fence sitting statements are not enough," one exasperated alumnae wrote. "For the sake of justice, *do* something."[27]

Preserving the Fabric of Queen's

This was the mood of the campus when David Smith – himself the son of an overseas missionary and husband of a United Church minister – became principal in the summer of 1984. Smith was also a labour economist, whose inclination was always to seek rational solutions to complex problems. Such a solution on the divestment issue would, however, prove elusive; emotion and rationality seldom mingled well. Two years later, Smith would confess to the Senate that divestment had caused him "greater personal concern" than any other issue during his principalship.[28] He shared the universal sentiment on Queen's campus that apartheid was an "evil," but he doubted whether outright divestment would in any way correct South Africa's abhorrent racism. Forced divestment brought on by one concerted group, he also worried, would set the dangerous precedent of letting one viewpoint have suzerainty over all others on a campus where diversity of opinion was supposed to be the norm.

As principal, Smith had also to look beyond the philosophical landscape and be mindful of the ongoing cohesiveness and collegiality of the Queen's community. His wife, Mary, recalls many a sleepless night as her husband wrestled with what increasingly seemed the insoluble problem of divestment. Smith's primal anxiety was that "the fabric of the university would only take so much stress and strain, and once you passed that point, you're in danger of ripping the social fabric of the university, and when that happens, you're doing more damage [than good]."[29]

The pressure proved relentless. The AMS established a working committee dedicated to keeping divestment top-of-mind on campus, as did the Graduate Students' Society. With the trustees standing firm on divestment, the AMS committee explored other anti-apartheid options. A referendum asked students to approve a fee to bring South African students to study at Queen's – 64 per cent approved. When the Board met, students mounted an information picket outside Richardson Hall, handing out leaflets calling for a pullout from South Africa. The AMS Assembly endorsed all these initiatives.[30] Faculty echoed the effort. Since their only access to the Board of Trustees was through its social-responsibility committee, faculty sought to bring the issue before the Senate. In 1986, for instance, Professor Merlin Donald of psychology wrote to Smith to argue that the Senate was "the only body which is truly representative of the university community," and therefore should be the crucible of the divestment debate. The Senate's agenda committee disagreed, saying the issue did not "directly affect the [academic] operation of the university."[31] Donald retorted that here was "a blurring of responsibility" between the Senate and the Board and that the Board could not claim the power to dictate what was and was not in the best interest of the university.

There was no precise way of knowing just how representative of the whole student or faculty population at Queen's these voices of opposition were. What was undeniable, by 1986, was that there was determined and persistent substantial minority opinion against apartheid at Queen's. That May, the Board devoted an entire day to the issue. By now, cracks were appearing in its consensus. Trustee Helen Cooper was joined by then-rector Richard Powers in moving that the university divest itself of all its South African holdings. Cooper praised the persistence and moral rectitude of the student divestment campaign and urged her colleagues on the Board to cease seeing the issue as one of "financial integrity." Powers said that he had "never seen an issue attract such widespread support at Queen's ... these future graduates were speaking now." AMS President Jim Hughes, who had observer status at Board meetings, chimed in. Queen's, he said, was profiting from the immorality of apartheid. Divesting would make a strong public statement about Queen's values and would satisfy the call for support from black leaders in South Africa. The Graduate Students' Society threatened to withhold its pledge to the Queen's Appeal.

Despite sensing the hardening of opinion, Alan Broadbent reiterated that his committee had been monitoring the issue for five years and was still against "total divestment." Richard Stackhouse, as chair of the Board's finance committee, argued that divestment would lower Queen's investment inflow at a time when the university was in deficit. Other Board members worried that divestment was politicizing the Board and pulling it away from equally pressing issues relating to the future of the university. If the Board gave in to this pressure, they fretted, what might be next – a debate on the morality of nuclear weapons?

In the midst of this growing rancour, Principal Smith felt swelling unease. Queen's storied ability to find consensus and act collegially seemed to be disintegrating on his watch. Nevertheless, he made one more attempt to find the middle ground. Addressing the Board, he began by commending the students and faculty who had so ardently brought the issue before the university. First, Smith, donning his economist's hat, noted that the stakes were not high: income from Queen's investment in eighteen South Africa–active companies totalled only about $7,500 a year. The university's holdings were "miniscule." Queen's had, he pointed out, divested itself of its one holding (Dominion Textiles) that had not willingly subscribed to the Sullivan principles. To divest the rest would have an "insignificant, if not perverse" impact – perverse because the shares might be bought up by investors who cared nothing for human rights. Smith went on to point out that only two of Canada's seventy-nine colleges and universities had divested their South African investments, and that only four top-tier universities in the United States had done so. Queen's could, he argued, show leadership by retaining its shares and using its proxies to discipline companies in South Africa. That would give Queen's a "voice" in a significant way. Divestment was the "easier way out." Members of the Queen's community would be better advised to act as *individuals*, rather than adopting a collective course of action that not all would find ethically palatable. He quoted University of Chicago president Hannah Gray: "I do not believe that the university should be the surrogate for our taking action as individuals in the public forum." With that, the Board voted on Helen Cooper's divestment motion, defeating it twenty-two to nine. Smith abstained. The Board then unanimously passed a motion condemning apartheid. The debate that Saturday had lasted four and a half hours. Significantly, core support for divestment came from Board members most closely tied to Queen's students and Kingston – Councillor Cooper, Mayor John Gerretsen, former mayor George Speal, the rector, and *Whig-Standard* publisher Michael Davies.[32]

Even though spring-term classes were over, reaction to the Board vote came quickly and angrily. Proponents of divestment vigorously countered the Board's arguments for retention, one alumnus describing them as "sanctimonious crap" and another saying she would never give money to Queen's

Kingston *Whig-Standard* publisher Michael Davies (BA 1959): Queen's and Kingston had a long-standing relationship. Many Kingston mayors and councillors had Queen's degrees. Davies sat on the Board of Trustees and frequently voiced his dissatisfaction with "instant traditions," such as heedless orientation practices that blighted town-gown relations.

again.[33] By late summer, Principal Smith was agonizing over how the acrimony might be calmed. He began drafting a long "report" to the trustees, recounting the genesis of the divestment debate. It was probably the most heartfelt document he wrote during his tenure in Richardson Hall. With a draft of the report in hand, Smith addressed the first Senate meeting of the fall term, again setting out his thoughts on the complexity of the situation. The Senate, however, was not in a discursive mood. Michelle Lally, a student senator from Arts and Science and AMS commissioner for university affairs, upbraided the principal, saying that pressure through educational seminars and proxy voting would never budge apartheid. This was a moral issue, plain and simple. Others tried to support Smith. Dean Rod Fraser spoke of the "impossibility of being a purist about divestment" and warned of the danger of cleaving the Senate by forcing a minority to vote against the majority. However, when Lally moved that the Senate endorse divestment, the vote carried twenty-eight to nineteen. Smith said that he would report the result to the trustees.

The October 1986 meeting of the trustees brought further tumult. On the Friday evening,

Smith tabled his now-completed report, *Queen's and South Africa: A Report to the Board of Trustees*, and asked the Board if it would reconsider its May decision to shun divestment. He stated that he hoped for a "closer consensus" of Queen's opinion. He said that he had received 1,200 mail-in cards from students, calling for divestment. The trustees balked, preferring to trust the judgment of the social-responsibility committee. As soon as this inclination became clear, a noisy group of about sixty protesters flooded into the Collins Room and announced that they would stage a sit-in. Board chair Walter Light reluctantly adjourned the meeting, leaving the protesting students to occupy the senators' seats and to stage a mock board meeting.* When the Board reconvened on Saturday morning, trustee George Speal said that there was no avoiding the "ground swell" of student opinion on the issue around Kingston. Nonetheless, the Board reaffirmed its willingness to trust the judgment of the social-responsibility committee and then turned to a rather unfocused debate on improving communications with students.[34]

---

*University Secretary Alison Morgan was left as the only university administrator in the Collins Room after the trustees adjourned their meeting and hastily vacated the room. The situation was tense and uneasy. The protestors went through the motions of deliberating as a mock Senate meeting, castigating apartheid. Morgan, however, adeptly managed to enlist the good will of the occupiers by asking them to help tidy up the room, which they willingly did – a Queen's version of the famous "Stockholm syndrome," when captors and captives merge their sensitivities. After that, with little else to do, the protestors departed.

Divesting in the Interests of Harmony

The issue festered through the winter of 1986–87. Smith reported back to the Senate, candidly admitting his "frustration and uncertainty about the steps now open to them." He confessed his anxiety that divestment would set a terrible precedent in the governance of Queen's, one that would permanently restrict "free intellectual inquiry and expression." The *Whig-Standard* praised Smith's "amazing self-control." Alan Broadbent's social-responsibility committee continued to try to build a bridge with the Senate and the student body, but could only report that it encountered "frustration and dissatisfaction with the vote of the Board of Trustees" against divestment and a simmering sense among students that the Board was high-handed and oblivious to student wishes. The faculty association, QUFA, already in testy negotiation with the administration over salaries, voiced its backing of divestment. A referendum showed that almost 60 per cent of voting faculty supported divestment. Queen's had never seen a campus standoff of such intransigence and duration.[35] Any sense of student and faculty deference to the trustees' authority seemed to have evaporated. Divestment was also tending to transfix all other strategic matters facing the university. Smith's anxiety over rending the fabric of the university intensified.

In September, the tension broke. While he never lost his belief that working with corporations from within offered the most effective means of curbing the evil of apartheid, Alan Broadbent realized that the time had come for pragmatism. The Senate's vote for divestment, he confided to Smith, posed a deadly danger to Queen's ingrained culture of bi-cameral governance. If trust was lost between the bricks-and-mortar authority of the trustees and the academic jurisdiction of the Senate, Queen's would risk an acrimonious paralysis. At the September meeting of the trustees, Broadbent announced that his committee was now prepared to support divestment from South Africa – it had become the only collegial course to take. "In my view," he told his Board colleagues, "the faculty are the centre of the university. You cannot have a good university without good faculty." Harmony on campus trumped all else, even if it meant chilling academic freedom on campus. Smith reluctantly agreed. Other Board members admitted that the "wearing and divisive" debate had ground them into submission and that the university must move on, regardless of philosophical considerations. When Helen Cooper once again moved her motion for divestment, the trustees surrendered their long-held position and voted nineteen to five to divest. Within a year, Queen's had stripped all South African exposure out of its endowment portfolio.[36]

AMS president Anthony Carty told the *Journal* that he was "elated," but dismayed that some trustees had voted simply to "just get rid of the issue." In the same issue, James McHugh, a doctoral student in political science, expressed his admiration of the new-found student élan at the university. Queen's, he said, had a proud tradition of collegiality, but had now recognized that "there are things in this world more important than serene institutional relations and social conformity in the interests of the 'Queen's spirit.'"[37] What had begun in Chile and ended in South Africa represented a fundamental adjustment of the balance of governance at Queen's. The old deference shown the Board of Trustees could no longer be automatically expected. Queen's students, backed by faculty, had asserted a new active citizenship. And they had done so by working *within* the established consensual norms of governance at Queen's.

What had been initiated in 1968 with the election of the first student senators had now reached fruition in a concerted campaign to interrogate the central moral and pedagogic purposes of the university. Deference had been fully replaced by critical inquiry and discourse. Student dissatisfaction over investment in countries with dubious moral legitimacy found voice and tactics that eventually provoked corrective action, however symbolic it might have been. Unlike the handful of student "radicals" at Queen's in the sixties, with their call to eradicate capitalism and its lackeys in the Collins Room of Richardson Hall, the eighties divestment crusaders had asserted their right to inclusion in university decision making, thereby changing the policies of the institution, and not the institution itself. Divestment had brought forth a new empowered citizenship in Queen's students, particularly in many student leaders who sought to shape their fellow students' commitment to the institution where they studied and the world that lay beyond graduation.

"Cultivating a Courteous and Gentlemanly Demeanour"

The divestment controversy emphasized the ability of the Queen's community in the 1980s and early 1990s to engage in a constructive, socially responsible dialogue. Paradoxically, the same years saw the emergence of socially destructive, anti-social behaviour spawned in first-year orientation and transmitted through raucous Homecoming street parties, beery weekend behaviour, and slovenly housekeeping in the student apartment district adjacent to the university, behaviours which corroded Queen's once copasetic relations with the city that surrounded it. "Town and gown" relations in these years shed their once quaint, peaceable aura and became the subject of friction and acrimony among students, university administrators, and often-irritated local citizens. Problems were readily apparent, but solutions would prove elusive. At root, the deterioration of town-and-gown relations reinforced the realization that Queen's was no longer the well-regulated, introverted, and cohesive community it had seemed for so long, but had in fact come to reflect the fragmented, atomized, and multi-layered Canadian society that lay beyond its boundaries. The border between college and community now existed on many levels, often overlapping and sometimes blurring. Negotiating that border required Queen's to chart new norms of behaviour and new mechanisms of control and acculturation among its students.

Town-gown relations have a very long lineage in western civilization. Very few other aspects of university life – the institution of tenure, perhaps – have been so long-lived. From the outset, universities were communities within communities. One thinks of Plato's academy, embedded within the walls of Athens. By medieval times, the presence of scholarly enclaves nestled in the midst of larger communities was widely accepted in cities such as Padua, Cambridge, Oxford, Bologna, Salamanca, and Paris. While these early universities looked upon the communities that surrounded them as a kind of protection, at the same time they zealously asserted the right to conduct their own affairs, often under the protection of the church or the monarch. Hence, the tradition of wearing an academic *gown* as a kind of uniform materialized to provide outward differentiation of scholars from townsfolk. Similarly, newcomers to the university – "freshmen," a term used as early as the 1590s at Cambridge – were ritualistically initiated into the privileges and distinct culture of their new alma mater, so as to perpetuate the distinction between scholar and "townie." From medieval times, freshmen were subjected to a "rush" (a word denoting a scrimmage between new college entrants and their second-year, or sophomore, mentors) to orient them to their new world of privilege.

Such differentiation inevitably led to tensions. Town-gown relations were by their very nature symbiotic. The "townies" thrived off the daily commerce generated by the scholars, while scholars benefited from the infrastructure of the adjacent town. But that delicate chemistry could easily go septic. Each party could readily find reason to resent the other – the cocky, entitled behaviour of young scholars rubbing up against the prerogatives of local property and commerce. Sometimes the results were spectacular: in 1355, an argument in an Oxford tavern erupted into a two-day running street battle that saw killing and destruction of property. The so-called

Queen's maintained many convivial ties with the city that surrounded it. Each winter Queen's students participated in heritage hockey (right) on the harbour ice in front of City Hall. On the inner harbour, Queen's students combined with local oarsmen at the Kingston Rowing Club under the guidance of coach John Armitage (opposite left). Kingstonians could also tune into Studio Q, the weekly student-produced cable television show (opposite right).

Battle of St Scholastica Day would come to typify a persistent theme of town-gown relations – to wit, the destabilizing combination of adolescent hormones and alcohol. The periodic collision of *gaudeamus igitur* and notions of local respectability and property ownership have provoked endless efforts to regularize and regulate town-gown relations: codes of conduct and jurisdictional boundaries have been drawn up over the centuries. But the instability inherent in having two starkly different cultures in close proximity has usually defied such attempts at normalization.

In its early years, Queen's conformed closely to this pattern of symbiosis. Local burghers and Church of Scotland ministers eagerly pressed for the establishment of a college within their environs. A college would flatter their material ambitions as Kingston vied for provincial dominance with its Lake Ontario rival, Toronto. At the same time, a college would satisfy the strongly-felt desire for denominational acknowledgment of Presbyterians in the face of the colony's "established" Anglican Church. Once chartered, Queen's College sought to assert its autonomy, establishing its precinct on two-and-a-half hectares of land in Lot 24 on the outskirts of the town. In 1860, for instance, the Queen's Senate mandated that all professors and students go about their academic duties in black gown and cap. The young college construed its suzerainty over its student body seriously, seeing itself as acting *in loco parentis*, endowing its Senate with the ultimate disciplinary authority over its student body. As early as 1850, Vice-Principal James Williamson, drew up a code of student conduct. Seven years later, the Senate instructed Williamson "to impress strongly on the students who are boarders the duties of cultivating a courteous and gentlemanly demeanour towards the families with whom they reside."[38]

Queen's took another step towards asserting some further control over its students in 1858: the students took charge of their own internal affairs under the umbrella of the Alma Mater Society. Out of this Magna Carta decision flowed a system of student self-discipline under the AMS Court, a student newspaper, and an annual cycle of student socialization that focused student culture around the college's tight campus. There were no fraternities at

Queen's. Fraternities were seen as notorious incubators of noxious civic behaviour. For instance, members of Yale's secretive Skull and Bones fraternity, founded in the 1830s, were notorious for their rite of "crooking" – winning campus kudos by heisting mementoes from town landmarks. Queen's "no fraternities" injunction had been upheld and given official sanction in the mid-1930s by the AMS Court when medical students attempted to assert a separate identity by affiliating with an American fraternity. The court, and a subsequent student referendum, crushed their ambitions.

A ban on fraternities did not, however, mean that Queen's students were civic angels. Most years, Halloween gave Queen's students an excuse to cause a ruckus in the neighbourhoods adjacent to the campus. Fences were toppled, effigies hung in trees, and costumes donned. Such revelry was usually passed off by Kingstonians as youthful hijinks. Throughout most of the year, Queen's students found themselves under the watchful eye of their boarding-house landladies, their professors, and, if some misdemeanour was deemed sufficiently deviant, the AMS Court or, ultimately, the university Senate. In nineteenth-century Kingston, taverns abounded. Intoxication on a downtown street could bring judgment from the Senate on a student for offending "moral propriety and good discipline."[39] On the whole, Queen's evolved along self-regulated, inward-looking lines. The city remained at arm's length, allowing the university a wide measure of autonomy. Kingston occasionally signalled its pleasure at having an institution of higher learning within its boundaries. In 1903, for instance, the city underwrote the cost of the New Arts Building on the Lower Campus, a building thereafter known as Kingston Hall.

For its part, the campus provided Kingstonians with a venue for cultural events, such as musical concerts in Grant Hall and the annual Dunning Trust lectures. By the 1950s, the city had initiated a tradition of generously contributing to Queen's fundraising campaigns. Local citizens – such as the Abramsky, Etherington, Connell, Carruthers, and Rosen families – echoed this generosity by financing buildings and academic activities. City councillors and mayors were elected to sit on the Board of Trustees to give voice to city concerns. Queen's reciprocated. Economist Clifford Curtis, an urban planner by training, served as Kingston mayor from 1948 to 1952. In 1952 English professor James Roy supplied the city with a readable history of itself, *Kingston: The King's Town*. Roy's rambling narrative linked Queen's and its host community in many ways – from the annual productions of the Faculty Players to the illicit ministrations of local bootleggers like Barriefield's colourful "Dollar Bill." On other occasions, Queen's lent its talents and facilities to the broader community. When Kingston celebrated its tercentenary in 1973, Queen's art conservators refurbished the art collection in City Hall. Three years later, Queen's residences were used to house Olympic sailors who were competing at nearby Portsmouth harbour. Queen's students displayed similar engagement. In the sixties, students undertook outreach programs to address the problem of poverty and inadequate housing in North Kingston; in the seventies a Student Volunteer Bureau connected students with the day-to-day requirements of Kingstonians in need of social support.

Economic Symbiosis

The bottom line of the Queen's-Kingston partnership was undeniably economic. Queen's was a big spender, rivalled only by Kingston's sprawling military base and a few large industrial employers such as Alcan and DuPont. The campus had a direct impact on the local economy through its spending on construction, ongoing maintenance, provisions, and real-estate acquisition. In 1969, for instance, Principal Deutsch supplied the City Commissioner of Industries with the welcome news that Queen's spending on new buildings would total $48 million over the next five years. The prospective health-sciences centre, he suggested, would add another $80 million. By 1975, Principal Watts estimated that $65 million of Queen's annual budget of $90 million trickled down into the local economy.[40] Money from Queen's also percolated into the local economy through the spending of wages by faculty and administrative staff, not to mention the impact of a relatively well-paid labour force on Kingston's real-estate market. Further economic momentum was added by students living in the community; by 1975, Watts estimated that 60 per cent of Queen's students lived at large in the Kingston community, spending money on food, rent, and entertainment each year.*

---

*As a student in Arts '72, the author recalls the standing belief at the time that Kingston was the only city in Ontario where sales at the local beer and liquor stores actually went *down* in the Christmas season.

Precisely measuring Queen's economic impact on Kingston did not receive intensive investigation until the 1990s. In 1994, Ken Snowdon, the university's chief resource planner, reported to the trustees that Queen's total spending in the local economy was $316.6 million. When economic multipliers (that is, the ripple effect of each dollar spent) were added into the equation, that impact swelled to $500 million. Queen's students, Snowdon estimated, pumped almost $110 million into the local community, while faculty and staff spent another $117 million in Kingston. An AMS report three years earlier – "Limestone and Learning" – had reached much the same conclusion as had Kingston city planners, who believed that Queen's "was the heart of the future of the Kingston economic base."[41]

A relationship of such magnitude was not without its frictions. With the high concentration of academic, military, and governmental activity within its borders, Kingston suffered from an unusually high level of tax exemption on publicly owned properties. The city therefore argued that it was being persistently shortchanged and underfinanced. In 1970, Mayor Val Swain told the provincial treasurer that the situation was "intolerable." Furthermore, the city alleged that even those taxes the university did pay – on its non-academic facilities – suffered from lagging assessment values, and therefore the university was annually paying less and less of its fair share in supporting municipal operations. Queen's was sympathetic to the city's case, acknowledging, that, if the province wanted a university system, it could not burden host communities unduly. Except, Queen's immediately added, the money could not come out of the university's nearly empty pockets. This impasse was eventually overcome by the introduction of a system of provincial payments to municipalities in lieu of taxes – the so-called "heads and beds" tax. Thus, for every full-time student attending Queen's, the city would receive a compensatory annual stipend from the province. In 1987, this was set at $75 per student. Equitable in its design, the system was vulnerable to inflation and political

A cartoon from the 6 March 1968 issue of the *Queen's Journal* reflects students' sense of entitlement in Kingston. A small provincial city, Kingston depended heavily on the economic input of military and academic spending, something that tended to give some students a sense of unbridled licence in their day-to-day behaviour.

neglect – no change in the amount per student has been made from that year down to the present.

There were also periodic inflammations of relations with the city when Queen's students sowed their wild oats beyond the campus. The city generally took these incidents in good humour, understanding that bouts of adolescent turmoil were a small price to pay for the larger benefit of a money-making institution like Queen's in its midst. When, for instance, medical students dislodged the two Britannic lions from the fountain outside the Frontenac Courthouse, the university paid $500 to the city for their restoration.[42] In 1974, the university and city established a standing liaison committee to help identify and channel mutual problems. Since the late sixties, the trustees and city council had hosted annual exchange visits to open friendly lines of communication – what Mayor Val Swain liked to call "fraternization." The university's de facto jurisdiction over its campus (except in areas of criminal justice) was respected by the city. Constables of the AMS, the AMS Court for student misdemeanours, and the Senate grievance procedures were left to oversee the communal life of the campus. In 1974, Principal Watts established a protocol with Kingston's chief of police governing any emergencies on campus – telephone alerts would be given to senior university administrators before police were dispatched. And, as if to stoke the fire of friendship, an annual city-student dinner, attended by AMS and city officials, was staged every year.

Within this relationship, Queen's developed an essentially introverted communal culture. Student life revolved around the fast-expanding residence precinct. Students living off campus came to campus not only for their classes, but also for their recreation and diversion. Within this cocoon of culture, Queen's built a remarkably hermetic society that for decades had only passing impact on the Kingston community that surrounded it. Within this culture, Queen's conducted an annual cycle of events, ranging from fall football games to the annual winter Snowball with minimal impact on the Kingston community.

The two most-structured and intensive events on this calendar were the September orientation of freshman and the late-fall alumni reunion. Orientation encapsulated the transmission of tradition at Queen's: the inoculation of newcomers with the serum of traditional ways. Its label had changed over the years from "rushing," to "hazing" to, by the sixties, the more innocuous "orientation." Over time, the university had tweaked orientation to temper it to the tenor of the times; in the early sixties, the Senate had, for instance, instructed the faculties to moderate the "violence" of their initiations – the throwing of engineering frosh into Lake Ontario came to an end. Through all this, the city saw and heard relatively little of orientation. During orientation week, frosh might be loosed on the town as shoe-shine fundraisers and clean-up volunteers, and, occasionally, on scavenger hunts.

Since the mid-1920s, Queen's had also hosted an annual autumn reconnection with its alumni. American universities had staged "homecomings" since the mid-nineteenth century, and now, as Canadian universities grew, the tradition crossed the border. Like orientation, the central purpose of alumni reunions was the passing on of the faith. Queen's graduates were invited back to their alma mater not only to reconnect with their classmates but also to mingle with the current crop of undergraduates. The old would transmit tradition to the young, but at the same time the young would connect bygone generations with the changing face of Queen's. This peculiar chemistry of noblesse oblige and adolescent exuberance was neatly contained *within* the campus boundaries. Richardson Stadium and Grant Hall anchored the weekend. Framed against the fall beauty of eastern Ontario, the weekend's highlight was always the football game that saw the Gaels pitted against one of their perennial rivals – McGill, the University of Toronto, or Western. Around the Saturday-afternoon match were arrayed a Saturday-morning parade that allowed year societies to salute the alumni; a principal's post-game tea; a Saturday-evening dinner; and a Sunday-morning church service in Grant Hall. Undeniably, the weekend was never exactly a tea party – stronger beverages usually found their way into Richardson Stadium and many a hotel room or student apartment, but the overall demeanour was convivial, affirmative, and controlled. When advertising executive and Commerce '58 grad Laird O'Brien returned to Queen's for his class reunion in 1985, he caught the mood of it all: "Reunions are celebrations of nostalgia … a strange and not always comfortable blending of today and yesterday, a groping for connections to the past while laden with the baggage of today."[43]

Tectonic Shifts in Student Life

The equilibrium of student life at Queen's began to shift in the late sixties. One cannot pinpoint the precise moment when the equipoise faltered or quantify its magnitude. But, cumulatively, a number of factors served to dramatically alter student culture at Queen's over the next two decades. First and foremost, Queen's grew. From 1961 to the end of the century, the university experienced more growth than it had in its initial 120 years of its existence. By 1971, for instance, at almost ten thousand students, Queen's was three times the size it had been a decade earlier. Given Queen's highly regarded reputation among graduating high-school students, the pace of growth slackened little through the remaining decades of the century. Queen's consciously tried to moderate its enrolment growth, usually managing to hold its expansion below that of most Ontario universities. Nonetheless, by the year 2000, total enrolment had surged to 17,773.

Such growth had two immediate implications. First, it strained Queen's original campus with its rigid boundaries to breaking point. More students posed the dual challenge of building additional academic facilities and expanding residence capacity. Over the rest of the century, the trustees wrestled with the dilemma of shoehorning new buildings into rapidly depleting geography. Academic and residential needs squeezed out recreational space. The old football stadium and hockey arena disappeared. To alleviate the pressure, the West Campus was developed in the 1970s, but its very nature bifurcated Queen's once-cohesive landscape. Home to the education faculty and site of the new football stadium and new residences, the West Campus never formed a communal tie with the main campus culture. Those on main campus came to regard their western campus confreres as distant cousins.

Growth in size also unavoidably made life at Queen's a more anonymous experience. The old coziness faded. An anonymity crept into student life; for instance, by the 1990s, registration each fall was done by computer rather than by queuing in a jostling lineup with one's future classmates. Queen's expansion to over seventeen thousand students also diversified the campus population. The forced growth of graduate studies after the sixties introduced a large cohort of students who had generally never bonded with the university as its undergraduates had done. Graduate students were often married and focused on specialized professionalized studies, and were inclined to different leisure pursuits than undergraduates. In 1962, Queen's graduate students had formed their own society, which coexisted uneasily within the AMS until 1981, when graduate students in a referendum voted to secede from the AMS. Graduate students resented paying activity fees geared to undergraduate passions (to support intercollegiate sports, for instance), nor did they always share the AMS's enthusiasm for affiliation with national student organizations. In 1976, graduate students, for instance, opened their own pub at the corner of Union and Barrie streets.

There were also jurisdictional problems: did graduate students come under the sway of AMS constables? This differentiation was more keenly felt by Queen's law students, who saw little affinity with undergraduate agendas. In 1998, the Law Students' Society also separated from the AMS in acrimonious fashion. (The departure of the law students immediately deprived the AMS of a ready source of budding legal talent for AMS Court hearings.) Graduate and law students subsequently banded together in the Society of Graduate and Professional Students in 1998 and began offering services better tailored to their more-mature interests. The Grad Pub, for example, continues to be a convivial point of graduate student socialization at Queen's.

The diversification of Queen's student demographics was accompanied by geographic dispersal. The old campus simply could not contain the university's surging population. New residences – Victoria, Gordon-Brockington, Acton, to name a few – managed to soak up the annual flood of first-year students, but upper-year students increasingly migrated off campus into rental accommodation within walking distance, usually in Sydenham Ward immediately to the north and east. Most rented apartments; the old boarding houses faded as students embraced a more independent lifestyle. The old turn-of-the-century Queen Anne–style houses of Sydenham Ward lent themselves to subdivision into apartments, so that soon streets such as

The birth of the Ghetto. Throughout the 1970s, Queen's growing student population spilled into Sydenham Ward to its north and east. On many blocks, students quickly came to outnumber Kingstonian homeowners, as an adolescent rental culture emerged. The area acquired the label of "the Ghetto," possibly in emulation of the sprawling student suburb to the east of McGill University.

Frontenac, Alfred, and University lost their sedate residential character and became bustling off-campus dormitory areas for university students.

The fulcrum of this transition came when student rentals started to outweigh established family residences. Like any neighbourhood where one demographic group became preponderant, the character of the areas around Queen's began to change. Although the AMS had introduced a "Bus-It" system, funded by a student fee, to provide year-round, ticketless bus ridership, hoping the students would move deeper into the city, the students themselves preferred the convenience of walking to campus, and continued to settle in Sydenham Ward. Sometime in the 1970s, students began to refer to the streets immediately north of the campus in Sydenham Ward as "the student Ghetto." As the usage of the term emerged in the pages of the *Journal*, in AMS minutes, and on the street, it was clear that the term "ghetto" was not in any way meant to be pejorative, but instead almost affectionate, as if to indicate that this is "our district." The cumulative effect of this dispersal was to diminish the long-standing introversion of campus life at Queen's. In effect, the border between university and city became fuzzy and variable.

As Queen's students increasingly assumed the identity of residential citizens in Kingston, other influences pushed them further away from the once powerfully conformist culture of their campus. As the number of female undergraduates grew – in 1975–76, females became the majority of Arts and Science undergraduates – so did the gender balance of the student population alter. At the same time, Queen's was beginning to reflect the swelling multicultural nature of Canadian society. *Oil Thigh* culture was thus no longer exclusively driven by male WASP values. The students of the late-twentieth century had been raised in baby-boom prosperity; by the 1990s their parents were likely to be second-generation baby boomers, accustomed to urban affluence and comfortably insulated by the welfare state. The 1982 Charter of Rights and Freedoms had capped the demise of the once-pervasive and powerful *in loco parentis* culture that had seen university students placed under the watchful eye of administrators and deans. Students were now full citizens with inalienable rights.

This sense of entitlement quickly permeated Canadian student society. University students were courted by credit-card companies, were welcomed at the beer store, and were free to pursue whatever sexual orientation they wished. They also tended to be affluent. Although access to the Ontario Student Assistance Program (OSAP) was a matter of keen concern to many Queen's students (about 30 per cent of whom annually relied on such support), the university tended to attract well-heeled students who came to Kingston in the expectation of living "the good life" as students. As the saying went, "we're here for a good time, not a long time." While it is dangerous to generalize, residence in the Ghetto tended to loosen students' filial connection with Queen's. One went to campus for classes and study, but returned to the other world of the Ghetto, where life was unfettered.

This liberation was facilitated by a fundamental confusion about disciplinary jurisdiction over students who chose to live off campus. There had never been any doubt that any non-academic misbehaviour by a student taking place on campus fell under the purview of the AMS constables and AMS Court. (Academic infractions such as plagiarism were fed into a separate system that culminated in a Senate deliberation.) This demarcation became blurry when students moved into the Ghetto. There was an unexamined assumption that AMS authority did in fact extend off campus into the Ghetto or, indeed, into any precinct that could be loosely related to the life of the university, such as a football game in another city. The Kingston police generally obliged this assumption and proved reluctant to intervene in the Ghetto, preferring to believe that it was in fact an extension of university territory.

The Ghetto therefore, in particular, came to exist in a kind of grey jurisdictional zone, falling between two stools of authority. In effect, the swelling student community in the Ghetto existed ambiguously between academic and civic control. This was particularly true at a time when the AMS non-academic justice system was trying to cope with the phenomenon of students as fully-fledged citizens empowered by the Charter. Canadian society was becoming increasingly litigious – "my rights vs your rights" was the new ethos of citizenship. Students were no longer generally willing to slip into a deferential persona. Some began appearing before the AMS Court accompanied by outside counsel, who often quickly exposed the looseness of the AMS system of natural justice. Others short-circuited the whole campus-justice system by appealing directly to the Ontario

Human Rights Commission when their rights were perceived to be infringed upon by campus justice. While a 1988 case before the Supreme Court of Ontario had indicated that a university might be legally construed as "specific community," even when its members erred off campus, a 1990 joint review of student discipline by the AMS and the administration found that complex cases still confounded the imprecise nature of non-academic discipline. There was a danger, the panel concluded, that such cases might fall between jurisdictions where neither felt the confidence to usurp the other's authority.[44] Life in the Ghetto by the 1980s was tending in this direction.

Life in the Ghetto

This dilution of the old cohesiveness of Queen's was accentuated by the ease with which students could now leave Kingston for the lusher weekend fields of Toronto, Montreal, or even American cities to the south. The AMS again lived up to its pledge of providing better student services by offering "Tricolour Express" coaches each weekend to whisk students away from Kingston to visit home or friends in other cities. The once-centrifugal pull of the campus on students' social life thus declined. There were fewer dances and concerts; electronic entertainment could be had cheaper and more instantaneously at home in the Ghetto. Student pubs ceased to be the popular watering holes they had once been; AMS-run Alfie's became a perennial drain on student coffers. Students began to party in their apartments – it was less expensive and there were no AMS constables. Keg parties, fuelled by capacious, rented beer kegs, became prevalent.

At the same time, Queen's student culture became more porous. With better transportation and the dawn of social media, Queen's, and particularly the Ghetto, gained a reputation as a mecca of fun for local high-school students and even students from farther afield in pursuit of good times worthy of a beer commercial. By the late 1980s, Queen's was acquiring a reputation as a "party school." Linda Frum's much-read *Guide to Canadian Universities* said as much. So did Queen's law professor Mark Weisberg, who lived on Frontenac Street just north of campus. His street, he wrote to the Queen's principal, was a "mixed block," which had traditionally been "quiet, pleasant and neighbourly," but was now under siege by students. Thursday nights had become "drinking night," on which "a culture of alcohol and disrespect" reigned. Kingston police, he complained, were unresponsive to older residents' concerns. A resident of nearby Albert Street reported that young children were shocked by the spectacle of Queen's rugby players performing their "Zulu rite" on his lawn in their underwear. This part of Queen's "heritage," he concluded, had become a "criminal act," and he was therefore moving to the suburbs.[45]

The looser, rapidly transforming student culture of the late-twentieth century posed another threat to Queen's. At times, it defied the university's ongoing attempt to groom its image as one of Canada's leading national universities. Universities, like many other institutions in Canadian society, were learning to "brand" themselves and their values in the hope of attracting the cream of each year's high-school graduates, while at the same time putting alumni and potential donors in a generous frame of mind. Queen's had long enjoyed a readily identifiable brand across the nation – football, bands, Ottawa mandarins, and ivy-covered, limestone buildings – that had made recruitment and fundraising a matter of ease. Press reports of unseemly incidents and controversy on the Queen's campus in the late 1980s and 1990s tarnished this image. Headlines splashing the news that Queen's was now the site of unseemly controversy around feminist attempts to instill the message that "No Means No" and unruly keg parties catastrophically undermined the power of received tradition at Queen's. The dilemma lay in the fact that the inputs to the making of Queen's tradition were no longer as malleable as they had

The Ghetto quickly bred its own traditions, particularly on weekends. Patterns of behaviour incubated during first-year residence life – floor parties, late-night hijinks – blossomed in the unchaperoned ethos of the Ghetto. Given the student density in Sydenham Ward, Queen's acquired a reputation as a "party school."

once been. The university was now plagued with what Kingston publisher Michael Davies told the trustees were "instant traditions," traditions that were dysfunctional, in that they gnawed at the reputation of the university as a progressive and cohesive community.[46] Nowhere would this process be more evident than in the deterioration, and eventual correction, of orientation and Homecoming, two traditions which had by the eighties been pulled off their moorings by such instant traditions.

At a meeting of the Senate in early 1988, Principal Smith rather somberly told his colleagues that, in his mind, orientation was a central tradition of the university. It was the portal through which the majority of members of the Queen's community first encountered their alma mater. Orientation week, he believed, should involve all "estates of the university," including the Kingston community. Smith's comments triggered much discussion. Law dean John Whyte reminded the Senate that orientation was a "socialization" process. University chaplain Brian Yealland likened it to "an explosion of experience." One common theme emerged: orientation at Queen's had drifted away from its original, benign purpose. It had become, Yealland argued, an "indoctrination to a cult." Whyte agreed: orientation, for many, was now a "frightening" experience. Vice-president of the AMS Caroline Field concurred: orientation was creating a "mass mentality" that failed to help students orient themselves to their new university world.[47] Such comments became sadly typical during the waning decades of the century at Queen's. Orientation thus provides a telling example of yet another Queen's tradition that had drifted from its initial purpose and would subsequently have to be leveraged back onto its proper foundation.

Seeking a New Orientation in September

It was easy to identify what had gone wrong by the late 1980s. Orientation had become a kind of *Animal House* bacchanalia, which had little connection with the culture of the four years of study and residency that lay ahead at Queen's. To begin with, it overemphasized the group at the expense of the individual. Faculty rivalry permeated the week. Students were obliged to don distinctive garb colour-keyed to faculty – T-shirts, overalls, pseudo-kilts, and other such apparel. The Queen's tam (worn pulled down over the ears) was the only common item of apparel. From the moment students arrived on the Sunday of orientation week, they were taught to hurl abuse at students in other faculties. Within each faculty, students were divided into frosh-group subsets and put under the leadership of a second-year student – a Gael in Arts and Science, a Boss in Commerce, a FREC in Engineering, and so on. Chants and gestures mocked competing faculties, often in the crudest fashion. In many ways, such behaviour had reverted to the rough-and-tumble of 1920s "rushes" on campus, when students were baptized in mud and abuse.

Interfaculty rivalry culminated in the Tindall Field games, games predicated on out-shouting and out-pulling other faculties, while excelling in gross behaviour. Applied Science students bore the worst of all this: they were obliged to style their hair in outlandish colours and spiked, helmet-like mounds, wear demeaning costumes, and, climactically, plunge into the famous Barriefield grease pit. Sociologically, the purpose of all this was to diminish the sense of individuality and to build up group identity. Some revelled in it; many bore the trial in quiet humiliation and discomfort. University had been sold them as an opportunity to "find oneself," but the first week of that experience seemed to be dedicated to self-effacement and loss of individuality. Similarly, orientation seemed barren of any introduction to the academic challenges that lay ahead or the more mundane, but daily important, business of living in residence. Many students never met a professor until their first class in the week *after* orientation.

In its procrustean passion for group identity, orientation seemed oblivious to those on the margin who did not fit its predetermined trajectory. First-year students, many from Kingston itself, who were not destined to live in residence often found themselves as hangers-on. Others were sidelined by the cost of orientation – year societies collected several hundred dollars from each frosh to cover the week's activities. Given the strong heterosexuality of Queen's student life, incoming students who were gay or lesbian or simply wrestling with their sexual identity often felt ill-at-ease during orientation, some opting out completely. As AMS education commissioner Kam Rao (herself openly lesbian) noted in 1990: "Orientation ritualizes domination."[48] Adolescent sexual awakening permeated the week. Lewd slogans were scrawled onto T-shirts and overalls. Raunchy posters – "Kiss your virginity goodbye" – were draped over the main entrances of women's residences. Homophobic lyrics slipped into faculty chants – many could not resist the rhyming of "queer" and "engineer." And the week was awash in alcohol. For many freshmen, this was the first week of adult freedom, and it was easy to equate that freedom with unfettered access to beer and spirits, especially if second-year group leaders implied that this was the Queen's norm.

Perhaps one of the most insidious instant traditions to install itself in orientation was the frosh house party. Most Gaels, Bosses, and FRECs had themselves just made the transition from residence to apartment life in the Ghetto or elsewhere off campus. Their apartments represented sites of unbridled freedom. Thus, noisy, alcohol-fuelled exuberance spread off campus, much to the annoyance of local citizens, who now found their streets littered with broken glass and blighted by late-night revelry. In 1984, the Senate committee on non-academic discipline put its finger on the new pulse of off-campus living: students had quickly adopted the attitude that "the Ghetto area belongs to us and nobody is going to stop us from having a good time in our sphere of influence."[49]

By the mid-eighties, orientation had thus become very effective at transmitting anti-social, group-think attitudes – nineteen-year-old upper-class students transferred and legitimized dubious attitudes and behaviours to impressionable minions who were but a year younger. The fall of 1984 perhaps best illustrated the subversion of orientation at Queen's: a grease-pole disaster that sent scores to hospital, a campus festooned with lewd banners, and Dean of Women Elspeth Baugh complaining that "alcohol abuse in Victoria Hall had never been higher."[50] As history professor Geoff Smith suggested, the term began "with a party that continued for six weeks."[51] Indeed, the behaviour legitimized that September in orientation resurfaced late in September on Molson Field at McGill University, at the notorious "Kill McGill" riot.*

---

*It bears mention that, despite the growing dysfunction of Orientation Week, first-year newcomers to Queen's continued to be capable of altruism in the first days of their university life. Frosh conducted a "charity day," which saw them shining shoes on Princess Street. Engineering students sold peanuts door-to-door for good causes and offered their labour as Kamikaze Fix 'n' Clean Teams to Kingstonians.

Orientation has deep sociological roots in western universities. In the 1970s, it drifted away from its useful purpose of acculturating newcomers to the rhythms of academic life. Queen's orientation increasingly became a week-long bacchanalia of reckless self-indulgence that had little to do with productive communal and intellectual endeavour. The line between youthful exuberance and thoughtless behaviour was crossed.

By the mid-eighties, there seemed to be widespread consensus that orientation needed dramatic correction. The determination straddled town and gown. Whether viewed from the principal's office, from the desk of the AMS president, or from the City Council chamber, orientation was seen to have succumbed to an anti-social virus and needed an inoculation of new values. Sociologically, orientation offered a unique opportunity for social re-engineering. It had the characteristics of a controlled psychological experiment: a cohort of impressionable newcomers to an institution, naively willing – at least for their first, wide-eyed week on campus – to submit to the behaviours placed before them as acceptable by their mentors. Change the inputs, and future behaviour might be altered. The key would be to break the cycle, which saw bad tradition passed from one year to the next. As trustee (and future chancellor) Jim Leech perceptively noted: "Once a [negative] reputation like that of the Mariposa Festival or Fort Lauderdale was acquired it was hard to get rid of it."[52] So much of Queen's constructive tradition had been transmitted from undergraduate class to undergraduate class, and then transmitted back when frosh eventually became alumni and dispatched their offspring to Queen's or came back for Alumni Weekend. Now it was clear that this storied process could contain malevolent elements – for example, upper-class students (nicknamed "pseudos") bent on reliving their wild week of orientation with the next year's wave of freshmen.

Through the late 1980s, pressure for reform grew. Central to this push for change was a recognition that, while the purpose of orientation was university-centric, its delivery was a city-wide problem. Two people who were instrumental in driving this message home were Kingston mayors John Gerretsen (1980–88) and Helen Cooper (1988–93). In 1987, Gerretsen told the Board of Trustees that they must see orientation as a "shared problem" not a "city problem" that left city police and bylaw officers to tackle any student misdemeanours whenever they spilled over the campus boundary.⁵³ Cooper, a Sydenham Ward councillor during Gerretsen's tenure as mayor, was vigorous in her attempts to link the interests of the university and those of her constituents. Cooper calculated that 65 per cent of the people in her ward were students and feared that they had come to see orientation and its hijinks as "somewhat of a sacred cow" – a cow that her other constituents increasingly disliked.

From that flank, Cooper came under direct pressure from disgruntled citizens who coalesced into lobby groups such as the Sydenham Ward Ratepayers' Association and eventually STAND (Student Area Neighbourhood Development group). Cooper warned the trustees that the Kingstonians resented hearing anti-social behaviour during orientation being passed off as "Queen's spirit," a term she felt had "a very shallow meaning for much of the internal community and had connotations of arrogance for outsiders." The members of STAND agreed. The group bluntly informed the trustees that they were "blissfully unaware or wilfully blind to the mounting cost to both the university and the Kingston community" of student behaviour in their ward.⁵⁴ Both Gerretsen and Cooper worked hard to channel such discontent into constructive dialogue with Queen's leaders. In this, they were singularly fortunate to strike a liaison with a remarkable string of AMS presidents in the eighties, student politicians who shared the city's concern over the misguided evolution of orientation. AMS presidents such as Donna Finley, Barbie Grantham, Sue Rooks, John Lougheed, and Innes van Nostrand, to name a few, were willing to reach out to the city to alleviate crises and, more importantly, to adjust student behaviours through consultation. Other dialogues took place with city police in an effort to establish protocols around when the police would supersede campus authority in the Ghetto.

Establishing a New Orientation

Richardson Hall, the trustees, and the Senate willingly abetted these town-gown contacts. In 1988, the Senate Committee on Non-academic Discipline revamped its statement of non-academic discipline to emphatically disclaim the notion that AMS justice in any way overrode the law of the land. On or off campus, Queen's students could not consider themselves a law unto themselves. In the wake of the fall 1984 orientation debacle, the administration and the AMS agreed to create an Orientation Activities Review Board (OARB), with a joint student-faculty membership. It would oversee the tenor of each year's orientation by meeting late each fall to review the previous September's activities and to suggest constructive changes for the next year. The board's role was not punitive, but instead advisory, intended to nudge orientation organizers in each faculty to temper their activities and to focus them on adaptation to college life rather than on inculcating riotous habits. In its first report in the fall of 1985, the board praised Applied Science for a more orderly and injury-free grease pole, but scolded it for the abundance of alcohol at events such as the Thundermug race (a chaotic street chase using wheeled toilets), the scavenger hunt, and house crawls in the Ghetto. Kudos went to Arts and Science for bringing in humanitarian and former politician Stephen Lewis to speak at Grant Hall.⁵⁵ Paralleling the board's oversight, the administration launched a task force on alcohol awareness to investigate the often-volatile mix of students and drink. Should, for instance, large breweries be given exclusive rights to cater university social events?

The orientation week was tweaked in other respects. Frosh group-leaders were subjected to screening interviews and training sessions, eventually being obliged to sign contracts which stipulated their duties. Professors were encouraged to participate in the week; small groups of freshman were invited to informal dinners with faculty members.

An orientation "hotline" was established in 1989 to allow Kingstonians to file complaints about student behaviour. In 1990, a mini-course dubbed "Queen's 101" was introduced to give first-year arrivals a rounded appreciation of the university experience that lay ahead of them. At the same time, orientation began to devote the first days of a new Queen's student to the joys and obligations of living in residence. Eventually, Orientation Week itself was shortened by several days. The implacable uniformity of orientation was also broken. Alternative events were introduced to provide students less keen on group activities with alternatives. Efforts were made to draw students not living in residence into the orientation agenda. The Muslim Students' Association hosted frosh events for Muslim students. There was a "Wimmin's Frosh Week."

There were, however, no quick fixes for orientation. "It takes time to change traditions and attitudes," OARB chairman Dag Nyhof told the *Journal* late in 1986, "but we're working on it." There were still outbursts of obnoxious behaviour: boisterous house parties, homophobic chants, and trash on residential streets. From the outset, there had always been a division of opinion over how orientation reform should be tackled. There were hard-liners, such as *Whig-Standard* publisher Michael Davies, who advocated a tough-love approach and looked to the city to treat students as it would any other citizen. Change would only come through punitive action. After seven years in office as mayor, John Gerretsen by 1987 was inclined to believe tough rather than soft love was the solution: if people repeatedly break the law in the streets then the police should be called into action. After all, it was his municipal budget that absorbed the additional costs of policing orientation. It was Gerretsen who called for the shortening, by two or three days, of the orientation week, in the belief that the less time students had before classes began, the less mischief there would be. More prevalent, however, was the inclination to trust in the gradual effect of persuasion and education. Principal Smith and his colleagues in the Senate applied the well-worn Queen's formula of consultation, co-operation, and consensus. Over time, gradual reform would break the cycle of bad orientation and seed the beginnings of a new, more constructive, orientation. Open-house discussions, pamphlets, and sexual-awareness sessions and guidelines offered the best path to redemption.

By 1990, the philosophical split came to a head, perhaps because the horrendous "No Means No" crisis of the previous fall had demonstrated that sexist attitudes were proving very durable at Queen's. At a December 1990 Senate meeting, political-studies professor C.E.S. "Ned" Franks, long a participant in town-gown matters, voiced dismay over his observation that student behaviour had steadily declined at Queen's over the last fifteen years. "Piecemeal" action had, in his opinion, not stemmed the tide. "Direct action" was now needed. That direct action came in the form of a special committee report that had been set in motion by Principal Smith the preceding spring. Chaired by business professor Rick Jackson, the committee was stocked with contingents of students and university administrators, with students in the majority. Acknowledging that there were "no easy solutions or panaceas," the committee underscored the reality that what happened in frosh week often echoed through a student's entire university career. The report pulled no punches. Queen's "spirit" had been perverted by recent decades of orientation into something that was "unthinking, shallow, narcissistic, and arrogant." Little of the traditional altruism and public spirit for which Queen's was famous was evident in that first week on campus. Hedonism, scofflaw behaviour, and cult-like mindlessness instead prevailed. Graduates of orientation possessed an attitude of unbridled entitlement The Jackson Report emphasized the clear and present dangers still embedded in the week: excessive alcohol consumption might easily lead to deaths.

The Jackson Report prescribed strong medicine for the healing of orientation. Jackson urged that the week must place more emphasis on *university* life, as opposed to *faculty* rivalries – for example, welcoming the whole incoming cohort of undergraduates in one grand ceremony. Group leaders must drop the "best-buddy persona" with the frosh and adopt a more socially responsible role – no drinking on the job, for instance. Indeed, the FRECS, Gaels, and Bosses must treat their duties as a "job," with contractually defined duties and penalties for non-performance. At the same time, Kingston police should not hesitate to enforce city bylaws on the streets around the university. Orientation must be more inclusive, welcoming all student lifestyles. In true Queen's tradition, the Jackson Report urged Queen's students to become "stakeholders" in their own destiny. They must salvage what was good and decent in orientation and eliminate the flaws. If they engaged this challenge wholeheartedly, they might avoid "radical surgery" on a tradition that had roots stretching back into the nineteenth century.[56]

In the wake of all the bad press provoked by sexist signs on Leonard Field, the Jackson Report was eagerly debated by the AMS, the Board of Trustees, and the Senate. There was a willingness to endorse its recommendations so as to accelerate the pace of piecemeal reform already evident in the late eighties. And the pace of reform did pick up. The first days of orientation were devoted to the process of adjusting to life in residence, in the hope that residence would cease to be seen as nothing more than a bed, regular meals, and periodic eruptions of partying. More alternative programs were developed – a coffee house for conversation, for example. The Tindall Field games were made less belligerent and more downright fun. Overalls were still worn, but without lewd slogans scrawled on their bottoms. The grease pit contained less vile detritus and the frosh were now bombarded with softer projectiles, like marshmallows. (It was, some complained, now a "puppy pole.") The AMS also engaged Mayor Cooper's task force on city-university relations. And at the same time, the Senate established its own Orientation Activities Review Board to supersede the old OARB. In the fall of 1991, it reported "significant progress" had been made in that year's orientation. From City Hall, Mayor Cooper wrote that the university had done "a superb job in recognizing many of the very deeply rooted problems that had become so-called traditions in the past."[57]

In less than a decade then, Queen's had turned an errant tradition around and had not only repaired its values but also rebuilt its once-friendly and constructive relations with the city that surrounded it. Success stemmed from two sources. First, Orientation Week presented a laboratory-like opportunity – a defined cohort of neophytes, whose behaviours might be conditioned if the inputs governing their activities were realigned with the intrinsic purposes of university life. Secondly, orientation changed course because *all* the parties affected by its faltering performance – student government, faculty societies, university administrators, and city officials – could see the conjugal purpose in doing so. The cycle was broken and new values introduced. There would, as in any human drama, be some recidivism in the years to come – adolescent hormones are sometimes irrepressible – but a new course had been set. However, the challenge of purging Homecoming – an event coming just six weeks after orientation each year – of its toxins would prove much harder for Queen's to achieve.

Party Time on University Avenue

Principal Smith declared that it was the largest Homecoming Queen's had ever hosted. Everything seemed to fall nicely into place that weekend in late-October 1984 – the weather was autumnally idyllic and the program full of familiar events – football, receptions, a grand dinner in Grant Hall, and the colourful parade of faculty floats down Union Street. Things soon, however, got out of hand.

On Friday evening, open-air rock music serenaded alumni and students in the university core around the intersection of Union and University. The mood was initially convivial. Floats for the

The true spirit of Homecoming perverted: alumni exchange greetings with freshmen at a Homecoming football game (top). Begun in the 1920, "alumni weekend" was intended to allow tradition to be transmitted from alumni to Queen's newcomers. Alumni wore their faded faculty jackets and paraded around the infield of the stadium under colourful umbrellas. By the 1980s, the tradition became fractured by spontaneous, beer-fuelled street parties that offended Kingstonians and alumni like. A tradition thus lost its core purpose and descended into near hooliganism.

next morning's parade were receiving their last touches, and conversation turned to the next day's football contest with the Carleton Ravens. Around midnight, the mood shifted. Crowd behaviour is always hard to dissect, but most agreed that, as the alumni, many of whom had travelled to Kingston that day, headed for their hotel rooms, a younger and much more exuberant cohort came into ascendancy. Swelled by arrivals from nearby Ghetto apartments and the residence precinct to the south, the crowd quickly transformed itself into a mob. Darkness bestowed anonymity on the partiers, so that it was difficult to discern who was who. Most observers soon realized that this was more than a Queen's event – local high schools and fun-seekers from other universities and cities seemed to have got the word that a good time was to be had "at Queen's," even though the party now spilled into streets well outside the Queen's enclave. Beer flowed freely. Bottles were smashed on the pavement. The tone of the crowd turned from festive to belligerent, ribald, and skittish. The police arrived, prompted by calls of complaint from local residents. Kingston Deputy Police Chief William Hackett reported that "hundreds and hundreds" of arrests were made and fines levied. Over two-thirds of these perpetrators, Principal Smith later claimed, were not in any way attached to the Queen's student body. Nonetheless, some Queen's students complained that the police had roughed them up and verbally abused them. It was, in short, a night of strained tempers and excited reactions.[58]

The next day things got worse. In the afternoon, the Gaels lost to their Ottawa rivals, the Carleton Ravens, in a close 37–32 contest. That evening the previous night's street party spontaneously reconvened in a free-wheeling, boozy bash. Over the two evenings, AMS president, Jim Hughes, estimated that over eight thousand people attended the Homecoming street party.[59] More arrests, more trash, and more infuriated citizens followed. It fell to Principal Smith and AMS President Hughes to write the post-mortem of the weekend's frenzy. Smith told the trustees and the Senate that only a "minority" of those present were responsible for the "reprehensible acts" that had prompted police intervention. Nonetheless, the Homecoming events had become "too large" and "had lost their Queen's character." Hughes stressed that the unruliness was "spontaneous" and the product of a "relatively few people."

Smith nonetheless acknowledged that it was "secondary" whether the upheaval had taken place "off campus." The event had been initiated by Queen's and was therefore its problem.

With the university's big Queen's Appeal campaign under way, the bad press generated by the fracas might damage fundraising. Some, Smith admitted, were calling for the university to summarily cancel Homecoming and thereby staunch the public-relations wound. Smith resisted this, arguing that the problem would be delivered into the hands of Queen's "accepted procedures and decision making bodies." The Senate Committee on Non-academic Discipline (SONAD) was asked to solicit opinions and propose reforms. Its chair, Professor Bill Reeve, immediately struck up a dialogue with the AMS to isolate problems with student discipline at Queen's, especially the seeming inability of the AMS justice system to assert its authority at off-campus events.[60] The next spring, Smith expanded the contemplation of what had gone wrong with a tried-and-true Queen's tradition. He asked his vice-principal, services, Jim Bennett, to head a task force to review the whole question of Homecoming, and he tapped Vice-Principal Duncan Sinclair to chair a Senate ad-hoc committee on crowd and alcohol control at Richardson Stadium, the epicentre of much of the liquor-fuelled misbehaviour.

All those tasked with dissecting Homecoming immediately discovered how much more slippery a problem it was than orientation. Frosh week's problem had hinged almost exclusively on a definable group of pliable newcomers to Queen's, whose behaviour could be tilted for better or worse during a highly structured week. The inputs to Homecoming were more varied – and much less controllable. The weekend was dedicated to alumni, some of whom returned to their alma mater full of nostalgia and a desire to reconnect with days gone by. Each Homecoming welcomed selected class years as they met benchmark anniversaries. They were saluted at halftime in the football game as they paraded around the stadium under yellow umbrellas. More recently graduated alumni also made the journey back to Kingston to indulge in the kind of undergraduate revelry that had typified their lives at Queen's only a few years before. Indeed, it was suggested that these newest alumni returned with messianic fervour, perpetuating a culture of boozy good times. The intent of the weekend had long been to promote communion between alumni and current Queen's students. The ambition here was to transmit Queen's lore and habits from the old to the new. But, given the proximity of the now-teeming Ghetto, Homecoming gatherings, particularly in the evening, stood a better chance of transmitting the *wrong* kind of tradition – outrageous self-indulgence with little regard to civic decorum. Time and again, the point was made that Homecoming's excesses were powerfully misshaped by upper-class students who – perhaps because of an exposure to such attitudes during their orientation – carried the virus of misbehaviour to the streets every Homecoming. Added to this mix was a polyglot of outsiders – high-school kids, out-of-towners – who hankered after a proverbial good time on somebody else's turf.

As with orientation, all realized the key to bringing Homecoming back onto a more traditional footing was breaking the cycle of bad behaviour. The challenge with Homecoming was that the university had far less leverage on the participants than it had with the eighteen-year-olds of orientation. Other factors complicated the Homecoming dilemma. A rainy weekend could make it seem as if the problem was solved. It was also extremely difficult to stop the dissemination of the wrong kind of information surrounding Homecoming. By the late 1980s, the internet was beginning to make the circulation of digital mythologies fast and broadly democratic. The emergence of social media a decade later would only accelerate the message – of good times at Queen's Homecoming. No amount of on-campus education could stem the flow of off-campus rumours of street parties open to all who chose to come to Kingston. Compounding the situation was the ongoing confusion and indecision around jurisdiction over the now-spreading footprint of Homecoming events. There was no doubt that the university and the AMS with its constables had purview over activities on campus and at Richardson Stadium. But there was far less certainty when Homecoming spilled into Sydenham Ward.

In some ways, the city still wished to abide by the old understanding that Queen's would take care of its own by posting AMS constables to keep the peace or by ultimately administering a slap on the wrist through the AMS Judicial Committee. But these remedies seemed to buckle under the pressure of eight-thousand-plus street partiers, especially because it was often impossible to tell a Queen's student from a high-school student from, say, Brockville. Down at City Hall, there was growing resentment of Homecoming and related student hijinks were costing the city dearly in police overtime and clean-up costs. Even more hard-line were citizen groups such as STAND, which complained of growing tired of the university's habitual "fine-tuning" of student behaviour.[61]

Principal Smith responded to such criticism by saying that the university was "wrestling" with the problem. Diagnosis of the symptoms began arriving in the spring of 1987. The review task force under Jim Bennett reported that Homecoming's traditional dedication to "a marvellous sense of community" had been twisted into something that carried a "negative connotation." It had become a "lightning rod" for local resentment of the university. Even if it was only a minority of hell-raisers, the discredit redounded against the reputation of the overall university. The solution was to attack the underlying behaviour that led to the October outbursts. Many Queen's students saw themselves as unconstrained by normal social decorum. The AMS justice system in the face of so large and insidious a problem was "ineffectual." Two things must immediately be done. First, students should be made to understand that they were subject to both the university's code of conduct and the law of the land. Secondly, a student-administration Alumni Weekend Advisory Board should be established to oversee the weekend and to push the event's agenda back towards the alumni and away from student entertainment. The focus of the weekend should be educational and celebratory. An effort should therefore be made to curtail big outdoor events on Friday and Saturday nights. Events should be decentralized and emphasis placed on small-group interaction. The report was savvy enough to realize that students would resist overt attempts by the administration to reprogram their behaviour. Instead, the key would be self-awareness through enlightenment. "We're all in this together," the Bennett Committee concluded.[62]

The trustees approved an Alumni Weekend Review Board with alacrity, stocking it with students, faculty, and administrators, and it set to work trying to change the attitude surrounding Homecoming. It too debated cancelling the event or moving it to a climatically colder calendar slot, but concluded that such symptomatic change would not root out the base attitudinal problem. It did determine to devise a "communications strategy," designed to underscore what was "unacceptable behaviour" at Queen's.[63] For its part, the AMS reiterated its belief that its authority extended off campus if behaviours there could be related to the "specific" university community. It also bolstered its student justice policy by specifying that its jurisdiction extended to "non-sponsored events" (such as street parties) and instructed the chief constable that such was the case.

Facilitating both these moves was the fact that, in 1984, Principal Smith had created the post of vice-principal, institutional relations. This was to be a wide-ranging assignment, involving everything from carrying the Queen's message to politicians in Toronto to smoothing relations with the various constituencies in Kingston affected by Queen's. Smith appointed two seasoned administrators to the post – former deans Duncan Sinclair, until 1986, and then Tom Williams. Each man found the job infuriatingly slippery and nebulous, but for the first time Queen's had a point man in matters of relations with local stakeholders. Hitherto, such relations had rested on the shoulders of the principal, who sought to curry local goodwill through his informal ties with Kingston politicians and opinion leaders. Now town-gown relations had become a permanent, institutionalized facet of running Queen's.

"Building Bridges": Repairing Homecoming

The moment Tom Williams donned the mantle of vice-principal, institutional relations, he felt the heat over Homecoming. On the one flank, there was much pressure from the city, angry ratepayers, and even members of the Queen's Senate for a "heavy hand" in dealing with street parties. Send in the police, fill up the downtown jail, and mete out stiff justice went the rhetoric. On the other hand, others called for patience and suasion. Williams had seen student confrontation before: as a young educational theorist working in Chicago in the late 1960s he had witnessed the upheaval brought on by students staring down the authority of Mayor Richard Daley. As Dean of Education at Queen's from 1976 to 1986, Williams had overseen the preparation of teachers whose challenge was to make adolescents come to their education rather than be brought to it. Consequently, his attitude to the challenge of reshaping and redirecting Homecoming was to persuade rather than to push. Change, he argued, would have to come "through negotiation" and proceeding in a "non-confrontational way."⁶⁴ He would come to say that his *bête noire* as vice-principal, institutional relations, was managing the tension between the Queen's tradition of respecting student self-government and obliging the calls for tighter control over events that were unquestionably damaging the university's reputation in its Kingston community and the broader Canadian community.

To manage this tension, Williams dedicated himself to "building bridges" with the varied stakeholders involved in Homecoming. He conceived of his role as a kind of roving ambassador for the university, making contact with affected parties, finding their thresholds, and patching together some sort of consensus. He became, for instance, an unusual ally of Kingston police chief, William Hackett, convincing him that law and order could be just as well served on Homecoming weekends through gentle-but-firm pressure as through heavy-handed crowd control. Similarly, Williams worked closely with Kingston mayor John Gerretsen and the Sydenham Ward ratepayers to open up lines of communication to anticipate and alleviate frictions, a pattern paralleled by AMS presidents. At the same time, Williams reached out to the AMS, sending his able assistant Kathy Beers to every AMS Assembly meeting to pick up the mood of student government. Williams quickly sensed that there was a willingness to change Homecoming on all fronts; the trick was to identify mutually agreeable mechanisms of change and to adopt a pace of change that would end the hellish street parties.

Slowly, changes crept into the culture of Homecoming. In 1987, as a result of Duncan Sinclair's investigation of alcohol and crowd behaviour, Queen's football games became "boozeless," as the *Journal* phrased it. The AMS constables would confiscate wineskins (long the favoured method of getting liquor into the stands) from football fans. "This should be a good test of Queen's spirit," AMS internal-affairs commissioner, Dave Pick, asserted.⁶⁵ Later that fall, the AMS Assembly decided to put a stop to all "out of committee" settlements in its judicial process, thereby ending the ability of students to strike one-off deals to wangle their way out of disciplinary charges. Williams and the AMS staged open meetings to air out the problems of Homecoming. On one thing, Williams was emphatic: illegal street parties were not, and never had been, part of the Queen's tradition. On Homecoming weekends in the late 1980s, Williams took to riding around the Ghetto in Chief Hackett's patrol car. When he spotted a clutch of students on some street with beer in hand, Williams leapt out of the squad car and sprinted up to the students. "Listen, I'm telling you guys," he warned them, "you've got about five minutes to cool things down before he's [pointing to the chief in the car] gonna bring in the troops." (On one such occasion Williams unexpectedly accosted his own daughter, a first-year student, who was innocently standing on a porch!)[66] To bolster such vigilance, a volunteer corps of faculty, alumni, and other well-wishers was organized to walk the streets around Queen's on Homecoming nights to calm the partying mood. They sported red baseball caps to distinguish themselves and lend some authority to their mission – hence the tag "red caps" (later changed to white caps to enhance recognition). Despite this suasion, Kingston police did not hesitate to lay charges against anyone who chose to act out in public. Drunks were usually placed in a tank in the city jail and released into the cold, sober light of the next day. The next week there was an inevitable tally of the arrests in the local paper– how many were associated with the university and how many were not. Usually, Queen's students were a minority. Back on campus, a "campus observation room" was opened in 1990 to provide medical oversight for intoxicated students; that year it was open for sixteen days and admitted sixty-three students.[67] Students found guilty of outrageous behaviour, Williams announced, could be evicted from university-owned housing.

By the late 1980s, Homecoming was becoming a tamer, more convivial, affair. In 1988 and 1989, there were no raucous street parties. The *Tricolour* yearbook published pictures of alumni and undergraduates mingling and emitting exuberant *Oil Thighs*. The *Journal* reported in 1989 that "students [and] alumni team up for Homecoming success."[68] Homecoming appeared to be returning to its roots. But there was no underestimating the power of a street party: the right weather, the right combination of rumour and exuberance, and the presence of even a small clutch of determined unruly revellers could bring a street party to life. With the Ghetto ever-present to the north of the campus, there was always a ready reservoir of party animals when the call came. (Eighties students, for example, doted on the film antics of John Belushi – playing "Bluto" Blutarsky – and his fellow frat-house buffoons in the ever-popular 1978 film, *National Lampoon's Animal House*.) By the early nineties, it became apparent that street parties were more like an undulant fever than a passing flu, a fever that peaked and waned, but never totally disappeared. With the right conditions, if the university let down its defences, the fever would return with a vengeance.

In October 1990, that fever returned to Queen's. Ali Velshi, the AMS campus activities commissioner, reported with dismay that Homecoming that year had been punctuated by "beer-bottle throwing, fridge tossing, turf ripping, window smashing, fighting, brawling, vomiting, urinating, and defecating in public, damaged and stolen property."[69] This grim news immediately provoked a return to familiar hard-line prescriptions: send in the police, send the bill to Queen's, and cancel the whole event. Unfortunately, this would become the recurrent tension surrounding Homecoming – an alternating wave of hope and despair. Then, by 1994, Homecoming had returned to a more placid footing. The *Journal* called Homecoming that year a "quiet success," with the only problem, according to the police, being the storming of the football field after a Gaels loss to the Bishop's Gaiters.

Unlike orientation, with its concentration on a single, controllable cohort, Homecoming never proved susceptible to a one-time adjustment in behaviour. There were too many variables dictating its demeanour. Containing its possible deleterious effects would require constant vigilance and adjustment. In 1994, for instance, the AMS converted its external-affairs portfolio into a municipal-affairs commission with a mandate to manage the society's relations with Kingston politicians and citizens. The new commission opened the way to a constructive dialogue with the city, overseeing everything from waste collection, participation in the annual United

Way, and monitoring tenant-landlord relations in the Ghetto. (When frustration over poor-quality student housing persisted, in 2006 the AMS subsequently instituted its Golden Cockroach Award to annually "honour" the city's worst student landlord.) Thus, the unavoidable conclusion was that the cycle had not been broken. And, to anticipate just a bit, in 2003 the virus resurfaced in a new location: Aberdeen Street, just north of the athletic centre. A short street in the Ghetto, entirely peopled by student renters, Aberdeen offered a boulevard-like ambiance for partying. By midnight, the party that year turned into a mob. The *Journal* facetiously reported that the street party had been "a smashing affair," with broken bottles and litter everywhere. When a clean-up crew arrived at four in the morning, students pelted them with beer bottles.[70] Unlike the more controllable culture of orientation week, Homecoming would remain a persistent virus, brought to the surface by an unpredictable mixing of weather, social media, and transmitted campus lore.

Managing Queen's

The persistence of these Homecoming shenanigans underscored the realization that, over the last decades of the twentieth century, Queen's had ceased to be a tightly bound, cohesive, and in many ways insular community. Dramatic changes in Canadian demographics and the Charter rights accorded every citizen had made the university a more porous community, open to the greater diversity of Canada and at the same time less susceptible to the power of a once-strong internal culture. Students were now citizens in the fullest sense, subject to the impulses of a consumerist, rights-driven society. Their lives had increasingly become multi-layered, no longer entirely tied to their existence as university learners. New diversions entered their lives – part-time employment, the seductions of an ever-expanding popular culture, and engagement with issues of socio-political import, ranging from the cost of their education to the evils of apartheid in South Africa.

Sometimes the outcomes were positive, as the concerted effort to oblige the university "to wash its hands" of investments which, in the protestors' eyes, were tainted. At other times, the results – street parties, turmoil in the Ghetto – were less than edifying. Through all this transition, the challenge for Queen's as a broadly defined community was to preserve its distinct identity and the values and processes it supported. Just as the university had belatedly been obliged to open up its ethnic identity to the reality of a multicultural Canada, so too did it have to understand that its old paternalistic ways would not serve it well in an age of pluralism. Queen's now lived in a world of active citizenship, in which all its constituents expected a voice in setting the course of the institution. Whatever the ultimate right or wrong of shedding investments in Chile and South Africa, the exercise of arriving at the divestment decision had obliged Queen's to think hard about its moral compass.

Every facet of Queen's life felt the shift. The AMS rejigged its mandate to accommodate the new sensibilities of its student members, while at the same time reaching out to the community surrounding it. There was wide recognition that Queen's must maintain its precious tradition of student self-regulation, even if this meant dramatically altering the nature of student justice. In a sense, Queen's had always treated its students as fully fledged citizens, by delegating power over their daily lives to their own keeping as early as 1858. Now that autonomy had to be updated. Students also needed to recognize that with modern rights came modern responsibilities – reaching out to the city to smooth the rough edges of orientation and Homecoming. And these responsibilities were ongoing, always in need of fine-tuning and modernization. Hence, the AMS's creation in 1994 of a municipal-affairs commission.

The same process of active citizenship infiltrated the ranks of faculty in the late-twentieth century. Not only were faculty members edging ever closer to collective bargaining, but, as the divestment debate had shown, the faculty also wanted a more decisive voice in deciding the overall purposes of the institution. This desire extended beyond faculty's traditional sway over the academic governance of the university into areas of its socio-political management. This was an era of "social responsibility" in which they were determined to participate.

The view from Richardson Hall also changed dramatically in these years of lively debates and frequent confrontation. More than any other principal, David Smith had been obliged to align Queen's with the world that surrounded it. Queen's no longer had the luxury of resting on its Presbyterian laurels of public service and late-Victorian liberalism. Issues of diversity, ethics, and pluralism now obliged it to adopt an active citizenship of its own. Hence, the creation of a vice-principalship for institutional relations in 1984. Queen's would now thrive or shrivel according to its willingness to engage the world around it, and it would have to do it while preserving – yet adapting – its rooted sense of community and shared responsibility. Queen's would have to be managed to new and more-inclusive standards.

One can recall the note sent to Smith in 1984 by his friend and dean of graduate studies Maurice Yeates: "The schedule you have set yourself can be completed only by a person with a stout heart and quick legs."[71] Smith's legs did not always keep up with the pace of change, as "No Means No" would illustrate. But under his watch, Queen's in many ways donned a modern garb of pluralism and consultation. The experience was not always smooth and consensual, but in the end Queen's preserved its cohesion, even if old relationships had been shed. By the time Smith stepped down in 1994, two implications of this transformation were apparent. First, the reputation of the university now had to be managed actively, year in and year out, from issue to issue. And, secondly, the span of authority, persuasion, and engagement expected of a principal had been tremendously stretched. On any one day, the principal might be expected to act as the university's minister of external affairs, its chief fundraiser, the chair of its Senate, and confidant of the student rector. After Smith, many wondered how Queen's could sustain the strain of balancing the demands of the ivory tower and the world beyond. The university would find a possible answer to this dilemma in a vice-principal's office at McGill University in Montreal, a city that, more than any other in Canada, had felt the stresses and strains of modern Canada.

10

"To Chart a Different Course"
William Leggett and the New Millennium, 1994–2004

Preparing leaders and citizens for a global society.
Motto on Queen's University letterhead, 1999

I believe there is a ceiling to how much a student should pay for a Queen's education, and that we are coming dangerously close to it.
Rector Michael Kealy, 2000

[There are] no magic bullets.
William Leggett, 2002

Decision at Hawkridge Farm

The Kingston *Whig-Standard* takes pride in being "Canada's oldest daily newspaper." Born as the *British Whig* in 1834, the paper was a mouthpiece of Reform sentiment in the 1830s. In the 1920s, it was acquired by Rupert Davies, who merged it with the *Daily Standard* and used it as a platform for a family publishing dynasty. Son Robertson went to Queen's, where he wrote for the *Queen's Journal* before embarking on a career that would bring him fame as a playwright, novelist, and editor of the Peterborough *Examiner*. Robertson's brother Arthur and nephew Michael stayed with the *Whig-Standard*. In 1976, Michael, Queen's class of 1959, assumed sole ownership of the paper and, thanks to brilliant editors such as Neil Reynolds, built it into a model community newspaper.[1] From his publisher's desk, Michael Davies kept a keen eye on the university, scolding its students for rowdiness in the city's streets, praising its academic achievements, and going to bat for it with the provincial government. In 1978, Davies was appointed to the Board of Trustees, joining the always-assertive Kingston city contingent. Davies, for example, labelled the raucous Homecoming street parties that erupted in the 1980s as corrosive behaviour that undermined town-and-gown relations.

Yet, for all its patina, the times turned against the *Whig*. Small-city newspapers struggled in an increasingly electronic and mass-market media world. In 1990, Davies shocked Kingston by selling the paper to the Southam chain. Most experts saw the sale as inevitable. Davies was now free to turn his attention to philanthropy, sailing his beloved yacht the *Archangel*, and tending his farm, *Hawkridge*, north of Kingston. Davies remained active on the Queen's Board, finding a parallel with his own publishing journey in the university's challenges – tight budgets, student accessibility, and wavering reputation. In 1993, as David Smith's second term as principal drew to a close, Davies was called upon not only to join the search for a successor, but also to play the role of that secretive process's host. Eager to shield their deliberations from curious eyes, the committee was delighted with Davies's invitation to use his rural home to interview finalists for the key Queen's post.

That spring, the Board launched its standing procedure for selecting a new principal: namely, a joint committee of eighteen members drawn from the Board and Senate, together with two staff members in support. Chaired by Chancellor Agnes Benidickson, the committee had stellar potential: business executives such as accountant Richard Stackhouse and Air Canada's Anne Bodnarchuck, politician and social activist Rosemary Brown, journalist Jeffrey Simpson, business dean David Anderson, and professors such as Catherine Harland from English and Marvin Baer from law, plus, in that now-central Queen's tradition, four student senators.[2] There was a natural tentativeness in the committee's first meetings; not everyone knew one another. There was consequently no preconception of what the ultimate appointee might look like. Two imperatives quickly emerged: the committee must find a person well-equipped to face the challenges pressing on Queen's – strained finances, a money-losing castle in the English countryside, and the continuing need to bring social and cultural diversity to the campus. Secondly, the committee was also aware that Queen's had drawn its last five principals from what seemed to many a privileged bailiwick of political scientists and economists. Nonetheless, the committee readily determined that the ultimate summons would go the *best* person available, regardless of lineage. The search began in February 1993.

Agnes Benidickson sat ably in the chair: she had been a model chancellor, quietly working behind the scenes with Principal Smith in support of Queen's fundraising and "friendraising" ambitions. Under her guidance, the joint committee adopted an activist approach to its mandate. Across Canada, senior academic appointments no longer emerged out of a chummy informality; consultants were now hired to guide the search and massage the candidate dossiers. Perhaps the leading such recruiter was Janet Wright of Toronto's Landmark Group. However, she had just agreed to aid the University of Western Ontario in its quest for a new president. Wright did come to Kingston to sit down with the committee over dinner to prime its members for the search ahead. In the absence of Wright, the committee engaged George Connell, a former president of both Western and Toronto, to facilitate its external relations.

The committee also sat down to dinner with the outgoing David Smith to ascertain his parting perspective on the principalship. Smith was frank. He bemoaned the fact that in recent years he had been obliged to be away from campus often: the presidency of the Council of Ontario Universities and the frequent necessity of battling the fiscal constriction of the NDP-imposed Social Contract had magnetically pulled him to Queen's Park. As a consequence, Smith felt that he had become detached from a close daily ministering to his campus – something Queen's principals had always seen as central to their suc-

Baptism of fire. Newly installed principal Bill Leggett (right) meets with Ontario minister of finance Floyd Laughren in early 1995. Leggett's tenure in Richardson Hall would be marked by strenuous financial negotiations with Queen's Park, first with the NDP government of Bob Rae and, after 1995, with the Conservative "common-sense" government of Mike Harris. In each case, the focus was on seeking a formula that would balance government austerity, inflation, and equitable fees for students.

cess. Campus morale was poor, perhaps exemplified by the faculty's pronounced tilt toward collective bargaining and griping about the financial toll of "the castle." The new principal, the committee concluded, would have fences to mend and a new balance to strike between the internal and external demands on his or her time.[3] Nonetheless, the new principal would inherit significant shifts in attitude and policy at Queen's on issues pertaining to such matters as equity, gender, and student orientation, shifts that he or she would be expected to promote.

Eager to tap into the mood of the campus, the committee broke into subgroups and fanned out to harvest a "micro-grained" sample of opinion. Members of the subgroup visited 155 departments on campus – from academic units to maintenance shops. Two "open" meetings were held in Grant Hall. The results were frank and startling. Morale was indeed low – the Social Contract had bitten deep, Herstmonceux Castle in England seemed an extravagance. There was also pronounced sentiment that Queen's storied reliance on political scientists and economists for leadership had exhausted itself. The science-oriented faculties harboured the feeling that they had for decades been given short shrift, particularly since funded research in the sciences was now a powerful driving force on Canadian campuses. Particularly forceful in this respect was David Canvin, the respected, one-time head of biology and dean of Graduate Studies and Research. Queen's, Canvin argued, was missing the boat in national research. The committee also became aware of the emerging trend in North American universities to appoint outsiders – either from other universities or from outside the academic realm – to their senior positions. (Biochemist Shirley Tilghman, a 1968 Queen's BA in chemistry, would, for instance, be appointed president of Princeton in 2001 after coming to that university from the University of Pennsylvania some years earlier.) Queen's long habit of organically growing its leaders seemed increasingly out of kilter with the times. Despite such trends and sentiments, the committee formed a determination to select the best candidate available. It was also mindful of its mandate to arrive at "a virtually unanimous choice."

Meanwhile, nominations – some two hundred of them – flooded into the office of the university secretary, Margaret Hooey. Through the summer of 1993, a core group of the committee winnowed the crop. By September, the choice had come down to a handful of candidates and the time had arrived to take up Michael Davies's invitation to adjourn to *Hawkridge* to meet the front-runners.

"Bulldozer Bill"

In the end, the committee faced an agonizing choice. Although four candidates came up to the farm, each for an intensive tête-à-tête with the committee, the choice narrowed to two men: an insider – Rod Fraser, an economist who had served as Queen's dean of Arts and Science in the eighties and, since then, as its vice-principal, resources – and an outsider – biologist William Leggett, McGill's vice-principal, academic, and a former dean of science. Fraser brought a record of devoted service to Queen's to his application. He had been a productive member of Queen's renowned department of economics, a solid dean of Arts and Science and, most crucially, as vice-principal, resources, had been tasked with squeezing money out of the university's operating budget in the grim years of the Bob Rae Social Contract. Fraser had chosen to pare budgets across the campus equitably – 2 per cent across the board. Rather than trying to practise surgery on selected units, Fraser opted for procrustean austerity, medicine he delivered fairly and forthrightly. Many resented his therapy, but few doubted his integrity and transparency. When quizzed by the committee about the university's recent policies, Fraser defended his, and by implication David Smith's, record without wavering. Tough times necessitated tough measures. This was perceived as an honourable stance, but left Fraser as the familiar, inside candidate, whose potential was already linked to Queen's distinctive ethos.

When George Connell, sniffing around for potential candidates for the Queen's job first called him at McGill, Bill Leggett dismissed the notion of his applying out of hand. Queen's, he told Connell, always hired its own. The search committee, he surmised, was simply looking for a straw man, a candidate who might be set up to demonstrate the intrinsic superiority of the inside candidate. Connell, however, persisted. Leggett was in truth feeling somewhat restless. Now in his mid-fifties, he had been at McGill since the late sixties, first completing his doctorate in marine biology, before embarking on an academic career that had seen him rise from assistant professor, through departmental head, to dean of science, and, finally in 1991, to vice-principal, academic. En route, Leggett polished his academic and administrative skills. As head of biology, he proved a meticulous administrator, attentive to the myriad small details – vetting research applications, grooming promotion dossiers – that built productivity and collegiality in his unit.

All the while, Leggett maintained his own vigorous program of research in fish ecology, amassing a handsome list of publications and a strong track record of winning grants from external agencies. As dean and then vice-principal, he was mentored by the energetic leadership of David Johnston, McGill's dynamic principal from 1979 to 1994. Now, as his term as vice-principal neared its completion, Leggett found himself pondering what he would do with the last decade of his academic career. A return to intensive research? Or perhaps, Connell urged, a university presidency. Leggett now became interested in Queen's, discussing the prospect with his wife, Claire. Queen's, he admitted, had always intrigued him. He had admired from afar its dedication to balancing teaching and research. Born in Orangeville, Ontario, he had also long yearned to return to the friendliness of small-town Ontario. Leggett therefore eventually decided to throw his cap into the ring.[4]

In some ways, Leggett conformed to established patterns of leadership at Queen's. Like Mackintosh, Corry, and Deutsch, he had emerged from small-town Canada. His father ran an auto-body shop and a bowling alley. The family was by no means prosperous; in primary school, young Bill did double duty as school janitor. He was initially more

Bill Leggett was the first principal of Queen's to emerge from a science background since Robert Wallace, a geologist, took the post in 1936. Leggett accelerated Queen's commitment to funded research. Here Dr Sherryl Taylor of the Department of Pathology researches the gene believed to cause Huntington's disease.

inclined to sports than book learning. His grades in school were lacklustre. Only a stern lecture from his father on the wisdom of earning a living by one's "head" rather than one's "hands" sufficiently bucked Bill up to gain entry to Waterloo University, where his interest in biology was aroused. A master's degree at Waterloo followed, and then the doctorate at McGill in 1969. Hard work in the classroom, committee room, and research lab became his lodestar.[5] As a student at Waterloo, he had found summer employment as a heavy-equipment operator and, when his colleagues in McGill's biology department learned this, they tagged him with the nickname "Bulldozer Bill" – indicative of his ability to do things in a forceful-yet-collegial way.

Leggett arrived at *Hawkridge* farm having done his homework. He understood, for instance, the costly predicament presented by Herstmonceux Castle – how to turn a medieval building into a modern educational facility. He prepared more than answers; he prepared *perspectives* on Queen's strengths and weaknesses. For all the red ink filling its moat, Herstmonceux, Leggett told the committee, offered Queen's an opportunity to internationalize itself – to engage a world that was increasingly conceiving of itself as a global entity. Queen's students must begin to look beyond the comfort zone of the Old Strand. Similarly, Queen's must shake off the complacency of what Leggett called the "Queen's way" – the assumption that Queen's genetically knew the right way to proceed.[6] In particular, this meant finding ways to revitalize the fabled quality of Queen's undergraduate education, while at the same time energizing Queen's enterprise in research in what was becoming across Canada a very competitive grants economy. The committee was impressed. Leggett seemed to be offering worldly, dynamic leadership, yet offering it with very solid, ongoing academic credentials. That same year, Leggett had, for instance, won major funding from the Natural Sciences and Engineering Research Council (NSERC) for oceanographic research. If Queen's was to enhance its research presence, there would be advantage and prestige in having a scientist of accomplishment as head of its team. On a less tangible basis, Leggett – "Bill" to all who met him – exuded a genial confidence. He was tall and extroverted, projecting a more activist personality than many of his low-key predecessors, a departure from the leadership style of an institution that had been tended by its own kith and kin for almost a half century. Finally, Leggett would bring with him from Montreal twenty-five years of experience in one of Canada's largest and most diverse cities. Diversity and cultural tolerance, values that Queen's was only now hurriedly trying to absorb, had been on the agenda in Montreal and McGill for centuries.

Leggett left *Hawkridge* late that September Saturday feeling that he had done well, and energized by the intriguing prospect of pushing Queen's in new directions, while at the same time striving to preserve its intrinsic virtues. Nonetheless, he continued to think that old ways died hard and that some competent insider would get the call. That evening, back in Kingston, Leggett got a call from committee member journalist Jeffrey Simpson, who was staying at the same bed-and-breakfast. Leggett and Simpson sat for several hours on the porch chatting about Leggett's fit with Queen's. Simpson as yet had no idea of the committee's ultimate disposition, but liked what he heard. The next morning confirmed his intuition. The committee voted unanimously to nominate Leggett as Queen's seventeenth principal. "Queen's students," it reported to the Board of Trustees, "will find Bill Leggett equally at home in the laboratory, the classroom, the administrative office, and the Quiet Pub."[7] When Agnes Benidickson telephoned Leggett on Monday morning to convey the good news, Leggett was so "shocked" that he accepted the post without negotiation. A central Queen's tradition had been set aside; for the first time since geologist Robert Wallace arrived in Kingston in 1936 from the University of Alberta there would be an unfamiliar face in the corner office at Richardson Hall.

There was a painful and awkward corollary to the committee's decision. While the committee had unanimously endorsed Leggett's selection, it regarded Rod Fraser with equal esteem. Their ultimate decision had hinged on a keenly felt desire for change and a sense that that change might best come from away. Those closest to Queen's culture immediately knew that the decision would have a devastating impact on Fraser, who had been as devoted to Queen's as any of its senior administrators had ever been. In the weeks following the decision, a small contingent of members of the selection committee paid a call on Fraser to assure him of their regard for his abilities. They found him crestfallen. One of their number, alerted to the fact that the University of Alberta president Paul Davenport might soon leave his post, quietly put the word out that Alberta-born Fraser would be a top-notch candidate to head that university and that Queen's had found nothing wanting in his candidacy. This, along with the other compelling aspects of his curriculum vitae, would soon make Fraser president of the University of Alberta, a post he would hold from 1995 to 2005.

Prodding the "Queen's Way"

There are a trove of jokes about the ironic difference between the experience of a job interview and the day-to-day reality of the actual job. As soon as Bill Leggett arrived in Kingston in the summer of 1994, he began to measure that ironic tension. His impression of Queen's from afar had always been that it was a university that had struck a commendable balance between teaching and research and that, unlike universities such as Toronto and McGill, in the maw of big cities, it had maintained a strong sense of community and intimacy amongst its staff and students. In this respect, Queen's did not disappoint. "I discovered very quickly that Queen's really was a community," he would later recall, and that "people really reacted well and had a strong sense of pride in the place, [and] the students and the alumni had a real sense of belonging and were proud of their association." Queen's was "a vibrant humming place." Years later, in retirement, Leggett found himself standing outside the University Club on a torrentially wet day, pondering his chances of getting across campus to a meeting without an umbrella. A Physical Plant dump truck pulled up in front of him: "Hi, Bill. Where you going? Hop in," the driver called out. Such collegiality, Leggett sensed from his first days on campus, was "a wonderful and very valuable attribute, something thrilling to be part of, so very rewarding personally."[8]

But ingrained collegiality can be dysfunctional. The university, Leggett now sensed, suffered from a kind of comfortable myopia. As he surveyed the senior administrators who surrounded him in Richardson Hall, he concluded that the corporate culture of the place was "a little hidebound, a little conservative." Their default position was invariably the "Queen's way." This genetic predisposition had been nurtured for decades, Leggett concluded, by "a long history of hiring its own." His predecessors, Ron Watts and David Smith, had encountered and perhaps encouraged the same attitude, but were probably too steeped in the ethos of the place to grow impatient with its habitual reliance on gradualism and consultation to challenge the mindset. Leggett was less patient. At McGill, he had served as dean under Principal David Johnston (1979–94) and had witnessed a decisive university head in action. A corporate lawyer by training, Johnston had served on the boards of large corporations, such as Southam, and understood that effective leadership required a delicate balance of assertiveness and consensus-building. Leggett brought a similar attitude to Queen's: a university president or principal, he believed, must be a combination of "coach" and "cheerleader." Queen's, Leggett concluded, had of late had a little too much cheerleading and too little tough coaching.

The new principal was fifty-five years old. As he surveyed the departmental heads in the Faculty of Arts and Science, he was struck by the fact that virtually all of them were older than he was. Similarly, for all the recent talk of gender and equality at Queen's, there was not one woman in charge of a department.* He was also struck by how inward-looking Queen's was; there was still an expectation that Queen's somehow acquired its reputation intrinsically. As a successful scientist coming from a cosmopolitan university in Canada's second-largest city (surveys consistently revealed that McGill was Canada's most readily recognized university beyond its borders), Leggett understood that universities had to *make* their own reputation on the international stage. In this respect, Leggett concluded that Queen's researchers needed more impetus to get onto the national and international stage. Since the 1960s, Queen's had bracketed graduate studies and research together under one dean. The reality here was that the now-much-expanded graduate program, with its incessant annual cycle of demands,

---

*A handful of women – Hilda Laird in German, Kathleen Morand in art history, and Marie Surridge in French – had been department heads in previous years.

had come to dominate 90 per cent of any dean's time, making the promotion of research the "weaker sister" of the mandate. At a time when funded research was becoming an ever-larger slice of a university's fiscal pie, a more concerted orchestration of campus research was becoming imperative. Faculty had to be groomed to succeed in attracting research monies from government agencies, corporations, and private foundations. Leggett's personal track record in funding his oceanographic research taught him the importance of such assertiveness.

Similarly, if Queen's faculty had to better equip themselves for the national and international stage, the same applied to Queen's students. Leggett found it "unusual" for a university of Queen's stature and self-image to be so lightly connected with the world beyond Ontario's borders. In a nation that had just entered a world of North American free trade and was heavily dependent upon the export of its natural resources to economies as far away as the Far East, Queen's provided few opportunities for its students to "globalize" themselves. Here, Leggett was adamant that the potential of its trans-Atlantic campus at Herstmonceux Castle, despite all its initial travails, must be realized. Equally important, Leggett concluded that, if the world for young university graduates was becoming increasingly global and competitive, then the quality of a Queen's undergraduate education must be protected – protected from fiscal starvation and from being overwhelmed by uncontrolled growth.[9]

A New Suite of Vice-Principals

Bill Leggett never professed to be a believer in strategic-planning exercises; elaborate and often hypothetical long-range planning did not lend itself to universities, where tenure prevailed and long-entrenched academic departmentalization introduced tremendous rigidities. Leggett preferred a more pragmatic approach to the "roadblocks" he perceived were holding Queen's back from crafting a new institutional personality and a purpose better suited to the times. He was inclined to avoid the commendable, but time-consuming, exercise of appointing principal's task forces, which had characterized the last few decades as Queen's had modernized. Such task forces did cast a wide net in drawing the wider Queen's community into discussion of strategic matters – the status of women, for instance – but they seldom led to decisive action and sometimes even delayed the application of solutions until a problem had spun out of control – as had happened in 1989 with the "No Means No" blow-up. Instead, Leggett determined to work within the more closely defined parameters of power allotted to his office – his power to appoint the people most immediately associated with his decision making. Over the first eighteen months of his tenure, Leggett dramatically reorganized the top deck of Queen's senior management. "You try to build a great team and cheer them on," he later reflected. Here Leggett displayed a canny sense for putting the right person in the right position. He only did so, however, after sounding out opinion in the Queen's community. Within weeks of taking office, Leggett circulated a letter to all staff, saying that he was "concerned that the current Vice-Principal structure does not adequately address the challenge that Queen's is likely to meet in the future." Principal Smith had sensed the same need, but, except for creating a new vice-principal, advancement, to expedite the university's Challenge Fund, had held back on any decisive reordering of function in deference to his soon-to-be-announced successor.

Leggett now made it clear that the time had arrived. As news of his impressive record at McGill began to filter into Kingston that fall, some suggested that "Bulldozer Bill" had not broken stride in changing jobs. The new principal called for staff input into the restructuring. Within six weeks of arrival, he visited every faculty on campus to engage the views of deans and faculty. Out of this, there emerged an agenda of refurbishing the quality of undergraduate education at Queen's, meeting ongoing financial stringency, and improving relations with government. There were plenty of more-focused ideas. Some recommended restoring the position of vice-principal, academic, dormant since the early 1970s, as a way to bolster the quality of undergraduate education. Others put forth the idea of an umbrella office for all student services, again a return to a dormant office – the dean of student affairs. To orchestrate such ideas, Leggett appointed a principal's advisory committee on vice-principals, giving it a focused mandate and tight schedule to draw up a blueprint for change. While impatient for movement, Leggett was not oblivious to his new university's predisposition to collegial consultation. The president of the faculty association, Annette Burfoot, and of the staff association, Mark Publicover, were asked to join the advisory committee, as were representatives of the AMS and the graduate students' association.

Throughout that fall, the advisory group deliberated over a new configuration for senior management at Queen's. As new positions materialized, smaller advisory groups were appointed to craft the fine details of the appointments. Results came quickly. In November, Leggett announced that the vice-principal, academic, would be resurrected. The post would serve to coordinate all academic matters on campus among deans, directors, and the Senate. The vice-president, academic, would transmit a signal that teaching was still paramount at Queen's. At the same time, the new vice-principal would be expected to look outward, conducting a kind of educational diplomacy with the federal and provincial governments in matters of educational standards and support. Leggett stressed that teamwork would be the central tenet of the new position; he wanted "no confrontational egomaniacs."[10] In December, Leggett announced that the old Research and Graduate Studies portfolio would be broken in two, with a dean assuming the graduate-studies bailiwick and a new vice-principal taking sole charge of the increasingly important research mandate. The vice-principal, research, Leggett stressed, must "create a climate and conditions in the university which will ensure that Queen's remains among the top set of leading research institutions in Canada." The dean of graduate studies would act as the "facilitator" within the university, ensuring the smooth interlocking of research and graduate endeavours.

Finally, Leggett understood that financial constriction would continue to be the main bugbear of Ontario university management. Since peaking in the mid-1970s, provincial support of post-secondary education had steadily declined, to the point that Queen's Park now described the provincial university as a "provincially assisted" system. Ontario now ranked amongst the lowest per-capita funders of post-secondary education among Canadian provinces (indeed in all of North America), a tumble from its generosity in the heyday of the sixties. While the province clung to its devotion to accessibility to post-secondary education (admittedly, Ontario did have one of the highest university participation rates in the country), annual operating grants to universities remained driven by what Leggett came to call the "bums in seats" basic-income-unit formula for calculating that support. Increasingly, the annual flow of cash from Queen's Park to Richardson Hall had been hit by freezes and even clawbacks that reflected the reduced ability of the provincial government to finance its many obligations. That constriction had become acute in the economically trying early 1990s. As vice-principal, resources, Rod Fraser had been saddled with the arduous task of meting out the Social Contract's tough medicine. Fraser understandably opted for an across-the-board cut to all intrauniversity budgets – painful, but equitable. Such cuts did little, however, to allow the university to restructure its priorities. By the mid-1990s, the provincial government was beginning to variegate its university funding – maintaining the BIU income formula, but at the same time initiating funding programs tied to specific educational purposes, such as the promotion of technological innovation, while also entertaining the possibility that certain fee structures, particularly those in professional programs, might be deregulated. Detecting the first stirrings of this shift and the reality that university finances would continue to be a perennially delicate balancing act, Leggett therefore realized that Queen's, with an operating budget of $180 million in the year he arrived, needed nimble financial management.

The appointment of a vice-principal, advancement, by David Smith had already indicated that more non-governmental income was a growing necessity. Now the university needed a financial ringmaster who could coordinate overall finances and organizational change. By December, Leggett was calling this position the vice-principal, operations and finance. He told his advisory committee that "there will be even greater financial challenge during the next five years." Queen's needed the ability "to think and act creatively in the area of finance particularly in the way we carry out our work. It will be necessary to become more efficient and effective in what we do." By the end of 1994, searches were under way for all three new positions. Leggett repeatedly used the term "team" in describing what he hoped would be the end result of this process. He told his advisory committee that his goal was to create "an environment of trust which will lead to more time creativity." He wanted a group that would not have sharp boundaries," thereby encouraging the vice-principals to find common ground.[11] Like anyone who had spent time administering a university, Leggett understood that turf wars over jurisdiction, fanned by ambition, bred paralysis.

In the spring of 1995, Leggett and his hiring committees harvested a remarkable crop of administrative talent. In one sweep on 22 March, he unveiled his new team. For vice-principal, academic, the nod went to David Turpin, a talented biologist who had been dean of Arts and Science since 1993. Trained at the University of British Columbia, Turpin was, like Leggett, an oceanographer. He had been at Queen's since 1981 and knew its ways. Inheriting the headship of the biology department from David Canvin, Turpin nurtured the department's star reputation in the Arts and Science faculty before becoming dean.[12] His reference painted a portrait of him as decisive, crisp in administration, a solid scholar, and attuned with the computer age. Similar characteristics described Suzanne Fortier, who garnered the post of vice-principal, research. Leggett had insisted that the person assuming this post have an "entrepreneurial" bent, capable of deciphering the increasingly complex world of funded research and grooming Queen's faculty for such competition. Fortier was a McGill-trained chemist, who had come to Queen's in 1982 after research experience in the United States and at the National Research Council in Ottawa. She came to Queen's not only as a crystallographer but also as a Québécoise, who took a keen interest in promoting French and Quebec culture on the campus. Fortier had been the associate dean of graduate studies since 1991. Like Turpin, she took an active interest in the application of computers to academic research and was cross-appointed to the department of computing and information science.

Having brought two insiders onto his team, Leggett's search committee looked to an outsider to take on the operations-and-finance portfolio – John Scott Cowan, a psychologist from the University of Ottawa. Cowan had made a reputation as a hard-nosed expert in academic labour relations, first as one of the instigators behind the certification of that university's faculty association in 1976, then as an advisor to the Association of Universities and Colleges of Canada, and finally as vice-rector of human resources and planning at the University of Ottawa. Cowan was tough and frontal in his manner. Duncan Sinclair, a seasoned administrative hand around Queen's, saw Cowan as "a problem solver … very tough, but very fair. We can use that."[13] Cowan's appointment also reflected the one surprise that awaited Leggett when he had arrived a year earlier to take up his duties.

Amid all the sweetness and light that had informed Leggett's interview at *Hawkridge* farm, one salient challenge facing the new principal went unmentioned – the fact that an unhappy faculty were on the verge of seeking union certification. Leggett had never, as an academic himself, been philosophically inclined to the unionization of faculty, but this was offset by a realization that the preservation of collegiality on his new campus was imperative. As will be seen, Leggett launched a last-ditch attempt at conciliation with the faculty association, an initiative that paralleled his fall 1994 rejigging of the university's executive cadre. When it became apparent that amicable consultation would no longer sustain faculty salary negotiation, Leggett immediately acknowledged that collective bargaining was unavoidable. With this in mind, he determined that the administration must equip itself with the best possible talent to negotiate the transition. Cowan, with his experience in Ottawa on both sides of the negotiating table, was that man.

Deep Strength in Faculty Leadership

What Leggett envisioned in 1994 became reality by the fall of 1995 – every Monday morning he presided over a weekly meeting of vice-principals. To these and other meetings, Leggett brought a crisp, decisive manner; trustee, and later board chair, John Rae, remembered him as a "good report" – someone who absorbed information readily, processed it quickly, and then moved to action.[14] This gave testament to a new spirit of focused collegiality at Queen's. (All three of the new vice-principals, like Rod Fraser before them, would go on to occupy a presidential office – Turpin at the University of Victoria, Fortier at McGill, and Cowan at the Royal Military College.) The new ethos spread beyond Richardson Hall. In the spring of 1995, a search was launched for a new dean of Education. After a report by outside consultants, Leggett announced that the successful candidate would have to better connect the faculty with the local secondary-school teaching community and at the same time engage new pedagogic technologies. Furthermore, it was imperative that the main and west campuses stop regarding each other as distinct "silos," and that the new dean must strive to connect the two solitudes. In March 1995, the job went to Rena Upitis, the specialist in teaching mathematics using electronic games, who had come to the university as a Queen's National Scholar. That September, Leggett announced a spate of new deans. The newly redefined post of dean of Graduate Studies went to Ron Anderson, a specialist in dynamics in the department of mechanical engineering. When David Anderson unexpectedly stepped down as dean of the School of Business, a search committee was tasked with finding a replacement who would continue to expand the school's external presence – for instance, through its executive MBA, its outreach to Asian business, and its executive training programs. The choice was Margot Northey, a specialist in effective business communication and author of the best-selling *Making Sense: A Student's Guide to Writing and Style* (1983). She would be the first woman appointed as dean of a major Canadian business school. Northey brought a soft, behaviouralist approach to the school's direction, but the overall thrust of connecting the Kingston school with the globalizing world of business remained.[15] As dean, Northey also quickly determined to provide the school with accommodation worthy of its aspirations – in short, to extract it from its dated and cramped quarters in Dunning Hall.

The two faculties at the fulcrum of Queen's undergraduate education also received new deans near the start of the Leggett era. Robert Silverman, a criminologist from the University of Alberta, arrived in late 1995 to take charge of the Faculty of Arts and Sciences, the workhorse of undergraduate teaching. The next spring, Tom Harris, an alumnus and chemical engineer hired in the eighties as a Queen's National Scholar, took over the deanship of Applied Science. These two faculties were the front line of the university's reputation for superior teaching. Ironically, they were also the first to feel the squeeze of any fiscal constriction on the university.

Their reliance on straightforward BIU funding tended to be at the root of anxiety over the slippage in the quality of a Queen's education. Neither Silverman nor Harris practised passive leadership and, in keeping with Leggett's expectation, exerted an activist pressure in university decision making.

Over in the Faculty of Law, Dean Don Carter continued to construct a more collegial and productive culture in the wake of the traumas of the late eighties. In the fall of 1996, Barry Smith took on the double crown of dean of medicine and vice-principal, health sciences. Smith, a Queen's-trained physician with experience in children's hospitals in Boston and Toronto, faced the challenge of further integrating the varied branches of medical science clustered across Queen's and the local hospitals. Smith would oversee two seismic shifts in the way medicine was taught and practised in Kingston. Late in 1996, in the wake of a report by Kingston lawyer and former Queen's administrator David Bonham, the constellation of medical services offered to the community were dovetailed into one coordinated entity. Each component of the new "single-governed" entity was designated to perform a specialty. Kingston General Hospital, for instance, took on intensive care and cancer treatment. The arrangement smoothed longstanding inter-institution rivalries. Then, a year later, Queen's embraced similar symmetry by combining its medical, nursing, and rehabilitation programs into a single School of Medicine. The amalgamation produced interprofessional efficiencies which soon bore fruit in the introduction of new programs, such as a doctorate in rehabilitation science and a BNSc in Aboriginal nursing. The amalgamation also allowed the vice-principal, health sciences, the dean, and his associate deans to better divide their energies between the internal management of the school and its complex external funding arrangements with the provincial government and professional regulatory bodies.

Over at the Stauffer Library, University Librarian Paul Wiens continued his vigorous transformation of the university library system from a purveyor of books to a diversified system of printed pages and electronic portals. Wiens conducted a delicate diplomacy between maintaining a book library and the burgeoning demands of the electronic-information revolution. Wiens liked to describe the internet as "the new volume on the shelf." With this in mind, the Stauffer embarked on new methods of collecting information for users: a consortia agreement, for instance, with other university libraries for acquiring "e-resources" to aid teaching, research, and learning. In 2002, Queen's joined the Scholars Portal, in an agreement that provided all twenty-one Ontario university libraries with a common electronic infrastructure for sharing information and facilitating interlibrary loans. *In toto*, the library's lifeblood acquisitions budget grew to $9 million by 2004. Changing conduits of knowledge, coupled with the impact of technology, saw the library's staff fall from 207 in 1991 to a trim 153 by 2004.[16] The library thus joined the university-wide effort to broaden the learning experience at Queen's. In 2004, this culminated in the decision to create a "learning commons" in the library that furnished students with one-stop assistance in honing their skills in writing, learning strategies, and information technology. In short, the Queen's library became a remarkably more productive and multi-faceted instrument of education.

Leggett set one last stone in place in the leadership arch he was constructing: a resurrected dean of student affairs. Briefly employed in the heady days of student unrest at Queen's in the Deutsch years, the dean of student affairs had then been intended to act as an interlocutor between administration and student body. When Deutsch concluded that the best intentions of the dean of student affairs seemed to result in a mixed message being sent to students, the role was allowed to slip into abeyance. Leggett determined to revive the post, but to give it better definition, wider functions, and budgetary clout. Since the early 1970s, students had become more entitled and assertive in their expectations of university life. Leggett acknowledged that students had "legitimate needs." A newly recreated dean of student affairs would coordinate the dialogue of administration and student body; it would give the students a voice at the weekly meeting of vice-principals and deans. The focus would be on service functions and, to this end, the new dean was given suzerainty over twelve campus units, ranging from food services and health and counselling on through to athletics and CFRC radio.[17] Some wondered whether the new office trespassed on the age-old prerogative of the Alma Mater Society – whether it was conceived as a critique of the state of student discipline and culture around Queen's. The official response to this anxiety was that matters of judicial surveillance remained in the hands of the AMS Judicial Committee and that students would continue to run their own associational life and to finance it through student-approved fees. Leggett viewed Queen's students as "very supportive" and "very understanding," and believed that the new dean would be there to facilitate relations with the students, not police their behaviour. "Mutual respect is a very important thing in life," he noted.[18] To fill the post, Leggett appointed Bob Crawford, a congenial professor of computing and associate dean of studies in Arts and Science, who, much as Chaplain Brian Yealland had been doing, conceived of his role as an ombudsman and ambassador for student concerns. Crawford began holding regular meetings with the AMS executive, as did Leggett and the vice-principals. He also dedicated himself to building bridges between the residential and academic life of Queen's students, commissioning studies by former Queen's administrators Margaret Hooey and Jill Harris to examine ways by which student residential communities might be linked to the "intellectual life" of the university.[19]

By Christmas 1996, not yet a year and a half into his mandate, Bill Leggett had remodelled the senior management of the university in a forceful and clear-sighted fashion. Some might suggest that he had acted with a very un-Queen's imperative. He was, after all, "Bulldozer Bill," with a reputation from McGill of decisiveness. Yet his vigour was rooted in a firm belief that Queen's was in the throes of a transition for which it was ill-equipped in form and function. Before proceeding, Leggett wanted the assurance that he had competent men and women around him, not to do his bidding, but instead to aid and abet his vision of a university guarding its heritage and at the same time aware that the world that had shaped that parochial reputation was rapidly changing. Queen's thus approached the millennium with as strong a cadre of progressive managers as it had ever enjoyed. But, in the interim, two matters of unfinished business demanded the new principal's attention: the unionization of his faculty and the fate of Queen's dean of women.

Crossing an Inevitable Watershed: The Faculty Unionizes

Universities, with their genetic predisposition to conciliation and consensus, are ill-equipped for confrontation in labour relations. Left in the dark by those who interviewed him for the job, Leggett arrived at Queen's to discover that labour relations on his new campus were far from harmonious – hardly the tranquil stereotype he had harboured of the place when he was in Montreal. That spring, a nasty strike between the Marriott Corporation, which provided the university with catering services in its residences, and its workers, many of them part-time employees, had broken out and gripped the Queen's community. Queen's was confronted by the unfamiliar sight of picketers on Queen's Crescent. Not only did the conflict paralyze food service in the campus residences, but it also provoked heated discussion of the university's responsibility to those working on its campus, even if not directly in its employ. Many students and faculty sympathized with the low-paid service workers. Adding to the pressure, the strike erupted just as the university prepared for its spring examinations. Consequently, the university sought a court injunction to ensure that student routines were not disrupted by the strike. Outgoing Principal David Smith confessed that Queen's suffered from a "degree of inexperience in dealing with labour conflict."[20] Some on campus – particularly CUPE local 229 representing campus maintenance workers – alleged that the university's injunction was an infringement on the strikers' freedom of speech, especially since university security personnel were said to be videotaping the picket line. The Senate Committee on Operations Review noted that the strike provoked a consideration of "basic values" on campus – the clash between workers' freedoms and the university's obligation to provide services to its students.

Leggett inherited the Marriott strike as it reached its ugliest point. There were anonymous letters threatening contamination of student food. A student filmmaker was arrested for troublemaking. The AMS Assembly urged the university to intercede. The new principal nonetheless resisted pressure to intervene, noting that the university was no longer *in loco parentis*, and therefore was not obliged to coddle its students in trying times. Finally, after six months of picketing, the strike was settled in late October, with workers winning guaranteed hours of work during the academic year.[21] In terms of Queen's culture, the sight of picketers daily parading up and down Queen's Crescent upset the comfortable notion that Queen's was a world apart from the sometimes hard realities of social inequality in Canadian life.

The same awakening could be said to apply to the gradual erosion of contractual relations between Queen's faculty and the administration. By 1994, the collegial give-and-take in the setting of faculty compensation that had prevailed since the seventies had all but collapsed. The Consultative Group established by Ron Watts had by the mid-1990s seen its credibility in the eyes of faculty eroded by inflation, university austerity, and a sense that professors elsewhere in the province were pulling away from their Queen's counterparts on paydays. On several occasions, unable to arrive at mutual agreement,

Principal Smith had imposed a salary package by fiat. Toronto's imposition of the Social Contract further bruised faculty sensibilities. By 1993, under pressure from the Queen's University Faculty Association (QUFA), Smith agreed to engage in a discussion of some sort of "special plan" or "dispute-resolution mechanism" tailored to Queen's specific needs that would supersede the uncertainty and informality of the Consultative Group. Smith delegated Vice-Principal Rod Fraser and Applied Science dean, David Bacon, to represent the administration; QUFA sent its president, Grant Amyot, and soon-to-be-president, Allan Manson. Later, university planner Ken Snowdon and QUFA executive Annette Burfoot rotated into the group.

Progress towards a special plan through the winter and spring of 1994 was, to quote the QUFA newsletter *QUFacts*, "rocky." There were many bones of contention, all given compression by the Social Contract pressing down on the Ontario public sector. A fundamental fault line opened up between the two sides: the administration favoured the retention of some form of internal mechanism of dispute resolution, while QUFA looked off-campus for binding arbitration overseen by a third party. Any internal process, QUFA argued, would not make faculty an "equal partner" in a process that would leave final authority in the hands of the Board of Trustees. The QUFA surveys of its membership now consistently indicated that there was little trust left in the old ways. The association fuelled this disposition by releasing figures that indicated that Queen's faculty salaries, in real purchasing terms, would fall by 11 per cent between 1992 and 1996, well behind compensation offered at other Ontario universities.[22]

Leggett arrived on campus just as the task force tried to package its disagreements in a report due to the trustees in September. He quickly suppressed his personal aversion to faculty unionization in favour of trying to restore the collegiality he believed was so central to "the Queen's way." A reservoir of ill will had built up around the compensation issue that needed to be drained if Queen's were to move forward on the other challenges that Leggett was convinced needed addressing. Leggett therefore did two things. He asked QUFA to agree to a postponement of the dispute-resolution report in the hope that the group, now joined by the new principal, might feel its way to a mutually acceptable method of settling faculty compensation, and QUFA, now led by sociologist Annette Burfoot, agreed to re-engage the consultation, but only "for a short time."[23] As a gesture of goodwill, Leggett agreed to settle QUFA's long-standing complaint to the Ontario Pay Equity Commission over gender-driven salary inequity at Queen's; lump-sum payments were consequently dispersed to women faculty who had worked at the university in the years prior to the complaint. This brought Queen's into line with pay-equity norms at many other Canadian universities. Nonetheless, Leggett at the same time, sensing that the die was cast, quietly began looking for a new vice-principal who would be adept at collective bargaining if his hunch proved correct. If there was to be a union, then the administration would come to the table well-represented. That man would be John Cowan, Leggett's newly appointed vice-principal, operations and finance.

Early in October, the reconstituted task force got down to work. Its four members – Leggett and Bacon for the administration and Amyot and Burfoot for QUFA – agreed that the group would shun public pronouncements about their deliberations. Indeed, there was a striking civility about their dialogue. Both sides seemed to agree that Queen's had to get rid of its "we-they" problem.[24] Communication between the two parties was cordially punctuated with "dear Bill" and "dear Annette" salutations. But, despite the civility, hard-core differences remained. Dean Bacon maintained that the old-style collegial approach still had "possibilities." Amyot of the QUFA countered by pointing out that binding arbitration was the most widely practised norm in the private and public sectors. Non-binding arbitration, Amyot argued, was rooted in the assumption that the university administration was motivated by an a priori institutional altruism attuned to the interests of all parties on campus. This, Amyot contended, had not of late been the association's experience. Sensing the chasm of difference, Leggett urged the panel to act "in the interests of the entire university."

Not surprisingly, on 20 October the QUFA executive voted to suspend the deliberation, citing a fundamental "lack of common ground" on the issue. The QUFA president Annette Burfoot resisted Leggett's plea to sustain the dialogue until Christmas, emphatically stating that "the status quo is not good enough." Leggett began to acknowledge the intransigence of the situation. His primary objective now shifted to resolving "the current problem of unhappiness" and creating "a culture of trust." In December, the task force issued an interim report that made it clear that the polarity of binding and non-binding arbitration was as wide as ever. Still hopeful that some sort of deal could be worked out, Leggett nonetheless agreed to hold a number of town-hall meetings to allow the issue to be aired out before the entire university community.[25] These meetings took place in January of the new year, 1995. That same month, QUFA championed binding arbitration to its membership. The association disparaged the administration's advocacy of an internal model of arbitration that would see the principal send a final compensation offer to the trustees for a decision. This was a "heads I win, tails you lose" scheme; the trustees were hardly objective "outsiders." In mid-February, QUFA put the matter to a membership vote. On a 48-per-cent turnout, two-thirds backed binding arbitration administered by a third party, while the only a third favoured a Queen's-centric internal system.

The Board of Trustees seemed less willing than the principal to acknowledge what now appeared inevitable. At its March meeting, despite a briefing from Leggett arguing that faculty were determined to be treated as "equal partners" in matters of compensation, the trustees voted to create their own task force to review the options. Its May 1995 report to the Board seemed to be couched in a nostalgia for the now-defunct Consultative Group – "good history to build upon." Board chair Donald Elliott acknowledged that there were "entrenched views" on the dispute-resolution front and the Board task force recognized the need for a "fair and equitable" process. Nonetheless, the board opted to champion the internal model, slightly tweaked to allow an outside mediation consultant to devise a final offer if faculty and administration became stalemated. That report would go to the principal, who would then submit it to the Board for ratification.[26]

The Board's hard-line reaction struck the QUFA as a "mockery" of two years of constructive engagement with university administration. The fact that the Board unanimously endorsed the revamped non-binding model "stunned" the QUFA executive. A gauntlet had been thrown down. QUFA angrily pointed out that Queen's was one of only two Ontario universities (the other being Western) at which faculty had no formal rights in salary negotiation. At a special meeting, QUFA subsequently won endorsement from its membership to seek certification under the terms of the Ontario Labour Relations Act. When that application was made on 18 September, the QUFA's newsletter proclaimed "We did it!"[27]

At the Brink: 3:15 a.m., 6 December 1995

On 27 and 28 September, the Ontario Labour Relations Board conducted a certification vote at Queen's. Seven hundred and thirty professors duly voted, with 57 per cent of them agreeing to form a union. There were voices of dissent: a group called Professors for a Better Queen's argued that unionization was unprofessional. For many faculty, however, the Board's obdurate attitude seemed to close the door to any further negotiation with Richardson Hall. The annual general meeting of QUFA in November approved the fact that its membership was now a "bargaining unit" operating under the Rand formula, which obliged all faculty to contribute dues to its operations. President Annette Burfoot celebrated the moment as "a significant transition in university affairs at Queen's."[28] As 1996 dawned, QUFA faced its first round of collective bargaining with its "employer." Remarkably, the negotiation went smoothly. By now, John Cowan had assumed his role as vice-principal, operations and finance, and thus became the university's chief negotiator. Cowan was tough (he had given a speech to the Canadian Association of University Business Officers, arguing that dealing with faculty was like "herding sacred cows") and well-versed, but was equally prepared to engage the union in constructive negotiation. Nonetheless, the negotiation was more informed by Leggett's desire to establish a new norm of harmonious labour relations than any desire to stare down the union. Indeed, Leggett was impressed by how "amicable" the negotiations proved to be. To some degree, both parties' willingness to strike an expeditious deal reflected the fact that Ontarians had just elected a cost-cutting Conservative government under Mike "Common Sense" Harris and that draconian austerity seemed to be in the wind.

Like most labour negotiations, the bargaining came down to the wire. A new labour agreement was needed to supersede the one that would terminate at the end of the year. Through the evening and night of 5–6 December, the teams from QUFA and the administration holed up in a conference room in Richardson Hall. Upstairs in his office, the new principal paced anxiously. There was one last sticking point: where would the intellectual property rights of faculty reside? Gratified by the lucrative success of PARTEQ, its office for commercializing university innovation, the administration was eager to capitalize on bright ideas emerging from faculty brains. The faculty naturally fought to retain its proprietary rights. In the end, a compromise was arrived at, fashioned on the famous Gatorade accord at the University of Florida.* At 3:15 a.m., weary negotiators emerged to announce that Queen's faculty had its first collective agreement. It was a thick, utilitarian document, its provisions ranging from merit and scale increases in compensation to the study of a process by which layoffs might take place under conditions of extreme financial exigency. Some matters remained to be ironed out. For instance, in what ways did collective bargaining rights impinge on the traditional authority of the Senate over academic governance at Queen's? Beyond these issues, the agreement had two immediate outcomes: the contract promised three years of labour stability at Queen's and an end to the acrimony of the early 1990s.

Annette Burfoot, a staunch advocate of collective bargaining, admitted that the smooth culmination of the process had in fact seemed "anti-climactic." On 11 January 1997, the Board, now no longer able to postpone the inevitable, met in closed session to approve the contract. Leggett confessed his "clear and unequivocal support for what was a very good agreement." He was particularly pleased with the "normative provisions of the agreement since these could endure for a long time." Leggett estimated that over its three-year term the agreement would cost Queen's $12.2 million in salaries and benefits. A 20-per-cent hike in tuition over the same period, he believed, would cover this expenditure. There was, however, little other costing out of the university's new fiscal relationship with its faculty. Dean Don Carter of law noted that the new contract would strip the Senate of its oversight of the terms of academic employment, but that it would still hold sway over the academic standards. At the same time, other aspects of the agreement slipped through with little incisive interrogation. The agreement did contain an article for final-offer arbitration by an outside mediator as a last-step default if all other negotiation failed. Under another provision, the management of the faculty pension plan, hitherto overseen by a bipartisan committee, now, for instance, became a bargainable right, something that might over time have severe liability implications as faculty demographics shifted and investment markets gyrated. The Board nonetheless ratified the contract and agreed to have three QUFA appointees join its future meetings.[29]

Similarly satisfied, QUFA proceeded to reorganize itself in order to embrace the opportunities opened up by collective bargaining. A new QUFA constitution, fashioned under the presidency of law professor Marvin Baer, was approved in 1997. To make the association more receptive to its members' wishes, a Council of Representatives was formed out of the thirty units of librarians, archivists, and faculty represented by QUFA. An executive committee would act as a cabinet, and an array of standing committees would groom the association's affairs and image. A political-action committee would, for instance, carry the concerns of Queen's faculty into the broader provincial and national arena, something that seemed crucial as the Harris government's "common-sense" revolution broke over the province. Ties were maintained with external bodies, such as the Ontario Confederation of Faculty Associations. An ad hoc committee on salary was mandated to oversee the crucial business of preparing for the annual negotiation with the university over salary scale and merit. By 1998, the new labour climate at Queen's seemed to have established itself with few problems. There was, *QUFacts* happily reported, "little posturing, excess

---

*Gatorade, a "power" drink designed to replenish hydration levels in sun-drenched athletes, was formulated by a team of medical researchers in the mid-1960s for the University of Florida Gators football team. Highly effective, the drink became the centre of a struggle between its inventors and the university that had made their research possible. Eventually, a deal was struck whereby the researchers garnered 20 per cent of the proceeds from the patent and the rest went to the university. Gatorade, the rights of which were later sold to Quaker Oats and PepsiCo, made millions for both parties.

rhetoric, public threats, or rancor from either side."[30] Subsequent three-year collective agreements were negotiated in 1999 and 2002 with the same facility. But there could be no denying that the old collegiality that underlay the relations of faculty and administration were a thing of the past. Labour relations at Queen's acquired a new, confrontational demeanour on the campus. Vice-Principal John Scott Cowan, the university's point man for collective bargaining, epitomized the new ethos – his brusque and domineering style frequently caused irritation, not only amongst faculty but throughout the administration. In 1999, Cowan left Queen's to become principal of the nearby Royal Military College.

"Equity for All" vs "Moral Suasion" – The Dean of Women

University presidencies are never hermetic affairs. Every new incumbent inevitably inherits baggage from their predecessors. For Bill Leggett, this was acutely apparent in the realm of gender and equity rights. The stigma of the "No Means No" debacle still tarnished Queen's image, an unsavoury legacy periodically revived by sexist outbursts in student newspapers or orientation excesses. Nonetheless, the Office of Human Rights under Irène Bujara was credibly establishing itself at the crossroads of the university's social existence as an impartial broker of the rights of students, faculty, and administrators. Coming from Montreal, where cultural values were constantly in play and hotly contested, Leggett was under no illusions that Queen's could aspire to exist as a back eddy of Canada's rights revolution. As the university had reluctantly and sometimes painfully learned since the 1970s, some of its most persistent traditions – football, residence life, and faculty recruitment, for instance – had been framed by gender exclusivity that was increasingly out of kilter with the times. More than any other Canadian university, Queen's had sustained itself on tradition that buttressed its central ethos of community and public service, but the last decades had furnished evidence that malfunctioning or outmoded traditions could prove dysfunctional. From "Kill McGill" football outbursts to sexist stereotypes chanted during orientation, David Smith's principalship had been punctuated by the evidence of the gap between received values and behaviours at Queen's, and of Canada's new mood of social equality and transparency. Bill Leggett was determined not to repeat that experience. "I am strongly committed to developing a system appropriate to the needs of the institution," he declared shortly after taking office, "which will ensure the protection of the rights of all individuals who work and study here."[31] This would not be as easy and clear cut as it seemed.

Since 1911, Queen's had maintained a commitment to the special needs of women in its midst. That year, Principal Daniel Gordon had acknowledged the need for an advisor to women, then still a slim minority of its students. The post, he wrote in his *Principal's Report*, would "be one of influence rather than authority, in which, by sympathy and counsel, not by command, she [for it was assumed that the role would be assigned to a woman] might aid the women students" in their studies and their development as citizens.[32] In 1918, the advisor became the dean of women, but the dedication to mentorship remained central to its mission. Thus, the position of dean of women at Queen's was founded, not to bolster tradition, but to slowly buck its hegemony by nurturing (a word that would persistently be employed to describe the post by its advocates over the years) in women a spirit of worth and independence amid a campus society that was powerfully male in orientation. Unlike her companion deans, the dean of women was equipped with few specific powers, and a meagre budget. She would oversee the management of women's residences. Indeed, the dean of women lived in the women's residence – first in Ban Righ Hall and later in Victoria Hall. Only a handful of staffers – an assistant dean, a residence business manager, and a secretary – reported directly to her. She oversaw the selection of residence dons and worked with the Women's Residence Council. But beyond such specified duties, the dean dwelt only in the realm of moral suasion. As a 1960s description of her portfolio noted: "She assists students in thinking through changing ideologies and values and personal problems." While her mandate may have appeared to be focused on women in residence, the dean of women was in fact dedicated to the needs of *all* women on Queen's campus, a constituency that expanded considerably in the wake of late-sixties growth in professional and graduate studies, not to mention the increasing number of women living off-campus.

Given the latitude provided them by their loose mandate, the incumbents of the dean's office chose to pursue tremendously varied priorities over the middle decades of the twentieth century. Alice Vibert Douglas (1939–59) chose to use her stature as a world-renowned astrophysicist as a role model for Queen's women, intellectually mentoring them away from traditional gendered values of society. University education was not about acquiring a "Mrs," but instead about getting a BA and, perhaps, an MA or even a PhD. Nonetheless, Douglas perpetuated many of the received norms of a women student at Queen's: Sunday-afternoon teas in the Ban Righ common room, Levana formals, residence curfews, and a skirts-mandatory policy at dinner. Douglas's successor, Beatrice Bryce (1959–71) felt the accentuated tension of old norms and the tremendous pressure of growth on Queen's campus and in women's consciousness across Canadian society. "Dean Bryce can be viewed as the transitional Dean," historians Maureen Garvie and Jennifer Johnson have eloquently noted, "coolly holding her white-gloved finger in the dyke as the wave of the 1960s crested."[33] Under Bryce, any pretense that undergraduate women lived a cloistered, protective existence on Queen's campus evaporated. Coed dining arrived, as did visitation hours for males. While Bryce may have tried to preserve elements of the old feminine mystique, she also acknowledged the need for progressive change – better health counselling, birth-control advice, and, in 1969, the integration of the men's and women's residence management.

Bryce's successor from 1971 to 1980, Evelyn Reid, accelerated the process of constructive engagement with the times. Although she had studied religion at Columbia in New York, Reid had no formal academic credentials, a fact that diminished her in the eyes of the academic deans with whom she worked day-by-day. Indeed, feminists on campus, such as the members of the Association of Women Teaching at Queen's, drawing inspiration from second-wave feminism's insistence on women's need to penetrate the world of credentialed success, called for a dean with academic weight. Reid nonetheless brought new activism to the dean's role. She reached out to the growing number of Queen's women who came and went to the university every day without ever experiencing residence life. As if to make her mission evident, Reid daily cycled to and fro across the campus. She took an active role in the founding of the Ban Righ Foundation. She established an oral-history project to capture the experiences of bygone women at Queen's before it was lost. She acknowledged new problems, such as recreational-drug use on campus. She brought contemporary culture into residence life through concerts, lectures, and theatre. A floor in Victoria Hall was designated French-only. Despite all this, Reid became caught in a pincher movement: her erstwhile colleagues in administration tended to think of her as an agitator who stirred up controversy, while on the other flank some feminists felt she lacked focus on hard-core feminist issues. This tension became evident in 1975 when Reid became eligible for a second term. Principal Watts appointed an advisory committee to guide the decision. Across Canada, many universities were scrapping the role of dean of women, reasoning that women now wanted equal treatment, not separate status. At Queen's such opinion was heard, but others championed the office as a means of further nurturing women's rights. Many women faculty argued that the dean should stay, but suggested that the incumbent should bring more-stalwart academic credentials to her mission. Battling a gnawing deficit, Watts chose to dodge the issue and took his committee's lukewarm recommendation to renew Reid for three more years.

Watts could not escape the issue forever. Despite pro-tem extensions of Reid's appointment, a 1979 advisory committee recommended that Queen's still needed a deanship dedicated to the "particular needs of women." It soon became apparent that the administration did not consider Reid a likely occupant of that position. She was not even informed that an advertisement of the post would be placed in *University Affairs*. A divisive debate followed, Reid's critics arguing that she had failed to take a hard feminist line on issues such as sexual harassment and her defenders declaring that she was not all about "coziness and culture," but instead about creating a "challenging academic environment" for Queen's women.[34] Although Reid was interviewed, the appointment went to Dr Elspeth Baugh, a clinical psychologist with strong Queen's roots. Baugh not only had a Queen's BA and a Marty Scholarship, which had supported her graduate studies in Michigan, but her father had been Principal Wallace. Now she returned to Queen's with a York PhD and much worldly experience as a mother and practising psychologist.[35] Baugh immediately brought a focused vigour to her mission. Upon arrival, she found her alma mater's gender inequality disturbing and archaic. Thus, from the outset, she dedicated herself to enhancing "the diversity of human experience" at Queen's.[36] She maintained the established role of mentor and nurturer to women students, but at the same time became a forceful voice for structural change in university policies and attitudes. She moved her office to the more-centrally-located Mackintosh-Corry Building and won membership on innumerable university committees. In 1988, she assumed the role of director of all Queen's residences. Baugh also taught a graduate course in clinical psychotherapy and championed the adoption of a women's-studies program. Her relations with Principal David Smith, whom she suspected of being a laggard on issues such as sexual harassment, were at times strained. This coolness became frosty after Smith's clumsy handling of the "No Means No" incident. In short, Baugh conducted herself as if she believed that her office carried "an implicit power" to act on feminist matters.[37]

In parallel with Baugh's activism on behalf of women, Queen's witnessed the emergence of a complementary, and at times competing, system of equity rights. Throughout the 1980s and into the 1990s, a series of external pressures and internal shocks provoked the university into a broader activism on the human-rights front. With the 1982 Charter of Rights and Freedoms in place, the federal government began insisting that its spending and employment practices oblige fundamental rights of gender, race, and religion. Federal research funding was, for instance, tied to institutional acknowledgement of Charter rights. The provincial government in Toronto imposed pay equity on Ontario employers. In 1989, for instance, Queen's instituted an Employment Equity Council. These new rights umbrellas also opened over student life. Articles of dubious gender sensitivity could now be challenged through complaint to the Ontario Human Rights Commission. Daily life on campus became more closely governed by updated codes of student and faculty behaviour. Sexual harassment was given sharper definition. Anti-racism and the perplexingly labelled anti-heterosexualism (that is, challenging the view that only heterosexual relations were "normal") coordinators were soon to be appointed. Grievance procedures were updated.

Nonetheless, the looseness of this emerging web of rights and responsibilities was made apparent in the university's lethargic response to the "No Means No" crisis. Recognition of this dysfunction led in 1991 to the creation of Queen's Human Rights Office with its mandate to act as the university's central agency for the inculcation and regulation of human respect on campus. Two things were evident in this gradual shift. First, there was a gravitational tendency to centralized oversight of human rights and responsibilities on the campus, a conscious shift away from having pockets of control dedicated to particular constituencies, whether they be students in residence or faculty in the classroom. Second, the university's administrators wanted to diminish their role as the final arbiters of questions of rights. They wanted no more slippage between the cracks, no more student sit-ins, and no more overlapping authority. They wanted an objective, systematic adjudication on rights on the Queen's campus.

The forceful activism of the dean of women was eventually bound to collide with the university's increasing assertion of a centralized rubric of rights. This became increasingly apparent in 1993 when Baugh retired and was replaced by Pamela Dickey Young, who had come to Queen's in 1985 to teach theology. An ordained United Church minister, she had earned a doctorate in religious studies from Southern Methodist University in Texas. In 1991, when Baugh had first indicted her desire to step down, Dickey Young had served on an advisory committee set up by the principal and ominously instructed to review the "future" role of the dean of women. In doing so, Dickey Young sensed a clear desire on the part of the administration to bring the office to a quiet conclusion. Indeed, while Dean Baugh's appointment had been extended, her mandate was curtailed – she would, for instance, lose her supervision of the residences. When Baugh, worn down by the precariousness of her circumstances, finally retired in 1993, Dickey Young somewhat reluctantly agreed to take the position.

In doing so, she made it clear that she would take up Baugh's mantle and push for structural change in the university's gender orientation. For instance, she became active in pushing for better daycare on campus; in 1994 expanded child-care facilities enabled women students to attend evening classes. At the same time, Dickie Young maintained the deanship's long-standing mentoring of women students. She used residence "fireside chats" to showcase women such as federal politician Mary Collins and Kingston mayor Helen Cooper as role models for young undergraduates. But it soon dawned on Dickie Young that she had little influence in the actual crucible of Queen's decision making. Her advocacy of a policy of spousal hiring (giving consideration to academically qualified spouses for employment at the same university), for instance, gained no traction. She also lamented the continuing looseness in Queen's equity policies: "I continue to be concerned that there are a large number of avenues of access to policies of a disciplinary nature that may issue quite different penalties." In her 1994 activities report, she described her role as "elusive." Lacking much hard authority and denied a meaningful budget, she found herself engaged in what she described as "shuttle diplomacy" between the various powers-that-be at Queen's.[38] Dickie Young increasingly came to the realization that, as important as mentoring young women was, she was impotent in affecting real policy change at Queen's. Her only power remained "moral suasion."[39] Months after Bill Leggett assumed the principalship, Dickie Young submitted her resignation and planned her return to the classroom.

Leggett understood that his ability to alter Queen's direction crucially depended on harmony in the workplace. Hence, his relatively quick surrender to the inevitability of collective bargaining with the faculty. Early in 1995, he sent a questionnaire to all members of the Queen's community, quizzing them about their workplace environment. In this, he relied upon the long-standing Principal's Advisory Committee on the Status of Women (PACSOW). Since the time of John Deutsch, the advisory committee had provided policy suggestions and statistical benchmarking of the progress of women at Queen's. Leggett told Sandi Carey, the chair of the group, that he considered it a "cornerstone" of Queen's approach to equity. This said, Leggett soon detected that a fundamental choice lay ahead: to perpetuate the work of the dean of women or to embrace a more decisive and holistic approach to matters of campus equity. Unlike his predecessor,

The cessation of the post of dean of women in 1996 wrenched the Queen's community. The administration argued that the university must embrace an all-in-one approach to human rights, while others defended the need for a special champion for women. In 1999, the launch of a book celebrating the nurturing role of the dean of women since 1911 drew the attendance of three former incumbents: (left to right) Evelyn Reid (1971–80), Elspeth Baugh (1980–90) and, Pamela Dickey Young (1993–96).

Leggett was not predisposed to push the issue to the back burner, however contentious it might prove to be. To feel out his options, the principal quietly wrote to his counterpart presidents at other major Canadian universities. How, he asked them, had they coped with the matter of ensuring equity? A consensus readily materialized: most universities had chosen to centralize the function. David Strangway at the University of British Columbia reported that his university had just created the office of associate vice-president, equity, a position buttressed by individual equity officers in each faculty. Robert Pritchard at the University of Toronto similarly reported that his campus had established a central Equity Issues Advisory Group. Susan Mann at York sagely advised that equity was a "philosophical issue" that would undoubtedly stir debate at Queen's, but that she herself favoured integrating equity into "all the activities of the university."[40]

Early in February 1995, Leggett acted. The time had come, he wrote to all staff, for a comprehensive review of all human-rights and equity matters at Queen's. To this end, a consultant – Mary Baetz, a psychologist with Western Management Consultants in Toronto – had been employed to facilitate the inquiry. Margaret Hooey, the able secretary of the Senate, would assist in the process. Open meetings were promised, and one-on-one consultation with Baetz was welcomed. Almost immediately, heated debate materialized. Pamela Dickey Young, who would stay on as dean until the end of the year, urged the principal to embed gender consciousness in the job descriptions of all the new vice-principal positions being advertised. Geographer Audrey Kobayashi told Leggett (whom she had known as a faculty member at McGill) that she was "deeply concerned about the current climate for women faculty members at Queen's." There were, she said, too few women in senior management. The prospect of losing the dean of women would only heighten the distrust and cynicism. If Queen's was serious about equity, she advised, there needed to be more explicit responsibility and accountability if equity was ever to have teeth at Queen's. Leggett generally agreed: "I am personally of the view that we will never succeed in this mission if we adopt the approach of a single individual with whom responsibility for advancement is lodged."[41] Across the campus, the debate was engaged by groups united in a concern for equity – the AMS Committee against Racism and Ethnic Discrimination and the Council of Employment Equity each brought their message to Baetz.

Baetz tabled her report just before Christmas 1995. Queen's, she reported, was at a "fork in the road." Commendable progress had been made on gender and equity issues, but the gains had been eroded by too little coordination, too much volunteerism, and a lack of accountability. The time had now come for a more "fundamental" approach to the problems of inequity. What Queen's lacked was an "integrated, strategic focus to meeting its well-articulated equity vision."[42] The clear implication of the Baetz report was that the function of the dean of women had become an outlier to the central purpose of equity at Queen's and that coordination of equity required central oversight unrestrained by gender demarcations. There was, after all, now a dean of student affairs who functioned regardless of gender. The report was challenged by some as "extremely general and vague," lacking in specific remedies.[43]

Wary of committing himself on the basis of one report alone, Leggett had also appointed an advisory committee on the office of the dean of women, which began its deliberations that November. Membership in the group drew on the faculty, the AMS, the graduate-student association, the alumni, the newly minted dean of student affairs, and the Board of Trustees. Leggett sat as its chair. Most assumed from the labelling of the advisory group that the appointment of a new dean was still on the table and that the challenge would be to rejig her mandate and office's authority. Leggett, however, was now becoming convinced that he would have to spend "political capital" to move this issue forward. Division became ever more evident as the committee deliberated. No easy consensus emerged. Leggett was now heavily inclined to pursue the advice he had received from his fellow university presidents – central equity services. Sensing this unavoidable outcome, two female members of the advisory group – Roberta Hamilton of sociology and Virginia Walker of biology – quit the committee rather than be party to what they considered its forgone conclusions.

The April report of the advisory committee sounded the death knell for the dean of women's role at Queen's. Ultimate authority for equity would be vested in the new vice-principal, academic, for all questions of academic hiring and tenure. The human-resources implications of equity would rest with the new vice-principal, operations and finance.

Backstopping these authorities would be a new University Equity Advisor, who would serve the equity interests of all students, staff, and faculty. More resources would be devoted to line equity functions such as the work of the sexual-harassment coordinators in handling complaints. Given this centralized scaffold, there could be no room for alternative avenues of equity advancement and redress, such as the dean of women had so ably offered since 1911. The long-standing status of women advisory committee would also cease its deliberations; its "good work" had often been conveniently overlooked because it had come to be seen as too closely connected to the principal's office. A new Senate committee on equity and the Council on Employment Equity would now monitor the equity situation at Queen's and chivvy the vice-principals if progress was deemed too slow.[44]

"No Slam Dunk": From Dean to Equity Advisor

An era was ending. And it was ending with an alacrity uncharacteristic of Queen's. Leggett instinctively believed that Queen's had to move forward on the equity front. It had to conform to national patterns. For too long matters of gender and equity had been allowed to drift amid a sea of consultation and gradualism, periodically spilling over into crises that had insidiously eroded Queen's sense of community. On 23 May 1996, Leggett took the recommendations of his advisory committee to the Senate. The appointment of deans was the principal's prerogative, but "out of respect" for the Senate he felt obliged to explain his purpose to its members. Conscious that the matters at hand affected the whole campus, he asked that his remarks be taped, so that there be no misinterpretation of his rationale. His ambition since arriving at Queen's, he said, had been to ensure "equity for everybody." Despite Queen's reputation as a "welcoming, sympathetic, understanding, and supportive" community, he had been struck by "an unease at Queen's" on the topic of equity. He had resolved to study the issue before acting, to consult in the university's inimitable fashion. "This is a serious issue," he admitted, "and I was not prepared to 'slam dunk' it." His "holistic" survey had convinced him that centralization was the way ahead. Not everyone, he admitted, agreed. He noted that his committee had sadly shed discontented members. But there could be no going back: an end had to be put to a "climate here which reverberates with dissatisfaction, with frustration, with anger, and with suspicion." There was a frankness to his sentiment: "I can give you absolutely no assurance that what I am doing is right and I am prepared to be proven wrong." Making such decisions, he confided, underlined his sense that university presidents found life "lonely at the top."[45]

The decision did not rest easy with many at Queen's. A venerable tradition was being laid to rest. Some complained about the process. Professor Kobayashi noted that the advisory committee had wandered far from its seeming mandate of examining the "office" of the dean of women into a wholesale revamping of equity services at Queen's. Many others bemoaned the loss of the dean's personal, nurturing touch in the lives of so many Queen's women over the years. "Let's be true to the spirit of 1911," Gail Ward Stewart of Arts '54 wrote in the *Queen's Alumni Review*. Diane McKenzie, a nursing grad of 1964, recalled how the dean's door was always open to women in need of a personal touch of support, "or, as my son calls it, a 'Mom-fix.'"[46] Many departments petitioned the principal to reverse his decision. Chaplain Brian Yealland called for the dean's reinstatement. Frank Burke, the president of QUFA, agreed. Trustees Mary Collins and Rosemary Brown questioned whether, since women were still in so many ways systematically disadvantaged in society, a single, designated woman could turn the tide. Broader initiatives, they suggested, might be more effective. A rally in June expressed the opinion that the loss of the dean of women in effect "demoted" women's equity needs. "The basic rationale for equity services," it was argued, "should be to address the needs of those who experience inequality."[47]

But Leggett stood by his decision. Attention now turned to the all-important appointment of the new University Advisor on Equity. Even the critics of Leggett's decision agreed that the position had to have teeth and a pervasive mandate. Realizing that he had spent a good deal of "political capital" in getting to this point, Leggett knew that the appointment had to have broad credibility. Through the fall and winter of 1996, open meetings and Senate and AMS committees, culminating in a principal's advisory committee, teased out the terms of reference for the position. There were many wrinkles: was the position primarily dedicated to addressing *individual* instances of inequity or to eradicating *systemic* inequity? Was the position to play an activist role in tackling equity challenges or was it to be a more passive and neutral arbiter of cases brought before it. Similarly, there was debate over exactly what "equity" meant: was it a static concept that simply benchmarked equal treatment for all or did it entail a proactive interventionism? Most favoured a continuation of the activism of an Elspeth Baugh or the Association of Women Teaching at Queen's. All the while, the Senate Committee on Operations Review worked on the wording of an overarching mission statement conveying the university's commitment to equity for all its members. By the spring of 1997, a tripartite strategy supporting equity at Queen's had fallen into place: the new equity advisor at its centre, supported on the flanks by a new Senate committee on educational equity and the existing Council on Employment Equity, would act as the fulcrum of a more-equitable Queen's.[48] In effect, what had begun with the opening of the Human Rights Office in 1992 had now unfolded into a full umbrella of human and equity rights at Queen's. It had been, Leggett reflected, "an emotional struggle for all."[49]

In April 1998, Leggett announced that Mary Margaret Dauphinee had been appointed as the University Advisor on Equity. Dauphinee brought twenty-five years of equity policy and implementation experience to her new assignment, most recently at Dalhousie University but previously with the City of Toronto and the federal government. She told the *Queen's Gazette* that equity involved "fairness for everybody" and warned that equity required both a "communal effort" and "the dedication of a lifetime – it is a process."[50] Dauphinee approached her duties with protean vigour. To underscore her central role in his administration, Leggett put Dauphinee in a Richardson Hall office. Her challenge was twofold: first, to push the equity message into every nook and cranny of the Queen's community, and then to benchmark the progress of equity in terms of balance and distribution through its ranks. She sat on hiring committees. She worked with the Coordinator of Faculty Recruitment and Retention (a post recently created by the vice-principal, academic) to ensure that faculty found Queen's and Kingston a harmonious environment. In compliance with the new QUFA collective agreement, she conducted equity surveys of the faculty to monitor whether Queen's reflected national benchmarks of diversity. There were seminars on making post-secondary education more accessible to students with disabilities or of low-income backgrounds. Dauphinee also connected with the Four Directions Aboriginal Student Centre to help Native Canadians adapt to the unfamiliar world of higher education.

Not all was sweetness and light, however. At times, the equity message seemed slow to penetrate. Dauphinee complained that only 35 per cent of faculty returned their equity surveys. Similarly, national rankings of universities by *Maclean's* and the *Globe and Mail* continued to rank Queen's poorly on the criteria of diversity. Nonetheless, together with Irène Bujara in the Human Rights Office, Dauphinee helped Queen's turn a crucial corner – the rancours of the previous decades over rights and equity now fell under the purview of what Dauphinee called "managed diversity." "Ten years ago – and 150 years before that," the *Queen's Journal* observed, "the student most likely to be seen strolling down University Avenue had blue eyes, fair skin, and a last name that began with 'Mac.'"[51] Perhaps emblematic of changing times at Queen's, students elected a Muslim, Taz Pirmohamed, as AMS president in 1994. Ahmed Kayssi, a Muslim undergraduate born in the Middle East, followed as student rector in 2002.[52] A remarkable photograph taken at convocation would capture the shift: Rector Kayssi, Chancellor Baillie, and Principal Leggett all decked out in kilts.

Bill Leggett's first eighteen months in office might thus well be described as a process of tidying up his inheritance as principal. He had acted with dispatch to reorder the senior administrative cadre, building a stellar team of colleagues, each with a cleanly defined strategic goal. He had acknowledged the inevitability of collective bargaining with Queen's faculty and had helped to launch its first contract onto untroubled waters. And now, he had aligned Queen's with contemporary attitudes and prescriptions for equity and diversity. The dean of women was gone, but a dean of student affairs and an equity advisor had been created. There had been traditional Queen's consultation in all this, but there had also been a decisiveness unfamiliar to Queen's in recent years propelling his agenda. Now, Leggett's focus shifted to adapting Queen's to broader tendencies unfolding in the twilight of the twentieth century – a world increasingly characterized by sometimes glib but powerful prescriptions: globalization, privatization, fiscal "common sense," branding, and accountability. Despite the oversimplification of such nostrums, Queen's would have to adjust its traditions to their ethos if it was to remain a nationally esteemed, viable, and competitive university in the new millennium.

Herstmonceux: A Castle of Dreams

Queen's principals since John Deutsch had wrestled with the challenge of making the university's West Campus more than a convenient annex for the education faculty and a residential precinct for accommodating the university's swelling undergraduate population. Bill Leggett would, however, be the first principal to contend with the reality of Queen's *east* campus – Herstmonceux, the moated medieval castle in East Sussex, England, thousands of kilometres, not just blocks, away. The castle had been the generous, if unexpected, 1993 gift of Alfred and Isabel Bader. Bader's motive extended far beyond any egotistical desire to celebrate his worldly success in business; it was, instead, a reflection of his vision to see Queen's assert itself on the international stage, thereby exposing its students to the world beyond Canada's cloistered boundaries. Bader's own youth had seen his values and entrepreneurial drive formatively shaped by a globe-trotting adolescence that took him from Europe to Canada and eventually to America. He was now intent on reversing that trajectory for young Canadians by giving them an inviting avenue into Europe.

But things at Herstmonceux had not gone exactly according to expectations. At his first meeting as principal in late September 1994, Leggett bore discouraging news from England. A few weeks earlier, the castle has welcomed its first students. But here were only forty-seven of them, all from Arts and Science. Estimates had suggested that the International Study Centre (ISC) – the less-medieval name now accorded the castle – would need at least 175 students a year to meet its costs. When Maurice Yeates, the former dean of Graduate Studies and now executive director of the ISC, explained that it would cost a first-year student $8,000 to spend a year in England, it became apparent that the centre, despite the forty courses it had on offer and its proximity to the rich cultural life of London, was meeting consumer resistance. Faculty were similarly not showing much enthusiasm for transatlantic pedagogy – library resources at Herstmonceux were, for instance, slim. The university accountants completed the gloomy picture: the frantic construction over the last year to ready the small, new campus was woefully over-budget and often shoddy in execution. Herstmonceux was, after all, hundreds of years old and did not lend itself to modern technologies and standards of comfort. A new residence, again generously funded by the Baders, was under construction. But costs were outstripping money. Asbestos had, for instance, to be stripped out of the castle's rooms. Trapped by their initial hasty embrace of the project, the trustees had little alternative but to pay the mounting bill. They approved an $18-million line of credit, from which $2 million had already been drawn. Yeates estimated that the centre would need about $1.3 million a year to operate and that the ink was likely to stay red for several years to come.

Leggett, echoing the university's upbeat press releases,[53] tried to put roseate gloss on the situation by praising the renovations that had been completed, but few on Queen's Kingston campus were convinced. Faculty members were still in the austere grip of the province's Social Contract, which had capped their salary hike that year at a mere 1 per cent. Departmental budgets had been trimmed, from faculty hiring to paper clips. Queen's students were in an equally sour mood. Undergraduate fees had been pushed to the maximum ceiling allowed by the province. Special per-course levies had been tacked onto normal fees. The AMS president, Katherine Philips, told the trustees that four thousand students had "opted-out" of their contribution to the AMS's pledge to support the university's ambitious Challenge Fund campaign.[54] Against this backdrop, a castle in the English countryside seemed like an extravagance. Rector David Baar bitterly noted to the trustees that "the financial viability of the Castle depended on factors only marginally associated with the Queen's mission."[55] Ironically, in these same months, the Stauffer Library – Queen's on-campus Gothic castle – was nearing completion. To be inaugurated on the day of Leggett's installation, the Stauffer was seen by all as a *useful* addition to the university's mission. Herstmonceux was not.

But Bill Leggett begged to differ. Like the critics, he too was deeply concerned by the escalating costs across the Atlantic. He could see also that the project had been entered into with Pollyanna-ish optimism and an ill-conceived business plan. In particular, he was troubled that the castle had initially been conceived of as a stand-alone addition to the university, rather than an integral part of its academic mission. He was also acutely aware that the castle's viability and the long-standing munificence of Alfred Bader were intimately connected. The facts suggested that the easiest option might have been to walk away from the castle, mend fences with Dr Bader, and then refocus on the university's home patch.[56] But two factors persuaded Leggett to give the International Study Centre a reprieve. First, he visited the castle and looked beyond the construction chaos and skimpy enrolment to see its long-term potential. He told the trustees that Herstmonceux was "a window of opportunity" for Queen's – an opportunity for the university to break out of the comfortable-but-parochial bailiwick in which it had existed for much of its existence. Yes, Queen's inured culture had brought esteem and success, but it was now in danger of a stasis that would cut it off from the rapidly globalizing possibilities challenging post-secondary education.

And here was his second intuition: Queen's must internationalize its ambitions if it was to attract the best and brightest of faculty and students. In particular, research and graduate studies would only thrive at Queen's if the university was attached to international flows of ideas and talent. In the fall of 1994, registrar Alison Morgan reported that Queen's had attracted only 278 international students to its first-year undergraduate programs.[57] Since the early 1990s, the number of international graduate students had also been steadily falling, driven lower by Ontario's decision to withdraw health coverage from foreign students and by scholarship parsimony on the part of federal agencies like CIDA.[58] Leggett was not alone in his perception that Queen's must stretch beyond its established reputation as a national university intent on becoming an international university. Queen's International Centre had been ministering to foreign students on campus since the 1960s. Now, under director Wayne Myles, it was increasingly involved in inducing Queen's students to think about study abroad through exchange programs. Leggett shared the ambition, telling the trustees that there was "a rapid awakening in Canada" to the need to attract foreign students and at the same time dispatch our own to foreign shores.[59] Herstmonceux offered Queen's a strategic perch on Europe's doorstep and a stepping stone to global awareness.

The struggle to save and then reorient Herstmonceux would prove arduous. Leggett initially decided to stay the course – to try to incubate the castle as an off-shore learning centre for Queen's that would be financially self-sustaining and would add lustre to the university's image. In keeping with his approach to his management team in Richardson Hall, he enlisted forceful leadership for the ISC, calling upon Don Macnamara, a retired Canadian Forces brigadier general, who was now teaching in the Queen's business school. A decisive military style and an interest in international studies made Macnamara a solid choice. He relocated to England and gave Leggett the straight goods on the Herstmonceux situation. By the spring of 1995, Macnamara was reporting that student numbers were creeping upward – "100-per-cent customer satisfaction," he reported – but that the budget was still sour – a projected $1.6-million deficit for the upcoming year. By September, he reported that attendance was up another 50 per cent, particularly since students from twenty-nine other universities were now eligible to take courses at Herstmonceux. The crucial problem, he now frankly admitted, was that the castle's 1994 business plan was simply unworkable and had been predicated on projections that were not "accurate." The break-even point for the ISC would have to be pushed back another year.[60]

The castle's faltering progress was compounded by political news from home base in Ontario. The election in June 1995 of a provincial government led by Progressive Conservative premier Mike Harris extended the financial gloom and uncertainty that had hung over post-secondary education in the province since the early decade. Harris's promise of a "common-sense revolution" in provincial finances soon translated into draconian cuts in spending, including a $400-million "diet" for post-secondary education. Initial projections by Vice-Principal Cowan and the university's senior planner, Ken Snowdon, indicated that this would slice as much as $20 million out of Queen's operating grant from Queen's Park. Against this ominous backdrop, any thought of shouldering further deficits in England seemed reckless. With the prospect of further boosts in student fees and continued capping of faculty salaries, the castle became a touchstone of discontent. Behind the scenes, the finance committee of the Board of Trustees grappled with the deterioration of the university's finances; in February 1996, projections for the 1995–96 budget under the strain of the Harris cuts showed a looming deficit of over $600,000. This cast Queen's ambitions in England in a stark new light. However flawed the project's initial goals may have been, one benchmark persisted: that Herstmonceux should never be a net drain on the university's operating budget. That dedication was now in tatters. So were the hopes that the castle could be sustained by fundraising in England and by selling its courses as the chance for an interesting interlude in Europe. However, there was acute anxiety that an abandonment of the ISC might damage the university's three-decade-long philanthropic relationship with Alfred Bader. Admittedly, Bader had at the outset said that the university would be free to sell the property if it was not financially viable, but this, everybody agreed, was not a message the university wanted to deliver to its most generous benefactor.

On 29 February, Leggett braced himself for what now seemed inevitable and addressed the Senate. He had no alternative but to close the centre. The cost of its acquisition had risen to $22.4 million, and its accumulated debt was nearing $14.7 million. The university could see no way to covering the castle's ongoing $500,000 annual maintenance bill. Queen's, he said, as if to salve his own ambition for the castle, would find other ways to extend its international outreach. Don Macnamara made an "impassioned plea for Herstmonceux." If, he said, "in these matters the 'head' must have its way, the 'heart' must have its say." Macnamara went on to enumerate "the loss" that closing the castle would represent. He cited the enthusiastic experience of those students who had come across the Atlantic – they had seen the cosmopolitan majesty of London, walked the beaches of Normandy, seen Anne Frank's hideaway home, and heard Shakespeare in the homeland of the bard. Queen's, he concluded, must understand that the castle "returns dividends in a way no balance sheet can measure." Macnamara's sentiment echoed beyond the Senate chamber: "Students at castle, surprised, saddened," ran the *Journal* headline a day later.

The Friday-afternoon meeting of the Senate segued immediately into a Board of Trustees meeting the next day. Few trustees' meetings have generated such passionate, heart-rending, and agonizing debate. Anticipating such intensity, Chair Donald Elliott said that debate would be limited to three minutes a person. After, that was, the principal had stated his case. Leggett opened the discussion with an incisive declaration that the castle had failed to live up to any of the initial assumptions underlying its acquisition. It *was* impinging on the university's operating budget. It had not sustained fundraising in England, and there was little prospect of it reporting a surplus in the near future. Queen's had, he frankly admitted, embarked on a project for which

The vision and generosity of Isabel and Alfred Bader, seen here on the ramparts of Herstmonceux under a fluttering Queen's flag, allowed the castle, despite its rocky start, to serve as a beachhead for Queen's internationalization.

it had little previous experience. For instance, the castle's initial business plan made no allowance for currency fluctuations between the dollar and the pound. Perhaps most disappointing, the centre was failing to attract enough students to sustain its 410-student annual capacity. Indeed, the castle was acquiring a reputation as a place which attracted only well-heeled students; other students found it too costly and too much of a disruption from their normal degree programs. Leggett then reminded the trustees that Dr Bader had said that he would not object to the jettisoning of the castle if it proved financially or academically unviable. With this in mind, Leggett had flown to Milwaukee to apprise Dr Bader of the situation. Privately, Leggett told friends that it was the most agonizing duty he had as yet performed on the university's behalf. Bader, he reported, was "concerned and upset," but nonetheless understanding.

Leggett then told the trustees that the university must "phase out" the ISC. A task force would define the "optimal exit strategy," and the doors would close in September 1996. He asked that people not "look back and point fingers." Even if it had stumbled in this sally, Queen's must still fix its gaze on the international horizon. Kim Sturgess, a Calgary business executive and chair of the finance committee, then declared that her committee backed the principal's reasoning. It was a stunning moment – Queen's was admitting defeat and planning a retreat. Leggett asked all concerned "to proceed in a constructive spirit," but the mood in the Collins Room had turned undeniably taut.*

Then the tide turned. As long as the castle had stumbled along piling up deficits, it had served as a convenient lightening rod for campus discontent. But now that its death knell had been sounded, people thought twice. At other times and for other

---

*The Collins Room, site of so many Board and Senate meetings, was named after Everett Alfred Collins, a Queen's engineering graduate of 1905 who became an executive with Inco and later a Queen's trustee. Collins gave generously to his alma mater. He also harboured virulent anti-Semitic views. When these views, expressed in correspondence with Principal Wallace in 1944, were uncovered by Queen's history professor Gordon Dueck in 2009, the trustees voted, after much pressure, to remove Collins's name from the room, given its role as a central forum for campus opinion. The room was subsequently renamed in honour of one-time Queen's chancellor Peter Lougheed.

causes, Leggett reminded his Queen's colleagues of the title of Hilda Neatby's history of the university's earliest years: *To Strive, to Seek, to Find, and Not to Yield*. Suddenly, Herstmonceux seemed to fit into that mould. People began to see potential, not liability, in the faraway castle. The Board had just agreed to admit its first two students to its deliberations – in April, Dean Campbell, a fourth-year philosophy student would take his seat in their midst. Student sensitivities had long been recognized in the right of outsiders to pose questions to the trustees. Following a last-ditch appeal by Don Macnamara to look beyond the dollars, students began to make their views known to the trustees. They complained that there had been no advance notice, let alone discussion, of the closure. Veterans of Herstmonceux courses told how the experience had opened their minds. A commerce student, Julie Breen, told the Board that she understood what the numbers were saying, but urged them to consider the powerful, less-tangible possibilities of allowing Queen's students to slip their parochial bonds. Going to the castle was not just about book-learning in England; it was about a *total* experience – about going to Paris to walk the galleries of the Louvre, about visiting the Great Hall in Ghent. Even though Leggett had broken the news of the closure only a day before in the Senate, student petitions had already been gathered and were now presented. Many of the students spoke with passion. The principal and many of the trustees were moved: "I had tears in my eyes," Leggett later admitted. "Honest to God."[61] Leggett would later describe this sudden transformation of negativism into diehard support as "my single greatest lesson in human behaviour."[62]

Taken aback by the students' fervour, the trustees paused to reconsider their options. Dan Burns, perhaps recalling his own student activism of the sixties, asked if the real-estate side of the problem might be separated from the question of perpetuating international studies. Toronto publisher Donna Scott suggested that the closure task force also be charged with looking into possible partnerships with other universities and better marketing of the castle. Many trustees fretted openly about letting Queen's reputation down by denying students a chance to connect with the greater world. Many, like businessmen John Rae and Jim Leech, said they understood the fiscal needs of the university, but feared the effects of admitting failure on the institution's psyche. Other trustees, such as Rosemary Brown, said that they wanted a fuller appreciation of where faculty and deans stood on the issue. Greg Frankson, AMS president, similarly called for more student input, especially since Herstmonceux was so clearly out of the financial reach of most students. As the debate wore on, a consensus began to emerge. It was perhaps best captured by trustee Dr Andy Pipe, another veteran of Queen's student politics in the late sixties, who suggested that the exit-strategy task force be asked to consider a "whole range of options," some of which might entail throwing a lifeline to the ISC. The Board could not make this decision simply on the grounds of bricks and mortar; more time and options were required.

As was their routine, the trustees met again on the Saturday morning. After a night of mulling the issue over, they decided to withdraw the bald motion to exit the English countryside. Chairman Don Elliott apologized for the "unseemly haste and seemingly skimpy information" behind the original motion. Leggett seemed pleased, but reminded the Board that time was still of the essence. A new motion with more latitude was introduced: the Board recognized that Herstmonceux was "not financially viable," and empowered the principal to convene a task force to explore either a means of correcting the "current financial situation" or "for exiting the business." That task force must report at the Board's next meeting in May. When quizzed about what the task force would look like, Leggett, reflecting the tenor of the foregoing debate, said that it would surely contain a student who had been to Herstmonceux, faculty members from Arts and Science and Business (the two most heavily involved faculties at the ISC), and an alumnus with marketing know-how. A week later, Leggett told the Senate that that person would be Greg Watson. A Queen's commerce grad from the 1980s and a partner at PriceWaterhouse, he would advise the task force on "restructuring" the ISC.[63]

In May, the Board convened with trepidation. The contentious fate of the dean of women and a proposal to fund early retirement buyouts of faculty headed the agenda, with Herstmonceux as a denouement. Leggett had the castle restructuring report in hand, but announced that it would remain confidential, because it contained sensitive financial data. He had chaired the group, ably assisted by physics professor and one-time dean of Graduate Studies, Bill McLatchie. But its analysis was clear. The ISC had been "flawed" from the outset. The notion that it could exist as a "stand-alone operation" was untenable. Students would not come if the ISC offered an "unfocused" curriculum that was marginal to degree programs back in Kingston. The key to the future was to "integrate" the castle's offerings with Queen's academic programs – to make Herstmonceux a satellite campus in a real sense. Along with this dovetailing, the ISC needed to find partners who might send their students to England to bolster enrolment. Leggett reported that a special meeting of the Senate two days before had endorsed this reorientation of the castle's mission. In future, the ISC's operations would be less top-down in direction and would involve greater faculty involvement. Further good news came from Milwaukee: Dr Bader had generously bolstered the castle's operating expenses with an additional million dollars, plus monies for bursaries. The Board joined in the common pull, agreeing to look into a one-time writing off of $11 million of the centre's debt. Perhaps counterintuitively, it also voted to boost fees at the centre. Leggett would later describe the arduous decisions over Herstmonceux in the spring of 1996 as "a defining point" in Queen's history: the university committed itself to international exposure, and in doing so found a way to "differentiate" itself in a globalizing world.[64] That fall, *Maclean's* annual survey of Canadian universities ranked Queen's first, citing its "remarkable achievement for a University set in a small town away from the centres of power." Leggett told the trustees that he chalked this up to Queen's "repeated willingness to chart a different course." Herstmonceux, he implied, was putting Queen's closer to the centre of things.

By November, the news from England was turning positive. As was his wont, Leggett relied on decisive appointments to shape the castle's future. Macnamara remained as executive director in England, with Bill McLatchie serving as the principal's special advisor and ISC coordinator back in Kingston. With others, they sat on a steering committee to guide the castle's management. McLatchie had solid experience in managing the multiversity that had built the neutrino laboratory in Sudbury. Now, a similar consortium arrangement was created for Herstmonceux – the Canadian Universities Study Abroad Program (CUSAP). Students at CUSAP colleges would be able to take ISC courses and accredit them to degree programs on their home campuses. Western and the universities of British Columbia and Toronto had already signed on. McLatchie was confident that such affiliation would allow the centre to operate at capacity. Royal Bank President Allan Taylor – a trustee – was heading a committee to explore sustaining corporate affiliations for the ISC. The faculty was drawn into planning the curriculum offered at the centre, while an academic director resident at the castle was appointed to ensure its smooth pedagogic operation. Faculty such as Greg Lessard, a member of the French department, eagerly took up the post. Thus, the old moat of resentment surrounding the castle began to drain. The turnaround was hardly instantaneous; in 1998, the centre still lost $1.4 million, mainly due to currency fluctuations. In 2000, fees were raised to $10,200. But enrolment climbed – in 2003, Vice-Principal Suzanne Fortier reported that there were 191 students registered at Herstmonceux.

"Preparing Leaders and Citizens for a Global Society"

As the new millennium dawned, Herstmonceux began to live up to Alfred Bader's expectation of it as a springboard onto the international stage for Queen's students. In 1999, the university imprinted its stationery with a new letterhead: "Preparing Leaders and Citizens for a Global Society." Principal Leggett had presaged this shift in an essay published in the Queen's Gazette the previous May. Queen's, he argued, found itself in an era of "fundamental change" driven by new technologies, contracting government support for universities, increasing interdisciplinary research and teaching, and the breakdown of traditional international boundaries. Queen's no longer had the option of retreating into "the comfort and security of customary practices, attempting to resolve the challenges" that came its way "in an ad hoc fashion." Queen's must therefore shed its parochialism and open new vistas to its students. This ambition at Queen's would focus on creating a "broader learning environment," which would "enhance opportunities for community service, cultural growth, and personal development as a means of facilitating the acquisition of the life and leadership skills required for a global society."[65] Leggett was determined to bring substance to such ambitions. Others at Queen's shared his passion. During the momentous debate over the castle's fate in 1996, Margot Northey, the dean of Business, had, for instance, urged the trustees to look to the Far East and deeper into the United States if they wanted to sharpen the world view of Queen's students.[66] Cumulatively, internationalization permeated the university as the century wound down.

First and foremost, Queen's students began to go abroad. The survival of Herstmonceux, Leggett would later reflect, "was probably the greatest single stimulus to Queen's rapid transition to a position of leadership in the proportion of its student body." At the beginning of his principalship, only about 1 to 2 per cent of Queen's students went abroad to study; by the early 2000s that number had risen to 15 per cent. Business students became especially peripatetic, with 70 per cent of undergraduate

Queen's students travelled many roads to innovation and internationalization in the late-twentieth century. A multidisciplinary team of students developed a series of solar-powered cars, which were entered in competitions that took them as far afield as the World Solar Challenge across the Australian outback.

commerce students studying abroad for some part of their four-year degree program.[67] Queen's students explored the world in other ways: engineering students took their campus-designed-and-built solar cars to competitions around the world, for instance racing across the sun-drenched Australian outback. Starting in 1995, Queen's students and staff from rehabilitation therapy and family medicine, directed by Dr Ruth Wilson, worked with the University of Sarajevo to establish better primary health care for the people of Bosnia in the wake of a civil war that had ripped the former Yugoslavia apart.[68] Queen's subsequently created an International Centre for the Advancement of Community-based Rehabilitation, thereby carrying its expertise as far afield as South America and Russia. The Queen's Engineering Society channelled student skills and commitment to social justice into the Queen's Project on International Development (QPID), which undertook projects in less-developed countries, such as Guyana and Burkina Faso. The multidisciplinary Research Centre for Southern Africa dedicated itself to the problems of South Africa as it struggled to free itself of the legacy of apartheid, winning, for instance, in 2002 a three-million-dollar grant from the British government to study AIDS there. Queen's was thus teaching itself to think across borders and across disciplines; a university that had long prided itself on being national was now slowly donning an international mantle.

At the same time, a bid was made to attract foreign students to Queen's; graduate fees were, for instance, lowered and scholarships increased. The number of international students slowly rose. By 2002, Queen's had 1,031 international students, its undergraduate programs boasting students from 76 countries. (At the same time, 1,117 of its students were studying abroad.) Attracting international students to Kingston was often a tough sell; small provincial cities were not the magnets that Toronto and Montreal were to new Canadians. To lubricate the flow of students and faculty between Kingston and the world beyond, Leggett, often accompanied by deans and academic specialists, toured extensively in search of academic-exchange agreements and research-cooperation concords. Such deals were signed with universities in such far-flung places as Perth, Australia, and Fudan, China. The internationalization of Queen's was soon evident in more than letterhead slogans and official globetrotting. In 1999, the director of marketing and communications, Richard Seres, advised the trustees to start "branding" their university as one dedicated to global outreach, as a place offering "a broader learning experience and international opportunities."[69] Not surprisingly, images of a moated castle in the idyllic English countryside soon began appearing on the university's promotional literature.

"Living in an Age of Discontinuity": Financing Queen's

The agonizing debate over the fate of Herstmonceux underscored one abiding lesson: the university's bills had to be paid. And in the nineties that was becoming an ever more arduous task. In the summer of 1994, Bill Leggett had arrived on a campus in the grip of the Social Contract imposed by the NDP government of Premier Bob Rae, a government that had gyrated between Keynesian deficit spending and draconian belt tightening. Tough budgets delivered by Vice-Principal Rod Fraser had consequently exacted sacrifices in every nook and cranny of the campus. Not only was less money coming in from Queen's Park, but the provincial government was also demanding better accountability of how universities spent their annual endowment from the taxpayers. Some fixes were easy – Queen's had already, for instance, created an audit committee on its Board of Trustees – but in other respects calculating productivity in academic endeavour proved tricky. How did one quantify effective teaching? Was the imposition of such benchmarks a breach of academic freedom? Faculty complained that "accountability" was the thin edge of an insidious wedge that would see universities eventually "run by government." Board members, weary of endless task forces and discussions of accountability, concluded that there would never be a consensus on the issue and that corporate indicators of performance simply did not translate into university affairs.[70] But the underlying reality remained: there had been a steady relative decline in provincial funding of post-secondary education in Ontario since the 1970s. The province's universities were chronically underfunded and ranked near the bottom of almost every province-by-province indicator of support.

Yet, through all this decline, Ontario had maintained the mantra of accessibility – insisting that this was a university system dedicated to the social and economic improvement of Ontario's citizens. By the late 1990s, Queen's received only about 41 per cent of its revenue from the provincial coffers; 24 per cent now came from funded research, 20 per cent from tuition, 7 per cent from donations, and 6 per cent from endowment earnings.[71] The bare cupboard of Ontario post-secondary education was made evident when, in the summer of 1996, former Queen's principal David Smith was asked by John Snobelen, the minister of education and training, to head an advisory panel on the "future directions" of the Ontario university system. Smith worked with expedition and reported that fall, perhaps to the minister's discomfort, that the system was indeed chronically underfunded and the situation was being exacerbated by the province's failure to compensate research overhead costs, or indeed to set out any coherent policy on how it would fund research on campuses.[72] The Smith Report joined a library of previous studies on the condition of the province's universities; few ever seemed to produce much change. The reality was that post-secondary education was invariably squeezed aside in the political agenda by the public's increasing preoccupation with health-care services and the economic health of the province.

Closer to home, the fiscal news was equally grim. Leggett was fortunate in that the Queen's Board of Trustees contained a group of very astute members drawn from the top echelons of Canadian business – people such as John Rae of Power Corporation, the TD Bank's Barbara Polk, Toronto financier (and future chancellor) Jim Leech, and PriceWaterhouse accounting's Tom O'Neill. These were businesspeople who were well versed in fiscal contours and who could see the strategic implications of dysfunctional budgets. At one Saturday theme session of the Board in 1995, for instance, former Queen's professor and now federal deputy-minister of finance, David Dodge, joined another Queen's grad, Dan Burns, provincial deputy-minister of municipal affairs and housing, to lay out a worrisome scenario of further federal austerity and provincial contraction. In the session, moderated by *Globe and Mail* columnist and alumnus Jeffery Simpson, the trustees heard that heightened university fees alone could not stabilize university budgets. Federal transfers for post-secondary education might, for instance, be cut as the Chrétien government embraced austerity. The old calculation of provincial-grant-plus-fee revenue would no longer serve to pace university operations.

The future now depended on a more complex set of variables: deregulating fees, chasing funded research, engaging in intense fundraising competition with other universities, and rejigging academic programs to public demand were some of the main possibilities. These changes would come with "greater intensity" than ever before. Burns would warn the trustees that Ontario was "living in an age of discontinuity." Leggett drew his own central conclusion: "There must be freedom of tuition, which will cause an enormous differentiation of Ontario universities."[73] The now decades-old "bums in seats" BIU formula, as he called it, would no longer sustain Queen's or the university system as a whole. To drive home the point that the system was ailing, Jennifer Lewington, the *Globe's* education columnist, was later asked to instruct the trustees in how the public perceived the universities. There was, she told them, a "credibility gap" between the universities' sense of their "entitlement" and the broader society which "now thinks in terms of restructuring and downsizing." To win public confidence, the universities needed to display "transparency, openness and provision of useful knowledge ... For the gum-chewing public, the test will be whether what you say will be what they see."[74]

That challenge had grown considerably in June 1995, when Ontario voters endorsed the "Common Sense revolution" of the Conservative party under Mike Harris, whose no-nonsense talk of tax cuts, privatization, and "workfare" reform of the welfare rolls captured the public mood of discontent with government. In the 1990s, Ontario thus appeared to have abandoned its long-standing addiction to moderate, centrist governance – first NDP gyration and now Tory austerity. High on the Harris agenda was a $400-million cut in the annual post-secondary education budget. This accentuated and accelerated the slow decline evident since the 1970s. In December 1995, Ken Snowdon, the associate vice-principal, planning, briefed the board on the implication of the Harris revolution. "The government," he reported, "has done exactly what it had said." Even with the 10-per-cent fee increase allowed to universities that year, the province's universities would be $280 million poorer. For Queen's, that boiled down to a cut of $14.6 million, or the equivalent of chopping 85 faculty and 137 staff positions.[75] And, Snowdon emphasized, the government seemed absolutely determined to balance the provincial budget by 2000. It would not impose restructuring on the universities; instead the onus was on the universities to remake themselves. Vice-Principal Cowan chimed in that some universities might fail under such restraint, but Queen's, if it chose the right "methodology," would "survive." Faced with such a dire prognostication, Leggett, the trustees, and the broader Queen's community began a serious conversation about change.

Initially, the Leggett administration pursued a traditional Queen's approach to austere times. Still showing its Presbyterian roots, the university had an aversion to deficits. At times, as it had in the lean seventies, it had endured short-term deficits when all else had failed. At the same time, the Watts tradition of broad consultation across campus still prevailed. With this in mind, Leggett set up a task force on budget planning in the wake of the Harris election. Since government input to the university budget was now contracting, attention focused on things more within the university's control: labour costs, operating expenses, and students fees. Since labour costs constituted 75 per cent of the university's operating spending, shedding faculty had an immediate bottom-line attraction, but there was quick agreement that there would be no forced retirement. Attempts to define the conditions under which financial exigency might allow the university to declare positions redundant had long proved fruitless. So, in early 1996, a voluntary early retirement policy was announced. In an effort to protect the core strength of departments, the university exercised the right to vet applicants and deny early departure to some. By the spring of 1997, $15.5 million had been dispersed to fund these early exits from academic life, a steep one-time expenditure that would bring long-term savings in compensation costs. The trustees eased the pain of this extraordinary spending, and that of the built-up debt at Herstmonceux, by transferring almost $10 million from the university's endowment fund into the operating budget, another reluctant departure from Queen's frugal heritage.[76] The thinning of faculty ranks was accompanied by the perpetuation of the across-the-board austerity that had become familiar under the Social Contract. Responding to the Harris cuts, vice-principal, academic, David Turpin, asked all deans to trim their budgets by as much as 12 per cent, suggesting that they eliminate small classes, employ more adjuncts, initiate co-operative programs with other universities, and start thinking about making Queen's more of a "laptop" university.[77]

Other short-term fixes were discussed. An attempt to draw surplus funds out of the pension fund foundered when agreement could not be found with

In the late decades of the twentieth century, there was ample evidence that the cost of a post-secondary education was outstripping inflation. The AMS was obliged to open a food bank for financially challenged students. The administration adopted a policy of ploughing back 30 per cent of fee increases into student assistance. Students nonetheless made their financial discomfort apparent, as this 2002 protest demonstrates.

the five bargaining groups that now constituted the university community. There was even fleeting consideration of whether Queen's might privatize itself and establish a strategy of setting its own fees and building up its endowment as a kind of "Harvard of the North." Most thought this "impractical" and likely to provoke internecine conflict between Ontario's large, established universities and postwar newcomers. When trustee Tom O'Neill, the chartered accountant, pointed out that to privatize Queen's would need a capital base of $2 billion, the idea faded. There was greater agreement on longer-term adjustments more within the established purview of university governance: increased student fees and enhanced fundraising. Over the last decade, the provincial government had shown willingness to let tuition for professional programs slip out from under government regulation and reflect what the market would bear, while at the same time allowing mainstream undergraduate fees some latitude in the hands of individual universities. Queen's highly successful, market-driven MBAs testified to this potential. Elsewhere, Queen's, aware of its strong reputation, had annually used this opening to boost its fees to the maximum allowable ceiling. In April 1996, the proposed 1996–97 university budget contained an average tuition hike of 19.7 per cent. The university had cushioned the impact of such steady, creeping escalation in undergraduate fees by setting aside 30 per cent of fee revenue for student assistance. A task force created by Leggett underscored this commitment in late 1995. So did a report entitled *Navigating the Storm*, produced by the AMS's Government Issues Committee in the wake of the Harris cuts. The students adamantly opposed any deeper cuts to post-secondary education and demanded that fee increases be married to a revamping of student aid. Any further deregulation of fees, they argued, should be negotiated and differentiated by degree program. Student loans, the AMS report advocated, should be contingent on future income – pay back the loan when your post-graduation income could sustain the burden.[78] It was clear that relying on an ever-increasing flow of student fees had direct consequences.

In 1996, 39 per cent of Queen's students were drawing support from the Ontario Student Assistance program (OSAP). More alarmingly, 3 per cent were said to be on the rolls of the Kingston Food Bank; a year later, a food bank opened on campus. The AMS president also reported that many cash-strapped students were opting out of non-mandatory student activity fees. Despite such hardship, there seemed to be a recognition among students that there was a trade-off between stiffer fees and bolstering the quality of post-secondary education. Nonetheless, the fiscal tolerance of Queen's students was reaching "saturation point," as a student delegation told the trustees. Many faculty began to speak out in Senate on the financial squeeze confronting students. When, in February 1997, the Senate debated a motion to ask the trustees to freeze tuition, over a thousand students gathered outside Richardson Hall. Over six hundred of them then staged a silent, fifteen-minute procession through the Senate chamber in support of the motion. "They're steamed," the *Journal* reported, suggesting that this was the largest student demonstration ever seen at Queen's. The motion was defeated (fees were, after all, a matter for the trustees to decide), and the 7-per-cent fee hike now proposed for 1997–98 stood. A fifty-seven-hour sit-in in the principal's office followed in March – "rally cries still echoing," in the words of the *Journal*.[79]

Advancement to the Fore: The Campaign for Queen's

As evidence that reliance on fee-driven revenue placed increasing strain on the Queen's community, attention shifted to the prospect of invigorating Queen's capital fundraising, deregulating more of its student fees, and pursuing more funded research. Here were three activities beyond the reach of lock-step regulation and, if deftly managed, they offered a lucrative enhancement of the university's revenues. By the spring of 1996, Queen's was garnering 9.9 per cent of its operating budget from fundraising, the highest ratio in Ontario. While its alumni base was deep and broad, Queen's had never enjoyed exceptional financial support from its alumni, but the powerful legacy of big donors such as Alfred Bader and Joseph Stauffer gave hope that more large donors, both private and corporate, could be harnessed to Queen's future. Oversight of the university's fundraising had traditionally been provided by the Queen's Fund Council, until recently headed by Agnes Benidickson, but now chaired by trustee Jim Leech.

More recently, the university had come to see fundraising not just as a series of episodic campaigns overseen by a fundraising director and an ad hoc staff. At times, the results had been flattering, particularly when the campaign was chaired by a prominent outsider – bankers like Allan Taylor of the Royal Bank and Bill Mulholland of BMO had each done stalwart work for Queen's in this respect. But reports from outside consultants, like the Ketchum group in Toronto, suggested that Queen's was still more in the game of "friend-raising" than fundraising. The alumni database was woefully inadequate. With such criticism in mind, fundraising was given prominence under a vice-principal, advancement, as a permanent, professional function. For this, Principal Smith had hired Florence Campbell, from the Conference Board in Ottawa. Aggressive fundraising would now allow the university to top up the endowment fund, making it a more reliable and substantial contribution to the operating budget, particularly since the monies, unencumbered by any government rubric, might be deployed whenever and wherever needed.

In the spring of 1997, besieged by news of debt and Queen's Park austerity, the trustees mulled over launching a capital campaign in the fall of 1998. A steering committee was formed. Leggett stressed that the campaign must be dedicated to the university's core mission of quality teaching and research. The prospect of a concerted fundraising effort met with trustee enthusiasm. The Harris government had already signalled its willingness to help universities that helped themselves: the Ontario Student Opportunity Trust Fund had been established to provide bursaries for Ontario university students based on Toronto, matching every dollar raised by a university. Queen's had immediately applied to have its McLaughlin graduate scholarships matched by Toronto. Trustees quickly produced a laundry list of commendable projects to place before would-be donors – a new athletic complex topped the list. There were also voices of caution. Competition would be stiff; other universities were in the hunt for donor dollars. (The Advancement Office already knew, for instance, that corporations were more inclined to support universities in their Toronto environs, rather than in distant eastern Ontario). Others, like the AMS's president Greg Frankson, pointed out that morale was low on campus and that students in particular might opt out of supporting an alma mater that had just hoisted their fees. Leggett agreed, but suggested that the best tonic for low morale was a campaign that could "underwrite some dreams."[80]

Initial enthusiasm did not, however, translate into initial progress. A year later, the vice-principal, advancement, reported that traditional steps were being taken to activate the campaign: assembling alumni volunteers, identifying key donors, and dispatching the principal on a coast-to-coast tour to spread the word. Key themes had been developed: broadening the student experience at Queen's, bolstering student assistance, renewing outdated facilities, such as the university's antiquated chemistry labs, and supporting niched academic programs. Campbell estimated that these projects might warrant a campaign target aimed as high as $150 million.[81] But there was tentativeness about the blueprint. It lacked precision and vigour. And, particularly in light of the university's tight finances, it seemed lethargic. This became especially clear to the deans, who were relying on the putative campaign to pump funds into their pet projects. When her five-year appointment came up for renewal later in 1998, Campbell opted to resign. This left Leggett with an empty executive office and a campaign barely under way.

Faced with this prospect, Leggett reverted to the initial assessment he had formed of Queen's corporate culture when he arrived in 1994: the place had great inner strength and tradition, but it was all too often lulled by its insularity into familiar, comfortable patterns. If the ambitious capital campaign envisaged by the trustees was to succeed, forceful leadership and new ideas were in order. He found that leadership in George Hood. From the outset, Leggett recognized a kindred spirit in Hood. On the one hand, Hood, a 1978 graduate from Queen's in political science, liked to boast that "no one could out-Queen's him." His father had gone to Queen's and had known the likes of Alfie Pierce (to whom he had conveyed cigarettes in his digs under the stadium) and Jean Royce, Queen's beloved registrar. A large, gregarious, and exuberant man, Hood had been an avid hockey player and was steeped in Queen's student culture – "fries in the Union" dominated his diet and centred his social life. On the other hand, Hood came to sense Queen's weaknesses. He disliked its "tribalism," its parochialism, and its tendency to regard the outside world in introverted terms. This recognition had been sharpened by Hood's experience away from Queen's in the eighties. An MA thesis on federal-provincial relations at the University of Western Ontario (followed by an MA in public administration at Queen's in 1981) led to employment in the Saskatchewan government of NDP premier Allan Blakeney, where he quickly acquired a reputation as a "turnaround" expert for troubled government projects. This culminated in his management of the $200-million Rafferty-Alameda dam project, a project requiring a deft touch in coping with conflicting jurisdictions, environmental interest groups, and construction delays. The title of Hood's published account of the project – *Against the Flow* – seemed to convey a sense of the complexity of the achievement.

George Hood's "Big Ask"

By 1991, Hood was restless in Saskatchewan. A call from Queen's political scientist Stewart Fyfe brought him back to Queen's as a Skelton-Clark fellow. From there, his reputation for stickhandling his way through the labyrinth of federal and provincial agencies and bringing momentum to stalled initiatives earned him the directorship of Queen's Centre for Resource Studies and the delicate challenge of finding consensus among bureaucrats, academics, and mining companies (who employed many Queen's engineers). In many ways, Hood displayed a boldness not usually found in academics. In Montreal, shortly after Bill Leggett had been named incoming principal in 1994, Hood called on the principal-elect and spent several hours imparting his assessment of Queen's to his soon-to-be colleague. Once at Queen's, Leggett, and his new vice-principal, research, Suzanne Fortier, were drawn to Hood's keen competitive instinct and his knack for navigating all the tributaries of funded research. Fortier asked him to become her associate vice-principal. The unfolding nexus of funded research in Canada – federally, provincially, and privately financed – demanded that academics become more entrepreneurial in their pursuit of knowledge. "Grantsmanship" was now of the essence. Hood brought this to his new assignment. He set up shop in a university-owned house on Albert Street and went to work connecting Queen's with corporate and bureaucratic Canada. The university could not afford to let intellectually and financially lucrative opportunities slip by its gates. Hood's bullish approach to such matters was in stark contrast with the university's genetic gentility. Nonetheless, Hood held one abiding tenet: he must always connect with the academic sensibilities of the university. Research would only shine if it reflected the intrinsic interest and abilities of the faculty around him. Hood, for instance, came to rely upon English professor and associate vice-principal, academic, Les Monkman –

Vice-principal George Hood (right) embraces long-time and much-respected Queen's custodian Rick Primeau. Hood's ebullient and hard-driving personality brought new verve to the challenge of raising money over and above government's annual grant. Hood's style did not always fit Queen's staid culture, but the Campaign for Queen's brought an unprecedented $262 million to Queen's coffers.

"my shepherd" – to keep lines of communication open with faculty.[82]

Ever restless, Hood told Leggett in the spring of 1998 that he was hankering for a new challenge and was thinking of leaving Queen's. Leggett asked him to stay, perhaps mindful that an opening in the advancement office might soon materialize. Campbell's resignation opened that door. Hood hesitated to apply. He had no fundraising expertise per se; his was a turnaround expertise for organizations that were in trouble. He sought out the opinion of people across campus. He especially wanted to know if the deans would be onside with him. Hood even took a Myers-Briggs personality test; it gave him an "ENTJ" rating, indicating an extroverted persona, probably a positive trait in fundraising. Eventually, he applied. So did others. A June interview led to an offer. He accepted, but insisted that he be able to take three able staffers from his research office with him to prime the new advancement pump with their expertise in accounting and policy. Waiting for the

October start of his appointment, Hood used the summer to scope out his plan for a capital campaign without precedent at Queen's. With his habitual panache, Hood tagged the exercise "Project Red Horse," named for a lighthouse near his beloved family cottage in the nearby Thousand Islands. Perhaps most importantly, in August he struck up an acquaintance with trustee Tom O'Neill, who liked what he saw and immediately offered his Bay Street perspective on Hood's mandate.

By the time Hood walked through the advancement-office door on October 1, he had a plan for a broad-front, aggressive campaign. The campaign would begin with a "quiet phase," lasting until the official kickoff in October 1999, during which the philosophy and mechanics of the campaign would be fine-tuned. Hood took a holistic, almost militaristic, approach to the whole exercise. His managerial style was distinctly at odds with the usually gradualist, hesitant style of university administration; he was emphatic in his ambition. The campaign must be "embedded" (a favoured word) throughout the whole university, from professors in their offices to alumni and supporters stretched across the nation. Again and again, he stressed that "it's about the organization." He worked to find what he called "academic champions" on campus – deans and professors who could connect academic needs with donors. People would be more likely to give if they were shown the exciting prospect of what their money would incubate at Queen's. Hood interviewed every member of the advancement office's eighty-strong staff. He connected with them, creating a sense of a team. (As research associate dean, Hood had famously hosted lively parties for his staff.) Some were let go. Others bucked at his forceful style. Outsiders were brought in for their expertise – Richard Seres for "branding," for example. Hood quickly realized that American fundraisers were years ahead of Canada in their techniques and success rates, so he headed south to pick the brains of professional fundraisers such as Marts and Lundy in New Jersey. He also picked the brains of Queen's grads who had grown prominent in the administration of American universities – scholar-administrators such as Tom Kinnear at Michigan and Shirley Tilghman at Princeton. Potential donor lists were drawn up, dividing the market into large, medium, and small segments. Campaigns worked if major donors – "the big ask" in advancement parlance – displayed their faith in the campaign at its outset; smaller donors tended to fall into line once they saw such benevolence.

George Hood was clearly a galvanic force. He consciously forsook the leisurely old ways of fundraising at Queen's –"little old ladies with rinse in their hair and cucumber sandwiches," he would lightheartedly observe – and many reacted to his determined manner. It was not that Queen's no longer valued its loyal alumni; it was that in order to survive in the fiscal chill of the late-twentieth century, Queen's needed unprecedented amounts of donated capital from deep pockets. Hood reflected a seismic shift in Canadian post-secondary education in the nineties – universities were now *managed* by hands-on experts, who, if they were smart, attempted to blend the strength of traditional culture with the imperatives of a highly competitive and cost-conscious outside world. Hood was no revolutionary in this respect; people such as Jim Courtright, athlete-turned-oil-man-turned-Queen's-development-vice-principal twenty years earlier, had seen the need. Hood now forced the pace. Coming from a family of Queen's grads, Hood was determined to preserve the best of the old at Queen's, while ensuring that the university equipped itself with the wherewithal necessary for the new century. Hood's determination soon took shape as the Campaign for Queen's, a project that won the Board's stamp of approval at its October and December meetings. Leggett underscored the "mission" of the campaign: to ensure that Queen's entered the twenty-first century in a position to support its core attributes – quality teaching for both undergraduates and graduates, superb research and scholarship, and exemplary service to the community.

None of this would be possible without a large injection of capital. Such fundraising, Leggett said, would take place in the "new context" of globalization, volatility, deregulation, ever-stingier provincial support, new technologies, and students who now conceived of themselves as consumers of education. The target would be breathtaking (at least for Queen's): $180 to $200 million. Bob Paterson, a Science '59 grad and now CEO of Imperial Oil, would chair the campaign, supported by O'Neill, John Rae of Power Corporation, and George Watson of TransCanada Pipelines.[83]

Drawing on this talent pool, a campaign cabinet and leadership council were created to provide ongoing guidance to the unfolding Campaign for Queen's. These spearheaded what Hood called the next stage of the campaign, its "internal" phase, designed to secure large donations from corporations and foundations. These would set the tone and foundation of the campaign. The campaign cabinet, for instance, steered the campaign toward potential $1-million-plus donors. By the time the campaign went public in the fall of 2000, a remarkable $160 million in "nucleus" gifts had thus already been committed to Queen's. Included in this was an ongoing $3-million pledge from Queen's students, who in an AMS 1999 referendum approved a $60 annual contribution from every Queen's student, a remarkable testament of faith by Queen's students in their alma mater. The Queen's Fund then went into a "public phase," dedicated to pushing the campaign to its target on the strength of widespread giving by alumni and the general public.

By the spring of 2000, Hood could tell the trustees that the advancement function at Queen's had been "retooled." Hood built a real professional élan into his staff. The onus was on being a "team player" who saw the campaign not in terms of bailiwicks but as an amalgam of "flexible and adaptable behaviours." The campaign rested on a decentralized, university-wide foundation that tapped down into the core of the university. There were, for example, development officers in all the faculties, academics who could carry faculty projects forward to the fundraisers and hence to potential donors. Faculty advisory committees were also established. The signature and image of the campaign was, however, tightly centralized. For instance, Queen's embraced the idea of "branding" itself, so as to ensure that a consistent, progressive image of the place was transmitted. Queen's thus became dedicated to grooming "citizens for global society" by offering a "broadened learning environment." To emphasize the message, Queen's restyled its famous stylized swash "Q" logo by combining it with the university crest. Not everybody at Queen's was comfortable about such labelling of the academic experience. Branding seemed to be the thin end of a wedge of corporatization, a denial of the intrinsic diversity and latitude of university life. In these same years, for instance, students complained that the university was awarding exclusive distribution rights on campus to companies such as Coca-Cola. The AMS struck a committee on corporate involvement on campus that warned of a growing loss of autonomy.[84] In response, the administration, and some AMS voices, pointed out that such arrangements brought hundreds of thousands of scholarship dollars and athletic support to the campus. Much the same rationale applied to branding. Universities could no longer rely on the loosely defined, warmly felt nostalgia and generosity of their alumni for sustaining support. They had to establish a carefully tuned and forceful identity in the broader marketplace of public opinion.

The results were unprecedented. In May 2003, Principal Leggett invited four hundred of the people most crucially involved in the campaign to an afternoon tea under a sprawling tent on Benidickson Field to declare the campaign over. The campaign had spurted past its original goal of $200 million and had come to rest at a grand total of $261,990,286. Well over half – $148.5 million – came from major gifts from corporations, foundations, and wealthy donors. Planned giving, such as bequests, brought in another $50 million, while more-traditional annual giving contributed $34.7 million. Gifts in kind garnered $28 million. This munificence was deployed over a wide range of projects – new buildings, student aid, faculty support, endowed chairs, and the library – all of which brought substance to the campaign's aim of enhancing the "broad learning environment" at Queen's. At the same time, the university's endowment – its all-important nest egg for future growth – had been fattened over the seven years of the campaign by 36 per cent, to $413 million.[85] Attention now focused on making advancement at Queen's a "continuous" function. The Queen's Fund Council was converted into the board's new Advancement Committee, charged with "advancing" Queen's on a broad front of change. The next year, Hood, reappointed as vice-principal for another five years, talked of the permanence of the "advancement funding model" at Queen's. Queen's students picked up on this mood, launching an ongoing "ThankQ" campaign that asked graduating fourth-year students to express an ongoing generosity to the university they were about to leave. Leggett's salute to the fundraisers that spring day in 2003 caught the mood of "can-do" optimism that the campaign had brought to Queen's, a headiness that would spill over into other thrusts of policy as the new millennium dawned.

"Weathering the Storm": Fees, Food Banks, and Deregulation

Despite the fact that almost $63 million of the Campaign for Queen's was earmarked for student assistance, the cost of education to the student continued to be a matter of festering concern. About 65 per cent of fees at Queen's remained under some sort of control from Queen's Park. The so-called privatization of fees for professional programs, such as the tremendously successful executive MBA program, acknowledged that certain types of post-secondary education could be market driven – post-graduation compensation would justify a student's investment in time spent at Queen's. But at the undergraduate level, Ontario's decades-old political commitment to accessibility persisted, dedicating university education to broad social and economic betterment. Few contested this dedication. The problem lay in making such a philosophy fiscally sustainable. By the mid-nineties, the BIU system that was providing the main fiscal injection to the annual operating budgets of Ontario universities had been eroded by inflation, by Queen's Park's diminishing budgetary allocation to the post-secondary sector, and by occasional bouts of outright austerity. The Rae government's Social Contract had provided the latest reminder of the financial vulnerability of Ontario's universities.

This slow strangulation had many side effects. Desperate to skimp on expenditures, universities, for instance, put off scheduled maintenance on their campuses. Queen's limestone heritage may have helped build the university's brand, but it also served to fatten a swelling unaddressed bill for deferred maintenance. More fundamentally, the growing gap between fee revenue and the provision of academic services introduced ongoing uncertainty for student and administrator alike in planning the future. Queen's Park seldom revealed its annual spending priorities in sufficient time for universities to look even one academic year ahead with any certainty. Consequently, students were never able to project the costs of their education over the four-year span of their programs. Trusting in its strong reputation, Queen's nonetheless usually opted to push its fee schedule to the maximum allowable hikes of between 7 and 10 per cent a year through the nineties.

The advent of the Mike Harris government with its resolve to balance the provincial budget by 2000 only exacerbated an already-deteriorating situation. The imposition of a procrustean $400-million cut in post-secondary spending, arriving on the heels of the Social Contract and a decade of persistent pressure from Toronto on the universities for greater spending accountability, pushed Queen's into severe retrenchment. From the heady days of the sixties, when previous Conservative governments had preened themselves as the universities' fiscal friends, Queen's Park downplayed its ardour for what it now called a "provincially assisted" university system. No wonder more-aggressive fundraising and the chase for funded research moved quickly to the top of the trustees' agenda. While former principal David Smith had worked on his 1996 *Future Direction* report, with its conclusion that Ontario was a parsimonious laggard in national post-secondary education, current principal, Bill Leggett, found himself more and more travelling Highway 401 to Queen's Park, directly carrying a message of financial exhaustion.

When Premier Harris publicly mused that social-science degrees seemed to contribute little to the province's well-being, Leggett wrote reminding him that many Queen's grads were in fact running the provincial bureaucracy and that this comment had created "unease" on campus.[86] (In December 1997, Harris was slated to cut the ribbon on Queen's new Biosciences Building. A thousand Queen's protesters awaited him, only to learn to their chagrin that a family illness had kept the premier away.) Leggett kept up the pressure. At the same meeting at which George Hood's appointment as vice-principal, advancement, was announced in late 1998, Leggett reported that he had lobbied no less than six deputy-ministers in Toronto for fiscal relief from the government's austerity. The good news, he reported, was that there would be no further cuts. The worrisome news was that there would be only meagre increases in spending, and the government would now "steer" its post-secondary spending towards "highly targeted funds," funds earmarked not for broad operational support of the universities, but for specific programs.[87]

By 1999, severe cost cutting on campus had whittled a projected deficit of $443,000 down to a balanced budget. Yet, the spring of 2000 brought news of another budget shortfall – this time $350,000, or about a half a per cent of Queen's operating capital. There was some good news:

PARTEQ, the university's arm's-length agency for commercialization of innovative ideas, was finally returning a steady profit to the university. The provincial coffers were also looking healthier, but this did not bring any direct relief to provincial campuses. The Harris government's spring 2000 budget announced that the province would cap increases in its operating grants to universities at 2 per cent and would require that fee increases conform to the same 2-per-cent ceiling. For Queen's, this was hardly fiscal relief – in 1999, its operating expenses, driven by nearly 3-per-cent national inflation, had grown by 3.7 per cent. Any further transfers to the universities from Toronto would be "performance driven," that is, universities would have to demonstrate their eligibility for funding by satisfying criteria of accountability and productivity. Such targeted funding represented a fundamental shift in Toronto's traditional undifferentiated across-the-board support of universities. What had begun in the early nineties with naive attempts to impose "value-for-money" concepts on university budgets had evolved into the erection of competitive wickets, through which universities had to pass in order to obtain additional support from the state. From the policy point of view in Toronto, this turnstile approach had the benefit of allowing the government to target its post-secondary spending to desirable objectives – the encouragement, for instance, of a "knowledge-based" economy, or bilingualism, or services for Northern Ontario.

Ontario's embrace of performance-driven funding had many faces. University budgeting now unfolded in a world of acronyms. In 1998, the Access to Opportunity Program (ATOP) offered additional operating support to universities enhancing their capacity in electrical engineering and computing. An Ontario Student Opportunity Trust Fund (OSOTF) program offered matching provincial funds for university bursaries established to assist academically competent but financially needy students. The largest of these focused spending programs was the SuperBuild program, designed to apply government money to infrastructure enhancement in key sectors of the provincial economy and society. Here the universities were well-positioned: educational reform in secondary education had mandated the abolition of Ontario's old Grade 13, with the result that, in 2003, a "double cohort" of high-school graduates was heading to university campuses. Residence beds and lecture halls, not to mention more professors, were needed to meet that surge.

In this new fiscal environment, Queen's acted with alacrity and did well, to some degree a reflection of the university's parallel success in finding private donors to join the funding of such projects. By late 2000, the SuperBuild had brought $121 million to Queen's, monies eagerly applied to such strategic initiatives as a new chemistry building, an integrated learning centre for science students, and the renovation of old Victoria school building into a state-of-the-art business school.[88] After much pressure by the Council of Ontario Universities, Queen's Park eventually provided a one-time additional grant to all universities to soften the anomaly of the double cohort. Accompanying these purpose-driven funding programs, the Ontario government also imposed broad-ranging benchmarks on its financial support of universities. Operating grants driven by BIUs were geared to the proportion of students successfully graduated by individual campuses since 1991. Payments were linked to the proportion of a university's graduates that had found gainful employment. At the same time, Quality Assessment Boards were established to review the intrinsic content of academic programs across campuses. Such simplistic calibration of academic productivity rightly provoked criticism in the Queen's Senate, but there was no doubt that the university's apron strings were now more and more tied to such performance-defined rationales.

Targeted funding did not ease the fundamental strain on Queen's. The 2-per-cent cap on fees and operating grants created a systemic constriction on the university budget. In the spring of 2000, Leggett wrote to Diane Cunningham, the provincial minister of training, colleges, and universities, praising the new funding programs but complaining that they did not alleviate "the harsh reality of increased operating costs associated with inflation and other expenses" pressuring the university's day-to-day operations. By way of example, Leggett pointed out that inflation and the falling value of the Canadian dollar were squeezing the library's budget dramatically as foreign journals and books became more costly. More publicly, the university issued a press release confessing that the province's below-inflation, 2-per-cent increase in its grant was "a serious disappointment to us," one that would impede Queen's ability to react to the double cohort, while at the same time maintaining its quality. Within a year, Leggett was telling the trustees that Queen's was facing "an acute budget crisis," one exacerbated by 4-per-cent inflation. Just to maintain the status quo, Queen's needed an additional $8.5 million a year.[89]

The new fiscal reality on Ontario campuses seemed to be that Queen's Park was prepared to spend on targeted niches of post-secondary education, but resolutely refused to engage in any discussion of reforming the boilerplate operating costs and fees. The political mantra of accessibility was still chanted. In the words of trustee Bill Young, a Queen's grad of the seventies and now a Boston financier: "The formula no longer works and radical thinking is necessary."[90] To reinforce the point, Leggett noted that Queen's had surrendered the first-place standing it had enjoyed in the *Maclean's* annual ranking of Canadian universities when he became principal in 1994; Ontario universities, he also noted, had collectively been drifting to the bottom of the charts in most of *Maclean's* rankings.[91]

Increasingly trapped in what Leggett described as a downward fiscal "spiral," the trustees had little option but to squeeze the existing tuition system for every dollar it could be obliged to surrender. Undergraduate fees were automatically hiked to the 2-per-cent ceiling allowed by Queen's Park. Steeper increases were taken in undergraduate programs, such as Commerce and Applied Science, where partial deregulation of fees was permitted. Outside the corral of regulated fees, fees for professional programs were pushed as high as the market would bear: the Executive MBA, for instance, saw its fees rise to $64,000, while its cousin in science and technology rose to $45,000. A full year at Herstmonceux cost $10,200 by 2000. In the space of five years, medical tuition had quintupled.[92] Queen's students did not endure such inflationary pressure supinely. Principal Leggett increasingly found himself alternatively pleading at Queen's Park for financial relief and trying to allay bitter student complaints on his campus over the cost and what they saw as the declining quality of their education. The pivotal student-faculty ratio at Queen's had, for instance, slipped from 14:1 in 1990 to an unflattering 22:1 by 2001.[93] The AMS and faculty societies channelled such frustration into protests ranging from referenda opposing further fee deregulation to mass pickets outside Board and Senate meetings. Other groups – the 1997 Anti-Tuition Hike Coalition, for instance – sprang into more spontaneous action, sometimes occupying the principal's office or flooding the Board with e-mails of protest and demands to be heard in person. The AMS reminded the Board that it had been obliged to open a food bank on campus and reported that an ever-growing number of students showed up at the doors every week. To drive home the point, students served Kraft Dinner to members of the Senate as they assembled for their monthly meeting in the Policy Studies Building in late 1997. The AMS president Greg Frankson told the crowd that students were not "big cows" to be milked for funds.[94]

The students were not without sympathizers. In 1998, physics professor Eugene Zaremba put forward a motion in the Senate that the university freeze tuition increases until some sort of predictable, long-term tuition policy was put in place to give students some sense of financial security. Arts and Science dean Bob Silverman sympathized, but noted that a freeze would cost the university

Leggett's outgoing, hands-in-pockets, forthright manner won respect from the student body in tough financial times. Encountering a student protest en route to a Senate meeting in 1998, Leggett jumped up into the protesters' pick-up truck and assured students that, if fees went up, so too would financial assistance.

$5 million a year. Others argued that a freeze would only further cripple the university's ability to deliver a quality education and would not get at the root of underfunding. The motion was defeated, principally because the regulation of fees was not within the Senate's authority.[95] When fifty students picketed the next Senate meeting to protest the outcome, Leggett, never shy of controversy and dialogue, jumped up on the back of a truck and told the protesters that he put the quality of their education first, but that accessibility and quality in university education had to be constantly balanced.

Appeals to balance and dialogue did not quell the rising tide of resentment among students. Medical students and graduate students closed ranks with the undergraduates represented by the AMS, arguing that their fees also must be constrained and kept from entering the financial stratosphere of the Queen's MBA. The AMS affiliated with the multi-university Coalition for the Preservation of Post-Secondary Education. While many students acknowledged that modest fee increases were understandable, there was universal agreement that the ad hocery of Queen's fee setting had to be replaced by "a commitment to predictability and planning."[96] With two students now sitting as members of the Board of Trustees, joining their more-numerous confreres who sat in the Senate, a meeting of these bodies seldom passed without some sort of student delegation making its case for action on the tuition front. Leggett's sense of foreboding crested in 2000, when it became clear that wholesale financial relief would not be forthcoming from Queen's Park. That November, an Arts and Science Society–sponsored referendum, drawing a strong 44-per-cent voter turnout, voiced a 91-per-cent rejection of any further tuition deregulation at Queen's.[97] The time, Leggett sensed, had arrived for some "radical thinking."

Through the summer of 2000, Leggett pondered the roadblock Queen's faced. He did so by drawing some of his closest colleagues into a cabal dedicated to solving the conundrum of preserving accessibility, ensuring quality, and expanding horizons on an increasingly precarious budget. Given the already apparent success of the Campaign for Queen's, George Hood and key members of his advancement team, such as statistician Kathy Wood, were naturals for the group. Hood thrived on big-ticket projects. Vice-principals David Turpin, David Anderson (appointed to replace Cowan in operations and finance), and Kerry Rowe (appointed to replace Fortier in research after she had been appointed academic vice-principal) rounded out the circle. By the fall, they had arrived at a general statement of strategic direction. The September issue of the *Queen's Alumni Review* carried an article authored by Leggett with the manifesto-like title of "Queen's at the Crossroads." Leggett forcefully restated his "vision" for Queen's: a broader learning environment that would allow Queen's to attract the best and the brightest students, offer them exposure to top-notch scholars, and open international vistas to them, all the while fostering cutting-edge research. In short, Queen's must aspire to be the Princeton or Stanford of Canada. To do so, it must have the "freedom" to set its own benchmarks in class sizes, teaching ratios, information technology, and other crucial indicators of pedagogic excellence. "Some people will accuse me of dreaming in techno colour," he realized. The key, he suggested to his alumni readers, would be marshalling the "financial resources" to meet these benchmarks. Policies of "stretching ourselves and our resources to the limit" had wrought much achievement, but Queen's was now "at a crossroads" – new and more reliable revenue streams had to be found. Leggett praised the alumni for making Queen's $335-million endowment one of the largest in Canada, but immediately pointed out that it was less than 4-per-cent of the Princeton endowment. Growing Queen's endowment, he concluded, was a "central element" in realizing Queen's ambitions in the twenty-first century.[98]

Breaking with the Past:
The Pathfinder Proposal

What Leggett's exhortation did not mention was fees. As reassuring as a bountiful endowment might be, state support and tuition constituted the year-to-year lifeblood of a university. If Queen's was to traverse the crossroad into the new century, Leggett and his cabal of advisors concluded in the autumn of 2000 that the strictures of state support had to be broken if Queen's was enjoy "the freedom to innovate," a phrase he used in an interview with *Policy Options*, a magazine for policy wonks. In this, Leggett was reconnecting with a decades-old Queen's tradition: taking the lead among Ontario universities in the way that tuition was calibrated and distributed. John Deutsch in the sixties had, for instance, engineered the basic income unit, as a means of respecting university autonomy and providing predictable and equitable injections of government funding. In the late eighties under David Smith, Queen's planners had led the way in establishing the "corridor" system of allocating and making more predictable the annual influx of enrolment on Ontario campuses. In these same years, Principal David Smith's *Blueprint for Action* had attempted to redress the balance of accessibility and fiscal viability on Ontario campuses by trading off large, phased-in tuition hikes in exchange for bolstered student aid. Smith's initiative succumbed to political lethargy and interuniversity jealousies. In all these initiatives, Queen's had taken on the role of proposing and pioneering reform in the interest of *all* Ontario universities. The unveiling of Queen's *A Pathfinder Program for Ontario Universities* in June 2001 was framed in the same way.

The *Pathfinder* initiative was unfurled in June 2001. There was a bold, forthright tone to its rhetoric. Its goal was the "full deregulation of tuition in all programs currently subject to regulation." Let universities set their own tuition levels and let the increased revenues enhance the quality of the learning environment – new faculty, lower student-teacher ratios, increased internationalization, the embrace of new technologies – on the condition that a generous part of the revenue windfall reverberate into student support. Ontario universities would thereby be equipped with the financial wherewithal to meet the levels of competitiveness and productivity that the government's recent shift to performance-geared funding – ATOP, OSOTF, and other programs were explicitly cited – had aspired to, while at the same time maintaining equality of access and predictability of the financial burden of a university education. To ensure that Ontario's devotion to accessibility was obliged, Pathfinder proposed that all university admissions be conducted on a "means blind" basis – that applicants be scanned only on the basis of their abilities, not their financial resources. Once admitted, poorer students would be eligible for a university's more-generous

bursaries and scholarships. As quality improved, universities would also be better placed to encourage the private sector to participate in their support programs and students on a dollar-for-dollar matching basis. *Pathfinder* emphasized that this prescription was not one written solely for Queen's; all universities could avail themselves of the liberated fee formula, matching their fees to their own ambitions. Queen's was, however, prepared to serve as a "pilot project" for the new tuition culture. Indeed, Queen's, with its vision of broadened student experience – Herstmonceux, global citizenry, education geared to the internet – would be an "ideal candidate for testing the Pathfinder program." *Pathfinder* rounded out its appeal by stressing Queen's longstanding role as an innovator in post-secondary education in Ontario. The deregulation of fees would be "true to tradition" at Queen's, a university that had, amongst many initiatives, pioneered extension courses in western Canada in the 1880s and launched the first fully privatized MBA in Canada.[99]

In October, a five-year implementation plan for *Pathfinder* was unveiled. Beginning in the fall of 2002, Queen's would boost its tuition fees in hitherto-regulated degree programs by 10 per cent a year for four years. By year four, for instance, a student in Arts and Science would pay almost $6,000 to attend Queen's. In return, however, that student would encounter smaller classes, new faculty expertise, a broadened system of student assistance, state-of-the-art technology, and new-found predictability in the cost of their education over time. Not only would 30 per cent of the tuition hike be set aside for student assistance, but, the plan projected, an additional 30-per-cent top-up would be forthcoming from "private-sector partners" prepared to back Queen's rising quality. The implementation plan had a business-like precision – $12.9 million to hire new professors, teaching assistants, and technicians, for instance. The political bottom line was boldly emphasized: dramatically improved quality of education, no additional base spending by government, and no diminution of accessibility.[100]

Throughout its preparation, there had been a conscious effort to make *Pathfinder* palatable to those it would ultimately affect, to give it credibility. Politically, the sensibilities of the Harris government – competitiveness, cost paring, continued accessibility, and enhanced accountability – were highlighted. Similarly, Leggett engaged in a diplomacy designed to sell the proposal to Ontario's other universities and the Council of Ontario Universities, their collective embodiment. The fear here was that *Pathfinder* might be perceived as a Trojan horse, put forth by Ontario's more "established" universities to allow them to pursue an elitist image at the expense of the province's newer and smaller universities. Initial response was positive, with the University of Toronto, McMaster, Waterloo, Western Ontario, and Brock all showing interest. They were, after all, facing the same fiscal pinch as Queen's. Back at Queen's, Leggett realized that the plan had to be sold to his colleagues. The trustees, long fed on a diet of grim financial news, needed little persuasion. Although the trustees ultimately set the fee schedule at Queen's, the backing of the academic staff who delivered the pedagogic goods at Queen's and the students who received them was crucially important.

In January 2002, Leggett, eager to gain wide support for his initiative, placed *Pathfinder* before the Senate. Reaction was mixed. Annette Burfoot, one-time QUFA president and now a senator, rightly described deregulation of all fees as a "watershed," and, as such, it deserved thorough discussion. She moved that any further deregulation of fees be opposed for the time being. Not everyone agreed. David Walker, dean of the Faculty of Health Sciences, argued that deregulation was the only way to place Queen's on a sustainable financial even keel. Dean Silverman of Arts and Science concurred: years of lobbying Toronto had brought no relief, and the time for "creative alternatives to chronic underfunding" had arrived. History professor James Carson pointed to public apathy over the state of Ontario's universities and said that a postponement would "handcuff" the administration at a crucial juncture. Leggett agreed, lamenting "the low level of intellectual debate on the issue and lack of reference to concrete data on the subject." "Current realities," he said could not be ignored. Burfoot said that she had no animus against the principal and understood that the university's back was "up against the wall." The motion was defeated and the Senate came onside.[101]

Student reaction was harder to gauge. Obviously, a student body of almost eighteen thousand was unlikely to be of one opinion. Fees had risen steadily through the late nineties.[102] A November 2000 ASUS student referendum had decisively panned any further deregulation of tuition. Student debt was an increasing anxiety. Many Queen's students were, for instance, exercising their right to opt out of the pledge to support the Campaign for Queen's. However, many commerce and engineering students argued that deregulated fees would enhance the quality of their education and consequently better prepare them for the professions that lay ahead of them. In January 2001, the *Journal* had happily reported that the Harris government would stick with its 2-per-cent cap on tuition for the next five years. Splinter student groups, such as the Coalition Against Deregulation, were still strident, arguing that all the talk of "quality" in education was but a smokescreen for a money grab from students. The March announcement that undergraduate commerce fees would rise by 20 per cent over the next two years reignited the debate over fees. All this took place against a backdrop of internecine unrest in the AMS, some students arguing that their government had become detached from their sensibilities. Early in 2001, the AMS rejoined the Ontario Undergraduate Student Association (OUSA), thereby aligning it with that organization's province-wide opposition to fee deregulation.[103] That spring the OUSA announced its fall slogan: "Back to school, back to debt." The unveiling of the *Pathfinder* initiative was therefore seen by most students as a turn in the wrong direction by the administration. Newly elected AMS president Scott Courtice was, however,

❖ *"The Good Ship AMS"* ❖

In 1986, AMS president Innes Van Nostrand launched a tradition: he bought a large picture of a sailing ship, placed it in the president's office, and put his signature on the back of it. "Steer a good course" was the implication transmitted to future incumbents. Since then, every outgoing AMS president has followed suit. Like the university that surrounded it, the AMS in the late twentieth century learned to sail a more strategic, more outgoing, and more enterprising course. It came to style itself as the "faculty of broader learning," a title it franked on an honorary diploma it awarded to Bill Leggett.

After seeking advice from consultants KPMG, the AMS in 1996 produced its "Vision 2000" strategic plan, replete with a mission statement dedicating the society to "student empowerment and personal development." With the departure of the Law Students Society in 1998, the AMS became an exclusively undergraduate body, and students became the majority on its board of directors. Greater student control over the John Deutsch Centre was similarly negotiated with the administration, culminating in a $1.3-million renovation of the centre in 1999. More student services were added, most notably the Common Ground coffee shop – "run by Queen's students for Queen's students" – in 2000. A year earlier, an $83-a-year dental plan was made available to AMS members, joining the prescription-drug benefit available since 1989. In 2003, the society took over financial responsibility for Canada's second-oldest radio station, CFRC. Within its own offices, the society rationalized the job descriptions, salaries, and benefits of its permanent employees. In 1994, it hired Claude Sherren, a retired military officer, who brought year-to-year, hands-on expertise to the society's management as its general manager. Every year, for instance, the AMS brought into its employ over fifteen hundred students, who served their fellow students in functions as varied as bartender and daycare supervisor. As with any enterprise, not everything always went smoothly: the AMS's two pubs – Alfie's and the Queen's Pub – habitually ran in the red.

The AMS also became more proactive in representing student concerns with other university stakeholders. As of 1995, students sat on the Board of Trustees and the Senate. In 1994, a municipal-affairs portfolio was added to the AMS commission system to provide a town-and-gown linkage with the city. Other commissions addressed issues such as equity, sustainability, and social issues. The AMS coordinated the use of the Grey House on Bader Crescent as a home for groups (such as the Ontario Public Interest Research Group) dedicated to increasingly diverse student needs. As tuition rose, the AMS responded by lobbying the Board of Trustees and, sadly, opening a food bank for cash-strapped students. Even when rankled by rising fees, the society was prepared to engage the broader Queen's community in support of large initiatives such as the Queen's Centre. Traditional services were maintained: AMS constables still patrolled pubs and football games, while the AMS Judicial Committee still dispensed its brand of natural justice (although sexual harassment now fell under broader campus jurisdisdiction). Permanent staff, such as Greg McKellar, its information and policy officer, ensured continuity from one elected AMS slate to the next. Each year, McKellar briefed incoming student politicians on their portfolios. On the whole, the AMS eschewed participation in provincial and national student lobby groups, preferring its own brand of activism: "Let Queen's speak for Queen's." In short, the AMS remained an activist democracy, molding its mandate to the times through dedicated fees, referenda, elections, and the weekly voice of the *Journal*. Go to: myams.org and queensjournal.ca.

prepared to entertain the proposal's potential for broader student assistance and better quality in the classroom, especially with the ominous double cohort looming on the horizon.

By the fall of 2001, the deregulation debate was raging across the campus. Leggett told a *Journal* reporter that the administration had never stopped pursuing deregulation at Queen's Park and that *Pathfinder* now offered relief from debt anxiety and falling educational quality. At an open meeting on the issue, Dean Silverman said: "We should be in this together. What happens in the next few months will change Queen's unequivocally." A 28 November rally begged to differ. Two hundred students on University Avenue chanted "We are not Harvard North." Leggett came out of Richardson Hall and talked with the protesters for an hour. Take your case, he suggested, to Queen's Park.[104] When, in January, a small group of students staged a noisy protest on the lawn of the principal's private home, dean of students, Bob Crawford, hurried over from the campus and persuaded them to desist. When an even smaller group occupied Leggett's office for five days, Leggett simply asked campus security to monitor the situation. In both protests, the AMS and ASUS executives remained stand-offish, suggesting that the majority of students were caught on the horns of the accessibility-quality dilemma.[105]

In the end, *Pathfinder* came to naught. This was not because of student opposition, but because it hit the same political wall that had stymied earlier Queen's attempts to break down the obdurate attitude, so long prevalent in Ontario political circles, that accessibility and unqualified growth was the essence of post-secondary education. By early 2002, *Pathfinder* had the support of about a third of Ontario universities and had been seriously discussed by the Ontario cabinet. A sizable number of Ontario's senior bureaucrats were Queen's graduates (trustee Dan Burns, deputy-minister of health, being a good example) and were favourably inclined to perpetuate the university's reputation as a shaper of public policy. But then fate intervened. In October, Premier Harris had announced his retirement and grew increasingly unwilling to bequeath a contentious issue to his successor. Following him in January, Finance Minister Ernie Eves resigned and went into the private sector. A leadership race unfolded, one that attracted Eves back into the political fold. Eves won the leadership support of training, colleges, and universities minister, Dianne Cunningham, who was said to be cool on the dynamics of the *Pathfinder* proposal. It was easy to conceive how the total deregulation of university fees could be spun by opposition politicians into an elitist abandonment of an Ontario birthright. At Harris's last cabinet meeting, *Pathfinder* was put on the back burner. Leggett told the trustees that Cunningham had written to tell him that deregulation would not go forward "at this time."[106] Trying to keep hope alive, Leggett told the trustees that he had met with Liberal leader Dalton McGuinty. But it was clear that Queen's and its fellow universities would remain mired in financial uncertainty, a point conveyed to the trustees in Leggett's projection of a 3-to-5-per-cent cut in the university's 2002–03 budget.

Perhaps the only encouraging news in *Pathfinder's* demise was Toronto's tacit acknowledgment that the freedom won for professional and certain niched undergraduate fees would remain in the universities' domain. The making of university budgets would remain a nervous, year-to-year calculation, as chronic underfunding inexorably whittled away pedagogic excellence and, paradoxically, student accessibility. "There is no magic bullet," Leggett would tell the trustees in 2003.[107] Making Queen's financially viable would require constant ingenuity and reliance on an ever-widening array of inputs. Deregulated fees and unprecedented fundraising had already offered an enticing indication of such fiscal diversification. Hikes in deregulated fees, such as those in Business and Law, would be reinvested in the university – 49 per cent to faculty, 30 per cent to student aid, and 30 per cent to the central budget. As the millennium dawned, the boom in funded research amplified that diversification.

"Think Research, Think Queen's"

On a May day in 1998, Bill Leggett did something all university presidents like doing: he cut a ribbon. The ribbon was not in Kingston, but instead hundreds of kilometres to the north in the mining town of Sudbury. There, buried two kilometres underground in an old mine shaft, Queen's, as head of a multiuniversity consortium, had built a neutrino observatory. Subatomic neutrino particles bombard the earth from space and, if observed in isolation deep below ground, can allow scientists to probe the origins of the universe. The $61-million project had drawn large injections of federal research support, as well as expertise from Canada, the United States, and Britain. Queen's physics professor Art McDonald acted as project director. The neutrino sensor tank constructed in the mine cavern contained a thousand tons of heavy water, which would refract neutrinos into pinpoints of light that could be analyzed free of any earthy contamination. The presence of special guests such as Cambridge physicist Stephen Hawking indicated that the scientific eyes of the world were that day on Sudbury.[108]

The powerful emergence of funded research on Canadian university campuses in the late-twentieth century had many stimuli. At root, the maturation and diversification of academic disciplines provided the intellectual impetus. Scholars no longer saw their careers solely in terms of teaching, with fitful adventures into research when time and meagre research funds allowed. Queen's professors were by the nineties invariably equipped with doctorates and less frequently tended to calibrate their academic progress only in terms of their teaching prowess on campus, but also in terms of their output and connection with fellow scholars in their field, who were scattered around the world. Such academic achievement now sat at the centre of the tenure-and-promotion process. The university in turn used such research achievements to polish its brand; seldom did a week or month go by without the *Queen's Gazette* or *Alumni Review* touting the faculty's research prowess. The Board of Trustees meetings now opened – after its age-old habit of saying a prayer – with a report from the dean of Graduate Studies and Research reporting on the university's success in attracting funded research. Conscious of this lucrative flow, Leggett had acted promptly in 1995 to divide the research and graduate-studies functions at Queen's. Administration of graduate studies was time-consuming, driven by the incessant annual cycle of new students and their funding and supervision. The cultivation of funded research was more strategic, more geared to a kaleidoscope of external opportunities. If graduate students had to be groomed for success in SSHRC and NSERC scholarship competitions, now so too did faculty have to be prepped for their entry into the arena of federal, provincial, corporate, and private funded research competitions. Under deans Ron Anderson and, after 2001, Ulrich Scheck, Queen's School of Graduate Studies and Research grew steadily. There was, for instance, a pronounced effort to attract more full-time graduate students, so that by 2004 the university had 2,575 full-time graduate students, up from 2,089 in 1994. As if to recognize this new, more-focused dedication to graduate studies, the Graduate Students' Society, which had exited the AMS in 1981, blended in 1998 with the Law Students' Society, which had also cast off from the AMS, to form the Society of Graduate and Professional Students (SGPS). Just as the faculty in these same years had embraced collective bargaining, the SGPS increasingly engaged the administration in hard-nosed bargaining. Queen's teaching assistants, for instance, had always received less pay than their big-city counterparts at York and Toronto. Despite the SGPS working with the dean to close this gap, a certification vote by teaching assistants in 2004 won 54-per-cent support for affiliation with the Public Service Alliance of Canada, an affiliation that would eventually take place in 2010.[109]

Leggett entrusted the new position of vice-principal, research, to chemist Suzanne Fortier, who had temporarily worn the old combined Graduate Studies and Research hat in the interregnum between Smith and Leggett. The decision reflected Leggett's own experience as a research scientist at McGill and his appreciation that obtaining research funds required concentrated effort. As head of McGill's biology department, Leggett had personally tweaked every application for external support submitted by his colleagues. The results were impressive. Leggett arrived at Queen's at a pivotal time. The traditional federal granting agencies – SSHRC, NSERC, and the Medical Research Council of Canada (to become the Canadian Institute of Health Research in 2000) – were on the verge of being augmented by an array of federal and provincial research initiatives. Public policy in Canada was coming alive to the reality of globalization and the so-called "knowledge economy." Ontario, for instance, responded with its Access to Opportunity, Research and Development, and SuperBuild programs, aimed at priming the province's technology pump. But it was the federal government in Ottawa that weighed most heavily into the field of funded research. Since the Second World War, Ottawa's support of Canadian universities had been largely indirect, usually in the form of per-capita-derived transfer payments to the provinces. From Ottawa's point of view, such transfers brought little political recognition to the national government. Programs of direct funded research, particularly if they were linked to the crucial national challenges such as genome research and the electronic revolution, had the double appeal of direct control and consequent political credit. The linchpin of the federal effort was unveiled in early 1997 with the launch of the Canadian Foundation for Innovation (CFI). It would support up to 40 per cent of the infrastructure costs of projects designed to place Canada on the cutting edge of what was increasingly labelled as "world class" research. The rhetoric suggested that scientific research was most favoured. In 2000, the CFI initiative was complemented by the Canada Research Chair program, designed to place the best Canadian university brains at the forefront of campus research. The chairs would be competitively selected upon nomination by individual campuses. The creation of Networks of National Centres of Excellence became embedded in Ottawa's agenda of national development.

As vice-principal, research, Fortier hailed the CFI program with its $800-million, five-year budget as a "fantastic opportunity" for Queen's. Here was a chance to build up Queen's research infrastructure at a time when the regulated university budget of operating grant and fees was strained to the limit. There were, nonetheless, formidable challenges: grant applications often needed evidence of matching funds to be successful. Queen's, situated as it was in eastern Ontario, was relatively poorly placed to attract industrial partners in this respect. Attention also had to be paid to those areas of university inquiry that seemed marginal to the CFI's interest in future-oriented, applied research. Nonetheless, Fortier excelled in grooming Queen's for the CFI challenge. She appointed a director of research services to facilitate the application process and research affiliations with other universities and formed an executive committee to oversee the application process at Queen's. She also appointed faculty coordinators to help seek out likely projects for CFI support, and created a Research Ethics Board to protect researchers' integrity and intellectual-property rights when outside money supported their work. The results were impressive. In the 1997–98 budget year, Fortier reported, 24 per cent of the university's $262.5-million budget was derived from research. In 1998, for instance, the dean of Applied Science, Tom Harris, reported signing an agreement with the

Ontario government and the National Research Council for the funding of a Centre for Automotive Materials and Manufacturing to pioneer "greener" cars and roads.[110]

Queen's reinforced the big funded thrusts of the new research culture. It created a series of Chancellor's Research Awards to honour productive researchers on campus. It put forward prominent and productive Queen's scholars for national awards: in 1996, for instance, Donald Akenson of history won the Molson Prize of the Canada Council for his work on the Irish diaspora, while pathologist Robert Kisilevsky won a Beaubien Award for his work on Alzheimer's disease. Dedicated chairs, usually supported by outside money, were set up to highlight Queen's expertise. The Purvis Professorship in Economics was established to perpetuate Queen's involvement in public policy and to commemorate the tragically shortened life of economist Douglas Purvis.

In the dying years of the twentieth century, Queen's thus became a factory for funded research. Fortier reported in great detail the university's success in Canada's funded-research league. Benchmarks of success were established: in 1997, for instance, an extraordinary 96.7 per cent of Queen's applications to NSERC for operating grants were successful. The aim was always for Queen's to match or exceed the national success rate in such competitions. There were crinkles in the new culture of research: the granting agencies would not permit the application of funded-research monies to normative university functions such as library acquisitions. The allocation of research overheads – who paid for the janitors and the heating bill? – continued to be a bone of contention; individual researchers garnered outside financial support, leaving the university to absorb the costs of housing that research. There was also an ongoing tension generated by the fact that so much of the new research culture was tilted towards the sciences. In 2001, it was remarked that only 20 per cent of the new Canada Research Chairs had been allocated to the Arts and Science faculty; the administration attempted to offset this imbalance by dedicating a preponderance of Queen's National Scholar appointments to that faculty over the next five years.[111] Even Chancellor Peter Lougheed admitted his anxiety that the chase for funded research might be "skewing" the university's integrity, eroding its freedom of unbridled inquiry. In the Senate, there were comments that the new research culture was too "quantitative" – too fixated on the gross flow of grant payments – and not enough concerned with the qualitative nature of the inquiry.[112] Few, however, could deny that funded research was giving the university a measure of financial freedom that its persistent visits to Queen's Park had not delivered.

In 2000, academic vice-principal David Turpin accepted the presidency of the University of Victoria, a post he would hold for thirteen years. As the new millennium dawned, Canadian university administrators were becoming a more-mobile cadre, deploying their talents where required. Turpin's role at Queen's was taken by Suzanne Fortier (who herself would in 2006 take up the presidency of NSERC in Ottawa). The vice-principal, research, post was consequently given to Kerry Rowe, an Australian-born civil engineer with a prolific research record at the University of Western Ontario and much experience on NSERC selection committees and in professional associations. Rowe took up Fortier's quest to establish Queen's as a research-intensive university. Rowe's mission was facilitated by the fact that the Liberal government of Paul Martin in Ottawa reinforced the federal CFI initiative by announcing that an additional $750 million would be devoted to the fund over the next ten years. Ottawa had also announced special millennium scholarships to bolster undergraduate study and enhanced budgets for its funding agencies in support of graduate study and research. Ontario's dedication to targeted support of research was at the same time manifest in its Super-Build decisions to fund new university facilities. In

2002, Rowe was able to announce that Queen's had been able to attract $129.6 million in research funding, an achievement embellished by strong showings in such awards as Killam Fellowships. Downstream from this success, PARTEQ thrived by commercializing ideas into patents, aiding start-up companies, and in generating commercial revenue in support of cancer research on campus. In 2003, Rowe was also able to report that Ottawa had finally agreed to permanently cover the indirect cost of research on Canadian university campuses, something that he estimated would bring $6.7 million to Queen's.[113]

This expansive environment bred creativity at Queen's. In 2001, Rowe and the Advisory Research Committee set out a strategic plan for research at Queen's. The goal was to make Queen's an internationally recognized centre for research that was concentrated in eight research "clusters" – areas of expertise ranging from material sciences to Queen's traditional strength in public policy.[114] Funding would be channelled into these bailiwicks of excellence and reinforced by intensified graduate programs. Research was also to be increasingly conceived of along interdisciplinary and interuniversity lines: centres were established or expanded in areas such as human mobility, primary medical care, Southern African studies, law in the contemporary workplace, fuel-cell research, and water and the environment, all with generous external funding from bodies such as NSERC and the Medical Research Council, as well foundations, corporations, and private donors.

When asked in 2004 to brief the trustees on her work as director of research services, Sandra Crocker titled her remarks: "Think Research, Think Queen's." Few could disagree. The increasingly prevalent annual rankings that calibrated Canadian universities' performance benchmarked Queen's rise as a research-intensive university. According to Re$earch Infosource Inc., Queen's scholars found themselves among the elite fifteen of Canada's research-intensive universities. The intensification of funded research under Leggett was indeed a shrewd, and probably inevitable, strategy; it alleviated the fiscal strain on the university by attaching it to a revenue stream unfettered by strictures of accessibility, while at the same time allowing it to enhance its distinctive brand. As a by-product, funded research promoted new spirit and inventiveness in Queen's faculty, allowing them opportunity to pursue their research inclinations. Take, for instance, the research of Canada Research Chair in environmental change, John Smol of the biology department: his dedication to probing the impact pollution and climatic change had on lakes and seashores allowed Queen's to address society's growing alarm over environmental deterioration in the new millennium. Scholars such as Smol (who would eventually garner an Order of Canada and a Killam Prize for his work) gave the university a new breed of academic celebrities, whose achievements could be used to project an image of progressiveness and connected Queen's with the broader Canadian society.

Indirectly, however, this fundamental rebalancing intensified the slow diminution of Queen's grand tradition of excellence in the classroom. Fame and academic fortune – and the tenure and promotion that flowed from it – now increasingly led away from the lecture hall and towards the annual grant announcements that flowed from Ottawa and Toronto. The same university rankings that polished Queen's reputation as a place of research now also reported that Queen's classes were growing larger and that fewer senior professors took on undergraduate courses as they headed for the lab or the research trip. Doctoral students – some promising, most as yet poorly equipped for pedagogy – took their place behind the podium. The 2003 *Maclean's* survey of thirty-eight Canadian universities, for instance, ranked Queen's #1 in "school spirit," but #20 in teaching-assistant quality and #19 in class size. As Principal Leggett had noted, there were no "magic bullets."

"You Don't Build It Until You Can Pay for It": Bricks and Mortar

In 1989, Queen's had successfully negotiated with Queen's Park over its ideal size. Still mindful of John Deutsch's wisdom of achieving a "steady state," Queen's had agreed that its "corridor" of enrolment would hover between 11,400 and 11,500 undergraduate students. This it had maintained, so that in 1994 Bill Leggett found 11,331 full-time undergraduates on campus, joined by 3,458 part-timers. Graduate students swelled the university's full enrolment to 17,510. Despite Queen's traditional dedication to calibrated growth, there was no avoiding the emerging dynamics of new-century growth. First, a surge in would-be university students eighteen to twenty-four loomed in the first decade of the new century. In 1999, a PriceWaterhouseCoopers consultant, Michael Gourley, told the trustees about the enrolment projections he was doing for the Council of Ontario Universities. The participation rate for eighteen- to twenty-four-year-olds would steadily increase by between 2 and 8 per cent a year. Echoing this scenario, the COU reported in October that admissions across the province had jumped that fall by 6.6 per cent, the highest such increase in a decade.[115]

The situation looked like a repeat of the sixties. Exacerbating the pressure was the fact that seismic shifts were taking place in *what* students wanted to study – life sciences, for instance, continue to boom, a trend accommodated by the new Biosciences Building, constructed in 1997. Other factors weighed in the balance. Leggett's growing dedication to a "broader learning experience" at Queen's suggested that attention would have to be paid to facilities outside the classroom – student services, a year at Herstmonceux, athletic facilities. Would opening the double-cohort domestic floodgate crowd out hoped-for international students? There was also an increasing trade-off between teaching facilities and research infrastructure. In this milieu, Queen's debated its ambitions and capacities. What would be the "right size" for Queen's in meeting this bulge? How many new professors, classrooms, and labs would be in order? Most importantly, how would they be financed?

A 1999 task force, chaired by Vice-Principal Turpin, provided some answers to these questions. Queen's traditional caution in matters of growth once again emerged.[116] The university's constrained geography and its wariness around the uneasy relation of growth and quality asserted themselves. Queen's was a residential university, and its residence system was already at 98-per-cent capacity, Turpin told the trustees. Trustees cited the recently completed report by Montreal Canadiens hockey star Ken Dryden on the university's athletics program, which had highlighted the shortfall in Queen's facilities. There was, he remarked, no field house and no student activity centre, and existing student services were strained.[117] Coupled with the cloud of financial austerity hanging over the campus, such considerations served to cool enrolment expansion at Queen's. Despite the allure of a windfall in tuition, Richardson Hall resisted Toronto's pressure to expand, even when the government relented to COU pressure and offered Ontario universities one-time adjustment relief for the upcoming double cohort.

As a result, the Leggett years saw steady-but-not-headlong growth in admissions at Queen's. Under Leggett, total enrolment at the university grew to 20,391 by 2004, up almost 3,000 over the decade. In the fall of 2003, registrar Jo-Anne Brady reported that the first wave of double-cohort students had arrived. That year, the university had received almost 40,000 applications for first-year places; only 3,450 were offered admission, a 2-per-cent increase over 2002. Those who were successful boasted average high-school grades of 88.9 per cent. Brady noted that one effect of the double cohort had been to give Queen's a remarkably young freshman class – many under nineteen years of age. Thus, by 2004, Queen's had for the first time broken above 20,000 in enrolment, but it had done so in a characteristically controlled fashion, protecting its standards and image.

Even such controlled growth required space and new facilities. In 1994, Leggett had inherited a worrisome list of bricks-and-mortar problems. The old Douglas Library needed kitting out as the compendium resource centre for the university's precious special collection and for the centralization of branch libraries such as engineering. The Agnes Etherington Art Centre needed expansion, as did the Donald Gordon Centre. Queen's chemistry labs in the Frost Wing, which jutted out behind Gordon Hall, were woefully out of date. To make the point, Leggett marched the trustees over to the wing after one of their meetings to horrify them with its decrepit ventilation system and to suggest that it would take $50 million to once again give Queen's a respectable reputation in the discipline. At the same time, construction of the Biosciences Building with its modern labs and classrooms provided a glimpse of what had been done for the life-science disciplines. Hovering above all this was the university's accumulating deferred-maintenance deficit, estimated by 2000 to be as high as $90 million and rising precipitously.[118]

Two factors governed Queen's careful approach to expansion during the Leggett years. First, there was the determination to abide by the university's 1994 Master Plan, which set out principles for the aesthetically harmonious and functional environment. Chaired by Dan Burns, a veteran of Queen's student politics in the sixties and now a senior Ontario civil servant, the Campus Planning and Development Committee dedicated itself to maintaining the quality and process initiated by the construction of the Stauffer Library. There could be no backsliding into the dark, brutalist days of Queen's building in the decades preceding that breakthrough, no return to "institutional grey and ugly," as one senator insisted. Architects would be carefully selected, and constant thought would be given to making Queen's

what Jeanne Ma, the university planning officer, called a "livable campus." The goal, Burns habitually told the trustees, was a built environment at Queen's that projected an image of "quality" – quality that would attract new undergraduates and faculty, while at the same time prompting alumni to dig deep to support their alma mater.[119]

The actual decision to commit to new buildings and facilities remained with the trustees, and here Queen's genetic frugality persevered. Throughout the Leggett years, there was an unspoken, underlying assumption that the university must avoid debt at all costs. Government support for universities was falling behind inflation and was increasingly predicated on specific ends, so the onus for raising the money for capital projects fell more and more on the university itself to ensure that it was walking a fiscally viable path. The endowment must be protected and expanded; this was being addressed by the Campaign for Queen's. At the same time, major capital projects must be securely financed before a shovel touched the ground. Time and again, Leggett and members of the Board's finance committee recited the credo "don't build it until you can pay for it." This dedication required delicate, multiparty financing, as monies for any one project were negotiated through programs such as the SuperBuild and skimmed out of endowment earnings or the proceeds of fundraising, student support, and the generosity of lead sponsors. Aided by persuasive salesmen such as Vice-Principal George Hood, Board chairs Don Elliott and John Rae, and chancellors Agnes Benidickson, Peter Lougheed, and Charles Baillie, Queen's more and more looked to outside philanthropy to move it forward. The highly visible commitment of generous donors gave credibility and momentum to university projects, thereby inviting other partners, small and large, to participate. "You can sell a dream," Leggett liked to say, "but you can't sell a mortgage." Finally, hours of deliberation by the Board's planning, finance, and investment committees rounded out the process of ensuring that sustainable financing was in place before the trustees gave the final nod to letting the tender on any new university project.

Room to Breathe: Art, Chemistry, Integrated Learning, and Business

The results of this judicious combination of master planning and careful financial husbandry were impressive. Between 1998 and 2000, for instance, the Agnes Etherington Art Centre received a thorough $7.2-million renovation and expansion. Triggered in 1995 by donor Alfred Bader's decision to donate more of his fine collection of Dutch Masters paintings to Queen's, the modernizing of the old Etherington house on University Avenue and the addition of new gallery space was initially underwritten by the federal and Ontario governments, but when the cash-strapped Ontario government pulled back, Bader once again stepped into the breach with the gift of $3 million that kept the project alive. When "the Agnes" reopened in 2000, it made Queen's a cultural hub of eastern Ontario. In gratitude, a new exhibition wing of the gallery was named after Bader. Four years later, when Bader turned eighty, Queen's Crescent outside the gallery was renamed Bader Lane.[120]

Chemistry was next. The dysfunctional Frost Wing was demolished. Gordon Hall next door was renovated, a project that included restoring its handsome original gabled roofline, a roofline lost to the clumsy addition of a fourth floor in the sixties. In 1998, initial planning for a new chemistry building was authorized, and a site to the west of Stirling Hall was chosen. A daunting estimate of almost $60 million was attached to the project. Indicative of the complex financing of such capital projects, the university looked in several directions for the wherewithal to begin construction of the five-storey building. The Ontario SuperBuild contributed a crucial foundation of $27 million. Other significant support was obtained from the CFI in Ottawa and Ontario's Innovation Trust. But the tipping point came when, in the spring of 2000, Calgary energy entrepreneur Michael Chernoff stepped forward with a donation of $12 million. Chernoff had graduated from Queen's in 1959 with a degree in geological engineering. A lad of humble origins from Saskatchewan, he had attended Queen's on a full scholarship and, like Bader, had never forgotten its impact on his life. His son Bruce had followed in his father's footsteps, graduating from Queen's in chemical engineering in 1987. Chernoff's support put a halo around the project, an inducement for smaller donors to fall into line. The sod turning for the new Chernoff Building in the fall of 2000 was timed to coincide with the kick-off of the public phase of the Campaign for Queen's. Two years later, the fourteen-thousand-square-metre building, with its array of "wet" (laboratory) and "dry" (administrative and lecturing) facilities was inaugurated, just as the campaign was cresting at $261 million.

Similar continuing loyalty to their alma mater was demonstrated by Donald Munro, a civil engineer who had graduated in 1952, and Robert Beamish a graduate of mechanical engineering in 1960. Each had prospered in life – Munro in heavy equipment and construction and Munro in petrochemicals. Beamish's son and daughter had followed in his footsteps to Queen's. In 2000, Munro and Beamish, had each harkened to Queen's call for help in altering the pedagogic dynamics of its engineering curriculum. Professional accreditation review of the Faculty of Applied Science had urged the adoption of a more "outcomes-oriented" curriculum, one that helped students to bridge the gap between textbook and workplace. Tom Harris, the dean, briefed the trustees on this need. Arguing that his faculty needed a facility that would serve as a "living laboratory in itself ... flexible, visible, stimulating, and interactive,"[121] Harris called for an "integrated learning centre" that would straddle all the separate departments in which engineers were trained at

Queen's. He suggested that a building would require about $30 million.

Once again, the baseplate funding was supplied by Ontario's SuperBuild, with a contribution of $12 million. The rest of the eventual $24.8-million price tag was met by monies generated by the Campaign for Queen's (which *in toto* contributed $63.5 million to new buildings at Queen's) and outside foundations. But it was the signature donations, totalling $9 million, given in the name of the Beamish family and of Donald and Mary Munro, that capped the process. When the new centre opened at the corner of Union and Division in 2004, Queen's took possession of one of Canada's most environmentally sensitive buildings, one in which a waterfall in the foyer (dedicated to Bill Leggett) cleansed the air used in the building. Not coincidentally, the student-run, eco-friendly Queen's Tea Room (named for the smoky, convivial emporium that had stood on the same corner decades before) soon opened in that same foyer.

Further west along Union Street, the School of Business had been agitating for new space for more than a decade. Since the late 1950s, the school had operated out of Dunning Hall, a building that it had long shared with economics. Now increasingly cramped, Dunning also seemed out of kilter with the business school's new image as a cutting-edge purveyor of MBAs oriented to the executive, public-sector, and science and high-tech markets, not to mention an undergraduate program geared to a globalized market. The school hankered after a facade and facilities that reflected its expanding mission. As well, if tuition was to be uncoupled from government regulation, business education had to project a keen, entrepreneurial image. Dean John Gordon had angled to get the prime location at the corner of Union and University, but that had gone to the Stauffer Library. His successor got little further. With no major outside backer and the long-time simmering rivalry of the business school and the economics department (David Smith's home base) over such issues as the teaching of foundation economics, a stasis stilled any attempt to relocate the burgeoning business school.[122] The arrival of an activist principal, Bill Leggett, and the appointment of a new dean of business, Margot Northey, changed that.

In 1991, Queen's had purchased the old Victoria School on the corner of Albert and Union for $1.7 million from the local school board. The property offered Queen's the opportunity of breaking out of the spatial box that had so long confined its expansion. The Romanesque-style school was a grand example of late-Victorian architecture, designed by one of Kingston's premier architects, William Newlands, to honour Canada's twenty-fifth anniversary in 1892. There was, therefore, no question of demolishing the handsome brick edifice; heritage vigilance was too strong in the city, and in the university's official plan.[123] Initially, the Victoria School was slated for use by the registrar's office, but the booming success of the business school's privatized programs and the arrival of Margot Northey in 1999 turned the tide. That year, the university commissioned a $250,000 study of the building's potential, which led in 2000 to the decision to renovate the old school as a new home for business education at Queen's, one that handsomely combined the high-ceilinged Victorian elegance of the building with a spacious new wing containing the latest teaching and conferencing technologies of the dawning century. The cost was estimated at $25 million.[124] Whereas the original acquisition of the old school had been financed through a creative mix of parking revenues and endowment profits, the renovation required much more substantial support. Once again, a willing and generous member of the alumni stepped forward to provide the lead donation, one that would prime the pump of government support and a broadening private base of giving. Thus, in 2001, warmed to the opportunity by Dean Northey and long-time marketing professor Dan Monieson, Melvin "Mel" Goodes pledged

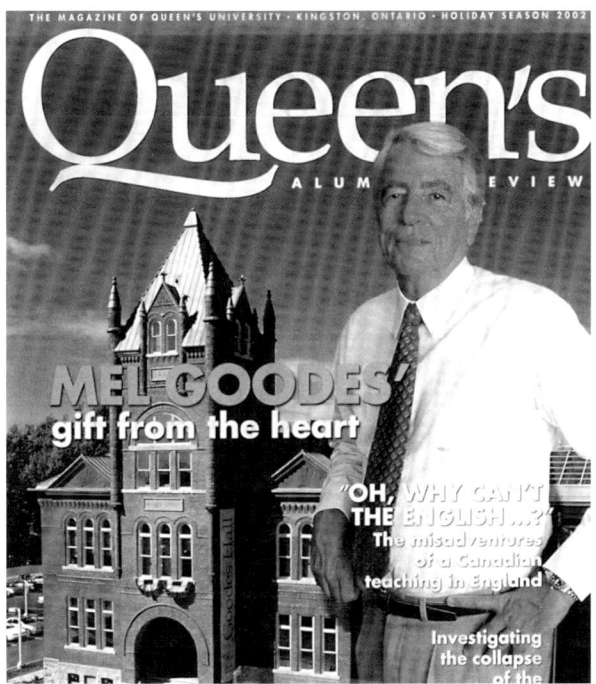

The cover of the *Queen's Alumni Review* celebrates the generosity of Queen's commerce graduate and Warner-Lambert CEO Mel Goodes in giving the Queen's business school its first purpose-built building. Goodes Hall combined the elegance of nineteenth-century local architecture with the needs of a modern business faculty.

a crucial $10 million to the project. Goodes had graduated in Queen's commerce in 1957 and gone on to a stellar career, which culminated in his position as CEO of the huge American pharmaceutical company Warner-Lambert. In the 1990s, he had returned to Queen's to sit on its board. As with the Beamish and Munro donations, Goodes dedicated his gift to the memory of his family, particularly his father, who had sacrificed much to put his son through Queen's. When Goodes Hall opened in the fall of 2003, Queen's finally had a facility that was both aesthetically alluring (an elegant complement to its neighbour, the Stauffer Library) and at the same time tuned to the needs of twenty-first-century business.[125]

One Roof Fits All: The Birth of the Queen's Centre

From the day he arrived on Queen's campus, Bill Leggett sensed that Queen's was a community bound by tradition and cohesion, more so than any other university he had encountered. Central to that cohesion was the harmonious connection of Queen's student life with those who taught and administered the place. Like all his immediate predecessors, Leggett obliged that connection. In 1995, for example, he allowed himself to be auctioned off in a principal-for-a-day raffle; Applied Science student Jennifer Kao filled his boots in Richardson Hall for a day, while he lived the life of a student. As his tenure unfolded, Leggett developed the habit of standing on the steps of his office to take a visual survey of the student body as it flowed up and down University Avenue. This he called the "Leggett cultural index," an admittedly unscientific means of checking the mood and diversity of the student body.[126] As a result, Leggett and his colleagues were not oblivious to the fraying of this cohesion, as spiralling tuition costs, accommodation shortages, and the upward creep of class sizes gnawed at students' bond with their university. Whether being served Kraft Dinner by debt-worried students outside a Senate meeting or seeing his office occupied by protesters against fee deregulation, Leggett realized that something had to be done to bolster student morale at Queen's. The Campaign for Queens and the *Pathfinder* initiative were conceived as means to reinforce the quality of Queen's teaching with better buildings, cutting-edge technology, and more student financial assistance. But there was also a commitment to improving the day-to-day quality of student life at Queen's. This focused on investing time and money in "broadening the learning environment" for those attending the university, something that would, to use Leggett's own words, "mesh with the social fabric of Queen's."[127] By the end of Leggett's principalship, this ambition became vested in what was to be Queen's largest-ever building project – something initially dubbed the "student life centre," but subsequently shortened into the more integrative "Queen's Centre." As the leitmotif of Queen's in the new millennium, the Queen's Centre would come to both inspire and haunt its community well into that new age.

Many pressures pushed the university towards the Queen's Centre. In the nineties, Queen's had begun taking an exit poll of its graduating undergraduate classes. Despite its idiosyncratic nature (the survey, for instance, only sampled those who had persevered at Queen's to graduation), the poll consistently reported that students valued the education they got at Queen's and were departing in the knowledge that they had been well prepared for life. However, the poll also consistently revealed that Queen's left much to be desired in catering to the day-to-day needs of students – athletics, food services, retail amenities. The annual *Maclean's* ranking of Canadian universities echoed this finding. At a time when many universities were centralizing their student services in mall-like emporiums – the McMaster Student Centre, for instance – Queen's students still found themselves scurrying between buildings for a textbook bought here and a coffee enjoyed there. In the nineties, the AMS and the administration had rejigged the constitution of the John Deutsch Centre to streamline its layout and services and to deliver more control of the building into student hands. Despite this shift, the JDUC, as it was popularly called, remained a cramped, low-ceilinged seventies concrete bunker.

Particularly irksome to students (and many faculty) were Queen's overstretched athletic facilities. Since the Milliken Report of 1971, Queen's had dedicated itself to a wide-based participatory sports culture. The university had come to boast the widest array of intramural sports programs in Canada. At the same time, Queen's continued to field teams in intercollegiate sports, an endeavour that every year saw over a thousand Gael athletes board buses and planes to take to fields, courts, or pools across the nation. The 2002 *Tricolour*, for example, listed forty-five competitive varsity teams and thirty-one recreational intramural teams at Queen's. Under all this pressure, the university athletic facilities were buckling. The Physical Education Centre (PEC), built in the early seventies, was by the end of the century handling as many as eighteen thousand visits a week. Some 89.6 per cent of Queen's students were estimated to make annual use of the university's athletic facilities, but they found them hot, smelly, and outdated. "The PEC Sucks," a *Journal* feature reported in 2002.[128]

Ken Dryden's 1997 report on Queen's sports facilities reaffirmed the Milliken philosophy: participatory sport was a Queen's "hallmark." However, facilities, Dryden concluded, were woefully overloaded: a multipurpose field house would alleviate the strain. Similarly, he noted that athletic subsidies assigned by the University Council on Athletics were inadequate: big intercollegiate teams were well-supported, while smaller intramural programs in sports such as judo and curling got a stingy 17 per cent of their operating needs.[129] Queen's tradition, which included a strong sporting bent, was under duress. It was not just that "jocks" liked to kick balls around and slap pucks into nets. Fitness culture was pervading Canada. Students pondering their choice of university increasingly looked for modern workout facilities on the campuses they inspected, and most concluded that Queen's did not measure up. Vice-Principal John Cowan revived the idea that a multi-million-dollar field house might do the trick. Alumni joined the chorus of concern: trustee and former Gaels football star Kent Plumley championed the idea of a more extensive, centrally located student-services hub.

Student Affairs Dean Bob Crawford reported that it was not just aerobics that students wanted. Queen's also lacked what he rather grandly labelled places for "informal intellectual exchange" – quiet lounges and coffee shops, places where laptop computers could pick up the internet or where study groups could convene. In addition, as the student ghetto grew to the north of campus, there was an evident need for better retail space where student might pick up milk, bread, and other staples on their way home. Queen's inadequacies in these respects added up to more than a lack of facilities. A campus which failed to bring its students together on common ground stood the danger of losing cohesion and a sense of shared experience. A 1998 Principal's Advisory Committee on Student Life Facilities, chaired by Tom Williams of the School of Policy Studies, confirmed the prognosis that Queen's was failing its students in their daily needs.

In 1999, Bob Crawford was asked to chair a task force to scope out what a solution might look like. Crawford worried that the university was facing a credibility gap between its storied brand as one of Canada's most popular universities and the deficiencies of day-to-day life on its campus. "Queen's," he fretted "was better than the sum of its parts."[130] What Queen's needed, he reported, was a "student life centre," a gathering place where students could congregate and satisfy practical and social needs ranging from treadmills to cappuccino. Such advice found Queen's in a heady, can-do mood. The Campaign for Queen's was surging towards unprecedented fundraising success. Construction cranes dominated the campus as new academic and gallery facilities sprouted, to be followed shortly by two new student residences. The advancement office under George Hood it seemed now stood on a competent, permanent footing, ready to respond to new initiatives. Through its SuperBuild program, the provincial government had demonstrated its willingness to back projects that conformed to its agenda of targeted growth. On campus, the mantra of enhancing the quality of education and the services supporting it was enthusiastically endorsed by trustees and AMS Assembly alike.

In May 2001, the trustees listened to what Crawford and the Campus Planning Committee, presciently chaired by Dan Burns, had to say. They were enthusiastic. In keeping with past precedent, the Board voted a small budget to allow the dimensions of the project to be probed – location, design, cost, and so on. Two governing factors were immediately apparent, again reflecting recent and past experience. First, the Board's traditional fiscal caution was voiced: "it was difficult to proceed further without the required funding." In effect, line up the financing before signing up the contractors. And, secondly, the project would need a lead sponsor: "The Student Life Centre facility needs a champion."[131] The clinching factor in the procurement of the expanded art gallery and the new chemistry and business buildings had been the willingness of benefactors like Bader, Chernoff, and Goodes to inspire confidence in the projects through their generosity. Initial discussions of the new student centre assumed the same trajectory.

In the fall of 2001, the consensus for a new student centre firmed up. Scott Courtice, the AMS president, urged the trustees to act with expedition, calling for a project leader to be appointed and warning that students did not want to see the project "languish." Responding to this message, Leggett asked vice-principal, advancement, George Hood, to take charge of the project in late 2001; the Campaign for Queen's had just surged past $200 million, and Hood's galvanic style seemed ideally suited to pushing the as-yet-nebulous student centre forward. The next year saw the centre begin to take tangible shape. Taking a page from his advancement blueprint, Hood determined that Queen's should ape "best practices" evident elsewhere in North America. As an advisor, he took on Richard Strong, a Harvard-trained Toronto architect renowned for his urban renewal work in Boston and Toronto. With Strong, he studied about twenty recent architectural projects around the continent that might provide a blueprint for Queen's student centre ambition. To help define that ambition, Hood used an online survey of the Queen's community to pin down exactly what was expected: 2,759 respondents gave general support to the idea of a centralized, integrated student-life and athletic centre, a "gathering place" in

Hood's words. To help bring precision to this consensus, Queen's employed the Boston design firm of Sasaki and Associates (Strong's one-time affiliates). The Sasaki team visited Queen's, walking through the Ghetto and around campus to gauge the rhythm and needs of student life. The trustees backed this approach, voting another $300,000 for planning the centre and, at its October 2002 meeting, listening to a forceful presentation by AMS president Michael Lindsay and other students calling for the centre as a means of renewing student involvement in their university. Lindsay assured that Board that Queen's undergraduate body would put its money where its mouth was by approving a mandatory fee in support of the project. To confirm the point, Lindsay accompanied the trustees on a tour of the tatty JDUC and rundown PEC to drive home the message that the status quo was no longer acceptable.[132]

By the spring of 2003, the physical and financial contours of the project were beginning to take shape. It was at this point that the "student learning centre" was rechristened the Queen's Centre. In March, Hood unveiled the conceptual dimensions of the project. The centre would devour the entire block encompassed by Union, University, Division, and Earl streets. The intention was to make the facility the epicentre of student life at Queen's – "one functional community," in Hood's words. While elements of existing facilities, such as the JDUC, would be incorporated into the complex, it was the scope of the new additions that was breathtaking. Totalling 72,000 square metres, the Queen's Centre would contain a 2,500-seat multipurpose facility, a four-court gym, an indoor track, a pool, a sprawling fitness centre, a rowing tank, an expanded hockey rink, space for club rooms, a climbing wall, and even a sports hall of fame. All this would be arranged around a central indoor "street," along which coffee shops and a multitude of student-friendly services would be arrayed. Adding an active academic component, the centre would also act as the hub of the university's School of Physical and Health Education (soon to be renamed the School of Kinesiology and Health Studies), a logical co-location.

Anticipating the trustees' genetic concern for cost, Hood said that the centre could be financed by a combination of philanthropy, sponsorships, student contributions, university revenues, and support from granting agencies. Certainly, if anyone at Queen's had a reputation for finding dollars to fulfill aspirations, it was Hood. Nonetheless, the total estimated cost of the project came in at a stunning $175 million, by far the largest price tag ever put on a Queen's project. To soften the sticker shock, Hood said that the project would be tackled in phases over a decade and that, when complete, it would cover its own operating costs through "revenue-generating mechanisms," such as user fees and space rental.[133] A go-ahead decision, he concluded, would be needed at the May 2003 meeting of the Board.

Bill Leggett not only believed in the Queen's Centre, but he also had come to rely on George Hood's directness and ability. In May, Leggett opened the trustees' debate by stressing that the Queen's Centre was about the "whole community" at Queen's, not just one privileged enclave of it. Improving the quality of student life at Queen's would wash through the university in powerful ways, ranging from stronger admission demand to strengthened student government. Leggett's sentiment was reinforced by that year's president of the AMS, Chrissie Knitter, who said that the students saw the centre as "an essential community-building tool." To demonstrate this faith, the AMS had voted $300,000 for the renovation of the JDUC. To ensure this communality, Leggett announced that the project would be shaped by a Queen's Centre Working Group, which would contain membership from every sector of the campus community. The AMS, for example, nominated two members. Taking another page from the Stauffer project, an executive committee headed by alumnus Dr Andy Pipe would then guide the strategic direction of the project, while a management committee would oversee the actual construction and operation of the centre. There were some voices of partial dissent. Law professor Sue Miklas wanted more consultation, suggesting that a project so daunting needed as broad a consensus as possible. Lawyer Don Bayne, a former Gaels quarterback, pointed out that the centre proposal did not include a field house and seemed oblivious to the needs of field sports. Such concerns aside, the mood of the Board was strongly tilted towards initial approval, trusting that the finer details would be sorted out as the planning proceeded.

The affirmation of the project was most crucially influenced by the financial assurances given the Board. Tom O'Neill, chair of the newly formed advancement committee, reported that he and his colleagues had agonized over the centre's financial projections. They had turned to Marts and Lundy, the American consultants who had so ably assisted the just-complete capital campaign, and had been assured that "there was absolutely no reason to doubt the University's ability to generate funds required over a period of time to support the concept." Bill Young, who chaired the Board's finance committee, agreed. "A variety of viable financial options existed," he said. One factor behind this confidence was the Board's groundbreaking decision a year earlier to finance the university's expansion through debenture financing. Informed at their May 2003 meeting that Queen's capital needs over the next four and a half years might total $130 million, the Board had instructed the university's financial managers to explore the possibility of short-term loans financed by annual cash flow or longer-term debenture borrowing. By August 2003, the idea of unsecured debentures seemed to have the upper hand, even though it would be unprecedented for Queen's. Underwriters had assured the finance committee that $60 to $70 million might be raised at an advantageous rate, just above the interest rate paid on federal bonds. Queen's would probably garner a respectable AA+ rating for creditworthiness.

Throughout the late summer of 2002, the best financial brains available to Queen's – men such as board chair John Rae and Royal Bank CEO Gordon Nixon – studied and endorsed the idea, backed by legal opinion from Toronto lawyers McCarthy Tetrault. The timing seemed propitious. Seven other Canadian universities had issued debentures. The financial markets were strong and likely to oversubscribe the issue. Since much of the money sought would be applied to the construction of two new residences, servicing the debt could rely on residence fees to pay the interest. In October, advised by Tom Thayer in the university's financial group that $90 million in debentures might be had at 6.4-per-cent interest over thirty years, the Board gave its nod. The money immediately proved useful, helping, for instance, to pay the final bills on Chernoff Hall. Despite all the due diligence, Queen's had crossed over into unfamiliar territory – its financial well-being to some degree was now hostage to external forces over which it had no direct control.[134]

Other factors buoyed the tide of initial confidence in the Queen's Centre. Queen's undergraduates harkened to the call. In October 2003, George Hood spoke before the AMS Assembly and, in his inimitably direct manner, exhorted them to contribute. They would, he said, be paying "more than you've ever paid before for anything else."[135] Nonetheless, the quality of their life at Queen's would undeniably benefit from the centre. The students did not need much prompting. The AMS president, Chrissie Knitter, and her successor, Tyler Turnbull, reminded their constituents that student monies had contributed to such Queen's centre-pieces as Grant Hall and the JDUC, and that the torch was now in their hands. The March 2005 AMS general meeting held in Grant Hall – the largest open meeting in its history – duly approved a mandatory annual fee on all its members to support the capital cost of the centre. This prospective student investment of $25.5 million now bolstered the project.[136] It was the largest capital pledge ever made by a Canadian student body. Student support was, however, not unanimous: mindful that the centre was primarily predicated on undergraduate needs, graduate and professional students at Queen's were cool on the project and decided against supporting it. Similarly, faculty remained largely neutral on the Queen's Centre, some seeing the project's potential to squeeze the university's pedagogic budget over time.

The optimistic launch of the Queen's Centre culminated in the designation of B + H Architects, a Toronto-based firm with an international reputation, as the primary architects of the project, aided by Sasaki Associates in Boston and Shoalts and Zaback of Kingston. The working group that made the selection was drawn from faculty, staff, and students, and, like the consultation on the Stauffer, played a hands-on role in fleshing out the design principles. The group, for instance, travelled to Boston to inspect state-of-the-art community centres. This buzz of architectural creativity gave Bill Leggett considerable satisfaction as he prepared to step down as principal in the summer of 2004 – the mooted centre offered solid proof that Queen's was ministering to the quality of its students' journey through its campus. Against the backdrop of a healthy national economy and the emergence of the more-viable, if rather pragmatic, funding formula underlying Queen's operations, there was justifiable reason for such optimism. But, as some remarked, the capstone of that optimism had yet to fall into place in the arch of the Queen's Centre. There was as yet no lead sponsor, no confidence-inspiring benefactor whose munificence would secure the centre's ascent. There were shadowy rumours of such support, but as yet no hard commitment. Without such a buy-in, the Queen's Centre remained a chimera. There was salutary wisdom in Bill Leggett's aphorism that "you can sell a vision, but you can't sell a mortgage."

Farewell to "a Coach and a Cheerleader"

Shortly after Bill Leggett assumed the principalship, the trustees had received news that one-time Queen's great football halfback John "Johnny" Munro had died. In 1934, Munro had kicked a single point that had given Queen's victory over Varsity and the Yates Cup. After leaving the gridiron and Queen's, John had gone on to success in the Toronto business community, rising to a senior position in Canada Life. It was reported that Munro had been buried with a Queen's pin on his lapel. The trustees passed an appropriate motion honouring a life well spent.[137] Johnny Munro epitomized the values of the old Queen's – a world of manly excellence and national reputation.

It was a world that Bill Leggett recognized and respected as central to the ethos of Queen's. He also recognized that, if Queen's were to thrive in the approaching millennium, he would have to reshape that ethos and align it with contemporary social and pedagogic values. In doing so, he saw himself in the role of "coach and cheerleader," someone who at times had to make "tough decisions" breaking old habits, while all the while building a "great team and cheering them on."[138]

As in a football game, recent principals of Queen's were usually given the opportunity to play two halves – a second term in Richardson Hall being approved after a process of evaluation and rededication by the trustees. Ron Watts and David Smith had enjoyed such extended tenure. So too would Bill Leggett. Throughout his ten years as principal, he faced the challenge of preserving the "old" at Queen's, while at the same time forcefully defining the "new." "Bulldozer Bill" arrived at Queen's at a propitious juncture and pushed Queen's in positive directions. He appreciated that the university had developed a unique sense of collegiality – "the Queen's Way" – over the decades, but at the same time feared that it had become too insular and smug.

Leggett enjoyed a close working relationship with three activist chancellors – Agnes Benidickson, Peter Lougheed, and Charles Baillie. Here, the principal and Chancellor Lougheed join in pre-game football festivities. As chancellor, Lougheed, a one-time Canadian football star and former Alberta premier, reflected Queen's national reach.

With this in mind, he dedicated himself to shoring up Queen's tradition of excellent teaching – the best of the old – while at the same time vigorously trying to open the institution and its students to the wider world – to make them "global citizens." In this light, persevering with Herstmonceux was a bold act of faith. Under Leggett, Queen's learned to reach out and embrace the world in ways beyond traditional academic realms. Queen's medical expertise touched the beleaguered people of Bosnia, while that same time Queen's engineering students drove their solar car across Canada from coast-to-coast and into the Guinness Book of Records.

Leggett and the capable administrators he assembled also helped attune Queen's to the changing relationship of university and state. The provincial government, long the dominant patron of Ontario's universities, slowly receded in the role of *assisting* post-secondary education. At the same time, Queen's Park demanded more of its universities: accountability, equity, and mandated outcomes for financial support. All this unfolded against an almost relentless backdrop of austerity and below-inflation financing. The Leggett years saw Queen's perforce develop a new model of sustaining itself – a hybrid mix of continuing government subsidy combined with the deregulation of tuition in professional programs, the pursuit of funded research, generous benefactors, and aggressive fundraising. It was a delicate formula needing constant vigilance. But it served to bring balance to Queen's revenue mix. Queen's never became the "Harvard of the North" under Leggett, but it did manage to assert its autonomy in distinctive ways – perhaps best illustrated by the success of its privatized MBA programs and the growing prestige of its law and medical programs. It was also able to bolster the day-to-day quality of education through initiatives such as the Integrated Learning Centre and the state-of-the-art Chernoff chemistry labs.

The emergence of the new model was by no means painless. Tuition outstripped inflation, squeezing student resources and straining their faith in post-secondary education. Leggett tried to alleviate the strain by augmenting Queen's student-aid policy. His *Pathfinder* initiative failed to break down Ontario's virtuous-but-poorly-maintained commitment to accessibility. Universities increasingly lived in a world in which economic expediency and other public priorities, such as maintaining the health of an aging population, trumped the educational needs of younger Ontarians. By 2004, it was possible to suggest that Queen's had become an *enterprise*, a carefully managed institution dependent on its ability to navigate varied streams of support and expectation. It was no longer the tight, inward-looking, and self-defining institution it had been under Principal Corry four decades before. It had become a looser, more disparate, constellation of groups with varying degrees of exposure to the world beyond Kingston.

Queen's changed its social hue in the Leggett years. After the fissures over gender and diversity in the eighties, Queen's became a kinder and gentler place. Leggett unfolded an umbrella of equality over the campus. As painful a decision as it was, he understood that the dean of women had to be displaced by human-rights policies that catered to all on campus, without regard to gender, race, or creed. At the same time, in appointing Suzanne Fortier as a vice-principal, Leggett brought women higher into the inner sanctum of decision making at Queen's than ever before. Under Leggett, women served as deans of law, business, and education. For the first time, a woman, Jean Stairs, served as principal of the Theology College. Other women, such as philosopher Christine Overall, family physician Sarita Verma, and School of Nursing professor Marianne Lamb, served as associate deans. Women, such as sociologist Roberta Hamilton, regularly sat as heads of department, a striking departure from the days of male patriarchy in the academic precinct. Women continued to serve in key administrative positions: Jo-Anne Brady followed in the footsteps of Alison Morgan as university registrar.

Leggett also understood that the time had passed when Queen's could settle issues of compensation and faculty rights through chummy committees and pragmatic consensus. Like diversity, collective bargaining for faculty needed to be admitted to campus. The campus came to respect such tough decisions. As he prepared to step down, the Senate saluted Leggett's "style that facilitates dialogue and fairness." Students, staff, and faculty now sat on both the Senate and the Board, the fullest measure of participatory democracy Queen's had ever experienced. In 2003, the AMS appointed the outgoing principal as its honorary president for the year. At his last Board meeting, the trustees voted to name the university's new 336-room residence after the outgoing principal (its companion residence honoured Ronald Watts). Board chair John Rae noted that Leggett had always "energized" the Board's meetings, a singular achievement in a body that many traditionally associated with languid, if thoughtful, deliberation.

Given the new diversity of Queen's, choosing a successor to Bill Leggett proved arduous. The usual joint Board-Senate committee was appointed and placed under Chancellor Charles Baillie's chairmanship. As was the custom, the group deliberated in secrecy and sought unanimity. It is often suggested that universities face fundamental choices in such situations: find someone who can maintain the pace of change or opt for someone who will stabilize the institution, giving it time to plateau and find a new equilibrium. Whatever its inclination, this selection committee had difficulty in finding consensus. Usually the appointment decision was announced late in the year preceding the changeover. In

December 2003, however, Baillie announced that the committee was still deliberating "enthusiastically and diligently." A new external executive search consultant had been hired. Finally, in early May 2004, Baillie told the trustees that they had a unanimous nominee: Dr Karen Hitchcock. Hitchcock certainly projected a hint of the new at Queen's: she would be the first woman – and first American-born – principal. But she was also another scientist. Hitchcock's academic journey had begun close at hand to Queen's: she attended St Lawrence University (a campus of the same 1840s vintage as Queen's) in nearby Canton, New York, before obtaining a doctorate in anatomy at the University of Rochester. A specialist in cell development, she had taught at Tufts, Texas, and Illinois before joining the SUNY system in Albany in 1991. In announcing the appointment, Baillie rather vaguely cited "the synchronous fit between the candidate's strengths and the mission and vision for Queen's University at this point in its history." The news that Queen's had its eighteenth principal brought "cheerful applause" from the trustees.[139] For Bill Leggett, it marked an end to the "richest ten years" of his career.[140]

Afterword
In the Fall of 2004

Dancing with Change.
Principal Karen Hitchcock, October 2004

The beginnings and endings of all human undertakings are untidy.
John Galsworthy, *Over the River* (1932)

Plus ça Change?

Fall reawakens familiar seasonal rhythms at any university. In late August 2004, a buzz of activity returned to the Queen's campus as professors readied course outlines and revitalized lectures. Graduate students burned the midnight oil to meet the impending autumn deadline for thesis defences. Deans welcomed new faculty members. Construction crews worked frantically to lay asphalt and complete projects before the crush of classes began. A year earlier that autumnal urgency had focused on completing two new student residences, named for former principals Watts and Leggett. In 2003, Queen's had absorbed its share of Ontario's "double cohort," a surge of unusually young undergraduates who had truncated their secondary education by jumping straight into university from Grade 12 without the now-defunct Grade 13. For 2004, a "shadow" of double-cohort students followed, as part of a hefty wave of 3,300 new undergraduates arriving on campus. Of this cohort, 26 per cent would be less than seventeen years old. In anticipation of their arrival, upper-year students selected to act as orientation leaders began drifting back into Kingston, ready to shepherd the frosh through their baptism into university life. On warm, late-August evenings, would-be Gaels, FRECs, Bosses, and other orientation leaders could be seen sitting on their porches in the Ghetto, beers in hand, regaling each other with tales of the traditions that they themselves had acquired only a year earlier. In a week, they would pass the torch of tradition to the latest generation of frosh.

For the frosh of 2004, life at Queen's began in earnest on the Sunday before Labour Day – "Move-in" Day – when convoys of minivans and station wagons descended on the university residences to deposit eager, but trepidatious, newcomers at their residence halls. The *Journal* described it as a day of "organized chaos."[1] Across the street from Victoria Hall, the student-run Common Ground Café set up a booth and dispensed free coffee to frazzled parents. Upper-year engineering students provided an accompanying chorus by chanting "Say good-bye to Mommy." Many of those delivering their progeny to Kingston were Queen's alumni – as always, the university generated a strong intergenerational loyalty. How familiar would the ways of Queen's in 2004 have been to a freshman of 1961 returning to Queen's almost a half-century later? At first glance, much would have seemed to have changed. A campus once dotted with amply-spaced buildings was now tightly packed, with academic, recreational, and residential buildings pushing at the seams of a campus now encircled by dense urban development. Drab, weather-stained concrete had in many places usurped limestone. Parking lots had conquered much of the green space left between the bricks and mortar. For some alumni parents, there would have been the discovery of the West Campus, with its education faculty, its residence complex, and its football stadium. Queen's had clearly pushed the envelope of its tightly confined nineteenth-century boundaries.

A graduate of the 1960s would, however, happily observe that the Lower Campus remained a swath of green, a monument to student, faculty, and alumni opposition to placement of the new physics building in the earlier decade. There was, on the other hand, much to admire in Queen's new density – the soaring neo-Gothic splendour of the Stauffer

"Move-in day": Goodbye, Mom. Hello, residence.

Library and the airy atrium of the Biosciences Complex. Beyond geography and architecture, there was evidence of more fundamental change in the definition of the Queen's community. Queen's now had a new-found invisible identity on the internet. Computers, both personal and institutional, abounded. A website – Common Room@Queens.ca – linked 10,000 alumni and friends of the university, allowing them to visit their old campus without actually going there. With Queen's alumni cresting 142,000 in number in 2004, that electronic constituency was certain to balloon.

The campus would also have struck graduates from the 1960s as unusually full of students. There were over 20,000 of them – undergraduate, graduate, and part-time – and 958 professors, plus librarians, technicians, and maintenance workers, who now went about their daily business at Queen's. The university guaranteed every first-year student a bed in a university residence: Bader Lane and University Avenue were thus alive with students transiting between classes, library, and residence home. A shuttle bus ferried students and staff between the main and West campuses. Graduate and professional students gave the campus a more "mature" look; there had been a very few graduate students in 1961, and only a "school" (as opposed to a fully fledged faculty) to cater to their needs. Pulling onto University Avenue, the graduate of the 1960s would have immediately been struck – perhaps even shocked – by the appearance of the once-shady arterial, divided by its central island of trees. The cathedral of stalwart elms and silver maples long synonymous with Queen's image as post-secondary arcadia had been denuded by the effects of years of auto pollution and road salt. That May, the trustees had reluctantly agreed to remove the remaining trees and a central median on University Avenue. A broad, new cobble-stoned boulevard now created the effect of a *grande allée*. New trees would be planted along the littoral of the new esplanade, but all knew that it would be decades before a new umbrella of shade materialized.

To returning alumni, the campus also now seemed distinctly divided into precincts – Law, Business, and Medicine all had their own bailiwicks clustered around the traditional campus core of Arts and Science and Applied Science. The old coziness of a tightly concentrated academic community seemed overwhelmed by numbers and specialization. Alumni of the 1960s would also have been struck by the diversity of undergraduate programs set before their offspring. Choice was now the order of the day. The perimeters of traditional disciplines had broken down, so that an incoming student of 2004 might concentrate on women's studies, global development studies, Aboriginal studies, or perhaps environmental studies, sensing that these new avenues of inquiry were more connected to their globalized world view than the more orthodox study of, say, English literature or physics. Within disciplines there was now a dizzying diversity of specializations. Political studies, for instance, had in 1961 been largely dedicated to the study of Canadian federal-provincial relations; now "political science" was perceived through the prism of international relations, Marxist analysis, conflict theory, and a multiplicity of other approaches. In 1961, arriving undergraduates were told – usually in a brief, friendly interview with Registrar Jean Royce – what they would study in first year. Now they were presented with an ample, and at times confusing, menu of academic opportunities.

Whatever their academic bent, students early in the twenty-first century would have appeared to their alumni parents as more casual in attire and demeanour than they had ever dared to be. The old deference was gone. In 1961, jeans seemed more suited to manual labour than library study. Now cut-offs and tank tops were almost *de rigueur* for coeds in the late-summer heat. White shirts, ties, and dresses were reserved for graduation day. Males sported longer hair and beards. Perhaps most striking, the university's residences were largely coeducational. Women were no longer obliged to wear skirts to dinner or to dine in feminine exclusivity. Clearly, the view of Queen's from a laden minivan on that September Sunday in 2004 brought into focus the question of just how Queen's and its culture had weathered the challenges and upheavals of the late-twentieth century. How had its traditions moved with the times? How fervently had it clung to established ways?

Becoming Acquainted with Queen's, 2004 Style

With the departure of parents and grandparents, orientation for the "class of 2008" began in earnest. The ritual was perhaps tamer and more intellectually uplifting than the harrowing antics experienced by their parents, but nonetheless still redolent of Gaelic chants, outlandish costumes, and tams pulled down over freshman ears. Applied Science frosh no longer endured the ignominy of shaved heads, but still sported ersatz tartan kilts made of curtain material and sporrans made of whisk brooms. Other aspects of the first week of university life were more conspicuously updated. The time-consuming irritation of on-campus academic registration in the humid confines of the arena was gone, replaced by QCARD electronic registration. Orientation now had a more deliberate academic slant; since the 1990s, incoming students took Queen's 101, a first-week primer on the fundamentals of academic and residence life. Special get-to-know-you dinners were arranged with faculty during orientation.

Orientation was also more inclusive. The once-strident heterosexuality of orientation – *"What's the sport of kings? Queen's, Queen's, Queen's"* – had been tempered to reflect new sensibilities. Gay and lesbian students no longer found themselves as marginalized by the hegemony of "straight" sexuality. A "Queerientation" opened the door to "queer-friendly" Kingston by offering barbeques, dances, and films to incoming gay and lesbian students.[2] And, with almost 60 per cent of Queen's students now female, gender sensibilities had tempered the once-unbridled maleness of orientation, even in faculties such as engineering, where only a quarter of undergraduates were women.[3] The Levana Society and the dean of women were gone, but a Human Rights Office provided to all those at Queen's an assurance of their rights and awareness of their responsibilities. The AMS-sponsored Grey House on Bader Lane offered an array of services dedicated to student well-being. Birth control, a taboo subject in the early 1960s, was now a normal aspect of the Queen's dialogue. Gender equity and diversity were now an acknowledged facet of Queen's life. There were, for instance, far more women professors; indeed for the first time Queen's was on the eve of installing its first woman principal – cell biologist Karen Hitchcock.

The cavalcade of minivans on Move-in Day revealed another new reality at Queen's. One in ten Queen's students was now foreign-born. In the sixties, Queen's "foreignness" had been largely confined to the International Centre in the Students' Union. Otherwise, the sixties' student body pro-

By the early twenty-first century, women were a vital and majoritarian force in many aspects of Queen's life. In the 1980s, Applied Science Dean David Bacon launched a concerted effort to attract women into engineering. By the 2000s, almost a quarter of engineering students were women. While Dean Bacon believed that women would have a "civilizing influence" on the faculty, women students seemed to embrace the storied male traditions, including climbing the grease pole.

jected an indelibly WASP persona. Names starting with "Mc" and "Mac" dominated the listings in the annual *Who's Where*. Canada's subsequent embrace of multiculturalism in the Trudeau years registered slowly at Queen's, but by 2004 the student body possessed a diversity that reflected not just more foreign-born students, but also a much broader racial and ethnic mix among native-born Canadians. The graduate school boasted students from seventy-three countries. Now one might hear snatches of Hindi, Chinese, and French on any stroll down University Avenue. The campus club culture, long ingrained in student life at Queen's, mirrored the shift. The *Tricolor* each year carried profiles of groups as diverse as the Sikh Student Association, the Spanish and Latin American Students' Association, and the Philippine Cultural Association. A Chinese-language newspaper, *The Empress*, had been promoting Chinese culture on campus and in Kingston for ten years. In the fall of 2004, a student group called "Campus Chat" distributed buttons that encouraged the beholder to "talk to me in Arabic" and sixteen other languages. The campus radio station, CFRC, on air since 1922, echoed Queen's new diversity with programs such as "Aboriginal Voices" and "Mandarin Orange." Diversity was, however, a complex construct, and Queen's still in many ways lagged behind emerging new Canadian norms. The 2003 *Maclean's* survey of Canadian universities ranked Queen's very near the bottom of its "cultural diversity" survey. The challenge of adjusting Queen's to Canada's multicultural society would persist.

At the end of orientation week, older traditions reasserted themselves. On Friday, the Frosh streamed into downtown Kingston and raised $23,500 for cystic fibrosis in their annual Shinerama blitz. Engineering students fanned out into the Kingston community to undertake voluntary clean-up assignments. An evening of rock music followed. On Saturday morning, the same engineering frosh were bused out to a field in nearby Barriefield for the annual rite of the grease pole, a tradition grafted onto the engineering faculty in the 1950s. That tradition had been tempered after the annual scramble in the oily pit had led to injuries in the previous decades. Less-insidious muck and less verbal abuse from upperclassmen were now the order of the day. When Science '08 snatched the tam off the top of the pole in a brisk thirty-one minutes, there were complaints that the challenge had become "too tame" and was therefore sapping class solidarity. "Preserve the grease pole," editorialized the *Journal*: the ritual was "good-spirited" and promoted class spirit.[4]

On Saturday afternoon, the climax of orientation began, as a ragtag army of frosh departed the main campus and moved westward along Union Street to Richardson Stadium, where football had been played since the old, main-campus stadium had been sacrificed in the name of expanding the academic precinct in the early 1970s. Nestled behind the buildings of the Education faculty on the West Campus, the new Richardson Stadium had never been as popular as its main-campus predecessor. It was out of sight and, except for crucial games, out of mind. Attendance had dropped steadily. But the new stadium had, nonetheless, been home to some illustrious teams. The inimitable Frank Tindall had stopped coaching the Gaels in the mid-1970s after over thirty years pacing up and down the sidelines chomping his cigar. He died in 1993 – "fourteen years into overtime," as one obituary put it. His place had been taken by Doug "Professor Pigskin" Hargreaves, who had guided the team not only to national championships in 1978 and 1992 but also to an array of Yates, Dunsmore, Atlantic, and Churchill bowls. In 1992, Hargreaves had even taken the team to England, where it clobbered an English football team, the Brighton B-52s. Many Queen's stalwarts on Richardson Field had gone on to the Canadian Football League, and a handful had even graduated to America's National Football League. When Hargreaves retired in 1994, his shoes were filled first by Bob Howes and, after 2002, by Pat Sheahan. Under Sheahan, the team had wound up its winning 2003 season with a wrenching, double-overtime loss to the Laurier Golden Hawks.[5]

The omens were not, however, promising on this Saturday in 2004. Torrential rain and stiff winds scoured the field as the tail end of Hurricane Frances lashed Kingston. Moreover, a week earlier, the Gaels had lost their first game of the season by a narrow margin at the University of Windsor. Now the opponents were the University of Guelph Gryphons, usually an easy mark. Despite the weather, the traditional mood of a Queen's football game prevailed. The Queen's Bands grandly entered the stadium – a troupe of 120 musicians, flag-bearers, cheerleaders, and sword dancers.[6] The "Bandsies" were on the eve of celebrating their centenary. In many ways, the bands were as close to a fraternity as Queen's students got – they contained hierarchies and clandestine rituals, such as indulging in risqué ditties and pre-game tots of sherry on the bus to the game.[7] The bands were also Queen's most recognized ornament, frequently on display to the nation. Eager to see the bands properly kitted out, outgoing Principal Bill Leggett and his wife, Claire, generously topped up a fund dedicated to buying new uniforms for the whole ensemble. The Leggetts were not alone in sensing that the bands were Queen's premier hallmark: sociologist and the dean of Arts and Science, Robert Silverman, frequently picked up his alto sax, donned a kilt, and joined the band. He once proudly marched with the band in Boston's St Patrick's Day parade. The Gaelic tradition thus remained at the centre of the Queen's ethos. A piper led every convocation procession. At what other university could there have been an earnest exchange of letters over what the plural of "kilt" was, as there was in the *Queen's Alumni Review* that fall?

Accompanying the Bandsies was Boo-Hoo the bear, the Queen's mascot since the 1920s. Once a live animal (who had on occasion been joined by greased pigs let loose onto the field), Boo-Hoo was now a human cavorting in a fuzzy bear suit. The stadium beer tent was named in his honour. The Boo-Hoo Lounge in fact represented the reinstitution of a Queen's tradition. Since the sixties, Queen's had recognized that students, liquor, and football were not always a fortuitous combination. All sorts of injunctions and prohibitions ensued, usually ineffectual. Now, the Boo-Hoo Lounge represented the controlled reintroduction of beer at the stadium. "Where there's beer, students will follow," political-science doctoral student Jeremy Clark confidently declared to the *Journal*. In case beer was not a sufficient inducement for fans, the game's ceremonial kickoff was performed by Gord Sinclair and Rob Baker of The Tragically Hip, a Kingston rock band that had begun its ascendancy to global popularity when its founding members first practised in Queen's Waldron student residence. Baker had a Queen's degree in fine arts and Sinclair one in history.

On that rainy Saturday in early September, pipe bands, beer, and rock celebrity would not, however, propel the Golden Gaels to victory. Quarterbacks Ryan Sheahan and Ali Clarkson performed adequately, but threw costly interceptions. Running back Bryan Crawford chalked up 118 yards on the ground. It was not enough. The Gaels took foolish penalties and the Gryphons scored on big passing plays. In the end, the Gaels fell by a single point, 27–26. "The cheers were weaker after the football's disappointing loss," the *Journal* reported under a photograph of deflated cheerleaders. Coach Sheahan framed the loss by saying that the team was on a "learning curve."[8] The curve would get steeper; Queen's would go on to a dismal 2–6 record in 2004. But better years would return; in 2009 the Gaels would again be national champions.

There was, however, a sense that the football tradition at Queen's was weakening. Not only was the stadium on the margins of the campus geography, but the student body was perhaps less inclined to savour gridiron contests. A majority of students were now female, and many came from multicultural backgrounds detached from the WASP manliness of moving a pigskin up and down a muddy field. Besides, other sports had taken root at Queen's. Since the Milliken Report of 1971, the focus had been on participatory sports open to the whole campus population, not just a male few. In this regard, Queen's teams in other sports began to work their way into campus culture; a month later the Queen's baseball team would win the national championship. Hockey – both men's and women's – flourished. Basketball, which Tindall had coached in the winter, persisted, played with equal vigour

The Queen's bands remained the university's most recognized ambassador in 2004. Perhaps the closest thing to a fraternity on a campus where "frats" were banned, the bands possessed both musical talent, camaraderie, and an irrepressible youthful exuberance.

by men and women. Sports thus began to reflect Queen's new-found gender diversity: women's rugby, competitive cheerleading, and cricket were redefining what it meant to excel at Queen's.

Millennials Arrive

Autumn brought other Queen's traditions to life – some burnished by time and others invented to satisfy new sensibilities. September, for instance, witnessed an expedient new Queen's tradition: the Aberdeen Olympics. Aberdeen Street, just north of the campus in the Ghetto, became the site of an impromptu, beer-fuelled funfest, in which students staged zany races and competitions. The "appliance toss" drew a boisterous crowd. The Olympics went late into the night, were raucous, and left mounds of debris. They smacked of self-indulgence and abused town-gown relations. One-time city councillor Don Rogers launched a vigorous citizens' campaign against this invented tradition. Rogers soon mounted a website chronicling Queen's students' unneighbourly conduct.

Late October heralded Homecoming, a tradition rooted in the 1920s and one under siege in changed times. Once called Alumni Weekend, Homecoming offered a bridge that connected two primordial poles of the Queen's community – students imbibing the culture of the university and alumni whose lives had been shaped by their years spent on the campus. The inaugural emphasis had been on conviviality and fun – parades, football, dances, and social gatherings. In short, Homecoming was about the transmission and smoothing of tradition. Since the 1980s, however, Homecoming had been bedevilled by an uneasy tension between its old-style conviviality and a new-born spirit of student hedonism. A Queen's tradition thus found itself in the midst of contention. For many, the alumni weekend remained a time to connect with past Queen's generations. On the Saturday of the 2004 Homecoming, there was, for instance, a ceremony to rededicate a memorial room honouring Queen's students killed in World War Two. That afternoon at Richardson Stadium, alumni paraded around the infield under multi-colour umbrellas to be saluted by a crowd of over ten thousand. In the evening, a "ceilidh" in the John Deutsch University Centre welcomed students and alumni alike.

For many students, however, Homecoming had become an opportunity for unbridled partying that had little to do with the past and everything to do with present entitlement. For them, the day began with "pancake keggers," early morning gatherings in Ghetto apartments predicated on flapjacks and hops. By noon, the pancakes disappeared, as straightforward "keggers" gained momentum. Then it was off to Richardson Stadium. By evening, undeterred by the Gaels' loss to Western on the gridiron, the partying gravitated to Aberdeen Street, now synonymous with beery good times. The crowd was predominantly young, but was sprinkled with people wearing Queen's jackets from years gone by. The previous week, Kingston police had sent letters to all residents of Aberdeen Street, setting out the penalties for outdoor consumption of liquor. Such cautions had little effect; by early Sunday morning, the police had arrested 19, ticketed 126, and warned another 400 partiers, many of whom had no direct tie to Queen's.

Homecoming had thus become a clash of traditions – one long in gestation and the other instant and purely hedonistic. Predictably, city councillors, AMS executives, and university officials roundly condemned the Aberdeen bacchanalia. The national press reported on the "drunken brawl" at Queen's. Alumni protested to the Advancement Office, the principal, and the *Queen's Alumni Review*. Plans were floated to create a squad of volunteer "peacekeepers" to patrol the street in future years. Yet the party tradition had its defenders. Earl St Denis of Science '64 and a one-time resident of Aberdeen Street reminded readers of the *Journal* that Queen's students had a long tradition of rowdiness: "[Aberdeen Street] looks just as shitty now as it was then. For Homecoming back in my day, we used to park cars across the top and bottom and close the street off." Others tried to find a middle ground: *Journal* photo editor, Emily MacLaurin King, wrote that, despite all the unseemly shenanigans, "we should raise our glass to Homecoming and what it says about the longevity of Queen's spirit."[9]

Aberdeen Street had become a test of Queen's ability to arbitrate its own behaviour, a challenge to the sense of community that had steadied it, pushed it forward, and preserved its cohesiveness over the many decades since its frail birth in 1841. Homecoming, once the transmitter of Queen's brand of loyalty, now seemed in part to have detached itself from the mechanisms and values that had for so long bound student, faculty, and alumni into a sustainable model of communal life. For the next few years, Queen's would struggle to reconcile the two divergent strains of "Queen's spirit." The proven elixirs of consultation and liberal persuasion failed to stunt the growth of this unruly new manifestation of the Queen's community. The pervasive reach of social media accentuated the dissolution. Keith Macleod of Meds '59 wrote to express his disgust that "the administration and student government are unable to control an annual problem that dishonours Queen's ... Drinking has always been part of university life but not hooliganism."[10]*

Perpetuating Limestone Liberalism

From the historian's point of view, the imbroglio over Homecoming opens an inviting window on the way the Queen's community had governed itself and adjusted its traditions since the mid-twentieth century. The Aberdeen Street contretemps stands as a jarring exception to the gradualist, consensual ethos that sat at the heart of Queen's culture. The street party's uncharacteristically obdurate nature

---

*To look ahead, in 2009, an exasperated Queen's administration cut the Gordian knot by announcing that it would attempt to break the Aberdeen cycle by suspending Homecoming entirely, thereby truncating the life of the dysfunctional new tradition. In its place, Queen's would try to create a replacement tradition of its own – a "spring reunion," with an emphasis on opening up the university's pedagogic treasures to the inquiring minds of alumni. In 2013, the old tradition of a convivial Homecoming was cautiously reintroduced. The hope was that the tradition might be reattached to its genetic purpose – connecting alumni with Queen's neophytes. In 2014, Brad McVey, pipe sergeant of the Queen's Bands remarked on the restoration of an old-style Homecoming that Queen's has "a miraculous ability to breathe new life into many of these old traditions." *QJ*, 29 July 2014.

❖ Leather-bound Tradition ❖

In 1884, the AMS president and the captain of the football team selected the tricolour – scarlet red, royal blue, and gold – to give Queen's a distinctive look on the gridiron. The urge has persisted ever since. In the early twentieth century, tricolour sweaters and scarves were sported across campus. Jeweller-designed class pins and Levana buttons were popular. In 1925, the Highland tam was adopted as standard garb at Queen's. The colour of the torrie – pompom – atop the tam denoted a student's faculty. In 1937, the AMS adopted a blazer and crest. Loyalty to Queen's thus came to have a sartorial flair.

Veterans enrolling after the Second World War enhanced the tradition. Accustomed to the camaraderie generated by military uniforms with all their identity-affirming insignia, Applied Science students in the late 1940s fashioned golden silk jackets emblazoned with their faculty, year, and a university crest. The accelerated engineering class of '48½ resulted in a jacket oddity. Silk became nylon and eventually leather in the late 1950s. The tradition spread. Red Arts jackets, blue Meds jackets, and, later, burgundy for Commerce, midnight blue for Nursing, black for Computing, and so on, followed. Shoulder flashes or "bars" indicating discipline appeared. Jacket rituals emerged: the university crest was affixed as a rite of passage at the end of first year as "a pass crest." Varsity athletes wore a red-and-gold "Q" on their backs. Each class designed its year crest, the only stipulation being that it contain a stylized Q and the tricolour. Jackets became *de rigueur* student wear at Queen's. Even through the hippie-heavy 1960s, Queen's students donned their jackets with pride. Away from the campus, the jackets became a kind of walking advertisement for loyalty Queen's-style. Every Homecoming became a fashion show of bygone classes sporting their heritage jackets. Over time, students embellished their jackets with personalized details – a small flag on the rear hem denoting their native land or ethnicity. In the 1980s, as the number of woman students in engineering finally began to rise, Dean David Bacon of Applied Science opined that women would exert a "civilizing effect" on the male culture of the faculty. Perhaps they would, but women engineers proved every bit as eager as their male counterparts to don the faculty's unique uniform.

Queen's engineering students took the jacket culture to new heights. First-year students were barred from wearing their jackets until their Christmas examinations were complete. Before that magic day arrived, they were forbidden to even touch the sacred leather. Ever inventive, frosh engineers collected their new jackets and kicked them home along the streets of Kingston. Exams over, the annual "jacket slam" – a day-long pummelling of the jackets into instant antiques – followed on the sidewalk outside Clark Hall, the Engineering Society's roost. Esteemed professors, such as geology professor John Hanes, were asked to drive their cars over their novice students' new wardrobe. Finally, a coat of gentian dye (said to honour the engineers who perished on the RMS *Titanic*) rounded out the *look*.

Traditions can turn dysfunctional. Jackets had initially been created to enhance faculty cohesiveness and allegiance to Queen's. By the turn of the twenty-first century, some jackets were, however, becoming billboards for anti-social behaviour. Particularly among Applied Science students, shoulder bars bragging of risk taking and hedonism began appearing. Alcohol consumption and sexual adventure acquired jacket-borne kudos – "Ritual," "Blue Light," and, "XXX." Some new shoulder patches did convey more altruistic achievement – "Kamikaze" for neighbourhood cleanup in Kingston. Nonetheless, for many students a jacket had become a statement of *personal* indulgences rather than adherence to faculty honour. Letters to the *Journal* suggested that a Queen's tradition had been betrayed.

draws ironic attention to the university's remarkable record of adjusting its traditions at a time of unprecedented and sustained social, intellectual, and economic change in Canada. From 1961 to 2004, the years covered by this history, Queen's experienced an almost sevenfold growth in its enrolment, from 3,100 to just over 20,000. Such bald figures disguised the quality of Queen's growth.

In these years, Queen's moved from being a small, well-regarded provincial university to being an internationally recognized institution – what some would call a *multiversity* – with expertise stretching from undergraduate instruction through to highly focused graduate and professional endeavour. In 1961, the university enjoyed a national reputation for excellence in teaching and dedication to public service. It was essentially an undergraduate institution, flanked by a struggling medical school, a puny graduate enterprise, and a fledgling law school. By 2004, its kudos rested on international success in medical, business, and legal professional training. Funded research had become a feedstock of its annual existence. At the undergraduate level, new disciplines – sociology, film studies, environmental studies, and computing, for instance – had provided new pedagogic momentum. Beyond its classrooms and residences, Queen's had enhanced its reputation for providing students with a "broader learning experience." International exchange agreements allowed Queen's students to explore a world that had become "globalized." A Queen's flag fluttered over a moated castle in the Sussex countryside. Every summer, Queen's art-history students explored the beauties of Venice. Queen's Engineers Without Borders (QEWB) connected young engineers with global concerns, ranging from the environment to fair trade, and Queen's doctors and nurses ministered to communities in distress around the world. The historian is left to isolate the central values and processes of Queen's culture that made this protean transition possible and, at times, sadly impeded it.

Queen's age-old penchant for seeing itself in Gaelic terms is hard to resist. While a good deal of the university's Scottishness was invented and transfused over time, Queen's did retain certain primordial Scottish-Presbyterian values present from its birth in 1841. There is no accidental coincidence in the fact that Glasgow-born John A. Macdonald – destined to become Canada's first prime minister – began his political career as a Kingston alderman in the same decade as Queen's College received its charter. As a young lawyer in Kingston, Macdonald had lent his name to the agitation for a sectarian college in his city. Later, his inveterate pragmatism, his ability to craft political alliances, brought disparate French and English colonists together in the world's first post-colonial nation in 1867. Macdonald's overriding insistence on political pragmatism and loyalty found an echo in the character of the fledgling college as it struggled to survive in the same years that the Canadian Confederation strove to bind itself into a viable nation.

If there is one phrase that has perennially been employed to capture the manner by which Queen's conducts its affairs, it is "the Queen's way." The expression is employed as if its meaning were automatically and genetically understood by all in the Queen's community. In most minds, the phrase connotes an innate understanding that Queen's relies on a code of communal precedence to chart its course. Words such as "loyalty," "spirit," "respect," and "dialogue" frequently accompany evocations of the "Queen's way." While the college jettisoned its sectarian affiliation in 1912, Presbyterian moral and social purpose has lingered in its institution's culture. The Queen's community has retained a remarkable cohesiveness and collegiality ever since. Calvinistic notions of worldly activism, democratic inclusion, and even predestination shimmer below the surface of most celebrations of the Queen's way.

The Scottish connection once again perhaps best elucidates the fealty of Queen's graduates to their alma mater. Beyond its ceremonial reliance on kilts,

If there is one word that permeates the Queen's experience, it is "loyalty." That loyalty manifests itself in many ways, from doing *Oil Thighs* in exotic locales to mailing an annual donation to the alma mater. Here engineering students (above) paint their year crest on a campus sidewalk. Faculty often displayed the same loyalty to the Old Strand: Political Studies professor John Meisel came to Queen's in 1949, bonded with the place, and remains beloved to many former students.

bagpipes, and *Oil Thighs*, Queen's sees itself rooted in the values of Scottish clanship. The Scottish clan system rested on the Gaelic notion of *duthchas* – a sense of belonging and connection to those who shared communal lands. A clan was bound together by the obligations of kinship, whereby the head of the clan ruled, not by force of heredity, but by the moral authority of benevolent leadership. While the arrival in Scotland of hierarchical feudalism and its emphasis on private land ownership would erode the egalitarianism of the Highland clans, the social ethos of clansmanship persisted in Scottish culture.

The Kingston Highlands

In many ways, that same ethos has permeated the life of Queen's University. Most readily, it surfaces in the institutional structure of the place. Presbyterianism is marked by its flat authority structure – no bishops – and its governance relies heavily on church elders drawn from the ranks of the lay congregation. The 1858 birth of the Alma Mater Society provides striking evidence of this inclination to inclusion and self-governance. Students at Queen's College were never perceived as passive participants in their learning experience; instead they were acknowledged as being capable of intelligent self-governance, as charter members of the community in which they studied. The AMS's constitution smacked of clannish devotion and Calvinistic uplift: "to preserve the attachment of the alumni to the University, and their interest in it ... to serve as a bond of union between the different classes of students, to cultivate a literary taste, and to further the general interests of the University." Similarly, the university's founders deliberately drew on the Scottish university model of governance evident on ancient Hibernian campuses such as Edinburgh and St Andrew's for inspiration. The "principal" was to be a low-keyed *primus inter pares*, not an imperious "president." He would maintain his connection with the academic mission by sitting as chair of the university Senate, while at the same time being the only member of the university administration present at the meetings of its

Queen's great tradition of service to the nation has been perpetuated in many ways. Here students participate in a 2003 model parliament in the actual House of Commons in Ottawa, a privilege arranged by long-serving federal Speaker Peter Milliken, who served as AMS Speaker in the late 1960s.

trustees, where the material well-being of the institution was nurtured – Scottish pragmatism at its best. Over time, the trustees have had the continuing wisdom to open their deliberations to representatives of Queen's student body, its faculty, and its administrative staff.

The principal, in the inimitable words of Principal Mackintosh, acted as "a very narrow isthmus" to connect trustees and faculty. The principal's authority lay in his power of suasion over a university that historian Frederick Gibson likened to "one big fraternity," not in any hard and fast authority. "This familial atmosphere," Gibson wrote, "tempered the formal authoritarianism of government at Queen's, breathing into the corporation the spirit of a clan and making the principal a kind of chieftain. The same atmosphere tended to make the university tolerant of dissenters in their midst, and this encouraged the development of a liberal tradition of respect for freedom of thought and expression." I have chosen to brand this intrinsic latitude in Queen's culture "limestone liberalism," a dedication to the slow-but-persistent amelioration of the human condition through a balancing of an individual's sense of self-interest with the imperatives of a inclusive, egalitarian society. Queen's was no stranger to such social chemistry: at the turn of the twentieth century, Queen's scholars such as Adam Shortt, Oscar Skelton, and William Clark had provided a blueprint for the conversion of hard-edged nineteenth-century, laissez-faire market liberalism into a model of liberalism predicated on the brokering of competing segments of society. That ethos worked its way through the so-called Queen's-educated "Ottawa men" into the genetic code of the unfolding Canadian welfare state, while at the same time inhabiting the culture of the university that gave birth to its philosophy.[11]

Queen's instinct for inclusiveness was reinforced by other Scottish importations. The 1870s witnessed the creation of a University Council drawn from alumni, to act as kind of sounding board for university policy – in effect, an annual meeting of the clan. That same decade saw a chancellor appointed to assume the university's ceremonial duties and guide the selection of principals. This circle of advocacy and advice was rounded out in 1912 with the creation of the post of student rector, an elected representative of student opinion. These participatory and representational institutions sat atop the university's bicameral reliance on Senate and Board of Trustees, thereby bringing under one collegial umbrella all the academic, ceremonial, and material decisions governing Queen's well-being. This nexus of governance has served Queen's remarkably well.

The clannishness of Queen's echoes through the period from 1961 to 2004. John Rae (Arts '67), a lad from Ottawa and later chairman of the Board of Trustees from 2000 to 2005, reflected on his first impressions of Queen's in the early 1960s. He was immediately struck by the "intimacy" of the university. In subsequent years, as a student of political studies, he came to revere the tradition of "dialogue and respect" that existed between teachers and taught. Queen's, he soon appreciated, bred "an almost reciprocal loyalty" in its graduates. As editor of the *Queen's Journal*, Rae found himself at a crossroad from which he could see all the intersections of the Queen's community. "One of the most important features of the creative university community," he wrote from his editor's chair, "is the eradication of social hierarchies between students and the faculty, because the very existence of social barriers prevents the free communication that is so vital to the development of any creative community."

A decade later, George Hood of Arts '78 arrived on campus eager to study political science. From his father, George (Sci. '43), George junior had already imbibed the Queen's spirit, but his own student years there and his subsequent return to the university in the 1990s to head its advancement effort instilled in him an abiding awareness of the "inherent tribalism of Queen's." Those who had come to Queen's became devotees, bound by cords of loyalty to the Old Strand – the old faith. Being attached to Queen's, Hood would quip, was like jazz – "if you have to ask, you don't get it."[12] Almost every issue of the *Queen's Alumni Review* re-echoes the sentiment. Padre A.M. "Marsh" Laverty, whose career and dedication to Queen's straddled four decades of postwar growth and adjustment, understood that, for most of its graduates, going to Queen's became a life sentence: "There was life *before* Queen's, life *at* Queen's, and life *after* Queen's – the last was the most important."

Loyalty to Queen's and adherence to the "Queen's way," however, was more than the residue of a comfortable clannishness. It reflected the *way* Queen's did things, and this was abidingly connected to its system of governance and decision making. For student and professor alike, the Queen's community has been marked by an abiding collegiality. In the 1960s, a daily camaraderie prevailed among faculty: over lunch in the makeshift faculty club in the Students' Memorial Union professors from disparate disciplines indulged in academic gossip and discussed their teaching strategies in the rapidly growing university. Later in the decade, the administration acquired a splendid home on King Street overlooking the lake and turned it into a fully fledged faculty club, so that Queen's professors could have a centre for their social interaction. There, on Fridays after classes, professors – almost all of them male – gathered for beer and kibitzing.

In these years, there was little sense of demarcation between faculty and administration. Most of Queen's administrators had risen organically from the ranks of faculty. Some, such as Bill Mackintosh and John Deutsch, were Queen's born and bred, but had done stints in the federal civil service before smoothly reintegrating into their alma mater. On any day, the principal or a dean might join faculty members for lunch. Almost every new faculty member in the 1960s and 1970s was personally welcomed to Queen's by Principals Corry or Deutsch. When David Smith arrived at Queen's to teach economics in 1961, he was immediately struck by the fact that "the direct lines of communication were strong and unique at Queen's." "Cohesiveness," Smith concluded, was Queen's "competitive advantage."[13]

The principal's presence at every meeting of the Board of Trustees extended that cohesiveness to the oversight of the university's material fortunes. The tight and trusting relationship of the principal and the chair of the Board of Trustees is indispensable in explaining Queen's success in managing its affairs in the late-twentieth century. In these years, the chair of the trustees was invariably drawn from the ranks of Queen's alumni who had prospered in the world beyond Queen's. Lawyers such as Norman McLeod Rogers, engineers such as Walter Light, bankers such as Douglas Gibson, and business executives such as Donald Elliott and John Rae brought their worldly expertise to the table back at Queen's and blended it with their intuitions about the Queen's way. A principal served by such men (Queen's would not have its first woman chair until 2013, when Barbara Polk of TD Canada Trust took on the role) could be confident that he might act with prudence and foresight. At other times, activist trustees enhanced the relationship by chivvying the university in progressive directions – for instance, Dan Burns's campaign for campus planning and competitive architectural design in the late 1990s. The principal's prowess at Queen's was rounded out by the presence of chancellors who not only supplied a ceremonial elegance to the university's affairs but also served as ambassadors for its reputation and needs in the world beyond Kingston. Chancellors of the quality and dedication of Bert Stirling, Agnes Benidickson, and Peter Lougheed were active in advancing Queen's interests far beyond the graduation platform in Grant Hall. With little exception, the triumvirate of principal, board chair, and chancellor gave Queen's a bulwark in these years.

The principal also sat as chairman of the Senate, comfortable in the belief that he was there both as a faculty member *and* as an administrator. Only in matters of compensation did the principal sensibly absent himself from the Senate, sensing that his presence would crimp free discussion of salary expectations. Every spring, the Queen's University Faculty Association invited the principal to address its annual meeting, in the expectation of a frank assessment of the university's prospects. Much the same candid rapport existed between Richardson Hall and the university's administrative staff. It was not uncommon for gardeners and carpenters to be on a first-name basis with the principal. In short, there was seldom little sense of "them" and "us" on the university campus. A similar intimacy existed between students and the administration. The Alma Mater Society had weight in the eyes of the administration. During the sixties, the last vestiges of paternalistic control over the AMS were shed by the administration – the Society's secretary-treasurer ceased being a cross-appointed university administrator. At the same time, the AMS made itself modern by incorporating and dedicating itself to the provision of useful services to its members. With the opening of the John Deutsch University Centre in the mid-1970s, the AMS had offices in the heart of the campus. The naming of the centre after Deutsch seemed to epitomize the bond between student, professor, and administrators at Queen's; Deutsch had lived each of these roles in his forty-year association with the university.

Although the university retained a stake in the management of the JDUC, there was no doubt that the AMS stood as a central, active component of the Queen's community. This recognition in a crucial way explains why Queen's remained largely immune to the student radicalism in that decade of protest, the 1960s, with its root-and-branch rejection of established authority. Queen's students shared in the university's culture of inclusion. Nothing better epitomized this culture than the unhesitating decision of Principal John Deutsch – fondly nicknamed "Johnny Dutch" by the students – to appoint four (later sixteen) student senators in the fall of 1968. Students also found the door opened to participation in their more immediate academic life with the creation of departmental student committees, where their input into curricula and regulations was sought. At Queen's, students therefore found themselves *inside* the corridors of decision making before a momentum of protest could form on the *outside*. Students reciprocated this bond of trust by annually appointing someone outside student ranks – a supportive professor, for instance – as the honorary president of the AMS. Queen's was never an "imagined community" – a compendium of manipulated traditions orchestrated to preserve a false sense of identity. Instead, its culture hinged on a vibrant process of constant negotiation and interaction between administration, alumni, faculty, students, and staff. The university's vaunted traditions tapped deep into its inclination to hear and embrace all of its constituents. That inclination rippled through the entire university – into the AMS General Assembly, into the Senate, into the University Council, and even into department committees.

The Politics of Inclusion

Queen's was, however, no student nirvana. Inclusion did not mean an absence of contention. Ideological difference over the relation of the university and the broader Canadian society emerged between some Queen's students and the administration, as the allegations of graduate student Charles "Chuck" Edwards so vividly illustrated in the late 1960s. Similarly, students frequently contested the financial burdens of their education; the last decade of the century would be punctuated by stalwart student opposition to fee inflation. Nonetheless, the channels of dialogue remained open. The "Edwards affair" of 1969–70 was addressed with openness and due process. Student delegations voicing concern over issues as disparate as the putative closing of Herstmonceux Castle and student debt levels were received in the Senate and Board of Trustees. Students found themselves sitting in on and voting in virtually every deliberative committee on campus – from the selection of a new principal to the crafting of campus master plan.

Queen's principals shrewdly understood that it was in their interest to stay connected with student opinion. Principal Ronald Watts made a point of having coffee every Wednesday morning with the president of the AMS to ascertain what was on the mind of the student body. Since 1969, students have insisted upon electing one of their own as their rector to carry their concerns into the inner sanctum of the Board of Trustees. Subsequently, the Board's instinct that inclusion served the university better than exclusion has opened the way to the election of six student, staff, and faculty members to their number. Sixteen student senators fulfill a similar function at deliberations of academic policy.

Queen's unfolding dynamic of broad inclusion has been incubated by its own distinctive manner of making decisions. Whether on academic questions of curriculum, academic discipline, and academic tenure and promotion or on bricks-and-mortar issues pertaining to buildings, pensions, and government relations, Queen's has habitually approached decision making with a dedication to creeping inclusion and consensus. Queen's has never been a place of abrasive confrontation. Both the Senate and the Board of Trustees sit atop scaffolds of committees which probe issues confronting the university and attempt to groom policy positions palatable to as many members of the Queen's community as possible. The emphasis has been on gradualism through consultation, not precipitous, authoritarian action. Reading the minutes of the Queen's Senate in these years often creates the impression of twin escalators, conveying drafts of committee reports up for Senate discussion and then delivering them back to committees for further grooming. The same relationship frequently seemed manifest in the reciprocity between the Board of Trustees and its committees. A similar yo-yoing of deliberation has prevailed at the faculty board level and indeed in the debates of the AMS Assembly. "At Queen's," one-time dean of Education and vice-principal Tom Williams has remarked, "there is no such thing as a definitive solution; there is always going to be some sort of

The Board of Trustees flanks Principal Leggett in 2004. Younger and more gender-balanced, the Board was distinctly more diversified than its 1960s predecessor. Faculty and staff now sat at its meetings and outsiders came from varied walks of life. Board Chairman John Rae (bottom row on right) maintained Queen's connection with long-standing corporate Canada, while at the same time drawing on his own roots as editor of the *Queen's Journal*.

appeal after appeal."[14] Armed with such an intuition, Williams would serve as Queen's principal from 2008 to 2009.

The university's governance offers an uncanny parallel to the delicacy of federal-provincial relations in Canada. All five Queen's principals from 1951 to 1994 – Mackintosh, Corry, Deutsch, Watts, and Smith – were steeped in the political and economic realities of Canadian federalism and Canada's genetic inclination to consensus and equipoise. Each in his own way applied an expertise acquired in observing how the Canadian political and economic system at large operated. In 1988, as government pushed for more "accountability" in the way public monies were spent, the Board of Trustees called upon former principal Watts to brief them on the essence of Queen's governance. Watts warned the trustees that "a neat and tidy mind" was "a crippling disability in any effort to understand the processes of internal governance at Queen's. It is not based on a clear and hierarchical structure, but on the dispersion of decision making among multiple bodies at various levels and upon complex and interlocking relationships between these bodies which involve the whole range of constituent communities within the University." "Collegiality" was "the Queen's way." To drive home his point in a tongue-in-cheek fashion, Watts supplied a sheet of diagrammatic depictions of how various nations – America, the Vatican, France, South Africa – hierarchically organized themselves. Besides these, Queen's

Afterword: In the Fall of 2004 519

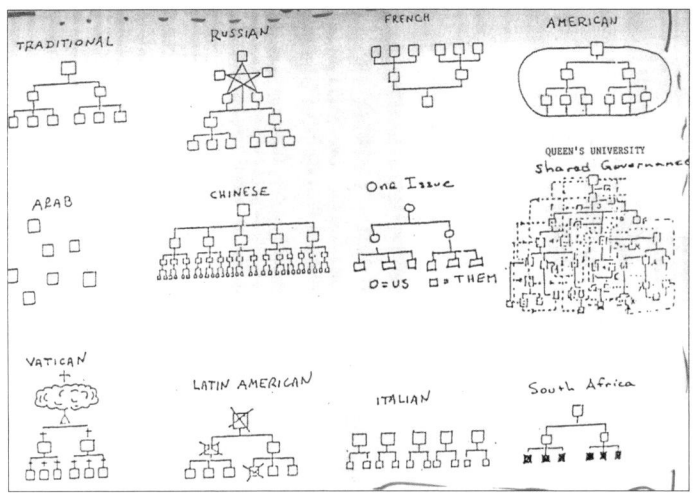

Former Principal Watts's simple guide to organizations – including Queen's.

model of "shared governance" was depicted as a scramble of cross-wiring with no immediately apparent logic.[15]

But, of course, the principal *was* the centre of governance at Queen's. He was the "isthmus" that connected the constituent elements of the Queen's community. Queen's principals possessed little tangible power in any conventional, corporate sense. Their power lay in their mastery of suasion, their ability to convince faculty, students, and staff that the interest of the whole of the Queen's community was always greater than that of its parts. A Queen's principal had to be a person of infinite patience. An effective principal could, of course, facilitate this by exercising the influence and power that was readily at his command: shrewd appointments to vice-principalships, close working relations with the chancellor and the chair of the trustees, weekly coffee with the AMS president, or a sampling of alumni opinion at the University Council. Throughout Queen's tumultuous growth in the late-twentieth century, the adroit use of a principal's advisory committee or task force became the favoured mechanism for identifying problems, analyzing them through broad consultation, and plotting the university's subsequent direction. Their reports provide perhaps a revealing prism of Queen's progress through these years. A "PAC" bought a principal time in almost Mackenzie King fashion – better to deliberate at leisure than to act in haste. But a PAC also drew upon the rich storehouse of campus expertise, thereby encouraging inclusion. Subsequent discussion of such reports by Senate and AMS committees served to educate the campus on the problem and smooth the way to plausible outcomes.

Through all this, a principal had to act as the university's lead emissary in its all-important relations with government funders of post-secondary education, its ambassador to the communities the university served, and salesman to its alumni and benefactors. Principals understandably sought to ease the pressure of such multi-tasking by applying a little humour: David Smith likened the necessity of being constantly "responsive" to so many disparate groups to "being an air traffic controller for a swarming beehive." Amongst friends, he quoted one-time University of Toronto President Sidney Smith as saying that a university president had "to be a ball of fire by day and a bag of wind by night." To survive, a university principal, he also added, needed "the stomach of a goat."

Cumulatively, a principal's shrewd suasion could move Queen's forward. Alex Corry's appointment of history professor Frederick Gibson as vice-principal, academic, in 1966 opened the way to a broadening of campus democracy; Gibson's PAC on Senate reform enhanced the role of the Senate as an engine of academic reform in the 1970s. Similarly, John Deutsch acknowledged the pressure of second-wave feminism by striking a PAC on the status of women at Queen's. Ronald Watts countered the debilitating fiscal austerity of the 1970s by convening the Consultative Group composed of administrators and faculty to adjudicate faculty compensation. David Smith used his suasion to promote the "quality" of a Queen's education, whether that entailed privatizing the MBA degree, unveiling a campus master plan, or rationalizing the remuneration of the medical faculty.

Most dramatically, Smith deployed a PAC with a wide mandate to investigate alleged racism at

Queen's. Bill Leggett in some ways represented a break from the federalist school of Queen's governance; he was a scientist, not a political scientist or an economist, and he was an outsider. His style was perhaps more impatient and decisive. Yet, he too soon came to rely on Queen's genetic inclination to consensus: he used his suasion to convince the university community to internationalize its ambitions. At the same time, Leggett bowed to the inevitability of collective bargaining at Queen's and recognized equity rights as a fundamental right of all members of the Queen's community. Like David Smith, Leggett confirmed his intuitions about Queen's by simply walking about the campus, buttonholing students and faculty alike about their sense of belonging to the community about them.

If the Queen's way habitually veered towards slow-forming and comfortable consensus, its culture occasionally required bold strokes. Alex Corry's decision to parachute the forceful Harry Botterell into the deanship of the medical school in 1962 saved a faculty that was teetering on the edge of collapse. Amid immense provincial pressure for the expansion of post-secondary education, John Deutsch stubbornly steered Queen's on a course towards "steady state" expansion, regulating its enrolment intake so as to maintain its quality brand. At the same time, Deutsch realized that universities had to plan their future and, with advisors such as Bernard Trotter, devised the basic-income-unit formula by which all Ontario universities could be equitably metered in their expansion. When financial austerity pinched the university's ability to renew its faculty in the late 1970s and early 1980s, Ronald Watts devised the Queen's National Scholars program as a way of attracting the best and the brightest. David Smith enhanced the program by tilting its hiring priorities towards women scholars. Bill Leggett too was capable of decisive strokes: the International Study Centre at Herstmonceux Castle in England was saved largely because the principal addressed the issue head-on. Similarly, Leggett's decision to terminate the post of dean of women courted controversy, but at the same time brought an end to the long tension between rights-for-all and affirmative action for particular groups within the campus community.

Tradition as Inaction

The vaunted Queen's way could also at times have dysfunctional tendencies. The belief that Queen's had a hereditary ability to muddle through to a better future could at times breed complacency and myopia. As strongly imbued as it was with its Gaelic aura of tradition and its reputation for excellence in the classroom and loyalty from its alumni, Queen's culture entered the late-twentieth century with some remarkable blind spots. It was a distinctly gendered society that gave unthinking primacy to males. Even as second-wave feminism swirled around its perimeters in the 1960s and 1970s, Queen's remained a bastion of male bonhomie. From the chummy conviviality of the faculty club to admissions strategies and the wording of course descriptions, women's interests and ambitions remained an afterthought at Queen's. Only in enclaves such as the registrar's office and the library did women enjoy any ascendancy. Glass ceilings remained firmly in place over the heads of women faculty and administrators. Few women reached senior administration posts. Fewer still headed departments or became full professors. Most faculty women were relegated to sessional teaching posts.

The surge of baby-boom students arriving at Queen's in the late 1960s reflected the changing geography of gender in Canada long before Queen's official attitudes and policies shifted. The annual injection of new undergraduate blood washed new social patterns and attitudes into a university whose culture had been shaped by faculty and administrators who had come to maturity decades before. For the first time in 1976–77, women entering first year at Queen's outnumbered men, most of this majority emanating from the Faculty of Arts and Science.

The demise of the Levana Society in the late 1960s indicated that Queen's women undergraduates already shared the emerging expectations of second-wave feminism. Women routinely occupied the presidency of the AMS, wrote strident editorials in the *Journal*, and agitated for an end to the entrenched maternalism of residence life. Remarkable women such as Krista Maeots, Jan Lichty, and Bronwen Wallace emerged from Queen's in the 1960s, women impatient to change gender politics both at Queen's and across Canada. Such ambitions were slower to register at the faculty level. In 1976–77, only 10.5 per cent of full-time faculty at the university were women. Men invariably earned more than women of the same rank and were more generously treated under the university pension plan. Only in the realm of sessional teaching did women have any weight, and here they had little security of employment or entitlement to benefits. The skewed gender balance of teaching washed through to the graduate school, where in 1976–77 only 23.9 per cent of students were women.

At Queen's, it would consequently require persistent pressure from groups such as the Association of Women Teaching at Queen's to alter the university's gender balance. From John Deutsch onwards, a standing committee on the status of women reported on the situation of women at Queen's, but seldom agitated overtly for affirmative action. Change in the gender balance at Queen's thus did not come quickly; by 1989–90, the proportion of full-time women faculty had crept up to just over 15 per cent of all faculty. The Queen's National Scholar initiative was, however, beginning to tilt the gender table at Queen's, and, more significantly for the long-term prospects of women professors, well over a third of doctoral graduates at Queen's were now women. In the day-to-day culture of Queen's, it took crises such as the disastrously handled "No Means No" controversy in 1989 to rattle Queen's complacency over women's rights in society. Many Canadians found it hard to reconcile their perception of Queen's as a leading national university with sexist behaviour on campus that ran so much against the grain of modern Canadian society. After 1989, the notion that "boys will be boys" faded at Queen's. By the early twenty-first century, women finally came to occupy senior departmental and administrative posts in numbers sufficient to ensure better, but not yet perfect, gender equality at Queen's.

A similar lulling complacency segregated Queen's from Canada's unfolding multiculturalism. In 1961, the university was still predominantly dependent on eastern Ontario as a catchment area for its students, a fact so eloquently captured in the regular "My father sent me down to Queen's" column in the alumni magazine. Up to the 1960s, Queen's essentially conceived of itself as an Anglo-Presbyterian enclave. It was never, however, dedicated to hermetic exclusivity, as Alfred Bader's happy experience at the university or the presence of Québécoise Suzanne Fortier in the ranks of its senior administration amply illustrated. "Queen's taught me," Bader confessed later in life, "that I would be judged as an individual, that I did not have to be a member of an IN group; even an alien Jew would be treated fairly by these Scottish Presbyterians."[16] Nonetheless, Queen's formidable wall of tradition tended to isolate it from the coming of multicultural diversity to the country at large. Queen's, after all, was situated in a small eastern-Ontario town, out of the mainstream of Canadian immigration.

For many outsiders, the university projected an aura of WASP dedication. Its high-school recruiters (usually headed by the loquacious Padre Laverty), for instance, instinctively headed for the pockets of established Canadian excellence – Forest Hill and the Town of Mount Royal rather than, say, the "new Canadian" Jane-Finch corridor. In this sense, Queen's was "national" in its appeal, drawing more promising applicants from beyond Ontario than other provincial universities. Yet, despite generous levels of student financial assistance, the university had difficulty attracting a student body that reflected Canada's shifting ethnic demographic. Queen's, at the same time, struggled in these decades to attract international students; the allure of large metropolitan campuses outshone that of a university that seemed to sit on the edge of Canada's urban epicentre.

Becoming Diverse – Slowly

Queen's thus came to reflect Canada's new racial and ethnic diversity slowly. It took a conjuncture of pressures to shift the complexion of the Queen's community. Some of the pressure came from without. The 1982 Charter of Rights and Freedoms redefined the entire social demeanour of Canada. Governments began mandating explicit policies of equity and human-rights protection. These surfaced at Queen's in initiatives such as the creation of the Human Rights Office in 1992 and the AMS committees on gender issues, human rights, and equity. Crises and frictions added to the momentum. There were occasional outbursts of virulent racism – hateful, anonymous posters on campus walls and racial slurs yelled in the night – that provoked action. The creation in 1990 of a presidential advisory committee on race relations under psychologist John Berry pulled the curtains back from the topic of racism at Queen's. Berry's committee contained a rainbow of Queen's and Kingston representation (from poets to professors) and dedicated itself to free-wheeling open meetings to canvass sensibilities and experience.

The evidence opened ears, eyes, and minds at Queen's. There seemed little evidence that Queen's suffered from unbridled, conscious racism, but most recognized that racial attitudes had systematically crept into how Queen's conducted its day-to-day routines. The Berry committee, for instance, heard from a Caribbean student hoping to study modern Commonwealth literature that his faculty advisor bluntly informed him: "We don't do that sort of thing at Queen's."[17] The bent of instruction in many other departments was Eurocentric and often dismissive of other racial heritages. It soon became

In 2002, Queen's students elected Iraqi-Canadian Ahmed Kayssi as their rector. Kayssi's activism did much to elevate the profile of the rectorship, a tradition dating back to 1912 and held by a student since 1969. Kayssi, seen here with Sir George Bain, the principal of Queen's University, Belfast, proved an adept ambassador for Queen's. Kayssi convinced Bain to raise the Kingston Queen's flag over his bailiwick as a fundraising promotion. Kayssi would go on to medical studies at the University of Toronto and Harvard before coming a vascular surgeon.

clear that Queen's suffered from systemic myopia in matters of race – its student recruitment, curriculum, faculty hiring, library holdings, and student services all needed reorientation. In his report, Professor Berry suggested that the fulcrum of the problem was not overt racism but a better balancing of equity and human rights at Queen's. Spurred by this prescription, Queen's adopted a new openness to Canada's diversity – Black history month was, for instance, celebrated every February. By the end of the decade, the shift was slowly becoming evident:

a black student had served as AMS president and a Muslim student was elected rector.

Other Queen's traditions were tested in the closing decades of the twentieth century. When activist trustees questioned why concrete brutalism was beginning to dominate the campus streetscape, sullying Queen's majestic limestone heritage, the Board of Trustees voted to revitalize the university's aesthetic vigilance. Architectural imagination and competition returned to Queen's, as did a rediscovery of limestone. The Stauffer Library, with its cladding of Queenston limestone and cherry-wood interior finishing, served as a beacon as the university entered the twenty-first century. At the same time, the prevailing chaos of campus planning was replaced by far-sighted deliberation. The 1994 campus plan set out an esthetic road map dedicated to maintaining the human scale of campus life. "Preserve the best, enhance the rest" became Queen's mantra when considering spatial changes.

Coping with Parsimony

Once-workable traditions were also gradually eroded. The 1960s were the golden years of post-secondary education in Ontario – new universities sprang to life and old universities were generously funded to expand. The 1970s brought stagflation and a shift in public opinion and funding. As government's one-time dominant funding role in Ontario post-secondary education steadily slipped in the last decades of the century, leaving Ontario as one of the least-supportive provincial jurisdictions in the country (indeed, on the continent), Queen's sought to redefine its fiscal circumstances. Principals Smith and Leggett presented bold prescriptions for the rejigging of provincial funding of universities, in effect trying to break the debilitating connection of constant government austerity and the sacrosanct creed of accessibility that persistently kept revenues lagging behind capital and operating expenses. Fees, Queen's suggested, could be deregulated, thereby bringing in new revenue that would allow universities to enhance their programs, while at the same allowing them to bolster student assistance.

When these initiatives failed to overcome entrenched political orthodoxy, Queen's altered course, pioneering the deregulation of fees for professional studies and pushing its undergraduate fees to the maximum allowable limits. Even without fee deregulation, Queen's maintained its tradition of generous student assistance. Nonetheless, like all Ontario universities, Queen's continued to walk a fiscal tightrope in the early twenty-first century. With 65 per cent of its fees still regulated by the provincial rubric of accessibility, and the newly elected Liberal government of Premier Dalton McGuinty committed to freezing undergraduate tuition in the province, Queen's returned to all-too-familiar deficit territory as the century turned. One of Principal Leggett's last duties was to inform the trustees that the McGuinty fee freeze would create a whopping $10-million shortfall in university revenues.

Four decades of fiscal precariousness dictated by the provincial mantra of accessibility to post-secondary education and government's increasingly parsimonious and often unpredictable support of the province's universities brought about a seismic shift in Queen's pedagogic orientation. In these years, Queen's went – many would say sadly – from being an institution dedicated to excellence in undergraduate instruction – "the Princeton of the North" – to what *Maclean's* now labels a medical-doctoral university, offering a full spectrum of undergraduate, graduate, and professional programs predicated on ever-diminishing state support, the deregulation of tuition in market-oriented programs, and the burgeoning possibilities of funded research. After the heyday of the 1960s, when public opinion and Queen's Park coffers generously and almost unquestioningly supported the growth of post-secondary education, the willingness, and ability, of provincial governments to fund university education steadily retreated, as other demands of the mature welfare state, particularly health care, expanded.

It was a testament to the perspicacity of John Deutsch, a principal seasoned by years in the senior civil service, that he saw the downturn in state support coming. Deutsch shrewdly applied the brakes to Queen's growth in the early 1970s, thereby ensuring that the university would continue to attract the best and brightest undergraduates and at the same time not have to engage in a headlong chase for BIUs in order to shore up overextended programs. The tenure of Principal Ronald Watts was marked by an arduous fiscal climate of paring expenses and combatting deficits. That climate persisted with varying intensity to the end of the century. Again and again, Queen's principals returned from lobbying Queen's Park with the news of austerity, freezes on tuition, and demands for greater financial accountability. In the face of such imposed stringency, universities looked for revenue streams that afforded some latitude beyond the straitjacket of formula funding – the annual mathematics of totting up BIU entitlements. Funded research and aggressive fundraising offered that opportunity.

From the Lecture Hall to the Laboratory

Over and above its storied reputation for moulding young minds in the lecture and seminar room, Queen's had long responded to society's demand for research that delved into the social, economic, and technological thrusts that propelled society forward. As early as the 1890s, the university had obliged the province by providing a home for the Ontario School of Mining and Agriculture in Carruthers Hall. Queen's-trained mining engineers subsequently fanned out across the Canadian mining frontier. Early in the twentieth century, Queen's political economists engaged the problems of the young Canadian state. Adam Shortt, for instance, studied the inner workings of the Canadian banking system. Bill Mackintosh and Frank Knox would later edit *The Canadian Banker*, the journal of the bankers' association, for years. But it would take the pressures of the mature social-welfare state and the emergence of corporate industrialism to institutionalize university research into sustained and systematic activity. The years bracketing this history witnessed the birth or aggrandizement of federal and provincial granting agencies – the Social Sciences and Humanities Research Council in the 1970s or the Canadian Institutes of Health Research in 2000 – dedicated to financing on-campus research. At the same time, private research foundations and sponsored corporate research looked to universities to provide answers to their concerns – curing cancer, building better microchips, understanding multicultural societies. Universities reacted with alacrity, not only because these venues activated the intellectual curiosity of their scholars, but also because funded research offered financial leeway to cash-strapped campuses. Funded research also added allure to a campus's reputation and bolstered its graduate programs by furnishing supervisors with the wherewithal to undertake research that not only drew MA and doctoral students, but also provided them with monies for research assistantships. Access to funded research was also a drawing card for young faculty, who increasingly saw greater prospects for academic career advancement in research than in traditional teaching.

Throughout the late twentieth century, the culture of research was in the ascendancy at Queen's. Initially, graduate studies and research were seen as close cousins and placed under the purview of a separate dean. But, by the last decade of the century, the relationship had diverged. The pursuit of research and its subsidization gave birth to a culture that was highly entrepreneurial and competitive. The grooming of research applications had become an intensive business; seminars were offered to new scholars on "launching research careers." Financial systems had to be developed for the disbursement of funds received and formulas for the recovery of university overheads developed. Universities began to report their success with granting agencies in much the same fashion as big-league sports reported their results. Consequently, graduate studies, with its more normative mandate of steering graduate students through the cycle of degree programs, and research, with its more free-wheeling ethos, were pulled apart at Queen's. Principal Leggett, with his own strong background in research, understood the crucial importance of funded research. His appointment of chemist Suzanne Fortier and then civil engineer Kerry Rowe to the position of vice-principal, research, paid a rich dividend to Queen's. In 2003–04, for instance, the university reported $149 million in funded research, a 119-per-cent increase over the last five years. Queen's researchers were gaining national and international reputations. Physicist Arthur McDonald was, for instance, awarded the 2003 Gerard Herzberg Gold Medal by NSERC – with its cheque for $1 million – for his work in coordinating the Sudbury Neutrino Observatory. That same year, environmental biologist John Smol won NSERC's Award of Excellence. Many others excelled.

Indicative of the expanding stature of funded research, both the Board of Trustees and the Senate now placed the report of the vice-principal, research, at the top of their agendas. Queen's, they were often informed, frequently exceeded national averages of success in the crucial competitions of federal and provincial granting agencies. The university's promotional literature increasingly employed the iconography of research – big computers, hard-hatted geologists at mine sites, interviewers on doorsteps – to project the progressive impression of a university engaged by society's problems. As the slogan went: "*Think Research, Think Queen's.*"

Consequently, Queen's faculty gradually reoriented their career ambitions towards funded research, the securing of which could be readily calibrated in dollars secured, teaching releases won, and articles published. In 1961, the culture of Queen's faculty had been strongly introverted, focused on teaching and the daily luncheon table at the faculty club. By 2004, faculty culture was much more extroverted, measured by success with external grant agencies, consultancies undertaken, and conferences attended. Size, academic specialization within disciples, two-career marriages, the advent of social media, the internet, and the increasing complexity of pedagogy completed the inevitable transformation of a professor's life at Queen's. Perhaps indicative of the emerging looser culture of the university, the faculty club, losing money and eager to broaden its constituency, in 1994 changed its name to the University Club, thereby welcoming anybody who desired membership.

In the Tradition of Frank Knox?

Meanwhile, back in classrooms across the campus, the business of teaching went on year after year. In some senses, Queen's maintained its Princeton-like reputation for quality teaching. Undergraduates still reported that Queen's had not disappointed their expectations. The *Maclean's* annual rankings of Canadian universities reported in 2003 that Queen's had a nation-leading first-place standing in thirteen categories. Jo-Anne Brady, the university registrar, reported in 2003 that the university had received an astonishing 40,000 applications for 3,400 undergraduate places. The medical school reported an even-more-daunting ratio of applications for its 125 places each year. Those accepted obviously liked what they encountered at Queen's: in 2003, the university enjoyed the highest undergraduate retention rate among Canadian universities – 90.2 per cent of Queen's undergraduates stayed the course to graduation; the provincial average was 73 per cent.

And, in the tradition of Frank Knox, George Whalley, and Fred Joliffe, Queen's still possessed some extraordinary professors, professors who inspired students not just by their textbook erudition but by the enthusiasm they brought to the life of the mind. In 1975, the Alumni Association established a $5,000 annual award for excellence in teaching. In 2004, Professor Donato Santeramo of the department of Spanish and Italian won the award for his galvanic teaching. Santeramo drew students into a mastery of Italian not just by lecturing, but by singing and acting out snippets of opera, showing Italian films, taking them to an Italian grocery store, and even preparing Italian dishes for their delectation. Santeramo was described by the *Alumni Review* as being very "*contento*" as a university lecturer. Over in the department of geological science and engineering, Professor John Hanes annually faced as many as six hundred first-year students in his course on the "earth's physical environment." Hanes disabused many of these neophyte engineers of their narrow view that engineering was simply about digging up the earth. The earth, Hanes stressed, was a "system," not just a bottomless pit of resources. He strived to equip would-be geologists with an "earth scientist's toolbox." In one famous assignment, he asked them to undertake an environmental assessment of the production of a central instrument of Canadian nationalism – the hockey stick. He often used a hockey stick as an unconventional pointer during his lectures. The stardom of "Hockey Stick" Hanes extended to his role as goalie on the department hockey team. Hanes too would win the Alumni Teaching Award, as well as a "Golden Apple" from engineering students inspired by his teaching.

Santeramo and Hanes were by no means alone. Over in the medical faculty, Professor Jackie Duffin, the holder of the Hannah Chair in medical history, connected would-be doctors with the evolutionary roots of their trade. On warm autumn afternoons, Duffin gathered her first-year charges *en plein air* on the Summerhill lawn and introduced them to their illustrious forebears – pioneers like Linnaeus and Laennec – in spirited lectures. Duffin even supplied her own textbook – a "scandalously short" (but immensely readable) introduction to the history of medicine.[18] Law students were similarly aroused to the wide-ranging implications of their unfolding careers by Professor Beverley Baines, a constitutional expert intrigued by the play of equality rights and religious freedom in an era of Charter rights. Baines reinforced her vigorous classroom erudition with frequent radio and television appearances, commenting, for instance, on the balance between polygamy and gender rights. Another Queen's voice frequently heard on the airwaves was that of Professor Ken Wong of the Business School. In and out of the classroom, Wong spoke with authority and enthusiasm about the nuances of modern marketing and strategic planning. Named "teacher of the year" several times in the executive MBA program that he himself had helped to create, Wong had also displayed his teaching skills in stints at Harvard and Cornell.

Despite such virtuosity, there were problems in campus classrooms. In 2003, Queen's was ranked an unflattering nineteenth by *Maclean's* in class size. The old intimacy of a Queen's class was being squeezed aside by the university's growing enrolment and perpetual budgetary constraint. Large classes brought in lucrative BIUs. Ronald Weisman of psychology complained to Principal Smith, that a professor at Queen's had become "a tiny figure at the front of the hall about the size of my thumb."[19] Fewer seasoned senior professors taught first-year courses; more graduate students – some promising, many unpolished – took over at the podium. Large classes also prompted the adoption of new methods that made coping with large courses more manageable. While some defended their effectiveness, multiple-choice examinations, for instance, tended to reduce learning to a mechanistic exercise.

Inevitably, larger classes introduced anonymity to undergraduate teaching; many students never knew the name of their professor. In 1990, Queen's boasted a student-to-professor ratio of 14.1; by 2001 this had slipped to 22:1.[20] Principal Leggett seemed acutely aware of this "downward spiral" and strove to shore up Queen's reputation for teaching. Initiatives such as the Instructional Development Centre for faculty and the Integrated Learning Centre for students were launched. By the dawn of the new century, the whole question of how teaching was delivered at Queen's was being further changed by the rapid evolution of the internet and the expanding media it might sustain. Courses could now be "live streamed" on the internet, and professors could open up live "chat rooms" on the internet during the course of a lecture. There was no doubt that the internet could further brighten teaching and make it more interactive; the problem increasingly would lie in finding a business model that would allow the university to sustain itself in the face of this "internet age" and all its implications.

Straining Old-Style Collegiality

Other traditions in the Queen's culture were tested to a point of diminishing return in these years and had to adapt to new circumstances. The collegiality of faculty and administration in matters of labour relations had been remarkably amicable in the 1960s and 1970s, but by the late decades of the century was not sustained in an increasingly complex work world. The university had expanded hugely, and the employer-employee relationship was now freighted with far more than the calculation of an annual salary – by matters of equity, academic tenure, promotion, and discipline. Queen's adoption of collective bargaining in 1995 recognized the collapse of a once-workable tradition and its unavoidable replacement by a mechanism better suited to the times.

Despite the relatively smooth negotiation of Queen's first collective agreement with faculty, there was no denying that the collegiality that had so happily prevailed in the 1960s and early 1970s had hardened into a more confrontational relationship. Queen's had become a sprawling enterprise that could no longer rely on a trust in collegiality to sustain its affairs. It had become a more contractual society. Matters that had traditionally been arbitrated by the Senate – academic appointment, tenure, and promotion, for instance – now came under the purview of collective bargaining. By the late 1990s, the Senate seemed to have slipped back from the pivotal role it had played in the 1970s in determining the academic life of the university. Paralleling this evolution was a realization that Queen's venerable tradition of organically grooming its own leadership might not necessarily hold up in an era when the one-time *art* of guiding a post-secondary institution had become a managerial *science*. Through five principalships since 1951, Queen's had been ably led by men who had percolated out of its culture, thereby bringing an intimacy with Queen's tradition to their mandate.

By the last decade of the century, Queen's began to recognize that managing a university at times required the importation of managerial skills. Principal Smith complained, for instance, that his time had become increasingly dominated by the university's external relations – with currying the understanding and favour of outside stakeholders, ranging from politicians and bureaucrats at Queen's Park who decided the provincial government's annual subsidization of universities to potential corporate and private benefactors who might make or break a fundraising campaign. The dramatic recognition in the 1990s that fundraising was now central to the university's fiscal well-being provoked Queen's into creating a full-time dedicated advancement office. The $262-million success story of that office's first concerted capital campaign in the new century confirmed that wisdom. The Leggett years can consequently be seen as a time of emerging concern for the way in which Queen's was managed. Queen's had become an *enterprise* that required skills hardly imagined in 1961.

Leggett, himself an outsider, devoted much time to getting his executive suite right. Graduate studies and research, traditionally rolled into one seemingly synonymous bundle, were broken apart into separate bailiwicks. The pursuit of funded research and its subsequent administration required distinct policies and skills; graduate studies entailed more normative, cyclical, administrative skills. The advancement function under George Hood epitomized the need for concerted effort and wily strategizing. Similarly, the arrival of collective bargaining with faculty necessitated Richardson Hall's acquisition of negotiating talent at the vice-principal level. Hence, John Cowan's arrival as a vice-principal, with his experience at CAUT and with faculty unions elsewhere, was designed to broaden the expertise of Queen's senior administration.

The resurrection of the office of dean of student affairs in 1995 at the same time reflected recognition that, in an age of Charter rights, the status of students on a university campus had become far more contractual than ever before. Matters of student discipline, well-being, and financial sustenance had become far more complex than they had ever been in the 1960s. Even the AMS had been obliged to rethink the way it managed itself; its commission structure now resembled that of a corporation, addressing such matters as environmental sustainability, social equity, and municipal affairs. Who in the 1960s could have envisaged that by the turn of the twenty-first century the AMS would be managing a food bank or a walk-home service? Indeed, in the 1960s the AMS had principally catered to the associational needs of students at Queen's – arranging a cycle of social events throughout the year, while at the same time maintaining a system of natural justice through its own court and nurturing the emergence of students as citizens by supporting model parliaments and an eloquent student newspaper. By 2004, the AMS had become almost a welfare state unto itself, offering health and dental care to its members and lending its voice to social and ethical issues that extended far beyond the campus. Through all this transition, Queen's students displayed remarkable initiative and social conscience. In 2006, for instance, Michele Romanow of Sci. '07 spearheaded the drive to open the environmentally-sustainable Queen's Tea Room nestled into the just-opened Beamish-Munro Hall. Operated under

Perhaps the most stalwart of Queen's traditions has been the determination of its students to chart their own course through the Alma Mater Society, a tradition initiated in 1858. Here the successful AMS executive team of Chrissie Knitter, Erik Gaustad, and Mike Jones celebrate their 2003 victory at the polls.

the auspices of the Engineering Society, the initiative showed how old Queen's traditions could be realigned to modern sensibilities. In 2008, Romanow was given a Tricolour Award, an annual recognition of service by students for students.

Through all this modernization, the AMS maintained its core mission – to provide students with as broad a measure of self-regulation as possible. This has been one of Queen's most abiding achievements. Although the parameters of that autonomy had shifted – the natural justice at the heart of the AMS Court had, for instance, suffered in an age of litigiousness and Charter rights – Queen's continued to enjoy one of the most vibrant student governments in the country. In 2003–4, the AMS reported financial operations totalling $8.5 million and employed fifty salaried officials to oversee its mandate. Over two hundred student clubs, for instance, flourished under AMS subsidization. Greg McKellar, the AMS's long-serving and devoted information officer, has suggested that, if one combined all the salaried appointees and volunteers associated with AMS governance, one would discover that 1,500 Queen's undergraduates – about 10 per cent of their cohort – are annually involved in making student government work at Queen's.

Every year, Queen's students were presented with a slate of referendum questions, seeking their approval of levies that were tacked onto (or sometimes removed from) their student service fee. This constituted a vigorous form of responsible government that allowed students to judge and support those services that impinged on their life on campus – the weekly publication of the *Queen's Journal*, the display of student art in Union Gallery, and the broadcasts of CFRC radio, to name just three. Thus, when the university asked for student input into the purpose and design of the new Queen's Centre in 2003, the AMS constructively obliged, not only with ideas but also with a vote at its spring 2004 general meeting that pledged long-term student fee support for the venture. Throughout these years, the AMS thus remained devotedly attached to the notion that students at Queen's were undeniably also *citizens* of Queen's. Implicit in this recognition was a realization that the boundary between student autonomy and the prerogatives of university administration – protecting the university's "brand" – would forever be in healthy contention. Over time, each party learned to adjust its course in the interest of the betterment of the whole community. One of the most durable and vital of Queen's traditions was that the principal's door was always open to the AMS president or the students' rector. In 1986, AMS president Innes Van Nostrand bought a large framed painting of a windjammer under full sail and put it on the wall of his office in the JDUC. He gave the picture a title: "The Good Ship AMS." Every year thereafter, the AMS's outgoing president added his or her signature to the back of the painting – a new tradition thus reinforced a venerable tradition that stretched back to the 1850s.

Queen's "Inherent Tribalism" Lives On

The "inherent tribalism" of Queen's, so strong in 1961, thus proved capable of bending with the times. Queen's liberalism by 2004 exhibited greater latitude and less rigid devotion to received wisdom. There seemed to be an innate appreciation that institutions that do not modify their traditions in the face of changing sensibilities run the real danger of ossifying, becoming irrelevant, and collapsing. Queen's had lived up to Cardinal Newman's challenge of being a vital community, of being "a place where enquiry is pushed forward and discoveries perfected and verified and rashness rendered innocuous and exposed by the collision of mind with mind and knowledge with knowledge." At Queen's, "the collision of mind with mind" had been conditioned by a strong sense of tradition, tradition that at times braked recklessness but at other times impeded timely, progressive change. At his 1968 installation as principal, John Deutsch saluted Queen's "rational and civilized way" of dealing with problems "in this time of explosive change and tension." The "Queen's way" thus entailed persistent consultation and inclusion. Change at Queen's consequently almost always came at a conservative pace. The university resisted faddish change; Deutsch's "steady state" policy of reluctant, measured growth was a masterstroke of going against the provincial grain. "Throughout her history," Watts-era vice-principal Jim Courtright aptly noted in the *Queen's Alumni Review*, "Queen's has adapted to change. At our university there is a civility and openness to differing views on internal and external questions of the day and a polite unwillingness to be bullied into precipitate action by strident policies from any single sector."[21]

At the same time, Queen's has not hesitated to build on its strengths – its bent for public policy, for instance, became embodied in these years in a School of Policy Studies and an Institute of Intergovernmental Relations. Nor was Queen's blinded by caution from seizing the initiative when opportunity knocked; its pioneering of a market-priced MBA vaulted it into the forefront of North American business-executive education. In the same decade of the 1990s, its medical staff and students carried their community health and rehabilitation skills into war-torn former Yugoslavia. Herstmonceux Castle, thanks to a timely nudge from Alfred Bader, further pushed Queen's onto the international stage. The vigorous expansion of graduate studies and funded research helped Queen's engage a Canadian society increasingly hungry for higher learning and applied knowledge. New traditions thus emerged at Queen's as old ones slipped into the shadows.

The same pattern of constantly testing tradition prevailed in the social fabric of the university. Some venerable values endured the test of the times. Student self-government reworked itself into an adept provider of services, while at the same time adjusting to a society of Charter rights in which students were no longer citizens-in-training, but instead fully fledged citizens by the time they set foot on campus. Queen's storied tradition of public service also persevered. Queen's dedication to the nation materialized in royal commission research and outspoken pronouncements on policies ranging from public health to tax reform. The informed voices of Queen's graduates have frequented the pages of the national press and filled the airwaves of networks as diverse as the BBC, Al Jazeera, and the CBC. The impulse of public service and good citizenship continues to manifest itself in Queen's daily life – a day seldom passes without a student club selling muffins outside the physical recreation centre to aid children suffering from cancer or rescue stray dogs. The Science '44 Co-op continues its six-decade tradition of allowing students to live in a co-operative and environmentally sustainable fashion in twenty-one houses clustered around their campus. Principal George Grant would have viewed the perpetuation of such initiative and altruism with pride. Queen's students, he fervently believed, had a duty to the world they had inherited. Other social and attitudinal traditions at Queen's proved stickier and at times regressive. When Queen's failed to live up to this Grantian call of duty, as it did in its lethargic awakening to issues of gender equality and social diversity, the price was at times steep and embarrassing.

At her installation as Queen's eighteenth principal in October 2004, Karen Hitchcock seemed to recognize that the arduous process of testing tradition would continue on her watch. For many crowding into the Harty Arena, the rhetoric of installing a new principal had a familiar ring: "I, Karen Hitchcock, promise to uphold the traditions and maintain the principles and purposes of Queen's University." Although an outsider to Queen's culture whose academic career had been entirely rooted in the United States, Hitchcock intuitively understood that her new university had been "dancing with change," citing a poem by Nigerian poet Ben Okri. Hitchcock described the ongoing challenge facing Queen's: balancing "our natural resistance to change" against the "value of change." As its motto had long suggested, "wisdom" and "stability" were at the heart of the university's mission. Queen's, Hitchcock assured her audience, must continue to be "an institution embedded in our society – deeply committed to basic academic values, yet able to configure itself in ways which are responsive to the society which supports it." It must preserve "an environment of collegiality, inclusiveness, and inventiveness." Principal Grant would have nodded in agreement with these cardinal values. Hitchcock's living predecessor principals – Ronald Watts and Bill Leggett – who were present that day, would have endorsed another of her observations that afternoon. The process of testing tradition in a venerable institution such as Queen's often required "difficult decisions to sustain it." This was, however, a worthy price to pay for community.[22]

Forty years before, the sage of Queen's English department, George Whalley, had taken pen in hand and written the introduction to a book of essays entitled *A Place of Liberty* about the challenges facing the modern university. "The *raison d'être* of the academic community is not what it does, or makes, but that it exists in a vital form, generating influence which can be neither predicted nor formulated."[23] By engaging the at-times-tense but cumulatively constructive process of testing its traditions in the protean years after 1961, Queen's had ensured that it remained "vital" as a community. It had "danced with change." In doing so, it had perpetuated its storied national presence as a force of liberalism – "limestone liberalism" – in Canadian society, while at the same time shedding its parochial bonds and stepping out onto a less-familiar, more-global stage. The "Queen's way" had been reformulated to fit the times. Maintaining this delicate dialectic between preserving worthwhile tradition and inventing new tradition would be Queen's challenge in the new millennium.

Tricolour photographer Harrison Smith brilliantly captured a mosaic of Queen's tradition on a football Saturday in 2003: the flags of Scotland, Ontario, Kingston, the United Kingdom, and Canada mingle behind the university colours.

Acknowledgments

Books are like pyramids – an author depends entirely on the solidity of the layers of support below him. In this respect, *Testing Tradition* rests on a sure foundation. My first and foremost thanks go to Principal Daniel Woolf, who came to his office at Queen's in 2009 determined to see the third volume of Queen's history written. It had been over three decades since the initial two volumes of the university's history had appeared, narratives covering the years from its founding in 1841 to the eve of Ontario's golden age of university expansion in 1961. A historian by training, Daniel understood how institutions are nurtured by their history and culture. Preparatory to being interviewed for the principal's position, Daniel read the treatment of Queen's evolution over its first century by historians Hilda Neatby, Roger Graham, and Fred Gibson, allowing the insights gained therein to shape his sense of what might be strategically possible in Queen's future. Once in office, he resolved to bequeath a similar legacy to his successors.

That resolve was enthusiastically shared by the Board of Trustees, who empowered the principal to select a suitable historian for the task. That assignment happily fell to me. Queen's previous historians had been of two genres. Hilda Neatby, on the one hand, had been a complete outsider to Queen's when she arrived in Kingston from the University of Saskatchewan in the early 1970s. Her perspective on Queen's was therefore fresh, untainted by years of experience in the ranks of its faculty and administration and thus open to what was both good and bad in the university's culture. Fred Gibson, on the other hand, had been lovingly attached to Queen's since his undergraduate years there in the early 1940s. Fred knew every nook and cranny of the place and brought a preconditioned sensibility to his task. As the third university historian, I am very much a hybrid – educated at Queen's in the 1970s as a historian and sprung from a family associated with Queen's since its founding in 1841, yet absent from its rhythms for over forty years, working in government, in think tanks, and at Carleton University in the interim. Queen's was thus distantly familiar to me, while its recent past – the years I was to explore – was experienced only from afar. My thanks therefore go to Daniel for his initial vision and ongoing interest in the project. Always supportive and curious, he was never interventionist and, given his own work as a historiographer, ever ready to proffer useful advice. Daniel's persuasion also brought the Richardson family, long attached to Queen's by their service and financial generosity, on board the project. My thanks therefore to the Chancellor Richardson Memorial Trust for its sustaining of my work and, in particular, Hartley Richardson, who clearly understands the vital impulse given Queen's by its history. Without such generous initial support, this book would never have been written.

It would also never have been possible without the existence of the Queen's University Archives. Since 1961, the university archives has been the repository not only of Queen's administrative records, but also of its audio, visual, and material history. It is superbly managed, its archivists and conservation specialists impeccably professional and helpful. I will hardly be the first historian to praise the Queen's Archives as, without question, the best university archives in the country. My sincere thanks therefore go to University Archivist Paul Banfield and his most excellent staff. In particular, front-line archivists Jeremy Heil, Heather Home, and Deirdre Bryden ministered to my myriad daily requests for documents and guidance with incredible friendliness and knowledge of their respective fields. Susan Office, Margaret Bignell, Heather Wolsley, and Shan Jin rounded out this experience of being in a historian's paradise. My days in the archives were also blessed by the presence of Amelia Wilkinson, my crackerjack research assistant, whose meticulous investigation of the *Queen's Journal* proved invaluable.

I have benefited from the diligent and insightful reading of this manuscript by a small group of readers, all of whom have long acquaintance with Queen's and its ways. Robert "Bob" Little, one-time AMS president and now a distinguished Kingston lawyer, chaired our small reading circle with friendly efficiency. Ken Cuthbertson, a Queen's graduate from the 1970s, long-time editor of the *Queen's Alumni Review*, and an author in his own right, applied his intimate knowledge of the university's life over the last three decades. Alison Morgan, an economist who served Queen's in a number of central functions, supplied her perspective, as did business professor and eloquent football historian Mervin "Merv" Daub, University Archivist Paul Banfield, and medical historian *extraordinaire* Jacalyn "Jackie" Duffin. I could not have had better advice and feedback. Their insights were augmented by the wisdom of a number of old Queen's hands. Greg McKellar, the AMS's long-serving Information Officer, freely lent his knowledge of Queen's primordial tradition of student self-government. His devotion to the university's student culture is inspiring. Ken Snowdon contributed his provincially admired understanding of university funding and finances. Many professors, active and retired, informed my understanding of Queen's, but none more so than political scientist John Meisel, whose devotion to Queen's has stretched well past a half-century.

Cheryl Lewis in the Principal's Office and Peggy Watkin in the Provost's Office promptly and effectively oversaw many of the administrative necessities of this project. At the McGill-Queen's University Press, Philip Cercone, Ryan Van Huijstee, Julia Monks, and Elena Goranescu efficiently expedited my manuscript into print. Fortune smiled on me when Patricia Kennedy in Toronto was asked to copyedit the manuscript. I had worked with Pat on a previous book and my admiration for her brilliant touch has only grown with re-acquaintance.

From the outset, I have encountered wonderful co-operation from the broader Queen's community; there was always curiosity and a willingness to lend a willing ear or entertain an inquiry. Thanks, therefore, to: Rachel Abs, Bernard Adell, Don Akenson, Jan Allen, George Anderson, Allan Armit, Alfred Bader, Beverley Baines, Gillian Barlow, Henry Becker, Alvan Bergman, John Berry, Mike Blair, Alicia Boutilier, Victor Bradley, Alan Broadbent, Judith Brown, Bruce Buchan, Irène Bujara, Annette Burfoot, Dan Burns, Blake Butler, James Carson,

Paul Christenson, Susan Cole, Sean Conway, Jacquelyn Coutré, Robert Crawford, Caroline Davis, David de Witt, Wilf Day, Helena Debnam, Cathy Dickison, Henry Dinsdale, Gordon Dueck, Peter Dorn, Karl Duttle, Tom Evans, Dorothy Farr, Nick Francis, C.E.S. "Ned" Franks, Paul Fritz, Stewart Fyfe, Lin Good, Stewart Goodings, Doris Goheen, David Gordon, Jan Graves, Charlotte Gray, Andrea Gunn, Roberta Hamilton, John Hanes, Tom Harris, Joan Harcourt, Agnes Herzberg, George Hood, Edward Turner Horton, Adnan Husain, Diana Inkster, John Isbister, Heather Jamieson, Ahmed Kayssi, Mark Kerr, Carl Keijzers, Daniel LaJoie, William Leggett, James Leith, Greg Lessard, Stephen Lougheed, Anne MacDermaid, James MacIntyre, Pamela Manders, Steven Maynard, Daniel McConnachie, Christopher McCreery, Deirdre McDade, Bob McGraw, Ross McGregor, John McLatchie, Pat McNally, John Metcalfe, Georgina Moore, Augusto Morales, Ruben Nelson, Lisa Newton, Brian Osborne, Christine Overall, Joseph Petric, James Pritchard, John Rae, Kam Rao, Chris Redmond, Anne Richard, Hilary Richardson, Brian Rogers, Jonathan Rose, Celia Russell, David Russo, Claude Sherren, Joan Sherwood, Robert Silverman, Jeffrey Simpson, Duncan Sinclair, John Smart, Pat Smart, Geoff Smith, Harrison Smith, Mary Smith, Harry Smith, James Stayer, Pat Sullivan, Mary Surridge, Doris Sweet, Barbara Teatero, Krista Hanna Thompson, Hugh Thorburn, Bernard Trotter, Gerald Tulchinsky, David Walker, Ronald Watts, Martha Whitehead, Paul Wiens, Tom Williams, Ian Wilson, Robert Wolfe, Ken Wong, Brian Yealland, and William Young. My sincere apology to anyone I have overlooked.

Authors devote perhaps eight hours a day on average to the task of research and writing. The rest of the day is spent with family and friends. For me, those hours have always proved a time of contentment. My wife, Sandy Campbell, is not only a skilled and erudite editor, but is also a Queen's historian in her own right, her biography of Queen's-educated and nationally renowned Canadian publisher Lorne Pierce – *Both Hands* – having been published by McGill-Queen's in 2013. To Sandy, Paget, and Lily, thank you for your constant support and for upholding, and seldom testing, our happy tradition.

Illustration Credits

The illustrations for this history are almost exclusively taken from the extensive image collection at the Queen's University Archives (archives@queensu.ca). To facilitate identification of the images, the following abbreviations have been used:

KWS	Kingston *Whig-Standard*
QAR	*Queen's Alumni Review*
QAR Coll	*Queen's Alumni Review* Collection at QUA
QG	*Queen's Gazette*
QJ	*Queen's Journal*
QUA	Queen's University Archives
TRI	*Tricolor* (*Tricolour* after 1978)

All references are keyed to page numbers in the volume.

Frontispiece "No Means No" protest window, QAR Coll, box 14.
- 2 Grant Hall, QUA, A ARCH V28-B-Grant-51
- 6 *Song Book*, QUA Printed Collection
- 8 Principal Grant, QUA, A ARCH V28 P-34.1
- 10 1923 Grey Cup football, QUA
- 15 Band on field, TRI, 1962, 91
- 17 Coach Tindall, TRI, 1962, 208
- 19 Orientation car wash, QAR Coll, box 14
- 24 Professor Jolliffe lecturing, TRI, 1964, p. 242
- 25 Professor Whalley, QUA, A ARCH V28 P-444
- 27 Professor Ward Cornell on rounds, QUA, A ARCH V28 P-496.4
- 29 Mackintosh, Corry, and Deutsch, QAR Coll, box 13
- 39 "Keep Queen's Green," QUA, A ARCH V28 Soc-Rel 1972 and Stirling Hall, QAR Coll, box 6
- 43 Board of Trustees, QUA, A ARCH V28 BT–undated–1.1 c. 1967
- 46 Jean Royce, QAR Coll, box 15
- 52 Corry on stage, QUA, A ARCH V28 P-417.2
- 57 Art donation, QUA, V28 Cer-28.1
- 59 Corry with Richardson, QUA, A ARCH V28 P-417.1
- 69 Harry Botterell, TRI, 1964, 100
- 80 Diefenbaker cuts ribbon, TRI, 1961, 95
- 89 Royce and Stirling, TRI, 1969 (note: not all *Tricolors* are paginated)
- 92 Watson Hall, QUA, A ARCH V28 B-Wat-3
- 95 Deutsch as rock star, QUA, A ARCH V28 P-50.12
- 97 Computer terminals, TRI, 1970
- 103 Senate in session, QUA, A ARCH V28 Sen-1.1
- 105 Deutsch with Vanier, QUA, A ARCH V28 P-50.9
- 114 Cartoon of "profs," QAR, May–June, 1963
- 125 Etherington art opening, QAR Coll, box 4
- 131 Deutsch with Davis, TRI, 1972
- 134 Watts on bike, TRI, Nov.–Dec. 1974 cover
- 137 Bertha Bailey's house, QAR Coll, box 6
- 140 CFRC, TRI, 1968, 116
- 141 "Missing the Boat," QJ, 19 Oct. 1968
- 144 Freshettes in T-shirts, QAR Coll, box 14, and grease pole, TRI, 1963, 105
- 145 Candle lighting, TRI, 1969, 187
- 153 Buller and McGregor, TRI, 1970
- 161 Victoria Hall, QUA, A ARCH V28-B-VIC 8 of 10
- 169 Sod girls, TRI, 1972
- 170 Faculty club, QAR Coll, box 9
- 172 Professor Clench, TRI, 1969, 171
- 182 Mackintosh-Corry Building, QAR Coll, box 5
- 184 Billboard, QUA, A ARCH V28 STUD-23
- 186 Map of Queen's, QAR Coll, box 15
- 189 Trudeau, TRI, 1969, 163
- 191 Krista Maeots, TRI, 1967
- 197 Tent-in, KWS, Sept. 14, 1968

198 Sheep cartoon, QUA, Queen's Printed Collection, from *AMS Forum*, Sept. 1968
199 Protestors with signs, TRI, 1969, 180
203 Edwards testifying, TRI, 1970
205 Engineers confront protesters, KWS, 12 March 1970
207 Clowns, KWS, 3 April 1970
208 Wallace Hall meeting, QUA, A ARCH V28 Stud-49, and AMS constable, TRI, 1970
213 Elrond architect, QUA, A ARCH V28 B-Elro-3.2
216 Elrond College, TRI, 1973
221 Abbie Hoffman, TRI, 1985, 134
225 Deutsch and Watts with coats, TRI, 1975
227 Streakers, TRI, 1974, and medical variety show, TRI, 1979, 120
229 Concert, TRI, 1979, 84
237 Student protest with signs, TRI, 1978
244 Library protest, TRI, 1982, p. 143
248 Mullan, TRI, 1980, 149
252 Greer, TRI, 1977
255 Michener kicks ball, QUA, V28 P-168.9
274 Watts at AMS party, TRI, 1984, 32
280 Cheerleaders, TRI, 1985, 56
285 Cartoon of Smith, QJ, Oct. 24, 1984
285 Smith on lawn, TRI, 1973
290 Student protest over Bovey, TRI 1985, 14
295 Challenge Fund, QUA, A ARCH V28 BT-1992-1.1
297 Royal visit, TRI, 1992, 17; football coach, TRI, 1990, 128; and players with trophy, TRI, 1992, 19
322 Smith at castle, QAR Coll, box 5
324 Rembrandt image supplied by Agnes Etherington Art Centre
328 Policy Studies Building, QUA A ARCH V28 Cer-44.1
331 Project Green crane, TRI, 1976
337 Stauffer Library, QUA, QAR Coll, box 6
343 Lakeshore service, TRI, 1975, and bike race, QUA A ARCH V28 p-5.4
354 Abramskys, QUA, A ARCH V28 Cer-42
358 Aboriginal dance, QUA, Queen's Photographer fonds, Black negatives
361 Women's studies, QAR Coll, box 15
363 Roberta Hamilton, QAR Coll, box 9
371 Student picketers, QAR Coll, box 15
373 "No Means No" window, QAR Coll, box 14
375 "No Means No" window, QAR Coll, box 14
378 QAR, cover, Mar.–April 1990
387 Mossman, TRI, 1970
391 Anti-apartheid, TRI, 1992, 95
398 Sutherland plaque, QAR Coll, box 13
400 Bus, TRI, 1987, 14
405 Professor Rawlyk, QUA, A ARCH V28 people "R," P-204
409 South Africa protesters, TRI, 1987, 173
413 Mayor at desk, TRI, 1983
416 Hockey, TRI, 1981, 164; rowing, TRI, 1991, 163; and CFRC, TRI, 1988, 95
419 Cartoon, QJ, 8 March 1968
421 Houses off-campus, TRI, 1982, 32
424 Chainsaw, TRI, 1991, 33; and party jocks, TRI, 1986, 44
430 Handshake, TRI, 1999, 44, and street party, TRI, 1987, 33
439 Leggett and Laughren, QAR Coll, box 1
441 Researcher with chart, QAR Coll, box 15
458 Deans of women, QUA, A ARCH V28 Cer-47
465 Baders on castle roof, taken with permission from Alfred Bader, *Adventures of a Chemist Collector* (London: Weidenfeld and Nicolson, 1995)
468 Solar car, QAR Coll, box 9
472 Tuition protesters, TRI, 2002, 58
475 George Hood, QUA A ARCH V28 P-702
481 Leggett on truck, QUA, A ARCH V28 P-609.8
495 Mel Goodes, QAR cover, fall 2002
501 Lougheed and Leggett, QUA, A ARCH V28 P-609
505 Move-in day, TRI, 1997, 3
507 Women on grease pole, QAR Coll, box 9
510 Band at football game, TRI, 2004, 89
514 Painting sidewalk, QUA, A ARCH V28 Stud-80; and Professor Meisel, QUA, A ARCH V28 P-476.3
515 Model parliament, QUA, A ARCH V28 B-2-2004-1
519 Board of Trustees, QUA, A ARCH V28 BT-2004-1
520 Watts schema, QUA, Minutes of the Board of Trustees, 14–15 May 1989
523 Men in kilts, image supplied by Ahmed Kayssi
529 AMS executive with cigars, TRI, 2003, 43
532 Gaelic dancer with flags, photo by Harrison Smith, TRI, 2005, cover

Notes

ABBREVIATIONS
AMS Alma Mater Society
AMSM Alma Mater Society Minutes
GW *Golden Words*
KWS Kingston *Whig-Standard*
MBT Minutes of the Board of Trustees
MUS Minutes of the University Senate
OPF Office of the Principal Files
QAFA Queen's Alumni Faculty Association
QAR *Queen's Alumni Review*
QJ *Queen's Journal*
QUA Queen's University Archives
RAQ Retirees' Association of Queen's

INTRODUCTION
1 Eric Hobsbawm and Terence Ranger, eds., *The Invention of Tradition* (Cambridge: Cambridge University Press, 1983), 1.
2 Benedict Anderson, *Imagined Communities: Reflections on the Origin and Spread of Nationalism* (London: Verso, 1983), 49.
3 *Queen's University Song Book* (Toronto & Winnipeg: Whaley, Royce & Co., 1903), 18.
4 D.D. Calvin, *Queen's University at Kingston: The First Century of a Scottish Canadian Foundation, 1841–1941* (Kingston: Queen's University Board of Trustees, 1941), 299.
5 Hilda Neatby, edited by Frederick W. Gibson and Roger Graham, *Queen's University, Volume I, 1841–1917: To Strive, to Seek, to Find, and Not to Yield* (Montreal: McGill-Queen's University Press, 1978).
6 Frederick W. Gibson, *Queen's University, Volume II, 1917–1961: To Serve and Yet Be Free* (Kingston & Montreal: McGill-Queen's University Press, 1983). Gibson invented the title, after consulting with former principal Alex Corry, to capture the spirit of his analysis – Queen's hybrid mission to serve society while always protecting its autonomy.

CHAPTER ONE
1 See: Arthur Zimmerman, *In the Shadow of the Shield: The Development of Wireless Telegraphy and Radio Broadcasting in Kingston and at Queen's University* (Kingston: Privately published, 1991), 144–5, and Queen's University Archives, "Ninety Years of Queen's Radio," http://archives.queensu.ca/Exhibits/cfrc.html. The call sign CFRC was assigned by Ottawa in 1923, *before* Queen's had won its three national championships.
2 See: Mervin Daub, *Gael Force: A Century of Football at Queen's* (Montreal & Kingston: McGill-Queen's University Press, 1996).
3 See: *Queen's University Song Book* (Toronto & Winnipeg: Whaley, Royce & Co. Ltd., 1903).
4 See: "The Story of Alfie Pierce," www.stoneskingston.ca. Pierce's origins and role at Queen's have been clouded by misinformation and, at times, controversy. Pierce died in 1951.
5 *Queen's Journal* [hereafter QJ], 15 Nov. 1960.
6 *Queen's Review*, Sep.-Oct. 1961. The *Review* did not become the *Queen's Alumni Review* until the 1970s. Montreal *Gazette* sportswriter Dink Carroll called Skypeck "the best passer ever to appear in Canadian college ranks." See: "Skypeck Shoots Down Gaels with a Shotgun Offence," Kingston *Whig-Standard* [hereafter KWS], 13 Nov. 1961.

7 *QJ*, 22 Nov. 1961.
8 *WS*, 20 Nov. 1961, and Alma Mater Society Minutes, Queen's University Archives [hereafter QUA] Locator #3621, 21 Nov. and 5 Dec. 1961.
9 Quoted in Herb Hamilton, *Queen's Queen's Queen's* (Kingston: Alumni Association of Queen's University, 1977), 5.
10 Lindy Mechefske, "Queen's Radio Has a Long History but an Uncertain Future," 13 Feb. 2013.
11 Edward Shils, *Tradition* (Chicago: University of Chicago Press, 1981), 33.
12 Office of the Principal Files [hereafter OPF], QUA, locator #1252, box 9, file: freshman.
13 John Meisel, *A Life of Learning and Other Pleasures: John Meisel's Tale* (Yarker: Wintergreen Studios Press, 2012), 162 and 173.
14 Retirees' Association of Queen's/Queens' University Archives Oral History project [hereafter RAQ interviews]: Ted Hodgetts, July 2008.
15 RAQ interviews: Brian Osborne, July 2009.
16 RAQ interviews: Grant Sampson, July 2008.
17 Interview with author, 2 Aug. 2011.
18 Norman Miller, *Lest We Forget* (Kingston, np, 1969), located in QUA, Queen's 6-L.
19 Queen's University Faculty Association [hereafter QUFA] *Newsletters, 1965–*, QUA, Queen's Printed Collection, QUFA, box 1.
20 Hugh Thorburn, Faculty Dinner speech, 29 March 1962, and minutes of QUFA meeting with Corry, 13 April 1962, QUA, OPF, locator #1250, box 10.
21 J.A. Corry, *My Life and Work: A Happy Partnership* (Queen's University: Kingston, 1981), 170.
22 See, for instance: S.F. Wise, "A Personal View of Kingston," *Historic Kingston* 22, March 1974, 1–8, and Ken Cuthbertson, "Queen's and Kingston – For Better, For Worse, For Poorer," *Kingston Life*, Fall 2002.
23 R. Watts to A.R.C. Duncan, 2 Nov. 1981, QUA, OPF, locator #1254, box 7, file: staff general.
24 Ronald L. Watts, foreword to F.W. Gibson, *Queen's University, Volume II, 1917–1961: To Serve and Yet Be Free* (Montreal & Kingston: McGill-Queen's University Press 1983), xiii.
25 Quoted in *Queen's Alumni Review*, Jan.-Feb. 1984, 5.
26 J.A. Corry, "The University in a Changing Society," reprinted in the *Queen's Journal*, 27 Oct. 1961. The spelling of Corry's first name often varies between "Alex" and "Alec" in many publications and much of his correspondence. "Alex" is used here, mainly because this is the form used in Corry's memoir.
27 John Henry Newman, *The Idea of a University* (originally published in 1854, Cambridge: Cambridge at the University Press, 1931), xxxiii and 26.
28 Hamilton, *Queen's*, 139, and Minutes of the Board of Trustees, 14 and 15 October 1966.
29 Cited in Hilda Neatby, *Queen's University, Volume I, 1841–1917: To Strive, To Seek, To Find, and Not To Yield* (Montreal & Kingston: McGill-Queen's University Press, 1978), 59.
30 Supplementary brief: Queen's University to Minister of Education, 21 Dec. 1949, OPF, QUA, locator #1250, box 10. Italics in original.
31 See: James Axtell, *The Making of Princeton University: From Woodrow Wilson to the Present*, (Princeton: Princeton University Press, 2006). There were many inviting parallels between Queen's and Princeton: Presbyterian roots, engrained student traditions, a culture of club life (like the famous Princeton eating clubs), student self-government (e.g., Princeton's Honor Code), and dedication to public service. Principal David Smith in the late twentieth century fell into the habit of likening Queen's to "the Harvard of the North," a less applicable association.
32 Author interview, 19 Nov. 2014.
33 A.W. Jolliffe, "All the History of Man," in Edward Sheffield, ed. *Teaching in the Universities: No One Way* (Montreal & Kingston: McGill-Queen's University Press, 1974), 86.
34 RAQ interviews: C.E.S. Franks, June 2010, and author interview, 15 March 2012.
35 RAQ interviews: Duncan Sinclair, June 2008, and author interview, 15 Oct. 2012.
36 *Queen's Alumni Review*, Sep.-Oct. 1981.
37 Fred Colwell in Michael D. Moore, ed., *George Whalley Remembered* (Kingston: Quarry Press, 1989), 126.
38 Ibid., 121.
39 See: A.A. Travill, *Just a Few Queen's Medical Profiles* (Kingston: Faculty of Medicine, Queen's University, 1992).
40 See: Mark Walters, "'Let Right be Done': A History of the Faculty of Law at Queen's University," *Queen's Law Journal*, vol. 32, #2 (Spring 2007), 314–88.
41 *Queen's Alumni Review* [hereafter QAR], May-June 1978, 19.
42 John Isbister unpublished memoir, *My Life: A Composition in Four Movements*, Chapter Seven: "Queen's." Copy in QUA.
43 RAQ interviews: Ned Franks.
44 "Honorary Degrees," OPF, locator #1250, box 12.
45 See: J.L. Granatstein, *The Ottawa Men: The*

Civil Service Mandarins, 1935–1957 (Toronto: Oxford University Press, 1982).
46 See: Sandra Campbell, *Both Hands: A Life of Lorne Pierce of Ryerson Press* (Montreal & Kingston: McGill-Queen's University Press, 2013).
47 *Report of the Principal of Queen's University to the Board of Trustees: 1961–62* (Kingston: Queen's University 1962). See also Mary Chown, Melva Eagelson, and Thelma Boucher, eds., *A Generous Loyalty: The Queens' Alumnae Memory Book* (Kingston: Queen's Alumni Association, 1992).
48 *Queen's Review*, "My Father Sent Me Down to Queen's," Jan.-Feb. 1962 and Jan.-Feb. 1964; author interview with Robert Little, 21 Nov. 2012.
49 Registrar's Report, *Report of the Principal ... 1961–62*.
50 Jean Royce memo to J.A. Corry, "The Changing Character of the University," QUA, OPF, locator #1252, box 15, file: Registrar.
51 RAQ interviews: Bob Crandall, Aug. 2008.
52 Author interview, 5 May 2011.
53 Senate Office Minutes, 9 Oct. 1850, QUA, locator #1240, box 1, file 1.
54 Neatby, *To Strive ...*, 313.
55 *The Freshman's Handbook, 1959–60*, QUA, Queen's Printed Collection.
56 See: AMS Court files, QUA, locator #3621, box 1, file #8.
57 *The Freshman's Handbook, 1959–60*.
58 AMS Court files, QUA, locator #3621, file #8.
59 See: F.W. Gibson, *To Serve ...*, 105–7.
60 Author interview with James MacIntyre (BA 1995), 27 Sept. 2011.
61 Women at the University of Toronto were subjected to a similar ritual.
62 RAQ interviews: Marilyn Bennett, June 2009, and Meisel, *A Life of Learning*, 275.
63 *Report of the Principal*, 134–7, and file #24: Building Fund Committee, QUA, locator #3621, box 1.
64 Shirley Ross to W.A. Mackintosh, 19 March 1961, QUA, OPF, locator #1250, box 14, file: new physics building.
65 Secretary, Kingston Alumni Branch, 11 March 1961, ibid.
66 Minutes of the Board of Trustees [hereafter MBT], 21 March 1961, and Mackintosh to Corry, 7 April 1961, QUA, locator #1251, box 1, file: Mackintosh-Corry correspondence 1951–61.
67 Price Waterhouse, "Summary of the Review of the Administrative Organization and the Accounting and Administrative Practices – October 1958," QUA, OPF, locator #1251, file: Price Waterhouse.
68 The federal amendment to the Queen's charter stated that the university's vice-chancellor "may or may not be the Principal." When Mackintosh stepped down from the vice-chancellor role in 1965, the titles of principal and vice-chancellor were reunited.
69 Roberta Hamilton, *Setting the Agenda: Jean Royce and the Shaping of Queen's University* (Toronto: University of Toronto Press, 2002), 10.
70 RAQ interviews: Bud Cornelius, July 2009.
71 R.L. Watts, "The Operation of Internal Governance within Queen's University," QUA, MBT, 13 and 14 May 1988.
72 See: QUA, OPF, locator #1252, box 18, file: J.B. Stirling.
73 See: QUA, OPF, locator #1250, box 22, file: University Council 1950–65.
74 W.A.M. Mackintosh to R.H. Common, 6 Aug. 1958, QUA, OPF, locator #1250, box 20, file: Senate, 1931–65.
75 Gibson, *To Serve ...*, 434.
76 Author interview with R.L. Watts, 13 June 2011.
77 Gibson, *To Serve ...*, 432.
78 Ibid., 430.
79 Arthur Keppel-Jones, *A Patriot in Search of a Country* (Kingston: Privately published, 2003), 349.
80 RAQ interviews: John Coleman, July 2009.
81 Cited in RAQ interviews: Jim Brown, May 2010.
82 RAQ interviews: Vivian and Pamela Abrahams, June 2010.
83 Quoted in *Queen's Alumni Review*, Jan.-Feb. 1984, 13.
84 Ibid.
85 Jean Royce, "Changing Nature of the University," QUA, OPF, locator #1252, box 15, file: registrar.
86 RAQ interviews: Merv Daub.
87 RAQ interviews: Barry Batchelor, August 2008.
88 Maureen McCallum Garvie and Jennifer L. Johnson, *Their Leaven of Influence: Deans of Women at Queen's University, 1916–1996* (Kingston: Queen's Alumni Association, 1999), 12.
89 Queen's University Faculty Women's Club collection, QUA, locator #3640, boxes 1 and 2.
90 Janette Hospital Turner, "A Safe Little Bourgeois Cage," in Mary Alice Downie and M.A. Thompson, eds., *Written in Stone: A Kingston Reader* (Kingston: Quarry Press, 1993), 226.
91 Jim Hilborn to author, e-mail of 16 Aug. 2012.

92 *Queen's Journal*, 16 February and 4 October, 1960, and Ed Lauer to author, e-mail of 7 Aug. 2012.
93 Corry, *My Life*, Chap. 8.

CHAPTER TWO

1 C.T. Bissell, ed., *National Conference of Canadian Universities, Proceedings: Canada's Crisis of Higher Education* (Toronto: University of Toronto Press, 1957). In 1957, the NCCU would add "and Colleges" to its title.
2 Douglas Owram, *Born at the Right Time: A History of the Baby-Boom Generation* (Toronto: University of Toronto Press, 1996), Chap. 1.
3 E.F. Sheffield, "Canadian University and College Enrolment Projected to 1965," in *National Conference of Canadian Universities, Proceedings 1955* (Toronto: University of Toronto Press, 1956), 39–45. See also: Paul Axelrod, *Scholars and Dollars: Politics, Economics, and the Universities of Ontario, 1945–1980* (Toronto: University of Toronto Press, 1982), 23.
4 E.F. Sheffield, "A Special Report on our Booming College Campuses," *Canadian Business*, March-April 1959.
5 Bissell, *National Conference*, 19.
6 Ibid., 4–5.
7 Ibid., 249–57.
8 RAQ interviews: John Coleman, July 2009.
9 Axelrod, *Scholars and Dollars*, 4.
10 Garbutt to Corry, 3 July 1965, QUA, OPF, locator #1252, Box 9, file: Gordon Garbutt.
11 Alexrod, *Scholars and Dollars*, 3.
12 J.A. Corry and J.E. Hodgetts, *Democratic Government and Politics* (Toronto: University of Toronto Press, revised 1959), 25 and 63.
13 Ibid., 41.
14 A.B. McKillop, *Matters of the Mind: The University in Ontario, 1791–1950* (Toronto: University of Toronto Press, 1994), 549 and 558.
15 Axelrod, *Scholars and Dollars*, 78.
16 Roger Graham, *Old Man Ontario: Leslie M. Frost* (Toronto: University of Toronto Press, 1990), 387.
17 Mackintosh to Hon. W.J. Dunlop, 25 Sep. 1956, QUA, OPF, locator #1250, Box 11, file: Government Grants (Ontario) 1951–57. Remarkably, Mackintosh was able to convey the entire financial operation of Queen's in eleven double-spaced pages.
18 Mackintosh to G.E. Hall (University of Western Ontario president), 14 March 1960, QUA, OPF, locator #1251, Box 14, file: Government Grants, 1957–61.
19 Corry to John P. Robarts, 21 Dec. 1960, QUA, OPF, locator #1251, Box 14, file: Government Grants, 1957–61, and Corry to Charles Lightbody, 14 Dec. 1965, QUA, OPF, locator #1251, Box 3, correspondence file.
20 Corry to Benson, 8 June 1964, QUA, OPF, locator #1252, Box 3, file: E.J. Benson.
21 Frost to Claude Bissell, 20 Nov. 1963, QUA, OPF, locator #1251, Box 18, file: Advisory Committee of University Affairs.
22 Paul Axelrod's *Scholars and Dollars* provides an excellent chronicle of the unfolding complexity of government-university relations in these years.
23 CPUO Memo to Premier John Robarts, 23 Nov. 1963, QUA, OPF, locator #1251, Box 18, file: Advisory Committee on University Affairs.
24 Corry to Frost, 31 Jan. 1963, QUA, OPF, locator #1251, Box 14, file: Government Grants, 1963–.
25 In 1975, Queen's gave an honorary degree to writer Margaret Laurence. In her novel *The Diviners*, Laurence had suggested that a "Presbyterian is someone who always looks cheerful, because whatever happens, they've expected something much worse."
26 MBT, 8 and 9 Feb., 1963.
27 Corry to Frost, 18 March 1963, QUA, OPF, locator #1251, Box 14, file: Government grants 1963–.
28 MBT, 18 and 19 Oct. 1963, and *Queen's University, Report of the Principal*, 1963–64, 191.
29 Corry to Robarts, 13 Nov. 1963, QUA, OPF, locator #1251, Box 14, file: Government grants, 1963–.
30 See: Duncan McDowall, *The Sum of the Satisfactions: Canada in the Age of National Accounting* (Montreal & Kingston: McGill-Queen's University Press, 2008).
31 See: J.L. Granatstein, *Ottawa Men: The Civil Service Mandarins, 1935–1957* (Toronto: Oxford University Press, 1982).
32 RAQ interviews: Bernard Trotter, July 2008.
33 Anecdotes abound about Deutsch's canny ability to manage people who initially mistook his manner as ineffectual. Pat Sims, his secretary at the Economic Council of Canada, recalled that in the council's start-up phase, a bumptious young economist insisted on an immediate meeting with Council Chairman Deutsch. Why, he demanded, did he not have a carpet in his office, like all the other young economic wizards hired by Deutsch? The chairman quietly weathered this outburst of umbrage and, after a moment's pause, simply said: "Why not take mine?" The young economist beat a sheepish retreat.

34 RAQ interviews: John Bannister, July 2009.
35 RAQ interviews: Bob Crandall, Aug. 2008.
36 QUA, OPF, locator #1252, file: Computer (electric) 1959–.
37 See: *Report of the Royal Commission on Higher Education*, June 1962, 102–3, in QUA, John Deutsch papers, locator #1022, Box 44, file: New Brunswick: Royal Commission on Higher Education in New Brunswick.
38 See: Corry to Frost, 8 Jan. 1964, QUA, OPF, Box 14, file: Government grants, 1963–.
39 Axelrod, *Scholars and Dollars*, 93. The Deutsch projections coincided almost exactly with projections done a year earlier by Professor R.W. Jackson, soon to be appointed as the first director of the Ontario Institute for Studies in Education.
40 Frost to R.D. Harkness, 22 May 1963, QUA, OPF, locator #1252, Box 9, file: Leslie Frost.
41 One notes the remarkable coincidence of Ontario's university funding debate with the national debate over universal medicare in Canada in these same years. In each instance, the crucial issues were accessibility for all citizens, equitable treatment for both user and provider, and the buffering of the autonomy of providers of the service, whether medical or academic.
42 Corry to Robarts, 25 Nov. 1963, QUA, OPF, locator #1252, Box 18, file: Advisory Committee on University Affairs.
43 J.A. Corry, "The University in the Modern State," in J.A. Corry, *Farewell the Ivory Tower: Universities in Transition* (Montreal & Kingston: McGill-Queen's University Press, 1970), 24.
44 Frost to Corry, 10 Feb. 1964, QUA, OPF, locator #1252, Box 12, file: J.R. McCarthy, Superintendent of Curriculum.
45 RAQ interviews: Bernard Trotter, July 2008; interview with author, 16 Feb. 2011; and J.A. Corry, *My Life and Work: A Happy Partnership* (Kingston: Queen's University, 1981), 178.
46 Corry, *My Life and Work*, 178.
47 Ibid., 214.
48 Corry to E.D. Hall [President of the University of Western Ontario], 9 Nov. 1964, QUA, OPF, locator #1251, Box 19, file: AUCC.
49 Corry was getting an honorary degree at Western. QUA, OPF, locator #1252, Box 20, file: University of Western Ontario.
50 See: A.A. Travill, *Just a Few: Queen's Medical Profiles* (Kingston: Queen's Faculty of Medicine, 1991), 8–13.
51 See: Margaret Angus, *Kingston General Hospital: A Social and Institutional History* (Montreal & Kingston: McGill-Queen's University Press, 1973) and Jessie V. Deslauriers, *Hotel Dieu Hospital, 1845–1995: The House of Tender Care – Continuing to Serve* (Kingston: Brown & Martin, 1995).
52 See: Jacalyn Duffin, *History of Medicine: A Scandalously Short Introduction* (Toronto: University of Toronto Press, 1999).
53 *Report of the Principal of Queen's University to the Board of Trustees, 1961–62*, 55.
54 Dr Robert More [head of pathology] to Corry, 27 October 1961, QUA, OPF, locator #1251, Box 15, file: Dean of Medicine.
55 Agnew, Peckham and Associates, "A Study of the Intern and Residency Situation at the Kingston General Hospital," Kingston General Hospital Archives, President and CEO fonds. This would appear to be the only existent copy of the report in Kingston.
56 Mackintosh to Bingham, 15 Feb. 1956, QUA, OPF, locator # 1252, file; Dr D.D.C. Bingham. See: Travill, *Just a Few*, 14–21.
57 Stuart Vandewater, "November 22, 1962: Future of Queen's Medical School: Resurrection or Bury It? A Memoir," QUA, Vandewater Papers, locator #2014.4 SE.
58 MBT, 15 June 1962.
59 Agnew, Peckham and Associates, "A Study …"
60 Donald B. Jennings, ed., *A Scrapbook of Memories, 1954–2004: An Historical Tribute to the Sesquicentennial* (Belleville: Epic Press, 2004), 221.
61 MBT, 15 June 1962.
62 John Hamilton to Corry, Sept. 1961, and J.A. MacFarlane to Corry, 5 Oct. 1961, QUA, OPF, locator #1252, Box 15, file: Dean of Medicine.
63 See: Edward Shorter, *Partnership for Excellence: Medicine at the University of Toronto and Academic Hospitals* (Toronto: University of Toronto Press, 2013), 80–5.
64 Vandewater, "November 22, 1962" [memoir].
65 RAQ interviews: Bernard Trotter, 15 July 2008. David Walker, a young English medical student who arrived in 1965, tells the story of how Botterell recruited him to Queen's. Walker's father had known Botterell in wartime England, and thereby Botterell met David on a visit to England in the summer of 1965. Walker had been toying with the idea of immigrating to Canada. "If you're going to come away eventually, why don't you come now and go to medical school?" Botterell propositioned him. Walker replied that this couldn't be "easy." A nonplussed Botterell responded: "I'm the dean; it's that easy." Four decades later, David Walker would become Dean

of Medicine at Queen's. RAQ interviews: David Walker, 26 July 2011.
66 RAQ interviews: Dr Vivian and Pamela Abrahams, 14 June 2010.
67 For an example of the setting out of these terms to individual faculty members, see Corry to Dr R. McGaughey, c. 1965, QUA, OPF, locator #1251, Box 3.
68 Botterell to Corry, 20 Jan. 1965, QUA, OPF, locator #1252, Box 15, file: Faculty of Medicine 1965–66.
69 MBT, 17 and 18 Nov. 1967.
70 For a synopsis, see: E. Harry Botterell, "Recent Developments in the Faculty of Medicine, 1962–1966," MBT, 14 and 15 Oct. 1966.
71 RAQ interviews: David Symington, 12 Aug. 2008, and Roy Walmsley, 16 June 2010.
72 *Report of the Principal ... 1961–62*, 66; QUA, OPF, locator #1252, Box 13, file: School of Nursing and Box 16, file: Nursing School, 1964–68. See also: E. Jean Hill and Rondalyn Kirkwood, *Breaking Down the Barriers: Nursing Science at Queen's University* (Kingston: School of Nursing, Queen's University, 1991).
73 Weir to Corry, 27 Jan. 1964, QUA, OPF, locator #1252, Box 16, File: Nursing School 1964–68.
74 R.J. Hand, "The Case for Graduate Education in Business," *Queen's Quarterly* 68 (Autumn 1961): 474 and 479.
75 See: Mervin Daub and P. Bruce Buchan, *Getting Down to Business: A History of Business Education at Queen's, 1889–1999* (Kingston: McGill-Queen's University Press, 1999).
76 RAQ interviews: Bob Crandall, Aug. 2008.
77 Daub and Buchan, *Getting Down to Business*, 48.
78 RAQ interviews: Bruce Buchan, July 2009, and author's interview, 7 November 2011. See: Daub and Buchan, *Getting Down to Business*, 54.
79 RAQ interviews: Pat Galasso, 18 June 2010.
80 Basmajian to Corry, 2 Oct. 1964, QUA, OPF, locator #1250, Box 18, file: School of Physical and Health Education 1946–65.
81 M.L. Howell to Basmajian, 5 Jan. 1965, ibid.
82 See: file, School of Physical and Health Education, 1966–72, QUA, OPF, locator #1254, Box 3.
83 James Brown, "Brownian Years at Queen's: A Brief Review by J.H. Brown," RAQ interviews files, 2010.
84 George Richardson, *Queen's Engineers: A Century of Applied Science, 1893–1993* (Kingston: Faculty of Applied Science, 1992), 71.
85 RAQ interviews: Jim Whitley, July 2010.
86 File: Mining Department, QUA, OPF, locator #1251, Box 8.
87 See: R.H. Clark Papers, QUA, locator #5096.3.
88 File: Faculty of Law 1963–64, QUA, OPF, locator #1250, Box 14.
89 Quoted in Mark Walters's excellent article, "'Let Right Be Done': A History of the Faculty of Law at Queen's University," *Queen's Law Journal* 32 (2007): 332.
90 RAQ interviews: Bob Little, June 2009.
91 RAQ interviews: Dennis Magnusson, Sept. 2010.
92 Corry to R.H. More, 10 Dec. 1963, QUA, OPF, locator #1250, Box 18, file: Department of Pathology.
93 George Harrower to Corry, 9 Nov. 1962, OPF, locator #1250, Box 11, file: School of Graduate Studies, and Corry to Donald Gordon, OPF, locator #1252, Box 9, file: Donald Gordon.
94 "Address by Hon. John Robarts, Prime Minister and Minister of Education, 10 Sept. 1962," QUA, OPF, locator #1250, Box 11, file: School of Graduate Studies.
95 See: Corry, *My Life*, 216–19.
96 *Report of the Principal ... 1967–68*, 107.
97 Corry to W.J.S. Melvin, 23 Aug. 1965, QUA, OPF, locator #1252, file: Athletics – Intercollegiate. The GSS initially affiliated with the AMS, but would eventually break away, realizing, as Corry had foreseen, their differentness.
98 Ernest Sirluck, "The Future Development of Graduate Programmes in Ontario," *Queen's Quarterly*, Summer 1968, 195–207.
99 Interview with Hilary Richardson, 22 Sept. 2011. I am indebted to Hilary Richardson for her many superb vignettes of Douglas Library history published in the library's house newsletters, *Factotum* and *Shelf Life*.
100 RAQ interviews: Lin Good, July 2008, author interview with Lin Good, 14 May 2012, and RAQ interviews: Barbara Aitken, July 2010.
101 Interview with Lin Good, 5 March 2013.
102 *Report of the Principal ... 1967–68*, 121.
103 Roberta Hamilton, *Setting the Agenda: Jean Royce and the Shaping of Queen's University* (Toronto: University of Toronto Press, 2002), 10.
104 See Alfred Bader, *Chemistry and Art: Further Adventures of a Chemist Collector* (London: Weidenfeld & Nicolson, 2008), 216–17. While at Queen's, Bader benefited from scholarships awarded by Royce's office.
105 Corry to all department heads, 8 Oct.1965, QUA, OPF, locator #1251, Box 12, file: Arts and Science Faculty, 1965– .
106 *Report of the Principal ... 1961–62*, 13.
107 Garbutt to Corry, 4 July 1965, QUA, OPF, locator #1252, Box 9, file: Garbutt.

108 S.L.G. Chapman, Richview Collegiate Institute, to Corry, 13 Feb. 1962, QUA, OPF, locator #1252, Box 15, file: Registrar.
109 Corry to Alan Cameron, 24 Oct, 1967, QUA, OPF, locator #1252, Box 4.
110 Conn to Corry, 14 April 1966, QUA, OPF, locator #1252, Box 15, file: Registrar.
111 Corry to Cameron, 24 Oct. 1967, QUA, OPF, locator #1252, Box 4.
112 Royce to Conn, 30 April 1965, QUA, OPF, locator #1252, Box 15, file: Registrar.
113 RAQ interviews: Margaret Hooey, July 2008.
114 Robin Ross, "Report on the Office of the Registrar, Queen's University," 15 July 1966, QUA, OPF, locator #1252, Box 15, file: Registrar.
115 Words of Eleanor Smith, an old friend who met Royce on a downtown street shortly thereafter, as quoted in Hamilton, *Queen's, Queen's, Queen's* (Kingston: Alumni Association of Queen's University), 158.
116 MBT, 25 and 26 Oct. 1968, and Hamilton, *Queen's* ..., 158.
117 Hamilton, *Queen's* ..., 143–5.
118 [Bernard Trotter], *Queen's University, 1963–1968: Some Facts and Figures* (Kingston: Queen's University, Office of Academic Planning, 1968).

CHAPTER THREE
1 MBT, 1 Nov. 1969.
2 *QJ*, 12 Sept. 1969.
3 Deutsch to Trudeau, 23 Nov. 1968, QUA, OPF, locator #1252, Box 1.
4 Vancouver *Province*, 13 Jan. 1969.
5 MBT, 17 and 18 Feb., 1967.
6 *Tricolor*, 1969, 29.
7 Deutsch to L.B. Pearson, 10 Oct. 1967, QUA, John Deutsch Papers, locator #1022, Series 1, Box 8.
8 Deutsch to Gordon Gibson, 8 April, 1968, ibid.
9 Donald Gordon to Corry, 3 May 1967, QUA, OPF, locator #1252, Box 9, file: Donald Gordon.
10 MBT, 26 and 27 May 1967.
11 Deutsch to Forde, 26 Sept. 1968, John Deutsch Papers, locator #1022, Series 1, Box 8. Forde had been Australian High Commissioner to Canada in the 1950s.
12 Deutsch installation speech, 8 November 1968, QUA, OPF, locator #1252, Box 5, file: Deutsch installation.
13 See "Deutsch Installation" file, ibid.
14 Mers Kutt was appointed director of the computing centre in 1965 after employment in companies like IBM and Honeywell. Much of his energy at Queen's was expended on managing access to the university's mainframe computer. For faculty and students, this meant hours of punching computers and booking time on the mainframe, often in the middle of the night. Sensing that the future of computing lay in placing processing capacity on the user's desktop, not in some distant centre, Kutt would leave Queen's late in 1968 and create what would later be called a "start-up company" dedicated to building a personal computer. This he did by 1971, when his pioneering MCM/70 micro-computer was unveiled. See Zbigniew Stachniak, *Inventing the PC: The MCM/70 Story* (Montreal & Kingston: McGill-Queen's University Press, 2011).
15 Published in 1970 under AUCC auspices in Ottawa.
16 Author interview with Jayant Lele, 4 April 2013.
17 Helen Robinson to Deutsch, 15 Dec. 1967, QUA, John Deutsch Papers, locator #1022, Series 1, Box 8. See Howard Adelman, ed., *The University Game* (Toronto: Anansi Press, 1968).
18 MBT, 26 and 27 Feb. 1966.
19 J.A. Corry, *My Life and Work: A Happy Partnership* (Kingston: Queen's University, 1981), 199.
20 MBT, 26 and 27 Feb. 1966.
21 RAQ interviews: Joan Webster, July 2009.
22 Gibson to Corry, 5 Dec. 1966, QUA, OPF, locator #1252, Box 19, file: VP (Academic). See also: James Perkins, *The University in Transition* (Princeton, NJ: Princeton University Press, 1966).
23 *University Governance at Queen's: 1/ Report of the Joint Committee on University Government & 2/ Second Report of the Committee on Structure of the Senate* (Kingston: Queen's University at Kingston, 1969).
24 F.W. Gibson, in his history of Queen's from 1917 to 1961, *To Serve and Yet Be Free*, notes that the trustees had at times paid lip service to the idea of consulting faculty on the choice of a principal (a gesture forced on them by Charlotte Whitton when Principal Wallace was selected in the 1930s). In 1960, the trustees, anxious to retain Corry's talents for Queen's, dispensed with a formal search committee altogether.
25 Royce's appointment as the committee's secretary would seem to indicate that she remained in the university's inner circle just months before her fateful February 1968 meeting with Corry, at which the principal clumsily announced her accelerated resignation. Surely, if there had been an ongoing plot to oust the registrar she would never have been invited to take such an instrumental role in Corry's restructuring committee.

26 Corry, *My Life*, 203.
27 Ibid., 204.
28 Corry to Gordon, 2 March 1968, QUA, OPF, locator #1252, Box 9, file: Donald Gordon.
29 R.L. Watts, "The Operation of Internal Governance within Queen's University," MBT, 13 and 14 May 1988.
30 Deutsch to Knox, 9 Dec. 1968, John Deutsch Papers, locator #1022, Series 1, Box 8.
31 Author interview, 6 Nov. 2012.
32 AMS President Charles "Chuck" Edwards in 1968.
33 RAQ interviews: Cathy Perkins, June 2009.
34 RAQ interviews: Stephanie Deutsch, June–July 2008.
35 Deutsch to Howard Ross, 11 Sept. 1968, QUA, OPF, locator #1252, Box 1, correspondence file. See Doug Owram, *Born at the Right Time: A History of the Baby-Boom Generation* (Toronto: University of Toronto Press, 1996), 184.
36 *Report of the Principal's Committee on Teaching and Learning* (Kingston: Queen's University, October 1969), foreword.
37 "Speaking Frankly," 27 March 1969, reproduced in part in *Campus*, vol. 5, #2 (March 1969).
38 Ross McGregor to author, e-mail of 12 Nov. 2012.
39 All preceding quotations from *Report of the Principal's Committee...*
40 See: "Arts Students Gain a Voice in Curriculum," *Tricolor*, 1969.
41 Minutes of the Arts and Science Faculty Board, 17 Oct. and 12 Dec. 1969.
42 Ibid.
43 Arthur Keppel-Jones. *A Patriot in Search of a Country* (Kingston; privately published, 2003), 354.
44 See Martin L. Friedland, *The University of Toronto: A History* (Toronto: University of Toronto Press, 2002), 531–3.
45 See, for instance: RAQ interviews: Brian Osborne, July 2009.
46 Bruce [Buchan?] to Deutsch, 1 May 1980, QUA, OPF, locator #1254, Box 22, file: Spring convocation, 1980.
47 Barott, Marshall, Merritt and Barott Master Plan, May 1961, QUA, OPF, locator #1252, Box 12, file: Master Plan for Campus Development.
48 *Academic Development at Queen's University: Report #1, September 1969*, supplement to *Queen's Gazette*, Vol. 1, #31.
49 *The Implications of Constant Student Enrolment During the Period 1975–80*, supplement to *Queen's Gazette*, Vol. 4, #34.
50 Deutsch to Colin Mackay, 16 Dec. 1968, QUA, OPF, locator #1252, Box 1, correspondence.
51 Dean Jim Brown of Applied Science, a champion of modernizing the university, contested the wisdom of this policy in 1965. An on-campus interview, he argued, might obviate the possibility of hiring a "grossly unattractive man, the man with poor hearing, sloppy habits ..." See: QUA, OPF, locator #1252, Box 7, file: Department of Civil Engineering.
52 RAQ interviews: Stewart Fyfe, May 2009.
53 RAQ interviews, Albert Fell, May 2009.
54 RAQ interviews: Madan Joneja, June 2009.
55 RAQ interviews: David Bonham, June 2009.
56 Author interview with Mervin Daub, 5 May 2011.
57 Author interview with C.E.S. Franks, 15 March 2012.
58 See: Donald Wright, *The Professionalization of History in English Canada* (Toronto: University of Toronto Press, 2005), Chap. 5.
59 QUA, OPF, locator #1251, Box 7, File: Department of History.
60 MBT, 9 and 10 May 1969.
61 QUA, OPF, locator #1250, Box 19, file: Sabbatical years, 1931–64.
62 *Statement of Academic Freedom and Tenure*, supplement to *Queen's Gazette*, 20 May 1969.
63 See: Senate Committee on Appointment, Promotion, Tenure and Leave, *Report to Senate: Regulations Governing Appointments, Tenure and Dismissal*, supplement to *Queen's Gazette*, 26 April 1977.
64 *Reports on the Appointment of Deans and Department Heads*, supplement to *Queen's Gazette*, 14 December 1971.
65 J.J. Deutsch installation speech, Nov. 1968, QUA, OPF, locator #1252, Box 5, file: Deutsch installation.
66 *Report of the Senate Committee on Grievance, Discipline and Related Matters, May 1971*, Supplement to *Queen's Gazette*, 22 June 1971.
67 RAQ interviews: Margaret Hooey, July 2008; and Jill Harris, June 2009.
68 *Queen's University Parking Policy, Sept. 1970*, supplement to *Queen's Gazette*, 31 Aug. 1970.
69 RAQ interviews: David Bonham, June 2009.
70 RAQ interviews: Mabel Corlett, June 2009. Corlett was actually appointed to the Faculty of Arts and Science, but since geologists in that faculty were cross-appointed to Applied Science, she became the first woman to break the glass ceiling in engineering.
71 Alexandra Johnston, as recounted to the author, Aug. 2015.

72 See, for instance, the career of Barbara Aitken (BA 1961) in various Kingston libraries. Aitken's husband, George, was a professor of electrical engineering at Queen's. RAQ interviews: Barbara Aitken, July 2010.
73 RAQ interviews: Jill Harris, July 2009.
74 RAQ interviews: Elizabeth Greene, June 2009.
75 RAQ interviews: Marion Meyer, May 2009.
76 Author interview with Lin Good, 12 May 2012, and RAQ interviews: Lin Good, July 2008. Lower revelled in his reputation for what he described in his memoir as "blunt plain-speaking," although he acknowledged that he suffered from a "lack of foresight in estimating the effect of words on others ..." See: A.R.M. Lower, *My First Seventy-five Years* (Toronto: Macmillan, 1969), 312. See also: Roberta Hamilton, *Setting the Agenda: Jean Royce and the Shaping of Queen's University* (Toronto: University of Toronto Press, 2002), 118.
77 Author interview with Beverley Baines, 4 May 2012.
78 RAQ interviews: Bettyanne Gargaro, June 2011. Gargaro would stay thirty-six years at Queen's.
79 Charles Lightbody to Corry, 25 Feb. 1964, QUA, OPF, locator #1250, file: History Department, 1935–.
80 QUA, OPF, locator #1250, Box 21, file: trustees 1963.
81 RAQ interviews: Lin Good, July 2008.
82 Author interview, 14 May 2012.
83 Neatby had arrived from the University of Saskatchewan as a full professor and was therefore not really the product of Queen's faculty promotion ladder. Other women, like physicist Alice Vibert Douglas, had earlier attained the rank of full professor by climbing the Queen's promotion ladder.
84 All statistics and quotations taken from *Report of the Principal's Committee on the Status of Women at Queen's University*, supplement to *Queen's Gazette*, 28 Feb. 1974.
85 RAQ interviews: Eveline Flint, June 2010.
86 RAQ interviews: John Coleman, July 2009.
87 QUA, Association of Women Teaching at Queen's fonds, locator #2303.9.
88 Dorothy Farr and Natalie Luckyj, *From Women's Eyes: Women Painters in Canada* (Kingston: Agnes Etherington Art Centre, 1976). See also: *Queen's Alumni Review*, March-April 1976. Author interview, Dorothy Farr, 13 May 2013.
89 See George Rawlyk and Kevin Quinn, *The Redeemed of the Lord Say So: A History of Queen's Theological College, 1912–1972* (Montreal & Kingston: McGill-Queen's University Press, 1980).
90 Rawlyk & Quinn, *The Redeemed of the Lord*, 188–9.
91 QUA, OPF, locator #1254, Box 3, file: Theology College, 1968–72.
92 MBT, 12 and 13 May 1973.
93 Gow to Deutsch, 5 Jan. 1968, QUA, OPF, locator #1251, Box 8, file: Political Studies Department.
94 Deutsch to F.A. Milligan (Canada Council), 12 Nov. 1968, QUA, OPF, locator #1252, Box 1, file: correspondence.
95 MBT, 28 Sept., 1968.
96 MBT, 25 and 26 Oct., 1968.
97 Author interview, Allan Armit, 23 Nov. 2012.
98 QUA, OPF, locator #1252, Box 12, file: McArthur College of Education 1961–65. MBT, 28 Aug. 1964.
99 Ready to Deutsch, 27 Jan. 1971, QUA, OPF, locator #1254, Box 2, file: McArthur College of Education.
100 Author interview with Tom Williams; and RAQ interviews: Tom Williams, June 2011.
101 Armit interview.
102 Minutes of the University Senate [hereafter MUS], 27 April 1972 and 27 Sept., 1973.
103 See Gordon Bertram, *The Contribution of Education to Economic Growth*, Staff Study # 12 (Ottawa: Economic Council of Canada, 1966), 63–4.
104 David Dodge, *Returns to Investment in University Training: The Case of Canadian Accountants, Engineers and Scientists* (Kingston: Queen's Industrial Relations Centre, 1972), 113. See also Paul Axelrod, *Scholars and Dollars: Politics, Economics, and the Universities of Ontario, 1945–1980* (Toronto: University of Toronto Press, 1982), Chap. 8.
105 MBT, 14 and 15 May 1971.
106 MBT, 11 and 12 Feb. and 14 April 1972, and MUS, 21 Dec. 1972.
107 *New York Times*, 1 Jan. 1971.
108 MBT, 12 Oct. 1973.
109 Author interview with Chris Redmond, 23 Jan. 2012.
110 Author interview with Ron Watts, 19 April 2013.

CHAPTER FOUR

1 Author interview, Bill Sirman, 29 May 2013.
2 See: H.P. "Herb" Dickey, "Bertha Bailey and Her Boys," *Queen's Alumni Review*, March-April 1984. The Bailey row house was bought by

Queen's in the mid-1970s, restored, and eventually moved around the corner to Alfred Street to allow the construction of the Stauffer Library. The restoration won a national heritage award.

3   See: T.H.B. Symons and R.L. Watts, "The Residence Hall and The University," *Queen's Quarterly* 64 (Winter 1957–58), 557.

4   Mary Chown, Melva Eagleson, and Thelma Boucher, eds., *A Generous Loyalty: The Queen's Alumnae Book* (Kingston: Queen's Alumni Association, 1992).

5   "Report to the Ban Righ Board by B.E. Bryce – 6 April 1963," QUA, OPF, locator #1252, Box 3, file: Ban Righ Board 1938–70. Buried in her report was an acknowledgment that not everything was rosy under her watch: that year there had been four pregnancies, an attempted suicide, and a nervous breakdown.

6   Catherine Perkins, "Life in Adelaide Hall," in Chown, et al., *A Generous Loyalty*, 48.

7   Author interview, Claude Sherren, 26 Nov. 2012.

8   AMS Minutes [hereafter AMSM], 31 Oct. 1961, QUA, Collection #3621.

9   *QJ*, 10 Nov. 1961.

10 RAQ interviews: Christine Fleig-Hamm, July 2008.

11 RAQ interviews: Brian Osborne, July 2009.

12 RAQ interviews: Roy Walmsley, June 2010.

13 Gérard Bessette, *Le Semestre* (Montreal: Québec/Amérique 1979).

14 RAQ interviews: Carlos Prado, May 2010.

15 See: David Helwig, *The Name of Things: A Memoir* (Erin, Ontario: Porcupine's Quill, 2006), 97.

16 RAQ interviews: Fred Euringer, May 2009, and Erdmute Waldhauer, *Drama at Queen's: From Its Beginnings to 1991* (Kingston: Typecast, 1991).

17 See: QUA, OPF, locator #1250, Box 10, file: Faculty Association 1945–62 and QUA, Queen's Printed Collection, QUFA Box 1, file: Newsletters 1965– .

18 Corry in the 1963 QUFA Annual Report, in QUA, OPF, locator #1250, Box 10, file: Faculty Association 1945–62.

19 See: Doug Owram, *Born at the Right Time: A History of the Baby-Boom Generation* (Toronto: University of Toronto Press, 1996), Chap. 9. Owram warns of oversimplifying the homogeneity of "youth radicalism" in the sixties.

20 *QJ*, 31 Oct. 1961.

21 AMSM, 16 Feb. 1962. A "Q" could only be added to a Queen's jacket by certified participants in intercollegiate sports.

22 *QJ*, 22 Nov. 1962.

23 *QJ*, 16 Feb. 1962, and AMSM, 23 Jan. 1962.

24 *QJ*, 19 Oct. 1963.

25 AMSM, 1 March 1966.

26 *QJ*, 26 Nov. 1965. See Richard Harris, *Democracy in Kingston: A Social Movement in Urban Politics* (Montreal & Kingston: McGill-Queen's University Press, 1988), 67–70.

27 QUA, AMS Papers, locator #3621, Box 3, file #66: Kingston Community Project.

28 *QJ*, 4 March 1966.

29 Author interviews, Chris Redmond, 23 Jan. 2012, and Wilf Day, 16 Feb. 2012.

30 *QJ*, 1 Oct. 1968.

31 *QJ*, 21 Sept. 1966 and 8 Nov. 1968.

32 *QJ*, 27 October 1967.

33 *QJ*, 6 Oct. and 24 Nov. 1966.

34 *QJ*, 27 Oct. 1961.

35 *QJ*, 18 Nov. 1960.

36 AMSM, 8 March 1966.

37 Author interview, Chris Redmond, 23 Jan. 2012.

38 *QJ*, 10 Nov. 1961. Susie's name was variously spelled with a "z" and an "s."

39 FREC stood for Frosh Regulation Enforcement Committee. See: Josef Reeve, "Pillar of Wisdom," NFB Documentary, 1970.

40 See: Joy Parr, ed., *Still Running: Personal Stories by Queen's Women Celebrating the Fiftieth Anniversary of the Marty Scholarship* (Kingston: Queen's University Alumnae Association, 1987).

41 Arts and Science Undergraduate Society papers, QUA, locator #3643, Box 6, file: merger.

42 *QJ*, 22 Nov. 1963.

43 *QJ*, 2 Feb. 1967. In the 30 January plebiscite, 411 members of Levana approved the merger and 103 opposed it. Males in the Arts Society overwhelmingly approved it.

44 *QJ*, 25 Sept. 1969.

45 AMSM, 30 Sept. 1969.

46 *QJ*, 19 Oct. 1971.

47 See: Marney McDiarmid, "From Mouth to Mouth: An Oral History of Lesbians and Gays in Kingston from World War II to 1980," MA thesis, Queen's University, 1999.

48 *Golden Words* [hereafter GW], 26 Sept. 1973, and *QJ*, 2 Oct. 1973.

49 McDiarmid, "From Mouth to Mouth," 70.

50 *The Body Politic*, March/April 1974, 23.

51 AMSM, 2 Oct. 1975.

52 *QJ*, 1 Oct., 1971 and Minutes of the Queen's Senate, 25 Sept. 1971.

53 *QJ*, 2 Feb. 1967.

54 G. Watt to Corry, 5 Nov. 1965, OPF, locator #1251, Box 11, file; AMS 1965–66.

55 AMSM, 4 Oct. 1966.

56 MBT, 14 and 15 Oct. 1966.

57 *QJ*, 22 Sept. and 27 Oct. 1967.
58 *QJ*, 16 Feb. 1968.
59 *QJ*, 15 March 1968.
60 *QJ*, 6 Nov. 1969. Only 664 voted for retention.
61 *QJ*, 13 Nov. 1967.
62 AMSM, 2 Oct. 1967.
63 Author interview, Dan Burns, 5 Nov. 2012.
64 AMSM, 23 Jan. and 5 Feb. 1968.
65 *QJ*, 16 Feb. 1968.
66 *QJ*, 8 March 1968.
67 Author interview, Ross McGregor, 6 Nov. 2012, and *QJ*, 11 Feb. 1969.
68 AMSM, 4 March, 1969.
69 Author interview, Brian Rogers, 5 Nov. 2012.
70 *QJ*, 6 and 13 Nov. 1969.
71 AMS *Forum*, Sept. 1968.
72 Author interviews, Alan Broadbent, 6 Nov. 2012, and Dan Burns, 5 Nov. 2012.
73 *QJ*, 12 March 1970.
74 *Alma Mater Matter*, 18 March 1970. The *Matter* was the new name of the AMS newsletter.
75 MUS, 9 Feb. 1970.
76 MUS, 28 May 1970.
77 MBT, 16 and 17 Oct. 1970. When it became apparent that past AMS presidents (often now living far from campus) found it difficult to attend meetings, the Board allowed current AMS vice-presidents to sit as student observers with their president.
78 *Tricolor 1973* provides a comprehensive synopsis of AMS activities in 1972–73.
79 *The Principal's Report, 1973–74*, 15.
80 *QJ*, 15 Feb. 1972.
81 AMSM, 31 May and 4 July 1973.
82 AMSM, 22 Nov. 1973.
83 AMSM, 6 May 1973.
84 Marvin Bloos, *How to Lose a Million: A Report of AMS Business Practices and Other Matters*, 12 Sept. 1973, QUA, AMS Records, locator #3621, Box 8.
85 See: Box 10, file: Restructuring the AMS, 1973–74.
86 MBT, 1 Nov. 1968.
87 MBT, 17 and 18 Nov. 1967.
88 *QJ*, 18 March 1968.
89 See: Maureen McCallum Garvie and Jennifer Johnson, *Their Leaven of Influence: Deans of Women at Queen's University, 1916–1996*, Kingston: Alumni Association of Queen's University, 1999, Chap. 7.
90 MBT, 15 and 16 Oct. 1965, and 27 and 28 Oct. 1967.
91 Speech notes on student housing problem, QUA, OPF, Box 25, file: invitations accepted and speeches 1980–81, and AMS President Donna Finley to Alderman Lois Miller, Sept. 1980, ibid., Box 15, file: AMS general 1980–84.
92 *QJ*, 8 March 1968.
93 D.H. Upton to Corry, April 1965, QUA, OPF, locator #1251, box 8, file: Student Health Services.
94 MBT, 9 April 1964, and QUA, OPF, locator #1251, Box 8, file: Student Health Services.
95 *Report of the Principal of Queen's to the Board of Trustees, 1965–66*, 123–4, and RAQ interviews: Marilyn Bennett, June 2009.
96 *QJ*, 2 March 1967.
97 Author interview, Diana Inkster, 24 May 2011.
98 Author interview, Dr Hans Westenberg, 5 Feb. 2013, and RAQ interviews: Marilyn Bennett, June 2009.
99 QUA, OPF, locator #1251, Box 15, file: Medical Faculty 1967.
100 QUA, OPF, Box 9, file: Leonard Foundation.
101 MBT, 19 Nov. 1971.
102 QUA, OPF, locator #31252, Box 10, file: Leonard Foundation. See also: James Rattray Memorial Trust, MBT, 19 Sept. 1975.
103 *Report of the Senate Committee on Grievance, Discipline, and Related Matters*, Supplement to the *Queen's Gazette* Vol. 3, #21, 1971.
104 QUA, AMS Records, locator #3621, Box 8, file: Brief to Senate Discipline Committee on AMS Constables, March 1970.
105 Ibid., unsigned memo of 1969–70, Box 9, file: Judicial Commission 1969–70.
106 *QJ*, 13 April, 1971.
107 Alexander to Watts, 13 Feb. 1975, QUA, OPF, locator #1254, box 28.
108 See Merv Daub, *Gael Force: A Century of Football at Queen's* (Montreal and Kingston: McGill-Queen's University Press, 1996), and Hendrik Willem Pardoel, *A Compilation of Queen's Athletics and Sports Teams: 1873–2004*, 3 vols. (Kingston: Queen's Athletics and Recreation, 2005).
109 MBT, 1 Nov. 1969.
110 "Some Comparative Figures for Queen's University," QUA, OPF, locator #1254, Box 28, file: financing 1979–82, and "Queen's University, 1963–1968: Some Facts and Figures," produced 16 Dec. 1968, QUA, Merv Daub Papers, locator #1022.1.
111 MBT, 1 Nov. 1968.
112 John Meisel, *A Life of Learning and Other Pleasures: John Meisel's Tale* (Yarker, Ontario: Wintergreen, 2012), 169 and 177.
113 RAQ interviews: John Hartwick, May 2010.
114 See: Arthur Keppel-Jones, *A Patriot in Search of a Country* (Kingston: privately published, 2003), 333.

115 MUS, 28 Oct. 1971, and "Evolution of the Department of Family Medicine," in Donald B. Jennings, ed., *A Scrapbook of Memories, 1954–2004: An Historical Tribute to the Sesquicentennial* (Kingston: Faculty of Health Sciences, 2004), 189–95.
116 See: *Reports on the Appointment of Deans and Departmental Heads, Queen's Gazette*, Vol. III, #41, 1941.
117 "Queen's University, 1963–1968: Some Facts & Figures," 16 Dec. 1968, Merv Daub Papers, QUA.
118 Author interview, Daniel McConnachie, 17 Nov. 2011.
119 See: Robin Mathews and James Steele, eds., *The Struggle for Canadian Universities* (Toronto: New Press, 1969).
120 MBT, 25 and 26 Oct. 1968.
121 RAQ interviews: Christopher Crowder, July 2009.
122 Author interview, Geoff Smith, 12 Feb. 2013.
123 J.A. Corry to Queen's Faculty Association, QUA, OPF, locator #1250, Box 10, file: Faculty 1945–62.
124 MBT, 15 Sept. 1972.
125 "Statement on Academic Freedom and Tenure," *Queen's Gazette*, 3, 17, 20 May 1969.
126 Gosse to Corry, 31 March 1965, QUA, OPF, locator #1250, box 10, file: Faculty Association.
127 Queen's University Faculty Association *Newsletter*, Sept. 1965, in QUA, Queen's Printed Collection, QUFA, Box 1.
128 David Dodge, et al., QUFA Salary Brief, QUA, OPF, locator #1252, Box 8: Faculty Association, 1970.
129 Corry to Col. D.B. Weldon, 18 June 1965, QUA OPF, locator #1252, Box 20, file: University of Western Ontario.
130 QUFA *Newsletter/QUFacts*, October 1975, in QUA, Queen's Printed Collection, QUFA, Box 1.
131 "Master Plan for Campus Development, May 1961," Barott, Marschall, Merrett & Barott, QUA, OPF, locator #1250, Box 12, file: Master Plan.
132 MBT, 17 and 18 Nov. 1968.
133 For a complete inventory of Queen's buildings, see: *Heritage Study: Heritage Policy – Inventory and Evaluation*, Kingston: Queen's University Campus Planning and Development and Commonwealth Historic Resource Management Ltd., 1998.
134 QAR, May–June 1970.
135 See: Mackintosh-Corry Hall Collection, QUA, locator #5059.
136 QJ, 24 Sept. 1974.
137 Author interview, Allan Armit, 23 Nov. 2012.
138 QAR, Sept.–Dec. 1968.
139 RAQ interviews: F.R.C. Clarke, May 2009.
140 Author interview, Dorothy Farr, 13 May 2013.
141 See: *Permanent Collection 1968* (Kingston: Agnes Etherington Art Centre, 1968).
142 MBT, 16 and 17 Oct. 1970. See: Alfred Bader, *Chemistry and Art: Further Adventures of a Chemist Collector* (London: Weidenfeld & Nicolson, 2008).
143 J. Douglas Stewart and Ian E. Wilson, *Heritage Kingston* (Kingston: Agnes Etherington Art Centre, 1973).
144 MBT, 1 Nov. 1968.
145 QAR, May–June 1971.
146 QJ, 9 Feb.1971.

CHAPTER FIVE

1 QUA, OPF, Locator #1252, Box 5, file: Deutsch installation, 8 Nov. 1968; *Tricolor*, 1969; *Globe and Mail*, 9 Nov. 1968; QJ, 12 Nov. 1968; and author interview, Ross McGregor, 6 Nov. 2012.
2 KWS, 9 Nov. 1968.
3 QJ, 8 and 12 Nov. 1968.
4 Deutsch to Trudeau, 23 Nov. 1968, QUA, OPF, locator #1252, Box 1, correspondence file.
5 See: A.R.M. Lower, *This Most Famous Stream: The Liberal Democratic Way of Life* (Toronto: Ryerson Press, 1954).
6 J.A. Corry, *My Life and Work: A Happy Partnership* (Kingston: Queen's University, 1981), ix.
7 Barry Ferguson, *Remaking Liberalism: The Intellectual Legacy of Adam Shortt, O.D. Skelton, W.C. Clark and W.A. Mackintosh, 1890–1925* (Montreal & Kingston: McGill-Queen's University Press, 1993), 235 and 246. See also: S.E.D. Shortt, *Search for an Ideal: Six Canadian Intellectuals and Their Convictions in an Age of Transition, 1890–1930* (Toronto & Buffalo: University of Toronto Press, 1976).
8 QJ, 24 Nov. 1966.
9 See: Richard Harris, *Democracy in Kingston: A Social Movement in Urban Politics, 1965–1970* (Montreal & Kingston: McGill-Queen's University Press, 1988).
10 QJ, 16 Feb. 1968.
11 QUA, OPF, locator #1252, Box 7, file: Charles Edwards.
12 See: George Brandie, ed., *Queen's Chemical Engineering: Worth Celebrating* (Kingston: Department of Chemical Engineering, c. 2002).
13 Author interview, Henry Becker, 23 Aug. 2011.
14 AMSM, 12 March 1968.
15 Stuart Willoughby, "Closing Argument on Behalf of Dr. Henry Becker and the Department of Chemical Engineering," c. January 1970, QUA,

OPF, locator #1252, Box 7, file: Edwards case various documents.
16 Jan Lichty and Mark Elliott, "Our Commitment Is to a Socially Just Society," *QJ*, 24 Sept. 1968.
17 Michael Carley, Charles Edwards, and Tom Good to Deutsch, 27 Aug. 1968, and Deutsch to Michael Carley et al., QUA, OPF, locator #1254, Box 14, file: student accommodation, and residences general, 1969–72.
18 Michael Carley to Deutsch, 6 Sept. 1968, QUA, Bernard Adell Papers, locator #1241.1, Box 1, file: Edwards evidence II.
19 *KWS*, 14 Sept. 1968.
20 *QJ*, 10 Sept. 1968.
21 *QJ*, 15 Oct. 1968.
22 *Golden Words* [hereafter *GW*], 4 Nov. 1968.
23 The Deutschs did not in fact live at Summerhill. They opted to remain in their own Kingston home and to use Summerhill for official entertaining.
24 *QJ*, 13 and 17 Sept. 1968.
25 RAQ interviews: Joan Webster, 2009.
26 *QJ*, 4 Oct. 1968.
27 *GW*, 4 Nov. 1968.
28 *AMSM*, 22 Oct. 1968.
29 *QJ*, 1 Nov. 1968.
30 *The AMS Forum*, Sept. 1968.
31 *The Other Journal* 1, 2, n.d. (c. late 1968).
32 *QJ*, 6 Nov. 1969.
33 Report on the Master's Thesis Defence, statement of Professor B.W. Wojceichowski, 6 Sept. 1968, QUA, Bernard Adell Papers, locator #1241.1, Box 1.
34 See: QUA, OPF, locator #1252, Box 7, file: File prepared by Dr Clark.
35 Author interview, James Leith, 2 Aug. 2011.
36 "The Professional Engineer," *GW*, 20 Jan. 1970.
37 Much of the material used to reconstruct the events surrounding the interaction of the University with Charles "Chuck" Edwards from November 1969 through the spring of 1970 is taken from the report of the so-called Adell Commission published in the *Queen's Gazette* on 26 Feb. 1970, and from the verbatim sound recordings of the committee hearings. See: *Report of the Special Senate Committee Constituted to Investigate Allegations Relating to Mr. Charles Edwards* [hereafter Adell Report] and QUA, SR 4, 26 reels of testimony taken by the Adell Commission [hereafter Committee tapes].
38 See: QUA, OPF, locator #1251, Box 4, file: CAUT and "National Security and the Universities," *CAUT Bulletin*, Dec. 1967, Vol. 16, #2, Dec. 1967.
39 File prepared by Dr Clark, QUA, OPF, locator #1251, Box 4, file: CAUT.
40 *QJ*, 14 October 1969, and MUS, 25 Sept. 1969.
41 Becker to E.J. Kennedy, 21 Nov. 1969, QUA, OPF, locator #1252, Box 7, File: File prepared by Dr R. Clark.
42 Author interview, Henry Becker, 23 Aug. 2011.
43 Stuart Ryan, "Cops on Campus," *This Paper Belongs to the People*, Vol. 1, #10, 3 Dec. 1969.
44 Tom Good and Glenn MacDonell to "friends," 2 Dec. 1969, QUA, OPF, locator #1252, Box 7, file: File prepared by Dr R. Clark.
45 Author interview, Bernard Adell, 11 July 2011.
46 See: Adell Report and Committee tapes, QUA, SR 4.
47 See: the *Globe & Mail*, 6 Jan. 1970.
48 Poster, QUA, OPF, locator #1252, Box 8, file: Edwards case correspondence.
49 All subsequent quotations from Adell Report.
50 Author interview, Bernard Adell, 11 July 2011.
51 *GW*, 3 March 1970. For extensive media coverage of these events, see QUA, OPF, locator #1252, Box 7, file: Edwards case clippings.
52 *QJ*, 5 March 1970.
53 *QJ*, 12 March 1970.
54 Becker and Adell interviews.
55 Yoshihoro Tsurumi to Deutsch, 6 April 1970, QUA, OPF, locator #1252, Box 8, file: Charles Edwards correspondence.
56 F.W. Gibson to Deutsch, 12 March 1970, QUA, OPF, locator #1252, Box 8, file: Charles Edwards correspondence, Feb.1970.
57 "Senate Votes: Edwards Stays," *QJ*, 6 April, 1970.
58 "Special Meeting of the Queen's Senate, April 3, 1970," QUA, OPF, locator #1252, Box 7, file: Charles Edwards; and *QJ*, 6 April 1970.
59 *QJ*, 6 April 1970.
60 A.R.M. Lower to Deutsch, 1 June 1970, QUA, OPF, locator #1252, Box 8, file: Edwards correspondence, Feb. 1970.
61 McIlraith to Deutsch, 4 June 1970, QUA, OPF, locator #1252, file: Charles Edwards.
62 Deutsch to Brian Scully, 17 Feb. 1970, QUA, OPF, locator #1252, Box 8, file: Charles Edwards correspondence, Feb. 1970.
63 QUA, J.J. Deutsch Papers, locator #1022, Series 1, Box 9.
64 See: *Report of the Senate Committee on Grievance, Discipline, and Related Matters*, May 1971, supplement to the *Queen's Gazette*, 22 June 1971.
65 J.J. Deutsch to Michael Carley et al., 6 Sept. 1968, QUA, OPF, locator #1252, Box 1, file: correspondence.
66 See: *The Need for Student Housing: A Case Study Related to Queen's University at Kingston, Ontario*, Oct. 1968, QUA, OPF, locator #1252, Box 1, file: correspondence.

67 See: W.J. Pardy, "The Science '44 Co-op: Memories of the Past" scrapbook (2006), available in QUA, and author interview, Dan Burns, 5 Nov. 2012.
68 Howard Adelman et al., eds., *The University Game* (Toronto: Anansi, 1968), 79.
69 MBT, 25 and 26 Oct. 1968, and author interview, Dan Burns, 5 Nov. 2012.
70 See: Paul Barron, "Cooped up? Go Co-op!" *QJ*, 11 March 1969.
71 KWS, 21 Feb. 1973.
72 McGregor interview, 6 Nov. 2012.
73 Deutsch to Peters, Dec. 1970, QUA, Elrond College Collection, locator #1114, Box 1.
74 Author interview, Ross McGregor, 1 March 2012.
75 Author interview, Ross McGregor, 6 Nov. 2012.
76 McGregor to Deutsch, 15 Oct. 1969, QUA, Elrond Collection, locator #1114, Box 1.
77 MBT, 12 Aug. 1970.
78 See: "The Student Co-op Mess," *Globe and Mail*, 9 Sept. 1974.
79 "A $3.3 Million Mixture of Whimsy and Business Sense," KWS, 21 Feb. 1973.
80 Elrond College Inc. Interim Report on Operations, 16 Feb. 1973, QUA, Elrond College Collection, locator #1114, Box 3, file: agendas.
81 *QJ*, 9 Feb. 1974.
82 Author interview, William Young, 6 June 2013.
83 MBT, 4 and 5 Feb., and 15 April 1977. "Elrond Struggling – but It Will Survive," *QJ*, 18 Feb. 1977.
84 MBT, 12 and 13 May 1978, and 14 Sept. 1979.
85 Jack E. Smith, "Elrond: An Architectural Study," QUA, Elrond College Collection, locator #1114, Box 3.
86 See: Harris, *Democracy in Kingston*, and Pat Smart, "Queen's History Department and the Birth of the Waffle Movement," in M. Athena Palaeologu, ed., *The Sixties in Canada: A Turbulent and Creative Decade* (Montreal: Black Rose Books, 2009), 310–18.
87 Author interview, Roberta Hamilton, 19 March 2013.
88 Author interview, Brian Rogers, 5 Nov. 2012.

CHAPTER SIX

1 *QJ*, 23 Nov. 1976.
2 Richard Simeon, ed., *Must Canada Fail?* (Montreal & Kingston: McGill-Queen's University Press, 1977). See also: R.M. Burns, ed., *One Country or Two?* (Montreal: McGill-Queen's University Press, 1971).
3 *QJ*, 30 Nov. 1976.
4 MBT, 13 and 14 May 1977.
5 MBT, 7 April 1978.
6 QUA, OPF, locator #1254, Box 22, file: Convocation, Fall 1979.
7 T.H.B. Symons and R.L. Watts, "The Residence Hall and the University," *Queen's Quarterly* 64 (Winter 1957–58), 552–68.
8 R.L. Watts, *New Federations: Experiments in the Commonwealth* (Oxford: Clarendon Press, 1966).
9 See: Thomas Courchene, ed., *The Federal Idea: Essays in Honour of Ronald L. Watts* (Kingston & Montreal: McGill-Queen's University Press, 2011).
10 RAQ interviews: Ron Watts, 15 June 2008, and author interviews, 4 Feb. 2011, 13 June, 2011, and 19 April 2013.
11 Symons and Watts, "The Resident Hall," 568.
12 MBT, 10 and 11 May 1974.
13 R.L. Watts to Cathy Morton, 29 March 1976, QUA, OPF, locator #1254, Box 10, file: Administrative files, 1970–77.
14 Ronald L. Watts, "Profile of a Decade: Queen's University, 1974–84," privately published, c. 1984.
15 Ronald L. Watts, "Freedom with Responsibility: Universities, Governments and the Public," *Queen's Quarterly* 82, 1 (Spring 1975), 14.
16 *Queen's Review*, July-August 1975.
17 *Montreal Gazette*, 20 March 1976.
18 MUS, 24 March 1976.
19 QUA, OPF, locator #1254, Box 24, file: Dr. J.J. Deutsch 1974–80.
20 MBT, 29 Nov. 1974.
21 James Auld to V.C. Abrahams, 22 Jan. 1975, QUA, OPF, locator #1254, Box 6, file: Staff 1973–74.
22 *Globe and Mail*, 11 April, 1975, and MBT, 11 April 1975.
23 See: Hilda Neatby, *Queen's University, Volume I, 1841–1917: To Strive, to Seek, to Find, and Not to Yield* (Montreal & Kingston: McGill-Queen's University Press, 1978).
24 Neatby, *Queen's University*, 156.
25 *Alumni Review*, Jan.-Feb. 1975.
26 "Report of the Principal's Committee on Financial Restraint," *Queen's Gazette* 7, 20 (22 May 1975), 1.
27 Ibid., 2.
28 Harrower to Watts, 12 Feb. 1975, QUA, OPF, locator #1254, Box 7, file: Salaries 1975–76.
29 MUS, 22 May 1975.

30 MUS, 24 Oct. 1974.
31 MBT, 24 and 25 Oct. 1975.
32 Author interview, Tom Williams, 23 Jan. 2013, and RAQ interviews: Tom Williams, 27 June 2011.
33 See: Mervin Daub and P. Bruce Buchan, *Getting Down to Business: A History of Business Education at Queen's, 1889-1999* (Montreal & Kingston: McGill-Queen's University Press, 1999), and QUA, OPF, locator #1254, Box 5, file: Dean of the School of Business Dr John R.M. Gordon 1977–78.
34 QUA, OPF, locator #1254, Box 5, file: Advisory Committee for Dean of Graduate Studies and Research.
35 See: Maureen McCallum Garvie and Jennifer L. Johnson, *Their Leaven of Influence: Deans of Women at Queen's University, 1916–1996* (Kingston: Alumni Association of Queen's University, 1999), Chap. 7.
36 QUA, OPF, locator #1254, Box 28, file: OCUA Briefs, 1974.
37 "Progress Report to the Principal PAGORP – July 1977," QUA, OPF, locator #1254, Box 17, file: Principal's Advisory Committee on Resource Planning PAGORP.
38 MBT, 20 and 21 Feb. 1976.
39 MBT, 9 April 1976 and 15 April 1977.
40 These figures are taken from Watts's "Profile of a Decade," appendices, 12. In 1974–75, there had been a surplus of $339,000 carried forward, which offset the next year's cumulative deficit.
41 MBT, 12 and 13 May 1978.
42 QUA, OPF, locator #1254, Box 29, file; OCUA 1978–79.
43 MUS, 28 April 1977.
44 MBT, 14 Sept. 1979.
45 MBT, 1 and 2 Feb. 1980.
46 Duncan Sinclair to Watts, 2 Feb. 1976, QUA, OPF, locator #1254, Box 17, file: Principal's Advisory Committee on Resource Planning.
47 Adell to Watts, 21 Dec. 1978, QUA, OPF, locator #1254, Box 18, file: Budget & Salaries, 1979–80.
48 QUA, OPF, locator #1254, Box 10, file: Retreat Opinicon, 1976–77.
49 R.L. Watts, "The Operation of Internal Governance within Queen's University," MBT, 13 and 14 May 1988.
50 Sinclair to Watts, 9 Sept. 1980, QUA, OPF, locator #1254, Box 18, file: Budget preparation, 1980–81.
51 MBT, 22 and 23 Oct. 1982.
52 MBT, 22 and 23 Oct. 1976. QUA, OPF, locator #1006, unnumbered box, file: QUFA – Memorandum of Understanding.
53 MBT, 4 and 5 Feb. 1977.
54 Sinclair to Watts, 25 June 1976, QUA, OPF, locator #1254, file: Faculty Association Consultative Group, 1977– .
55 Ibid., QUA, OPF, locator #1254, Consultative Group Minutes, 15 Feb. 1977.
56 QUFA Salary Brief, Feb. 1980, QUA, OPF, locator #1254, Box 7, file: Consultative Group, 1977– .
57 Watts, "Profile of a Decade," 3 and 29. This was a constant-dollar calculation.
58 MBT, 4 Dec. 1981.
59 Ibid., appendices. 12.
60 *QUFacts*, Nov. 1979.
61 QUFA Brief on Salary and Related Matters, 20 Nov. 1981, QUA, OPF, locator #1254, Box 7, file: Consultative Group, 1981–82.
62 *QUFacts*, Oct. 1981.
63 *QUFacts*, Feb. 1983.
64 Memorandum of Understanding between Queen's University and QUFA as to the Status of the Association in relation to the University, 10 Jan. 1984, QUA, OPF, locator #1254, Box 7a, File: Consultative Group, 1983–84; and MBT, 30 March 1984.
65 RAQ interviews: Bud Cornelius, July 2009.
66 RAQ interviews: Eveline Flint, June 2010.
67 Eveline Flint to Flora MacDonald, 10 April 1975, QUA, OPF, locator #1254, Box 6, file: Queen's University Staff Association, 1973– .
68 Memo of 2 March 1981, QUA, locator #1254, Box 18, file: Budget, 1981–82.
69 MBT, 23 and 24 Oct. 1981.
70 MBT, 15 and 16 May 1982.
71 Memo by Duncan Sinclair, 4 Jan. 1982, QUA, OPF, locator #1254, Box 18, file: Budget, 1983–84.
72 MUS, 14 Dec. 1978; and MBT, 8 Dec. 1978.
73 "Brief to the OCUA by Principal of Queen's Ronald Watts, February 1980," MBT, 1 and 2 Feb. 1980.
74 MBT, 11 and 12 April 1980.
75 MUS, 27 Sept. 1977.
76 MUS, 26 Sept. 1978.
77 Watts, "Profile," 14.
78 Ibid., appendices, 1.
79 MBT, 8 Dec. 1978.
80 Hand to Watts, 9 May 1979, QUA, OPF, locator #1254, Box 10, file: Donald Gordon Retreat, October 1979.
81 MBT, 13 and 14 May 1977; and MUS, 26 May 1977.

82 MUS, 27 Jan. 1977.
83 Michael MacMillan, *The Academic Cloister* (Queen's Campus Films), QUA, MI 202. MacMillan would go on to create Atlantis Films and in 1984 win an Academy Award for his short film *Boys and Girls*.
84 "Study-in Address: Provincial Day of Protest Against Government Underfunding," QUA, OPF, locator #1254, Box 28, file: Ministry of Colleges and Universities, 1979–82.
85 Norman to Stephenson, 14 March 1983, QUA, OPF, locator #1254, Box 7, file: Faculty Association, 1981–84.
86 Colin Norman, *The Queen's English* (Kingston: Department of English, 1975). MBT, 22 and 23 Oct. 1976; and *Queen's Alumni Review*, Nov-Dec. 1976.
87 Watts, "Profile," appendices, 10, and "Status of Women at Queen's," Report of Principal's Advisory Review Committee on the Status of Women 1979, *Queen's Gazette*, 11 March 1980.
88 MBT, 29 Nov. 1974. Margaret Hooey from the Senate Office was called upon to assist the committee.
89 Crowe to Watts, 27 Oct. 1978, QUA, OPF, locator #1254, Box 23, file: State of the University Addresses.
90 B. Baines, K. Herman, and M. Maxwell to Watts, 1 Dec. 1978, QUA, OPF, Box 7, file: AWTAQ, 1978–79.
91 "Report of the Principal's Committee on Appointment and Promotion of Women Members of the Academic Staff at Queen's University, 15 March, 1978," *Queen's Gazette* Vol. 10, #37, 19 Sept. 1978.
92 "The Status of Women at Queen's, 1979," *Queen's Gazette*, 15 March 1980 12, 10.
93 1980 AWTAQ memo, QUA, Beverley Baines fonds, file: Status of Women at Queen's, 1974–87.
94 See: QUA, Association of Women Teaching at Queen's fonds, locator #2303.49, various files.
95 MBT, 13 Dec. 1979.
96 MUS, 28 Feb. 1985.
97 Author interview, Christine Overall, 22 August, 2011.
98 QUA, OPF, locator #1001.31 and 1006, Box 9, file: 1986–87 Queen's National Scholars competition.
99 *QJ*, 19 Oct. 1984.
100 Dana Johnson to Watts, 9 Oct. 1974 and Sinclair to Watts, 16 July 1974, QUA, OPF, locator #1254, Box 4, file: Dean of Graduate Studies, 1974.
101 See: J.A.W. Gunn, John Matthews, D.M. Schurman, and M.G. Wiebe, eds., *Benjamin Disraeli Letters, 1815–34*, Vol. I (Toronto & Buffalo: University of Toronto Press, 1982).
102 "Working Paper on the Review of Graduate Studies," April 1977, chaired by R.L. McIntosh, QUA, OPF, locator 1254, Box 2, file: School of Graduate Studies, 1968–72.
103 McLatchie to Watts, 31 May 1977, ibid.
104 Watts, "Profiles," 20-2.
105 MBT, 9 Dec., 1983; and T. Geoffrey Flynn, "The Discovery at Queen's of Hormones in the Heart," in Donald Jennings, ed., *A Scrapbook of Memories, 1954–2004* (Belleville: Epic Press, 2004), 111–16.
106 MBT, 5 and 6 Feb. 1982.
107 Ibid.
108 MBT, 3 and 4 Feb. 1983.
108 QUA, OPF, locator 1006, unnumbered box, files: Office of Research Services & Overhead Policy. Author interview, Ken Snowdon, 9 Jan. 2012.
110 MBT, 3 and 4 Feb. 1983.
111 MUS, 24 June 1976.
112 MUS, 23 Nov. 1978.
113 Hilary Richardson, "GEAC and the Library, 1980–1988," private manuscript. Author interviews with Hilary Richardson, Barbara Teatero, and Martha Whitehead, 22 Sept. 2011 and 12 March, 2012.
114 MBT, 11 and 12 May 1984.
115 QUA, OPF, locator #1254, Box 1, file: Arts & Science – Department and Staff and Box 2, file: McArthur College of Education.
116 MBT, 30 March, 11 and 12 May 1984.
117 QUA, OPF, locator #1254, Box 30, file: "Universities in the Information Revolution." Queen's film professor William Nichols spoke at the conference on digitalization and "stand-alone microcomputers."
118 Watts, "Profile," 23-4.
119 QUA, OPF, locator #1254, Box 13, file: Industrial Relations Centre, 1978–83.
120 "Proposal for the Establishment of a School of Public Policy, June 1984," QUA, OPF, locator #1006, unboxed; and MUS, 28 June 1984.
121 QUA, OPF, locator #1254, file: Graduate Studies, 1983–84.
122 QUA, OPF, locator #1254, Box 2, file: Bromley visit 1982.
123 Watts, "Profile," 21-2.
124 MUS, 24 April, 1975 and 24 March 1977.
125 MUS, 24 March 1977.
126 QUA, OPF, locator #1254, Box 15, file: Botterell Hall opening and 125th anniversary of medical faculty, October 1979.
127 See: Margaret Angus, *Kingston General Hospi-*

tal: A Social and Institutional History, Volume II: 1965–1992 (Kingston: Kingston General Hospital, 1994).
128 S.L. Vandewater to D. MacIntyre, 22 Oct. 1968, QUA, OPF, locator #1254, Box 3, file: "Old" medical faculty, 1968– ."
129 MBT, 21-22 Feb. 1976.
130 QUA, OPF, locator #1254, Box 15, file: QUAF-HOP City Liaison, 1971– .
131 MBT, 20 and 21 Feb. 1976.
132 See: Jason Albert Hannah fonds, QUA, locator #2318.
133 Symington to Watts, 5 July, 1975 and Powles to Watts, 24 June 1975, QUA, OPF, locator #1254, file: Dean of Medicine, 1975.
134 MBT, 4 and 5 Feb. 1977.
135 Watts, "State of the University Address, 1979," *Queen's Gazette*, 23 Oct. 1979.
136 QUA, OPF, locator #1254, Box 15, file: Botterell Hall opening and 125th anniversary of medical faculty.
137 MBT, 5 and 6 Dec. 1980.
138 Duncan Sinclair, author interview, 25 Oct. 2013.
139 MBT, 12 and 13 May 1978.
140 QUA, OPF, locator #1254, Box 4, file: Institute of Intergovernmental Government Relations, 1969–74.
141 MBT, 13 and 14 May 1988.
142 QAR, July-Aug. 1987. Courtright was speaking on the occasion of being awarded the Montreal Alumni Medal.
143 *Maclean's*, 18 March 1980.
144 E.R. Yendt to Watts, 5 June 1975, QUA, locator #1254, Box 5, file: Dean of Medicine, 1975.
145 RAQ interviews: Ken Snowdon, Aug. 2011; and author interview, Ken Snowdon, 15 April 2011 and 9 Jan. 2012.
146 MBT, 3 and 4 Feb., 30 March, and 11 and 12 May 1984; and MUS, 14 Aug. 1984.
147 MBT, 8 and 9 Feb. 1985.
148 MBT, 8 April 1983, and 3 and 4 Feb 1984.
149 MBT, 6 July 1983.

CHAPTER SEVEN
1 QJ, 30 Oct. 1984.
2 Ibid.
3 QJ, 21 Sept. 1984.
4 AMSM, 11 Oct. and 22 Nov. 1984.
5 MBT, 23 and 24 Oct. 1987.
6 MUS, 27 Sept. 1984.
7 MBT, 7 Dec. 1984.
8 MBT, Oct. 25 and 26 1985.
9 Ibid.
10 MBT, 6 and 7 Feb. 1987.
11 MUS, 28 May 1987.
12 QJ, 24 Oct. 1984.
13 David Smith, *Values at Queen's*, Special Supplement to the *Queen's Alumni Review*, March 1990, S4 and S6.
14 Ibid.
15 RAQ interviews: John Hartwick, May 2010.
16 Ibid.
17 Author interview with Mary Smith, 22 Nov. 2013.
18 Ibid.
19 MBT, 7 and 8 Feb. 1986.
20 MBT, 23 and 24 Oct. 1987.
21 MBT, 17 and 18 Oct. 1986.
22 MBT, 8 and 9 May 1987.
23 MBT, 29 and 30 Jan. 1988.
24 MBT, 9 and 10 May 1986.
25 MBT, 8 and 9 May 1987.
26 MBT, 5 Dec. 1986.
27 MUS, 14 August 1984.
28 MUS, 24 October 1985.
29 MUS, 26 Oct. 1989.
30 MUS, 17 Dec. 1985.
31 MBT, 2 April 1986.
32 MBT, 10 and 11 May 1985 and 2 April 1986; Alison Holt, "Facing the Financial Crunch," *Queen's Alumni Review,* July-Aug. 1989, 12.
33 David Smith, *A Principal's Report: Qualities of a Queen's Education*, 1989–90, QUA, Queen's printed Collection. Queen's had stopped publishing an annual Principal's Report in the mid-1970s. The university had become too large to encompass it comfortably in a single compendium. Cancellation saved costs. The *Queen's Gazette*, published since 1969, also served to convey information to faculty, staff, and students.
34 Smith, *Report*, 20.
35 Ibid.
36 Queen's University at Kingston, *Ontario Universities: A Blueprint for Action*, March, 1989, QUA, Queen's printed Collection, Misc. Reports, Box 4.
37 MBT, 3 and 4 March 1989.
38 AMS Assembly, 9 March 1989, and *Queen's Alumni Review*, July-Aug. 1989, 14.
39 MBT, 5 and 6 Oct. 1990.
40 MBT, 1 and 2 March 1991.
41 Richard Allen to Smith, 29 May 1991, QUA, OPF, locator #1001.31, Box 15, file: Race relations general, 1991– .
42 Smith to Allen, July 1991, QUA, OPF, locator #1001.31, Box 15, file: QUFA – Minutes/Agenda 1991.
43 MBT, 1 and 2 March 1991.

44 MUS, 26 Sept. 1991.
45 Stackhouse to Rae, 29 Nov. 1991, QUA, OPF, locator #1001.31, Box 15, file: provincial government.
46 MBT, 4 and 5 Dec. 1992.
47 *Queen's Gazette*, 3 Feb. 1992.
48 MBT, 8 and 9 May 1992.
49 QUA, OPF, locator #1006, unboxed, file: PARTEQ.
50 OECD, *Financing Higher Education: Current Patterns* (Washington & Paris: OECD, 1992).
51 Association of Universities and Colleges in Canada, *Prosperity in the Knowledge Age: The Role of Canada's Universities* (Ottawa: AUCC, 1992).
52 *Time*, 29 April 1992, and *Toronto Star*, 6 August 1992.
53 Jeffrey Simpson, "Accountability in Higher Education," speech to the AUCC, March 1992, in QUA, OPF, locator #1006, Box 15, file: PATFORI.
54 Sinclair to Smith and Vice-Principals, 4 May, 1992, QUA, OPF, locator #1006, Box 15, File: PATFORI misc.
55 Ibid.
56 MBT, 7 and 8 Dec. 1990.
57 MBT, 4 and 5 Oct. 1991.
58 *QUFacts*, Jan. 1989.
59 Snowden to Baer, 15 Dec. 15 1990, QUA, OPF, locator #1001.31, Box 15, file: QUFA 1990–91.
60 *QUFacts*, March 1990
61 Smith, *Values at Queen's*, S2.
62 *Report of the Principal's Panel to Review Faculty Women's Salaries*, Oct. 1991, QUA, OPF, locator #1001.31, Box 16, file: PAC on Faculty Women's Salaries.
63 Jack Hughes, memo to Support Staff Review Committee, 8 Feb. 1988, QUA, locator #1006, unnumbered box, file: Support Staff Review Committee.
64 MUS, 30 March, 1989.
65 RAQ interviews: Bud Cornelius, August 2008.
66 Ibid. The strike lasted only a weekend and would never have been called if news of the successful contract had been more expeditiously communicated to union rank and file on the Friday afternoon when it was concluded.
67 Ibid.
68 QUA, OPF, locator #1006, unnumbered box, file: staff – unions.
69 John Platt, Allan McPhail, and Arlie Redmond to Smith, 26 Feb. 1992, QUA, locator #1006, unnumbered box, file: March P/VP meetings.
70 *QUFacts*, Oct. 1989 and Jan. 1990.
71 *QUFacts*, fall 1990.
72 *QUFacts*, October 1992.
73 Author interview, Annette Burfoot, 13 Dec. 2012.
74 *QUFacts*, March/April 1992.
75 Stayer to David Smith, 10 Jan. 1990, QUA, OPF, locator #1001.31, Box 15, file: QUFA financial restraints correspondence, 1990.
76 Baxter to W. McCreamy, 19 Jan. 1990, QUA, OPF, locator #1001.31, Box 15, file: QUFA financial restraints correspondence, 1990.
77 Purvis to Baer, 25 Jan. 1990, QUA, OPF, locator #1001.31, Box 15, file: QUFA financial restraints correspondence, 1990.
78 QUFA *Salary Bulletins #4 and #5*, May & July 1992, QUA, Queen's Printed Collection, Box 1: QUFA.
79 QUA, OPF, locator #1006, unnumbered box, file: QUFA general and QUFA Information Bulletin #6, April 1993.
80 Sinclair to QUFA Executive Committee, 1 June 1992, QUA, OPF, locator #1006, file: QUFA faculty salary July 1992.
81 Grant Amyot to Smith, 26 April 1993, QUA, OPF, locator #1006, unnumbered box, file: QUFA general.
82 *QUFacts*, February 1993.
83 Smith to Amyot, 7 June 1993, QUA, OPF, locator #1006, unnumbered box, file: QUFA general.
84 MBT, 14 and 15 May 1993, and Bob Little to A.H. Jeeves, 14 June 1993, QUA, OPF, locator #1006, unnumbered box, file: QUFA general.
85 QUA, AMS Assembly minutes, 16 Sept. 1993.
86 See W.H. Broadhurst, *University Accountability: A Strengthened Framework* (Toronto: Task Force on University Accountability, 1993).
87 MBT, 3 and 4 Dec. 1993.
88 *QUFacts*, Jan. 1994.
89 See Carol Armstrong, "The Moose Factory Experience: A Privilege Unique to Nurses of This University," *Queen's Alumni Review*, March-April 1984, and Alison Sayers. "The Moose Factory Connection," *Queen's Alumni Review*, Nov.-Dec. 1990.
90 See: Paul Rosenbaum, S.E.D. Shortt, and D.M.C. Walker, "Alternative Funding for Academic Medicine: Experience at a Canadian Health Sciences Centre," *Academic Medicine* 79, 3: (March 2004) 197–204.
91 See: Duncan G. Sinclair, "The Alternative Funding Plan (AFP): Changing the Financing of the School of Medicine," in Donald B. Jennings, ed., *A Scrapbook of Memories, 1954–2004* (Kingston: School of Medicine, Faculty of Health Sciences, 2004), 233–9.
92 See: Jacalyn Duffin, *History of Medicine: A Scan-*

93 Sinclair to Smith, 24 January 1991, QUA, OPF, locator #1006, unnumbered box, file: Alternative Funding Plan – Faculty of Medicine.
94 "Proposal for an Alternative Organization and Funding Model for the Faculty of Medicine," February 1991, QUA, OPF, locator #1006, unnumbered box, file: Alternative Funding Plan – Faculty of Medicine.
95 MBT, 1 and 2 March 1991.
96 MBT, 12 and 13 May 1989.
97 MBT, 13 and 14 Dec. 1991.
98 QUA, OPF, locator #1006, unnumbered box, file: Medicine 1992.
99 KWS, 10 Feb. 1984.
100 QUA, OPF, locator #1006, unnumbered box, file: Medicine 1992.
101 MBT, 29 and 30 Jan. 1988, and MUS, 2 March 1989.
102 MUS, 27 June 1991.
103 Mervin Daub and Bruce Buchan, *Getting Down to Business: A History of Business Education at Queen's, 1889–1999* (Montreal & Kingston: McGill-Queen's University Press, 1999), 85–6.
104 MUS, 28 April 1994.
105 MBT, 13 and 14 May 1994. "Business School," *Globe and Mail*, 8 March 1994, and "Class Warfare," *Canadian Business*, April 1994.
106 Ken Wong, "The New MBA: More Than Just a Price Tag," *Queen's Alumni Review*, March/April 1994.
107 It is worth noting that not all MBA fees went into the business school's coffers; the university "taxed back" part of the fees as a charge-back on facilities used and employee benefits.
108 *QJ*, 1 Oct. 1985 and 27 Oct. 1988.
109 The official opening of the International Centre in 1966 featured an eclectic evening of steel bands, Zulu dances, sitar solos, and Scottish reels. QUA, OPF, locator #1251, Box 15, file: International Centre.
110 QUA, OPF, locator #1006, unnumbered box, file: International Centre.
111 MUS, 27 Feb. 1986.
112 QUA, OPF, locator #1006, unnumbered box, file: Committee of Vice-Principals and Deans – agendas, 1992– .
113 See Irving Abella and Harold Troper, *None Is Too Many: Canada and the Jews of Europe, 1933–1948* (Toronto: University of Toronto Press edition, 2012).
114 Alfred Bader, *Adventures of a Chemist Collector* (London: Weidenfeld & Nicolson, 1995), Chaps. 1–2; David McTavish, "Alfred Bader," *Queen's Alumni Review*, Nov.-Dec. 1983; and Sara Beck, "A Word and a Missing Suitcase," *Queen's Alumni Review*, March-April 2011.
115 This contentious issue is more fully discussed in F.W. Gibson, *Queen's University, Volume II 1917–1961: To Serve and Yet Be Free* (Kingston & Montreal: McGill-Queen's University Press, 1983), 199–203.
116 See: Roberta Hamilton, *Setting the Agenda: Jean Royce and the Shaping of Queen's University* (Toronto: University of Toronto Press, 2002), 93–5.
117 Bader to Wallace, 6 March 1945, QUA, OPF, locator #1252, Box 10, file: Hillel Foundation.
118 Bader, *Adventures*, Chap. 7.
119 McTavish, "Bader," 9.
120 Conversation with David de Witt, Bader Curator of European Art, Agnes Etherington Art Centre, Nov. 2013. See also Alfred Bader, *Chemistry and Art: Further Adventures of a Chemist Collector* (London: Weidenfeld & Nicolson, 2008).
121 QUA, OPF, locator #1254, Box 5, file: Art Centre: Principal's Advisory Committee for Director, 1982–83.
122 MBT, 16 and 17 Oct. 1970. Bader would also help to finance the construction of chemistry labs, and fund student scholarships at Queen's. In later years, he would also underwrite the cost of curatorial appointments at the art centre.
123 Bader to McTavish, 5 March 1993, QUA, OPF, locator #1006, unnumbered box, file: Agnes Etherington Art Centre. See David de Witt, *The Bader Collection: Dutch and Flemish Paintings* (Kingston: Agnes Etherington Art Centre, 2008).
124 QUA, OPF, locator #1006, unnumbered box, file: Committee of Vice-Principals and Deans – agendas, 1992– .
125 MBT, executive committee, 14 Dec. 1992.
126 MBT, 4 and 5 Dec. 1992.
127 MBT, 1 and 2 Oct. 1993.
128 MBT, 30 Sept. and 1 Oct. 1994.
129 Author interview, William Leggett, 24 Sept. 2012, and MBT, 30 Sept. and 1 Oct. 1994.
130 Soberman to Bennett, 7 March 1986, QUA, OPF, locator #1001/31, Box 15, file: School of Public Policy, 1986–87
131 QUA, OPF, locator #1006, file: New Technology Building project.
132 Joe Berridge to Karl Van Dalen, 22 April 1986, private files of Professor David Gordon, Queen's School of Urban and Regional Planning.
133 MUS, 25 June 1987.
134 MBT, 5 Dec. 1987.

135 Author interview, Alan Broadbent, 6 Nov. 2012.
136 MBT, 13 and 14 May 1988. See also "Planning for Campus Development: 'Where Will All the Buildings Go?'" Supplement to the *Queen's Gazette,* 1 Dec. 1987.
137 Margaret Angus, *The Old Stones of Kingston: Its Buildings before 1867* (Toronto: University of Toronto Press, 1966).
138 QUA, OPF, locator #1006, unnumbered box, file: Union Street houses, and MBT, 1 and 2 March 1991.
139 "The 1993 Campus Plan (draft)" and "1994 Queen's University Campus Plan," Sept. 1994, in MBT, 1 and 2 Oct., 1994.
140 MUS, 27 June and 24 Oct. 1985; 27 Oct. 1988; and 26 Oct, 1989.
141 "The Library of the 21st Century: Report of the Task Force," Supplement to the *Queen's Gazette,* 31 Oct. 1989, and QUA, OPF, locator #1006, unnumbered box, file: Stauffer Library.
142 Author interview, Barbara Teatero, 29 Jan. 2014.
143 MBT, 7 and 8 Dec. 1990.
144 *Globe and Mail,* 22 Dec. 1990.
145 Meisel to Wiens, 10 Feb. 1992, QUA, OPF, locator #1006, unnumbered box, file: Douglas Library, and author interview, Paul Wiens, 12 April 2012.
146 *Globe and Mail,* 29 Oct. 1994.
147 Yeates to Smith, 23 Dec. 1983, QUA, OPF, locator #1254, box 2, file: Grad Studies, 1983–84.
148 QUA, OPF, locator #1006, unnumbered box, file: Speeches, 1988–94. He also added that a principal had to have "a stomach of a goat."

CHAPTER EIGHT

1 Steve Parry to Padre and Mrs A.M. Laverty, 15 Nov. 1973, QUA, A.M. Laverty fonds, locator #1186, Box 6, file: Student thank you letters.
2 RAQ interviews: Joan Wright, May 2011.
3 MBT, 8 and 9 Feb. 1985.
4 Author interview, Brian Yealland, 24 Oct. 2012.
5 MBT, 29 March 1985.
6 QUA, OPF, locator #1006, unnumbered box, file: churches on campus.
7 MUS, 28 March 1980.
8 Ibid.
9 MUS, 23 Jan. 1981.
10 *Globe and Mail,* 11 Feb. 1981.
11 Laverty to Kennedy, 29 Jan. 1981, QUA, Laverty fonds, locator #1186, Box 3, file: convocation – religious elements.
12 Ryan to Laverty, note of Jan. 1980, QUA, Laverty fonds, locator #1186, Box 3, file: convocation – religious elements.
13 KWS, 11 Feb. 1981.
14 Bader to Bater, 16 Feb. 1981, QUA, OPF, locator #1254, Box 22, file: Prayers at convocation.
15 *Toronto Star,* 24 Jan. 1981.
16 Cunningham, Little, Bonham & Milliken to Vernon Ready, 25 Feb. 1981, QUA, OPF, locator #1254, Box 22, file: Prayers at convocation.
17 Tulchinsky to Watts, 28 April 1981, QUA, OPF, locator #1254, Box 22, file: Prayers at Convocation.
18 MUS, 19 March 1981.
19 MUS, 24 Sept. 1981.
20 MUS 22 and 26 April 1982.
21 KWS, 3 May 1982.
22 QUA, OPF, locator #1254, Box 22, file: Prayers at Convocation 1982–84.
23 MUS, 22 April 1976.
24 QAR, July-Aug. 1975.
25 QJ, 13 November 1987.
26 MUS, 24 Jan. 1985.
27 MBT, 23 and 24 Oct. 1987.
28 Linda Frum, *Linda Frum's Guide to Canadian Universities* (Toronto: Key Porter, 1987).
29 AMS Assembly minutes, 14 Jan. 1988.
30 Author interview, Mary Smith, 22 Nov. 2013. Mary Smith, David's widow, talked of "the pain" – sleepless nights, nervous digestion – that her husband daily internalized in coping with the stresses of a university community grown restless and dissatisfied in its social orientation and cohesiveness.
31 See: Sarah Beck, "A Question of Treason," *Queen's Alumni Review,* #1, 2008.
32 See: F.W. Gibson, *Queen's University, Volume II: 1917–1961: To Serve and Yet Be Free* (Montreal & Kingston: McGill-Queen's University Press, 1983), 275–84.
33 Jacalyn Duffin, "The Jews of Queen's: Religion, Race and Change in Twentieth-Century Canada," *Canadian Journal of History*, 49, no. 3 (Winter 2014): 370–94.
34 See: Roberta Hamilton, "A Kindness Long Remembered," *Queen's Alumni Review* 3, 2014.
35 Author interview, Gerald Tulchinsky, 11 March, 2011.
36 See: Stanley B. Frost, *McGill University: For the Advancement of Learning, Vol. II, 1895–1971* (Montreal & Kingston: McGill-Queen's University Press, 1980) and Martin L. Friedland, *The University of Toronto: A History* (Toronto: University of Toronto Press, 2000).
37 While Queen's eschewed quotas, it was not immune to the pervasive anti-Semitism frequently voiced in inter-war WASP Canadian society. In

1919, Principal R. Bruce Taylor told a meeting of Queen's Montreal alumni branch that he was proud that Queen's, unlike McGill, was not inundated by Jews. Only five Jews were attending Queen's. Jews, he confided to his audience, lowered the tone of Canadian university life. They had, for instance, shirked their wartime duty by not enlisting. To their credit, some alumni protested these sentiments. See: Gerald Tulchinsky, *Canada's Jews: A People's Journey* (Toronto: University of Toronto Press, 2008), 132–3.

38 Ibid., 320.
39 See: Gordon Dueck, "The Origins of Beth Israel, Kingston's First Synagogue," *Historic Kingston*, 57 (2009): 26–31.
40 Tulchinsky to Smith, 23 Dec. 1988, QUA, locator #1006, unnumbered box, file: History.
41 G. Tulchinsky, *Taking Root: The Origins of the Jewish Community in Canada* (Toronto: Lester, 1992) and *Branching Out: the Transformation of the Canadian Jewish Community* (Toronto: Stoddard, 1998).
42 MBT, 29 and 30 Sept. 1989, and 1 and 2 Oct. 1993.
43 *Towards Diversity and Equity at Queen's: A Strategy for Change – Final Report of the Principal's Advisory Committee on Race Relations*, 28 Feb. 1991, supplement to the *Queen's Gazette* 23 (8 April 1991), 7.
44 January 1992 Queen's Employment Equity Workforce, QUA, OPF, locator #1006, unnumbered box, file: March P/VP meetings.
45 See: www.queensu.ca/fdasc.
46 Alison Morgan, memo, 14 March 1995, QUA, locator #1001.31, Box 16, file: General – equity 1994–96. Calculating the actual number of Aboriginal students was difficult in an age of Charter rights; applicants to Queen's might "self-identify" their racial origin or remain racially anonymous.
47 MUS, 23 Jan. 2003.
48 *QJ*, 30 Jan. 2004.
49 *QJ*, 10 Feb. 2004.
50 See, for instance: MUS, 25 June 1992.
51 *Towards Diversity*, 14.
52 Author interview, Beverley Baines, 4 May 2012.
53 MBT, 14 and 15 Oct. 1983.
54 *QAR*, Jan.-Feb. 1986.
55 Ad hoc Committee for the Establishment of a Chair of Woman's Studies, QUA, OPF, locator #1006, unnumbered box, file: Women's Studies 1991– .
56 Minutes of the Arts and Science Faculty Board, 13 Dec. 1985. Resistance, nonetheless, continued. A year later, a letter by a post-doctoral student in geological sciences was widely circulated on campus. In it, the writer suggested that the "feminist problem" at Queen's had little to do with equality and everything to do with getting access to power and the nepotism that came with it. Privileging one group over another, he concluded, smacked of Nazism's assault on free thought in the 1930s. Letter of D.J. Toogood, Nov. 1986, QUA, Baines fonds, file: McIntyre memo, 1986.
57 MBT, 26 Sept. 1985, and 23 Jan. 1986.
58 Beverley Baines, "A Brief History of Women's Studies at Queen's University," talk given on the twentieth anniversary of Women's Studies, 6 March 2008, and author interviews: Christine Overall, 22 Aug. 2011; Beverley Baines, 4 May 2012; and Roberta Hamilton, 19 March 2013. See also: Beverley Baines fonds, QUA, locator #1039.1.
59 MBT, 4 and 5 Oct. 1991.
60 Baines interview.
61 *Tricolor*, 1989.
62 QUA, Baines fonds, Locator #1039.1, file: torts 1989–90.
63 *QJ*, 17 Oct. 1986. Ms Cohen persevered and graduated in 1988.
64 Pickard to search committee, 20 Nov. 1986, QUA, OPF, locator #1001.3, box 3, file: law general (decanal search).
65 Sheila McIntyre, "Gender Bias Within the Law School: 'The Memo' and Its Impact," *Canadian Journal of Women and the Law*, 2 (1987), 369 and 373. McIntyre was not alone in her protest. At the annual Canadian Association of Law Teachers meeting in June 1986, Dalhousie law professor Christine Boyle had provoked attendees with a paper entitled "Teaching Law As If Women Really Mattered, or What about the Washrooms?"
66 McIntyre, "Gender," 372.
67 Ron Price to all members of faculty, 5 Aug. 1986, Baines fonds, file: McIntyre memo.
68 *KWS*, 21 Oct. 1986.
69 *Toronto Star*, 24 Oct. 1986.
70 Kay Herman to Smith, 17 Oct. 1986, Baines fonds.
71 MUS, 23 Oct. 1986.
72 *QJ*, 31 Oct. 1986.
73 Bala memo of 29 Oct. and Soberman memo of 27 Oct. 1986, Baines fonds.
74 Magnusson to all staff, 2 Nov. 1986, QUA, Baines fonds, locator #1039.1., and MUS, 27 Nov. 1986.

75 Anne Kershaw, "Law School Confidential," KWS, 16 July 1988.
76 Memo of 18 Jan. 1989, QUA, Baines fonds, locator #1039.1, file: Feminist legal studies.
77 Petition organized by Patrick Hawkins, Law '89, QUA, Baines fonds, locator #1039.1.
78 Mark D. Walters, "'Let Right Be Done': A History of the Faculty of Law at Queen's University," *Queen's Law Journal* 32 (2007), 357.
79 Adell to Watts, 22 July 1982, QUA, OPF, locator #1254, box 2, file: Faculty of Law, 1970–77.
80 QUA, OPF, locator #1001.31, Box 16, file: Status of Women – sexual assault 1986 Gaskin Report.
81 MBT, 29 and 30 Jan. 1988.
82 QJ, 11 Oct. 1990.
83 AMS Assembly minutes, 19 Jan. 1990.
84 See: Lucia Nixon, "Rituals and Power: The Anthropology of Homecoming," *Queen's Quarterly* 94, 2 (Summer 1987).
85 QJ, 4 March 1986 and 23 Jan. 1990. It was difficult to know whether the perpetrators of such harassment were members of the Queen's community or outsiders eager to bring hatred to the campus.
86 QJ, 14 March 1986.
87 MUS, 27 March 1986.
88 AMS Assembly minutes, 29 Sept. 1988.
89 QJ, 21 Nov. 1986.
90 QUA, OPF, locator #1006, unnumbered box, file: Surface. *Globe and Mail*, 11 March 1994.
91 *Queen's Alumni Review*, May-June 1990.
92 AMS Assembly minutes, 26 Oct. 1989.
93 QJ, 13 Oct., 1989.
94 QUA, OPF, locator #1001.1, box 9, file: Gordon House Sign Incident – 1989. Gordon House is now referred to as a "hall."
95 Author interview, Mary Smith, 22 Nov. 2013.
96 QJ, 17 Oct. 1989.
97 Author interview, Deirdre McDade, 26 April 2012, and QJ, 17 Oct. 1989.
98 QJ, 26 Oct. 1989.
99 QUA, OPF, locator #1001.1, Box 16, file: Gender Issues Group.
100 *Queen's Alumni Review*, Jan.-Feb. 1990. See: Susan Donaldson and William Kymlicka, "No Thaw in Chill Campus Climate," *Globe & Mail*, 28 Nov. 1990.
101 AMS Assembly, 23 Nov. 1989.
102 MUS, 23 Nov. 1989, and MBT, 1 and 2 Dec. 1989.
103 Penelope Hutchinson, "'No' Now Really Does Mean 'No,'" *Queen's Alumni Review*, #1, 2010, 7.
104 Author interview, Kam Rao, 9 April 2014.
105 MUS, 22 Nov. 1990.
106 MUS, 26 Sept. 1991.
107 QAR, March-April 1990, S8.
108 Quoted in Katherine Govier, "A Time To Be Just," *Queen's Alumni Review*, March-April 1990, 16.
109 *Tricolour*, 1991.
110 W.M. Zuk to Smith, 29 Jan. 1990, QUA, OPF, locator # 1001.1, box 9, file: Gordon House Sign Incident 1991– .
111 MUS, 28 March 1991.
112 MBT, 1 and 2 March 1991, and 2 and 3 Oct. 1992.
113 Reported in MUS, 22 Sept. 1983.
114 MUS, 23 May, 1991; 21 Jan. 1993; and 24 March, 1994.
115 See, for instance: QJ, 16 Jan. 1992.
116 See, for instance: Marvin McInnis to Smith, 13 April 1993, QUA, OPF, locator #1001.31, box 15, file: race relations.
117 MUS, 27 May 1993.
118 MUS, 12 Dec. 1991.
119 Author interview, Irène Bujara, 12 August 2014.
120 MUS, 24 June 1993.
121 QUA, OPF, locator #1001.31, box 15, file: Race relations responses – Senate Committees.
122 See, for instance: Chris Veldhoven, "Report on the Needs of Lesbian, Gay and Bisexual Faculty, Staff and Students at Queen's University," Human Rights Office, Queen's University, January 1995, copy in MUS, 2 March 1995.
123 See Richard Elliott, "An Overlooked Constituency, A Broader View of Equality: Employment Equity for Lesbians, Gay Men and Bisexual Women and Men," a report submitted to Dr Joan Geramita, Associate Vice-Principal, Human Services, 1992.
124 *Globe and Mail*, 11 March 1994.
125 QJ, 8 Feb. 1991.
126 See, for instance: Sheila McIntyre to women friends and women they trust, memo 12 Dec. 1989, QUA, Baines fonds, unprocessed, file: Law faculty misogyny incident, 1989–90.
127 Quoted in MUS, 24 March 1990.
128 See: Bronwyn Drainie, "Trials and Errors: In the Case of the Women vs. the Men at Osgoode Law School, the Jury Is Still Out," *Toronto Life*, August 1991.
129 Katherine Monteith, "A Report Card on Canada's Law Schools," *The Canadian Lawyer*, Feb. 1991. Queen's law professor Susan Miklas in the *Queen's Alumni Review* (March-April 1991) attacked the survey, arguing that her faculty was "constantly evolving" and that this was a healthy sign.
130 See: QUA, OPF, locator #1001.31, file: law-general (decanal search 1991).
131 "Job Offer Sparks Brouhaha," KWS, 5 Feb. 1993.

132 Sadinsky to Smith, 24 Feb 1993, QUA, OPF, #1006.31, file: law general (decanal search 1991).
133 Gold to Smith, 12 April 1993, QUA, OPF, locator #1006, unnumbered box, file: Graduate Studies and Research.
134 See: Walters, "'Let right,'" 364–76.
135 Sedgwick to Smith, 25 Jan. 1993, QUA, OPF, locator #1001.31, file: law general 1993.
136 Senate Committee on Appointments, Promotion, Tenure and Leave, 17 Jan. 1992, QUA, OPF, locator #1001.31, file: Race relations responses to May 8 memo.
137 RAQ interviews: Batchelor, 14 Aug. 2008; Joneja, 4 June 2009; and Kumar, 25 May 2011.
138 Alexander Lamoire to W. Leggett, 12 March 1997, QUA, OPF, locator #1006, unnumbered box, file: student affairs.
139 QJ, 5 Nov. 1985.
140 QJ, 3 Oct. 1989.
141 Monture to Smith, 25 Feb. 1987, QUA, OPF, locator #1006, unnumbered box, file: student complaints.
142 QJ, 4 April 1985.
143 QJ, 27 March 1985.
144 Bujara interview and Ekta Singh, "Abandoning Equity Policy: (Re)membering the Queen's University 1991 Principal's Advisory Committee on Race Relations," MEd thesis, Queen's University, 2010.
145 See: *Hearts of Hate*, a film made by Queen's-educated filmmaker Peter Raymont in 1995, which focuses on the insidious nature of groups like the Heritage Front.
146 QJ, 24 Nov. 1989.
147 QJ, 24 Sept. 1987.
148 AMS Assembly, 28 Sept. 1989.
149 QJ, 6 April 1990.
150 AMS Assembly, 22 Nov. 1990.
151 Author interview, John Berry, 8 Oct. 2013.
152 MBT, 1 & 2 Dec. 1989.
153 Pickard to Smith, 11 Jan. 1990, QUA, OPF, locator #1001.31, Box 16, file: race relations – grievance officers.
154 *Towards Diversity and Equity at Queen's: A Strategy for Change – Final Report of the Principal's Advisory Committee on Race Relations*, 28 Feb. 1991, supplement to Queen's *Gazette*, 8 April 1991.
155 All quotations from QUA, OPF, locator #1001.31, box 15, various file: race relations responses to 8 May memo.
156 QJ, 2 Feb. 1996. Frankson's vice-presidential colleague was Annette Paul, a Malaysian-born student in women's studies.
157 QJ, 29 March 1996.
158 QJ, 17 Jan. 1997.
159 Lamoire to Leggett, 12 March 1997, QUA, OPF, locator #1006, unnumbered box, file: student affairs.

CHAPTER NINE

1 RAQ interviews: Stephanie Deutsch, June-July 2008.
2 QJ, 27 Oct. 1978.
3 RAQ interviews: David McLay, 18 May 2010.
4 MBT, 13 and 14 May 1977.
5 Christie to Powis, 2 Nov. 1977, QUA, OPF, locator #1254, Box 20, file: CRR correspondence 1977–78.
6 MUS, 24 Nov. 1977, and Travill to R.W. Southam (chair of the Board of Trustees), 31 Jan. 1978, QUA, OPF, locator #1254, Box 20, file: CRR correspondence, 1977–78.
7 A.J. Petrina to Senate, 6 March 1978, MUS 23 March 1978.
8 MBT, 20 Oct. 1989.
9 Derek Bok, *Beyond the Ivory Tower: Social Responsibility of the Modern University* (Cambridge, MA: Harvard University Press, 1982), Chap. 1.
10 QUA, OPF, locator #1254, Box 20, file: CSR 1981.
11 Rawlyk to Collins, 30 Jan. 1980, QUA, OPF, locator #1254, Box 20, file: CSR 1981, file: CSR 1980.
12 School of Business Working Paper 79-6, April 1979 copy in QUA, OPF, locator #1254, Box 20, file: open meeting, 6 Nov. 1980.
13 McGregor to Editor, *Alumni Review*, 26 Aug.1980.
14 QJ, 21 Oct. 1980.
15 MBT, 5 and 6 Dec. 1980.
16 QJ, 4 Feb. 1983.
17 Bannister to Buchan, 29 March 1978, QUA, OPF, locator #1254, box 20, file: Social Responsibility Committee 1977–78.
18 KWS, 1 Feb. 1982.
19 MBT, 13 and 14 May 1983
20 Author interview, Alan Broadbent, 6 Nov. 2012.
21 QUA, OPF, locator #1254, box 20, file: CSR meeting 13 May 1982.
22 Kenneth Hilborn to *Queen's Alumni Review*, 28 July 1983, and Graham Davis to *Queen's Alumni Review*, 30 Aug. 1983, QUA, OPF, locator #1254, box 20, file: CSR meeting 14 Oct. 1983.
23 Alfred Bader to Hartland Paterson, 7 Jan. 1982, QUA, OPF, locator #1254, Box 20, file: CSR, Jan.–Dec. 1982.

24 *QJ*, 2 Nov. 1982.
25 *QJ*, 4 Feb. 1983.
26 Walter Williams, "Beware the Well-intentioned," *New York Times*, 15 May 1983.
27 Jean Christie to *Queen's Alumni Review*, 3 Aug. 1983, QUA, OPF, locator #1254, box 20, file: CSR meeting 14 Oct. 1983.
28 David Smith, "Queen's and South Africa: A Draft Report to the Board of Trustees by the Principal," MUS, 25 Sept. 1986.
29 RAQ interviews: Mary Smith, 8 June 2008, and author interview with same, 22 Nov. 2013.
30 See, for instance: *QJ*, 6 March 1986.
31 MUS, 26 June 1986.
32 MBT, 9 and 10 May 1986.
33 *QJ*, 13 May 1986. This was the opinion of a Queen's medical graduate, Isaac Sobol, who was dedicating his energies to ministering to Canada's Aboriginal peoples.
34 MBT, 17 and 18 Oct. 1986.
35 MUS, 27 May 1987.
36 MBT 3 Sept. 1987 and 21–22 Oct. 1988.
37 *QJ*, 11 Sept. 1987.
38 See: Hilda Neatby, "Queen's University: Town and Gown to 1877," in Gerald Tulchinsky, ed., *To Preserve and Defend: Essays on Kingston in the Nineteenth Century* (Montreal & Toronto: McGill-Queen's University Press, 1976), 331–41.
39 See: Hilda Neatby, *Queen's University, Volume I, 1841–1917: To Strive, to Seek, to Find, and Not to Yield* (Montreal & Kingston: McGill-Queen's University Press, 1978).
40 See: QUA, OPF, locator #1254, box 15, files: City of Kingston, 1969–75 and City of Kingston, 1976.
41 MBT, 3 and 4 March 1994.
42 QUA, OPF, locator #1254, box 15, file: City of Kingston, 1969–75.
43 Laird O'Brien, "What We Were: A Return to Old Friends and Old Halls," *Imperial Oil Review*, #3, 1985, reprinted in *Queen's Alumni Review*, Nov.–Dec. 1985: 4–7.
44 AMS Assembly, 29 Sept. 1988, and MBT, 1 and 2 March 1991.
45 Weisberg to W. Leggett, 14 Aug, 1995, QUA, OPF, locator #1006, file: student complaints & Albert Street resident to David Smith, 30 Sept. 1991, QUA, OPF, locator #1006, file: physical and health education.
46 MBT, 23 and 24 Oct. 1987.
47 MUS, 28 Jan. 1988.
48 *QJ*, 19 Jan. 1990.
49 MUS, 25 Oct. 1984.
50 See: *QJ*, 14 and 18 Sept. 1984.
51 MUS, 25 Oct. 1984.
52 MBT, 23 and 24 Oct. 1987.
53 Ibid.
54 MBT, 6 and 7 Feb. 1987; 11 and 12 May 1990.
55 *QJ*, 21 Nov. 1985.
56 MUS, 22 Nov. 1990.
57 MUS, 26 Sept, 1991.
58 *QJ*, 28 and 31 Oct. 1986, and MUS, 27 Nov. 1986.
59 AMS Assembly, 6 Nov. 1986.
60 AMS Assembly, 15 Jan. 1987.
61 MBT, 5 and 6 Oct. 1990. STAND stood for Student Area Neighbourhood Development.
62 MUS, 28 May 1987.
63 MBT, 4 and 5 Dec. 1987.
64 RAQ interviews: Tom Williams, 27 June 1911, and author interview, 23 Jan. 1913.
65 *QJ*, 11 Sept. 1987.
66 RAQ interviews: Tom Williams.
67 QUA, OPF, locator #1001.31, box 16, file: PAC on alcohol awareness, 1989– .
68 *QJ*, 24 Oct.1989.
69 *QJ*, 25 Oct.1990.
70 *QJ*, 7 Oct. 2003.
71 Yeates to Smith, 19 Sept. 1983, QUA, OPF, locator #1254, file: Grad Studies 1983–84.

CHAPTER TEN

1 See: Douglas Fetherling, *A Little Bit of Thunder: The Strange Inner Life of the Kingston Whig-Standard* (Toronto: Stoddard, 1993).
2 MBT, 12 and 13 March 1993, and MUS, March 25 and April 22 1993.
3 Author interview, Jeffrey Simpson, 2 June 2014.
4 Author interviews, William Leggett, 24 Sept. 2012 and 29 May 2014.
5 See: Ross H. Paul, *Leadership under Fire: The Challenging Role of the Canadian University President* (Montreal & Kingston: McGill-Queen's University Press, 2011), especially 274–7.
6 RAQ interviews: William Leggett, 24 May 2011.
7 MBT, 12 Oct. 1993.
8 RAQ interviews: William Leggett, 24 May 2012.
9 Author interviews, William Leggett, 24 Sept. 2012 and 29 May 2014.
10 QUA, OPF, locator #1001.31, box 6, file: VP Academic, 1994–95.
11 Ibid., plus file: Minutes Operations and Finance.
12 The biology department had always had a strong collegiality and performance. See: B.N. Smallwood, H.M. Good, and A.S. West, *Queen's Biology: An Academic History of Innocence Lost and Fame Gained, 1858–1965* (Kingston: Queen's Department of Biology, 1991).
13 QUA, OPF, locator #1001.31, Box 6, file: Minutes Operations and Finance.

14 Author interview, John Rae, 19 Nov. 2014.
15 See: Mervin Daub and P. Bruce Buchan, *Getting Down to Business: A History of Business Education at Queen's, 1899–1999* (Kingston & Montreal: McGill-Queen's University Press, 1999), 88–97.
16 Author interview, Paul Wiens, 11 April 2012.
17 MBT, 24 Nov, 1994, and 26 Nov. 1998.
18 RAQ interviews: William Leggett, 24 May, 2011.
19 See, for instance: The Barriefield Group, *Re-Thinking Queen's Residential Communities*, April 2000, QUA, Margaret Hooey fonds, uncatalogued.
20 MUS, 28 April 1994.
21 MUS, 22 Sept. 1994, and *QJ*, 23 Sept. and 25 Oct. 1994.
22 *QUFacts*, June 1994.
23 Ibid., Sept. 1994.
24 QUA, OPF, locator #1006, file: Task Force on Dispute Resolution.
25 Ibid.
26 MBT, 12 and 13 May 1995.
27 *QUFacts*, Aug. 1995.
28 *QUFacts*, Nov. 1995, and author interview, Annette Burfoot, 13 Dec. 2012.
29 MBT, 10 Jan. 1997. See also: Sandra Rastin, "Queen's University Faculty Association's Certification Drive: A Case Study," MA thesis in sociology, Queen's University, 1996.
30 *QUFacts*, July 1998.
31 Leggett to Rector Peter Gallant, 14 Dec. 1994, QUA, OPF, locator #1001.31, box 16, file: general – equity, 1994–96.
32 See: Maureen McCallum Garvie and Jennifer L. Johnson, *Their Leaven of Influence: Deans of Women at Queens' University, 1916–1996* (Kingston: Alumni Association of Queen's University, 1999), 12.
33 Ibid., 119.
34 Jo Vellacott to Elspeth Baugh, 25 Jan. 1980, QUA, OPF, locator #1254, box 14, file: Ban Righ Board, 1980–81.
35 See: Joy Parr, ed., *Still Running ... [Personal Stories by Queen's Women Celebrating the Fiftieth Anniversary of the Marty Scholarship.]* (Kingston: Queen's Alumnae Association, 1987), 97–107.
36 Baugh to Smith, 10 June 1991, QUA, OPF, locator #1001.31, file: Employment Equity Council.
37 McCallum and Johnson, *Their Leaven of Influence*, 107. Heavy reliance has been placed on this excellent analysis of an office in constant transformation.
38 MUS, 24 March 1994.
39 *QJ*, 26 Oct. 1995.
40 See: QUA, OPF, locator #1001.31, Box 16, file: Review: equity and human rights at Queen's.
41 Kobayashi to Leggett, 16 Feb. 1995, and Leggett to Kobayashi, 6 March 1995, QUA, OPF, locator # 1001.31, Box 16, file: Review: equity and human rights at Queen's, file: general – equity, 1994–95.
42 Mary Baetz, "Queen's University Review of Equity Services," 18 Dec. 1995, copy in QUA, OPF, locator #1001.31, Box 16, file: Review: equity and human rights at Queen's.
43 Robert Hudson to Leggett, 29 March 1996, QUA, OPF, locator #1001.31, Box 15, file: Baetz report; Report of Equity Structures, Dec. 1995.
44 *Penultimate Report to Principal William C. Leggett on the Office of the Dean of Women*, April 1996, QUA, OPF, locator #1001.31, Box 16, file: general – equity, 1994–96.
45 MUS, 23 May 1996.
46 McKenzie to Leggett, 15 May 1996, QUA, OPF, locator #1001.31, file: general – equity 1994-96, Box 15, file: equity.
47 Kobayashi to Leggett, 17 Oct. 1996, QUA, OPF, locator #1001.31, Box 16, file: status of women – mandate & membership.
48 QUA, OPF, locator #1001.31, Box 15, file: university advisor on equity e-mail responses, 1997.
49 MBT, 9 and 10 May 1997.
50 MUS, 30 April 1998, and *Queen's Gazette*, 6 April and 14 Sept. 1998.
51 *QJ*, 12 Sept. 1997.
52 See: Ahmed Kayssi, "Challenging the 'Culture of Whiteness,'" *QJ*, 5 April 2007.
53 See: *Queen's Alumni Review*, Sept.-Oct. 1994.
54 MBT, 3 and 4 March 1994.
55 MBT, 30 Sept. and 1 Oct. 1994.
56 RAQ interviews: William Leggett, 24 May 2011.
57 MUS, 22 Sept. 1994.
58 See, for instance: MUS, 29 Feb. and 7 March 1996.
59 MUS, 24 Nov. 1994. See also: Paul, *Leadership under Fire*, 276–7.
60 MBT, 12 and 13 May and 29 and 30 Sept. 1995.
61 RAQ interviews: William Leggett, 24 May 2011.
62 Ibid.
63 MBT, 1 and 2 March 1996, and MUS, 7 March 1996.
64 MUS, 9 May 1996, and MBT, 10 and 11 May 1996.
65 William Leggett, "Leaders and Citizens for a Global Society," supplement to the *Queen's Gazette*, 20 May, 1998.
66 MBT, 10 and 11 May 1996.
67 RAQ interviews: William Leggett, 24 May 2011.

68 MBT, 2 and 3 March 2001.
69 MBT, 3 and 4 Dec. 1999.
70 MBT, 2 Dec. 1994.
71 MBT, 6 and 7 March 1998.
72 David Smith, chair, *Report of the Advisory Panel on the Future Directions for Post-secondary Education* (Toronto: Ministry of Education and Training, 1996).
73 MBT, 29 and 30 Sept. 1995 and 1 and 2 Dec. 1995.
74 MBT, 4 and 5 Dec. 1998.
75 MBT, 1 and 2 Dec. 1995.
76 MBT, 7 and 8 March 1997.
77 MBT, 1 and 2 Dec. 1995.
78 QJ, 26 Oct. 1995.
79 QJ, 28 Feb. and 7 March 1997.
80 MBT, 7 and 8 March 1997.
81 MBT, 6 and 7 March 1998.
82 Author interviews, George Hood, 26 Sept. 2012 and 10 June 2014.
83 MBT, 2 and 3 Oct. and 4 and 5 Dec. 1998.
84 AMS Assembly minutes, 6 April, 2000.
85 MBT, 19 and 20 Sept. 2003, and George Hood, "Campaign for Queen's – End of Campaign Report," May 2004, QUA, Hood fonds, locator #2409.
86 MUS, 10 Dec. 1997.
87 MBT, 2 and 3 Oct. 1998.
88 MBT, 3 and 4 March and 1 and 2 Dec. 2000.
89 MBT, 28 and 29 Sept. 2001.
90 MBT, 13 and 14 Oct. 2000.
91 MBT, 1 and 2 Dec. 2000.
92 For one treatment of the impact of higher tuition, see: Jacalyn Duffin, "What Goes Around, Comes Around: A History of Medical Tuition," *Canadian Medical Association Journal*, 164 (Jan. 2001): 50–6.
93 MUS, 4 Oct. 2001.
94 QJ, 14 March 1997.
95 MUS, special meeting, 10 Feb. 1998.
96 QJ, 26 Nov. 1998 and 4 Nov. 1999.
97 AMS Assembly, 23 Nov. 2000.
98 William Leggett, "Queen's at the Crossroads," QAR, Sept.-Oct. 2000, 13–15. See also: William Watson, "The Freedom to Innovate: An Interview with William Leggett," *Policy Options* (Sept. 2000): 13–18.
99 "A Pathfinder Program for Ontario Universities," Queen's University, 25 June 2001, copy in QUA, George Hood fonds, locator #2409.
100 "Implementing a Queen's Pathfinder Program," 12 October 2001, QUA, George Hood fonds, locator #2409.
101 MUS, 31 Jan. 2002.
102 See: Nick Treanor, Stephanie Relic, and Matt Aaronson, "For a Few Dollars More ... The Buck Must Stop Here," *Queen's Alumni Review*, May-June 1998.
103 AMS Assembly, 8 March 2001, and QJ, 9 March 2001.
104 QJ, 30 Nov. 2001.
105 QJ, 18 and 22 Jan. 2001.
106 MBT, 1 and 2 March, 2002.
107 MBT, 7 and 8 March, 2003.
108 "A New Eye on the Universe," *Queen's Alumni Review*, July-August, 1998.
109 MUS, 28 and 29 Sept. 2003, and QJ, 24 Feb. 2004.
110 MBT, 6 and 7 March and 4 and 5 Dec. 1998.
111 MUS, 19 April 2001.
112 MBT, 2 and 3 Oct. 1998, and MUS, 25 Sept. 2003.
113 MBT, 7 and 8 March 2003.
114 MUS, 25 Jan. 2001.
115 MBT, 4 and 5 March 1999, and MUS, 21 Oct. 1999.
116 *Enrolment Planning Task Force Discussion Paper, Queen's Gazette*, 15 Sept. 1999.
117 MBT, 1 and 2 Oct. 1999, and MUS, 23 Sept. 1999.
118 MBT, 1 and 2 Dec. 2000.
119 Author interview, Dan Burns, 5 Nov. 2012.
120 MBT, 4 and 5 March 1995, 1 and 2 Dec. 1995, 8 and 9 May 1998, 5 and 6 March 1999, and 8 May 2004; QUA, OPF, locator #1006, file: Agnes Etherington Art Centre.
121 MBT, 3 and 4 March 2000.
122 See: Daub and Buchan, *Getting Down to Business*, 86–8.
123 See: Queen's University Campus Planning and Development Committee and Commonwealth Resource Management Ltd., *Heritage Study – Heritage Planning, Inventory and Evaluation* (Kingston: Queen's University, 1998).
124 MBT, 1 and 2 Oct. 1999 and 6 May 2000.
125 See: Christine Ward, "A Gift from the Heart," QAR, Holiday Season, 2002.
126 MBT, Sept. 29 and 30 1995, and RAQ interviews: William Leggett, 24 May 2011.
127 MBT, 7 and 8 March 2003.
128 QJ, 18 Jan. 2002.
129 MBT, 3 and 4 Oct. 1997.
130 Author interview, Bob Crawford, 6 Feb. 2015.
131 MBT, 11 and 12 May 2001.
132 MBT, 10 and 11 May and 4 and 5 Oct. 2002.
133 MBT, 7 and 8 March 2003.
134 MBT, 10 and 11 May, 13 Aug., teleconference, 4 and 5 Oct., and 29 Oct. teleconference 2002.
135 QJ, 9 Oct. 2003.

136 *QJ*, 26 March 2004.
137 MBT, 2 Dec. 1994, and see: the website of the Queen's Football Hall of Fame.
138 RAQ interviews: William Leggett, 24 May 2011.
139 MBT, 8 May 2004.
140 RAQ interviews: William Leggett, 24 May 2011.

AFTERWORD

1 *QJ*, 10 Sept. 2004.
2 *QJ*, 14 Sept. 2004.
3 *Queen's Gazette*, 12 July 2004.
4 *QJ*, 10 Sept. 2004.
5 See: Hendrik Willem Pardoel, *A Compilation of Queen's Athletes and Sports Teams: 1873–2004*, Vol. II (Kingston: Queen's Athletics and Recreation, 2005).
6 *QJ*, 14 Sept. 2004.
7 Author interview, James MacIntyre, 27 Sept. 2011.
8 *QJ*, 14 Sept. 2004.
9 *QJ*, 26 Oct. 2004.
10 *QAR*, 26 Oct. 2004.
11 See: Barry Ferguson, *Remaking Liberalism: The Intellectual Legacy of Adam Shortt, O.D. Skelton, W.C. Clark, and W.A. Mackintosh, 1890–1925* (Montreal & Kingston: McGill-Queen's University Press, 1993) and J.L. Granatstein, *The Ottawa Men: The Civil Service Mandarins, 1935–1957* (Toronto: Oxford University Press, 1982).
12 Author interview, George Hood, 26 Sept. 2012.
13 QUA, OPF, locator #1006, unnumbered box, file: Speeches 1988–94.
14 RAQ interviews: Tom Williams, 13 July 2011.
15 R.L. Watts, "The Operation of Internal Governance within Queen's University," in MBT, 13 and 14 May 1988.
16 *QAR*, Jan.-Feb. 1987, 18.
17 Author interview, John Berry, 8 Oct. 2013, and "Towards Diversity and Equity at Queen's: A Strategy for Change," Queen's University, 28 Feb. 1991, a supplement to the *Queen's Gazette*, 8 April 1991.
18 Jacalyn Duffin, *History of Medicine: A Scandalously Short Introduction* (Toronto: University of Toronto Press, 1999).
19 Ronald Weisman to D.C. Smith, 18 April 1992, OPF, locator #1001.31, Box 7, file; Psychology 1992–96.
20 William McLatchie, MUS, 1 March 2001.
21 *QAR*, July-Aug. 1987, 16.
22 *Queen's Gazette*, special edition, 28 Oct. 2004, and "The Changing Face of Queen's," *QAR*, Summer 2004.
23 George Whalley, ed., *A Place of Liberty: Essays on the Government of Canadian Universities* (Toronto: Clark & Irwin, 1964), introduction.

Index

Abella, Rosalie, 352
Aberdeen Street, 435, 510–11
Aboriginal Council, 357–8
Aboriginal Teacher Education Program, 357–8
Aboriginals at Queen's, 356–9, 396; admission criteria, 359; BNSc for Aboriginals, 448
Abrahams, Vivian, 45, 69, 230, 404
Abramsky, Harry and Ethel, 351, 354, 417
Abramsky Hall, 354
Access to Opportunity Program, 479, 483, 488
accountability, 296, 301, 309, 469–70, 519
Adell, Bernard, 79, 222, 353, 367, 386; chairs Edwards inquiry, 203–5; dean of law, 233, 238; religious elements, 347–8; report on Edwards inquiry, 204–7
Adelman, Howard, 211
Adelman, Howard Tzvi, 356
Advancement Office, 374, 474, 511; retooled by Hood, 477
Aesculapian Society, 34, 37; Medical House, 37, 386
Agnes Etherington Art Centre, 36, 56–7, 184, 265, 268, 340, 354, 492–3; *From Women's Eyes* exhibition, 124–5; *Heritage Kingston* exhibit, 185; Raymond Moriyama extension, 338; support from Alfred Bader, 185, 324, 493
Agnew, Peckham and Associates, 67–8
Aitkins, Craig, 102
Akenson, Donald, 489
Alcan, 408, 418
Alexander, Bruce, 35
Alexander, Jean, 254

Alexander, Lamoire, 392
Allan, Ralph, 107
Allen, Richard, 296–7
Allende, Salvador, 402–8
Alma Mater Matter, 156
Alma Mater Society (AMS), 9, 11, 18, 22, 33, 98, 100–2, 112, 138, 192, 416, 514; AMS court system, 35, 37, 116, 151, 167, 200, 282, 371–2, 375, 379, 416–17, 419, 422, 431–2; bilingualism, 140; birth control information, 158, 165; Board of Trustees, 103, 154, 485; "Bus-It," 158, 421; changing role in 1960s, 138–9, 148–50; commemorates Robert Sutherland, 397–8; commission system of governance, 153, 434–5, 485, 529; committee on corporate involvement, 477; committee on racism and ethnic relations, 352, 393, 397, 458; Common Grounds coffee shop, 485, 505; compensates McGill, 281; concerts, 159; condemns candle-lighting ceremony, 145; constables, 35, 116, 157, 167–8, 205, 208, 221, 371, 419, 421–2, 432; dean of student affairs, 449; direct election of executive, 150–1, 154, 193, 529; Earle Report, 148; embodiment of limestone liberalism, 190, 514, 517; Edwards accusations, 202–8; Edwards-Lichty resignation, 196; "fair share" demands, 154; fee strike of 1973, 158; Gender Issues Committee, 335, 379; Golden Cockroach award, 435; "Good Ship AMS," 485, 530; Grey House, 154, 485, 507; honorary presidents, 143; housing crisis in 1968, 210–19; incorporation in 1969, 152, 157, 401; jacket/tam tradition, 512;

Knox teaching award, 25; Lesbian and Gay Issues Committee, 372; liquor bylaws, 140; Marriott strike, 449–50; *Navigating the Storm* report on cutbacks, 472; near bankruptcy in early 1970s, 159; no fraternities, 12, 37, 510; non-academic discipline, 115–16; offices, 170; 125th anniversary, 274; opens food bank, 473, 529; press council, 386, 369; *Queen's Journal*, 142; rector, 149–50; referendum on fee deregulation, 481; relations with principal, 104, 147, 152, 155, 518; Social Contract, 309–10; social responsibility referenda, 404, 406–7, 411; social responsibility seminars, 410; sponsors course evaluations, 175; Stauffer Library support, 335–6; Student Assistance Levy referendum, 308; student fees collected, 34, 158, 170, 401; student pubs, 154, 158–9, 160, 275; student services expanded, 154, 158–9; supports of *Blueprint for Action*, 294; support of new university centre, 170; support of Queen's Centre, 498–500; support of student clubs, 34, 138, 140–1, 320, 351, 393; supports PATFORI, 299; tricolour, 107, 512; Tricolour Express bus, 400, 423; *Vision* 2000 plan, 484; Walkhome service, 401, 529; women's issues committee, 360
Alternate Funding Plan/SEAMO, 312–13
alumni, 4, 31–2, 34, 185, 222, 342, 378, 404, 411, 430, 505–6, 510; "pseudos," 426; yellow umbrellas, 431. *See* Homecoming
Alumni Association, 185, 257, 288
Alumni Association Award for

Excellence in Teaching, 248–9; winners, 526–7
Alumni Weekend Review Board, 432
American Assembly of Collegiate Schools, 320
Amyot, Grant, 242, 305–7, 450–1
Anderson, Benedict, 6, 518
Anderson, David, 262, 315–20, 438, 482; replaces Cowan as vice–principal, operations and finance, 482
Anderson, Doris, 250
Anderson, George, 142, 192
Anderson, Marian, 342
Anderson, Ron, 447
Andras, Robert, 214
Andrews, Elias, 125–6
Andrews, Graham, 111
Anglican Church, 404
Angus, Margaret, 183
Anishinaabe peoples, 356–7
Anti-Tuition Hike Coalition, 481
April Fool's pranks, 180, 370–1
Archer, John, 84
architecture: Queen's shifts away from limestone buildings, 181, 267–8, 524
Armit, Allan, 183
Armitage, John, 416
Arts and Sciences Undergraduate Society, 109, 143–4, 370, 372, 383
Arts Society, 34, 37
Association for Tenants' Action in Kingston, 193
Association of Universities and Colleges of Canada, 63, 97–8, 265, 299, 446
Association of Women Teaching at Queen's, 124, 179, 251–2, 254–5, 256–7, 259, 359, 362, 363, 365, 384, 460
Athletic Board of Control, 168, 369; Colour Night, 168
Atwood, Margaret, 279–80, 339
Auld, James, 230
Avis, James, 235
Axelrod, Paul, 54

B + H Architects, 500
Baar, David, 326, 462
Bacon, David, 78, 223, 292, 345, 450–1; microcomputing, 264; women in engineering, 369, 507, 512
Bader, Alfred: art collector and benefactor, 185, 323–4, 336, 340, 473, 493, 497; early life and education, 321–3, 354, 522; career as chemist, 323, 325; initial acceptance at Queen's, 86, 321–3; Herstmonceux Castle, 461–7; religious elements controversy, 348
Bader, Isabel, 324, 462
Bader Lane, 493, 505
Baer, Marvin, 303, 305–6, 388, 438, 453

Baetz, Mary, 459–60
Bailey, Bertha, 135, 137, 161, 336
Baillie, Charles, 461, 492
Bain, Sir George, 523
Baines, Beverley, 119, 252, 254, 359, 361, 363–5, 384, 527
Bala, Nick, 366, 389
Ban Righ Board, 163, 256
Ban Righ Centre for Continuing University Education, 124
Ban Righ Foundation, 256, 455
Ban Righ Hall, 31, 256, 454
Bank of Montreal, 263
Bannister, John, 59, 406, 408
Barott, Marshall, Merrett and Barott, 111
Bartlett, Fred, 75
Bartlett Gym, 168
Bartley, Virginia, 364, 386–9
basic income unit (BIU), 60–3, 72, 93, 112, 125, 130, 132, 229, 231, 237, 289, 445, 470, 478, 480, 521, 525, 527; corridor planning of enrolment, 290–1, 491
Basmajian, John, 65, 71, 76
Batchelor, Barry, 45, 303, 346, 390, 392–4, 404
Bater, Robert: divestment, 404; religious elements controversy, 347–9
Baugh, Elspeth, 373, 376, 384, 394, 425, 456, 458, 460
Baumgart, Alice, 118, 233, 252, 259, 277, 396; becomes vice-principal, human services, 304, 376
Baxter, Peter, 306
Bayne, Don, 92, 499
Beal, John, 261
Beamish-Munro Hall, 494, 529
Beamish, Robert, 493–4
Beaton, Gary, 407
Beck, Stan, 367
Becker, Gary, 131
Becker, Henry, 78, 194, 199–201, 203–8, 219, 222
Beckett, Tom, 142
Beckman, Margaret, 333
Beer, Charles, 84
Beers, Kathy, 377, 433
Bell, Michael, 124
Bell Northern Research, 265
Benidickson, Agnes, 253–5, 327, 438, 442; activist chancellor, 284–5, 492
Benidickson Field, 477
Bennett, Jim, 121, 328–9, 378, 431
Bennett, Marilyn, 166
Bennett, Richard, 42, 149
Benson, Edgar, 55, 95, 214
Beridge, Lewinberg, 329, 331
Bernabei, Wilma, 253
Bernard, D.T., 264, 326, 335
Berry, John: report on racism and diversity, 356, 359, 394–7, 523

Bessette, Gérard, 139–40
Bessette, Irene, 79, 364
Beveridge, James, 81
Bieler, André, 57, 90, 184–5
Bingham, Dermid, 65–6, 70
Biosciences Complex, 338, 479, 491–2
Biotechnology Board, 277
Bissell, Claude, 63
Black, Edwin, 224
Blainey vs *Ontario Hockey Association*, 369
Blake, Diana, 85
Blanchard, John, 215, 221
Block V project, 268
Bloos, Marv, 159–60
"blue light" stations, 368
Blueprint for Action, 292–5, 302, 318, 339, 483
Blyth, Sam, 325
Boag, Tom, 233, 272, 310
Board of Graduate Studies, 23, 81
Board of Library Curators, 83–4,
Board of Trustees, 33, 98; advancement committee, 478; Ban Righ residence, 256; attitude to 1960s growth, 56–7; board task forces, 1980s, 288–9; chairmanship, 283, 288, 517; collective bargaining with faculty, 450–4; composition in 2004, 519; divestment controversy in Chile, 402–8, and in South Africa, 408–11; duty of financial oversight, 402; early 1960s problems in medical faculty, 68, 71; Herstmonceux Castle, 325–6; housing crisis of late 1960s, 210–19; Jackson Report on orientation, 429; Leech Report on revenue enhancement, 293–4; long-term planning committee, 180, 268; Lower Campus protest, 1960, 38–9; nature of its authority, 43–4; Queen's Centre, 495–500; rector as *de facto* member, 155; selection process for principal, 96, 101; social responsibility, 402–8; social responsibility sit-in, 413; student, staff and faculty observers and members, 157, 485, 518; theme sessions, 289; women on, 43, 120, 517, 519; worried about Americanization of faculty, 176
Bodnarchuck, Anne, 259, 299, 438
Bok, Derek, 274, 340, 406
Bonham, David, 80, 113, 159, 217; report on medical services in Kingston, 448; vice-principal, finance, 232, 236
Boo-Hoo, the bear, 16, 509
Boo-Hoo lounge, 509
Booz, Allen & Hamilton, 269–70
Botterell, Harry, 166, 232, 268, 273, 310, 521; early career, 68–9; appointed dean and subsequent reforms, 69–70, 71–2, 73, 91, 98;

crucial staff appointments, 175; health-sciences complex, 133; Senate reform, 157; support of nursing school, 72
Botterell Hall, 186, 273
Bovey, Edmund, 276–7, 283–4, 289, 291, 294; student protests against report, 290
Bracken, Franklin, 271
Bracken Library, 271, 311
Brackley, G.A. & Co., 56
Brady, Jo-Anne, 491, 502, 526
Brant, Clare, 357
Brebner, Arthur, 100
Brecht, Bertolt, 199
Breen, Julie, 466
Brent, Gail, 121
Brereton, Steve, 158, 160
Broadbent, Alan, 149, 213, 222, 263, 302, 328, 331, 336, 534; "Dormouse" column, 155; heads Board committee on social responsibility, 409–14; Queen's architecture, 328, 331, 336; runs for rector, 155–6
Brockington, Leonard, 22, 38, 42, 98, 149, 155
Brockington Hall, 161
Brockington Visitorship, 224, 400
Bromley, Allan, 266
Brown, Rev. George, 43
Brown, Gordon, 125
Brown, James, 77; Edwards affair, 205–9; revamping of Applied Science, 77–8, 87, 91
Brown, Malcolm, 26, 261
Brown, Norman, 228, 349; opposes women's studies, 361
Brown, Rosemary, 370, 438, 460, 466
Browne, Reg, 77
Brutalism, 267
Bryce, Beatrice, 46, 118, 137, 143, 455
Buchan, Bruce, 74, 405
Bujara, Irène, 381–2, 454, 461
Buller, Robert, 288, 396
Burfoot, Annette, 306, 445, 450–1, 453, 484
Burge, John, 259
Burney, Derek, 30
Burns, Dan, 211–12, 218, 222, 331, 334, 466, 470, 486; chairs Campus Planning and Development Committee, 492, 497
Burns, Robert, 128
Burns, Ron, 63
Buttars, John, 102, 209

Calvin, Dileno Dexter, 7, 10, 90
Campaign for Queen's, 473, 475–8, 482, 484, 492–5, 497, 528
Campbell, "Cartwheel Jane," 183
Campbell, Dean, 466
Campbell, Florence, 301, 446, 473–4

Campling, C.H.R. "Chuck": religious elements committee, 346–7
Campus Information Network System, 334
Canada-Asia Business Relations Centre, 316, 320
Canada Council, 174, 184, 261
Canada Mortgage and Housing Corporation, 161, 193, 211–19
Canada Pension Plan, 161, 177
Canada Research Chair Program, 488, 490
Canada Student Loan Program, 63
Canadian Association of University Teachers, 50, 98, 115, 139, 177, 200, 209, 254, 529
Canadian Banker, 25, 525
Canadian Centre for Guided Ground Transport, 78
Canadian Charter of Rights and Freedoms, 254, 282, 339, 348, 364, 368, 389, 393, 422, 435, 456, 523, 527, 529
Canadian Council of Professional Engineers, 76
Canadian Foundation for Innovation, 318, 488–9
Canadian Institutes of Health Research, 525
Canadian International Development Agency, 312, 463
Canadian Lawyer, 386
Canadian Medical Association, 65
Canadian Microelectronics Corporation, 262
Canadian Nursing Association, 71
Canadian Officer Training Corps, 167
Canadian Radio-Television Commission, 183
Canadian Union of Public Employees, 245, 266, 304–5, 449; CUPE 1302, 121
Canadian Union of Students, 147, 150–1, 153–4, 195, 197, 401
Canadian University Press, 142
Cancer Research Group, 272, 310
Canvin, David, 202, 439, 446
Cappon, James, 8, 23
Carr, Shirley, 253, 262, 280
Carrie, Sandi, 457
Carruthers family, 417
Carson, George, 102, 148, 150
Carson, James, 484
Carter, Donald, 387–9, 389, 448
Cartwright, Meredith, 385
Carty, Anthony, 414
Cassidy, Gordon, 316
Cat's Meow, 146
Central Admissions Office, 87
Central Mortgage and Housing Corporation. See Canada Mortgage and Housing Corporation

Centre for Automotive Materials and Manufacturing, 318, 489
Centre for International Relations, 266
Centre for Knowledge-based Enterprise, 318
Centre for Metal and Mineral Sciences, 78
Centre for Resource Studies, 266
Centre for Studies in Molecular Neuroscience, 318
CFRC, 15, 18, 106–7, 138, 140, 183–4, 485, 530
Challenge Fund, 295–6, 298, 340, 444
Chancellor: creation of role, 41, 515, 517; Baillie, 462, 492, 501; Benidickson, 284; Lougheed, 465, 492, 501; Michener, 134, 228; Stirling, 42, 228
Chapler, Christopher, 299
Charles, Prince of Wales, 297, 336
Chernoff, Bruce, 493
Chernoff, Michael, 493, 497
Chernoff Building, 493, 502
Chile, 402–8. *See* social responsibility
Chown, Edwin, 148
Chown, May, 137
Chrétien, Jean, 31, 470
Christie, Hugh, 404–5
Churcher, Margaret, 249
Churchill, Ed and Anna, 319
Clark, F.R.C., 36, 173, 184, 279
Clark, Lorenne, 387
Clark, Reg, 194, 199–200, 203–8, 219, 222; "Man, Science, and Nature" course, 78
Clark, W.C., 192, 515
Clarke, George Elliott, 398
Clarkson, Ali, 509
Clayton, John, 224
Clench, Ralfe, 87, 133, 143, 171
Clevenger, Gene, 264
Clinical Learning Centre, 310
clinical teaching units, 70, 106
Coalition Against Deregulation, 484
Coalition for the Preservation of Post-Secondary Education, 482
Cocks, Jacqui, 189, 210
Code of Conduct, 116, 167, 282, 363, 368, 377, 416
Cohanin, Moussa, 353
Cohen, Sharon, 364
Coleman, John, 45, 52, 114, 123
Collins, Everett Alfred, 465
Collins, Mary, 253, 457, 460; heads Board committee on social responsibility, 405–6
Committee of Presidents of Provincially-Assisted Universities of Ontario (CPUO), 55, 58, 60–1, 63, 82–3
computing at Queen's, 60, 74, 96–7, 263–5; FORTRAN, 77; QUIK/LAW, 81; IBM 3081, 263; internet streaming, 528; Library of the Twenty-first

Index 569

Century, 337; personal computers, 334; User Code of Ethics, 264
Conference Board of Canada, 474
Conn, Hugh, 62, 72, 76, 87, 129; as vice-principal, administration, 77, 79
Connell, George, 438, 440
Connell, Walter "Ford," 26–7, 33, 67
Connell, Walter Thomas, 26, 65, 417
Connor, C.W. "Cal," 17
Consultative Group on Faculty Compensation, 240–2, 276, 282, 302, 307, 310, 450–1; facilitates daycare and maternity leave, 302; final breakdown, 450–1; introduces merit and progress-through-the-ranks salary adjustment, 302
Conway, Jill, 280
Conway, Sean, 295
Cooke, Dave, 317
Cooper, Helen, 329, 332, 336, 412, 414, 426–7, 457
Coordinator of Faculty Recruitment and Retention, 461
Corlett, Mabel, 119
Cornelius, Bud, 41, 243, 245, 304
Corry, J.A., 3, 80; appoints Harry Botterell as dean of medicine, 68–9; celebrates Queen's 125th anniversary, 90; champions individual rights, 200; dealings with Queen's Park, 55–7, 61–2, 94; early life, 14, 32, 59; early years at Queen's, 15, 72; end of old paternalistic culture, 177; faculty association, 139; favours "orderly planning," 180; initiates administrative reforms, 40, 98, 520; modernizing Applied Science, 76–8; modernized physical education, 76; *My Life and Work* memoir, 89, 191; philosophy as principal, 20, 22, 31, 33, 36, 42, 61, 64, 99, 102, 140, 155, 200, 520; Queen's as national university, 220; Queen's history, 7, 90; reaction to Duff-Berdahl report, 99, 103, 104, 147; relations with Jean Royce in 1960s, 86–8; teaches Politics 2, 24, 114; student health services, 165
Costellano, Marlene, Brant, 357
Council of Ontario Universities (COU), 63, 82, 115, 201, 230–1, 236, 301, 438, 484, 491; *Order on Campus* report, 201
Council on Employment Equity, 303, 458
Courchene, Thomas, 316
Courtice, Scott, 484, 497
Courtright, Jim, 186, 257, 275, 476, 530
Cousins, Marney, 121
Cowan, John Scott, 447, 451, 452, 454, 471; appointed vice-principal, operations and finance, 446, 529; Queen's Centre, 496
Craine, Agnes, 65, 351
Crandall, Robert, 32, 60, 74, 235

Crawford, Bob, 449, 486; Queen's Centre, 496–500
Crawford, Bryan, 509
Creighton, Donald, 224
Crocker, Sandra, 490
Cronk, Bruce, 26
Crowder, Christopher, 176
Crowe, Arlene, 251–2
Crowe, Harry, 177
Crown, Robert, 142, 148
Cunningham, Diane, 480, 486
Cunningham & Cunningham, 36
Cunningham, Swan, Carty, Little and Bonham, 308
Curtis, Clifford, 36, 82, 168, 417
Curtis, Guy, 15
Cuthbertson, Ken, 378

Darling and Downey, 339
Daub, Merv, 32, 45, 74, 407
Dauphinee, Mary Margaret, 461
Davies, Arthur, 36
Davies, Michael, 281, 289, 412–13, 423, 428, 437–8, 440
Davies, Robertson, 36, 437
Davies, Rupert, 437
Davis, Sam, 272
Davis, William, 56, 130–1, 158, 238, 274, 277
Day, James, 166
Day, Wilf, 141–2, 151, 195–6
deans: role of, 45, 115, 238–9
dean of student affairs, 100, 148, 196, 445, 448–9, 461, 486, 529
dean of women, 46–7, 100, 118, 123, 136, 143–4, 162–3, 166, 234, 254, 343, 373–4, 394, 424, 449, 454–5, 457–61, 467, 502, 507, 521
Debating Union, 28
De Bold, Adolfo, 262
Defence Research Board, 78
Delisle, Ron, 79
Department of Anaesthesiology, 70, 313
Department of Anatomy, 65, 75, 113, 270–3, 312, 381
Department of Art History, 109, 171, 184, 325, 359–60, 443, 513
Department of Biology, 56, 126, 180–1, 202, 261, 338, 439, 446, 459, 490
Department of Chemical Engineering, 28, 76, 78, 151, 181, 192, 194, 200, 202–4, 209, 222, 259
Department of Chemistry, 23–4, 54, 78, 81, 86, 179, 249, 323, 325, 361, 439, 474, 480, 492–3, 497, 502
Department of Civil Engineering, 22, 77, 100, 111, 181, 246, 303, 346, 391, 404
Department of Classics, 47, 97, 246
Department of Computing and Information Science, 77, 96
Department of Drama, 30, 109, 126, 139, 280

Department of Economics, 10, 15, 18, 20, 24–5, 28, 30, 50, 59, 73–4, 77, 80–2, 96–7, 106, 110, 127, 173, 175, 179, 190, 222, 233, 285–86, 289, 306–7, 334, 337, 440, 489, 494, 516; Richard Lipsey appointed, 175, 286
Department of Economics and Political Studies, 73, 278, 519
Department of Electrical Engineering, 265–6, 319, 493
Department of English, 8, 23, 25, 30, 40, 47, 72, 77–8, 84–5, 92, 96, 106–7, 109, 118–19, 139, 157, 183, 202, 249–50, 255, 260, 360–1, 394, 396, 402, 417, 438, 475, 506, 531
Department of Extension, 23
Department of Family Medicine, 68, 70, 173–4, 254, 310, 469
Department of Film Studies, 106, 249
Department of French/ French Studies, 138–40, 219, 253, 255, 363, 443, 455, 467
Department of Geography, 20, 82, 91, 106, 138, 180, 211, 261, 266; graduate programs approved, 173
Department of Geological Sciences, 24, 78, 118, 527
Department of German, 47, 90, 118, 396, 443
Department of History, 10–11, 30, 39, 45, 62, 91, 97, 100, 106, 109, 114, 119, 128, 130, 142, 183, 190, 198, 199, 207, 219–20, 224, 234, 260, 280, 299, 306, 347–8, 353, 356, 361, 368, 390, 399, 404–6, 425, 465, 484, 489, 520, 523
Department of Mathematics, 22–3, 45, 52, 74, 77, 82, 114, 123, 172, 181, 215, 380, 447
Department of Medicine, 26–7, 67, 261, 311, 353
Department of Mechanical Engineering, 45, 72, 77, 85, 261, 351, 447, 493
Department of Mining Engineering, 32, 47, 78, 82, 181, 369, 404
Department of Paediatrics, 173, 254
Department of Pathology, 65, 70, 81, 175, 272, 312, 441
Department of Physics, 38–9, 52, 56, 78, 109, 137, 81, 190, 226, 261–2, 359, 403, 467, 481, 487, 505–6
Department of Physiology, 45, 70, 76, 106, 230, 233, 249, 268, 280, 351, 354, 404
Department of Political Studies, 15, 20, 73, 78, 80–2, 96–7, 109, 134, 172–3, 215, 223–5, 241, 244, 280, 285, 337, 410, 428, 506, 514, 516; Sir Edward Peacock Professor, 175
Department of Psychiatry, 80, 166, 272, 311
Department of Psychology, 74–5, 106, 180–1, 356, 394, 396, 411, 527

Department of Russian, 91
Department of Sociology, 74–5, 91, 97, 106, 119, 121, 124, 128, 154, 164, 173, 176, 199, 201, 252, 255, 306, 356, 360, 364, 459, 513; Sociology 331; on women, 121
Department of Spanish and Italian, 527
Department of Surgery, 26, 66, 70, 136, 311, 313, 429, 440
Departmental Student Committees, 151
Deutsch, John J.: appointed vice-principal, administration, 40, 57, 60, 62, 73, 94; attitude to 1960s post-secondary growth, 64, 93, 525; collegiality, 516; corporate directorships, 95, 203; creates Committee on Financial Constraint, 231; creates Committee on the Status of Women at Queen's, 121, 123, 360; creates Committee on Teaching and Learning, 106, 108; death, 225, 228; devises basic income unit, 60–1, 91; early life, 32, 58–9, 72, 93, 346; education faculty, 129–31; foresees economic downturn in 1970s, 133; handling of Edwards affair, 202–9; housing crisis of late 1960s, 210–13; "Johnny Dutch," 95, 105, 517; as Ottawa mandarin, 11, 29, 58, 62, 105, 110, 191; personality, 59, 94, 104, 133, 399; philosophy as principal, 96, 104–6, 111, 114, 116–17, 121, 152, 188, 200, 246, 274, 279, 530; reaction to student radicalism, 198, 202–8; rector, 150; renegotiates status of Theology College, 124–7; "steady state" policy, 94, 98, 111–12, 133, 146, 160, 246–7, 313–14, 491; university centre plans, 170
Deutsch, Stephanie, 59, 105
Dexter, Grant, 84
Diana, Princess of Wales, 297
Dick, Susan, 361
Diefenbaker, John, 64, 79–80, 214; Bill of Rights, 355
Disraeli Project, 260–1
Divestment. *See* social responsibility
Dodge, David, 131–2, 179, 286, 470
"Dollar Bill" (William Allen), 417
Domino Theatre, 139
Donald, Merlin, 411
Donald Gordon Centre, 492
Dorn, Peter, 107
"double cohort," 480, 491, 504
Douglas, Alice Vibert, 46, 118, 143, 455
Douglas, James, 83, 333, 336
Douglas Library, 56, 83–4, 85, 234, 249, 277, 333, 337, 492; arrival of computers, 263–4, 337; expansion and modernization in 1960s, 84–5; librarians recognized as professionals, 177, 242; Special Collections, 84; women in, 118–19, 121

Downie, John, 78
Drew, George, 54
Dryden, Ken: study of athletics, 491, 496
Dubos, René, 96
Dueck, Gordon, 465
Duff, David, 410
Duff-Berdahl Report, 91, 98–100, 139, 147, 149, 151, 179, 305
Duffin, Jacalyn, 65, 311, 353, 355, 527
Dumas, Genevieve, 370
Duncan, A.R.C. "Sandy," 249; as dean of Arts, 27, 72, 106, 225
Dunning, Charles, 28, 551
Dunning Hall, 73, 75
Dunning Trust Lectures, 28, 224, 250, 353, 369, 417
DuPont, 418
Du Prey, Pierre, 335
Dupuis, Nathan, 2, 8–9, 23
Du Toit, Allsopp, Hillier, 332
Duttle, Karl, 330
Dymond, Matthew, 72

Eady, Ron, 143
Eagleson, Melva, 83
Eamon, Keith "Skip," 92
Earl, Rollo, 225, 351
eastern Ontario: influence on Queen's, 7, 9, 11, 21, 23, 30, 32–3, 43, 55, 72, 74, 81, 95, 120, 122, 125, 146, 159, 166, 174, 184, 192, 233, 247, 253, 271–2, 311, 315, 320, 327, 339, 344–5, 350, 355, 362, 474, 488, 493, 522
Easton, David, 175
École Polytechnique de Montréal, 376
Economic Council of Canada, 73, 94–5, 131
Edwards, Charles "Chuck," 192, 400, 518; academic career at Queen's, 194; elected AMS president, 151–2, 194–5; evidence before Adell inquiry, 201–8; Free Socialist Movement, 198; graduate studies, 199–200; post-Queen's career, 220–2; resignation as AMS president, 196–7; runs for rector, 155; spearheads social activism, 196; tent-in on Summerhill lawn, 196–7; visits Paris, 195; Wallace Hall meeting, 207–9
Edwards Defence Committee, 205
Eikelboom, Jenny, 306
Elliott, Donald, 452, 464, 466, 492, 517
Elliott, Mark, 188, 195
Ellis, Douglas, 44
Elrond College, 158, 193, 212–19, 221–2, 267; becomes Princess Towers, 217
Emergency Committee for Student Housing, 193, 195, 210
emergency medicine, 68
Employment Opportunity Officer, 253, 275, 352, 456
Empress, The, 508

endowment, 21, 31, 41, 55–8, 66, 68–9, 78, 81, 159, 193, 228–30, 239, 241, 247, 254, 257, 263, 283, 291, 293, 340, 402, 410, 482
Engineering Society, 142, 359, 369, 376, 469, 512; brewing competition, 370; Clark Hall pub, 369; founding, 34; Golden Apple award, 527; jacket tradition, 512; Tea Room, 529
Equity Office, 382
Estall, Martyn, 100
Etherington, Agnes, 184
Etherington, Brian, 387–8
Etherington, Frederick, 184, 417
Ettinger, George Harold "Curly": dean of medicine, 28, 65, 68
Euringer, Fred, 109, 139
Eves, Ernie, 486
Expo 67, 213

faculty: British bias, 176; burden of committee work, 174; growing emphasis on research, 267; impact of 1960s inflation, 178; male bias, 114, 122, 443; pre-1970s informal appointment process, 112, 114; profile of in 1961–71 period, 171; profile in 1974–76, 239; profile in 2004, 505; worry over Americanization, 176
Faculty Association. *See* Queen's University Faculty Association
faculty boards, 41, 44, 98, 100–2, 108, 116, 274, 323, 346, 348, 360, 362
Faculty Club, 20, 174, 226; moves to King Street, 170, 172, 516; in Wallace Hall, 139, 171
Faculty of Applied Science, 50, 56, 122, 143, 261, 439, 493; first woman professor, 370; FRECS, 143; Harris appointed dean, 447–8; male domination, 250; microcomputing, 264, 334; "plumbers," 163; revamping curriculum in 1960s, 76–8; solar car, 468, 501; women faculty, 253
Faculty of Arts and Science, 86, 91, 97, 102, 106, 108, 233, 310, 334, 443, 521; Blue Book report on teaching and learning, 108–9, 110, 181; Silverman appointed dean, 447
Faculty of Education: created, 129–31; growth, 162, 508; Kenya project, 320; Upitis appointed dean, 448; Vernon Ready as dean, 130; Williams appointed dean, 233, 433
Faculty of Graduate Studies and Research, 81, 162, 234, 439, 487; Advisory Research Committee, 490; Anderson appointed dean of graduate studies, 447, 487; Bromley Report, 1982, 266–7; Director of Research Services, 490; enrolment in 1990s, 487; growing emphasis on research in 1970s, 174–5, 260, 265–7, 513, 525; Kerry Rowe as dean, 489–90, 531;

Index 571

separation of graduate studies and research functions, 267, 445, 447, 525, 528; *Think Research, Think Queen's*, 526; Ulrich Scheck as dean, 487
Faculty of Law, 122, 233; gender wars in late 1980s, 362–7, 383–89; "Hound Dogs," 383; library, 80, 311; profile in 1961, 26; under Dean Adell, 233; under Dean Carter, 387–90, 448; under Dean Lederman, 79–81; under Dean Soberman, 81, 211
Faculty of Medicine, 7, 310, 448; accreditation, 313; dean/vice-principal split authority in 1970s, 233; health-sciences building project, 268, 270–3; library, 270–1; pressure on admissions, 526; profile of faculty in 1961, 26, 64–6; reformed by Harry Botterell, 68–9, 70–3, 91, 173, 268; unification of medicine, nursing, and rehabilitation, 313, 448
Faculty Players, 139
Fagan, Drew, 406
"Fair Share" Report, 156–7, 206
Family Care Unit, 173
Farr, Dorothy, 124
Federal-Provincial Fiscal Arrangements Act, 229
Fell, Albert, 113
Ferguson, Barry, 192
Findley, Donna, 427
Fisher, H.K., 277
Fleig-Hamm, Christiane, 138
Fleming, Sandford, 9, 29
Fletcher, Douglas, 213
Flint, Eveline, 121; as Staff Liaison Officer, 123, 244
Folwell, Rod, 156, 158, 206, 209
football, as tradition at Queen's, 15, 17, 363, 500, 508–11; interest of Mackintosh and Corry in, 16–17; "Kill McGill," 281, 425, 454; Yates Cup win in 1968, 92; effect of 1970 Milliken Report, 168, 509
Forde, Francis, 96
Forsey, Eugene, 224
Fortier, Suzanne, 361, 447, 467, 475, 522; appointed vice-principal, research, 446, 488, 526; to NSERC, 489
Fotheringham, Allan, 223, 275
Four Directions Aboriginal Centre, 357–8, 461
Fowler, Daniel, 185
Frank, 367
Franks, C.E.S. "Ned," 24, 113, 181, 215–16, 218, 428
Frankson, Greg, 397–8, 466, 474, 481
Fraser, Rod, 277–8, 286, 289–90, 294, 296–9, 302, 304, 326, 355, 360, 387, 413, 445, 450; candidate for principalship, 440, 442; president of University of Alberta, 442, 447
Freedman, Adele, 336

Free Socialist Movement, 198–9, 202–9, 219–20, 401
Freidan, Betty, 120
Friends of Queen's, Inc., 31
Frost, Grenville, 54–5, 61
Frost, Leslie, 54, 56–7, 63, 238
Frost Wing, 492
Frum, Linda, 423
Frye, Northrop, 96
Fuller, Buckminster, 218
fundraising, 8, 56, 128, 132, 134, 136, 185–6, 219, 255, 257–9, 264, 276, 288, 293–5, 301, 336, 339–40, 343, 348, 350, 374, 378, 417, 423, 431, 438, 464, 470, 472–3, 475–7, 479, 486, 492, 497, 501, 523, 525, 528
Fur Cup, 371
Fyfe, Stewart, 113
Fyfe, William Hamilton, 10, 14

Galbraith, John Kenneth, 90
Galsworthy, John, 504
Garbutt, Gordon, 52, 87
Gargaro, Bettyanne, 119
Garvie, Maureen, 455
Gaskin, Paul, 368
Gaustad, Erik, 529
gay/lesbian sexuality, 145–6, 367, 369–72, 375, 507; homophobia, 425
Gay Men's Caucus, 367
GEAC, 263–4
geographical full-time status, 69, 272, 310–12; overage, 310
George, Graham, 173, 189
George T. Richardson Memorial Fund, 184
Geramita, Joan, 303
Gerretsen, John, 281, 412, 426–8, 433
"Ghetto," 163, 268, 276, 421–5, 427, 429, 431, 434–5, 505, 510
Gibson, Frederick W., 7, 9, 12, 42–5, 84, 91, 109, 198, 515; Senate reform in 1960s, 100–3, 104, 116, 194, 220, 520
Gibson, Gordon, 95
Gibson, James Douglas, 13, 134, 228, 517
Gill, Ernest, 30, 44, 185
Gill, Murray, 257
Globe and Mail, 230, 317, 336, 338, 372, 383, 403–4, 461, 470
Gold, Alan D., 388
Golden Words, 142, 146, 196, 199, 368–9, 376, 379
Good, Harold, 180
Good, Jacqui, 155
Good, Lin, 83–4, 119, 259, 333; sits on Ontario Council of University Affairs, 253; work and report of Committee on the Status of Women at Queen's, 121–3
Good, Tom, 198, 201, 203, 210, 222
Goodes Hall, 494–5

Goodes, Mel, 315, 494–5, 497
Gordon, Daniel, 454
Gordon, David, 330
Gordon, Donald, 44, 50, 70, 96, 104
Gordon, John, 233, 315, 494
Gordon, Roy, 76
Gordon House (now Hall), 161, 372–5, 378
Gorsky, Morley, 203
Gosse, Richard, 100, 178
Gould, Glenn, 38
Govier, Katherine, 378
Gow, Donald, 128
Graduate Students' Society, 148, 299, 396, 406, 411–12, 420–1; Grad Pub, 421
Graham, Roger, 9
Grant, George, 211
Grant, George Munro, 2, 8–9, 10, 274, 350; as fundraiser, 12, 21, 230; the Grant tradition, 11, 72, 531; muscular Christian, 25, 125; *Ocean to Ocean*, 29; *Queen's Quarterly*, 128
Grant Hall, 2, 9, 90, 96, 149, 153, 188–9, 279–80, 331, 342, 376, 417, 420, 499; candle-lighting ceremony, 145, 370; tradition service, 20
Grantham, Barbie, 427
Gray, Hannah, 289, 406, 412
Gray, John, 206
grease pole tradition, 19, 143, 281, 284, 425, 429, 507–8
Green, Alan, 121; Stauffer Library, 334–38
Greene, Elizabeth, 119, 360
Greene, Lorne, 30–1, 191
Greenidge, Herbert, 166
Greer, Germaine, 252
Gregor, Frances Helen, 228
Grey Cup, 10, 15–16, 169, 183
Griffiths, Peter, 152–3, 156
Grossman, Irving, 212, 214–15
Guide to Canadian Universities, 352
Gundy, H. Pearson, 84–5, 89–90, 119, 166
Gunn, Jock, 260
Gunn, Ken, 235, 246

Hall, Emmett, 64, 71, 269
Halperin, Israel, 353
Hamilton, A.C., 396
Hamilton, Herb, 31, 138, 185; resigns as AMS secretary-treasurer, 148
Hamilton, Roberta, 97, 269, 361, 363, 375, 502
Hammett, John, 30, 44, 70
Hand, Richard, 73–4, 91, 113, 233, 286
Hanes, John, 527
Hanley, John, 342
Hannah, Jason, 30; funds chair in medical history, 271
Hardin, Garrett, 289

572   Index

Hare, Kenneth, 94, 198
Hargreaves, Doug, 297, 508
Harkness, Robert D., 44, 61, 101, 106, 210
Harkness Hall, 161
Harland, Catherine, 438
Harris, Jill, 119, 253–4, 449
Harris, Michael: "Common Sense Revolution," 452–3, 461, 464, 471, 474, 478–9, 484, 486
Harris, Tom, 259, 447–8; Integrated Learning Centre, 493
Harrison, Eric, 109
Harrower, George, 100, 129, 134, 208, 232; Blue Book report, 108–9, 110–11, 154; chairs Committee on Teaching and Learning, 106, 108; favours clustering of academic units, 180–1
Hartwick, John, 172–3, 286
Harvison Young, Alison, 389
Hatcher, Donald, 268
Haudenosaunee peoples, 356–7
Hawking, Stephen, 487
Hawkridge Farm, 437–8, 441–2, 446
heads and beds tax, 163, 418
heads of department, 172; become managers, 174; long tenure, 114–15
health-sciences building, 268–9. See also Botterell Hall
Heap, Dan, 404
Heffalump, 158–9
Helwig, David, 139
Hennessy, Peter, 24
Heritage Front, 392, 397
Herman, Kay, 97, 121, 124, 252, 365; prize in women's studies, 361
Herstmonceux Castle, 321, 324–7, 439, 441, 444, 462–7, 483, 491, 518, 531
Highway 401, 147, 152
Hill, Jean, 72–3, 118, 121, 233
Hillel House, 354–5
Hinton, Ralph, 40
Hitchcock, Karen; appointment, 502–3, 507; early career, 503; installation, 503, 531
Hobsbawm, Eric, 5, 7, 15
hockey, 14, 30, 136, 169, 188, 369, 371, 416, 420, 474, 491, 498, 509, 527
Hodgetts, J.E. "Ted," 20, 113–14
Hodgkinson, Ruth, 271
Hoffman, Abbie, 192, 220–1
Holt, Alison, 379
Homecoming, 185, 198, 281, 415, 419–20, 423, 431–3, 510–11; campus observation room, 434; "pseudos," 426; "red caps," 434; street/keg parties, 423–4, 429–31; (1984), 510–11
Hood, George, 474, 482, 492; appointed vice-principal, advancement, 475, 529; Campaign for Queen's, 476–8; early life and career, 474–5, 516; Project "Red Horse," 476; Queen's Centre, 497–500
Hood, Marilyn, 352
Hooey, Margaret, 87, 117, 119, 376, 439, 449, 458
Hotel Dieu Hospital, 65, 67, 70–1, 174, 311, 424; joins health-sciences complex project, 269
Houston, Stuart and John, 185
Howes, Bob, 508
Hsu, James, 78
Hughes, Jim, 412, 430
Humacher, Carl, 299
Humanities House, 277
Human Rights Office, 381–2, 396–7, 454, 456, 460–1, 507; "positive space" policy, 382
Hunt, Constance, 386
Hutchinson, Penelope, 376

IDEA Foundation, 262
Illich, Ivan, 212
Instructional Development Centre, 527
Integrated Learning Centre, 493, 502, 527
Institute of Industrial Relations, 74, 127; becomes School of Industrial Relations, 265–6
Institute of Intergovernmental Relations, 127, 266, 273, 530
Institute of Local Government, 127
Inter-Faith Council, 345, 382, 397
International Centre, 319, 351, 390, 403, 463
International Centre for the Advancement of Community-based Rehabilitation, 312, 320, 469
International Programs Office, 319–21; *The International Dimension of Queen's University*, 321
international students, 247, 319–20, 339, 390, 463, 468–9
International Study Centre, 462–3, 465–7, 521; Canadian Universities Study Abroad Program, 467
Isbister, John, 28, 135, 138

jackets, 18–19, 511–12
Jackson, Rick, 377, 428–9
James, Cyril, 16–17
Janzen, Charlene, 379
Japan, 262; Japan Society, 320
Japanese language, 262
Jean Royce Hall, 162
Jeeves, Alan, 299
Jewett, Pauline, 30, 120
Jews at Queen's, 353–6
Jock Harty Arena, 136, 168, 180, 186, 279
John Deutsch Centre Council, 398
John Deutsch Institute for the Study of Economic Policy, 228, 266
John Deutsch University Centre, 154, 229, 496, 498, 510, 517; Arthur Erickson as architect, 171; initial planning, 170; named for Deutsch, 228
Johnson, Jennifer, 455
Johnston, David, 280–1, 440, 443
Jolliffe, Alfred "Fred": teaches Geology 100, 23–4, 526
Joneja, Madan, 113, 391; 1992 report on human rights at Queen's, 381, 396
Jones, Caroline, 374
Jones, Mike, 529
Jordan, W. Dennis, 336
Jordan, William, 8

Kalin, Rudy, 396
Kanter, Rosabeth Moss, 376
Kao, Jennifer, 495
Kaufman, Nate, 70–1, 175, 272
Kayssi, Ahmed, 461, 523
Kealy, Michael, 437
Kelly, H. Garfield "Gub," 26, 70, 232–3, 270
Kelso, Charis, 376
Kennedy, Russell, 215, 232
Keppel-Jones, Arthur, 45, 109–10, 114
Kerr, Clark, 4–5
Ketchum Ltd., 295, 301, 473
Keyes, Ken, 272
King, Alice, 85
King, Cecil, 357
King, Cheryl, 259
King, William Lyon Mackenzie, 11, 29, 100, 274
Kingston, 146, 320, 329; boarding houses, 235–6, 400; capital pledges to Queen's, 258; CKWS radio station, 36; economic impact of university on city, 418–19; frictions over university expansion, 179; the "Ghetto," 421–2; heads and beds tax, 163, 418; *Heritage Kingston* exhibit, 185; impact of Elrond College, 215–16, 218; James Roy's history of city, 417; Jews, 355; Kingston Hall, 417; Kingston police, 281, 378, 422–3, 429, 430, 433–4; labour pool, 243, 245; Lesbian and Gay Association of Kingston, 372; liaison committee, 419; local families, 417; Loyalist character of city, 21; North Kingston, 141, 151, 219, 418; queer community, 145–6, 371; rental accommodation, 161, 403; Rotary Club, 319, 342, 390; STAND, 427, 432; Student Volunteer Bureau, 143; Sydenham Ward, 158, 163, 329, 377, 399, 421, 424, 427, 433, 510; taverns, 400; town-gown relations, 36, 138, 172, 281, 377, 401, 415–19, 421–2, 426, 428, 432; *Whig-Standard*, 165, 183, 189, 195, 212, 218, 281, 289, 313, 347, 350, 365, 367, 374, 384, 410, 413–14, 423, 428–30, 437

Index 573

Kingston Arts and Music Club, 185
Kingston Conference (1960), 30
Kingston General Hospital, 26–7, 65–7, 71, 311, 448; Family Care Unit, 173–4; joins health-sciences complex project, 269–70
Kingston Hall, 36, 56
Kingston Psychiatric Hospital, 269–70
Kingston Rowing Club, 416
Kingston Symphony Orchestra, 173
Kinnear, Tom, 476
Kisilevsky, Robert, 489
Knitter, Chrissie, 498–9, 529
Knowlan, Scott, 292
Knox, Frank, 32, 190, 247, 526; AMS teaching award, 25; early life, 24; teaches ECON 4, 24, 233; edits *Canadian Banker*, 25, 525
Kobayashi, Audrey, 458, 460
Koestler, Arthur, 96
Kostuik, John, 405
Kropp, Ben, 353
Krishna, Vern, 386
Kumar, Pradeep, 341, 391
Kutt, Mers, 96
Kuwabara Payne McKenna Blumberg, 335–6
Kuyek, Don, 203

Ladd, Stewart, 331–2
Lahey, Kathleen, 259, 366, 389
Laird, Hilda, 47, 90, 119, 443
Lake Opinicon retreat, 108–9, 110
Lally, Michelle, 413
LaMarsh, Judy, 120
Lamb, Marianne, 502
Lambert, Phyllis, 335
Landmark Group, 438
Larass, Michael 207
Lash, Stanley, 128
Laughren Floyd, 308, 439
Laverty, A.M., 31, 38, 125, 341–2, 347, 516, 522
Laverty, Frances, 341
Lawford, Hugh, 79; QUIK/LAW, 81
Lawson, George, 330
Law Students' Society, 346–7, 379, 386; separates from AMS, 412, 487
Lawyer's Weekly, 365
Laxer, James, 142, 219–20
Leadlay, Frank "Pep," 15
Lebensold, Fred, 38
LeBlanc, Greg, 158
Lederman, William, 367; dean of law, 26–7, 78–81, 83, 113, 127; early life and career, 26
Lee, Dennis, 211
Leech, George, 88–90
Leech, James, 288, 399, 426, 466, 470; report on revenue enhancement, 292–5
Leggett, Claire, 440, 509

Leggett, William; adjusts vice-principal structure, 444–7; AMS honorary president, 502; "Bulldozer Bill," 441, 444, 449, 500; champions "broader" learning environment, 482, 491; collective bargaining, 447, 450–2; commemorates Robert Sutherland, 398; commitment to internationalize Queen's/Herstmonceux, 441, 444, 462–8, 483, 501, 513, 531; coping with Social Contract austerity, 470–2, 478–9; dean of women, 454–60, 502; early life and career, 440–1, 444, 488; enrolment, 491; hires George Hood, 475; Leggett cultural index, 494; Marriott strike, 449–50; *Pathfinder Program for Ontario Universities*, 483–7, 495, 524; philosophy as principal, 441–2, 447, 454, 492, 500, 502, 531; Principal's Advisory Committee on Student Life Facilities, 497–500; purchases new band uniforms, 509; *Queen's at the Crossroads*, 482; Queen's Centre, 495–500; residence named for, 502; resurrects dean of student affairs, 448–9; selection as principal, 438–43; shifting fee structure, 478, 481; student assistance, 483–7, 502; student sit-in in office, 473; University Advisor on Equity, 460
Leighton, David, 284, 331
Leith, James, 20, 199
Lele, Jayant, 97
Lemmon, Hazlett, 50, 402
Lenard, Al, 168
Leonard, Col. R.W., 136, 166
LeRoy, Barry, 102
Lesbian and Gay Association of Kingston, 372
Lessard, Greg, 467
Levana Society, 34–5, 120, 143, 167, 194, 370, 455, 507, 522; candle-lighting ceremony, 37, 370; demise, 144
Lewington, Jennifer, 470
Lewis, Stephen, 427
Lewis, W. Bennett, 262
Lichty, Jan, 145, 151–2, 194–6, 522; feminist, 198; resignation as AMS vice-president, 197
life sciences, 269
Light, Walter, 258, 262, 278, 283–4, 288–9, 291, 294, 405, 413, 517
Lilles, Heino, 92
"limestone liberalism," 99, 104, 188, 190–2, 198, 221, 220–2, 511–13, 515, 532
Lindsay, Michael, 498
Lindsey, Jane, 217
Lindsley, Thayer, 78
Lipsey, Richard, 175, 286
Little, Robert "Bob," 32, 38, 127, 345

Little, Walter, 32, 132
Lougheed, John, 281, 427
Lougheed, Peter, 465, 492
Love, Morris, 232
Low, James, 71
Lower, A.R.M., 11, 13, 28, 31, 33, 39, 119, 209; embodiment of limestone liberalism, 190
Lower Campus, 38–9, 42, 136, 170, 190, 417, 505
Luckyj, Natalie, 124

Ma, Jeanne, 331–2, 492
MacCallum, Elizabeth, 29
Macdonald, Donald, 287
MacDonald, Donald C., 30
MacDonald, Flora, 244–5, 272, 313
Macdonald, Sir John A., 29, 36, 90, 513
MacDonell, Glenn, 153, 198, 201, 203
Macdonnell, James M., 44
MacIntyre, Donald, 269
Mackay-Lassonde, Claudette, 379
Mackintosh-Corry Building, 181–2, 271, 328, 330, 456; Ron Thom as architect, 181–2, 268, 328
Mackintosh, Donald, 76, 168
Mackintosh, Jean, 41
Mackintosh, William A., 14–15, 30, 36, 101, 525; collegiality, 516; dealings with medical school, 66; dealings with Queen's Park, 54, 60; death, 30; early life and Ottawa civil service, 11, 14, 29, 32, 127–8, 191, 223; Elrond College, 215; gender attitudes, 82; Lower Campus protests of 1960, 38–9; mentor to students, 28, 35, 38; on nature of principalship, 42–3, 62, 72, 99; on Queen's parochialism, 12, 45; retains vice-chancellor's role in 1960s, 40, 59; writes 1945 "white paper," 191
MacLaurin-King, Emily, 511
Macleans's, 223, 275, 300, 461, 467, 480, 490, 496, 524, 526–7
MacLeod, Keith, 511
MacMillan, Michael: *The Academic Cloister*, 249
Macnamara, Donald, 463–4, 466
Macphail, Sandy, 22
Macpherson, Lawrence, 73–4, 113
Maeots, Krista, 142, 151, 189, 219–20, 522
Magnusson, Denis, 80–1, 364–6
Main Campus Residence Council, 373–4
Malony, Rita, 312
Mann, Susan, 458
Manson, Allan, 306, 309, 317, 389, 450
Marcuse, Herbert, 199
Markus, Terry Ellen, 347
Marriott Corporation, 449–50

574   Index

Marshall, Tom, 28, 139
Martin, Bill, 142, 197
Martin, Paul, 489
Marts and Lundy, 476, 499
Marty Scholarship, 456
Mathers, Donald, 126-7, 345
Mathers, Helen, 256
Matheson, John, 30
Matthews, Bruce, 68
Matthews, John, 260
Maudsley, Robert, 312
Maxwell, Mary, 97, 121, 124, 360
McAdams, Nancy, 335
McAlister, Dan, 331
McArthur, Duncan, 130
McArthur College. *See* Faculty of Education
McBurney, Margot, 234, 263, 337
McCarney, Hal "Moose," 18
McCarthy Tetrault, 499
McCorriston, James, 70
McCready, William, 306
McDonald, Arthur, 487, 526
McGill-Queen's University Press, 107, 128-9, 223-4, 410
McGregor, Ross, 104-5, 152-3, 154-6, 160, 197-8, 202, 206, 212-14, 219-20, 222; "Fair Share" committee, 156; Ketchum Ltd., 295, 301; social responsibility, 407
McGuinty, Dalton, 486, 524
McHugh, James, 399, 414
McIlraith, George, 209
McIntosh, Robert, 234, 260
McIntyre, John, 142, 197
McIntyre, Sheila, 363-7, 384
McKellar, Greg, 3, 485, 529
McKenna, Katherine, 360
McKenzie, Diane, 460
McKeough, Darcy, 236
McKillop, A.B., 54
McKinnon, James, 286
McKinnon, Kelley, 386
McLatchie, William, 261, 335, 467
McLaughlin, Earle, 30, 56, 402
McLaughlin, R.S. "Sam," 23, 82, 342-3, 350
McLay, David, 109, 201; divestment controversy, 403-8
McLeod, D.I., 342
McLeod, Lynn, 289
McNeill, William, 280
McNeill, William Everett, 10, 40, 85, 256
McSherry, James, 372
McTavish, David, 324
McVey, Brad, 511
Medical Advisory Committee, 70
Medical Care Act, 64, 163
Medical Research Council of Canada, 174, 261, 488, 490
Medical Variety Show, 227, 369

Medland, Mary, 105, 119
Mein, Katherine, 119
Meisel, John, 113, 127, 141, 191, 224, 280, 337; arrival at Queen's, 20, 172, 514; mentoring students, 31; offers course on Quebec, 140; teaches sociology, 97
Men's Residence Board, 162
Meyer, Marion, 119
Michener, Norah, 134
Michener, Roland, 134, 228, 255
Miklas, Sue, 499
Miller, Willet, 23
Milliken, John "Jack," 26; 1970 report on athletics, 168, 496, 509
Milliken, Peter, 515
Minde, Thomas, 392
Model Parliament, 28, 400, 515
Molloy, John, 298
Mongillo, Antoinette, 381
Monieson, Dan, 74, 494
Monkman, Les, 475
Montreal Gazette, 228
Monture, Patricia, 364, 392
Moore, Emily, 368
Moose Factory, 72
Morand, Kathleen, 253, 443
More, Robert, 81
Morgan, Alison, 299, 357, 397, 413, 502
Morgentaler, Henry, 369
Moriyama, Raymond, 338
Morley, William, 84
Morris Hall: becomes coeducational, 162
Morton, Mary, 124, 360, 364
Mossman, Mary Jane, 119, 386-7
Muir, William, 405
Mulholland, William, 258, 473
Mullan, David, 248; working group on sexual harassment, 379-80
Mulroney, Brian, 316, 410
multiculturalism, 344-5, 349-50, 362, 381, 390, 507, 522-3; Multi-Heritage Collective at Queen's, 392
Munro, Donald, 493-4
Munro, John "Johnny," 500
Murray, Mary-Alice, 79, 364
Muslim Students' Association, 428
Mustard, Fraser, 276, 278
Must Canada Fail?, 223
Myerson, Martin, 96
Myles, Wayne, 319, 463

Nabisco Foundation, 291
National Federation of Canadian University Students, 142
National Research Council, 78, 82, 174, 489
National Students' Union, 158
Native Students' Association, 357
Natural Sciences and Engineering Research Council, 261-2, 488-90

Neatby, Hilda, 7, 9-10, 129, 187, 245, 466
Nelson, Rob, 151
New Democratic Party, 219, 295-6, 306, 308, 318; Waffle Manifesto, 219-20
New Left, 141, 150, 155, 193, 210
Newman, Cardinal John Henry, 4, 9-10, 22, 226, 338, 530
Newman, Joan, 193, 196, 219
Newman, Peter, 94
Newman Club, 187, 341-2
Nicol, William, 23
Nixon, Gordon, 499
"No Means No," 367-80, 389, 394, 401, 423, 436, 454, 456, 522; Gordon House nine, 379; Montreal massacre, 370, 376, 381, 383-4; Principal's Working Group on Gender Issues, 376
Noonan, Sheila, 364, 366
Noranda Mines, 402-8; Alf Powis, 404; Andacollo copper mine, 403
Norman, Colin: *The Queen's English*, 249
Norman, Dan, 170, 249, 268
Northern Telecom, 262, 264-5
Northey, Margot, 447, 468
Nuechterlein, James, 347
Nyhof, Dag, 428

O'Brien, Laird, 420
Ochs, Phil, 141
Office of Academic Planning, 111
Office of Research Services, 261, 300
O'Hara, Terry, 198, 202-5, 208, 222
O'Leary, Grattan, 91, 149-50, 152, 155, 210
Ondaatje, Michael, 26, 28, 139
O'Neill, Tom, 470, 472, 476-7, 499
Ontario; adoption of BIU system, 60-3; post-secondary education relations with, 53-5, 71, 229, 235-6, 241, 283-4, 287, 289-91, 296-8, 314, 339, 445, 479-80, 501, 524; Queen's reliance on eastern Ontario, 32, 146; support of Stauffer Library, 336; University Excellence Fund, 291
Ontario Academic Credits, 314
Ontario Confederation of University Faculty Associations, 179, 453
Ontario Council of Graduate Studies, 246, 260, 265, 318
Ontario Council of University Affairs, 63, 231, 235-6, 245, 253, 277; *System on the Brink* report, 236, 260, 294-5
Ontario Environmental Review Commission, 389
Ontario Federation of Students, 158
Ontario Graduate Fellowship, 82
Ontario Hall, 56

Ontario Hospital Services Commission, 65
Ontario Human Rights Code, 355, 381
Ontario Human Rights Tribunal, 392, 456
Ontario Labour Relations Act, 307, 452
Ontario Labour Relations Board, 245, 305
Ontario Medical Association, 313
Ontario Pay Equity Commission, 451
Ontario Public Interest Research Group, 485
Ontario Research and Development Fund, 318, 488
Ontario Scholars, 249, 292
Ontario School of Mining and Agriculture, 525
Ontario Student Assistance Program, 147, 422, 472
Ontario Student Housing Corporation, 161, 215
Ontario Student Opportunity Trust Fund, 474, 479, 483
Ontario Undergraduate Student Association, 484
orientation, 19, 143–4, 280–1, 419, 423, 426, 434, 504–7; charity day, 425, 508, 512; "instant tradition," 281; Jackson Report, 428–9; late 1960s attempt at reform, 154, 164; late 1980s reforms, 427–9; "Move-in Day," 505–7; Orientation Activities Review Board, 377, 427–9; Queerientation, 507; sexist language, 255, 425, 507; Tindall Field Games, 424, 429; University 101/Queen's 101, 377–8, 507; Wimmin's Frosh Week, 428. *See also* grease pole
Orr, John, 162
Osborne, Brian, 20, 138–9
Ottawa Journal, 149
Overall, Christine, 259, 288, 357, 502
Owram, Douglas, 50

Pakrul, David, 189, 197, 210–12
Parker, Charles, 127
Parnell, Ted, 195
Parr, Joy, 361
Parrott, Harry, 270–1
PARTEQ, 298, 338, 452, 479, 490
Paterson, Bob, 477
Pathfinder Program for Ontario Universities 483–7, 502
pay equity, 296, 303–5, 381, 451, 456
Peacock, Sir Edward, 30, 33, 175, 286
Pearson, Mike, 61, 63, 95, 200; Royal Commission on the Status of Women, 120
pensions, 177, 242, 336, 363, 518
Pepin, Patti, 388
Perkins, Cathy, 137, 341, 378
Peters, Dave, 212–14, 218
Peterson, David, 278, 290, 295

Peterson, Ed, 75
Philips, Katherine, 309, 462
Phillips, Ted, 85
Physical Education Centre, 76, 496
Pick, David, 433
Pickard, Michael, 385
Pickard, Toni, 81, 341, 364, 394–6
Pierce, Alfie, 16, 160, 391, 474
Pierce, Lorne, 30, 33; Edith and Lorne Pierce Collection, 84
Pike, Robert, 97
Pinochet, Augusto, 403
Pipe, Andrew, 109, 149, 154, 165, 189, 197, 466; Queen's Centre, 498–500
planning, 62, 91, 327–9; deterioration of campus in 1970s, 268; idea of clustering academic units, 180–1; joint Senate-Trustees Campus Planning Committee, 268, 330–1, 339, 492, 497; lack of master plan, 180; limestone *vs* Modernist/brutalist architecture, 181–3, 267; Master Plan of 1994, 332, 338, 492
Playboy, 368
Plewes, Campbell "Pappy," 28, 78, 194
Plumb, Alfred, 90
Plumley, Kent, 17, 496
Politics Club, 28
Polk, Barbara, 470, 517
Porter, John, 97
Powis, Alf, 404–5, 407
Powles, William, 272
Prado, Carlos, 139
Presbyterian Church: influence on Queen's, 7, 10, 12–13, 18, 22, 28, 31, 33–4, 44, 56–7, 86, 112, 124–5, 166, 185, 211, 231, 257, 276, 342–3, 397, 401, 416, 436, 513–14, 522
Primeau, Rick, 474
Primohamed, Taz, 462
Princeton University, 439
principal: balance of consensus and decisiveness, 521; nature of role, 42–4, 73, 177, 239, 279, 436, 514–15, 517, 520; shared governance, 520; use of advisory committees, 117, 121
Principal's Advisory Committee on Resources Issues, 298, 302; *Meeting the Challenges*, 300–2
Principal's Development Fund, 276, 355
Pritchard, Robert, 458
Project Green, 330–1
Publicover, Mark, 445
Purvis, Douglas, 286, 306, 489
Purvis Professorship in Economics, 489

Quarry, 139
Queen's Afro-Caribbean Club, 392
Queen's Alumnae Association, 31, 143, 256
Queen's Alumni Law Association, 386
Queen's Alumni Review, 23, 31–2, 86,

114, 134, 185, 230, 256, 342, 348, 377–8, 410, 482, 495, 509, 511, 516, 530
Queen's Appeal, 258, 412, 431
Queen's bands, 5, 15–16, 18, 37, 52, 138, 148, 183, 280, 423, 509–11; new uniforms, 509
Queen's Centre, 485, 495–500, 530
Queen's Centre for Resource Studies, 475
Queen's Centre Working Group, 498
Queen's Choral Ensemble, 228
Queen's Counsel, 367
Queen's Engineering Society, 469
Queen's Engineers Without Borders, 513
Queen's Fund Council, 473, 478
Queen's Gazette, 117, 157, 461
Queen's Homophile Association, 145–6, 369, 372
Queen's Journal, 9, 16–17, 30, 32, 38, 94, 138, 140–2, 143, 148–9, 150, 154, 159, 162, 170, 186, 189, 192, 195, 197–8, 209, 216, 221, 223, 284–5, 342, 364–6, 369, 371, 375, 383, 392, 397, 410, 433–5, 461, 473, 484–6, 496, 505, 509, 511–2, 516, 530
Queen's-Kingston Health Sciences Complex Council, 270–2
Queen's Law Lesbians and Gays, 367, 379
Queen's National Scholars, 258–9, 275, 288, 292–3, 300, 305, 359, 363, 366, 447, 489, 521
"Queen's Ottawa men," 29, 33, 57–8, 127, 191–2, 266, 287, 515
Queen's Project on International Development, 469
Queen's Quarterly, 7, 73, 107, 128, 225
Queen's Quest, 258, 263–4
Queen's spirit, 5, 13, 30, 45, 72–3, 102, 104–5, 153, 183–4, 186–7, 190, 211, 245, 274, 441, 443, 450, 500, 511, 513, 532; blind spots, 521; inclination to consensus, 521, 530
Queen's Student and Community Assault Centre, 368
Queen's Student Services, 158
Queen's summer school, 23
Queen's Tea Room, 20, 171, 494, 529
Queen's University: administrative reform in late 1950s, 40–1; becomes a multiversity, 4, 513; centenary in 1941, 6–7; chancellor, 9; charter, 90; collegiality at Queen's, 20–1, 22, 513, 527; dedication to public service, 22, 29; deferred maintenance, 492; "distinctly Christian" clause, 348, 353; early reliance on eastern-Ontario enrolment/"poor boys' university," 32–3, 43, 159, 171, 344, 362; 1841 enrolment levels in early 1960s, 12;

Gaelic traditions, 5–6, 7–8, 11, 13, 18, 20–1, 22, 28, 41, 90, 98, 136, 140, 164, 512–13; growth by 2004, 513; inclusive society, 518; male ethos, 12; motto, 4, 107, 287, 437, 468; as a national university, 32, 288, 292, 531; nature of leadership at, 72, 232; 125th anniversary celebration, 90; removal of trees on University Avenue, 505; support staff, 243–4; a teaching university, 9, 20, 23, 527; tricolour flag, 107. *See also* Board of Trustees
Queen's University and Affiliated Hospitals Council, 269–70
Queen's University Archives, 10, 84
Queen's University Faculty Association, 20, 139, 178, 209, 240, 248–9, 252, 302, 309, 317, 379, 382, 445, 450, 461, 484, 517; affiliates with librarians and archivists, 242; collective bargaining, 242, 451–2, 454, 527; considers alternative negotiation mechanisms, 179, 240, 242–3, 450–1; Council of Representatives, 453; new constitution, 453; Professors for a Better Queen's, 452; *QUFacts*, 303, 450, 453; referendum on divestment, 414; Salary Committee, 179
Queen's University Song Book, 6, 391
Queen's University Staff Association, 244, 304, 445
Queen's way. *See* Queen's spirit
Queen's Women and the Law, 384, 386
Queen's Women's Association, 120
Queen's Women's Centre, 372–3
Quinton, Natalie, 373

Race Relations Officers, 394–5
racism, 390–7, 520, 523; Principal's Advisory Committee on Race Relations, 393–5; Student Committee Against Racism, 394; *Towards Diversity and Equity at Queen's: A Strategy for Change*, 395
Rae, Bob, 295–7, 298, 338, 439, 470; Social Contract, 308–9, 438–40, 469, 478
Rae, John, 23, 31, 142, 447, 466, 477, 492, 499, 502, 516–17
Ranger, Terence, 5
Rao, Kam, 376, 393, 425
Rawlyk, George, 219, 224, 234, 280, 399, 405–7
Read, John, 164
Ready, Vernon, 130–1, 233, 407
rector, 6, 381; creation and initial incumbents, 42, 98, 516; first female rector, 386; late 1960s referendum on role, 149–50
Redmond, Chris, 186–7
Redmond, Donald, 85, 234; recognizes librarians as professionals, 177

Reeve, William, 396
Registrar's Office, 83, 235; changing role in 1960s, 86; Ross Report, 88. *See also* Royce, Jean
Reid, Evelyn, 118; work as dean of women, 234, 455–6, 458
religious elements controversy, 345–9
Rembrandt, *Head of an Old Man in a Cap*, 324
research: shift of faculty focus from teaching to research in 1970s, 174–5, 234, 441, 513
Research Centre for Southern Africa, 469
Research Ethics Board, 488
Reynolds, Neil, 365, 437
Rhodes Scholarship, 300; Charles Galunic, 319; Steven Beke, 319
Rice, Christine, 259
Rice, W.B., 45
Richardson Hall, 39–40; Collins Room, 41, 102–3, 465
Richardson, James: senior, 184, 254; son, 59, 169, 214
Richardson Stadium, 184, 420, 508; new stadium opened, 168
Rickerd, David, 316
Ridout, Godfrey, 90
Rigsby, David, 284
Riley, Patrick, 158
Robarts, John, 55–6, 58, 61, 79, 129
Robinson, Svend, 369
Rochdale College, 211, 215
Roche, Edmund, 126–7
ROFF, 373–4; occupies principal's office, 374–5
Rogers, Brian, 221
Rogers, Gordon, 510
Rogers, Janet, 156, 206
Rogers, Norman McLeod, 59, 157, 283, 404–5, 517
Rogers, Shelagh, 184
Romanow, Michelle, 529
Rooks, Sue, 254
Roosevelt, Franklin D., 10
Rose, Dave, 151
Rosen, David, 70–1
Rosen, Irving and Regina, 356, 417; lecture series, 356
Ross, Robin, 88
Rowe, Kerry: appointed vice-principal, research, 482, 489–90, 526
Roy, James, 417
Royal Canadian Mounted Police, 116, 177, 200–1, 204, 209, 322
Royal College of Physicians and Surgeons, 67
Royal Military College, 21, 167
Royce, Jean, 32, 102, 117, 119, 162, 166, 185, 189, 251, 256, 321, 323, 474, 506; administrative offices held, 86; career and forced retirement in 1960s, 85–91, 166; early life and

career, 40, 72, 85–6; honorary degree, 1968, 89–90; later life, 90; praise from Corry, 86; on Queen's changing character, 45–6; Ross Report, 88
Ruggles, Richard: art conservation, 138, 173, 265
Rutenberg, David, 319
Ryan, Claude, 224
Ryan, Frank, 273
Ryan, Kathleen, 10, 273
Ryan, Robin, 210
Ryan, Stuart, 39, 347, 367; career before Queen's, 26; teaching reputation, 26, 79
Ryan, Stuart (son), 201, 203, 222

sabbaticals, 177; 1937 policy, 114
Sadinsky, Stanley, 386, 388
Safdie, Moshe, 218, 335
St Denis, Earl, 511
St Lawrence College, 270
St Mary's of the Lake Hospital, 269–70, 311
Sandwell, B.K., 42
Santeramo, Donato, 526–7
Sasaki and Associates, 498, 500
Saturday Club, 20, 47, 84, 171, 340, 363
School of Business, 233, 247, 263, 286, 391; David Anderson as dean, 315; doctoral studies, 260; early history, 23; full-cost MBA, 315–19, 472, 480–2, 501, 531; growth in 1960s, 73; international outreach, 319–20, 339; introduction of MBA, 73–5; John Gordon as dean, 315, 494; Margot Northey as dean, 447, 494; Mel Goodes, 315, 494–5; separate faculty, 74; Victoria School renovated, 494
School of English, 23, 350–1
School of Environmental Studies, 318, 362
School of Graduate Studies, 82; growth in 1960s, 82
School of Music, 106, 173, 184, 279, 362
School of Nursing, 71–2, 102, 118, 233–4, 310, 312, 502; unification with medicine, 448
School of Physical and Health Education, 75, 498
School of Policy Studies, 266, 328, 362, 530
School of Public Administration, 128, 266
School of Rehabilitation Therapy, 71, 272, 310, 313; community-based rehabilitation, 310, 531
School of Urban and Regional Planning, 128
Schurman, Donald, 260
Schwartz, Margot, 348

Index 577

Science'44 Co-op, 136–7, 158, 211, 531
Science formal, 189
Scott, Donna, 409, 466
Sedgwick, Gordon, 386–7, 389
Senate, 33, 82, 117, 284, 517; codification of tenure and promotion, 175; dean of women, 459–60; debates fee deregulation, 481; forms of gender address, 361; handling of Adell Report, 204–5; impact of collective bargaining, 453, 528; long-term planning committee, 180, 268; "No Means No," 375; non-academic discipline, 115, 164, 167, 200, 208, 431; reform of role in 1960s, 98, 100–1, 104, 110, 194, 220; role and powers, 41, 43; Senate Budget Committee, 304; Senate Committee on Academic Development, 110–11, 112–14, 246, 257, 266, 276, 291, 308, 314, 317; Senate Committee on Academic Procedures, 396; Senate Committee on Appointment, Promotion, Tenure, and Leave, 110, 115, 178, 248; Senate Committee on Computing, 264; Senate Committee on Fine Arts and Public Lectures, 183; Senate Committee on Grievance, Discipline, and Related Matters, 116–17, 167, 206, 209; Senate Committee on Operations Review, 450, 460; Senate Committee on Student Affairs, 201; Senate Library Committee, 335; Senate Office, 119; social responsibility, 411, 414; *Statement on Academic Freedom and Tenure*, 115; student senators, 1968, 102, 104, 155, 157, 198, 414, 484, 485, 517; Tenure Appeal Committee, 178; town-gown relations, 428–9
Seres, Richard, 469, 476
Sexual Assault Centre, 372
Sexual Harassment Complaint Board, 380; policy in place, 382
Shannon, Kathleen, 259
Sharp, Tilbe, Irwin + Partners, 338
Sheahan, Pat, 508–9
Sheahan, Ryan, 509
Sherren, Claude, 221, 485
Shils, Edward, 19
Shoalts and Zaback, 500
Shortt, Adam, 9, 23, 127, 192, 223, 362, 515, 525
Sikh Student Association, 508
Silverman, Robert, 447–8, 481, 484, 486, 509
Simeon, Richard, 223
Simmons, Gordon, 202
Simpson, Jeffrey, 106, 116, 205, 222, 297, 299, 438, 442, 470
Sinclair, Duncan, 25, 32, 232–3, 238–9, 240, 245, 260, 281, 288, 313, 343–4, 349, 446; amalgamation of medicine, nursing, and rehabilitation, 318; creates task force on medical faculty compensation, 311; dean of medicine and vice-principal, health services, 311, 313; examines admissions policy, 551; Southeastern Ontario Medical Organization/alternate funding plan conceived, 311–14, 339; Homecoming, 431–3
Sinclair, Gord, 509
Sir John A. Macdonald Building, 80, 365
Sirluck, Ernest, 83
Skelton. O.D., 9, 11, 29–30, 42, 58, 127, 191–2, 223, 362, 515
Slater, David, 82, 274; Edwards affair, 205–9, 222
Smart, John, 207, 219
Smart, Pat, 219
Smith, David: appointment as principal, 278, 285, 287; *Blueprint for Action*, 293–5, 318, 339, 524; chairs Council of Ontario Universities task force on fees, 291; collegiality, 516; corridor enrolment system, 290; creates Principal's Working Group on Gender Issues, 376; department head in economics, 173, 285–6; early life and career, 285–6, 411; era of Charter rights, 282; fiscal condition of Queen's, 283, 291, 296–8, 309, 339–40; Herstmonceux Castle, 321–2, 324–7, 339; installation, 280; Principal's Advisory Committee on Resource Issues, 298, 302; "No Means No" controversy, 367–80; philosophy as principal, 285–6, 288, 340, 436, 443, 520, 528; *Queen's and South Africa: A Report to the Board of Trustees*, 413; Queen's National Scholar scheme, 258–9; *Queen's University: Strategy, 1985-90*, 320; race-relations inquiry, 393–4; report on future direction of Ontario universities, 470; Royal Commission on the Economic Union, 278; social responsibility issue, 411–15; steady state, 314; stresses quality of a Queen's education, 292, 520; *Values at Queen's*, 300, 313, 389, 394
Smith, Geoff, 176, 368, 425
Smith, Harrison, 532
Smith, Jack, 218
Smith, Mary, 411
Smith, Sidney, 51, 92, 520
Smol, John, 490, 526
Snoblen, John, 470
Snodgrass, William, 7, 21, suggests chancellor, 41
Snowdon, Ken, 276, 289, 299–300, 302, 418, 450, 464, 471
Soberman, Daniel, 81, 206, 233, 240, 328, 353, 386
Social Contract, 308–9, 438–9, 445, 450, 462, 469
social responsibility, 402, 415, 435–6; AMS referenda, 404, 406; Chile, 402–8, 410, 414; Dominion Textiles, 406, 412; Investor Responsibility Research Centre, 405; Kingston Anti-Apartheid Coalition, 410; South Africa, 406, 408–15; Student Action Committee, 404, 407–8; Sullivan Principles, 405–6, 408, 412; Task Force on the Churches and Social Responsibility, 408
Social Sciences and Humanities Research Council, 260–1, 488, 525
Society of Graduate and Professional Students, 487–8; affiliates with Public Service Alliance of Canada, 488
solar car, 468, 501
South Africa. *See* social responsibility
Southam, Robert W., 228, 405
South-East Asian Womyn's Collective, 383
Spanish and Latin American Students' Association, 508
Speal, George, 412–13
Stackhouse, John, 281, 372
Stackhouse, Richard, 296–7, 412, 438
staff, 5, 21, 26, 46, 56, 62, 66–8, 71–2, 75–6, 81, 83–5, 87–8, 114–16, 118–19, 121–3, 139, 159, 171, 177–80, 182, 224, 227, 230–1, 241–5, 251–3, 255, 264, 283, 299, 303–5, 309, 339, 346, 392, 394–5, 404, 407, 418, 438, 443–5, 448, 459, 471, 502, 515, 517–19
Staff Liaison Officer, 244
Staff Training and Development Coordinator, 244
Stairs, Jean, 502
status of women at Queen's, 43, 46–8, 137, 143, 366, 443, 454, 502, 507, 521–2; adjunct professors, 303; Alexander Report, 1980, 254, 303; centennial of women at Queen's, 1984, 259; corrective pay hike, 303; enrolment grows, 247, 250; "freshettes," 143–4; gender codes, 162; intense heterosexuality of Queen's, 145–6; Morand-Surridge Report, 1978, 253; Mullan report on sexual harassment, 380, 382; Pearson's royal commission on status of women, 120; as presidents of faculty societies, 359; Principal's Advisory Committee on the Status of Women, 117–24, 250, 360, 457; second-wave feminism, 145; sexist language, 255; Susie-Q Week, 138, 143, 145, 181; "Take Back the Night" marches, 368; women on administrative staff, 243, 521–2
Stauffer, Joseph S., 336

Stauffer Foundation, 291, 328–9, 337
Stauffer Library, 137, 332–9, 398, 448, 473, 492, 505, 524; adopts e-resources/learning commons, 448
Stayer, James, 355
"steady state" policy. See Deutsch, John J.
Stephenson, Bette, 238, 277
Stewart, Gail Ward, 460
Stirling, John, 30, 80, 89, 134, 228; Stirling Hall named for, 39
Stirling Hall, 39, 52, 190, 210, 493
Strangway, David, 458
Strong, Richard, 497–8
Student Action Committee. See social responsibility
Student Area Neighbourhood Development (STAND) group, 427, 432
Student Assistance Levy, 308, 326
Student Awards Office, 159
Student Christian Movement, 138, 141, 403
Student Committee Against Racism, 394
Student Health Services, 165–6
Student Union for Peace Action, 141–2, 192
Student Volunteer Bureau, 143, 158, 418
Students for a Democratic Society, 189, 192
Students for a New University, 195–6, 210
Students' Memorial Union, 38, 136, 154, 161, 170, 516
Sudbury Neutrino Observatory, 295, 467, 487, 526
Studio Q, 416
Sturgess, Kim, 465
Sullivan, Leon, 405
Summerhill, 330, 399; 1962 historic plaque, 45; restoration in 1982, 268; tent-in on lawn, 1968, 196–7, 210
SuperBuild, 480, 488–9, 493, 497
Surface, 372, 383
Surridge, Marie, 253, 363, 443
Sutherland, Robert, ix, 351, 397–8
Swain, Val, 418–9
Swash Q, 107, 477
Sydenham Ward Ratepayers' Association, 427
Symington, David, 71, 272

Taylor, Allan, 295, 467, 473
Taylor, Bruce, 3, 7
Taylor, Sherryl, 441
Teatero, Barbara, 338
Technology Centre (Walter Light Hall), 329
Teepell, Raymond, 133
Teertsta, Margaret, 256
television, 180
Tett, Eleanor, 119

Thank-Q, 478
Theological College, 3, 37, 102, 124–7, 173, 347, 404, 502
This Paper Belongs to the People, 198, 201
Thobani, Sunera, 382
Thom, Ron, 181, 212–13, 328
Thomson, Graham, 39
Thorburn, Hugh, 20–1, 191
Thorsell, William, 383
Tilghman, Shirley, 439, 476
Tindall, Frank, 135, 169, 297; basketball coach, 168, 509; early life, 16–18; Yates Cup win in 1968, 92; retirement in 1976, 168, 508–9
Tolkein, J.R.R., 212
Toronto Star, 365, 374
town-gown relations. See Kingston
Tragically Hip, The, 509
Traversy, Val, 202
Travill, Tony, 271, 404
Treatment and Rehabilitation (T & R) grants, 310, 313
Tricolor/Tricolour, 94, 138–9, 140, 183, 189, 383, 434, 496, 508, 532
Tricolour Award, 529
Trotter, Bernard, 62, 111, 180, 521; report on television teaching, 180
Trotter, Bruce, 159
Truch, Bill, 335
Trudeau, Pierre, 59, 89, 93–5, 100, 120, 147, 150, 192–3, 224, 404; honorary degree, 187–8
Tugwell, Tony, 142
Tulchinsky, Gerald, 348, 353–5; Holocaust course, 355–6
Turnbull, Tyler, 499
Turpin, David, appointed vice-principal, academic, 446, 471, 482, 491; to University of Victoria, 489
Tyendinaga Mohawks, 356

Uffen, Robert, 234, 261
Ukrainian Studies, 362
Union Gallery, 530
University Advisor on Equity, 460–1
United Church of Canada, 125–7, 407; Chambers United Church, 125
University Club, 443, 526
University Council, 9, 520; 1874 creation, 42, 515; on 1970 socio-economic profile of Queen's students, 147
University Council on Athletics, 168, 496; proliferation of sports, 509–10
University Health Officer, 165
Upitis, Rena, 259, 288
Upton, Donald, 166
Urquhart, M.C. "Mac," 20
Usher, Dan, 286

Van der Rohe, Mies, 213
Vandewater, Stuart, 70, 272

Vanier Cup, 92, 169, 297
Vanier, Jean, 105
Van Loon, Richard, 97
Van Nostrand, Innes, 427, 430, 530
Vaughan, Michael, 212, 214
Velshi, Ali, 393, 434
Verma, Sarita, 502
Victoria Hall, 161, 425, 454–5, 505; goes coed, 386
Victoria School, 332
Vroom Construction, 214–15

Waldron Tower, 509
Walker, David, 116, 484
Walker, Virginia, 459
Wallace, Bronwen, 141, 145, 202, 219, 256, 522
Wallace, Robert, 10, 72, 274, 442, 465; Halperin case, 353–4; Jewish "problem," 322–3
Walmsley, Roy, 139
Walters, Mark, 364
Warren, Jake, 258
Watkins, Mel, 220
Watson, George, 477
Watson, Greg, 467
Watson, John, 8, 192
Watson Hall, 91–2
Watts, Donna, 225, 274
Watts, Gordon, 147–8
Watts, Ronald, 7, 11, 21, 29, 127; appointed dean of Arts and Science, 109–10; appointed principal, 134, 224, 226; capital campaigns, 258; chairs Senate Committee on Grievance, Discipline, and Related Matters in 1970, 116–17; collegiality, 226, 274; early life and career, 224–6, 519; Elrond College, 217; faculty renewal, 257; fiscal constraint in 1970s, 227, 229–31, 235–6, 238–9, 241, 251, 268, 525; health sciences building project, 270–3; Institute for Intergovernmental Relations, 225, 273; Japan, 262; philosophy as principal, 227, 239, 245, 246, 257, 273–5, 443, 518–19, 531; Principal's Advisory Group on Resource Planning, 235; Principal's Advisory Committee on Teaching Effectiveness, 249; promotes consultative approach to salary negotiation, 179, 231, 237, 239–41; on Queen's governance, 41, 104, 520; Queen's National Scholar scheme, 258–9; streamlines senior administration, 232; "Rainbow Proposals," 241; relations with AMS, 226, 518; relations with Queen's Park, 225, 230; reliance on advisory committees, 231; residence named for, 502; School of Public Policy proposal, 266; strategic planning, 239; Task Force on National Unity, 224, 273, 519

Wattsford, George, 62, 90
Waugh, Douglas, 233, 270, 310
Webster, Stewart, 100, 104
Webster Foundation, 257
Weir, Jennie, 71–2
Weisberg, 346, 348
Weisman, Ronald, 527
West Campus, 130, 162, 332, 505–6, 508; new football stadium, 168
Wever, Henrik, 261
Whalley, George: early life, 25, 72, 109; *A Place of Liberty*, 531; Senate reform, 157; Swash Q, 107; teaching reputation, 25, 28, 92, 96, 247, 526
Wheare, Kenneth, 225
Whistler, Jane, 325
Whitley, Jim, 77, 218
Whitton, Charlotte, 9–10, 30, 191
Whole Earth Catalogue, 212
Who's Where, 507
Whyte, John, 224, 364, 366, 378, 384–7, 389, 396
Wiebe, Mel, 260
Wiens, Edith, 338
Wiens, Paul, 337–8, 448; embraces e-resources, 448
Williams, Dorothy, 148
Williams, Tom, 288, 299, 351–2, 375, 385, 432–4; early career, 433; Queen's Centre, 497; Queen's ethos, 518–19
Williamson, James, 8, 416
Willoughby, Stu, 203–4
Wilson, Beverley. *See* Baines, Beverley
Wilson, Ian, 84
Wilson, Laurence, 67, 310, 313
Wilson, Lois, 259
Wilson, Ruth, 469
"Winsom," 394
Wiwa, Ken, 398
Wolff family, 322
Wolman, Tony, 160
women at Queen's. *See* status of women
Women's Residence Council, 455
Women's Studies, 301, 359–62; first course, 360–1
Wong, Ken, 316–17, 527

Wood, Donald, 74
Wood, Kathy, 482
Woolf, Daniel, 375
Wright, Douglas, 62; Wright Commission/*The Learning Society*, 132, 158
Wright, Janet, 228

Yates Cup, 16–18, 32, 189, 500, 508
Yealand, Brian, 344–5, 376, 382, 397, 424, 449
Yeates, Maurice, 180, 234, 261, 266–7, 326, 340, 436, 462
Young, Alison, 317
Young, Pamela Dickey, 457–9
Young, William, 217, 219, 222; Queen's Centre, 499

Zacks, Samuel and Ayala, 57, 185
Zaremba, Eugene, 481